PHILIP'S

D0453538

STREET ATLAS
Surrey

Dorking, Epsom, Guildford, Leatherhead, Reigate, Woking

www.philips-maps.co.uk
First published in 1996 by
Philip's, a division of
Octopus Publishing Group Ltd
www.octopusbooks.co.uk
Endeavour House, 189 Shaftesbury Avenue
London WC2H 8JY
An Hachette UK Company
www.hachette.co.uk

Fifth colour edition 2010
First impression 2010

SUREA

978-1-84907-093-5 (spiral)

© Philip's 2010

Ordnance Survey®

This product includes mapping data licensed
from Ordnance Survey® with the permission
of the Controller of Her Majesty's Stationery
Office. © Crown copyright 2010. All rights
reserved. Licence number 100011710.

Speed camera data provided by
PocketGPSWorld.com Ltd

Post Office is a trade mark of Post Office Ltd in
the UK and other countries.

Printed in China

Contents

II	Mobile safety cameras
III	**Key to map symbols**
IV	**Key to map pages**
VI	**Route planning**
VIII	Major administrative and Postcode boundaries

| 1 | **Street maps** at 3½ inches to 1 mile |
| 219 | **Street maps** of Dorking, Epsom, Guildford, Kingston upon Thames, Leatherhead and Woking at 7 inches to 1 mile |

| 222 | **Index** of towns, villages, streets, hospitals, industrial estates, railway stations, schools, shopping centres, universities and places of interest |

Digital Data

The exceptionally high-quality mapping found in this atlas is available as digital data in TIFF format, which is easily convertible to other bitmapped (raster) image formats.

The index is also available in digital form as a standard database table. It contains all the details found in the printed index together with the National Grid reference for the map square in which each entry is named.

For further information and to discuss your requirements, please contact
philips@mapsinternational.co.uk

Mobile safety cameras

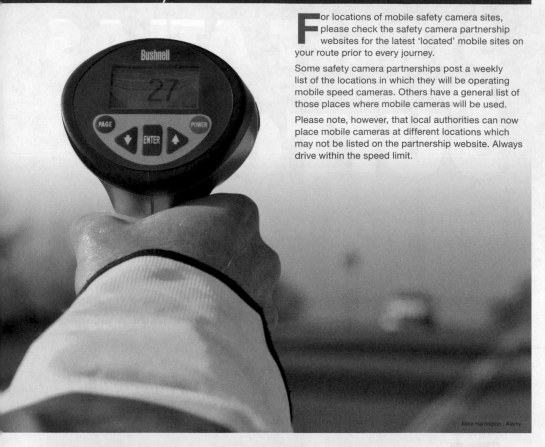

Mike Harrington / Alamy

For locations of mobile safety camera sites, please check the safety camera partnership websites for the latest 'located' mobile sites on your route prior to every journey.

Some safety camera partnerships post a weekly list of the locations in which they will be operating mobile speed cameras. Others have a general list of those places where mobile cameras will be used.

Please note, however, that local authorities can now place mobile cameras at different locations which may not be listed on the partnership website. Always drive within the speed limit.

Useful websites

Surrey Safety Camera Partnership
www.surrey-safecam.org

Sussex Safer Roads Partnership
www.sussexsaferroads.gov.uk

Kent and Medway Safety Camera Partnership
www.kmscp.org

London Safety Camera Partnership
www.lscp.org.uk

Hampshire and Isle of Wight Safer Roads Partnership
www.saferroadspartnership.co.uk

Further information
www.dvla.gov.uk

www.thinkroadsafety.gov.uk

www.dft.gov.uk

www.road-safe.org

Key to map symbols

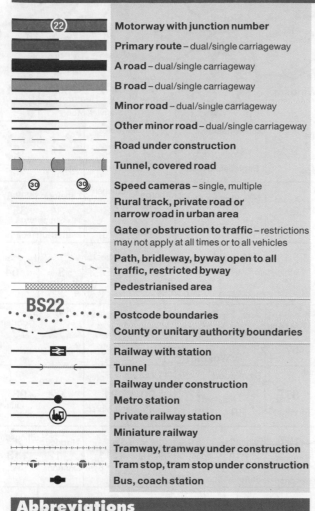

	Motorway with junction number
	Primary route – dual/single carriageway
	A road – dual/single carriageway
	B road – dual/single carriageway
	Minor road – dual/single carriageway
	Other minor road – dual/single carriageway
	Road under construction
	Tunnel, covered road
	Speed cameras – single, multiple
	Rural track, private road or narrow road in urban area
	Gate or obstruction to traffic – restrictions may not apply at all times or to all vehicles
	Path, bridleway, byway open to all traffic, restricted byway
	Pedestrianised area
BS22	Postcode boundaries
	County or unitary authority boundaries
	Railway with station
	Tunnel
	Railway under construction
	Metro station
	Private railway station
	Miniature railway
	Tramway, tramway under construction
	Tram stop, tram stop under construction
	Bus, coach station

◆	Ambulance station
◆	Coastguard station
◆	Fire station
◆	Police station
✚	Accident and Emergency entrance to hospital
H	Hospital
+	Place of worship
i	Information centre – open all year
P	Shopping centre, parking
P&R PO	Park and Ride, Post Office
Ⓧ	Camping site, caravan site
▶ ✕	Golf course, picnic site
Church ROMAN FORT	Non-Roman antiquity, Roman antiquity
Univ	Important buildings, schools, colleges, universities and hospitals
	Woods, built-up area
River Medway	Water name
	River, weir
	Stream
	Canal, lock, tunnel
	Water
	Tidal water
58 87 246	Adjoining page indicators and overlap bands – the colour of the arrow and band indicates the scale of the adjoining or overlapping page (see scales below)

The dark grey border on the inside edge of some pages indicates that the mapping does not continue onto the adjacent page

The small numbers around the edges of the maps identify the 1-kilometre National Grid lines

Enlarged maps only

	Railway or bus station building
	Place of interest
	Parkland

Abbreviations

Abbr	Full	Abbr	Full
Acad	Academy	Meml	Memorial
Allot Gdns	Allotments	Mon	Monument
Cemy	Cemetery	Mus	Museum
C Ctr	Civic centre	Obsy	Observatory
CH	Club house	Pal	Royal palace
Coll	College	PH	Public house
Crem	Crematorium	Recn Gd	Recreation ground
Ent	Enterprise	Resr	Reservoir
Ex H	Exhibition hall	Ret Pk	Retail park
Ind Est	Industrial Estate	Sch	School
IRB Sta	Inshore rescue boat station	Sh Ctr	Shopping centre
Inst	Institute	TH	Town hall / house
Ct	Law court	Trad Est	Trading estate
L Ctr	Leisure centre	Univ	University
LC	Level crossing	W Twr	Water tower
Liby	Library	Wks	Works
Mkt	Market	YH	Youth hostel

The map scale on the pages numbered in blue is 3½ inches to 1 mile
5.52 cm to 1 km • 1: 18 103

0	¼ mile	½ mile	¾ mile	1 mile

0	250m	500m	750m	1km

The map scale on the pages numbered in red is 7 inches to 1 mile
11.04 cm to 1 km • 1: 9051

0	220yds	440yds	660yds	½ mile

0	125m	250m	375m	500m

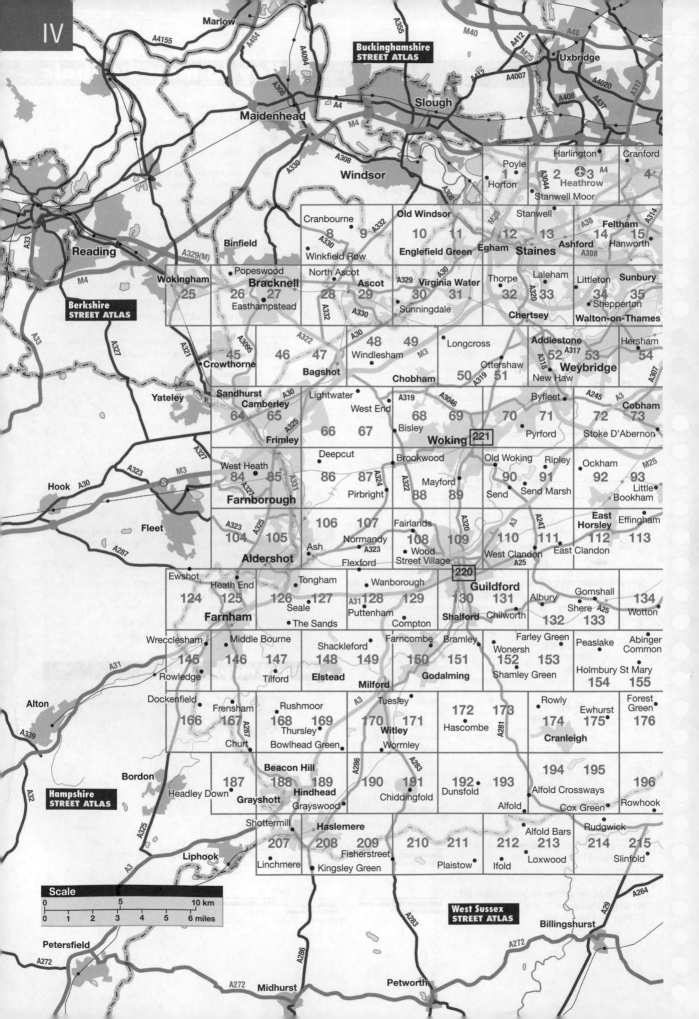

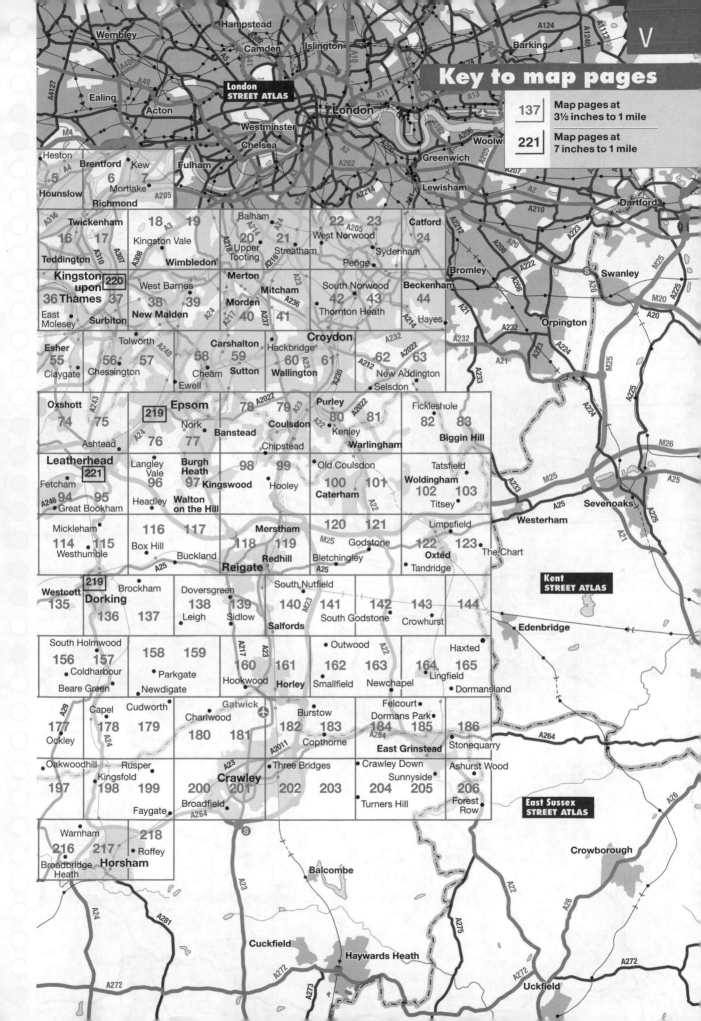

Key to map pages

137	Map pages at 3½ inches to 1 mile
221	Map pages at 7 inches to 1 mile

Wembley Hampstead Camden Islington Barking

London STREET ATLAS

Ealing Acton London Westminster Chelsea Woolwich Greenwich Lewisham Dartford

Heston Brentford Kew Fulham Hounslow Mortlake Richmond

Twickenham **16** **17** **18** **19** Balham **22** **23** Catford **24** Teddington Kingston Vale **20** Upper Tooting **21** Streatham West Norwood Sydenham Penge Bromley Swanley

Kingston upon **220** Thames **36** **37** West Barnes **38** **39** Merton Mitcham **42** **43** Beckenham **44** Orpington Morden **40** **41** Thornton Heath South Norwood Hayes

East Molesey Surbiton New Malden Croydon

Esher **55** **56** **57** Tolworth Carshalton **58** **59** Hackbridge **60** **61** **62** **63** Claygate Chessington Cheam Sutton Wallington New Addington Selsdon Ewell

Oxshott **74** **75** **219** Epsom Nork **78** **79** Purley **80** **81** Fickleshole **82** **83** Ashtead **76** **77** Banstead Coulsdon Kenley Warlingham Biggin Hill Chipstead

Leatherhead **221** Fetcham **94** **95** Langley Vale **96** Burgh Heath **97** Kingswood **98** **99** Old Coulsdon **100** **101** Woldingham **102** **103** Tatsfield Great Bookham Headley Walton on the Hill Hooley Caterham Titsey

Mickleham **114** **115** **116** **117** Merstham **120** **121** Limpsfield Westhumble Box Hill **118** **119** Godstone **122** **123** Buckland Redhill Bletchingley Oxted The Chart Reigate Tandridge

Kent STREET ATLAS

Westcott **135** Brockham Doversgreen **138** **139** South Nutfield **140** **141** **142** **143** **144** Dorking **136** **137** Leigh Sidlow South Godstone Crowhurst Salfords Edenbridge

South Holmwood **156** **157** **158** **159** Outwood Haxted Coldharbour **160** **161** **162** **163** **164** **165** Beare Green Hookwood Horley Smallfield Newchapel Lingfield Dormansland

Capel Cudworth Gatwick Burstow Felcourt Dormans Park **177** **178** **179** Charlwood **182** **183** **184** **185** **186** Ockley **180** **181** Copthorne East Grinstead Stonequarry

Oakwoodhill Rusper Three Bridges Crawley Down Ashurst Wood Kingsfold Crawley Sunnyside **197** **198** **199** **200** **201** **202** **203** **204** **205** **206** Faygate Broadfield Turners Hill Forest Row

East Sussex STREET ATLAS

Warnham **218** Roffey **216** **217** Horsham Crowborough Broadbridge Heath

Balcombe

Cuckfield Haywards Heath Uckfield

Route planning

Major administrative and Postcode boundaries

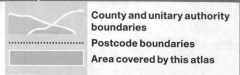

County and unitary authority boundaries

Postcode boundaries

Area covered by this atlas

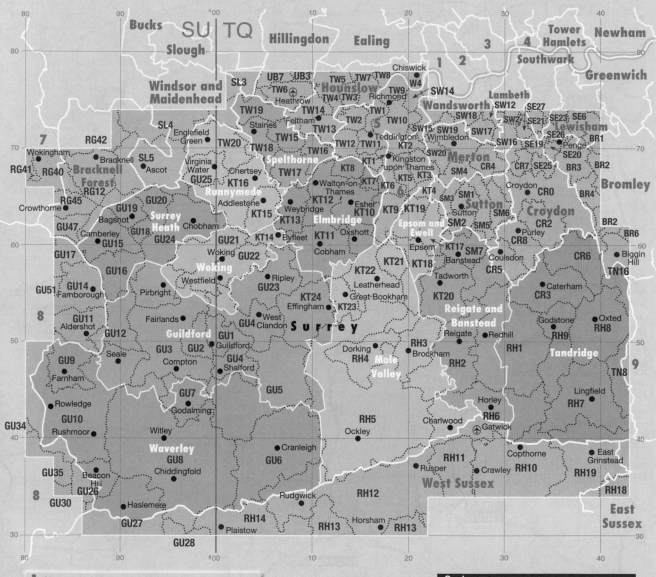

1 Hammersmith and Fulham
2 Royal Borough of Kensington and Chelsea
3 City of Westminster
4 City of London
5 Richmond upon Thames
6 Kingston upon Thames
7 Wokingham
8 Hampshire
9 Kent

Scale

0   5   10   15 km

0   5   10 miles

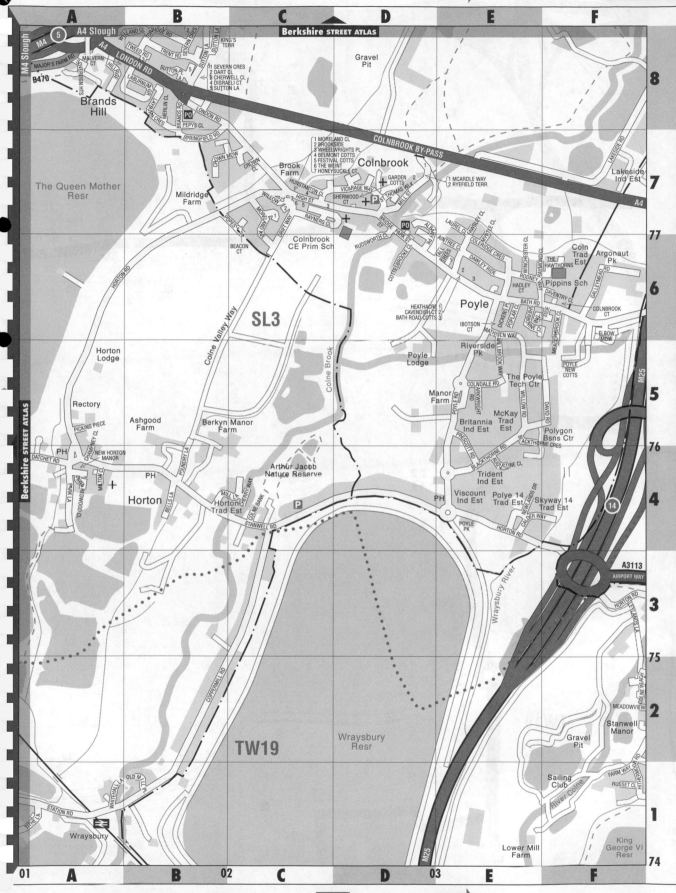

Berkshire STREET ATLAS

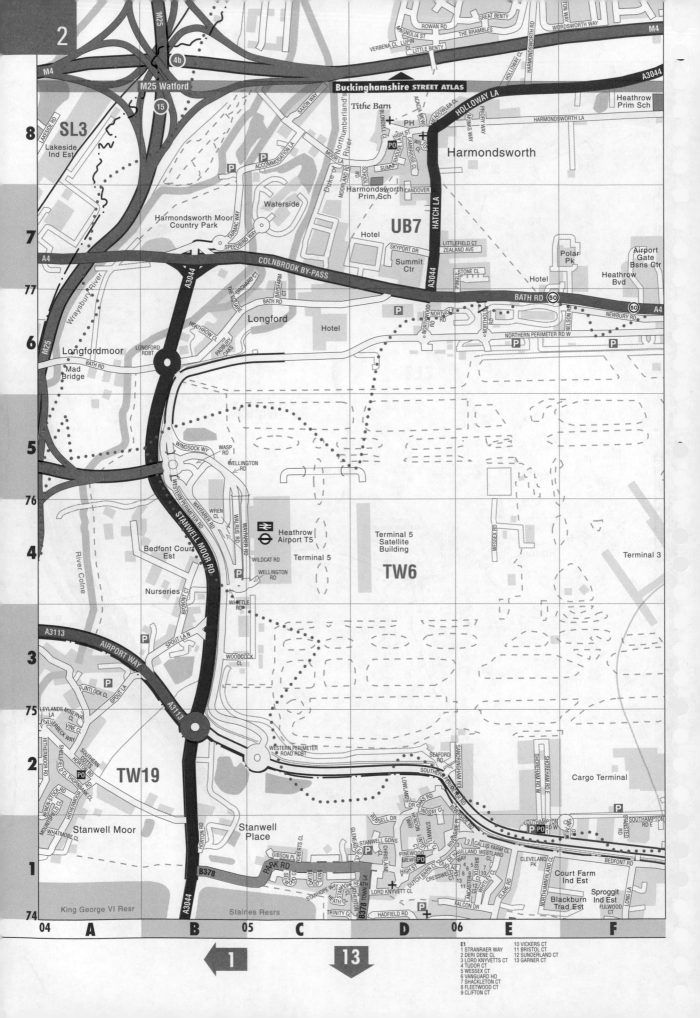

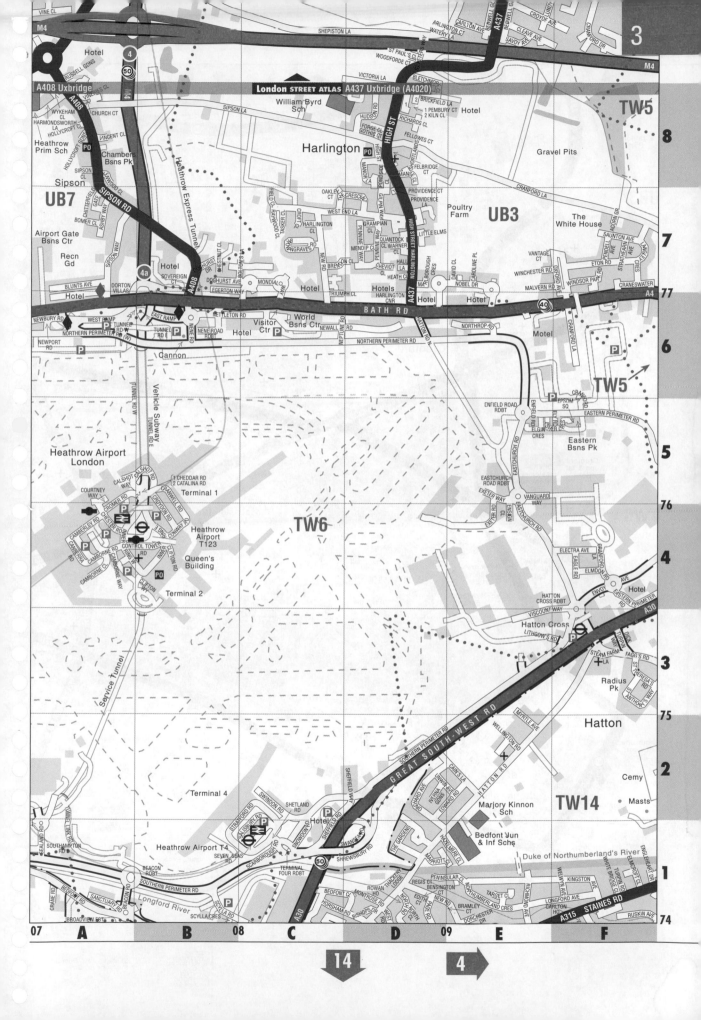

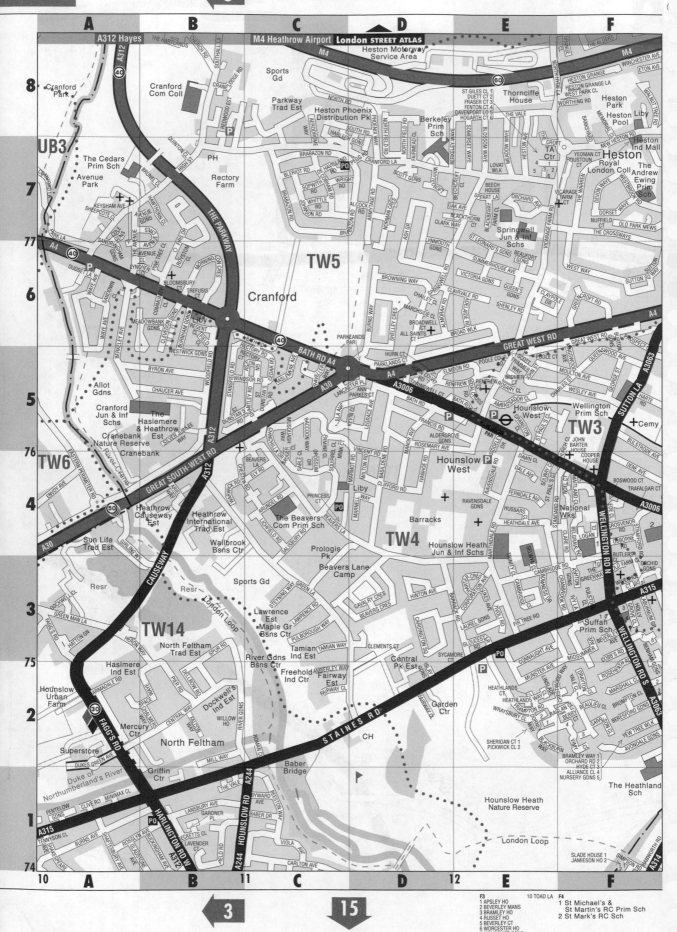

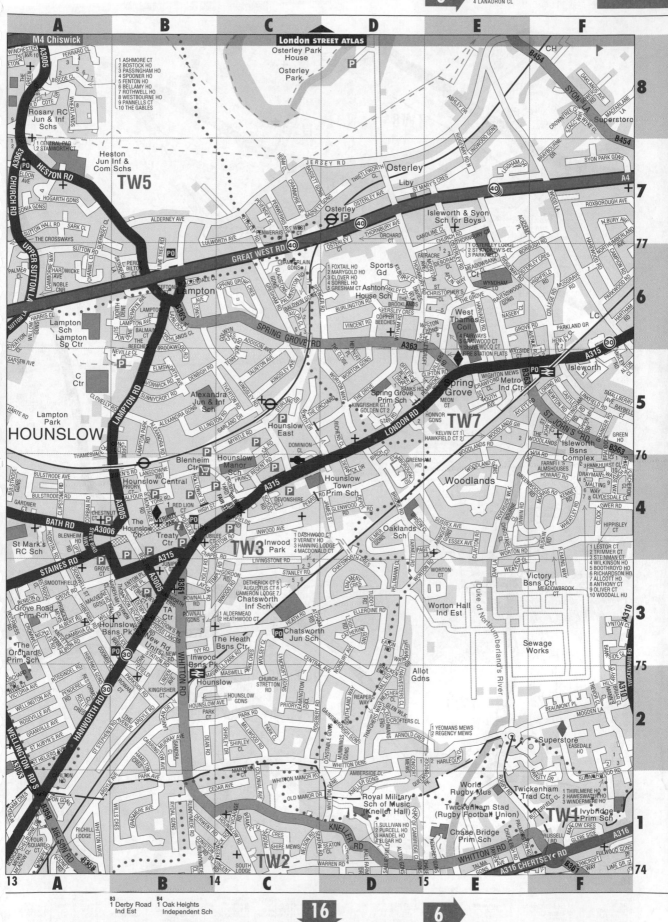

6

F5
1 OVERTON CL
2 THURZA CT
3 PRIMROSE PL
4 LANADRON CL

F6
1 NORTHUMBERLAND AVE
2 BEECHEN CLIFF WAY

5

B3
1 Derby Road
Ind Est

B4
1 Oak Heights
Independent Sch

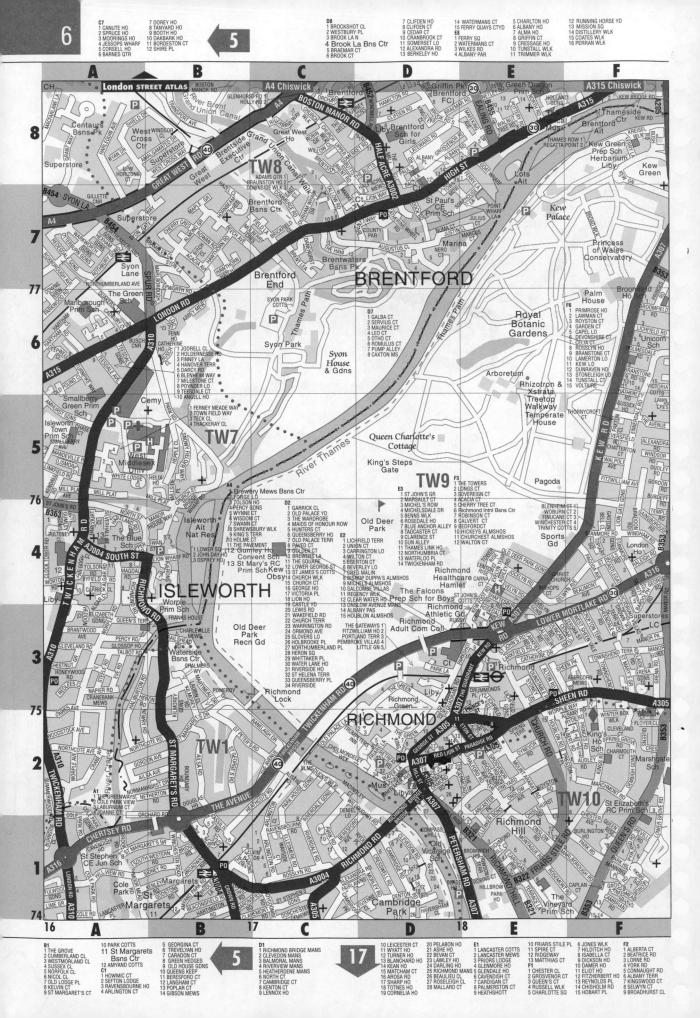

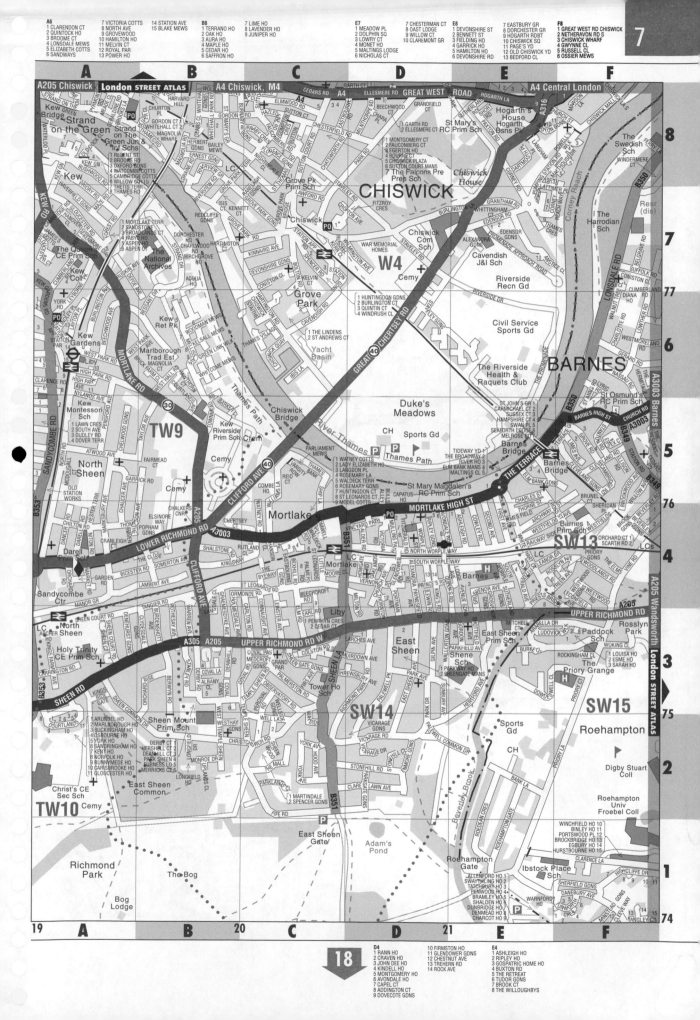

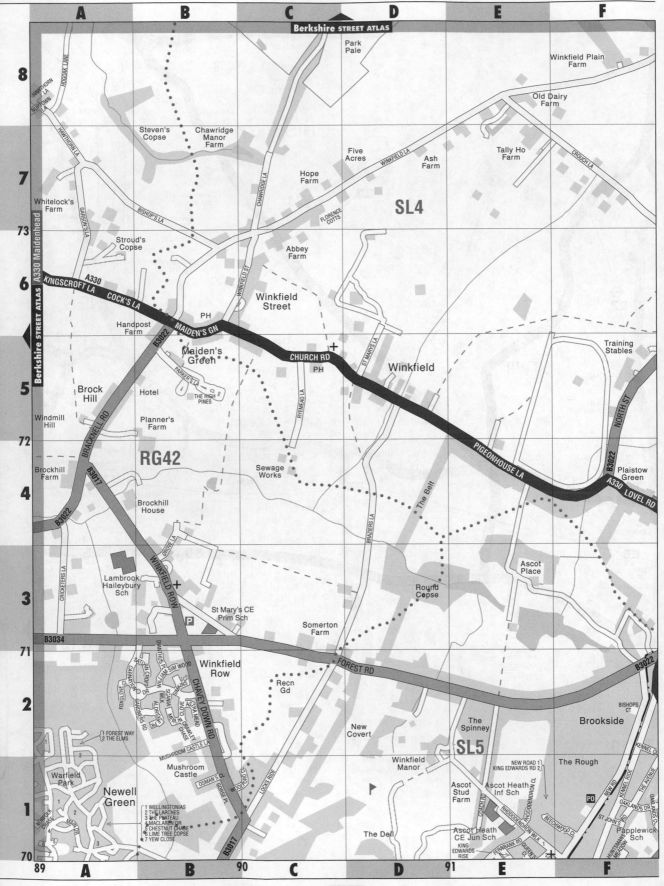

Berkshire STREET ATLAS

A B C D E F

8
7
73
6
5
72
4
71
3
2
1
70

89 A B 90 C D 91 E F

Berkshire STREET ATLAS

A330 Maidenhead

HAWTHORN LA
NUPTOWN LA
HOGOAK LANE
Park Pale
Winkfield Plain Farm
Old Dairy Farm
Steven's Copse
Chawridge Manor Farm
Five Acres
Winkfield La
Ash Farm
Tally Ho Farm
CROUCH LA
Hope Farm
SL4
HAWTHORN LA
GARSON'S LA
BISHOP'S LA
CHAWRIDGE LA
WINKFIELD ST
Whitelock's Farm
Stroud's Copse
Abbey Farm
FLORENCE COTTS
A330
KINGSCROFT LA
COCK'S LA
Handpost Farm
MAIDEN'S GN
Winkfield Street
PH
Training Stables
Maiden's Green
CHURCH RD
PH
ST MARY'S LA
Winkfield
Brock Hill
Hotel
PARKER'S LA
THE HIGH PINES
RYEMEAD LA
Windmill Hill
Planner's Farm
BRACKNELL RD
B3017
B3022
RG42
Brockhill Farm
Sewage Works
PIGEONHOUSE LA
B3022
Plaistow Green
A330 LOVEL RD
NORTH ST
Brockhill House
GROVE LA
The Belt
BRAZIERS LA
Ascot Place
CRICKETERS LA
Lambrook Haileybury Sch
WINKFIELD ROW
Round Copse
St Mary's CE Prim Sch
P
Somerton Farm
B3034
FOREST RD
B3022
Winkfield Row
CHAVEY DOWN RD
Recn Gd
BISHOPS CT
The Spinney
Brookside
CARNATION DR
DIANTHUS PL
SATURN CROFT
SIM WOOD
GARDNERS RD
SCANIA WLK
ALDRICH CT
MERLIN CHASE
CRAWLEY DR
FRAMEAD
New Covert
SL5
KENNEL CL
New Road
KING EDWARDS RD
The Rough
1 FOREST WAY
2 THE ELMS
FLYDYKE
MUSHROOM CASTLE LA
Winkfield Manor
Ascot Heath Inf Sch
RHODODENDRON WLK
RHODODENDRON CL
BEECHWOOD CL
NEW RD
THE AVENUE
Warfield Park
Mushroom Castle
OSMAN'S CL
GORSE PL
WOOD FORD CT
LOCKS RIDE
Ascot Stud Farm
COACH RD
PO
OAKLANDS CL
KENNEL RIDE
Newell Green
NORFOLK CHASE
MJR DR
1 WELLINGTONIAS
2 THE LARCHES
3 THE PLATEAU
4 MACLAREN DR
5 CHESTNUT CHASE
6 LIME TREE COPSE
7 YEW CLOSE
B3017
The Dell
Ascot Heath CE Jun Sch
KING EDWARDS RISE
FERNBANK RD
QUEEN'S
ST JOHN'S RD
HUNTSMANS MEADOW
Papplewick Sch

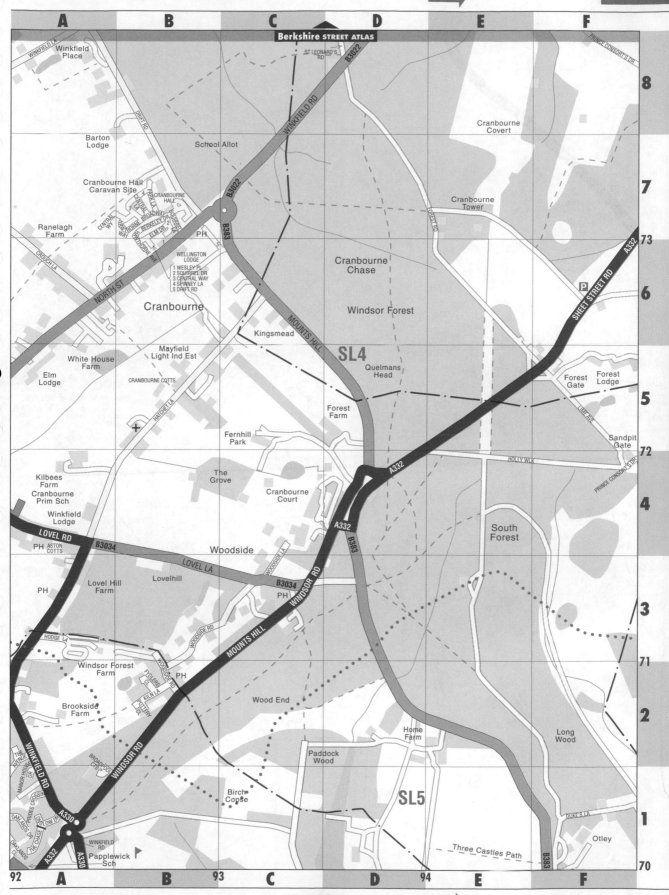

Berkshire STREET ATLAS

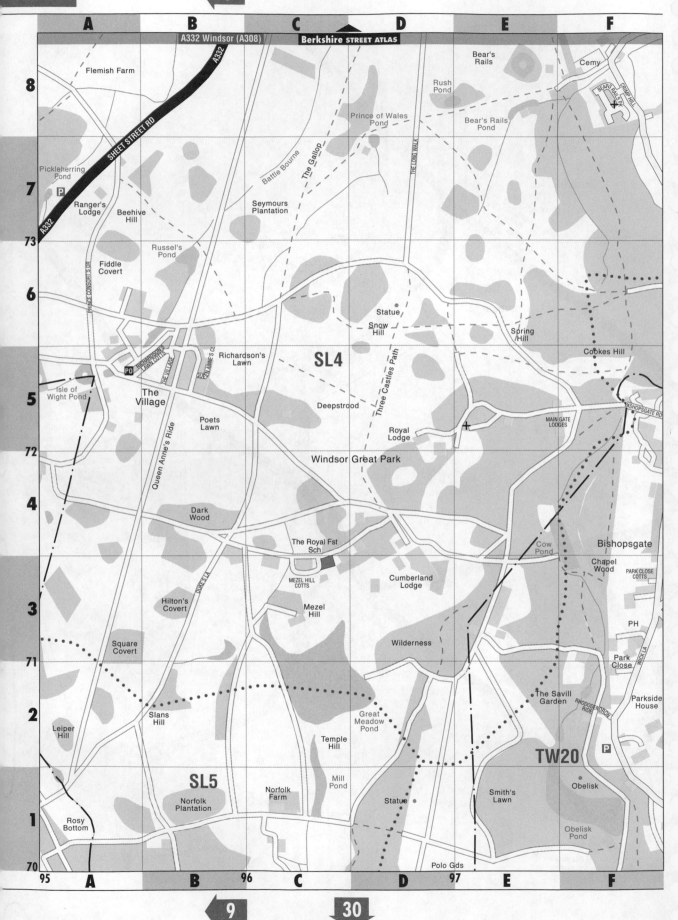

A332 Windsor (A308)
Berkshire STREET ATLAS

A **B** **C** **D** **E** **F**

8

Flemish Farm

Bear's
Rails

Cemy

Rush
Pond

Bear's Rails
Pond

Prince of Wales
Pond

SHEET STREET RD

7

Pickleherring Pond

P

A332

Ranger's
Lodge

Beehive
Hill

Russel's
Pond

Battle Bourne

The Gallop

The Long Walk

73

6

PRINCE CONSORT'S DR

Fiddle
Covert

Seymours
Plantation

Statue

Snow
Hill

Spring
Hill

Cookes Hill

BISHOPSGATE RD

Richardson's
Lawn

SL4

Three Castles Path

RICHARDSON'S LAWN COTTS

PO

THE VILLAGE

QUEEN ANNE'S CL

5

Isle of
Wight Pond

The Village

Poets
Lawn

Deepstrood

Royal
Lodge

MAIN GATE
LODGES

72

Queen Anne's Ride

Windsor Great Park

4

Dark
Wood

Cow
Pond

Bishopsgate

Chapel
Wood

PARK CLOSE
COTTS

DUKES LA

The Royal Fst
Sch

MEZEL HILL
COTTS

Cumberland
Lodge

3

Hilton's
Covert

Mezel
Hill

Wilderness

PH

Park
Close

WICK LA

Square
Covert

RHODODENDRON RIDE

71

2

Leiper
Hill

Slans
Hill

Great
Meadow
Pond

The Savill
Garden

Parkside
House

TW20

P

Temple
Hill

SL5

Mill
Pond

Obelisk

1

Rosy
Bottom

Norfolk
Plantation

Norfolk
Farm

Statue

Smith's
Lawn

Obelisk
Pond

70

Polo Gds

A **B** **C** **D** **E** **F**

12

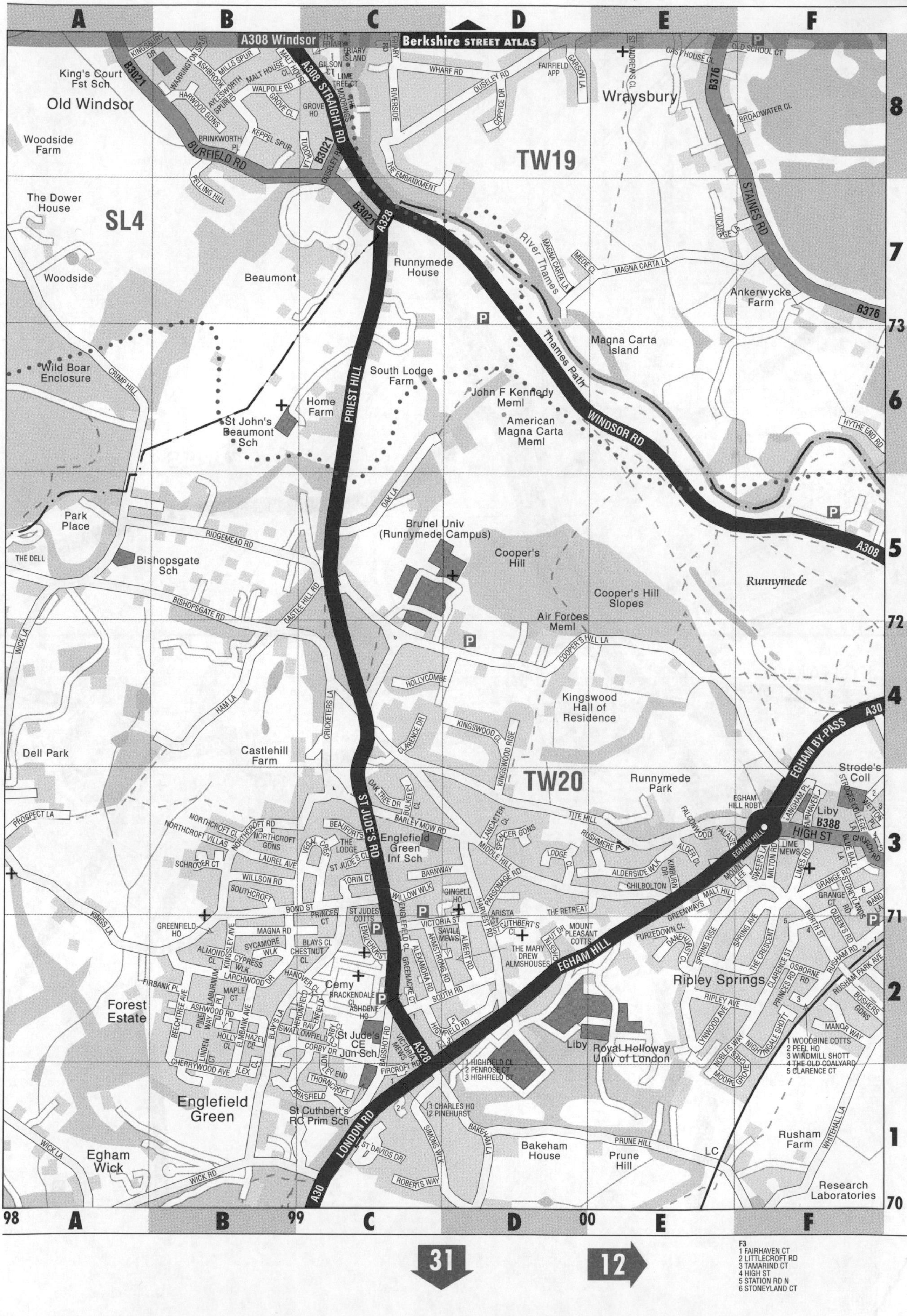
A
B
C
D
E
F
A308 Windsor
Berkshire STREET ATLAS
King's Court Fst Sch
Old Windsor
Woodside Farm
The Dower House
SL4
Woodside
Beaumont
Runnymede House
Wraysbury
TW19
River Thames
Thames Path
Magna Carta Island
Ankerwycke Farm
Wild Boar Enclosure
South Lodge Farm
Home Farm
St John's Beaumont Sch
John F Kennedy Meml
American Magna Carta Meml
PRIEST HILL
WINDSOR RD
A308 STRAIGHT RD
BURFIELD RD
STAINES RD
B3021
A328
B376
A308
Park Place
Bishopsgate Sch
RIDGEMEAD RD
BISHOPSGATE RD
Brunel Univ (Runnymede Campus)
Cooper's Hill
Cooper's Hill Slopes
Air Forces Meml
Runnymede
Kingswood Hall of Residence
Dell Park
Castlehill Farm
TW20
Runnymede Park
Strode's Coll
EGHAM BY-PASS
HIGH ST
Liby
Englefield Green Inf Sch
ST JUDE'S RD
EGHAM HILL
The Mary Drew Almshouses
Ripley Springs
Forest Estate
Cemy
St Jude's CE Jun Sch
Royal Holloway Univ of London
Englefield Green
St Cuthbert's RC Prim Sch
LONDON RD
A30
Egham Wick
Bakeham House
Prune Hill
Rusham Farm
Research Laboratories
1 WOODBINE COTTS
2 PEEL HO
3 WINDMILL SHOTT
4 THE OLD COALYARD
5 CLARENCE CT
1 HIGHFIELD CL
2 PENROSE CT
3 HIGHFIELD CT
1 CHARLES HO
2 PINEHURST
8
7
73
6
5
72
4
3
71
2
1
70
98
99
00

31

12

F3
1 FAIRHAVEN CT
2 LITTLECROFT RD
3 TAMARIND CT
4 HIGH ST
5 STATION RD N
6 STONEYLAND CT

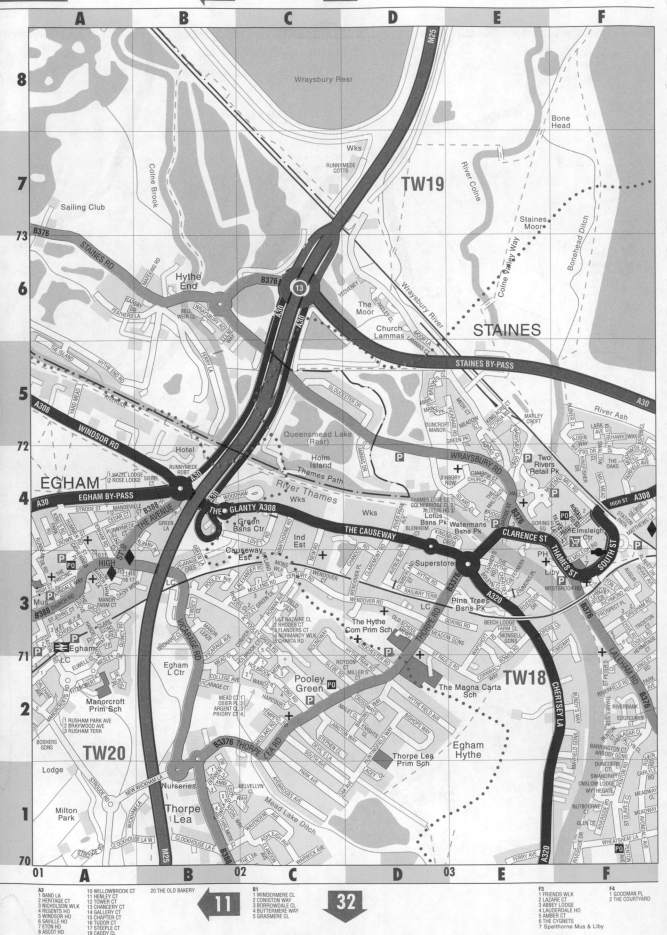

A3
1 BAND LA
2 HERITAGE CT
3 NICHOLSON WLK
4 REGENTS HO
5 WINDSOR HO
6 SAVILLE HO
7 ETON HO
8 ASCOT HO
9 MANOR FARM
10 WILLOWBROOK CT
11 HENLEY CT
12 TOWER CT
13 CHANCERY CT
14 GALLERY CT
15 CHAPTER CT
16 TUDOR CT
17 STEEPLE CT
18 CADDY CL
19 TUDOR CT
20 THE OLD BAKERY

B1
1 WINDERMERE CL
2 CONISTON WAY
3 BORROWDALE WAY
4 BUTTERMERE WAY
5 GRASMERE CL

F3
1 FRIENDS WLK
2 LAZARE CT
3 ABBEY LODGE
4 LAUDERDALE HO
5 AMBER CL
6 THE CYGNETS
7 Spelthorne Mus & Liby

F4
1 GOODMAN PL
2 THE COURTYARD

11

32

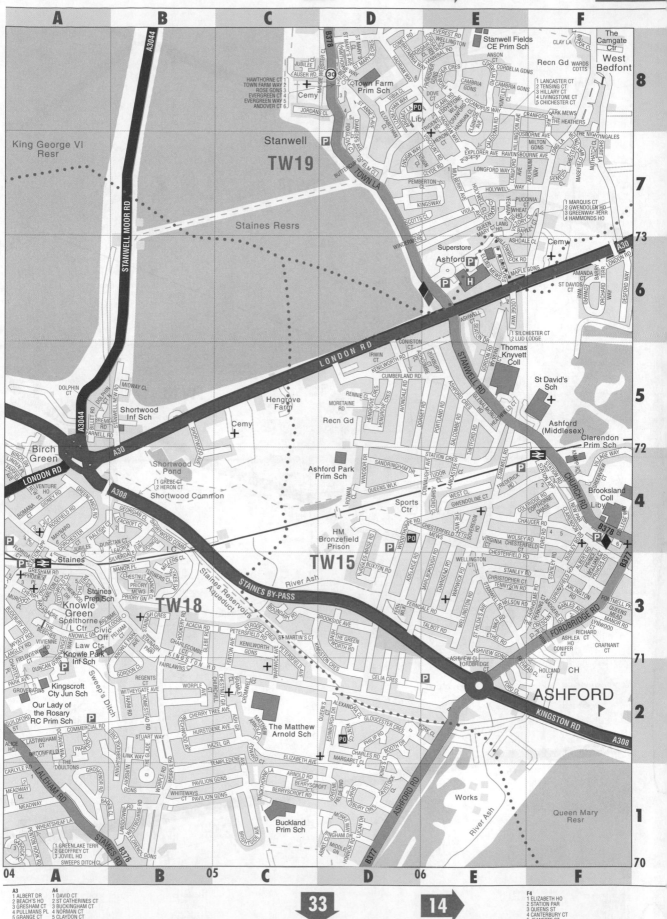

A3
1 ALBERT DR
2 BEACH'S HO
3 GRESHAM CT
4 PULLMANS PL
5 GRANGE CT

A4
1 DAVID CT
2 ST CATHERINES CT
3 BUCKINGHAM CT
4 NORMAN CT
5 CLAYDON CT
6 GREENLANDS CT

F4
1 ELIZABETH HO
2 STATION PAR
3 QUEENS ST
4 CANTERBURY CT
5 JEANETTE CT
6 CHURCH PAR

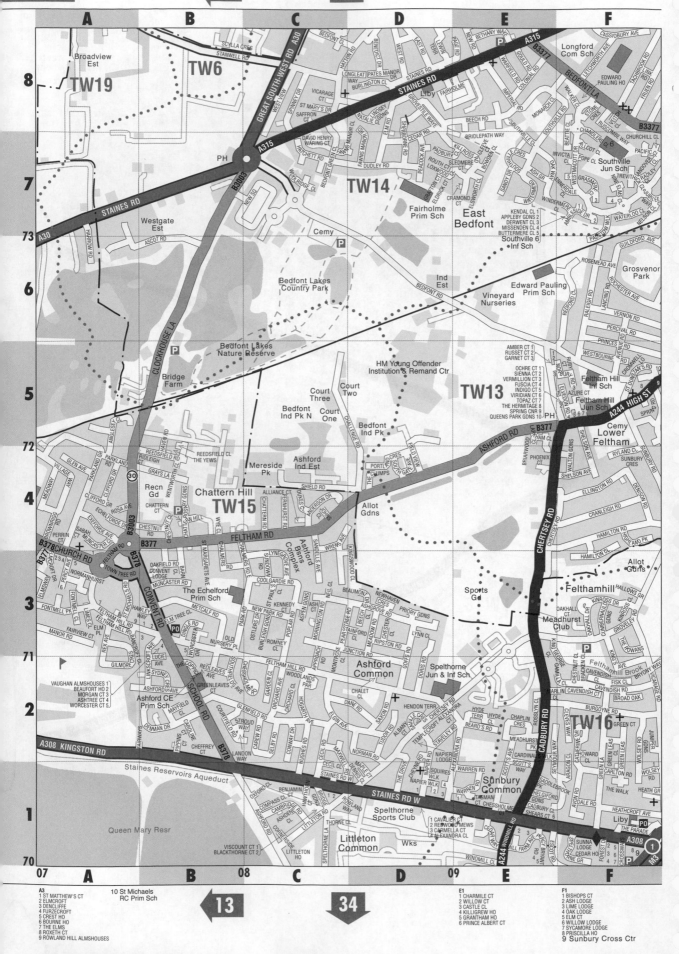

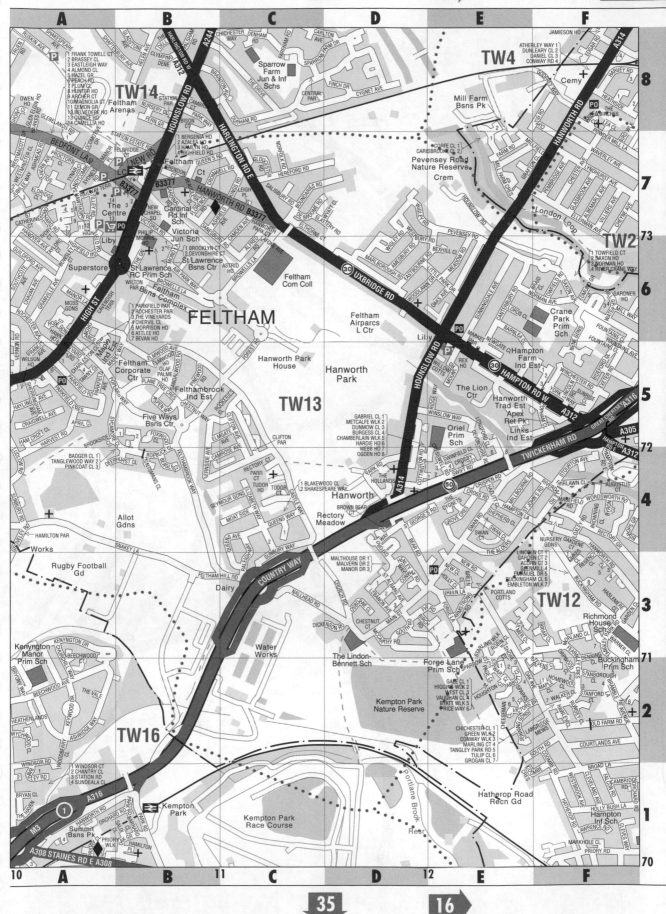

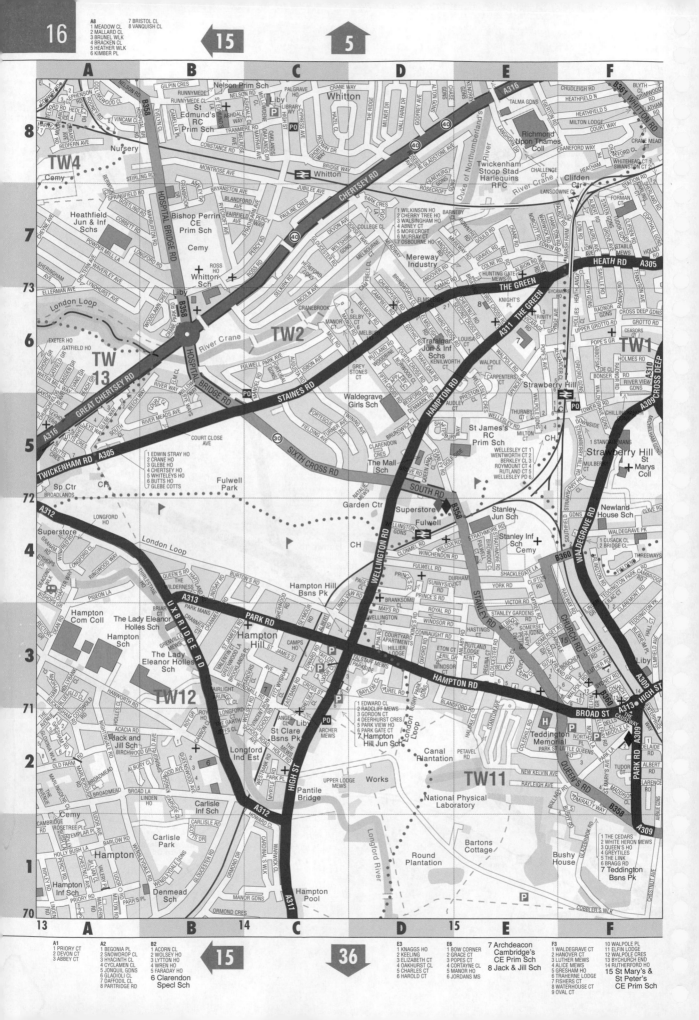

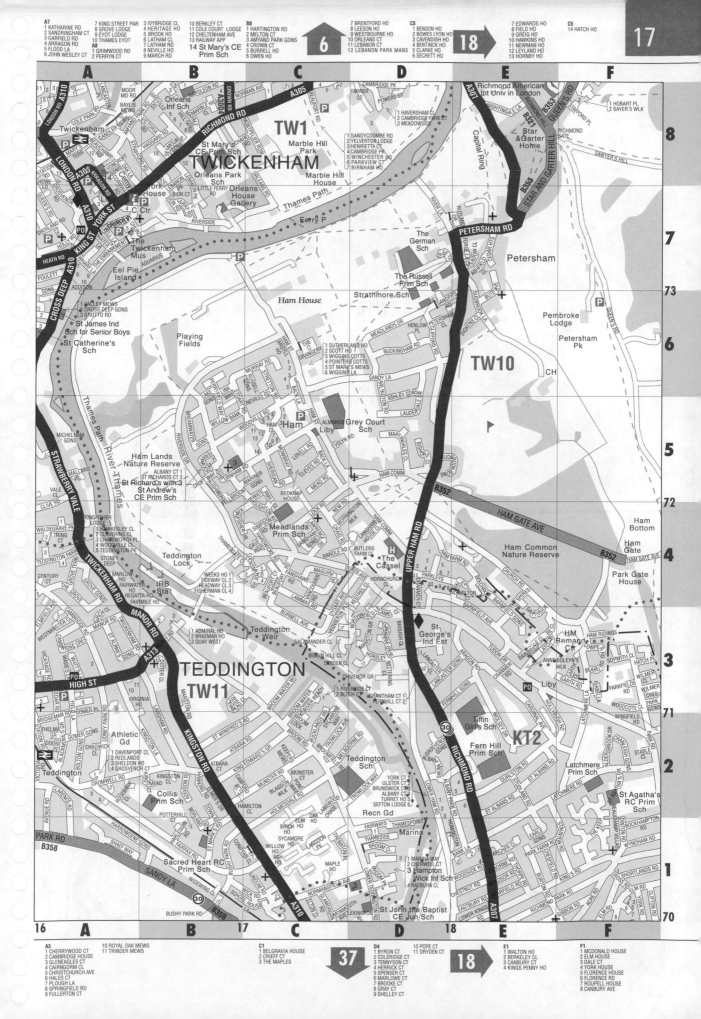

A1
1 QUEEN'S CT
2 ST GEORGES RD
3 PARK ROAD HO
4 DAGMAR RD
5 TAPPING CL
6 ARTHUR RD
7 BOROUGH RD
8 BELVEDERE CT
9 BRAYWICK CT

10 DEAN CT
11 ROWAN CT
12 RICHMOND CT
13 SUNNINGDALE CT
14 HAWKER CT
15 CROMWELL CT
16 KINGS CT

18 St Paul's CE
Jun Sch
19 Park Hill Sch

17 Alexandra
Inf Sch

B1
1 BRAMLEY HO
2 ABINGER HO
3 THURSLEY HO
4 RIDGE HO
5 THE CLONE
6 MOUNT CT
7 HILLSIDE CT
8 HILL CT
9 ROYAL CT

B2
1 GODSTONE HO
2 HAMBLEDON HO
3 KINGSWOOD HO
4 LEIGH HO
5 MILTON HO
6 NEWDIGATE HO
7 FARLEIGH HO

10 LAKESIDE
11 HIGH ASHTON

8 OCKLEY HO
9 EFFINGHAM HO
10 DUNSFOLD HO
11 PIRBRIGHT HO
12 CLANDON HO
13 RIPLEY HO

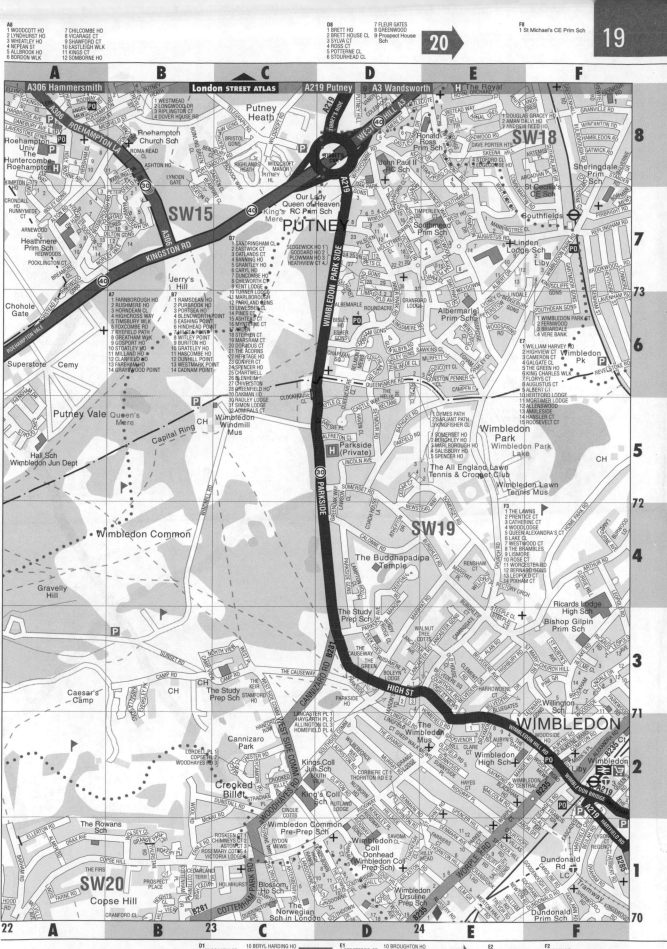

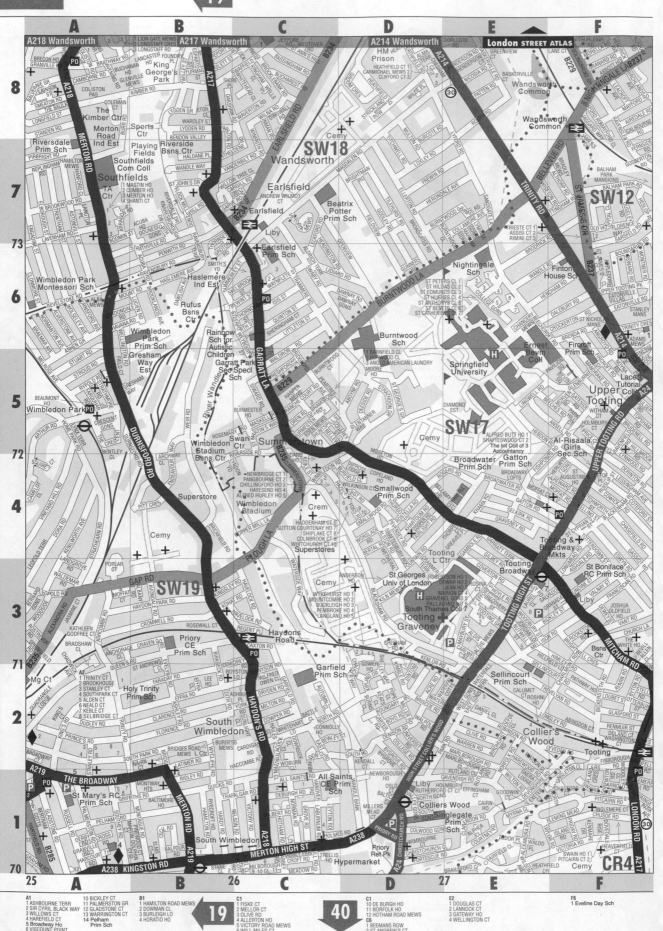

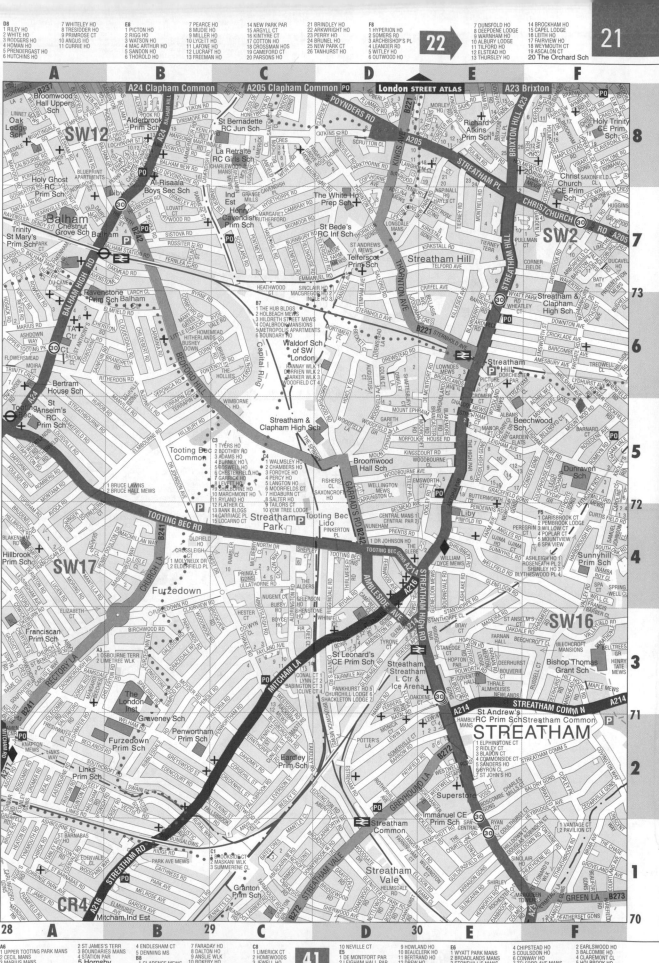

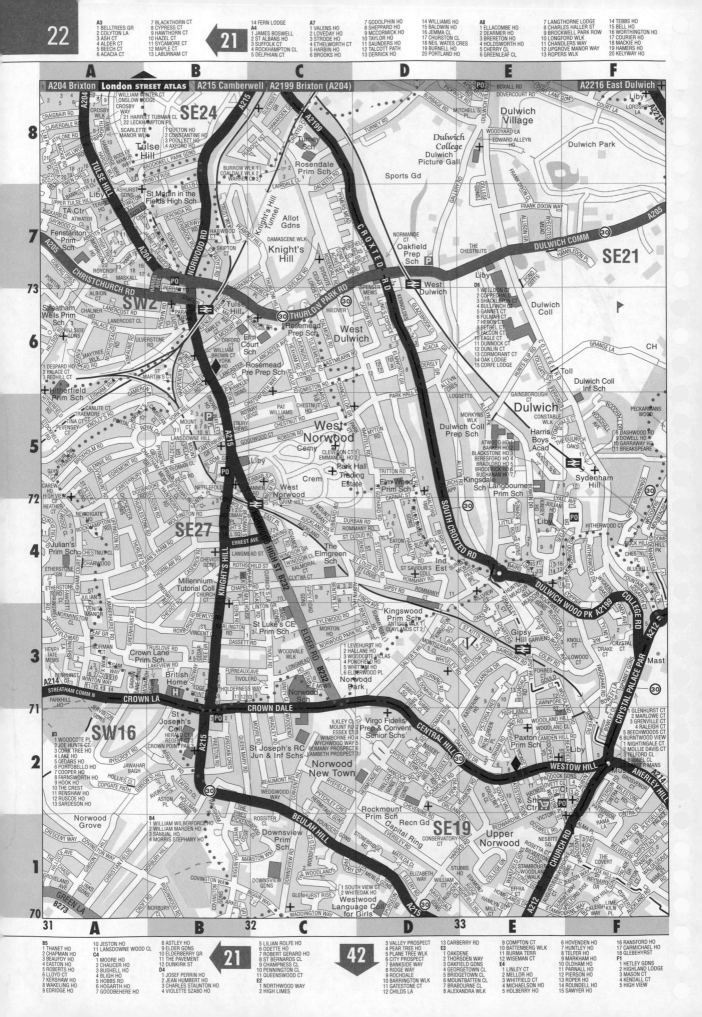

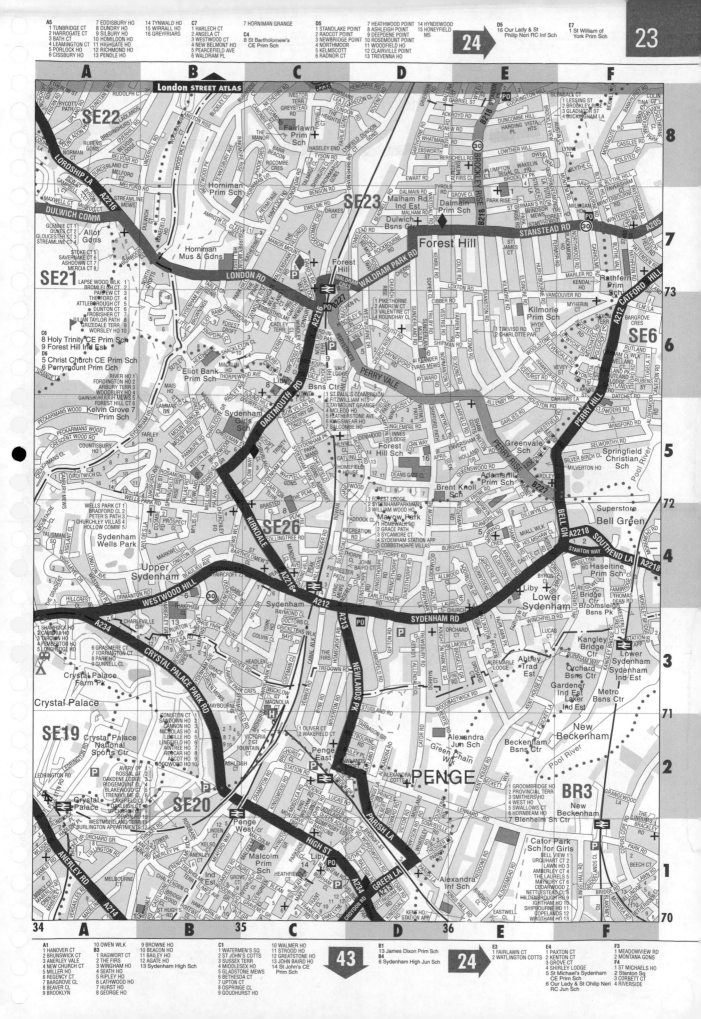

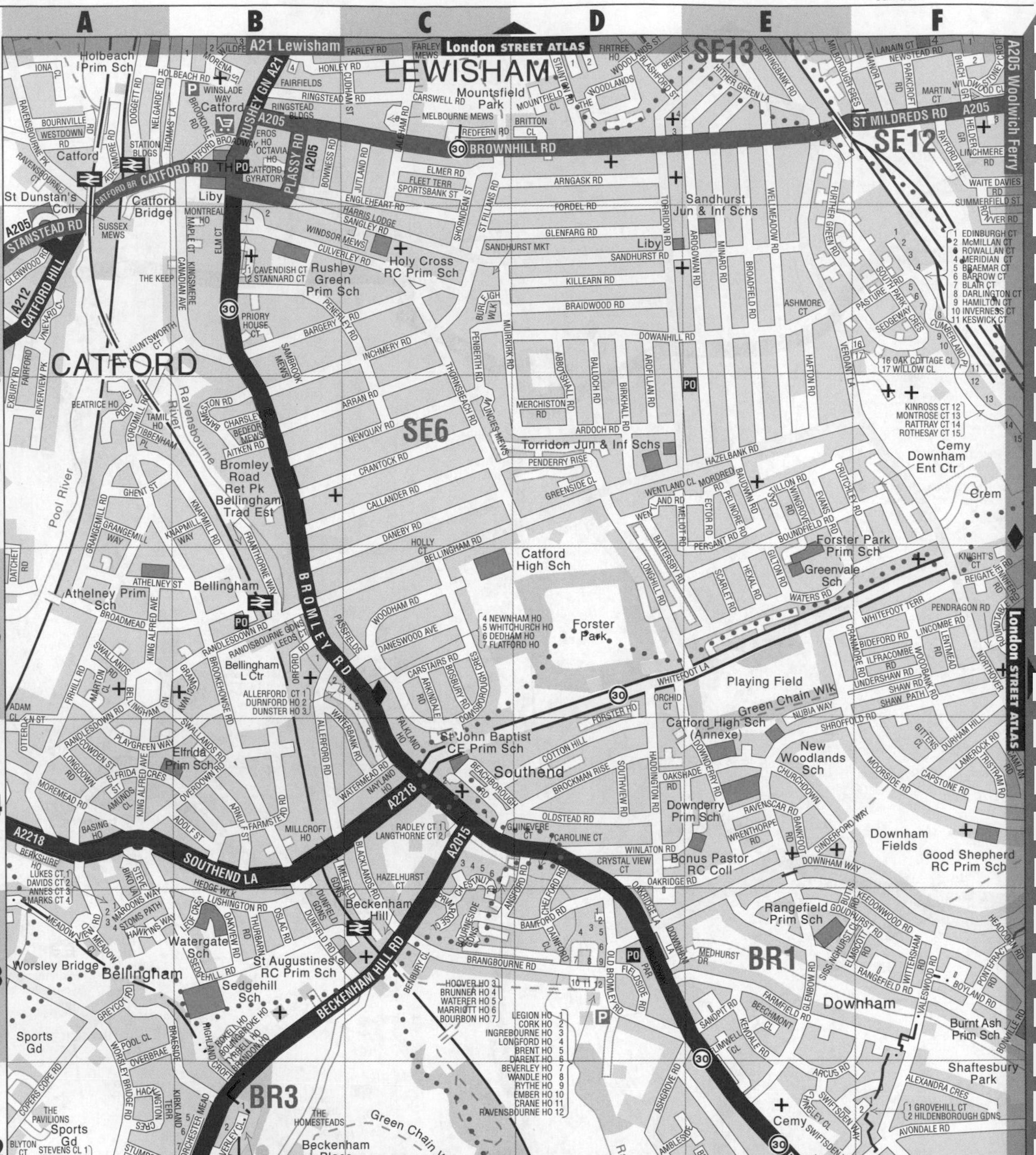

London STREET ATLAS

LEWISHAM

CATFORD

SE6

SE13

SE12

BR1

BR3

BR2

Downham

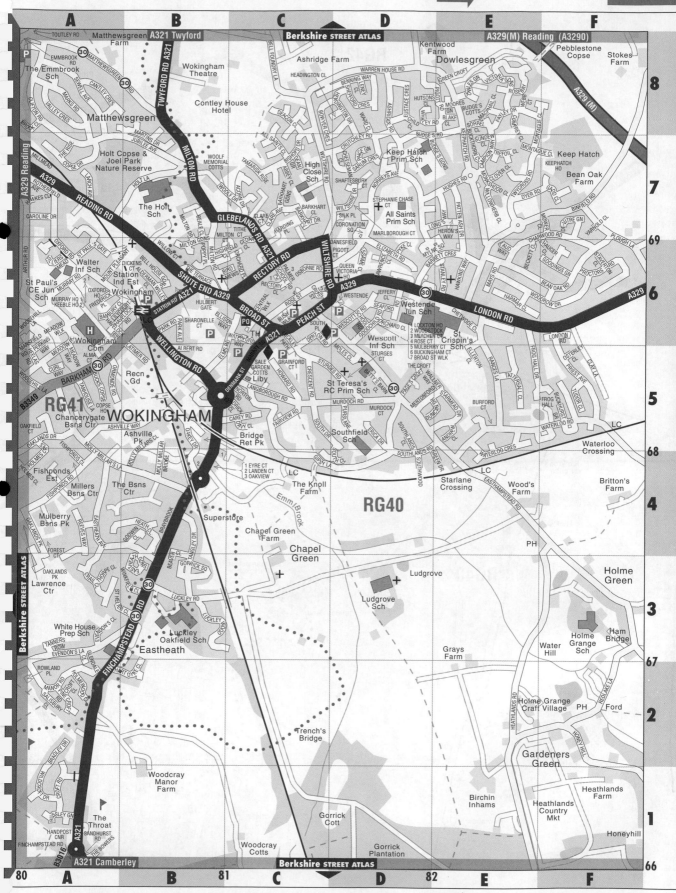

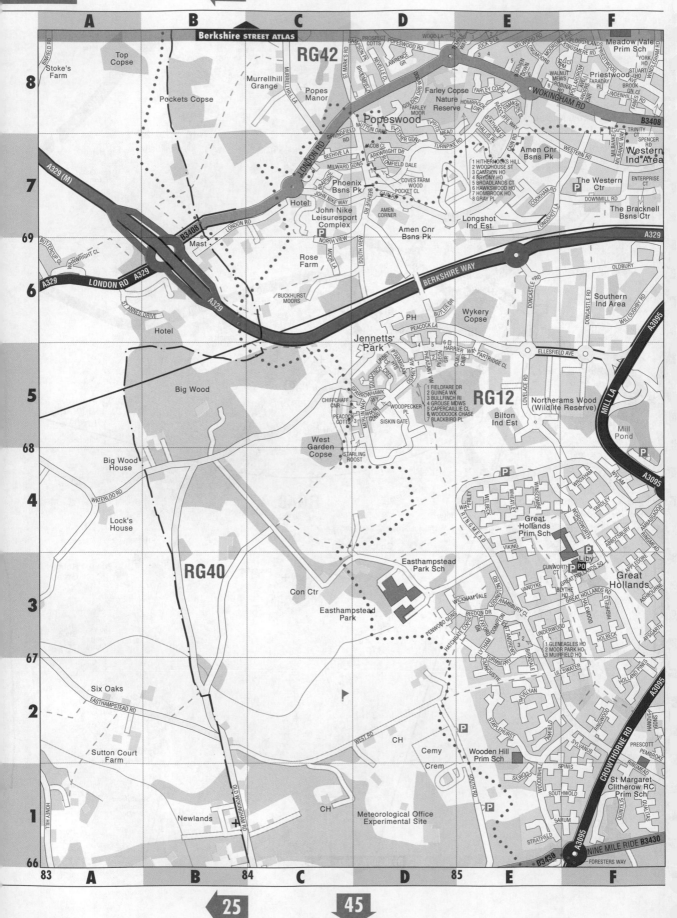

Berkshire STREET ATLAS

RG42

RG12

RG40

Stoke's Farm

Top Copse

Pockets Copse

Murrellhill Grange

Popes Manor

Popeswood

Farley Copse Nature Reserve

Wokingham Rd

Meadow Vale Prim Sch

Priestwood

Western Ind Area

Amen Cnr Bsns Pk

The Western Ctr

Enterprise Ct

The Bracknell Bsns Ctr

1 HITHERHOOKS HILL
2 WOODHOUSE ST
3 CAMPION HO
4 BRYONY HO
5 BROADLANDS CT
6 HAWKSWOOD HO
7 HOMBROOK HO
8 GRAY PL

Phoenix Bsns Pk

Hotel

John Nike Leisuresport Complex

Amen Corner

Amen Cnr Bsns Pk

Longshot Ind Est

Mast

North View

Rose Farm

Buckhurst Moors

Berkshire Way

Southern Ind Area

Oldbury

Hotel

Wykery Copse

PH

Peacock La

Jennetts Park

Butler Dr

Ellesfield Ave

Northerams Wood (Wildlife Reserve)

Mill Pond

Mill La

Big Wood

1 FIELDFARE DR
2 GUINEA WK
3 BULLFINCH RI
4 GROUSE MDWS
5 CAPERCAILLIE CL
6 WOODCOCK CHASE
7 BLACKBIRD PL

CHIFFCHAFF CNR

PEACOCK COTTS

Sparrowhawk

Woodpecker Pl

Siskin Gate

West Garden Copse

Starling Roost

Bilton Ind Est

Big Wood House

Ringmead

Great Hollands Prim Sch

Liby
PO

Great Hollands

Lock's House

Waterloo Rd

Viking

Easthampstead Park Sch

Con Ctr

Easthampstead Park

Wickham Vale

1 GLENEAGLES HO
2 MOOR PARK HO
3 MUIRFIELD HO

Six Oaks

EASTHAMPSTEAD RD

Sutton Court Farm

CH

West Rd

Cemy

Crem

Wooden Hill Prim Sch

St Margaret Clitherow RC Prim Sch

Newlands

CH

South Rd

Meteorological Office Experimental Site

NINE MILE RIDE B3430

FORESTERS WAY

Crowthorne Rd

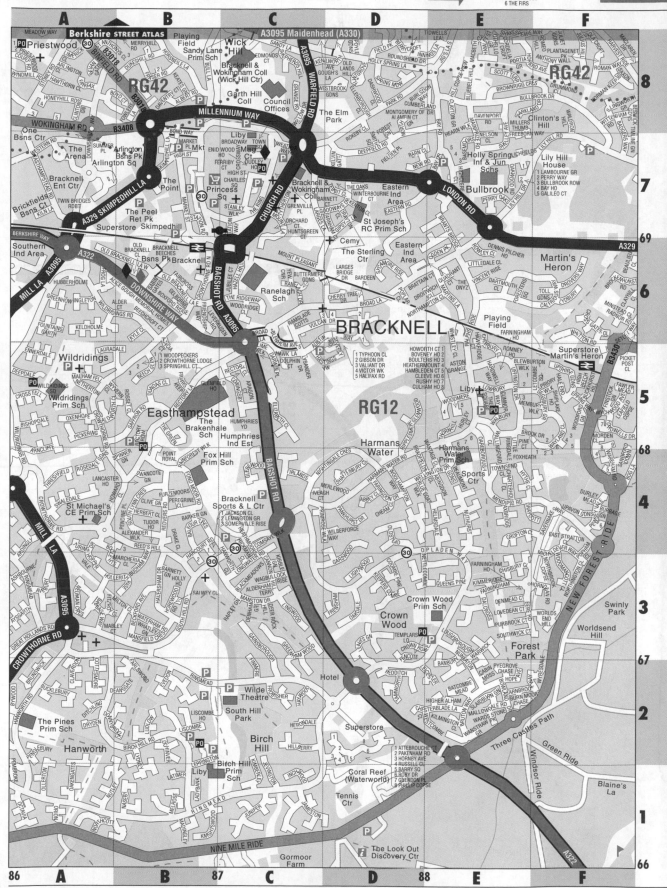

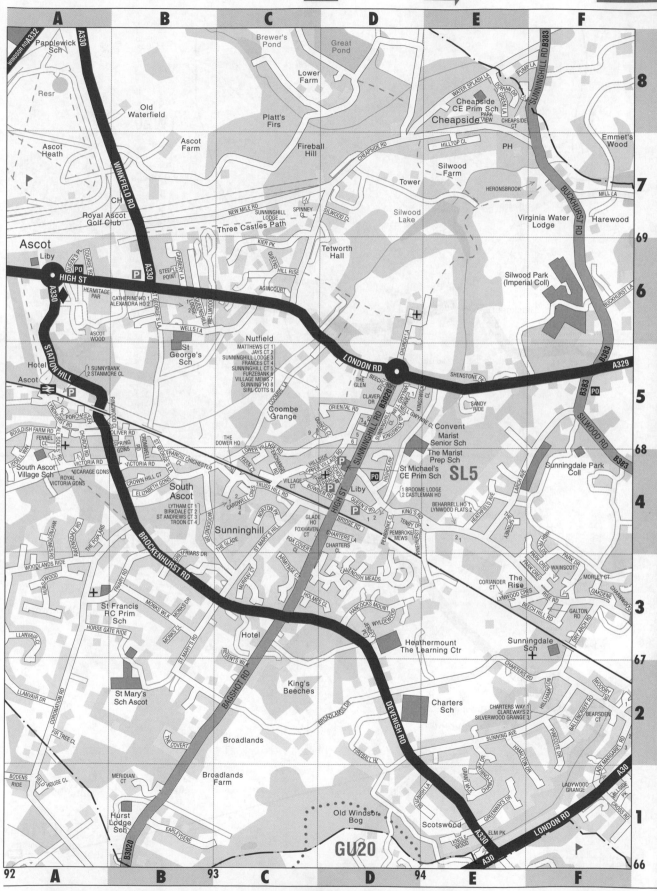

A B C D E F

8

7

69

6

5

68

4

3

67

2

1

66

Papplewick Sch
WINDSOR RD A332
A330
Old Waterfield
Resr
Ascot Heath
Ascot Farm
Brewer's Pond
Great Pond
Lower Farm
Platt's Firs
Fireball Hill
Water Splash La
Cheapside CE Prim Sch
Cheapside
PUMP LA
GREEN LA
SUNNINGHILL RD B383
PARK VIEW
CHEAPSIDE CT
HILLTOP CL
PH
Silwood Farm
Tower
HERONSBROOK
Emmet's Wood
MILL LA
Virginia Water Lodge
Harewood
BUCKHURST RD
CH
WINKFIELD RD
Royal Ascot Golf Club
NEW MILE RD
Three Castles Path
SUNNINGHILL LODGE
SPINNEY CL
SILWOOD CL
KIER PK
QUEENS HILL RISE
Tetworth Hall
Silwood Lake
Silwood Park (Imperial Coll)
BUCKHURST LA
B383
A329
Ascot
Liby
PO
HIGH ST
A330
QUEEN'S PL
COURSE RD
CARBERY LA
ST GEORGE'S LA
STEEPLE POINT
AGINCOURT
LONDON RD
BEECHCROFT CL
SHENSTONE PK
SANDY RIDE
A330
Hermitage Par
CATHERINE HO 1
ALEXANDRA HO 2
COOMBE LA
CLAVER DR
B3020
WELL GWYNNE CL
KINGSWICK CL
KINGSWICK DR
Convent Marist Senior Sch
The Marist Prep Sch
SL5
Sunningdale Park Coll
B383
PO
Hotel
Ascot
STATION HILL
RINGWOOD RD
1 SUNNYBANK
2 STANMORE CL
QUEENSHILL
WELLS LA
St George's Sch
Nutfield
MATTHEWS CT 1
JAYS CT 2
SUNNINGHILL LODGE 3
FRANCES CT 4
SUNNINGHILL CT 5
FURZEBANK 6
VILLAGE MEWS 7
SUNNING HO 8
SIRL COTTS 9
Coombe Grange
THE GLEN
ORIENTAL RD
DUKES CL
SUNNINGHILL RD
WELL GWYNNE
CL
St Michael's CE Prim Sch
SILWOOD RD
1 BROOME LODGE
2 CASTLEMAN HO
LARCH AVE
HARTFIELD AVE
1
2
PORCHESTER RD
OLIVER RD
SPRING GDNS
CROMWELL RD
ST FRANCIS CHICHESTER CL
THE DOWER HO
LOWER VILLAGE RD
FARM CL
UPPER VILLAGE RD
MILLSIDE
VILLAGE CT
P
HIGHCLERE
PEMBROKE CL
THE SPINNEY
BOULDISH FARM RD
ALL SOULS RD
CHURCH RD
FENNEL CL
VICTORIA RD
ST FRANCIS CL
VICTORIA RD
CROWN HILL CT
ELIZABETH GDN
CARDWELL CRES
TRUSS HILL RD
NORTON PK
BOWDEN RD
TERRACE
HIGH ST
PO
Liby
QUEEN'S RD
1
2
KING'S RD
PEMBROKE MEWS
TENBY DR
PINEHURST
BEHARRELL HO 1
LYNWOOD FLATS 2
2
1
South Ascot Village Sch
LIDDELL WAY
VICARAGE GDNS
ROYAL VICTORIA GDNS
South Ascot
LYTHAM CT 1
BIRKDALE CT 2
ST ANDREWS CT 3
TROON CT 4
Sunninghill
THE GLADE
ST MARY'S HILL
WOODEND
GLADE HO
FOXHAVEN CT
FOX COVERT CL
BRIDGE RD
CHARTERS LA
CHARTERS CL
JERSEY
CORIANDER CT
The Rise
LYNWOOD CRES
RISE RD
BEECH HILL RD
PARK CRES
PARK DR
WAINSCOT
MORLEY CT
OAKDENE
CHARNWOOD
GALTON RD
DRY ARCH RD
WHITMORE'S RIDE
WOODLANDS RIDE
HIRST WOOD
THE POPLARS
RAMSDALE RD
FRIARY RD
FRECKFRIARS DR
BROCKENHURST RD
St Francis RC Prim Sch
HORSE GATE RIDE
MONKS WLK
MONKS DR
MONKS CL
REGENTS WLK
ST MARY'S RD
WYGRAM CL
ARMITAGE CT
HOLMES CL
HANCOCKS MOUNT
WYLDEWOOD
Heathermount The Learning Ctr
CHARTERS RD
Sunningdale Sch
CHARTERS RD
WOODBY
LANVAIR CL
LLANVAIR DR
CORONATION RD
FIR TREE CL
BODENS RIDE
FIELD HOUSE CL
MERIDIAN CT
St Mary's Sch Ascot
BAGSHOT RD
B3020
THE COVERT
Hotel
King's Beeches
Broadlands
Broadlands Farm
DEVENISH RD
BROADLANDS DR
FIREBALL HILL
Old Windsor Bog
GU20
Scotswood
BASINGSHILL
GREENWAY'S DR
GRANT WAY
HAMILTON DR
KNOLE WOOD
ELM PK
A330
A30
LONDON RD
Charters Sch
SUNNING AVE
CHARTERS WAY 1
CLAREWAYS 2
SILVERWOOD GRANGE 3
HILLMARTIN RD
HILL MARGARET RD
LADY MARGARET RD
PINECOTE DR
BALLENCRIEFF RD
BEARSDEN CT
LADYWOOD GRANGE
HILLSIDE PK
CROSS RD
A30
Hurst Lodge Sch
EARLEYDENE
67

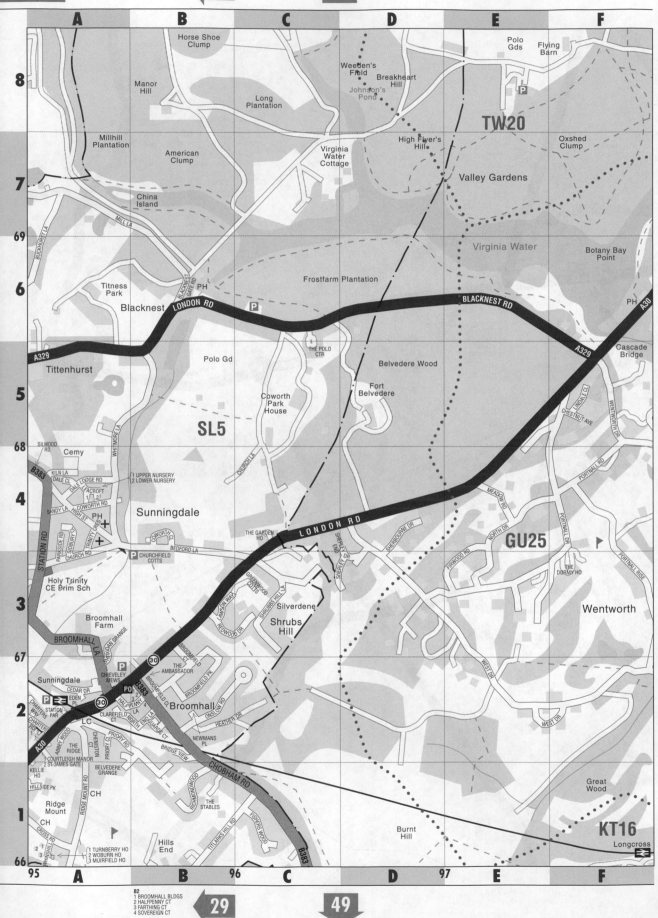

B2
1 BROOMHALL BLDGS
2 HALFPENNY CT
3 FARTHING CT
4 SOVEREIGN CT

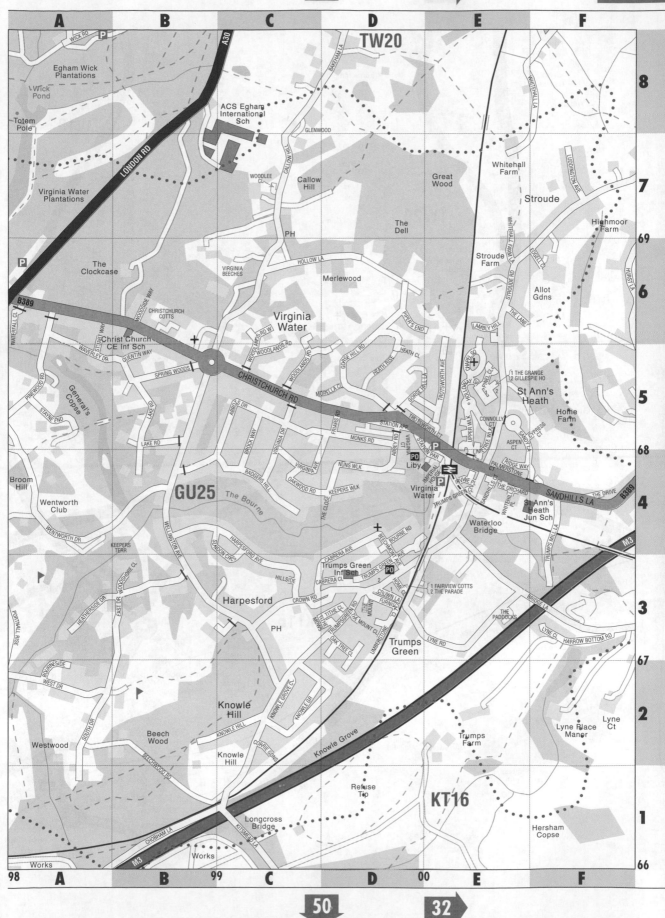

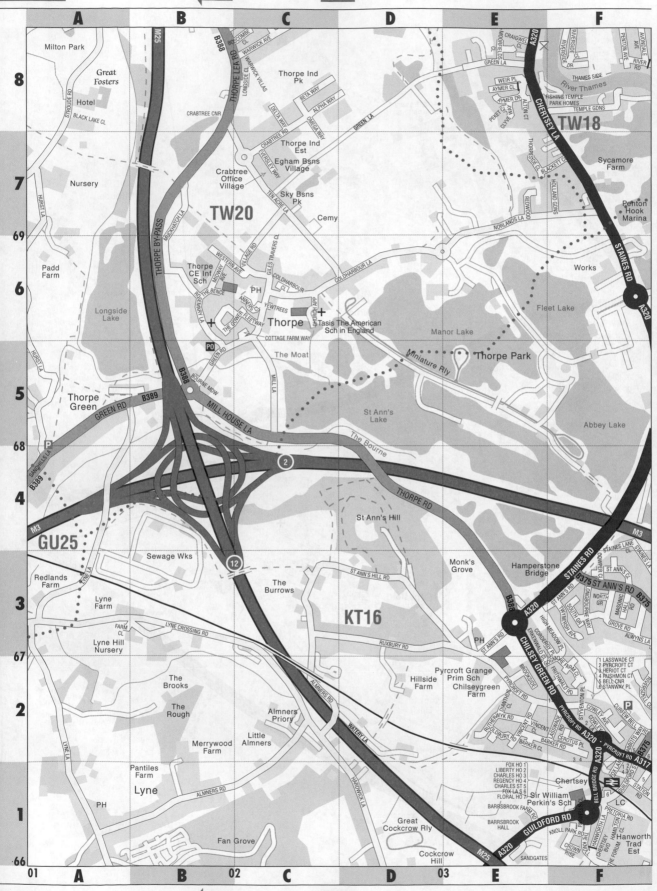

A2
1 FOUNDRY MEWS
2 RIVERSDELL CL
3 BURWOOD PAR
4 BEOMONDS ROW
5 BEOMONDS
6 GALSWORTHY RD
7 CHERTSEY WLK

A3
1 ONSLOW MEWS
2 WINDSOR PL
3 ALWYNS CL
4 ALWYNS LA
5 WILLATS CL
6 DEAN CT
7 SPIRES CT

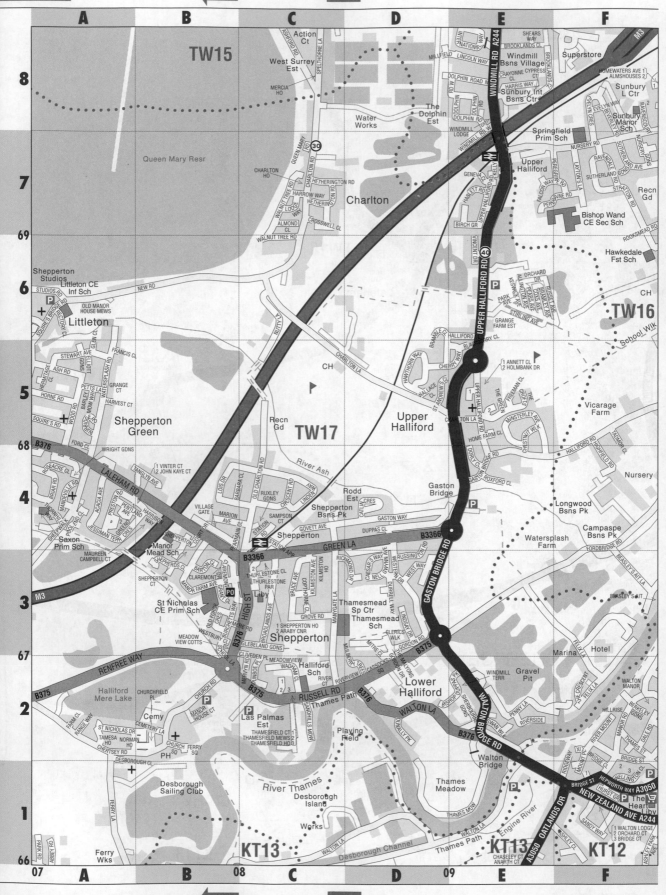

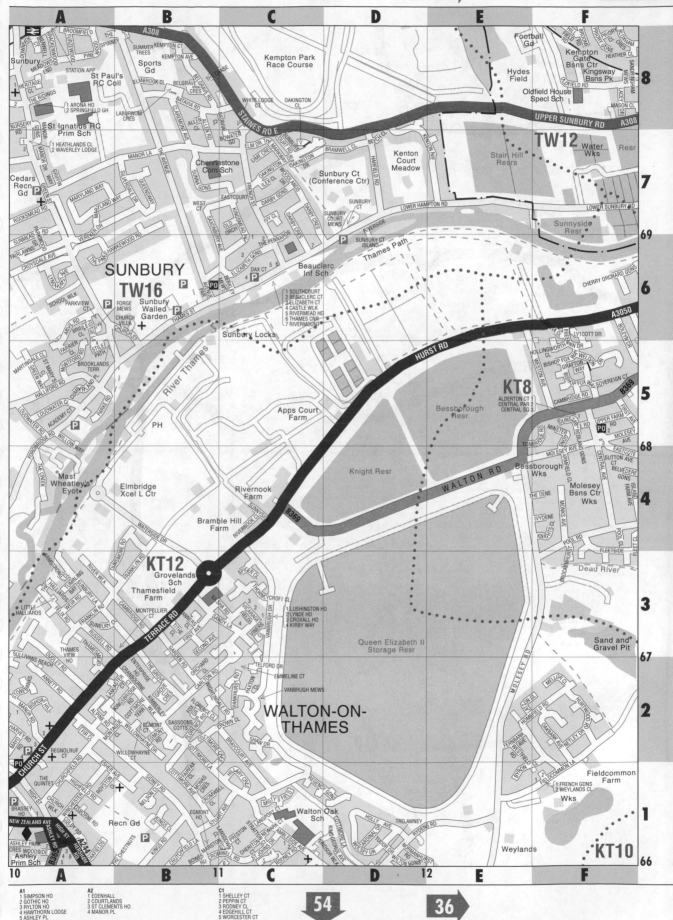

A1
1 SIMPSON HO
2 GOTHIC HO
3 RYLTON HO
4 HAWTHORN LODGE
5 ASHLEY PL
6 BLATCHFORD CT

A2
1 EDENHALL
2 COURTLANDS
3 ST CLEMENTS HO
4 MANOR PL

C1
1 SHELLEY CT
2 PEPPIN CT
3 RODNEY CL
4 EDGEHILL CT
5 WORCESTER CT
6 DUNBAR CT

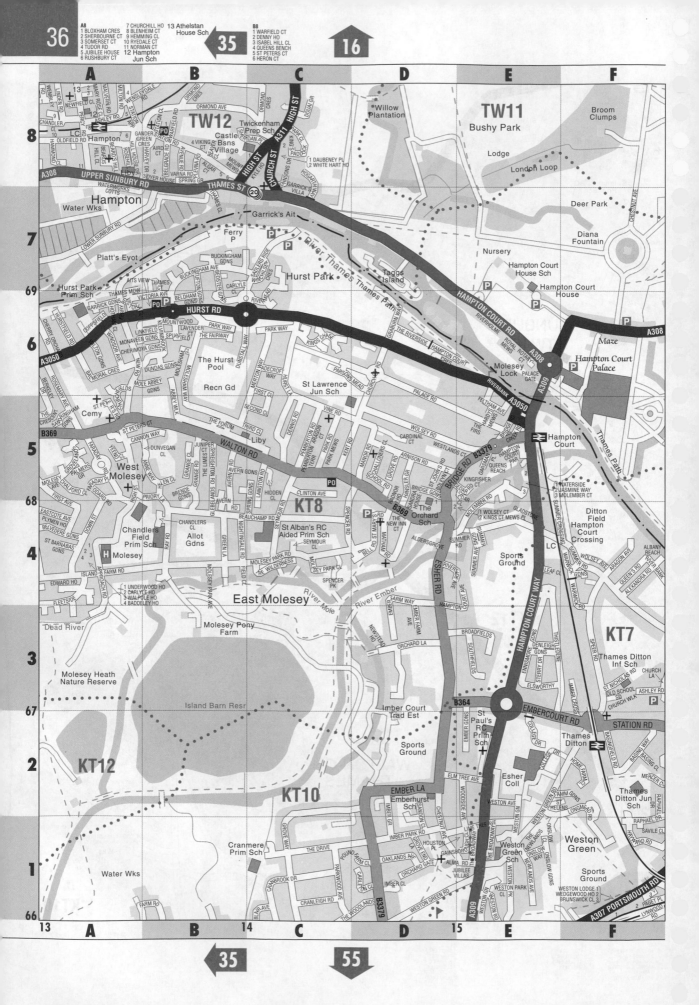

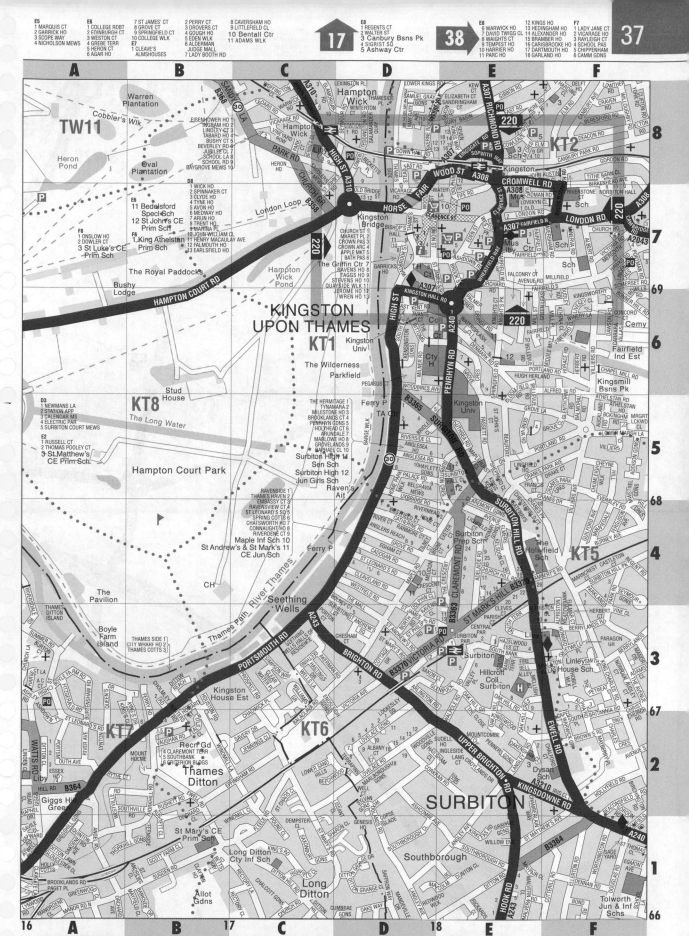

E5	E6	7 ST JAMES' CT	2 PERRY CT	8 CAVERSHAM HO	E8	E8	12 KINGS HO	F7
1 MARQUIS CT	1 COLLEGE RDBT	8 GROVE CT	3 DROVERS CT	9 LITTLEFIELD CL	1 REGENTS CT	6 WARWICK HO	13 HEDINGHAM HO	1 LADY JANE CT
2 GARRICK HO	2 EDINBURGH CT	9 SPRINGFIELD CT	4 EDEN WLK	10 BENTALL CTR	2 WALTER ST	7 DAVID TWIGG CL	14 ALEXANDER HO	2 VICARAGE HO
3 SCOPE WAY	3 WESTON CT	10 COLLEGE WLK	5 GOUGH HO	11 ADAMS WLK	3 CANBURY BSNS PK	8 WAIGHTS CT	15 BRAMBER HO	3 RAYLEIGH CT
4 NICHOLSON MEWS	4 GREBE TERR		6 ALDERMAN		4 SIGRIST SQ	9 TEMPEST HO	16 CARISBROOKE HO	4 SCHOOL PAS
	5 HERON CT	E7	JUDGE MALL		5 ASHWAY CTR	10 HARRIER HO	17 DARTMOUTH HO	5 CHIPPENHAM
E5	6 AGAR HO	1 CLEAVE'S	7 LADY BOOTH RD			11 PARC HO	18 GARLAND HO	6 CAMM GDNS
		ALMSHOUSES						

A2	5 LEANDER CT	15 WINTON CT	E1	4 PANDORA CT	E4	10 STRATTON CT	19 AUSTIN HO	F3
1 RALEIGH HO	6 CLINTON HO	16 SYDENHAM HO	1 ASH TREE CL	5 WELLINGTON CT	EFFINGHAM	11 MORAY HO	20 WENTWORTH CT	1 PERCY CT
2 LEICESTER HO	7 HOLLINGSWORTH	17 CAROLINE CT	2 THE SHRUBBERY	6 GLENBUCK CT	LODGE	12 DULVERTON CT	21 THE PRIORY	2 HOLMWOOD
3 GRESHAM HO	8 GLOUCESTER CT	18 ELLSWOOD CT	3 MALVERN CT	7 LEIGHTON HO	2 MAPLE HO	13 WESTERHAM	22 THE SHERATON	3 MIDDLE GREEN CL
4 WHITE GATES	9 PALMERSTON CT	19 MASEFIELD CT	4 GATE HOUSE	8 OAKHILL CT	3 CHANNON CT	14 HILL CT	23 WAGNER MEWS	
	10 REDWOOD CT		5 YEW TREE HO	9 DOWNS VIEW LODGE	4 FALCONHURST	15 ASSHETON-BENNETT HO	24 CHRISTOPHER CT	F4
D2	11 HURSLEY CT			10 OSBORNE CT	5 FERNDOWN	16 HATFIELD HO	25 HOBART HO	1 WOODLEIGH
1 NAPIER CT	12 WESTMORLAND CT		E3	11 CLAREMONT CT	6 VICEROY LODGE	17 OXFORD CT	26 ST MARK'S HTS	2 HIGHCROFT
2 DARLINGTON HO	13 LAWSON CT		1 STATION APP	12 ST JAMES' CT	7 FRENSHAM HO	18 PENNINGTON LODGE		3 CAERNARVON CT
3 CHARMINSTER CT	14 ALEXANDER CT		2 SOUTH BANK LODGE	13 ASHBY HO	8 KINGSLEY HO			4 REGENCY CT
4 MULBERRY CT			3 BRAMSHOTT CT		9 RANNOCH CT			

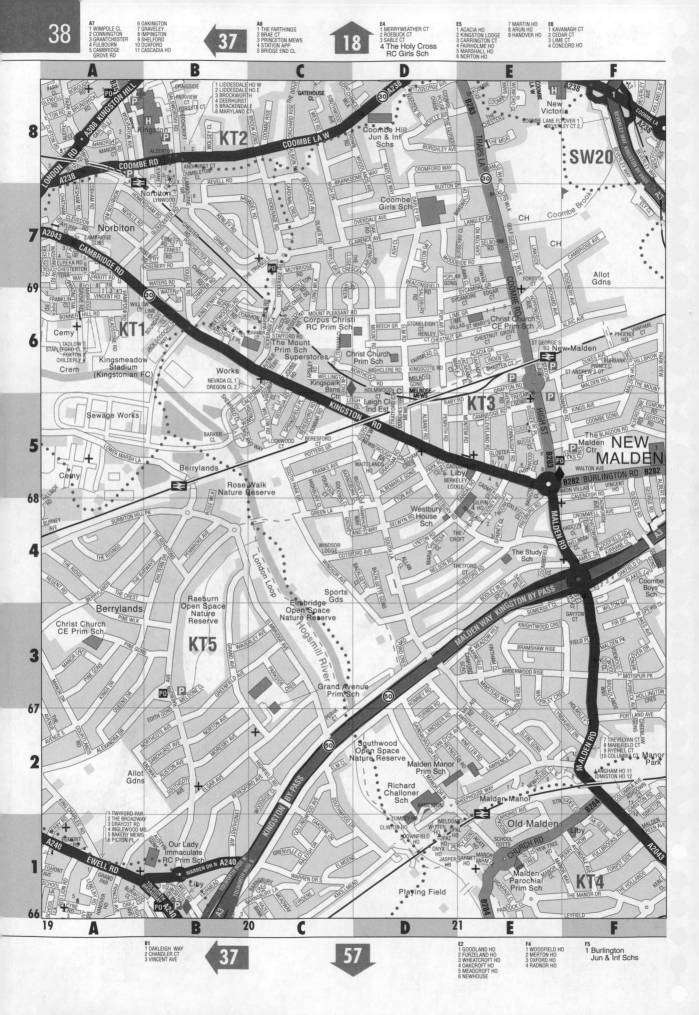

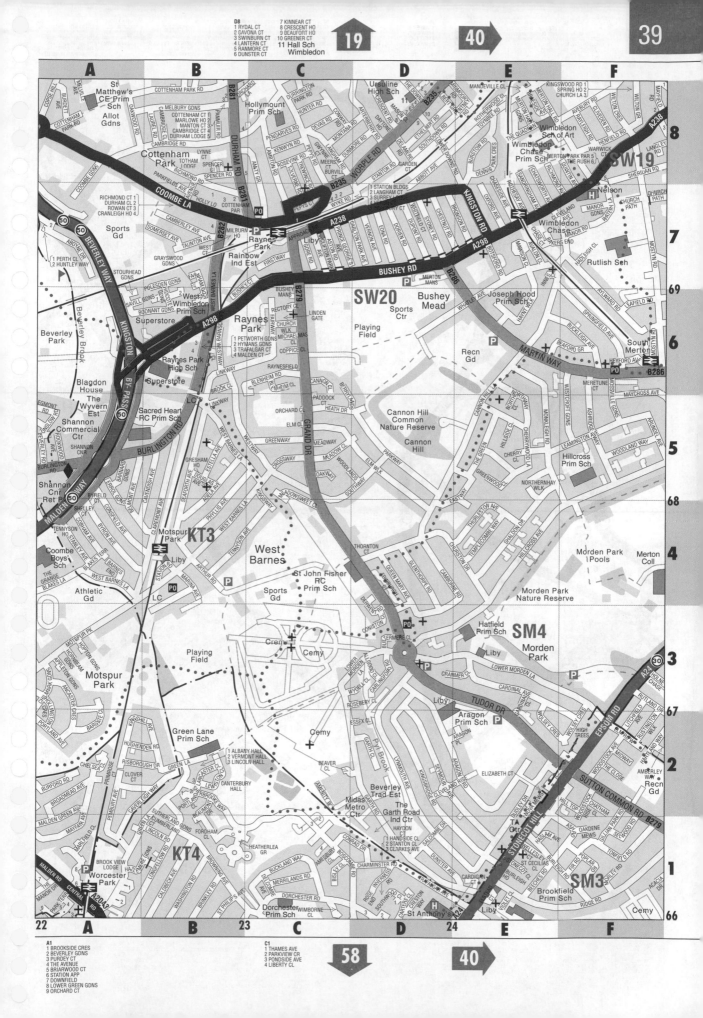

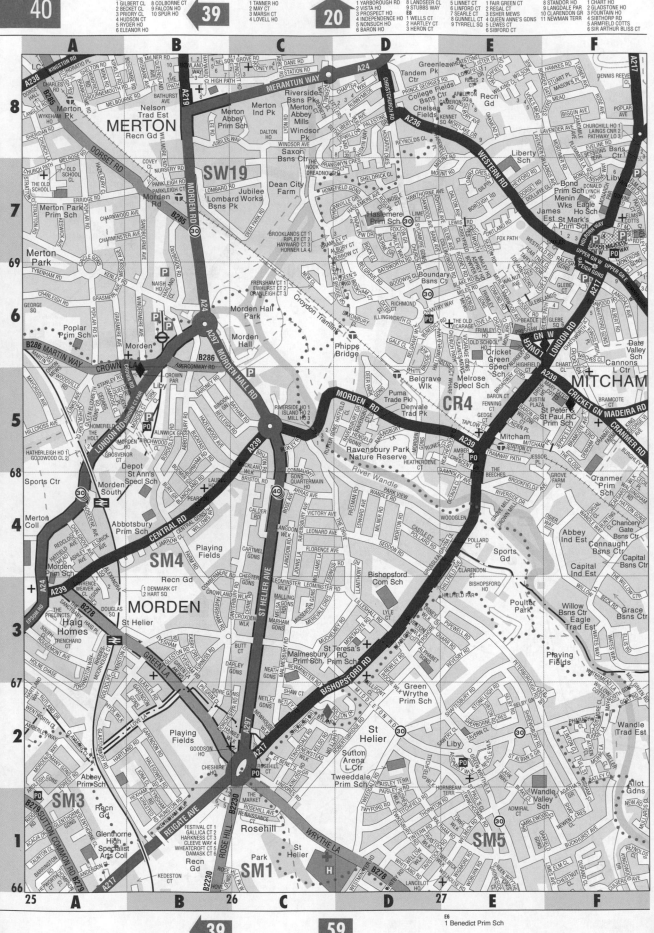

39

20

39

59

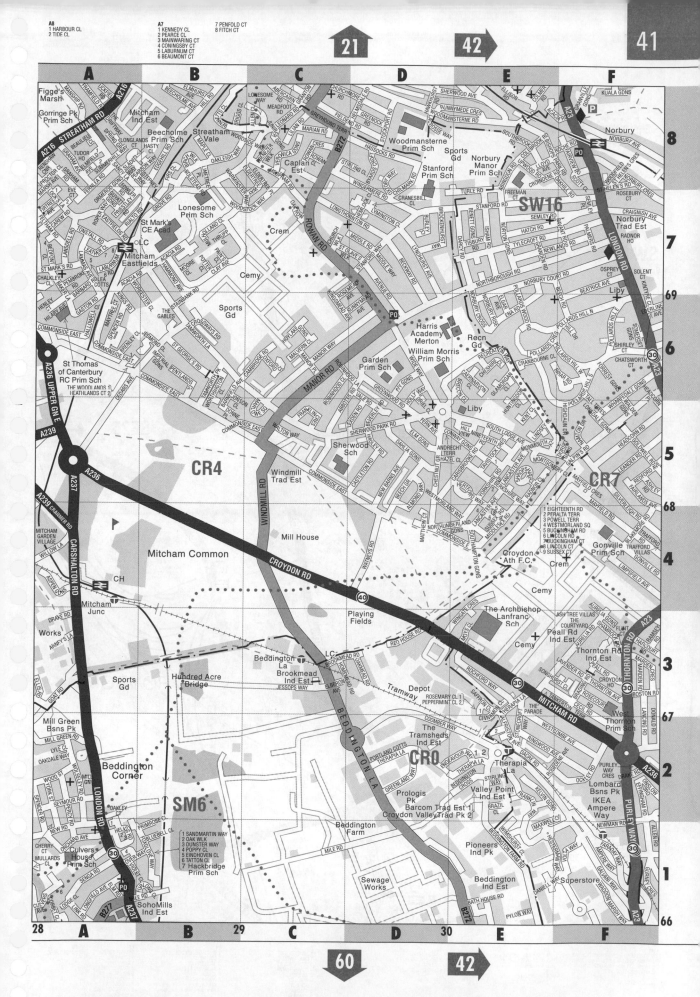

Map grid columns: A B C D E F
Map grid rows: 8 7 69 6 68 5 4 67 3 2 66

Norbury Park
Norbury Manor Bsns & Ent Coll for Girls
Norbury
Kensington Avenue Prim Sch
Sports Gd
SW16
Sports Gd
St James The Great RC Prim Sch
CR7
Winterbourne Jun Girls' & Boy's Schs
Winterbourne Inf Sch
Thornton Heath
Thornton Heath Coll
Bensham Manor Specl Sch
Ecclesbourne Jun & Inf Schs
Thornton Heath
Mayday University
Broad Green
Elmwood Jun & Inf Schs
Liby
Kingsley Prim Sch
TA Ctr

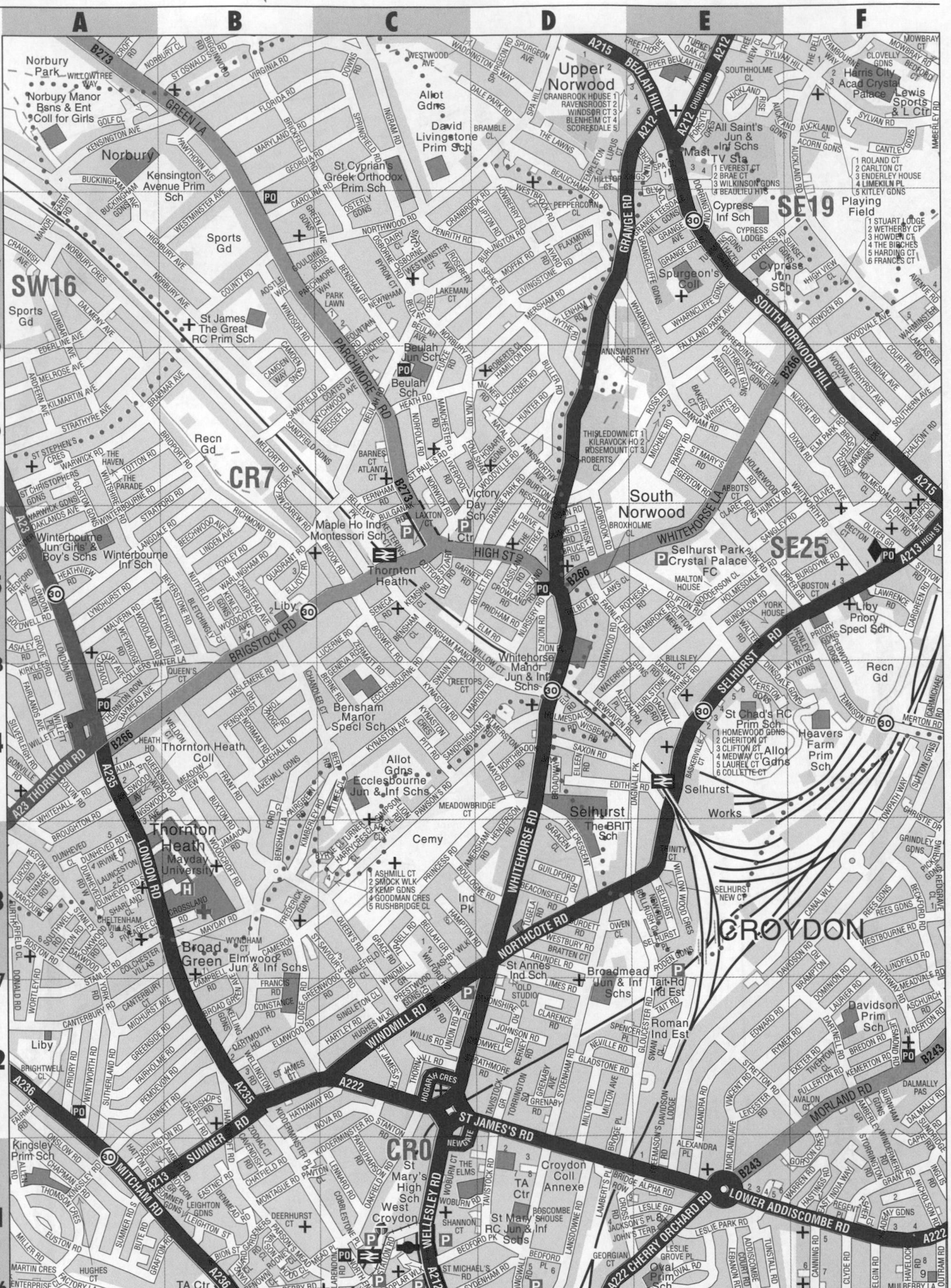

St Cyprian's Greek Orthodox Prim Sch
David Livingstone Prim Sch
Upper Norwood
Cranbrook House
Ravensroost
Windsor CT
Blenheim CT
Scoresdale
Beulah Jun Sch
Beulah Sch
Victory Day Sch
Maple Ho Ind Montessori Sch
Whitehorse Manor Jun & Inf Schs
Allot Gdns
Cemy
Ind Pk
St Annes Ind Sch
Broadmead Jun & Inf Schs
Windmill Bridge Ho
St James's RD
CRO
St Mary's High West Croydon
St Mary RC Jun & Inf Scts
Croydon Coll Annexe
TA Ctr

Mast
SE19
Cypress Inf Sch
Cypress Lodge
Cypress Jun Sch
Spurgeon's Coll
South Norwood
Selhurst Park Crystal Palace FC
SE25
Liby Priory Specl Sch
Recn Gd
St Chad's RC Prim Sch
Heavers Farm Prim Sch
Selhurst Works
Selhurst
The BRIT Sch
CROYDON
Davidson Prim Sch
Selhurst New CP
Roman Ind Est
Tait Rd Ind Est
Lower Addiscombe Rd
Oval Prim Sch
Al Khair Prim & Sec Sch

Harris City Acad Crystal Palace
Lewis Sports & L Ctr
Playing Field
All Saint's Jun & Inf Schs
TV Sta

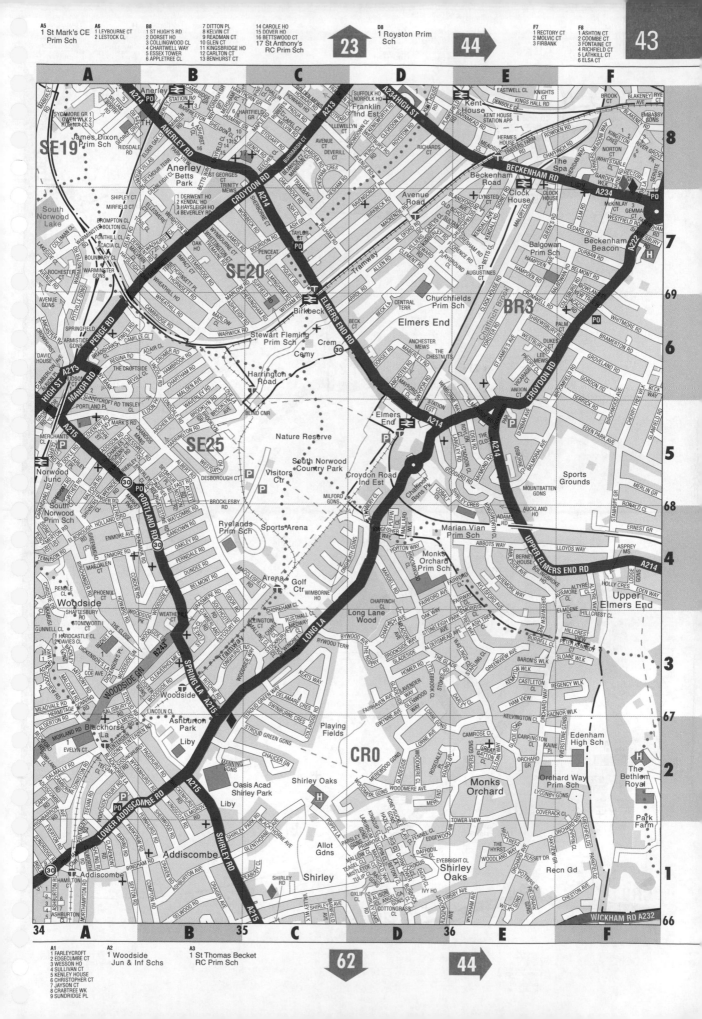

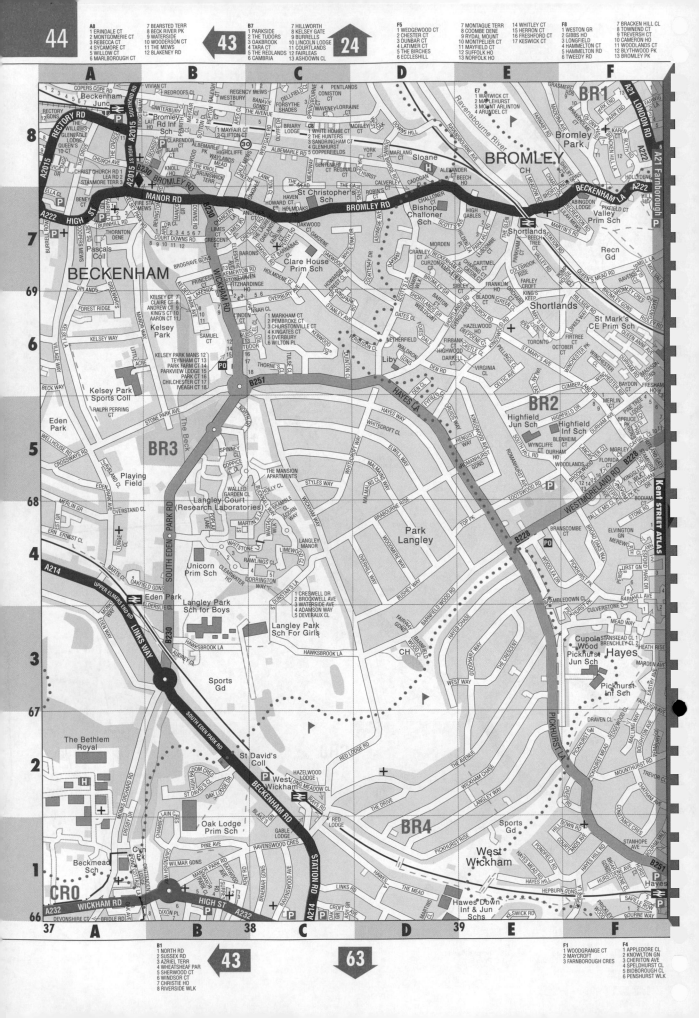

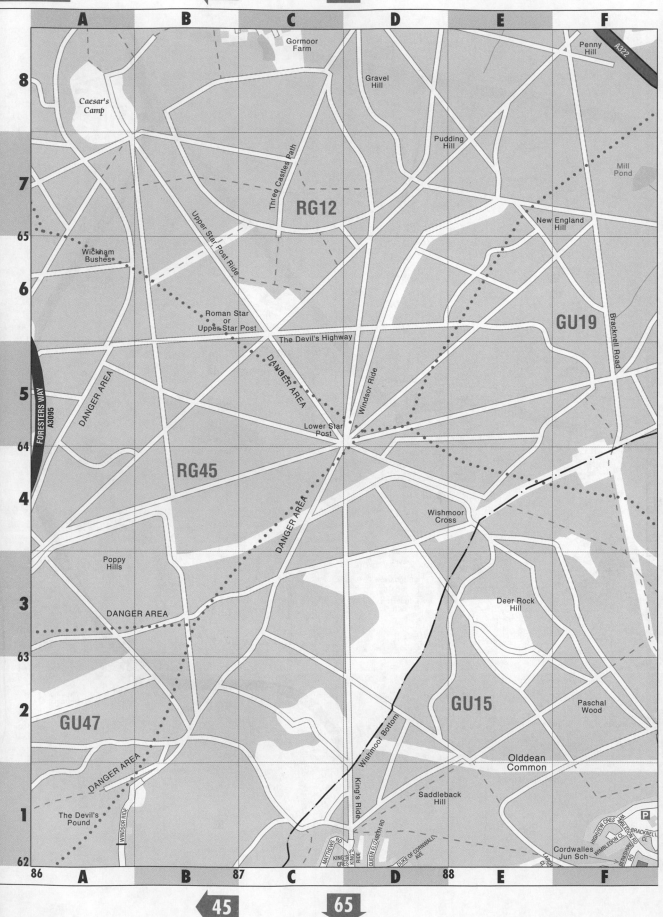

A B C D E F

8

Gormoor
Farm

Caesar's
Camp

Gravel
Hill

Penny
Hill

A322

7

Three Castles Path

Pudding
Hill

RG12

Mill
Pond

65

Wickham
Bushes

6

New England
Hill

Upper Star Post Ride

GU19

Roman Star
or
Upper Star Post

Bracknell Road

The Devil's Highway

DANGER AREA

5

DANGER AREA

Windsor Ride

FORESTERS WAY A3095

Lower Star
Post

64

RG45

4

Wishmoor
Cross

DANGER AREA

3

Poppy
Hills

Deer Rock
Hill

DANGER AREA

63

2

GU15

Paschal
Wood

GU47

Olddean
Common

DANGER AREA

Wishmoor Bottom

Saddleback
Hill

1

The Devil's
Pound

WINDSOR RIDE

King's Ride

Cordwalles
Jun Sch

MATTHEWS RD
KING ST
KING'S CRES
QUEEN ELIZABETH RD
DUKE OF CORNWALL AVE
LARCH CL
HIGHVIEW CRES
WIMBLEDON CL
MALEDON RD
BRACKNELL CL
BERKSHIRE RD

P

62

86 A B 87 C D 88 E F

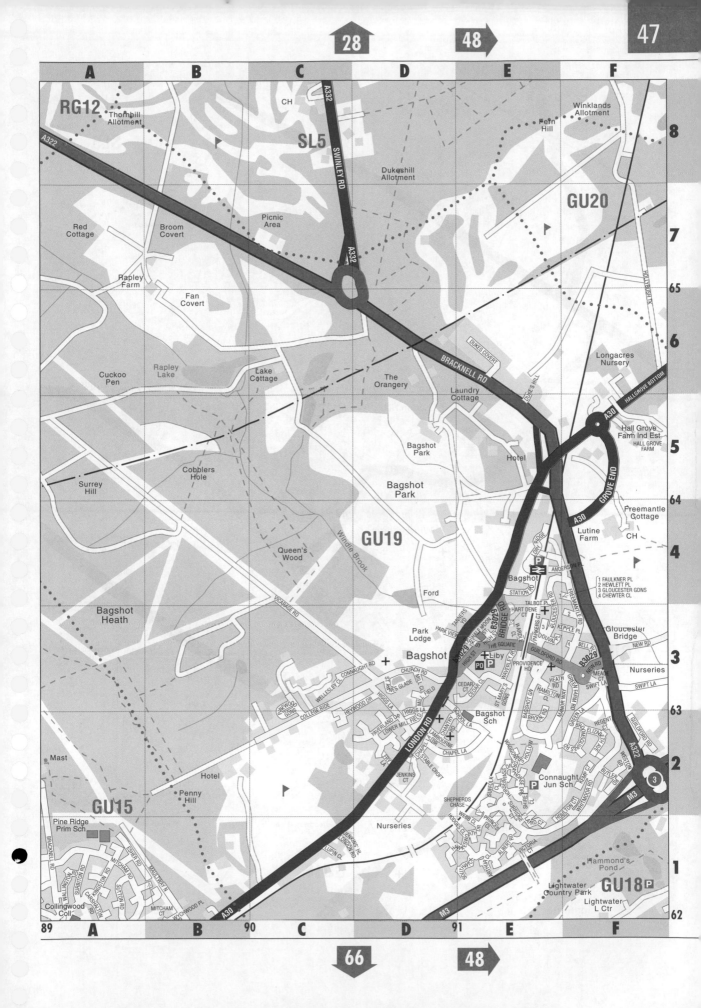

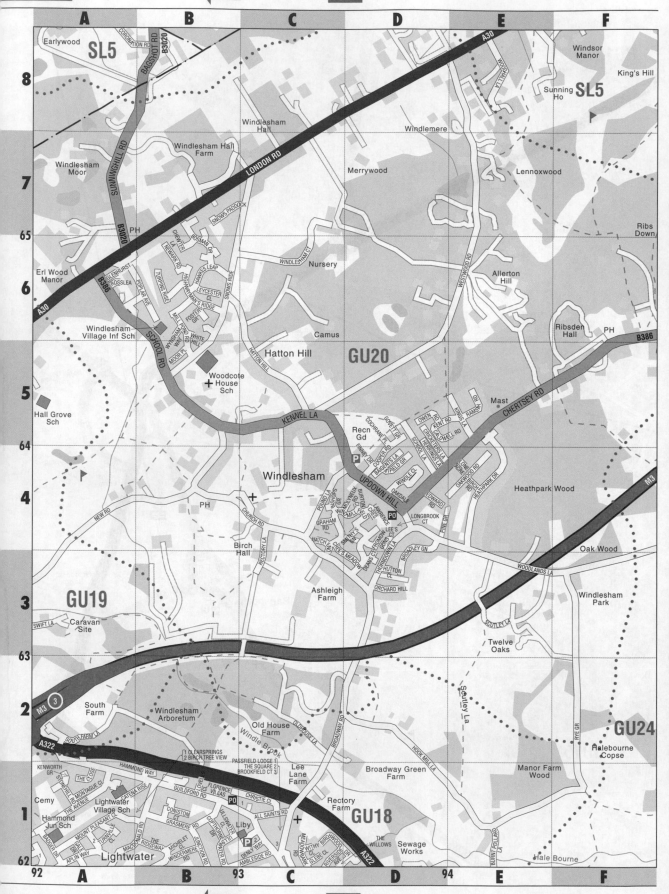

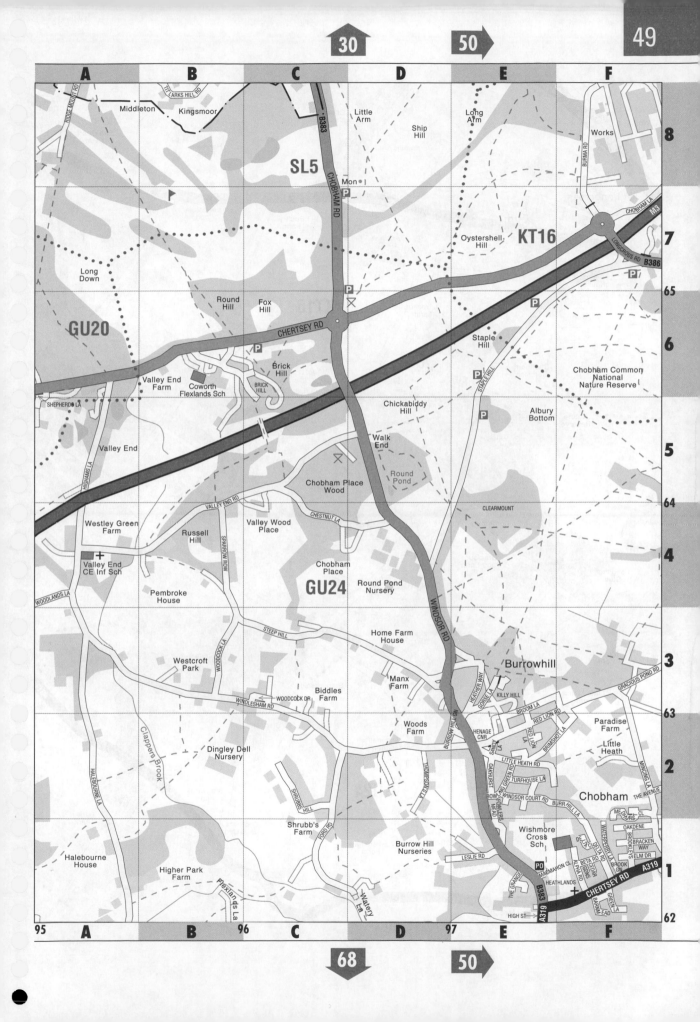

A   B   C   D   E   F

Works

CHOBHAM LA

M3

Longcross

8

Works

Barrowhills

Chertsey
Common

KITSMEAD LA

Hersham
Farm

Fan
Court

Fan Court
Farm

TRYS HILL   B386

HOLLY CL

B386

'BURY CT

TANGLEWOOD CL

7

LONGCROSS RD

Poultry
Farm

Flutters
Hill

Longcross
Lodge

Longcross
House

65

Lilypond
Farm

KT16

CH

6

Chobham
Common

Pipers Green
Stud

The
Lodge

ACCOMMODATION RD

Fox
Hills

The
Dower
House

Budds
Cottage

Nature
Reserve

Gracious
Pond

Childown

5

64

GRACIOUS POND RD

Langshot
Stud

Butts
Hill

Gracious
Pond Farm

P

STONEHILL CRES

STONEHILL RD

Stonehill

Fern Hill

CH

4

Mossat
Farm

Rambridge
Farm

Stannershill
Farm

Stanners
Hill

A319

3

Little Manor
Farm

63

Dunstall
Green

Stanners
Hill

THE AVENUE

CHOBHAM PARK LA

GU24

Stanyards
Farm

BONSEY'S LA

Berwin
Park

2

Chobham Park
Farm

Larkenshaw

Larkenshaw
Farm

Chobham
Bsns Ctr

Nurseries

A319

OLD CHERTSEY RD

CHERTSEY RD

YOUNGSTROAT LA

JESSAMY
LA

London Aerial
Photo Liby

Fairoaks
Airport

1

Sow Moor

62

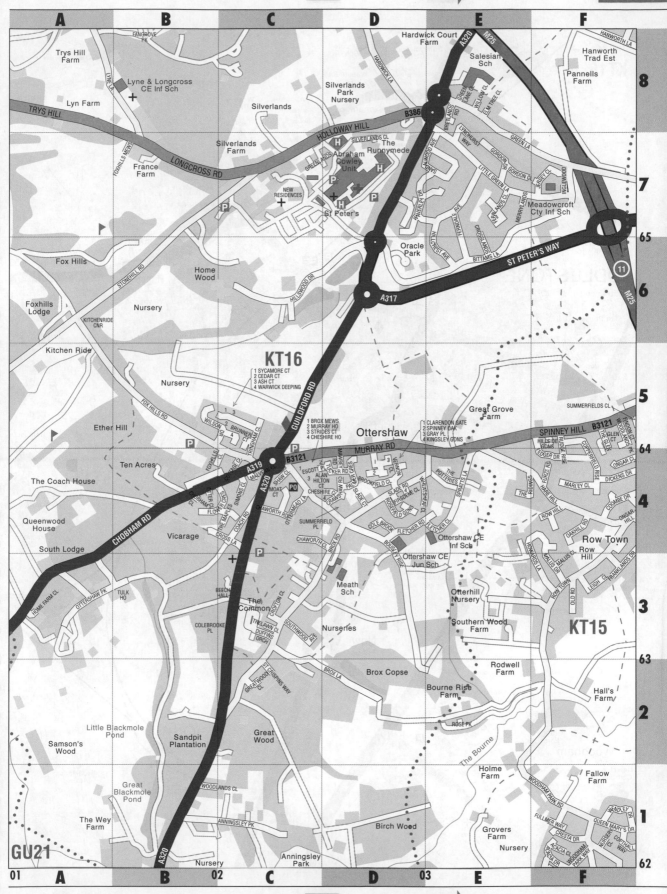

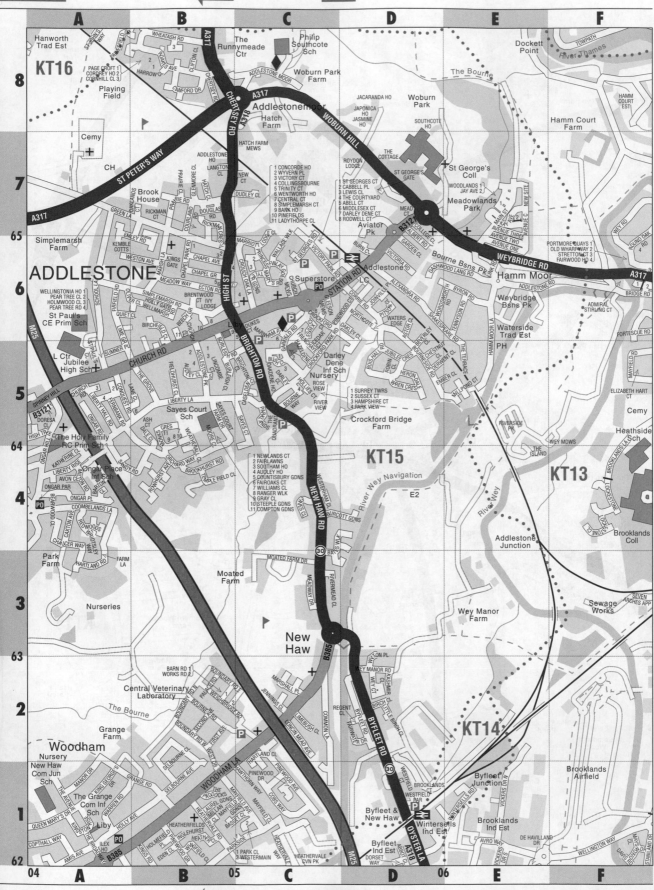

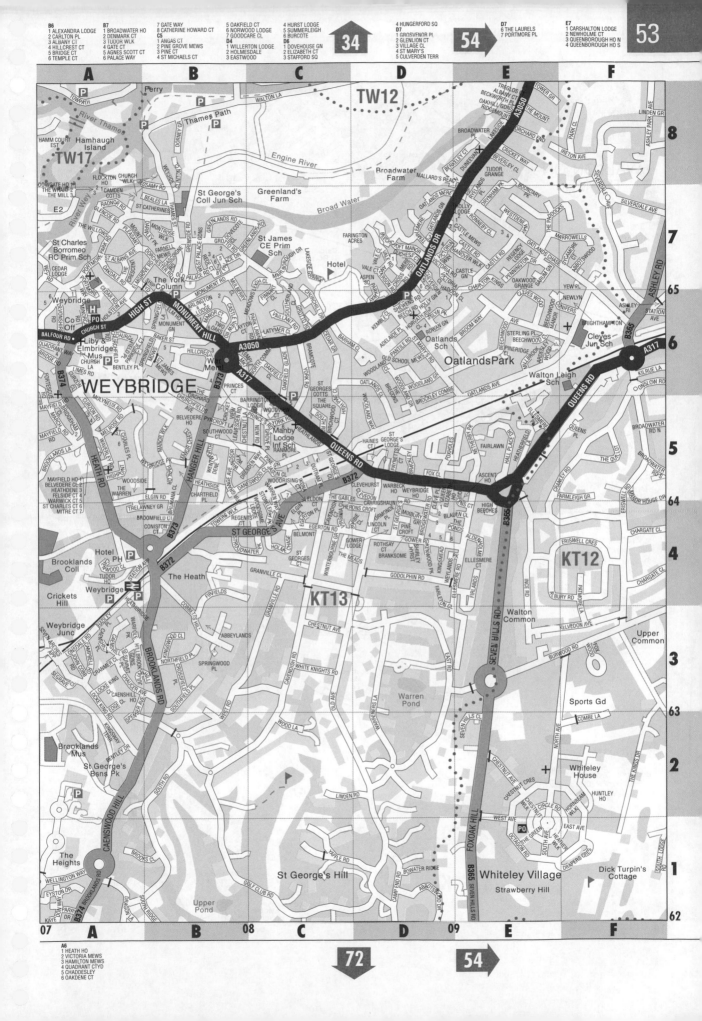

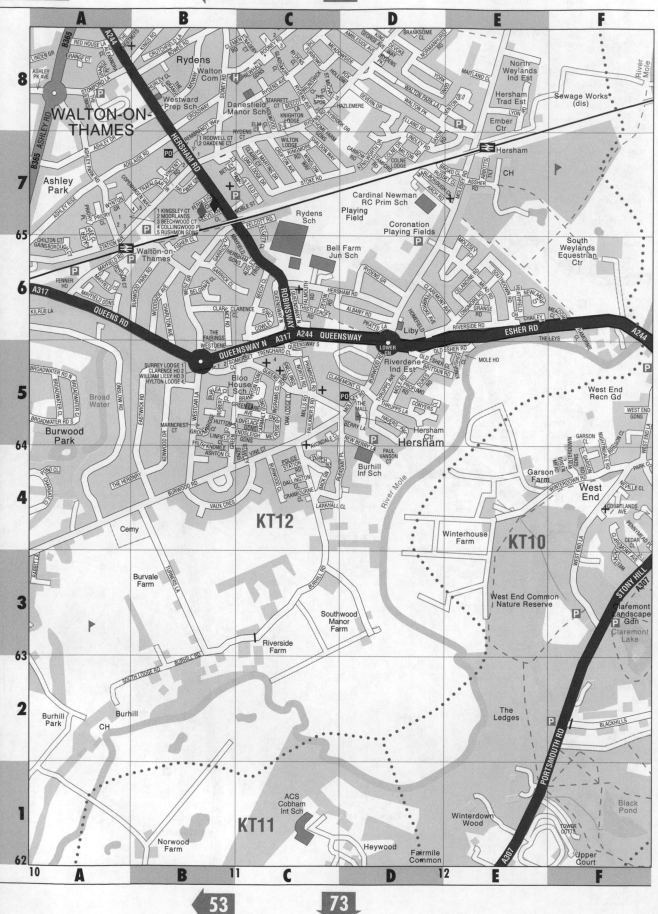

C8
1 INWOOD CT
2 WORCESTER CT
3 RODNEY GN

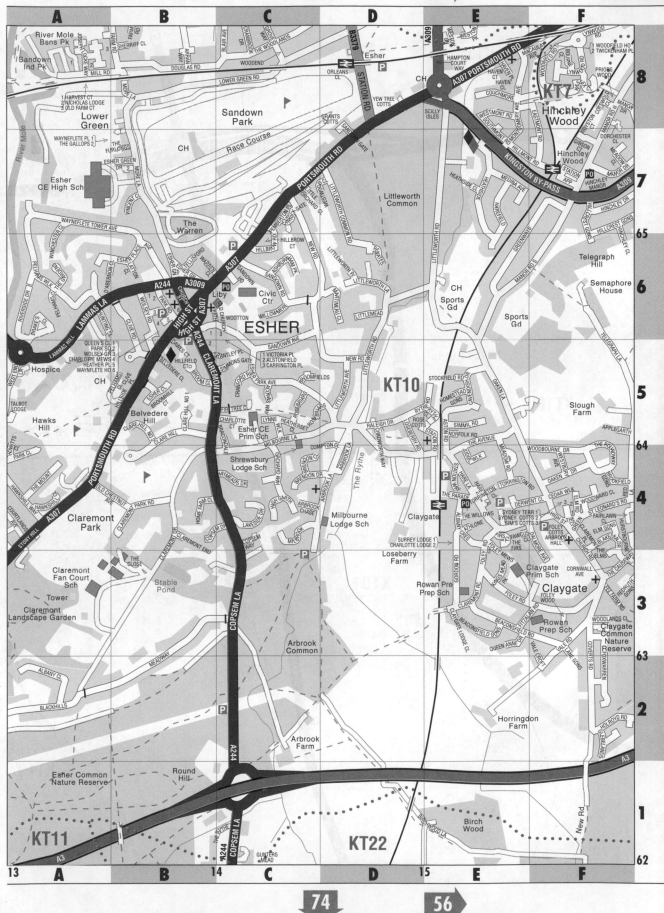

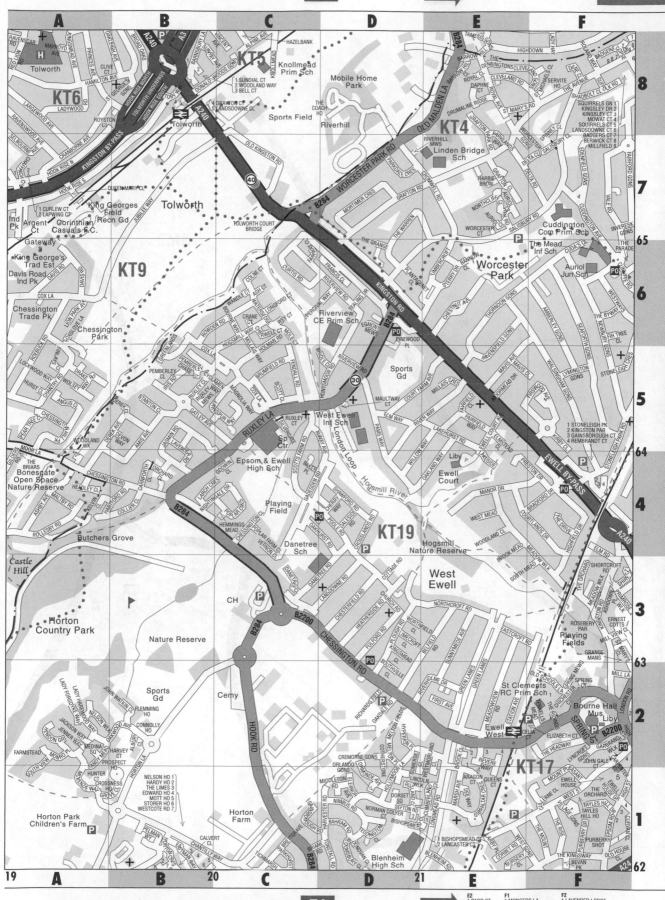

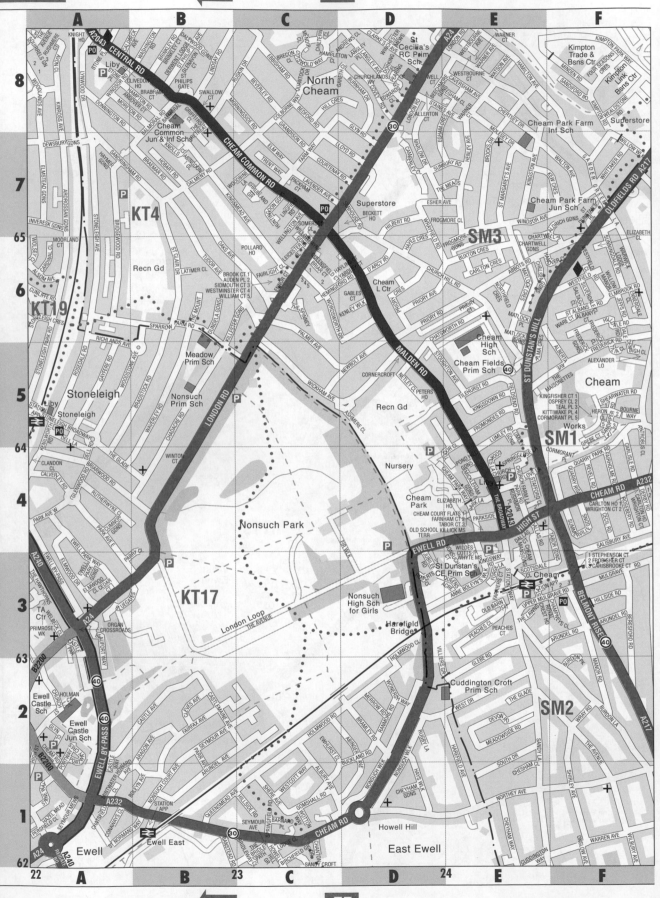

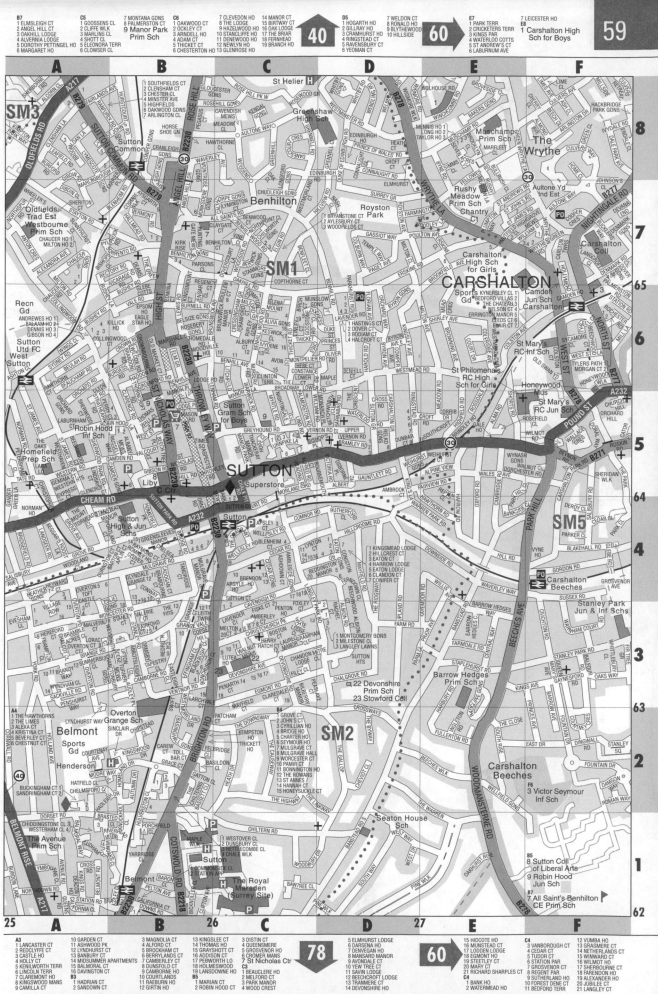

B7
1 Elmsleigh Ct
2 Angel Hill Ct
3 Oakhill Lodge
4 Alvernia Lodge
5 Dorothy Pettingel Ho
6 Margaret Ho

C5
1 Goossens Cl
2 Cliffe Wlk
3 Marlins Cl
4 Shott Cl
5 Eleonora Terr
6 Clowser Cl

7 Montana Gdns
8 Palmerston Ct
9 Manor Park Prim Sch

C6
1 Oakwood Ct
2 Ockley Ct
3 Arndell Ho
4 Adam Ct
5 Thicket Ct
6 Chesterton Ho

7 Clevedon Ho
8 The Lodge
9 Hazelwood Ho
10 Stancliffe Ho
11 Denewood Ho
12 Newlyn Ho
13 Glenrose Ho

14 Manor Ho
15 Birtway Ho
16 Oak Lodge
17 The Briar
18 Fernhead
19 Branch Ho

D5
1 Hogarth Ho
2 Gillray Ho
3 Cramhurst Rd
4 Ringstead Ct
5 Ravensbury Ct
6 Yeoman Ct

7 Weldon Ct
8 Ronald Ho
9 Blythewood
10 Hillside

E7
1 Park Terr
2 Cricketers Terr
3 Kings Par
4 Waterloo Ct
5 St Andrew's Ct
6 Laburnum Ave

7 Leicester Ho
E8
1 Carshalton High Sch for Boys

A3
1 Lancaster Ct
2 Redclyffe Ct
3 Castle Ho
4 Holly Ct
5 Kenilworth Terr
6 Lincoln Terr
7 Claremont Ho
8 Kingswood Mans
9 Camilla Ct

10 Garden Ct
11 Ashwood Pk
12 Lyndhurst Ct
13 Banbury Ct
14 Midsummer Apartments
15 Balmoral Ct
16 Davington Ct

B3
1 Hadrian Ct
2 Sandown Ct

B4
1 Magnolia Ct
2 Alford Ct
3 Brockham Ct
4 Berrylands Ct
5 Bromley Ct
6 Dunsfold Ct
7 Camborne Ho
8 Courtlands
10 Raeburn Ho
11 Girtin Ho

B5
1 Marian Ct
2 Robin Hood Ct

C6
13 Kingslee Ct
14 Thomas Ho
15 Grayshott Ct
16 Pebworth Lo
17 Pebworth Lo
19 Lansdowne Ct

C3
3 Distin Ct
4 Queensmere
5 Grosvenor Ho
6 Cromer Mans

C2
1 Beauclere Ho
2 Melford Ct
3 Park Manor
4 Wood Crest

D5
5 Elmhurst Lodge
6 Darsena Ho
7 Denvegan Ho
8 Mansard Manor
9 Avondale Ct
10 Yew Tree Ct
11 Savin Lodge
12 Beechcroft Lodge
13 Tranmere Ct
14 Devonshire Ho

15 Hidcote Ho
16 Munstead Ct
17 Lodden Lodge
18 Egmont Ho
19 Steetley Ct
20 Mary Ct
21 Richard Sharples Ct

C4
1 Bank Ho
2 Watermead Ho

C4
4 Vanborough Ct
5 Cedar Ct
6 Tudor Ct
7 Grosvenor Ct
8 Regent Par
9 Sutherland Rd
10 Forest Dene Ct
11 Bedford Terr

12 Vumba Ho
13 Grasmere Ct
14 Netherlands Ct
15 Winward Ct
16 Wilmot Ho
17 Sherbourne Ct
18 Farendon Ho
19 Alexander Ho
20 Jubilee Ct
21 Langley Ct

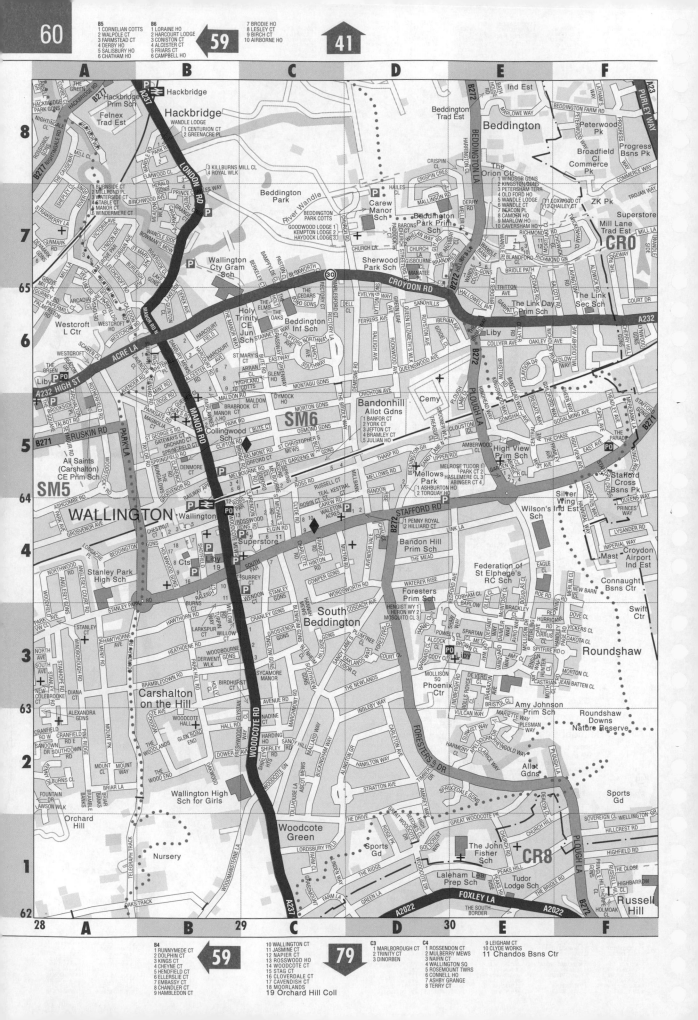

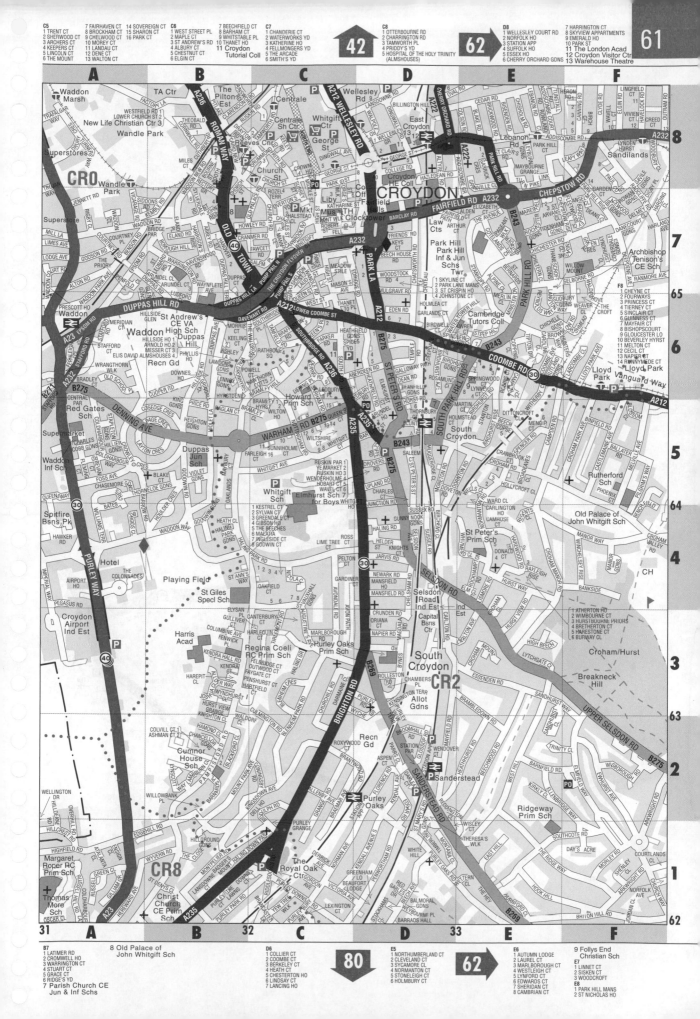

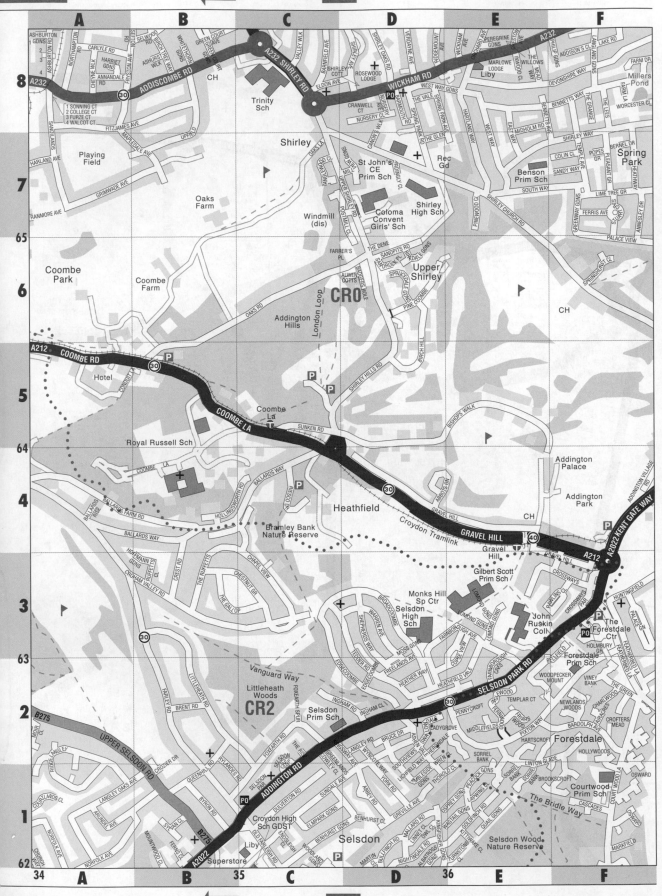

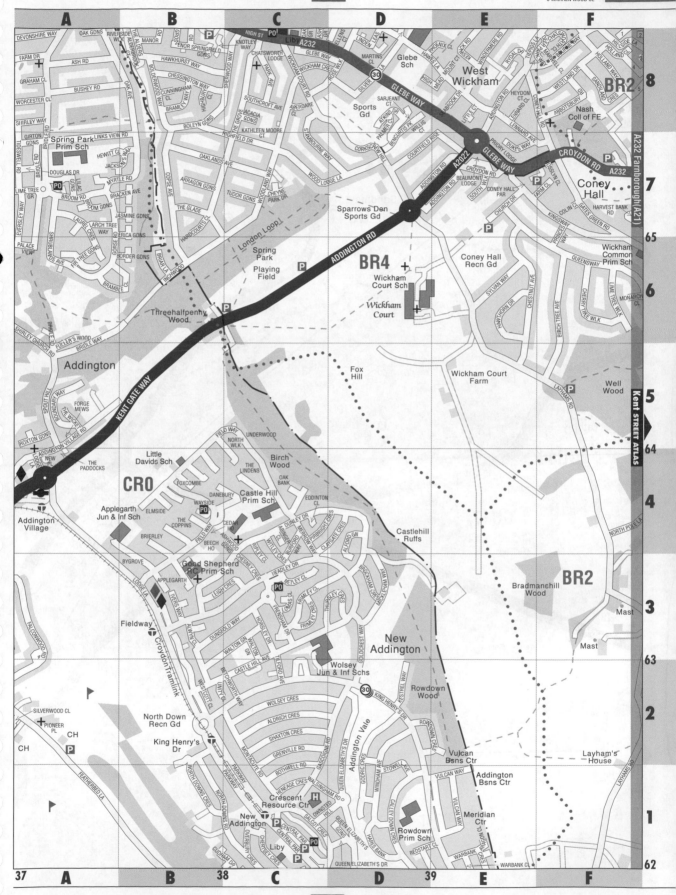

D8
1 MULBERRY CL
2 MAY CL
3 SHRIVENHAM CL
4 CENTURION CL
5 CHAFFINCH CL
6 TARBAT CT
7 ROCKFIELD WAY
8 BALINTORE CT

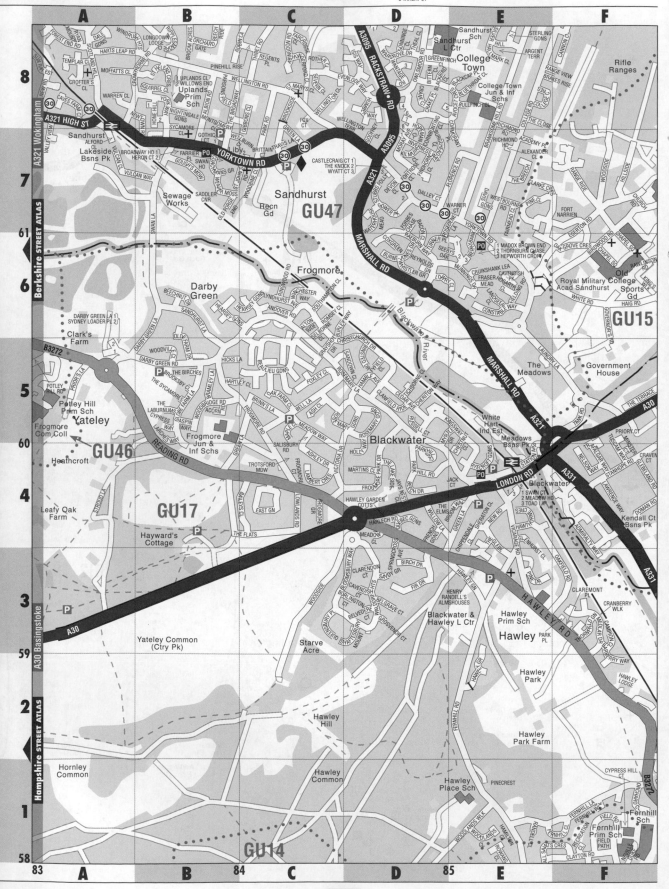

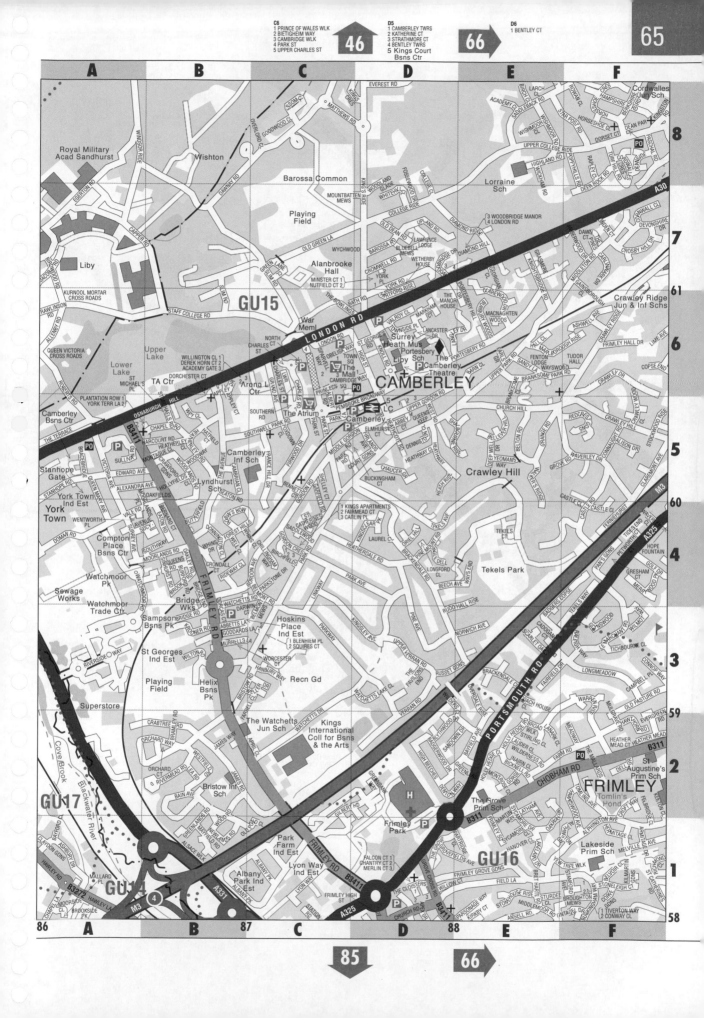

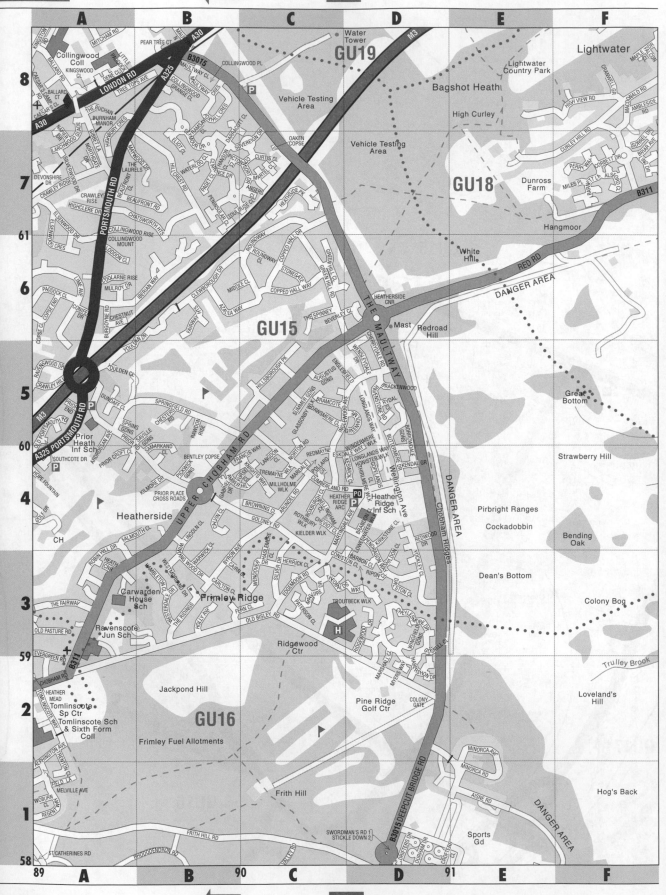

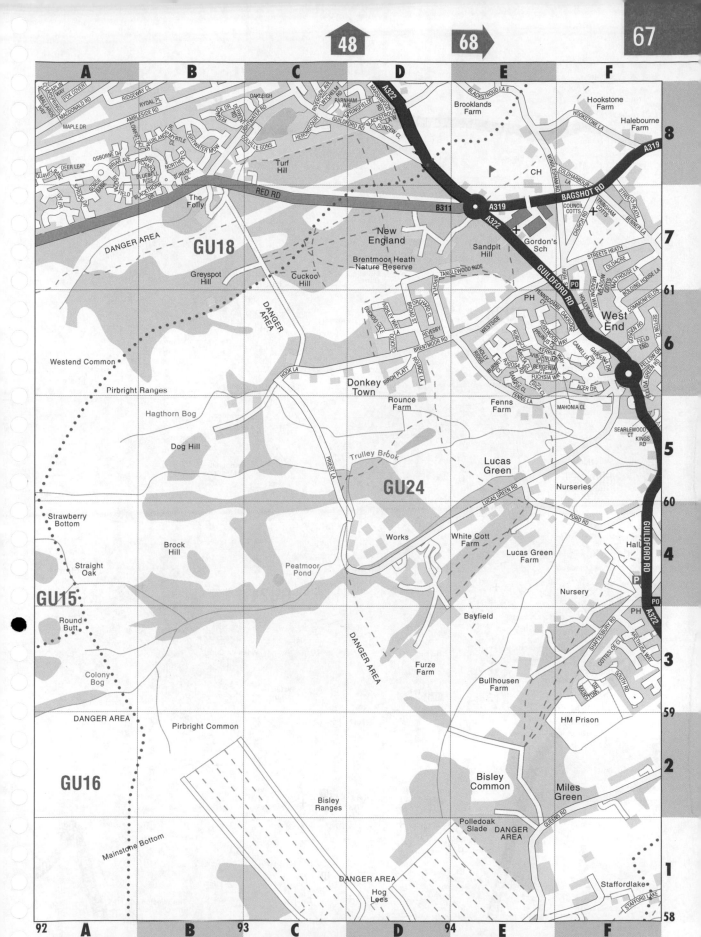

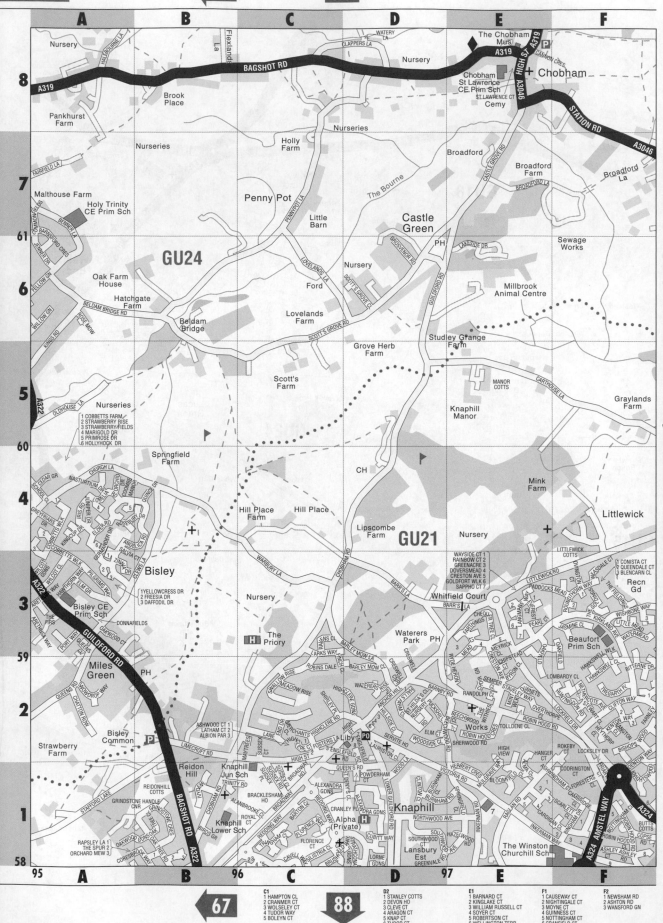

67
49

C1
1 Hampton Cl
2 Cranmer Ct
3 Wolseley Ct
4 Tudor Way
5 Boleyn Ct

D2
1 Stanley Cotts
2 Devon Ho
3 Cleve Ct
4 Aragon Ct
5 Knap Ct
6 Tudor Ct
7 Anchor Cres
8 Kings Gate

E1
1 Barnard Ct
2 Kinglake Ct
3 William Russell Ct
4 Soyer Ct
5 Robertson Ct
6 Wellington Terr

7 St John's Cty
Prim Sch

F1
1 Causeway Ct
2 Nightingale Ct
3 Moyne Ct
4 Guinness Ct
5 Nottingham Ct
6 Cranfield Ct
7 St Johns Waterside
8 Capstans Wharf
9 Barrack Path

F2
1 Newsham Rd
2 Ashton Rd
3 Wansford Gn

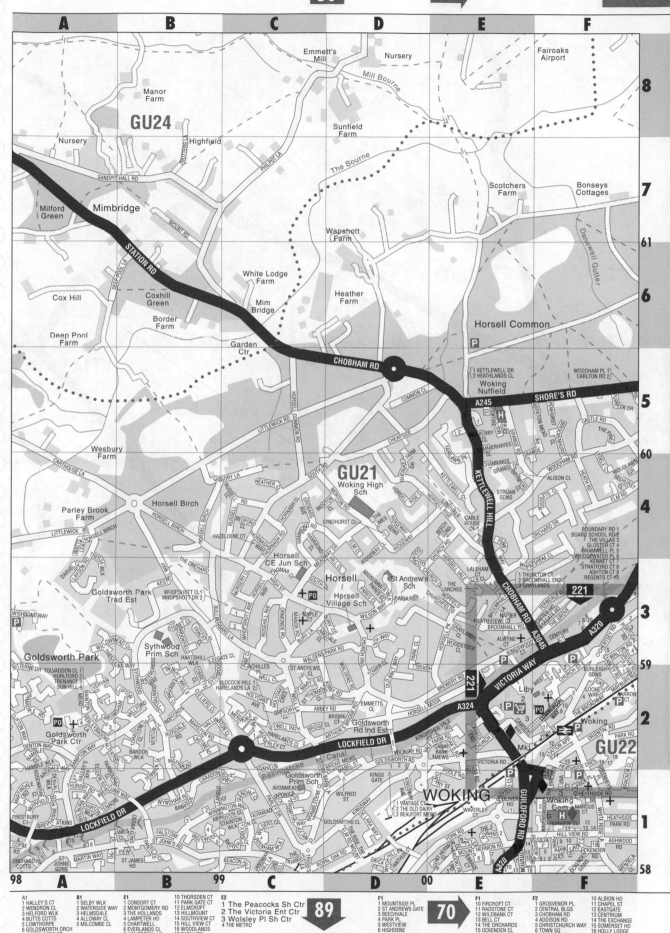

A1
1 HALLEY'S CT
2 WENDRON CL
3 HELFORD WLK
4 BUTTS COTTS
5 LOWTHORPE
6 GOLDSWORTH ORCH
7 WOODLANDS CT
8 ROSLYN CT
9 WINDERMERE CT

B1
1 SELBY WLK
2 WATERSIDE WAY
3 HELMSDALE
4 ALLOWAY CL
5 MILCOMBE CL

E1
1 CONSORT CT
2 MONTGOMERY RD
3 THE HOLLANDS
4 LAMPETER HO
5 CHARTWELL
6 EVERLANDS CL
7 HOMEBEECH HO
8 HOMEWORTH
9 CARMEL CL

10 THORSDEN CT
11 PARK GATE CT
12 ELMCROFT
13 HILLMOUNT
14 SOUTHVIEW CT
15 HILL VIEW CT
16 WOODLANDS
17 PARK HTS

E2
1 The Peacocks Sh Ctr
2 The Victoria Ent Ctr
3 Wolsley Pl Sh Ctr
4 THE METRO

F1
1 MOUNTSIDE PL
2 ST ANDREWS GATE
3 BEECHVALE
4 PARK PL
5 WESTVIEW
6 HIGHDENE
7 MEADSIDE
8 PINEHURST
9 QUEENS CT

10 FIRCROFT CT
11 RADSTONE CT
12 WILDBANK CT
13 BELL CT
14 THE ORCHARDS
15 OCKENDEN CL
16 ABINGDON CT

F2
1 GROSVENOR PL
2 CENTRAL BLGS
3 CHOBHAM RD
4 ADDISON RD
5 CHRISTCHURCH WAY
6 TOWN SQ
7 WOLSEY WLK
8 MERCIA WLK
9 CHURCH PATH

10 ALBION HO
11 CHAPEL ST
12 EASTGATE
13 CENTRUM
14 THE EXCHANGE
15 SOMERSET HO
16 HOLLY LODGE
17 COPPER BEECH HO
18 OAK HO

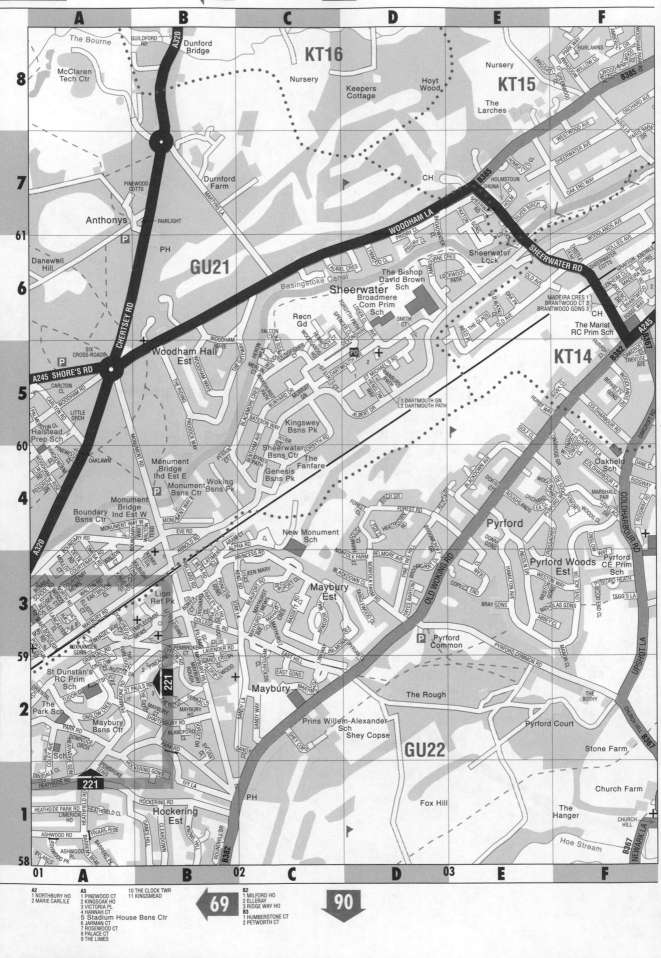

A2
1 Northbury Ho
2 Marie Carlile

A3
1 Pinewood Ct
2 Kingsoak Ho
3 Victoria Pl
4 Hannah Ct
5 Stadium House Bsns Ctr
6 Jarman Ct
7 Rosewood Ct
8 Palace Ct
9 The Limes
10 The Clock Twr
11 Kingsmead

B2
1 Milford Ho
2 Elleray
3 Ridge Way Ho

B3
1 Humberstone Ct
2 Petworth Ct

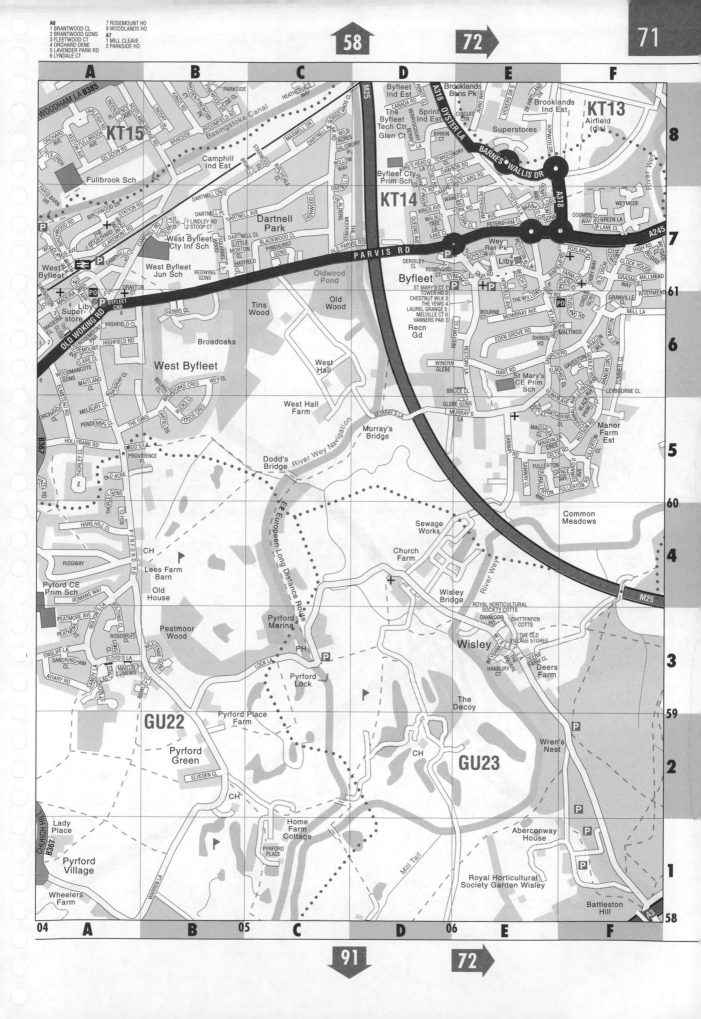

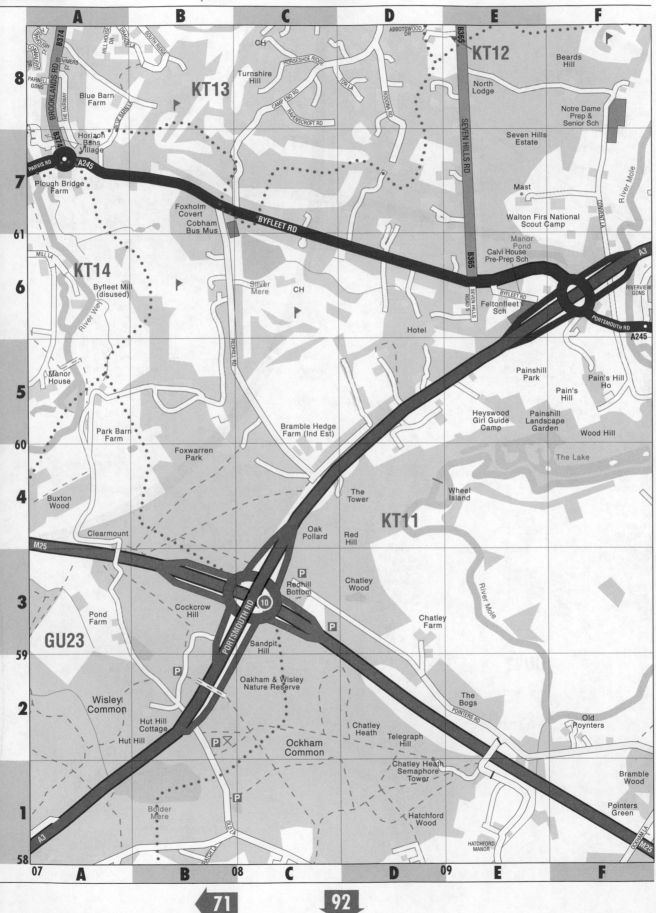

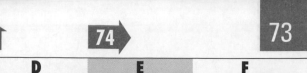

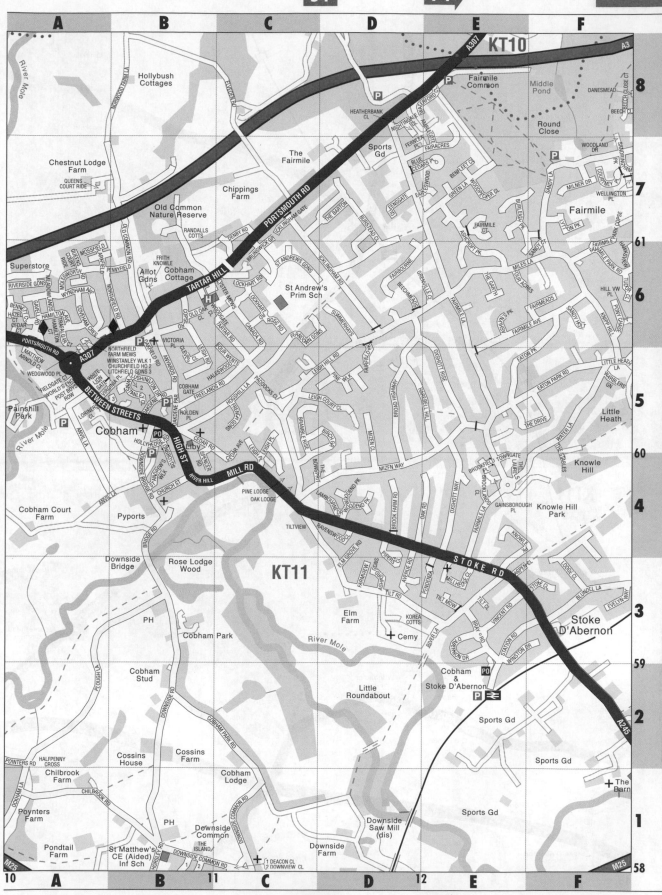

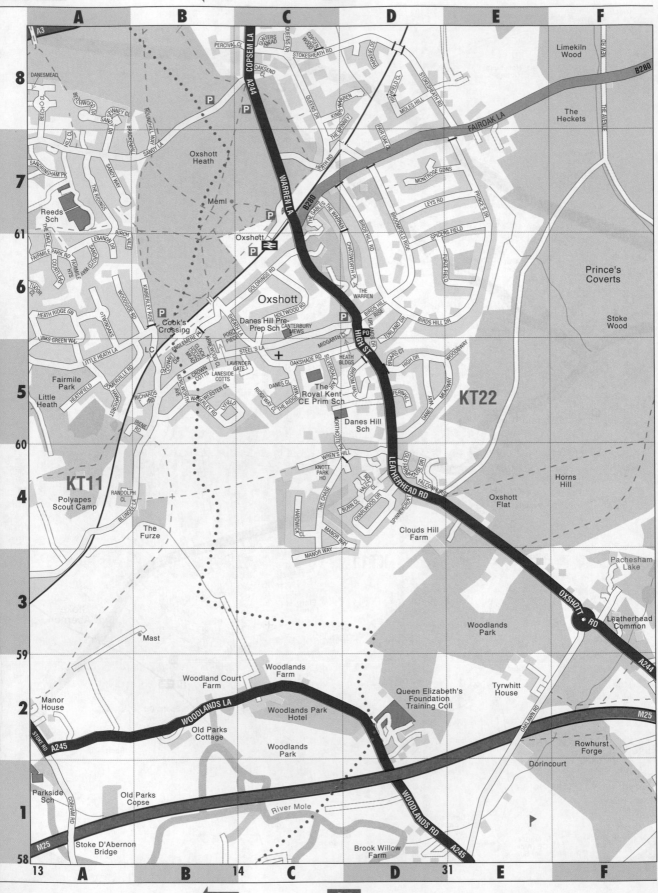

E1
1 Downsend Sch -
  Ashtead Lodge
2 CHARLOTTE CL

F1
1 St Giles CE
  Inf Sch

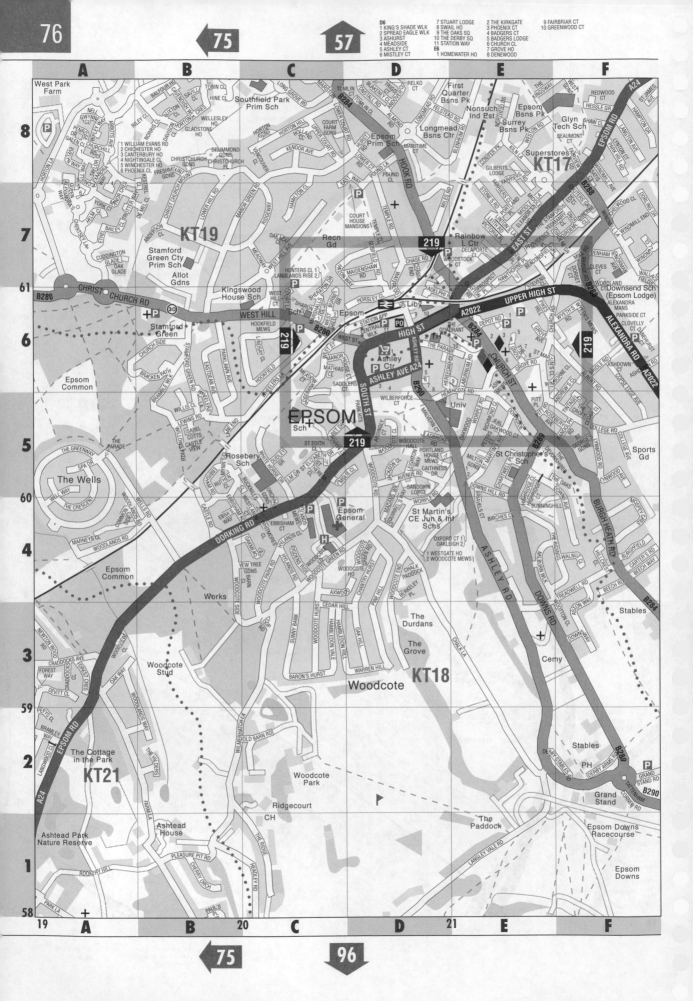

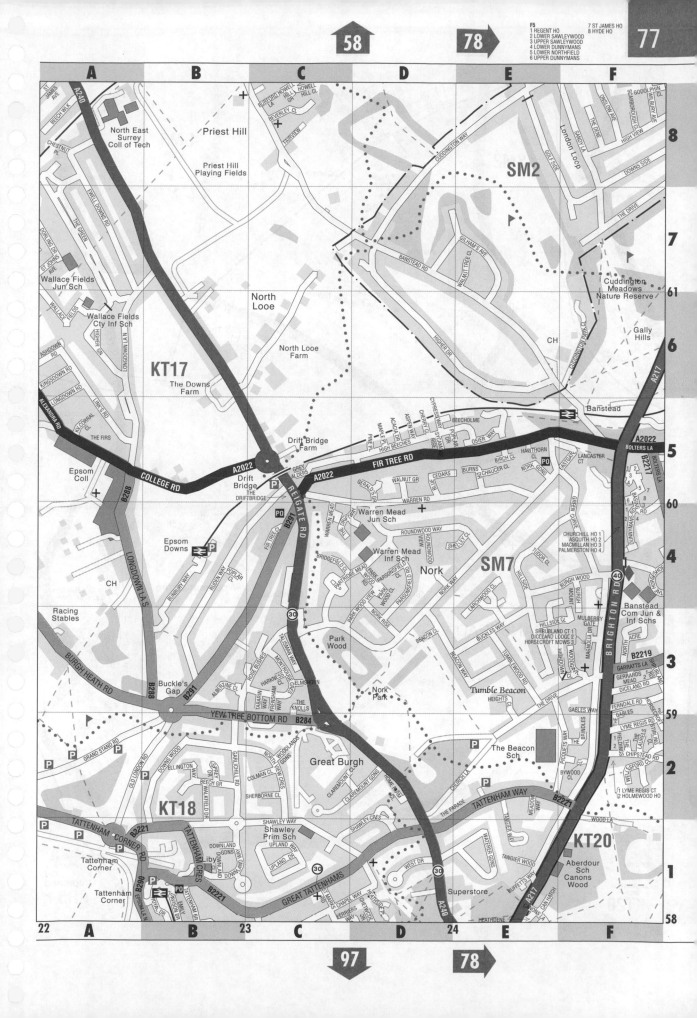

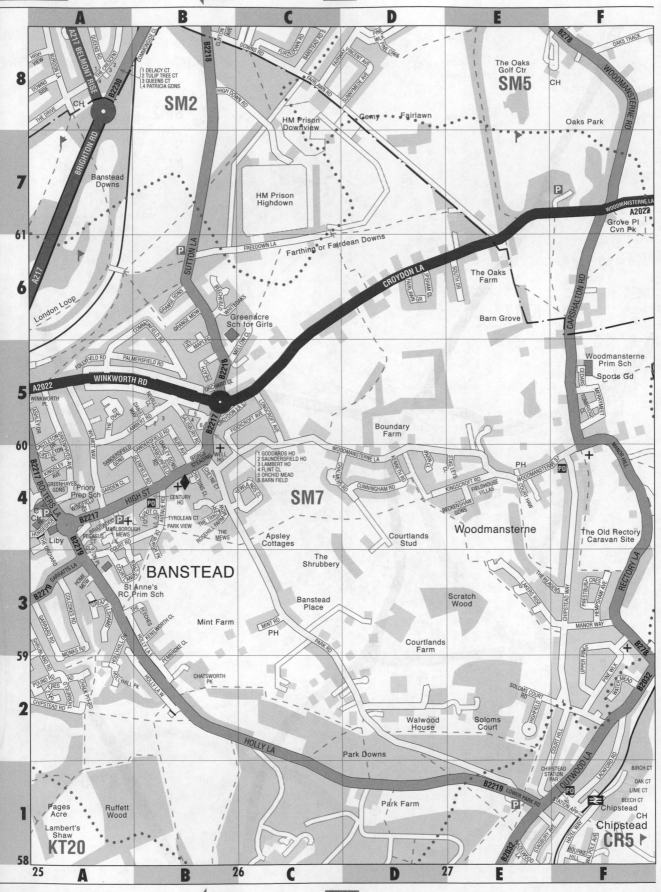

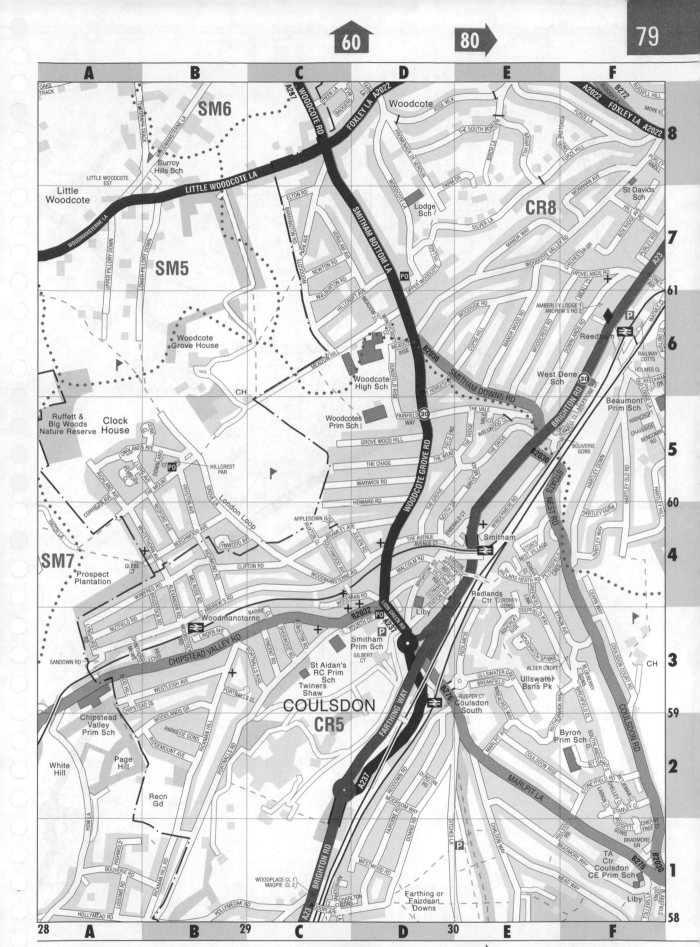

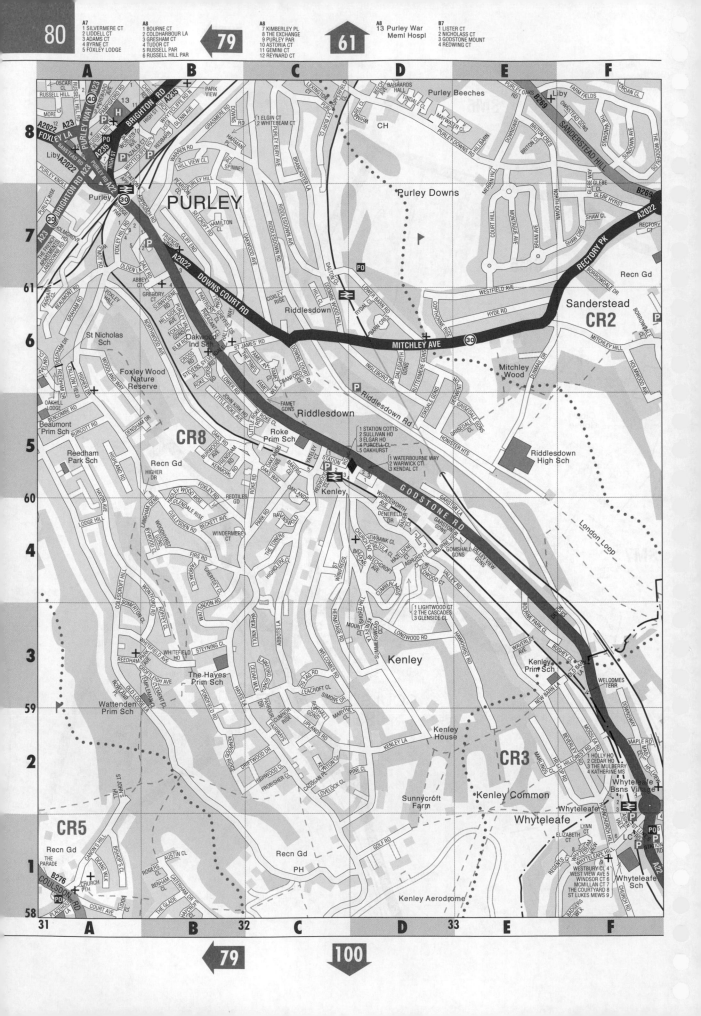

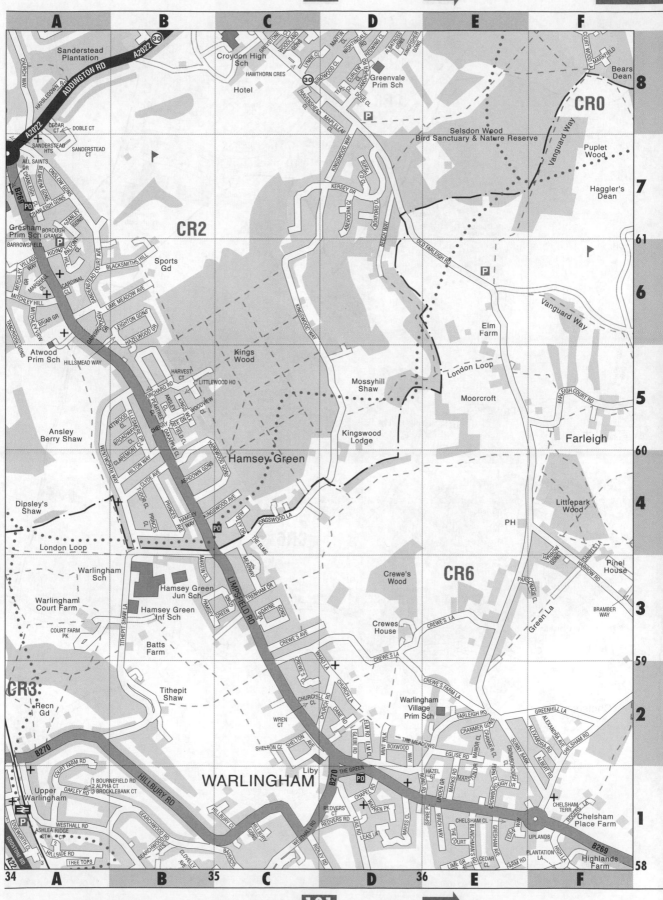

81
63

A B C D E F

8 Bears Wood
Frith Wood
CR0
Hutchinson's Bank Nature Reserve
FARLEIGH DEAN CRES
OVERBURY CRES
CHERTSEY CRES
CUDHAM DR
CLEVES RD
ST BERNARD'S GDNS
ST MATTHEW'S GDNS
HUTCHINSON'S RD
FRYLANDS CT
THORPE CL
FLORA GDNS
LEVERET CL
CALLEY DOWN
REDS WAY
WARBANK CL
WARBANK
VALENTYNE CL
Kennels
ARNHEM DR
UVEDALE CRES
UVEDALE CL
MILNE PK W
MILNE PK E
LEIGH CT
CATOR CL
CATOR CRES
WALSH CRES
COMPORT GN
KING HENRY'S DR
LAVIHAMS RD
BR2

7 Farleigh Dean
Frylands Wood
FEATHERBED LA
KENNEL WOOD CRES
HOMESTEAD WAY
CORBETT CL
FAIRCHILDES AVE
Fairchildes Prim Sch
THISTLEWOOD CRES
COMPORT GN
Addington High Sch
JEWELS HILL

61 CH
Dumpsy Derry
Crab Wood
Fairchildes Cotts

6 Limekiln Shaw
Coldblow Shaw
Chapel Hill
PARK RD
BLACKMAN'S LA
SKID HILL LA

5 Vanguard Way
FARLEIGH COURT RD
Little Farleigh Green Farm
HIGH HILL RD
Fickleshole Farm
PH
Fairchildes Farm
Fickleshole

60 Farleigh Court

4 Greatpark Wood
Cemy
The Gripes
ASPEN HO
SYCAMORE HO
WILLOW HO
TOWERs PL
EAST PARKSIDE
WEST PARKSIDE
Five Acre Shaw
SCOTSHALL LA
CR6
Greathill Shaw
FAIRCHILDES RD
Honeyoak Wood

3 PARKSIDE MEWS
LODGE WLK
BRIAR CL
Warlingham Park Sch
HARROW RD
Holt Wood
HOLT WOOD
CHURCH LA
Midgley Shaws
HESIERS RD

59 PH
CHELSHAM COMMON RD
HENLEY WOOD
Ledgers Farm
HESIERS HILL

2 Chelsham
Henley Wood
Vanguard Way
LEDGERS RD
WASHPOND LA
Chelsham Court
Chelsham Court Farm
CHELSHAM COURT RD
Broom Lodge Farm
BEDDLESTEAD LA
Owls Wood

1 Mast
Cony Crook
White Bank

58 LIMPSFIELD RD
B269
BEECH FARM RD

37 A B 38 C D 39 E F

81
102

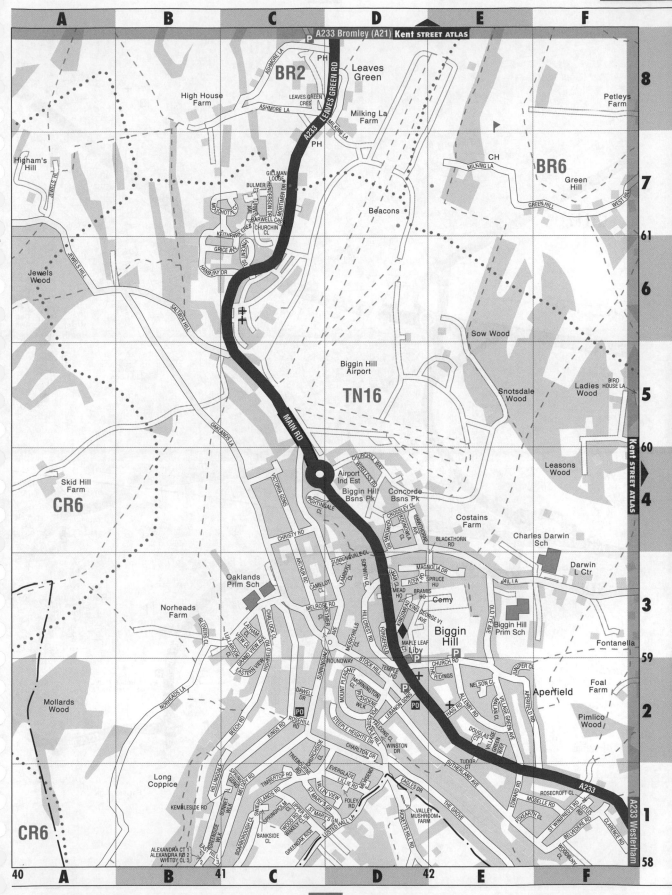

D5
1 HAMILTON GDNS
2 GRANTHAM DR
3 MULBERRY WY
4 WHETSTONE RD

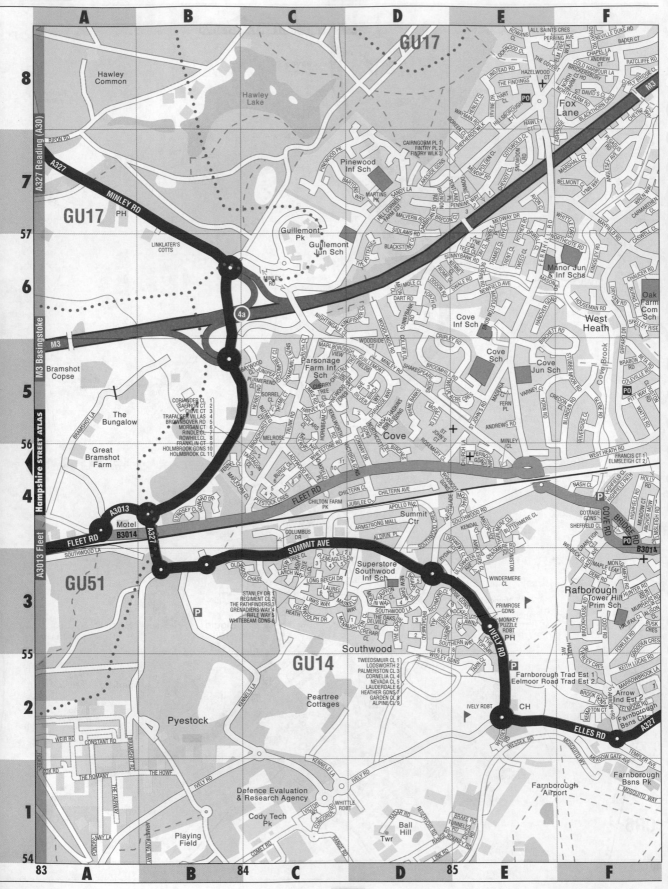

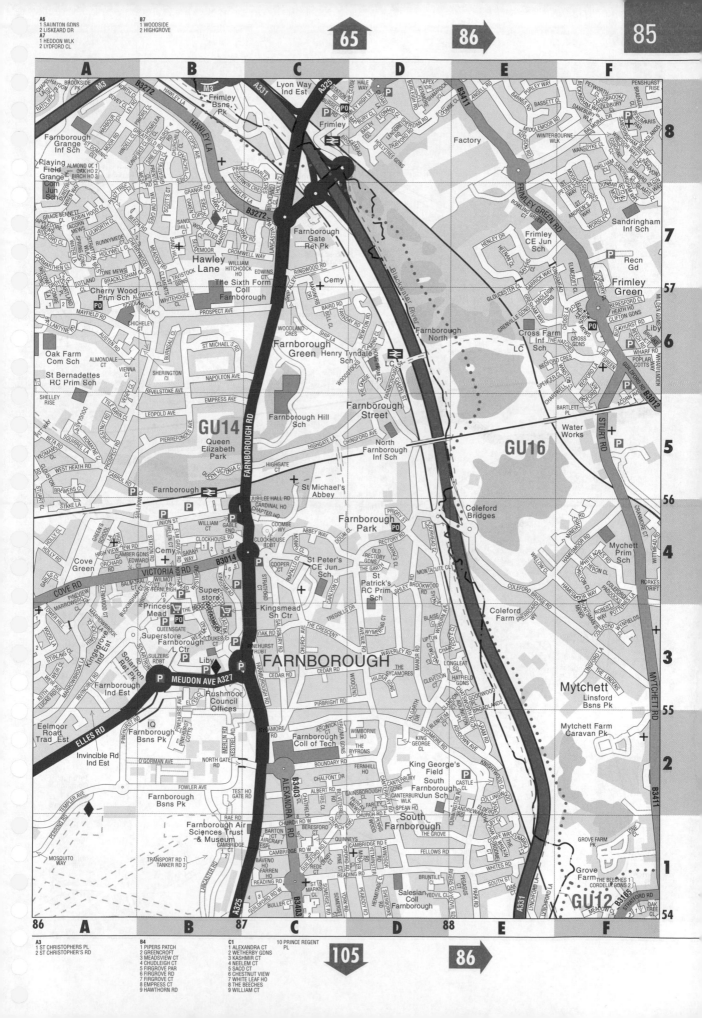

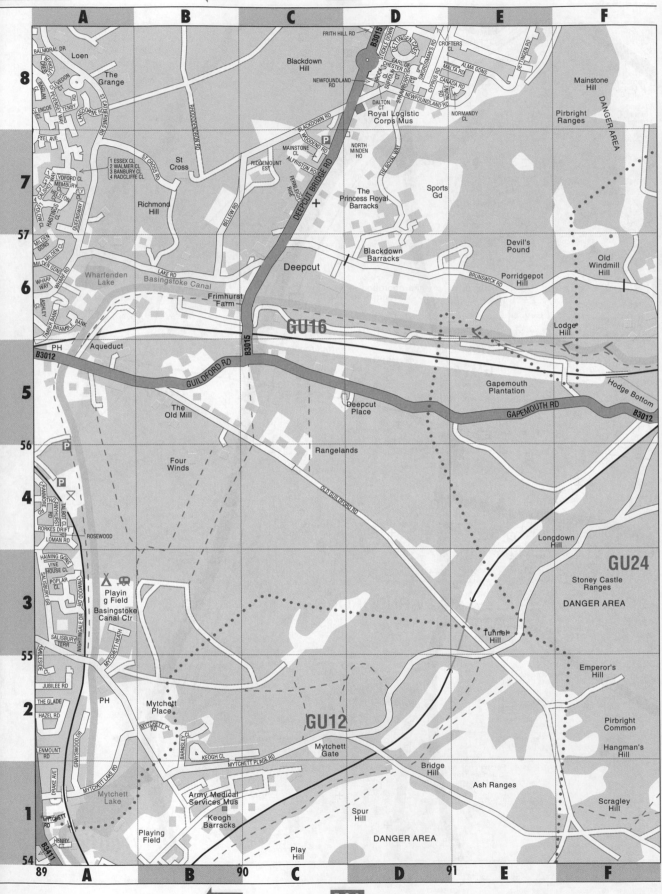

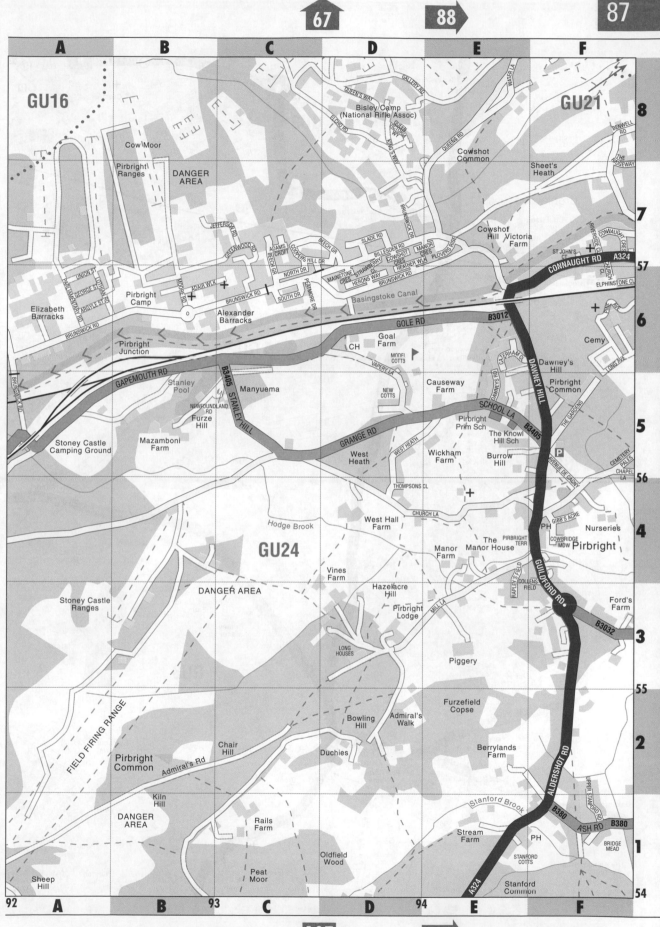

A   B   C   D   E   F

8

7

57

6

5

56

4

55

2

1

54

GU16

GU21

Cow Moor

Pirbright
Ranges

DANGER
AREA

Queen's Way

Bisley Camp
(National Rifle Assoc)

Cowshot
Common

Sheet's
Heath

GALLERY RD

QUEEN'S RD

WATER LA

BENWELL
RD

THE
RIDGEWAY

Elizabeth
Barracks

Pirbright
Camp

Alexander
Barracks

JEFFERSON RD
GREENWOOD RD
ADAMS
CROFT
BEECH GR
NORTH DR
SOUTH DR
COOPERS HILL DR
PENFORD DR
BRUNSWICK DR

BEECH GR
SLADE RD
BILLESDEN RD
COWSHOT
CRES
HEATHER WLK
MANOR
CRES
PLOVERS RISE

Cowshot
Hill
Victoria
Farm

ST JOHN'S
CT
RIVERSIDE CL
CHURCH
CL
ELPHINSTONE CL
CONNAUGHT CRES

CONNAUGHT RD   A324

UNION ST
LOTHIAN RD
GEORGE ST
ARGYLE ST
PARLIAMENTARY RD

MOORE RD
ADAIR WLK
BRUNSWICK RD

MAINSTONE
CRES
STRAWBERRY
CL
HERONS WAY
BRUNSWICK RD

Basingstoke Canal

B3012

Cemy

Cemy

BRUNSWICK RD

Pirbright
Junction

GAPEMOUTH RD

Stanley Pool

B3405

STANLEY HILL

Manyuema

NEWFOUNDLAND
RD
Furze
Hill

GOLE RD

Goal
Farm

CH

VAPERY LA

MODFI
COTTS

NEW
COTTS

Causeway
Farm

CATERHAM CL
DAWNEY'S RD

DAWNEY HILL

Dawney's
Hill

Pirbright
Common

THE GARDENS

LONG AVE

PILE AVE

B3012

Stoney Castle
Camping Ground

Mazamboni
Farm

GRANGE RD

West
Heath

WEST HEATH

Pirbright
Prim Sch

SCHOOL LA

B3405

The Knowl
Hill Sch

Burrow
Hill

Wickham
Farm

AVENUE DE CAGNY

P

CEMETERY
PALES

CHAPEL
LA

GU24

Hodge Brook

THOMPSONS CL

CHURCH LA

West Hall
Farm

The
Manor House

PIRBRIGHT
TERR

PH

Manor
Farm

GIBB'S ACRE

COWBRIDGE
MDW

Pirbright

Nurseries

Stoney Castle
Ranges

DANGER AREA

Vines
Farm

Hazelacre
Hill

Pirbright
Lodge

MILL LA

RAPLEY'S FIELD
COLLENS
FIELD

GUILDFORD RD

Ford's
Farm

B3032

LONG
HOUSES

Piggery

FIELD FIRING RANGE

Chair
Hill

Admiral's Rd

Pirbright
Common

Duchies

Bowling
Hill

Admiral's
Walk

Furzefield
Copse

ALDERSHOT RD

UPPER STANFORD RD

Kiln
Hill

DANGER
AREA

Rails
Farm

Oldfield
Wood

Berrylands
Farm

B380

Stanford Brook

B380

ASH RD

BRIDGE
MEAD

Sheep
Hill

Peat
Moor

Stream
Farm

PH

STANFORD
COTTS

Stanford
Common

A324

C8
1 PARR CT
2 HOWARD CT
3 KATHERINE CT
4 HAMPTON CL

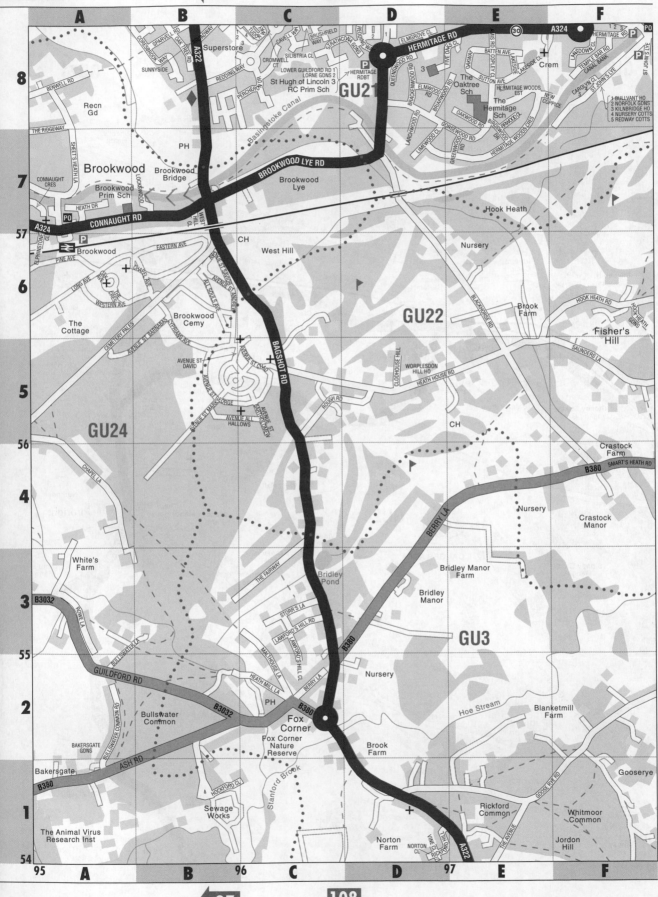

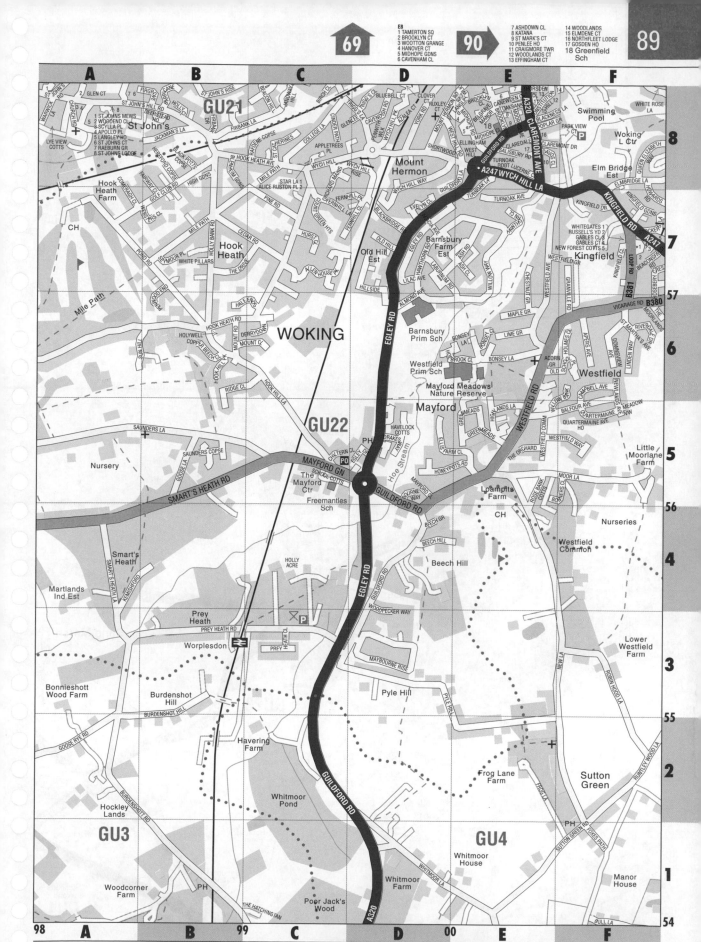

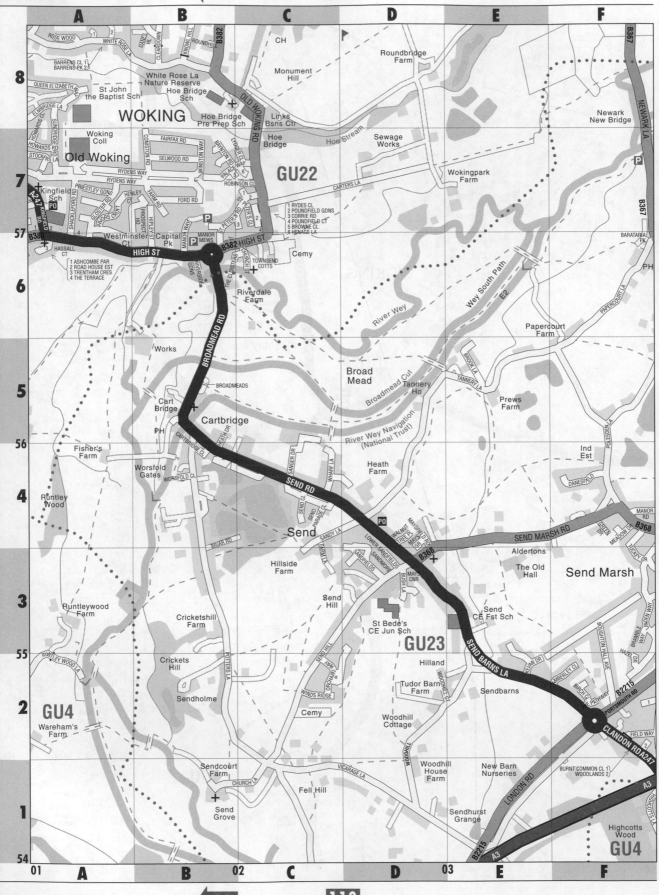

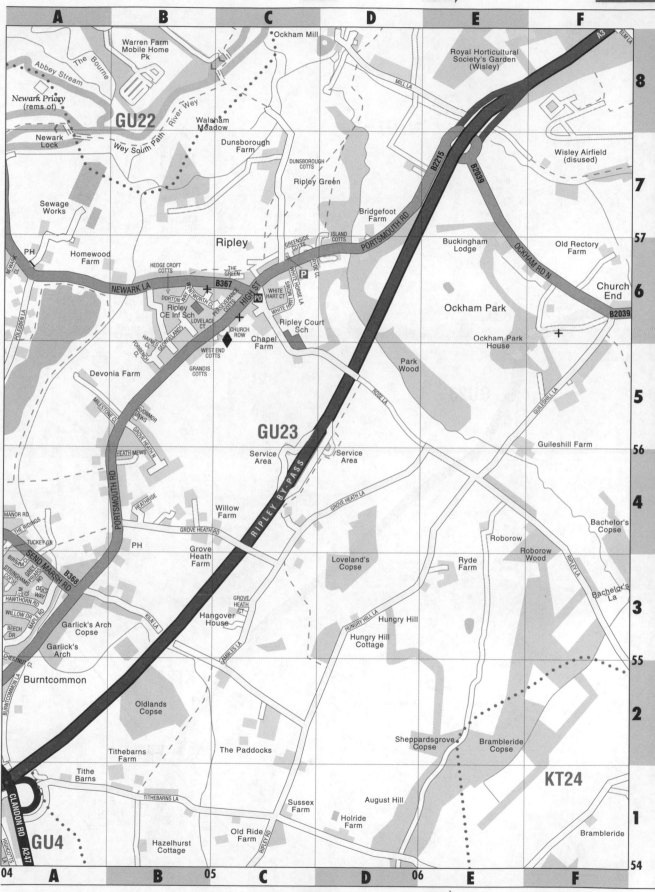

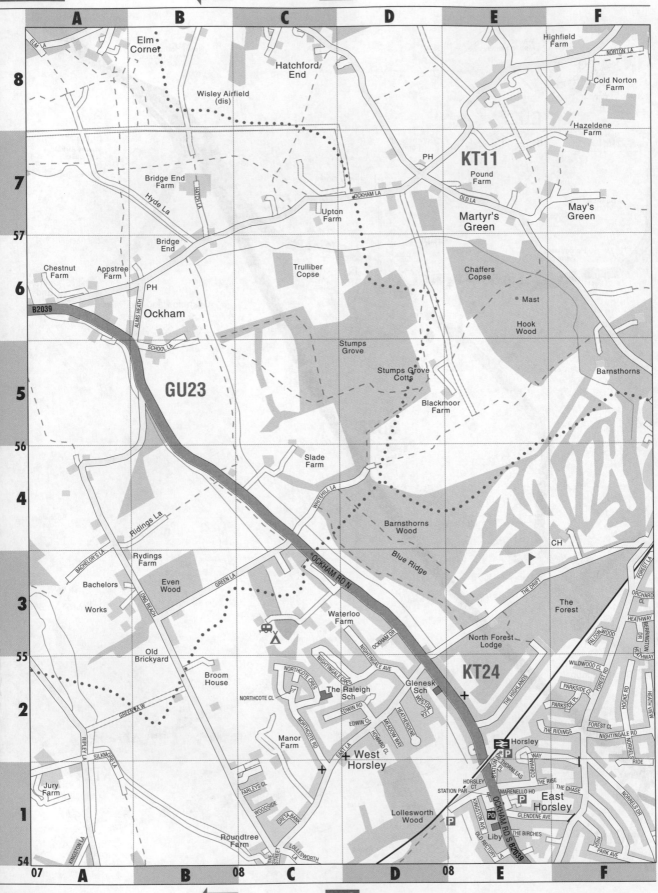

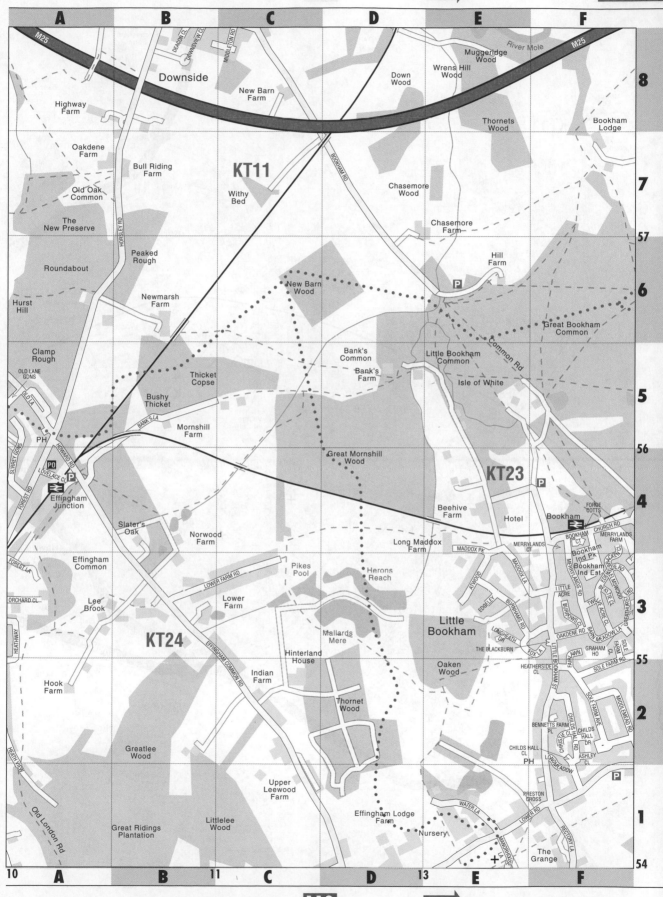

A **B** **C** **D** **E** **F**

M25

Downside

Highway Farm

Oakdene Farm

Bull Riding Farm

Old Oak Common

The New Preserve

Roundabout

Hurst Hill

Clamp Rough

OLD LANE GDNS

PH

PO

LOVELACE CL

P

Effingham Junction

SURREY GDNS

FOREST RD

HOWARD RD

OLD LA

HORSLEY RD

New Barn Farm

KT11

Withy Bed

Peaked Rough

Newmarsh Farm

Thicket Copse

Bushy Thicket

BANK'S LA

Mornshill Farm

Slater's Oak

Norwood Farm

Effingham Common

Lee Brook

ORCHARD CL

HEATHWAY

Hook Farm

HEATH VIEW

Old London Rd

Great Ridings Plantation

KT24

FOREST LA

Lower Farm

LOWER FARM RD

Littlelee Wood

Greatlee Wood

EFFINGHAM COMMON RD

Indian Farm

Hinterland House

Pikes Pool

Mallards Mere

Thornet Wood

Upper Leewood Farm

New Barn Wood

Bank's Common

Bank's Farm

Great Mornshill Wood

Herons Reach

Effingham Lodge Farm

Nursery

Down Wood

Muggeridge Wood

Wrens Hill Wood

River Mole

M25

Thornets Wood

Chasemore Wood

Chasemore Farm

Hill Farm

P

Great Bookham Common

Little Bookham Common

Common Rd

Isle of White

KT23

P

Beehive Farm

Hotel

Long Maddox Farm

MADDOX PK

Little Bookham

Oaken Wood

Bookham Lodge

FORGE COTTS

Bookham

CHURCH RD

Bookham CT

Bookham Ind Pk

Bookham Ind Est

MERRYLANDS CT

MADDOX LA

ATWOOD

EDGELEY

BURNHAMS RD

LONGHEATH DR

FOX LA

THE BLACKBURN

MERRYLANDS RD

Merrylands Farm

LITTLE ACRE

BEATTIE CL

TWEACRE CL

BURROWS

OAKDENE RD

LITTLE BOOKHAM ST

HEATHERSIDE CL

PARK WAY

OAK MEADOW LA

BARN MEADOW LA

LONGSWOOD CL

ELMSWOOD CL

GRAHAM HO

SOLE FARM CL

SOLE FARM RD

BENNETTS FARM PL

CHILDS HALL PL

CHSHO

CHILDS HALL RD

CHILDS HALL CL

PH

LONGMEADOW

SOLE FARM AVE

ASHLEY CL

MIDDLEMEAD RD

P

Preston Cross

WATER LA

LOWER RD

RECTORY LA

MANORHOUSE LA

+

The Grange

8

7

57

6

5

56

4

55

3

2

1

54

A **B** **C** **D** **E** **F**

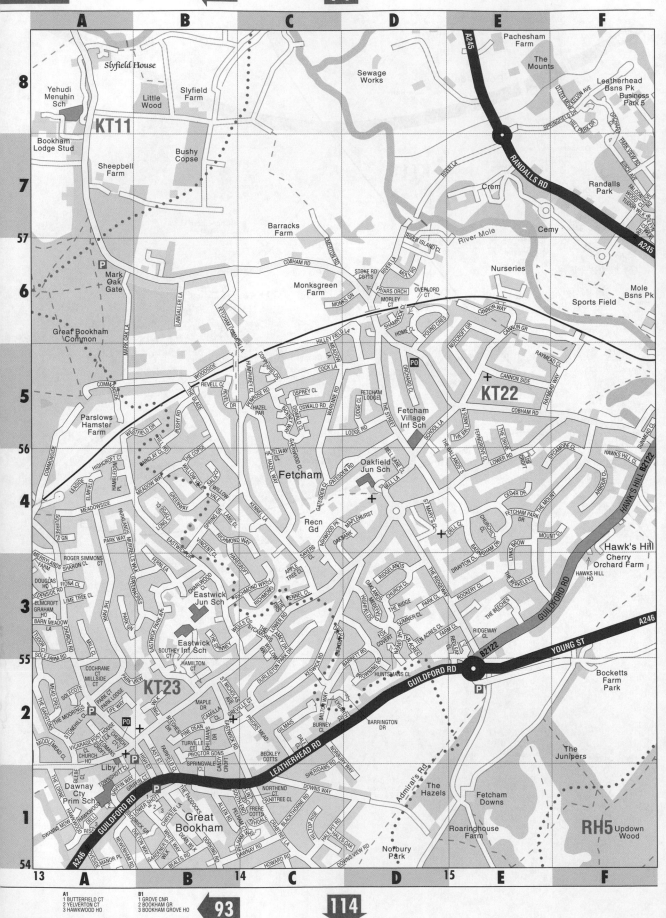

A1
1 BUTTERFIELD CT
2 YELVERTON CT
3 HAWKWOOD HO

B1
1 GROVE CNR
2 BOOKHAM GR
3 BOOKHAM GROVE HO

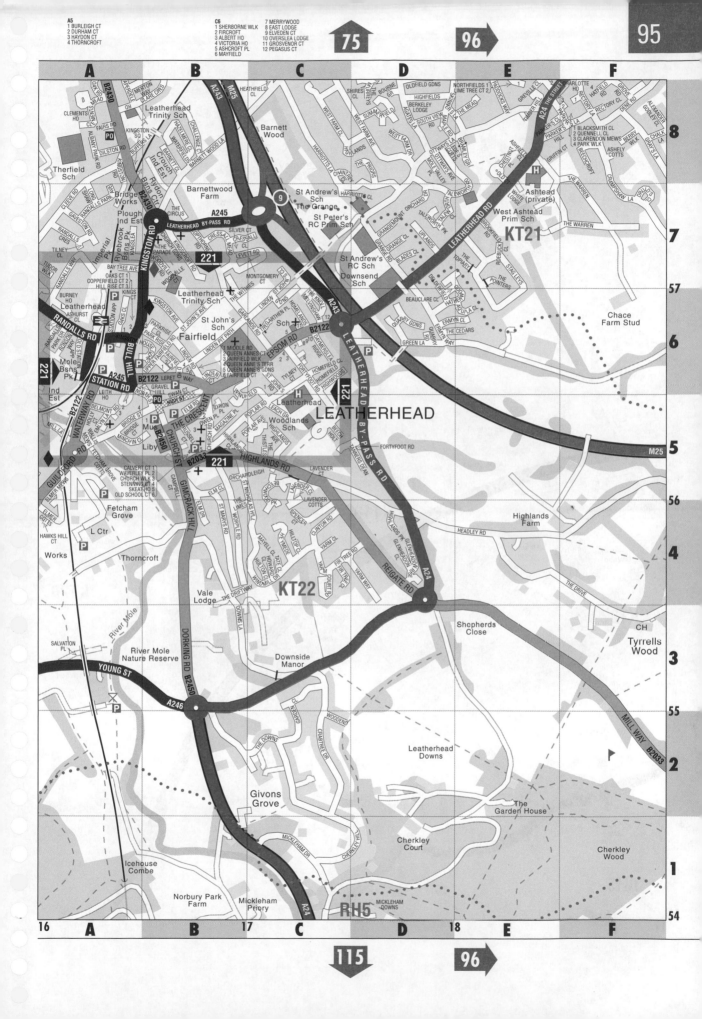

A B C D E F

8

7

57

6

5

56

4

3

55

2

1

54

19 A B 20 C D 21 E F

City of London Freemen's Sch

KT21 Ashtead Park

CHALK LA
RALLIWOOD RD
GRAY'S LA
OAKEN COPPICE
PARK LA
FARM LA
CRAMPSHAW LA

PIPE'S A

HEADLEY RD
CHALK PIT
DOWNS RD

Larch Field

Tudor Croft

SHEPHERDS' WLK
CRADDOCKS AVE

Thirty Acre Barn

PEBBLE LA

Gilletts Cotts

HEADLEY RD
WALTON RD

Langley Bottom Wood

MILLERS COPSE
GROSVENOR MEWS
GROSVENER MEWS
LANGLEY VALE RD
ROSEBERY RD
GROSVENOR RD
HARDING RD
BEACONSFIELD RD
SADDLERS WAY
STRAND CL
HAYES
MAINMEAD
MANN
MEAD
STABLE CL
VALE CL
TILER

Langley Vale

The Vale Prim Sch

Langley Vale Farm

The Warren

Walton Downs

Nohome Farm

Downs View Wood

Downs View

EBRISHAM LA

Addlestead Wood

Addlestead Farm

Fourfield Close

SHEEP WLK

Hurst Farm

Little Hurst Wood

Round Wood

M25

56

Hambleton Wood

HEADLEY RD

Headley Court

DALE VIEW

TILLEY LA

Headley Park

FARRIERS

HURST LA

Twistwood

Edes Barn Cotts

HURST RD

KT20

KT18

KT22

THE DRIVE

Court Farm

CUNLIFFE CL

CLAY LA

HURST CL

Hookwood Cotts

Hook Wood

Great Hurst Wood

Sandhill Wood

Oyster Hill

Nower Wood

Langley Lane

SLOUGH LA

TUMBER ST

CHURCH LA

PH

P

Costal Wood

HOWARD CL

B2033

MILL WAY

P

Nature Reserve

LEECH LA

LODGEBOTTOM RD

CRABTREE LA

THE SPINNEY

BROOK LA

Headley

Heath House

B2033

Heath Farm

Manor House

Walton Park Wood

M25

Love Lane

RH5

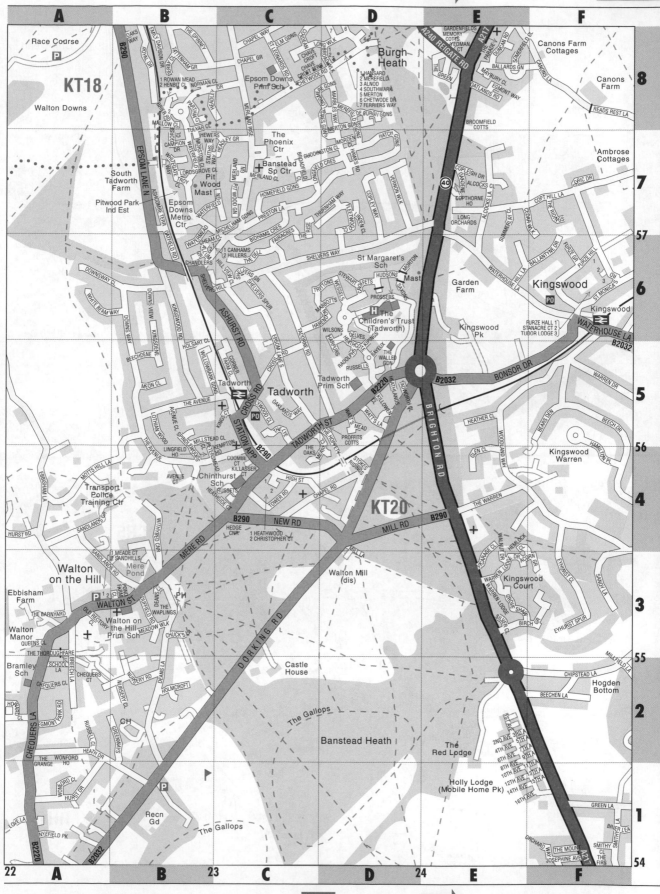

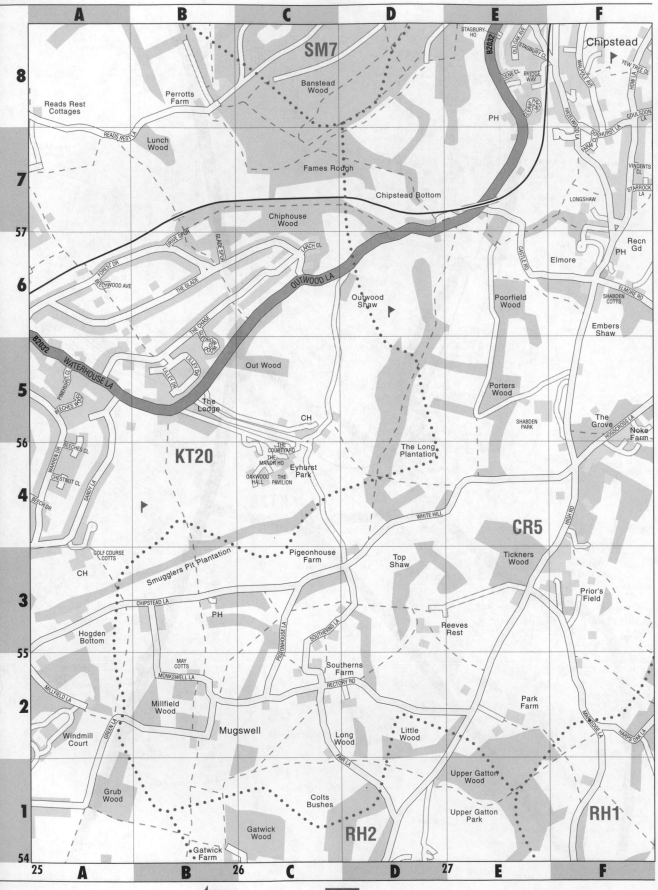

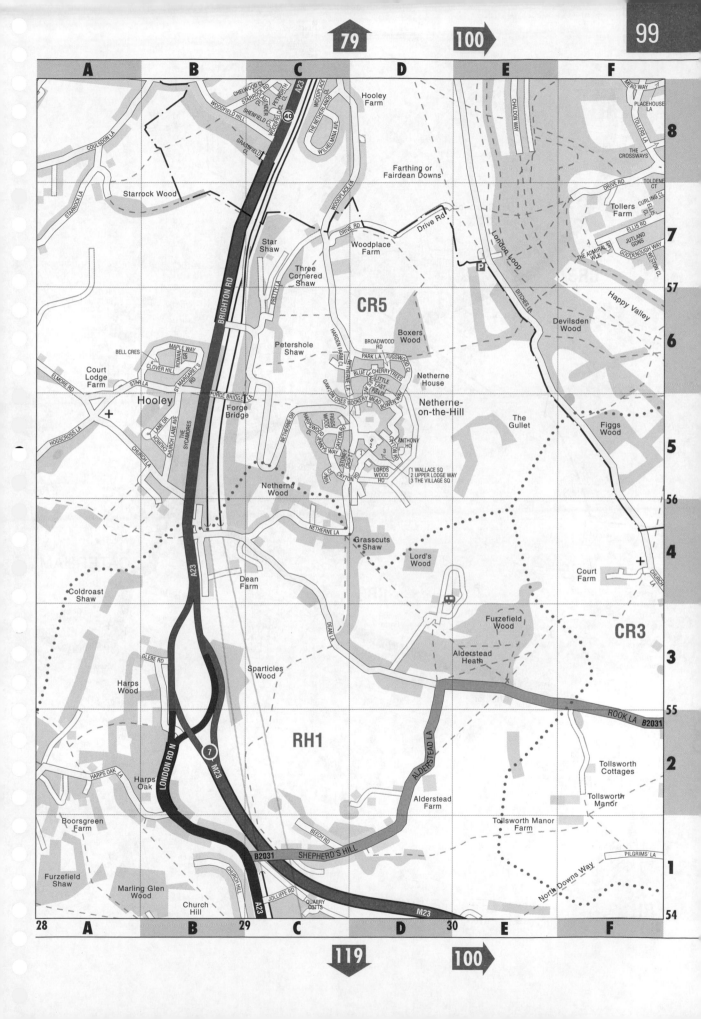

99

C6
1 NEWLANDS CT
2 HUNTSMANS CT
3 ALMA CT

80

D5
1 LE PERSONNE HOMES
2 THE FIRS
3 CHATFIELD CT
4 CHRISTIE WLK
5 CEDAR CT
6 HOLM CT

A B C D E F

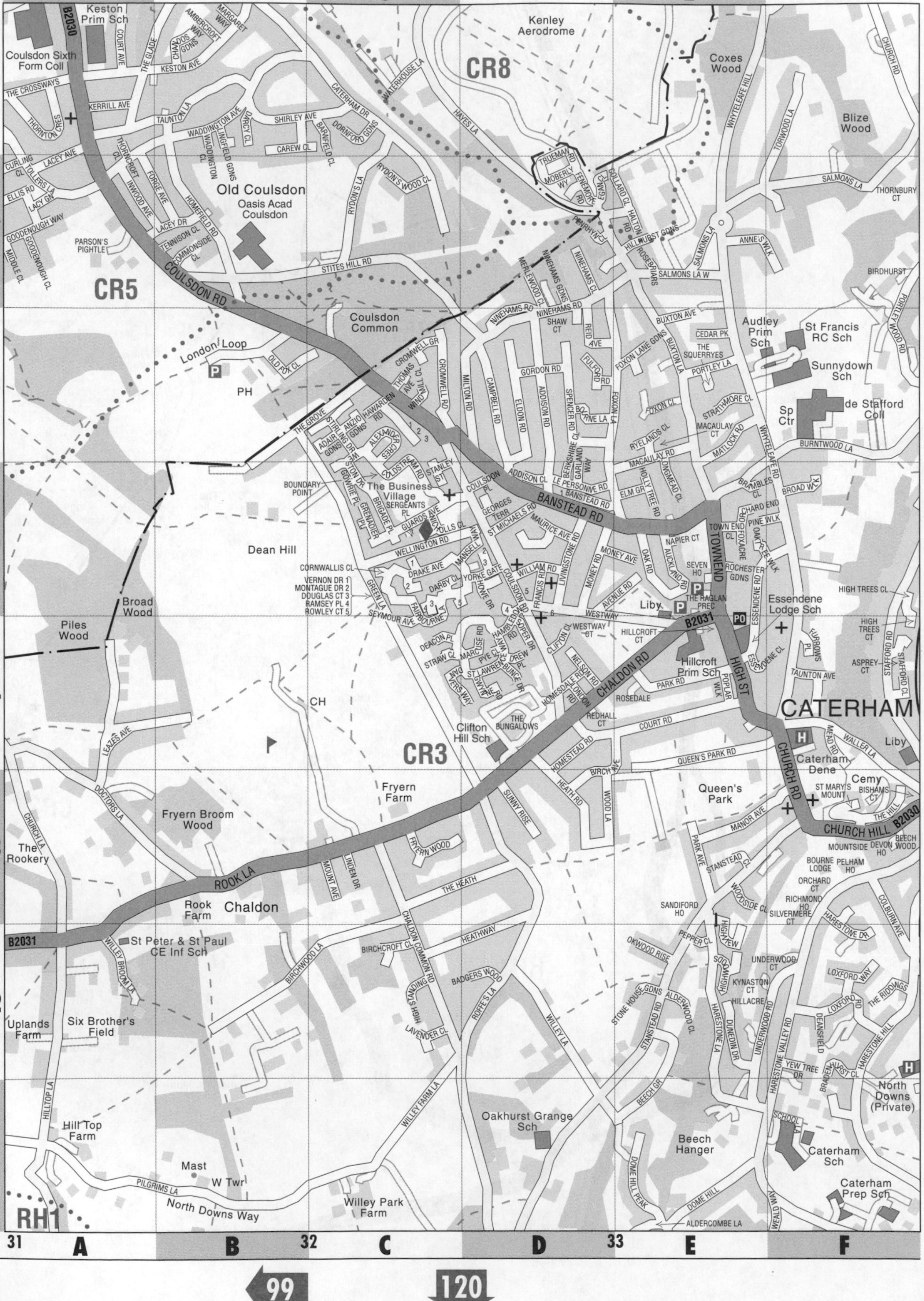

8
7
57
6
5
56
4
3
55
2
1
54
B2030
Keston Prim Sch
Coulsdon Sixth Form Coll
COURT AVE
THE GLADE
CHANDOS WAY
AMBERCROFT WAY
MARGARET WAY
KESTON AVE
THE CROSSWAYS
KERRILL AVE
THORNTON CRES
TAUNTON LA
WADDINGTON AVE
WADDINGTON CL
INGFIELD GDNS
DARCY CL
SHIRLEY AVE
CAREW CL
BARNFIELD CL
DORNFORD GDNS
CATERHAM DR
WATERHOUSE LA
HAYES LA
Kenley Aerodrome
CR8
Coxes Wood
WHYTELEAFE HILL
TORWOOD LA
Blize Wood
CHURCH RD
SALMONS LA
THORNBURY CT
CURLING CL
LACEY AVE
TOLLERS LA
ELLIS RD
LACY GN
GOODENOUGH WAY
GOODENOUGH CL
MIDDLE CL
THORNCROFT
INWOOD AVE
FORGE AVE
HOMEFIELD RD
LACEY DR
TENNISON CL
COMMONSIDE CL
Old Coulsdon
Oasis Acad Coulsdon
PARSON'S PIGHTLE
CR5
RYDON'S LA
RYDON'S WOOD CL
TRUEMAN RD
MOBERLY WY
FENEMORE RD
EGAN CL
BOLLARD CL
HALTON RD
PENRHYN CL
HILLHURST GDNS
ROSEBRIARS
SALMONS LA W
ANNE'S WLK
BIRDHURST
PORTLEY WOOD RD
STITES HILL RD
COULSDON RD
Coulsdon Common
London Loop
OLD FOX CL
P
PH
MERLEWOOD CL
NINEHAMS GDNS
NINEHAMS CL
NINEHAMS RD
SHAW CT
BUXTON AVE
Audley Prim Sch
St Francis RC Sch
CEDAR PK
THE SQUERRYES
PORTLEY LA
Sunnydown Sch
Sp Ctr
de Stafford Coll
CROMWELL GR
CROMWELL RD
THOMAS AVE
WINDMILL CL
MILTON RD
CAMPBELL RD
ELDON RD
GORDON RD
ADDISON RD
REID AVE
FULFORD RD
FOXON LANE GDNS
BUXTON LA
FOXON LA
FOXON CL
STRATHMORE CL
RYELANDS CL
MACAULAY CT
MACAULAY RD
MATLOCK RD
WHYTELEAFE RD
BURNTWOOD LA
THE GROVE
HAWARDEN RD
ANZIO GDNS
STIRLING DR
ADAIR GDNS
ALEXANDER CRES
COLDSTREAM RD
STANLEY ST
BOUNDARY POINT
The Business Village
SERGEANTS PL
GOWRIE PL
GRENADIER PL
BRIGADE PL
GUARDS AVE
NICHOLLS CL
COULSDON PL
GEORGES TERR
ST MICHAELS RD
ADDISON CL
BERKSHIRE CL
GARLAND WAY
SPENCER RD
BORNE LA
LE PERSONNE RD
BANSTEAD RD
ELM GR
HOLLY TREE RD
LONGMEAD CL
BRAMBLES CL
BROAD WLK
TOWN END CL
CHARD END
PINE WLK
FOXACRE
OAKTREE WLK
NAPIER CT
Dean Hill
WELLINGTON RD
MAURICE AVE
LIVINGSTONE RD
MONEY RD
MONEY AVE
OAK RD
AUCKLAND RD
SEVEN HO
TOWNEND
ROCHESTER GDNS
ESSENDENE RD
HIGH TREES CL
CORNWALLIS CL
VERNON DR 1
MONTAGUE DR 2
DOUGLAS CT 3
RAMSEY PL 4
ROWLEY CT 5
DRAKE AVE
MANSELL WAY
DARBY CL
YORKE GATE
HOWE DR
COULSDON RD
FRANCIS RD
WILLIAM RD
AVENUE RD
Liby
THE RAGLAN PREC
Essendene Lodge Sch
Broad Wood
Piles Wood
GREEN LA
SEYMOUR AVE
FAIRBOURNE
WESTWAY
WESTWAY CT
B2031
PO
HIGH TREES CT
HILLCROFT CT
DEACON PL
MARCUSE RD
HAMBLEDON RD
COPPER DR
STRAW CL
PYE CL
DREW PL
ST LAWRENCE WAY
BUNCE DR
CLIFTON CL
NELSON RD
ESSENDENE CL
FURROWS PL
STAFFORD RD
STAFFORD CL
ASPREY CT
CHALDON RD
Hillcroft Prim Sch
HIGH ST
POPLAR WLK
TAUNTON AVE
PARK RD
HOMESDALE RD
LONDON RD
ROSEDALE
CH
THE BUNGALOWS
REDHALL CT
CATERHAM
COURT RD
Clifton Hill Sch
CR3
HOMESTEAD RD
QUEEN'S PARK RD
H
MEAD RD
WALLER LA
Liby
CHURCH RD
Caterham Dene
LEAZES AVE
DOCTORS LA
Fryern Farm
BIRCH AVE
HEATH RD
WOOD LA
Queen's Park
ST MARY'S MOUNT
Cemy
BISHAMS CT
THE HILL
SUNNY RISE
MANOR AVE
CHURCH HILL
B2030
Fryern Broom Wood
CHURCH LA
The Rookery
FRYERN WOOD
MOUNTSIDE
DEVON HO
BEECH WOOD
PARK AVE
STANSTEAD CL
BOURNE LODGE
PELHAM HO
ROOK LA
MOUNT AVE
LINDEN DR
THE HEATH
ORCHARD CT
Rook Farm
Chaldon
SANDIFORD HO
WOODSIDE CL
RICHMOND HO
SILVERMERE CT
HARESTONE DR
COLBURN AVE
B2031
St Peter & St Paul CE Inf Sch
WILLEY BROOM LA
BIRCHWOOD LA
BIRCHCROFT CL
HEATHWAY
CHALDON COMMON RD
OKWOOD RISE
PEPPER CL
HIGHVIEW
UNDERWOOD CT
BADGERS WOOD
SOUTHWOOD
KYNASTON CT
LOXFORD WAY
THE RIDINGS
HIGH STANDING
ROFFE'S LA
STONE HOUSE GDNS
ALDERWOOD CL
HILLACRE
LOXFORD RD
Uplands Farm
Six Brother's Field
LAVENDER CL
WILLEY LA
STANSTEAD RD
HARESTONE LA
DUNEDIN DR
UNDERWOOD RD
HARESTONE VALLEY RD
DEANSFIELD
HARESTONE HILL
YEW TREE DR
BRADENHURST CL
H
North Downs (Private)
HILLTOP LA
WILLEY FARM LA
BEECH GR
Oakhurst Grange Sch
Beech Hanger
SCHOOL LA
Caterham Sch
Hill Top Farm
Mast
W Twr
PILGRIMS LA
North Downs Way
Willey Park Farm
DOME HILL PEAK
DOME HILL
ALDERCOMBE LA
WEALD WAY
Caterham Prep Sch
RH1
31
32
33

A B C D E F

99

120

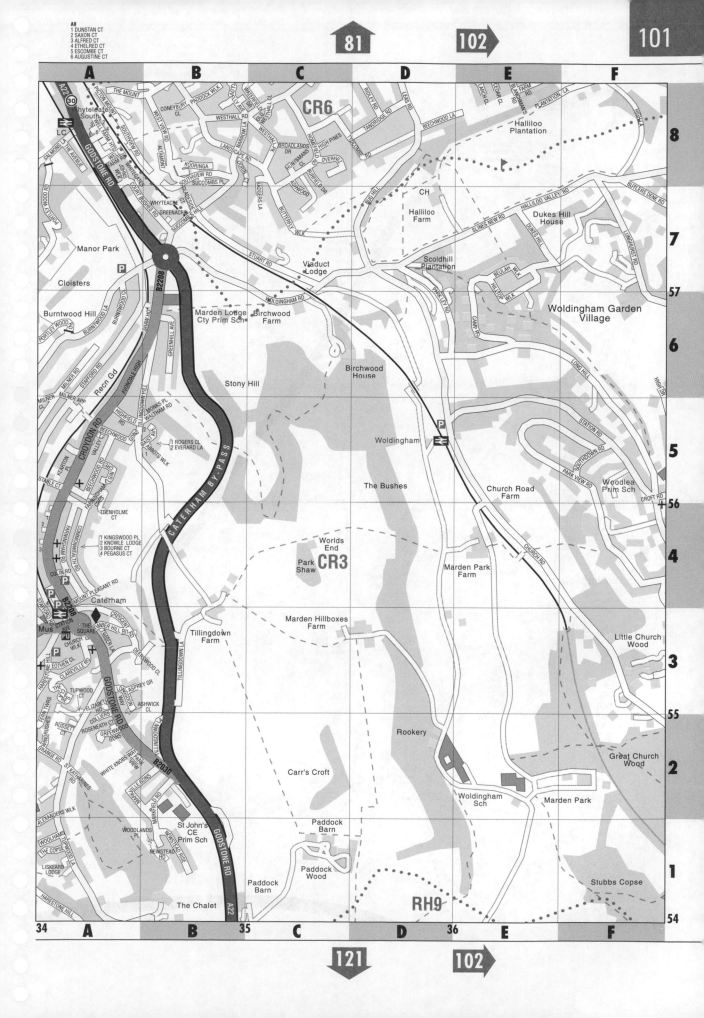

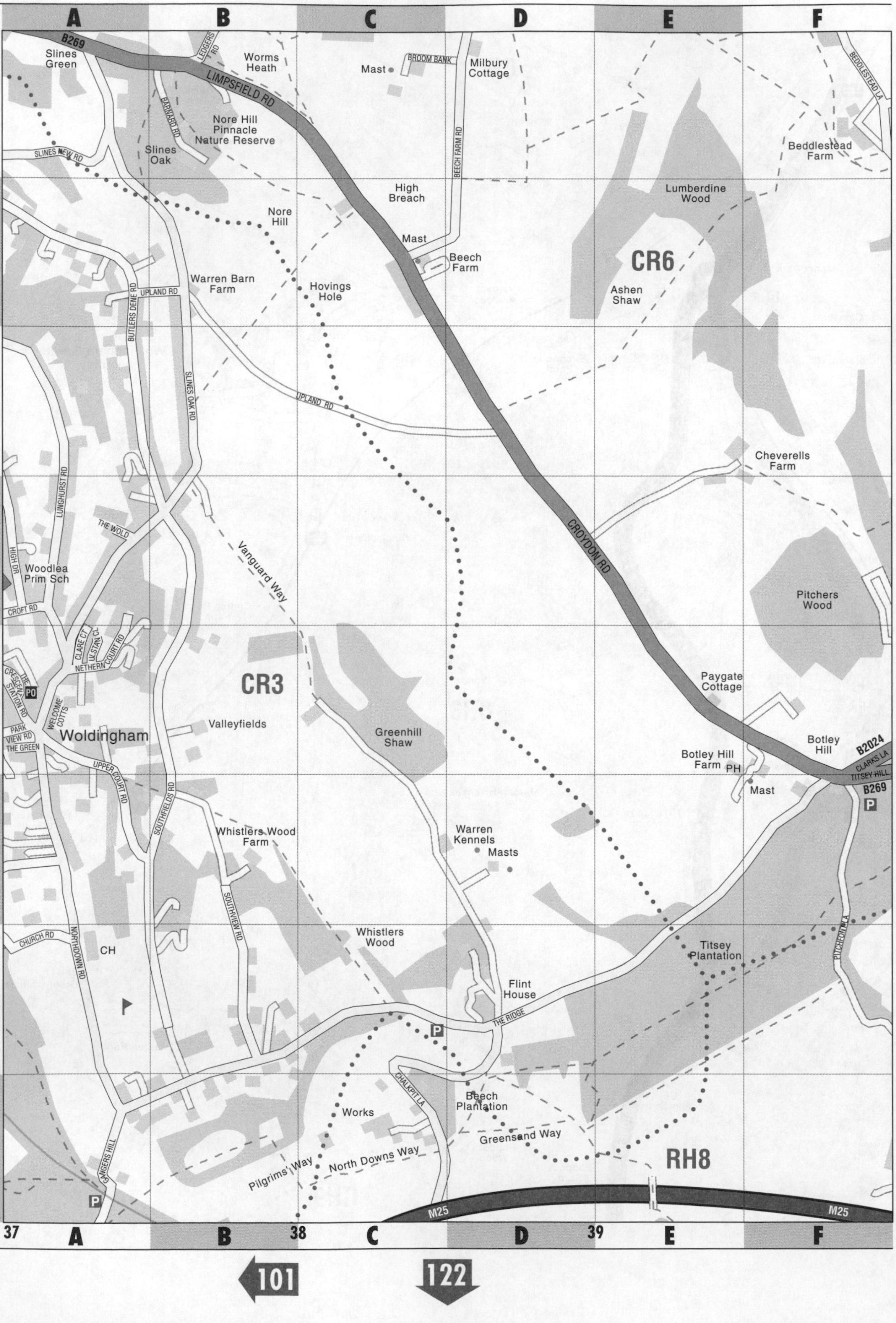

A B C D E F

8

7

57

6

5

56

4

3

55

2

1

54

37 A B 38 C D 39 E F

B269

Slines Green

Worms Heath

Mast

Broom Bank

Milbury Cottage

LIMPSFIELD RD

Nore Hill Pinnacle Nature Reserve

Slines Oak

SLINES NEW RD

BARNFIELD RD

LEDGERS RD

High Breach

BEECH FARM RD

Beddlestead Farm

BEDDLESTEAD LA

Nore Hill

Mast

Lumberdine Wood

CR6

Warren Barn Farm

Hovings Hole

Beech Farm

Ashen Shaw

BUTLERS DENE RD

UPLAND RD

SLINES OAK RD

UPLAND RD

Cheverells Farm

THE WOLD

LUNGHURST RD

Vanguard Way

CROYDON RD

Pitchers Wood

HIGH DR

Woodlea Prim Sch

CLARE CT

VISTAN CT

NETHERN COURT RD

CROFT RD

CR3

Paygate Cottage

Botley Hill

B2024

CLARKS LA

CRESCENT RD

STATION RD

PO

WELCOME COTTS

Valleyfields

Greenhill Shaw

Botley Hill Farm

PH

TITSEY HILL

B269

PARK VIEW RD

THE GREEN

Woldingham

UPPER COURT RD

SOUTHFIELDS RD

SOUTHVIEW RD

Whistlers Wood Farm

Warren Kennels

Masts

Mast

PITCHFONT LA

CHURCH RD

NORTHDOWN RD

CH

Whistlers Wood

Titsey Plantation

THE RIDGE

Flint House

CHALKPIT LA

Works

Beech Plantation

Greensand Way

RH8

SANDERS HILL

P

Pilgrims' Way

North Downs Way

M25

M25

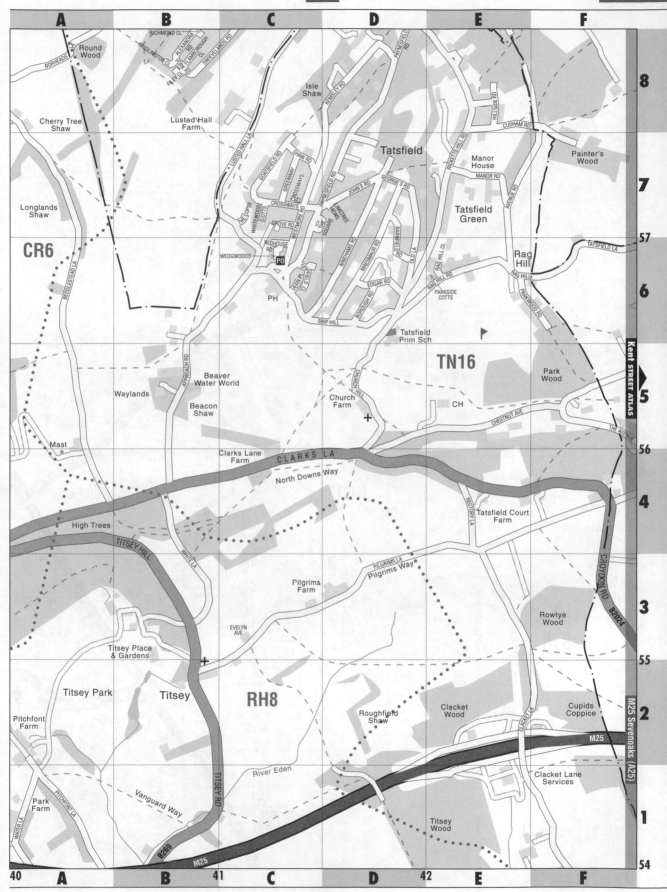

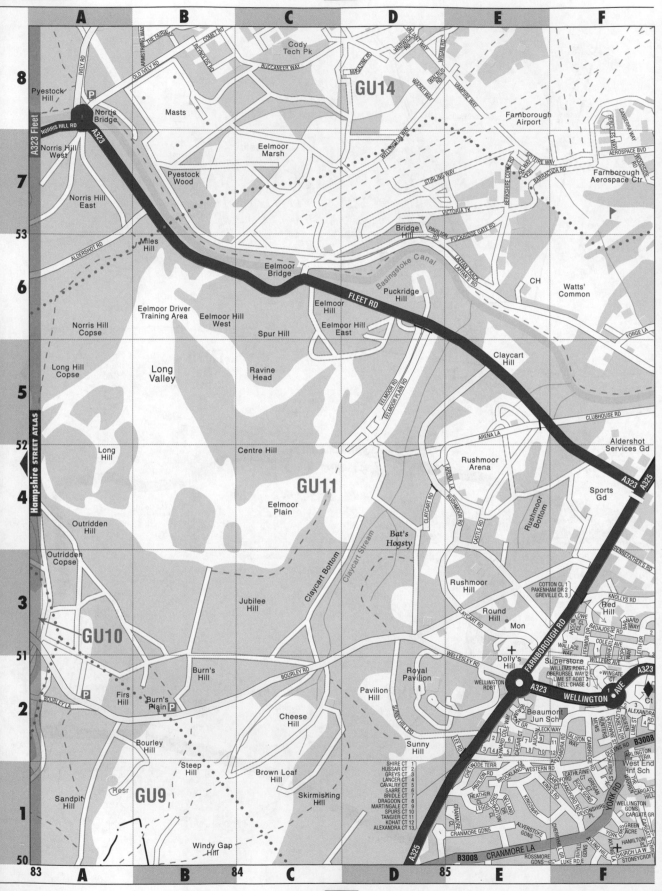

Hampshire STREET ATLAS

A323 Fleet

GU14

Pyestock Hill

Norris Bridge

P

Masts

Cody Tech Pk

BUCCANEER WAY

COMET RD

THE FAIRWAY

OLD IVELY RD

IVELY RD

FERNDALE RD

Armstrong Way

MAGAZINE RD

Farnborough Airport

WARWICK RD

VALIANT WAY

WICAN RD

VAMPIRE WAY

WALRUS RD

WELLINGTON WAY

Farnborough Aerospace Ctr

CANBERRA WAY

HERCULES WAY

AEROSPACE BVD

WOODSIDE RD

Norris Hill RD

A323

Norris Hill West

Norris Hill East

ALDERSHOT RD

Miles Hill

Pyestock Wood

Eelmoor Marsh

STIRLING WAY

VICTORIA TK

Bridge Hill

PAVILION RD

SKI WAY

BARRACUDA RD

SPITFIRE WAY

BERKSHIRE COPSE RD

B3035

Basingstoke Canal

Eelmoor Bridge

Puckridge Hill

FLEET RD

CH

Watts' Common

LAFFAN TRACK

LAFFAN'S RD

FORGE LA

Eelmoor Driver Training Area

Eelmoor Hill West

Spur Hill

Eelmoor Hill

Eelmoor Hill East

Claycart Hill

CLUBHOUSE RD

Aldershot Services Gd

Norris Hill Copse

Ravine Head

EELMOOR RD

EELMOOR PLAIN RD

ARENA LA

A323

A325

Long Hill Copse

Long Valley

Centre Hill

GU11

Eelmoor Plain

Rushmoor Arena

Sports Gd

Long Hill

Outridden Hill

Claycart Bottom

Claycart Stream

Bat's Hogsty

CASTLE RD

CLAYCART RD

RUSHMOOR RD

ARENA LA

Rushmoor Bottom

BENNEFATHER'S RD

Red Hill

Outridden Copse

GU10

Jubilee Hill

Rushmoor Hill

Round Hill

Mon

FARNBOROUGH RD

KNOLLYS RD

BARNARD WAY

ANSON RD

BADAJOS RD

LOWE

COLE RD

Burn's Hill

BOURLEY RD

CLAYCART RD

WALLACE WAY

WILLEMS AVE

LEITH DR

Firs Hill

P

Burn's Plain

P

WELLESLEY RD

Dolly's Hill

Royal Pavilion

WELLINGTON RDBT

Superstore

WILLEMS RDBT 1
OBERURSEL WAY 2
LIME ST RDBT 3
BELL CHASE 4

WINGATE CT

A323

Ct

BOURLEY LA

Bourley Hill

Cheese Hill

Pavilion Hill

SUNNY HILL RD

LEE RD

A323

A323

WELLINGTON AVE

ALEXANDRA RD

Beaumont Jun Sch

HOWARD COLE WAY

CAESAR CT

AUCHINLECK WAY

ALISON WAY

B3008

West End Inf Sch

YORK RD

Sandpit Hill

Steep Hill

GU9

Brown Loaf Hill

Skirmishing Hill

Sunny Hill

SHIRE CT 1
HUSSAR CT 2
GREYS CT 3
LANCER CT 4
CAVALRY CT 5
SABRE CT 6
BRIDLE CT 7
DRAGOON CT 8
MARTINGALE CT 9
SPURS CT 10
TANGIER CT 11
KOHAT CT 12
ALEXANDRA CT 13

CHERNODE TERR

PAVILION RD

BROOKLANDS RD

WESTERN RD

HEATHER CL

KINGSWAY

KING'S RD

LEGGE CRES

WELLAND RD

CAMBRIDGE RD

QUEENS RD

DEVONSHIRE RD

ALVERSTOKE GDNS

CHERHILL LGR

AYLING HILL

Resr

Windy Gap Hill

Bourley Hill

B3008

CRANMORE LA

CRANMORE GDNS

ROSSMORE GDNS

York RD

WELLINGTON GDNS

CARGATE GR

GREEN ACRE

HAMILTON PL

CHURCH LA W

Stoneycroft

C8
1 HAWTHORN CT
2 SHAFTESBURY CT
3 PRINCESS CT

85

106

D8
1 SYLVAN CT
2 GROSVENOR HO
3 ARNELLA CT
4 THE FERNS
5 KINGDOM HO

F5
1 STIRLING CL
2 WYVERN CL
3 BALMORAL HO
4 HATFIELD HO

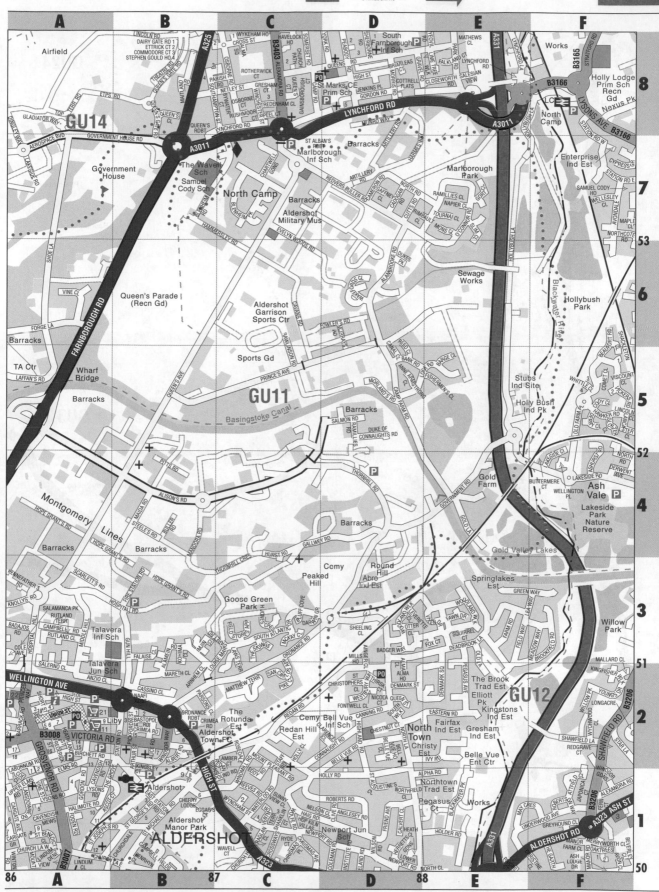

A1
1 LABURNUM CL
2 LABURNUM PAS
3 PARK HO
4 WOLSELEY RD
5 CULLENS MEWS
6 SALES CT
7 BURLINGTON CT
8 CHASEWATER CT
9 GARRETT MEWS
10 EDWARD CT
11 HEREFORD HO
12 HEATHER CT
A2
1 UPPER UNION ST
2 EDWARD ST
3 NELSON ST
4 LOWER NELSON ST
5 UPPER UNION TERR
6 CROSS ST
7 UNION TERR
8 WELLINGTON ST
9 LITTLE WELLINGTON ST
10 COURT RD
11 The Arcade
   Sh Ctr
12 STRATFIELD HO
13 PHOENIX CT
14 FIR TREE ALLEY
15 MOUNTBATTEN CT
16 SEFTON HO
17 WILLIAM FARTHING CL
18 HIGH VIEW LODGE
19 NELSON HO
20 IONA HO
21 The Wellington
   Sh Ctr
22 Princes Hall
   Theatre

B1
1 MANOR WLK
2 BOULTERS RD
3 WELLESLEY GATE
4 ST DAVIDS CT
5 HERALD CT
6 ST GEORGE'S RD E
7 HARRIET CT
8 BEECHNUT RD
9 Beechnut Ind Est

B2
1 ARTILLERY RD
2 ENTERPRISE HO
3 EMARC HO
4 WALPOLE HO
5 LONDON HO
6 GABLE END
7 AVERY CT

C1
1 WINDMILL CT
2 Manor Pk Ind Est
3 BEMBRIDGE CT
4 BROADHURST MEWS
5 PEMBURY PL

F1
1 OAKTREES CT
2 WOODLANDS PK
3 Walsh Memorial CE Inf Sch

A **B** **C** **D** **E** **F**

GU24

8 Nexus Pk
Play Hill
DANGER AREA
Furze Hill
Lookout Hill
Ranges
Romping Downs
Scarp Hill
Cleygate Common

Ash Vale
Greatbottom Flash
Pit Hill
Peatmoor Hill

7 Great Bottom
Bastion Hill

53 Fox Hill West

Steel Hill
Ash Common
Fox Hills
6 Dukes Hill
Ranges

DANGER AREA

Heather Cl

Stony Hill
Ricochet Hill
Wyke Common
5 Gorselands Cl
Dolleyshill
GU3

52 Milton Grange
Normandy Hill
Normandy Lodge Farm

DANGER AREA
Roughs Farm
4 GU12
Surprise Hill
Gravelpit Hill
Rand's Plantation
Wyke Prim Sch
PIRBRIGHT RD
A324

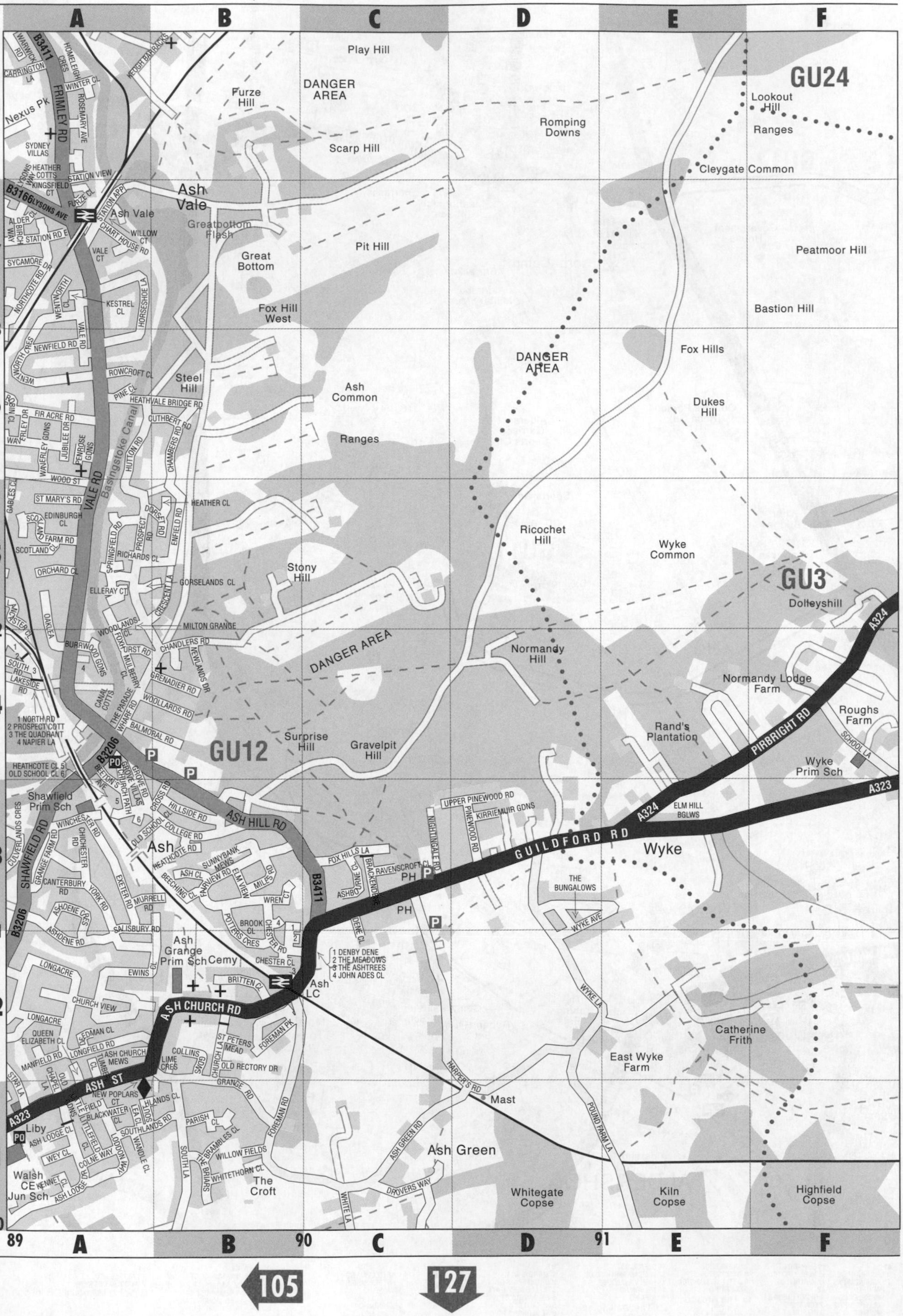

Shawfield Prim Sch
Upper Pinewood Rd
Kirriemuir Gdns
A324
ELM HILL BGLWS
A323
3 Ash
ASH HILL RD
Fox Hills La
GUILDFORD RD
Wyke
B3411
Ravenscroft Cl
THE BUNGALOWS
PH

51 Ash Grange Prim Sch Cemy
Chester Rd
1 Denby Dene
2 The Meadows
3 The Ashtrees
4 John Ades Cl
Ash LC
Wyke La
2 ASH CHURCH RD
Catherine Frith
East Wyke Farm

ASH ST
A323
Mast
Liby
1 Walsh CE Jun Sch
Ash Green
Whitegate Copse
Kiln Copse
Highfield Copse
The Croft
Drovers Way

50 89 **A** **B** 90 **C** **D** 91 **E** **F**

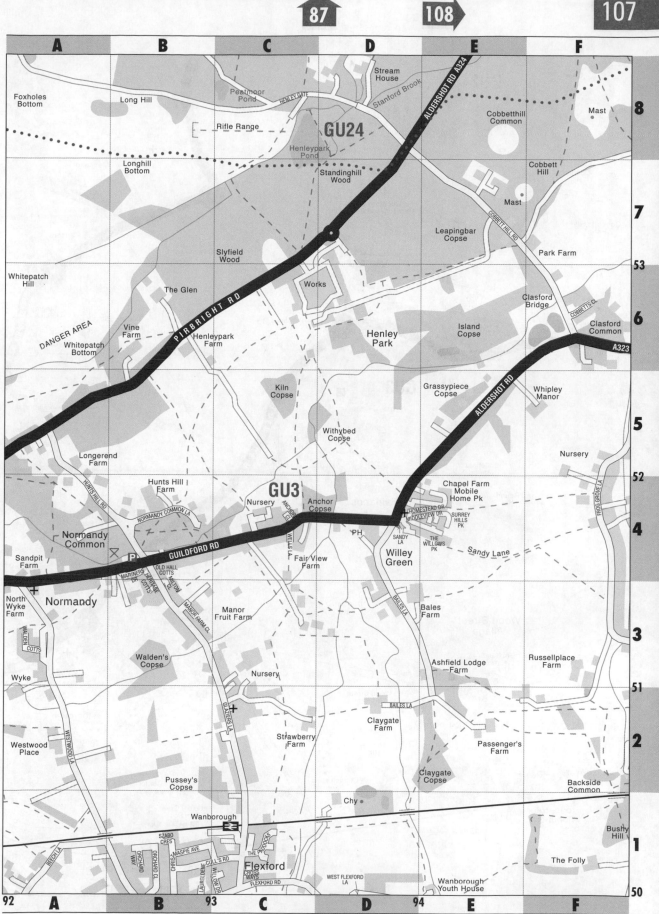

A B C D E F

Foxholes Bottom

Long Hill

Peatmoor Pond

Stream House

Stanford Brook

GU24

Cobbetthill Common

Mast 8

Rifle Range

Henleypark Pond

Longhill Bottom

Standinghill Wood

Cobbett Hill

Mast 7

Whitepatch Hill

The Glen

Slyfield Wood

Works

Leapingbar Copse

Park Farm

53

DANGER AREA

Vine Farm

PIRBRIGHT RD

Henleypark Farm

Henley Park

Island Copse

Clasford Bridge

COBBETT HILL RD

Clasford Common

COBBETT'S CL

6

Whitepatch Bottom

Kiln Copse

Grassypiece Copse

ALDERSHOT RD

Whipley Manor

A323

Longerend Farm

Withybed Copse

Nursery

5

HUNTS HILL RD

Hunts Hill Farm

GU3

Nursery

Anchor Copse

Chapel Farm Mobile Home Pk

52

FROG GROVE LA

Normandy Common

NORMANDY COMMON LA

WELLS LA

ANCHOR CL

PH

HOMESTEAD DR MIDDLEVIEW DR

Surrey Hills Pk

4

Sandpit Farm

P

GUILDFORD RD

Fair View Farm

Willey Green

SANDY LA

THE WILLOWS PK

Sandy Lane

North Wyke Farm

Normandy

MARINERS DR

OLD HALL COTTS

MILTON COTTS

HERITAGE COTTS

MANOR FARM CL

Manor Fruit Farm

BALES LA

Bales Farm

3

WALDEN COTTS

Wyke

Walden's Copse

Nursery

Ashfield Lodge Farm

Russellplace Farm

51

Westwood Place

WESTWOOD LA

GLAZIERS LA

Strawberry Farm

BAILES LA

Claygate Farm

Passenger's Farm

2

Pussey's Copse

Claygate Copse

Backside Common

Wanborough

SZABO CRES

MASPIE AVE

ORCHARD WAY

ORCHARD CL

CHRIS...

CULL'S RD

LAUREL DENE

WILLOW RD

THE PADDOCKS

CROSS WAYS

Chy

Bushy Hill

The Folly

1

BEECH LA

Flexford

FLEXFORD RD

WEST FLEXFORD LA

Wanborough Youth House

50

92 A B 93 C D 94 E F

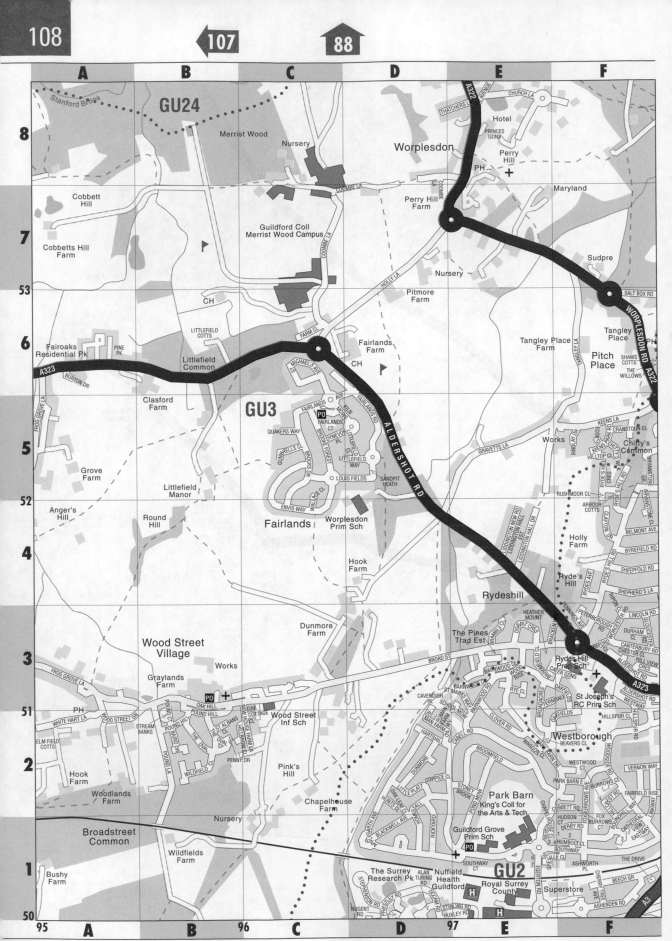

8   Stanford Brook   GU24   Merrist Wood   Nursery   Worplesdon   Hotel   CHURCH LA   PRINCES GDNS   THATCHERS

Cobbett Hill   Perry Hill   Maryland

7   Cobbetts Hill Farm   Guildford Coll Merrist Wood Campus   COOMBE LA   Perry Hill Farm   PH   Sudpre

53   CH   HOLLY LA   Pitmore Farm   Nursery   SALT BOX RD   WORPLESDON RD

6   Fairoaks Residential Pk   PINE PK   LITTLEFIELD COTTS   FARM CL   Fairlands Farm   Tangley Place Farm   Tangley Place   Pitch Place   SHAWS COTTS   THE WILLOWS   A322

A323   BURTON DR   Littlefield Common   ST MICHAEL'S AVE   CH

Clasford Farm   GU3   FAIRLANDS AVE   FAIRLANDS RD   ALDERSHOT RD   Works   KEENS LA   CRANSTOUN CL   Chitty's Common

5   FROG GROVE LA   QUAKERS WAY   PO   FAIRLANDS CT   KILN   DYNEVOR PL   GRAVETTS LA   HILLTOP CL   FINDLAY DR   BRYANSTONE GR

GUMBRELLS CL   BROOKS DR   BROOME FOREST   LITTLEFIELD WAY   RYDE'S HILL RD   BRANSTONE CL

52   Anger's Hill   Grove Farm   Littlefield Manor   WALLACE CL   LOUIS FIELDS   SANDPIT HEATH   RUSHMOOR CL   CLAYTON DR   ARBOUR COTTS   BELMONT AVE

4   Round Hill   ENVIS WAY   Worplesdon Prim Sch   Fairlands   Holly Farm   RYDE'S AVE   BYREFIELD RD   SHEEPFOLD RD

Hook Farm   Ryde's Hill   SHEPHERD'S AVE

Rydeshill   PETERBOROUGH RD   LINCOLN RD

Dunmore Farm   HEATHER MOUNT   FENNINGS AVE   DURHAM CL

3   FROG GROVE LA   Wood Street Village   Works   BROAD ST   The Pines Trad Est   BRAMBLE CL   BRACKEN CL   Rydes Hill Prep Sch   CHESTER CL   HILL VIEW CRES   A323   ALDERSHOT RD

Graylands Farm   PO   OAK HILL   BARNWOOD RD   CATER GDNS   St Joseph's RC Prim Sch   WESTWAY

51   PH   WHITE HART LA   WOD STREET GN   POUND HILL   NEW HOUSE FARM LA   Wood Street Inf Sch   CAVENDISH PL   ST MARYS WAY   SCHOOL MDW   CLOVER RD   HILLSPUR RD   Westborough   HILLSPUR CL

ELM FIELD COTTS   THE OVAL   ST ALBANS CL   OAK COTTAGE CL   HARTSHILL   OAKFIELDS   BEAVERS CL

2   POUND LA   WILDFIELD CL   PENNY DR   Pink's Hill   BROOMFIELD   WAGGON CL   WESTWOOD CT   Park Barn   PARK BARN E   BURROWS CL   FAIRFIELD RISE   VERNON WAY

Hook Farm   Chapelhouse Farm   LITTLE PLATT   COPPICE CL   STONEY BROOK   King's Coll for the Arts & Tech   COBBETT RD   FOX BURROWS CT   RUNDHILL WAY

Woodlands Farm   Nursery   OAK LEAF CL   HUNT'S CL   RICKYARD   POND FARM   Guildford Grove Prim Sch   PO   HUDSON CT   DERBY RD   CATHEDRAL VIEW   EASTWAY

1   Broadstreet Common   Wildfields Farm   The Surrey Research Pk   ALAN TURING RD   Nuffield Health Guildford   SOUTHWAY   GU2   HUMBOLT CL   THE DRIVE

Bushy Farm   STEPHENSON RD   PRIESTLEY RD   OCEANO RD   STIRLING RD   Royal Surrey County   EGERTON RD   Superstore   ASHWORTH PL   CHERRY TREE   BEECH GR   ASHENDEN RD   A3

50   NUGENT RD   HUXLEY RD   H

E1
1 HOPTON CT
2 BARGATE CT
3 FARLEIGH CT
4 SHACKLETON WLK
5 ANSTON CT
6 PURBECK CT
7 EGERTON CT

F1
1 WEALDON CT
2 FRANKLIN CT
3 COACHLADS AVE

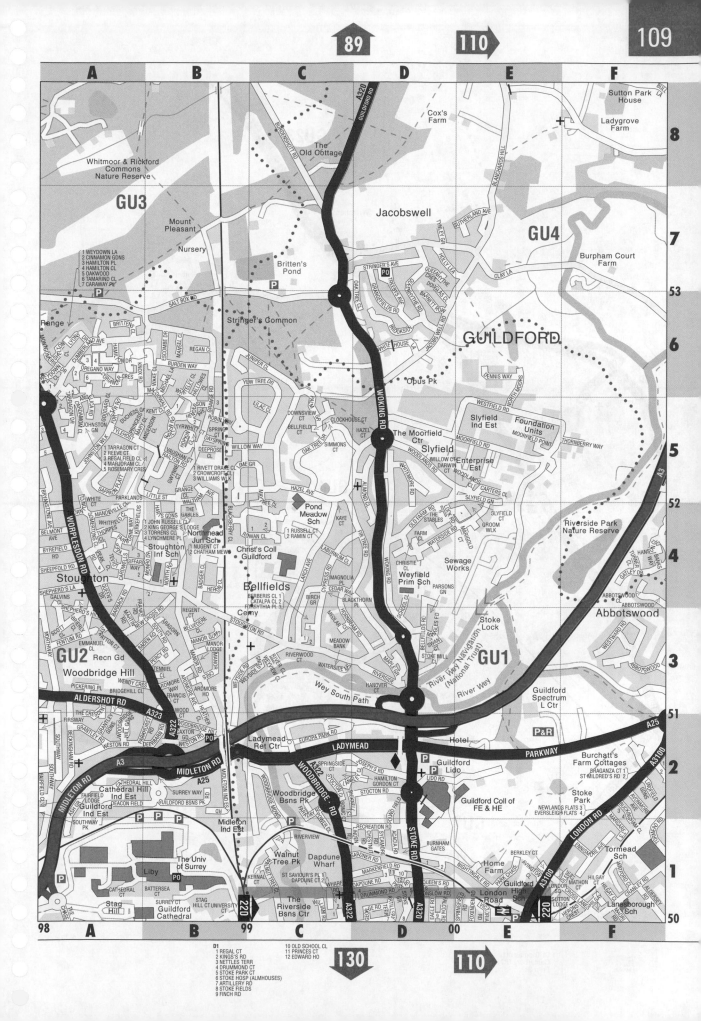

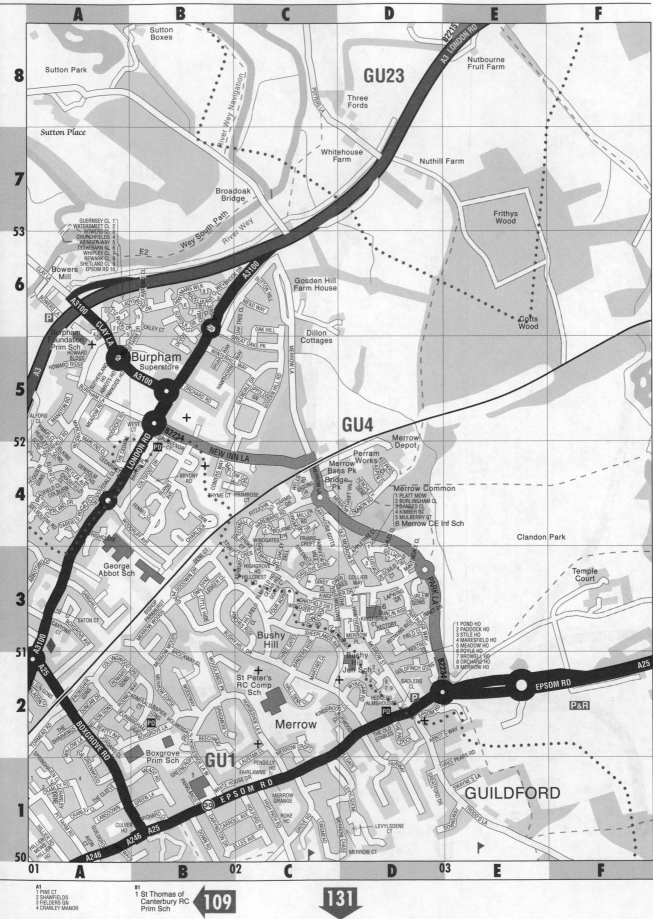

A1
1 PINE CT
2 SHAWFIELDS
3 FIELDERS GN
4 CRANLEY MANOR

B1
1 St Thomas of
Canterbury RC
Prim Sch

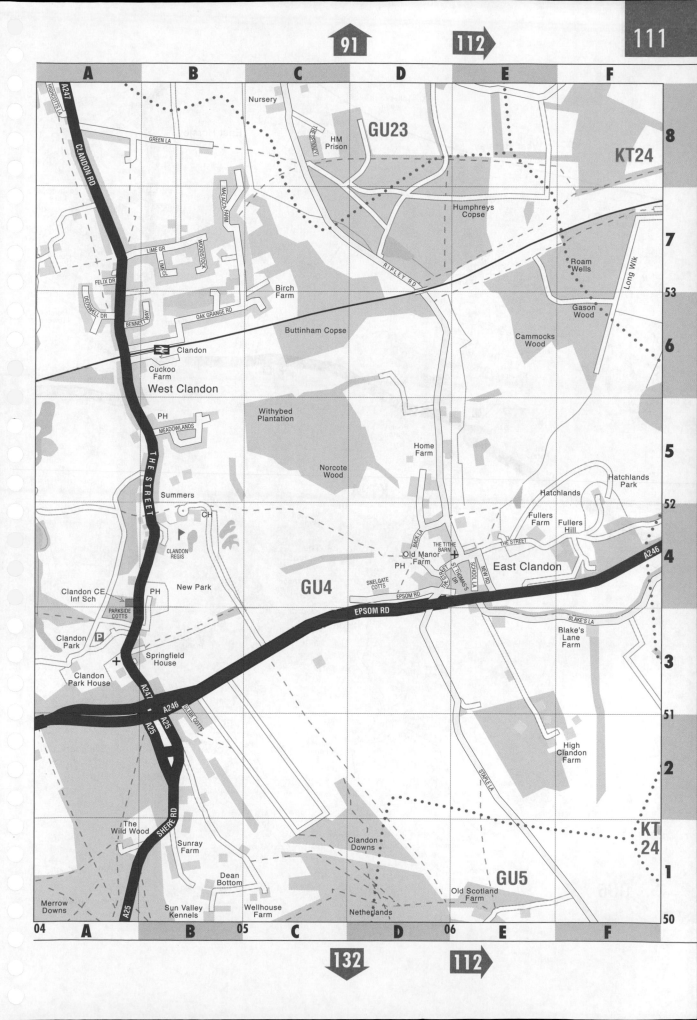

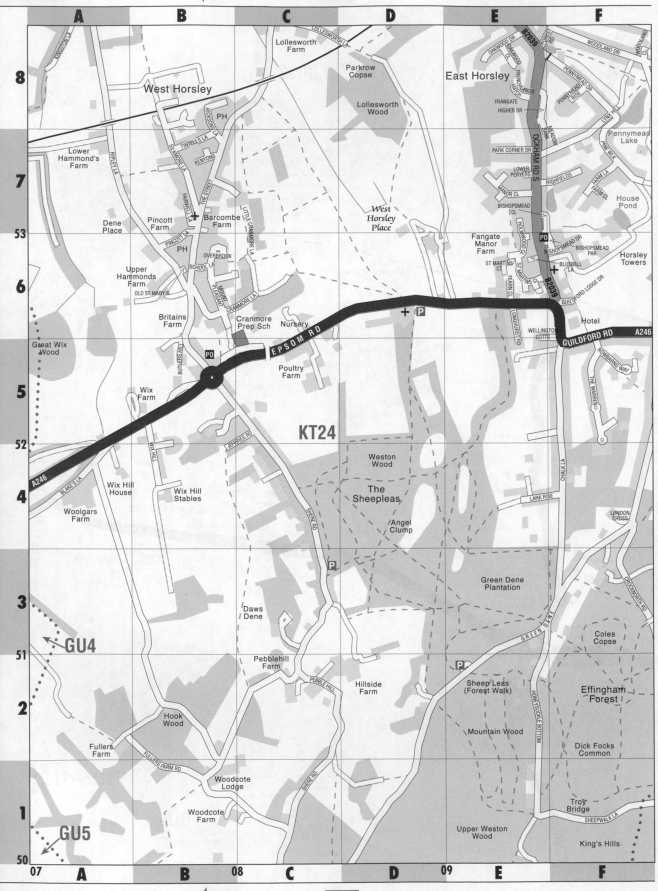

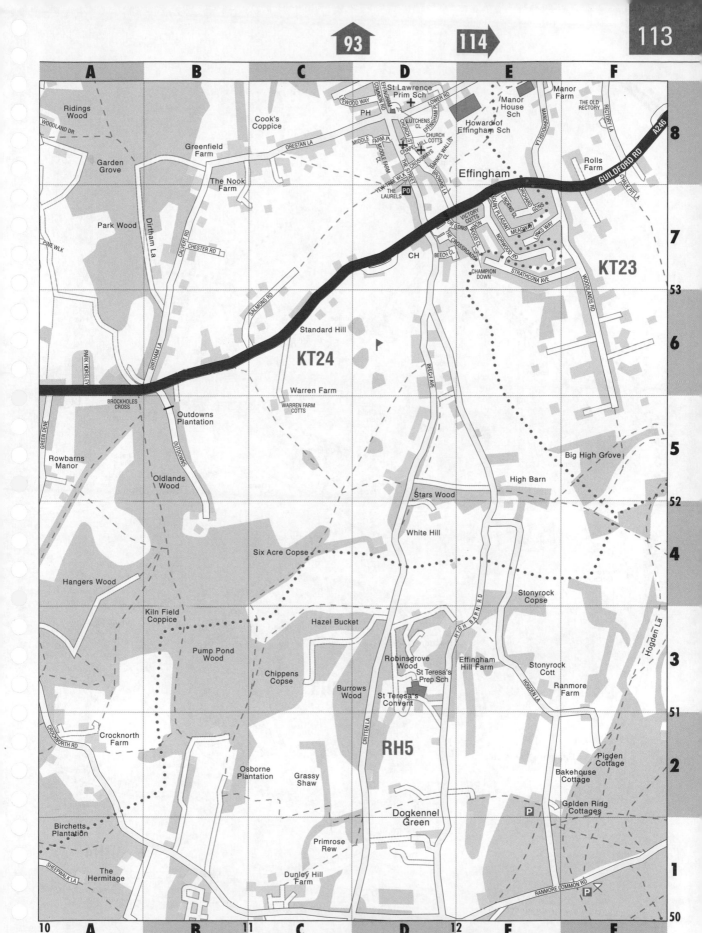

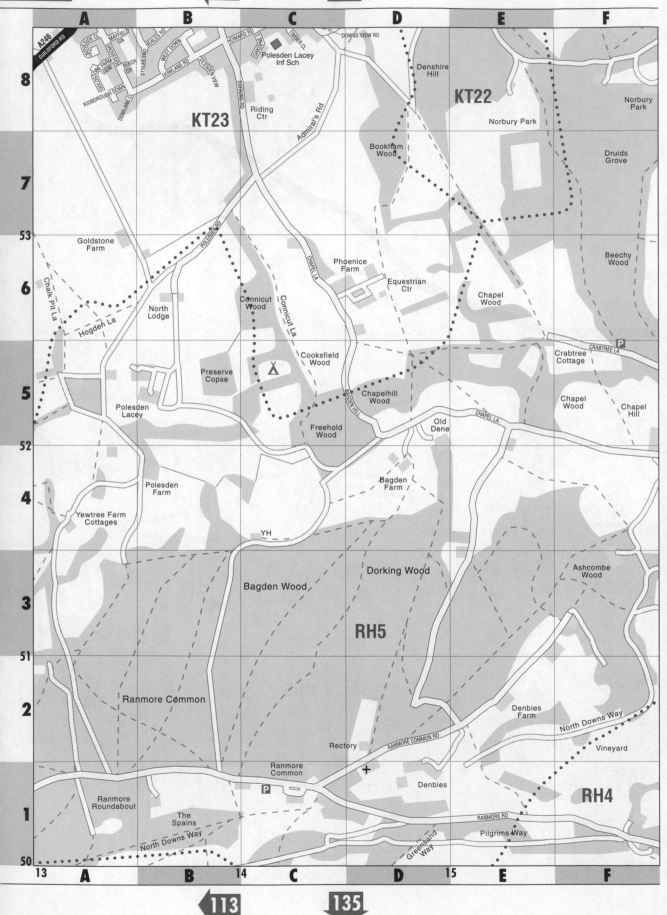

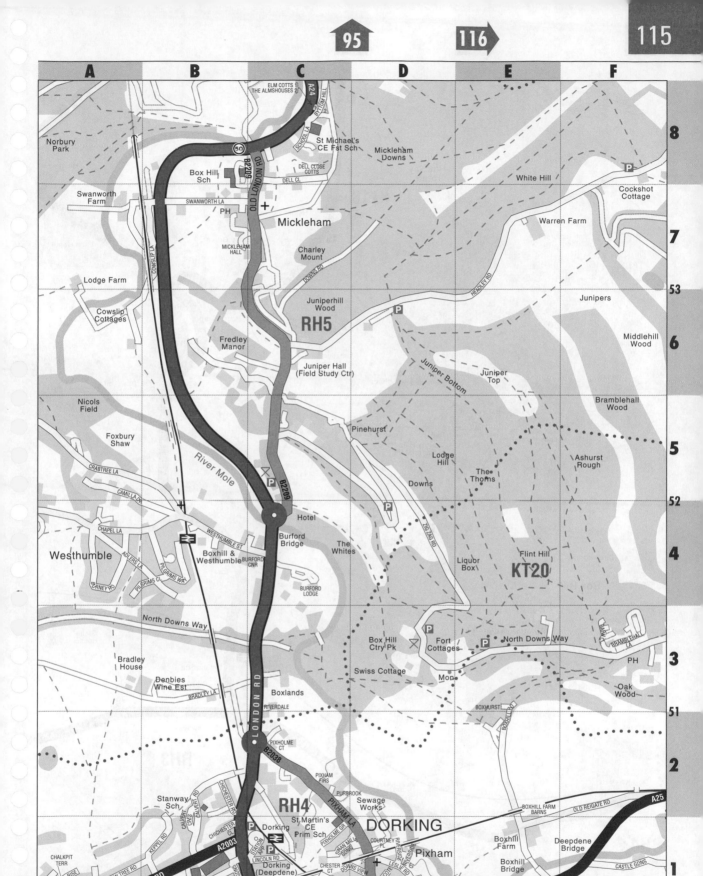

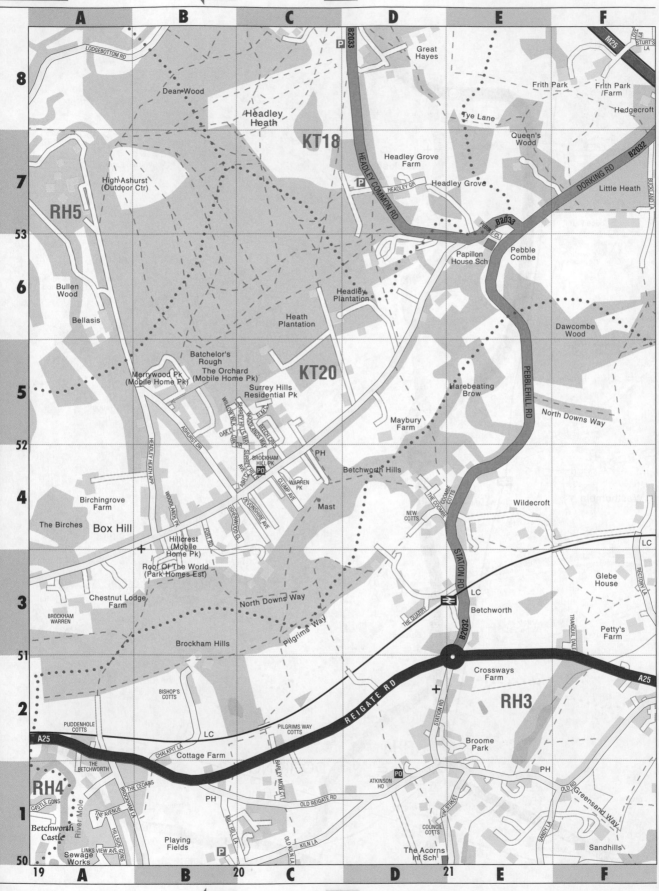

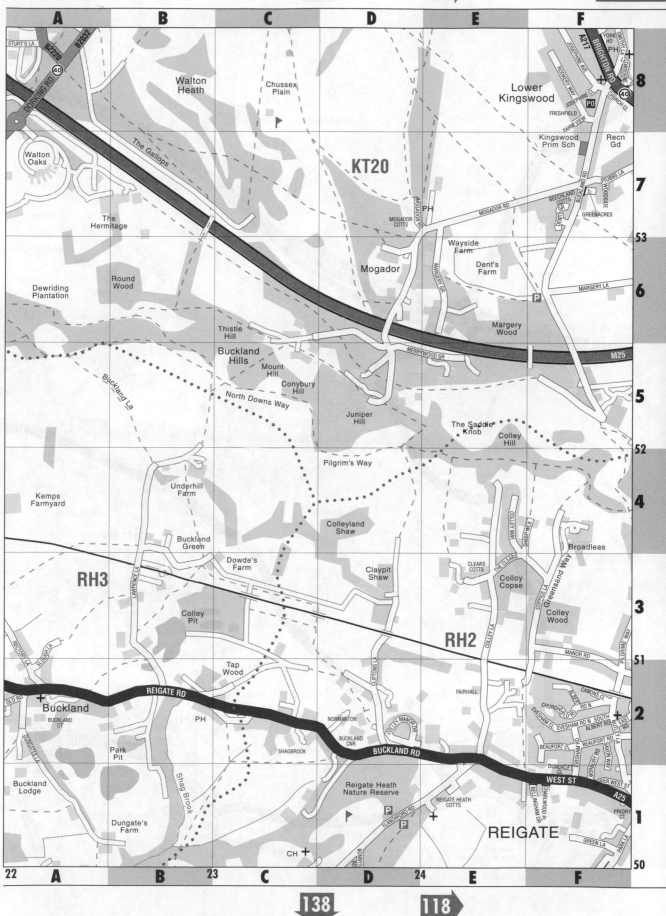

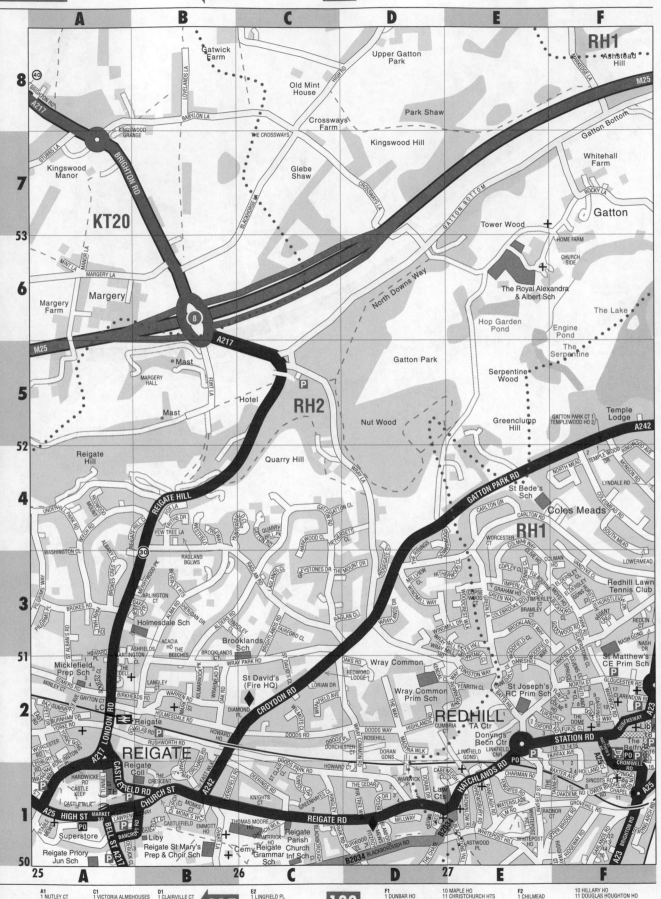

RH1
Ashstead Hill
M25

Gatwick Farm

Upper Gatton Park

Old Mint House

Crossways Farm

Park Shaw

Gatton Bottom

Whitehall Farm

THE CROSSWAYS

Glebe Shaw

Kingswood Hill

Rocky La
Gatton

KT20

Kingswood Grange

Kingswood Manor

MARGERY LA

Tower Wood
HOME FARM
CHURCH SIDE

Margery Farm
Margery

North Downs Way

The Royal Alexandra & Albert Sch

The Lake

8

Hop Garden Pond

Engine Pond

The Serpentine

Mast
Margery Hall

Hotel

RH2

Gatton Park

Serpentine Wood

Temple Lodge

A242

Mast

Quarry Hill

Nut Wood

Greenclump Hill

GATTON PARK CT 1
TEMPLEWOOD HO 2

Reigate Hill

Temple Wood

RINGWOOD AVE
MONSON RD

GATTON PARK RD

St Bede's Sch

NORTH MEAD

LYNDALE RD

REIGATE HILL

Coles Meads

COLESMEAD RD
SOUTH MEAD

RH1

Redhill Lawn Tennis Club

LOWERMEAD

Holmesdale Sch

Brooklands Sch

Wray Common

St Matthew's CE Prim Sch

Micklefield Prep Sch

St David's (Fire HQ)

Wray Common Prim Sch

St Joseph's RC Prim Sch

REDHILL
TA Ctr

REIGATE

Reigate Coll

CROYDON RD

Donyngs Recn Ctr

STATION RD

The Belfry

A25

Superstore

HIGH ST

CHURCH ST

A242

Law Cts

HATCHLANDS RD

REIGATE RD

B2034

Reigate Priory Jun Sch

Reigate St Mary's Prep & Choir Sch

Reigate Parish Church Inf Sch

Reigate Grammar Sch

B2034 BLACKBOROUGH RD

A23

BRIGHTON RD

A1
1 Nutley Ct
2 Slipshoe St
3 Churchfield Ct

A2
1 Somers Pl
2 Flanchford Ho
3 Clayhall Ho
4 Littleton Ho
5 Elvington Lodge

C1
1 Victoria Almshouses
2 Eversfield Ct
3 Hillbrow

D1
1 Clairville Ct
2 Highview Ct
3 Treeview Ct
4 Harlow Ct
5 Wraymill Ct

E2
1 Lingfield Pl
2 Chestnut Mead
3 Sandown Ct

F1
1 Dunbar Ho
2 Marston Ho
3 Cromwell Wlk
4 Edgehill Ho
5 Morriss Ct
6 Observatory Wlk
7 Waveney Ho
8 Grove Ho
9 Ely Ho

10 Maple Ho
11 Christchurch Hts
12 Glamis Ho
13 Atholl Ho
14 Dunvegan Ho
15 Stirling Ho
16 Market Field Rd

F2
1 Chilmead
2 Colne Ho
3 Tavy Ho
4 Rother Ho
5 Wandle Ho
6 Kennet Ho
7 Orwell Ho
8 Windrush Ho
9 Avon Ho

10 Hillary Ho
11 Douglas Houghton Ho
12 Squirrels Gn
13 Chilworth Ct
14 The Hollies
15 Cromwell Pl
16 Marylebone Ho
17 Abbey Bsns Ctr
18 The Harlequin

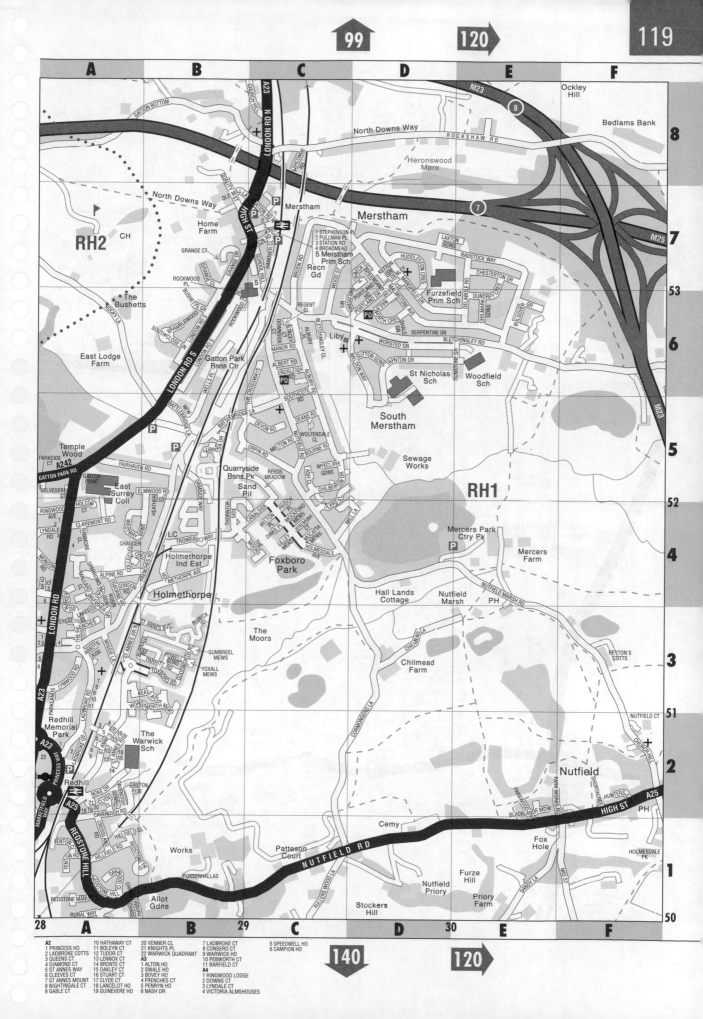

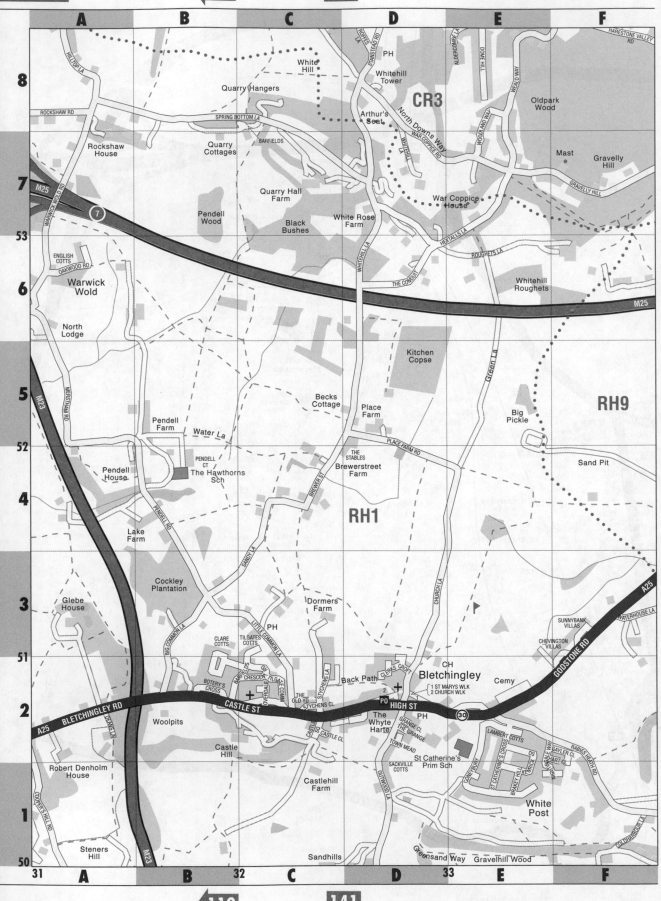

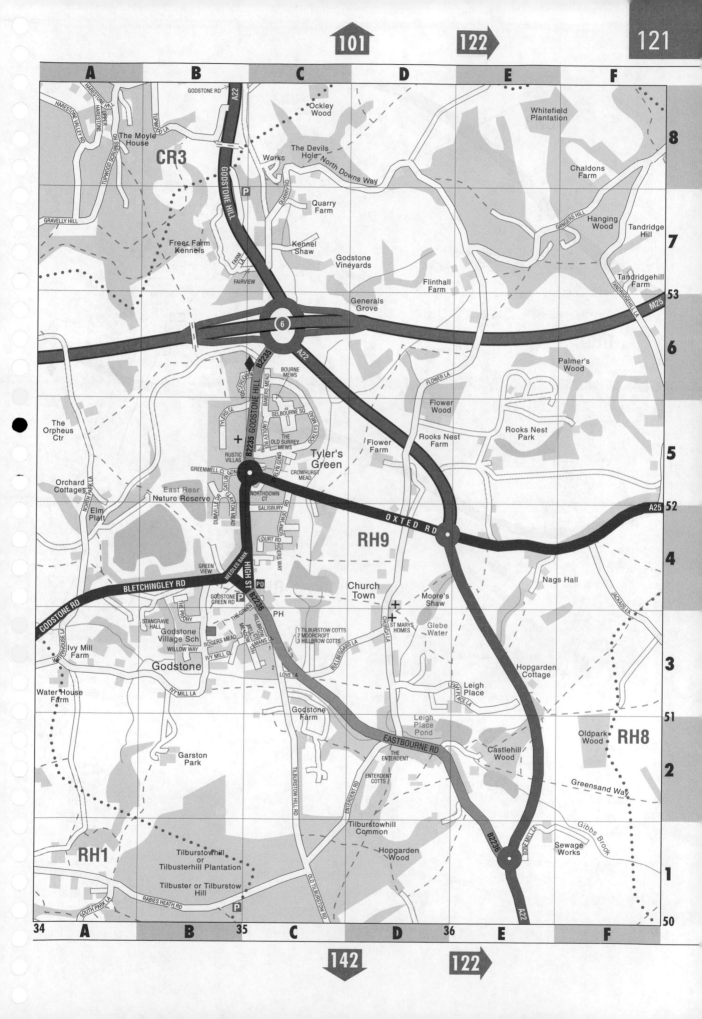

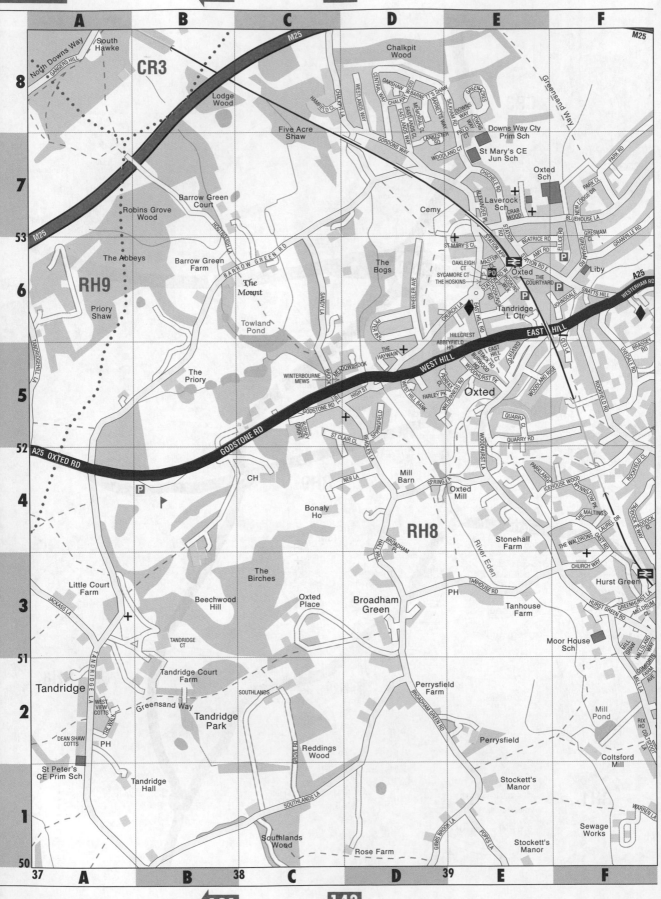

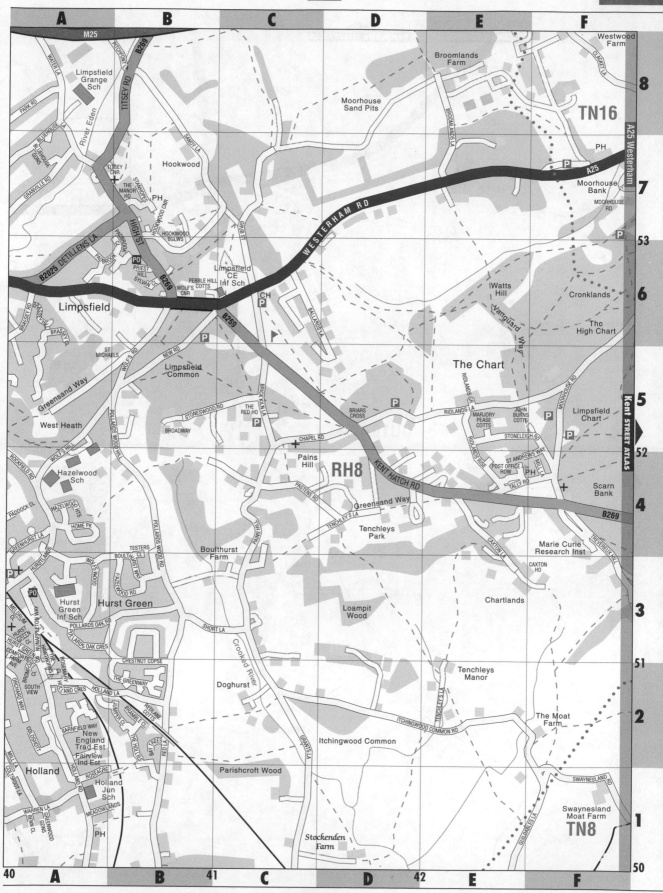

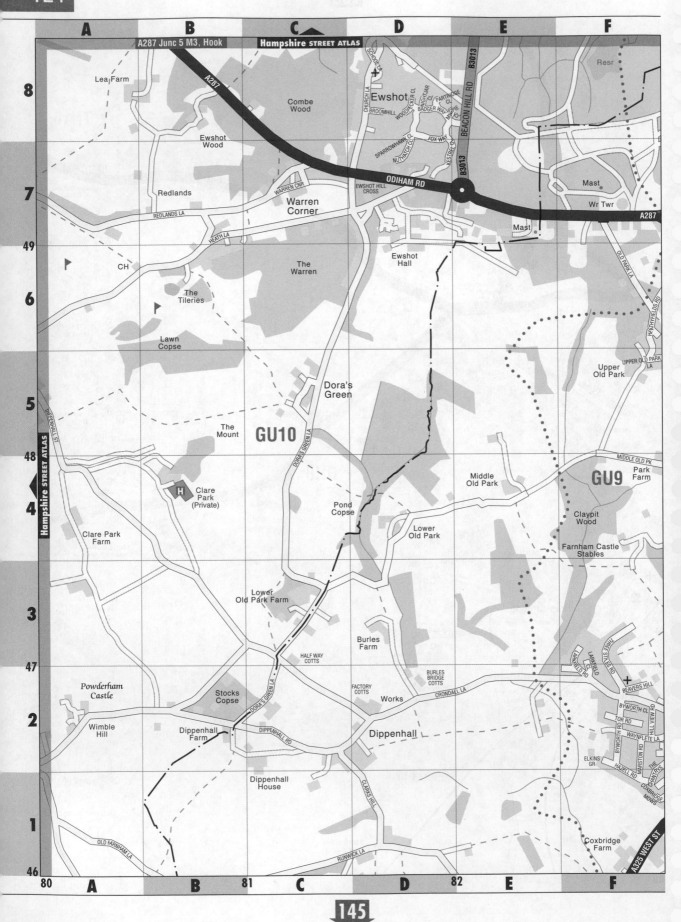

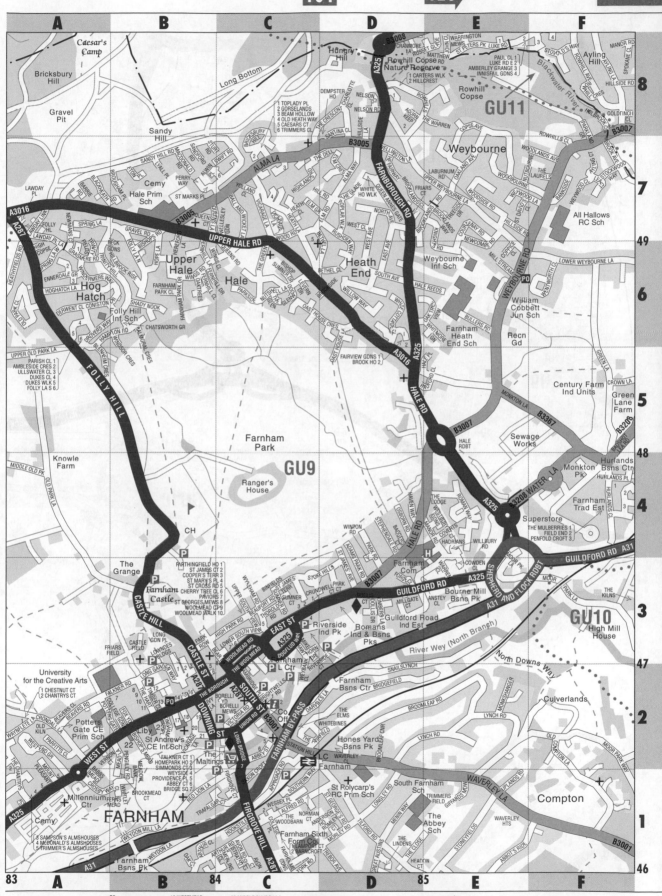

B2
1 LONG GARDEN WLK W
2 LONG GARDEN WLK E
3 LONG GARDEN MEWS
4 LONG GARDEN WLK
5 ST GEORGES YD
6 THE MEWS
7 AUSTIN'S COTTS
8 LOVETT HO
9 MOUNTBATTEN LODGE
10 WESTMEAD
11 COBBETTS MEWS
12 LION AND LAMB WAY
13 ARUNDELL PL
14 LION AND LAMB YD
15 HARTS YD
16 OLD KILN COURTYARD
17 CHURCH PAS
18 WEAVERS YD
19 UPPER CHURCH LA
20 MIDDLE CHURCH LA
21 LOWER CHURCH LA
22 Wilmer House
Mus of Farnham
23 Farnham Adult
Learning Ctr

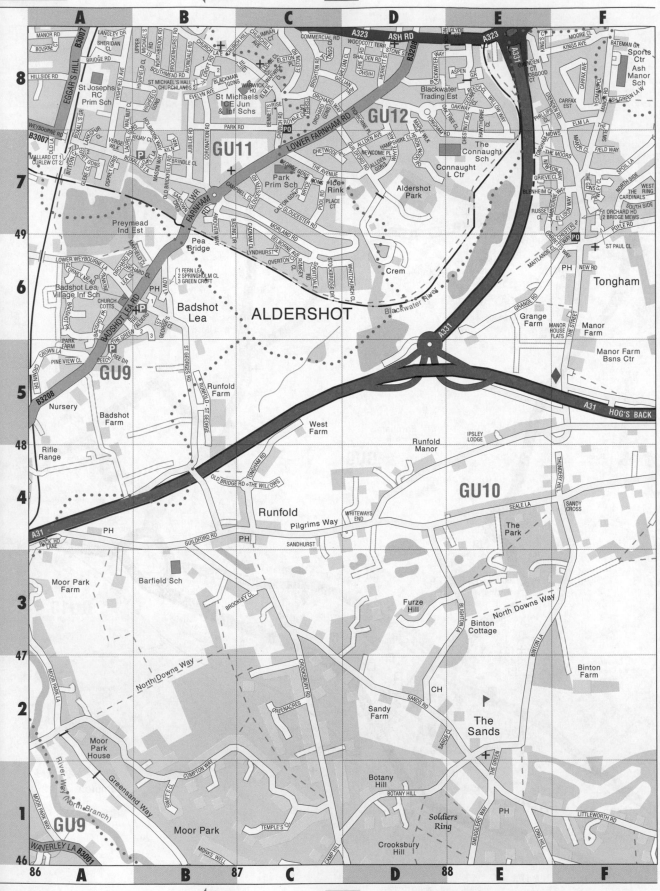

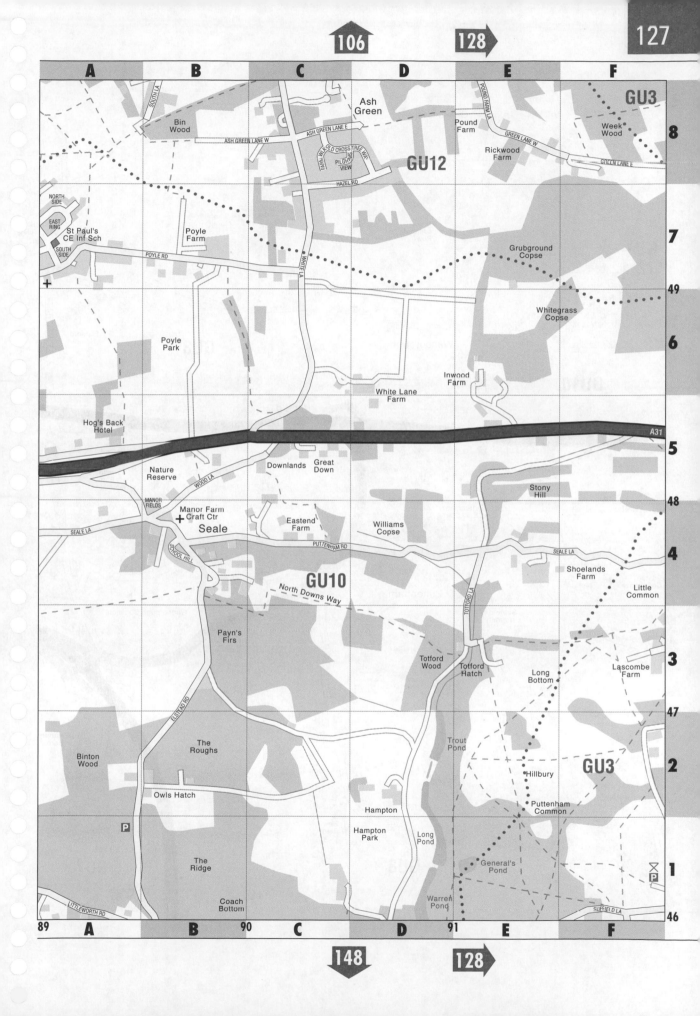

A   B   C   D   E   F

GU3

8   Bin Wood   Ash Green   Pound Farm   Week Wood
Ash Green Lane W   Ash Green Lane E   Green Lane W
FARM WK   OLD CROSS TREE WAY   GU12   Rickwood Farm   Green Lane E

NORTH SIDE   PILGRIMS VIEW
7   EAST RING   St Paul's CE Inf Sch   Poyle Farm   HAZEL RD   Grubground Copse
SOUTH SIDE   POYLE RD   WHITE LA

49   Whitegrass Copse

6   Poyle Park   Inwood Farm   Whitegrass Copse

White Lane Farm

Hog's Back Hotel   A31
5   Nature Reserve   Downlands   Great Down   Stony Hill

48   MANOR FIELDS   WOOD LA

4   SEALE LA   Manor Farm Craft Ctr   Seale   Eastend Farm   Williams Copse   SEALE LA   Shoelands Farm   Little Common
SCHOOL HILL   PUTTENHAM RD   TOTFORD LA

GU10
North Downs Way

3   Payn's Firs   Totford Wood   Totford Hatch   Long Bottom   Lascombe Farm

47   ELSTEAD RD

2   Binton Wood   The Roughs   Trout Pond   Hillbury   GU3
Owls Hatch   Hampton   Puttenham Common
P   Hampton Park   Long Pond   General's Pond

1   The Ridge   Warren Pond
LITTLEWORTH RD   Coach Bottom   SHUFFIELD LA

89   A   B   90   C   D   91   E   F   46

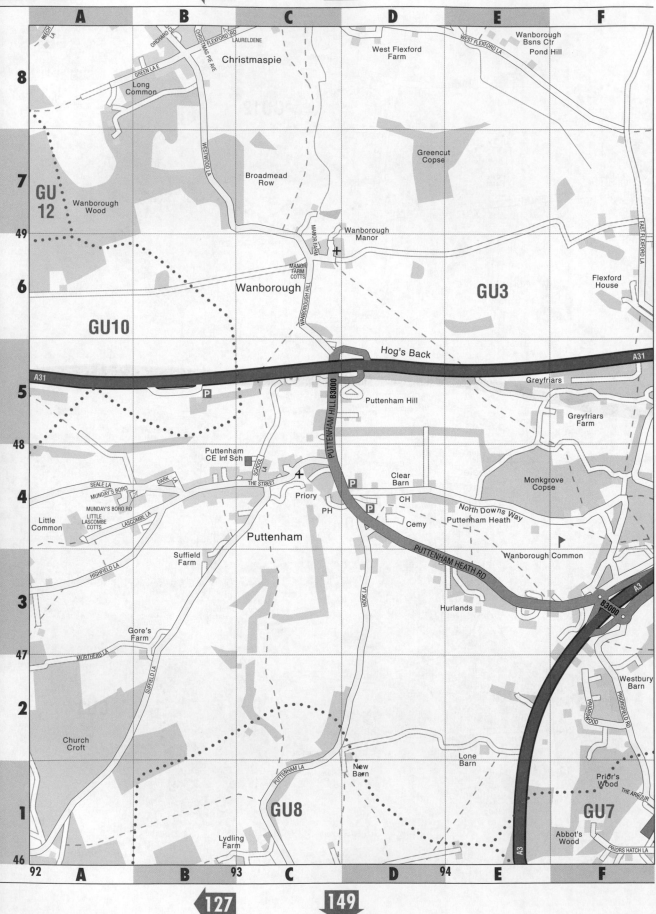

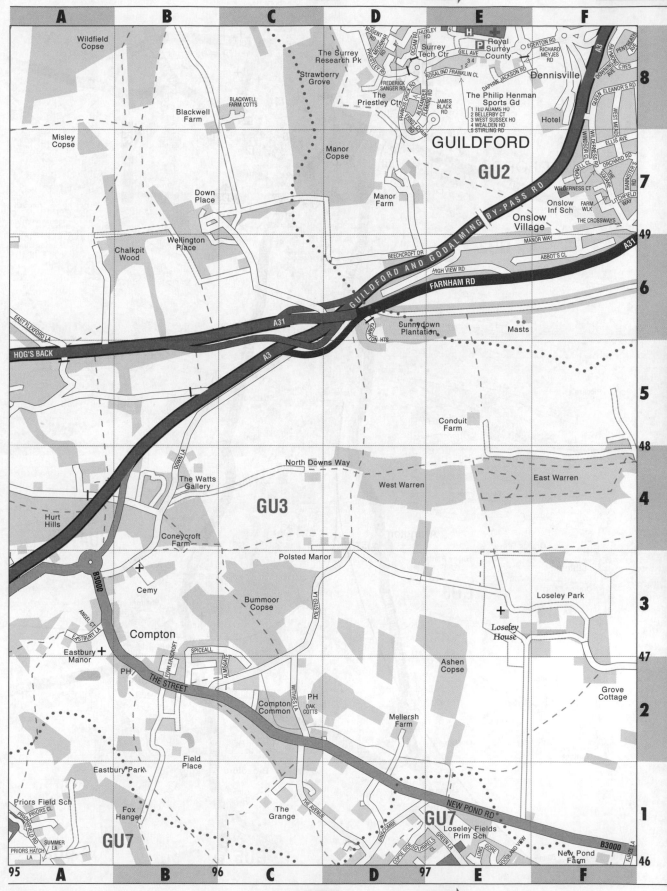

8

Wildfield Copse

The Surrey Research Pk

Strawberry Grove

Surrey Tech Ctr

Royal Surrey County

Dennisville

Blackwell Farm

Blackwell Farm Cotts

The Priestley Ctr

The Philip Henman Sports Gd
1 TED ADAMS HO
2 BELLERBY CT
3 WEST SUSSEX HO
4 WEALDEN HO
5 STIRLING RD

GUILDFORD

GU2

Hotel

7

Misley Copse

Manor Copse

Onslow Inf Sch

Down Place

Manor Farm

Onslow Village

Wilderness Ct

THE CROSSWAYS

49

Wellington Place

GUILDFORD AND GODALMING BY-PASS RD

A31

Chalkpit Wood

BEECHCROFT DR

MANOR WAY

ABBOT'S CL

6

HIGH VIEW RD

FARNHAM RD

EAST FLEXFORD LA

A31

A3

Sunnydown Plantation

Masts

HOG'S BACK

COMPTON HTS

5

Conduit Farm

48

North Downs Way

East Warren

The Watts Gallery

West Warren

GU3

4

Hurt Hills

DOWN LA

Coneycroft Farm

Polsted Manor

Loseley Park

3

Cemy

Bummoor Copse

POLSTED LA

Loseley House

B3000

Compton

ANGEL CT

EASTBURY LA

SPICEALL

ALMSGATE

Ashen Copse

47

Eastbury Manor

PH

THE STREET

FOWLERSCROFT

WITHIES LA

Grove Cottage

2

Compton Common

PH
OAK COTTS

Mellersh Farm

Field Place

THE AVENUE

Eastbury Park

Priors Field Sch

Fox Hanger

The Grange

GU7

Loseley Fields Prim Sch

NEW POND RD

1

PRIORS CL

SUMMER LA

PRIORS HATCH LA

GU7

DINGCOMBE

GREEN LA

LONG GORE

COPSE SIDE

BOURNELS CL

WOODLAND VIEW

New Pond Farm

B3000

FURZE LA

46

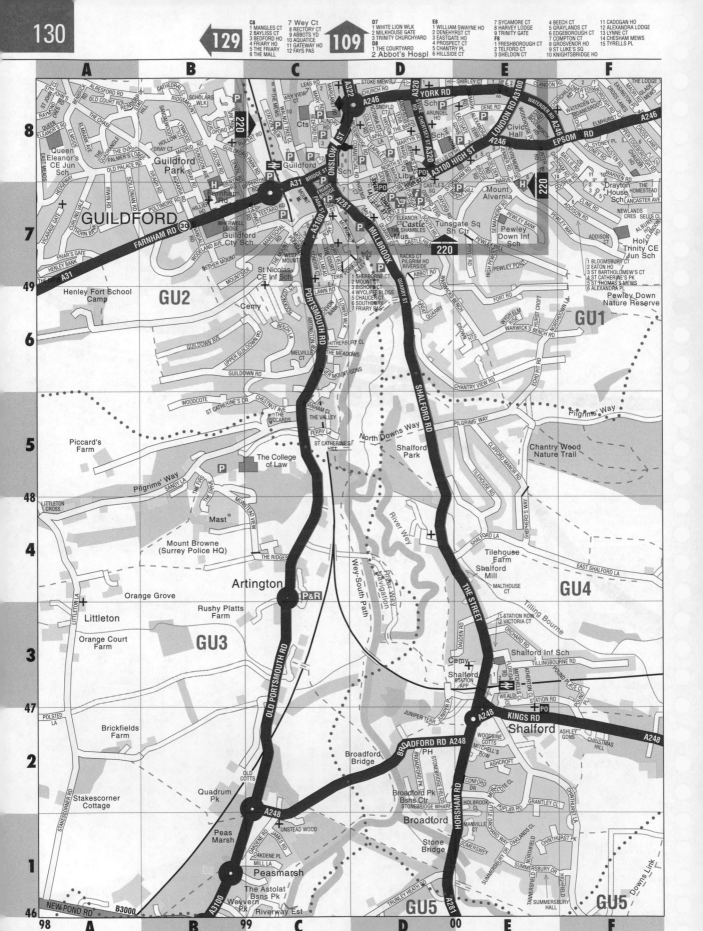

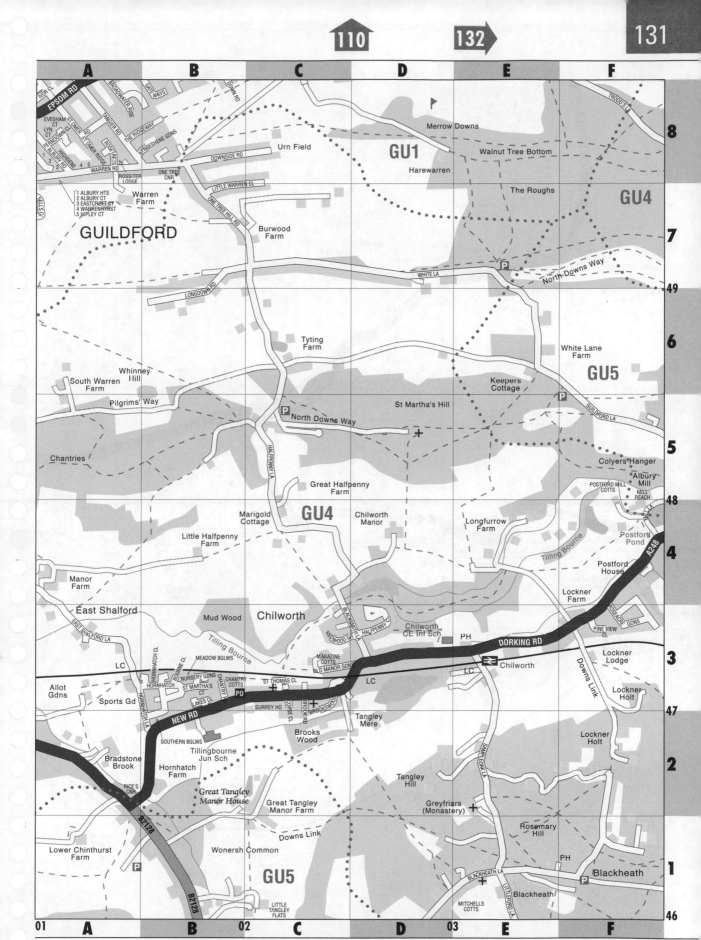

A B C D E F

8

7

49

6

5

48

4

3

47

2

1

46

01 A B 02 C D 03 E F

EPSOM RD

IVOR CL
EVESHAM CT
ST OMER CT
LYN CT
FERNDOWN CL
HIGHDENE
ALBURY RD
BELL'S CL
BROADWATER RISE
GATE WAYS
ST OMER RD
TANGIER RD
THE RIDGEWAY
LYNGESHENE GDNS
ROSS TREES
ALBURY HTS
HINGEVOLD
DOWN RD
DOWNSIDE RD
ONE TREE CNR
LITTLE WARREN CL
WARREN RD

1 ALBURY HTS
2 ALBURY CT
3 EASTCROFT CT
4 WARRENHYRST
5 HIPLEY CT

Urn Field

GU1

Merrow Downs

Walnut Tree Bottom

Harewarren

The Roughs

GU4

Warren Farm

GUILDFORD

Burwood Farm

ONE TREE HILL RD

LONGDOWN RD

White Lane Farm

GU5

Whinney Hill

Tyting Farm

South Warren Farm

WHITE LA

North Downs Way

Pilgrims' Way

Keepers Cottage

HALFPENNY LA

St Martha's Hill

GUILDFORD LA

Chantries

North Downs Way

Great Halfpenny Farm

Colyers Hanger
Albury Mill
POSTFORD MILL COTTS
MILL REACH

Marigold Cottage

GU4

Chilworth Manor

Longfurrow Farm

Postford Pond

Little Halfpenny Farm

Manor Farm

Tilling Bourne

Postford House

East Shalford

Mud Wood

Chilworth

Lockner Farm

A248

EAST SHALFORD LA

BLACKSMITH LA

HALFPENNY CT

Chilworth CE Inf Sch

PH

DORKING RD

ROSACRE GDNS
PINE VIEW CL

HORNHATCH CL

MEADOW BGLWS

REDWOOD GR

MAGAZINE COTTS
OLD MANOR GDNS

Chilworth

Downs Link

Lockner Lodge

LC

NURSERY GDNS
ST MARTHA'S CT
CHANTRY RD
CHANTRY COTTS
ST THOMAS CL

LC

LC

Lockner Holt

Allot Gdns

HORNHATCH LA

BOURNE CL

PO

SURREY HO

COPSE CL

BROOK RD

BROOKSIDE

Tangley Mere

LAKES CL

Sports Gd

NEW RD

Brooks Wood

SAMPLEOAK LA

Lockner Holt

SOUTHERN BGLWS

Tillingbourne Jun Sch

Hornhatch Farm

Bradstone Brook

RICE'S CNR

B2128

Great Tangley Manor House

Great Tangley Manor Farm

Tangley Hill

Greyfriars (Monastery)

Rosemary Hill

PH

Lower Chinthurst Farm

Downs Link

Wonersh Common

GU5

LITTLE TANGLEY FLATS

B2128

Blackheath

BLACKHEATH LA

LITTLEFORD LA

Blackheath

MITCHELLS COTTS

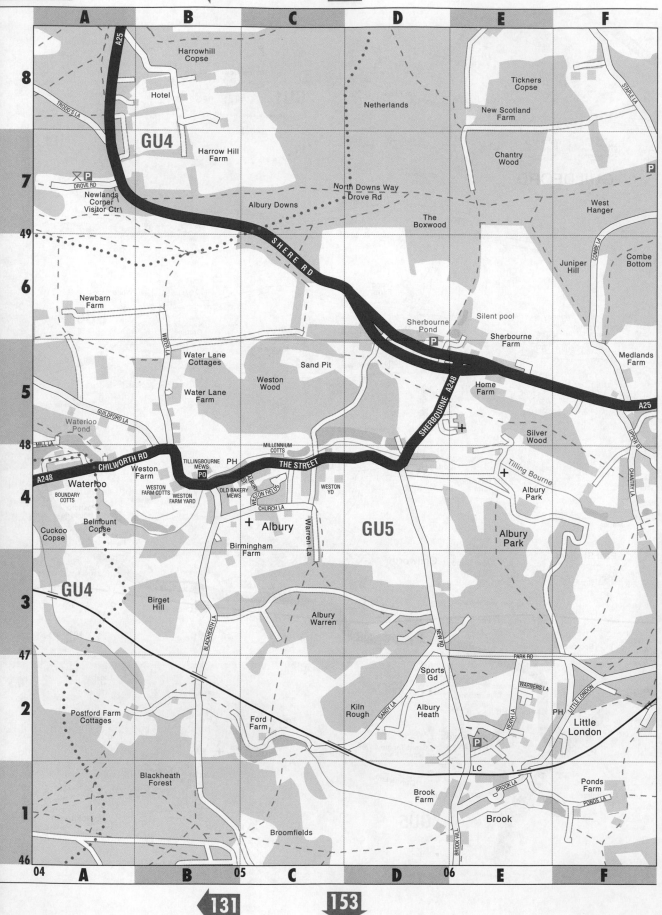

A B C D E F

8

7

49

6

5

48

4

3

47

2

1

46

GU4

Harrowhill Copse

Hotel

Harrow Hill Farm

TRODD'S LA

A25

Newlands Corner Visitor Ctr

DROVE RD

Albury Downs

North Downs Way
Drove Rd

Netherlands

Tickners Copse

New Scotland Farm

Chantry Wood

The Boxwood

West Hanger

Juniper Hill

Combe Bottom

SHERE RD

Newbarn Farm

WATER LA

Water Lane Cottages

Water Lane Farm

Weston Wood

Sand Pit

Sherbourne Pond

Silent pool

Sherbourne Farm

Medlands Farm

GUILDFORD LA

Waterloo Pond

MILL LA

A248

Waterloo

CHILWORTH RD

Weston Farm

Boundary Cotts

Belmount Copse

Cuckoo Copse

GU4

Birget Hill

BLACKHEATH LA

Postford Farm Cottages

Blackheath Forest

Weston Farm Cotts

Weston Farm Yard

TILLINGBOURNE MEWS

PO

PH

Old Bakery Mews

CHURCH LA

Albury

Birmingham Farm

MILLENNIUM COTTS

THE STREET

ALBURY ST

WESTON FIELDS

WARREN LA

Weston Yd

GU5

Albury Warren

Ford Farm

Kiln Rough

SANDY LA

Albury Heath

Home Farm

SHERBOURNE A248

Silver Wood

Tilling Bourne

Albury Park

Albury Park

NEW RD

Sports Gd

PARK RD

WARNERS LA

HEATH LA

LITTLE LONDON

PH

Little London

A25

UPPER ST

CHANTRY LA

COMBE LA

STAPLE LA

P

Brook Farm

BROOK HILL

LC

P

Brook

BROOK LA

PONDS LA

Ponds Farm

Broomfields

04 A B 05 C D 06 E F

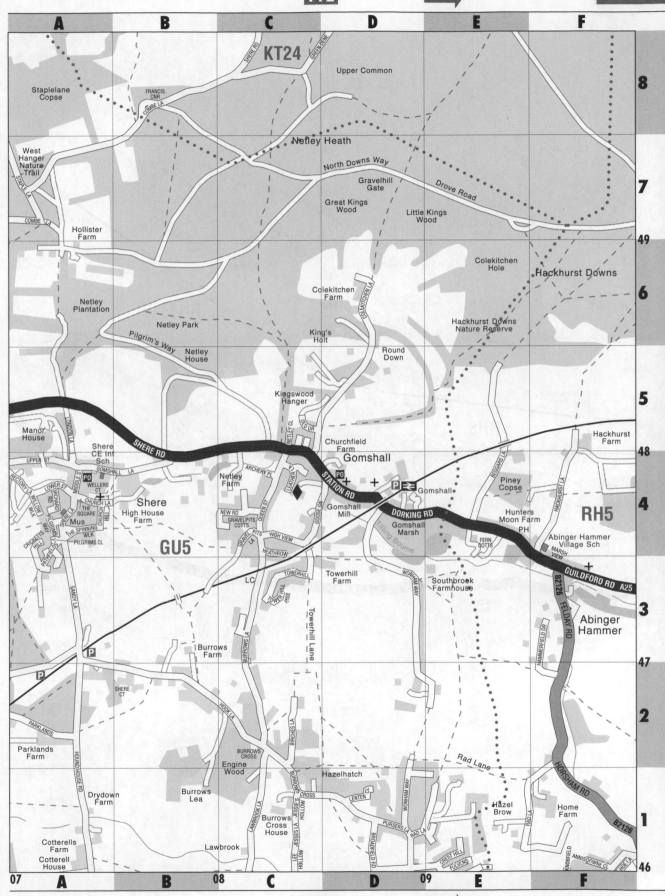

133
113

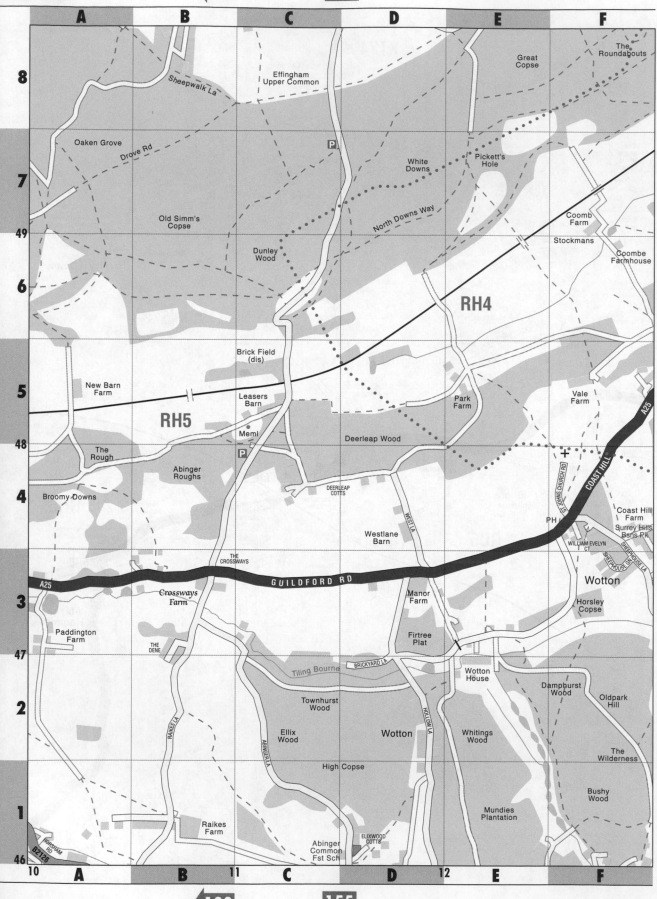

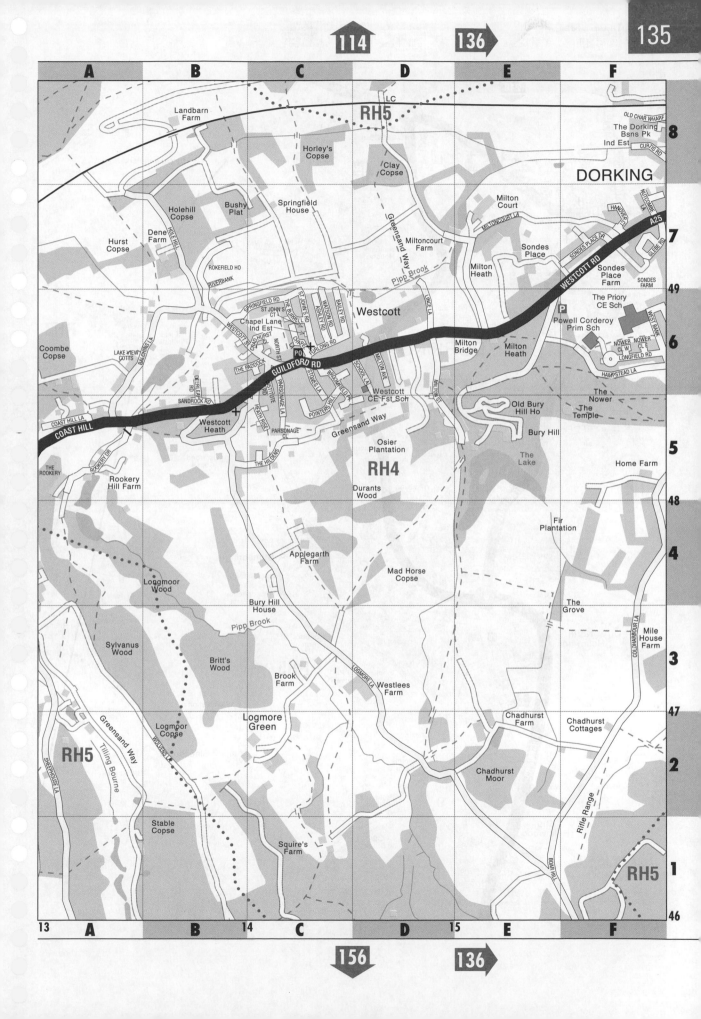

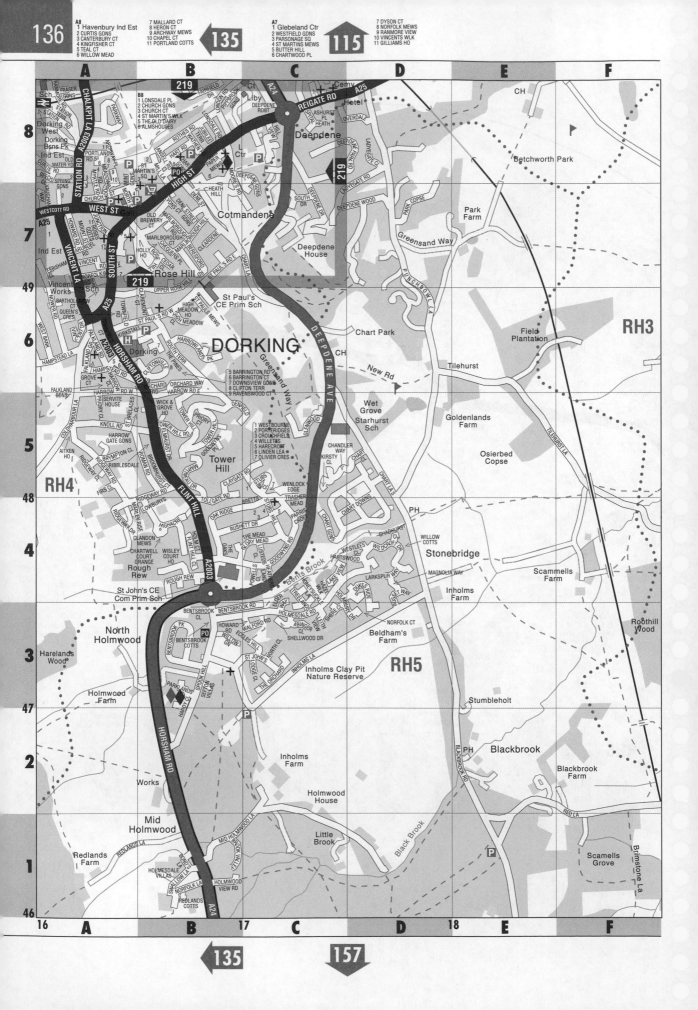

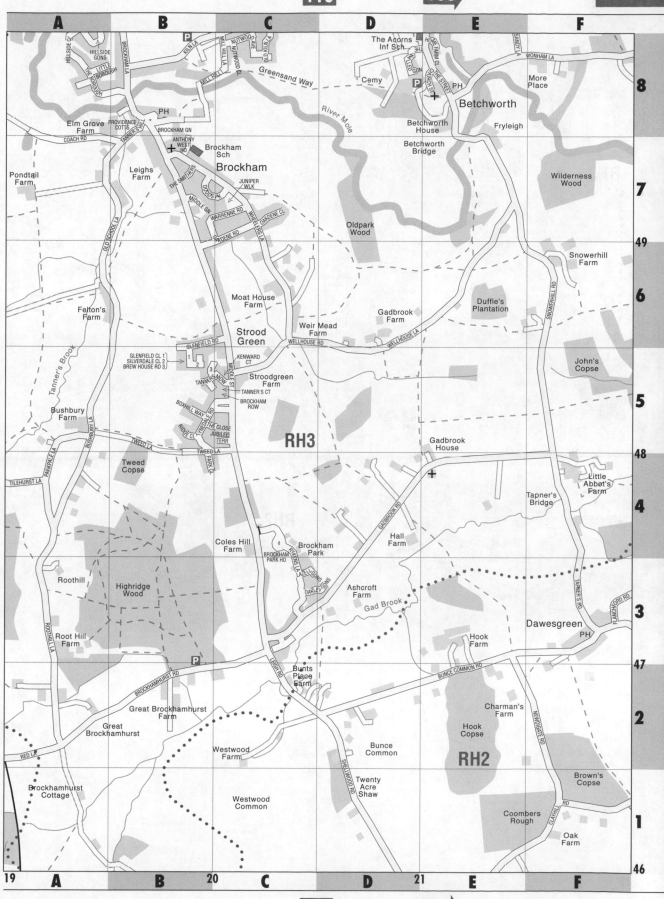

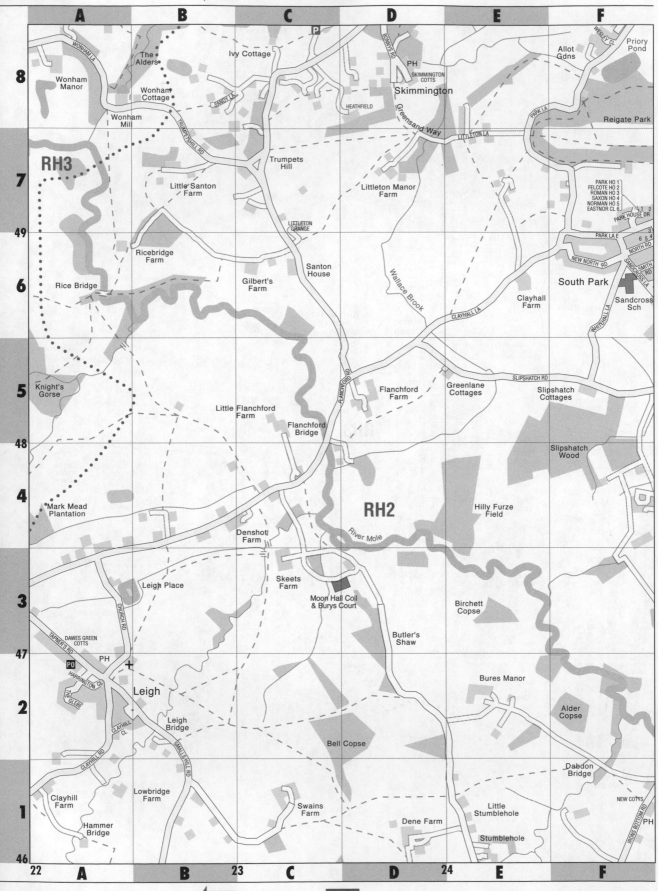

A   B   C   D   E   F

8

Wonham Manor
The Alders
Ivy Cottage
Wonham Cottage
WONHAM LA
Wonham Mill
SANDY LA
Skimmington
SKIMMINGTON COTTS
PH
HEATHFIELD
Greensand Way
Allot Gdns
Priory Pond
WESLEY CL
Reigate Park
PARK LA
LITTLETON LA

RH3

7

Trumpets Hill
Little Santon Farm
TRUMPETSHILL RD
Littleton Manor Farm
PARK HO 1
FELCOTE HO 2
ROMAN HO 3
SAXON HO 4
NORMAN HO 5
EASTNOR CL 6
PARK HOUSE DR

49

LITTLETON GRANGE
PARK LA E
NORTH RD

Ricebridge Farm
Santon House
South Park

6

Rice Bridge
Gilbert's Farm
Wallace Brook
CLAYHALL LA
Clayhall Farm
Sandcross Sch
WHITEHALL LA
SANDCROSS LA
SMITH RD
NEW NORTH RD

5

Knight's Gorse
Little Flanchford Farm
Flanchford Bridge
FLANCHFORD RD
Flanchford Farm
Greenlane Cottages
Slipshatch Cottages
SLIPSHATCH RD

48

Slipshatch Wood

4

Mark Mead Plantation
Denshot Farm
River Mole
Hilly Furze Field
RH2

3

Leigh Place
Skeets Farm
Moon Hall Coll & Burys Court
Birchett Copse
CHURCH RD
Butler's Shaw

47

TAPNER'S RD
DAWES GREEN COTTS
PH
PO
Leigh
Bures Manor
HARRINGTON CL
THE GLEBE

2

CLAYHILL CL
Leigh Bridge
SMALLS HILL RD
Alder Copse
Dabdon Bridge
NEW COTTS

1

Clayhill Farm
Lowbridge Farm
Swains Farm
Dene Farm
Little Stumblehole
CLAYHILL RD
Hammer Bridge
Bell Copse
Stumblehole
IRONS BOTTOM RD
PH

46

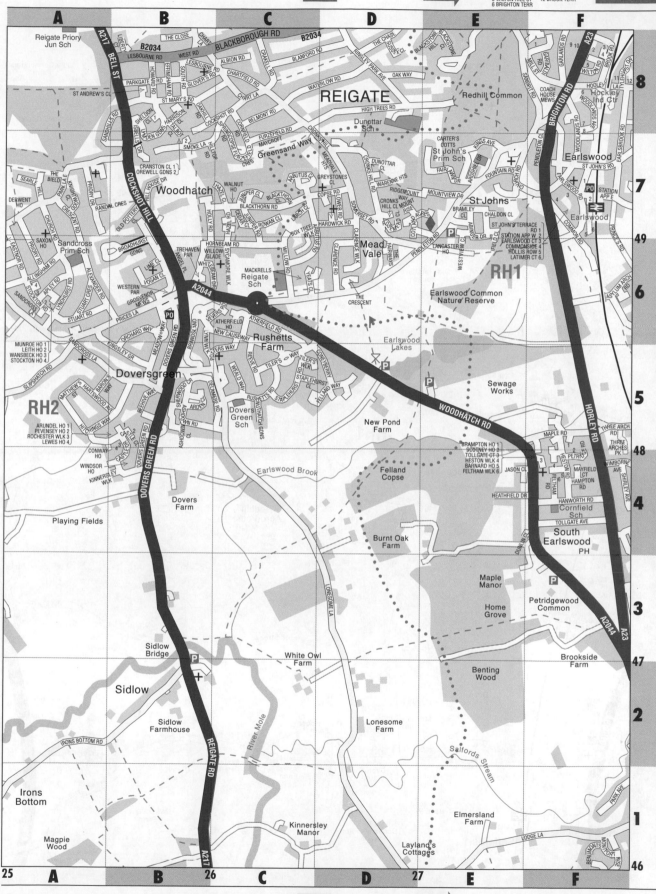

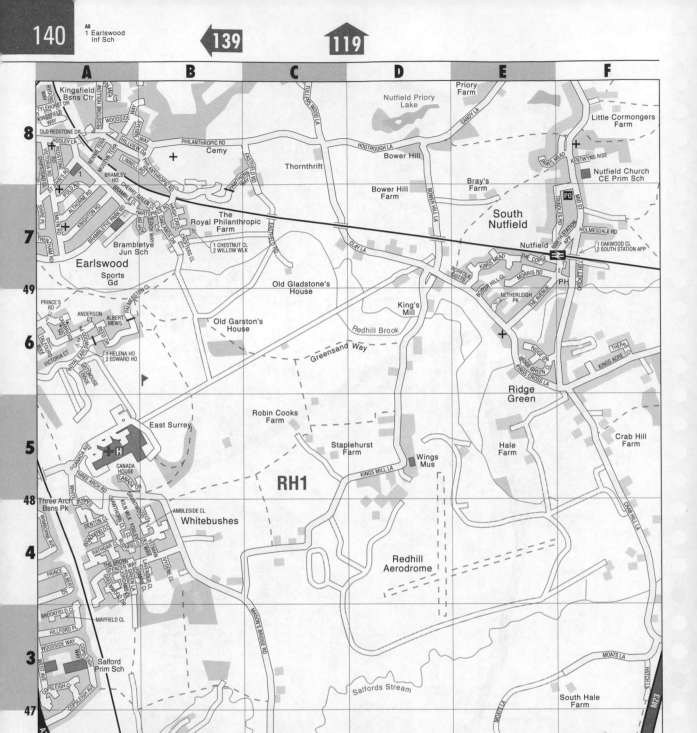

A   B   C   D   E   F

8

Kingsfield Bsns Ctr
RYDONS DR
RYDONS WAY
TYLEHURST DR
KINGSFIELD WAY
Old Redstone Dr
REDSTONE HOLLOW
PALMER CL
WOODSIDE
HILLVIEW DR
SUTTON WAY
Hooley La
Philanthropic Rd
Cemy
Thornthrift
Nutfield Priory Lake
Priory Farm
HOGTROUGH LA
Bower Hill
Little Cormongers Farm
SANDY LA
BRAYS MEAD
KENTWYNS RISE
Nutfield Church CE Prim Sch

VICTORIA RD
ST JOHN'S RD
CHIPSTEAD CL
FOLD RD
BRAMLEY HO
M W TERR
RENNIE TERR
LINNELL RD
CHERRY GREEN CL
EASTFIELD RD
HAWTHORN WAY
HIGH CL
PHILANTHROPIC RD
BRAMBLE CL
ALTHORNE RD
KNIGHTON RD
The Royal Philanthropic Farm
1 CHESTNUT CL
2 WILLOW WLK
Bower Hill Farm
Bray's Farm
South Nutfield
MID ST
TRINDLES RD
HOLMESDALE RD
PO

7
SHIRE RD
TREN THAM RD
EVLYN RD
BRAMBLETYE PARK RD
HARTSPIECE RD
OAKLANDS DR
CROFTERS CL
BIRCH WAY
HARTS GDNS
EASTFIELD RD
CLAY LA
BOWER HILL LA
Nutfield
NORFOLK COTTS
KINGS MEAD
Morris Rd
THE COPSE
1 OAKWOOD CL
2 SOUTH STATION APP
CRICKETT HILL
PH

Brambletye Jun Sch
Earlswood
Sports Gd

49
PRINCE'S RD
PALMERSTON RD
Old Gladstone's House
Old Garston's House
King's Mill
BOWER HILL CL
NETHERLEIGH PK
The Avenue
1 SOUTH STATION APP
2
KINGS ACRE
THE PO
KINGS CROSS LA

6
CAMBRIDGE SQ
SALFORD WAY
VICTORIA CT
ANDERSON CT
ALBERT MEWS
REED DR
COLOMAN ST
ROYAL EARLSWOOD
GATEHOUSE LODGE
1 HELENA HO
2 EDWARD HO
Redhill Brook
Greensand Way
RIDGE GN
RIDGE GREEN LA
Ridge Green
Crab Hill Farm

5
CANADA AVE
East Surrey
H
CANADA HOUSE
CANADA DR
Robin Cooks Farm
Staplehurst Farm
Wings Mus
KINGS MILL LA
Hale Farm

RH1

48
THREE ARCH RD
BUSHEY
Three Arch Bsns Pk
GRANTWOOD DR
HAWTHORNE CL
FOXLEY DR
AMBLESIDE CL
Whitebushes
CRAB HILL LA

4
WIMBORNE AVE
DENTON RD
EVERSFIELD RD
RATHGAR CL
KILN WALK
LAVENDER CL
IVYDENE CL
Redhill Aerodrome

PRINCE ALBERT SQ
THE BROW
SPENCER WAY
JORDANS CL
GREEN LA
GREENWOOD DR
MASON'S BRIDGE RD
MOATS LA

3
WEST AVE
WOODSIDE WAY
COPSLEIGH WAY
COPSLEIGH CL
COPSLEIGH AVE
Salford Prim Sch
MAYFIELD CL
HILLFORD PL
BROOKFIELD CL
Salfords Stream
MOATS LA
South Hale Farm
HATCH LA
M23

47
Honeycrock Ct
PH
HONEYCROCK LA

2
A23
BRIGHTON RD
Salfords Bridge
PO
Dean Farm
Mason's Bridge
Dairy House Farm
AXES LA
Axeland Park
Furzefield Wood
GREEN LA

1
LODGE LA
WHITE GLNS
STONE LODGE
OAK LODGE
MEAD AVE
SOUTHERN AVE
WESTMEAD DR
PARK VIEW RD
AUTUMN FARM
BRIGHTON RD
HONEYCROCK LA
WESTSIDE HO
DINRAVEN AVE
JUNE LA
WESTSIDE
Cyprus Farm
FAIRACRES
Axes Farm
Caravan Park
West View Farm
NEW HOUSE LA
ST GEORGE'S RD

Salfords
Salbrook Rd
Perrywood Bsns Pk
PICKETTS LA
Christmas Farm Kennels
Woolborough Hatch Farm

46
A23

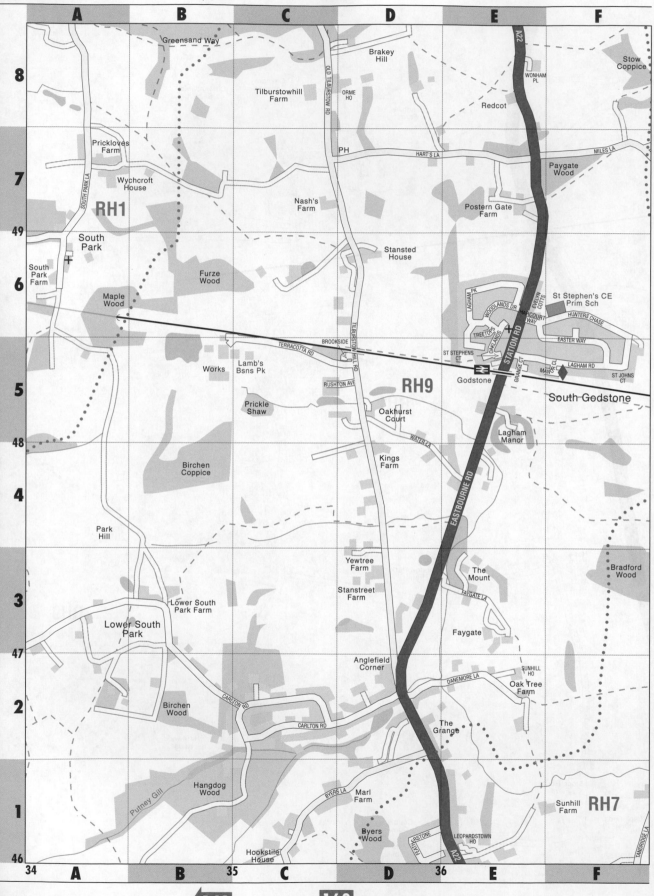

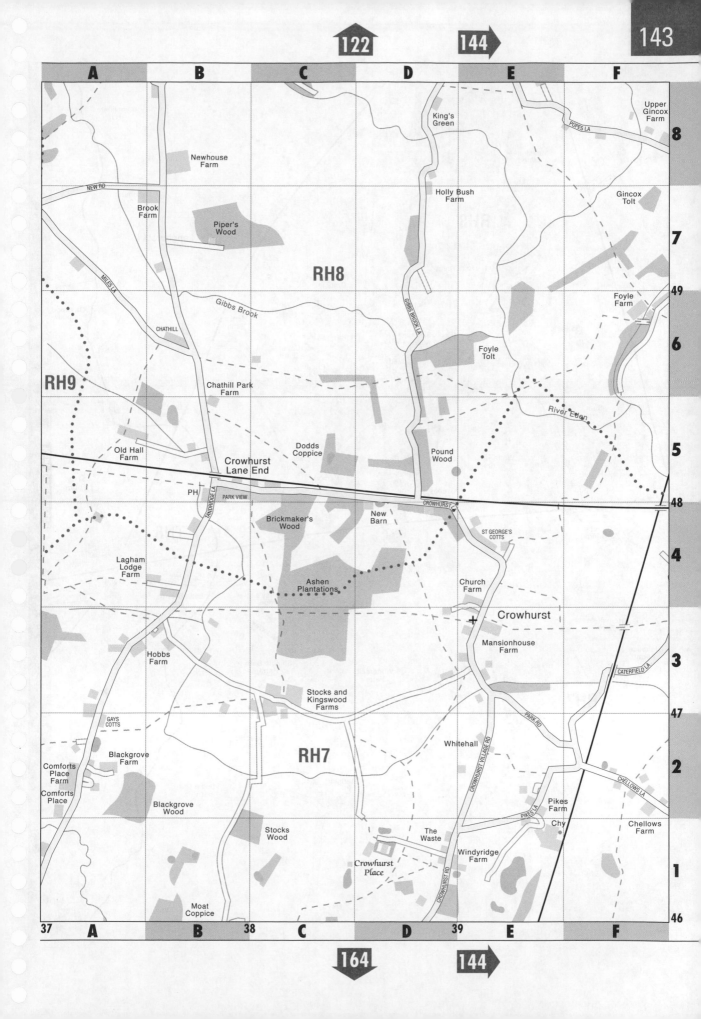

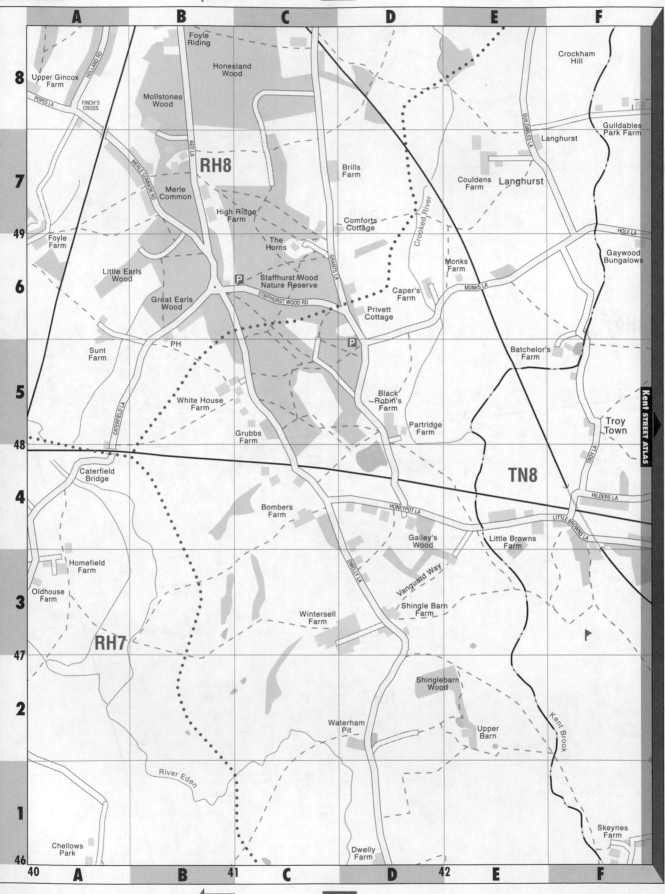

Hampshire Street Atlas

Cheeks Farm

Old Farnham La
Runwick La

Grover's Farm

Ridgway House

Willey Copse

Bunces Farm

Runwick La

Runwick House

Coxbridge Bsns Pk
ENDEAVOUR PL

A31

COXBRIDGE RDBT

Hill Farm

Hotel

Chandler La

Willey Place

Alton Rd

Passmore Bridge

KINGFISHER RD 1
HERON CL 2
THE BUNTINGS 3

THE HATCHES

8

Willey Mill House

River La

RIVER ROW COTTS

WRECCLESHAM RD

A325

Weydon La

Weydon Sch

GU9

Ganscombe Copse

BEARWOOD COTTS 1
WEAVERS GDNS 2
BRYN RD 3
STEWARDS RISE 4

Grovebell Ind Est

7

Northbrook Farm

Cromdall Rd

River Way

Sand Pit

Recn Gd

WESTFIELD

THE OLD VICARAGE

RINEDALE

BUTTERMER

DALE CL

THE STREET

ALLERTON WAY

CHURCH LA

PO

GREENFIELD RD

45

PH

A31

Wrecclesham

COVENOR WOOD

ST PETER'S GDNS

RURAL CL

KINGS LA

GRANTLEY CT

CHARTWELL

SHORTHEATH CREST

HEATHER CL

SHORTHEATH CREST

6

A31 Alton

A31

GRAVEL HILL RD

Grovelands Mill

Holt Pound La

GU10

COPSE WAY

BROADWELL RD

WOODCUT RD

POTTERY CT

GREYSTEAD PK

QUENNELLS HILL

COLESON HILL RD

HOLLY DR

HOLES WOOD

WRECCLESHAM HILL

B3384

ECHO BARN LA

B3384

CROWHOLT

THE CHASE

SANDROCK HILL RD

LAUREL LA

5

Holt Pound Farm

Wrecclesham Farm

BROWNS WLK

THORN CL

LAUREL LA

THORN CL

Cotton's Copse

PH

Manley Bridge

MANLEY RD

Manleybridge Farm

THE AVENUE

44

Holt Pound Inclosure

The Old Kiln Farm

Fairvalley Farm

ROSEMARY LA

HIGH ST

CHAPEL RD

CLARE MEAD

THE COPSE

BOUNDSTONE RD

SHRUBBS LA

SWITCHBACK

THE AVENUE

4

Holt Pound

FULLERS RD

THE SQUARE

THE AVENUE

MEADOW WAY

ORCHARD END

Forest Wlk

P

GRAVEL HILL RD

Bools Farm

FOREST GLADE

SCHOOL RD

Rowledge CE Prim Sch

P

RECREATION RD

PH

PO

PH

CHERRY TREE RD

HADLEYS

Rowledge

PROSPECT RD

THE LONG RD

PEAR TREE LA

HAWTHORN LA

3

PARK CL

Mast

Birdworld & Underwater World

CHURCH LA

P

CHERRY TREE WLK

Lickfolds Farm

LICKFOLDS RD

43

Alice Holt Lodge

Lodge Pond

P

Borderfield Farm

BOUNDARY RD

Hawthorn Farm

2

Plain Piece

Alice Holt Forest

Glenbervie Inclosure

West End

WEST END LA

1

THE GLADE

A325

Reeds Hatch Farm

West End House

42

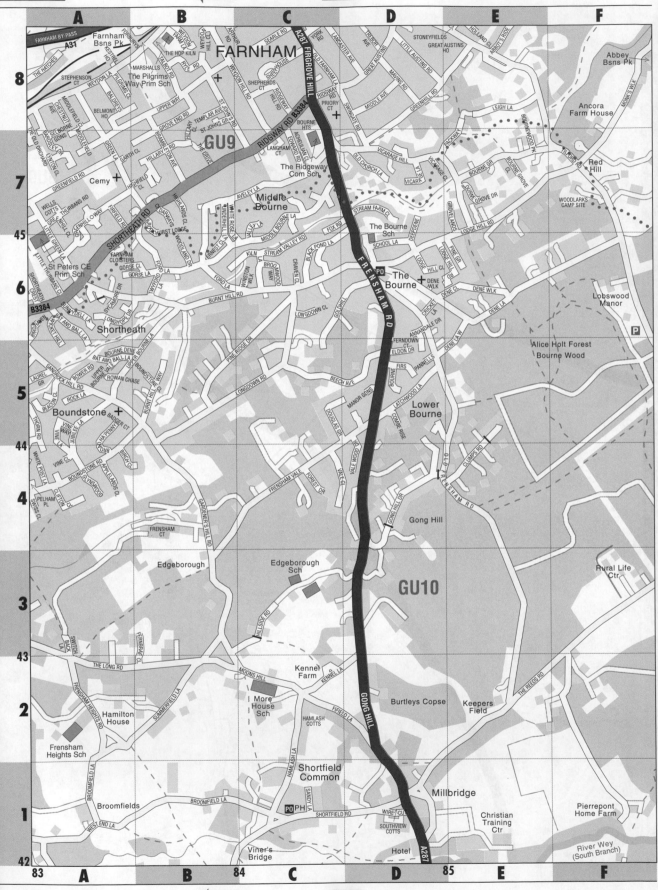

A B C D E F

FARNHAM

8

7

45

6

5

44

4

3

43

2

1

42

GU9

GU10

Farnham By-Pass
A31
Farnham Bsns Pk
Stephenson Ct
The Pilgrims Way Prim Sch
Marshalls
The Hop Kiln
Shepherds Ct
Searle Rd
York Rd
Lancaster Ave
Stoneyfields
Great Austins Ho
Abbey Bsns Pk

Cemy
Highfield Cl

Middle Bourne
The Ridgeway Com Sch

Red Hill

St Peters CE Prim Sch
Farnham Cloisters

Shortheath
Boundstone

The Bourne Sch
The Bourne

Lobswood Manor

Alice Holt Forest
Bourne Wood

Lower Bourne

Woodlarks Camp Site

Edgeborough
Edgeborough Sch

Gong Hill

Rural Life Ctr

Kennel Farm
More House Sch

Burtleys Copse
Keepers Field

Shortfield Common
Millbridge

Frensham Heights Sch

Broomfields

Christian Training Ctr
Pierrepont Home Farm

Viner's Bridge
Hotel
A287
River Wey (South Branch)

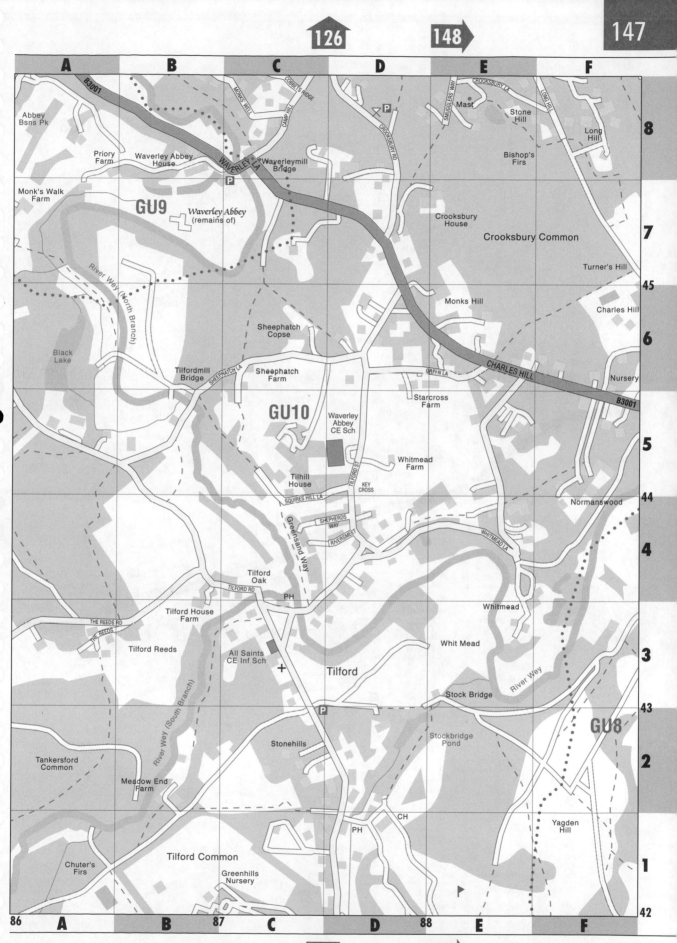

A B C D E F

8

GU10

Culverswell Hill

Littleworth Cross

The Warren

Puttenham Common Nature Trails

The Tarn

GU3

LITTLEWORTH RD

P

P

Cuttmill Pond

Cutt Mill House

The Marsh

7

SEALE RD

Britty Wood

Lower Puttenham Common

SUFFIELD LA

Broad Firs

LOMBARD ST

Gatwick

45

6

Fullbrook Farm

Broomfields

Sugarbaker Farm

CHARLES HILL B3001

Amina Heights

River Wey

Works

Woodside Farm

5

Charleshill

PH

Turner's Farm

FULBROOK LA

Polshot Manor

Thundry Farm

FARNHAM RD

44

GU8

Hankley Farm

The Mill House

PH

ELSTEAD GN

AVENUE ROW

HAM LA

LOWER HAM LA

Works

4

CEDAR MOUNT

BACK LA

BARN CT

BROADFIELD

HAZLEWOOD

MILFORD RD

P

Burford Lodge

STACEY'S MDW

HOPE'S

LITTLE GN THE SQUARE

ELORG'S CL

BURFORD LEA

Cemy

STACEY'S FARM RD

SPRINGFIELD

HILL CREST

UPPER SPRINGFIELD

SPRINGFIELD WAY

SHACKLEFORD RD

B3001

Westbrook

Westbrook Farm

WESTBROOK HILL

CHURCH GN

WEST HILL

BANKSIDE

SPRINGHALL

THE CROFT

HOOKLEY CL

SILVER BIRCHES WAY

Lex Farm

3

Hankley Cottages

THE GABLES

COPSE EDGE

DOWN

GUARDIAN CT

CL

VONES

ALLENDALE

Sunray Farm

St James CE Prim Sch

Springhaven

Royal Lodge

43

MOORS LA

ASH LA

PO

WOODSIDE COTTS

RED HOUSE LA

KINGSMEAD PK CVN PK

PEAT COMM

Great Hookley Farm

HOOKLEY LA

Guinea Common

2

THURSLEY RD

BEACON VIEW RD

Pot Common

The Moors

Red House Farm

Westbrook Moor

1

Tadmoor Cottage

Woolford's Farm

WOOLFORDS LA

Cemy

Elstead Common

42

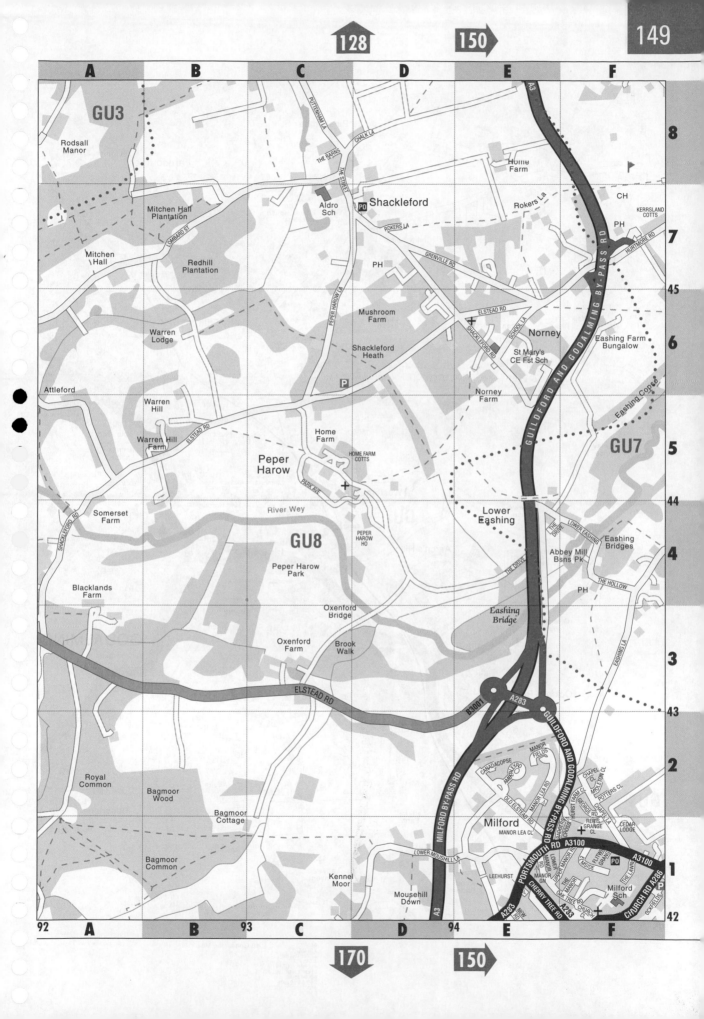

GU3

Rodsall Manor

Mitchen Hall Plantation

Mitchen Hall

LOMBARD ST

Redhill Plantation

Warren Lodge

Attleford

Warren Hill

Warren Hill Farm

ELSTEAD RD

PEPER HAROW LA

THE BARNS

THE STREET

PUTTENHAM LA

CHALK LA

Aldro Sch

PO

Shackleford

ROKERS LA

PH

GRENVILLE RD

Mushroom Farm

Shackleford Heath

P

Home Farm

Peper Harow

PARK AVE

River Wey

GU8

Somerset Farm

SHACKLEFORD RD

Blacklands Farm

Peper Harow Park

Oxenford Bridge

Oxenford Farm

Brook Walk

HOME FARM COTTS

PEPER HAROW HO

ELSTEAD RD

Royal Common

Bagmoor Wood

Bagmoor Cottage

Bagmoor Common

Kennel Moor

Mousehill Down

Home Farm

ROKERS LA

ELSTEAD RD

SCHOOL LA

SHACKLEFORD RD

Norney

St Mary's CE Fst Sch

Norney Farm

Lower Eashing

THE DRIVE

LOWER EASHING

Abbey Mill Bsns Pk

THE HOLLOW

PH

Eashing Bridge

THE DRIVE

Eashing Bridges

EASHING LA

GU7

Eashing Farm Bungalow

Eashing Copse

CH

PH

KERRSLAND COTTS

HURTMORE RD

GUILDFORD AND GODALMING BY-PASS RD

A3

B3001

A283

GUILDFORD AND GODALMING BY-PASS RD

MILFORD BY-PASS RD

A3

Milford

CANADACOPSE

MANOR FIELDS

OLD ELSTEAD RD

MANOR LEA RD

MANOR LEA CL

HURST FARM CL

GEORGE RD

CHAPEL LA

CHAPEL CL

MOLLISON CL

POTTIERS CL

RERTS GRANGE

CEDAR LODGE

PORTSMOUTH RD

A3100

A3100

PO

A283

NEW RD

A283

CHERRY TREE RD

CHURCH RD A286

Milford Sch

P

LEEHURST

LOWER MOUSHILL LA

UPPER MANOR RD

THE MANOR

OAK TREE CL

ROCKFIELDS

8
7
45
6
5
44
4
3
43
2
1
42

92   A   93   B   C   93   D   94   E   F

A   B   C   D   E   F

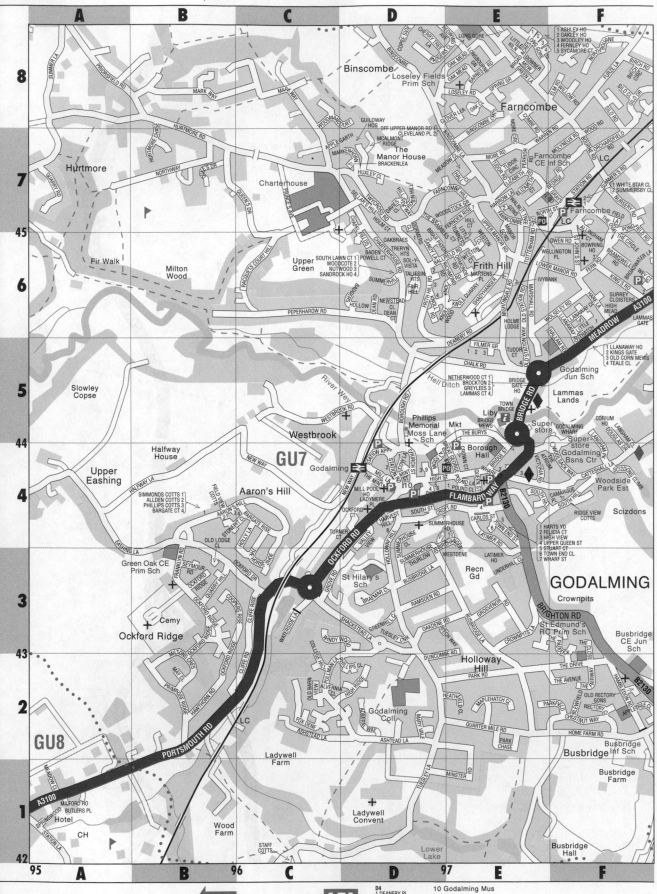

D4
1 DEANERY PL
2 CHESTER HO
3 THE FLAT
4 LOWER SOUTH ST
5 HENRY MARSHALL HO
6 BISHOPS HO
7 EDMUNDS GATE
8 HAZELWOOD COTTS
9 ANGEL CT

10 Godalming Mus

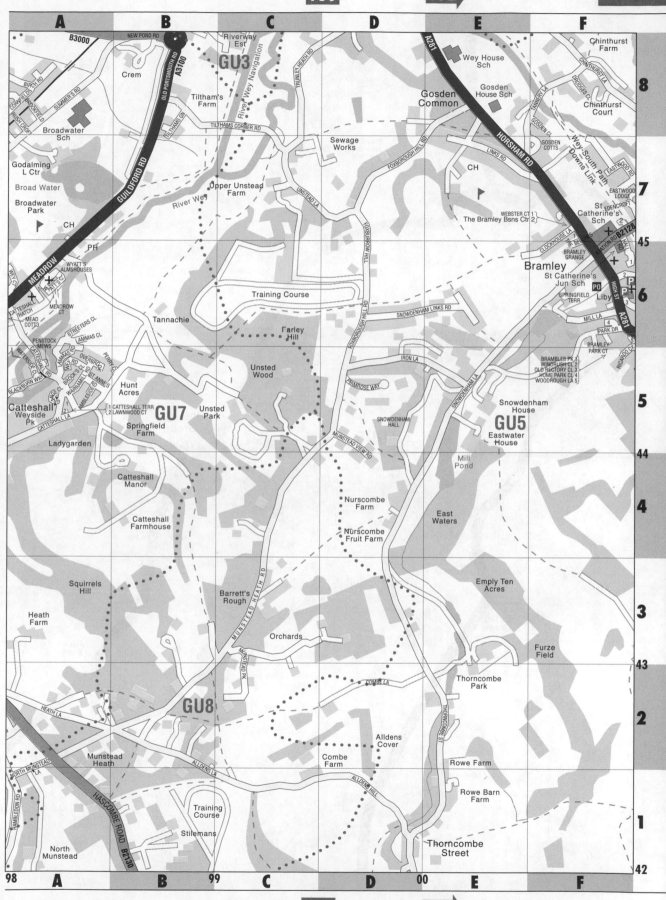

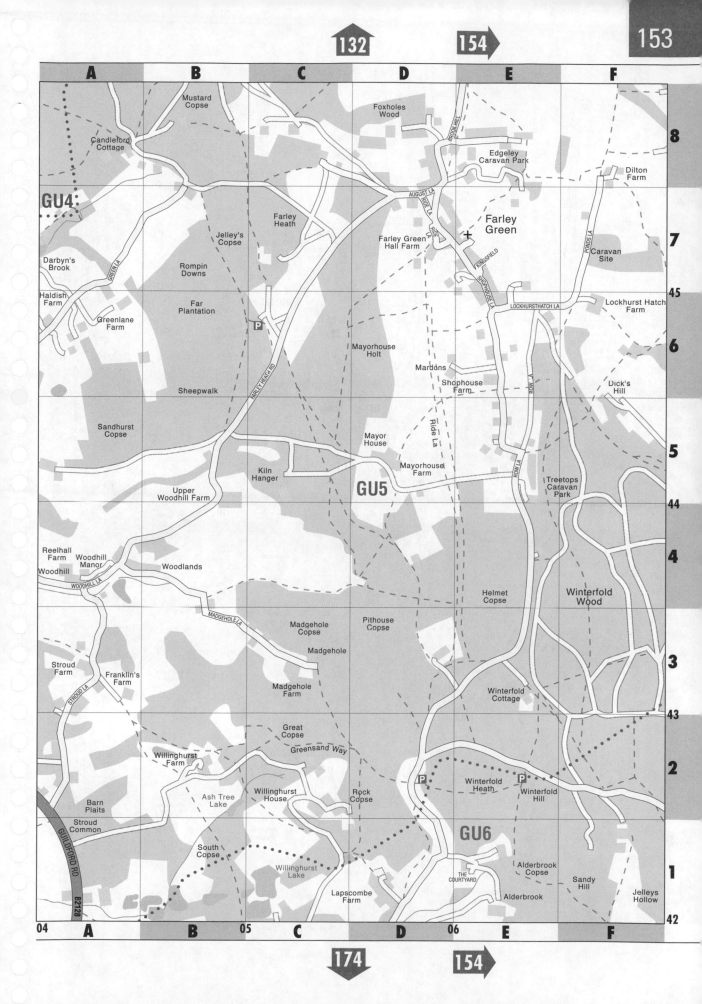

153
133

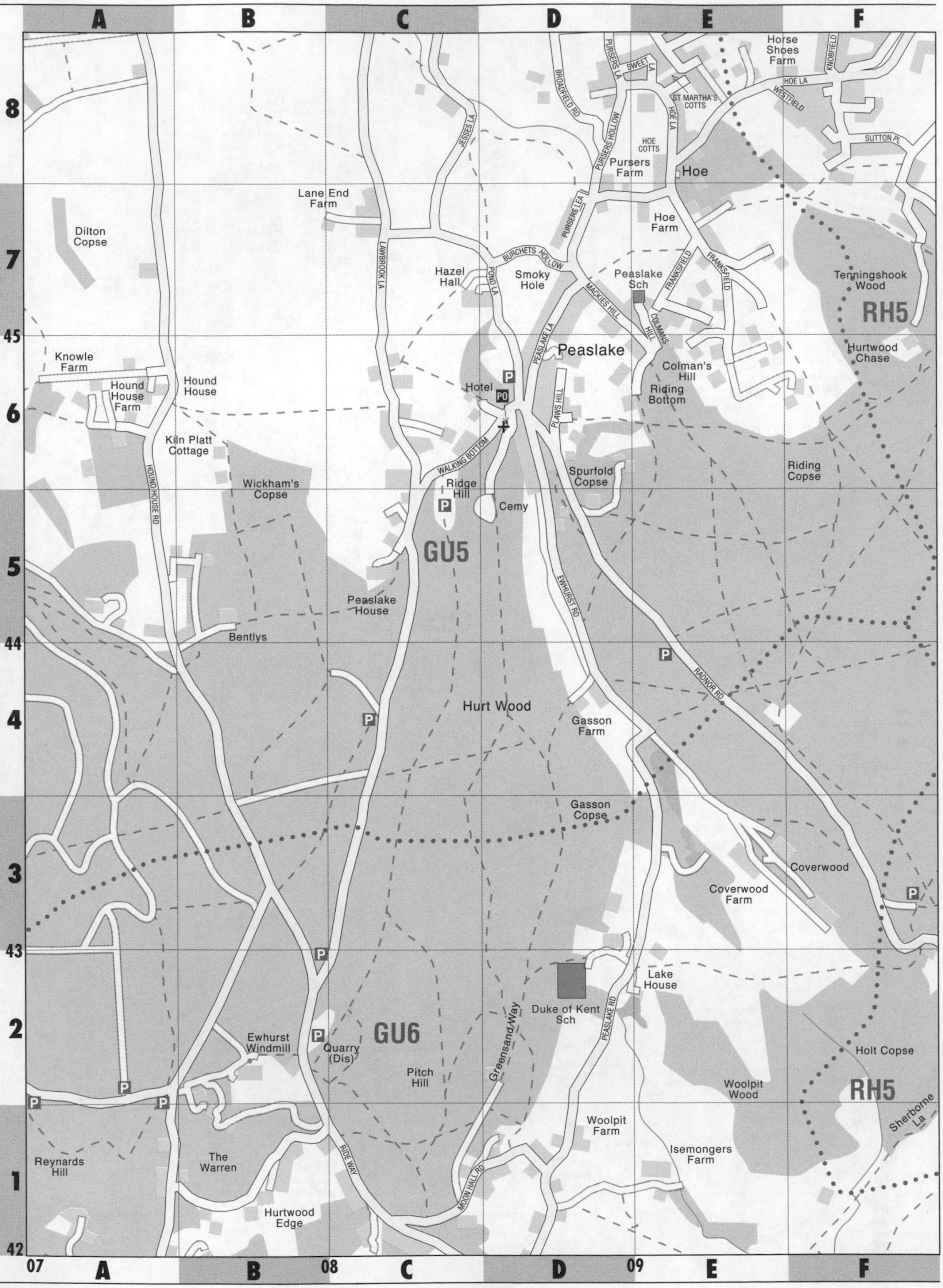

	A	B	C	D	E	F

8

Dilton Copse

Horse Shoes Farm

Lane End Farm

PURSERS LA
SWEET LA
BROADFIELD RD
PURSERS HOLLOW
HOE LA
HOE LA
WESTFIELD
KNOBFIELD
SUTTON PL
St Martha's Cotts
HOE COTTS

7

Knowle Farm

Hound House Farm
Hound House

Hazel Hall
Smoky Hole

BURCHETS HOLLOW
JESSES LA
LAWBROOK LA
POND LA
MACKIES HILL
PURSERS LEA
Pursers Farm
Hoe Farm
Hoe
Peaslake Sch
FRANKSFIELD
FRANKSFIELD

Tenningshook Wood

45

Kiln Platt Cottage

HOUND HOUSE RD
Hotel
PO
Peaslake
PEASLAKE LA
COLMANS HILL
Colman's Hill
Riding Bottom

RH5
Hurtwood Chase

6

Wickham's Copse

Ridge Hill
WALKING BOTTOM
Cemy
Spurfold Copse
Riding Bottom

Riding Copse

5

Peaslake House

GU5

Bentlys

EWHURST RD

44

Hurt Wood

Gasson Farm
RADNOR RD

4

P

Gasson Copse

Coverwood

3

Coverwood Farm

P

43

Lake House

2

Ewhurst Windmill
Quarry (Dis)
GU6
Pitch Hill
GREENSAND WAY
Duke of Kent Sch
PEASLAKE RD

Holt Copse

RH5

1

Reynards Hill
The Warren
Hurtwood Edge
RIDE WAY
MOON HALL RD
Woolpit Farm
Woolpit Wood
Isemongers Farm
Sherborne La

42

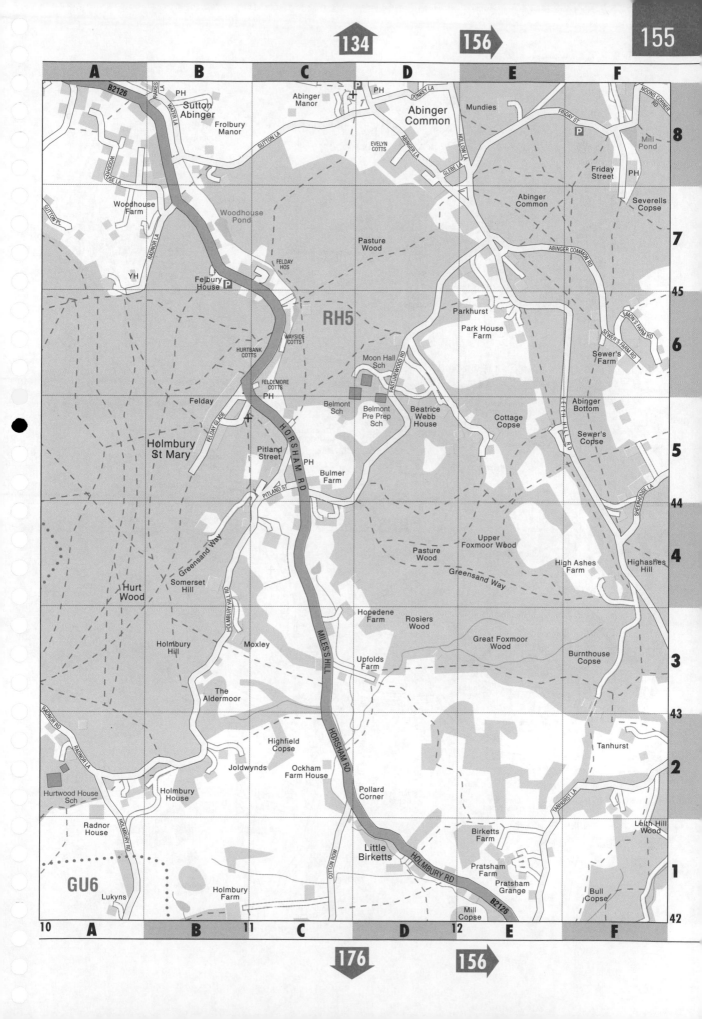

A B C D E F

8

7

45

6

5

44

4

43

3

2

1

42

NOONS CORNER RD
SHEEPHOUSE LA
Home Farm
Broadmoor
BROADMOOR COTTS
Severells Copse
Pond Cottage
WHITEBERRY RD
Simons Copse
Brookwick Copse
High Field
Collickmoor Farm
Robin Gate Cottage
Robbing Gate
RH4
Pondfield Copse
COLDHARBOUR LA
Upper Merriden Cottage
Leylands
SHEEPHOUSE LA
Shootlands Farm
Warren Farm
Tilling Springs
Leylands Farm
Greensand Way
Whiteberry Rd
Broadmoor Bottom
The Duke's Warren
Coldharbour Common
Waterden Wood
Whiteberry Hill
Whiteberry Gate
WOLVENS LA
Crockers Farm
Anstiebury Farm
PH Anstiebury
Coldharbour
Spring Copse
RH5
Wotton Common
Snakes Hill
ANSTIE LA
Kitlands Farm
Kitlands
East Lodge
Leith Hill
Leith Hill Tower
WEALD VIEW COTTS
The Landslip
Gill Wood
LEITH HILL RD
ABINGER RD
Cockshot Farm
Mosses Wood
BROOMEHALL RD
East Campfield Place
TANHURST LA
Bushy Copse
Smither's Copse
Broome Hall Farm
Leith Hill Place Wood
Broome Hall
Leith Hill Place
Leith Hill Place Farm
Hartshurst Farm
Fatting Hovel Copse
Nutfold Copse
Great Copse

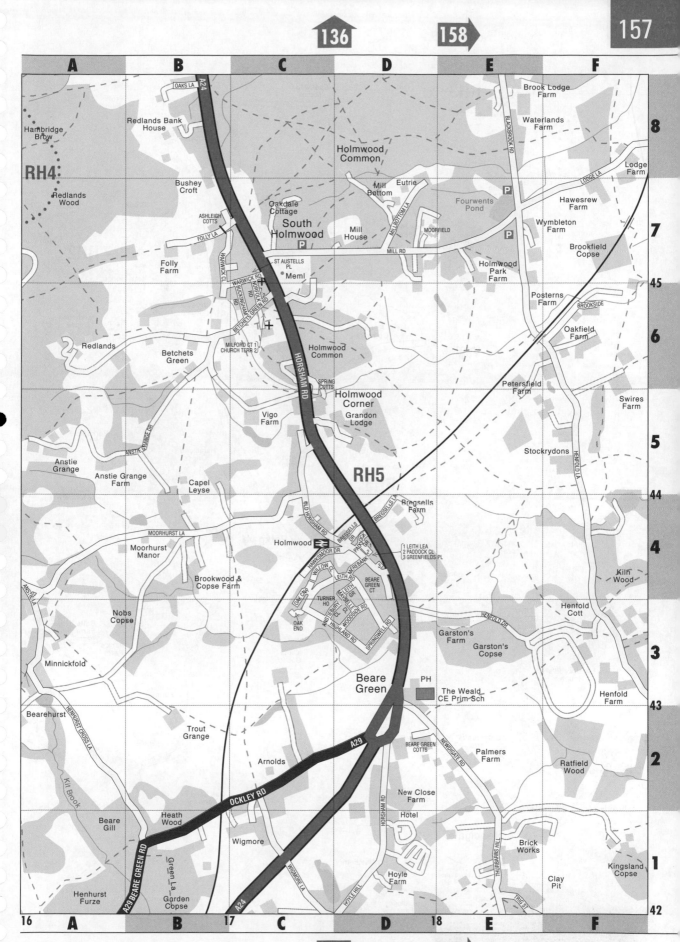

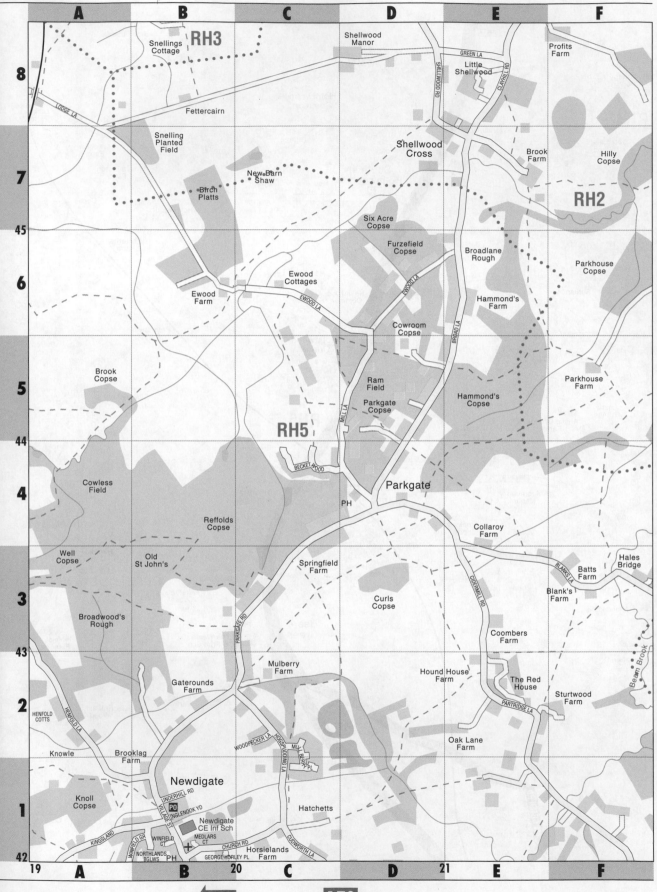

A   B   C   D   E   F

RH3

Snellings
Cottage

Shellwood
Manor

Profits
Farm

8

Little
Shellwood

GREEN LA

CLAPHILL RD

SHELLWOOD RD

LODGE LA

Fettercairn

Snelling
Planted
Field

Shellwood
Cross

Brook
Farm

Hilly
Copse

7

New Barn
Shaw

Birch
Platts

RH2

45

Six Acre
Copse

Furzefield
Copse

Broadlane
Rough

Parkhouse
Copse

6

Ewood
Cottages

EWOOD LA

EWOOD LA

Hammond's
Farm

Ewood
Farm

Cowroom
Copse

BROAD LA

5

Brook
Copse

Ram
Field

Parkgate
Copse

Hammond's
Copse

Parkhouse
Farm

RH5

MILL LA

44

Cowless
Field

BECKET WOOD

Parkgate

4

Reffolds
Copse

PH

Collaroy
Farm

Hales
Bridge

Well
Copse

Old
St John's

Springfield
Farm

BLANKS LA

Batts
Farm

3

Broadwood's
Rough

Curls
Copse

CUDWORTH RD

Blank's
Farm

Bean Brook

43

Mulberry
Farm

Coombers
Farm

PARKGATE RD

Gaterounds
Farm

Hound House
Farm

The Red
House

Sturtwood
Farm

2

Henfold
Cotts

HENFOLD LA

WOODPECKER LA

HOGSPUDDING LA

MULBERRY PL

PARTRIDGE LA

Knowle

Brooklag
Farm

Oak Lane
Farm

Newdigate

UNDERHILL RD

1

Knoll
Copse

VILLAGE ST

PO

INGLENOOK YD

Hatchetts

WINFIELD GR

WINFIELD CT

Newdigate
CE Inf Sch

MEDLARS
CT

CHURCH RD

CUDWORTH LA

KINGSLAND

NORTHLANDS
BGLWS

PH

GEORGE HORLEY PL

Horsielands
Farm

42

A B C D E F

8

Dulands
Copse

Deanoak
Bridge

Ashurst
Farm

Swains
Copse

Dean Oak
Farm

DEANOAK LA

IRONSBOTTOM

Nalderswood

RH2

Rigden
Farm

Mynthurst

Grove
Cottage

SOUTH LODGE
CT

7

Grove
Farm

Mynthurst
Farm

MYNTHURST FARM
COTTS

Little Mynthurst

Bush House
Copse

Herons Head
Farm

45

Fortune
Farm

SMALLS HILL RD

Deanoak Brook

Nutley Dean
Bsns Pk

Collendean
Copse

6

Orchard Four Acre
Plantation

Little Mynthurst
Farm

Nutley Dean
Farm

Rookery
Wood

Norwood Place
Farm

5

Dowces
Farm

Cherry Tree
Farm

Rose Cottage
Farm

Collendean
Farm

COLLENDEAN LA

44

RH5

Chantersluer
Farm

Rowgardenswood

4

Chantersluer
Wood

RH6

PH

+

Norwood
Hill

Brittleware
Farm

Rickettswood
Farm

Norwood Hill
Orchards

3

Ricketts
Wood

NORWOOD HILL

NORWOODHILL RD

43

BLANKS LA

2

Highworth Farm

Edolph's Copse
Nature Reserve

Rainbow
Wood

SPENCERS LA

Pockmires
Wood

Beggars Gill

STAN HILL

Edolphs
Farm

1

Stanhill Court

Johnson's
Common

Beggars Gill

42

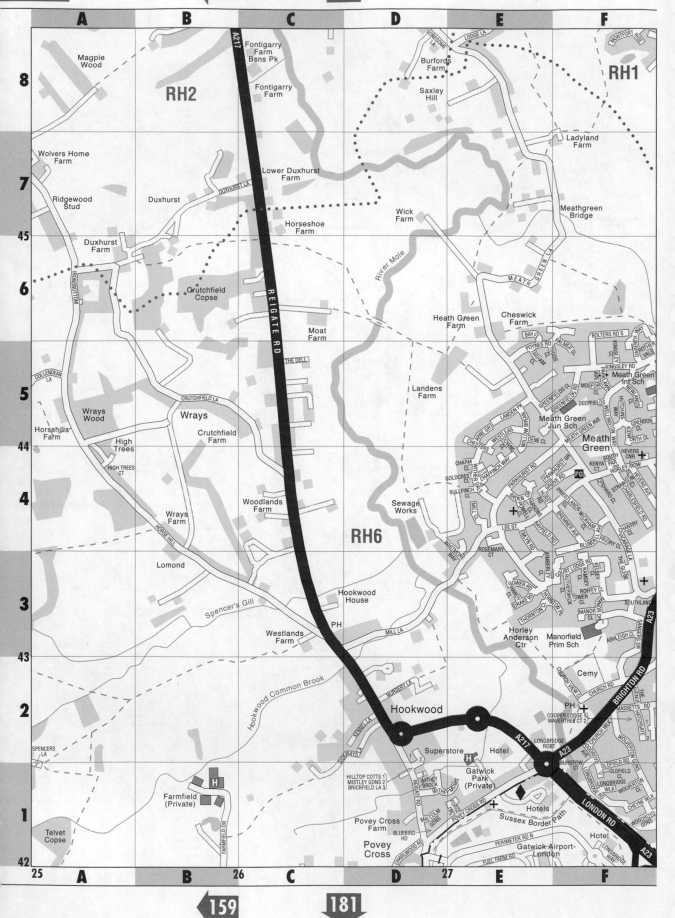

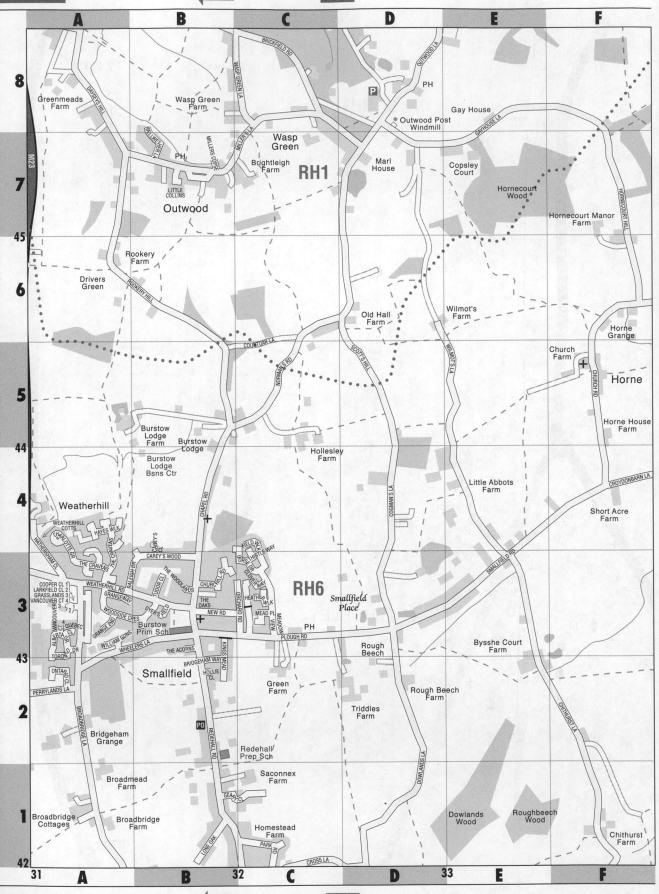

8

Greenmeads
Farm

Wasp Green
Farm

PH

Little
Collins

Outwood

Outwood Post
Windmill

Gay House

Wasp
Green

Copsley
Court

Hornecourt
Wood

Hornecourt Manor
Farm

Brightleigh
Farm

RH1

Marl
House

7

45

Rookery
Farm

Drivers
Green

ROOKERY HILL

Old Hall
Farm

Wilmot's
Farm

Church
Farm

Horne
Grange

6

COURTOAK LA

NORMAN'S RD

SCOTT'S HILL

WILMOT'S LA

Horne

5

Burstow
Lodge
Farm

Burstow
Lodge

Hollesley
Farm

Little Abbots
Farm

Horne House
Farm

CROYDONBARN LA

44

Burstow
Lodge
Bsns Ctr

COGMAN'S LA

Short Acre
Farm

4

Weatherhill

WEATHERHILL
COTTS

HAYES WLK

CHARLOTTE GR

THE CRAVENS

CAREY'S CL

CAREY'S WOOD

FIELD WLK

THISTLEY WAY

RH6

Smallfield
Place

HATHERSHAM CL

THE CRAVENS

RALEIGH DR

TUDOR CL

THE WOODLANDS

CHURCHILL RD

ORCHD DR

CLOVER WAY

SMALLFIELD RD

3

COOPER CL 1
LARKFIELD CL 2
GRASSLANDS 3
VANCOUVER CT 4

WEATHERHILL RD

GRANGEWAY

DYER'S FLD

THE OAKS

HEATHER
WLK

MEAD PL

PH

Bysshe Court
Farm

WOODSIDE CRES

GRANGE RD

NEW RD

MEADOW
VIEW

QUEBEC
CL

ALBERTA
DR

WILLIAM GDNS

WHEELERS LA

Burstow
Prim Sch

PLOUGH RD

Rough
Beech

Rough Beech
Farm

43

TORON
TO
CL

THE ACORNS

KINGS MEAD

BRIDGEHAM WAY

HOLLIE
CL

Smallfield

Green
Farm

Triddles
Farm

ONTARIO
CL

PERRYLANDS LA

BROADBRIDGE LA

REDEHALL RD

DOWLANDS LA

CHITHURST LA

2

Bridgeham
Grange

PO

Redehall
Prep Sch

Saconnex
Farm

Broadmead
Farm

GEA   CL

1

Broadbridge
Cottages

Broadbridge
Farm

Homestead
Farm

LONE OAK

PARK
RD

CROSS LA

Dowlands
Wood

Roughbeech
Wood

Chithurst
Farm

42

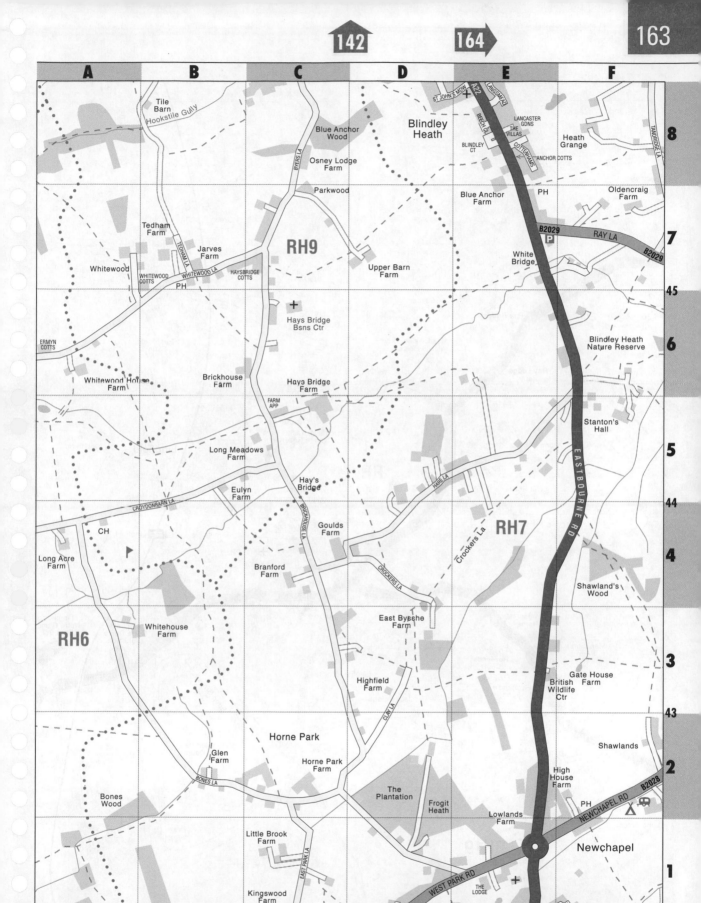

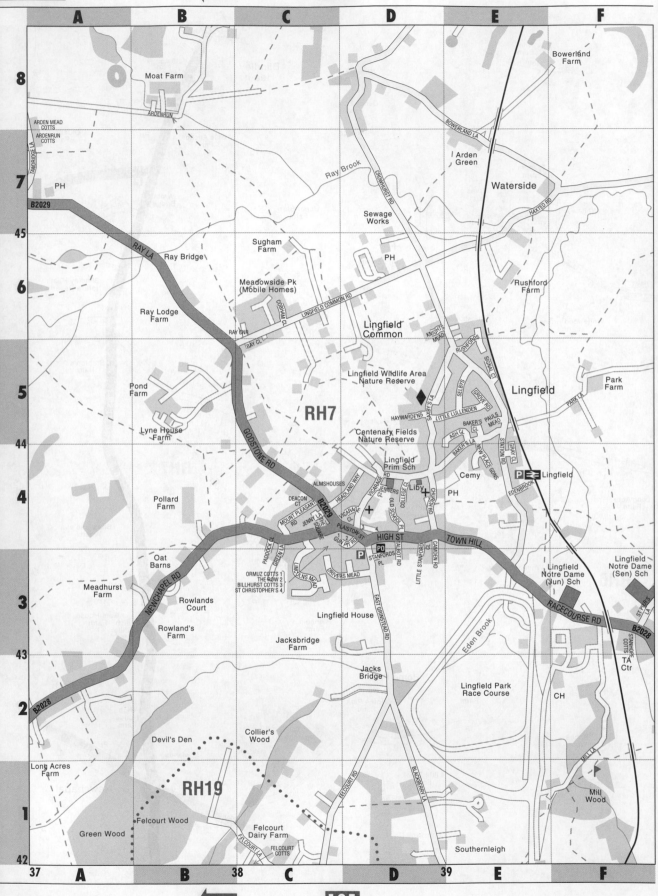

A B C D E F

8

ARDENRUN

Moat Farm

Bowerland Farm

ARDEN MEAD COTTS
ARDENRUN COTTS

BOWERLAND LA

7 PH

Arden Green

TANDRIDGE LA

B2029

Waterside

RAY LA

45 Ray Bridge

Ray Brook

HAXTED RD

CROWHURST RD

Sewage Works

Sugham Farm

Rushford Farm

6 Ray Lodge Farm

Meadowside Pk (Mobile Homes)

COBHAM CL

LINGFIELD COMMON RD

PH

Lingfield Common

RAY CNR

Knights Mead

RUSHFORDS

Park Farm

RAY CL

KNIGHTS MEAD

PARK LA

5 Pond Farm

Lingfield Wildlife Area Nature Reserve

SELBYS

SIGNAL CT

Lingfield

RH7

HAYWARDENS

SAMSBY'S LA

LITTLE LULLENDEN

GROVE RD

Lyne House Farm

Centenary Fields Nature Reserve

BAKER'S CL

PAULS MEAD

44 GODSTONE RD

ASH CL

NEW PLACE GDNS

STATION RD

GRAY CL

BAKER'S LA

EDENBROOK

P Lingfield

Lingfield Prim Sch

Pollard Farm

ALMSHOUSES

RD

Cemy

4 DEACON CT

HEADLAND WAY

VICARAGE MEWERS CL

OLD SCHOOL LA

COLLEGE CL

Liby

PH

MOUNT PLEASANT RD

B2029

JENNY LA

VICARAGE CL

CHURCH RD

PADDOCK CL

THE SQUARE

3

PLAISTOW ST

HIGH ST

TOWN HILL

GREEN LA

GULF PIT RD

LITTLE STANFORD

CAMDEN RD

Oat Barns

LINDENS MEAD

TALBOT RD

Lingfield Notre Dame (Jun) Sch

Lingfield Notre Dame (Sen) Sch

NEWCHAPEL RD

DRIVERS MEAD

PO

STANFORDS PL

EAST GRINSTEAD RD

Meadhurst Farm

P

ORMUZ COTTS 1
THE ROW 2
BILLHURST COTTS 3
ST CHRISTOPHER'S 4

3 Rowlands Court

Lingfield House

RACECOURSE RD

ST PIERS LA

B2028

Rowland's Farm

Jacksbridge Farm

STANHOPE COTTS

43 B2028

Eden Brook

Jacks Bridge

Lingfield Park Race Course

TA Ctr

2

Devil's Den

Collier's Wood

CH

Long Acres Farm

MILL LA

RH19

Mill Wood

1 Green Wood

Felcourt Wood

Felcourt Dairy Farm

FELCOURT LA

FELCOURT RD

BLACKBERRY LA

Southernleigh

FELCOURT COTTS

42

37 A 38 B C 38 D 39 E F

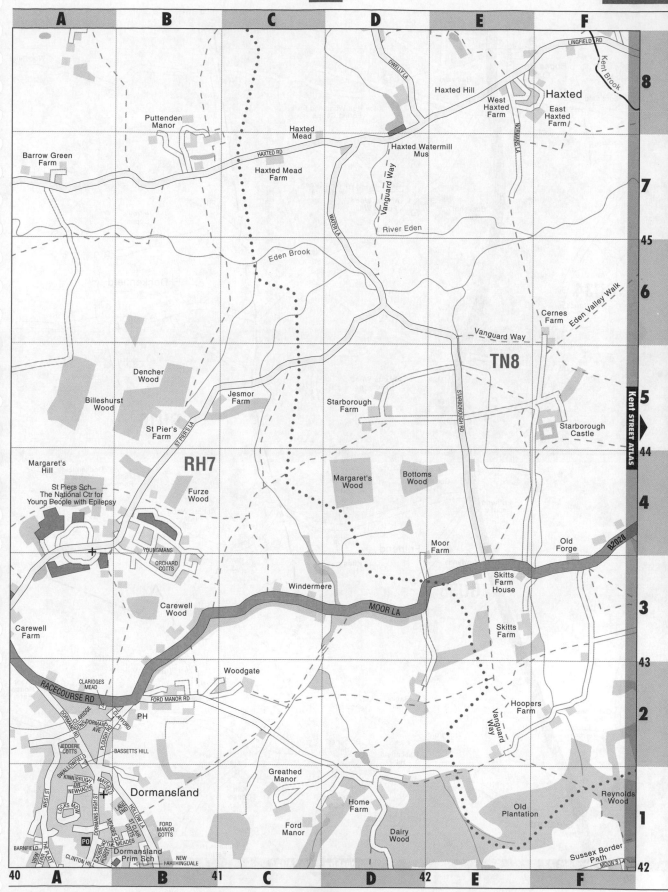

Kent Brook

LINGFIELD RD

8

Haxted Hill

West
Haxted
Farm

Haxted

DWELLY LA

East
Haxted
Farm

Puttenden
Manor

NORMANS LA

Barrow Green
Farm

Haxted
Mead

Haxted Watermill
Mus

HAXTED RD

Haxted Mead
Farm

Vanguard Way

7

45

River Eden

WATER LA

Eden Brook

6

Cernes
Farm

Eden Valley Walk

Vanguard Way

Dencher
Wood

TN8

Kent STREET ATLAS

5

Billeshurst
Wood

Jesmor
Farm

Starborough
Farm

STARBOROUGH RD

Starborough
Castle

44

St Pier's
Farm

ST PIERS LA

Margaret's
Hill

RH7

Margaret's
Wood

Bottoms
Wood

B2028

4

St Piers Sch
The National Ctr for
Young People with Epilepsy

Furze
Wood

Moor
Farm

Old
Forge

YOUNGMANS

ORCHARD
COTTS

Windermere

Skitts
Farm
House

3

Carewell
Wood

MOOR LA

43

Carewell
Farm

Skitts
Farm

Woodgate

RACECOURSE RD

CLARIDGES
MEAD

FORD MANOR RD

Hoopers
Farm

2

CLARIDGE
GDNS

DORMANS
AVE

PH

Vanguard
Way

DORMANS RD

CLAFORD

PLOUGH RD

BASSETTS HILL

JEDDERE
COTTS

SWALLONFIELD

KINNIBRUG
DR

Greathed
Manor

NEW HACHE

MAYFIELD

Dormansland

Home
Farm

Old
Plantation

Reynolds
Wood

1

WEST ST

LOCKS MDW

DORMANS HIGH ST

LAUR
END

HOLLOW LA

ST CLAIR
COTTS

THE MEADES

Ford
Manor
COTTS

Ford
Manor

Dairy
Wood

BARNFIELD

THE PLATT

VIEW TERR

LADBROKE
HURST

PO

Dormansland
Prim Sch

NEW
FARTHINGDALE

Sussex Border
Path

MOON'S

42

CLINTON HILL

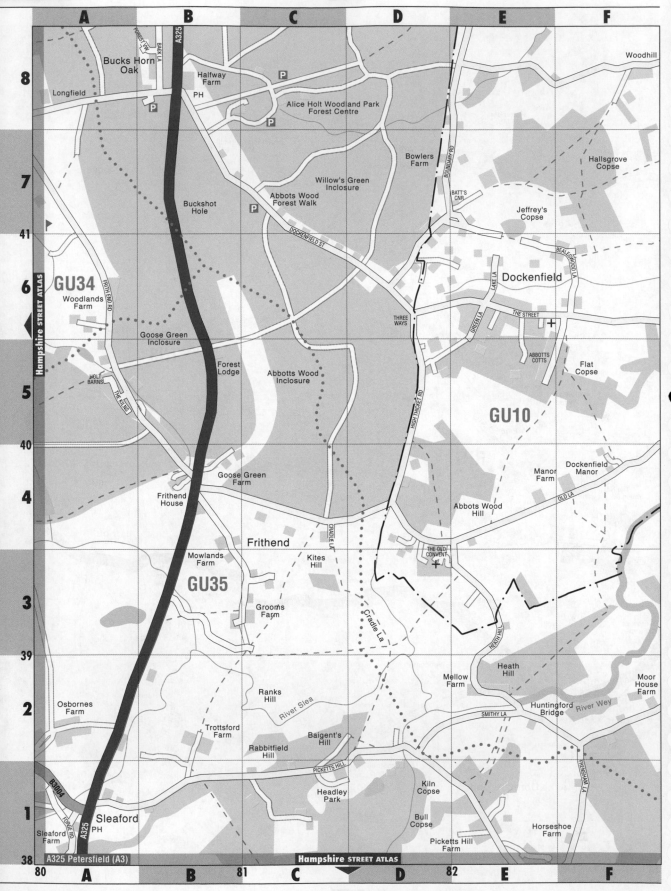

A B C D E F

8

7

41

6

GU34

5

40

4

3

39

2

1

38

80 A B 81 C D 82 E F

Hampshire STREET ATLAS

A325 Petersfield (A3)

Woodhill

Bucks Horn Oak

Longfield

Halfway Farm

PH

Alice Holt Woodland Park Forest Centre

Hallsgrove Copse

Bowlers Farm

Willow's Green Inclosure

Jeffrey's Copse

Buckshot Hole

Abbots Wood Forest Walk

BATT'S CNR

Dockenfield

DOCKENFIELD ST

Woodlands Farm

THREE WAYS

THE STREET

Goose Green Inclosure

ABBOTTS COTTS

Flat Copse

HOLT BARNS

Forest Lodge

Abbotts Wood Inclosure

GU10

Frithend House

Goose Green Farm

Manor Farm

Dockenfield Manor

OLD LA

Abbots Wood Hill

Mowlands Farm

GU35

Kites Hill

Frithend

THE OLD CONVENT

Grooms Farm

CRADLE LA

Cradle La

HEATH HILL

Heath Hill

Mellow Farm

Moor House Farm

Osbornes Farm

Ranks Hill

River Slea

Huntingford Bridge

River Wey

Trottsford Farm

Baigent's Hill

SMITHY LA

Rabbitfield Hill

PICKETTS HILL

Kiln Copse

FRENSHAM LA

B3004

Headley Park

Bull Copse

Horseshoe Farm

Sleaford Farm

FORGE RD

A325

Sleaford

PH

Picketts Hill Farm

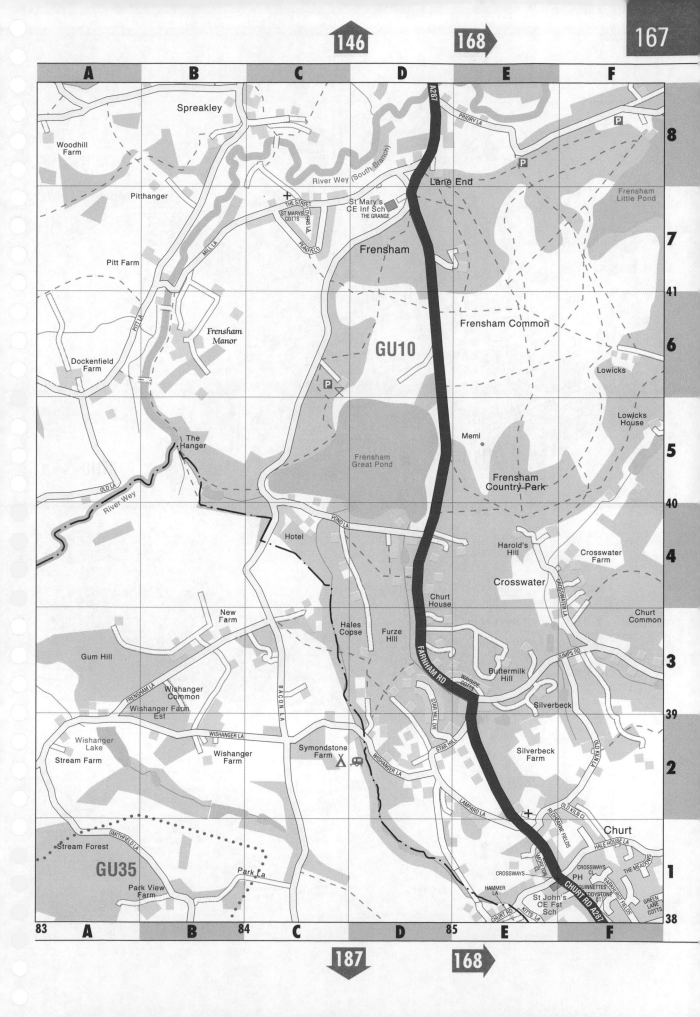

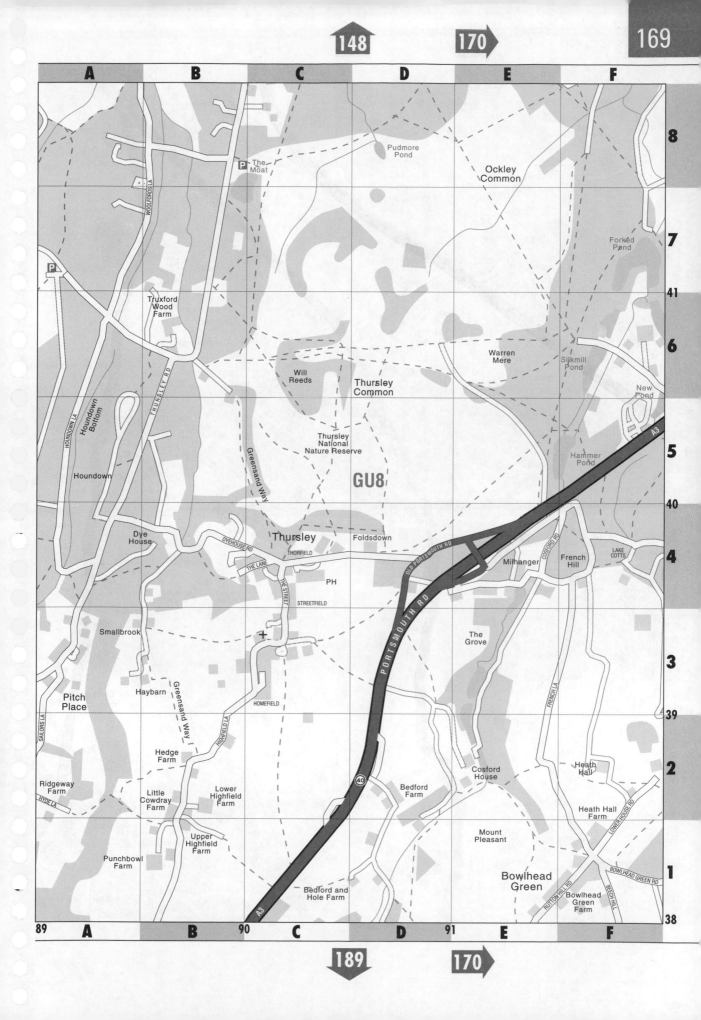

A B C D E F

8
Borough Farm
Mistlebrooks Wood
Mousehill Corner
MILFORD BY PASS RD
A283 PORTSMOUTH RD
Mousehill
A283
A286
NEW LA
GREEN LA
THE CEDARS
MOUSEHILL LA
LADYCROSS
PINKS MEWS
BROOK MEAD
DOWER COTTS
DOWER HOUSE
PILGRIM CT
BUSDENS WAY
BUSDENS LA
HIGHCROFT
BUSDENS CL
MILFORD LODGE

7
Rodborough Hill
PORTSMOUTH RD
A3
Cemy
MILFORD HEATH RD
SANDY LA
HEATH END COTTS
OXTED GN
OXTED GN
SWALLOW CL
WOODPECKERS
Rodborough Tech Coll
RAKE LA

41
WEBB RD
HEATHVIEW RD
MARTINS
WOOD
MERRY ACRES

6
Witley Common
GASDEN DR
KHARTOUM RD
YEW TREE RD
CRAMHURST LA
Cramhurst
PETWORTH RD
Wheelerstreet

Witley & Milford Commons
The Witley Centre (Visitor Ctr)
GASDEN LA
GASDEN COPSE
KESWICK RD
WILDCROFT WOOD
WHEELER LA
SUNNYHILL
BARNES CL
CLOVER
WILLOW MEWS
EASTFIELDS

5
HASLEMERE RD
LITTLE LONDON
CROFT RD
SUNNY DOWN
HALLHOUSE RD
DORLCOTE WAY
ROKE LA
ROKE LA COTTS
MIDDLE CL
CHICHESTER CL
WESTFIELDS
MILL LA
Crossways
Enton Mill Farm
MILTONS COTTS

GU8
Mare Hill
The Chandler CE Jun Sch
NEWLANDS EST
GEORGE ELIOT CL
Witley
NORTHFIELD

40
Milford Lodge
Heath House
Barrow Hills Sch
CHURCHFIELDS
Witley CE Inf Sch
PH

4
The Shrubbery
Stable Lake
Hazel Copse
Chestnut Copse
THE MOUNT

Thursley Lake
Home Pond

3
Witley Park
Winkford Farm
Culmer
CULMER LA

39
West Firs
CHURCH LA
CULMER HILL

2
Parsonage House
Parsonage Farm
Pond Coppice
PO
GURDON'S LA

Rockwoods
Banacle Common
King Edward's Sch
FRANKLIN CT
BRIDWELL CL
A283

1
Chocolates
Furzefield Wood
BONA MEAD GREEN RD
Heath Hills
Greensand Way
The Hill House
Sandhills
BANACLE HILL RD
BROOK RD
Wormley
ROBIN WY

Brook
PH
A286
STATION LA
COMBE LA

38
92 A 93 B 94 C D E F

A B C D E F

8
7
41
6
5
40
4
3
39
2
1
38

95 A B 96 C D 97 E F

Tuesley

STAFF COTTS

Milford

Tuesley Farm

Middle Lake

GU7

Clock Barn Farm

TUESLEY LA

P

LC

Milford

STATION LA

RAKE LA

Lower Enton Lake

Large Enton Lake

CH

Station Rd

STATION RD

Hydestile

Hydon Hill (Cheshire Home)

CLOCK BARN LA

Enton Green

HAMBLEDON RD

NEW PO

THE HEXONS

SALT LA

P

Mill Copse

Hydon Farm

HYDESTILE COTTS

Potter's Hill

Potter's Barn

POTTERS HILL

The Tolt

Hydon Heath

MILL LA

Great Enton

Horsehatches

Feathercombe

Hydon Ridge

Hydon's Ball

Hazel Copse

Old Enton

GU8

Hambledon Field

WATER LA

Great House

FEATHERCOMBE LA

Fourteen Acre Copse

Witley Ponds

CLOCK HOUSE COTTS

ENTON LA

CLOCK HOUSE APARTMENTS

Oak Ho

Parson's Hanger

Court Farm

CHURCH LA

Enton Hall

CULMER LA

ROSE COTTS

Sweetwater Pond

SWEETWATER LA

Buss's Common

PH

Greensand Way

Greensand Way

Hilltop Farm

Hambledon

Vann Hill

Buss's

St Dominic's Sch

Ashlands Copse

Hasledons

Stonepit Hill

Hambledon Common

MALTHOUSE LA

PADDOCK CL

Beech Hill

WOODLANDS RD

VANN LA

Gunter's Wood

Vann Moor

COMBE LA

PETWORTH RD

A283

WORMLEY

HAMBLEDON PK

THE EVERGREENS

CHERRYHURST

LANE END

PO

VANN LA

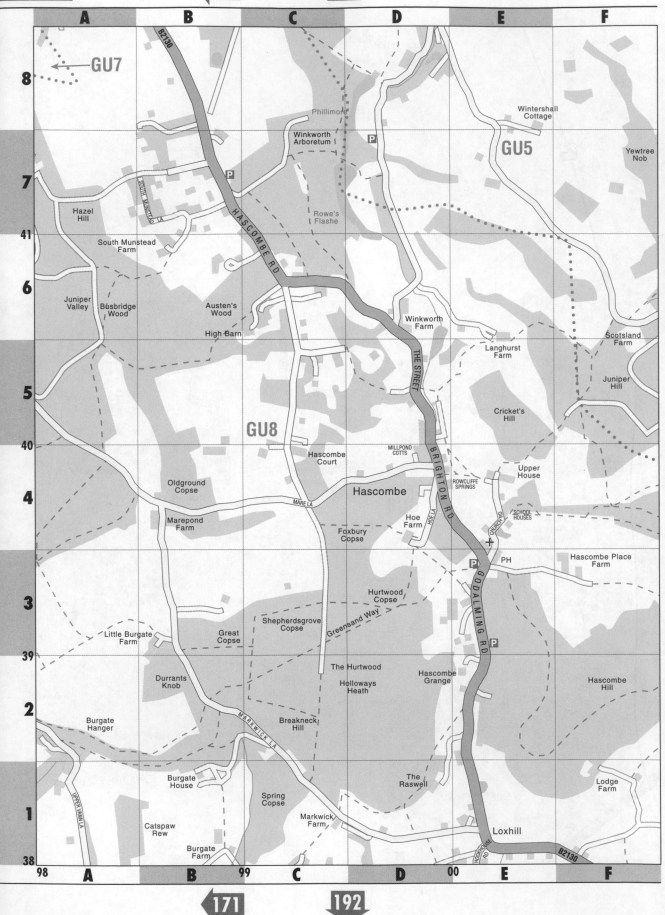

A   B   C   D   E   F

8

GU7

Phillimore

Winkworth
Arboretum

Wintershall
Cottage

GU5

Yewtree
Nob

7

41

Hazel
Hill

South Munstead
Farm

Rowe's
Flashe

6

Juniper
Valley

Busbridge
Wood

Austen's
Wood

Winkworth
Farm

Langhurst
Farm

Scotsland
Farm

High Barn

Juniper
Hill

5

GU8

Cricket's
Hill

40

Hascombe
Court

MILLPOND
COTTS

Upper
House

4

Oldground
Copse

MARE LA

Hascombe

ROWCLIFFE
SPRINGS

SCHOOL
HOUSES

Marepond
Farm

Foxbury
Copse

Hoe
Farm

Hascombe Place
Farm

PH

3

Little Burgate
Farm

Great
Copse

Shepherdsgrove
Copse

Hurtwood
Copse

Greensand Way

39

Durrants
Knob

The Hurtwood

Hascombe
Grange

Hascombe
Hill

2

Burgate
Hanger

MARKWICK LA

Breakneck
Hill

Holloways
Heath

The
Raswell

Lodge
Farm

Burgate
House

Spring
Copse

1

UPPER VANN LA

Catspaw
Rew

Markwick
Farm

Loxhill

B2130

Burgate
Farm

HOOKHOUSE RD

38

98   A   B   99   C   D   00   E   F

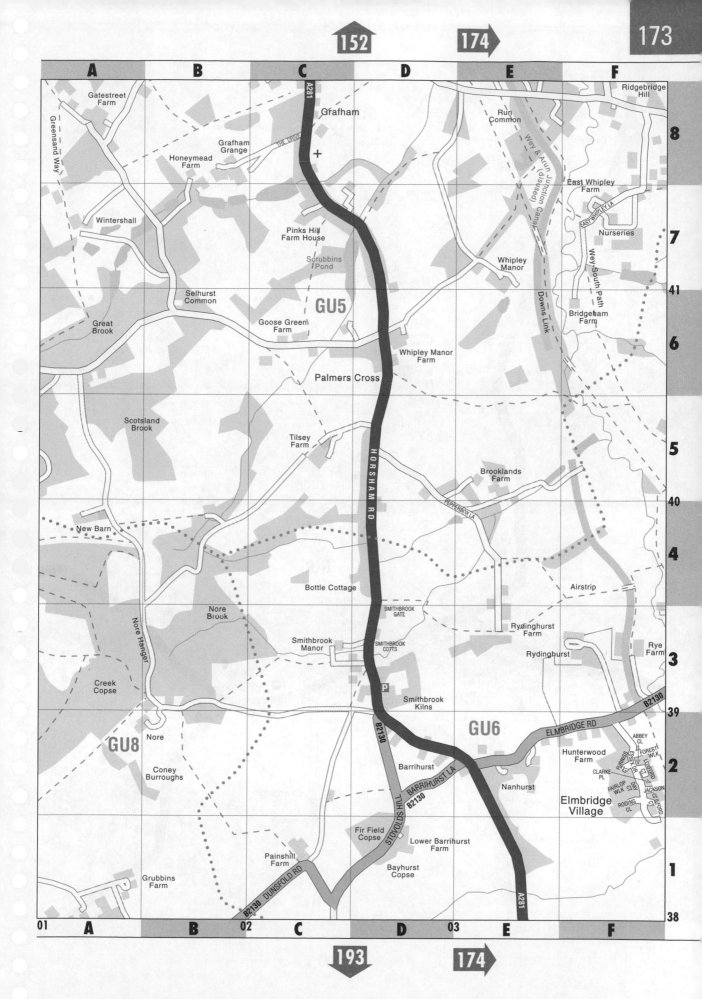

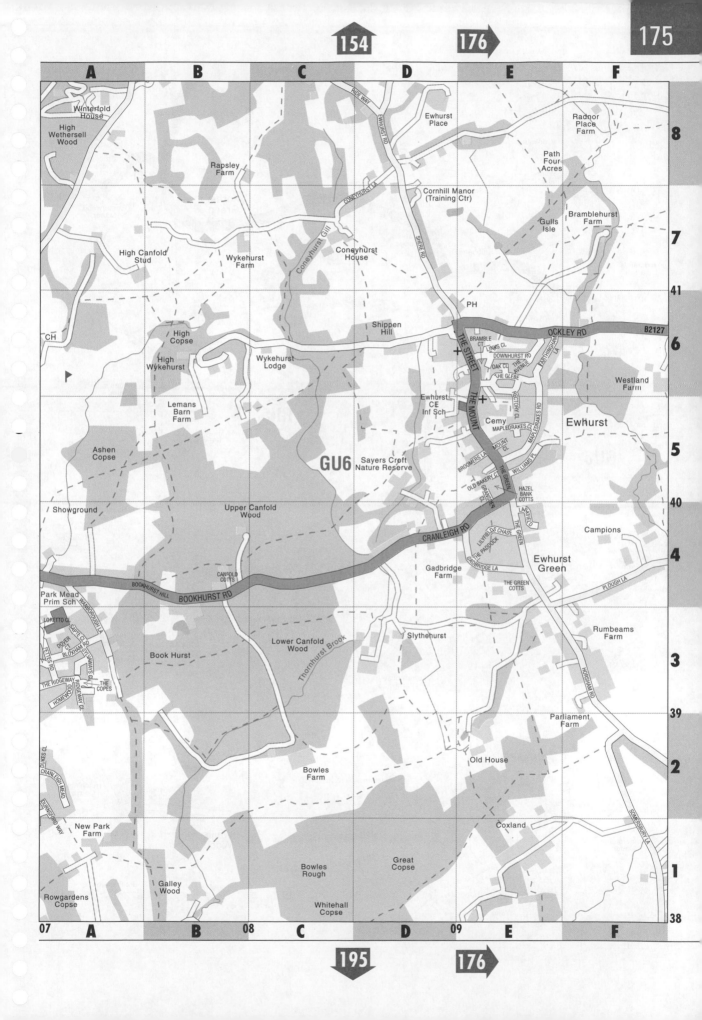

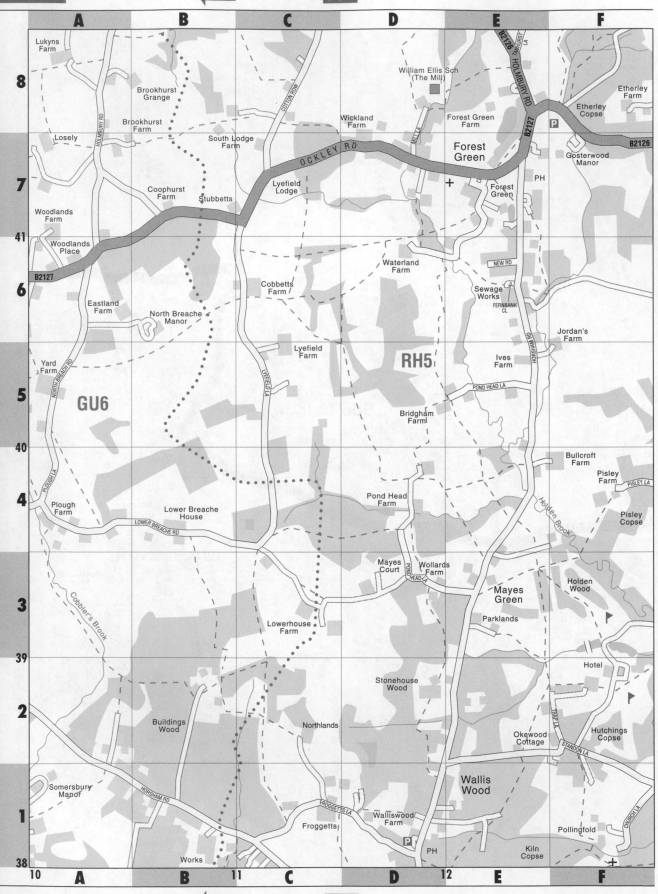

A   B   C   D   E   F

Church Wood

ABINGER RD

New Barn House

Meares Copse

Buckinghill Farm

Cherry Tree Lodge

A29

BEANE GREEN RD

Etherley Copse

ETHERLEY HILL

Pennsylvania Copse

BROOMEHALL RD

Highfield Wood

8

Goster Wood

COX CNR

OCKLEY RD

Aviary Barn

BURYWOOD HILL

Square Copse

Holms Gill

PARK LA

7

High Woods

Sheep Green

Aviary Copse

41

Wellspring Pond

LAKE RD

Hatch Park

COLE'S LA

+

Ockley Court

B2126

6

Home Farm

Jayes Park

Kissing Copse

Jayes Park

Courtbottom Wood

Church Copse

5

Woodstock House

Volvens Farm

MOLE ST

Castle Copse

B2126

PH

Weavers Pond

PH

PO

Ockley

Vann Farm

VANN FARM RD

Wickney Holt

40

Fishfold Farm

PISLEY LA

Parkland Farmhouse

Scott-Broadwood CE Inf Sch

STANE ST

PRIDEAUX GDNS

FRIDAY ST

Council Cotts

Vann House

Vann Lake

VANN LAKE

4

Sewage Works

CRICKETERS CL

ELMERS RD

PH

Elmers Farm

RH5

BRICKYARD COPSE

RECTORY CL

VANN LAKE RD

NEW BARN LA

CATHILL LA

New Barn

Cathill Wood

3

LEITH VALE COTTS

STANDON LA

Standon Homestead

Birches Wood

39

Leith Vale

Hannah Peschar Sculpture Gdn

Fir Copse

Sewage Works

Eversheds Farm

2

CHURCH LA

A29

Oakwood Mill Farm

WALEYS LA

Hopgardens Rue

WALEYS LA

MEARE ST

Waleys

1

13   A   14   B   C   15   D   E   F   38

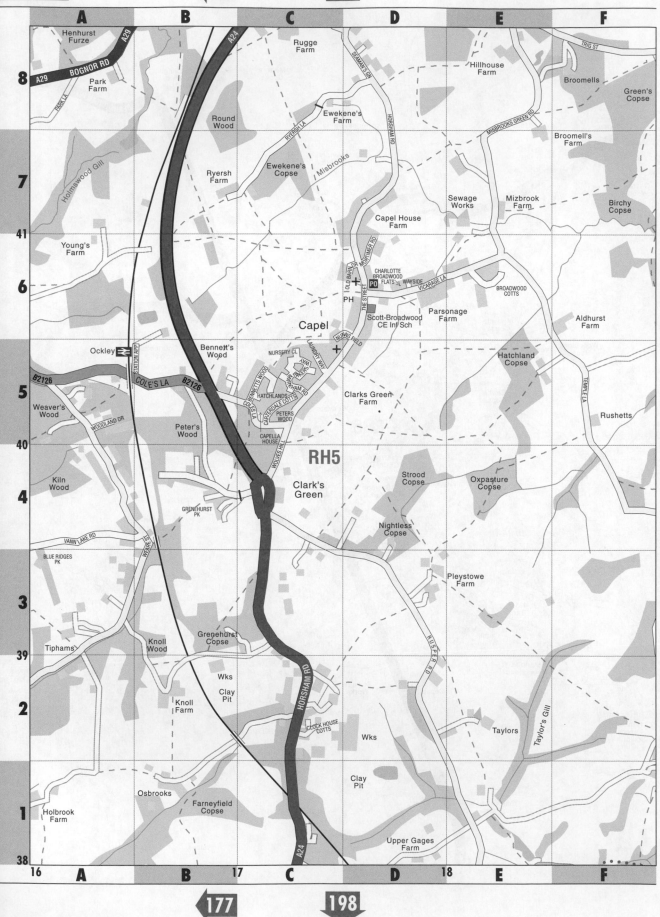

Henhurst Furze
A29
BOGNOR RD
A29
PARK LA
Park Farm
Round Wood
Rugge Farm
Ewekene's Farm
RYERSH LA
Hillhouse Farm
TRIG ST
Broomells
Green's Copse
Holmswood Gill
Ryersh Farm
Ewekene's Copse
Misbrooks
SEAMAN'S GN
HORSHAM RD
MISBROOKS GREEN RD
Broomell's Farm
Young's Farm
Capel House Farm
Sewage Works
Mizbrook Farm
Birchy Copse
MORTIMER RD
CHARLOTTE BROADWOOD FLATS
WAYSIDE
VICARAGE LA
BROADWOOD COTTS
OLD BARN DR
THE STREET
PO
PH
Scott-Broadwood CE Inf Sch
NUMS FIELD
Parsonage Farm
Aldhurst Farm
Ockley
STATION APP
Capel
Bennett's Wood
NURSERY CL
LAUNDRY WAY
Hatchland Copse
TEMPLE LA
COLE'S LA
B2126
BENNETTS WOOD
WH SHERWH
PRIORS
HORSHAM RD
HATCHLANDS
CARTERDALE COTTS
COLE'S LA
Clarks Green Farm
Rushetts
B2126
Weaver's Wood
WOODLAND DR
Peter's Wood
PETERS WOOD
CAPELLA HOUSE
RH5
WOLVES HILL
Strood Copse
Oxpasture Copse
Kiln Wood
GRENEHURST PK
Clark's Green
Nightless Copse
VANN LAKE RD
WEARE ST
BLUE RIDGES PK
Pleystowe Farm
B2126
Tiphams
Knoll Wood
Grenehurst Copse
RUSPER RD
Knoll Farm
Wks
Clay Pit
Osbrooks
Farneyfield Copse
HORSHAM RD
CLOCK HOUSE COTTS
Wks
Taylors
Taylor's Gill
Holbrook Farm
Clay Pit
Upper Gages Farm
A24

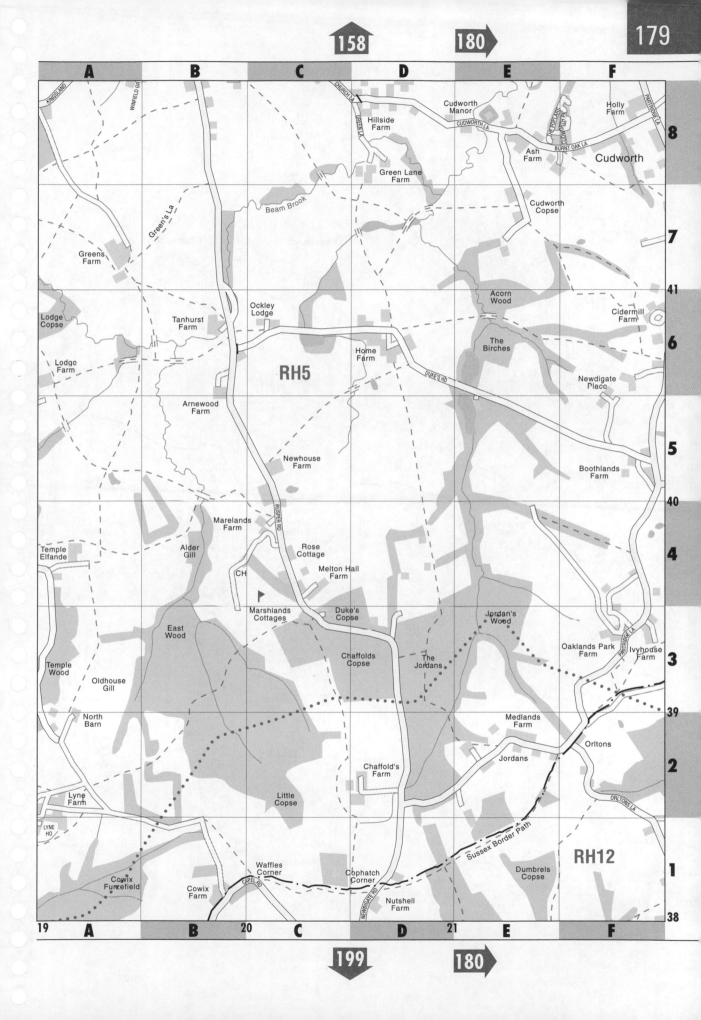

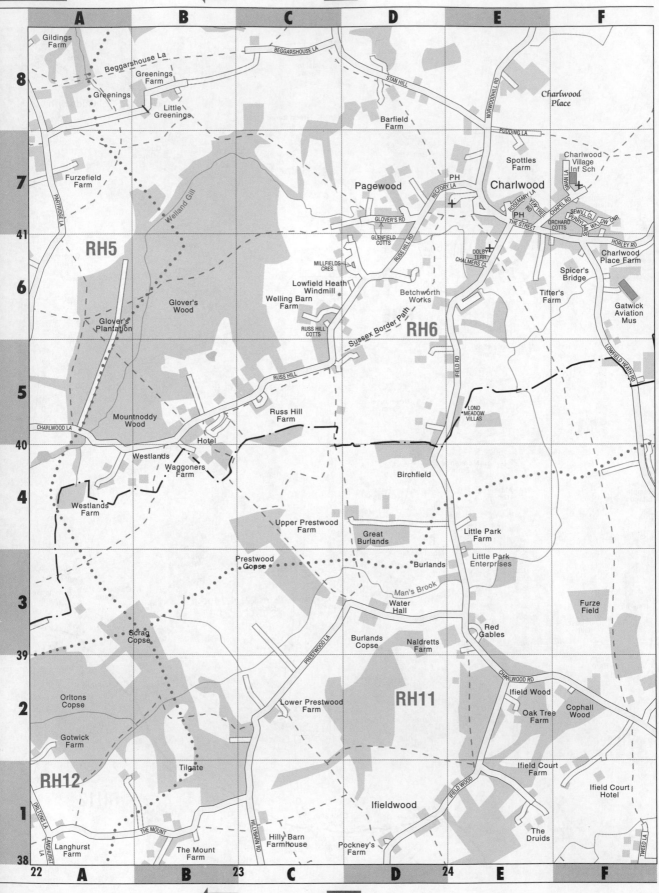

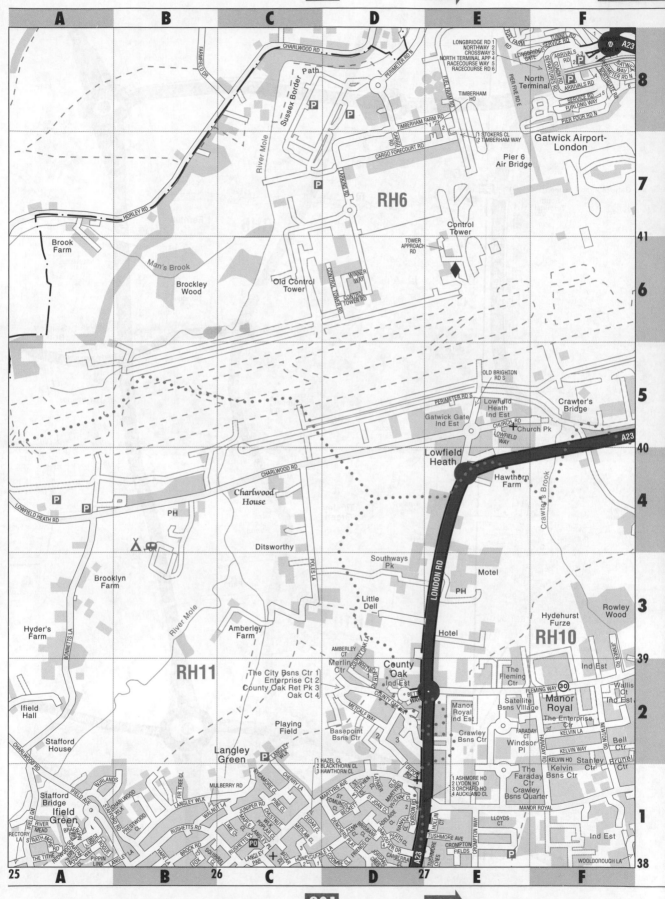
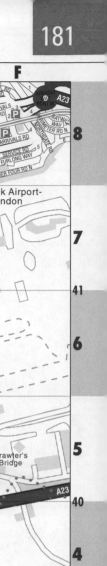

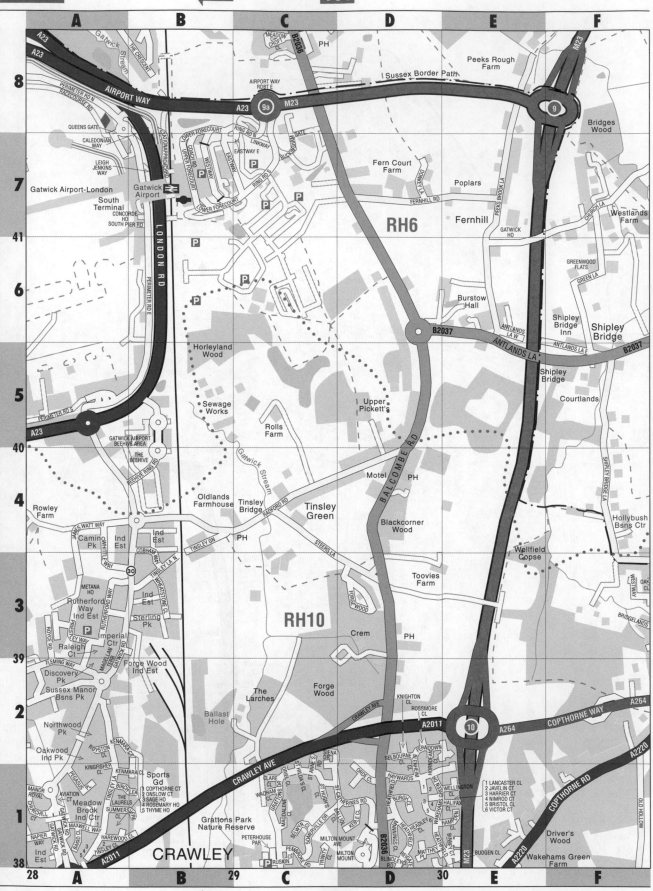

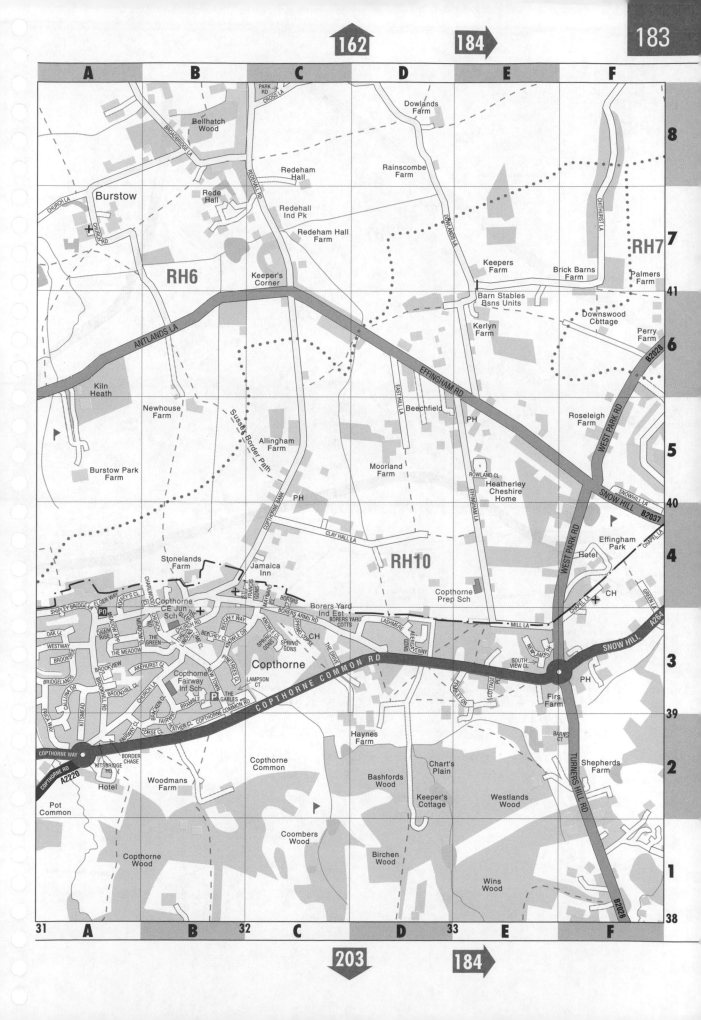

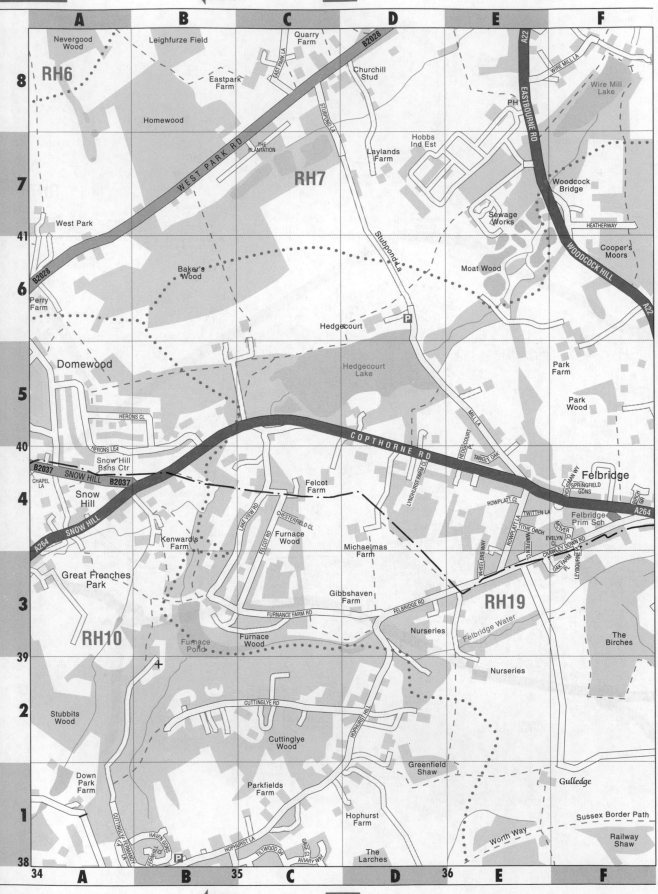

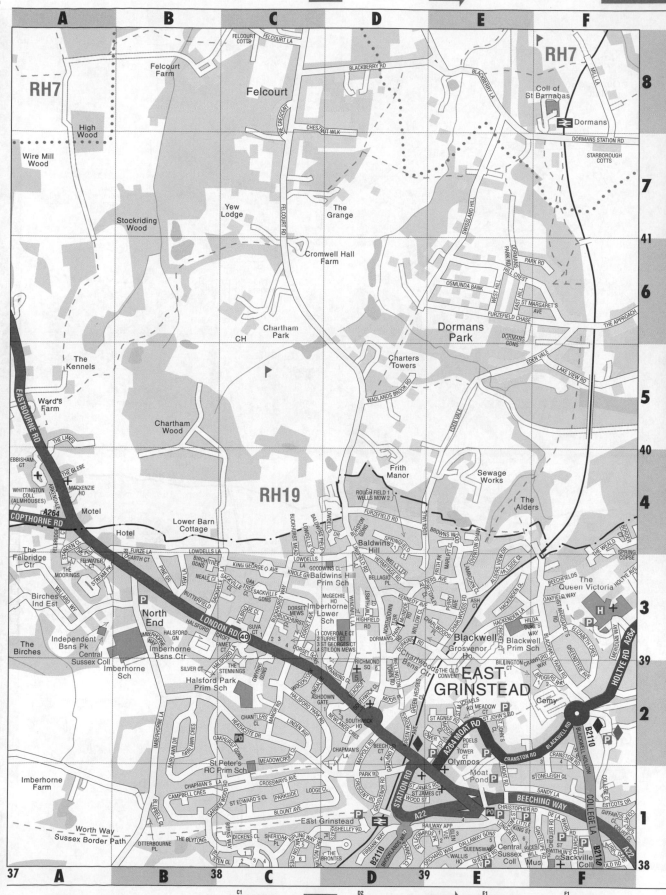

RH7

8

Coll of
St Barnabas

Dormans

DORMANS STATION RD

STARBOROUGH
COTTS

7

41

6

5

40

4

RH7

High
Wood

Wire Mill
Wood

Felcourt
Farm

FELCOURT
COTTS

FELCOURT LA

Felcourt

BLACKBERRY RD

BLACKWELL LA

MILL LA

Stockriding
Wood

Yew
Lodge

THE CRESCENT

CHESTNUT WLK

FELCOURT RD

The
Grange

SWISSLAND HILL

DORMANS
PARK RD

PARK RD

HILL CREST

WEST HILL

EAST HILL

ST MARGARET'S AVE

Cromwell Hall
Farm

OSMUNDA BANK

FURZEFIELD CHASE

THE APPROACH

The
Kennels

Ward's
Farm

CH

Chartham
Park

Charters
Towers

WADLANDS BROOK RD

Dormans
Park

DORMANS
GDNS

EDEN VALE

LAKE VIEW RD

EASTBOURNE RD

THE LIMES

Chartham
Wood

RH19

Frith
Manor

Sewage
Works

The
Alders

EDEN VALE

EBBISHAM
CT

THE GLEBE

MACKENZIE
HO

WHITTINGTON
COLL
(ALMHOUSES)

Motel

ARGOEDALE

A264

COPTHORNE RD

Lower Barn
Cottage

ROUGH FIELD 1
WELLS MDW 2

FURZEFIELD RD

Baldwins
Hill

BUCKHURST MEAD

LOWDELLS

LOWDELLS DR

LOWDELLS FIELD

ELMSTON
GDNS

LINGFIELD RD

SPRINGFIELD

BROWNS WD

EDEN VALE

THE WEALD

SPRING
COPSE

BORDER

The
Felbridge
Ctr

The
Moorings

STANDEN CL

THE PEAK

FURZE LA

REGARTH CT

PINE GR

LOWDELLS LA

BIRCHTREE
CL

KING GEORGE'S AVE

NEALE CL

BLACKWELL
HOLLOW

Baldwins Hill
Prim Sch

KNOLE GR

GOODWINS
CL

WELLS LEA

FRITH PK

MARLPIT CL

ALDERS VIEW DR

LAMBOURNE

BEECHFIELDS

The
Queen Victoria

HOLTYE AVE

OAKFIELD WAY

Birches
Ind Est

WILLARD WAY

STREAM PK

FELWATER
CT

Birches

The
Birches

Independent
Bsns Pk
Central
Sussex Coll

Imberhorne
Bsns Ctr

Imberhorne
Sch

SACKVILLE CL

OAK
TREE
CL

SACKVILLE GDNS

NEALE CL

SACKVILLE
CL

EDGE CL

BUTTERFIELD

BLACKWELL RD

BLACKWELL
HOLLOW

McGECHIE
HO

Imberhorne
Lower
Sch

DORSET
MEWS

WINDMILL LA

HIGHFIELD
RD

THRUSH'RD

MOSS'DOWN

DORMANS PARK RD

KENNEDY AVE

WILLOW CL

CHARLWOODS RD

PERRY
RD

ASH CL

HACKENDEN CL

HACKENDEN LA

ST MARGARET'S CT

ELIZABETH CRES

GREENSTEDE AVE

MERIDIAN WAY

CRAWFURD WAY

HILDA
DUKE'S
WAY

Blackwell
Prim Sch

Blackwell

Grosvenor
Ho

BADGERS
WAY

H

ST MICHAELS
RD

DORSET AVE

BLACKWOOD CL

North
End

LONDON RD

A40

IMBERHORNE
WAY

HALSFORD
CROFT

SILVER CT

FAME'T
CT

HALSFORD WAY

GWYNNE
GDNS

THE
STENNINGS

Halsford Park
Prim Sch

WOODSTOCK

ASHDOWN
GATE

MANNING CL

1 COVERDALE CT
2 TURRET CT
3 ST GEORGES CT
4 STILDON MEWS

RICHMOND
SQ

WELLINGTON RD

MOOR RD

Charlwoods
Bsns Ctr

THE OLD
CONVENT

EAST
GRINSTEAD

BILLINGTON
CT

BADGERS
WAY

Cemy

A264

HOLTYE

39

2

1

38

The
Stennings

IMBERHORNE LA

FAIRLAWN DR

FAIRLAWN CRES

CHANTLERS CL

HEATHCOTE DR

MANOR RD

LINDEN AVE

OAKHURST GDNS

MEADOWCROFT

MAYPOLE RD

SOUTHWICK
HO

NEWLANDS

SOUTHWICK

GREEN HEDGES

GREEN HEDGES AVE

ST AGNES
RD

MEADOW
CT

ST JOHN'S RD

ST JOHN'S

PODELS
CT

OLYMPUS
CT

P

Olympos

CRANSTON RD

CRANSTON CL

STONELEIGH CL

MOAT RD

A264

SANDY LA

Moat
Pond

BLACKWELL RD

COLLEGE LA

B2110

Imberhorne
Farm

St Peter's
RC Prim Sch

BLUEBELL CL

CHAPMAN'S LA

CAMPBELL CRES

GARDEN

ST EDWARD'S CL

CROSSWAYS AVE

PARKSIDE

LODGE GR

PARK RD

CRESCENT RD

GROSVENOR RD

STATION RD

ST JAMES RD

WOOD ST

ST JAMES CT

BEECHING WAY

A22

CHRISTOPHER RD

DE LA WARR RD

CANTELUPE RD

GIFFARDS
WAY

ESTCOTS DR

COLLEGE CT

A22

OLD RD

Worth Way

Sussex Border Path

OTTERBOURNE
PL

THE BLYTONS

BLUEBELL CL

BONNYS WAY

DICKENS CL

SHERIDAN CL

KIPLING WAY

KESHELLEY RD

FIRBANK WAY

BROOKLANDS WAY

B2110

East Grinstead

A22

RAILWAY APP

LEONARD RD

LONDON RD

KING ST

QUEENSWAY

DALLAWAY GDNS

WALLIS
HO

QUEEN'S RD

Central
Sussex
Coll

Mus

P

Sackville
Coll

WITHIN'S LA

ST JULIAN

OLD RD

THE BRONTES

STEN CL

C1
1 THE BROWNINGS
2 BYRON GR
3 CHAUCER AVE
4 TENNYSON RISE
5 THE SAYERS
6 WORDSWORTH RISE

D2
1 YEW CT
2 BEECH CL
3 ELM CT
4 ST CATHERINE'S CT
5 St Mary's CE Prim
Sch
6 CHETNOLE

E1
1 GLENSIDE
2 GREGORY CT
3 WARELAND HO
4 OVERTON CT
5 BROOKLAND HO
6 INSTITUTE WLK
7 CANTELUPE MEWS

F1
1 CANTELUPE HO
2 RUDGE HO
F2
1 ROBIN CL
2 EARLE HO
3 EASTCOURT VILLAS
4 THE OLD SURGERY
5 ST JULIAN
6 DRURY LO

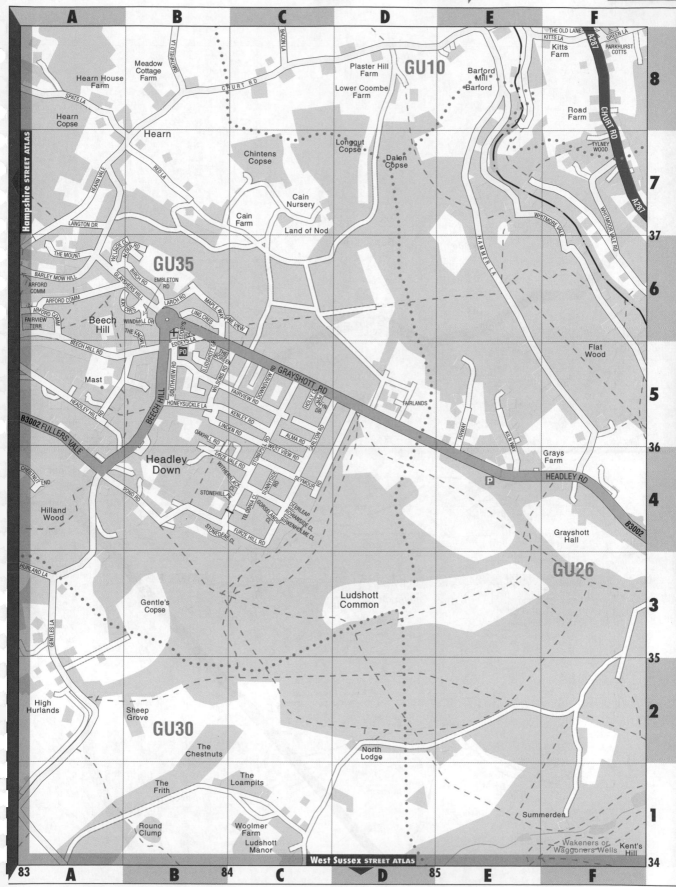

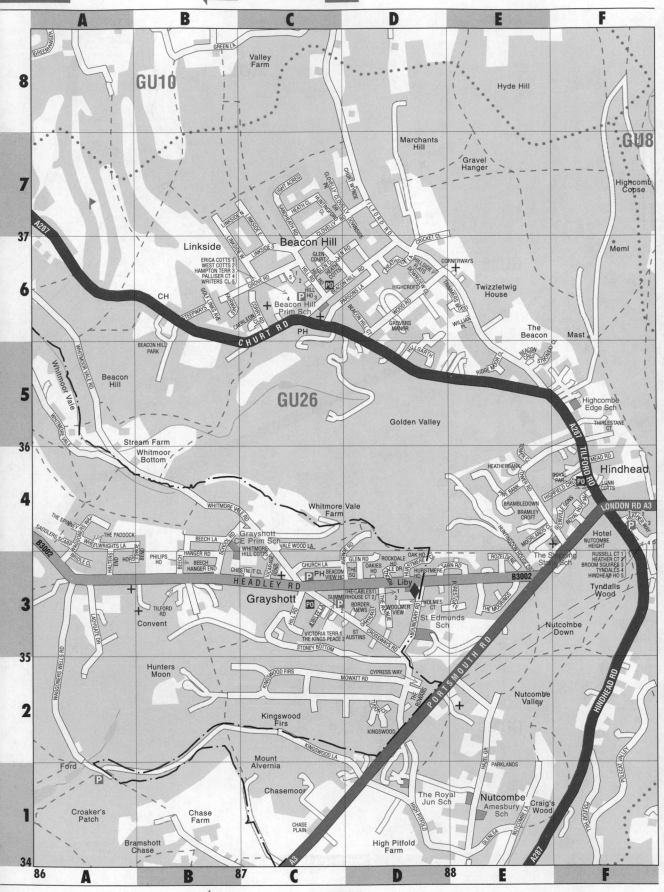

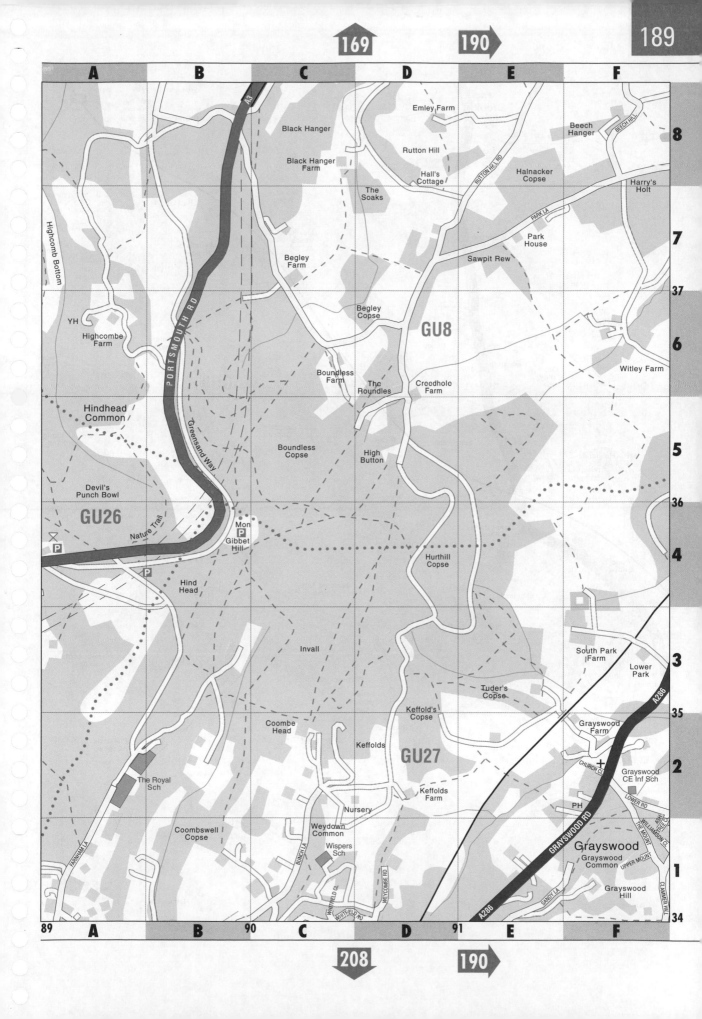

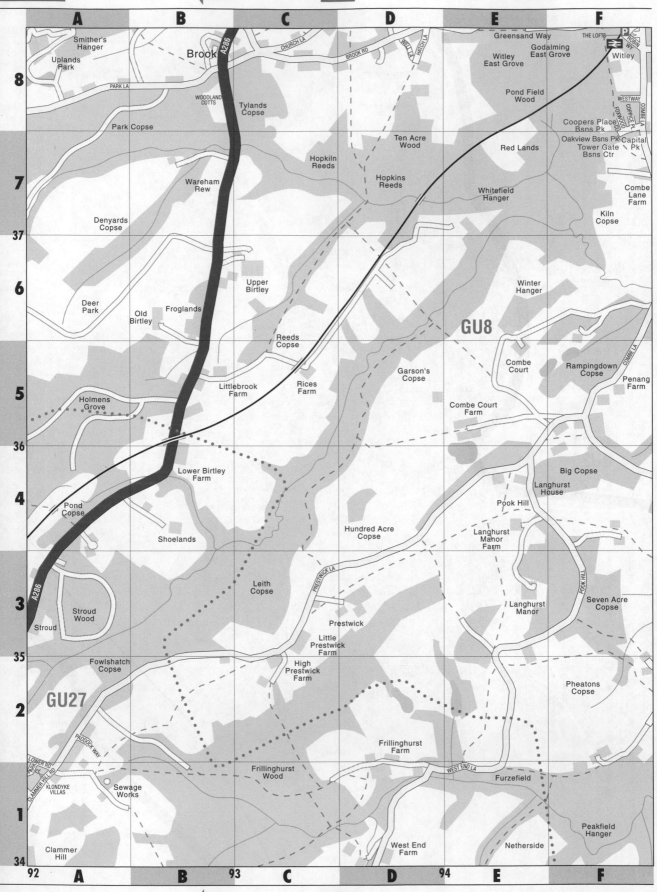

A   B   C   D   E   F

Smither's
Hanger
Uplands
Park
Brook
PARK LA
WOODLAND
COTTS
Tylands
Copse
Park Copse
CHURCH LA
BROOK RD
WELL LA
HATCH LA
Ten Acre
Wood
Greensand Way
Witley
East Grove
Godalming
East Grove
THE LOFTS
Witley
ROBIN
WESTWAY
COPPICE PL
FOXWOOD
COMBE LA
8

Wareham
Rew
Hopkiln Reeds
Hopkins
Reeds
Whitefield
Hanger
Pond Field
Wood
Red Lands
Coopers Place
Bsns Pk
Oakview Bsns Pk
Tower Gate
Bsns Ctr
Capital
Pk
Combe
Lane
Farm
Kiln
Copse
7

37

Denyards
Copse

Deer
Park
Old
Birtley
Froglands
Upper
Birtley
Reeds
Copse
Winter
Hanger
6

GU8

Holmens
Grove
Littlebrook
Farm
Rices
Farm
Garson's
Copse
Combe
Court
Combe Court
Farm
Rampingdown
Copse
Penang
Farm
COMBE LA
5

36

Pond
Copse
Lower Birtley
Farm
Big Copse
Langhurst
House
4

Shoelands
Hundred Acre
Copse
Pook Hill
Langhurst
Manor
Farm
POOK HILL
Stroud
Wood
Leith
Copse
PRESTWICK LA
Prestwick
Langhurst
Manor
Seven Acre
Copse
3

Stroud
A286
35

Fowlshatch
Copse
Little Prestwick
Farm
High
Prestwick
Farm
Pheatons
Copse
GU27
2

PADDOCK WAY
LOWER RD
PARK PL
CLAMMER HILL RD
KLONDYKE
VILLAS
Sewage
Works
Frillinghurst
Wood
Frillinghurst
Farm
WEST END LA
Furzefield
Netherside
Peakfield
Hanger
1

Clammer
Hill
West End
Farm
34

92   A   B   93   C   D   94   E   F

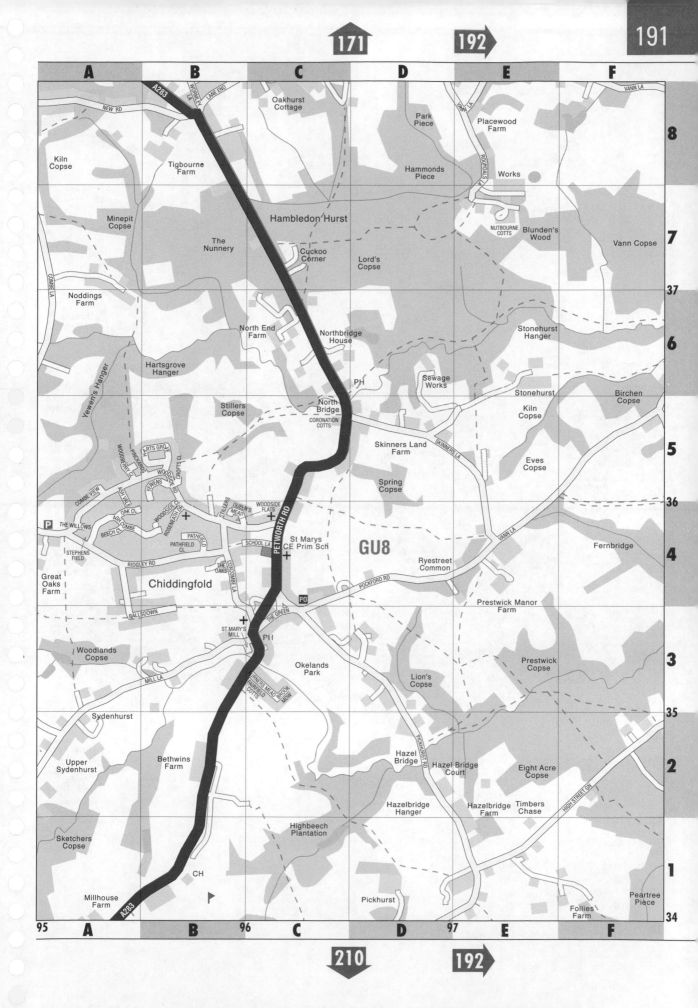

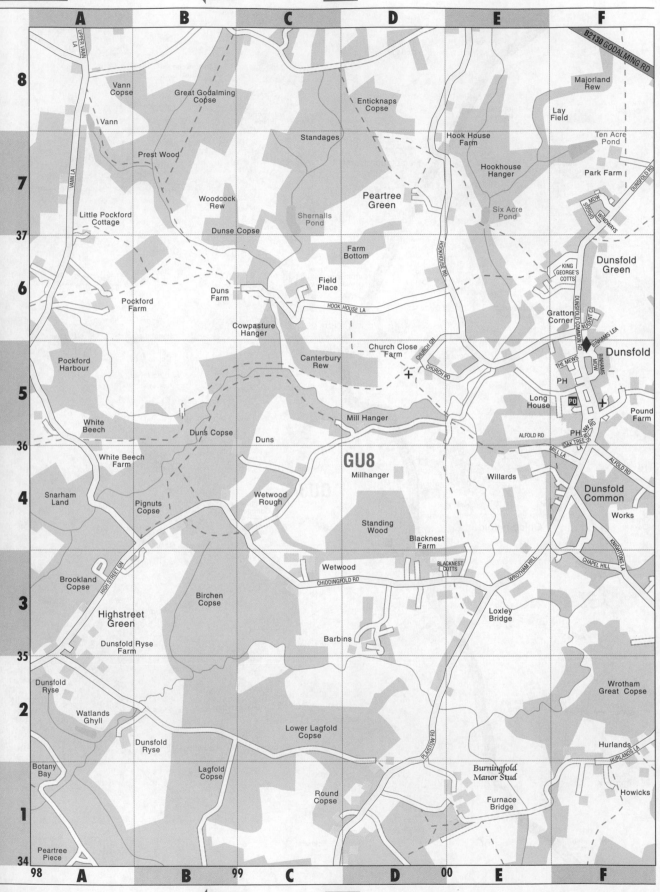

191
172

A B C D E F

8

7

37

6

5

36

4

3

35

2

1

34

98 A B 99 C D 00 E F

UPPER VANN LA

VANN LA

Vann Copse

Vann

Great Godalming Copse

Prest Wood

Woodcock Rew

Little Pockford Cottage

Dunse Copse

Pockford Farm

Duns Farm

Cowpasture Hanger

Canterbury Rew

Pockford Harbour

White Beech

Duns Copse

Duns

Mill Hanger

White Beech Farm

Snarham Land

Pignuts Copse

Wetwood Rough

GU8

Millhanger

Brookland Copse

HIGHSTREET GN

Highstreet Green

Dunsfold Ryse Farm

Birchen Copse

Wetwood

CHIDDINGFOLD RD

Standing Wood

Blacknest Farm

BLACKNEST COTTS

Loxley Bridge

Dunsfold Ryse

Watlands Ghyll

Dunsfold Ryse

Barbins

Lower Lagfold Copse

Botany Bay

Lagfold Copse

Round Copse

Peartree Piece

Enticknaps Copse

Standages

Shernalls Pond

Farm Bottom

Field Place

HOOK HOUSE LA

Church Close Farm

CHURCH GN

CHURCH RD

Peartree Green

Hook House Farm

Hookhouse Hanger

Six Acre Pond

HOOKHOUSE RD

King George's Cotts

Gratton Corner

The Mews

Long House

PO

PH

ALFOLD RD

Willards

Wetwood

Blacknest Farm

WROTHAM HILL

FLAXSTOW RD

Burningfold Manor Stud

Furnace Bridge

B2130 GODALMING RD

Majorland Rew

Lay Field

Ten Acre Pond

Park Farm

DUNSFOLD RD

GREEN MDW

WINDWAYS

Dunsfold Green

DUNSFOLD COMMON RD

CRESCENT CL

BINHAMS LEA

Dunsfold

MDW

PH

Pound Farm

OAK TREE

MILL LA

ALFOLD RD

Dunsfold Common

Works

KNIGHTONS LA

CHAPEL HILL

HURLANDS LA

Wrotham Great Copse

Hurlands

Howicks

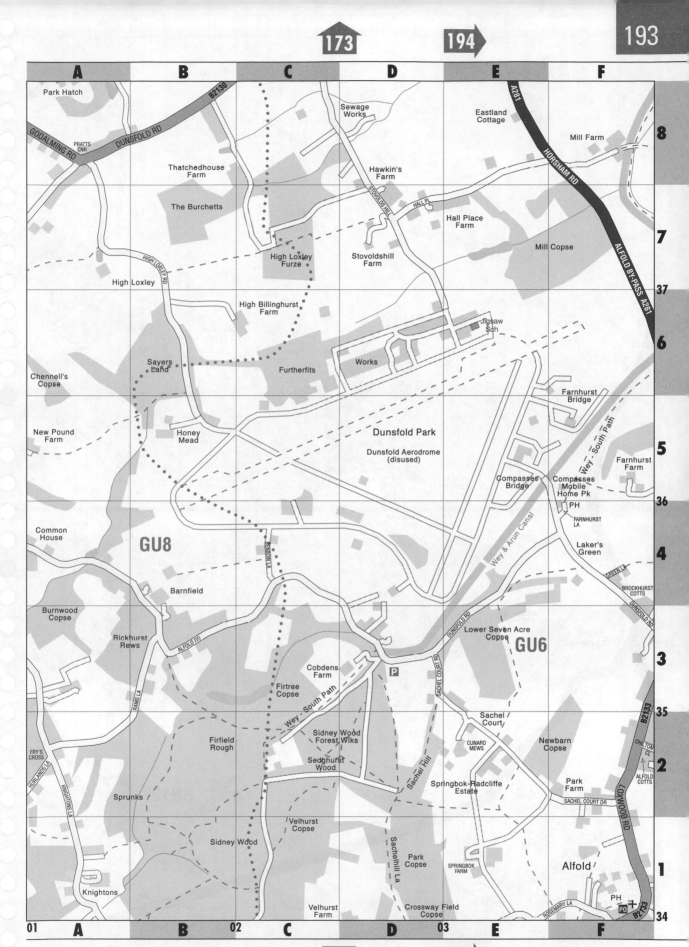

193 174

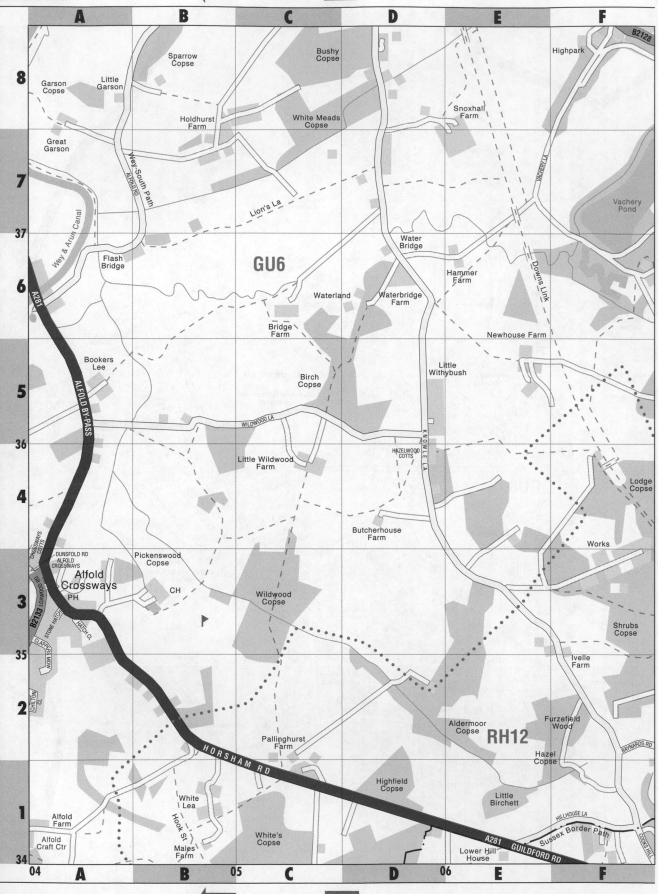

193 213

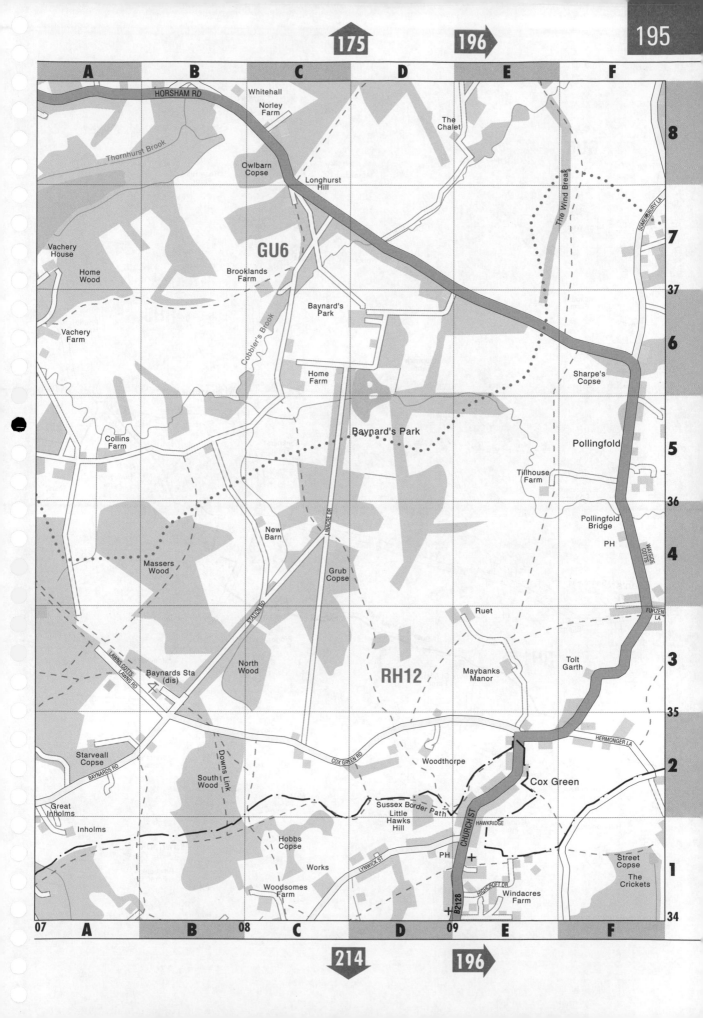

A   B   C   D   E   F

OAKFIELDS
Recn Gd

8

GU6

Somersbury Wood

Chapel House

Oakwood Hill

HORSHAM RD
HORSHAM RD

Abrahams

Rose Hill Farm

Nags Wood

Clay Pit

Smokejack Farm

7

Works

SMOKEJACK HILL

Wet Wood

37

Hillhouse Farm

RH5

Pound House

6

Hoopwick Farm

Exfold Furze Field

Broadstone Farm

HONEYWOOD LA

MONKS MANOR

Pollingfold Copse

Pinkhurst Farm

MONKS LA

5

Pink Hurst

Honeybush Farm

Sansomes Copse

HORSHAM RD

36

Furzen Cottage

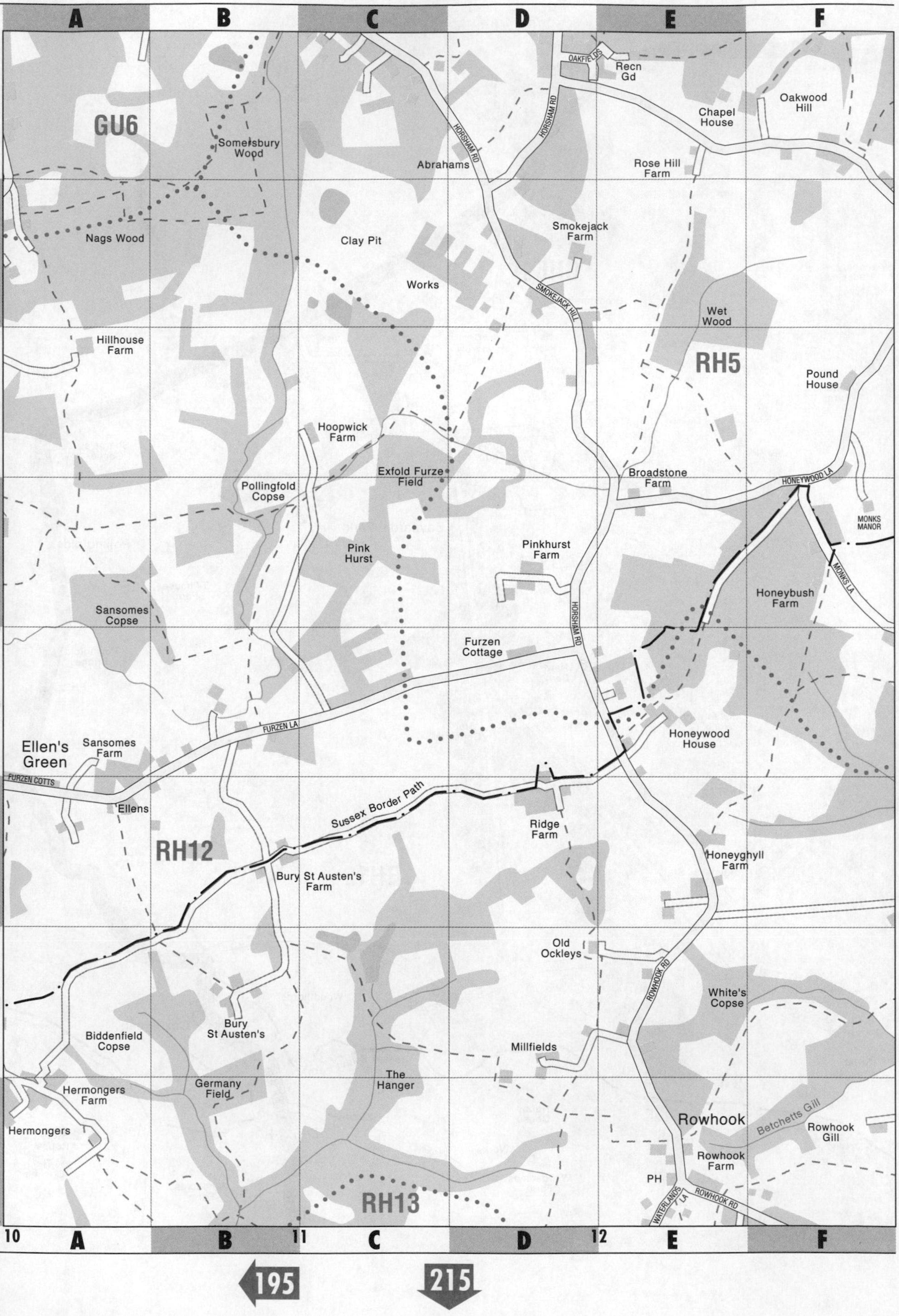

Ellen's Green

Sansomes Farm

FURZEN LA

Honeywood House

4

FURZEN COTTS

'Ellens

Sussex Border Path

Ridge Farm

Honeyghyll Farm

RH12

3

Bury St Austen's Farm

Old Ockleys

ROWHOOK RD

35

White's Copse

2

Biddenfield Copse

Bury St Austen's

Millfields

Rowhook

Betchetts Gill

Rowhook Gill

Germany Field

The Hanger

Rowhook Farm

Hermongers Farm

PH

Hermongers

RH13

WATERLANDS LA
ROWHOOK RD

1

34

10   A   B   11   C   D   12   E   F

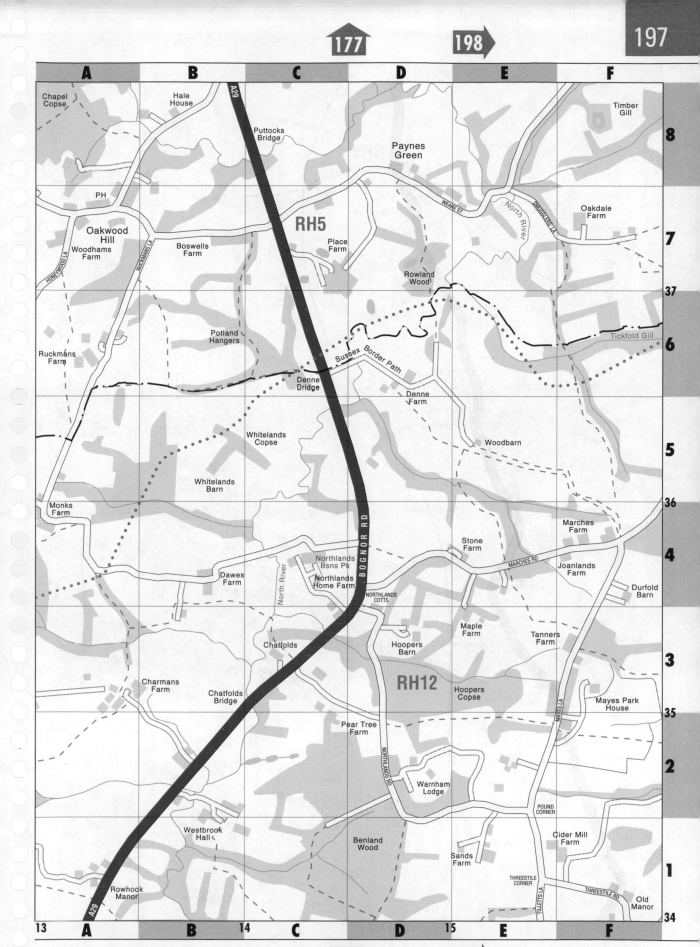

Chapel Copse

Hale House

Puttocks Bridge

Paynes Green

WEARE ST

North River

SLAUGHTERS LA

Oakdale Farm

Timber Gill

PH

Oakwood Hill

Woodhams Farm

HONEYWOOD LA

RUCKMANS LA

Boswells Farm

RH5

Place Farm

Rowland Wood

Ruckmans Farm

Potland Hangers

Sussex Border Path

Denne Bridge

Denne Farm

Tickfold Gill

Whitelands Copse

Woodbarn

Whitelands Barn

Monks Farm

Marches Farm

Dawes Farm

North River

Northlands Bsns Pk

Northlands Home Farm

BOGNOR RD

NORTHLANDS COTTS

Stone Farm

MARCHES RD

Joanlands Farm

Durfold Barn

Chatfolds

Hoopers Barn

Maple Farm

Tanners Farm

Charmans Farm

Chatfolds Bridge

RH12

Hoopers Copse

Mayes Park House

MAYES LA

Pear Tree Farm

NORTHLANDS RD

Warnham Lodge

POUND CORNER

Westbrook Hall

Benland Wood

Sands Farm

Cider Mill Farm

THREESTILE CORNER

TILLETTS LA

THREESTILE RD

Old Manor

Rowhook Manor

A29

197
178

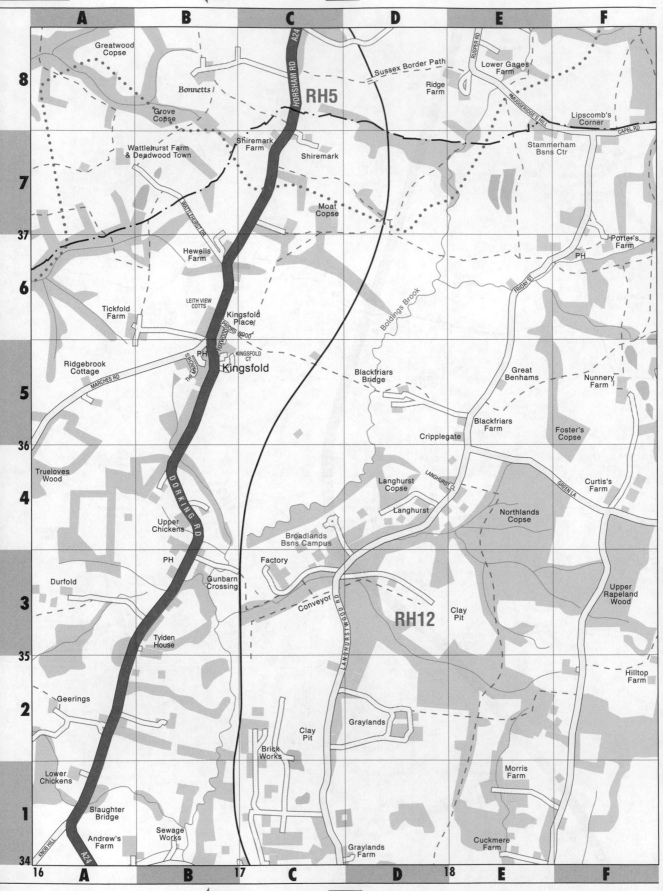

197
217

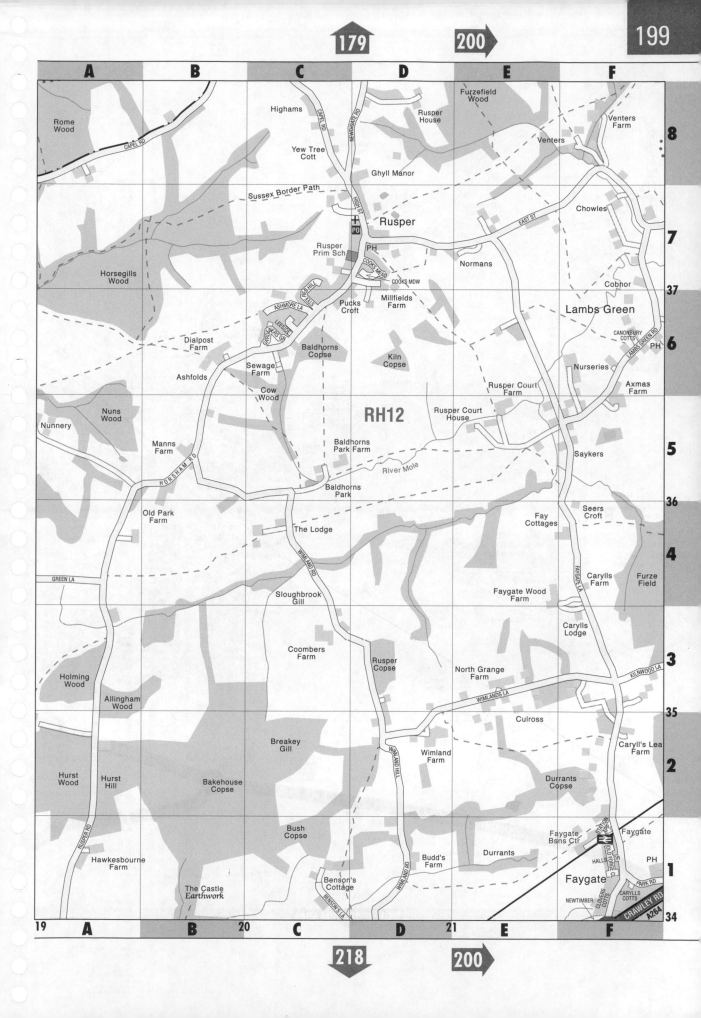

D5
1 THE COURTYARD
2 WALSTEAD HO
3 RAVENDENE CT
4 WILLOWFIELD
5 ASHWOOD
6 PARISH HO

7 PERRYFIELD HO
8 HANDSWORTH HO
9 GLENDON HO
10 ALEXANDRA CT
11 SPRING CL

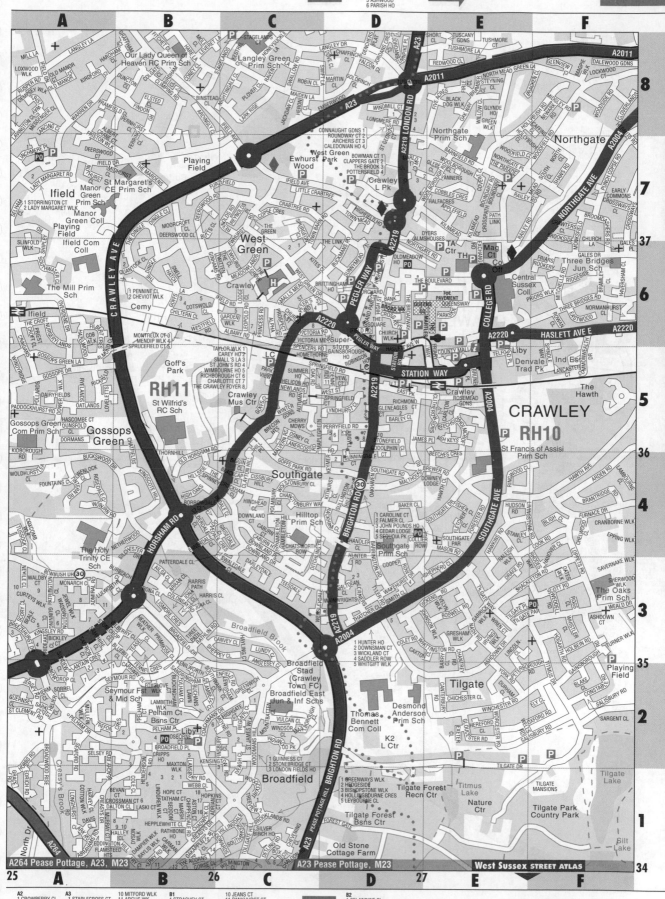

A2
1 CROWBERRY CL
2 BURDOCK CL
3 CHARLOCK CL
4 BORAGE CL

A3
1 STAPLECROSS CT
2 CHAILEY CT
3 PLAYDEN CT
4 MOLINS CT
5 BURNEY CT
6 PERKSTEAD CT
7 GLANVILLE CT
8 PEACOCK WLK
9 RUNSHOOKE CT

10 MITFORD WLK
11 ARGUS WK

B1
1 STRACHEY CT
2 GREENWOOD CT
3 SHINWELL WLK
4 WILKINSON CT
5 MORRISON CT
6 ADAMSON CT
7 KEIR HARDIE HO
8 SILKIN WLK
9 HERSCHEL WLK

10 JEANS CT
11 PANKHURST CT
12 RAMBLERS WAY
13 SHERATON CT
14 TIMBERLANDS
15 WOODING GR
16 THOMSON CT
17 RICHARDSON CT
18 RAMSEY CT

B2
1 CELANDINE CL
2 HENBANE CT
3 SELSEY CT
4 BROADFIELD BARTON
5 ATTLEE HO
6 BALMORAL CT
7 ISLINGTON HO

A   B   C   D   E   F

SANDY LA

HAZELWOOD CL 1
RUFWOOD 2
TURNERS HILL RD
B2028

King's
Wood

Little Rowfant
Farm

Kiln
Wood

8

Old
Rowfant

Blackpond
Shaw

Home
Farm

Sussex Border

Bushy
Wood

Path

Mill
Pond

Ley
House

OLD HOLTYE

Hazel
Shaw

Huntsland
House

Rowfant
House

7

Hayheath

Layhouse
Wood

WALLAGE LA

Mill

37

Horsepasture Wood

Worth Way

B2028

6

Works

Compasses
Wood

Hundred Acres

Rydal

Oaken Wood

Compasses
Corner

Rowfant
Bsns Ctr

TURNERS HILL RD

The
Burches

RH10

The
Gill

Miswells
House

5

Worth
Hall

MAJOR'S HILL

TURNERS HILL RD

Miswell
Wood

NORTH ST

36

B2028

Worth Hall
Farm

Tulleys
Farm

4

Stoney
Plats

Lodge
Wood

Butcher's
Wood

High
Lines

Quarry
Wood

CHURCH RD

B2110

Standinghall
Farm

STANDINGHALL LA

Grove
Farm

3

The
Grove

35

Coldharbour
Farm

Rough
Wood

PADDOCKHURST RD

Grove
Farmhouse

Threepoint Gill

2

Brickkiln
Wood

South Hill

BACK LA

MOUNT
NODDY

STONE
COTTS

Bulls
Copse

Worth Sch

Grove
Wood

Threepoint
Wood

1

B2110

Worth
Abbey

34

31   A   B   32   C   D   33   E   F

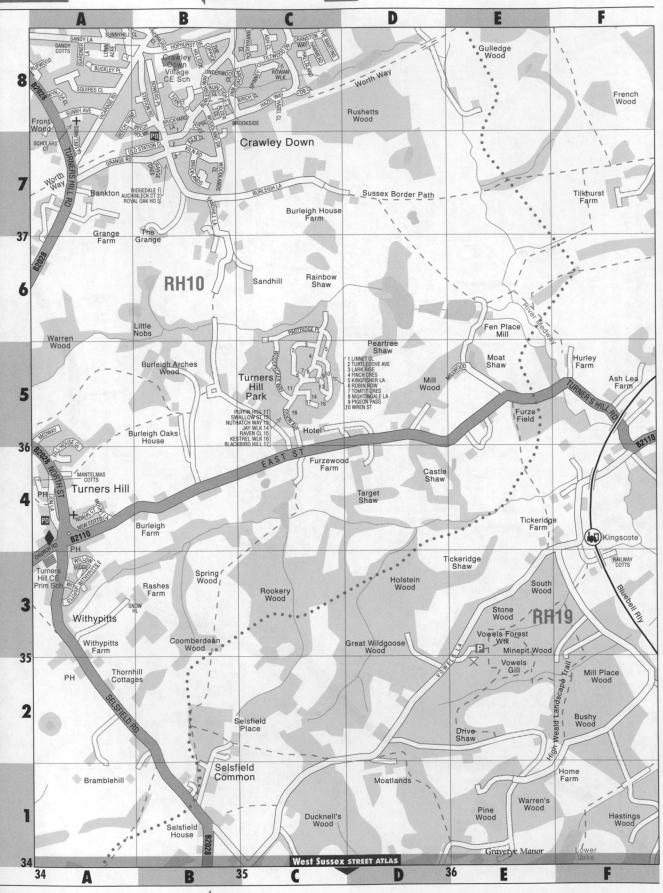

A   **B**   **C**   **D**   **E**   **F**

SANDY LA

SUNNYHILL CL

SANDY COTTS

GARDNER LA

HOPHURST DR

HILLSIDE

HOPHURST LA

THE COPPICE

HARWARDEN

ASH CL

CRANSTON WAY

THE MARTINS

HAMPSTEAD

CRANSTON WAY

RUFWOOD

Gulledge Wood

French Wood

8

BUCKLEY PL

LONG ACRE

Crawley Down Village CE Sch

FOREST CT

SPINNEY

ROWAN WLK

COB SQ

Worth Way

B2028

WYN LEA CL

SUNNY AVE

STATION RD

BOWERS PL

BEECH GDNS

BRICKYARD

ALDER

BIRCH CL

HAZEL WAY

HAZEL WAY

BROOKSIDE

Rushetts Wood

Front Wood

SCHOLARS' CT

+

PO

KILN CL

Crawley Down

GRANGE RD

OLD STATION CL

BRICKLANDS

KILN RD

WOODLANDS

7

Worth Way

Bankton

RIDGEDALE 1

AUCHINLECK CT 2

ROYAL OAK HO 3

BURLEIGH LA

SANDHILL LA

Burleigh House Farm

Sussex Border Path

Tilkhurst Farm

37

Grange Farm

The Grange

River Medway

RH10

Sandhill

Rainbow Shaw

6

Little Nobs

PARTRIDGE PL

Fen Place Mill

Moat Shaw

Hurley Farm

Warren Wood

Burleigh Arches Wood

WOODPECKER WAY

Peartree Shaw

1 LINNET CL

2 TURTLEDOVE AVE

3 LARK RISE

4 FINCH CRES

5 KINGFISHER LA

6 ROBIN ROW

7 TOMTIT CRES

8 NIGHTINGALE LA

9 PIGEON PASS

10 WREN ST

Mill Wood

MILLWOOD

Ash Lea Farm

TURNER'S HILL RD

5

Turners Hill Park

SISSINGH AVE

Furze Field

Burleigh Oaks House

PUFFIN HILL 11

SWALLOW ST 12

NUTHATCH WAY 13

JAY WLK 14

RAVEN CL 15

KESTREL WLK 16

BLACKBIRD HILL 17

Hotel

EAST ST

36

B2028

HILL HOUSE CL

MEDWAY

Furzewood Farm

Castle Shaw

B2110

MANTELMAS COTTS

NORTH ST

LION LA

Turners Hill

NOAHS CT

MOUNT LA

Target Shaw

Tickeridge Farm

Kingscote

4

PH

PO

+

NEW COTTS

Burleigh Farm

RAILWAY COTTS

B2110

PH

CHURCH RD

WILLOW RIDGE

WITHYPITTS E

PH

Tickeridge Shaw

Bluebell Rly

Turners Hill CE Prim Sch

Rashes Farm

SNOW HL

WITHYPITTS

Spring Wood

Rookery Wood

Holstein Wood

South Wood

3

Withypitts

Stone Wood

RH19

Withypitts Farm

Coomberdean Wood

Vowels Forest Wk

Minepit Wood

Thornhill Cottages

Great Wildgoose Wood

P

Vowels Gill

Mill Place Wood

35

SELSFIELD RD

VOWELS LA

High Weald Landscape Trail

PH

Drive Shaw

Bushy Wood

2

Selsfield Place

Bramblehill

Selsfield Common

Moatlands

Home Farm

Warren's Wood

1

Ducknell's Wood

Pine Wood

Hastings Wood

B2028

Selsfield House

Gravetye Manor

Lower Lake

34

A   34   **B**   35   **C**   **D**   36   **E**   **F**

185

206

205

F8
1 MIDDLE ROW
2 FOREST LODGE
3 SACKVILLE CT
4 GREAT HOUSE CT
5 PORTLAND HO
6 CORNWALL GDNS

7 NORMANDY CL
8 WILLOW MEAD
9 KINGS COPSE
10 REGAL DR
11 BECKETT WAY
12 TOLLGATE PL
13 FAIRVIEW CT

A   B   C   D   E   F

Great
Wood

Coles
Wood

CHAUCER AVE

TENNYSON RISE

SMOLLETTS

WALTON CRES

THE
CLOSE

COPYLAND RD

GARDEN WOOD RD

CHRISTIES

BROOKLANDS WAY

B2110

QUEEN'S RD

OLSEN'S RD

WEST ST

LANGRIDGE

PATON WAY

WEST HILL

WEST LA

WEST LA

THE DAKINS

THE JORDANS

DEXTER DR

ELMSTEAD

HIGH ST

JUDGES
CL

BELL
HAMMER

JUDGE'S
TERR

DALEDENE

B2110

FAIRFIELD RD

12 13

8

Hill Place
Farm

High
Grove

BROOK
MANOR

Brook House
Farm

EAST
GRINSTEAD

NIGHTINGALE CL

HURST FARM RD

HURST HILL

SHIP ST

PORTLAND RD

THE FIRS

THE RISE

ELM CT

CLASS CL

PORTLAND RD

KINGFISHER
RISE

HERMITAGE LA

LOWER MERE

MALLARD PL

HERONTYE DR

RICHMOND
AVE

YORK
AVE

TUDOR CL

Herontye

HERONTYE
HO

7

Crockshed
Wood

IMBERHORNE LA

TURNER'S HILL RD

ASHDOWN
VIEW

SOUTHLANDS

MUSSBRAE AVE

ACORN CL

MILL CL

The Meads
Prim Sch

PINE WAY

HOUSE RD

GARDEN
CL

VICTORIA WAY

STUART WAY

HAMPTON
WAY

37

Sunnyside

Bulrushes
Bsns Pk

MILL COTTS

THE MEADS

THE GODDENS

CORONATION RD

Dunnings Mill
Sports Club
PH

FOREST VIEW RD

STOCKWELL RD

DUNNINGS RD

STEPHENSON DR

CHESTERTON DR

MEWS
CT

FLEMING WLK

FARADAY AVE

F7
1 CROMWELL PL
2 CLARENCE DR
3 HARWOODS CL
4 COLLINGWOOD CL

6

HAZLEDEN
CROSS

Fonthill
Lodge
Sch

COOMBE HALL PK

COOMBE HALL RD

Coombe
Hall
Farm

Bulrushes
Farm

MEGWAY DR

Tobias Sch
of Art

Eurythmy
Sch

Artemis Sch of
Speech + Drama

LISTER AVE

NEWTON AVE

Bluebell Rly

Hazleden
Farm

Imberley

Dunning's
Wood

Sussex Border Path

Beechcroft
Towse

Boyles
Farm

Rushett's
Shaw

5

The
Plantation

RH19

SAINT HILL RD

Playing
Field

Rockwood
Park

Rockingshill
Wood

Jenkin's
Wood

36

High
Wood

P

Playing
Field

SAINT HILL
GN

WEST HOATHLY RD

Standen
Farm

Busses
Farm

4

The
Rough

Saint Hill
Manor

Hen Robin
Wood

Saint Hill
Farm

Standen
House

Jenhurst
Wood

Busses
Wood

3

Ridge Hill
Manor

Cock Robin
Wood

HARWOODS LA

High Weald Landscape Trail

35

Mary
Wood

River Medway

Mill Place
Farm

Bluebell Rly

Stone Hill
House

ADMIRAL'S BRIDGE LA

Weir Wood Resr

2

Pit
Shaw

Whillet's
Bridge

GRINSTEAD LA

SUSSEX BORDER PATH

Admiral's Bridge
Wood

Charlwood
Farm

Alder
Moors

1

Birch Farm
Nursery

P

LEGSHEATH LA

Weir Wood Resr
Nature Reserve

34

Neylands
Farm

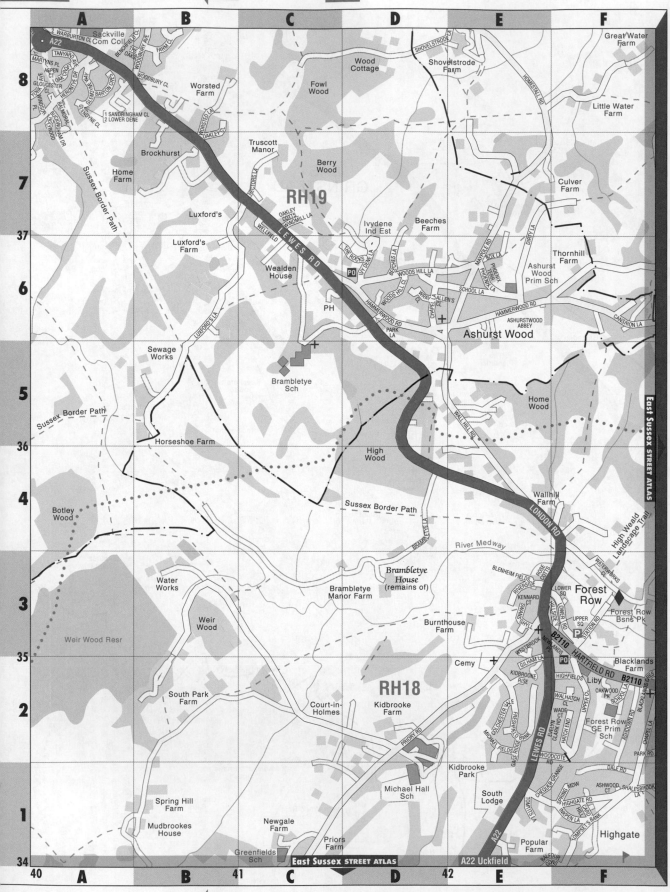

A B C D E F

8
7
37
6
5
36
4
35
3
2
1
34

A22
WARBURTON CL
Sackville
Com Coll
MARTYNS PL
ASPEN CT
GLOUCESTER
WINDSOR PL
TANYARD
HERIVOTS DR
OAK
BARTON CRES
BUCKINGHAM DR
BELMONT
RICKWOOD
CEDORNE CL
Home
Farm
Brockhurst
Woodbury Cl
Woodbury Cl
1 SANDRINGHAM CL
2 LOWER DENE
Worsted
Farm
Truscott
Manor
Luxford's
Luxford's
Farm
Sewage
Works
Horseshoe Farm

Sussex Border Path

Sussex Border Path

Wood
Cottage
Fowl
Wood
Berry
Wood

RH19

Wealden
House
PH

Brambletye
Sch

Botley
Wood

Water
Works
Weir
Wood

Weir Wood Resr

South Park
Farm

Spring Hill
Farm

Mudbrookes
House

Greenfields
Sch

Newgale
Farm

High
Wood

Sussex Border Path

Bramletye
Manor Farm

Bramletye
House
(remains of)

Court-in-
Holmes

Priors
Farm

Kidbrooke
Farm

RH18

Michael Hall
Sch

Kidbrooke
Park

River Medway

Shovelstrode
Farm

Wood
Hill

Ivydene
Ind Est

Beeches
Farm

Culver
Farm

Thornhill
Farm

Ashurst Wood
Prim Sch

Ashurstwood
Abbey

Ashurst Wood

Home
Wood

Wallhill
Farm

LONDON RD

Great Water
Farm

Little Water
Farm

Burnthouse
Farm

Cemy

Blenheim Fields

Forest
Row

Forest Row
Bsns Pk

B2110 HARTFIELD RD

Blacklands
Farm

B2110

Liby

Forest Row
CE Prim
Sch

South
Lodge

Popular
Farm

Highgate

East Sussex STREET ATLAS

A22 Uckfield

East Sussex STREET ATLAS

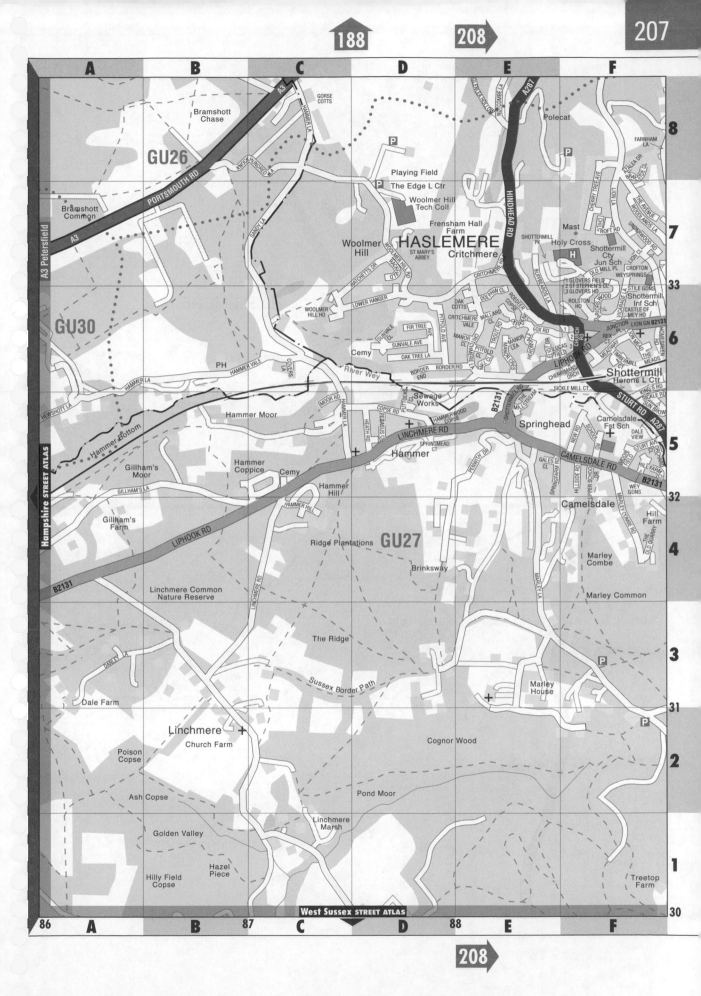

188
208

A B C D E F

GU26

Bramshott Chase

GORSE COTTS

PORTSMOUTH RD

KNOCK HUNDRED LA

A3

SANDY LA

Bramshott Common

A3 Petersfield

A3

GU30

HAMMER LA

PH

HAMMER VALE

HAMMER LA

HEWSHOTT LA

Hammer Bottom

Gillham's Moor

GILLHAM'S LA

Gillham's Farm

LIPHOOK RD

B2131

Dale Farm

DARLEY LA

Poison Copse

Linchmere

Church Farm

Ash Copse

Golden Valley

Hilly Field Copse

Hazel Piece

Playing Field
The Edge L Ctr
Woolmer Hill Tech Coll

P

Woolmer Hill

WOOLMER HILL RD

HATCHETTS DR

LOWER HANGER

Woolmer Hill Ho

Cemy

FIR TREE AVE
SUNVALE CL
SUNVALE AVE
OAK TREE LA

River Wey

PITFOLD AVE

Hammer Moor

MOOR RD

COPSE RD
PUTTICKS CL
PEGASUS CL
HEATH RD
HAMMER LA

Sewage Works

Hammer Coppice
Cemy

Hammer Hill

HAMMER HILL

LINCHMERE RD

LINCHMERE RD

Ridge Plantations

GU27

Linchmere Common Nature Reserve

The Ridge

Sussex Border Path

Cognor Wood

Pond Moor

Linchmere Marsh

HASLEMERE
Critchmere

ST MARY'S ABBEY

Frensham Hall Farm

CRITCHMERE HO

DOLPHIN CL
OAK COTTS
CRITCHMERE VALE
MALLARD CL
TROUT CL
MANOR LEA
MANOR CL
PITFOLD CL
MANOR CRES
BORDER END
BORDER RD

Hammer

SPRINGMEAD CT

Hammerwood Copse

Brinksway

FOX RD
ELIOT CL

RUDFORD COPSE
HERON WAY
LUCAS CL
CHERRIMANS ORCH

B2131

SHOTTERMILL RD
THE MILLSTREAM

Springhead

PENWITH DR

NEW RD
SCHOOL RD

GALES CL
SPRINGFARM RD
HILLSIDE RD
UPPER SCHOOL RD

CAMELSDALE RD

MARLEY LA

Marley House

Marley Combe

Marley Common

Marley House

P

P

NUTCOMBE LA
GLEN CRES HOLLOW

A287

HINDHEAD RD

Polecat

FARNHAM LA

P

Mast

Holy Cross

SHOTTERMILL PK

CHERRY TREE AVE
AZALEA DR
BAMPFYLDE CL
THE AVENUE
WOODLANDS LA
UNDERWOOD RD
CHILL LA
CROFT RD
LION LA

Shottermill Cty Jun Sch
H
CROFTON WEYSPRINGS

STILE GDNS
Shottermill Inf Sch
Castle of Mey Ho

VICARAGE LA
PRIORS WOOD
ROLSTON HO
1 GLOVERS FIELD
2 ST STEPHEN'S CL
3 GLOVERS HO

CHURCH RD

REX CL
LION GN
OLD MILL PL
JUNCTION PL
TIMBERMILL WAY
HEADLEY CL

B2131

THE MEADS
HOMEGREEN HO

LION MEAD

Shottermill

LIPHOOK RD

Herons L Ctr

SICKLE MILL CT

STURT RD

A287

KING'S RD
SICKLE MILL
SLUM BROW

Camelsdale Fst Sch

DALE VIEW

STURT AVE
HILL FARM

B2131

Camelsdale

WEY GDNS
MARLEY COMBE RD

Hill Farm

THE OLD QUARRY

P

P

Treetop Farm

Hampshire STREET ATLAS

West Sussex STREET ATLAS

86 A 87 B C 88 D E F

8 7 33 6 5 32 4 3 31 2 1 30

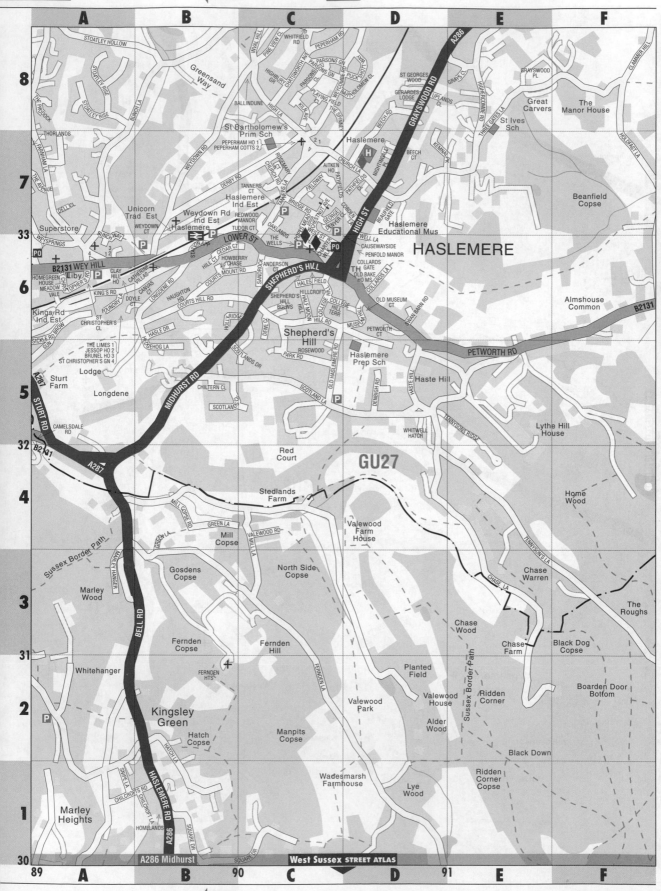

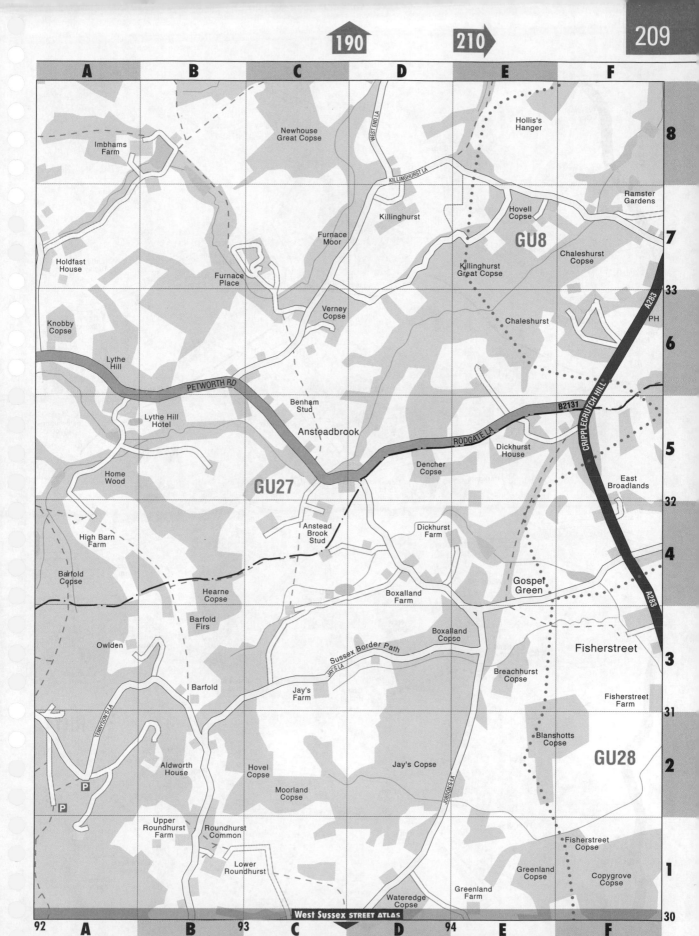

A   B   C   D   E   F

8

Imbhams Farm

Newhouse Great Copse

Hollis's Hanger

WEST END LA

KILLINGHURST LA

Killinghurst

Hovell Copse

Ramster Gardens

GU8

7

Holdfast House

Furnace Moor

Furnace Place

Killinghurst Great Copse

Chaleshurst Copse

A283

33

Verney Copse

Chaleshurst

PH

Knobby Copse

6

Lythe Hill

PETWORTH RD

Benham Stud

B2131

CRIPPLECRUTCH HILL

Lythe Hill Hotel

Ansteadbrook

RODGATE LA

Dickhurst House

5

Home Wood

GU27

Dencher Copse

East Broadlands

32

High Barn Farm

Anstead Brook Stud

Dickhurst Farm

4

Barfold Copse

Hearne Copse

Boxalland Farm

Gospel Green

A283

Barfold Firs

Boxalland Copse

Owlden

SUSSEX BORDER PATH

Fisherstreet

3

Barfold

JAY'S LA

Jay's Farm

Breachhurst Copse

Fisherstreet Farm

31

TENNYSON'S LA

Aldworth House

Hovel Copse

Jay's Copse

Blanshotts Copse

GU28

2

P

Moorland Copse

JOBSON'S LA

P

Upper Roundhurst Farm

Roundhurst Common

Fisherstreet Copse

Lower Roundhurst

Greenland Farm

Greenland Copse

Copygrove Copse

1

Wateredge Copse

92   A   B   93   C   D   94   E   F   30

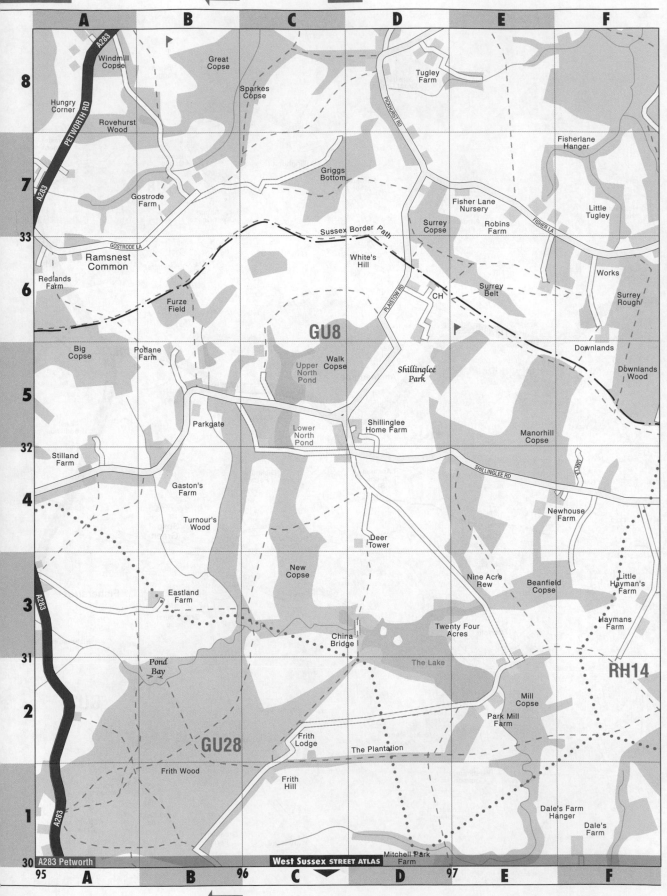

A B C D E F

8

Old Lands

Oaken Wood

Canterbury Copse

Ireland

Hurlands Copse

Tugley Wood

Oak Wood

Peartree Hanger

Burntwood Kennels

The Hatchetts

Upper Ifold

Inside Copse

GU8

Durfold Hall

Tidy's Copse

7

Durfold Hatch Cottage

Birch Copse

FISHER LA

Dungate Farm

Upper Ifold Wood

33

Oakhurst Farm

Durfold Wood Woodlands Wlks

Sussex Border Path

6

Fisherlane Wood

Durfold Wood

PLAISTOW RD

Weald Barkfold Copse

DURFOLD WOOD

Downlands Wood

Shortland Copse

DUNSFOLD RD

5

Barkfold Hanger

32

Winkins Wood Farm

RH14

Weald Barkfold

Oakhurst

4

SHILLINGLEE RD

Ashpark Wood

Short's Farm

Plaistow Place

Highbridge House

Works

Lyon's Farm

3

Kingspark Wood

COUNCIL COTTS

Plaistow & Kirdford Prim Sch

31

WELL BRI
ASHFIELD
ORCHARD
THE STREET
PACK LA
PH
PO
LOXWOOD RD

2

Birchfold Copse

Ifold Copse

Plaistow

Beggars Copse

BUSHFIELD

RICKMANS LA

GU28

Sparrwood Hangar

Rumbolds Farm

Rumbold Wood

1

Chilsfold Farm

30

98 A B 99 C D 00 E F

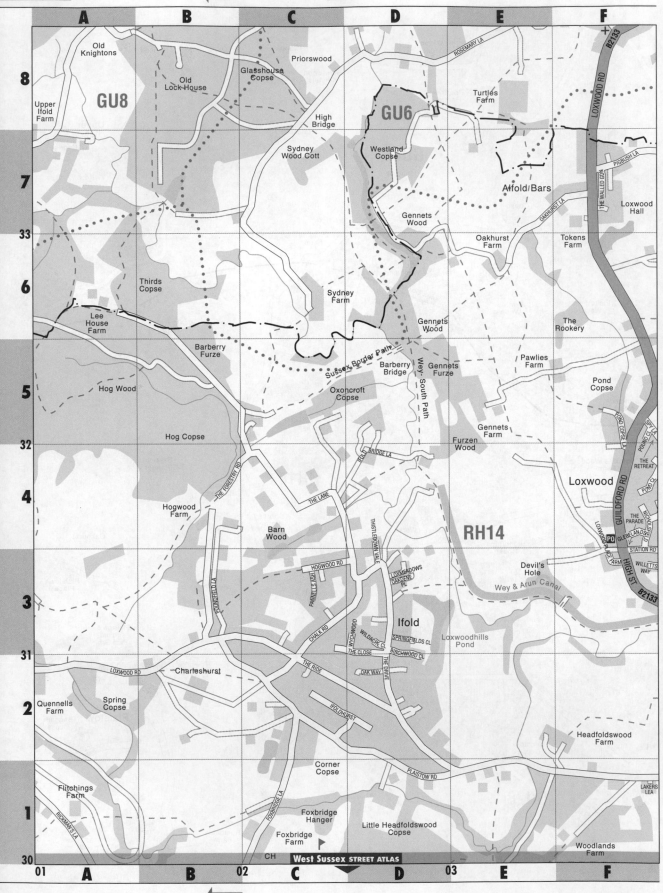

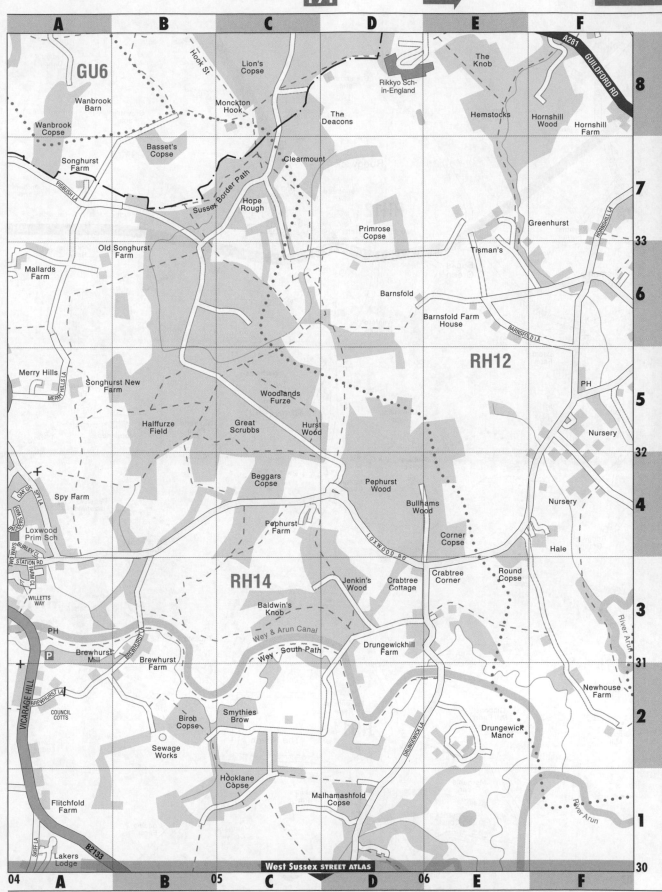

GU6

A281 GUILDFORD RD

8

Wanbrook Barn

Wanbrook Copse

Hook St

Lion's Copse

Monckton Hook

The Knob

Rikkyo Sch-in-England

The Deacons

Hemstocks

Hornshill Wood

Hornshill Farm

Songhurst Farm

PIGBUSH LA

Basset's Copse

Clearmount

7

Sussex Border Path

Hope Rough

Primrose Copse

Greenhurst

HORNSHILL LA

33

Old Songhurst Farm

Tisman's

Mallards Farm

Barnsfold

6

Barnsfold Farm House

BARNSFOLD LA

Merry Hills

MERRY HILLS LA

Songhurst New Farm

RH12

PH

5

MERRY

Halffurze Field

Great Scrubbs

Woodlands Furze

Hurst Wood

Nursery

32

Spy Farm

Beggars Copse

Pephurst Wood

Nursery

4

OAK GR
SPY LA

BADGERS W

Loxwood Prim Sch

WH WAYS
BURLEY CL
FARM CL

STATION RD

Pephurst Farm

Bullhams Wood

LOXWOOD RD

Corner Copse

Hale

WILLETTS WAY

RH14

Jenkin's Wood

Crabtree Cottage

Crabtree Corner

Round Copse

3

PH

Baldwin's Knob

Wey & Arun Canal

Drungewickhill Farm

31

P

Brewhurst Mill

BREWHURST L

Brewhurst Farm

Wey - South Path

Newhouse Farm

River Arun

VICARAGE HILL

BREWHURST LA

COUNCIL COTTS

Birob Copse

Smythies Brow

DRUNGEWICK LA

Drungewick Manor

2

Sewage Works

Hooklane Copse

Malhamashfold Copse

River Arun

1

Flitchfold Farm

SKIFF LA

B2133

Lakers Lodge

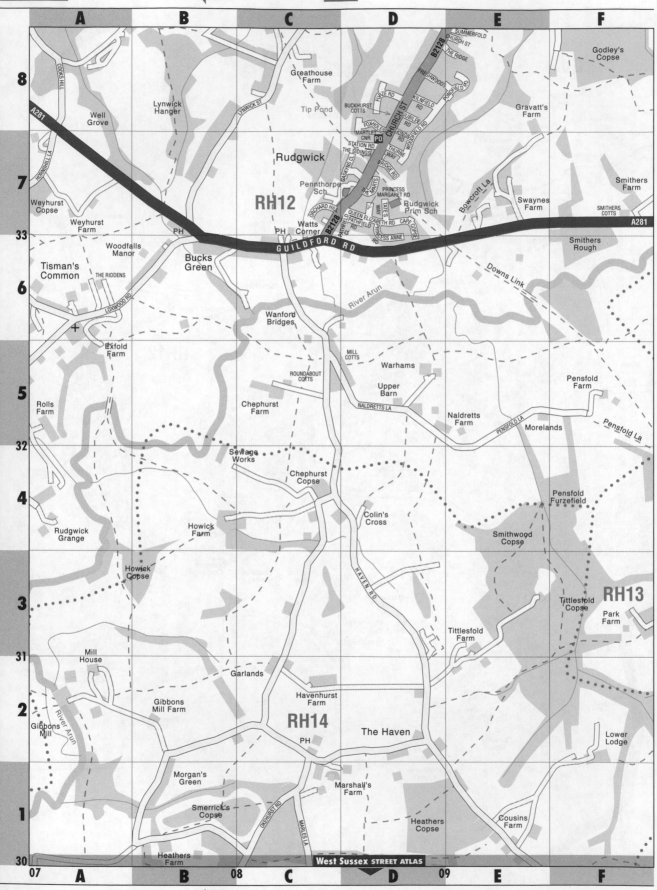

A B C D E F

8

COOKS HILL LA

A281

Greathouse
Farm

Lynwick Hanger

SUMMERFOLD
CHURCH ST
THE RIDGE

B2128
FRESHWOODS

FURZE RD

KILNFIELD
RD

PONDFIELD

Godley's
Copse

Well
Grove

LYNWICK ST

Tip Pond

BUCKHURST
COTTS

FOXHOLES
MARTLET
CNR

JUBILEE
RD

CHURCH ST

WOODFIELD RD

Gravatt's
Farm

7

HORNSHILL LA

Weyhurst
Copse

Rudgwick

PO

STATION RD
THE SIDINGS
CASKYN CL

THURNE
WAY

BRIDGE RD

ACE HARTS

Smithers
Farm

RH12

Pennthorpe
Sch

PRINCESS
MARGARET RD

Rudgwick
Prim Sch

Bowcroft La

Swaynes
Farm

SMITHERS
COTTS

Weyhurst
Farm

PH

PH

Watts
Corner

B2128

QUEEN ELIZABETH
RD
PATHFIELD
RD

TATE'S
WAY

PRINCESS ANNE

CAPE COPSE

A281

33

Woodfalls
Manor

Bucks
Green

GUILDFORD RD

Smithers
Rough

Tisman's
Common

THE RIDDENS

Downs Link

6

LOXWOOD RD

Wanford
Bridges

River Arun

Exfold
Farm

MILL
COTTS

Warhams

Pensfold
Farm

5

Rolls
Farm

Chephurst
Farm

ROUNDABOUT
COTTS

Upper
Barn

NALDRETTS LA

Naldretts
Farm

PENSFOLD LA

Morelands

Pensfold La

32

Sewage
Works

Chephurst
Copse

Pensfold
Furzefield

4

Rudgwick
Grange

Howick
Farm

Colin's
Cross

Smithwood
Copse

3

Howick
Copse

HAVEN RD

Tittlesfold
Farm

Tittlesfold
Copse

RH13

Park
Farm

31

Mill
House

Garlands

Havenhurst
Farm

RH14

Gibbons
Mill Farm

2

Gibbons
Mill

River Arun

PH

The Haven

Lower
Lodge

Morgan's
Green

Marshall's
Farm

1

Smerrick's
Copse

OKEHURST RD

MARLES LA

Heathers
Copse

Cousins
Farm

30

Heathers
Farm

07 A B 08 C D 09 E F

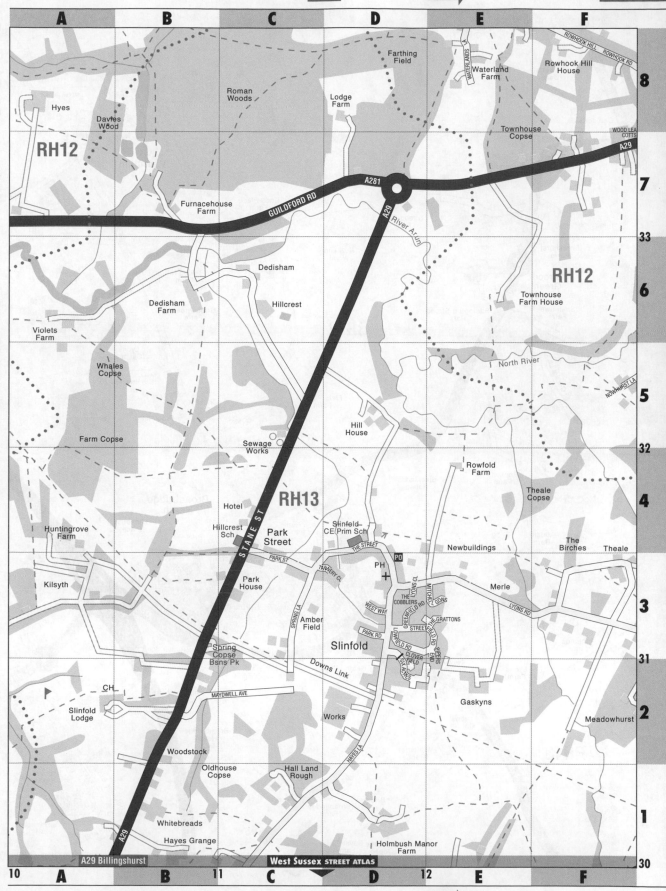

A   B   C   D   E   F

RH12

Hyes
Davies Wood

Roman Woods

Farthing Field

Lodge Farm

Waterlands La
Waterland Farm

ROWHOOK HILL
ROWHOOK RD
Rowhook Hill House

Townhouse Copse

WOOD LEA COTTS

A29

8

A281

GUILDFORD RD

Furnacehouse Farm

A29

River Arun

7

33

Dedisham

RH12

Townhouse Farm House

6

Dedisham Farm

Hillcrest

Violets Farm

North River

NOWHURST LA

5

Whales Copse

32

Farm Copse

Sewage Works

Hill House

Rowfold Farm

Theale Copse

4

RH13

Hotel

Hillcrest Sch

Park Street

Slinfold CE Prim Sch

THE STREET

Newbuildings

The Birches

Theale

Huntingrove Farm

PARK ST

TANNERY CL

PO
PH

LYONS CL
THE COBBLERS
GREENFIELD RD
MITCHEL GDNS
LYONS RD

Merle

STANE ST

Kilsyth

Park House

SPRING LA

Amber Field

WEST WAY
PARK RD

LOWFIELD RD
THE STREET
WESTFIELD RD
PIPERS END
THE GRATTONS

3

31

Spring Copse Bsns Pk

Downs Link

Slinfold

CLOVER FIELD
1ST ACRES

CH

MAYDWELL AVE

Gaskyns

Meadowhurst

2

Slinfold Lodge

Works

HAYES LA

Woodstock

Oldhouse Copse

Hall Land Rough

1

Whitebreads

Hayes Grange

Holmbush Manor Farm

A29

30

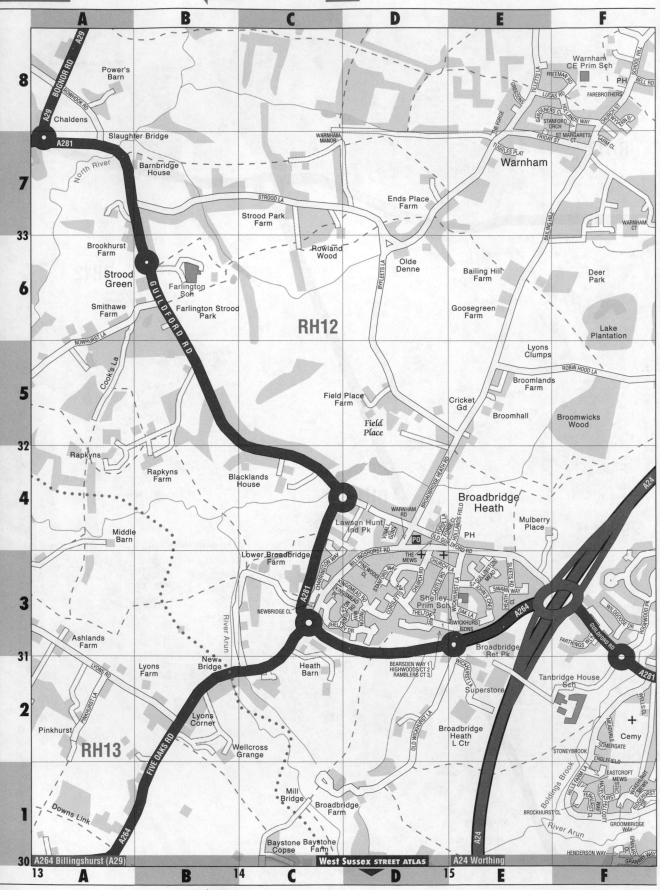

West Sussex STREET ATLAS

D5
1 WISTON CT
2 NUTBOURNE CT
3 ASHINGTON CT
4 MARLBOROUGH CL
5 WOODMANCOTE CT

← 198   218 →   217

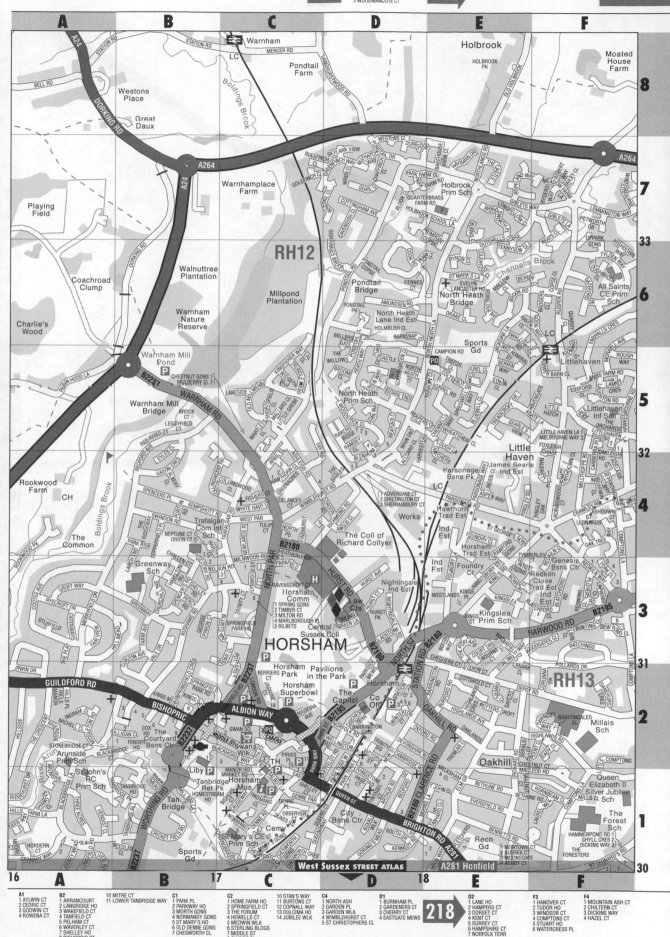

West Sussex STREET ATLAS

RH12

HORSHAM

RH13

Benson's Farm

Cow Barn

Castle Copse

Owlscastle Farm

Channells Brook

PH

Dobsongill Pond

Rookfield Pond

Beechwood

Middle Hill

Faygate Forest

A264

CRAWLEY RD

LC

Clovers Way

ROSE COTTS

Roffey Place (Christian Training Ctr)

Roffey Park

Newhouse Farm

Newhouse Bsns Ctr

Moorhead Farm

The Birches

Roffey Park

1 BUTTERMERE CL
2 GRASMERE GDNS

St Robert Southwell RC Prim

NEW MOORHEAD DR

High Wood

Beedingwood

Beedingwood Dr

Roffey Park Inst

Roffey

Woodside Farm

Stonelodge Plain

Roffey Hurst

FOREST RD

Cemy

Highbiroh Hill

Knights Strength

Northolmes Jun Sch

1 WOODBRIDGE CT
2 MANOR CT

Leechpool Prim Sch

The Orchard

Owlbeech Wood

Leechpool & Owlbeech Woods

Owlbeech PL

1 OWLBEECH CT
2 OWLBEECH LODGE

THE COURTYARD

Forest Grange Manor

Whitevane Hill

Whitevane Pond

Race Hill

HARWOOD RD

B2195

PO

Dogkennel Pond

Greenbroom Hill

Leechpool Wood

Townhouse Copse

St Leonard's Park Ho

St Leonard's Park

Home Farm

High Weald Landscape Trail

Lily Beds

Padwick Rd

Blackthorn

HAMPER'S LA

Sandpit Clump

Stew Pond

Dry Pond

Hamper's La

Comptons La

Sheepwash Wood

Scragged Oak

Scragged Oak Hill

Mick's Cross

Greenslade Wood

Heron Way Prim Sch

Brambling Rd

The Glen

Sunoak Plantation

DOOMSDAY GDN

A264

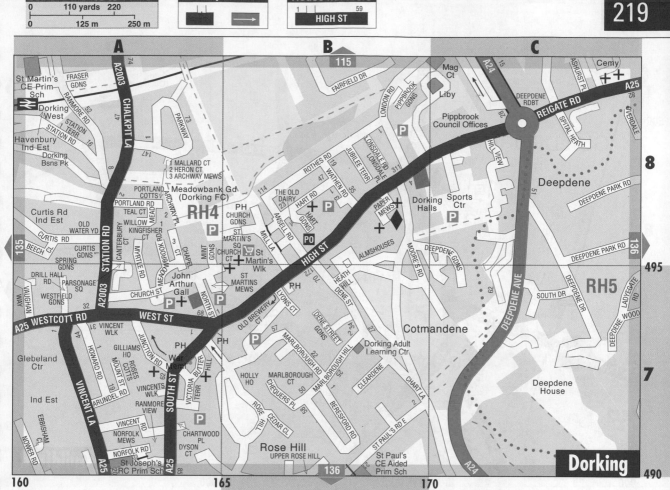

Dorking

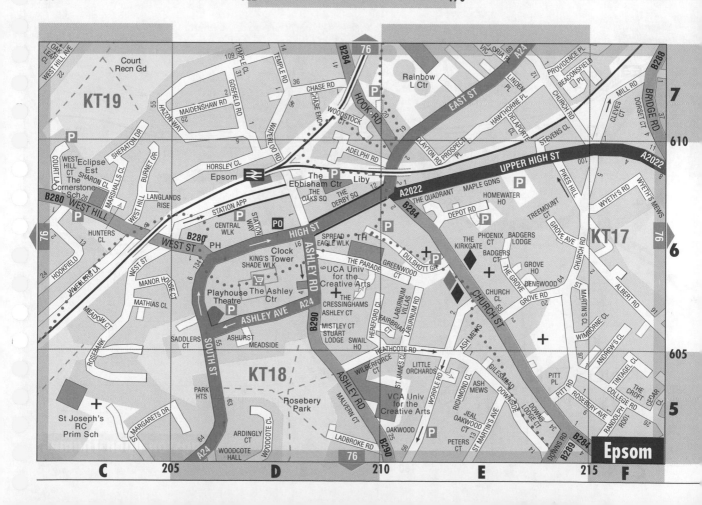

Epsom

Scale: 7 inches to 1 mile

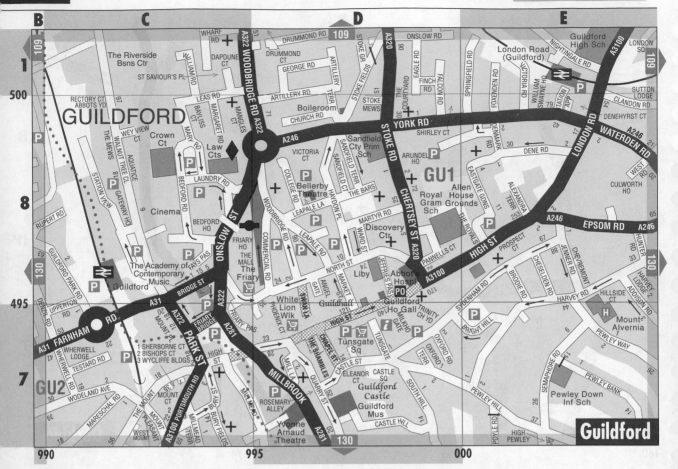

Guildford

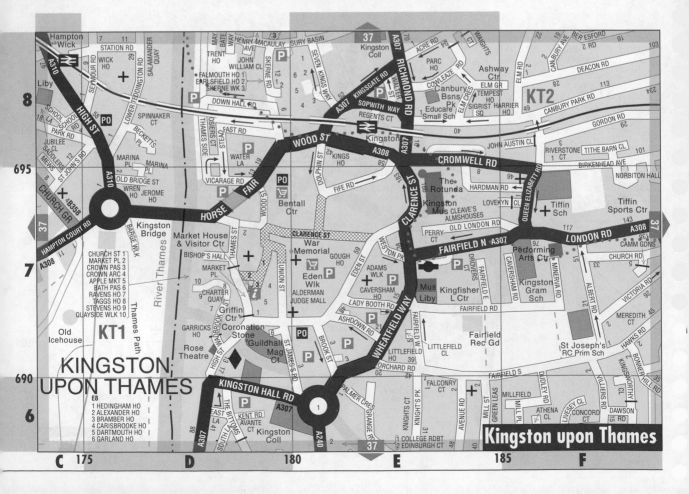

Kingston upon Thames

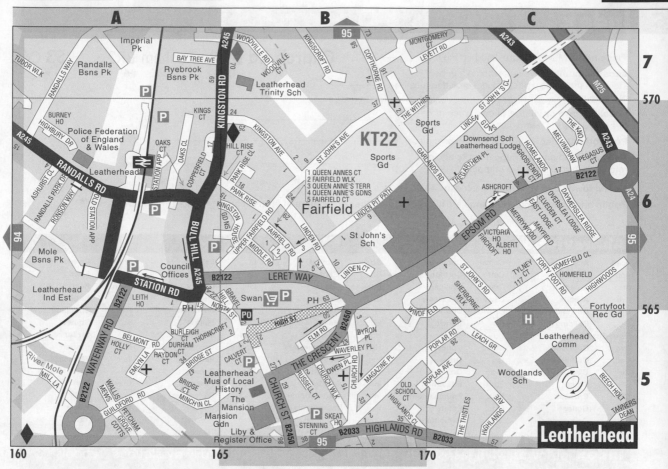

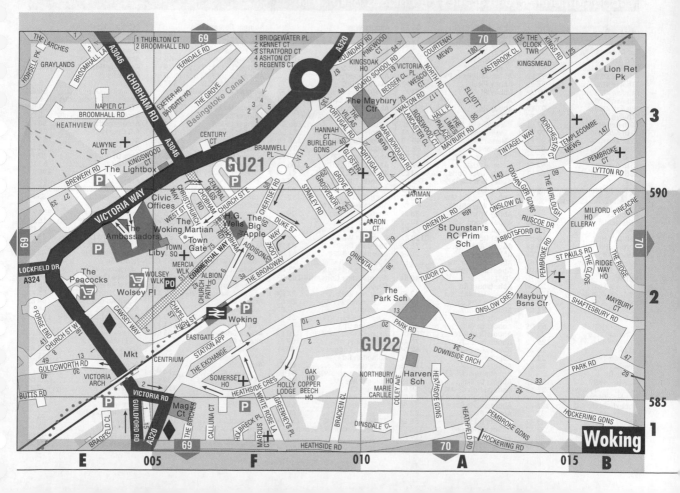

Index

Place name May be abbreviated on the map

Church Rd 6 Beckenham BR2..........**53** C6

Location number Present when a number indicates the place's position in a crowded area of mapping

Locality, town or village Shown when more than one place has the same name

Postcode district District for the indexed place

Page and grid square Page number and grid reference for the standard mapping

Cities, towns and villages are listed in CAPITAL LETTERS

Public and commercial buildings are highlighted in **magenta** **Places of interest** are highlighted in blue with a star★

Abbreviations used in the index

Acad	**Academy**	Comm	**Common**	Gd	**Ground**	L	**Leisure**	Prom	**Promenade**
App	**Approach**	Cott	**Cottage**	Gdn	**Garden**	La	**Lane**	Rd	**Road**
Arc	**Arcade**	Cres	**Crescent**	Gn	**Green**	Liby	**Library**	Recn	**Recreation**
Ave	**Avenue**	Cswy	**Causeway**	Gr	**Grove**	Mdw	**Meadow**	Ret	**Retail**
Bglw	**Bungalow**	Ct	**Court**	H	**Hall**	Meml	**Memorial**	Sh	**Shopping**
Bldg	**Building**	Ctr	**Centre**	Ho	**House**	Mkt	**Market**	Sq	**Square**
Bsns, Bus	**Business**	Ctry	**Country**	Hospl	**Hospital**	Mus	**Museum**	St	**Street**
Bvd	**Boulevard**	Cty	**County**	HQ	**Headquarters**	Orch	**Orchard**	Sta	**Station**
Cath	**Cathedral**	Dr	**Drive**	Hts	**Heights**	Pal	**Palace**	Terr	**Terrace**
Cir	**Circus**	Dro	**Drove**	Ind	**Industrial**	Par	**Parade**	TH	**Town Hall**
Cl	**Close**	Ed	**Education**	Inst	**Institute**	Pas	**Passage**	Univ	**University**
Cnr	**Corner**	Emb	**Embankment**	Int	**International**	Pk	**Park**	Wk, Wlk	**Walk**
Coll	**College**	Est	**Estate**	Intc	**Interchange**	Pl	**Place**	Wr	**Water**
Com	**Community**	Ex	**Exhibition**	Junc	**Junction**	Prec	**Precinct**	Yd	**Yard**

Index of towns, villages, streets, hospitals, industrial estates, railway stations, schools, shopping centres, universities and places of interest

1st–Acr

1st Ave KT20............ **97** E2
2nd Ave KT20............ **97** E2
3rd Ave KT20............ **97** E2
4th Ave KT20............ **97** E2
5th Ave KT20............ **97** E2
6th Ave KT20............ **97** E2
7th Ave KT20............ **97** F2
8th Ave KT20............ **97** F2
9th Ave KT20............ **97** F2
10th Ave KT20........... **97** F1
11th Ave KT20........... **97** F1
12th Ave KT20........... **97** F1
13th Ave KT20........... **97** F1
14th Ave KT20........... **97** F1
15th Ave KT20........... **97** F1
16th Ave KT20........... **97** F1

A

Aaron Ct
Beckenham BR3.......... **44** B6
Woking GU21............ **69** F2
AARON'S HILL............ **150** C4
Aaron's Hill GU7........ **150** B4
Abbess Cl SW2.......... **22** B7
Abbetts La GU15......... **65** B3
Abbey Cl
Bracknell RG12.......... **27** D4
Elmbridge Village GU6... **173** F2
Pyrford GU22............ **70** E3
Wokingham RG40........ **25** C7
Abbey Ct
Camberley GU15......... **65** D5
Chertsey KT16........... **33** B2
Farnham GU9........... **125** C2
1 Hampton TW12........ **16** A1
Laleham TW18........... **33** C5
Purley CR8............. **80** B7
Abbey Dr
Laleham TW18........... **33** C5
Upper Tooting SW17..... **21** A3
Abbeyfield Cl CR4........ **40** E7
Abbeyfield Ho RH8....... **122** E6
Abbeyfields Pk KT16..... **33** C2
Abbey Gdns KT16........ **33** A3
Abbey Gn KT16.......... **33** A3
Abbey Ind Est CR4...... **40** F4
Abbey La BR3........... **24** A1

Abbeylands KT13........ **53** B3
Abbey Lodge 3 TW18... **12** F3
Abbey Mdws KT16....... **33** C2
Abbey Mews
Brentford TW7........... **6** B6
Laleham TW18.......... **33** C5
Abbey Mill Bsns Pk GU7. **149** F4
Abbey Pk BR3.......... **24** A1
Abbey Pl KT16.......... **33** A6
Abbey Prim Sch SM4.... **40** A2
Abbey Rd
Chertsey KT16.......... **33** B2
Croydon CR0, CR9...... **61** B7
Lower Halliford TW17.... **34** A1
Merton SW19........... **40** C8
Selsdon CR2........... **62** D1
Virginia Water GU25..... **31** D5
Woking GU21........... **69** D2
Abbey River Cotts KT16.. **33** C3
Abbey Sch The GU9..... **125** D1
Abbey St GU9.......... **125** C2
Abbey Trad Est SE26.... **23** F3
Abbey Way GU14........ **85** C4
Abbey Wlk KT8......... **36** B5
Abbey Wood SL5....... **30** A2
Abbot Cl KT14.......... **71** D8
Abbot Rd GU1.......... **130** D7
Abbots Ave KT19....... **76** A8
Abbotsbury RG12....... **26** F4
Abbotsbury Ct RH13.... **217** E3
Abbotsbury Prim Sch
SM4................. **40** B4
Abbotsbury Rd
Coney Hall BR2, BR4.... **63** F8
Morden SM4, SW19..... **40** B5
Abbot's Cl GU2........ **129** F6
Abbots Ct SE25........ **42** E6
Abbots Dr GU25........ **31** C5
Abbotsfield Rd RH11... **200** D4
Abbotsford Cl GU22..... **70** A2
Abbots Gn CR0, CR2.... **62** D4
Abbotshall Rd SE6..... **24** D6
Abbots Ho GU4........ **110** A5
Abbot's Hospl★ 2 GU1. **130** D8
Abbots La CR8......... **80** C3
Abbotsleigh Cl SM2.... **59** B3
Abbotsleigh Rd SW16... **21** C3
Abbotsmede Cl TW1.... **16** F6
Abbots Pk SW2........ **22** A7
Abbots Rd SM1, SM3.... **58** E6
Abbot's Ride GU9...... **125** E1
Abbots Rise RH1....... **119** A3

Abbots Way
Beckenham BR3......... **43** E4
Chertsey KT16.......... **32** F2
Abbot's Way GU1....... **110** D2
Abbots Wlk CR3........ **101** B5
ABBOTSWOOD.......... **109** F3
Abbotswood
Guildford GU1......... **109** F3
Walton-on-Thames KT13.. **53** F7
Abbotswood Cl GU1.... **109** F4
Abbotswood Dr KT13.... **53** D1
Abbots Wood Forest Wlk★
GU10............... **166** C7
Abbotswood Rd SW16... **21** D5
Abbots Yd 9 GU1...... **130** C8
Abbott Ave SW20...... **39** D8
Abbott Ho SW12....... **20** F8
Abbotts Cotts GU10.... **166** E5
Abbotts Rd CR4, SW16.. **41** C5
Abbotts Tilt KT12...... **54** E7
Abelia Cl GU24........ **67** E6
Abell Ct KT15......... **52** C6
Abercairn Rd SW16.... **21** C1
Aberconway Rd SM4.... **40** B5
Abercorn Cl CR2....... **81** D7
Abercorn Mews TW10... **6** E3
Abercorn Way GU21.... **69** A1
Aberdare Cl BR4....... **63** C8
Aberdeen Rd CR0...... **61** D6
Aberdour Sch KT20.... **77** F1
Aberfoyle Rd SW16.... **21** D2
Abergavenny Gdns RH10 **183** D3
Abingdon Cl
Bracknell RG12......... **27** E4
Merton SW19........... **20** C2
Woking GU21........... **69** C1
Worcester Park KT4..... **58** B7
Abingdon Ct
Upper Tooting SW17..... **20** F2
16 Woking GU22....... **69** F1
Abingdon Lodge BR2... **44** F7
Abingdon Rd
Sandhurst GU47........ **45** C1
Thornton Heath SW16... **41** E8
Abinger Ave SM2....... **58** D2
Abinger Cl
Dorking RH5........... **136** C3
New Addington CR0..... **63** C4
Wallington SM6........ **60** E5
ABINGER COMMON...... **155** D8
Abinger Common Fst Sch
RH5................ **134** D1

Abinger Common Rd
RH5................ **155** F7
Abinger Ct
3 Thornton Heath CR0... **42** B2
Wallington SM6........ **60** E5
Abinger Dr RH1........ **139** E7
Abinger Gdns TW7....... **5** E4
ABINGER HAMMER...... **133** F3
Abinger Hammer Village Sch
RH5................ **133** F4
Abinger Ho 2 KT2...... **18** B1
Abinger Keep RH6..... **161** C4
Abinger La RH5........ **134** C2
Abinger Rd RH5....... **156** C3
Abinger Way GU4...... **110** B6
Abney Ct TW2......... **16** D6
Aboyne Dr SW20....... **39** A7
Aboyne Rd SW17....... **20** D5
Abraham Cowley Unit Hospl
KT16................ **51** D7
Abrahams Rd RH11.... **201** A1
Abro Ind Est GU11..... **105** D3
Acacia Ave
Brentford TW8.......... **6** B7
Littleton TW17......... **34** A4
Sandhurst GU47........ **45** D1
Woking GU22.......... **89** D7
Acacia Cl
Penge SE20........... **43** A7
Woodham KT15......... **51** F1
Acacia Ct
Bracknell RG12......... **27** B6
4 Richmond TW9........ **6** F3
6 West Norwood SW16... **22** A3
Acacia Dr
Banstead KT17......... **77** D5
Cheam SM3............ **40** A1
Woodham KT15......... **51** F1
Acacia Gdns BR4...... **63** C8
Acacia Gr
Dulwich SE21.......... **22** D6
Kingston upon Thames KT3. **38** E6
Acacia Ho
Cranleigh GU6........ **174** E2
1 New Malden KT3...... **38** E5
Reigate RH2.......... **118** A3
Acacia Mews UB7...... **2** D8
Acacia Rd
Beckenham BR3........ **43** F6
Guildford GU1......... **109** D1
Hampton TW12......... **16** A2
Mitcham CR4.......... **41** B7
Staines TW18.......... **13** B3

Acacia Rd continued
Thornton Heath SW16... **41** E8
Academy Cl GU15...... **65** E8
Academy Ct TW16...... **35** A5
Academy Gate GU15... **65** B6
Academy Gdns CR0.... **42** F1
Academy Pl
Isleworth TW7........... **5** E7
Sandhurst GU47........ **64** E7
Acad of Contemporary Music
The GU1............. **130** C8
Accommodation La UB7... **2** C8
Accommodation Rd KT16. **50** E6
A C Court KT7......... **37** A3
Ace Par KT9.......... **56** E7
Acer Cl RG42......... **28** A8
Acer Dr GU24......... **67** F6
Acer Rd TN16......... **83** D3
Acheulian Cl GU9..... **146** C7
Achilles Pl GU21...... **69** C2
Ackroyd Rd SE23...... **23** E8
Acorn Ave GU16....... **85** F5
Acorn Cl
East Grinstead RH19.... **205** E8
1 Hampton TW12........ **16** B2
Horley RH6........... **161** C4
Acorn Ct TW12........ **15** F3
Acorn Dr RG40........ **25** C7
Acorn Gdns SE19...... **42** F8
Acorn Gr
Kingswood KT20........ **97** F3
Woking GU22.......... **89** E6
Acorn Keep GU9...... **125** D8
Acorn Mews GU14..... **85** A7
Acorn Rd GU17........ **64** B5
Acorns RH13......... **218** A4
Acorns Inf Sch The RH3. **116** D1
Acorns The
Crawley RH11......... **201** B1
21 Putney SW19........ **19** D7
Smallfield RH6........ **162** B3
Acorns Way KT10...... **55** C5
Acorn Way
Beckenham BR3........ **44** C4
Forest Hill SE23....... **23** D5
Acqua Ho TW9.......... **7** B7
Acre La SM5.......... **60** A6
Acre Rd
Kingston upon Thames
KT2................ **37** F4
Mitcham SW19......... **20** D2
Acres Gdns KT20...... **97** D8
Acres Platt GU6...... **174** F4

ACS Cobham Inf Sch KT11 ... 54 C1
ACS Egham International Sch TW20 ... 31 C7
Action Ct TW15 ... 34 C8
Acuba Ho SW18 ... 20 B7
Acuba Rd SW18 ... 20 B6
Adair Cl SE25 ... 43 B6
Adair Gdns CR3 ... 100 C6
Adair Wlk GU24 ... 87 B6
Adam Cl SE6 ... 24 A5
Adam Ct 4 SM1 ... 59 C6
Adams Cl KT5 ... 37 F3
Adams Croft GU24 ... 87 C7
Adams Ct 3 CR8 ... 80 A7
Adams Ho 3 SW16 ... 21 C3
Adams Mews SW17 ... 20 F6
Adamson Ct 6 RH11 ... 201 B1
Adamson Way BR3 ... 44 C4
Adams Park Rd GU9 ... 125 D3
Adams Qtr TW8 ... 6 C8
Adams Rd BR3 ... 43 E4
Adamsrill Prim Sch SE26 ... 23 E5
Adamsrill Rd SE23, SE26 ... 23 E4
Adams Way SE25, CR0 ... 43 A3
Adams Wlk 11 KT1 ... 37 E7
Adare Wlk SW16, SW2 ... 21 F6
ADDINGTON ... 63 A5
Addington Bsns Ctr CR0 ... 63 E1
Addington Ct 8 SW14 ... 7 D4
Addington Gr SE26 ... 23 E4
Addington High Sch CR0 ... 82 E7
Addington Rd
Sanderstead CR2 ... 81 A8
Selsdon CR2 ... 62 C1
Thornton Heath CR0 ... 42 A1
West Wickham BR4, CR0 ... 63 D6
Addington Village Halt CR0 ... 63 A4
Addington Village Rd CR0 63 A5
ADDISCOMBE ... 43 B1
Addiscombe Ave CR0 ... 43 A2
Addiscombe Court Rd CR0, CR9 ... 61 E8
Addiscombe Halt CR0 ... 43 A1
Addiscombe Rd
Crowthorne RG45 ... 45 C4
Croydon CR0, CR9 ... 61 E8
Addison Ave TW3 ... 5 C6
Addison Cl CR3 ... 100 D5
Addison Ct
16 Belmont SM2 ... 59 B3
Guildford GU1 ... 130 F7
Twickenham TW1 ... 17 A7
Addison Gdns KT5 ... 37 F5
Addison Rd
Caterham CR3 ... 100 D6
Croydon SE25 ... 43 A5
Farnborough GU16 ... 85 E8
Guildford GU1 ... 130 F7
Teddington TW11 ... 17 B2
4 Woking GU21 ... 69 F2
Addison's Cl CR0 ... 62 F8
ADDLESTONE ... 52 A6
Addlestone Ho KT15 ... 52 B7
Addlestone L Ctr KT15 ... 52 A5
ADDLESTONEMOOR ... 52 C8
Addlestone Moor KT15 ... 52 C8
Addlestone Pk KT15 ... 52 B5
Addlestone Rd KT13, KT15 ... 52 E6
Addlestone Sta KT15 ... 52 D6
Adecroft Way KT8 ... 36 C6
Adela Ave KT3 ... 39 B5
Adelaide Cl
Crawley RH11 ... 181 D1
Horsham RH12 ... 217 F4
Adelaide Ct 15 BR3 ... 24 A1
Adelaide Pl KT13 ... 53 D6
Adelaide Rd
Ashford TW15 ... 13 D3
Heston TW5 ... 4 E6
Kingston upon Thames KT6 ... 37 E4
Richmond TW9 ... 6 F3
Teddington TW11 ... 16 F2
Walton-on-Thames KT12 ... 54 B7
Adelina Mews SW12 ... 21 D7
Adelphi Cl RH10 ... 202 D4
Adelphi Rd KT17 ... 76 D6
Adenmore Rd SE6 ... 24 A8
Adlers La RH5 ... 115 A4
Adlington Pl GU14 ... 85 E2
Admiral Ct SM5 ... 40 E1
Admiral Ho TW11 ... 17 B3
Admiral Rd RH11 ... 201 A3
Admiral's Bridge La RH19 ... 205 C2
Admirals Ct
Guildford GU1 ... 110 B2
32 Putney SW19 ... 19 D7
Admiral Stirling Ct KT13 ... 52 F6
Admiral's Wlk The CR5 ... 99 F7
Admiralty Rd TW11 ... 16 F2
Admiralty Way
Camberley GU15 ... 64 F4
Teddington TW11 ... 16 F2
Adolf St SE6 ... 24 B4
Adrian Ct RH11 ... 201 B1
Advance Rd SE27 ... 22 C4
Adversane Ct RH12 ... 217 D4
Adyar Ct 7 SW19 ... 19 E1
Aerodrome Way TW5 ... 4 C8
Aerospace Bvd GU14 ... 105 A7
Agar Cl KT6 ... 56 F8
Agar Ho 6 KT1 ... 37 E6
Agate Ho
New Malden KT4 ... 38 E1
12 Penge SE26 ... 23 B3
Agate La RH12 ... 217 F5
Agates La KT21 ... 95 D8
Agincourt SL5 ... 29 C6
Agnes Scott Ct 5 KT13 ... 53 B7
Agnew Rd SE23 ... 23 D8
Agraria Rd GU2 ... 130 B7
Ailsa Ave TW1 ... 6 B2
Ailsa Cl RH11 ... 201 B3
Ailsa Rd TW1 ... 6 B2
Ainger Cl GU12 ... 105 D2
Ainsdale Way GU21 ... 69 A1
Ainsworth Rd CR0, CR9 ... 61 B8
Aintree Cl SL3 ... 1 E6
Aintree Ho SE26 ... 23 B2
Aintree Rd RH10 ... 202 A4
Airborne Ho 10 SM6 ... 60 B6
Aircraft Espl GU14 ... 85 C1
Aird Ct TW12 ... 36 B8
Airedale Rd SW12 ... 20 F8
Air Forces Meml★ TW20 ... 11 D4
Air Park Way TW13 ... 15 B6
Airport Ho CR0 ... 61 A4
Airport Ind Esatate TN16 ... 83 D4
Airport Way
Horley RH6 ... 182 B8
Stanwell TW19 ... 2 A3
Airport Way Rdbt E RH6 ... 182 C8
Airport Way Rdbt W RH6 181 F8
Aisne Rd GU16 ... 66 E1
Aitken Cl CR4 ... 40 F2
Aitken Ho
Dorking RH4 ... 136 A5
Haslemere GU27 ... 208 C7
Aitken Rd SE6 ... 24 B6
Aits View KT8 ... 36 B6
Akabusi Cl SE25 ... 43 A3
Akehurst Cl RH10 ... 183 B3
Akehurst St SW15 ... 19 A8
Akerman Rd KT6 ... 37 C3
Alamein Rd GU11 ... 105 B3
Alanbrooke Cl GU21 ... 68 C1
Alanbrooke Rd GU11 ... 105 D6
Alan Hilton Ct KT16 ... 51 D4
Alan Rd SW19 ... 19 E3
Alan Turing Rd GU2 ... 108 D1
Albain Cres TW15 ... 13 E6
Alba Mews SW18 ... 20 A6
Albans Cl SW16 ... 21 E5
Albany Cl
Esher KT10 ... 55 A2
Mortlake SW14 ... 7 B3
Reigate RH2 ... 118 A3
Albany Cres KT10 ... 55 E4
Albany Ct
Ashford TW15 ... 14 D2
Cheam SM1 ... 58 F6
Kingston upon Thames KT2 ... 17 E2
Oatlands Park KT13 ... 53 E8
Richmond TW10 ... 17 B5
Surbiton KT6 ... 37 D2
3 Weybridge KT13 ... 53 B6
Albany Hall KT4 ... 39 B2
Albany Ho 6 TW8 ... 6 E8
Albany Mews
Kingston upon Thames KT2 ... 17 D2
Sutton SM1 ... 59 B5
Albany Par 4 TW8 ... 6 E8
Albany Park Ind Est GU15 65 C1
Albany Park Rd
Kingston upon Thames KT2 ... 17 E2
Leatherhead KT22 ... 95 A8
Albany Pas 14 TW10 ... 6 E2
Albany Pk
Frimley GU15 ... 65 C1
Poyle SL3 ... 1 D7
Albany Pl
Brentford TW8 ... 6 D8
Egham TW20 ... 12 B4
Albany Rd
Brentford TW8 ... 6 D8
Crawley RH11 ... 201 C6
Hersham KT12 ... 54 D6
New Malden KT3 ... 38 D5
Richmond TW10 ... 6 F2
Wimbledon SW19 ... 20 B3
Albany Reach KT7 ... 36 F4
Albany Terr 6 TW10 ... 6 F2
Albatross Gdns CR2 ... 81 D8
Albemarle SW19 ... 19 D6
Albemarle Ave TW2 ... 15 F7
Albemarle Gdns KT3 ... 38 D5
Albemarle Lodge SE26 ... 23 E3
Albemarle Pk BR3 ... 44 B8
Albemarle Rd BR2, BR3 ... 44 C8
Albermarle Prim Sch SW19 ... 19 E6
Alberta Ave SM1 ... 58 F5
Alberta Ct 1 TW10 ... 6 F2
Alberta Dr RH6 ... 162 A3
Albert Ave KT16 ... 33 A6
Albert Carr Gdns SW16 ... 21 E3
Albert Crane Ct RH11 ... 201 A8
Albert Ct 9 SW19 ... 19 E7
Albert Dr
Putney SW19 ... 19 E6
Sheerwater GU21, KT14 ... 70 D5
1 Staines TW18 ... 13 A3
Albert Gr SW20 ... 39 D8
Albert Ho 3 KT22 ... 95 C6
Albertine Cl KT17 ... 77 B3
Albert Mews RH1 ... 140 A6
Albert Rd
Addlestone KT15 ... 52 D6
Aldershot GU11 ... 105 B2
Ashford TW15 ... 13 F3
Ashtead KT21 ... 75 F1
Bagshot GU19 ... 47 E1
Albert Rd *continued*
Bracknell RG42 ... 27 B8
Camberley GU15 ... 65 C5
Carshalton SM1 ... 59 D5
Crowthorne RG45 ... 45 B5
Croydon CR0, SE25 ... 43 B5
Englefield Green TW20 ... 11 D2
Epsom KT17 ... 76 F6
Farnborough GU14 ... 85 C2
Hampton TW12 ... 16 C3
Horley RH6 ... 161 A3
Hounslow TW3 ... 5 A3
Kingston upon Thames KT1 ... 37 F7
Merstham RH1 ... 119 C6
Mitcham CR4 ... 40 F6
New Malden KT3 ... 38 F5
Penge SE20 ... 23 D2
Richmond TW10 ... 6 F2
Teddington TW11 ... 16 F2
Twickenham TW1 ... 16 F7
Warlingham CR6 ... 81 F2
Wokingham RG40 ... 25 B5
Albert Road N RH2 ... 117 F2
Albert Wlk RG45 ... 45 B5
Albery Cl RH12 ... 217 B4
Albion Cl RH10 ... 202 D5
Albion Ct
Streatham SW2 ... 22 A6
Sutton SM2 ... 59 D3
Albion Ho 10 GU21 ... 69 F2
Albion Par GU21 ... 68 C2
Albion Pl SE25 ... 43 A6
Albion Rd
Hounslow TW3 ... 5 A3
Kingston upon Thames KT2 ... 38 C8
Reigate RH2 ... 139 C8
Sandhurst GU47 ... 64 B8
Sutton SM2 ... 59 D3
Twickenham TW2 ... 16 E7
Albion St CR0, CR9 ... 42 B1
Albion Villas Rd SE23, SE26 ... 23 C5
Albion Way RH12 ... 217 C2
ALBURY ... 132 C4
Albury Ave
East Ewell SM2 ... 58 C1
Hounslow TW7 ... 5 F7
Albury Cl
Epsom KT19 ... 57 B2
Hampton TW12 ... 16 B2
Longcross KT16 ... 50 A7
Albury Ct
4 Croydon CR0 ... 61 C6
Guildford GU1 ... 131 A8
Mitcham CR4 ... 40 D7
Sutton SM1 ... 59 C6
Albury Ho GU1 ... 130 F7
Albury Hts GU1 ... 131 A8
Albury Keep RH6 ... 161 B4
Albury Lodge 10 SW2 ... 21 F8
Albury Pl RH1 ... 119 C6
Albury Rd
Chessington KT9 ... 56 E5
Guildford GU1 ... 131 A8
Hersham KT12 ... 53 F4
Merstham RH1 ... 119 C6
Albury St GU5 ... 132 C4
Alcester Ct 4 SM6 ... 60 B6
Alcester Rd SM6 ... 60 B6
Alcock Cl SM6 ... 60 D3
Alcock Rd TW5 ... 4 D7
Alcocks Cl KT20 ... 97 E7
Alcocks La KT20 ... 97 E7
Alcorn Cl SM3 ... 59 A8
Alcot Cl RG45 ... 45 B4
Aldeburgh Ho RH6 ... 161 A2
Alden Ct
South Croydon CR0 ... 61 D7
5 Wimbledon SW19 ... 20 A2
Aldenham Terr RG12 ... 27 C3
Aldenholme KT13 ... 53 E4
Alderbrook Ct BR4 ... 63 B8
Alderbrook Prim Sch SW12 ... 21 B8
Alderbrook Rd
Balham SW12 ... 21 B8
Cranleigh GU6 ... 174 C8
Alder Cl
Ash Vale GU12 ... 106 A7
Crawley Down RH10 ... 204 B8
Englefield Green TW20 ... 11 E3
Aldercombe La CR3 ... 100 E1
Alder Croft CR5 ... 79 F3
Alder Ct
Bracknell RG12 ... 27 B6
4 West Norwood SW16 ... 22 A3
Aldergrove Gdns TW4 ... 4 E5
Alderman Judge Mall 6 KT1 ... 37 E7
Alderman Willey Cl RG41 ... 25 B6
Aldermead TW3 ... 5 B3
Aldermoor Rd SE6 ... 23 F5
Alderney Ave TW5 ... 5 B7
Alder Rd
Headley Down GU35 ... 187 B6
Mortlake SW14 ... 7 D4
Alders Ave RH19 ... 185 E3
Aldersbrook Dr KT2 ... 17 F2
Aldersey Rd GU1 ... 109 F1
Aldersgrove KT8 ... 36 D4
ALDERSHOT ... 105 B1
Aldershot Garrison Sp Ctr GU11 ... 105 C6
Aldershot Military Mus★ GU11 ... 105 C7
Aldershot Rd
Ash GU12 ... 105 F1
Fairlands GU3 ... 108 D5
Aldershot Rd *continued*
Fleet GU14 ... 104 A6
Pirbright GU24 ... 87 F2
Wood St V GU3 ... 107 E5
Aldershot Sta GU11 ... 105 B1
Alderside Wlk TW20 ... 11 E3
Aldersmead Ave CR0 ... 43 D3
Aldersmead Rd BR3 ... 23 E1
Alders Rd RH2 ... 118 B3
Alderstead La RH1 ... 99 D2
Alders The
Badshot Lea GU9 ... 126 B6
Feltham TW13 ... 15 E4
Heston TW5 ... 4 F8
Streatham SW16 ... 21 C4
West Byfleet KT14 ... 71 C7
West Wickham BR4 ... 63 B8
Alders View Dr RH19 ... 185 E3
Alderton KT2 ... 38 B8
Alderton Ct KT8 ... 35 F5
Alderton Rd CR0 ... 43 A2
Alderwick Dr TW3 ... 5 D4
Alderwood Cl CR3 ... 100 E2
Aldingbourne Cl RH11 ... 200 F7
Aldis Mews SW17 ... 20 E3
Aldis St SW17 ... 20 E3
Aldous House TW18 ... 12 E4
Aldren Rd SW17 ... 20 C5
Aldrich Cres CR0 ... 63 C2
Aldrich Gdns SM3 ... 58 F7
Aldrich Terr SW18 ... 20 C6
Aldridge Pk RG42 ... 8 B2
Aldridge Rise KT3 ... 38 E3
Aldrington Rd SW16 ... 21 C4
Aldrin Pl GU14 ... 84 D4
Aldro Sch GU8 ... 149 C7
Aldwick Cl GU14 ... 85 A6
Aldwick Rd CR0 ... 60 F6
Aldworth Cl RG12 ... 27 A5
Aldworth Gdns RG45 ... 45 A5
Aldwych Cl RH10 ... 202 D4
Alexa Ct 3 SM2 ... 59 A4
Alexander Cl
Sandhurst GU47 ... 64 E7
Twickenham TW2 ... 16 F6
Alexander Cres CR3 ... 100 C6
Alexander Ct
Beckenham BR2 ... 44 D8
14 Surbiton KT6 ... 37 D2
Alexander Evans Mews SE23 ... 23 D6
Alexander Fleming Rd GU2 ... 129 D8
Alexander Godley Cl KT21 95 F8
Alexander Ho
14 Kingston upon Thames KT2 ... 37 E8
19 Sutton SM2 ... 59 C4
Alexander Lo SM1 ... 58 F5
Alexander Pl RH8 ... 122 E7
Alexander Rd
Coulsdon CR5 ... 79 B4
Egham TW20 ... 12 C3
Reigate RH2 ... 139 A6
Alexanders Wlk CR3 ... 101 A1
Alexander Wlk RG12 ... 27 B4
Alexandra Ave
Camberley GU15 ... 65 A5
Sutton SM1 ... 59 A7
Warlingham CR6 ... 81 F2
Alexandra Cl
Staines TW18 ... 13 D2
Walton-on-Thames KT12 ... 54 A8
Alexandra Cotts SE20 ... 23 D2
Alexandra Cres BR1 ... 24 F2
Alexandra Ct
Aldershot GU11 ... 104 E1
Biggin Hill TN16 ... 83 B1
10 Crawley RH10 ... 201 D5
1 Farnborough GU14 ... 85 C1
Alexandra Dr
Surbiton KT5 ... 38 A2
West Norwood SE19 ... 22 E3
Alexandra Gdns
Chiswick W4 ... 7 E7
Hounslow TW3 ... 5 B5
Knaphill GU21 ... 68 D1
Wallington SM5 ... 60 A2
Alexandra Ho SL5 ... 29 B6
Alexandra Inf Sch
17 Kingston upon Thames KT2 ... 18 A1
Penge BR3 ... 23 D1
Alexandra Jun & Inf Sch TW3 ... 5 B5
Alexandra Jun Sch SE26 ... 23 D2
Alexandra Lodge
12 Guildford GU1 ... 130 F8
1 Weybridge KT13 ... 53 B6
Alexandra Mans KT17 ... 76 F6
Alexandra Pl
Croydon CR0 ... 42 E1
Guildford GU1 ... 130 F7
South Norwood SE25 ... 42 D4
Alexandra Rd
Addlestone KT15 ... 52 D6
Aldershot GU11 ... 104 F2
Ashford TW15 ... 14 E2
Ash GU12 ... 105 F1
Biggin Hill TN16 ... 103 B8
12 Brentford TW8 ... 6 D8
Croydon CR0 ... 42 E2
Englefield Green TW20 ... 11 C2
Epsom KT17 ... 76 F6
Farnborough GU14, GU11 ... 85 C1
Hounslow TW3 ... 5 B5
Kingston upon Thames KT2 ... 18 A1
Mitcham CR4 ... 20 E1
Alexandra Rd *continued*
Mortlake SW14 ... 7 D4
Penge SE26 ... 23 D2
Richmond TW9 ... 6 F5
Thames Ditton KT7 ... 36 F4
Twickenham TW1 ... 6 C1
Warlingham CR6 ... 81 F2
Wimbledon SW19 ... 20 A3
Alexandra Sq SM4 ... 40 A4
Alexandra Terr GU1 ... 130 E8
Alexandra Way KT19 ... 76 A8
Alexandra Wlk 8 SE19 ... 22 E3
ALFOLD ... 193 F1
ALFOLD BARS ... 212 E7
Alfold By-Pass
Alfold Crossways GU6 ... 194 A5
Alfold GU6 ... 193 F7
Alfold Cotts GU6 ... 193 F2
Alfold Craft Ctr GU6 ... 194 A1
ALFOLD CROSSWAYS ... 194 A3
Alfold Crossways GU6 ... 194 A3
Alfold Rd
Cranleigh GU6 ... 194 B7
Dunsfold GU8 ... 193 B3
Alfonso Cl GU12 ... 126 C8
Alford Cl
Guildford GU4 ... 110 A4
Sandhurst GU47 ... 64 A7
Alford Ct 4 SM2 ... 59 B3
Alford Gn CR0 ... 63 D4
Alfred Butt Ho SW17 ... 20 F5
Alfred Cl RH10 ... 202 E5
Alfred Ct 3 CR3 ... 101 A8
Alfred Hurley Ho SW17 ... 20 C4
Alfred Rd
Croydon SE25 ... 43 A4
Farnham GU9 ... 125 C1
Feltham TW13 ... 15 C6
Kingston upon Thames KT1 ... 37 F6
Sutton SM1 ... 59 C5
Alfreton Cl SW19 ... 19 D5
Alfriston KT5 ... 37 F3
Alfriston Ave CR0 ... 41 E2
Alfriston Cl KT5 ... 37 F3
Alfriston Rd GU16 ... 86 C7
Algar Cl TW7 ... 6 A4
Algar Ct TW12 ... 36 B8
Algar Rd TW7 ... 6 A4
Algarve Rd SW18 ... 20 B7
Algernon Tollemache Almshos The TW10 ... 17 C5
Alice Gough Memorial Homes RG12 ... 27 B6
Alice Ho TW18 ... 13 A2
Alice Holt Woodland Park Forest Ctr★ GU10 ... 166 C8
Alice Mews 4 TW11 ... 16 F3
Alice Rd GU11 ... 105 B2
Alice Ruston Pl GU22 ... 89 C8
Alice Way TW3 ... 5 B3
Alicia Ave RH10 ... 202 C6
Alington Gr SM6 ... 60 D2
Alison Cl
Croydon CR0 ... 43 D1
Farnborough GU14 ... 84 F3
Woking GU21 ... 69 E4
Alison Dr GU15 ... 65 F5
Alison's Rd GU11 ... 105 B4
Alison Way GU11 ... 104 F2
Al Khair Prim & Sec Sch 8 CR0 ... 42 E1
Allan Cl KT3 ... 38 D4
Allbrook Cl TW11 ... 16 E3
Allbrook Ho 5 SW15 ... 19 A8
Allcard Cl RH12 ... 217 D4
Allcot Cl
Crawley RH11 ... 200 E3
East Bedfont TW14 ... 14 F7
Allcott Ho TW7 ... 5 F4
Allden Ave GU12 ... 126 D7
Allden Cotts GU7 ... 150 B4
Allden Gdns GU12 ... 126 D7
Alldens Hill GU5, GU8 ... 151 D1
Alldens La GU8 ... 151 B1
Allder Way CR2 ... 61 B3
Allenby Ave CR2 ... 61 C2
Allenby Rd
Biggin Hill TN16 ... 83 E2
Forest Hill SE23 ... 23 E5
Sandhurst GU15 ... 65 A6
Allen Cl
Mitcham CR4 ... 41 C8
Sunbury TW16 ... 35 B8
Allendale GU8 ... 148 C3
Allendale Cl
Forest Hill SE26 ... 23 D3
Sandhurst GU47 ... 45 A2
Allenford Ho SW15 ... 7 F1
All England Lawn Tennis & Croquet Club The★ SW19 ... 19 E5
Allen House Pk GU22 ... 89 C7
Allen Rd
Great Bookham KT23 ... 94 B1
Penge BR3 ... 43 D7
Sunbury TW16 ... 35 B7
Thornton Heath CR0 ... 42 A1
Allen's Cl RH19 ... 206 D6
Allenswood 12 SW19 ... 19 E7
Allerford Ct SE6 ... 24 B5
Allerford Rd SE6 ... 24 B4
Allerton Ct SM3 ... 58 D8
Allerton Ho 4 SW19 ... 20 C1
Alleyn Cres SE21 ... 22 D6
Alleyn Pk SE21 ... 22 E5

Alleyn Rd SE21....22 E5
Allgood Cl SM4....39 D3
All Hallows RC Sch GU9. 125 F7
Alliance Cl TW4....4 F2
Alliance Ct TW15....14 C4
Allingham Ct GU7....150 F7
Allingham Gdns RH12...218 B5
Allingham Rd RH2....139 A6
Allington Ave TW17....34 E6
Allington Cl SW19....19 D3
Allington Ct CR0....43 C3
Allison Gr SE21....22 E7
Alloway Cl **4** GU21....69 B1
All Saints' Benhilton CE Prim Sch **7** SM1....59 B7
All Saints (Carshalton) CE Prim Sch SM5....60 A5
All Saints CE Inf Sch GU10....147 C3
All Saint's CE Jun & Inf Schs SE19....42 E8
All Saints CE Prim Sch
  Horsham RH12....217 F6
  Merton SW19....20 C1
  Sutton SM1....59 C7
All Saints Cl RG40....25 C7
All Saints Ct TW5....4 D6
All Saints Dr CR2....81 A7
All Saints Prim Sch RG40. 25 D7
All Saints Rd
  Lightwater GU18....48 C1
  Merton SW19....20 C1
  Sutton SM1....59 C7
Allsmoor La RG12....27 F6
All Souls Ave GU24....88 B6
All Souls' Rd SL5....29 A5
Allum Gr KT20....97 B6
Allwood Cl SE26....23 D4
Allyington Way RH10....202 D5
Allyn Cl TW18....12 F2
Alma Cl
  Aldershot GU12....105 D2
  Knaphill GU21....68 E1
Alma Cres SM1....58 E5
Alma Ct
  3 Caterham CR3....100 C6
  Wokingham RG41....25 A5
Alma Gdns GU16....86 E8
Alma Ho
  Aldershot GU12....105 D2
  7 Brentford TW8....6 E8
Alma La GU9....125 C7
Alma Pl
  Penge SE19....22 F1
  Thornton Heath CR7....42 A4
Alma Rd
  Carshalton SM5....59 E5
  Headley Down GU35...187 C5
  Reigate RH2....118 B3
  Thames Ditton KT10, KT7..36 E1
Alma Sq GU14....105 C8
Alma Terr SW18....20 D8
Alma Way GU9....125 D7
Almer Rd SW20....19 A1
Almners Rd
  Chertsey KT16....32 C2
  Lyne KT16....32 B1
Almondale Ct GU14....85 A6
Almond Ave
  Carshalton SM5....59 F8
  Woking GU22....89 D6
Almond Cl
  Charlton TW17....34 C7
  Crawley RH11....201 A5
  Englefield Green TW20....11 B2
  Farnborough GU14....85 A7
  Feltham TW13....15 A7
  Guildford GU1....109 D5
Almond Gr TW8....6 B7
Almond Rd KT19....76 D8
Almond Way CR4....41 C5
Almorah Rd TW5....4 D6
Almsgate GU3....129 C2
Alms Heath GU23....92 B6
Almshouse La KT9....56 D2
Almshouses
  6 Dorking RH4....136 B8
  Lingfield RH7....164 C4
  Sunbury TW16....34 F5
Almshouses The RH5....115 C8
Alnod RH18....97 D8
Alnwick Gr SM4....40 B5
Alphabet Gdns SM5....40 D3
Alpha Ct CR6....81 A1
Alpha Hospl Woking (Private) GU21....68 D1
Alpha Rd
  Aldershot GU12....105 E1
  Chobham GU24....49 F1
  Crawley RH11....201 C6
  Croydon CR0....42 E1
  Surbiton KT5....37 F3
  Teddington TW11....16 D3
  Woking GU22....70 C4
Alpha Way TW20....32 C8
Alphea Cl SW19....20 E1
Alphington Ave GU16...65 F5
Alphington Gn GU16....65 F1
Alpine Ave KT5....57 C8
Alpine Cl
  Farnborough GU14....84 D3
  South Croydon CR0....61 E7
Alpine Rd
  Redhill RH1....119 A4
  Walton-on-Thames KT12..35 A2

Alpine View SM5....59 E5
Alresford Rd GU2....130 A8
Alric Ave KT3....38 F6
Al-Risaala Boys Sec Sch SW12....21 B8
Al-Risaala Girls Sec Sch SW17....20 F4
Alsace Wlk GU15....65 B1
Alsford Cl GU18....66 F7
Alsom Ave KT4....58 A6
Alston Cl KT7....37 B2
Alstonfield KT10....55 B5
Alston Rd SW17....20 D4
Altamont CR6....101 B8
Altdam Farm RH1....140 A2
Alterton Cl GU21....69 A2
Alt Gr SW19....19 E1
Althorne Rd RH1....140 A7
Althorp Rd SW17....20 F7
Alton Cl TW7....5 F5
Alton Ct
  19 Beckenham BR3....24 A1
  Egham TW18....32 E8
Alton Gdns
  Beckenham BR3....24 A1
  Twickenham TW2....16 D8
Alton Ho **1** RH1....119 A3
Alton Rd
  Croydon CR0, CR9....61 A7
  Farnham GU10, GU9...145 D7
  Richmond TW10, TW9....6 E3
  Roehampton SW15....19 A7
Alton Ride GU17....64 C6
Altyre Cl BR3....43 F4
Altyre Rd CR0, CR9....61 D8
Altyre Way BR3....43 F4
Alvernia Cl GU7....150 C2
Alvernia Lodge **4** SM1..59 B7
Alverstoke Gdns GU11..104 E1
Alverstone Ave SW18, SW19....20 A6
Alverstone Rd KT3....38 F5
Alverston Gdns SE25....42 E4
Alvia Gdns SM1....59 C6
Alway Ave KT19....57 D5
Alwen Cotts CR0....62 D6
Alwin Pl GU9....125 B7
Alwyn Cl CR0....63 B3
Alwyn Ct GU21....69 E3
Alwyne Mans SW19....19 F2
Alwyne Rd SW19....19 F2
Alwyns Cl **3** KT16....33 A3
Alwyns La KT16....33 A3
Amalgamated Dr TW8....6 B8
Amanda Ct TW15....13 F6
Aman Dalvi Ho SW18....19 E8
Ambassador RG12....26 F4
Ambassador Cl TW3....4 E5
Ambassadors The **2** GU21....69 E2
Ambassador The SL5....30 B2
Ambercroft Way CR5...100 B8
Amber Ct
  Aldershot GU12....105 C2
  Feltham TW13....14 E5
  Mitcham CR4....40 E5
  5 Staines TW18....12 F3
Amber Gdns GU14....85 A4
Amber Hill GU15....66 B4
Amberley Cl
  Crawley RH10....202 C6
  Horsham RH12....218 A6
  Send Marsh GU23....90 F2
Amberley Ct
  Beckenham BR3....23 F1
  Sutton SM2....59 C3
Amberley Dr KT15....70 F8
Amberley Gdns KT19....57 F6
Amberley Gr
  Croydon CR0....42 F2
  Forest Hill SE26....23 B3
Amberley Grange GU11. 125 E8
Amberley Lodge CR8....79 F6
Amberley Rd
  Horsham RH12....218 A6
  Milford GU8....149 E2
Amberley Way
  Heston TW4....4 C2
  Morden SM4....39 F2
Amberside Cl TW2....5 D1
Amberwood Cl SM6....60 E5
Amberwood Dr GU15...65 F7
Amberwood Rise KT3....38 E3
Amblecote KT11....73 E7
Ambleside
  Catford BR1....24 D2
  Crowthorne RG45....45 C4
  Godalming GU7....151 A5
  13 Putney SW19....19 E7
Ambleside Ave
  Beckenham BR3....43 E4
  Streatham SW16....21 D4
  Walton-on-Thames TW16.35 C1
Ambleside Cl
  Crawley RH11....200 D5
  Farnborough GU14....84 E3
  Mytchett GU16....86 A2
  Redhill RH1....140 B4
Ambleside Cres GU9...125 A6
Ambleside Dr TW14....14 F7
Ambleside Gdns
  Selsdon CR2....62 D1
  Streatham SW16....21 D3
  Sutton SM2....59 C4
Ambleside Rd GU18....67 B8
Ambleside Way TW20...12 B1
Ambrey Way CR8, SM6..60 D2

Ambrook Ct SM1....59 D5
Amen Cnr SW17....21 A2
Amen Corner Bsns Pk RG12....26 D7
Amenity Way SM4....39 C2
American Magna Carta Meml★ TW20....11 D6
Amersham Rd CR0....42 D3
Amesbury Ave SW2....21 F6
Amesbury Cl KT4....39 C1
Amesbury Rd TW13....15 D6
Amesbury Sch GU26...188 E1
Amey Dr KT23....94 C3
Amhurst Gdns TW7....6 A5
Amis Ave
  Chessington KT19....57 B5
  Woodham KT15....52 A1
Amis Rd GU21....88 E8
Amity Gr SW20....39 C8
Amlets La GU6....174 E5
Ampere Way CR0, CR9...41 F1
Amroth Cl SE23....23 B7
Amstel Way GU21....68 F1
Amundsen Rd RH12...217 D6
Amyand Cotts **12** TW1....6 B1
Amyand Park Gdns **3** TW1....17 B8
Amyand Park Rd TW1....17 A8
Amy Cl SM6....60 E3
Amy Johnson Prim Sch SM6....60 E3
Amy Rd RH8....122 E6
Anarth Ct KT13....34 E1
Ancaster Cres KT3....39 A3
Ancaster Dr SL5....28 E8
Ancaster Rd BR3....43 D6
Anchester Mews BR3....43 D6
Anchorage Cl SW19....20 A3
Anchor Cl GU21....69 A2
Anchor Cotts RH7....163 E4
Anchor Cres **7** GU21....68 D2
Anchor Hill GU21....68 D2
Anchor Mdw GU14....84 F4
Anders Cnr RG42....26 F8
Anderson Cl
  Cheam SM3....40 A1
  Epsom KT19....76 B7
Anderson Ct
  Haslemere GU27....208 C6
  Redhill RH1....140 A6
Anderson Dr TW15....14 C4
Anderson Ho
  Farnham GU9....125 D1
  Upper Tooting SW17....20 D3
Anderson Pl GU19....47 E4
Anderson Rd KT13....53 D7
Anderson's Pl TW3....5 B3
Andhurst Ct KT2....38 B8
Andon Ct BR3....43 E6
Andover Cl
  East Bedfont TW14....14 F7
  Epsom KT19....76 D8
Andover Ct
  North Cheam KT4....58 B8
  Stanwell TW19....13 D8
Andover Rd
  Blackwater GU17....64 C6
  Twickenham TW2....16 D7
Andover Way GU11....126 B7
Andrecht Terr CR4....41 D5
Andreck Ct BR3....44 C7
Andrewartha Rd GU14..85 E2
Andrew Ct RG40....25 E5
Andrew Ct
  Beckenham BR3....44 B6
  Farnborough GU14....84 F8
  Forest Hill SE23....23 D6
Andrewes Ho SM1....59 A6
Andrew Ewing Prim Sch The TW5....4 F7
Andrew Reed Ho SW18..19 E8
Andrews Cl KT4....58 D8
Andrew's Cl KT17....76 F6
Andrew's Ho CR8....79 F6
Andrews Rd GU14....84 E5
Andrew Wilmot Ct SW19.20 C7
Andromeda Cl RH11....200 E4
ANERLEY....43 B8
Anerley Ct SE20....23 B1
Anerley Gr SE19....22 F1
Anerley Hill SE19....22 F2
Anerley Park Rd SE20....23 B1
Anerley Pk SE20....23 B1
Anerley Rd SE20, SE19....43 B8
Anerley Sta SE20....43 B8
Anerley Station Rd SE20..43 B8
Anerley Vale **3** SE19....23 A1
Anfield Cl SW12....21 C8
Angas Ct **1** KT13....53 C5
Angela Ct **2** SE23....23 C7
Angel Ct
  Compton GU3....129 A3
  9 Godalming GU7....150 D4
Angelfield TW3....5 B2
Angel Gate GU1....130 D8
Angel Hill SM1....59 B7
Angel Hill Ct **2** SM1....59 B7
Angel Hill Dr SM1....59 B7
Angelica Gdns CR0....43 D1
Angelica Rd
  Bisley GU24....68 A4
  Guildford GU2....109 A5
Angell Cl RH10....202 C5
Angel Ho RH2....139 B6

Angel Rd KT7....37 A1
Angers Cl GU15....66 C7
Anglers Reach KT6....37 D4
Anglesea Ho KT1....37 D5
Anglesea Rd KT1....37 D5
Anglesey Ave GU14....84 F7
Anglesey Cl
  Ashford TW15....14 A5
  Crawley RH11....201 C2
Anglesey Court Rd SM5..60 A4
Anglesey Gdns SM5....60 A4
Anglesey Rd GU12....105 D1
Angles Rd SW16....21 E4
Anglo American Laundry SW17....20 C5
Angus Cl
  Chessington KT9....57 A5
  Horsham RH12....217 D4
Angus Ho **10** SW12....21 D8
Anlaby Rd TW11....16 E3
Annandale Dr GU10....146 D6
Annandale Rd
  Croydon CR0....62 A8
  Guildford GU2....130 B7
Anne Armstrong Cl GU11....105 D5
Anne Boleyn's Wlk
  Cheam SM3....58 E3
  Kingston upon Thames KT2.17 E3
Anne Compton Mews **2** SE12....24 F8
Anners Cl TW20....32 C6
Annes Ct SE3....24 A3
Annesley Dr CR0....62 F7
Anne's Wlk CR3....100 E7
Annett Cl TW17....34 E5
Annett Rd KT12....35 A2
Anne Way KT8....36 B5
Annie Brookes Cl TW18..12 D5
Anningsley Pk KT16....51 C1
Annisdowne Cl RH5....133 F1
Ann Parkes Ct TW5....4 D5
Annsworthy Ave CR7, SE25....42 D6
Annsworthy Cres CR7....42 D7
Ansell Gr SM5....41 A1
Ansell Rd
  Dorking RH4....136 B8
  Frimley GU16....65 E1
  Upper Tooting SW17....20 F5
Anselm Cl CR0....61 F7
Ansford Rd BR1, SE6....24 D4
Ansley Cl CR2....81 B5
Anslie Wlk **9** SW12....21 B8
Anson Cl GU11....104 F3
Anson Ct TW19....13 E8
ANSTEADBROOK....209 C5
Anstey Cl GU9....125 E3
Anstice Cl W4....7 E7
Anstiebury Cl RH5....157 C3
Anstie Grange Dr RH5...157 B5
Anstie La RH5....156 F4
Anston Ct **5** GU2....108 E1
Anthony Ct TW7....5 F4
Anthony Ho CR5....99 D5
Anthony Rd CR0, SE25....43 A3
ANTHONYS....70 A7
Anthony West Ho RH3...137 B7
Antigua Wlk SE19....22 D3
Antlands La RH6....182 E5
Antlands Lane E RH6....182 F5
Antlands Lane W RH6....182 E6
Anton Cres SM1....59 A7
Antrobus Cl SM1....58 F5
Anvil Cl SW16....21 C1
Anvil La KT11....73 A5
Anvil Rd TW16....35 A6
Anyards Rd KT11....73 B5
Anzio Cl GU11....105 A2
Anzio Gdns CR3....100 C6
Aostle Way CR7....42 B7
Apeldoorn Dr SM6....60 E2
Aperdele Rd KT22....75 A1
APERFIELD....83 F2
Aperfield Rd TN16....83 E2
Apers Ave GU22....89 F6
Apex Cl BR3....44 B8
Apex Dr GU16....65 D1
Apex Ret Pk TW13....15 F5
Apley Rd RH2....139 A6
Aplin Ct SM1....59 B4
Aplin Way
  Hounslow TW7....5 E6
  Lightwater GU18....48 A1
Apollo Pl GU21....89 A8
Apollo Rise GU14....84 D4
Apperlie Dr RH6....161 C1
Appleby Cl TW2....16 D6
Appleby Ct GU15....65 B6
Appleby Gdns SW14....14 F7
Appledore RG12....26 F3
Appledore Cl
  1 Hayes BR2....44 F4
  Upper Tooting SW12, SW17. 20 F6
Appledore Mews GU14..85 A7
Appledown Rise CR5....79 C4
Applefield RH10....201 E7
Applegarth
  Claygate KT10....55 F5
  New Addington CR0....63 B3
Apple Garth GU7....150 C7
Applegarth Ave GU2....108 D1
Applegarth Jun & Inf Schs CR0....63 B4
Apple Gr KT9....56 E6
Applelands Cl GU10....146 A4
Apple Mkt KT1....37 D7

Appleton Gdns KT3....39 A3
Appleton Sq CR4....40 E8
Appletree Ct
  Godalming GU7....150 F2
  6 Penge SE20....43 B8
Apple Tree Cl KT23....94 C3
Appletree Ct GU4....110 D3
Appletree Pl **4** RG42....27 A8
Appletrees Pl GU22....89 C8
Apple Tree Way GU47....45 D1
Appley Ct GU15....65 B6
Appley Dr GU15....65 B6
Approach Rd
  Ashford TW15....14 C2
  East Molesey KT8....36 A4
  Farnham GU9....125 C1
  Merton SW20....39 C7
  Purley CR8....80 B7
  Tatsfield TN16....103 B5
Approach The RH19....185 F6
April Cl
  Ashtead KT21....75 F1
  Camberley GU15....65 C2
  Feltham TW13....15 A5
  Horsham RH12....217 C4
April Glen SE23....23 D5
Aprilwood Cl KT15....70 F8
Apsley Cl
  Crawley RH11....200 F4
  Sutton SM2....59 C4
Apsley Ho **1** TW4....4 F3
Apsley Rd
  Croydon SE25....43 B5
  Kingston upon Thames KT3.38 C6
Aqua Ho KT16....33 C2
Aquarius TW1....17 B7
Aquarius Ct RH11....200 E4
Aquatice **10** GU1....130 C8
Aquila Cl KT21....95 E6
Arabella Dr SW15....7 E3
Araby Cnr TW17....34 C3
Aragon Ave
  Ewell KT17....58 B2
  Thames Ditton KT7....36 F4
Aragon Cl
  Ashford TW16....14 F1
  New Addington CR0....63 E1
Aragon Ct
  Bracknell RG12....27 C5
  East Molesey KT8....36 C5
  Epsom KT19....57 E1
  4 Knaphill GU21....68 D2
Aragon Pl SM4....39 E2
Aragon Prim Sch SM4....39 D2
Aragon Rd
  Kingston upon Thames KT2....17 E3
  West Barnes SM4....39 E2
Aragon Wlk KT14....71 F6
Aragorn Ct GU2....109 B3
Aram Ct GU22....70 B4
Arbor Cl BR3....44 B7
Arborfield Cl SW2....21 F7
Arbor Ct KT22....94 F4
Arbour Cotts GU2....108 F5
Arbour The GU7....128 F1
Arbrook Chase KT10....55 C4
Arbrook Ct KT9....56 D5
Arbrook Hall KT10....55 F4
Arbrook La KT10....55 D4
Arbury Terr SE26....23 B5
Arbutus Cl RH1....139 C7
Arbutus Rd RH1....139 C6
Arcade Sh Ctr The **11** GU11....105 A2
Arcade The **5** CR0....61 C7
Arcadia Cl SM5....60 A6
Arcadian Pl SW18....19 F8
Archbishop Lanfranc Sch The CR0....61 F7
Archbishop's Pl **3** SW2..21 F8
Archbishop Tenison's CE Sch CR0....61 F7
Archdale Pl KT3....38 B6
Archdeacon Cambridge's CE Prim Sch **7** TW2....16 C6
Archer Cl KT2....17 E1
Archer Ct TW13....15 A7
Archer Ho TW10....7 A3
Archer Mews TW12....16 C2
Archer Rd SE25....43 B5
Archers Ct
  Crawley RH10....201 D8
  3 Croydon CR2....61 C5
  10 Redhill RH1....139 F8
Archery Pl GU5....133 C4
Arch Rd KT12....54 D7
Archway Cl
  Wallington SM6....60 E7
  Wimbledon SW19....20 B4
Archway Mews **9** RH4..136 A8
Archway Pl RH4....136 A8
Archway St SW13, SW14....7 E4
Arcturus Rd RH11....200 E3
Arcus Rd BR1....24 E2
Arden **17** SW19....19 D7
Arden Cl
  Bracknell RG12....28 A7
  Reigate RH2....139 B5
Arden Mead Cotts RH7..164 A8
Arden Rd RH10....201 F4
Ardenrun RH7....164 B8
Ardenrun Cotts RH7....164 A7
Ardent Cl SE25....42 E6
Ardesley Wood SE13....53 E6
Ardfern Ave SW16....42 A6
Ardfillan Rd SE6....24 D6
Ardgowan Rd SE6....24 E7

Ardingly RG12 . . . 27 A4
Ardingly Cl
Crawley RH11 . . . 201 B8
South Croydon CR0 . . . 62 D7
Ardingly Ct KT18 . . . 76 D5
Ardleigh Gdns SM3 . . . 40 A2
Ardley Cl SE23, SE6 . . . 23 E5
Ardlui Rd SE27 . . . 22 C6
Ardmay Gdns KT6 . . . 37 E4
Ardmore Ave GU2 . . . 109 B3
Ardmore Ho GU2 . . . 109 B3
Ardmore Way GU2 . . . 109 B3
Ardoch Rd SE6 . . . 24 D6
Ardrossan Ave GU15 . . . 66 A5
Ardrossan Gdns KT4 . . . 58 A7
Ardshiel Dr RH1 . . . 139 E7
Ardwell Rd SW2 . . . 21 E6
Ardwick Ct GU14 . . . 85 C2
Arena Halt SE25 . . . 43 C4
Arena La GU11 . . . 104 E5
Arena L Ctr GU15 . . . 65 C6
Arenal Dr RG45 . . . 45 C3
Arena The RG12 . . . 27 A7
Arethusa Way GU24 . . . 67 F3
Arford Comm GU35 . . . 187 A6
Argent Cl TW20 . . . 12 C2
Argent Ct KT6 . . . 57 A7
Argent Terr GU47 . . . 64 E8
Argonaut Pk SL3 . . . 1 F6
Argosy Gdns TW18 . . . 12 F2
Argosy La TW19 . . . 13 D8
Argus Wlk 11 RH11 . . . 201 A3
Argyle Ave TW2, TW3 . . . 5 A1
Argyle Ct TW11 . . . 16 E3
Argyle Ho SM2 . . . 59 C4
Argyle Rd TW3 . . . 5 B2
Argyle St GU24 . . . 87 A6
Argyll Ct
Crawley RH11 . . . 201 D5
15 Streatham SW2 . . . 21 E8
Argyll Ho TW10 . . . 17 C6
Ariel Way TW4 . . . 4 B4
Arista Ct TW20 . . . 11 D2
Arkell Gr SE19 . . . 22 B1
Arkendale RH19 . . . 185 A4
Arkindale Rd SE6 . . . 24 C5
Arklow Mews 3 KT6 . . . 56 E8
Arkwright Dr RG42 . . . 26 D7
Arkwright Ho 22 SW2 . . . 21 E8
Arkwright Rd
Poyle SL3 . . . 1 E5
South Croydon CR2 . . . 61 F2
Arlington Bsns Pk RG42 . . 27 B7
Arlington Cl
Bracknell RG42 . . . 27 A8
Sutton SM1 . . . 59 A8
Twickenham TW1 . . . 6 C1
Arlington Ct
Reigate RH2 . . . 118 A3
4 Twickenham TW1 . . . 6 C1
Arlington Dr SM5 . . . 59 F8
Arlington Lodge KT13 . . . 53 B6
Arlington Rd
Ashford TW15 . . . 13 F3
Richmond TW10 . . . 17 D6
Surbiton KT6 . . . 37 D3
Teddington TW11 . . . 16 F4
Twickenham TW1 . . . 6 C1
Arlington Sq RG12 . . . 27 A7
Arlington Terr GU11 . . . 104 F2
Armadale Rd
Feltham TW14 . . . 4 A2
Woking GU21 . . . 69 A2
Armeston KT3 . . . 38 D2
Armfield Cl KT8 . . . 35 F4
Armfield Cotts 5 CR4 . . . 40 F7
Armfield Cres CR4 . . . 40 F7
Armistice Gdns SE25 . . . 43 A6
Armitage Ct SL5 . . . 29 C3
Armitage Dr GU16 . . . 65 F1
Armstrong Cl KT12 . . . 35 A3
Armstrong Mall GU14 . . . 84 D4
Armstrong Rd
Englefield Green TW20 . . . 11 C2
Feltham TW13 . . . 15 E3
Armstrong Way GU14 . . . 84 B1
Army Medical Services Mus★
GU12 . . . 86 B1
Armytage Rd TW5 . . . 4 D7
Arnal Cres SW18 . . . 19 E8
Arncliffe RG12 . . . 27 A4
Arndale Way TW20 . . . 12 A3
Arndell Ho 3 SM1 . . . 59 C6
Arne Cl RH11 . . . 200 F3
Arne Gr RH6 . . . 160 E5
Arnella Ct 3 GU14 . . . 105 D8
Arnewood Cl
Oxshott KT22 . . . 74 B5
Roehampton SW15 . . . 19 A7
Arney's La CR4 . . . 41 A3
Arnfield Cl RH11 . . . 200 E5
Arngask Rd SE6 . . . 24 D8
Arnhem Cl GU11 . . . 105 B2
Arnhem Dr CR0 . . . 82 D8
Arnison Rd KT8 . . . 36 D5
Arnold Cres TW7 . . . 5 D2
Arnold Dr KT9 . . . 56 D4
Arnold Ho CR0 . . . 61 B6
Arnold Rd
Mitcham SW17 . . . 20 F1
Sheerwater GU21 . . . 70 B4
Staines TW18 . . . 13 C1
Arnulf St SE6 . . . 24 B4
Arnull's Rd SW16 . . . 22 B2
Arona Ho TW16 . . . 35 A8
Arosa Rd 16 TW1 . . . 6 D1
Arragon Gdns
Streatham SW16 . . . 21 E1
Arragon Gdns *continued*
West Wickham BR4 . . . 63 B7
Arragon Rd
Twickenham TW1 . . . 17 A8
Wandsworth SW18 . . . 20 A7
Arran Cl
Crawley RH11 . . . 201 B3
Wallington SM6 . . . 60 C6
Arrancourt 1 RH12 . . . 217 B2
Arran Rd SE6 . . . 24 C6
Arran Way KT10 . . . 55 B8
Arras Ave SM4 . . . 40 C4
Arreton Mead GU21 . . . 69 F5
Arrivals Rd RH6 . . . 181 F8
Arrol Rd BR3 . . . 43 D6
Arrow Ind Est GU14 . . . 84 F2
Arrow Rd GU14 . . . 84 F2
Artel Croft RH10 . . . 202 A6
Artemis Pl SW18 . . . 19 F8
Artemis Sch of Speech &
Drama RH19 . . . 205 E6
Arterberry Rd SW20,
SW19 . . . 39 D8
Arthur Cl
Bagshot GU19 . . . 47 E1
Farnham GU9 . . . 125 B1
Arthur Ct CR0 . . . 61 D7
Arthur Jacob Nature
Reserve★ SL3 . . . 1 C4
Arthur Rd
Biggin Hill TN16 . . . 83 C3
Crawley RH11 . . . 200 E6
Farnham GU9 . . . 125 C1
Horsham RH13 . . . 217 D1
6 Kingston upon Thames
KT2 . . . 18 A1
West Barnes KT3 . . . 39 B4
Wimbledon SW19 . . . 20 A5
Wokingham RG41 . . . 25 A6
Arthur's Bridge Rd GU21 . 69 D2
Arthur St GU11 . . . 105 B2
Artillery Rd
1 Aldershot GU11 . . . 105 B2
Farnborough GU11, GU14 105 D8
7 Guildford GU1 . . . 109 D1
Artillery Terr GU1 . . . 109 D1
ARTINGTON . . . 130 C4
Artington Wlk GU2 . . . 130 C6
Arundale KT1 . . . 37 D5
Arundel Ave
Ewell KT17 . . . 58 B1
Merton SM4 . . . 39 F5
South Croydon CR2 . . . 62 A1
Arundel Cl
Crawley RH10 . . . 202 C6
Croydon CR0, CR9 . . . 61 B7
Hampton TW12 . . . 16 B3
Arundel Ct
4 Beckenham BR2 . . . 44 E7
Croydon CR0 . . . 61 B7
Arundel Ho
Croydon CR0 . . . 61 D5
Guildford GU1 . . . 130 D8
Reigate RH2 . . . 139 B5
Richmond TW10 . . . 7 A2
Arundell Pl 13 GU9 . . . 125 B2
Arundel Rd
Belmont SM2 . . . 58 F3
Dorking RH4 . . . 136 A7
Frimley GU15 . . . 66 C4
Hounslow TW4 . . . 4 C4
Kingston upon Thames KT1 . 38 C7
Thornton Heath CR0 . . . 42 D3
Arun Ho
8 New Malden KT3 . . . 38 E5
7 Teddington KT2 . . . 37 D8
Arunside RH12 . . . 217 A1
Arunside Prim Sch RH12 217 A2
Arun Way RH13 . . . 217 E1
Ascalon Ct 19 SW2 . . . 21 F8
Ascent Ho KT13 . . . 53 E5
Aschurch Rd CR0 . . . 42 F2
ASCOT . . . 29 A6
Ascot Ct GU11 . . . 105 A1
Ascot Heath CE Jun Sch
SL5 . . . 8 E1
Ascot Heath Inf Sch SL5 . . . 8 E1
Ascot Ho
8 Egham TW20 . . . 12 A3
Penge SE26 . . . 23 B2
Ascot Mews SM6 . . . 60 C2
Ascot Race Course SL5 . . 28 F6
Ascot Rd
East Bedfont TW14 . . . 14 B6
Mitcham SW17 . . . 21 A2
Ascot Sta SL5 . . . 29 A5
Ascot Towers SL5 . . . 28 F7
Ascot Wood SL5 . . . 29 A6
ASH . . . 106 B3
Ashbourne RG12 . . . 26 F3
Ashbourne Cl
Ash GU12 . . . 106 C3
Coulsdon CR5 . . . 79 C1
Ashbourne Rd CR4, SW17 . 21 A1
Ashbourne Terr 1 SW19 . 20 A1
Ashbrook Rd SL4 . . . 11 B8
Ashburnham Pk KT10 . . . 55 C6
Ashburnham Rd
Crawley RH10 . . . 202 A4
Richmond TW10 . . . 17 B5
Ashburton Ave CR0 . . . 43 B1
Ashburton Cl CR0 . . . 43 A1
Ashburton Gdns CR0 . . . 62 A8
Ashburton Ho SM6 . . . 60 D5
Ashburton Rd CR0, CR9 . . . 62 A8
Ashbury Cres GU4 . . . 110 C3
Ashbury Dr GU17 . . . 65 A1
Ashbury Pl SW19 . . . 20 C2
Ashby Ave KT9 . . . 57 A4
Ashby Ct RH13 . . . 217 E1
Ashby Grange 7 SM6 . . . 60 C4
Ashby Ho 13 KT6 . . . 37 E3
Ashby Way UB7 . . . 3 A7
Ashby Wlk CR0 . . . 42 C3
Ash Church Mews GU12 . 106 A2
Ash Church Rd GU12 . . . 106 B2
Ash Cl
Ash GU12 . . . 106 B3
Blackwater GU17 . . . 64 C5
Box Hill KT20 . . . 116 C4
Carshalton SM5 . . . 59 F8
Crawley Down RH10 . . . 204 C8
Kingston upon Thames KT3 . 38 D7
Lingfield RH7 . . . 164 E5
Merstham RH1 . . . 119 C5
Penge SE20 . . . 43 C7
Pyrford GU22 . . . 71 A4
Woking GU22 . . . 89 E7
Ash Combe GU8 . . . 191 A4
Ashcombe Ave KT6 . . . 37 D2
Ashcombe Cl TW15 . . . 13 E5
Ashcombe Par GU22 . . . 90 A7
Ashcombe Rd
Dorking RH4 . . . 115 A1
Merstham RH1 . . . 119 C8
Wallington SM5 . . . 60 A4
Wimbledon SW19 . . . 20 A3
Ashcombe Sch The RH4 . 115 B1
Ashcombe Sq KT3 . . . 38 C6
Ashcombe Terr KT20 . . . 97 B7
Ashcroft GU4 . . . 130 E2
Ashcroft Ct SE26 . . . 23 C5
Ashcroft Pk KT11 . . . 73 E6
Ashcroft Pl 5 KT22 . . . 95 C6
Ashcroft Rd KT9 . . . 56 F7
Ashcroft Rise CR5 . . . 79 E3
Ash Ct
Addlestone KT15 . . . 52 B5
Ashford TW15 . . . 14 C3
East Grinstead RH19 . . . 185 E3
9 Merton SW19 . . . 19 E1
Ottershaw KT16 . . . 51 C5
West Ewell KT19 . . . 57 C6
3 West Norwood SW16 . . . 22 A3
Ashdale KT23 . . . 94 C1
Ashdale Cl
Stanwell TW19 . . . 13 E6
Twickenham TW2 . . . 16 C8
Ashdale Way TW2 . . . 16 B8
Ashdene Cl TW15 . . . 14 C1
Ashdene Cres GU12 . . . 106 A3
Ashdene House TW20 . . . 11 C2
Ashdene Rd GU12 . . . 106 A2
Ashdown Ave GU14 . . . 85 E2
Ashdown Cl
13 Beckenham BR3 . . . 44 B7
Bracknell RG12 . . . 28 A7
Reigate RH2 . . . 139 B5
7 Woking GU22 . . . 89 E8
Ashdown Ct
Crawley RH10 . . . 201 F3
Dulwich SE22 . . . 23 A7
Epsom KT17 . . . 76 F6
Horsham RH13 . . . 217 F4
New Malden KT4 . . . 38 F2
Sutton SM2 . . . 59 C4
Ashdown Dr RH10 . . . 201 E3
Ashdown Gate RH19 . . . 185 D2
Ashdown Gdns CR2 . . . 81 B4
Ashdown Pl
Ewell KT17 . . . 57 F3
Thames Ditton KT7 . . . 37 A2
Ashdown Rd
Ewell KT17 . . . 77 A6
Forest Row RH18 . . . 206 F2
Kingston upon Thames KT1 . 37 E7
Reigate RH2 . . . 139 B5
Ashdown View RH19 . . . 205 E7
Ashdown Way SW17 . . . 21 A6
Ash Dr RH1 . . . 140 B7
Ashe Ho 21 TW1 . . . 6 D1
Ashely Cotts KT21 . . . 95 F8
Ashenden Rd GU2 . . . 108 F1
Ashen Gr SW19 . . . 20 A6
Ashen Vale CR2 . . . 62 D2
Asher Dr SL5 . . . 28 C8
Ashfield RH14 . . . 211 E2
Ashfield Ave TW13 . . . 15 B7
Ashfield Cl
Ashtead KT21 . . . 95 E8
Beckenham BR3 . . . 24 A1
Richmond TW10 . . . 17 E7
Ashfields RH2 . . . 118 B3
ASHFORD . . . 13 F2
Ashford Ave TW15 . . . 14 B2
Ashford Bsns Complex
TW15 . . . 14 C4
Ashford CE Prim Sch
TW15 . . . 14 B2
Ashford Cl TW15 . . . 13 E4
ASHFORD COMMON . . . 14 D2
Ashford Cres TW15 . . . 13 E5
Ashford Gdns KT11 . . . 73 D3
Ashford Hospl TW15 . . . 13 E6
Ashford Ind Est TW15 . . . 14 C4
Ashford Park Prim Sch
TW15 . . . 13 D4
Ashford Rd
Feltham TW13, TW15 . . . 14 E5
Littleton Common TW15,
TW17 . . . 14 C1
Staines TW18 . . . 33 D8
Ashford Sta TW15 . . . 13 F5
Ash Gr
East Bedfont TW14 . . . 14 E7
Guildford GU2 . . . 109 A2
Ash Gr *continued*
Heston TW5 . . . 4 D7
Penge SE20 . . . 43 C7
Staines TW18 . . . 13 C2
West Wickham BR4 . . . 44 C1
Ash Grange Prim Sch
GU12 . . . 106 B2
ASH GREEN . . . 106 C1
Ash Green Lane E GU12 . 127 C8
Ash Green Lane W GU12 . 127 C8
Ash Green Rd GU12 . . . 106 C1
Ashgrove Rd
Ashford TW15 . . . 14 D3
Catford BR1 . . . 24 D2
Ash Hill Rd GU12 . . . 106 B3
Ash Ho TW11 . . . 17 C1
Ashington Ct 3 RH12 . . . 217 D5
Ash Keys RH10 . . . 201 E5
Ash La GU8 . . . 148 C2
Ashlake Rd SW16 . . . 21 E4
Ashlea Ct CR6 . . . 81 A1
Ashlea Ho TW15 . . . 13 F3
Ashleigh Ave TW20 . . . 12 C1
Ashleigh Cl RH6 . . . 160 F3
Ashleigh Cotts RH5 . . . 157 B7
Ashleigh Ct SE26 . . . 23 B2
Ashleigh Gdns SM1 . . . 59 B8
Ashleigh Ho
1 Mortlake SW14 . . . 7 E4
Streatham SW16 . . . 21 F4
Ashleigh Point 8 SE26 . . . 23 D5
Ashleigh Rd
Horsham RH12 . . . 217 C4
Mortlake SW14 . . . 7 E4
Penge SE20 . . . 43 B6
Ashley Ave
Epsom KT18 . . . 76 D6
Morden SM4 . . . 40 A4
Ashley Cl
Frimley GU16 . . . 86 A6
Little Bookham KT23 . . . 93 F2
Oatlands Park KT12, KT13 . 34 F1
Ashley Ct
5 Epsom KT18 . . . 76 D6
Knaphill GU21 . . . 68 F1
Ashley Ctr KT18 . . . 219 D6
Ashley Dr
Banstead SM7 . . . 78 A5
Blackwater GU17 . . . 64 C4
Hounslow TW7 . . . 5 E8
Twickenham TW2 . . . 16 B7
Walton-on-Thames KT12 . . . 54 A7
Ashley Gdns
Richmond TW10 . . . 17 D6
Shalford GU4 . . . 130 F2
Ashley Ho GU7 . . . 150 E8
Ashley La CR0 . . . 61 B6
ASHLEY PARK . . . 54 A7
Ashley Park Ave KT12 . . . 53 F8
Ashley Park Cres KT12 . . . 35 A1
Ashley Park Rd KT12 . . . 54 A7
Ashley Pl 5 KT12 . . . 35 A1
Ashley Prim Sch KT12 . . . 35 A1
Ashley Rd
Epsom KT18 . . . 76 E4
Farnborough GU14 . . . 85 D4
Hampton TW12 . . . 36 A8
Knaphill GU21 . . . 68 F1
Richmond TW9 . . . 6 E4
Thames Ditton KT7 . . . 36 F3
Thornton Heath CR7 . . . 41 F5
Walton-on-Thames KT12 . . . 54 A8
Westcott RH4 . . . 135 C6
Wimbledon SW19 . . . 20 B2
Ashley Rise KT12 . . . 54 A7
Ashley Way GU24 . . . 67 D6
Ashling Rd CR0, CR9 . . . 43 A1
Ash Lodge 2 TW16 . . . 14 F1
Ash Lodge Cl GU12 . . . 106 A1
Ash Lodge Dr GU12 . . . 106 A1
Ashlyn's Pk KT11 . . . 73 E6
Ashlyns Way KT9 . . . 56 D4
Ashman Ct CR2 . . . 61 B2
Ash Manor Sch GU12 . . . 126 F8
Ash Manor Sp Ctr GU12 . 126 F8
Ashmead Rd TW14 . . . 15 A7
Ashmere Ave BR3 . . . 44 D7
Ashmere Cl SM3 . . . 58 D5
Ash Mews KT18 . . . 76 E5
Ashmill Ct CR0 . . . 42 C3
Ashmore Ct
Catford SE6 . . . 24 E7
Heston TW5 . . . 5 A8
Ashmore Ho RH11 . . . 181 D1
Ashmore La
Biggin Hill BR2 . . . 83 C8
Rusper RH12 . . . 199 C6
Ash Rd
Aldershot GU12 . . . 126 D8
Cheam SM3, SM4 . . . 39 F1
Crawley RH10 . . . 202 A8
Croydon CR0 . . . 63 A8
Littleton TW17 . . . 34 A5
Pirbright GU24 . . . 88 A1
Woking GU22 . . . 89 E7
Ashridge GU14 . . . 84 F7
Ashridge Gn 2 RG42 . . . 27 B8
Ashridge Rd RG40 . . . 25 D8
Ashridge Way
Ashford TW16 . . . 15 A2
Merton SM4, SW20 . . . 39 F5
Ash St GU12 . . . 106 A1
Ash Sta GU12 . . . 106 B2
Ashstead La GU7 . . . 150 C2
Ashstead Sta KT21 . . . 75 E3
ASHTEAD . . . 75 E1
Ashtead Ct 15 SW19 . . . 19 D7
Ashtead Hospl (Private)
KT21 . . . 95 E8
Ashtead La GU7 . . . 150 D2
Ashtead National Nature
Reserve★ KT21 . . . 75 D4
Ashtead Pk Nature Reserve★
KT21 . . . 76 A1
Ashtead Woods Rd KT21 . . 75 C3
Ashton Cl
Cheam SM1 . . . 59 A6
Hersham KT12 . . . 54 B4
Ashton Ct
1 Beckenham BR3 . . . 43 F8
Woking GU21 . . . 69 F3
Ashton Gdns TW4 . . . 4 F3
Ashton Ho SW15 . . . 19 B8
Ashton House Sch TW7 . . . 5 D6
Ashton Rd 2 GU21 . . . 68 F2
Ashtree Ave CR4 . . . 40 D7
Ash Tree Cl
Croydon BR3, CR0 . . . 43 E3
Farnborough GU14 . . . 84 C3
Grayswood GU27 . . . 189 F1
1 Surbiton KT6 . . . 37 E1
Ashtree Ct TW15 . . . 14 B3
Ashtrees GU6 . . . 174 E1
Ashtrees The GU12 . . . 106 B2
Ash Tree Villas CR0 . . . 41 F3
Ash Tree Way CR0 . . . 43 E3
Ashurst 3 KT18 . . . 76 D6
Ashurst Cl
Horsham RH12 . . . 218 A5
Kenley CR8 . . . 80 D4
Leatherhead KT22 . . . 95 A6
Penge SE20 . . . 43 B8
Ashurst Dr
Box Hill KT20 . . . 116 B5
Crawley RH10 . . . 202 D6
Littleton TW17 . . . 33 E5
Ashurst Gdns SW2 . . . 22 A7
Ashurst Pl RH4 . . . 136 C8
Ashurst Rd
Ash Vale GU12 . . . 105 F4
Tadworth KT20 . . . 97 C6
Ashurst Wlk CR0 . . . 62 B8
ASHURST WOOD . . . 206 E6
Ashurstwood Abbey
RH19 . . . 206 F6
Ashurst Wood Prim Sch
RH19 . . . 206 E6
ASH VALE . . . 106 B7
Ash Vale GU8 . . . 191 A5
Ashvale Rd SW17 . . . 20 F3
Ash Vale Sta GU12 . . . 106 A7
Ashview Cl TW15 . . . 13 E3
Ashview Gdns TW15 . . . 13 E3
Ashville Pk RG41 . . . 25 B5
Ashville Way RG41 . . . 25 A5
Ashway Ctr 5 KT2 . . . 37 E8
Ashwell Ave GU15 . . . 65 F6
Ashwell Ct TW15 . . . 13 E6
Ashwick Cl CR3 . . . 101 A3
Ashwood
5 Crawley RH11 . . . 201 D5
Warlingham CR6 . . . 101 C7
Ashwood Ct
Forest Row RH18 . . . 206 F1
Knaphill GU21 . . . 68 C2
Ashwood Gdns CR0 . . . 63 C4
Ashwood Pk
11 Belmont SM2 . . . 59 A3
Fetcham KT22 . . . 94 C4
Woking GU22 . . . 70 A1
Ashwood Pl GU22 . . . 70 A1
Ashwood Rd
Englefield Green TW20 . . . 11 B2
Woking GU22 . . . 70 A1
Ashworth Pl GU2 . . . 108 F1
Aslett St SW18 . . . 20 C8
Asmar Cl CR5 . . . 79 E4
Aspects SM1 . . . 59 B5
Aspen Cl
Guildford GU4 . . . 110 D4
Staines TW18 . . . 12 F5
Stoke D'Abernon KT11 . . . 73 E3
Aspen Ct
East Grinstead RH19 . . . 206 A8
11 Redhill RH1 . . . 139 F8
Richmond TW9 . . . 7 A7
South Croydon CR2 . . . 61 D2
Virginia Water GU25 . . . 31 E5
Aspen Gdns
Ashford TW15 . . . 14 C3
Mitcham CR4 . . . 41 A4
Aspen Gr GU12 . . . 126 E8
Aspen Ho
Chelsham CR6 . . . 82 B4
Richmond TW9 . . . 7 A7
Aspen Lo 1 SW19 . . . 19 F2
Aspen Sq KT13 . . . 53 D7
Aspen Vale CR3 . . . 80 F1
Aspen Way
Banstead KT17 . . . 77 D5
Feltham TW13 . . . 15 B5
Horsham RH12 . . . 217 E4
Aspinall Ho SW12 . . . 21 E7
Aspin Way GU17 . . . 64 B5
Asprey Ct CR3 . . . 100 F4
Asprey Gr CR3 . . . 101 A3
Asprey Ho CR4 . . . 40 E6
Asprey Mews BR3 . . . 43 F4
Asquith House SM7 . . . 77 F4
Assembly Wlk SM5 . . . 40 E2
Assher Rd KT12 . . . 54 E7

Assheton-Bennett Ho [15]
KT6 . . . . 37 E4
Assisi Ct SW12 . . . . 20 F7
Astede Pl KT21 . . . . 75 F1
Astleham Rd TW17 . . . . 33 E6
Astleham Way TW17 . . . 33 F6
Astley Ho [8] SE27 . . . . . 22 C4
Astolat Bsns Pk The
GU3 . . . . 130 C1
Aston Cl KT21 . . . . 75 C1
Aston Cotts SL4 . . . . 9 A4
Aston Ct
Crawley RH11 . . . . 201 B1
Wimbledon SW20 . . . . 19 C1
Aston Gn TW5 . . . . 4 C5
Aston Grange RG12 . . . . 27 E5
Aston Pl SW16 . . . . 22 B2
Aston Rd
Claygate KT10 . . . . 55 E5
Merton SW20 . . . . 39 C7
Astonville St SW18 . . . . . 20 A7
Aston Way KT18 . . . . . . 76 F3
Astor Cl
Addlestone KT15 . . . . . 52 D6
Kingston upon Thames KT2 . 18 B2
Astoria Ct [10] CR8 . . . . . 80 A8
Astoria Mans [18] SW16 . . 21 E5
Astoria Par SW16 . . . . . . 21 E5
Astra Bsns Ctr RH1 . . . 161 A7
Astra Mead RG42 . . . . . . 8 B2
Astrid Ho TW13 . . . . 15 C6
Astwood Pl RH1 . . . . . . 118 E1
Asylum Arch Rd RH1 . . 139 F6
Atalanta Cl CR8 . . . . 61 A1
Atbara Ct TW11 . . . . 17 B2
Atbara Rd TW11 . . . . 17 B2
Atcham Rd TW3 . . . . 5 C3
Atfield Gr GU20 . . . . 48 D4
Atheldene Rd SW18 . . . . 20 C7
Athelney Prim Sch SE6 . 24 A5
Athelney St SE6 . . . . 24 A5
Athelstan Cl RH10 . . . . 202 E6
Athelstan Ho KT1 . . . . . 37 F5
Athelstan House Sch [13]
TW12 . . . . 36 A8
Athelstan Rd KT1 . . . . . . 37 F5
Athena Cl KT1 . . . . 37 F6
Atherfield Ho RH2 . . . . 139 C6
Atherfield Rd RH2 . . . . 139 C6
Atherley Way TW4 . . . . . 15 F8
Atherton Cl
Shalford GU4 . . . . 130 E3
Stanwell TW19 . . . . 2 D1
Atherton Dr SW19 . . . . . 19 D4
Atherton Ho CR2 . . . . . . 61 E4
Athlone KT10 . . . . 55 E4
Athlone Ct [4] SE6 . . . . . 24 D8
Athlone Rd SW2 . . . . 22 A8
Atholl Ho [13] RH1 . . . . . 118 F1
Atkins Cl GU21 . . . . 69 A1
Atkins Dr BR4 . . . . 63 D8
Atkinson Ct RH6 . . . . . . 161 B2
Atkinson Ho RH3 . . . . . 116 D1
Atkinson Rd RH10 . . . . 202 C4
Atkins Rd SW4, SW12 . . . 21 D8
Atlanta Ct CR7 . . . . 42 C6
Atrebatti Rd GU47 . . . . . 45 C1
Atrium Sh Ctr The GU15 . 65 C5
Atrium The GU7 . . . . . . 150 E4
Attebrouche Ct RG12 . . . 27 D2
Attfield Cl GU12 . . . . . . 105 F1
Attleborough Ct SE21 . . 23 B6
Attlee Cl CR7 . . . . 42 C4
Attlee Ho
[5] Crawley RH11 . . . . 201 B2
Feltham TW13 . . . . 15 A5
Attwood Cl CR2 . . . . 81 B5
Atwater Cl SW2 . . . . 22 A7
Atwell Pl KT7 . . . . 37 A1
Atwood KT23 . . . . 93 E3
Atwood Ave TW9 . . . . 7 A5
Atwood Ho SE21 . . . . . . 22 E5
Atwood Prim Sch CR2 . . 81 A6
Aubyn Hill SE27 . . . . . . 22 D4
Auchinleck Ct RH10 . . . 204 B7
Auchinleck Way GU11 . . 104 E2
Auckland Cl
Crawley RH11 . . . . 181 D1
South Norwood SE19 . . 42 F8
Auckland Ct SE27 . . . . . 22 C4
Auckland Gdns SE19 . . . 42 F8
Auckland Hill SE27 . . . . 22 C4
Auckland Ho BR3 . . . . . . 43 E4
Auckland Rd
Caterham CR3 . . . . 100 E5
Kingston upon Thames KT1 . 37 F5
South Norwood SE19, SE25 . 42 F8
Auckland Rise SE19 . . . . 42 E8
Auden Pl SM3 . . . . 58 C6
Audley Cl KT15 . . . . 52 B5
Audley Ct
Surbiton KT5 . . . . 37 F3
Twickenham TW2 . . . . . 16 D5
Audley Dr CR6 . . . . 81 C4
Audley Firs KT12 . . . . . . 54 C6
Audley Ho KT15 . . . . 52 B5
Audley Pl SM2 . . . . 59 B3
Audley Prim Sch CR3 . . 100 F6
Audley Rd TW10 . . . . 6 F2
Audley Way SL5 . . . . 28 C6
Audrey Ho BR3 . . . . 44 B3
Audric Cl KT1 . . . . 38 A8
Augur Cl TW18 . . . . 12 F3
Augusta Cl KT8 . . . . 35 F6
Augusta Rd TW2 . . . . . . 16 C6

Augustine Cl SL3 . . . . 1 E4
Augustine Ct [6] CR3 . . . 101 A8
August La GU5 . . . . 153 D7
Augustus Cl TW8 . . . . 6 D7
Augustus Ct
Feltham TW13 . . . . 15 F4
Hounslow TW3 . . . . 5 C3
[8] Putney SW19 . . . . . . 19 E7
South Norwood SE19 . . 22 E1
Streatham SW16 . . . . . 21 D6
Augustus Gdns GU15 . . . 66 C5
Augustus Rd SW19 . . . . . 19 E7
Aultone Way
Carshalton SM5 . . . . . . 59 F7
Sutton SM1 . . . . 59 C8
Aultone Yard Ind Est SM5 . 59 F7
Aura Ho [3] TW9 . . . . 7 B6
Aurelia Gdns CR7 . . . . . 41 F3
Aurelia Rd CR0, CR7, CR9 . 41 F3
Auriol Cl KT4 . . . . 57 E7
Auriol Jun Sch KT19 . . . 57 F6
Auriol Park Rd KT4 . . . . 57 E7
Aurum Cl RH6 . . . . 161 B2
Austen Cl RH19 . . . . . . 185 B1
Austen Rd
Farnborough GU14 . . . . 85 A6
Guildford GU1 . . . . 130 F8
Austin Cl
Coulsdon CR8 . . . . 80 B1
Forest Hill SE23, SE6 . . . 23 F8
Twickenham TW1 . . . . . . 6 C2
Austin Ho [19] KT6 . . . . . 37 E4
Austin's Cotts [7] GU9 . . 125 B2
Austin Way RG12 . . . . . . 27 C5
Austyn Gdns KT5 . . . . . . 38 B1
Austyns Pl [2] KT17 . . . . 57 F2
Autumn Cl
Crawley RH11 . . . . 201 C5
Wimbledon SW19 . . . . . 20 C2
Autumn Dr SM2 . . . . 59 B2
Autumn Lodge [1] CR2 . . 61 E6
Avalon Cl SW20 . . . . 39 E7
Avalon Ct CR0 . . . . 42 F2
Avante Cl KT1 . . . . 37 D6
Avarn Rd SW17 . . . . 20 F2
Avebury RG12 . . . . 27 A3
Avebury Ct RH12 . . . . . 218 A7
Avebury Rd SW19 . . . . . 39 F8
Aveley La GU9 . . . . 146 C7
Aveling Cl
Crawley RH10 . . . . 202 C4
Purley CR8 . . . . 79 F6
Aven Cl GU6 . . . . 174 F3
Avening Rd SW18 . . . . . 20 A8
Avening Terr SW18 . . . . 20 A8
Avenue All Hallows GU24 . 88 B5
Avenue C KT15 . . . . 52 E7
Avenue Cl
Cranford TW5 . . . . 4 B6
Tadworth KT20 . . . . 97 B5
Avenue Cres TW5 . . . . . . 4 B7
Avenue Ct
Coulsdon CR5 . . . . 79 D4
Penge SE20 . . . . 43 C8
Tadworth KT20 . . . . 97 B4
Avenue De Cagny GU24 . 87 F5
Avenue Elmers KT6 . . . . 37 E4
Avenue Gdns
Cranford TW5 . . . . 4 B7
Horley RH6 . . . . 161 C2
Mortlake SW14 . . . . 7 E4
South Norwood SE25 . . . 43 A7
Teddington TW11 . . . . . 16 F2
Avenue One KT15 . . . . . . 52 E6
Avenue Par TW16 . . . . . . 35 B6
Avenue Park Rd SE21,
SE27 . . . . 22 B6
Avenue Prim Sch The
SM2 . . . . 59 A1
Avenue Rd
Banstead SM7 . . . . 78 B4
Belmont SM2 . . . . 59 A1
Caterham CR3 . . . . 100 E5
Cobham KT11 . . . . 73 D3
Cranleigh GU6 . . . . 174 F1
Egham TW18 . . . . 12 D3
Epsom KT18 . . . . 76 D5
Farnborough GU14 . . . . 85 D3
Feltham TW13 . . . . 14 F5
Grayshott GU26 . . . . . . 188 C3
Hampton TW12 . . . . . . 36 B8
Hounslow TW7 . . . . 5 F6
Kingston upon Thames KT1 . 37 E6
Mitcham SW16 . . . . 41 D7
New Malden KT3 . . . . . . 38 E5
South Norwood, Anerley
SE25 . . . . 43 A7
Tatsfield TN16 . . . . 103 E7
Teddington TW11 . . . . . 17 A2
Wallington SM6 . . . . . . 60 C3
Wimbledon SW20 . . . . . 39 B7
Avenue Rd Halt BR3 . . . . 43 D7
Avenue Row GU8 . . . . . . 148 D4
Avenue S KT5 . . . . 38 A2
Avenue St Andrew GU24 . 88 B6
Avenue St Barnabas GU24 . 88 B6
Avenue St Bartholomew
GU22 . . . . 88 C5
Avenue St Chad GU22 . . 88 C5
Avenue St David GU22 . . 88 B5
Avenue St George GU22 . 88 B5
Avenue St Mark GU22,
GU24 . . . . 88 C5
Avenue St Savior GU24 . 88 B5
Avenue Sucy GU15 . . . . . 65 B4
Avenue Terr KT3 . . . . . . 38 C6
Avenue The
Aldershot GU12 . . . . . . 126 C7

Avenue The continued
Beckenham BR3 . . . . . . 44 C8
Belmont SM2 . . . . 58 F2
Biggin Hill TN16 . . . . . 103 F5
Brockham RH3 . . . . . . 116 A1
Camberley GU15 . . . . . 65 B5
Chobham GU24 . . . . . . 50 A2
Claygate KT10 . . . . 55 E5
Compton GU3, GU7 . . . 129 C1
Coulsdon CR5 . . . . 79 D4
Cranford TW5 . . . . 4 A6
Crowthorne RG45 . . . . . 45 B5
Dormansland RH19 . . . 186 B6
Egham TW20 . . . . 12 B4
Ewhurst GU6 . . . . 175 E6
Godalming GU7 . . . . . . 150 F2
Grayshott GU26 . . . . . . 188 D3
Hampton TW12 . . . . . . 15 F2
Haslemere GU27 . . . . . 207 F7
Horley RH6 . . . . 160 F2
Hounslow TW3 . . . . 5 B2
Lightwater GU18 . . . . . 48 A1
[4] New Malden KT4 . . . 39 A1
North Ascot SL5 . . . . 8 F1
Oxshott KT22 . . . . 74 F8
Richmond TW9 . . . . 6 F5
Rowledge GU10 . . . . . . 145 F3
South Croydon CR0 . . . . 61 E7
South Nutfield RH1 . . . 140 E6
Staines TW18 . . . . 33 B8
Stoneleigh KT17, SM3 . . 58 C3
Sunbury TW16 . . . . 35 B7
Surbiton KT5 . . . . 37 F3
Tadworth KT20 . . . . 97 B5
Twickenham TW1 . . . . . . 6 B2
West Wickham BR4 . . . . 44 E2
Whyteleafe CR3 . . . . . . 101 A8
Woodham KT15 . . . . . . 52 A1
Worcester Park KT4 . . . 57 F8
Worplesdon GU3 . . . . . 88 E1
Avenue Three KT15 . . . . 52 E7
Avenue Two KT15 . . . . . 52 E6
Averil Gr SW16 . . . . 22 B2
Avern Gdns KT8 . . . . . . 36 B5
Avern Rd KT8 . . . . 36 B5
Avery Ct
[7] Aldershot GU11 . . . . 105 B2
Penge SE20 . . . . 23 B1
Aviary Rd GU22 . . . . 71 A3
Aviary Way RH10 . . . . . 184 C5
Aviation Ct RH10 . . . . . 182 A1
Aviator Pk KT15 . . . . . . 52 D7
Aviemore Cl BR3 . . . . . . 43 F4
Aviemore Way BR3 . . . . 43 E4
Avington Cl GU1 . . . . . . 109 E1
Avington Gr SE20 . . . . . 23 C1
Avoca Rd SW17 . . . . 21 A4
Avocet Cres GU47 . . . . . 64 E8
Avon Cl
Addlestone KT15 . . . . . 52 A4
Ash GU12 . . . . 105 F1
Farnborough GU14 . . . . 84 E7
Sutton SM1 . . . . 59 C6
Worcester Park KT4 . . . 58 A8
Avon Ct
Farnham GU9 . . . . 125 C1
Guildford GU1 . . . . 110 A1
Avondale KT15 . . . . 105 F7
Avondale Ave
Hinchley Wood KT10 . . . 56 A7
New Malden KT4 . . . . . . 38 F1
Staines TW18 . . . . 12 F1
Avondale Cl
Hersham KT12 . . . . 54 C5
Horley RH6 . . . . 161 A5
Avondale Ct [9] SM2 . . . . 59 C3
Avondale Gdns TW4 . . . . 4 F2
Avondale High CR3 . . . . 101 A6
Avondale Ho [6] SW14 . . . 7 D4
Avondale Rd
Aldershot GU11 . . . . . . 126 B8
Ashford TW15, TW19 . . . 13 D5
Bromley BR1 . . . . 24 F2
Mortlake SW14 . . . . 7 D4
South Croydon CR2 . . . . 61 C4
Wimbledon SW19 . . . . . 20 B3
Avon Ho
[9] Redhill RH1 . . . . . . 118 F2
[5] Teddington KT2 . . . . 37 D8
Avonmead GU21 . . . . . . 69 C1
Avonmore Ave GU1 . . . . 109 F2
Avonmor Mews GU23 . . 91 B5
Avon Path CR2 . . . . 61 C3
Avon Rd
Ashford TW16 . . . . 14 F1
Farnham GU9 . . . . 125 C1
Avonwick Rd TW3 . . . . . . 5 B5
Avro Way
Byfleet KT13 . . . . 52 E1
Wallington SM6 . . . . . . 60 E3
Axbridge RG12 . . . . 27 E4
Axes La RH1 . . . . 140 D2
Axford Ho SW2 . . . . 22 B7
Axwood KT18 . . . . 76 C4
Ayebridges Ave TW20 . . 12 C1
Ayjay Cl GU11 . . . . 126 A7
Aylesbury Ct SM1 . . . . . 59 C7
Aylesford Ave BR3 . . . . 43 E4
Aylesworth Spur SL4 . . . 11 B8
Aylett Rd
Croydon SE25 . . . . 43 B5
Isleworth TW7 . . . . 5 E5
Ayliffe Cl KT1 . . . . 38 A7
Ayling Ct SM4 . . . . 39 D2
Ayling Hill GU11 . . . . . . 104 F1
Ayling La GU11 . . . . 125 F8

Aylward Rd
Forest Hill SE23 . . . . . . 23 D6
Merton SW20 . . . . 39 F6
Aylwin Ct [1] RH12 . . . . 217 A1
Aymer Cl TW18 . . . . 32 E8
Aymer Dr TW18 . . . . 32 E8
Aysgarth RG12 . . . . 27 A3
Aysgarth Ct SM1 . . . . . . 59 B7
Aysgarth Rd SE21 . . . . . 22 E8
Ayshe Court Dr RH13 . . 217 E3
Azalea Ct
Purley CR8 . . . . 80 B8
Woking GU22 . . . . 89 D8
Azalea Dr GU27 . . . . . . 207 F8
Azalea Ho TW13 . . . . . . 15 B7
Azalea Way GU15 . . . . . 66 B6
Azriel Terr [3] BR4 . . . . 44 B1
Azure Ct TW13 . . . . 14 F5

B

Babbacombe Cl KT9 . . . . 56 D5
Babbage Way RG12 . . . . 27 A3
Babbs Mead GU9 . . . . . 125 A1
Baber Dr TW14 . . . . 4 C1
Babington Ct SW16 . . . . 21 D3
Babington Rd SW16 . . . . 21 D3
Babylon La KT20, RH2 . . 118 B8
Bachelor's La GU23 . . . . 92 A3
Back Gn KT12 . . . . 54 C4
Back La
Brentford TW8 . . . . 6 D8
Crawley RH10 . . . . 203 D1
East Clandon GU4 . . . . 111 D4
Elstead GU8 . . . . 148 D4
Frithend GU10 . . . . 166 B8
Plaistow GU8 . . . . 211 E2
Richmond TW10 . . . . . . 17 C6
Backley Gdns CR0 . . . . . 43 A3
Bacon Cl GU47 . . . . 64 D6
Bacon La GU10 . . . . 167 C3
Badajos Rd GU11 . . . . . 104 F3
Baddeley Ho KT8 . . . . . . 36 A4
Baden Cl TW18 . . . . 13 B1
Baden Dr RH6 . . . . 160 E4
Baden Powell Cl KT6 . . . 56 F8
Baden Powell Ct GU7 . . 150 D6
Baden Rd GU2 . . . . 109 B3
Bader Cl CR8 . . . . 80 D4
Bader Ct GU14 . . . . 84 F8
Badger Cl
Feltham TW13 . . . . 15 B5
Guildford GU2 . . . . 109 B4
Hounslow TW4 . . . . 4 C4
Badger Ct GU10 . . . . . . 146 A5
Badger Dr GU18 . . . . . . 48 A1
Badgers Cl
Ashford TW15 . . . . 13 F3
Farncombe GU7 . . . . . . 150 D8
Horsham RH12 . . . . . . 217 F6
Woking GU21 . . . . 69 C1
Badgers Copse
Frimley GU15 . . . . 65 E4
Worcester Park KT4 . . . 57 F8
Badgers Cross GU8 . . . 149 E1
Badgers Ct
[4] Epsom KT17 . . . . . . 76 E6
Farnham GU9 . . . . 125 C4
Badgers Hill GU25 . . . . 31 C4
Badgers Hole CR0 . . . . . 62 D6
Badgers Hollow GU7 . . . 150 D6
Badgers La CR6 . . . . . . 101 C8
Badgers Lodge [5] KT17 . 76 E6
Badger's Mount CR8 . . . 61 B1
Badgers Way
Bracknell RG12 . . . . . . 27 F7
East Grinstead RH19 . . 185 F2
Loxwood RH14 . . . . . . 213 A4
Badgers Wlk
Kingston upon Thames
KT3 . . . . 38 E7
Purley CR8 . . . . 79 C8
Whyteleafe CR3 . . . . . . 80 F1
Badgers Wood CR3 . . . . 100 D2
Badger Way
Aldershot GU12 . . . . . . 105 D3
Crondall GU10 . . . . 124 D8
Badgerwood Dr GU16 . . . 65 D2
Badingham Dr KT22 . . . . 94 E4
Badminton Rd SW12 . . . 21 A8
BADSHOT LEA 126 B6
Badshot Lea Rd GU11,
GU9 . . . . 126 A6
Badshot Lea Village Inf Sch
GU9 . . . . 126 A6
Badshot Pk GU9 . . . . . . 126 A6
Bagden Hill KT23, RH5 . . 114 D5
BAGSHOT 47 D3
Bagshot Gn GU19 . . . . . 47 E3
Bagshot Rd
Ascot SL5 . . . . 29 C2
Bracknell RG12 . . . . . . 27 C4
Brookwood GU21, GU22, GU24,
GU3 . . . . 88 C5
Englefield Green TW20 . . 11 C2
West End GU24 . . . . . . 68 C8
Bagshot Sch GU19 . . . . 47 E2
Bagshot Sta GU19 . . . . 47 E4
Bahram Rd KT19 . . . . . . 57 D1
Baigents La GU20 . . . . . 48 D4
Bailes La GU3 . . . . 107 D3
Bailey Cl
Frimley GU16 . . . . 85 D8
Horsham RH12 . . . . . . 217 F7
Bailey Cres KT9 . . . . . . 56 D3

Bailey Ho
Mitcham CR4 . . . . 40 E6
[11] Penge SE26 . . . . . . 23 B3
Bailey Mews W4 . . . . 7 B8
Bailey Pl SE26 . . . . 23 D2
Bailey Rd RH4 . . . . 135 C6
Baileys Cl GU17 . . . . 64 C4
Bailing Hill RH12 . . . . . 216 E7
Baillie Rd GU1 . . . . 130 F8
Bain Ave GU15 . . . . 65 B2
Bainbridge cl KT2 . . . . . 17 E3
Bainton Mead GU21 . . . . 69 A2
Baird Cl RH10 . . . . 182 A1
Baird Dr GU3 . . . . 108 B2
Baird Gdns SE19 . . . . . . 22 E4
Baird Rd GU14 . . . . 85 C6
Bakeham La TW20 . . . . . 11 D1
Bakehouse Barn Cl
RH12 . . . . 217 E7
Bakehouse Ct SL5 . . . . . 28 B8
Bakehouse Rd RH6 . . . . 161 A5
Baker Cl RH10 . . . . 201 D4
Baker La CR4 . . . . 41 A7
Baker Pl KT19 . . . . 57 C4
Bakers Cl CR8 . . . . 80 C5
Baker's Cl RH7 . . . . 164 E5
Bakers Ct
[9] Redhill RH1 . . . . . . 139 F8
South Norwood SE25 . . . 42 E6
Bakers End SW20 . . . . . 39 E7
Bakersgate Gdns GU24 . 88 A2
Bakers Gdns SM5 . . . . . 59 E8
Baker's La RH7 . . . . 164 E4
Bakers Mead RH9 . . . . . 121 C6
Baker St KT13 . . . . 53 B6
Bakers Way RH5 . . . . . 178 C5
Bakery Mews KT6 . . . . . 38 A1
Bakewell Dr KT3 . . . . . . 38 E7
Balaam Ho SM1 . . . . . . 59 A6
Balaclava Rd KT6 . . . . . 37 C2
Balchins La RH4 . . . . . . 135 B6
Balcombe Ct RH10 . . . . 202 D7
Balcombe Gdns RH6 . . . 161 C2
Balcombe Ho [3] SW2 . . . 21 F7
Balcombe Rd
Crawley, Tinsley Green RH6,
RH10 . . . . 182 D5
Crawley, Worth RH10 . . 202 D5
Horley RH6 . . . . 161 B2
Baldreys GU9 . . . . 146 A8
Baldry Gdns SW16 . . . . 21 F2
Baldwin Cl RH10 . . . . . 202 C3
Baldwin Cres GU4 . . . . . 110 C3
Baldwin Gdns TW3 . . . . . 5 C6
Baldwin Ho [15] SW2 . . . 22 A7
Baldwins Field RH19 . . . 185 C4
Baldwins Hill Prim Sch
RH19 . . . . 185 D3
Balfont Cl CR2 . . . . 81 A6
Balfour Ave GU22 . . . . . 89 F5
Balfour Cres RG12 . . . . 27 B4
Balfour Gdns RH18 . . . . 206 E1
Balfour Ho KT19 . . . . . . 76 B8
Balfour Rd
Croydon SE25 . . . . 43 A5
Hounslow TW3 . . . . 5 B4
Merton SW19 . . . . 20 B1
Wallington SM5 . . . . . . 59 F3
Weybridge KT13 . . . . . . 53 A6
Balgowan Cl KT3 . . . . . . 38 E5
Balgowan Prim Sch BR3 . 43 E7
Balgowan Rd BR3 . . . . . 43 F7
BALHAM 21 A7
Balham Gr SW12 . . . . . . 21 A8
Balham High Rd SW12,
SW17 . . . . 21 A7
Balham Hill SW12 . . . . . 21 B8
Balham L Ctr SW17 . . . . 21 B6
Balham New Rd SW12 . . 21 B8
Balham Park Mansions
SW12 . . . . 20 F7
Balham Park Rd SW12,
SW17 . . . . 21 A7
Balham Sta SW12 . . . . . 21 B7
Balham Station Rd SW12 . 21 B7
Balintore Ct [8] GU47 . . . 64 D8
Ballands N The KT22 . . . 94 E5
Ballands' S The KT22 . . . 94 E4
Ballantyne Dr KT20 . . . . 97 F6
Ballantyne Rd GU14 . . . 85 A6
Ballard Cl KT2 . . . . 18 D1
Ballard Ct GU15 . . . . . . 66 A8
Ballard Rd GU15 . . . . . . 66 A8
Ballards Farm Rd CR0,
CR2 . . . . 62 A4
Ballards Gn KT20 . . . . . 97 E8
Ballards La RH8 . . . . . . 123 C6
Ballards Rise CR2 . . . . . 62 A4
Ballards Way CR0, CR2 . . 62 C4
Ballater Rd CR2 . . . . . . 61 F5
Ballencrieff Rd SL5 . . . . 29 F2
Ballfield Rd GU7 . . . . . . 150 E6
Ballina St SE23 . . . . 23 D8
Ballindune GU27 . . . . . . 208 C8
Balliol Cl RH10 . . . . 182 D1
Balliol Way GU47 . . . . . . 45 E1
Balloch Rd SE6 . . . . 24 D6
Ballsdown GU8 . . . . 191 A3
Ball & Wicket La GU9 . . 125 C7
Balmain Ct TW3 . . . . 5 B6
Balmoral RH19 . . . . 206 A8
Balmoral Ave BR3 . . . . . 43 E5
Balmoral Cres
East Molesey KT8 . . . . . 36 A6
Hale GU9 . . . . 125 B6
Balmoral Ct
[15] Belmont SM2 . . . . . 59 A3
[6] Crawley RH11 . . . . . 201 B2

Balmoral Ct continued
Farnborough GU14 . . . . 85 B4
North Cheam KT4 . . . . 58 B8
West Norwood SE27 . . . . . 22 C4
Balmoral Dr
Frimley GU16. . . . . 85 F8
Woking GU22. . . . . 70 C3
Balmoral Gdns CR2 . . . . 61 D1
Balmoral Grange TW18. . . 33 B7
Balmoral Ho 3 GU12. . . . 105 F5
Balmoral Mans 3 TW1. . . . . 6 D1
Balmoral Rd
Ash GU12. . . . . 106 B4
Kingston upon Thames KT1 . 37 F5
North Cheam KT4 . . . . 58 B8
Balmoral Way SM2. . . . . 59 A1
Balquhain Cl KT21 . . . . 75 D2
Baltic Cl SW19. . . . . 20 D1
Baltimore Ho SW19. . . . . 20 B1
Balvernie Gr SW18. . . . . 20 A8
Bamford Rd BR1. . . . . 24 D3
Bampfylde Cl SM6 . . . . 60 C7
Bampton Rd SE23. . . . . 23 D5
Bampton Way GU21. . . . . . 69 A2
Banavie Gdns BR3. . . . . . . 44 C8
Banbury RG12 . . . . 27 E2
Banbury Cl
Frimley GU16. . . . . 86 A7
Wokingham RG41 . . . . 25 A6
Banbury Ct 13 SM2. . . . . . . 59 A3
Bancroft Cl TW15 . . . . 14 A3
Bancroft Rd RH2. . . . . 118 B1
Bancroft
Crawley RH10 . . . . 202 D5
Reigate RH2. . . . . 118 B1
Banders Rise GU1. . . . . . . 110 C2
Band La 1 TW20. . . . . 12 A3
BANDONHILL 60 D5
Bandon Hill Prim Sch
SM6 . . . . 60 D4
Bandon Rise SM6. . . . . 60 D5
Banfor Ct SM6. . . . . 60 C4
Bank Ave CR4. . . . . 40 D7
Bank Bldgs 13 SW16 . . . . . 21 C3
Bankfoot Rd BR1. . . . . 24 E4
Bank Ho
Addlestone KT15 . . . . 52 B6
1 Sutton SM1. . . . . 59 C4
Bankhurst Rd SE4, SE6. . . . 23 F4
Bank La
Crawley RH10 . . . . 201 D6
Kingston upon Thames KT2 . 17 E1
Roehampton SW15 . . . . 7 E2
Bank Mews SM1. . . . . 59 C4
Bank Rd GU11. . . . . 105 D5
Banks Ho TW7. . . . . 5 E5
Bankside
Heath End GU9 . . . . 125 F7
South Croydon CR2 . . . . . . 61 F4
Woking GU21. . . . . 69 B1
Bankside Cl
Biggin Hill TN16. . . . . 83 C1
Carshalton SM5. . . . . 59 E4
Elstead GU8. . . . . 148 D3
Isleworth TW7. . . . . 5 F3
Bankside Dr KT7. . . . . 56 B8
Bankside Way 7 SE19 . . . . 22 E2
Bank's La KT24. . . . . 93 B5
Banks Rd RH10 . . . . 202 C5
Banks Way GU1. . . . . 109 F4
Bannacle Hill Rd GU8 . . . 170 E1
Banning Ho 4 SW19 . . . . . 19 D7
Bannister Cl
Streatham SW2. . . . . 22 A7
Witley GU8. . . . . 170 F6
Bannister's Rd GU2 . . . . . 129 F7
Bannow Cl KT19 . . . . 57 E6
BANSTEAD 78 B3
Banstead Com Jun Sch
SM7 . . . . 77 F4
Banstead Inf Sch SM7. . . . 77 F4
Banstead Rd
Belmont KT17, SM7. . . . . . 77 D7
Caterham CR3 . . . . 100 A8
Purley CR8. . . . . 80 A8
Sutton SM5 . . . . 59 E3
Banstead Road S SM2 . . . . 59 D1
Banstead Sp Ctr KT20 . . . . 97 C7
Banstead Sta SM7 . . . . 77 F5
Banstead Way SM6. . . . . . . 60 E5
Bapel Ct BR3. . . . . 24 A1
Barataria Pk GU23. . . . . . . 90 F6
Barbara Ct TW17. . . . . 34 B4
Barber Cl RH10. . . . . 202 C2
Barber Dr GU6. . . . . 174 E4
Barberry Way GU17. . . . . . 64 F2
Barbon Cl GU15. . . . . 66 D3
Barclay Cl KT23. . . . . 94 B4
Barclay Rd CR0, CR9. . . . . . 61 D7
Barcombe Ave SW2. . . . . . 21 F6
Barcom Trad Est CR0. . . . . 41 E2
Bardeen Pl RG12. . . . . 27 D6
Bardney Rd SM4. . . . . 40 B5
Bardolph Ave CR0. . . . . 62 F2
Bardolph Rd TW9. . . . . 6 F4
Bardon Wlk GU21. . . . . 69 B2
Bardsley Cl CR0. . . . . 61 F7
Bardsley Dr GU9. . . . . 146 A7
Barfield Ct 11 RH1 . . . . . . 119 A3
Barfields
Bletchingley RH1. . . . . . . 120 C2
Redhill RH1. . . . . 120 C8
Barfield Sch GU10 . . . . . . 126 B3
Barfreston Way SE20. . . . . 43 B8
Bargate Cl KT3 . . . . 39 A2
Bargate Ct
Godalming GU7 . . . . 150 C4
2 Guildford GU2. . . . . 108 E1

Bargate Ho GU21 . . . . 69 F3
Bargate Rise GU7 . . . . 150 C4
Barge Cl GU11. . . . . 105 E5
Bargery Rd SE6. . . . . 24 B7
Bargrove Cl 7 SE20. . . . . . 23 A1
Bargrove Cres SE6. . . . . . . 23 F6
Barham Ct 8 CR0. . . . . 61 C6
Barham Rd
Croydon CR0, CR2. . . . . . . 61 C5
Wimbledon SW20 . . . . 19 A1
Barhatch La GU6. . . . . 174 F6
Barhatch Rd GU6. . . . . 174 F4
Baring Ct CR0, CR9. . . . . . . 43 A1
Barker Cl
Chertsey KT16. . . . . 32 E2
Kingston upon Thames KT3 . 38 B5
Richmond TW9 . . . . 7 B5
Barker Gn RG12. . . . . 27 B4
Barker Ho SE21. . . . . 22 E5
Barker Rd KT16. . . . . 32 F2
Barkers Mdw SL5 . . . . 28 D8
Barker Wlk SW16 . . . . 21 D5
Barkham Rd RG41. . . . . 25 A5
Barkhart Cl RG40 . . . . 25 C7
Barkhart Dr RG40 . . . . 25 C7
Barkhart Gdns RG40. . . . . . 25 C7
Barkis Mead GU47 . . . . 45 E2
Barley Cl RH10. . . . . 201 D5
Barley Ct TW19 . . . . 13 E7
Barleymead 6 RH6 . . . . . . 161 B4
Barley Mow Ct GU21 . . . . . 68 D2
Barley Mow Ct RH3 . . . . . 116 C1
Barley Mow Hill GU35 . . . 187 A6
Barley Mow La GU21 . . . . . 68 D3
Barley Mow Rd TW20. . . . . 11 C3
Barley Mow Way TW17 . . . 34 A5
Barlow Cl SM6. . . . . 60 E3
Barlow Rd
Crawley RH11 . . . . 200 D3
Hampton TW12 . . . . 16 A1
Barmeston Rd SE6 . . . . 24 B6
Barmouth Rd CR0. . . . . 62 D8
Barnard Cl
Frimley GU16 . . . . 85 F8
Sunbury TW16 . . . . 15 B1
Wallington SM6. . . . . 60 D3
Barnard Ct
1 Knaphill GU21 . . . . 68 E1
Streatham SW16 . . . . 21 F5
Barnard Gdns KT3 . . . . 39 A5
Barnard Ho RH1 . . . . 139 F4
Barnard Pl KT17 . . . . 58 C1
Barnard Rd
Chelsham CR6 . . . . 102 B8
Mitcham CR4 . . . . 41 A7
Barnards Pl CR2. . . . . 61 B2
Barnard Way GU11. . . . . . 104 F3
Barnato Cl KT14 . . . . 71 E7
Barnby Rd GU21. . . . . 68 D2
Barn Cl
Ashford TW15 . . . . 14 B3
Bracknell RG12 . . . . 27 D7
Camberley GU15 . . . . 65 E6
Crawley RH10 . . . . 202 D6
Epsom KT18. . . . . 76 C4
Tadworth KT20. . . . . 115 F3
Woodmansterne SM7 . . . . 78 D4
Barn Cres CR8. . . . . 80 D6
Barncroft GU9. . . . . 125 C1
Barn Ct GU8 . . . . 148 E4
Barneby Cl TW2 . . . . 16 E7
BARNES. 7 F6
Barnes Bridge Sta SW13 . . 7 F5
Barnes Cl GU14 . . . . 85 D4
Barnes Ct CR7 . . . . 42 C6
Barnes End KT3. . . . . 39 A4
Barnes High St SW13. . . . . . 7 F5
Barnes Hospl SW14. . . . . 7 E4
Barnes Mews 9 RH12. . . . 217 B2
Barnes Prim Sch SW13. . . . . 7 F4
Barnes Qtr 6 TW8 . . . . 6 C7
Barnes Rd
Farncombe GU7. . . . . 150 E8
Frimley GU16. . . . . 85 E8
Barnes Wallis Cl KT24. . . . 113 D8
Barnes Wallis Dr KT13,
KT14. . . . . 71 E8
Barnett Cl
Leatherhead KT22 . . . . 95 B8
Wonersh GU5 . . . . 152 C8
Barnett Ct RG12. . . . . 27 C7
Barnett Gn RG12. . . . . 27 B3
Barnett La
Lightwater GU18 . . . . 66 F7
Wonersh GU5 . . . . 152 C7
Barnett Row GU4 . . . . 109 D6
Barnett's Shaw RH8. . . . . 122 D8
Barnetts Way RH8 . . . . . . 122 D8
Barnett Wood Inf Sch
KT21. . . . . 75 D2
Barnett Wood La
Ashtead KT21, KT22 . . . . . 75 D1
Leatherhead KT22. . . . . . . 95 B8
Barnfield
Cranleigh GU6. . . . . 174 E3
Dormansland RH7 . . . . . . 165 A1
New Malden KT3 . . . . 38 E3
Barn Field SM7. . . . . 78 B5
Barnfield Ave
Croydon CR0. . . . . 62 C8
Kingston upon Thames KT2 . 17 E3
Mitcham CR4 . . . . 41 B6
Barnfield Cl
Coulsdon CR5 . . . . 100 C8
Wandsworth SW17 . . . . . . 20 C5
Barnfield Gdns KT2 . . . . . . 17 E3

Barn Field Pl RH19. . . . . . 186 A3
Barnfield Rd
Crawley RH10. . . . . 201 E2
South Croydon CR2 . . . . . . 61 E2
Tatsfield TN16 . . . . 103 D6
Barnfield Way RH8. . . . . . 123 A2
Barnfield Wood Cl BR3. . . 44 D3
Barnfield Wood Rd BR3 . . 44 D3
Barnhill Ave BR2. . . . . 44 F4
Barnlea Cl TW13. . . . . 15 E6
Barnmead GU24 . . . . 49 F1
Barn Meadow La KT23. . . . 93 F3
Barnmead Rd BR3. . . . . 43 E8
Barn Rd KT15. . . . . 52 B2
Barnsbury Cl KT3 . . . . 38 C5
Barnsbury Cres KT5. . . . . . 38 C1
Barnsbury La KT5. . . . . 38 C1
Barnsbury Prim Sch
GU22. . . . . 89 D6
Barnscroft SW20. . . . . 39 B6
Barns Ct RH10 . . . . 183 F2
Barnsfold La RH12 . . . . . . 213 E6
Barnsford Cres GU24. . . . . 68 A6
Barnsley Cl GU12 . . . . 86 B2
Barnsnap Cl RH12. . . . . . . 217 D6
Barn Stables Bsns Units
RH10. . . . . 183 E6
Barns The GU8. . . . . 149 C8
Barnway TW20. . . . . 11 C3
Barnwood Cl GU3 . . . . 108 E3
Barnwood Cl GU3 . . . . 108 E3
Barnwood Rd GU2, GU3 . . 108 E3
Barnwood Rd GU2, GU3 . . 108 E3
Barnyard The KT20. . . . . . . 97 A3
Baron Cl SM2. . . . . 59 B1
Baron Ct CR4. . . . . 40 E5
Baron Gr CR4. . . . . 40 E5
Baron Ho 6 SW19 . . . . 40 D8
Barons BR3. . . . . 44 B7
Barons Ct SM6 . . . . 60 D7
Baronsfield Rd TW1. . . . . . . 6 B1
Baron's Hurst KT18 . . . . . . 76 C3
Barons The TW1. . . . . 6 B1
Barons Way TW20. . . . . 12 D2
Baron's Way RH2 . . . . 139 A5
Baron's Wlk CR0. . . . . 43 E3
Barossa Rd GU15. . . . . 65 D7
Barracane Dr GU21. . . . . . . 89 B8
Barrack Path 9 GU21. . . . . 68 F1
Barrack Rd
Aldershot GU11. . . . . 105 A2
Guildford GU2. . . . . 109 A4
Hounslow TW4. . . . . 4 E3
Barracuda Rd GU11. . . . . . 104 E7
Barrads Hall CR2. . . . . 61 D1
Barr Beacon SE23. . . . . 23 C8
Barrens Brae GU22. . . . . . . 70 A1
Barrens Cl GU22. . . . . 90 A8
Barrens Pk GU22. . . . . 90 A8
Barrett Cres RG40. . . . . 25 E6
Barrett Rd KT22. . . . . 94 D3
Barrhill Rd SW2. . . . . 21 E6
Barricane GU21. . . . . 89 B8
Barrie Cl CR5 . . . . 79 C3
Barrie Rd GU9 . . . . 125 A7
Barrihurst La GU6. . . . . . . 173 D2
Barringer Sq SW17. . . . . . . 21 A4
Barrington Ct
Dorking RH4 . . . . 136 A6
Staines TW18. . . . . 12 F2
Barrington Dr KT22. . . . . . . 94 D2
Barrington Gate RH12. . . . 217 D2
Barrington Lodge KT13. . . . 53 C5
Barrington Rd
Cheam SM3. . . . . 40 A1
Crawley RH10 . . . . 201 D3
Dorking RH4 . . . . 136 A6
Horsham RH13 . . . . 217 E2
Purley CR8. . . . . 79 C7
Barrington Wlk 10 SE19 . . . 22 E2
Barrow Ave SM5. . . . . 59 F3
Barrow Ct SM5. . . . . 59 E3
Barrow Green Rd RH8. . . . 122 C6
Barrow Hedges Cl SM5. . . . 59 E3
Barrow Hedges Prim Sch
SM5 . . . . 59 E3
Barrow Hedges Way SM5. . 59 E3
Barrow Hill KT4. . . . . 57 F8
Barrow Hill Cl KT4 . . . . 57 F8
Barrow Hills Sch GU8 . . . 170 E4
Barrow Rd
Croydon CR0. . . . . 61 A5
Streatham SW16 . . . . 21 D2
Barrowsfield CR2. . . . . 81 A7
Barrsbrook Farm Rd KT16 32 E1
Barrsbrook Hall KT16 . . . . 32 E1
Barr's La GU21. . . . . 68 D3
Barry Cl RH10. . . . . 201 E3
Barry Sq RG12 . . . . 27 D2
Barry Terr TW15 . . . . 13 F6
Barsons Cl SE20 . . . . 23 C1
Barston Rd SE27. . . . . 22 C5
Barstow Cres SW2. . . . . . . 21 F7
Bartholomew Ct GU27 . . . 208 D8
Bartholomew Ct RH4. . . . . 136 A6
Bartholomew Way RH12. . 218 A7
Bartlett Cl RH10. . . . . 85 F5
Bartlett St CR0, CR2 . . . . . . 61 D5
Barton Cl
Addlestone KT15 . . . . 52 A4
Aldershot GU11. . . . . 104 E1
Knaphill GU21 . . . . 68 C1
Shepperton TW17 . . . . 34 B3
Barton Cres RH19. . . . . 206 A8
Barton Ct
Beckenham BR2. . . . . 44 D6

Barton Ct continued
Farnborough GU14 . . . . . . 85 C1
Sutton SM1. . . . . 59 B4
Barton Gn KT3. . . . . 38 D7
Barton Pl GU1. . . . . 110 B4
Barton Rd GU5. . . . . 152 A7
Bartons Way GU14 . . . . . . 84 D7
Barton The KT11. . . . . 73 D7
Barts Cl BR3. . . . . 44 A4
Barttelot Rd RH12. . . . . . . 217 D2
Barwell Bsns Pk KT9. . . . . . 56 D2
Barwell La KT9. . . . . 56 C3
Barwood Ave BR4. . . . . 44 B1
Basden Gr TW13 . . . . 16 A6
Basemoors RG12. . . . . 27 E7
Basepoint Bsns Ctr
RH11. . . . . 181 D2
Bashford Rd RH10. . . . . . . 202 D8
Basildene Rd TW4, TW5. . . . 4 D4
Basildon Cl SM2. . . . . 59 B2
Basildon Way RH11 . . . . . 200 E2
Basil Gdns
Croydon CR0. . . . . 43 D1
West Norwood SE27 . . . . . 22 C3
Basing Cl KT7. . . . . 36 F2
Basing Dr GU11. . . . . 126 B7
Basingfield Rd KT7. . . . . . . 36 F2
Basinghall Gdns SM2. . . . . 59 B2
Basing Ho SE6. . . . . 24 A4
Basing Rd SM7. . . . . 77 F4
Basingstoke Canal Ctr★
GU16. . . . . 86 A3
Basing Way KT7. . . . . 36 F2
Baskerville Ct
Croydon CR0. . . . . 42 E4
Wandsworth SW18 . . . . . . 20 E8
Baskerville Rd SW18 . . . . . 20 E8
Basset Cl KT15. . . . . 52 C1
Bassett Cl
Belmont SM2. . . . . 59 B2
Frimley GU16. . . . . 85 E8
Bassett Dr RH2 . . . . 118 A2
Bassett Gdns TW7 . . . . 5 C7
Bassett Rd
Crawley RH10 . . . . 202 D3
Woking GU22. . . . . 70 C3
Bassetts Hill RH7. . . . . 165 A2
Bassingham Rd SW18 . . . . 20 C8
Batavia Cl TW16 . . . . 35 C8
Batavia Rd TW16 . . . . 35 B8
Bat & Ball La GU10 . . . . . 146 A5
Batcombe Mead RG12. . . . 27 E2
Bateman Gr GU14. . . . . . . 126 F8
Batemans Ct RH10 . . . . . . 202 A3
Bates Cres
Croydon CR0. . . . . 61 A5
Streatham SW16 . . . . 21 C1
Bateson Way GU21. . . . . . . 70 C5
Bates Wlk KT15. . . . . 52 C4
Bath Ct 3 SF26. . . . . 23 A5
Bathgate Rd SW19 . . . . 19 D5
Bath House Rd CR0. . . . . . . 41 E1
Bath Pas KT1. . . . . 37 D7
Bath Rd
Camberley GU15 . . . . 65 D6
Cranford, Hounslow TW3, TW4,
TW5. . . . . 4 E5
Harlington TW6, UB7, TW5 . . 3 D6
Harmondsworth TW6, UB7 . . 2 E6
Poyle SL3, UB7, TW6 . . . . . . 1 E6
Bath Road Cotts SL3 . . . . . . 1 E6
Bathurst Ave SW19. . . . . . . 40 B8
Batley Cl CR4. . . . . 40 F2
Batsworth Rd CR4. . . . . 40 D6
Ratten Ave GU21 . . . . 88 E8
Battenberg Wlk 10 SE19. . 22 E2
Battersby Rd SE6 . . . . 24 D5
Battersea Ct GU2 . . . . 109 B1
Battlebridge La RH1 . . . . . 119 B5
Battle Cl SW19. . . . . 20 C2
Battlebridge La RH1 . . . . . 119 B5
Batts Hill RH2. . . . . 118 E3
Batty's Barn Cl RG40 . . . . . 25 D5
Baty Ho SW2 . . . . 21 F7
Baudwin Rd SE6. . . . . 24 E6
Baulk The SW18. . . . . 20 A8
Bavant Rd SW16 . . . . 41 F7
Baveno Ho GU14 . . . . 85 C1
Bawtree Cl SM2. . . . . 59 C1
Bax Cl GU6. . . . . 174 E2
Baxter Ave RH1. . . . . 118 F1
Baxter Cl RH10. . . . . 202 B4
Bayards CR6. . . . . 81 C1
Bay Cl RH6. . . . . 160 E6
Baydon Ct BR2. . . . . 44 F6
Bay Dr RG12. . . . . 27 E7
Bayeux KT20. . . . . 97 D5
Bayfield Ave GU16 . . . . 65 E2
Bayfield Rd RH6. . . . . 160 E4
Bayford Cl GU17. . . . . 65 A1
Baygrove Mews KT1 . . . . . 37 C8
Bayham Rd SM4. . . . . 40 C5
Bay Ho RG12. . . . . 27 E7
Bayhorne La RH6. . . . . 161 C1
Bayleaf Cl TW12 . . . . 16 D3
Baylis Mews TW1 . . . . 17 A8
Bayliss Ct 2 GU1 . . . . 130 C8
Baylis Wlk RH11. . . . . 201 B1
Baynards Rd RH12 . . . . . . 195 A2
Baynton Rd GU22 . . . . 90 B7
Bay Rd RG12. . . . . 27 E7
Bays Cl SE26 . . . . 23 C3
Baysfarm Ct UB7 . . . . 2 C6
Bay Tree Ave KT22 . . . . 95 A7
Bay Trees RH8. . . . . 123 B2
Baywood Cl GU14. . . . . 84 C5
Bazalgette Cl KT3. . . . . 38 D4

Bazalgette Gdns KT3 . . . . . 38 D4
Beachborough Rd BR1 . . . . 24 C4
Beach Gr TW13 . . . . 16 A6
Beach's Ho 2 TW18 . . . . . . 13 A3
Beachy Rd RH11. . . . . 201 A1
Beacon Cl
Banstead SM7 . . . . 77 D3
Rowledge GU10. . . . . 146 A5
Beacon Cres GU26 . . . . . . 188 E5
Beacon Ct
Colnbrook SL3 . . . . 1 C7
Horsham RH13 . . . . 218 A4
Beacon Gr SM5 . . . . 60 A6
BEACON HILL 188 C6
Beacon Hill
Dormansland RH7 . . . . . . 186 B8
Woking GU21. . . . . 89 C8
Beacon Hill Ct GU26. . . . . 188 D6
Beacon Hill Pk GU26 . . . . 188 B6
Beacon Hill Prim Sch
GU26. . . . . 188 C6
Beacon Hill Rd
Beacon Hill GU26. . . . . . . 188 D6
Crondall GU10 . . . . 124 E8
Beacon Ho 10 SE26. . . . . . . 23 B3
Beacon Pl SM6 . . . . 60 E7
Beacon Rd TW19, TW6. . . . . 3 A1
Beacon Rdbt TW6. . . . . 3 A1
Beacon Sch The KT20. . . . . 77 E7
Beaconsfield Cl RH10. . . . . 55 E3
Beaconsfield Pl KT17. . . . . 76 E7
Beaconsfield Rd
Claygate KT10 . . . . 55 E3
Kingston upon Thames KT3 . 38 D7
Langley Vale KT18 . . . . 96 E8
Old Woking GU22. . . . . 89 F7
Surbiton KT5 . . . . 37 F2
Thornton Heath CR0 . . . . . 42 D3
Twickenham TW1. . . . . 6 B1
Beaconshaw BR1. . . . . 24 E1
Beacon View Ho GU26. . . 188 C3
Beacon View Rd GU8 . . . . 148 C2
Beacon Way SM7. . . . . 77 E3
Beadle Ct CR4 . . . . 40 E6
Beadles La RH8. . . . . 122 D4
Beadlow Cl SM4 . . . . 40 D3
Beadman Pl SE27. . . . . 22 B4
Beadman St SE27. . . . . 22 B4
Beadnell Rd SE23. . . . . 23 D7
Beaford Gr SW20. . . . . 39 F6
Beagle Cl TW13 . . . . 15 B4
Beale Cl RG40 . . . . 25 B7
Beale Ct RH11 . . . . 201 A3
Beales La
Weybridge KT13 . . . . 53 B7
Wrecclesham GU10 . . . . . 145 F7
Beales Rd KT23. . . . . 94 B1
Bealeswood La GU10. . . . . 166 F6
Beam Hollow GU9 . . . . 125 C7
Bean Oak Rd RG40 . . . . 25 F6
Beardell St SE19 . . . . 22 F2
Beard Rd TW10 . . . . 17 F3
Beard's Hill TW12. . . . . 36 A8
Beards Hill Cl TW12. . . . . . 36 A8
Beard's Rd TW15, TW16. . . 14 E2
Beare Gn Rd RH5 . . . . 177 F8
BEARE GREEN 157 D3
Beare Green Cotts RH5. . . 157 D2
Beare Green Ct RH5. . . . . . 157 D4
Beare Green Rd RH5 . . . . . 157 B1
Bearfield Rd KT2. . . . . 17 E1
Bear Rd TW13 . . . . 15 D4
Bears Den KT20. . . . . 97 F5
Bearsden Ct SL5 . . . . 29 F2
Bearsden Way RH12. . . . . 216 D3
Bears Rail Pk SL4 . . . . 10 F8
Bearsted Terr 7 BR3. . . . . . 44 A8
Bearwood Ct KT15 . . . . 52 A4
Bearwood Cotts GU10 . . . 145 F7
Beasley's Ait La TW16,
TW17. . . . . 34 F3
Beatrice Ave SW16. . . . . . . 41 F7
Beatrice Ho SE6 . . . . 24 A6
Beatrice Rd
Oxted RH8 . . . . 122 E6
2 Richmond TW10. . . . . 6 F1
Beatrix Potter Prim Sch
SW18 . . . . 20 C7
Beattie Cl
East Bedfont TW14 . . . . . . 14 F7
Little Bookham KT23 . . . . . 93 F3
Beatty Ave GU1 . . . . 110 A2
Beauchamp Rd
East Molesey KT8 . . . . 36 C4
South Norwood CR7, SE25 . 42 D8
Sutton SM1 . . . . 59 A6
Twickenham TW1. . . . . 17 A8
Beauchamp Villas KT2 . . . . 17 F1
Beauclare Cl KT21. . . . . 95 D6
Beauclerc Ct TW13. . . . . . . 15 E4
Beauclerc Inf Sch TW16. . . 35 C6
Beauclere Ho 1 SM2. . . . . 59 C3
Beauclerk Cl TW13. . . . . . . 15 B7
Beauclerk Ho 10 SW16 . . . 21 E5
Beaufield Gate GU27 . . . . 208 D7
Beaufort Cl
Putney SW19 . . . . 19 B8
Reigate RH2. . . . . 117 F2
Woking GU22. . . . . 70 C3
Beaufort Ct TW10. . . . . 17 C4
Beaufort Gdns
Heston TW5 . . . . 4 E6
North Ascot SL5. . . . . 28 E8
South Norwood SW16 . . . . 21 F1

Beaufort Ho
Ashford TW15 .... 14 B3
9 Wimbledon SW20 ..... 39 D8
Beaufort Lodge CR2 ..... 61 D1
Beaufort Mews GU21 .... 69 D2
Beaufort Prim Sch GU21 . 68 F3
Beaufort Rd
Ash Vale GU12 .... 105 F6
Farnham GU9 .... 125 C3
Kingston upon Thames KT5,
KT6 .... 37 E5
Reigate RH2 .... 117 F2
Richmond TW10 .... 17 C4
Twickenham TW1 ...... 17 C8
Woking GU22 .... 70 C3
Beauforts TW19 .... 11 C3
Beaufort Way KT17 ...... 58 A3
Beaufoy Ho 3 SE27 ..... 22 B5
Beaufront Cl GU15 ...... 66 A7
Beaufront Rd GU15 ...... 66 B7
Beaulieu Ave SE26 ...... 23 B4
Beaulieu Cl
Bracknell RG12 .... 28 A6
Hounslow TW4 ....4 F2
Mitcham CR4 .... 41 A8
26 Twickenham TW1 .... 6 D1
Beaulieu Gdns GU17 .... 64 C5
Beaulieu Hts SE25 ...... 42 E8
Beaumaris Par GU16 .... 85 F8
Beaumont Ave TW9 ......6 F4
Beaumont Cl 3 RH11 ... 200 D1
Beaumont Ct
Ascot SL5 .... 28 F5
Ewell KT17 .... 76 F8
6 Mitcham CR4 .... 41 A7
5 Wimbledon SW20 .... 19 D1
Beaumont Dr
Ashford TW15 .... 14 D3
New Malden KT4 ...... 39 B2
Beaumont Gdns RG12 ... 27 E4
Beaumont Gr GU11 ..... 104 E2
Beaumont Ho
1 Streatham SW2 ..... 21 E7
Wimbledon SW19 ...... 20 A5
Beaumont Jun Sch GU11 104 F2
Beaumont Lodge BR4 ... 63 E7
Beaumont Pl TW7 ....5 F2
Beaumont Prim Sch CR8 . 80 A5
Beaumont Rd
Purley CR8 .... 80 A6
Putney SW15, SW19 ... 19 E8
South Norwood SE19 ... 22 C2
Beaumonts RH1 .... 139 F1
Beaumont Sq GU6 ..... 174 F3
Beaumont Terr 1 SE13 . 24 E8
Beaver Cl
Hampton TW12 .... 36 B8
Horsham RH12 .... 217 F6
8 Penge SE20 .... 23 A1
West Barnes SM4 ...... 39 C2
Wokingham RG41 ...... 25 B3
Beavers Cl
Farnham GU9 .... 125 A2
Guildford GU3 .... 108 E2
Beavers Com Prim Sch The
TW4 ....4 C4
Beavers Cres TW4 .... 4 D3
Beavers Hill GU9 .... 124 F2
Beavers La TW4 ....4 C4
Beavers Rd GU9 .... 125 A2
Beaver Water World *
TN16 .... 103 B5
Beck Ct BR3 .... 43 D6
BECKENHAM 44 A7
Beckenham Beacon Hill Sta
SE6 .... 24 C3
Beckenham Bsns Ctr BR3 23 E2
Beckenham Ct BR3 ...... 44 A8
Beckenham Gr BR2 ...... 44 D7
Beckenham Hill Rd BR3,
SE6 .... 24 C3
Beckenham Hospl BR3 .. 43 F7
Beckenham Junction Sta/
Halt BR3 .... 44 A8
Beckenham La BR2 ...... 44 F7
Beckenham Place Park
Nature Reserve * BR3 . 24 C2
Beckenham Place Pk BR3 24 B1
Beckenham Rd
Beckenham BR3 .... 43 E8
West Wickham BR3, BR4.. 44 C2
Beckenham Rd Halt BR3 . 43 E8
Beckenshaw Gdns SM7 .. 78 E4
Becket Cl
Croydon SE25 .... 43 A3
2 Merton SW19 .... 40 B8
Beckett Ave CR8 .... 80 B4
Beckett Cl
Streatham SW16 ...... 21 D6
Wokingham RG40 ...... 25 E6
Beckett Ho SM3 .... 58 D7
Beckett La RH11 .... 181 D1
Beckett Rd CR5 .... 99 D5
Becketts Cl TW14 ....4 B1
Becketts Pl KT1 .... 37 D8
Beckett Way 11 RH19 .. 205 E8
Beckett Wlk BR3 .... 23 E2
Becket Wood RH5 ...... 158 C4
Beckford Ave RG12 ..... 27 B3
Beckford Rd CR0 .... 42 F3
Beckford Way RH10 .... 202 B2
Beck Gdns GU9 .... 125 E3
Beckingham Rd GU2 ... 109 A2
Beck La BR3 .... 43 D6
Beckley Cotts KT23 ..... 94 C1

Beckmead Sch BR3 ...... 44 A1
Beck River Pk 8 BR3 ... 44 A8
Beck Way BR3 .... 44 A6
Beckway Rd SW16 ...... 41 D7
Beckworth Pl KT13 ..... 53 E8
Beclands Rd SW17 ..... 21 A2
Becmead Ave SW16 .... 21 D4
Becondale Rd SE19 ..... 22 E3
Bedale Cl RH11 .... 201 C4
BEDDIINGTON CORNER 41 A2
BEDDINGTON 60 E8
Beddington Cross CR0 .. 41 E2
Beddington Farm Rd
Croydon CR0 .... 60 F8
Wallington CR0, CR9 ... 41 E1
Beddington Gdns SM5,
SM6 .... 60 A4
Beddington Gr SM6 ..... 60 D5
Beddington Ind Est CR0 . 41 E1
Beddington Inf Sch SM6 . 60 C6
Beddington La CR0 ..... 60 E8
Beddington La Halt CR0. . 41 C3
Beddington Manor SM2 . 59 D4
Beddington Park Cotts
SM6 .... 60 D7
Beddington Park Prim Sch
CR0 .... 60 D7
Beddington Trading Est
CR0 .... 60 E8
Bedfordstead La CR6,
TN16 .... 103 A6
Bedelsford Specl Sch 11
KT1 .... 37 E6
Bedfont Cl
East Bedfont TW14 ......3 C1
Mitcham CR4 .... 41 A8
Bedfont Court Est TW19 ..2 B4
Bedfont Ct TW19 ....2 B3
Bedfont Green Cl TW14 . 14 C7
Bedfont Ind Pk TW15 ... 14 D5
Bedfont Ind Pk N TW15.. 14 C5
Bedfont Inf Sch TW14 ....3 E1
Bedfont Jun Sch TW14 ...3 E1
Bedfont La TW14, TW13 . 14 F8
Bedfont Lakes Ctry Pk*
TW14 .... 14 C6
Bedfont Rd
East Bedfont TW14, TW13.14 D6
Stanwell TW19 ....2 F1
Bedford Ave GU16 ...... 85 F5
Bedford Cl
13 Chiswick W4 ....7 E8
Woking GU21 .... 69 C4
Bedford Ct
9 Richmond TW9 ....6 F3
South Norwood SE19 ... 42 F8
Bedford Cres GU16 ..... 85 F6
Bedford Hill SW12, SW16,
SW17 .... 21 B6
Bedford Ho 3 GU1 .... 130 C8
Bedford La
Frimley GU16 .... 85 F6
Sunningdale SL5 .... 30 B4
Bedford Lakes Nature
Reserve* TW15 .... 14 B5
Bedford Pk CR0 .... 42 C1
Bedford Pl CR0 .... 42 D1
Bedford Rd
Guildford GU1 .... 130 C8
Horsham RH13 .... 217 D1
North Cheam KT4 ...... 58 C8
Twickenham TW2 ...... 16 D5
Bedford Terr 11 SM2 ... 59 C4
Bedford Villas SM5 ..... 59 F7
Bedgebury Gdns SW19 . 19 E6
Bedlow Cotts GU6 ..... 174 F3
Bedlow Way CR0 .... 60 F6
Bedser Cl
South Norwood CR7 .... 42 C6
Woking GU21 .... 70 A3
Bedster Gdns KT8 ...... 36 B6
Bedwardine Rd SE19 ... 22 E1
Beech Ave
Brentford TW8 ....6 B7
Camberley GU15 ...... 65 D4
Effingham KT24 ...... 113 D6
Farnham GU10 .... 146 C5
South Croydon CR2 .... 61 D1
Beech Cl
Aldershot GU12 ...... 126 E8
Ashford TW15 .... 14 D3
Blindley Heath RH7 ... 163 E8
Byfleet KT14 .... 71 E7
Carshalton SM5 .... 59 F8
Chiddingfold GU8 ..... 191 A4
Cobham KT11 .... 74 A8
Dorking RH4 .... 136 A8
2 East Grinstead RH19 . 185 D2
Effingham KT24 ...... 113 D7
Hersham KT12 .... 54 C6
Putney SW15 .... 19 A4
Stanwell TW19 .... 13 D8
Sunbury TW17 .... 35 D7
Wimbledon SW19 ...... 19 C2
Beech Close Ct KT11 ... 73 F8
Beech Copse CR2 ...... 61 E5
Beech Cres KT20 ...... 116 C5
Beechcroft
Ashtead KT21 .... 95 F8
Kingston upon Thames KT2 . 38 B8
Beechcroft Ave
Kenley CR8............ 80 D4
Kingston upon Thames KT1,
KT3 .... 38 C7
Beechcroft Cl
Ascot SL5............. 29 D5
Heston TW5............4 E7

Beechcroft Cl *continued*
Streatham SW16 ...... 21 F3
Beechcroft Ct RG12 .... 27 B6
Beechcroft Dr GU2 .... 129 D6
Beechcroft Lodge 12 SM2 59 C3
Beechcroft Manor KT13 . 53 D7
Beechcroft Mans SW16.. 21 F3
Beechcroft Rd
Chessington KT9 ...... 56 F7
Mortlake SW14 ....7 C4
Upper Tooting SW17 ... 20 E6
Beech Ct
Beckenham BR3 .... 23 F1
Chipstead CR5 .... 78 F1
East Grinstead RH19 . 185 D2
4 Guildford GU1 ..... 130 F8
5 West Norwood SW16 . 22 A3
Beechdene KT20 .... 97 B5
Beech Dr
Blackwater GU17 ...... 64 D4
Kingswood KT20 ...... 97 F5
Reigate RH2 .... 118 D1
Send Marsh GU23 ..... 91 A3
Beechen Cliff Way 2 TW7 .5 F6
Beechen La KT20 .... 97 F2
Beechen Pl SE23 .... 23 C6
Beeches Ave SM5 ...... 59 E3
Beeches Cl
Kingswood KT20 ...... 98 A4
Penge SE20 .... 43 C8
Beeches Cres RH10 ... 201 E4
Beeches Dr KT23 .... 94 B2
Beeches La RH19 ..... 206 D6
Beeches Mead RH19 .. 186 F5
Beeches Rd
Cheam SM3 .... 39 E1
Upper Tooting SW17 ... 20 F5
Beeches The
Ash Vale GU12 .... 85 F1
Banstead SM7 .... 78 B3
Bramley GU5 .... 151 F6
8 Farnborough GU14 .. 85 C1
Fetcham KT22 .... 94 E3
Hounslow TW3 ....5 B6
Mitcham CR4 .... 40 E4
Reigate RH2 .... 118 D2
South Croydon CR2 .... 61 C4
Staines TW18 .... 13 A3
Beeches Wlk SM2, SM5 . 59 E2
Beeches Wood KT20 ... 98 A5
Beechey Cl RH10 ..... 183 B5
Beechey Way RH10 ... 183 B3
Beech Farm Rd CR6 ... 102 E8
Beechfield SM7 .... 78 B6
Beechfield Ct 7 CR0 ... 61 C6
Beechfield Rd SE6 ..... 23 F7
Beechfields RH19 .... 185 F3
Beech Gdns
Crawley Down RH10 .. 204 A8
Woking GU21 .... 69 E4
Beech Glen RG12 ...... 27 B5
Beech Gr
Addlestone KT15 ...... 52 B6
Burgh Heath KT18 .... 77 B2
Caterham CR3 .... 100 E1
Great Bookham KT23 . 114 A8
Guildford GU2 .... 108 F1
Kingston upon Thames KT3 . 38 D6
Mitcham CR4 .... 41 D5
Pirbright GU24 .... 87 D7
Woking GU22 .... 89 D4
Beech Hall KT16 .... 51 C3
Beech Hanger End GU26 188 B3
BEECH HILL 187 A6
Beech Hill
Bowlhead Green GU8 . 189 D1
Headley Down GU35 .. 187 B5
Woking GU22 .... 89 D4
Beech Hill Rd
Headley Down GU35 .. 187 A5
Sunningdale SL5 ...... 29 F3
Beech Ho
Beckenham BR2 .... 44 E8
New Addington CR0 ... 63 B4
Beech Holme RH10 ... 204 B8
Beech Holt KT22 .... 95 C5
Beech House Rd CR0, CR9 . 61 D7
Beeching Cl GU12 .... 106 B3
Beeching Way RH19 .. 185 E1
Beech La
Flexford GU3 .... 107 A1
Grayshott GU26 ..... 188 B4
Guildford GU2 .... 130 C6
Beechland Cotts KT20 . 117 F7
Beechlawn GU1 ...... 130 F8
Beech Lodge TW18 .... 12 E3
Beechmeads KT11 ..... 73 D6
Beechmont Ave GU25 .. 31 D4
Beechmont Cl BR1 ..... 24 E3
Beechmore Gdns SM3.. 58 D8
Beechnut Dr GU17 ..... 64 B6
Beechnut Ind Est 9
GU12 .... 105 B1
Beechnut Rd 8 GU12 . 105 B1
Beecholme KT17 .... 77 E5
Beecholme Ave CR4 .... 41 B8
Beecholme Prim Sch CR4 41 B8
Beech Rd
Biggin Hill TN16 ...... 83 C2
East Bedfont TW14 ... 14 E8
Epsom KT18 .... 76 F4
Farnborough GU14 .... 85 A7
Frimley GU16 .... 85 F6

Beech Rd *continued*
Merstham RH1 .... 99 C1
Oatlands Park KT13 ... 53 D6
Reigate RH2 .... 118 A4
Thornton Heath SW16 . 41 F6
Beech Ride GU47 ...... 45 B1
Beechrow TW10 .... 17 C4
Beechside RH10 ...... 201 E5
Beechtree Ave TW20 ... 11 B2
Beech Tree Cl RH10 .. 201 D7
Beech Tree Ct BR2 ..... 44 E7
Beech Tree Dr GU9 ... 126 A5
Beech Tree La TW18 ... 33 B7
Beech Tree Pl SM1 ..... 59 B5
Beechvale 3 GU22 ..... 69 F1
Beechway GU1 .... 110 B2
Beech Way
Epsom KT17 .... 76 F4
Godalming GU7 ...... 150 D3
Selsdon CR2 .... 81 D7
Twickenham TW2 ..... 16 A5
Beech Wlk KT17 .... 77 A8
Beech Wood CR3 ..... 100 F3
Beechwood Ave
Ashford TW16 .... 15 A2
Kingswood KT20 ...... 98 A6
Oatlands Park KT13 ... 53 E6
Thornton Heath CR7 .. 42 B5
Wallington CR5 .... 79 B4
Beechwood Cl
Knaphill GU21 .... 68 E2
Long Ditton KT6 ...... 37 D2
North Ascot SL5 ....8 F1
Oatlands Park KT13 ... 53 E6
Beechwood Ct
Ashford TW16 .... 15 A3
Carshalton SM5 ...... 59 F6
Cheam SM1 .... 59 A5
Chiswick W4 ....7 D8
Sutton SM2 .... 59 B1
Walton-on-Thames KT12 . 54 A7
Beechwood Dr KT11 ... 74 A8
Beechwood Gdns CR3.. 101 A5
Beechwood La CR6 ... 101 D8
Beechwood Manor KT13.. 53 E6
Beechwood Pk KT22 ... 95 C5
Beechwood Rd
Caterham CR3 .... 101 A5
Knaphill GU21 .... 68 D2
South Croydon CR2 ... 61 E2
Wentworth GU25 ...... 31 B1
Beechwood Sch SW16 . 21 E5
Beechwoods Ct SE19 .. 22 F3
Beechwood Villas RH1 . 161 A7
Beecot La KT12 .... 54 C8
Beeding Cl RH12 ..... 218 A5
Beedingwood Dr RH12 . 218 E8
Beedon Dr RG12 .... 26 E3
Beehive La RG12 .... 26 C7
Beehive Rd
Bracknell RG12, RG42 . 26 D7
Staines TW18 .... 12 F3
Beehive Ring Rd RH6 .. 182 B4
Beehive The RH6 ..... 182 B4
Beehive Way RH2 .... 139 B5
Beeleigh Rd SM4 ...... 40 B5
Beemans Row 1 SW18 . 20 C6
Beeston Way TW14 ......4 C1
Beeton's Ave GU12 ... 106 A4
Beggarshouse La RH6 . 180 C8
Beggars La RH5 ...... 133 E4
Beggar's Roost La SM1.. 59 A4
Begonia 1 TW12 ...... 16 A2
Beharrell Ho SL5 ...... 29 E4
Behenna Cl RH11 .... 200 E5
Beira St SW12 .... 21 B8
Belcroft Cl BR1 .... 24 F1
Beldam Bridge Rd GU24.. 68 A6
Beldham Gdns KT8 .... 36 B6
Beldham Rd GU9 ..... 145 F7
Belenoyd Ct SW16 .... 21 F5
Belfast Rd SE25 .... 43 B5
Belfield Rd KT19 ...... 57 E2
Belfry Sh Ctr The RH1 . 118 F2
Belgrade Rd TW12 .... 36 B8
Belgrave Cl KT12 ...... 54 B6
Belgrave Cres GU15 ... 35 B8
Belgrave Ct GU17 ..... 64 D3
Belgrave Manor GU22 . 89 E8
Belgrave Rd
Barnes SW13 ....7 F7
Hounslow TW4 ....4 F4
Mitcham CR4 .... 40 D6
2 South Norwood SE25 . 42 F5
Sunbury TW16 .... 35 B8
Belgrave Wlk CR4 ..... 40 D6
Belgrave Wlk Halt CR4 . 40 D5
Belgravia Ct 1 RH6 ... 161 B3
Belgravia Gdns BR1 ... 24 E2
Belgravia Ho 1 TW11 . 17 C1
Belgravia Mews KT1 ... 37 D5
Bel La 2 TW13 .... 15 F5
Bellagio Pl RH19 ..... 185 D3
Bellamy Ho
Heston TW5 ....5 A8
Upper Tooting SW17 ... 20 D4
Bellamy Rd RH10 .... 202 C2
Bellamy St SW12 ...... 21 B8
Belland Dr GU11 ..... 104 E1
Bellasis Ave SW2 ...... 21 E6
Bell Bridge Rd KT16 ... 32 F1
Bell Cl GU14 .... 85 C6
Bell Cnr KT16 .... 32 F2
Bell Cres CR5 .... 99 B6

Bell Ct
Tolworth KT5 .... 57 B8
13 Woking GU22 ...... 69 F1
Bell Ctr RH10 .... 181 F2
Bell Dr SW18 .... 19 E8
Bellerby Ct GU2 ...... 129 E8
Bellever Hill GU15 ..... 65 E5
Belle Vue Cl
Aldershot GU12 ...... 105 D2
Staines TW18 .... 13 A8
Belle Vue Ent Ctr GU12 105 E2
Belle Vue Inf Sch GU12 105 D2
Bellevue Pk CR7 ...... 42 C5
Bellevue Rd
Kingston upon Thames
KT1 .... 37 E6
Upper Tooting SW17 ... 20 F7
Belle Vue Rd GU12 ... 105 D2
Bellew Rd GU16 .... 86 B7
Bellew St SW17 .... 20 C5
Bell Farm Jun Sch KT12.. 54 C6
Bellfield CR0 .... 62 F3
BELLFIELDS 109 C4
Bellfields Ct GU1 ..... 109 C5
Bellfields Rd GU1 .... 109 D3
Bell Foundry La RG40 . 25 C8
Bell Gn SE6 .... 23 F4
BELL GREEN 23 F4
Bell Green La BR3, SE26,
SE6 .... 23 F4
Bell Hammer RH19 ... 205 E8
Bell Ho 15 SW2 .... 22 A8
Bell House Gdns RG41.. 25 B6
BELLINGHAM 24 A3
Bellingham Cl GU15 ... 66 C4
Bellingham Dr RH2 ... 117 F1
Bellingham Gn SE6 .... 24 A5
Bellingham L Ctr SE6 .. 24 B5
Bellingham Rd SE6 .... 24 C5
Bellingham Sta SE6 ... 24 A5
Bellingham Trad Est SE6 . 24 B6
Bell La
Blackwater GU17 ...... 64 C5
Fetcham KT22 .... 94 D4
Rowledge GU10 ...... 145 E3
Twickenham TW1 ..... 17 A7
Bell Lane Cl KT22 ..... 94 D4
Bellmarsh Rd KT15 .... 52 B6
Bell Meadow
Dulwich SE19 .... 22 E4
Godstone RH9 .... 121 C3
Bellmore Ct 5 CR0 .... 42 F1
Belloc Ct RH10 ...... 202 C7
Belloc Ct RH13 ...... 218 A3
Bello Cl SE24 .... 22 B7
Bell Pl GU19 .... 47 F3
Bell Rd
East Molesey KT8 ..... 36 D4
Hounslow TW3 ....5 B3
Kingsley Green GU27 . 208 B3
Warnham RH12 ...... 217 A8
Bells La SL3 ....1 B4
Bell St RH2 .... 139 B8
Belltrees Gr 1 SW16 ... 22 A3
Bell Vale La GU27 .... 208 C4
Bell View BR3 .... 23 F1
Bellview Ct TW3 ....5 B3
Bell Vue Ho GU12 .... 105 D2
Bell Weir Cl TW19 ..... 12 B6
Bellwether La RH1 ... 162 B7
BELMONT 59 A2
Belmont Ave
Guildford GU2 .... 108 F4
West Barnes KT3 ..... 39 A5
Belmont Cl GU14 ...... 84 F7
Belmont Cotts SL3 ..... 1 C7
Belmont Ho GU9 ..... 146 A8
Belmont Mews
Camberley GU15 ..... 65 C3
Putney SW19 .... 19 D6
Belmont Pre Prep Sch
RH5 .... 155 D5
Belmont Rd
Beckenham BR3 ...... 43 F7
Belmont SM2 .... 59 A1
Camberley GU15 ..... 65 C4
Crowthorne RG45 .... 45 B6
Croydon SE25 .... 43 B4
Leatherhead KT22 ... 95 A5
Reigate RH2 .... 139 C8
Twickenham TW2 ..... 16 D6
Wallington SM6 ...... 60 C5
Belmont Rise SM1, SM2.. 58 F3
Belmont Sch RH5 .... 155 D6
Belmont Sta SM2 ...... 59 B1
Belmore Ave GU22 .... 70 D3
Belsize Gdns SM1 ..... 59 B6
Belsize Grange KT16 .. 33 C2
Belstone Mews GU14 .. 85 A7
Beltane Dr SW19 ...... 19 D5
Belthorn Cres SW12 ... 21 C8
Belton Rd GU15 .... 65 E5
Belvedere Ave SW19 .. 19 E3
Belvedere Cl
Esher KT10 .... 55 B5
Guildford GU2 .... 109 B3
Teddington TW11 ..... 16 E3
Weybridge KT13 ..... 53 A5
Belvedere Ct
Blackwater GU17 ..... 64 D3
Crawley RH10 .... 202 B7
8 Kingston upon Thames
KT2 .... 18 A1
Redhill RH1 .... 119 A5
Belvedere Dr SW19 ... 19 E3
Belvedere Gdns KT8 .. 36 A4
Belvedere Gr SW19 ... 19 E3

Belvedere Grange SL5 ... **30** A1
Belvedere Ho
Feltham TW13 ... **15** A7
Weybridge KT13 ... **53** B5
Belvedere Rd
Biggin Hill TN16 ... **83** F1
Farnborough GU14 ... **85** C2
Penge SE19 ... **22** F1
Belvedere Sq SW19 ... **19** E3
Belvoir Cl GU16 ... **65** F1
Belvoir Lodge SE22 ... **23** A8
Belvoir Rd SE22 ... **23** A8
Bembridge Ct 3 GU12 ... **105** C1
Benbow La GU8 ... **193** C4
Benbrick Rd GU2 ... **130** A8
Benbury Cl BR1 ... **24** C3
Bence The TW20 ... **32** B6
Bench Field CR2 ... **61** F5
Benchfield Cl RH19 ... **186** B1
Bencombe Rd CR8 ... **80** A5
Bencroft Rd SW16 ... **21** C1
Bencurtis Pk BR4 ... **63** D8
Bendon Valley SW18 ... **20** B8
Benedict Dr TW14 ... **14** D8
Benedict Prim Sch 1
CR4 ... **40** E6
Benedict Rd CR4 ... **40** D6
Benedict Wharf CR4 ... **40** E6
Benen-Stock Rd TW19 ... **2** A2
Benett Gdns SW16 ... **41** E7
Beney Ct BR3 ... **44** A7
Benfleet Cl
Cobham KT11 ... **73** E7
Sutton SM1 ... **59** C7
Benham Cl
Chessington KT9 ... **56** C4
Coulsdon CR5 ... **80** B1
Benham Gdns TW3, TW4 ... **4** F2
Benhams Cl RH6 ... **161** A5
Benhams Dr RH6 ... **161** A5
Benhill Ave SM1 ... **59** C6
Benhill Ct SM1 ... **59** D6
Benhill Rd SM1 ... **59** D6
Benhill Wood Rd SM1 ... **59** C6
BENHILTON ... **59** C7
Benhilton Ct SM1 ... **59** C7
Benhilton Gdns SM1 ... **59** B7
Benhurst Cl CR2 ... **62** D1
Benhurst Ct
13 Penge SE20 ... **43** B8
Streatham SW16 ... **22** A3
Benhurst Gdns CR2 ... **62** C1
Benhurst La SW16 ... **22** A3
Benin St SE13 ... **24** D8
Benjamin Ct TW15 ... **14** C1
Benjamin Mews SW17 ... **21** C8
Benjamin Rd RH10 ... **202** D4
Benn Cl RH8 ... **123** A1
Benner La GU24 ... **68** A7
Bennet Cl KT1 ... **37** C8
Bennets Ct SW19 ... **40** C8
Bennett Cl
Cobham KT11 ... **73** A6
Crawley RH10 ... **202** B2
Hounslow TW4 ... **4** E2
Bennett Ct GU15 ... **65** C5
Bennetts Ave CR0 ... **62** E8
Bennetts Cl CR4, SW16 ... **41** B8
Bennetts Farm Pl KT23 ... **93** F2
Bennetts Rd RH13 ... **217** E1
Bennetts Rise GU11 ... **126** C8
Bennett St 2 W4 ... **7** E8
Bennetts Way CR0 ... **62** F8
Bennetts Wood RH5 ... **178** C5
Bennett Way GU4 ... **111** B6
Benning Way RG40 ... **25** D8
Benns Wlk 5 TW9 ... **6** E3
Bens Acre RH13 ... **218** A2
Bensbury Cl SW15 ... **19** C8
Bensham Cl CR7 ... **42** C5
Bensham Gr CR7 ... **42** C7
Bensham La CR0, CR7 ... **42** B3
Bensham Manor Rd CR0,
CR7 ... **42** C5
Bensham Manor Specl Sch
CR7 ... **42** C4
Bensington Ct TW14 ... **3** D1
Benson Cl TW3 ... **5** A3
Benson Ho 1 TW10 ... **17** C5
Benson Prim Sch CR0 ... **62** E7
Benson Rd
Croydon CR0, CR9 ... **61** A7
Forest Hill SE23 ... **23** C7
Benson's La RH12 ... **199** C1
Bentall Sh Ctr KT2 ... **220** D5
Benthall Gdns CR8 ... **80** C2
Bentham Ave GU21 ... **70** C4
Bentinck Ho 4 TW10 ... **17** C5
Bentley Cl SW19 ... **20** A5
Bentley Copse GU15 ... **66** B4
Bentley Ct 1 GU15 ... **65** D6
Bentley Dr KT13 ... **53** A2
Bentley Pl KT13 ... **53** A6
Bentley Towers 4 GU15 ... **65** D5
Benton's La SE27 ... **22** C4
Benton's Rise SE27 ... **22** D3
Bentsbrook Cl RH5 ... **136** B3
Bentsbrook Cotts RH5 ... **136** B3
Bentsbrook Pk RH5 ... **136** B3
Bentsbrook Rd RH5 ... **136** B3
Benwell Ct TW16 ... **35** A8
Benwell Rd GU24 ... **88** A8
Benwick Ct SE20 ... **43** C8
Benwood Ct SM1 ... **59** C7
Beomonds 5 KT16 ... **33** A2
Beomonds Row 4 KT16 ... **33** A2
Berberis Cl GU1 ... **109** C3
Bere Rd RG12 ... **27** E3
Beresford Ave
Tolworth KT5 ... **38** C2
Twickenham TW1 ... **6** C1
Beresford Cl GU16 ... **85** F6
Beresford Ct
Farnborough GU14 ... **85** C1
Kingston upon Thames KT3 ... **38** C5
11 Twickenham TW1 ... **6** C1
Beresford Gdns TW4 ... **4** F2
Beresford Ho SE21 ... **22** E5
Beresford Rd
Belmont SM2 ... **58** F3
Dorking RH4 ... **136** B7
Kingston upon Thames KT2 ... **37** F8
Kingston upon Thames, Norbiton
KT3 ... **38** C5
Bergenia Ct GU24 ... **67** E6
Bergenia Ho TW13 ... **15** B7
Berkeley Ave TW4 ... **4** A5
Berkeley Cl
Crawley RH11 ... **200** E2
2 Kingston upon Thames
KT2 ... **17** E1
Stanwell TW19 ... **12** D6
Berkeley Cres GU16 ... **86** A8
Berkeley Ct
Ashtead KT21 ... **75** F1
3 Croydon CR0 ... **61** D6
Oatlands Park KT13 ... **53** E8
Wallington SM6 ... **60** C6
Berkeley Dr
Cranbourne SL4 ... **9** B7
East Molesey KT8 ... **36** A6
Berkeley Gdns
Claygate KT10 ... **56** A4
Pyrford KT14 ... **70** F5
Walton-on-Thames KT12 ... **34** F2
Berkeley Ho 13 TW8 ... **6** D8
Berkeley Lodge
Ashtead KT21 ... **95** D8
New Malden KT3 ... **38** E5
Berkeley Pl
Epsom KT18 ... **76** D4
Wimbledon SW19 ... **19** D2
Berkeley Prim Sch TW5 ... **4** D7
Berkeleys The KT22 ... **94** E3
Berkeley Waye TW5 ... **4** D7
Berkley Cl TW2 ... **16** E5
Berkley Ct
Guildford GU1 ... **109** E1
10 Twickenham TW1 ... **17** A8
Berkley Mews TW16 ... **35** C6
Berkshire Cl CR3 ... **100** D5
Berkshire Copse Rd
GU11 ... **104** E7
Berkshire Ho SE6 ... **24** A4
Berkshire Rd GU15 ... **65** F8
Berkshire Way
Bracknell RG12 ... **26** D6
Mitcham CR4 ... **41** E5
Bernard Ct GU15 ... **65** B4
Bernard Gdns 12 SW19 ... **19** F3
Bernard Rd SM6 ... **60** B6
Bernel Dr CR0 ... **62** F7
Berne Rd CR7 ... **42** C4
Bernersh Cl GU47 ... **45** C1
Berney Ho BR3 ... **43** E4
Berney Rd CR0 ... **42** D2
Berridge Rd SE19 ... **22** E3
Berrington Dr KT24 ... **92** F3
Berrybank GU47 ... **64** E6
Berrycroft RG12 ... **27** D8
Berry Ct TW4 ... **4** F2
Berry La
Hersham KT12 ... **54** D5
Pirbright GU3 ... **88** C2
West Norwood SE21, SE27 ... **22** D4
Woking GU22, GU3 ... **88** D4
BERRYLANDS ... **38** A3
Berrylands
Surbiton KT5 ... **37** F3
West Barnes SW20 ... **39** C5
Berrylands Ct 6 SM2 ... **59** B3
Berrylands Rd KT5 ... **37** F3
Berrylands Sta KT5 ... **38** B5
Berryman's La SE26 ... **23** D4
Berry Meade KT21 ... **75** F2
Berrymeade Wlk 6
RH11 ... **200** E5
Berryscourt KT14 ... **71** D8
Berryscroft Ct TW18 ... **13** C1
Berryscroft Rd TW18 ... **13** C1
Berry's La KT14 ... **71** D8
Berry Wlk KT21 ... **95** F8
Berstead Wlk 1 RH11 ... **200** F3
Bertal Rd SW17 ... **20** D4
Bertie Rd SE26 ... **23** D2
Bertram Cotts SW19 ... **20** A1
Bertram Rd KT2 ... **18** A1
Bertrand Ho 11 SW16 ... **21** E5
Bert Rd CR7 ... **42** C4
Bertrum House Sch SW17 ... **21** A6
Berwick Cl TW2 ... **16** A7
Berwick Ct KT4 ... **57** F8
Berwick Gdns SM1 ... **59** C7
Berwyn Ave TW3 ... **5** B6
Berwyn Rd
Mortlake SW14, TW10 ... **7** B3
Streatham SE24 ... **22** B7
Beryl Harding Ho 10
SW20 ... **19** D1
Berystede KT2 ... **18** B1
Besley St SW16 ... **21** C2
Bessant Dr TW9 ... **7** B6
Bessborough Rd SW15 ... **19** A7
Bessborough Wks KT8 ... **35** F4
Beswick Gdns RG12 ... **27** F8
Beta Rd
Chobham GU24 ... **49** F1
Farnborough GU14 ... **85** A5
Woking GU22 ... **70** B3
Beta Way TW20 ... **32** C8
Betchets Green Rd RH5 ... **157** C6
Betchley Cl RH19 ... **185** E3
BETCHWORTH ... **137** E8
Betchworth Cl SM1 ... **59** D5
Betchworth Sta RH3 ... **116** E3
Betchworth The RH4 ... **116** A1
Betchworth Way CR0 ... **63** C2
Betchworth Works RH6 ... **180** D6
Bethany Waye TW14 ... **14** E8
Bethel Cl GU9 ... **125** D6
Bethel La GU9 ... **125** D6
Bethersden Cl BR3 ... **23** F1
Bethesda Ct 6 SE20 ... **23** C1
Bethlem Royal Hospl The
BR3 ... **44** A2
Bethune Cl RH10 ... **202** D5
Bethune Rd RH13 ... **217** E1
Betjeman Cl CR5 ... **79** F2
Betley Ct KT12 ... **54** B7
Betony Cl CR0 ... **43** D1
Betts Cl BR3 ... **43** E7
Betts Way
Crawley RH10 ... **181** D2
Long Ditton KT6 ... **37** B1
Penge SE20 ... **43** B8
Bettswood Ct 16 SE20 ... **43** B8
Betula Cl CR8 ... **80** D4
Between Streets KT11 ... **73** A5
Beulah Ave CR7 ... **42** C7
Beulah Cres CR7 ... **42** C7
Beulah Gr CR0 ... **42** C3
Beulah Hill SE19, SW16 ... **22** C1
Beulah Inf Sch CR7 ... **42** C6
Beulah Jun Sch CR7 ... **42** C6
Beulah Rd
Merton SW19 ... **19** F1
South Norwood CR7 ... **42** C6
Sutton SM1 ... **59** A6
Beulah Wlk CR3 ... **101** E7
Bevan Ct
Crawley RH11 ... **201** B1
Croydon CR0 ... **61** A5
22 Twickenham TW1 ... **6** D1
Bevan Gate RG42 ... **27** A8
Bevan Ho TW13 ... **15** A5
Bevan Pk KT17 ... **57** F1
Beverley Ave
Hounslow TW4 ... **4** F3
Wimbledon SW20 ... **38** F8
Beverley Cl
Addlestone KT15 ... **52** D5
Ash GU12 ... **105** F1
Chessington KT9 ... **56** C6
East Ewell KT17 ... **77** C8
Frimley GU15 ... **66** D6
Oatlands Park KT13 ... **53** E8
Beverley Cotts SW15 ... **18** E5
Beverley Cres GU14 ... **84** F2
Beverley Ct
5 Belmont SM2 ... **59** A4
5 Hounslow TW4 ... **4** F3
Kingston upon Thames
SW20 ... **38** F8
Beverley Gdns
Barnes SW13 ... **7** F4
2 North Cheam KT4 ... **39** A1
Beverley Ho
Beckenham BR3 ... **24** C1
Catford BR1 ... **24** D3
Beverley Hts RH2 ... **118** B3
Beverley Hyrst 10 CR0 ... **62** A8
Beverley La KT2 ... **18** E1
Beverley Lodge 6 TW10 ... **6** E2
Beverley Mans 2 TW4 ... **4** F3
Beverley Mews RH10 ... **202** A5
Beverley Rd
Barnes SW13 ... **7** F4
Kenley CR3 ... **80** F2
Mitcham CR4 ... **41** D5
New Malden KT3 ... **39** A5
North Cheam KT4 ... **58** C8
Penge SE20 ... **43** B7
Sunbury TW16 ... **34** F8
Teddington KT1 ... **37** C8
Beverley Trad Est SM4 ... **39** D2
Beverley Way
Kingston upon Thames KT3,
SW20, KT2 ... **38** F8
Wimbledon KT3, SW20 ... **39** A6
Beverley Way Kingston By-Pass
Kingston upon Thames
KT3 ... **38** F8
West Barnes KT3, SW20 ... **39** A6
Beverly Rd RG12 ... **27** D5
Beverstone Rd CR7 ... **42** B5
Bevill Allen Cl SW17 ... **20** F3
Bevill Cl SE25 ... **43** A6
Bevington Rd BR3 ... **44** B7
Bevin Sq SW17 ... **20** F5
BEWBUSH ... **200** F3
Bewbush Comm Prim Sch
RH11 ... **200** F3
Bewbush Dr RH11 ... **200** F3
Bewbush Manor RH11 ... **200** E2
Bew Ct SE21 ... **23** A8
Bewley St SW19 ... **20** C2
Bewlys Rd SE27 ... **22** B3
Bexhill Cl TW13 ... **15** E6
Bexhill Rd
Forest Hill SE4 ... **23** F8
Mortlake SW14 ... **7** C4
Beynon Rd SM5 ... **59** F5
Bicester Rd TW9 ... **7** B4
Bickersteth Rd SW17 ... **20** F2
Bickley Ct
Crawley RH11 ... **201** A3
10 Wimbledon SW19 ... **20** A1
Bickley St SW17 ... **20** F3
Bicknell Cl GU1 ... **109** C2
Bicknell Rd GU16 ... **65** E2
Bickney Way KT22 ... **94** C5
Bicknoller Cl SM2 ... **59** B1
Bidborough Cl 5 BR2 ... **44** F4
Biddulph Rd CR2 ... **61** C2
Bideford Cl
Farnborough GU14 ... **85** A7
Feltham TW13 ... **15** F5
Bideford Rd BR1 ... **24** F5
Bidhams Cres KT20 ... **97** C6
Bidmead Ct KT6 ... **56** E7
Bield The RH2 ... **139** A7
Bietigheim Way 2 GU15 ... **65** C6
Big Apple The★ GU21 ... **69** F2
Big Common La RH1 ... **120** B3
Biggin Ave CR4 ... **40** F8
Biggin Cl RH11 ... **201** C4
BIGGIN HILL ... **83** E3
Biggin Hill SE19 ... **22** B1
Biggin Hill Airport TN16 ... **83** D5
Biggin Hill Bsns Pk TN16 ... **83** D4
Biggin Hill Cl KT2 ... **17** C3
Biggin Hill Prim Sch
TN16 ... **83** E3
Biggin Way SE19 ... **22** C1
Bigginwood Rd SW16 ... **42** B8
Bignor Cl RH12 ... **218** A7
Bilberry Cl RH11 ... **201** B3
Bilberry Manor SM2 ... **59** C3
Bilbets RH12 ... **217** C3
Billesden Rd GU24 ... **87** D7
Billet Rd TW18, TW19 ... **13** A5
Billhurst Cotts RH7 ... **164** D4
Billingshurst Rd RH12 ... **216** D3
Billington Ct RH19 ... **185** E2
Billinton Dr RH10 ... **202** B5
Billinton Hill CR0 ... **61** D8
Billockby Cl KT9 ... **56** F4
Billsley Ct SE25 ... **42** E5
Bilton Ind Est RG12 ... **26** E5
Binbury Row TW18 ... **12** E4
Bindon Gn SM4 ... **40** B5
Binfield Rd
Bracknell, Dowlesgreen
RG40 ... **25** F7
Bracknell, Priestwood RG42 ... **27** A8
Byfleet KT14 ... **71** E7
South Croydon CR2 ... **61** F5
Binfields GU9 ... **125** C3
Bingham Cnr CR0 ... **43** A1
Bingham Dr
Knaphill GU21 ... **68** F1
Staines TW18 ... **13** D1
Bingham Rd CR0, CR9 ... **43** B1
Bingley Rd TW16 ... **15** A1
Binhams Lea GU8 ... **192** F5
Binhams Mdw GU8 ... **192** F5
Binley Ho SW15 ... **7** F1
Binney Ct RH10 ... **182** E1
BINSCOMBE ... **150** D8
Binscombe Cres GU7 ... **150** E8
Binscombe La GU7 ... **150** E7
Binstead Cl RH11 ... **201** B8
Binsted Dr GU17 ... **64** D5
Binton La GU10 ... **126** E3
Birchanger GU7 ... **150** E4
Birchanger Rd SE25 ... **43** A4
Birch Ave
Caterham CR3 ... **100** D3
Leatherhead KT22 ... **94** F7
Birch Circ GU7 ... **150** F8
Birch Cl
Banstead SM7 ... **77** E5
Brentford TW8 ... **6** B7
Camberley GU15 ... **65** E8
Crawley Down RH10 ... **204** C8
Hounslow TW3 ... **5** D5
New Haw KT15 ... **52** D2
Rowledge GU10 ... **146** A4
Send Marsh GU23 ... **90** F2
Teddington TW11 ... **17** A3
Woking GU21 ... **89** C8
Birchcroft Cl CR3 ... **100** C2
Birch Ct
Ashtead KT21 ... **75** D2
Chipstead CR5 ... **78** F1
Croydon CR0 ... **61** F8
Sutton SM1 ... **59** C6
9 Wallington SM6 ... **60** B6
Birchdale Cl KT14 ... **71** C8
Birch Dr GU17 ... **64** D3
Birchend Cl CR2 ... **61** D4
Birches Cl
Epsom KT18 ... **76** E4
Mitcham CR4 ... **40** F6
Birches Ind Est RH19 ... **185** A3
Birches La GU5 ... **133** C2
Birches Rd RH12 ... **218** B5
Birches The
Blackwater GU17 ... **64** B5
5 Bromley BR2 ... **44** F5
Crawley RH10 ... **202** A7
East Horsley KT24 ... **92** E1
Farnborough GU14 ... **84** D4
South Norwood SE25 ... **42** F7
Twickenham TW4 ... **15** F8
Woking GU22 ... **69** F1
Birchett Rd
Aldershot GU11 ... **105** A2
Farnborough GU14 ... **84** E6
Birchetts Cl 1 RG42 ... **27** B8
Birchfield Cl
Addlestone KT15 ... **52** B6
Coulsdon CR5 ... **79** F3
Birchfield Gr KT17 ... **58** C1
Birchfields GU15 ... **65** C4
Birch Gn TW18 ... **13** A4
Birch Gr
Cobham KT11 ... **73** D5
East Grinstead RH19 ... **184** F4
Guildford GU1 ... **109** C4
Kingswood KT20 ... **97** F3
Lewisham SE12 ... **24** F8
Upper Halliford TW17 ... **34** E7
Woking GU22 ... **70** D4
BIRCH GREEN ... **13** A4
Birchgrove Ho TW9 ... **7** B7
BIRCH HILL ... **27** C2
Birch Hill CR0 ... **62** D5
Birch Hill Prim Sch RG12 ... **27** B1
Birch Hill Rd RG12 ... **27** B2
Birch Ho
Farnborough GU14 ... **85** A7
Teddington TW11 ... **17** C1
Birchington Rd KT5 ... **37** F2
Birch La
Purley CR8 ... **79** E8
West End GU24 ... **67** D7
Winkfield SL5 ... **28** A8
Birchlands Ave SW12 ... **20** F8
Birchlands Ct GU47 ... **45** E2
Birch Lea RH10 ... **182** A1
Birch Platt GU24 ... **67** D6
Birch Rd
Farncombe GU7 ... **151** A8
Feltham TW13 ... **15** D3
Headley Down GU35 ... **187** B6
Windlesham GU20 ... **48** E4
Birch Side RG45 ... **45** A6
Birch Tree Ave BR4 ... **63** F6
Birch Tree Gdns RH19 ... **185** B3
Birch Tree View GU18 ... **48** A1
Birch Tree Way CR0 ... **62** B8
Birch Vale KT11 ... **74** A6
Birch Way
Ash Vale GU12 ... **106** A7
Redhill RH1 ... **140** B7
Warlingham CR6 ... **81** E1
Birch Wlk
Mitcham CR4 ... **41** B8
West Byfleet KT14 ... **71** A7
Birchwood Ave
Beckenham BR3 ... **43** F5
Hackbridge SM6 ... **60** B7
Birchwood Cl
Crawley RH10 ... **202** C3
Horley RH6 ... **161** B4
Ifold RH14 ... **212** D3
Morden SM4 ... **40** B5
Birchwood Ct KT13 ... **53** C5
Birchwood Dr
Lightwater GU18 ... **48** C1
West Byfleet KT14 ... **71** A7
Birchwood Gr TW12 ... **16** A2
Birchwood La
Caterham CR3 ... **100** B2
Oxshott KT10, KT22 ... **55** E1
Birchwood Rd
Streatham SW17 ... **21** B3
West Byfleet KT14 ... **71** A7
Birdham Cl RH11 ... **201** B8
Birdhaven GU10 ... **146** A6
Birdhurst CR3 ... **100** F7
Birdhurst Ave CR2 ... **61** D6
Birdhurst Ct SM6 ... **60** C3
Birdhurst Gdns CR2 ... **61** D6
Birdhurst Rd
Mitcham SW19 ... **20** E2
South Croydon CR2 ... **61** E5
Birdhurst Rise CR2 ... **61** E5
Bird-in-Hand Pas SE23 ... **23** C6
Bird Mews RG40 ... **25** B6
Birds Gr GU21 ... **68** B1
Birds Hill Dr KT22 ... **74** D6
Birds Hill Rd KT22 ... **74** D6
Birds Hill Rise KT22 ... **74** D6
Birdswood Dr GU21 ... **88** E7
Birdwell Ct CR2 ... **61** D6
Bird Wlk TW2 ... **15** F7
Birdwood Cl
Selsdon CR2 ... **81** D8
Teddington TW11 ... **16** E4
Birdwood Rd GU15 ... **64** F6
Birdworld & Underwater World★ GU10 ... **145** B3
Birkbeck Hill SE21 ... **22** B7
Birkbeck Pl
Sandhurst GU47 ... **45** E1
West Norwood SE21 ... **22** C6
Birkbeck Rd
Penge BR3 ... **43** D7
Wimbledon SW19 ... **20** B2
Birkbeck Sta/Halt SE20 ... **43** C6
Birkdale RG12 ... **26** E2
Birkdale Ct SL5 ... **29** C4
Birkdale Dr RH11 ... **200** D5
Birkdale Gdns CR0 ... **62** D6
Birkenhead Ave KT2 ... **37** F8
Birkenholme Cl GU35 ... **187** C4
Birkhall Rd SE6 ... **24** D6
Birkheads Rd RH2 ... **118** A2
Birkin Ct KT14 ... **71** D8
Birkwood Cl SW12 ... **21** D8
Birnam Cl GU23 ... **91** A3
Birnham Ho TW1 ... **17** C8
Birtley Ctyd GU5 ... **152** B3

BIRTLEY GREEN 152 B3
Birtley Mews GU5 152 A3
Birtley Rd GU5 152 B4
Birtley Rise GU5 152 A5
Birtway Ct 15 SM1 59 C6
Biscoe Cl TW5 5 A8
Bisenden Rd CR0 61 E8
Bisham Cl
Carshalton CR4 40 F1
Crawley RH10 202 D3
Bishams Ct CR3 100 F3
Bishop Challoner Sch BR2 44 D7
Bishopdale RG12 27 A5
Bishop David Brown Sch The GU21 70 D6
Bishop Duppa's Almshouses 8 TW10 6 E2
Bishop Duppas Pk TW17 34 E2
Bishop Fox Way KT8 35 F5
Bishop Gilpin CE Prim Sch SW19 19 F3
Bishop Parkhurst GU1 110 B3
Bishop Perrin CE Prim Sch TW2 16 B7
Bishopric RH12 217 B2
Bishopric Ct 8 RH12 217 B2
Bishops Cl
Richmond TW10 17 D5
Sutton SM1 59 A7
Bishop's Cl CR5 80 A1
Bishop's Cotts RH3 116 B2
Bishopscourt 8 CR0 61 F8
Bishops Ct
1 Ashford TW16 14 F1
Guildford GU2 130 C7
Horsham RH12 217 C1
North Ascot SL5 8 F2
Richmond TW9 6 E4
Bishops Dr
East Bedfont TW14 3 D1
Wokingham RG40 25 C7
Bishopsford Com Sch SM4 40 D3
Bishopsford Ho SM4 40 E3
Bishopsford Rd SM4 40 D3
BISHOPSGATE 10 F4
Bishopsgate Rd TW20 11 B5
Bishopsgate Sch TW20 11 A5
Bishops Gr
Hampton TW12 15 F4
Windlesham GU20 48 C4
Bishop's Hall KT1 37 D7
Bishops Hill KT12 35 A2
Bishops Ho 6 GU7 150 D4
Bishop's La SL4 8 B7
Bishop's Mead GU9 125 B2
Bishopsmead Cl
East Horsley KT24 112 E7
Epsom KT19 57 D1
Bishopsmead Ct KT19 57 E1
Bishopsmead Dr KT24 112 F6
Bishopsmead Par KT24 112 F6
Bishops Park Rd SW16 41 E8
Bishop's Pl SM1 59 C5
Bishops Rd GU9 125 B7
Bishop's Rd CR0 42 B2
Bishops Sq GU6 174 F3
Bishopsthorpe Rd SE26 23 D4
Bishopstone Wlk RH10 201 C1
Bishop Sumner Dr GU9 125 C6
Bishops Way TW20 12 D2
Bishops Wlk CR0, CR9 62 E5
Bishops Wood GU21 68 F2
Bishop Thomas Grant Sch SW16 21 F3
Bishop Wand CE Sec Sch TW16 34 F7
BISLEY 68 B3
Bisley CE Prim Sch GU24 68 A3
Bisley Cl KT4 39 C1
Bisley Ho SW19 19 D6
Bison Ct TW14 15 B8
Bitmead Cl RH11 200 E5
Bittams La KT16 51 E6
Bittern Cl
Aldershot GU11 126 A7
Crawley RH11 200 D5
Sandhurst GU47 64 D8
Bitterne Dr GU21 69 A2
Bittoms The KT1 37 D6
Blackberry Cl
Guildford GU1 109 B4
Upper Halliford TW17 34 E5
Blackberry Farm Cl TW5 4 E7
Blackberry La RH7 185 E8
Blackberry Rd RH19, RH7 185 D8
Blackbird Cl GU47 64 D8
Blackbird Hill RH10 204 C5
Blackbird Pl RG12 26 D5
Blackborough Cl RH2 118 C1
Blackborough Rd RH2 118 D1
Blackbridge Ct RH12 217 A2
Blackbridge La RH12 217 A1
Blackbridge Rd GU22 89 D7
BLACKBROOK 136 E2
Blackbrook Rd
Dorking RH5 136 E2
South Holmwood RH5 157 E8
Blackburn The KT23 93 F3
Blackburn Trad Est TW19 2 F1
Blackburn Way
Godalming GU7 151 A5
Hounslow TW4 4 E2
Blackbush Cl SM2 59 B3
Blackcap Cl RH11 201 C4
Blackcap Pl GU47 64 E8
Black Cnr RH10 182 D4
Black Dog Wlk RH10 201 E8
Blackdown Ave GU22 70 E4
Blackdown Cl GU22 70 D3
Blackdown Rd GU16 86 C8
Blackenham Rd SW17 20 F4
Blackett Cl TW18 32 F7
Blackett Rd RH10 202 C5
Blackfold Rd RH10 202 A5
Blackford Cl CR2 61 B2
Blackham Ho SW19 19 E2
BLACKHEATH 131 F1
Blackheath RH10 202 D8
Blackheath Gr GU5 152 B8
Blackheath La
Albury GU5 132 B3
Wonersh GU5, GU4 152 C8
Blackheath Rd GU9 125 A7
Blackhills KT10 55 A2
Blackhorse La
Croydon CR0 43 A2
Lower Kingswood KT20, RH2 118 C7
Blackhorse Lane Halt CR0 43 A2
Blackhorse Rd GU21, GU22 88 E6
Black Horse Way RH12 217 C2
Black Lake Cl TW20 32 A8
Blacklands Cres RH18 206 F2
Blacklands Mdw RH1 119 E2
Blacklands Rd SE6 24 C4
Blackman Gdns GU11 126 B8
Blackman's La CR6 82 F5
Blackmeadows RG12 27 C3
Blackmoor Cl SL5 28 D7
Blackmoor Wood SL5 28 D7
Blackmore Cres GU21 70 C5
Blackmore Ho SE23 23 F7
Blackmore's Gr TW11 17 A2
Blackness La GU22 89 E8
BLACKNEST 30 B6
Blacknest Cotts GU8 192 E3
Blacknest Gate Rd SL5 30 B6
Blacknest Rd GU25, SL5 30 E6
Black Pond La GU10 146 C6
Black Potts Copse GU22 89 B8
Black Prince Cl KT14 71 F5
Blackshaw Rd SW17 20 D3
Blacksmith Cl KT21 95 F8
Blacksmith La GU4 131 D3
Blacksmiths Hill CR2 81 B6
Blacksmiths La KT16 33 A2
Blacksmith's La TW18 33 C6
Blackstone Cl
Farnborough GU14 84 D6
Reigate RH1 139 E8
Blackstone Hill RH1, RH2 118 E1
Blackstone Ho SE21 22 E5
Blackstroud Lane E GU18, GU24 67 E8
Blackstroud Lane W GU18 67 D8
Blackthorn Cl
Crawley RH11 181 C1
Horsham RH13 218 A2
Reigate RH2 139 C7
Blackthorn Cres GU14 84 F8
Blackthorn Ct
Heston TW5 4 E7
7 West Norwood SW16 22 A3
Blackthorn Dr GU18 67 B7
Blackthorne Ave CR0 43 C1
Blackthorne Cres SL3 1 E5
Blackthorne Ct TW15 14 C1
Blackthorne Rd
Great Bookham KT23 94 C1
Poyle SL3 1 E4
Blackthorn Pl GU1 109 C4
Blackthorn Rd
Biggin Hill TN16 83 E3
Reigate RH2 139 C7
BLACKWATER 64 D5
Blackwater Cl GU12 106 A1
Blackwater & Hawley L Ctr GU17 64 E3
Blackwater La RH10 202 D6
Blackwater Pk GU12 105 E1
Blackwater Sta GU17 64 E4
Blackwater Trad Est GU12 126 D8
Blackwater Way GU12 126 D8
BLACKWELL 185 E3
Blackwell Ave GU2 108 D1
Blackwell Farm Cotts GU3 129 C8
Blackwell Farm Rd RH19 185 F3
Blackwell Hollow RH19 185 F2
Blackwell Prim Sch RH19 185 E3
Blackwell Rd RH19 185 F2
Blackwood Cl KT14 71 C7
Bladen Cl KT13 53 E4
Blades Cl KT22 95 D7
Bladon Cl GU1 110 A2
Bladon Ct
Beckenham BR2 44 E7
Streatham SW16 21 E2
Blagdon Rd KT3 38 F5
Blagdon Wlk TW11 17 C2
Blair Ave KT10 55 C8
Blair Ct
Beckenham BR3 44 B8
Carshalton SM5 59 F7
Catford SE6 24 F7
Blairderry Rd SW2 21 E6
Blaise Cl GU14 85 D3
Blake Cl
Carshalton SM5 40 E1
Crawley RH10 201 F2
Crowthorne RG45 45 C4
Wokingham RG40 25 E8
Blake Ct CR0 61 B5
Blakeden Dr KT10 55 F4
Blakefield Gdns CR5 79 F1
Blakehall Rd SM5 59 F4
Blake Ho BR3 24 B2
Blake Mews 15 TW9 7 A6
Blakemore Rd
Streatham SW16 21 E5
Thornton Heath CR7 41 F4
Blakeney Ave BR3 43 F8
Blakeney Cl KT19 76 D8
Blakeney Rd
Beckenham BR3 43 F8
12 Beckenham BR3 44 A8
Blake Rd
Croydon CR0 61 E8
Mitcham CR4 40 E6
Blakes Ave KT3 38 F3
Blake's Gn BR4 44 C1
Blakes La KT3 38 F4
Blake's La GU4 111 F3
Blakes Terr KT3 39 A4
Blakewood Cl TW13 15 C4
Blakewood Ct SE20 23 B1
Blanchard Ho 13 TW1 6 D1
Blanchards Hill GU4 109 E8
Blanchland Rd SM4 40 B4
Blanchman's Rd CR6 81 E1
Blandfield Rd SW12 21 A8
Blandford Ave
Penge BR3 43 E7
Twickenham TW2 16 B7
Blandford Cl
Wallington CR0 60 E7
Woking GU22 70 B2
Blandford Rd
Penge BR3 43 D7
Teddington TW11 16 E3
Blane's La SL5 28 C3
Blanford Mews RH2 118 D1
Blanford Rd RH2 139 C8
Blanks La RH5, RH6 159 B2
Blashford St SE13 24 D8
Blatchford Cl RH13 217 F3
Blatchford Ct 6 KT12 35 A1
Blatchford Rd RH13 217 F3
Blays Cl TW20 11 C2
Blay's La TW20 11 B2
Blean Gr SE20 23 C1
Blegborough Rd SW16 21 C2
Blencarn Cl GU21 68 F3
Blendworth Point 4 SW15 19 B7
Blenheim 26 SW19 19 D7
Blenheim Ave RG12 27 C6
Blenheim Bsns Ctr CR4 40 F7
Blenheim Cl
Crawley RH10 182 D1
East Grinstead RH19 186 A3
Tongham GU10 126 E7
Wallington SM6 60 C3
West Barnes SW20 39 C6
West Byfleet KT14 70 F6
Blenheim Cres
Hale GU9 125 A5
South Croydon CR2 61 C3
Blenheim Ct
Bromley BR2 44 F5
Egham TW18 12 D4
Farnborough GU14 85 D2
8 Hampton TW12 36 A8
Richmond TW9 6 F4
South Norwood SE19 42 E8
Sutton SM2 59 C4
Blenheim Ctr TW3 5 B4
Blenheim Ctr SE26 23 D1
Blenheim Fields RH18 206 E3
Blenheim Gdns
Kingston upon Thames KT2 18 B1
Sanderstead CR2 81 A7
Wallington SM6 60 C3
Woking GU22 89 B8
Blenheim High Sch KT19 57 D1
Blenheim Ho TW3 5 A4
Blenheim Park Rd CR2 61 C2
Blenheim Pk GU11 105 C7
Blenheim Pl TW11 16 F3
Blenheim Rd
Epsom KT19 76 E8
Farnborough GU14 105 B7
Horsham RH12 217 D4
Penge SE20 23 C1
Sutton SM1 59 B7
West Barnes SW20 39 C6
Blenheim Way TW7 6 A6
Blenhiem Pl GU15 65 C3
Bleriot Rd TW5 4 C7
BLETCHINGLEY 120 D2
Bletchingley Cl RH1 119 C6
Bletchingley Rd
Godstone RH9 121 B4
Merstham RH1 119 E6
Nutfield RH1 120 A2
Bletchingly Cl CR7 42 B5
Bletchmore Cl UB3 3 D8
Blewburton Wlk RG12 27 E5
Blewfield GU7 150 F2
Bligh Cl RH10 201 F4
Bligh Ho 4 SE27 22 C4
Blighton La GU10 126 E3
Blincoe Cl SW19 19 D6
Blind Cnr SE25 43 B5
Blindley Ct RH7 163 E8
BLINDLEY HEATH 163 D8
Blindley Heath Nature Reserve* RH7 163 F6
Blindley Rd RH10 182 D1
Bloggs Way GU6 174 D3
Blomfield Dale RG42 26 D7
Blondell Cl UB7 2 D8
Bloo House Sch KT12 54 C5
Bloomfield Cl GU21 68 E1
Bloomfield Rd KT1 37 E6
Bloom Gr SE27 22 B5
Bloomhall Rd SE19 22 D3
Bloomsbury Cl KT19 57 D1
Bloomsbury Ct
Cranford TW5 4 B6
Guildford GU1 130 F7
Bloomsbury Way GU17 64 D3
Bloor Cl RH12 217 D7
Blossom Cl CR2 61 F5
Blossom House Sch SW20 19 C1
Blossom Waye TW5 4 E7
Blount Ave RH19 185 C1
Bloxham Cres TW12 35 F8
Bloxham Rd GU6 175 A3
Bloxworth Cl
9 Bracknell RG12 27 F5
Wallington SM6 60 C7
Blue Anchor Alley 7 TW9 6 E3
Blue Ball La TW20 11 F3
Blue Barn La KT13 72 A8
Bluebell Cl
Carshalton CR4 41 B1
Crawley RH11 201 B3
East Grinstead RH19 185 B1
Forest Hill SE26 22 F4
Horsham RH12 217 E5
Bluebell Ct GU22 89 D8
Bluebell Hill RG12 27 E8
Bluebell La KT24 112 E6
Bluebell Mews GU15 65 D7
Bluebell Rise GU18 67 B8
Blueberry Gdns CR5 79 F3
Bluebird Ho RH6 160 D1
Blue Cedars SM7 77 D5
Blue Cedars Pl KT11 73 D7
Blue Coat Wlk RG12 27 D4
Bluefield Cl TW12 16 A3
Bluegates
Stoneleigh KT17 58 A3
Wimbledon SW19 19 E3
Bluehouse Gdns RH8 123 A7
Bluehouse La RH8 122 F7
Blue Leaves Ave CR5 99 D6
Blueprint Apartments SW12 21 B8
Blue Ridges Pk RH5 178 A3
Blue Sch The TW7 6 A4
Bluethroat Cl GU47 64 E8
Bluff Cove GU11 105 C3
Blundel La KT11 74 B4
Blundell Ave RH6 160 F4
Blunden Rd GU14 84 F5
Blunt Rd CR0 61 D5
Blunts Ave UB7 3 A7
Blunts Way RH12 217 C3
Blyth Cl TW1 5 F1
Blythe Cl SE23 23 F8
Blythe Hill SE23, SE6 23 F8
Blythe Hill La SE23, SE6 23 F7
Blythe Ho RG12 26 F3
Blytheswood Pl SW16 21 F4
Blythe Vale SE23, SE6 23 F7
Blythewood 9 SM1 59 D5
Blythewood La SL5 28 E7
Blyth Rd BR1 44 F8
Blythwood Dr GU16 65 D2
Blythwood Pk 12 BR1 44 F8
Blyton Ct BR3 24 A2
Blytons The RH19 185 B1
Board School Rd GU21 69 F3
Boar Hill RH5 135 E1
Bocketts Farm Pk* KT22 94 F2
Bockhampton Rd KT2 17 F1
Boddicott Cl SW19 19 E6
Bodens Ride SL5 28 F1
Bodiam Cl RH10 202 C6
Bodiam Ct
Carshalton SM1 59 D6
Hayes BR2 44 F5
Bodiam Rd SW16 21 D1
Bodicea Mews TW4 5 A1
Bodley Cl KT3 38 E4
Bodley Manor Way SE24 22 A8
Bodley Rd KT3 38 E4
Bodmin Gr SM4 40 B4
Bodmin St SW18 20 A7
Bodnant Gdns SW20 39 B6
Bog La RG12 28 A5
Bognor Rd RH12, RH5 197 D4
Boileroom* GU1 130 D8
Bois Hall Rd KT15 52 D5
Bolderwood Way BR4 63 B8
Bolding House La GU24 67 F7
Boleyn Ave KT17 58 B1
Boleyn Cl
Crawley RH10 202 D3
Egham TW18 12 E3
Boleyn Ct
East Molesey KT8 36 D5
5 Knaphill GU21 68 C1
11 Redhill RH1 119 A2
Boleyn Dr KT8 35 F6
Boleyn Gdns BR4 63 B8
Boleyn Lodge SW19 19 D3
Boleyn Wlk KT22 94 F7
Bolingbroke Gr SW11 20 F8
Bolingbroke Ho
Beckenham BR3 43 E4
Catford BR3 24 B3
Bolney Ct
Crawley RH11 200 F3
Kingston upon Thames KT6 37 C4
Bolsover Gr RH1 119 E6
Bolstead Rd CR4 41 B8
Bolters La SM7 78 A4
Bolters Rd RH6 161 A5
Bolters Road S RH6 160 F6
Bolton Cl
Chessington KT9 56 E4
Penge SE20 43 A7
Bolton Dr SM4 40 D2
Bolton Gdns
Bromley BR1 24 F2
Teddington TW11 17 A2
Bolton Rd
Chessington KT9 56 E4
Chiswick W4 7 C7
Crawley RH10 202 C2
Boltons Cl GU22 71 A3
Bolton's La
Harlington UB3 3 B7
Pyrford GU22 71 A3
Bomer Cl UB7 3 A7
Bonaly Ho RH8 122 C4
Bonchurch Cl SM2 59 B3
Bond Gdns SM6 60 C6
Bond Prim Sch CR4 40 F7
Bond Rd
Mitcham CR4 40 F7
Surbiton KT6 56 F8
Warlingham CR6 81 E1
Bond's La RH5 136 B1
Bond St TW20 11 C3
Bond Way RG12 27 B8
Bonehurst Rd RH1, RH6 161 A7
Bone Mill La RH9 121 E1
Bonesgate Open Space Nature Reserve* KT19 57 B3
Bones La RH6, RH7 163 B2
Bonner Hill Rd KT1 38 A6
Bonners Cl GU22 89 F5
Bonnetts La RH11 181 A3
Bonnington Ho 11 SM2 59 B4
Bonnys Rd RH2 138 D8
Bonser Rd TW1 16 F6
Bonsey Cl GU22 89 E6
Bonsey La GU22 89 E6
Bonsey's La GU24, KT16 50 F2
Bonsor Dr KT20 97 E5
Bonus Pastor RC Coll BR1 24 E4
Bonville Rd BR1 24 F3
Bookham Ct
Little Bookham KT23 93 F4
Mitcham CR4 40 D6
Bookham Gr 2 KT23 94 B1
Bookham Grove Ho 3 KT23 94 B1
Bookham Ind Est KT23 93 F3
Bookham Ind Pk KT23 93 F4
Bookham Rd KT11 93 D7
Bookham Sta KT23 93 F4
Bookhurst Hill GU6 175 A4
Bookhurst Rd GU6 175 B4
Boole Hts RG12 27 A4
Boothby Ho 2 SW16 21 C3
Booth Dr TW18 13 D2
Booth Ho 9 TW8 6 C7
Booth Rd
Crawley RH11 200 E3
Croydon CR0, CR9 61 B8
Boothroyd Ho TW7 5 F4
Booth Way RH13 217 E3
Borage Cl 4 RH11 201 A2
Border Chase RH10 183 A2
Border Cres SE26 23 B3
Border Ct RH19 185 F4
Border End GU27 207 D6
Border Gate CR4 40 F8
Border Gdns CR0 63 B6
Border Mews GU26 188 D3
Border Rd
Forest Hill SE26 23 B3
Haslemere GU27 207 D6
Bordesley Rd SM4 40 B5
Bordeston Ct 11 TW8 6 C7
Bordon Wlk 6 SW15 19 A8
Boreen The GU35 187 B5
Borelli Mews GU9 125 C2
Borelli Yd GU9 125 C2
Borers Arms Rd RH10 183 C3
Borers Cl RH10 183 C4
Borers Yard Cotts RH10 183 C3
Borers Yard Ind Est RH10 183 C3
Borland Rd TW11 17 B1
Borough Grange CR2 81 A7
Borough Hill CR0, CR9 61 B7
Borough Rd
Godalming GU7 150 D5
Hounslow TW7 5 F6
7 Kingston upon Thames KT2 18 A1
Mitcham CR4 40 E7
Tatsfield TN16 103 D6
Borough The
Brockham RH3 137 A8
Farnham GU9 125 B2
Borrowdale Cl
Crawley RH11 201 B4
Sanderstead CR2 80 F6
3 Thorpe Lea TW20 12 B1
Borrowdale Dr CR2 80 F7
Borrowdale Gdns GU15 66 D4
Bosbury Rd SE6 24 C5

Boscombe Cl TW20 .... 32 C8
Boscombe Gdns SW16 ... 21 E2
Boscombe House CR0 .... 42 D1
Boscombe Rd
  Merton SW19 .... 40 B8
  Mitcham SW17 .... 21 A2
  North Cheam KT4 ..... 39 D1
Bosham Rd RH10 ..... 202 C3
Boshers Gdns TW20 .... 11 F2
Bosman Dr GU20 ...... 48 B6
Bostock Ave RH12 .... 218 A5
Bostock Ho TW5 ...... 5 A8
Boston Ct
  South Norwood SE25 ... 42 F5
  Sutton SM2 .... 59 C3
Boston Gdns W4 .... 7 E8
Boston Manor Rd
  Brentford TW8 .... 6 B8
  Brentford TW8 .... 6 C8
Boston Rd CR0 .... 42 A3
Boswell Ho 5 SW16 ... 21 C3
Boswell Rd
  Crawley RH10 .... 201 E3
  Thornton Heath CR7 ... 42 C5
Boswood Ct TW4 ...... 4 F4
Botany Hill GU10 ..... 126 D1
Botery's Cross RH1 ... 120 B2
Bothwell Rd CR0 ...... 63 C1
Bothy The GU22 ...... 70 F2
Botsford Rd SW20 .... 39 E7
Boucher Cl TW11 ..... 16 F3
Boughton Ave BR2 .... 44 F2
Boughton Hall Ave GU23 . 90 F3
Bouldish Farm Rd SL5 ... 29 A5
Boulevard The
  Crawley RH10 .... 201 E6
  4 Upper Tooting SW17 ... 21 A6
Boullen Ct SM1 ...... 59 C6
Boulogne Rd CR0 ..... 42 C3
Boulters Rd RG13 ..... 27 E5
Boulters Rd 2 GU11 ... 105 B1
Boulthurst Way RH8 ... 123 B3
Boundaries Mans 3
  SW12 .... 21 A7
Boundaries Rd
  Feltham TW13 .... 15 C7
  Upper Tooting SW12, SW17 21 A7
Boundary Bsns Ct CR4 ... 40 D6
Boundary Bsns Ctr GU21 . 70 A4
Boundary Cl
  Crawley RH10 .... 201 E7
  Kingston upon Thames KT1 . 38 B6
  Penge SE20 .... 43 A7
Boundary Cotts GU4 ... 132 A4
Boundary Ho
  6 Balham SW12 ...... 21 B7
  Twickenham TW1 ..... 6 B2
Boundary Pk KT13 .... 53 E7
Boundary Point CR3 ... 100 C5
Boundary Rd
  Crawley RH10 .... 201 E7
  Dockenfield GU10 .... 166 D7
  Farnborough GU14 .... 85 C2
  Grayshott GU26 ..... 188 D3
  Mitcham SW19 .... 20 D2
  Rowledge GU10 ...... 145 E2
  Staines TW15 .... 13 C3
  Wallington SM5, SM6 ... 60 A3
  Woking GU21 .... 70 A4
Boundary Road E KT15 ... 52 B2
Boundary Road N KT15 ... 52 B2
Boundary Road W KT15 ... 52 B2
Boundary Way
  Addington CR0 ...... 63 A5
  Woking GU21 .... 70 A4
Boundfield Rd SE6 .... 24 E6
BOUNDSTONE 146 A5
Boundstone Cl GU10 ... 146 B5
Boundstone Rd GU10 ... 146 A4
Bourbon Ho SE6 ...... 24 C4
Bourdon Rd SE20 ..... 43 C7
Bourg-de-Peage Ave
  RH19 .... 186 A1
Bourke Hill CR5 ...... 78 F1
Bourley La GU9 ...... 104 A2
Bourley Rd
  Aldershot GU11 ..... 104 C2
  Crondall GU10 .... 104 C2
Bourne Ave KT16 ..... 33 A6
Bourne Bsns Pk KT15 ... 52 E6
Bourne Cl
  Chilworth GU4 ...... 131 B3
  Hinchley Wood KT7 ... 55 F8
  Hounslow TW7 .... 5 E4
  West Byfleet KT14 .... 71 B6
Bourne Ct
  Aldershot GU11 ...... 126 A8
  Caterham CR3 .... 101 A4
  Chiswick W4 .... 7 C8
  1 Purley CR8 .... 80 A8
  West Byfleet KT14 .... 71 E6
Bourne Dene GU10 .... 146 A5
Bourne Dr CR4 .... 40 D7
Bournefield Rd CR3 ... 81 A1
Bourne Firs GU10 .... 146 D5
Bourne Gr
  Ashtead KT21 .... 95 D8
  Farnham GU10 ...... 146 E7
Bourne Grove Cl GU10 . 146 E7
Bourne Grove Dr GU10 . 146 E7
Bourne Hall Mus* RH7 . 57 F2
Bourne Ho 6 TW15 ... 14 A3
Bourne Hts GU9 ...... 146 C8
Bourne La CR3 .... 100 D6
Bourne Lodge CR3 .... 100 F3
Bourne Mdw TW20 .... 32 B5
Bourne Mews RH9 .... 121 C6

Bourne Mill Bsns Pk
  GU9 .... 125 E3
Bournemouth Ct SM1 ... 59 C5
Bournemouth Rd SW19 ... 40 A8
Bourne Park Cl CR8 ... 80 E3
Bourne Rd
  Farncombe GU7 ..... 150 F7
  Merstham RH1 ...... 119 C5
  Virginia Water GU25 ... 31 D4
  Woodham KT15 ...... 52 B2
Bourne Sch The GU10 ... 146 D6
Bourneside GU25 ..... 31 A2
Bourneside Gdns SE6 ... 24 C3
Bourneside Rd KT15 ... 52 D5
Bourne St CR0, CR9 ... 61 B8
Bourne Vale BR2 ..... 44 F1
Bournevale Rd SW16 ... 21 E4
Bourne View CR8 ..... 80 D4
Bourne Way
  Addlestone KT15 ..... 52 C5
  Cheam SM1 .... 58 F5
  Coney Hall BR2, BR4 ... 63 F8
  West Ewell KT19 ..... 57 C6
  Woking GU22 .... 89 D5
Bournewood Pk GU10 . 146 E7
Bourns Ct RH13 ...... 217 E3
Bournville Rd SE13, SE6 . 24 A8
Bousley Rise KT16 .... 51 D4
Bouverie Ct SW16 .... 21 E3
Bouverie Gdns CR8 ... 79 F5
Bouverie Rd CR5 ..... 79 A1
Boveney Ho RG12 ..... 27 E5
Boveney Rd SE23 ..... 23 D8
Bovey Ho 3 RH1 ..... 119 A3
Bovill Rd SE23 .... 23 D8
Bovingdon Sq CR4 .... 41 E5
Bowater Gdns TW16 ... 35 C7
Bowater Rd RH10 .... 202 C3
Bowater Ridge SL5 .... 53 D1
Bow Corner 1 TW2 ... 16 E6
Bowden Cl TW14 ..... 14 E7
Bowden Rd SL5 ...... 29 D4
Bowen Dr SE21 ...... 22 E5
Bowen Way CR5 ..... 99 D5
Bower Ct GU22 ...... 70 B3
Bower Hill Cl RH1 .... 140 E6
Bower Hill La RH1 .... 140 D7
Bowerland La RH7 .... 164 E7
Bower Rd GU10 ...... 146 A5
Bowers Cl GU4 ...... 110 A6
Bowers Farm Dr GU4 ... 110 B5
Bowers La GU4 ...... 110 A6
Bowers Pl RH10 ...... 204 B8
Bowers The RG40 .... 25 A1
Bowes Cl RH13 ...... 217 E3
Bowes Lyon Ho 2 TW10 . 17 C5
Bowes Rd
  Egham TW18 .... 12 E2
  Walton-on-Thames KT12 . 54 B8
Bowfell Rd SW4 ...... 21 D8
Bowland Dr RG12 ..... 27 E2
Bowley Cl SE19 ...... 22 F2
Bowley La SE19 ...... 22 F2
BOWLHEAD GREEN 169 E1
Bowlhead Green Rd GU8 170 B1
Bowling Green Cl SW19 . 19 B8
Bowling Green Ct GU16 . 85 E7
Bowling Green La RH12 217 D3
Bowling Green Rd GU24 . 49 E2
Bowlings The GU15 ... 65 C6
Bowman Ct RH10 .... 201 D7
Bowman Mews SW18 ... 19 F7
Bowmans Lea SE23 ... 23 C8
Bowman's Mdw SM6 ... 60 B7
Bowness Cl 7 RH11 ... 200 D5
Bowness Cres SW15 ... 18 E3
Bowness Dr TW4 ..... 4 E3
Bowness Rd SE6 ..... 24 B8
Bowry Ho GU7 .... 150 F6
Bowsley Ct TW13 .... 15 A4
Bowsprit The KT11 ... 73 C4
Bowyer Cres RG40 ... 25 C8
Bowyer Ho CR4 ...... 40 E6
Bowyers Cl KT21 ..... 75 F1
Bowyer Wlk SL5 ..... 28 E8
Boxall Rd SE21 ...... 22 E8
Boxall's Gr GU11 ..... 126 A8
Boxall's La GU11 ..... 126 A7
Boxall Wlk RH13 ..... 217 D1
Box Cl RH11 .... 201 C1
Boxford Cl CR2 ...... 81 D7
Boxford Ridge RG12 ... 27 B6
Boxgrove Ave GU1 .... 110 A3
Boxgrove La GU1 ..... 110 B2
Boxgrove Prim Sch GU1. 110 B2
Boxgrove Rd GU1 .... 110 A2
BOX HILL 116 A4
Box Hill Ctry Pk* KT20 . 115 D3
Boxhill Farm Barns RH4. 115 C2
Boxhill Rd RH4 ...... 115 C3
Box Hill Sch RH5 ..... 115 B8
Boxhill Way RH3 ..... 137 B5
Boxhill & Westhumble Sta
  RH5 .... 115 B4
Boxhurst RH4 .... 115 C3
Box La RH19 .... 206 E6
Boxley Rd SM4, SW19 ... 40 C5
Box Ridge Ave CR8 ... 79 F7
Box Tree Wlk RH1 .... 139 C7
Boxwood Way CR6 .... 81 D2
Boyce Ho SW16 ...... 21 C3
Boyd Cl KT2 .... 18 A1
Boyd Ct RG42 .... 27 A8
Boyland Rd BR1 ..... 24 F3
Boyle Farm Rd KT7 ... 37 A3
Brabazon Ave SM6 ... 60 E3

Brabazon Rd TW5 ..... 4 D7
Brabham Ct KT4 ..... 58 B8
Brabon Rd GU14 ..... 84 F5
Brabourne Cl 7 SE19 ... 22 E3
Brabourne Ct SM2 ... 59 B4
Brabourne Rise BR3 .. 44 D4
Brabrook Ct SM6 ..... 60 B5
Bracebridge GU15 .... 65 A5
Bracewood Gdns CR0 . 61 F7
Bracken Ave
  Balham SW12 .... 21 A8
  West Wickham CR0 ... 63 B7
Bracken Bank SL5 .... 28 C8
Bracken Cl
  Ashford TW16 ...... 14 F2
  Copthorne RH10 .... 183 B2
  Little Bookham KT23 ... 93 F3
  4 Twickenham TW2 ... 16 A8
  Woking GU22 .... 69 F1
  Wonersh GU5 .... 152 B6
Brackendale KT1 ..... 38 B7
Brackendale Ct 2 BR3 . 24 A1
Brackendale Rd GU15 . 65 D4
Brackendene GU12 ... 106 C3
Brackendene Cl GU21 ... 70 A4
Bracken End TW7 ..... 5 D2
Bracken Gr RH12 .... 218 B5
Brackenhill 1 RH1 ... 74 B7
Bracken Hill Cl 7 BR1 . 44 F8
Bracken Hill La BR1 ... 44 F8
Brackenlea GU7 ..... 150 D7
Bracken Path KT18 ... 76 B6
Brackens The RG45 ... 45 A7
Bracken Way
  Chobham GU24 ...... 49 F1
  Guildford GU3 ...... 108 E3
Brackenwood
  Cranleigh GU6 ...... 174 B3
  Frimley GU15 .... 66 D5
  Sunbury TW16 ...... 35 A8
Brackenwood Rd GU21. 88 D8
Bracklesham Cl GU14 . 85 A7
Bracklesham Ho GU21. 68 C1
Brackley KT13 .... 53 D5
Brackley Cl SM6 ..... 60 E3
Brackley Rd BR3 ..... 24 A1
BRACKNELL 27 D6
Bracknell Beeches RG12 27 B6
Bracknell Bsns Ctr The
  RG12 .... 26 F7
Bracknell Cl GU15 .... 46 F1
Bracknell Enterprise Ctr
  RG12 .... 27 A7
Bracknell Rd
  Bracknell RG19 ..... 47 E5
  Camberley GU15 .... 47 A1
  Crowthorne RG45 ... 45 D6
  Winkfield RG42 ..... 8 A5
Bracknell Sp & L Ctr
  RG12 .... 27 C4
Bracknell Sta RG12 ... 27 B6
Bracknell Wlk RH11 ... 200 E3
Bracknell & Wokingham Coll
  RG12 .... 27 C8
Bracknell & Wokingham Coll
  (Wick Hill Ctr) RG12 ... 27 C8
Bracondale KT10 ..... 55 C5
Bradbury Ct SW20 ... 39 C7
Bradbury Rd RH10 ... 202 C3
Braddock Cl TW7 ..... 5 F5
Braddon Rd TW9 ..... 6 F4
Bradenhurst Cl CR3 ... 100 F2
Bradfield Cl
  Guildford GU4 ...... 110 A4
  Woking GU22 .... 69 E1
Bradfields RG12 ..... 27 D4
Bradford Cl SE26 .... 23 B4
Bradford Dr KT19 .... 57 F4
Brading Rd
  Streatham SW2 ..... 21 F8
  Thornton Heath CR0 . 41 F3
Bradley Cl SM2 ...... 59 B1
Bradley Ct CR0 ...... 61 A6
Bradley Dr RG40 .... 25 A2
Bradley La RH4, RH5 ... 115 B3
Bradley Mews SW12 ... 20 F7
Bradley Rd SE19 ..... 22 C2
Bradmore Gn CR5 .... 79 F1
Bradmore Way CR5 ... 79 F1
Bradshaw Cl SW19 ... 20 A2
Bradshaws 3 SE25 ... 43 A6
Bradsole Ho 13 BR3 ... 24 A1
Bradstock Rd KT17 ... 58 B5
Braeburn Rd RH11 ... 181 A1
Brae Ct
  2 Kingston upon Thames
  KT2 .... 38 A8
  South Norwood SE25 ... 42 E8
Braemar Ave
  South Croydon CR2 ... 61 C2
  Thornton Heath CR7 . 42 B6
  Wimbledon SW18, SW19 20 A6
Braemar Cl
  Frimley GU16 ...... 85 F8
  Godalming GU7 ..... 150 D3
Braemar Ct
  5 Brentford TW8 ..... 6 D8
  Catford SE6 .... 24 F7
Braemar Gdns BR4 ... 44 C1
Braemar Ho TW11 ... 17 B3

Braemar Rd
  Brentford TW8 ...... 6 D8
  North Cheam KT4 ... 58 B7
Braeside
  Beckenham BR3 .... 24 B3
  Bracknell RG12 ..... 26 C7
  Horley RH6 .... 161 A3
  Woodham KT15 ..... 71 B8
Braeside Ave SW19 ... 39 E8
Braeside Cl GU27 .... 207 F8
Braeside Rd SW16 ... 21 C1
Braes Mead RH1 .... 140 E8
Brafferton Rd CR0 ... 61 C6
Braganza St GU1 .... 109 F2
Bragg Rd TW11 ..... 16 F2
Braid Cl TW13 ...... 15 F6
Braidwood Ho 2 CR7 . 42 A8
Braidwood Rd SE6 ... 24 D7
Brailsford Cl CR4 .... 20 E1
Brainton Ave TW14 ... 15 C8
Brakenhale Sch The RG12 27 B5
Brake Rd GU14 ...... 84 E1
Brakes Rise GU47 .... 64 E8
Brakey Hill RH1 ..... 120 E1
Bramber Cl
  Crawley RH10 ...... 201 E8
  Horsham RH12 ..... 218 B5
Bramber Ho 15 KT2 ... 37 E8
Bramber Way CR6 ... 81 F3
Bramble Acres Cl SM2 . 59 A3
Bramble Bank GU16 ... 86 A6
Bramble Banks SM5 ... 60 A2
Bramble Cl
  Beckenham BR3 .... 44 C4
  Copthorne RH10 .... 183 B3
  Croydon CR0 .... 63 B6
  Guildford GU3 ...... 108 E3
  London SE19 .... 42 D8
  Oxted RH8 .... 123 B2
  Redhill RH1 .... 140 A7
  Upper Halliford TW17 . 34 D6
Bramble Ct GU6 ..... 175 E6
Brambledene Cl GU21 . 69 C1
Brambledown
  Hindhead GU26 .... 188 E4
  Staines TW18 ...... 33 B8
Brambledown Cl BR2, BR4 44 E4
Brambledown Rd
  South Croydon CR2 ... 61 E3
  Wallington SM5, SM6 ... 60 B8
Bramblegate RG45 ... 45 A6
Bramblehall La KT20 . 115 F3
Bramble Hedge Farm (Ind
  Est) KT11 .... 72 C5
Bramble La TW12 .... 15 F2
Bramble Rise KT11 ... 73 C5
Brambles Cl
  Ash GU12 .... 106 B1
  Brentford TW7, TW8 ... 6 B7
  Caterham CR3 ...... 100 E5
Brambles Pk GU5 .... 151 F6
Brambles The
  Farncombe GU7 ..... 150 D7
  8 Wimbledon SW19 ... 19 F3
Brambleton Ave GU9 . 146 B7
Bramble Twitten RH19 186 A1
Brambletye Jun Sch
  RH1 .... 140 A7
Brambletye La RH18 . 206 D4
Brambletye Park Rd
  RH1 .... 140 A7
Brambletye Rd RH10 . 202 A5
Brambletye Sch RH19 . 206 C5
Bramble Way GU23 ... 90 F3
Bramble Wlk KT18 ... 76 B6
Bramblewood RH2 ... 119 B6
Bramblewood Cl SM5 . 40 E1
Brambling Cl RH13 ... 218 A1
Brambling Ct 4 SE25 . 42 F5
Brambling Rd RH13 ... 218 A1
Bramcote
  Frimley GU15 ...... 66 C5
  Weybridge KT13 .... 53 C6
Bramcote Ave CR4 ... 40 F5
Bramcote Ct CR4 .... 40 F5
Bramerton Rd BR3 ... 43 F6
Bramham Gdns KT9 ... 56 D6
Bramis Ho TN16 ..... 83 D3
BRAMLEY 151 F6
Bramley Ave
  Coulsdon CR5 ...... 79 C4
  Upper Halliford TW17 . 34 E6
Bramley Bank Nature
  Reserve* CR0 ...... 62 C4
Bramley Bsns Ctr The
  GU5 .... 151 F7
Bramley CE Inf Sch GU5 152 A5
Bramley Cl
  Chertsey KT16 ..... 33 B1
  Crawley RH10 ...... 201 F6
  Croydon CR2 .... 61 C5
  Redhill RH1 .... 139 E7
  Staines TW18 ...... 13 C2
  Twickenham TW2 ... 5 C1
Bramley Croft GU26 . 188 E4
Bramley Ct
  Feltham TW14 ..... 3 E1
  Mitcham CR4 .... 40 D7
  Redhill RH1 .... 118 C3
  Wallington SM6 .... 60 C5
Bramley Gr RG45 .... 95 E8
Bramley Grange GU5 . 151 F6
Bramley Hill CR0, CR2 . 61 C6
Bramley Ho
  3 Hounslow TW3 ..... 4 F3
  1 Kingston upon Thames
  KT2 .... 18 B1
  Redhill RH1 .... 140 A8

Bramley Ho continued
  Roehampton SW15 ... 7 F1
Bramleyhurst CR2 .... 61 C5
Bramley La BR1 ..... 64 B5
Bramley Park Ct GU5. 151 F6
Bramley Rd
  Camberley GU15 .... 65 B2
  Carshalton SM1 .... 59 D5
  East Ewell SM2 ..... 58 D2
Bramley Sch KT20 ... 97 A2
Bramley Way
  Ashtead KT21 ...... 75 F2
  Hounslow TW4 ..... 4 F2
  West Wickham CR0 ... 63 B8
Bramley Wlk RH6 .... 161 C3
Brampton Gdns KT12 . 54 C5
Brampton Ho RH1 ... 139 F5
Brampton Rd CR0 .... 42 F3
Bramshaw Rise KT3 ... 38 E3
Bramshot La GU14 ... 84 A5
Bramshot Rd GU14 ... 84 A2
Bramshott Ct 3 KT6 ... 37 E3
Bramston Rd SW17 ... 20 C5
Bramswell Rd GU7 ... 150 F6
Bramwell Cl TW16 ... 35 D7
Bramwell Pl 69 F3
Brancaster La CR8 ... 80 C8
Brancaster Rd SW16 . 21 E1
Branch Ho 19 SM1 ... 59 C6
Brandon Cl
  Crawley RH10 ...... 202 D4
  Frimley GU15 ...... 66 D4
Brandon Ho BR3 .... 24 B3
Brandon Rd SM1 .... 59 B6
Brandreth Rd SW17 ... 21 B6
Brandries The SM6 ... 60 D7
BRANDS HILL 1 A8
Brandsland RH2 .... 139 B6
Brands Rd SL3 ...... 1 B8
Brandy Way SM2 ... 59 A3
Brangbourne Rd BR1 . 24 C3
Brangwyn Cres SW19 . 40 D7
Branksome KT13 .... 53 D4
Branksome Cl
  Camberley GU15 .... 65 E6
  Teddington TW11 ... 16 D4
  Walton-on-Thames KT12 . 54 D8
Branksome Hill Rd GU47 64 E8
Branksome Park Rd GU15 65 E6
Branksome Rd SW19 . 40 A8
Branksome Way KT3 ... 38 D8
Bransby Rd KT9 ..... 56 E4
Branscombe Ct BR2 ... 44 E4
Branstone Ct 9 TW9 ... 6 F6
Branstone Rd TW9 ... 6 F6
Brantridge Rd RH10 ... 201 F4
Brants Bridge RG12 ... 27 E7
Brantwood Ave TW7 ... 6 A3
Brantwood Cl 1 KT14 . 71 A6
Brantwood Ct KT14 ... 70 F6
Brantwood Dr KT14 ... 70 F6
Brantwood Gdns 2 KT14 . 71 A6
Brantwood Rd CR2 ... 61 D2
Branxholme Ct BR1 ... 44 F8
Brassey Cl
  East Bedfont TW14 ... 15 A7
  Limpsfield RH8 ..... 123 A6
Brassey Hill RH8 .... 123 A6
Brassey Ho KT12 .... 35 A1
Brassey Rd RH8 ..... 123 A6
Brasted Cl
  Belmont SM2 .... 59 A1
  Forest Hill SE26 .... 23 C4
Brasted Lodge 11 BR3. 24 A1
Brathway Rd SW18 ... 20 A8
Brattain Ct RG12 .... 27 D6
Bratten Ct CR0 ...... 42 D3
Braunston Ho TW8 ... 6 C8
Bravington Cl TW17 ... 33 F4
Braxted Pk SW16 .... 21 F2
Braybourne Dr TW7 ... 5 F7
Braybrook RG41 .... 25 A6
Braybrooke Gdns SE19 . 22 E1
Bray Cl RH10 .... 202 D4
Braycourt Ave KT12 ... 35 C2
Bray Ct
  Chessington KT9 ... 56 F5
  Streatham SW16 ... 21 E3
Braye Cl GU47 ...... 45 C1
Bray Gdns GU22 .... 70 E3
Bray Rd
  Guildford GU2 ...... 130 B8
  Stoke D'Abernon KT11 . 73 E3
Braywick Ct 9 KT2 ... 18 A1
Braywood Ave TW20 . 12 A2
Braziers La RG42, SL4 . 8 D4
Brazil Cl CR0 .... 41 E2
Breakfield CR5 ...... 79 E3
Breakspeare SE21 .... 22 F5
Breamore Cl SW15 ... 19 A7
Breamwater Gdns TW10 . 17 B5
Brecon Cl
  Farnborough GU14 ... 84 D7
  Mitcham CR4 .... 41 E6
  North Cheam KT4 ... 58 C8
Brecon Ho SW18 .... 20 A8
Brecon Hts RH11 .... 201 C5
Brecons The RH13 ... 53 D6
Bredhurst Cl SE20 ... 23 C2
Bredinghurst SE22 ... 23 A8
Bredon Rd CR0 ..... 42 F2
Bredune CR8 .... 80 C4
Breech La KT20 ..... 97 A2
Breech The GU47 .... 64 E7
Breezehurst Dr RH11 . 200 F3

Bregsells Dr RH5 . . . . 157 D4
Bregsells La RH5 . . . . 157 D4
Bremer Rd TW18, TW19 . . . 13 A5
Bremner Ave RH6 . . . . 160 F4
Brenchley Cl BR2 . . . . 44 F3
Brenda Rd SW17 . . . . 20 F6
Brende Gdns KT8 . . . . 36 B5
Brendon Cl
　Esher KT10 . . . . 55 C4
　Harlington UB7 . . . . 3 C7
Brendon Dr KT10 . . . . 55 C4
Brendon Rd GU14 . . . . 84 D7
Brenley Cl CR4 . . . . 41 A6
BRENTFORD 6 D7
Brentford Bsns Ctr TW8 . . . 6 C7
BRENTFORD END 6 C7
Brentford Ho [7] TW1 . . . . 17 B8
Brentford Sch for Girls
　TW8 . . . . 6 D8
Brentford Sta TW8 . . . . 6 C8
Brent Ho BR1 . . . . 24 D3
Brent Knoll Sch SE26 . . . . 23 D5
Brent Lea TW8 . . . . 6 C7
Brent Rd
　Brentford TW8 . . . . 6 C8
　South Croydon CR2 . . . . . 62 B2
Brentside TW8 . . . . 6 C8
Brentside Executive Ctr
　TW8 . . . . 6 B8
Brentwaters Bsns Pk TW8 . 6 C7
Brent Way TW8 . . . . 6 D7
Brentwood Ct KT15 . . . . . . 52 B6
Brereton Ho [3] SW2 . . . . 22 A8
Bret Harte Rd GU16 . . . . . 65 E1
Bretherton Ct CR2 . . . . . . 61 E4
Bretlands Rd KT16 . . . . . . 51 E8
Brettgrave KT19 . . . . 57 C1
Brett Ho [1] SW15 . . . . . . 19 D8
Brett House Cl [2] SW15 . . 19 D8
Brettingham Cl RH11 . . . . 200 E3
Bretts RH4 . . . . 136 C4
Brewer Rd RH10 . . . . 201 E4
Brewers Cl GU14 . . . . 85 A5
Brewers La [10] TW9 . . . . . 6 D2
Brewer St RH1 . . . . 120 C4
Brewery La KT14 . . . . 71 E6
Brewery Mews Bsns Ctr [1]
　TW7 . . . . 6 A4
Brewery Rd GU21 . . . . 69 E2
Brew House Rd RH3 . . . . . 137 B5
Brewhurst La RH14 . . . . . 213 A2
Breydon Wlk RH10 . . . . . . 202 B4
Brian Ave CR2 . . . . 80 E7
Briane Rd KT19 . . . . 57 C1
Briar Ave
　Lightwater GU18 . . . . 67 A8
　South Norwood SW16 . . . 21 F1
Briar Banks SM5 . . . . 60 A2
Briar Cl
　Chelsham CR6 . . . . 82 A3
　Crawley RH11 . . . . 181 C1
　Hampton TW12 . . . . 15 F3
　Isleworth TW7 . . . . 5 C2
　West Byfleet KT14 . . . . . 71 C8
Briar Ct
　Cheam SM3 . . . . 58 C6
　Hampton TW12 . . . . 16 B3
Briardale SW19 . . . . 19 F7
Briar Gdns BR2 . . . . 44 F1
Briar Gr CR2 . . . . 81 A6
Briar Hill CR8 . . . . 79 E8
Briar La
　Croydon CR0 . . . . 63 B6
　Wallington SM5 . . . . 60 A2
Briarleas Ct GU14 . . . . . . 105 D8
Briar Patch GU7 . . . . 150 D6
Briar Rd
　Littleton TW17 . . . . 34 A4
　Send GU23 . . . . 90 B4
　Thornton Heath SW16 . . 41 F6
　Twickenham TW2 . . . . . . 16 E7
Briars Cl GU14 . . . . 84 D3
Briars Cross RH8 . . . . 123 D5
Briars Ct KT22 . . . . 74 D5
Briars The
　Ash GU12 . . . . 106 B1
　Chessington KT9 . . . . . . 57 A4
Briars Wood RH6 . . . . 161 C4
Briarswood Cl RH10 . . . . . 202 D8
Briar The [17] SM1 . . . . . . 59 C6
Briar Way GU4 . . . . 110 B5
Briar Wlk KT14 . . . . 71 A7
Briarwood SM7 . . . . 78 A4
Briarwood Cl TW13 . . . . . 14 E5
Briarwood Ct [5] KT4 . . . . 39 A1
Briarwood Rd
　Knaphill GU21 . . . . 88 D8
　Stoneleigh KT17 . . . . . . 58 A4
Briary Lodge BR3 . . . . 44 C8
Briavels Ct KT18 . . . . 76 E4
Brickersbury Ho GU14 . . . 84 F8
Brickfield Ct TW8 . . . . 6 C7
Brickfield La
　Harlington UB3 . . . . 3 D8
　Hookwood RH6 . . . . 160 D1
Brickfield Rd
　Outwood RH1 . . . . 162 C8
　South Norwood CR7, SW16 . 42 B8
　Wimbledon SW19 . . . . . . 20 B4
Brickfields Bsns Ct RG12 . 27 A7

Brick Hill GU24 . . . . 49 C6
Brickhouse La RH7, RH9 . 163 E4
Brick Kiln La RH8 . . . . 123 C5
Bricklands RH10 . . . . 204 B7
Bricksbury Hill GU9 . . . . . 125 C7
Brickwood Cl SE26 . . . . . . 23 B5
Brickwood Rd CR0 . . . . . . 61 E8
Brickyard Copse RH5 . . . 177 C4
Brickyard La
　Crawley Down RH10 . . . 204 B8
　Wotton RH5 . . . . 134 D2
Brideake Cl RH11 . . . . . . 201 A3
Bridge Barn La GU21 . . . . 69 D1
Bridge Cl
　Byfleet KT14 . . . . 71 F7
　Lower Halliford KT12 . . . 34 F1
　Staines TW18 . . . . 12 E4
　Teddington TW1 . . . . . . 16 F4
　Woking GU21 . . . . 69 C2
Bridge Cotts GU6 . . . . . 174 B3
Bridge Ct
　Leatherhead KT22 . . . . . 95 A5
　Walton-on-Thames KT12 . 34 F1
　[5] Weybridge KT13 . . . . 53 B6
　Woking GU21 . . . . 69 D2
　Wrecclesham GU10 . . . 145 F7
Bridge End GU15 . . . . 65 B4
Bridge End Cl [5] KT2 . . . . 38 A8
Bridgefield GU9 . . . . 125 D3
Bridgefield Cl SM7 . . . . . . 77 C4
Bridgefield Rd SM1 . . . . . 59 A4
Bridge Gate Ho GU7 . . . . 150 E5
Bridge Gdns
　East Molesey KT8 . . . . . 36 D5
　Littleton Common TW15 . 14 C1
Bridgeham Cl KT13 . . . . . 53 A5
Bridgeham Way RH6 . . . . 162 B2
Bridgehill Cl GU2 . . . . . . 109 A3
Bridge Ho
　Chertsey KT16 . . . . 33 C2
　[4] Sutton SM2 . . . . 59 B4
Bridge Ind Est RH6 . . . . . 161 B3
Bridge La GU25 . . . . 31 F3
Bridgelands RH10 . . . . . . 183 A3
Bridgelands Cl BR3 . . . . . 23 F1
Bridge L Ctr SE26 . . . . . . 23 F4
Bridgeman Rd TW11 . . . . 17 A2
Bridgemead GU16 . . . . . . 85 D8
Bridge Mead GU24 . . . . . 87 F1
Bridge Mews
　Godalming GU7 . . . . 150 E4
　Tongham GU10 . . . . 126 F7
　Woking GU21 . . . . 69 D2
Bridge Par
　Croydon CR0 . . . . 61 B7
　Purley CR8 . . . . 80 A7
　Streatham SW16 . . . . . . 21 E3
Bridge Pk GU4 . . . . 110 C4
Bridge Pl CR0 . . . . 42 D1
Bridge Rd
　Aldershot GU11 . . . . . . 126 A8
　Ascot SL5 . . . . 29 D4
　Bagshot GU19 . . . . 47 E3
　Camberley GU15 . . . . . . 65 B3
　Chertsey KT16 . . . . 33 B2
　Chessington KT9 . . . . . . 56 E5
　Cobham KT11 . . . . 73 B4
　Cranleigh GU6 . . . . 174 E3
　East Molesey KT8 . . . . . 36 E5
　Epsom KT17 . . . . 76 F7
　Farnborough GU14 . . . . 84 F4
　Farncombe GU7 . . . . . . 150 E5
　Haslemere GU27 . . . . . 208 C7
　Isleworth TW3, TW7 . . . . 5 D4
　Penge BR3 . . . . 23 F1
　Rudgwick RH12 . . . . . . 214 D7
　Sutton SM2 . . . . 59 B4
　Twickenham TW1 . . . . . . 6 B1
　Wallington SM6 . . . . 60 C5
　Weybridge KT13 . . . . . . 52 F6
Bridge Ret Pk RG40 . . . . . 25 B5
Bridge Row CR0 . . . . 42 D1
Bridges Cl RH6 . . . . 161 D3
Bridges Ct RH12 . . . . 218 A5
Bridges La CR0 . . . . 60 E6
Bridge Sq GU9 . . . . 125 C2
Bridges Rd SW19 . . . . . . 20 B2
Bridges Road Mews SW19 20 B2
Bridge St
　Colnbrook SL3 . . . . 1 D7
　Godalming GU7 . . . . . . 150 E4
　Guildford GU1 . . . . 130 C8
　Leatherhead KT22 . . . . . 95 A5
　Richmond TW10 . . . . 6 D2
　Staines TW18 . . . . 12 E4
　Walton-on-Thames KT12 . 34 F2
Bridgetown Cl [5] SE19 . . 22 E3
Bridge View SL5 . . . . 30 B2
Bridgewater Pl GU21 . . . . 69 F3
Bridgewater Rd KT13 . . . . 53 D4
Bridge Way
　Chipstead CR5 . . . . 98 E8
　Twickenham TW2 . . . . . . 16 C8
Bridge Wharf KT16 . . . . . 33 C2
Bridge Wharf Rd TW7 . . . . 6 B4
Bridgewood Cl SE20 . . . . 23 B1
Bridgewood Rd
　North Cheam KT4 . . . . . 58 A6
　Streatham SW16 . . . . . . 21 D1
Bridge Works
　Camberley GU15 . . . . . . 65 B3
　Leatherhead KT22 . . . . . 95 A8
Bridgford St SW17, SW18 . 20 C5
Bridle Cl
　Grayshott GU26 . . . . . . 188 A3
　Kingston upon Thames KT1 . 37 D5
　Sunbury TW16 . . . . 35 A6
　West Ewell KT19 . . . . . . 57 D5

Bridle Ct GU11 . . . . 104 E2
Bridle La TW1 . . . . 6 B1
Bridle Path CR0 . . . . 60 E7
Bridle Path The KT17 . . . . 58 C1
Bridlepath Way TW14 . . . . 14 E7
Bridle Rd
　Addington CR0 . . . . 63 A6
　Claygate KT10 . . . . 56 B4
　Epsom KT17 . . . . 76 F6
Bridle Rd The CR8 . . . . . . 60 E1
Bridle Way
　Crawley RH10 . . . . 202 D7
　Croydon CR0 . . . . 63 A6
Bridleway Cl KT17 . . . . . . 58 C1
Bridleway The SM6 . . . . . 60 C5
Bridlington CT TN16 . . . . 103 B8
Bridport Rd CR7 . . . . 42 B6
Bridwell Cl GU8 . . . . 170 F1
Brier Lea KT20 . . . . 97 F1
Brierley CR0 . . . . 63 B4
Brierley Cl SE25 . . . . 43 A5
Brierley Rd SW12 . . . . . . 21 C6
Brierly Cl GU2 . . . . 109 A3
Brigade Pl CR3 . . . . 100 C5
Brier Rd KT20 . . . . 97 B8
Briggs Cl CR4 . . . . 41 B8
Brighthampton KT13 . . . 53 F6
Bright Hill GU1 . . . . 130 E7
Brightlands Rd RH2 . . . . 118 C3
Brightman Rd SW18 . . . . 20 D7
Brighton Cl KT15 . . . . 52 C5
Brighton Rd
　Addlestone KT15 . . . . . . 52 C5
　Aldershot GU11 . . . . . . 126 C8
　Banstead KT20, SM2, SM7 . 77 F3
　Belmont SM2 . . . . 59 B2
　Coulsdon CR5, CR8 . . . . 79 D4
　Crawley RH11 . . . . 201 D4
　Croydon CR2, CR8 . . . . 61 C3
　Godalming GU7 . . . . . . 150 E3
　Hascombe GU8 . . . . . . 172 D4
　Hooley CR5, RH1 . . . . . . 99 B6
　Horley RH6 . . . . 160 F2
　Horsham RH13 . . . . 217 E1
　Kingston upon Thames KT6 . 37 D3
　Kingswood KT20 . . . . . . 97 E5
　Lower Kingswood KT20 . 117 F8
　Purley CR8 . . . . 80 B8
　Redhill RH1 . . . . 139 F8
　Salfords RH1 . . . . 140 A2
　South Croydon CR2 . . . . 61 C3
Brighton Terr [6] RH1 . . . 139 F8
Brightside Ave TW18 . . . . 13 C1
Brightwell CT CR0 . . . . . . 42 A1
Brightwell Cres SW17 . . . 20 F3
Brightwells Rd GU9 . . . . 125 C2
Brigstock Par [1] CR7 . . . 42 A4
Brigstock Rd
　Coulsdon CR5 . . . . 79 B3
　Thornton Heath CR7 . . . 42 B5
Brimshot La GU24 . . . . . . 49 E2
Brindle Cl GU11 . . . . 126 B7
Brindles The SM7 . . . . . . 77 F2
Brindley Ho
　Carshalton SM1 . . . . . . 59 E5
　[21] Streatham SW12 . . . 21 E8
Brine Ct KT6 . . . . 37 D4
Brinkley Ct KT4 . . . . 58 B8
Brinkley Rd KT4 . . . . 58 B8
Brinkworth Pl SL4 . . . . . . 11 B8
Brinn's La GU17 . . . . 64 C5
Brinsworth Cl TW2 . . . . . 16 D6
Brisbane Ave SW19 . . . . . 40 B8
Brisbane Cl RH11 . . . . . . 181 D1
Briscoe Rd SW19 . . . . . 20 D2
Brisson Cl KT10 . . . . 54 F4
Bristol Cl
　Crawley RH10 . . . . 182 D1
　[7] Hounslow TW4 . . . . . 16 A8
　Stanwell TW19 . . . . 2 E1
　Wallington SM6 . . . . 60 E3
Bristol Ct [11] TW19 . . . . . 2 E1
Bristol Gdns SW15 . . . . . 19 C8
Bristol Rd SM4 . . . . 40 C4
Bristow Inf Sch GU15 . . 65 B2
Bristow Rd
　Camberley GU15 . . . . . . 65 B3
　Hounslow TW3 . . . . 5 C4
　Wallington SM6 . . . . 60 E6
　West Norwood SE19 . . . 22 E3
Britannia Ind Est SL3 . . . 1 E5
Britannia Rd KT5 . . . . 37 F2
Britannia Way TW19 . . . . 13 D8
British Home & Hospl for
　Incurables SE27 . . . . . 22 B3
British Wildlife Ctr★
　RH7 . . . . 163 E3
Briton Cl CR2 . . . . 80 E8
Briton Cres CR2 . . . . 80 E8
Briton Hill Rd CR2 . . . . . . 61 F1
BRIT Sch The SE25 . . . . 42 D3
Brittain Ct GU47 . . . . 64 C7
Brittain Rd KT12 . . . . 54 D5
Britten Cl
　Ash GU12 . . . . 106 B2
　Crawley RH11 . . . . 200 F3
　Horsham RH13 . . . . 218 B4
Brittens Cl GU2, GU3 . . . 109 A6
Britton Cl SE6 . . . . 24 D8
Brixton Hill SW2 . . . . 21 E8
Brixton Hill Pl SW2 . . . . . 21 E8
Broadacre GU18 . . . . 13 A3
Broad Acres GU7 . . . . . . 150 E8
BROADBRIDGE HEATH . 216 E4
Broadbridge Heath L Ctr
　RH12 . . . . 216 E2

Broadbridge Heath Rd
　RH12 . . . . 216 D4
Broadbridge La
　Burstow RH6 . . . . 183 B8
　Smallfield RH6 . . . . 162 A2
Broadbridge Ret Pk
　RH12 . . . . 216 E3
Broad Cl KT12 . . . . 54 E7
Broadcoombe CR2 . . . . . 62 D3
Broadeaves Cl
　Croydon CR0 . . . . 61 E5
　South Croydon CR2 . . . . 61 E5
BROADFIELD 201 C1
Broadfield Barton [4]
　RH11 . . . . 201 B2
Broadfield Cl
　Burgh Heath KT20 . . . . . 97 C7
　Croydon CR0 . . . . 60 F8
Broadfield Dr RH11 . . . . . 201 B3
Broadfield East Jun & Inf
　Schs RH11 . . . . 201 C2
Broadfield Pl RH11 . . . . . 201 B2
Broadfield Rd
　Catford SE6 . . . . 24 E7
　Peaslake GU5 . . . . 154 D8
Broadfields KT8 . . . . 36 E3
Broadfield Stadium (Crawley
　Town FC) RH11 . . . . . . 201 C2
BROADFORD 130 D1
Broadford La GU24 . . . . . 68 E7
Broadford Pk GU4 . . . . . 130 D2
Broadford Pk Bsns Ctr
　GU4 . . . . 130 D2
Broadford Rd GU4 . . . . . 130 D2
Broadgates Rd SW18 . . . 20 D7
Broad Green Ave CR0 . . . 42 B2
BROADHAM GREEN . . . 122 D3
Broadham Green Rd
　RH8 . . . . 122 D2
Broadham Pl RH8 . . . . . . 122 D4
Broad Ha'penny GU10 . . 146 A5
Broad Highway KT11 . . . . 73 D5
Broadhurst
　Ashtead KT21 . . . . 75 E3
　Farnborough GU14 . . . . 84 C5
Broadhurst Cl [9] TW10 . . 6 F2
Broadhurst Gdns RH2 . . . 139 B6
Broadhurst Mews [4]
　GU12 . . . . 105 C1
Broad La
　Bracknell RG12 . . . . 27 D6
　Hampton TW12 . . . . 16 A2
　Parkgate RH2, RH5 . . . . 158 E6
Broadlands
　Farnborough GU14 . . . . 85 E2
　Feltham TW13 . . . . 16 A5
　Frimley GU16 . . . . 85 F8
Broadlands Ave
　Shepperton TW17 . . . . . 34 C3
　Streatham SW16 . . . . . . 21 E6
Broadlands Bsns Campus
　RH12 . . . . 198 C4
Broadlands Cl SW16 . . . . 21 E6
Broadlands Ct
　Bracknell RG42 . . . . 26 E8
　Richmond TW9 . . . . 7 A7
Broadlands Dr
　Sunningdale SL5 . . . . . . 29 D2
　Warlingham CR6 . . . . . . 101 C8
Broadlands Mans [2]
　SW16 . . . . 21 E6
Broadlands Way KT3 . . . . 38 F3
Broadley Gn GU20 . . . . . 48 D4
Broadmead
　Ashtead KT21 . . . . 75 F2
　Catford SE6 . . . . 24 A5
　Farnborough GU14 . . . . 84 D3
　Hampton TW12 . . . . 16 A2
　Horley RH6 . . . . 161 C4
　Merstham RH1 . . . . 119 C7
Broadmead Ave KT4 . . . . 39 A2
Broadmead Cl TW12 . . . . 16 A2
Broadmead Inf Sch CR0 . 42 D2
Broadmead Jun Sch CR0 . 42 D2
Broadmead Rd GU23 . . . . 90 B5
Broadmeads GU23 . . . . . 90 B5
Broadmere Com Prim Sch
　GU21 . . . . 70 D6
Broadmoor Cotts RH5 . . 156 A8
Broadmoor Est RG45 . . . 45 E5
Broadmoor Hospl RG45 . 45 E5
Broadmoor Prim Sch
　RG45 . . . . 45 D4
Broad Oak TW16 . . . . 14 F2
Broad Oaks KT6 . . . . 57 B8
Broadoaks Cres KT14 . . . 71 B6
Broad Oaks Way BR2 . . . 44 F4
Broadpool Cotts SL5 . . . . . 9 A1
Broad St Wlk RG40 . . . . . 25 C6
Broad St
　Guildford GU3 . . . . 108 D3
　Teddington TW11 . . . . . . 16 F2
　West End GU24 . . . . 67 D6
　Wokingham RG40 . . . . . 25 C6
Broadview Est TW19 . . . . 14 A8
Broadview Rd SW16 . . . . 21 D1
Broadwater Cl
　Hersham KT12 . . . . 54 A5
　Sheerwater GU21 . . . . . 70 D7
　Wraysbury TW19 . . . . . . 11 E8
Broadwater Ho [1] KT13 . 53 B7
Broadwater La GU7 . . . . 150 F6
Broadwater Pl KT13 . . . . 53 E8
Broadwater Prim Sch
　SW17 . . . . 20 E4
Broadwater Rd SW17 . . . 20 E4
Broadwater Rise GU1 . . . 131 A8

Broadwater Road N KT12 . 54 A5
Broadwater Road S KT12 . 54 A5
Broadwater Sch GU7 . . . 151 A8
Broadway
　Bracknell RG12 . . . . 27 C7
　Cranbourne SL4 . . . . 9 B7
　Knaphill GU21 . . . . 68 C1
　Limpsfield RH8 . . . . 123 B5
　Tolworth KT6 . . . . 38 B1
Broadway Ave
　Thornton Heath CR0 . . . 42 D4
　Twickenham TW1 . . . . . . 6 B1
Broadway Cl CR2 . . . . . . 81 B5
Broadway Ct
　Beckenham BR3 . . . . . . 44 C6
　Wimbledon SW19 . . . . . 20 A2
Broadway Gdns CR4 . . . . 40 E5
Broadway Ho GU21 . . . . . 68 C1
Broadway Ho [5] SW19 . . 20 A1
Broadway Ho GU47 . . . . 64 B7
Broadway Lofts SW17 . . . 20 E4
Broadway Mkt SW17 . . . . 20 F4
Broadway Par BR1 . . . . . 24 D3
Broadway Pl [5] SW19 . . . 19 F2
Broadway Rd GU18, GU20 . 48 C2
Broadway The
　Cheam SM3 . . . . 58 E4
　Crawley RH10 . . . . 201 D6
　Laleham TW18 . . . . 33 C7
　Mortlake SW13 . . . . 7 E5
　Sandhurst GU47 . . . . . . 64 B8
　Sutton SM1 . . . . 59 C6
　Thames Ditton KT10 . . . 36 E1
　Tolworth KT6 . . . . 38 A1
　Wallington CR0 . . . . 60 E6
　Wimbledon SW19 . . . . . 19 F2
　Woking GU21 . . . . 69 F2
　Woodham KT15 . . . . 52 A1
Broadwell Ct TW5 . . . . . . 4 D6
Broadwell Rd GU10 . . . . 145 F7
Broad Wlk
　Burgh Heath KT18 . . . . . 97 D8
　Caterham CR3 . . . . 100 F5
　Cranleigh GU6 . . . . 174 F1
　Crawley RH10 . . . . 201 D6
　Frimley GU16 . . . . 65 E2
　Heston TW5 . . . . 4 E6
　Richmond TW9 . . . . 6 F7
Broadwood Cl RH12 . . . . 218 A5
Broadwood Cotts RH5 . . 178 E6
Broadwood Rd CR5 . . . . . 99 D6
Broadwood Rise RH11 . . 201 A3
Brockbridge Ho SW15 . . . 7 F1
Brock Cl GU16 . . . . 86 D8
Brockenhurst KT8 . . . . . . 35 F3
Brockenhurst Ave KT4 . . 38 E1
Brockenhurst Cl GU21 . . 69 F5
Brockenhurst Rd
　Aldershot GU11 . . . . . . 126 B8
　Ascot SL5 . . . . 29 B3
　Bracknell RG12 . . . . 28 A6
　Croydon CR0 . . . . 43 B2
Brockenhurst Way SW16 . 41 D7
BROCKHAM 137 C7
Brockham Cl SW19 . . . . . 19 F3
Brockham Cres CR0 . . . . 63 D3
Brockham Ct
　[5] Belmont SM2 . . . . . . 59 B3
　[8] Croydon CR2 . . . . . . 61 C5
Brockham Dr SW2 . . . . . . 21 F8
Brockham Gn RH3 . . . . . 137 B8
Brockham Hill Pk KT20 . . 116 C4
Brockham Ho [14] SW2 . . 21 F8
Brockham Keep RH6 . . . 161 C4
Brockham La RH3 . . . . . . 116 A1
Brockham Park Ho RH3 . 137 C4
Brockham Row RH3 . . . . 137 C5
Brockham Sch RH3 . . . . 137 B7
Brockham Warren KT20 . 116 A3
Brockholes Cross KT24 . 113 A6
Brockhurst Cl RH12 . . . . 216 F1
Brockhurst Cotts GU6 . . 193 F4
Brockhurst Lodge GU9 . 146 B7
Brocklebank Ct CR6 . . . . 81 A1
Brocklebank Rd SW18 . . 20 C8
Brocklesby Rd SE25 . . . . 43 B5
Brockley Combe KT13 . . . 53 D6
Brockley Pk SE23 . . . . . . 23 E8
Brockley Rise SE23 . . . . . 23 E8
Brockley View SE23 . . . . 23 E8
Brockman Rise BR1 . . . . 24 D4
Brock Rd RH11 . . . . 181 B1
Brock's Cl GU7 . . . . 151 A5
Brocks Dr
　Cheam SM3 . . . . 58 E7
　Fairlands GU3 . . . . 108 C5
Brockshot Cl [1] TW8 . . . . 6 D8
Brockton GU7 . . . . 150 E5
Brock Way GU25 . . . . 31 C5
Brockway Cl GU1 . . . . . . 110 B2
Brockwell Ave BR3 . . . . . 44 B4
Brockwell Ct [2] CR0 . . . . 42 B2
Brockwell Park Gdns
　SE24 . . . . 22 B8
Brockwell Park Row [9]
　SW2 . . . . 22 A8
Brockworth KT2 . . . . 38 B8
Broderick Ho SE21 . . . . . 22 E5
Brodie Ho [7] SM6 . . . . . 60 B6
Brodie Rd GU1 . . . . 130 E8
Brodrick Gr KT23 . . . . . . 94 A1
Brodrick Rd SW17 . . . . . 20 E6
Brograve Gdns BR3 . . . . 44 B7
Broke Ct GU4 . . . . 110 C4
Brokes Cres RH2 . . . . . . 118 A3
Brokes Rd RH2 . . . . 118 A3
Bromford Cl RH8 . . . . . . 123 A2

Bromleigh Ct SE21, SE22 . . 23 B6
BROMLEY 44 E8
Bromley Ave BR1 . . . . 24 E1
Bromley Cres BR2 . . . . 44 F6
Bromley Gdns BR1 . . . . 24 F1
Bromley Gdns BR2 . . . . 44 F6
Bromley Gr BR2 . . . . 44 D7
Bromley Hill BR1 . . . . 24 E2
BROMLEY PARK 44 F8
Bromley Pk 13 BR1 . . . . . . 44 F8
Bromley Rd
  Beckenham BR3 . . . . 44 B8
  Bromley BR2, BR3 . . . . . . 44 D7
  Catford SE6, BR1 . . . . . . 24 B5
Bromley Road Inf Sch
  BR3 . . . . 44 B8
Bromley Road Ret Pk SE6 24 B6
Brompton Cl
  Hounslow TW4 . . . . 4 F2
  Penge SE20 . . . . 43 A7
Bromwich Ho TW10 . . . . 6 E1
Bronson Rd SW20 . . . . 39 E7
Bronte Ct 14 RH1 . . . . . . 119 A2
Brontes The RH19 . . . . . . 185 D1
BROOK
  Guildford 132 E1
  Witley 170 B1
Brook Ave
  Ascot SL5 . . . . 28 F6
  Heath End GU9 . . . . 125 F7
Brook Cl
  Ash GU12 . . . . 106 B3
  Dorking RH4 . . . . 115 C1
  East Grinstead RH19 . . . 186 B1
  Epsom KT19 . . . . 57 E2
  Sandhurst GU47 . . . . 45 E1
  Stanwell TW19 . . . . 13 F8
  Upper Tooting SW17 . . . . 21 A6
  West Barnes SW20 . . . . . 39 B6
  Wokingham RG41 . . . . . . 25 A8
Brook Ct
  Beckenham BR3 . . . . 43 F8
  6 Brentford TW8 . . . . 6 D8
  Cheam SM3 . . . . 58 C6
  Horsham RH12 . . . . 217 B5
  7 Mortlake SW14 . . . . 7 E4
Brookdale Rd SE6 . . . . . . 24 B8
Brook Dr
  Ashford TW16 . . . . 14 E2
  Bracknell RG12 . . . . 27 E5
Brooke Ct
  Frimley GU16 . . . . 85 F6
  7 Kingston upon Thames
  KT2 . . . . 17 C4
Brooke Forest GU3 . . . . . 108 C5
Brookehowse Rd SE6 . . . . 24 B5
Brookers Cl KT21 . . . . 75 D2
Brookers Cnr RG45 . . . . . 45 C5
Brookers Ho KT21 . . . . . . 75 D2
Brookers Row RG45 . . . . . 45 C6
Brook Farm Rd KT11 . . . . . 73 D4
Brookfield
  Farncombe GU7 . . . . . . 151 A8
  Woking GU21 . . . . 69 B3
Brookfield Ave SM1 . . . . . 59 E7
Brookfield Cl
  Ottershaw KT16 . . . . 51 D4
  Redhill RH1 . . . . 140 A3
Brookfield Ct GU18 . . . . . 48 C1
Brookfield Gdns KT10 . . . 55 F4
Brookfield Pl KT11 . . . . . . 73 E4
Brookfield Prim Sch SM3 . 39 E1
Brookfield Rd
  Aldershot GU12 . . . . 105 F3
  Ashtead KT21 . . . . 95 E7
Brookfields Ave CR4 . . . . 40 E4
Brook Gdns
  Barnes SW13 . . . . 7 F4
  Farnborough GU14 . . . . . 84 F2
  Kingston upon Thames KT2 . 38 C8
Brook Gn
  Bracknell RG42 . . . . 26 F8
  Chobham GU24 . . . . 49 F1
Brook Hill
  Farley Green GU5 . . . . . 153 D8
  Oxted RH8 . . . . 122 C5
Brookhill Cl RH10 . . . . . . 183 A3
Brookhill Rd RH10 . . . . . . 183 A3
Brook Ho
  Cranleigh GU6 . . . . 174 F4
  Heath End GU9 . . . . 125 D6
  5 Twickenham TW1 . . . . 17 A8
Brookhouse 2 SW19 . . . . 20 A2
Brookhouse Rd GU14 . . . . 84 F3
Brookhurst Rd KT15 . . . . . 52 B4
Brook La
  Farley Green GU5 . . . . . 132 E1
  Faygate RH12 . . . . 218 C8
  Send GU23 . . . . 90 E5
Brookland Ho 5 RH19 . . . 185 E1
Brooklands GU11 . . . . 104 E1
Brooklands Ave SW18 . . . . 20 B6
Brooklands Cl
  Charlton TW16 . . . . 34 E8
  Heath End GU9 . . . . 125 D7
  Stoke D'Abernon KT11 . . . 73 E4
Brooklands Coll KT13 . . . . 52 F4
Brooklands Ct
  Kingston upon Thames
  KT1 . . . . 37 D5
  Mitcham CR4 . . . . 40 D7
  New Haw KT15 . . . . 52 D1
  Reigate RH2 . . . . 118 B3
Brooklands Ind Est
  Byfleet KT13 . . . . 52 E1
  West Byfleet KT13 . . . . . 71 E8
Brooklands La KT13 . . . . . 52 F4

Brooklands Mus ★ KT13 . . 53 A2
Brooklands Pl TW12 . . . . . 16 B3
Brooklands Rd
  Crawley RH11 . . . . 201 C1
  Heath End GU9 . . . . 125 E7
  Thames Ditton KT7 . . . . . 37 A1
  Weybridge KT13 . . . . 53 B3
Brooklands Sch RH2 . . . . 118 B3
Brooklands Terr TW16 . . . 35 A5
Brooklands The TW7 . . . . . . 5 D6
Brooklands Way
  East Grinstead RH19 . . . 205 D8
  Heath End GU9 . . . . 125 E7
  Redhill RH1 . . . . 118 E3
Brook Lane Bns Ctr 4
  TW8 . . . . 6 D8
Brook Lane N 3 TW8 . . . . . 6 D8
Brookley Cl GU10 . . . . . . 126 C3
Brookleys GU24 . . . . 49 F1
Brooklyn 9 SE20 . . . . 23 A1
Brooklyn Ave SE25 . . . . . . 43 B5
Brooklyn Cl
  Carshalton SM5 . . . . 59 E8
  Woking GU22 . . . . 89 E8
Brooklyn Ct
  Feltham TW13 . . . . 15 B6
  2 Woking GU22 . . . . 89 E8
Brooklyn Gr SE25 . . . . . . 43 B5
Brooklyn Rd
  Croydon SE25 . . . . 43 B5
  Woking GU22 . . . . 89 E8
Brook Manor RH19 . . . . . 205 D7
Brook Mdw GU8 . . . . 191 C3
Brookmead CR4 . . . . 41 C3
Brook Mead
  Milford GU8 . . . . 170 F8
  West Ewell KT19 . . . . . . 57 E4
Brookmead Ct
  Cranleigh GU6 . . . . 174 E2
  Farnham GU9 . . . . 125 B1
Brookmead Ind Est CR0 . . 41 C3
Brookmead Rd CR0 . . . . . 41 C3
Brook Rd
  Bagshot GU19 . . . . 47 E2
  Brook GU8 . . . . 190 D8
  Camberley GU15 . . . . . . 65 B4
  Chilworth GU4 . . . . 131 C3
  Horsham RH12 . . . . 217 E6
  Merstham RH1 . . . . 119 C7
  Redhill RH1 . . . . 139 F8
  Surbiton KT6 . . . . 56 E8
  Thornton Heath CR7 . . . . 42 C5
  Twickenham TW1 . . . . 6 A1
  Wormley GU8 . . . . 170 E1
Brook Road S TW8 . . . . 6 D8
Brooksby Cl GU17 . . . . . . 64 B5
Brook Sch The RH10 . . . . 202 C3
Brookscroft CR0 . . . . 62 E1
Brooks Cl KT13 . . . . 53 A1
Brooks Ho 6 SW2 . . . . . . 22 A7
BROOKSIDE 8 F2
Brookside
  Beare Green RH5 . . . . . 157 F6
  Chertsey KT16 . . . . 32 E2
  Colnbrook SL3 . . . . 1 C7
  Copthorne RH10 . . . . . . 183 A3
  Cranleigh GU6 . . . . 174 E1
  Cranleigh GU6 . . . . 174 E3
  Crawley Down RH10 . . . 204 B8
  Crawley RH10 . . . . 201 F7
  Guildford GU4 . . . . 109 D6
  Hale GU9 . . . . 125 D6
  Sandhurst GU47 . . . . 64 C8
  South Godstone RH9 . . . 142 D5
  Wallington SM5 . . . . 60 A5
Brookside Ave TW15 . . . . 13 D3
Brookside Cl TW13 . . . . . 15 A5
Brookside Cres 1 KT4 . . . 39 A1
Brookside Ct 1 SW16 . . . . 21 C1
Brookside Pk GU14 . . . . . 65 A1
Brookside Way CR0 . . . . . 43 D3
Brooks La W4 . . . . 7 A8
Brooksland Coll TW15 . . . 13 F4
Brooks Rd W4 . . . . 7 A8
Brook St KT1 . . . . 37 E7
Brookswood GU4 . . . . . . 131 G4
Brook Terr 12 RH1 . . . . . 139 F8
Brook The RH10 . . . . 201 D7
Brook Trad Est The
  GU12 . . . . 105 E2
Brook Valley RH5 . . . . . . 136 B1
Brookview RH10 . . . . 183 A3
Brook View Lodge KT4 . . . 39 A1
Brookview Rd SW16,
  SW17 . . . . 21 C3
Brook Way KT22 . . . . 75 A1
Brookwell La GU5 . . . . . . 152 B2
BROOKWOOD 88 A7
Brookwood 5 RH6 . . . . . 161 B4
Brookwood Ave SW13 . . . . 7 F5
Brookwood Ct BR2 . . . . . . 44 F5
Brookwood Ho RH6 . . . . 161 B6
Brookwood Lye Rd GU21,
  GU24 . . . . 88 C7
Brookwood Pk RH6 . . . . . 161 B2
Brookwood Prim Sch
  GU24 . . . . 88 A7
Brookwood Rd
  Farnborough GU14 . . . . . 85 D4
  Hounslow TW3 . . . . 5 B6
  Wandsworth SW18 . . . . . 20 A7
Brookwood Sta GU24 . . . . 88 A6
Broom Acres GU47 . . . . . . 45 B1
Broom Bank CR6 . . . . . . 102 C8
Broom Cl
  Esher KT10 . . . . 55 B5
  Teddington TW11 . . . . . . 17 D1
Broomcroft Cl GU22 . . . . . 70 D3

Broomcroft Dr GU22 . . . . 70 D3
Broomdashers Rd RH10 . 201 F7
Broome Cl
  Headley KT18 . . . . 96 C1
  Horsham RH12 . . . . 217 D5
Broome Ct 3 TW9 . . . . 7 A6
Broome Hall RH5 . . . . . . 156 D2
Broomehall Rd
  Coldharbour RH5 . . . . . 156 D2
  Ockley RH5 . . . . 177 E8
Broome Lodge
  Ascot SL5 . . . . 29 D4
  Staines TW18 . . . . 13 A3
Broome Rd TW12 . . . . 35 F8
Broomers La GU6 . . . . . . 175 E5
Broomfield
  Bracknell RG42 . . . . 26 D8
  Elstead GU8 . . . . 148 E4
  Guildford GU2 . . . . 108 E2
  Staines TW18 . . . . 13 A2
  Sunbury TW16 . . . . 35 A8
Broomfield Cl
  Guildford GU3 . . . . 108 E3
  Sunningdale SL5 . . . . 30 B2
Broomfield Cotts KT20 . . . 97 E8
Broomfield Ct
  Sunningdale SL5 . . . . 30 B3
  Weybridge KT13 . . . . 53 B4
Broomfield House Sch
  TW9 . . . . 6 F6
Broomfield La
  Farnham GU10 . . . . 146 C1
  Frensham GU10 . . . . . . 146 A1
Broomfield Pk
  Sunningdale SL5 . . . . 30 B2
  Westcott RH4 . . . . 135 C6
Broomfield Rd
  Beckenham BR3 . . . . 43 F6
  Richmond TW9 . . . . 6 F6
  Surbiton KT5 . . . . 37 F1
  Teddington TW11 . . . . . . 17 C2
  Woodham KT15 . . . . 71 B8
Broomfield Ride KT22 . . . 74 D7
Broomfields KT10 . . . . . . 55 C5
Broom Gdns CR0 . . . . 63 A7
BROOMHALL 30 B2
Broom Hall KT22 . . . . 74 D5
Broomhall Bldgs 1 SL5 . . 30 B2
Broomhall End GU21 . . . . 69 E3
Broomhall La
  Sunningdale SL5 . . . . 30 A3
  Woking GU21 . . . . 69 E3
Broomhall Rd
  South Croydon CR2 . . . . 61 D2
  Woking GU21 . . . . 69 E3
Broomhill Ct GU10 . . . . . 124 D8
Broomhill Ct KT10 . . . . . . 55 B5
Broomhill Rd GU14 . . . . . 84 D5
Broomhurst Ct RH4 . . . . . 136 B5
Broom La GU24 . . . . 49 E3
Broomlands La RH8 . . . . 123 E8
Broomleaf Cnr GU9 . . . . . 125 D2
Broomleaf Rd GU9 . . . . . 125 E2
Broomloan La SM1 . . . . . . 59 A8
Broom Lock TW11 . . . . . . 17 C2
Broom Pk KT1 . . . . 17 D1
Broom Rd
  Croydon CR0 . . . . 63 A7
  Richmond TW11 . . . . 17 C3
Broomsleigh Bsns Pk
  SE26 . . . . 23 F3
Broom Squires GU26 . . . 188 F4
Broomsquires Rd GU19 . . 47 F2
Broom Water TW11 . . . . . 17 C3
Broom Water W TW11 . . . 17 C3
Broom Way
  Blackwater GU17 . . . . . . 64 E4
  Oatlands Park KT13 . . . . 53 E6
Broomwood Cl CR0 . . . . . 43 D4
Broomwood Hall Sch
  SW16 . . . . 21 D5
Broomwood Hall Upper Sch
  SW12 . . . . 21 A8
Broomwood Way GU10 . . 146 C6
Broseley Gr SE26 . . . . . . 23 E3
Broster Gdns SE25 . . . . . 42 F6
Brougham Pl GU9 . . . . . . 125 B7
Brough Cl KT2 . . . . 17 D3
Broughton Ave TW10 . . . . 17 C4
Broughton Ho 10 SW19 . . 19 E1
Broughton Mews GU16 . . 65 F1
Broughton Rd CR7 . . . . . . 42 A3
Browell Rd GU4 . . . . 110 D2
Browells La TW13 . . . . . . 15 B6
Brown Bear Ct TW13 . . . . 15 D4
Brown Cl SM6 . . . . 60 E3
Browne Cl GU22 . . . . 90 C7
Browne Ho 9 SE26 . . . . . 23 B3
Browngraves Rd UB7 . . . . . 3 C7
Brownhill Rd SE6 . . . . . . 24 C8
Browning Ave
  Carshalton SM1 . . . . 59 E6
  North Cheam KT4 . . . . . . 39 B1
Browning Cl
  Crawley RH10 . . . . 202 C7
  Frimley GU15 . . . . 66 C4
  Hampton TW12 . . . . 15 F4
Browning Rd KT22 . . . . . . 94 D2
Brownings The 1 RH19 . . 185 C1
Browning Way TW5 . . . . . . 4 D6
Brownjohn Ct RH10 . . . . 202 A7
Brownlow Rd
  Redhill RH1 . . . . 118 E1
  South Croydon CR0 . . . . 61 F6
Brownrigg Cres RG12 . . . 27 E8
Brownrigg Rd TW15 . . . . . 14 A4
Brown's Hill RH1 . . . . . . 141 D2

Browns La KT24 . . . . 113 D8
Brownsover Rd GU14 . . . . 84 C4
Brown's Rd KT5, KT6 . . . . 37 F2
Browns Wlk GU10 . . . . . . 145 D5
Browns Wood RH19 . . . . . 185 E4
Broxholme Cl SE25 . . . . . 42 D5
Broxholm Rd SE27, SW16. 22 A5
Brox La KT15, KT16 . . . . . 51 D2
Brox Mews KT16 . . . . 51 C4
Brox Rd KT16 . . . . 51 D4
Broxted Rd SE23, SE6 . . . 23 F6
Bruce Ave TW17 . . . . 34 C3
Bruce Cl KT14 . . . . 71 E6
Bruce Dr CR2 . . . . 62 D2
Bruce Hall Mews SW17 . . 21 A4
Bruce Lawns SW17 . . . . . 21 A4
Bruce Rd
  Mitcham CR4 . . . . 21 A1
  South Norwood SE25 . . . 42 D5
Brudenell Rd SW17 . . . . . 21 A4
Brumana Cl KT13 . . . . . . 53 B4
Brumfield Rd KT19 . . . . . . 57 C5
Brunel Cl
  Cranford TW5 . . . . 4 B7
  South Norwood SE19 . . . 22 F2
Brunel Ctr RH10 . . . . . . 181 F2
Brunel Ct SW13 . . . . 7 F5
Brunel Dr RG45 . . . . 45 C8
Brunel Ho
  Haslemere GU27 . . . . . . 208 A6
  24 Streatham SW2 . . . . . 21 E8
Brunel Pl RH10 . . . . 201 E5
Brunel Univ (Runnymede
  Campus) TW20 . . . . 11 C5
Brunel Wlk 3 TW2 . . . . . . 16 A8
Brunner Ct KT16 . . . . 51 C5
Brunner Ho SE6 . . . . 24 C4
Brunswick RG12 . . . . 27 A2
Brunswick Cl
  Crawley RH10 . . . . 202 A4
  Thames Ditton KT7 . . . . . 36 F1
  Twickenham TW2 . . . . . . 16 D5
  Walton-on-Thames KT12 . 54 C8
Brunswick Ct
  Crawley RH10 . . . . 202 A4
  Kingston upon Thames KT2 . 17 D2
  2 Merton SW19 . . . . 19 E1
  2 Penge SE19 . . . . 23 A1
Brunswick Dr GU24 . . . . . 87 D7
Brunswick Gr KT11 . . . . . 73 C6
Brunswick Manor SM1 . . . 59 C6
Brunswick Mews SW16 . . 21 D2
Brunswick Pl SE19 . . . . . 23 A1
Brunswick Rd
  Kingston upon Thames
  KT2 . . . . 38 A8
  Pirbright, Alexander Barracks
  GU24 . . . . 87 C6
  Pirbright, Blackdown Barracks
  GU16, GU24 . . . . 86 E6
  Sutton SM1 . . . . 59 B6
Brunswick Terr BR3 . . . . . 44 B8
Bruntile Cl GU14 . . . . 85 D1
Brushfield Way GU21 . . . . 68 C1
Brushwood Rd RH12 . . . . 218 B6
Bruton Rd SM4 . . . . 40 C5
Bruton Way RG12 . . . . . . 27 E2
Bryan Cl TW16 . . . . 15 A1
Bryanston Ave TW2 . . . . . 16 B7
Bryanstone Ave GU2 . . . 109 A4
Bryanstone Cl GU2 . . . . . 108 F5
Bryanstone Ct SM1 . . . . . 59 C7
Bryanstone Gr GU2 . . . . 108 F5
Bryce Cl RH12 . . . . 218 A5
Bryce Gdns GU11 . . . . . . 126 C2
Bryden Cl SE26 . . . . 23 E3
Brympton Cl RH4 . . . . . . 136 A5
Brynford Cl GU21 . . . . . . 69 E4
Bryn Rd GU10 . . . . 145 F7
Bryony Ho RG42 . . . . 26 E8
Bryony Rd GU1 . . . . 110 B4
Bryony Way TW16 . . . . . . 15 A2
Buccaneer Way GU14 . . . 104 C8
Buchanan Ho
  Dulwich SE21 . . . . 22 E5
  Wandsworth SW18 . . . . . 20 A8
Buchan Ctry Pk ★ RH11 . 200 E1
Buchans Lawn RH11 . . . . 201 B2
Buchan The GU15 . . . . . . 66 A8
Bucharest Rd SW18 . . . . . 20 C8
Buckfast Rd SM4 . . . . 40 B5
Buckhurst Ave CR4, SM5 . 40 F1
Buckhurst Cotts RH12 . . 214 D8
Buckhurst Gr RG40 . . . . . 25 F5
Buckhurst Hill RG12 . . . . 27 F5
Buckhurst La SL5 . . . . 30 A4
Buckhurst Mead RH19 . . 185 C4
Buckhurst Moors RG12 . . 26 C6
Buckhurst Rd
  Ascot SL5 . . . . 29 F7
  Frimley GU16 . . . . 85 F6
  Buckhurst Way RH19 . . . 185 C3
Buckingham Ave
  East Molesey KT8 . . . . . . 36 B7
  Feltham TW14 . . . . 4 B1
  South Norwood CR7 . . . . 42 A8
Buckingham Cl
  Guildford GU1 . . . . 109 F2
  Hampton TW12 . . . . 15 F3
Buckingham Ct
  Belmont SM2 . . . . 59 A2
  Camberley GU15 . . . . . . 65 D5
  Crawley RH11 . . . . 201 B2
  Farnborough GU14 . . . . . 85 B4

Buckingham Ct continued
  Mitcham CR4 . . . . 41 E4
  3 Staines TW18 . . . . 13 A4
  Wokingham RG40 . . . . . . 25 C6
Buckingham Dr RH19 . . . 206 A8
Buckingham Gate RH6 . . 182 C7
Buckingham Gdns
  Hampton KT8 . . . . 36 B7
  South Norwood CR7 . . . . 42 A7
Buckingham Ho TW10 . . . . 7 A2
Buckingham La SE23 . . . . 23 E8
Buckingham Prim Sch
  TW12 . . . . 15 F3
Buckingham Rd
  Hampton TW12 . . . . 15 F3
  Kingston upon Thames KT1 . 37 F5
  Mitcham CR4 . . . . 41 E4
  Richmond TW10 . . . . 17 D6
  South Holmwood RH5 . . . 157 C6
Buckingham Way SM6 . . . 60 C2
BUCKLAND 117 A2
Buckland Cl GU14 . . . . . . 85 C7
Buckland Cnr RH2 . . . . . 117 D2
Buckland Ct RH3 . . . . . . 117 A2
Buckland Prim Sch TW18. 13 C1
Buckland Rd
  Chessington KT9 . . . . . . 56 F5
  East Ewell SM2 . . . . 58 D2
  Lower Kingswood KT20 . . 117 F7
  Reigate RH2 . . . . 117 D2
Bucklands Rd TW11 . . . . . 17 C2
Buckland Way KT4 . . . . . . 39 C1
Buckland Wlk SM4 . . . . . . 40 C5
Bucklebury RG12 . . . . . . 27 A2
Buckleigh Ave SW20 . . . . 39 F6
Buckleigh Ho SW19 . . . . . 20 D3
Buckleigh Rd SW16 . . . . . 21 E1
Buckleigh Way SE19 . . . . 22 F1
Bucklers' Way SM5 . . . . . 59 F7
Buckles Way SM7 . . . . . . 77 E3
Buckley Cl SE23 . . . . 23 B8
Buckley Pl RH10 . . . . 204 A8
Buckmans Rd RH11 . . . . . 201 D6
Bucknall Way BR3 . . . . . . 44 C4
Bucknills Cl KT18 . . . . . . 76 C5
Bucks Cl KT14 . . . . 71 B5
Bucks Copse RG41 . . . . . 25 A5
BUCKS GREEN 214 B6
Buckswood Dr RH11 . . . . 201 A4
Buckthorn Cl RG40 . . . . . 25 E7
Buddhapadipa Temple The
  SW19 . . . . 19 D4
Budebury Rd TW18 . . . . . 13 A3
Budge La CR4 . . . . 40 F2
Budge's Cl RH10 . . . . . . 182 D1
Budgen Dr RH1 . . . . 119 A3
Budge's Cotts RG40 . . . . 25 E8
Budge's Gdns RG40 . . . . 25 E7
Budge's Rd RG40 . . . . . . 25 D7
Budham Way RG12 . . . . . 27 B3
Budleigh Ho 6 SW2 . . . . . 78 B4
Buffbeards La GU27 . . . . 207 E6
Buffers La KT22 . . . . 95 A8
Bug Hill CR3, CR6 . . . . . 101 D7
Bugkingham Way GU16 . . 65 F1
Bulganak Rd CR7 . . . . . . 42 C5
Bulkeley Cl TW20 . . . . . . 11 C3
Bullard Rd TW11 . . . . 16 F2
Bullbeggars La
  Godstone RH9 . . . . 121 C3
  Woking GU21 . . . . 69 B3
BULLBROOK 27 E7
Bullbrook Dr RG12 . . . . . 27 F8
Bullbrook Row RG12 . . . . 27 E7
Buller Ct GU14 . . . . 85 C1
Buller Rd
  Aldershot GU11 . . . . 105 B4
  South Norwood CR7 . . . . 42 D6
Bullers Rd GU9 . . . . 125 E6
Bullfinch Cl
  Horley RH6 . . . . 160 E4
  Horsham RH12 . . . . 217 C7
  Sandhurst GU47 . . . . 64 E8
Bullfinch Ct 4 SE21 . . . . 22 D6
Bullfinch Rd CR2 . . . . 62 D1
Bullfinch Rise RG12 . . . . 26 D5
Bull Hill KT22 . . . . 95 A6
Bull La
  Bracknell RG42 . . . . 27 B8
  Woking GU4 . . . . 89 F1
Bullrush Cl
  Carshalton SM5 . . . . 59 E8
  Thornton Heath CR0 . . . . 42 E3
Bulls Alley SW14 . . . . 7 D5
Bullswater Common Rd GU24,
  GU3 . . . . 88 A2
Bullswater La GU24 . . . . . 88 A2
Bullvant Ho GU21 . . . . . . 88 F8
Bulmer Ct TN16 . . . . 83 C7
Bulrushes Bsns Pk RH19 205 D6
Bulstrode Ave TW3 . . . . . . 5 A4
Bulstrode Gdns TW3 . . . . . 5 A4
Bulstrode Rd TW3 . . . . 5 A4
Bunbury Way KT17 . . . . . . 77 B4
Bunce Common Rd RH2 . 137 E2
Bunce Dr CR3 . . . . 100 D4
Bunch La GU27 . . . . 208 A6
Bunch Way GU27 . . . . . . 208 A6
Bundy's Way TW18 . . . . . 12 F2
Bungalow Rd SE25 . . . . . 42 E5
Bungalows The
  Caterham CR3 . . . . 100 D4
  Mitcham SW16 . . . . 21 B1
  Normandy GU12 . . . . . . 106 D3
  Wallington SM6 . . . . 60 B5

Bunting Cl
Horsham RH13 . . . . 217 F3
Mitcham CR4 . . . . 40 F4
Buntings The GU9 . . . . 145 F8
Bunyan Cl RH11 . . . . 200 E3
Bunyard Dr GU21 . . . . 70 C5
Burbage Gn RG12 . . . . 27 F4
Burbage Rd SE21, SE24 . . . 22 D8
Burbank KT3 . . . . 38 F6
Burbeach Cl RH11 . . . . 201 B3
Burberry Cl KT3 . . . . 38 E7
Burbidge Rd TW17 . . . . 34 A5
Burbury Woods GU15 . . . . 65 E6
Burchets Hollow GU5 . . . 154 D7
Burchetts Way TW17 . . . . . 34 B3
Burcote 6 KT13 . . . . 53 D4
Burcote Rd SW18 . . . . 20 D8
Burcott Gdns KT15 . . . . 52 D4
Burcott Rd CR8 . . . . 80 A5
Burdenshot Hill GU3 . . . . . 89 B3
Burdenshott Ave TW10 . . . . .7 B3
Burdenshott Rd
Guildford GU4 . . . . 109 C8
Woking GU22, GU3, GU4 . . 89 A2
Burden Way GU2 . . . . 109 B6
Burdett Ave SW20 . . . . 39 A8
Burdett Cl RH10 . . . . 202 D5
Burdett Rd
Richmond TW9 . . . . .6 F4
Thornton Heath CR0 . . . . . . 42 D3
Burdock Cl
2 Crawley RH11 . . . . 201 A2
Croydon CR0 . . . . 43 D1
Lightwater GU18 . . . . 67 B8
Burdon La SM2 . . . . 58 F2
Burdon Pk SM2 . . . . 58 F2
Burfield Cl SW17 . . . . 20 D4
Burfield Dr CR6 . . . . 101 C8
Burfield Rd SL4 . . . . 11 B8
Burford Cnr RH5 . . . . 115 C4
Burford Ct RG40 . . . . 25 E5
Burford La KT17 . . . . 77 C8
Burford Lea GU8 . . . . 148 E4
Burford Lodge RH5 . . . . . 115 C4
Burford Rd
Camberley GU15 . . . . 65 B4
Forest Hill SE6 . . . . 23 F6
Horsham RH13 . . . . 217 E2
New Malden KT4 . . . . 39 A2
Sutton SM1 . . . . 59 A8
Burford Way CR0 . . . . 63 C4
Burge Cl GU14 . . . . 84 C4
Burgess Cl TW13 . . . . 15 E4
Burgess Mews SW19 . . . . . 20 B2
Burgess Rd SM1 . . . . 59 B6
Burges Way TW18 . . . . 13 A3
Burgh Cl RH10 . . . . 182 D1
Burghead Cl GU47 . . . . 64 D7
Burghfield KT17 . . . . 76 F4
BURGH HEATH 97 D8
Burgh Heath Rd KT17,
KT18 . . . . 76 F4
Burghill Rd SE26 . . . . 23 E4
Burghley Ave KT3 . . . . 38 D8
Burghley Ct SW19 . . . . 19 E3
Burghley Ho SW19 . . . . . . 19 E5
Burghley Pl CR4 . . . . 40 F5
Burghley Rd SW19 . . . . . . 19 E4
Burgh Mount SM7 . . . . 77 F4
Burgh Wood SM7 . . . . 77 F4
Burgos Cl CR0 . . . . 61 A4
Burgoyne Rd
Ashford TW16 . . . . 14 F2
Camberley GU15 . . . . 66 A6
South Norwood SE25 . . . . . 42 F5
Burham Cl SE20 . . . . 23 C1
Burhill Com Inf Sch KT12 . 54 D4
Burhill Rd KT12 . . . . 54 C3
Buriton Ho 9 SW15 . . . . . . 19 B7
Burke Cl SW15 . . . . .7 E3
Burlands RH11 . . . . 181 A1
Burlea Cl KT12 . . . . 54 B5
Burleigh Ave SM6 . . . . 60 B7
Burleigh Cl
Addlestone KT15 . . . . 52 B5
Crawley Down RH10 . . . . 204 B8
Burleigh Ct 1 KT22 . . . . . . 95 A5
Burleigh Gdns
Ashford TW15 . . . . 14 C3
Woking GU21 . . . . 69 F2
Burleigh Ho SM4 . . . . 39 E1
Burleigh La
Crawley Down RH10 . . . . 204 C7
North Ascot SL5 . . . . 28 E8
Burleigh Lo 3 SW19 . . . . . 20 B1
Burleigh Pk KT11 . . . . 73 E7
Burleigh Rd
Addlestone KT15 . . . . 52 B5
Cheam SM3, SM4 . . . . 39 E1
Frimley GU16 . . . . 85 D8
North Ascot SL5 . . . . 28 E7
Burleigh Way RH10 . . . . . 204 B8
Burleigh Wlk SE6 . . . . 24 C7
Burles Bridge Cotts
GU10 . . . . 124 D2
Burley Cl
Loxwood RH14 . . . . 213 A4
Mitcham SW16 . . . . 41 D7
Burley Orchard KT16 . . . . 33 A3
Burleys Rd RH10 . . . . 202 C6
BURLEYS WOOD 202 E7
Burley Way GU17 . . . . 64 C6
Burlingham Cl GU4 . . . . . 110 D3
Burlings The SL5 . . . . 28 F7
Burlington Apartments
SE20 . . . . 23 B1
Burlington Ave TW9 . . . . . . 7 A6
Burlington Cl TW14 . . . . . . 14 D8
Burlington Ct
7 Aldershot GU11 . . . . . . 105 A1
Blackwater GU17 . . . . 64 D3
Chiswick W4 . . . . 7 C7
Burlington Ho TW10 . . . . . . .6 F1
Burlington Jun & Inf Sch 1
KT3 . . . . 38 F5
Burlington La W4 . . . . .7 E8
Burlington Pl RH2 . . . . . . 118 A2
Burlington Rd
Hounslow TW7 . . . . 5 D6
New Malden KT3 . . . . 38 F5
South Norwood CR7 . . . . . . 42 D7
Burlsdon Way RG12 . . . . . . 27 E8
Burma Rd GU24, KT16 . . . . 49 F8
Burmarsh Ct SE20 . . . . 43 C8
Burma Terr 11 SE19 . . . . . . 22 E3
Burmester Ho SW17 . . . . . 20 C5
Burmester Rd SW17 . . . . . 20 C5
Burnaby Cres W4 . . . . 7 C8
Burnaby Gdns W4 . . . . .7 B8
Burnbury Rd SW12 . . . . . . 21 C7
Burn Cl
Addlestone KT15 . . . . 52 D6
Oxshott KT22 . . . . 74 D4
Burne-Jones Dr GU47 . . . . 64 D6
Burnell Ave TW10 . . . . 17 C3
Burnell Ho 19 SW2 . . . . 22 A7
Burnell Rd SM1 . . . . 59 B6
Burnet Ave GU1 . . . . 110 B4
Burnet Cl GU24 . . . . 67 E6
Burnet Gr KT19 . . . . 76 C6
Burney Ave KT5 . . . . 37 F4
Burney Cl KT23 . . . . 94 C2
Burney Ct 5 RH11 . . . . . . 201 A3
Burney Ho
Leatherhead KT22 . . . . 95 A6
4 Streatham SW16 . . . . . . 21 C3
Burney Rd RH5 . . . . 115 A4
Burnham Cl GU21 . . . . 68 D1
Burnham Dr
North Cheam KT4 . . . . 58 D8
Reigate RH2 . . . . 118 A2
Burnham Gates GU1 . . . . 109 D1
Burnham Gdns
Cranford TW5 . . . . 4 B6
Croydon CR0 . . . . 42 F2
Burnham Manor GU15 . . . . 66 A8
Burnham Pl 1 RH13 . . . . 217 D1
Burnham Rd
Knaphill GU21 . . . . 68 D1
Morden SM4 . . . . 40 B5
Burnhams Rd KT23 . . . . . . 93 E3
Burnham St KT2 . . . . 38 A8
Burnham Way SE26 . . . . . . 23 F3
Burnhill Rd BR3 . . . . 44 A7
Burn Moor Chase RG12 . . . 27 E2
Burnsall Cl GU14 . . . . 85 B6
Burns Ave TW14 . . . . 4 A1
Burns Cl
Farnborough GU14 . . . . 84 F6
Horsham RH12 . . . . 217 E7
Mitcham SW17 . . . . 20 D2
Wallington SM5 . . . . 60 A2
Burns Ct SM6 . . . . 60 B3
Burns Dr SM7 . . . . 77 E5
Burnside KT21 . . . . 75 F1
Burnside Cl TW1 . . . . 6 A1
Burnside Ct SM6 . . . . 60 A7
Burns Rd RH10 . . . . 202 C8
Burns Way
Crawley RH12 . . . . 200 C1
East Grinstead RH19 . . . . 185 C1
Heston TW5 . . . . 4 D6
Burnt Ash Prim Sch BR1 . 24 F3
Burnt Common Cl GU23 . . 90 F2
Burntcommon La GU23 . . . 91 A2
Burnt Hill Rd GU10 . . . . . 146 B6
Burnt Hill Way GU10 . . . . 146 B5
Burnt House La RH12 . . . . 200 A7
Burnt Oak La RH5 . . . . . . 179 F1
Burnt Pollard La GU24 . . . . 48 E1
Burntwood Cl
Caterham CR3 . . . . 101 A6
Wandsworth SW18 . . . . 20 E7
Burntwood Ct SW17 . . . . . . 20 C5
Burntwood Grange Rd
SW18 . . . . 20 E7
Burntwood La
Caterham CR3 . . . . 101 A6
Wandsworth SW17 . . . . 20 D6
Burntwood Sch SW17 . . . . 20 D6
Burntwood View SE19 . . . . 22 F3
BURPHAM 110 B5
Burpham Foundation Prim
Sch GU4 . . . . 110 A5
Burpham La GU4 . . . . 110 A5
Burrage Rd RH1 . . . . 119 A3
Burrell Cl CR0 . . . . 43 E3
Burrell Ct RH11 . . . . 200 F4
Burrell Ho 5 TW1 . . . . 17 B8
Burrell Rd GU16 . . . . 85 C8
Burrell Row BR3 . . . . 44 A7
Burrells 9 BR3 . . . . 44 B7
Burrell The RH4 . . . . 135 C6
Burr Hill La GU24 . . . . 49 F2
Burritt Rd KT1 . . . . 38 A7
BURROWHILL 49 E3
Burrow Hill Gn GU24 . . . . . 49 E2
BURROWS WOOD —
Burrows Cl
Guildford GU2 . . . . 108 F2
Little Bookham KT23 . . . . . 93 F3
Burrows Cross GU5 . . . . . 133 C2
Burrows La GU5 . . . . 133 C3
Burrow Wlk SE21 . . . . 22 C8
Burr Rd SW18 . . . . 20 A8
Burrwood Gdns GU12 . . . 106 A4
Burstead Cl KT11 . . . . 73 D7
Burston Gdns RH19 . . . . . 185 D4
BURSTOW 183 A7
Burstow Ct RH6 . . . . 160 F1
Burstow Ho RH6 . . . . 161 B6
Burstow Lodge Bsns Ctr
RH6 . . . . 162 B4
Burstow Prim Sch RH6 . . 162 B3
Burstow Rd SW20 . . . . 39 E8
Burtenshaw Rd KT7 . . . . . . 37 A3
Burton Cl
Chessington KT9 . . . . 56 D3
Horley RH6 . . . . 161 A2
South Norwood CR7 . . . . . . 42 D6
Windlesham GU20 . . . . 48 D4
Burton Ct KT7 . . . . 37 A3
Burton Dr GU3 . . . . 108 A6
Burton Gdns TW5 . . . . .4 F6
Burton Ho SE26 . . . . 23 B3
Burton Rd KT2 . . . . 17 E1
Burtons Ct 11 RH12 . . . . . 217 C2
Burton's Rd TW12 . . . . 16 C4
Burtwell La SE21, SE27 . . . 22 D4
Burvill Ct SW20 . . . . 39 C8
Burwash Rd RH10 . . . . . . 202 A5
Burway Cl CR2 . . . . 61 E4
Burway Cres KT16 . . . . 33 A5
Burwood Ave CR8 . . . . 80 B5
Burwood Cl
Guildford GU1 . . . . 110 D2
Hersham KT12 . . . . 54 C4
Reigate RH2 . . . . 118 D1
Tolworth KT6 . . . . 38 A1
Burwood Ct SE23 . . . . 23 C8
Burwood Ho RH8 . . . . 122 E5
Burwood Lo SW19 . . . . 19 F4
Burwood Par 3 KT16 . . . . . 33 A2
BURWOOD PARK 54 A5
Burwood Park Rd KT12 . . . 54 B6
Burwood Rd
Hersham, Burwood Park
KT12 . . . . 54 B4
Hersham KT12 . . . . 54 D5
Bury Cl GU21 . . . . 69 D3
Bury Fields GU2 . . . . 130 C7
Bury Gr SM4 . . . . 40 B4
Bury La GU21 . . . . 69 C3
Bury St GU2 . . . . 130 C7
Burys The GU7 . . . . 150 E5
Burywood Hill RH5 . . . . . . 177 E7
BUSBRIDGE 150 F2
Busbridge CE Jun Sch
GU7 . . . . 150 F2
Busbridge Inf Sch GU7 . . 150 F2
Busbridge La GU7 . . . . 150 E3
Busby Ho SW16 . . . . 21 C4
Busch Cl TW7 . . . . .6 B6
Busch Cnr TW7 . . . . .6 B6
Busdens Cl GU8 . . . . 170 F8
Busdens La GU8 . . . . 170 F8
Busdens Way GU8 . . . . . . 170 F8
Bushbury La RH3 . . . . 137 A5
Bush Cl KT15 . . . . 52 C5
Bushell Cl SW2 . . . . 21 F6
Bushell Ho 3 SE27 . . . . . . 22 C4
Bushetts Gr RH1 . . . . 119 B6
Bushey Cl CR3 . . . . 80 F3
Bushey Croft RH8 . . . . . . 122 C5
Bushey Ct SW20 . . . . 39 B7
Bushey Down SW12 . . . . . . 21 B6
Bushey La SM1 . . . . 59 A6
Bushey Mans SW20 . . . . . . 39 C6
BUSHEY MEAD 39 D6
Bushey Rd
Croydon CR0 . . . . 63 A8
Merton SW20 . . . . 39 D7
Sutton SM1 . . . . 59 A6
Bushey Way BR3 . . . . 44 D4
Bushfield RH14 . . . . 211 F2
Bushfield Dr RH1 . . . . 140 A4
Bush La GU23 . . . . 90 D3
Bushnell Rd SW17 . . . . 21 B5
Bush Rd
Littleton TW17 . . . . 33 F4
Richmond TW9 . . . . .6 F8
Bush Wlk RG40 . . . . 25 C6
Bushwood Rd TW9 . . . . .7 A8
Bushy Ct KT1 . . . . 37 C8
BUSHY HILL 110 C3
Bushy Hill Dr GU1 . . . . . . 110 C3
Bushy Hill Jun Sch GU1 . 110 D2
Bushy Park Gdns TW11 . . . 16 D3
Bushy Park Rd TW11 . . . . . 17 B1
Bushy Rd
Fetcham KT22 . . . . 94 B5
Teddington TW11 . . . . 16 F1
Bushy Shaw KT21 . . . . 75 C2
Business Ctr The RG41 . . . 25 B4
Business Pk 5 KT22 . . . . . 94 F8
Business Village The
CR3 . . . . 100 C5
Busk Cres GU14 . . . . 84 F3
Bute Ave TW10 . . . . 17 E6
Bute Ct SM6 . . . . 60 C5
Bute Gardens W SM6 . . . . . 60 C5
Bute Gdns SM6 . . . . 60 C5
Bute Rd
Thornton Heath CR0 . . . . . . 42 A1
Wallington SM6 . . . . 60 C6
Butler Dr RG12 . . . . 26 D6
Butler Rd
Bagshot GU19 . . . . 47 F2
Crowthorne RG45 . . . . 45 B6
Butlers Cl TW4 . . . . .4 F3
Butlers Dene Rd CR3 . . . . 102 A7
Butlers Farm Cl TW10 . . . . 17 D4
Butlers Hill KT24 . . . . 112 B5
Butlers Pl GU8 . . . . 150 A1
Butlers Rd RH13 . . . . 218 B4
Butt Cl GU6 . . . . 174 E4
Butt Ct SM4 . . . . 40 C3
Buttercup Cl RG40 . . . . . . 26 A6
Buttercup Sq TW19 . . . . . . 13 D7
Butterfield
Camberley GU15 . . . . 65 B4
East Grinstead RH19 . . . . 185 B3
Butterfield Cl TW1 . . . . .5 F1
Butterfield Ct 1 KT23 . . . . 94 A1
Butterfly Wlk CR6 . . . . . . 101 C7
Butter Hill
5 Dorking RH4 . . . . 136 A7
Hackbridge SM5, SM6 . . . . 60 A6
Buttermer Cl GU10 . . . . . 145 F7
Buttermere Cl
East Bedfont TW14 . . . . . . 14 F7
Farnborough GU14 . . . . . . 84 E4
Horsham RH12 . . . . 218 B6
West Barnes SM4 . . . . 39 D3
Buttermere Ct GU12 . . . . 105 F4
Buttermere Dr GU15 . . . . . 66 D4
Buttermere Gdns
Bracknell RG12 . . . . 27 C6
Sanderstead CR8 . . . . 80 D6
Buttermere Way 4 TW20 . 12 B1
Buttersteep Rise SL5 . . . . 28 C1
Butterworth Ct SW16 . . . . 21 E5
Butts Cl RH11 . . . . 201 B7
Butts Cotts
3 Feltham TW13 . . . . 15 F5
4 Woking GU21 . . . . 69 A1
Butts Cres TW13 . . . . 16 A5
Butts Ho TW13 . . . . 16 A5
Butts Rd
Catford BR1 . . . . 24 E3
Woking GU21 . . . . 69 E2
Butts The TW8 . . . . 6 D8
Buxton Ave CR3 . . . . 100 E6
Buxton Cl KT19 . . . . 76 B8
Buxton Cres SM3 . . . . 58 E6
Buxton Dr KT3 . . . . 38 D7
Buxton La CR3 . . . . 100 E6
Buxton Rd
Ashford TW15 . . . . 13 D3
4 Mortlake SW14 . . . . 7 E4
Thornton Heath CR7 . . . . . 42 B4
Byards Croft SW16 . . . . . . 41 D8
Byatt Wlk TW12 . . . . 15 E2
Bychurch End 13 TW11 . . . 16 F3
Bycroft St SE20 . . . . 23 D1
Bycroft Way RH10 . . . . . . 202 B8
Byerley Way RH10 . . . . . . 202 E7
Byers La RH9 . . . . 142 C1
Bye Ways TW2 . . . . 16 B5
Byeways The KT5 . . . . 38 B4
Byeway The SW14 . . . . 7 C4
Byfield Ct KT3 . . . . 39 A5
Byfield Rd TW7 . . . . 6 A4
BYFLEET 71 D7
Byfleet Cnr KT14 . . . . 71 A6
Byfleet Cty Prim Sch
KT14 . . . . 71 D8
Byfleet Ind Est KT14 . . . . . 71 D8
Byfleet & New Haw Sta
KT15 . . . . 52 D1
Byfleet Rd
New Haw KT14, KT15 . . . . . 52 D2
Weybridge KT11, KT13 . . . . 72 C7
Byfleets La RH12 . . . . 216 D6
Byfleet Tech Ctr The
KT14 . . . . 71 D8
Byfrons The GU14 . . . . 85 D2
Bygrove CR0 . . . . 63 B3
Bygrove Ct SW19 . . . . 20 D2
Bygrove Rd SW19 . . . . 20 D2
Byland Cl SM4 . . . . 40 D2
Bylands GU22 . . . . 70 A1
Byne Rd
Carshalton SM5 . . . . 59 E8
Penge SE20, E26 . . . . 23 C3
Bynes Rd CR2 . . . . 61 D3
By Pass Rd KT22 . . . . 95 B7
Byrd Rd RH11 . . . . 200 F3
Byrefield Rd GU2 . . . . 108 F4
Byrne Cl CR7 . . . . 42 C3
Byrne Ct 4 CR8 . . . . 80 A7
Byrne Rd SW12 . . . . 21 B6
Byron Ave
Carshalton SM1 . . . . 59 D6
Coulsdon CR5 . . . . 79 F3
Cranford TW4 . . . . 4 B5
Frimley GU15 . . . . 66 B3
West Barnes KT3 . . . . 39 A4
Byron Ave E SM1 . . . . 59 D6
Byron Cl
Crawley RH10 . . . . 202 B7
Forest Hill SE26 . . . . 23 E4
Hampton TW12 . . . . 15 F4
Horsham RH12 . . . . 217 E6
Knaphill GU21 . . . . 68 E2
Streatham SW16 . . . . 21 E2
Walton-on-Thames KT12 . . . 35 E1
Byron Ct
Dulwich SE21 . . . . 23 A7
1 Richmond TW10 . . . . 17 D4
South Norwood CR7 . . . . . . 42 C7
Byron Dr RG45 . . . . 45 B3
Byron Gdns SM1 . . . . 59 D6
Byron Gr 2 RH19 . . . . 185 C1
Byron Ho BR3 . . . . 24 B2
Byron Pl KT22 . . . . 95 B5
Byron Prim Sch CR5 . . . . . 79 F2
Byron Rd
Addlestone KT15 . . . . 52 E6
Byron Rd *continued*
South Croydon CR2 . . . . 62 B1
Byton Rd SW17 . . . . 20 F2
Byttom Hill RH5 . . . . 115 C8
Byward Ave TW14 . . . . 4 C1
Bywater Ct GU14 . . . . 105 C8
Byways The KT21 . . . . 75 D1
Byway The
Sutton SM2 . . . . 59 D2
Worcester Park KT19 . . . . . 57 F6
Bywood RG12 . . . . 27 A2
Bywood Ave CR0 . . . . 43 D3
Bywood Cl
Banstead SM7 . . . . 77 F2
Purley CR8 . . . . 80 B4
Bywood Terr CR0 . . . . 43 C3
Byworth Cl GU9 . . . . 124 F2
Byworth Rd GU9 . . . . 124 F2

C

Cabbell Pl KT15 . . . . 52 C6
Cabell Rd GU2 . . . . 108 E2
Caberfeigh Cl RH1 . . . . . . 118 E1
Cabin Moss RG12 . . . . 27 E2
Cable House Ct GU21 . . . . . 69 E4
Cabrera Ave GU25 . . . . 31 D3
Cabrera Cl GU25 . . . . 31 D3
Cabrol Rd GU14 . . . . 85 A5
Caburn Ct RH11 . . . . 201 C4
Caburn Hts RH11 . . . . 201 C4
Cackstones The RH10 . . . 202 D7
Cadbury Cl
Ashford TW16 . . . . 14 E1
Isleworth TW7 . . . . 6 A6
Cadbury Rd TW16 . . . . 14 E2
Caddy Cl 18 TW20 . . . . 12 A3
Cadley Terr SE23 . . . . 23 C6
Cadmer Cl KT3 . . . . 38 E5
Cadnam Cl GU11 . . . . 126 C6
Cadnam Point 14 SW15 . . . 19 B7
Cadogan Cl
Beckenham BR3 . . . . 44 D7
Teddington TW11 . . . . 16 E3
Cadogan Ct
Frimley GU15 . . . . 65 E3
New Malden KT3 . . . . 38 E5
Sutton SM2 . . . . 59 B4
Cadogan Ho 11 GU1 . . . . . 130 F8
Cadogan Pl CR8 . . . . 80 C2
Cadogan Rd
Farnborough GU11 . . . . . . 105 D7
Kingston upon Thames KT6 . 37 D4
Caenshill Ho KT13 . . . . 53 A3
Caenshill Pl KT13 . . . . 53 A3
Caenshill Rd KT13 . . . . 53 A3
Caenswood Hill KT13 . . . . . 53 A1
Caenwood Cl KT13 . . . . 53 A4
Caen Wood Rd KT21 . . . . . 75 C1
Caerleon Cl
Beacon Hill GU26 . . . . 188 C6
Claygate KT10 . . . . 56 B3
Caernarvon GU16 . . . . 85 F8
Caernarvon Cl CR4 . . . . 41 E6
Caernarvon Ct 3 KT5 . . . . . 37 F4
Caesar Ct GU11 . . . . 104 E2
Caesar's Camp Rd GU15 . . 66 A8
Caesar's Cl GU15 . . . . 66 A8
Caesars Ct GU9 . . . . 125 C7
Caesar's Way TW17 . . . . . . 34 D3
Caesars Wlk CR4 . . . . 40 F4
Caffins Cl RH10 . . . . 201 E8
Caillard Rd KT14 . . . . 71 E8
Cain Rd RG12 . . . . 26 D7
Cain's La TW14 . . . . .3 E2
Cairn Cl GU15 . . . . 66 B3
Cairndale Cl BR1 . . . . 24 F1
Cairngorm Cl 4 TW11 . . . . 17 A3
Cairngorm Pl GU14 . . . . . . 84 E7
Cairn Ho SW19 . . . . 20 E1
Cairo New Rd CR0, CR9 . . . 61 B8
Caister Ho 11 SW12 . . . . . . 21 B8
Caistor Mews SW12 . . . . . . 21 B8
Caistor Rd SW12 . . . . 21 B8
Caithness Dr KT18 . . . . 76 D5
Caithness Rd CR4 . . . . 21 B1
Calbourne Rd SW12 . . . . . . 21 A8
Caldbeck Ave KT4 . . . . 39 B1
Caldbeck Ho 7 RH11 . . . . 200 F3
Calderdale Cl RH11 . . . . . 201 B4
Calder Rd SM4 . . . . 40 C4
Calder Way SL3 . . . . 1 E4
Caldwell Rd GU20 . . . . 48 D5
Caledonian Ho RH10 . . . . 201 D8
Caledonian Way RH6 . . . . 182 B7
Caledonia Rd TW19 . . . . . . 13 E7
Caledon Pl GU4 . . . . 110 A4
Caledon Rd SM6 . . . . 60 A6
Calendar Mews 3 KT6 . . . . 37 D3
Calfridus Way RG12 . . . . . . 27 F6
California Cl SM2 . . . . 59 A1
California Ct SM2 . . . . 59 B1
California Rd KT3 . . . . 38 C6
Callander Rd SE6 . . . . 24 C6
Calley Down Cres CR0 . . . . 63 D1
Callis Farm Cl TW19 . . . . . . .2 E1
Callisto Cl RH11 . . . . 200 E3
Callow Field CR8 . . . . 80 A6
Callow Hill GU25 . . . . 31 C7
Calluna Ct GU22 . . . . 69 F1
Calluna Dr RH10 . . . . 183 A3
Calmont Rd BR1 . . . . 24 E2
Calonne Rd SW19 . . . . 19 D4
Calshot Rd TW6 . . . . .3 B5
Calshot Way
Frimley GU16 . . . . 86 A7
Harlington TW6 . . . . 3 A5

Calthorpe Gdns SM1 . . . . . 59 C7
Calton Gdns GU11 . . . . . 126 C7
Calumet Ct SW17 . . . . . 20 E2
Calverley Cl BR3 . . . . . 24 B2
Calverley Ct BR3 . . . . . 44 D7
Calverley Rd KT17 . . . . . 58 A4
Calvert Cl
  Aldershot GU12 . . . . . 105 D1
  Epsom KT19 . . . . . 57 B1
Calvert Cres RH4 . . . . . 115 B1
Calvert Ct
  Leatherhead KT22 . . . . . 95 B5
  8 Richmond TW9 . . . . . 6 F3
Calvert Rd
  Dorking RH4 . . . . . 115 B2
  Effingham KT24 . . . . . 113 B7
Calvi House Pre-Prep Sch
  KT11 . . . . . 72 E6
Calvin Cl GU15 . . . . . 66 B4
Calvin Wlk RH11 . . . . . 200 E3
Camac Rd TW2 . . . . . 16 D7
Camargue Pl GU7 . . . . . 150 F4
Camber Cl RH10 . . . . . 202 C6
CAMBERLEY 65 D6
Camberley Ave SW20 . . . . . 39 B8
Camberley Bsns Ctr GU15 65 A5
Camberley Cl SM3 . . . . . 58 D7
Camberley Ct **7** SM2 . . . . . 59 B3
Camberley Inf Sch GU15 . 65 C5
Camberley Rd TW6 . . . . . 3 A4
Camberley Sta GU15 . . . . . 65 D5
Camberley Theatre The★
  GU15 . . . . . 65 C5
Camberley Twrs **1** GU15 . 65 D5
Cambisgate SW19 . . . . . 19 E3
Camborne Cl TW6 . . . . . 3 A4
Camborne Ho **9** SM2 . . . . . 59 B3
Camborne Rd
  Belmont SM2 . . . . . 59 B3
  Croydon CR0 . . . . . 43 A2
  Wandsworth SW18 . . . . . 20 A8
  West Barnes SW20 . . . . . 39 D4
Camborne Road S TW6 . . 3 A4
Camborne Way
  Harmondsworth TW6. . . . . 3 A4
  Heston TW5. . . . . 5 A6
Cambray Rd SW12 . . . . . 21 C7
Cambria **6** BR3 . . . . . 44 B7
Cambria Cl TW3 . . . . . 5 A3
Cambria Ct
  Feltham TW14 . . . . . 15 B8
  Staines TW18. . . . . 12 E4
Cambria Gdns SW19 . . . . . 13 E8
Cambria Ho SE26 . . . . . 23 A4
Cambrian Cl
  Camberley GU15 . . . . . 65 B5
  West Norwood SE27 . . . . . 22 B5
Cambrian Ct **8** CR2 . . . . . 61 E6
Cambrian Rd
  Farnborough GU14 . . . . . 84 D7
  Richmond TW10 . . . . . 6 F1
Cambridge Ave KT3, SW20 38 F7
Cambridge Cl
  Harmondsworth UB7. . . . . 2 D8
  Hounslow TW4. . . . . 4 E3
  Knaphill GU21 . . . . . 68 F1
  Wimbledon SW20 . . . . . 39 B8
Cambridge Cotts TW9 . . . . 7 A8
Cambridge Cres TW11 . . . 17 A3
Cambridge Ct
  Farnborough GU14 . . . . . 85 C1
  7 Twickenham TW1 . . . . . 6 D1
  Wimbledon SW20 . . . . . 39 B8
Cambridge Gdns KT1 . . . . 38 A7
Cambridge Gr SE20 . . . . . 43 B8
Cambridge Grove Rd
  Kingston upon Thames
  KT1 . . . . . 38 A6
  5 Kingston upon Thames,
  Norbiton KT1 . . . . . 38 A7
CAMBRIDGE PARK 6 D1
Cambridge Park Sta TW1 . 17 D8
Cambridge Pk TW1 . . . . . 6 C1
Cambridge Pl GU9 . . . . . 125 C2
Cambridge Rd
  Aldershot GU11 . . . . . 104 F2
  Barnes SW13. . . . . 7 F5
  Carshalton SM5. . . . . 59 E5
  Crowthorne RG45 . . . . . 45 C4
  Croydon SE20, SE25 . . . . . 43 B6
  East Molesey KT8 . . . . . 35 F5
  Hampton TW12 . . . . . 15 F1
  Horsham RH13 . . . . . 217 D2
  Hounslow TW4. . . . . 4 E3
  Kingston upon Thames KT1. 38 A7
  Littleton Common TW15,
  TW17 . . . . . 14 C1
  Mitcham CR4 . . . . . 41 C6
  New Malden KT3 . . . . . 38 E5
  Richmond TW9 . . . . . 7 A7
  Sandhurst GU47 . . . . . 45 E1
  Teddington TW11 . . . . . 17 A3
  Twickenham TW1 . . . . . 6 D1
  Walton-on-Thames KT12. . 35 B3
  Wimbledon SW20 . . . . . 39 B8
Cambridge Road E GU14 . 85 D1
Cambridge Road W GU14. 85 C1
Cambridge Sq
  Camberley GU15 . . . . . 65 C6
  Redhill RH1 . . . . . 140 A6
Cambridge Tutors Coll
  CR0 . . . . . 61 E6
Cambridge Wlk **3** GU15. 65 C6
Camden Ave TW13 . . . . . 15 C7
Camden Cotts KT13 . . . . . 53 A7
Camden Gdns
  South Norwood CR7 . . . . . 42 B6

Camden Gdns *continued*
  Sutton SM1 . . . . . 59 B5
Camden Hill Rd SE19 . . . . 22 E2
Camden Ho SM6 . . . . . 60 E7
Camden Jun Sch SM5 . . . 59 F6
Camden Rd
  Carshalton SM5 . . . . . 59 F6
  Lingfield RH7 . . . . . 164 D4
  Sutton SM1 . . . . . 59 B5
Camden Way CR7 . . . . . 42 B6
Cameford Ct **19** SW12 . . 21 E8
Camel Cl KT2 . . . . . 17 D3
Camellia Ct
  21 Beckenham BR3 . . . . . 24 A1
  West End GU24 . . . . . 67 F6
Camellia Ho TW13 . . . . . 15 A7
Camellia Pl TW2 . . . . . 16 B8
Camelot Cl
  Biggin Hill TN16 . . . . . 83 C3
  Wimbledon SW19 . . . . . 20 A4
Camelot Ct RH11 . . . . . 200 E6
Camelsdale Fst Sch
  GU27 . . . . . 207 F5
Camelsdale Rd GU27. . . . 207 F5
CAMELSIDE. 207 F4
Cameron Cl GU6 . . . . . 174 E1
Cameron Ct **3** SW19 . . . 19 E7
Cameron Ho **10** BR1. . . . 44 F8
Cameron Lodge TW3. . . . 5 C3
Cameron Pl SW16 . . . . . 22 A5
Cameron Rd
  Farnborough GU11 . . . . . 105 D7
  Forest Hill SE6. . . . . 23 F6
  Thornton Heath CR0 . . . . 42 B3
Cameron Sq CR4 . . . . . 40 E8
Camgate Ctr The TW19 . . 13 F8
Camilla Cl
  Ashford TW16 . . . . . 14 F2
  Great Bookham KT23. . . . 94 B2
Camilla Ct **1** SM2 . . . . . 59 A3
Camilla Dr RH5 . . . . . 115 A5
Camille Cl SE25 . . . . . 43 A6
Camino Pk RH10 . . . . . 182 A4
Camlan Rd BR1 . . . . . 24 F4
Camm Gdns
  6 Kingston upon Thames
  KT1 . . . . . 37 F7
  Thames Ditton KT7 . . . . 36 F2
Camomile Ave CR4 . . . . . 40 F8
Campaspe Bsns Pk TW16. 34 F4
Campbell Cl
  Aldershot GU11 . . . . . 126 C7
  Streatham SW16 . . . . . 21 A4
  Twickenham TW2 . . . . . 16 D7
  West Byfleet KT14 . . . . . 71 D7
Campbell Cres RH19 . . . . 185 B1
Campbell Ct
  Dulwich SE21. . . . . 23 A7
  Leatherhead KT22 . . . . . 95 B5
Campbell Fields GU11 . . . 105 B1
Campbell Ho **6** SM6 . . . . 60 B6
Campbell Pl GU16 . . . . . 65 F3
Campbell Rd
  Aldershot GU11 . . . . . 105 A3
  Caterham CR3 . . . . . 100 D6
  Crawley RH10 . . . . . 202 C5
  Thornton Heath CR0 . . . . 42 B3
  Twickenham TW2 . . . . . 16 D6
  Weybridge KT13 . . . . . 53 A3
Campden Rd CR0, CR2 . . 61 E5
Campen Cl SW19. . . . . 19 E6
Camp End Rd KT11, KT13. 72 C8
Camp Farm Rd GU11 . . . 105 D5
Camp Hill GU10. . . . . 147 C8
Camphill Ct KT14 . . . . . 71 A7
Camphill Ind Est KT14 . . 71 B8
Camphill Rd KT14, KT15. 71 B7
Campion Cl
  Blackwater GU17 . . . . . 64 F3
  South Croydon CR2 . . . . 61 E6
Campion Dr KT20 . . . . . 97 B7
Campion Ho
  Bracknell RG42 . . . . . 26 E8
  6 Redhill RH1. . . . . 119 A4
Campion Rd
  Horsham RH12 . . . . . 217 E5
  Hounslow TW7. . . . . 5 F6
Campion Way RG40 . . . . 25 E7
Camp Rd
  Farnborough GU14 . . . . . 105 C8
  Wimbledon SW19 . . . . . 19 C3
  Woldingham CR3 . . . . . 101 E6
Camps Ho TW12 . . . . . 16 C3
Camp View SW19 . . . . . 19 B3
Camrose Ave TW13 . . . . 15 C4
Camrose Cl
  Croydon CR0 . . . . . 43 E2
  Morden SM4 . . . . . 40 A5
Camrose Ct CR2 . . . . . 61 E4
Canada Ave RH1 . . . . . 140 A5
Canada Copse GU8. . . . . 149 E2
Canada Dr RH1 . . . . . 140 A5
Canada Rd RH1 . . . . . 140 A5
Canada Ho
  Byfleet KT14 . . . . . 71 D8
  Cobham KT11. . . . . 73 C6
  Frimley GU16 . . . . . 86 E8
Canadian Ave SE6. . . . . 24 B7
Canal Bank GU21 . . . . . 88 F8
Canal Bank Mews GU21 . 69 E2
Canal Cl GU11 . . . . . 105 D5
Canal Cotts GU12 . . . . . 106 A4
Canalside RH1 . . . . . 119 B4
Canal Wlk
  Croydon CR0 . . . . . 42 F3
  Forest Hill SE26. . . . . 23 C3
Canberra Cl RH11 . . . . . 181 D1

Canberra Pl RH12 . . . . . 217 F4
Canberra Rd TW6 . . . . . 3 A4
Canberra Way GU14. . . . 104 F8
Canbury Ave KT2 . . . . . 37 F8
Canbury Bsns Pk **3** KT2. 37 E8
Canbury Ct **3** KT2 . . . . . 17 E1
Canbury Mews SE26. . . . 23 A5
Canbury Park Rd KT2 . . . 37 F8
Canbury Sch KT2 . . . . . 18 B2
Candler Mews TW1 . . . . 17 A8
Candlerush Cl GU22. . . . 70 B2
Candover Cl UB7. . . . . 2 D7
Candy Croft KT23 . . . . . 94 B2
Canewden Cl GU22. . . . . 89 E8
Canfold Cotts GU6 . . . . . 175 B4
Canford Dr KT15 . . . . . 52 B8
Canford Gdns KT3 . . . . . 38 E3
Canford Pl TW11 . . . . . 17 B2
Canham Rd SE25. . . . . 42 E6
Canhams KT20 . . . . . 97 B6
Can Hatch KT20. . . . . 77 E1
Canmore Gdns SW16. . . . 21 C1
Canning Rd
  Aldershot GU12 . . . . . 105 D2
  Croydon CR0, CR9 . . . . . 61 F8
Cannizaro Rd SW19 . . . . 19 D3
Cannon Cl
  Hampton TW12 . . . . . 16 B2
  Sandhurst GU47 . . . . . 64 F8
  West Barnes SW20 . . . . . 39 C6
Cannon Cres GU24 . . . . . 68 E8
Cannon Gr KT22 . . . . . 94 E6
Cannon Hill RG12 . . . . . 27 C3
Cannon Hill Comm Nature
  Reserve★ SW20 . . . . . 39 D5
Cannon Hill La KT3, SM4,
  SW20 . . . . . 39 E5
Cannon Ho SE26 . . . . . 23 B2
Cannon Mews SL5 . . . . . 28 B8
Cannon Side KT22 . . . . . 94 E5
Cannons L Ctr CR4 . . . . . 40 F6
Cannon Way
  East Molesey KT8 . . . . . 36 B5
  Fetcham KT22 . . . . . 94 E6
Cannon (West End of
  General Roy's Base Line)★
  TW6 . . . . . 3 B6
Canonbie Rd SE23 . . . . . 23 C8
Canonbury Cotts RH12 . . 199 F6
Canons Cl RH2 . . . . . 117 F2
Canon's Hill CR5 . . . . . 80 A1
Canons La KT20 . . . . . 97 F8
Canon's Wlk CR0 . . . . . 62 D7
Canopus Way SW19 . . . . 13 E8
Cansiron La RH19 . . . . . 206 F6
Cantelupe Ho **1** RH19. . 185 F1
Cantelupe Mews **7**
  RH19 . . . . . 185 F1
Cantelupe Rd RH19 . . . . 185 F1
Canterbury Cl BR3 . . . . . 44 B8
Canterbury Ct
  4 Ashford TW15 . . . . . 13 F4
  3 Dorking RH4. . . . . 136 A8
  South Croydon CR2 . . . . 61 C3
  Thornton Heath CR0 . . . . 42 A3
Canterbury Gdns GU14 . . 85 D2
Canterbury Gr SE27, SW16 22 A5
Canterbury Hall KT4 . . . . 39 B2
Canterbury Ho KT19. . . . 76 A8
Canterbury Mews KT22. . 74 C6
Canterbury Rd
  Ash GU12. . . . . 106 A3
  Crawley RH10 . . . . . 201 E2
  Farnborough GU14 . . . . . 85 D2
  Feltham TW13 . . . . . 15 E6
  Guildford GU2 . . . . . 108 F3
  Morden SM4 . . . . . 40 C3
  Thornton Heath CR0, CR7. 42 A2
Canterbury Wlk GU14 . . . 85 D2
Canter The RH10. . . . . 202 E7
Cantley Cres RG41 . . . . . 25 A8
Cantley Gdns SE19 . . . . . 42 F8
Canute Ct SW16 . . . . . 22 A5
Canute Ho **1** TW8 . . . . . 6 C7
Canvas St SE17 . . . . . 208 B6
Canvey Cl RH11 . . . . . 201 C3
Capatus Ho SW14 . . . . . 7 D5
Cape Copse RH12 . . . . . 214 D7
CAPEL 178 C6
Capel Ave SM6. . . . . 60 F5
Capel Ct
  7 Mortlake SW14 . . . . . 7 D4
  Penge SE20 . . . . . 43 C8
Capel La RH11 . . . . . 200 F5
Capella House RH5 . . . . . 178 C4
Capel Lodge
  5 Richmond TW9 . . . . . 6 F6
  15 Streatham SW2 . . . . 21 F8
Capel Rd RH12 . . . . . 199 A8
Capercaillie Cl RG12 . . . . 26 D6
Capern Rd SW18 . . . . . 20 C7
Capital Bsns Ctr
  Mitcham CR4 . . . . . 40 F4
  South Croydon CR2 . . . . 61 D3
Capital Ind Est CR4 . . . . . 40 F4
Capital Pk
  Old Woking GU22. . . . . 90 B6
  Wormley GU8. . . . . 190 F7
Capitol The★ RH12. . . . . 217 D2
Caplan Ct TW10. . . . . 6 F1
Caplan Est CR4 . . . . . 41 C8
Capper Rd GU15 . . . . . 65 A7
Capricorn Cl RH11 . . . . . 200 E4
Capri Rd CR0 . . . . . 42 F2
Capsey Rd RH11 . . . . . 200 E5
Capstans Wharf **8** GU21. 68 F1
Capstone Rd BR1 . . . . . 24 F4

Caradon Cl GU21 . . . . . 69 B1
Caradon Ct **7** TW1 . . . . . 6 C1
Caraway Cl RH11 . . . . . 201 B2
Caraway Pl
  Guildford GU2 . . . . . 109 A6
  Hackbridge SM6 . . . . . 60 B7
Carberry Rd **13** SE19 . . . 22 E2
Carbery La SL5 . . . . . 29 B6
Cardamom Cl GU2 . . . . . 109 A5
Card Hill RH18 . . . . . 206 F1
Cardigan Cl GU21 . . . . . 68 F1
Cardigan Ct
  North Cheam KT4 . . . . . 39 E4
  7 Richmond TW10 . . . . 6 E1
Cardigan Rd
  Richmond TW10 . . . . . 6 E1
  Wimbledon SW19 . . . . . 20 C2
Cardinal Ave
  Kingston upon Thames
  KT2 . . . . . 17 E2
  West Barnes SM4 . . . . . 39 E3
Cardinal Cl
  Sanderstead CR2 . . . . . 81 A6
  West Barnes SM4 . . . . . 39 E3
  Worcester Park KT4 . . . . 58 A6
Cardinal Cres KT3. . . . . 38 C7
Cardinal Ct KT8 . . . . . 36 D5
Cardinal Dr KT12 . . . . . 35 D1
Cardinal Ho GU14 . . . . . 85 C4
Cardinal Newman RC Prim
  Sch KT12 . . . . . 54 D7
Cardinal Rd TW13 . . . . . 15 B7
Cardinal Road Inf Sch
  TW13 . . . . . 15 B7
Cardinals The GU10 . . . . 126 F7
Cardinal's Wlk
  Ashford TW16 . . . . . 14 E2
  Hampton TW12 . . . . . 16 C1
Cardingham GU21 . . . . . 69 B2
Cardington Sq TW4 . . . . . 4 D3
Cardwell Cres SL5 . . . . . 29 C4
Cardwells Keep GU2 . . . . 109 A4
Carew Cl CR5 . . . . . 100 B8
Carew Ct SM2 . . . . . 59 B2
Carew Ho SW16 . . . . . 22 A5
Carew Manor Sch SM6 . . 60 D7
Carew Rd
  Ashford TW15 . . . . . 14 C2
  Mitcham CR4 . . . . . 41 A7
  Thornton Heath CR7 . . . . 42 B5
  Wallington SM6 . . . . . 60 C4
Carey Ho RH11 . . . . . 201 C6
Carey Rd RG40 . . . . . 25 C5
Carey's Cl RH6 . . . . . 162 B4
Carey's Wood RH6 . . . . . 162 B3
Carfax RH12 . . . . . 217 C2
Carfax Ave GU10 . . . . . 126 F8
Carfax Est GU10. . . . . 126 F8
Cargate Ave GU11 . . . . . 105 A1
Cargate Gr GU11 . . . . . 105 A1
Cargate Hill GU11 . . . . . 104 F1
Cargate Terr GU11 . . . . . 104 F1
Cargill Rd SW18 . . . . . 20 C7
Cargo Forecourt Rd
  RH6 . . . . . 181 D7
Cargo Rd RH6 . . . . . 181 D7
Cargreen Rd SE25 . . . . . 42 F5
Carholme Rd SE23 . . . . . 23 F7
Carisbrook Ct **1** SW16. . 21 F5
Carisbrooke GU16. . . . . 85 F8
Carisbrooke Cl TW4. . . . 15 E8
Carisbrooke Ct SM2. . . . 58 F3
Carisbrooke Ho
  16 Kingston upon Thames
  KT2 . . . . . 37 E8
  Richmond TW10 . . . . . 7 A2
Carisbrooke Rd CR4. . . . 41 E5
Carleton Ave SM6. . . . . 60 D2
Carleton Cl KT10 . . . . . 36 D1
Carling Ct TW1 . . . . . 16 F7
Carlingford Gdns CR4 . . . 21 A1
Carlingford Rd SM4 . . . . 39 D3
Carlington Ho CR0 . . . . . 61 E5
Carlin Pl GU15 . . . . . 65 C4
Carlinwark Dr GU15 . . . . 65 F7
Carlisle Cl KT2 . . . . . 38 A8
Carlisle Inf Sch TW12 . . . 16 B2
Carlisle Rd
  Cheam SM1 . . . . . 58 F4
  Hampton TW12 . . . . . 16 B1
  Rushmoor GU10. . . . . 168 C6
Carlisle Way SW17 . . . . . 21 A3
Carlos St GU7 . . . . . 150 E4
Carlton Ave
  Feltham TW14 . . . . . 4 C1
  South Croydon CR2 . . . . 61 E3
Carlton Cl
  Chessington KT9 . . . . . 56 D4
  Crawley RH10 . . . . . 201 E5
  Frimley GU15 . . . . . 66 B3
  Woking GU21 . . . . . 70 A5
Carlton Cres SM3 . . . . . 58 E6
Carlton Ct
  Horley RH6 . . . . . 161 A5
  12 Penge SE20 . . . . . 43 B8
  South Norwood SE19. . . . 42 F8
  Staines TW18. . . . . 13 A3
Carlton Gn RH1 . . . . . 118 E4
Carlton Ho
  Cheam SM1 . . . . . 58 F4
  Feltham TW14 . . . . . 3 F1
  Hounslow TW4. . . . . 5 A1
Carlton Park Ave SW20 . . 39 D7
Carlton Pl **2** KT13 . . . . . 53 B6
Carlton Rd
  Ashford TW16 . . . . . 14 E1
  Blindley Heath RH9 . . . . 142 C1
  Headley Down GU35 . . . . 187 C5

Carlton Rd *continued*
  Kingston upon Thames KT3 . 38 E7
  Mortlake SW14 . . . . . 7 C3
  Redhill RH1, RH2 . . . . . 118 E4
  South Croydon CR2 . . . . 61 D3
  Walton-on-Thames KT12 . . 35 B2
  Woking GU21 . . . . . 70 A5
Carlton Terr SE26 . . . . . 23 C4
Carlton Twrs SM5 . . . . . 59 F7
Carlton Tye RH6 . . . . . 161 C3
Carlwell St SW17 . . . . . 20 E3
Carlyle Cl KT8 . . . . . 36 B7
Carlyle Ct RG45 . . . . . 45 C5
Carlyle Ho KT8. . . . . 36 A4
Carlyle Rd
  Croydon CR0 . . . . . 62 A8
  Staines TW18. . . . . 13 A1
Carlyon Cl
  Farnborough GU14 . . . . . 85 C4
  Mytchett GU16. . . . . 85 F4
Carlys Cl BR3 . . . . . 43 D7
Carmalt Gdns KT12 . . . . 54 C5
Carman Wlk RH11 . . . . . 201 B1
Carmarthen Cl GU14 . . . . 85 A7
Carmel Cl **9** GU22 . . . . . 69 E1
Carmella Ct TW15. . . . . 14 D1
Carmichael Ct SW13 . . . .7 F5
Carmichael Ho **17** SE21. . 22 E4
Carmichael Mews SW18. . 20 D8
Carmichael Rd SE25. . . . 43 A5
Carminia Rd SW17 . . . . . 21 B6
Carnac St SE21, SE27 . . . 22 D5
Carna Ct TW9. . . . . 6 E4
Carnation Cl RG45 . . . . . 45 B8
Carnation Dr RG42 . . . . .8 B2
Carnegie Cl KT6 . . . . . 56 F8
Carnegie Pl SW19 . . . . . 19 D5
Carnforth Cl KT19. . . . . 57 B4
Carnforth Rd SW16 . . . . 21 D1
Carnoustie RG12 . . . . . 26 E2
Carole Ho **14** SE20 . . . . 43 B8
Carolina Rd CR7 . . . . . 42 C8
Caroline Cl
  Hounslow TW7. . . . . 5 E7
  South Croydon CR0 . . . . 61 E6
  Streatham SW16 . . . . . 21 F5
Caroline Ct
  Ashford TW15 . . . . . 14 B2
  Catford SE6 . . . . . 24 D4
  Crawley RH11 . . . . . 201 D4
  17 Surbiton KT6 . . . . . 37 D2
Caroline Dr RG41 . . . . . 25 A7
Caroline Pl UB3. . . . . 3 E7
Caroline Rd SW19 . . . . . 19 F1
Carolyn Cl GU21 . . . . . 88 F8
Carpenter Cl KT17 . . . . . 57 F2
Carpenters Ct TW2. . . . . 16 E6
Carrara Villas KT1 . . . . . 37 F6
Carriage Pl **14** SW16 . . . 21 C3
Carrick Cl TW7 . . . . . 6 A4
Carrick Gate KT10. . . . . 55 C7
Carrigshaun KT13. . . . . 53 D4
Carrington Ave TW3. . . . .5 B2
Carrington Cl
  Croydon CR0 . . . . . 43 E2
  Redhill RH1 . . . . . 118 F2
Carrington Ct **3** KT3. . . . 38 E5
Carrington Ho **7** SW19. . 20 A1
Carrington La GU12. . . . 106 A8
Carrington Lodge **3** TW10 .6 F2
Carrington Pl KT10. . . . . 55 C6
Carrington Rd TW10 . . . .7 A3
Carroll Ave GU1. . . . . 110 B1
Carroll Cres SL5 . . . . . 28 C5
Carrow Rd KT12 . . . . . 54 D7
CARSHALTON 59 E7
Carshalton, Beddington &
  Wallington War Memorial
  Hospl SM5 . . . . . 59 F4
CARSHALTON BEECHES . 59 E2
Carshalton Beeches Sta
  SM5 . . . . . 59 F4
Carshalton Coll SM5 . . . . 59 F7
Carshalton Gr SM1 . . . . . 59 D5
Carshalton High Sch for Boys
  1 SM5. . . . . 59 E8
Carshalton High Sch for Girls
  SM5 . . . . . 59 F7
Carshalton Lodge **1**
  KT13. . . . . 53 E7
CARSHALTON ON THE
  HILL. 60 B3
Carshalton Park Rd SM5. . 59 F5
Carshalton Pl SM5 . . . . . 60 A5
Carshalton Rd
  Camberley GU15 . . . . . 47 A1
  Carshalton SM1, SM5 . . . 59 D5
  Mitcham CR4 . . . . . 41 A4
  Wallington SM7 . . . . . 78 F6
Carshalton Sta SM5 . . . . 59 F6
Carson Rd SE21 . . . . . 22 D6
Carstairs Rd SE6. . . . . 24 C8
Carswell Rd SE6 . . . . . 24 C8
Cartbridge Cl GU23 . . . . 90 B4
Carterdale Cotts RH5 . . . 178 C5
Carter Rd
  Crawley RH10 . . . . . 202 D3
  Mitcham SW19 . . . . . 20 D2
Carters Cl
  Guildford GU1 . . . . . 109 E5
  North Cheam KT4 . . . . . 39 D1
Carter's Cotts RH1 . . . . . 139 E7
Carters La
  Forest Hill SE23. . . . . 23 F5
  Woking GU22 . . . . . 90 D7

Cartersmead Cl RH6 161 B4
Carter's Rd KT17 76 F4
Carters Wlk GU9 125 D8
Carthouse Cotts GU4 110 C4
Carthouse La GU21 68 E5
Cartmel Cl RH2 118 E3
Cartmel Ct BR2 44 E7
Cartmel Gdns SM4 40 C4
Carwarden House Sch GU15 66 A3
Caryl Ho 6 SW19 19 D7
Carylls Cotts RH12 199 F1
Cascades CR0 62 F1
Cascades Ct SW19 19 F1
Cascadia Ho 11 KT1 38 A7
Caselden Cl KT15 52 C5
Casewick Rd SE27 22 B4
Casher Rd RH10 202 C3
Cassel Hospl The TW10 17 D4
Cassilis Rd TW1 6 B1
Cassino Cl GU11 105 B2
Cassiobury Ave TW14 14 F8
Cassland Rd CR7 42 D5
Casslee Rd SE6 23 F8
Cassocks Sq TW17 34 D2
Castillon Rd SE6 24 E6
Castlands Rd SE6 23 F6
Castle Ave KT17 58 B2
Castle Bsns Village TW12 36 B8
Castle Cl
- Beckenham BR2 44 E6
- Bletchingley RH1 120 C2
- Camberley GU15 65 F4
- 3 Charlton TW16 14 E1
- Farnborough GU14 85 E2
- Reigate RH2 139 B5
- Wimbledon SW19 19 D5
Castlecombe Dr SW19 19 D8
Castlecraig Ct GU47 64 D7
Castle Ct
- Belmont SM2 59 A4
- Forest Hill SE26 23 E4
- Morden SM4 40 D4
Castledine Rd SE20 23 B1
Castle Dr
- Horley RH6 161 C2
- Reigate RH2 139 B4
Castle Field GU9 125 B3
Castlefield Ct RH2 118 B1
Castlefield Rd RH2 118 A1
Castlegate TW9 6 F4
Castle Gdns RH4 115 F1
Castle Gn KT13 53 E7
CASTLE GREEN 68 D7
Castle Grove Rd GU24 68 E7
Castle Hill
- Farnham GU9 125 B3
- Guildford GU1 130 D7
Castle Hill Ave CR0 63 C2
Castle Hill Prim Sch
- Chessington KT9 56 F5
- New Addington CR0 63 C4
Castle Hill Rd TW20 11 C5
Castle Ho 3 SM2 59 A3
Castle Keep RH2 118 A1
Castlemaine Ave
- Ewell KT17 58 B2
- South Croydon CR0, CR2 61 F5
Castleman Ho SL5 29 D4
Castle Mews KT13 53 E7
Castle of Mey Ho GU27 207 F6
Castle Par KT17 58 A3
Castle Rd
- Aldershot GU11 104 E4
- Broadbridge Heath RH12 216 D3
- Camberley GU15 65 F4
- Epsom KT18 76 B4
- Isleworth TW7 5 F5
- Kingswood CR5 98 E6
- Oatlands Park KT13 53 E7
- Woking GU21 69 F5
Castle Sq
- Bletchingley RH1 120 C2
- Guildford GU1 130 D7
Castle St
- Bletchingley RH1 120 C2
- Farnham GU9 125 B3
- Guildford GU1 130 D7
Castle The RH12 217 E7
Castleton Cl
- Banstead SM7 78 A4
- Croydon CR0 43 E3
Castleton Ct KT5 37 F4
Castleton Dr SM7 78 A5
Castleton Rd CR4 41 D5
Castle View KT18 76 B5
Castle View Rd KT13 53 B6
Castle Way
- Ewell KT17 58 A2
- Feltham TW13 15 C4
- Wimbledon SW19 19 D5
Castle Wlk
- Reigate RH2 118 A1
- Sunbury TW16 35 C6
Castle Yd 19 TW10 6 D2
Caswell Cl GU14 84 F6
Catalina Rd TW6 3 B5
Catalpa Cl GU1 109 C3
Catena Rise GU18 48 B1
Caterfield La
- Crowhurst RH7 143 F3
- Oxted RH7, RH8 144 A5
Cater Gdns GU3 108 F3
CATERHAM 100 F4
Caterham By-Pass CR3 101 B4
Caterham Cl GU24 87 E6
Caterham Dene Hospl CR3 100 F4
Caterham Dr CR5 100 C8
Caterham Prep Sch CR3 100 F1
Caterham Sch CR3 100 F1
Caterham Sta CR3 101 A3
Caterways RH12 217 A3
CATFORD 24 A7
Catford Br SE6 24 A8
Catford Bridge Sta SE6 24 A8
Catford Broadway SE6 24 B8
Catford Gyratory SE6 24 B8
Catford High Sch SE6 24 C5
Catford High Sch (Annexe) BR1 24 E4
Catford Hill SE6 24 A7
Catford Rd SE6 24 A8
Catford Sh Ctr SE6 24 B8
Catford Sta SE6 24 A8
Cathedral Cl GU2 130 B8
Cathedral Ct GU2 109 A1
Cathedral Hill GU2 109 A2
Cathedral Hill Ind Est GU2 109 A2
Cathedral View GU2 108 F1
Catherine Baird Ct 13 SW12 21 B8
Catherine Cl KT14 71 F5
Catherine Ct
- Aldershot GU11 104 F1
- 3 Wimbledon SW19 19 F3
Catherine Dr
- Ashford TW16 14 F2
- Richmond TW9 6 E3
Catherine Gdns TW3 5 D3
Catherine Ho
- Ascot SL5 29 B6
- Isleworth TW7 6 B6
Catherine Howard Ct 8 KT13 53 B7
Catherine Rd KT6 37 D4
Catherine Villas GU27 208 B6
Catherine Wheel Rd TW8 6 D7
Cathill La RH5 177 C3
Cathles Rd SW12 21 C8
Catlin Cres TW17 34 D4
Catling Cl SE23 23 D5
Catlin Gdns RH9 121 B5
Caton Ct BR2 44 E7
Cator Cl CR0 82 E8
Cator Cres CR0 82 E8
Cator La BR3 43 F8
Cator Park Sch for Girls BR3 23 E1
Cator Rd
- Penge SE20, SE26 23 D2
- Wallington SM5 59 F5
CATTESHALL 151 A5
Catteshall Hatch GU7 151 A6
Catteshall La GU7 150 F4
Catteshall Rd GU7 151 A5
Catteshall Terr GU7 151 A5
Causeway
- Feltham TW14, TW4 4 B3
- Horsham RH12 217 C1
Causeway Ct 1 GU21 68 F1
Causeway Est TW20 12 C4
Causewayside GU27 208 D6
Causeway The
- Carshalton SM5 60 A8
- Claygate KT10 55 F3
- Egham TW18, TW20 12 D4
- London SW19 19 D3
- Sutton SM2 59 C2
- Teddington TW11 16 F2
- Wimbledon SW19 19 C3
Cavalier Ct TW15 14 D1
Cavalier Way RH19 205 F7
Cavalry Cres TW4 4 D3
Cavalry Ct GU11 104 E2
Cavans Rd GU11 105 C6
Cavell Way
- Crawley RH10 202 C5
- Epsom KT19 76 A8
- Knaphill GU21 88 C8
Cavendish Apartments The 4 BR1 24 F1
Cavendish Ave KT3 39 B5
Cavendish Cl
- Ashford TW16 14 F2
- Horsham RH12 217 D7
Cavendish Ct
- Ashford TW16 14 F2
- Blackwater GU17 64 D3
- Catford SE6 24 B7
- Poyle SL3 1 E6
- 6 Richmond TW10 6 E1
- 17 Wallington SM6 60 B4
- Weybridge KT13 53 C4
Cavendish Dr KT10 55 E5
Cavendish Gdns RH1 119 A2
Cavendish Ho
- 3 Richmond TW10 17 C5
- Twickenham TW1 6 A1
Cavendish Jun & Inf Sch W4 7 E7
Cavendish Meads SL5 29 D3
Cavendish Mews
- Aldershot GU11 105 A1
- Sutton SM1 59 C8
Cavendish Par TW4 4 E5
Cavendish Pk GU47 64 E6
Cavendish Pl
- Guildford GU2 108 D3
- Streatham SW12 21 C7
Cavendish Rd
- Aldershot GU11 105 A1
Cavendish Rd *continued*
- Ashford TW16 14 F2
- Balham SW12 21 B8
- Chiswick W4 7 C6
- Mitcham SW19 20 E1
- New Malden KT3 38 F5
- Redhill RH1 119 A2
- Sutton SM2 59 C3
- Thornton Heath CR0 42 B1
- Weybridge KT13 53 C3
- Woking GU22 89 D8
Cavendish Terr TW13 15 A6
Cavendish Way BR4 44 B1
Cavendish Wlk KT19 76 B8
Cavenham Cl 6 GU22 89 E8
Cave Rd TW10 17 C4
Caverleigh Way KT4 39 B2
Caversham Ave SM3 58 E8
Caversham Ho
- 8 Kingston upon Thames KT1 37 E7
- Wallington SM6 60 E7
Caversham Rd KT1 37 F7
Caves Farm Cl GU47 64 A8
Cawnpore St SE19 22 E3
Cawsey Way GU21 69 E2
Cawston Ct 12 BR1 24 F1
Caxton Ave KT15 52 A4
Caxton Cl RH10 201 E3
Caxton Gdns GU2 109 B2
Caxton Ho RH8 123 F3
Caxton La RH8 123 E4
Caxton Mews 8 TW8 6 D7
Caxton Rd SW19 20 C3
Caxton Rise RH1 119 A2
Caxtons Ct GU1 110 A3
Caygill Cl BR2 44 F5
Cayton Rd
- Coulsdon CR5 99 D5
- Hooley CR5 99 C5
Cearn Way CR5 79 F4
Ceasors Ct TW2 16 F6
Cecil Cl
- Ashford TW15 14 C1
- Chessington KT9 56 D6
Cecil Ct 12 CR0 61 F8
Cecil Lodge KT9 56 D6
Cecil Mans 2 SW17 21 A6
Cecil Pl CR4 40 F4
Cecil Rd
- Ashford TW15 14 C2
- Cheam SM1 58 F4
- Hounslow TW3 5 C5
- Merton SW19 20 B1
- Thornton Heath CR0 41 F3
Cedar Ave
- Blackwater GU17 64 D5
- Cobham KT11 73 C4
- Twickenham TW2 5 C1
Cedar Cl
- Aldershot GU12 126 E8
- Bagshot GU19 47 E3
- Crawley RH11 181 C1
- Dorking RH4 136 B7
- East Molesey KT8 36 E5
- Epsom KT17 76 F5
- Esher KT10 54 F3
- Horsham RH12 217 C3
- Kingston upon Thames KT2 18 D4
- Laleham TW18 33 C6
- Reigate RH2 139 C7
- Wallington SM5 59 F4
- Warlingham CR6 101 E8
- West Norwood SE21 22 C6
- Wokingham RG40 25 C6
Cedarcroft Rd KT9 56 F6
Cedar Ct
- Addlestone KT15 52 C5
- Bagshot GU19 47 E3
- 9 Brentford TW8 6 D8
- 5 Caterham CR3 100 D5
- Cobham KT11 73 A6
- Egham TW20 12 A4
- Haslemere GU27 208 B6
- 2 Kingston upon Thames KT3 38 E6
- Mortlake SW14 7 C3
- Ottershaw KT16 51 C5
- Sanderstead CR2 81 A8
- Stoneleigh KT17 58 A3
- 4 Sutton SM2 59 C4
- Wimbledon SW19 19 D5
Cedar Dr
- Fetcham KT22 94 E4
- Sunningdale SL5 30 A2
Cedar Gdns
- Chobham GU24 49 F1
- Sutton SM2 59 C4
- Woking GU21 69 B1
Cedar Gr
- Bisley GU24 68 A4
- Weybridge KT13 53 C6
Cedar Hill KT18 76 C3
Cedar Ho
- Charlton TW16 14 F1
- Guildford GU4 110 C3
- New Addington CR0 63 B4
- 5 Richmond TW9 7 B6
- Whyteleafe CR3 80 F2
Cedar Hts TW10 17 E7
Cedarhurst 1 BR1 24 E1
Cedar La GU16 85 D8
Cedarland Terr SW20 19 B1
Cedar Lodge
- Crawley RH11 201 D4
- Weybridge KT13 53 A7
Cedar Mount GU8 148 D4
Cedar Pk CR3 100 E6
Cedar Rd
- Cobham KT11 73 B5
- Cranford TW5 4 C5
- Croydon CR0, CR9 61 E8
- East Bedfont TW14 14 D7
- East Molesey KT8 36 E5
- Farnborough GU14 85 C3
- Sutton SM2 59 C4
- Teddington TW11 17 A3
- Weybridge KT13 53 A6
- Woking GU22 89 C7
Cedars
- 2 Bracknell RG12 27 F5
- Woodmansterne SM7 78 F5
Cedars Ave CR4 41 A6
Cedars Ct GU1 110 A4
Cedars Ho 5 SW27 22 B3
Cedars Prim Sch The TW5 4 A7
Cedars Rd
- Barnes SW13 7 F5
- Beckenham BR3 43 F7
- Morden SM4 40 A5
- Teddington KT8 37 C8
- Wallington CR0 60 E6
Cedars The
- Ashtead KT22 95 D6
- Brockham RH3 116 A1
- Byfleet KT14 71 F7
- Guildford GU1 110 A4
- Milford GU8 170 E8
- Reigate RH2 118 D1
- Teddington TW11 16 F2
- Wallington SM6 60 C6
Cedar Terr TW9 6 E3
Cedar Tree Gr SE27 22 B3
Cedarville Gdns SW16 21 F2
Cedar Way
- Charlton TW16 14 E1
- Guildford GU1 109 C4
Cedarways GU9 146 B7
Cedar Wlk
- Claygate KT10 55 F4
- Kenley CR8 80 C3
- Kingswood KT20 97 E7
Cedarwood BR3 23 F1
Cedric Ct 2 RH12 217 A1
Celandine Cl
- 1 Crawley RH11 201 B2
- Crowthorne RG45 45 C6
Celandine Rd KT12 54 E6
Celia Cres TW15 13 D2
Celia Ct
- Ewell KT17 57 F2
- 7 Richmond TW9 6 F6
Celtic Ave BR2 44 E6
Celtic Rd KT14 71 F5
Cemetery La TW17 34 B2
Cemetery Pales
- Brookwood GU24 88 A6
- Pirbright GU24 87 F5
Centaurs Bsns Pk TW7 6 A8
Centenary Ct BR3 44 C8
Centenary Fields Nature Reserve* RH7 164 D5
Central Ave
- East Molesey KT8 35 F4
- Isleworth TW3, TW7 5 C3
- Wallington SM6 60 E5
Central Blgs 2 GU21 69 F2
Central Ct KT15 52 B6
Centrale Halt CR0 61 C8
Centrale Sh Ctr CR0 61 C8
Central Gdns SM4 40 B4
Central Hill SE19 22 D2
Central La SL4 9 B7
Central Mans SW16 21 E4
Central Par
- Croydon CR0 61 A6
- East Molesey KT8 35 F5
- Feltham TW14 15 C8
- Heston TW5 5 A7
- Kingston upon Thames KT6 37 E3
- New Addington CR0 63 C1
- Penge SE20 23 D1
- Streatham SW16 21 E4
Central Pk Est TW4 4 D3
Central Rd
- Morden SM4 40 B4
- North Cheam KT4 58 A8
Central Sq KT8 35 F5
Central Sussex Coll
- Crawley RH10 201 E6
- East Grinstead RH19 185 A3
- East Grinstead RH19 185 E1
- Horsham RH12 217 D3
Central Terr BR3 43 D6
Central Veterinary Laboratory KT15 52 B2
Central Way
- Cranbourne SL4 9 B7
- Feltham TW14 4 B2
- Oxted RH8 122 D8
- Sutton SM5 59 E3
Central Wlk
- Epsom KT19 76 D6
- Wokingham RG40 25 C6
Centre Court Sh Ctr 3 SW19 19 F2
Centre The TW13 15 B7
Centrium 13 GU22 69 F2
Centurion Cl 4 GU47 64 D8
Centurion Ct SM6 60 B8
Century Ct
- Teddington TW11 17 A4
- Woking GU21 69 F3
Century Farm Ind Units GU9 125 F5
Century Ho SM7 78 B4
Century Rd TW18, TW20 12 C3
Century Way GU24 87 D8
Century Yd SE23 23 C6
Cerne Rd SM4 40 C3
Cerotus Pl KT16 32 F2
Chadacre Rd KT17 58 B5
Chaddesley 5 KT13 53 A6
Chadhurst Cl RH5 136 D4
Chadwick Ave SW19 20 A2
Chadwick Cl
- Crawley RH11 201 B1
- Roehampton SW15 18 F8
- Teddington TW11 17 A2
Chadwick Pl KT6 37 C3
Chadworth Way KT10 55 D5
Chaffers Mead KT21 75 F3
Chaffinch Ave CR0 43 D3
Chaffinch Bsns Pk BR3 43 D5
Chaffinch Cl
- Crawley RH11 201 D8
- Croydon CR0 43 D3
- Horsham RH12 217 D7
- 5 Sandhurst GU47 64 D8
- Tolworth KT6 57 A7
Chaffinch Rd BR3 43 E8
Chaffinch Way RH6 160 E4
Chagford Ct SW19 20 E1
Chailey Cl
- 2 Crawley RH11 201 A3
- Heston TW5 4 D6
Chailey Ct CR0 60 E7
Chailey Pl KT12 54 E6
Chalcot Cl SM2 59 A3
Chalcot Mews SW16 21 E5
Chalcott Gdns KT6 37 C1
CHALDON 100 B3
Chaldon Cl RH1 139 E7
Chaldon Common Rd CR3 100 C2
Chaldon Rd
- Caterham CR3 100 D4
- Crawley RH11 201 C1
Chaldon Way CR5 79 E1
Chalet Cl TW15 14 D2
Chale Wlk SM2 59 B2
Chalfont Dr GU14 85 C2
Chalfont Rd SE25 42 F6
Chalford Cl KT8 36 A5
Chalford Ct KT6 37 F2
Chalford Rd SE21 22 D4
Chalgrove Ave SM4 40 A4
Chalgrove Rd SM2 59 D3
Chalice Cl SM6 60 D4
Chalkenden Cl SE20 23 B1
Chalkers Cnr SW14 7 B4
Chalk La
- Ashtead KT21 96 A8
- East Horsley KT24 112 F4
- Epsom KT18 76 E3
- Shackleford GU8 149 D8
Chalkley Cl CR4 41 A7
Chalk Paddock KT18 76 D4
Chalkpit La
- Brockham RH3 116 B2
- Dorking RH4 115 A1
- Oxted RH8 122 D8
- Woldingham CR3, CR8 102 C1
Chalk Pit La KT23 113 F8
Chalk Pit Rd
- Banstead SM7 78 A2
- Langley Vale KT18 96 C8
- Sutton SM1 59 C4
Chalkpit Terr RH4 115 A1
Chalkpit Wood RH8 122 D8
Chalk Rd
- Farncombe GU7 150 E5
- Ifold RH14 212 C3
Chalky La KT9 56 D1
Challen Ct RH12 217 B3
Challenge Ct
- Leatherhead KT22 95 B8
- Twickenham TW2 16 E8
Challenge Rd TW15 14 D5
Challice Way SW2 21 F7
Challin St SE20 43 C8
Challis Pl RG42 26 E8
Challock Cl TN16 83 C3
Challoner Ct BR2 44 D7
Challoners Cl KT8 36 D5
Chalmers Cl RH6 180 E6
Chalmers Rd
- Ashford TW15 14 B3
- Banstead SM7 78 C4
Chalmers Rd E TW15 14 C3
Chalmers Way
- Feltham TW14 4 B2
- Twickenham TW1 6 B3
Chamber La GU10 145 C7
Chamberlain Cres BR4 44 B2
Chamberlain Gdns TW3 5 C6
Chamberlain Way KT6 37 E2
Chamberlain Wlk TW13 15 E4
Chambers Bsns Pk UB7 3 A8
Chambers Ho 2 SW16 21 C4
Chambers Pl CR2 61 D3
Chambers Rd GU12 106 B6
Chamomile Gdns GU14 84 C5
Champion Cres SE26 23 E4
Champion Down KT24 113 E7
Champion Rd SE26 23 E4
Champness Cl 9 SE27 22 D4
Champney Cl SL3 1 A4
Champneys Cl SM2 58 F3
Chancellor Gdns CR2 61 B2
Chancellor Gr SE21 22 C5
Chancery Ct 13 TW20 12 A3
Chancerygate Bsns Ctr RG41 25 A5

Chancery Gate Bsns Ctr
CR4 . . . . **40** F4
Chancery La BR3 . . . . **44** B7
Chancery Mews SW17 . . . **20** E6
Chanctonbury Chase
RH1 . . . . **119** A1
Chanctonbury Dr SL5 . . . **29** E1
Chanctonbury Gdns SM2 . **59** B3
Chanctonbury Way
RH11 . . . . **201** C4
Chanderie Ct ◼ CR0 . . . **61** C7
Chandler CE Jun Sch The
GU8 . . . . **170** F5
Chandler Cl
Crawley RH10 . . . . **201** D4
Hampton TW12 . . . . **36** A8
Chandler Ct
◼ Horley RH6 . . . . **161** B3
Thornton Heath CR7 . . . **42** B4
◼ Tolworth KT5 . . . . . . **38** B1
◼ Wallington SM6 . . . . . **60** B4
Chandlers KT20 . . . . **97** B6
Chandlers Cl
East Bedfont TW14 . . . . **14** F8
East Molesey/East Molesey
KT8 . . . . **36** B4
Chandlers Field Prim Sch
KT8 . . . . **36** B4
Chandlers Rd GU12 . . . . **106** B4
Chandlers Way ◼ SW2 . . **22** A8
Chandler Way RH5 . . . . **136** C5
Chandon Lodge SM2 . . . . **59** C3
Chandos Bsns Ctr ◼ SM6 **60** C4
Chandos Gdns CR5 . . . . **100** B8
Chandos Mans CR0 . . . . . **43** A5
Chandos Rd TW18 . . . . . . **12** D3
Channel Cl TW5 . . . . **5** A6
Channings GU21 . . . . **69** E4
Channon Ct ◼ KT6 . . . . . **37** E4
Chantilly Way KT19 . . . . **57** B1
Chantlers Cl RH19 . . . . . **185** C2
Chanton Dr SM2 . . . . **58** C1
Chantrey Cl KT21 . . . . . . **95** C8
Chantrey Rd RH10 . . . . . **201** E3
Chantry Cl
Horley RH6 . . . . **160** F4
Sunbury TW16 . . . . **15** A1
Chantry Cotts GU4 . . . . **131** B3
Chantry Ct SM5 . . . . **59** E7
Chantry Ct GU16 . . . . **65** D1
Chantry Hurst KT18 . . . . **76** D4
Chantry La GU5 . . . . **132** F4
Chantry Pl ◼ GU1 . . . . . **130** E8
Chantry Rd
Bagshot GU19 . . . . **47** D2
Chertsey KT16 . . . . **33** C2
Chessington KT9 . . . . . . **57** A5
Chilworth GU4 . . . . **131** B3
Chantrys Ct GU9 . . . . . . **125** A2
Chantrys The GU9 . . . . **125** A1
Chantry View Rd GU1 . . **130** E6
Chantry Way CR4 . . . . . . **40** D6
Chantry Wood Nature Trail★
GU1 . . . . **130** C3
Chapel Ave
Addlestone KT15 . . . . . . **52** B6
Brookwood GU24 . . . . . . **88** B6
Chapel Cl GU8 . . . . **149** F2
Chapel Ct ◼ RH4 . . . . . **136** A8
Chapel Farm Mobile Home
Pk GU3 . . . . **107** E4
Chapel Fields GU7 . . . . **150** D7
Chapel Gr
Addlestone KT15 . . . . . . **52** B6
Burgh Heath KT18 . . . . . **97** C8
CHAPEL GREEN **25** C4
Chapel Hill
Dunsfold GU8 . . . . **192** F3
Effingham KT24 . . . . . . **113** D8
Chapelhouse Cl GU2 . . . **108** E1
Chapel La
Ashurst Wood RH19 . . . **206** D6
Bagshot GU19 . . . . **47** D2
Copthorne RH10 . . . . . **183** F4
Farnborough GU14 . . . . . **84** F8
Forest Row RH18 . . . . . **206** F2
Great Bookham KT23 . . . **114** C6
Milford GU8 . . . . **149** F2
Pirbright GU24 . . . . **88** A4
Westcott RH4 . . . . **135** C6
Westhumble RH5 . . . . . **114** E5
Chapel Lane Ind Est
RH4 . . . . **135** C6
Chapel Mill Rd KT1 . . . . . **37** F6
Chapel Park Rd KT15 . . . **52** B6
Chapel Rd
Camberley GU15 . . . . . . **65** B5
Charlwood RH6 . . . . . . **180** F7
Hounslow TW3 . . . . **5** B4
Limpsfield RH8 . . . . . . **123** C5
Redhill RH1 . . . . **118** F1
Rowledge GU10 . . . . . . **145** E3
Smallfield RH6 . . . . **162** B4
Tadworth KT20 . . . . **97** D4
Twickenham TW1 . . . . . . **17** B8
Warlingham CR6 . . . . . . **81** D1
West Norwood SE27 . . . . **22** B4
Chapel Sq
Sandhurst GU15 . . . . . . **64** F6
Virginia Water GU25 . . . . **31** E5
Chapel St
Farnborough GU14 . . . . . **85** D6
Guildford GU1 . . . . **130** D7
◼ Woking GU21 . . . . . . **69** F2
Chapel View CR2 . . . . . . **62** C3
Chapel Way KT18, KT20 . . **77** C1
Chaplain's Hill RG45 . . . . **45** D4
Chaplin Cres TW16 . . . . . **14** E2

Chapman Ho ◼ SE27 . . . **22** B5
Chapman Rd
Crawley RH10 . . . . **202** C2
Thornton Heath CR0 . . . . **42** A1
Chapman's La RH19 . . . **185** B1
Chapman Sq SW19 . . . . . **19** D6
Chapter Ct ◼ TW20 . . . . **12** A3
Chapter Ho GU14 . . . . . . **85** C4
Chapter Way TW12 . . . . . **16** A4
Chara Pl W4 . . . . **7** D8
Charcot Ho SW15 . . . . **7** F1
Chargate Ct KT12 . . . . . . **54** A4
Charing Ct BR2 . . . . **44** E7
Charlbury Cl ◼ RG12 . . . **27** F5
Charlecombe Ct TW18 . . . **13** B3
Charlecote Cl GU14 . . . . . **85** D3
Charlecote Gr SE26 . . . . . **23** B5
Charles Babbage Cl KT9 . **56** D3
Charles Cobb Gdns CR0 . **61** A5
Charles Ct
South Croydon CR2 . . . . **61** D5
◼ Teddington TW11 . . . . **17** A1
Charles Darwin Sch TN16 **83** F3
Charles Dickens Ct TW18 **13** B3
Charlesfield Rd RH6 . . . . **160** F4
Charles Haller St ◼ SW2 **22** A8
CHARLESHILL **148** A5
Charles Hill GU10 . . . . . **147** E6
Charles Ho
Chertsey KT16 . . . . **32** F1
Englefield Green TW20 . . **11** C1
Charles Lesser KT9 . . . . . **56** D5
Charles Mills Ct SW16 . . . **21** E2
Charles Rd
Merton SW19 . . . . **40** A8
Staines TW18 . . . . **13** D2
Charles Sq RG12 . . . . **27** C7
Charles St
Chertsey KT16 . . . . **32** F1
Croydon CR0, CR9 . . . . . **61** C7
Hounslow TW3 . . . . **4** F5
Mortlake SW13, SW14 . . . **7** E5
Charles Staunton Ho ◼
SE27 . . . . **22** D4
Charleston Cl TW13 . . . . . **15** A5
Charleston Ct RH10 . . . . **202** B3
Charleville Cir SE19, SE26 . **23** A3
Charleville Mews TW7 . . . . **6** B3
Charlmont Rd SW17 . . . . . **20** F2
Charlock Cl ◼ RH11 . . . **201** A2
Charlock Way GU1 . . . . . **110** B4
Charlotte Broadwood Flats
RH5 . . . . **178** D6
Charlotte Cl
◼ Ashtead KT21 . . . . . . **75** E1
Heath End GU9 . . . . . . **125** D8
Charlotte Ct
Crawley RH11 . . . . **201** C6
Esher KT10 . . . . **55** C5
Charlotte Gr RH6 . . . . . . **162** A4
Charlotte Ho KT21 . . . . . . **95** E8
Charlotte Lodge KT10 . . . **55** E4
Charlotte Mews
Esher KT10 . . . . **55** B6
Farnborough GU14 . . . . . **85** D5
Charlotte Par SE23 . . . . . **23** E6
Charlotte Rd
Barnes SW13 . . . . **7** F6
Wallington SM6 . . . . **60** C4
Charlotte Sq ◼ SW10 . . . . **6** F1
CHARLTON **34** D7
Charlton Ave KT12 . . . . . . **54** B6
Charlton Ct GU47 . . . . . . **45** D1
Charlton Dr TN16 . . . . . . **83** D2
Charlton Gdns CR5 . . . . . **79** C1
Charlton Ho
◼ Brentford TW8 . . . . . . **6** E8
Charlton TW17 . . . . **34** C7
Charlton Kings KT13 . . . . **53** E7
Charlton La TW17 . . . . . . **34** D5
Charlton Rd TW17 . . . . . . **34** C7
CHARLWOOD **180** E7
Charlwood CR0 . . . . **62** F2
Charlwood Cl
Copthorne RH10 . . . . . **183** B4
Little Bookham KT23 . . . . **94** B3
Charlwood Dr KT22 . . . . . **74** D4
Charlwood Ho
Richmond TW9 . . . . **7** B7
◼ Streatham SW2 . . . . . **21** F7
Charlwood La RH5 . . . . . **180** A5
Charlwood Pl RH2 . . . . . **117** F1
Charlwood Rd
Crawley RH6, RH11 . . . **181** C4
Hookwood RH6, RH11 . . **181** C8
Rusper RH11, RH6 . . . . **180** E2
Charlwoods Bsns Ctr
RH19 . . . . **185** D2
Charlwoods Pl RH19 . . . **185** E3
Charlwoods Rd RH19 . . . **185** E3
Charlwood Village Inf Sch
RH6 . . . . **180** F7
Charlwood Wlk RH11 . . . **181** B1
Charman Rd RH1 . . . . . . **118** E1
Charmans Cl RH12 . . . . . **218** B5
Charm Cl RH6 . . . . **160** E4
Charmile Ct ◼ TW16 . . . . **14** E1
Charminster Ave SW19 . . . **40** B7
Charminster Ct ◼ KT6 . . . **37** D2
Charminster Rd KT4 . . . . . **39** D1
Charmouth Ct TW10 . . . . . **6** F2
Charnwood SL5 . . . . **29** D3
Charnwood Ave SW19 . . . . **40** B7
Charnwood Cl KT3 . . . . . . **38** E5
Charnwood Rd SE25 . . . . . **42** D5
Charrington Rd ◼ CR0,
CR9 . . . . **61** C8

Charrington Way RH12 . . **216** C3
Charsley Rd SE6 . . . . **24** B6
Charta Rd TW20 . . . . **12** C2
Charta Road W TW20 . . . . **12** C3
Chart Cl
Bromley BR2 . . . . **44** E8
Croydon CR0 . . . . **43** C3
Dorking RH5 . . . . **136** D5
Mitcham CR4 . . . . **40** F5
Chart Downs RH5 . . . . . **136** D4
Charter Cres TW4 . . . . **4** E3
Charter Ct KT3 . . . . **38** E6
Charter Ho ◼ SM2 . . . . . **59** B4
Charterhouse GU7 . . . . . **150** C7
Charterhouse Cl RG12 . . . **27** E4
Charterhouse Rd GU7 . . . **150** D6
Charter Pl TW18 . . . . **13** A2
Charter Rd KT1 . . . . **38** B6
Charters Cl
Ascot SL5 . . . . **29** D4
West Norwood SE19 . . . . **22** E3
Charters Ct GU12 . . . . . . **126** C8
Charters La SL5 . . . . **29** D4
Charter Sq KT1 . . . . **38** B7
Charters Rd SL5 . . . . **29** D2
Charters Sch SL5 . . . . . . **29** D2
Charters Way SL5 . . . . . . **29** F2
Charter Wlk GU27 . . . . . **208** C6
Chartfield Pl KT13 . . . . . . **53** B5
Chartfield Rd RH2 . . . . . **139** C8
Chart Gdns RH5 . . . . . . **136** C4
Chartham Gr SE27 . . . . . . **22** B5
Chartham Rd SE25 . . . . . . **43** B6
Chart Ho ◼ CR4 . . . . **40** F7
Chart La
Dorking RH4 . . . . **136** C7
Reigate RH2 . . . . **139** C8
Chart La S RH5 . . . . **136** D5
Charts Cl GU6 . . . . **174** E2
CHART THE **123** E5
Chartway RH2 . . . . **118** B1
Chartwell
Frimley GU16 . . . . **85** F6
◼ Putney SW19 . . . . . . **19** D7
◼ Woking GU22 . . . . . . **69** E1
Wrecclesham GU9 . . . . **145** F6
Chartwell Cl ◼ SE9 . . . . . **42** D1
Chartwell Court Grange
RH4 . . . . **136** B4
Chartwell Gdns
Cheam SM3 . . . . **58** E6
Farnborough GU11 . . . . **105** C7
Chartwell Lodge ◼ BR3 . . **24** A1
Chartwell Pl
Cheam SM3 . . . . **58** F6
Epsom KT18 . . . . **76** E5
Chartwell Way ◼ SE20 . . . **43** B8
Charwood SW16 . . . . **22** A4
Charwood Rd RG40 . . . . . **25** F7
Chase Bridge Prim Sch
TW2 . . . . **5** E1
Chase Ct
Isleworth TW7 . . . . **6** A5
Merton SW20 . . . . **39** E7
Chase End KT19 . . . . **76** D7
Chasefield Cl GU4 . . . . . **110** A4
Chasefield Rd SW17 . . . . **20** F4
Chase Gdns TW2 . . . . **16** D8
Chase La GU27 . . . . **208** E3
Chaseley Ct KT13 . . . . . . **34** E1
Chasemore Cl CR4 . . . . . . **40** F2
Chasemore Gdns CR0 . . . **61** A5
Chase Plain GU26 . . . . . **188** C1
Chase Rd KT17, KT19 . . . . **76** D7
Chaseside Ave SW20 . . . . **39** E7
Chaseside Gdns KT16 . . . **33** B2
Chase The
Ascot SL5 . . . . **9** A1
Ashtead KT21 . . . . **75** C1
Coulsdon CR5 . . . . **79** D5
Crawley RH10 . . . . **202** A5
Crowthorne RG45 . . . . . **45** A6
East Horsley KT24 . . . . . **92** F1
Farnborough GU14 . . . . . **85** D6
Guildford GU2 . . . . **130** A8
Kingswood KT20 . . . . . . **98** B6
Oxshott KT22 . . . . **74** C4
Reigate RH2 . . . . **139** D8
South Norwood SW16 . . . **22** A1
Sunbury TW16 . . . . **35** B8
Wallington SM6 . . . . **60** F5
Chasewater Ct ◼ GU11 . . **105** A1
Chateau The SM5 . . . . . . **59** F7
Chatelet Cl RH6 . . . . **161** B4
Chatfield Cl GU14 . . . . . . **85** C2
Chatfield Ct ◼ CR3 . . . . **100** D5
Chatfield Dr GU4 . . . . . . **110** C3
Chatfield Rd CR0 . . . . **42** B1
Chatfields RH11 . . . . . . **201** B4
Chatham Ave BR2 . . . . . . **44** F2
Chatham Cl SM3 . . . . **39** F2
Chatham Ho ◼ SM6 . . . . . **60** B5
Chatham Mews GU2 . . . . **109** B4
Chatham Rd KT1, KT2 . . . . **38** A7
Chathill RH8 . . . . **143** B6
Chatley Heath Semaphore
Tower★ KT11 . . . . **72** D1
Chatsfield KT17 . . . . **58** A1
Chatsworth Ave
Haslemere GU27 . . . . . **208** C8
Merton SW20 . . . . **39** C7
Chatsworth Cl BR2, BR4 . . **63** F8
Chatsworth Cres TW3, TW7 . **5** D4
Chatsworth Ct SW16 . . . . . **41** F6
Chatsworth Gdns KT3 . . . . **38** F4
Chatsworth Gr GU9 . . . . **125** B6

Chatsworth Ho KT6 . . . . . **37** D4
Chatsworth Hts GU15 . . . . **66** B7
Chatsworth Inf Sch TW3 . . . **5** C3
Chatsworth Jun Sch TW3 . . **5** C3
Chatsworth Lodge BR4 . . . **63** C8
Chatsworth Pk SM7 . . . . . **78** B2
Chatsworth Pl
Mitcham CR4 . . . . **40** F6
Oxshott KT22 . . . . **74** D6
Teddington TW11 . . . . . **17** A4
Chatsworth Rd
Cheam SM3 . . . . **58** E6
Chiswick W4 . . . . **7** C8
Croydon CR0, CR9 . . . . . **61** D7
Farnborough GU14 . . . . . **85** E3
Chatsworth Row RH11 . . **201** C4
Chatsworth Way SE27 . . . **22** C5
Chattern Ct TW15 . . . . . . **14** B4
CHATTERN HILL **14** B4
Chattern Hill TW15 . . . . . **14** B4
Chattern Rd TW15 . . . . . . **14** C4
Chatterton Ct TW9 . . . . . . **6** F5
Chatton Row GU24 . . . . . . **68** A2
Chaucer Ave
Cranford TW4 . . . . **4** B5
◼ East Grinstead RH19 . **185** C1
Richmond TW9 . . . . **7** A5
Weybridge KT13 . . . . . . **53** A3
Chaucer Cl
Banstead SM7 . . . . **77** E5
Wokingham RG40 . . . . . **25** F6
Chaucer Ct
Guildford GU2 . . . . **130** C7
Redhill RH1 . . . . **119** A4
Chaucer Gdns SM1 . . . . . **59** A7
Chaucer Gn CR0 . . . . **43** C2
Chaucer Gr GU15 . . . . . . **65** D5
Chaucer Ho
Guildford GU1 . . . . **130** F8
Sutton SM1 . . . . **59** A7
◼ West Norwood SE27 . . **22** C4
Chaucer Way
Addlestone KT15 . . . . . . **52** A4
Mitcham SW19 . . . . **20** D2
Chavasse Way GU14 . . . . **84** D5
Chave Croft KT18 . . . . . . **97** C8
Chave Croft Terr KT18 . . . **97** C8
CHAVEY DOWN **28** A8
Chavey Down Rd RG42 . . . **8** B2
Chaworth Cl KT16 . . . . . . **51** C4
Chaworth Rd KT16 . . . . . . **51** C4
Chawridge La SL4 . . . . **8** C7
CHEAM **58** F5
Cheam Cl
Bracknell RG12 . . . . **27** D4
Burgh Heath KT20 . . . . . **97** B6
Cheam Common Inf Sch
KT4 . . . . **58** B8
Cheam Common Jun Sch
KT4 . . . . **58** B8
Cheam Common Rd KT4 . . **58** B7
Cheam Court Flats SM3 . . **58** E4
Cheam Fields Prim Sch
SM3 . . . . **58** E5
Cheam High Sch SM3 . . . . **58** E6
Cheam L Ctr SM3 . . . . **58** D6
Cheam Mansions SM3 . . . **58** E3
Cheam Park Farm Inf Sch
SM3 . . . . **58** E7
Cheam Park Farm Jun Sch
SM3 . . . . **58** E7
Cheam Park Way SM3 . . . **58** E4
Cheam Rd
Cheam SM1 . . . . **59** A4
East Ewell KT17, SM2 . . . **58** C1
Cheam Sta SM2 . . . . **58** E3
Cheapside GU21 . . . . **69** D5
Cheapside CE Prim Sch
SL5 . . . . **29** E8
Cheapside Ct SL5 . . . . . . **29** E8
Cheapside Rd SL5 . . . . . . **29** D7
Cheddar Rd TW6 . . . . **3** B5
Cheeseman Cl
Hampton TW12 . . . . **15** E2
Wokingham RG40 . . . . . **25** D7
Cheffrey Ct TW15 . . . . . . **14** B2
Chelford Rd BR1, E6 . . . . . **24** D3
Chellows La RH7 . . . . . . **143** F2
Chelmsford Cl SM2 . . . . . **59** A2
Chelsea Cl
Hampton TW12 . . . . **16** C3
New Malden KT4 . . . . . . **39** A2
Chelsea Ct SM2 . . . . **59** B4
Chelsea Fields SW19 . . . . **40** D8
Chelsea Gdns SM3 . . . . . **58** E6
Chelsfield Gdns SE26 . . . **23** C5
CHELSHAM **82** A2
Chelsham Common Rd
CR6 . . . . **82** A2
Chelsham Court Rd CR6 . . **82** E2
Chelsham Rd
Croydon CR2 . . . . **61** D4
Warlingham CR6 . . . . . . **81** F2
Chelsham Terr CR6 . . . . . **81** F1
Cheltenham Ave ◼ TW1 . . **17** A8
Cheltenham Cl KT3 . . . . . **38** C6
Cheltenham Villas CR7 . . . **42** A3
Chelwood Cl
Coulsdon CR5 . . . . **99** C8
Crawley RH10 . . . . **201** F4
Ewell KT17 . . . . **76** F7
Chelwood Ct ◼ CR2 . . . . **61** C5

Chelwood Gdns TW9 . . . . . **7** A5
Cheney Ct
Crowthorne RG45 . . . . . **45** C5
Forest Hill SE23 . . . . . . **23** D7
Cheniston Cl KT14 . . . . . . **71** A6
Cheniston Ct SL5 . . . . **30** A2
Chennells Way RH12 . . . **217** E5
Chennestone Com Sch
TW16 . . . . **35** B7
Chepstow Cl RH10 . . . . . **202** E6
Chepstow Rd CR0 . . . . . . **61** F8
Chepstow Rise CR0 . . . . . **61** E7
Chequer Grange RH18 . . **206** E1
Chequer Rd RH19 . . . . . **185** F1
Chequers Cl
Horley RH6 . . . . **161** A4
Walton on the Hill KT20 . . **97** A2
Chequers Ct
◼ Croydon CR0 . . . . . . **42** F1
Horsham RH13 . . . . . . **217** E2
Walton on the Hill KT20 . . **97** A2
Chequers Dr RH6 . . . . . . **161** A4
Chequers La KT20 . . . . . . **97** A2
Chequers Pl RH4 . . . . . . **136** B7
Chequer Tree Cl GU21 . . . **68** E3
Cherbury Cl RG12 . . . . . . **27** E5
Cherimoya Gdns KT8 . . . . **36** B6
Cherington Way SL5 . . . . **28** E7
Cheriton Ave ◼ BR2 . . . . **44** F4
Cheriton Ct
South Norwood SE25 . . . **42** E4
Walton-on-Thames KT12 . . **35** C1
Cheriton Sq SW17 . . . . . . **21** A6
Cheriton Way GU17 . . . . . **64** D5
Cherkley Hill KT22, RH5 . . **95** D1
Cherrimans Orch GU27 . . **207** F6
Cherry Cl
Banstead KT17 . . . . **77** D5
Carshalton SM5 . . . . **59** F8
Merton SM4 . . . . **39** E5
◼ Streatham SW2 . . . . . **22** A8
Cherry Cres TW8 . . . . **6** B7
Cherry Ct
Carshalton CR4 . . . . **41** A1
◼ Horsham RH13 . . . . . **217** D1
Cherrydale Rd GU15 . . . . . **66** D5
Cherry Green Cl RH1 . . . **140** B7
Cherry Hill Gdns CR0 . . . **60** F6
Cherryhill Gr GU11 . . . . . **104** F1
Cherryhurst GU8 . . . . . . **171** B1
Cherry La RH11 . . . . **181** C1
Cherry Lodge
Aldershot GU12 . . . . . . **105** B1
Horley RH6 . . . . **161** B2
Cherry Mdws RH11 . . . . **201** C5
Cherry Orch
Ashtead KT21 . . . . **76** B1
Staines TW18 . . . . **13** A3
Cherry Orchard Gdns
◼ Croydon CR0 . . . . . . **61** D8
East Molesey KT8 . . . . . **35** F6
Cherry Orchard Rd
Croydon CR0 . . . . **42** E1
East Molesey KT8 . . . . . **36** A6
Cherry St GU21 . . . . **69** E1
Cherry Tree Ave
Guildford GU2 . . . . **108** C3
Haslemere GU27 . . . . . **207** F7
Staines TW18 . . . . **13** B2
Cherry Tree Cl
Crawley RH10 . . . . **202** D8
Farnborough GU14 . . . . . **84** C5
Farnham GU9 . . . . **125** C3
Sandhurst GU47 . . . . . . **45** D1
Cherry Tree Ct
Coulsdon CR5 . . . . **79** D5
◼ Richmond TW9 . . . . . . **6** F3
Cherry Tree Dr
Bracknell RG12 . . . . **27** D6
Streatham SW16 . . . . . . **21** E5
Cherry Tree Gn CR2 . . . . . **81** B5
Cherry Tree Ho TW2 . . . . . **16** D6
Cherry Tree La GU7 . . . . **150** D8
Cherry Tree Rd
Milford GU8 . . . . **149** E1
Rowledge GU10 . . . . . . **145** E3
Cherrytrees CR5 . . . . **99** D6
Cherry Tree Wlk
Beckenham BR3 . . . . . . **43** F5
Coney Hall BR4 . . . . **63** F6
Horsham RH12 . . . . . . **218** B6
Rowledge GU10 . . . . . . **145** E3
Cherry Way
Horton SL3 . . . . **1** C4
Upper Halliford TW17 . . . **34** E5
West Ewell KT19 . . . . . . **57** D4
Cherrywood Ave TW20 . . . **11** B1
Cherrywood Cl KT2 . . . . . **18** A1
Cherrywood Com Prim Sch
GU14 . . . . **85** A6
Cherrywood Ct ◼ TW11 . . **17** A3
Cherrywood La SM4, SW20 **39** E5
Cherrywood Rd GU14 . . . . **85** B7
CHERTSEY **33** B2
Chertsey Bridge Rd KT16,
TW18 . . . . **33** D2
Chertsey Bvd KT16 . . . . . **32** F1
Chertsey Cl CR8 . . . . **80** B4
Chertsey Cres CR0 . . . . . **63** C1
Chertsey Ct SW14 . . . . **7** B4
Chertsey Dr SM3 . . . . **58** E8
Chertsey Ho TW13 . . . . . . **16** A5
Chertsey La
Egham TW18 . . . . **12** F2
Epsom KT19 . . . . **76** A7

Chertsey Meads Nature
Reserve★ KT15 . . . . . 33 E1
Chertsey Mus★ KT15 . . . . 33 A3
Chertsey Rd
Addlestone KT15 . . . . 52 B8
Ashford TW15 , TW16 . . . . . 14 D2
Burrowhill GU20, GU24 . . . . 49 C6
Byfleet KT14 . . . . 71 D8
Chobham GU24, KT16,
GU21 . . . . 50 D1
Feltham, Ashford Common TW13,
TW16 . . . . 14 D2
Feltham TW13, TW16 . . . . . 14 E4
Lower Halliford TW17 . . . . . 34 A2
Shepperton TW17 . . . . 33 F2
Twickenham TW2 . . . . 16 D7
Windlesham GU20 . . . . 48 E5
Woking GU21 . . . . 69 F3
Chertsey St
Guildford GU1 . . . . 130 D8
Upper Tooting SW17 . . . . . 21 A3
Chertsey Sta KT16 . . . . 32 F1
Chertsey Wlk [7] KT16 . . . . 33 A2
Chervil Cl TW13 . . . . 15 A5
Cherwell Cl SL3 . . . . .1 B8
Cherwell Ct
Teddington KT1 . . . . 17 D1
West Ewell KT19 . . . . 57 C6
Cherwell Wlk RH11 . . . . . 200 F5
Cheselden Rd GU1 . . . . . . 130 E8
Cheseman St SE26 . . . . 23 B5
Chesfield Rd KT2 . . . . 17 E1
Chesham Cl SM2 . . . . 58 E1
Chesham Cres SE20 . . . . . 43 C8
Chesham Ct
Kingston upon Thames
KT6 . . . . 37 D3
Wandsworth SW18 . . . . . . 20 D8
Chesham Mews [14] GU1. . 130 F8
Chesham Rd
Guildford GU1 . . . . 130 F8
Kingston upon Thames KT1,
KT2 . . . . 38 A7
Mitcham SW17 . . . . 20 D2
Penge SE20 . . . . 43 C8
Cheshire Cl
Mitcham CR4, SW16 . . . . . 41 E6
Ottershaw KT16 . . . . 51 D4
Cheshire Gdns KT9 . . . . . 56 D4
Cheshire Ho
Cheam SM4 . . . . 40 B2
Ottershaw KT16 . . . . 51 D4
Chesney Cres CR0 . . . . 63 C3
Chessell Cl [4] CR7 . . . . . . 42 B5
Chessholme Ct TW16 . . . . 14 E1
Chessholme Rd TW15 . . . . 14 C2
CHESSINGTON 56 E4
Chessington Cl KT19 . . . . 57 C4
Chessington Com Coll
KT9 . . . . 56 D3
Chessington Hall Gdns
KT9 . . . . 56 D4
Chessington Hill Pk KT9 . . 57 A5
Chessington North Sta
KT9 . . . . 56 D5
Chessington Par KT9 . . . . 56 E5
Chessington Park KT9 . . . 57 A6
Chessington Rd KT19 . . . . 57 D3
Chessington South Sta
KT9 . . . . 56 E5
Chessington Trade Pk
KT9 . . . . 57 A6
Chessington Way BR4 . . . . 63 B8
Chessington World of
Adventures & Zoo★ KT9. 56 C1
Chester Ave
Richmond TW10 . . . . .6 F1
Twickenham TW2 . . . . 15 F7
Chesterblade La RG12 . . . . 27 E2
Chester Cl
Ashford TW15 . . . . 14 D3
Ash GU12 . . . . 106 B2
Dorking RH4 . . . . 115 C1
Guildford GU2 . . . . 108 F3
[1] Richmond TW10 . . . . . . .6 F1
Sutton SM1 . . . . 59 A8
Chester Ct
[2] Bromley BR2 . . . . 44 F5
Dorking RH4 . . . . 115 C1
Chesterfield Cl RH19 . . . . 184 C4
Chesterfield Ct
Ashford TW15 . . . . 13 E4
Kingston upon Thames KT6 . 37 E4
Chesterfield Dr KT10 . . . . 56 A8
Chesterfield Ho [6] SW16 . 21 C3
Chesterfield Mews TW15 . 13 E4
Chesterfield Rd
Ashford TW15 . . . . 13 E3
Chiswick W4 . . . . 7 C8
West Ewell KT19 . . . . 57 D3
Chester Gdns SM4 . . . . . . 40 C3
Chester Ho
[2] Godalming GU7 . . . . . 150 D4
Kingston upon Thames KT1 . 38 B7
Chesterman Ct [8] W4 . . . .7 E7
Chester Rd
Ash GU12. . . . . 106 B2
Effingham KT24 . . . . 113 B7
Harlington TW6 . . . . 3 A4
Hounslow TW4 . . . . .4 B4
Wimbledon SW19 . . . . 19 C2
Chesters RH6 . . . . 160 E5
Chesters Rd GU15 . . . . . . 66 B5
Chesters The KT3 . . . . 38 E8
Chesterton Cl RH19 . . . . . 205 F7

Chesterton Ct RH13 . . . . . 218 A4
Chesterton Dr
Merstham RH1. . . . . 119 E7
Stanwell TW19. . . . . 13 F7
Chesterton Ho
[5] Croydon CR0. . . . . 61 D6
[6] Sutton SM1. . . . . 59 C6
Chesterton Terr KT1 . . . . . 38 A7
Chester Way GU10 . . . . 126 F6
Chestnut Ave
Aldershot GU12 . . . . 126 E8
Camberley GU15 . . . . 66 A6
Coney Hall BR4 . . . . 63 E6
Farnham GU9. . . . . 146 A8
Guildford GU2 . . . . 130 C5
Hampton TW12 . . . . 16 A1
Haslemere GU27 . . . . 208 C7
Kingston upon Thames KT8,
KT11 . . . . 36 F7
[12] Mortlake SW14 . . . . . . 7 D4
Tatsfield TN16 . . . . 103 E5
Thames Ditton KT10 . . . . . 36 D1
Wentworth GU25 . . . . 30 F5
Weybridge KT13 . . . . 53 C3
Whiteley Village KT12 . . . . 53 E2
Worcester Park KT19 . . . . . 57 E6
Chestnut Chase RG42 . . . 8 A1
Chestnut Cl
Addlestone KT15 . . . . 52 D5
Ashford, Chattern Hill TW15 14 B4
Ashford, Felthamhill TW16 . 14 A7
Blackwater GU17. . . . . 64 E4
Carshalton SM5. . . . . 40 F1
Catford SE6 . . . . 24 C4
East Grinstead RH19 . . . . . 186 A1
Englefield Green TW20 . . . . 11 C1
Grayshott GU26. . . . . 188 C3
Harlington UB7 . . . . 3 B7
Kingswood KT20 . . . . 98 A4
Redhill RH1 . . . . 140 B7
Send Marsh GU23 . . . . 91 A3
West Norwood SE27 . . . . . 22 A4
Chestnut Copse RH8 . . . 123 B2
Chestnut Cres KT12 . . . . . 53 E2
Chestnut Ct
Aldershot GU12 . . . . 105 D2
Beckenham BR3. . . . . 24 A1
[6] Belmont SM2 . . . . 59 A4
[5] Croydon CR0. . . . . 61 C6
Farnham GU9. . . . . 125 A4
Feltham TW13 . . . . 15 D3
Horsham RH13 . . . . 217 E2
Hounslow TW3. . . . . 5 A4
Kingston upon Thames KT3 . 38 E6
Chestnut End GU35 . . . . . 187 A4
Chestnut Gdns RH12 . . . . 217 C5
Chestnut Gr
Balham SW12 . . . . 21 A7
Isleworth TW7. . . . . 6 A3
Kingston upon Thames KT3 . 38 D6
Mitcham CR4 . . . . 41 D5
Penge SE20 . . . . 23 B1
South Croydon CR2 . . . . . . 62 C3
Staines TW18. . . . . 13 C2
Woking GU22 . . . . 89 E7
Chestnut Grove Sch
SW12 . . . . 21 A7
Chestnut Ho
Crowthorne RG45 . . . . 45 C5
West Norwood SE27 . . . . . 22 C5
Chestnut La
Chobham GU24 . . . . 49 C4
Weybridge KT13 . . . . 53 B5
Chestnut Manor Cl TW18 . 13 B3
Chestnut Mead [2] RH1 . . 118 E2
Chestnut Pl
Ashtead Kt21 . . . . 95 E8
Dulwich SE26. . . . . 22 F4
Ewell KT17 . . . . 77 A8
Chestnut Rd
Ashford TW15 . . . . 14 B4
Farnborough GU14 . . . . . . 85 A5
Guildford GU1 . . . . 109 D1
Horley RH6 . . . . 161 B5
Kingston upon Thames KT2 . 17 E1
Merton SW20. . . . . 39 D7
Twickenham TW2 . . . . 16 E6
West Norwood SE27 . . . . . 22 C5
Chestnuts The
Dulwich SE21. . . . . 22 E7
Horley RH6 . . . . 161 A5
Penge BR3. . . . . 43 D6
Walton-on-Thames KT12 . . 54 A8
Chestnut Tree Gr GU14 . . . 84 C5
Chestnut View
Bramley GU5. . . . . 152 A4
Feltham TW13 . . . . 15 B5
Godalming GU7 . . . . 150 F2
Chestnut Wlk
Crawley RH11 . . . . 181 C1
Felcourt RH19 . . . . 185 C8
Upper Halliford TW17 . . . . 34 E5
West Byfleet KT14 . . . . 71 E7
Whiteley Village KT12 . . . . 53 E2
Cheston Ave CR0 . . . . 43 F1
Chesworth Cl [7] RH13. . . . 217 C1
Chesworth Cres RH13. . . . 217 C1
Chesworth Gdns RH13. . . . 217 C1
Chesworth La RH12,
RH13 . . . . 217 C1
Chetnole RH19 . . . . 185 D2
Chetwode Cl RG40 . . . . . . 25 E6
Chetwode Dr KT20 . . . . . . 77 D1
Chetwode Pl GU11 . . . . . . 126 C7
Chetwode Rd
Burgh Heath KT18, KT20 . . 97 C8

Chetwode Rd *continued*
Upper Tooting SW17 . . . . . 20 F5
Chetwode Terr GU11 . . . . 104 E1
Chevening Cl RH11 . . . . . 201 C1
Chevening Rd SE19 . . . . . . 22 D2
Chevington Villas RH1 . . . 120 F3
Cheviot Cl
Banstead SM7 . . . . 78 B4
Farnborough GU14 . . . . . . 84 E7
Frimley GU15 . . . . 66 C4
Harlington UB3 . . . . 3 D7
Sutton SM2 . . . . 59 D2
Cheviot Gdns SE27 . . . . . . 22 B4
Cheviot Rd SE27 . . . . 22 B3
Cheviot Wlk RH11 . . . . . . 201 B6
Chevremont GU1 . . . . 130 E8
Chewter Cl GU19. . . . . 47 F3
Chewter La GU20 . . . . 48 B6
Cheyham Gdns SM2 . . . . . 58 D1
Cheyham Way SM2. . . . . . 58 E1
Cheylesmore Dr GU16. . . . 66 D3
Cheyne Ave TW2. . . . . 15 F7
Cheyne Ct
Banstead SM7 . . . . 78 B4
[1] Croydon CR0. . . . . 61 F8
[4] Wallington SM6 . . . . . . 60 B4
Cheyne Hill KT5. . . . . 37 F5
Cheyne Park Dr BR4 . . . . 63 C7
Cheyne Rd TW15 . . . . 14 D2
Cheyne Way GU14. . . . . . . 84 F8
Cheyne Wlk
Croydon CR0 . . . . 62 A8
Horley RH6 . . . . 161 A1
Chichele Gdns CR0. . . . . . 61 E6
Chichele Rd RH8 . . . . 122 E7
Chicheley Ct GU14 . . . . . . 85 B6
Chichester Cl
Crawley RH10 . . . . 201 E2
Dorking RH4 . . . . 115 B1
Hampton TW12 . . . . 15 F2
Witley GU8 . . . . 170 E5
Chichester Ct
Ewell KT17 . . . . 57 F2
Stanwell TW19. . . . . 13 E7
Chichester Dr CR8 . . . . . . 79 F7
Chichester Ho KT19 . . . . . 76 A8
Chichester Mews SE27 . . . 22 A4
Chichester Rd
Ash GU12. . . . . 106 A3
Dorking RH4 . . . . 115 B2
South Croydon CR0 . . . . . . 61 E7
Chichester Terr RH12 . . . . 217 D2
Chichester Way TW14 . . . . 15 C8
CHIDDINGFOLD 191 B4
Chiddingfold Rd GU8. . . . 192 C3
Chiddingly Cl RH10 . . . . . 202 B5
Chiddingstone Cl SM2. . . . 59 A1
Chieveley Mews SL5 . . . . . 30 A2
Chiffchaff Corner RG12. . . 26 D5
Chilberton Dr RH1 . . . . . . 119 C5
Chilbolton TW20 . . . . 11 E3
Chilbrook Rd KT11 . . . . . . 73 A1
Chilchester Ct BR3 . . . . . . 44 B6
Chilcombe Ho [7] SW15. . . 19 A8
Chilcroft La GU27 . . . . . . 208 B1
Chilcroft Rd GU27. . . . . . 207 F7
Chilcrofts Rd GU27 . . . . . 208 A1
Child Cl RG40 . . . . 25 D8
Childebert Rd SW17. . . . . . 21 B6
Childerly KT1 . . . . 38 A6
Children's Trust (Tadworth)
The KT20 . . . . 97 D6
Childs Hall Cl KT23 . . . . . . 93 F2
Childs Hall Dr KT23 . . . . . . 93 F2
Childs Hall Rd KT23 . . . . . . 93 F2
Childs La [12] SE19 . . . . . . 22 E2
Chilham Cl GU16. . . . . 85 F8
Chillerton Rd SW17 . . . . . . 21 B3
Chillingford Ho SW17 . . . . 20 C4
Chillingham Way GU15 . . . 65 C4
Chillingworth Gdns TW1 . 16 F5
Chilmark Gdns
Merstham RH1. . . . . 119 E6
New Malden KT3 . . . . 39 A3
Chilmark Rd SW16 . . . . . . 41 D8
Chilmead [1] RH1 . . . . . . 118 F2
Chilmead La RH1 . . . . 119 D3
Chilsey Green Rd KT16 . . . 32 E2
Chiltern Ave
Farnborough GU14 . . . . . . 84 D4
Twickenham TW2 . . . . 16 A7
Chiltern Cl
Crawley RH11 . . . . 201 B6
Farnborough GU14 . . . . . . 84 D4
Haslemere GU27 . . . . 208 B5
North Cheam KT4 . . . . 58 C8
South Croydon CR0 . . . . . . 61 E7
Staines TW18. . . . . 13 A3
Woking GU22. . . . . 89 C5
Chiltern Ct [2] RH12 . . . . . 217 F4
Chiltern Dr KT5 . . . . 38 B4
Chiltern Gdns BR2 . . . . . . 44 F5
Chiltern Rd
Sandhurst GU47 . . . . 45 A1
Sutton SM2 . . . . 59 C1
Chilterns The SM2 . . . . . . 59 B2
Chilthorne Cl SE6 . . . . 23 F8
Chiltington Ct RH12 . . . . . 217 D4
Chilton Cl GU6. . . . . 193 F2
Chilton Ct KT12 . . . . 54 A6
Chilton Farm Pk GU14. . . . 84 C4
Chilton Rd TW9 . . . . 7 A4
Chiltons Cl SM7 . . . . 78 B4
CHILWORTH 131 C3

Chilworth CE Inf Sch
GU4 . . . . 131 D3
Chilworth Ct
[8] Putney SW19 . . . . 19 D7
[13] Redhill RH1. . . . . 118 F2
Chilworth Gdns SM1 . . . . . 59 C7
Chilworth Rd GU4, GU5 . . 132 A4
Chilworth Sta GU4 . . . . . . 131 E3
Chimneys Ct SW19 . . . . . 19 C1
China Mews SW2 . . . . 21 F8
Chine The GU10. . . . . 145 F5
Chingford Ave GU14. . . . . 85 D5
Chingley Cl BR1 . . . . 24 E2
Chinthurst La
Shalford GU4, GU5 . . . . . 130 F2
Wonersh GU5 . . . . 152 A7
Chinthurst Mews CR5 . . . . 79 A3
Chinthurst Pk GU4 . . . . . 130 C1
Chinthurst Sch KT20 . . . . . 97 C4
Chippendale Cl GU17. . . . 64 E4
Chippendale Rd RH11 . . . . 201 B1
Chippenham [5] KT1. . . . . 37 F7
CHIPSTEAD 78 F1
Chipstead Ave CR7. . . . . . 42 B5
Chipstead Cl
Belmont SM2 . . . . 59 B2
Coulsdon CR5 . . . . 79 A3
Penge SE19 . . . . 22 F1
Redhill RH1 . . . . 140 A7
Chipstead Ct GU21 . . . . . . 68 E2
Chipstead Ho [4] SW2 . . . . 21 E7
Chipstead La KT20 . . . . . . 98 B3
Chipstead Rd SM7 . . . . . . 78 A2
Chipstead Sta CR5 . . . . . . 78 F1
Chipstead Station Par
CR5. . . . . 78 F1
Chipstead Valley Prim Sch
CR5. . . . . 79 A3
Chipstead Valley Rd CR5 . . 79 B3
Chipstead Way CR5, SM7. . 78 F3
Chirton Wlk GU21. . . . . . . 69 A1
Chisbury Cl RG12 . . . . 27 E3
Chisholm Rd
Croydon CR0 . . . . 61 E8
[14] Richmond TW10. . . . . .6 F1
Chislehurst Rd TW10. . . . . .6 E2
Chislet Cl BR3 . . . . 24 A1
CHISWICK 7 D7
Chiswick Cl CR0 . . . . 60 F7
Chiswick Com Sch W4 . . . 7 D7
Chiswick Ho★ W4 . . . . 7 D7
Chiswick Lane S W4 . . . . . 7 F8
Chiswick Mall W4. . . . . . . 7 F8
Chiswick Plaza W4. . . . . . . 7 C8
Chiswick Quay W4 . . . . 7 C6
Chiswick Sq [10] W4. . . . . . 7 E8
Chiswick Sta W4. . . . . 7 C7
Chiswick Staithe W4 . . . . . 7 C6
Chiswick Village W4 . . . . . 7 B8
Chiswick Wharf [3] W4 . . . 7 F8
Chithurst La RH6, RH7 . . . 162 F2
Chittenden Cotts GU23 . . 71 E3
Chitterfield Gate UB7 . . . . 3 A7
Chitty's Wlk GU3 . . . . 108 F5
Chive Ct GU14 . . . . 84 C4
Chivelston [27] SW19 . . . . 19 D7
Chivenor Gr KT2 . . . . 17 D3
CHOBHAM 49 F2
Chobham Bsns Ctr GU24 . 50 E1
Chobham Cl KT16. . . . . . . 51 B4
Chobham Common National
Nature Reserve★ KT16 . 49 F6
Chobham Gdns SW19 . . . . 19 D6
Chobham La KT16, GU24 . . 50 A8
Chobham Mus The★
GU24. . . . . 68 E8
Chobham Park La GU24 . . 50 B2
Chobham Rd
Burrowhill GU24, SL5 . . . . 49 C7
Chobham GU21 . . . . 69 E3
Frimley GU16 . . . . 66 A2
Knaphill GU21 . . . . 68 D3
Ottershaw KT16. . . . . 51 B4
[3] Woking GU21 . . . . 69 F2
Woking, Horsell Common GU21,
GU24. . . . . 69 D5
Chobham St Lawrence CE
Prim Sch GU24 . . . . . . 68 E8
Choir Gn GU21. . . . . 68 E2
Cholmley Rd KT7 . . . . 37 B3
Cholmondeley Wlk TW9 . . 6 C2
Chrislaine Cl TW19. . . . . . 2 D1
Chrismas Ave GU12 . . . . . 105 C1
Chrismas Pl GU12 . . . . . . 105 C1
Christ Church TW9 . . . . . .6 E4
Christ Church Ave [5]
TW11 . . . . 17 A3
Christ Church CE Inf Sch
GU25 . . . . 31 B6
Christ Church CE Prim Sch
[5] Forest Hill SE23 . . . . . . 23 D6
Kingston upon Thames KT3 . 38 E6
Purley CR8. . . . . 61 B1
Streatham SW2 . . . . 21 F7
Surbiton KT5 . . . . 38 A3
Christchurch Cl SW19 . . . . 20 D1
Christchurch Cotts GU25 . 31 B6
Christchurch Dr GU47. . . . 64 D6
Christchurch Gdns KT19 . . 76 B8
Christchurch Ho [2] SW2 . . 21 E7
Christchurch Hts [11] RH2 . 118 F1
Christ Church Mount
KT19. . . . . 76 B7
Christchurch Pk SM2. . . . . 59 C3
Christchurch Pl KT19. . . . . 76 B8

Christ Church Prim Sch
KT3 . . . . 38 D6
Christchurch Rd
Mitcham SW19 . . . . 20 D1
Mortlake SW14 . . . . 7 C2
Purley CR8. . . . . 80 B8
Streatham SW2 . . . . 21 F7
Virginia Water GU25 . . . . . 31 C5
Christ Church Rd
Beckenham BR3. . . . . 44 A7
Epsom KT18. . . . . 76 A6
Surbiton KT5 . . . . 37 F3
Christchurch Way [5]
GU21 . . . . 69 F2
Christian Fields SW16 . . . . 22 A1
Christie Cl
Guildford GU1 . . . . 109 D4
Lightwater GU18. . . . . 48 C1
Little Bookham KT23 . . . . . 93 F3
Christie Dr SE25 . . . . 43 A4
Christie Ho [7] BR4 . . . . . . 44 B1
Christies RH19 . . . . 205 D8
Christie Wlk [4] CR3 . . . . . 100 D5
Christine Cl GU12 . . . . 105 F1
Christmas Hill GU4. . . . . . 130 F2
CHRISTMASPIE 128 C8
Christmaspie Ave GU3 . . . 107 B1
Christopher Ct
Ashford TW15 . . . . 13 E3
[6] Croydon CR0. . . . . 43 A1
[24] Kingston upon Thames
KT6 . . . . 37 E4
Sutton SM1 . . . . 59 A5
Tadworth KT20. . . . . 97 C4
Christopher Rd RH19. . . . 185 E1
Christ's CE Sec Sch TW10 . 7 A2
Christ's Coll Guildford
GU1. . . . . 109 C4
Christy Est GU12 . . . . 105 E2
Christy Rd TN16. . . . . 83 C4
Chrystie La KT23. . . . . 94 B1
Chuck's La KT20 . . . . 97 B3
Chudleigh Ct [4] GU14 . . . 85 B4
Chudleigh Gdns SM1. . . . . 59 C7
Chudleigh Rd TW2 . . . . . . 16 F8
Chulsa Rd SE26. . . . . 23 B3
Chumleigh Wlk KT5. . . . . . 37 F5
Church App
Dulwich SE21. . . . . 22 D5
Thorpe TW20 . . . . 32 C6
Church Ave
Beckenham BR3. . . . . 44 A8
Farnborough GU14 . . . . . . 85 C3
Mortlake SW14 . . . . 7 D4
Church Circ GU14. . . . . . . 85 C1
Church Cl
Addlestone KT15 . . . . 52 B6
[6] Epsom KT17 . . . . 76 E6
Fetcham KT22 . . . . 94 D3
Grayswood GU27. . . . . . . 189 F2
Hounslow TW4. . . . . .4 F5
Laleham TW18. . . . . 33 C6
Lower Kingswood KT20. . . 117 F8
Milford GU8 . . . . 149 F1
Pirbright GU24. . . . . 87 F6
Woking GU21 . . . . 69 E3
Church Cotts
Badshot Lea GU9. . . . . . . 126 A6
Effingham KT24 . . . . 113 D8
Churchcroft Cl SW12. . . . . 21 A8
Church Ct
[3] Dorking RH4 . . . . 136 B8
Forest Hill SE26. . . . . 23 E3
Great Bookham KT23 . . . . . 94 A2
Harmondsworth UB7 . . . . . 3 A8
Reigate RH2. . . . . 118 B1
[15] Richmond TW10. . . . . .6 D2
West Norwood SE27 . . . . . 22 B4
Churchdale GU12 . . . . 105 B1
Churchdown BR1 . . . . 24 E4
Church Dr BR4 . . . . 63 E7
CHURCH END 91 F6
Church Est Almshouses [11]
TW9 . . . . .6 F3
Church Farm La SM3. . . . . 58 E4
Churchfield Cotts SL5. . . . 30 B3
Churchfield Ct [3] RH2. . . 118 A1
Churchfield Ho RH13 . . . . 71 B5
Churchfield Pl
Lower Halliford TW17 . . . . 34 B2
Weybridge KT13 . . . . 53 A6
Churchfield Rd
Reigate RH2. . . . . 117 F2
Walton-on-Thames KT12 . . 35 A1
Weybridge KT13 . . . . 53 A6
Churchfields
East Molesey KT8 . . . . 36 A6
Guildford GU4 . . . . 110 A6
Witley GU8. . . . . 170 E4
Woking GU21. . . . . 69 E3
Churchfields Ave
Feltham TW13 . . . . 16 A5
Weybridge KT13 . . . . 53 B5
Churchfields Prim Sch
BR3. . . . . 43 D6
Churchfields Rd BR3 . . . . . 43 E7
Church Gdns
[2] Dorking RH4. . . . . 136 B8
Leatherhead KT22. . . . . . . 95 B7
Church Gn
Dunsfold GU8. . . . . 192 D5
Elstead GU8. . . . . 148 C3
Hersham KT12. . . . . 54 C4
Church Gr KT1. . . . . 37 C7
Church Hill
Aldershot GU11, GU12. . . 126 C8
Camberley GU15 . . . . 65 E5
Caterham CR3 . . . . 100 F3

Church Hill *continued*
Merstham RH1 99 B1
Nutfield RH1 119 F2
Purley CR8 60 E1
Pyrford GU22 71 A1
Shamley Green GU5 152 E4
Shere GU5 133 A4
Tatsfield TN16 103 D5
Wallington SM5 59 F5
Wimbledon SW19 19 F3
Woking GU21 69 D3
Church Hill Rd
Cheam SM3 58 E6
Kingston upon Thames KT6 37 E4
Church Ho KT23 94 A2
Churchill Ave
Aldershot GU12 126 C8
Horsham RH12 217 B3
Churchill Cl
East Bedfont TW14 14 F7
Farnborough GU14 85 B8
Fetcham KT22 94 E4
Warlingham CR6 81 D2
Churchill Cres GU14 85 B8
Churchill Ct
Crawley RH10 182 A1
Staines TW18 13 C2
Churchill Dr KT13 53 C6
Churchill Ho
7 Hampton TW12 36 A8
Mitcham CR4 40 F8
Churchill House SM7 77 F4
Churchill Lodge SW16 21 D3
Churchill Rd
Epsom KT19 76 A8
Guildford GU1 130 F8
North Ascot SL5 28 F7
Smallfield RH6 162 B3
South Croydon CR2 61 C3
Churchill Way
Ashford TW16 15 A2
Biggin Hill TN16 83 D4
Churchin Cl TN16 83 C7
Church La
Albury GU5 132 C4
Ascot SL5 29 D5
Ash GU12 106 B2
Bisley GU21, GU24 68 A4
Bletchingley RH1 120 D3
Broadbridge Heath RH12 216 D3
Brook GU8 190 C8
Burgh Heath KT18, SM7 77 E2
Burstow RH6 182 F7
Caterham CR3 100 A3
Chelsham CR6 82 C3
Chessington KT9 56 F4
Copthorne RH10 183 B3
Cranleigh GU6 174 E3
Crawley RH10 201 F6
Crondall GU10 124 D8
East Grinstead RH19 185 F1
Farnborough GU14 84 E4
Godstone RH9 121 D3
Grayshott GU26 188 C3
Hambledon GU8 171 D2
Haslemere GU27 208 D7
Headley KT18 96 C2
Hooley CR5 99 B5
Merton SW19 39 F8
Oxted RH8 122 E6
Pirbright GU24 87 D4
Rowledge GU10 145 E3
Send GU23 90 C1
Shere GU5 133 A4
Sunningdale SL5 30 B4
Teddington TW11 16 F3
Thames Ditton KT7 37 A3
Twickenham TW1 17 A7
Upper Tooting, Furzedown SW17 21 B4
Upper Tooting SW17 21 A3
Wallington SM6 60 D7
Wallis Wood RH5 176 F1
Warlingham CR6 81 D2
Weybridge KT13 53 A6
Witley GU8 170 E2
Worplesdon GU3 108 E8
Wrecclesham GU10 145 F7
Churchlands GU11 126 B8
Churchlands Way KT4 58 D8
Church Lane Ave CR5 99 B5
Church Lane Dr CR5 99 B5
Church Lane E GU11 126 B8
Church Lane W GU11 105 A1
Churchley Rd SE26 23 B4
Churchley Villas SE26 23 B4
Church Mdw KT6 56 C8
Church Mews KT15 52 C6
Churchmore Rd SW16 41 D8
Church Paddock Ct SM6 60 D7
Church Par 6 TW15 13 F4
Church Pas 17 GU9 125 B2
Church Path
Ash GU12 106 A3
Coulsdon CR5 80 A1
Farnborough GU14 105 C8
Merton SW19 40 A7
Mitcham CR4 40 E6
9 Woking GU21 69 F2
Church Pk RH6 181 E5
Church Pl CR4 40 E6
Church Rd
Addlestone KT15 52 B5
Aldershot GU11 126 C8
Ascot SL5 29 A5
Ashford TW15 13 F4
Ashtead KT21 75 D1
Bagshot GU19 47 D3
Church Rd *continued*
Barnes SW13 7 F5
Beckenham BR2 44 E6
Biggin Hill TN16 83 E2
Bracknell RG12 27 C7
Broadbridge Heath RH12 216 D3
Burstow RH6 183 A7
Byfleet KT14 71 E6
Caterham CR3 100 F3
Cheam SM3 58 E4
Claygate KT10 55 F3
Copthorne RH10 183 B3
Cranford TW5 4 B8
Crawley, Lowfield Heath RH6 181 E5
Crawley, Worth RH10 202 E6
Croydon CR0, CR9 61 C7
Dunsfold GU8 192 D5
East Molesey KT8 36 D6
Egham TW20 12 A3
Epsom KT17 76 E6
Feltham TW13 15 D3
Fetcham KT23 94 A3
Frimley GU16 65 D1
Guildford GU1 130 D8
Hascombe GU8 172 E4
Haslemere GU27 208 C7
Haslemere, Shottermill GU27 207 F6
Heston TW5 5 A7
Horley RH6 160 F2
Horley RH6 161 A3
Horne RH6 162 F5
Horsham RH12 218 B5
Hounslow TW7 5 E7
Kenley CR8 80 D4
Kingston upon Thames KT1 37 F7
Leatherhead KT22 95 B5
Leigh RH2 138 A3
Lingfield RH7 164 D4
Little Bookham KT23 93 F4
Long Ditton KT6 37 C1
Lower Halliford TW17 34 B2
Milford GU8 149 F1
Mitcham CR4, SW19 40 D7
Newdigate RH5 158 B1
New Malden KT4 38 E1
Purley CR8 60 E1
Redhill RH1 139 E7
Richmond, Ham TW10 17 E4
Richmond TW10, TW9 6 E2
Sandhurst GU15 64 F7
Sandhurst, Owlsmoor GU47 45 E1
South Norwood SE19 22 E1
Sunningdale SL5 30 A3
Teddington TW11 16 F3
Turners Hill RH10 204 A3
Wallington SM6 60 D7
Warlingham CR6 81 D2
West End GU24 67 F7
West Ewell KT19 57 D3
Whyteleafe CR3 100 F8
Wimbledon SW19 19 E4
Windlesham GU20 48 C4
Winkfield, Chavey Down SL5 28 B8
Winkfield SL4 8 C5
Woking, Horsell GU21 69 E4
Woking, St John's GU21 89 A8
Woldingham CR3 101 E4
Church Rise
Chessington KT9 56 F4
Forest Hill SE23 23 D6
Church Road E
Crowthorne RG45 45 B5
Farnborough GU14 85 D2
Church Road W
Crowthorne RG45 45 B4
Farnborough GU14 85 C1
Church Row GU23 91 C6
Church Side
Epsom KT18 76 B6
Gatton RH2 118 F6
Churchside Cl TN16 83 C2
Church Sq TW17 34 B2
Church St
Aldershot GU11 104 F2
Betchworth RH3 137 E8
Chiswick W4 7 F8
Cobham KT11 73 B4
Crawley RH11 201 C6
Crowthorne RG45 45 B4
Croydon CR0, CR9 61 C8
Dorking RH4 136 A7
Effingham KT24 113 D8
Epsom KT17, KT18 76 E6
Esher KT10 55 B6
Ewell KT17 58 A2
Godalming GU7 150 D4
Hampton TW12 36 C8
Isleworth TW7 6 B5
Kingston upon Thames KT1 37 D7
Leatherhead KT22 95 B5
Old Woking GU22 90 C6
Reigate RH2 118 B1
Rudgwick, Cox Green RH12 195 E1
Rudgwick RH12 214 E8
Staines TW18 12 E4
Sunbury TW16 35 B6
Twickenham TW1 17 A7
Walton-on-Thames KT12 35 A2
Warnham RH12 216 F8
Weybridge KT13 53 A6
Church Street E GU21 69 F2
Church Street Halt CR0 61 C8
Church Street W GU21 69 E2
Church Stretton Rd TW3 5 C2
Church Terr
22 Richmond TW10 6 D2
South Holmwood RH5 157 C6
Church Vale SE23 23 D6
Church View GU12 106 A2
Church View Cl RH6 160 F2
Churchview Rd TW2 16 D6
Church Villa TW16 35 B6
Church Way
Oxted RH8 122 F3
South Croydon CR2 81 A8
Church Wlk
Bletchingley RH1 120 D2
Brentford TW8 6 C8
Caterham CR3 101 A3
Chertsey KT16 33 A3
Crawley RH10 201 D6
Horley RH6 160 F2
Leatherhead KT22 95 B5
Mitcham SW16 41 C7
Reigate RH2 118 C1
14 Richmond TW10 6 D2
Thames Ditton KT7 36 F3
Walton-on-Thames KT12 35 A1
West Barnes SW20 39 C6
Weybridge KT13 53 A7
Churston Cl 17 SW2 22 A7
Churston Dr SM4 39 E4
Churstonville Ct BR3 44 B6
CHURT 167 F1
Churton Pl W4 7 B8
Churt Rd
Beacon Hill GU26 188 C6
Headley Down GU10, GU35 187 C8
Churt Wynde GU26 188 D7
Chuters Cl KT14 71 F7
Chuters Gr KT17 76 F7
Cibber Rd SE23 23 D6
Cidermill Rd RH5 158 E3
Cinderford Way BR1 24 E4
Cinder Path GU22 89 C8
Cinnamon Cl CR0 41 E2
Cinnamon Gdns GU2 109 A6
Cinque Cotts SW19 19 C2
Cintra Ct SE19 22 F2
Cintra Pk SE19 22 F1
Circle Gdns
Byfleet KT14 71 F6
Merton SW19 40 A7
Circle Hill Rd RG45 45 C5
Circle Rd KT12 53 E2
Circle The GU7 150 F6
Circuit Ctr KT13 71 E8
Circus The KT22 95 B7
Cirrus Cl SM6 60 E3
Cissbury Cl RH12 218 A6
Cissbury Hill RH11 201 C4
Cissbury Ho 6 SE26 23 A5
City Bsns Ctr RH13 217 D1
City of London Freemen's Sch KT21 96 A8
City Prospect 6 SE19 22 E2
City Wharf Ho KT7 37 B3
Clacket La TN16 103 E2
Claire Ct
Beckenham BR3 44 B6
Walton-on-Thames KT12 54 C7
Clairvale Rd TW5 4 E6
Clairview Rd SW16, SW17 21 B4
Clairville Ct 1 RH2 118 D1
Clairville Point 12 SE23 23 D5
Clammer Hill GU27 189 F1
Clammer Hill Rd GU27 190 A1
Clandon Ave TW20 12 C1
Clandon CE Inf Sch GU4 111 A4
Clandon Cl KT17 58 A4
Clandon Ct
Farnborough GU14 85 D3
Sutton SM2 59 D4
Clandon Ho
Guildford GU1 130 F7
12 Kingston upon Thames KT2 18 B2
Clandon Mews RH4 136 B4
Clandon Pk★ GU4 111 A3
Clandon Rd
Guildford GU1 130 E8
Send Marsh GU4, GU23 91 A1
West Clandon GU4, GU23 111 A8
Clandon Regis GU4 111 B4
Clandon Sta GU4 111 B6
Clanfield Ho 12 SW15 19 A7
Clanfield Ride GU17 64 D5
Clappers Gate RH10 201 D7
Clappers La GU24 68 D8
Clappers Mdw GU6 194 A3
Clare Ave RG40 25 C7
Clare Cl
Crawley RH10 182 C1
West Byfleet KT14 71 A6
Clare Cotts RH1 120 B3
Clare Cres KT22 75 B1
Clare Ct
Wimbledon SW19 19 E2
Wokingham RG40 25 C7
Woldingham CR3 102 A4
Claredale GU22 89 E8
Claredale Ct SM2 59 C3
Clarefield Ct SL5 30 A2
Clare Gdns TW20 12 A3
Clare Hill KT10 55 B5
Clare Hill (No 1) KT10 55 B5
Clare Hill (No 2) KT10 55 B5
Clare House Prim Sch BR3 44 C7
Clare Lawn Ave SW14 7 D2
Clare Mead GU10 145 F4
Claremont TW17 34 B3
Claremont Ave
Camberley GU15 65 F5
Esher KT10 54 F4
Hersham KT12 54 D6
Sunbury TW16 35 B8
West Barnes KT3 39 B4
Woking GU22 89 E8
Claremont Cl
Hamsey Green CR2 81 B4
Hersham KT12 54 D5
4 Streatham SW2 21 F7
Claremont Ct
Dorking RH4 136 B6
11 Kingston upon Thames KT6 37 E3
Claremont Dr
Esher KT10 55 B4
Shepperton TW17 34 B3
Woking GU22 89 E8
Claremont End KT10 55 B4
Claremont Fan Court Sch KT10 55 A3
Claremont Gdns KT6 37 E4
Claremont Gr 10 W4 7 E7
Claremont Ho 7 SM2 59 A3
Claremont La KT10 55 B5
Claremont Landscape Gdn★ KT10 54 F3
Claremont Lo 16 SW20 19 D1
CLAREMONT PARK 55 A4
Claremont Park Rd KT10 55 B4
Claremont Pl
Blackwater GU17 64 F3
Claygate KT10 55 F4
Claremont Rd
Claygate KT10 55 E3
Croydon CR0 43 A1
Egham TW18 12 D3
Kingston upon Thames KT6 37 E4
Redhill RH1 119 A4
Teddington TW11 16 F4
Twickenham TW1 6 C1
West Byfleet KT14 71 A7
Claremont Terr KT7 37 B2
Claremount Cl KT18 77 C2
Claremount Gdns KT18 77 D2
Clarence Ave
Kingston upon Thames KT3 38 D7
Streatham SW4 21 D8
Clarence Cl
Aldershot GU12 105 D2
Hersham KT12 54 B6
Clarence Ct
Egham TW20 11 F2
Horley RH6 161 D4
Clarence Dr
Camberley GU15 66 B7
2 East Grinstead RH19 205 F7
Englefield Green TW20 11 C4
Clarence Ho KT12 54 B5
Clarence La SW15 7 F1
Clarence Mews 1 SW12 21 B8
Clarence Rd
Biggin Hill TN16 83 F1
Hersham KT12 54 B6
Horsham RH13 217 E1
Reigate RH1 139 D6
Richmond TW9 7 A6
Sutton SM1 59 B5
Teddington TW11 17 A2
Thornton Heath CR0 42 D2
Wallington SM6 60 B5
Wimbledon SW19 20 B2
Clarence St
Egham TW20 11 F2
Kingston upon Thames KT1, KT2 37 E7
9 Richmond TW9 6 E3
Staines TW18 12 E4
Clarence Terr TW3 5 B3
Clarence Way RH6 161 D4
Clarence Wlk RH1 139 D6
Clarendon Cres TW2 16 D5
Clarendon Ct
Beckenham BR3 44 B8
Blackwater GU17 64 D3
Morden SM4 40 E4
1 Richmond TW9 7 A6
Clarendon Gate KT16 51 D4
Clarendon Gr 10 CR4 40 F6
Clarendon Mews KT21 95 F8
Clarendon Prim Sch TW15 13 F4
Clarendon Rd
Ashford TW15 13 F4
Croydon CR0, CR9 61 B8
Mitcham SW19 20 E1
Redhill RH1 118 F2
Wallington SM6 60 C4
Clarendon Specl Sch 6 TW12 16 B2
Clarens St
Forest Hill SE6 23 F6
London SE6 23 F6
Clare Park Hospl (Private) GU10 124 B4
Clare Rd
Hounslow TW4 4 F4
Stanwell TW19 13 E8
Clares The CR3 101 A3
Claret Gdns SE25 42 E5
Clareville Rd CR3 101 A3
Clareways SL5 29 F2
Clare Wood KT22 75 B1
Clarewood Dr GU15 65 E6
Clarice Way SM6 60 E2
Claridge Gdns RH7 165 A2
Claridges Mead RH7 165 A2
Clarke Cl CR0 42 C3
Clarke Cres GU15 64 E7
Clarke Ho 5 TW10 17 C5
Clarke Pl GU6 173 F2
Clarke's Ave KT4, SM3 58 D8
Clark Rd RH11 201 A1
CLARK'S GREEN 178 C4
Clarks Hill GU10 124 D1
Clarks La CR6, RH8, TN16 103 C4
Clark Way TW5 4 D7
Claudia Pl SW19 19 E7
Claverdale Rd SW2 22 A8
Claverdon RG12 27 A2
Claver Dr SL5 29 D5
Clavering Cl TW1 17 A4
Claverton KT21 75 E2
Clay Ave CR4 41 B7
Claycart Rd GU11 104 D4
Clay Cnr KT15 33 B1
Claydon Ct 5 TW18 13 A4
Claydon Dr CR0 60 E6
Claydon Gdns GU17 65 A1
Claydon Rd GU21 69 A3
Clayford RH7 165 B2
CLAYGATE 55 F3
Claygate Cl SM1 59 C7
Claygate Comm Nature Reserve★ KT10 56 A3
Claygate Cres CR0 63 D4
Claygate La
Hinchley Wood KT10 56 A8
Thames Ditton KT7 37 A1
Claygate Lodge Cl KT10 55 E3
Claygate Prim Sch KT10 55 E3
Claygate Rd RH4 136 B5
Claygate Sta KT10 55 E4
Clayhall Ho 3 RH2 118 A2
Clayhall La RH2 138 E6
Clay Hall La RH10 183 C4
Clayhanger GU4 110 C3
Clayhill Cl
Bracknell RG12 28 A6
Leigh RH2 138 A2
Clay Hill Ho GU27 208 A6
Clayhill Rd RH2 137 F1
Clay La
Guildford, Burpham GU4 110 A5
Guildford, Jacobswell GU4 109 E7
Headley KT18 96 B3
Horne RH7 163 D3
South Nutfield RH1 140 D7
Stanwell TW19 13 F8
Wokingham RG40 25 F5
Claylands Ct SE19 22 D3
Claymore Cl SM3, SM4 40 A2
Claypole Dr TW5 4 E6
Clays Cl RH19 205 E8
Clayton Dr GU2 108 F4
Clayton Gr RG12 27 E8
Clayton Hill RH11 201 C4
Clayton Ho KT7 37 B1
Clayton Mead RH9 121 B4
Clayton Rd
Chessington KT10, KT9 56 D6
Ewell KT17 76 E6
Farnborough GU14 64 F1
Isleworth TW7 5 E4
Cleardene RH4 136 B7
Cleardown GU22 70 B1
Clearmount GU24 49 E4
Clears Cotts RH2 117 E3
Clearsprings GU18 67 A8
Clears The RH2 117 E3
Clearwater Ho BR3 44 B4
Clear Water Ho 12 TW10 6 E2
Clear Water Pl KT6 37 C3
Cleaveland Rd KT6 37 D4
Cleave Prior CR5 98 E8
Cleaverholme Cl SE25 43 B3
Cleave's Almshouses 1 KT2 37 E7
Cleeve Ct TW14 14 E7
Cleeve Hill SE23 23 B7
Cleeve Ho RG12 27 E5
Cleeve Rd KT22 95 A7
Cleeves Ct 6 RH1 119 A2
Cleeve The GU1 110 A1
Cleeve Way
Cheam SM1 40 B1
Roehampton SW15 18 F8
Clement Cl CR8 80 B3
Clement Rd
Penge BR3 43 D7
Wimbledon SW19 19 E3
Clements Ct TW4 4 D3
Clements Ho KT22 95 A8
Clements Mead KT22 95 A8
Clements Rd KT12 54 B8
Clensham Ct SM3 59 A8
Clensham La SM1 59 A8
Clerics Wlk TW17 34 D3
Clerks Croft RH1 120 D2
Cleve Ct 3 GU21 68 D2
Clevedon KT13 53 D5
Clevedon Ct
2 Croydon CR0 61 E5
Farnborough GU14 85 D3
Frimley GU16 86 A8
West Norwood SE21 22 D5
Clevedon Gdns TW5 4 B6
Clevedon Ho 7 SM1 59 C6
Clevedon Mans 2 TW1 6 D1

Clevedon Rd
Kingston upon Thames
KT1 . . . . **38** A7
Penge SE20 . . . . **43** D8
Twickenham TW1 . . . . . **6** D1
Clevehurst KT13 . . . . **53** D5
Cleveland Ave
Hampton TW12 . . . . . . **15** F1
Merton SW20 . . . . **39** F7
Cleveland Cl KT12 . . . **54** B7
Cleveland Ct TW10 . . . . **6** F2
Cleveland Dr TW18 . . . **33** B8
Cleveland Gdns
Barnes SW13 . . . . **7** F5
Worcester Park KT4 . . . **57** F8
Cleveland Pk TW19 . . . . **2** E1
Cleveland Pl GU7 . . . **150** E7
Cleveland Rd
Barnes SW13 . . . . **7** F5
Isleworth TW7 . . . . **6** A3
New Malden KT3 . . . . . **38** E5
Worcester Park KT4 . . . **57** F8
Cleveland Rise SM4 . . **39** D2
Cleve Pl KT13 . . . . **53** D5
Cleves Ave KT17 . . . . . **58** B2
Cleves Cl KT11 . . . . . . **73** B5
Cleves Cres CR0 . . . . . **82** C8
Cleves Ct
Epsom KT17 . . . . **76** F7
Kingston upon Thames KT6 . **37** E3
Cleves Jun Sch KT13 . . **53** F6
Cleves Rd TW10 . . . . . **17** C5
Cleves Way
Ashford TW16 . . . . **14** F2
Hampton TW12 . . . . . . **15** F1
Cleves Wood KT13 . . . **53** E6
Clewborough Dr GU15 . **66** B6
Clews La GU24 . . . . . . **68** B3
Clifden Ct 8 TW16 . . . **6** D8
**Clifden Ctr (Richmond Adult
& Community Coll)** TW1 . **16** F7
Clifden Ho 7 TW8 . . . . **6** D8
Clifden Rd
Brentford TW8 . . . . **6** D8
Twickenham TW1 . . . . . **16** F7
Cliff End CR8 . . . . **80** B7
Cliffe Rd
Croydon CR2 . . . . **61** D5
Godalming GU7 . . . . . **150** C2
Cliffe Rise GU7 . . . . . **150** C3
Cliffe Wlk 2 SM1 . . . . **59** C5
Clifford Ave
Mortlake SW14, TW1,
TW9 . . . . **7** B4
Wallington SM6 . . . . . . **60** C6
Clifford Ct SW18 . . . . **20** D8
Clifford Gr TW15 . . . . . **14** A4
Clifford Ho BR3 . . . . . **24** B2
Clifford Manor Rd GU4 . **130** E5
Clifford Rd
Croydon SE25 . . . . **43** A5
Hounslow TW4 . . . . **4** D4
Richmond TW10 . . . . . . **17** D6
Clifton Ave
Feltham TW13 . . . . **15** C5
Sutton SM2 . . . . **78** B8
Clifton Cl
Caterham CR3 . . . . . . **100** D4
Chertsey KT15 . . . . **52** B8
Horley RH6 . . . . **161** D3
Rowledge GU10 . . . . . **146** A4
Clifton Ct
Beckenham BR3 . . . . . . **44** B8
South Norwood SE25 . . . **42** E4
9 Stanwell TW19 . . . . . . **2** E1
Clifton Gdns GU16 . . . **85** F6
Clifton Hill Sch CR3 . . **100** D4
Clifton Mews SE25 . . . **42** E5
Clifton Par TW13 . . . . **15** C4
Clifton Pk SM7 . . . . . . **78** A4
Clifton Pl SM7 . . . . . . **78** A4
Clifton Rd
Coulsdon CR5 . . . . **79** C4
Crawley RH10 . . . . **202** C6
Harlington TW6 . . . . **3** B4
Hounslow TW7 . . . . **5** E5
Kingston upon Thames KT2 . **37** F8
South Norwood SE25 . . . **42** E5
Teddington TW11 . . . . . **16** E4
Wallington SM6 . . . . . . **60** B5
Wimbledon SW19 . . . . . **19** D2
Wokingham RG41 . . . . . **25** A8
Cliftons La RH2 . . . . . **117** D2
Clifton Terr RH4 . . . . **136** B6
Clifton The KT6 . . . . . **56** E8
Cliftonville RH4 . . . . **136** B6
Clifton Way
Hounslow TW6 . . . . **3** B4
Woking GU21 . . . . **68** F2
Climping Rd RH11 . . . **201** B8
Cline Rd GU1 . . . . . . **130** F7
Clinton Ave KT8 . . . . . **36** C5
Clinton Cl
Knaphill GU21 . . . . **68** D1
Weybridge KT13 . . . . . . **53** B8
Clinton Hill RH7 . . . . **186** A8
Clinton Ho
New Malden KT3 . . . . . **38** D1
6 Surbiton KT6 . . . . . **37** D2
Clinton Rd KT22 . . . . . **95** C4
Clintons Gn RG42 . . . . **27** A8
Clinton Terr SM1 . . . . **59** C6
Clippesby Cl KT9 . . . . **56** F4
Clipstone Rd TW3 . . . . . **5** A4
Clitherow Gdns RH10 . . **201** E5

Clive Ct
Streatham SW16 . . . . . . **21** D3
Tolworth KT6 . . . . **57** A8
Cliveden Pl TW17 . . . . **34** C3
Cliveden Rd SW19 . . . . **39** F8
Clivedon Ho KT4 . . . . . **58** A8
Clive Gn RG12 . . . . . . **27** B4
Clive Ho
3 Croydon CR0 . . . . . **42** F1
Redhill RH1 . . . . **118** E3
Clive Pl KT10 . . . . **55** B5
Clive Rd
Aldershot GU12 . . . . . . **105** D1
Esher KT10 . . . . **55** B6
Feltham TW14 . . . . **4** A1
Mitcham SW19 . . . . . . **20** E2
Teddington TW1 . . . . . . **17** A4
West Norwood SE21, SE27 . **22** D5
Clive Way RH1 . . . . . . **202** C6
Clock Barn La GU8 . . . **171** F6
CLOCK HOUSE **79** A5
Clock House Apartments
GU8 . . . . **171** B3
Clockhouse Cl SW19 . . **19** C6
Clock House Cl KT14 . . . **71** F7
Clock House Cotts
Capel RH5 . . . . **178** C2
Enton Green GU8 . . . . . **171** B3
Clockhouse Ct GU1 . . . **109** C5
Clock House Ct BR3 . . . **43** E7
Clockhouse La
Ashford TW14, TW15 . . . **14** B5
Bramley GU5 . . . . **151** F7
East Bedfont TW14, TW15 . **14** B5
Clockhouse Lane E TW20 . **12** B1
Clockhouse Lane W TW20 **12** A1
Clock House Mead KT11 . **74** B5
Clock House Rd GU14 . . **85** B4
Clock House Sta BR3 . . . **43** E7
Clock Tower Rd TW7 . . . **5** F4
Clock Twr The 10 GU21 . **70** A3
Clodhouse Hill GU22 . . **88** D5
Cloister Cl TW11 . . . . . **17** B3
Cloister Gdns SE25 . . . **43** B3
Cloisters Ho 8 SW19 . . **20** A1
Cloisters The
Frimley GU16 . . . . **65** D1
Old Woking GU22 . . . . . **90** B6
Clone The 5 KT2 . . . . . **18** B1
Clonmel Rd TW11 . . . . **16** D4
Clonmore St SW18 . . . . **19** F7
Close The
Beckenham BR3 . . . . . . **43** E5
Brockham RH3 . . . . . . **137** B5
Cheam SM3 . . . . **39** F2
Croydon SE25 . . . . **43** A3
East Grinstead RH19 . . . **205** D8
Esher KT10 . . . . **55** B3
Farnham GU9 . . . . **125** D1
Frimley GU16 . . . . **85** C8
Godalming GU7 . . . . . **150** F3
Horley RH6 . . . . **161** C1
Hounslow TW7 . . . . **5** D5
Ifold RH14 . . . . **212** D3
Kingston upon Thames KT3 . **38** C7
Lightwater GU18 . . . . . . **48** A1
Mitcham CR4 . . . . **40** F5
Mortlake SW14 . . . . **7** B4
North Ascot SL5 . . . . . . **28** D7
Purley CR8 . . . . **61** B1
Purley, Russell Hill CR8 . . **60** F1
Reigate RH2 . . . . **139** B8
Sandhurst GU47 . . . . . . **64** E8
Surbiton KT6 . . . . **37** E3
Virginia Water GU25 . . . **31** D4
Wallington SM5 . . . . . . **59** E2
West Byfleet KT14 . . . . . **71** A6
Woking GU22 . . . . **70** B2
Wonersh GU5 . . . . **152** B7
Closeworth Rd GU14 . . **105** E8
Cloudesdale Rd SW17 . . **21** B6
Clouston Cl SM6 . . . . . **60** E5
Clouston Rd GU14 . . . . **84** F5
Clovelly Ave CR6 . . . . **101** B8
Clovelly Ct KT17 . . . . . **76** F6
Clovelly Dr GU26 . . . . **188** D7
Clovelly Gdns SE19 . . . **42** F8
Clovelly Pk GU26 . . . . **188** C7
Clovelly Rd
Beacon Hill GU26 . . . . **188** E4
Hounslow TW3 . . . . **5** B5
Clover Cl RG40 . . . . . . **25** E7
Clover Ct
New Malden KT4 . . . . . **39** A2
Sutton SM2 . . . . **59** B4
Woking GU22 . . . . **89** D8
Cloverdale Ct 16 SM6 . . **60** A8
Clover Field RH13 . . . **215** D3
Cloverfields RH6 . . . . **161** B4
Clover Ho TW3 . . . . **5** C6
Cloverlands RH10 . . . . **201** F8
Clover Lea GU7 . . . . . **150** E8
Clover Rd GU2 . . . . . . **108** E2
Clovers Cotts RH12 . . . **199** F1
Clovers End RH12 . . . . **218** A5
Clovers Way RH12 . . . . **218** D7
Clover Way
Carshalton CR4 . . . . . . **41** A1
Smallfield RH6 . . . . . . **162** C3
Clowders Rd SE6 . . . . . **23** F5
Clowser Cl 6 SM1 . . . . **59** C5
Clubhouse Rd GU11 . . . **104** F5
Club La RG45 . . . . **45** D5
Clump Ave KT20 . . . . **116** C4
Clumps Rd GU10 . . . . **146** E4

Clumps The TW15 . . . . **14** D4
Clyde Ave CR2 . . . . . . **81** B4
Clyde Cl RH1 . . . . **119** A2
Clyde Ct
Aldershot GU12 . . . . . . **126** E8
17 Redhill RH1 . . . . . **119** A2
Clyde Ho 3 KT2 . . . . . **37** D8
Clyde Rd
Croydon CR0 . . . . **61** F8
Stanwell TW19 . . . . **13** E7
Sutton SM1 . . . . **59** A5
Wallington SM6 . . . . . . **60** C4
Clydesdale Cl TW7 . . . . . **5** F4
Clydesdale Gdns TW10 . . **7** F2
Clyde Terr SE23 . . . . . **23** C6
Clyde Vale SE23 . . . . . **23** C6
Clyde Works 10 SM6 . . . **60** C4
Clymping Dene TW14 . . **15** B8
Clytha SE27 . . . . **22** C4
Clyve Way TW18 . . . . . **32** E8
Coach Ho The KT4 . . . . **57** D8
Coach House Cl GU16 . . **65** E3
Coach House La SW19 . . **19** D5
Coach House Mews RH1 . **139** D7
Coachlads Ave 3 GU2 . . **108** F1
Coachmans Dr
Crawley RH11 . . . . **201** B2
Sandhurst GU47 . . . . . . **64** B7
Coach Rd
Brockham RH3 . . . . . . **137** A7
Crawley, North Terminal
RH6 . . . . **181** D3
Crawley, South Terminal
RH6 . . . . **182** B7
Dorking RH4 . . . . **115** C1
North Ascot SL5 . . . . **8** E1
Ottershaw KT16 . . . . . . **51** C4
Coalbrook Mans 4 SW12 . **21** B7
Coaldale Wlk SE21 . . . . **22** C8
Coast Hill RH4, RH5 . . . **134** F4
Coast Hill La RH4 . . . . **135** A5
Coates Ct CR7 . . . . **42** C6
Coates Wlk 15 TW8 . . . . . **6** E8
Coatham Pl GU6 . . . . . **174** F3
Cobalt Cl BR3 . . . . **43** D5
Cobbets Ridge GU10 . . **147** C8
Cobbett Cl RH10 . . . . . **202** C8
Cobbett Hill Rd GU3 . . . **107** E7
Cobbett Rd
Guildford GU2 . . . . **108** F2
Twickenham TW2 . . . . . **16** A7
Cobbetts Cl
Woking GU21 . . . . **69** B2
Wood St V GU3 . . . . . . **107** F6
Cobbetts Farm GU24 . . . **68** A4
Cobbetts Hill KT13 . . . . **53** B3
Cobbetts Mews 11 GU9 . **125** B2
Cobbetts Way GU9 . . . . **145** F6
Cobbetts Wlk GU24 . . . . **68** A4
Cobblers The RH13 . . . **215** D3
Cobbler's Wlk TW11 . . . **16** F1
Cobbles Cres RH10 . . . **201** E7
Cobb's Rd TW4 . . . . **4** F3
Cobbsthorpe Villas SE26 . **23** D4
Cob Cl RH10 . . . . **204** C8
Cobden La GU27 . . . . . **208** D7
Cobden Mews SE26 . . . . **23** B3
Cobden Rd SE25 . . . . . **43** A4
COBHAM **73** B5
Cobham Ave KT3 . . . . . **39** A4
Cobham Bus Mus KT11 . **72** B7
Cobham Cl
Lingfield RH7 . . . . **164** C6
Wallington SM6 . . . . . . **60** E4
Cobham Cottage Hospl
KT11 . . . . **73** B6
Cobham Gate KT11 . . . . **73** B5
Cobham Park Rd KT11 . . **73** C2
Cobham Rd
Fetcham KT11, KT22 . . . **94** C6
Heston TW5 . . . . **4** C7
Kingston upon Thames KT1,
KT2 . . . . **38** A7
**Cobham & Stoke D'Abernon
Sta** KT11 . . . . **73** E2
Cobham Way
Crawley RH10 . . . . **182** B4
East Horsley KT24 . . . . . **92** E1
Twickenham TW2 . . . . . **16** D7
Cobnor Cl RH11 . . . . . **200** F4
Cobs Way KT15 . . . . . . **52** C1
Coburg Cres SW2 . . . . . **22** A7
Cob Wlk RH11 . . . . . . **201** A6
Cochrane Ct KT23 . . . . . **94** A2
Cochrane Pl GU20 . . . . **48** D5
Cochrane Rd SW19 . . . . **19** F1
Cock-A-Dobby GU47 . . . **45** A1
Cock La KT22 . . . . **94** C5
Cocks Cres KT3 . . . . . . **38** F5
Cockshot Hill RH2 . . . . **139** B7
Cockshot Rd RH2 . . . . **139** C8
Cock's La RG42 . . . . **8** A6
Codrington Ct GU21 . . . **68** F1
Codrington Hill SE23, SE4 . **23** E8
Cody Cl
Ash Vale GU12 . . . . . . **105** F5
Wallington SM6 . . . . . . **60** D3
Cody Rd GU14 . . . . **84** F3
Cody Tech Pk GU14 . . . **84** C1
Coe Ave SE25 . . . . **43** A3
Coe Cl GU11 . . . . **105** A1
Cogman's La RH6 . . . . **162** D4
Cokenor Wood GU10 . . **145** F6
Cokers La SE21 . . . . . . **22** C7
Colborne Ct 8 SW19 . . . **40** B8
Colborne Way KT4 . . . . **58** C8
Colburn Ave CR3 . . . . **100** F3
Colburn Cres GU4 . . . . **110** A4
Colburn Way SM1 . . . . **59** D7

Colby Rd
Dulwich SE19 . . . . **22** E3
Walton-on-Thames KT12 . . **35** A1
Colchester Vale RH18 . . **206** E2
Colchester Villas CR7 . . **42** A3
Colcokes Rd SM7 . . . . . **78** A3
COLDHARBOUR **156** E4
Coldharbour Cl TW20 . . **32** C6
Coldharbour La
Bletchingley RH1 . . . . . **120** F1
Dorking RH4, RH5 . . . . **135** F3
Egham TW20 . . . . **32** D6
Purley CR8 . . . . **61** A1
South Holmwood RH4, RH5 **156** F6
West End GU24 . . . . **67** F8
Coldharbour Rd
Croydon CR0 . . . . **61** A5
Pyrford GU22, KT14 . . . . **70** F4
Coldharbour Way CR0 . . **61** A5
Coldshott RH8 . . . . . . **123** A2
Coldstream Rd CR3 . . . **100** C5
Cole Ave GU11 . . . . . . **104** F3
Colebrook KT16 . . . . . . **51** D4
Colebrook Cl SW19 . . . . **19** D8
Colebrooke Pl KT16 . . . **51** C3
Colebrooke Rd RH1 . . . **118** E3
Colebrook Rd SW16 . . . **41** E8
Colebrook Rise BR2 . . . **44** E7
Cole Cl RH11 . . . . **201** B1
Cole Court Lodge 11 TW1 . **17** A8
Coleford Bridge Rd GU16 . **85** E4
Coleford Cl GU16 . . . . . **85** E3
Coleford Paddocks GU16 . **85** F4
Cole Gdns TW5 . . . . **4** A7
Colekitchen La GU5 . . . **133** D6
Coleman Cl SE25 . . . . . **43** A7
Coleman Ct SW18 . . . . . **20** A8
Coleman Rd GU12 . . . . **105** D1
Cole Park Gdns TW1 . . . . **6** A1
Cole Park Rd TW1 . . . . . **6** A1
Cole Park View 2 TW1 . . . **6** A1
Cole Rd TW1 . . . . **6** A1
Coleridge Ave
SM1 . . . . **59** E6
Coleridge Cl
Crowthorne RG45 . . . . . **45** C4
Horsham RH12 . . . . **217** E6
Coleridge Cres SL3 . . . . . **1** E6
Coleridge Ct 2 TW10 . . . **17** D4
Coleridge Rd
Ashford TW15 . . . . **13** F4
Croydon CR0 . . . . **43** C2
Colesburg Rd BR3 . . . . . **43** F7
Colescroft Hill CR8 . . . . **80** A4
Coleshill Rd TW11 . . . . **16** E2
Coles La RH5 . . . . **178** C5
Cole's La RH5 . . . . **178** B5
Colesmead Rd RH1 . . . **118** F4
Coleson Hill Rd GU10 . . **145** F5
Colet Rd RH11 . . . . . . **201** D3
Coleville Rd GU14 . . . . **84** F5
Coley Ave GU22 . . . . . . **70** A2
Colgate Cl RH11 . . . . . **201** B8
Colin Cl
Coney Hall BR4 . . . . **63** F7
Croydon CR0 . . . . **62** F7
Colin Ct
Forest Hill SE6 . . . . **23** F8
Streatham SW16 . . . . . . **21** D6
Colin Rd CR3 . . . . **101** A4
Coliston Pas SW18 . . . . **20** A8
Coliston Rd SW18 . . . . . **20** A8
Collamore Ave SW18 . . . **20** E7
Collard Cl CR3 . . . . **100** E7
Collards Gate GU27 . . . **208** D6
Collards La GU27 . . . . **208** D6
College Ave
Egham TW20 . . . . **12** B2
Epsom KT17 . . . . **76** F5
College Cl
Addlestone KT15 . . . . . . **52** D7
Camberley GU15 . . . . . . **65** D7
East Grinstead RH19 . . . **185** F1
Lingfield RH7 . . . . **164** D4
Twickenham TW2 . . . . . **16** D7
College Cres
Redhill RH1 . . . . **119** A4
Sandhurst GU47 . . . . . . **64** E8
College Ct CR0 . . . . **62** A8
College Dr KT7 . . . . **36** E2
College Fields Bsns Ctr
SW19 . . . . **40** E8
College Gdns
Dulwich SE21 . . . . **22** E7
Farnham GU9 . . . . **125** B2
New Malden KT3 . . . . . **38** F4
Upper Tooting SW17 . . . . **20** E6
College Gn SE19 . . . . . . **22** E1
College Hill
Godalming GU7 . . . . . **150** C2
Haslemere GU27 . . . . . **208** C6
College Hill Terr GU27 . . **208** C6
College La
East Grinstead RH19 . . . **185** F1
Woking GU22 . . . . **89** C8
College Pl GU9 . . . . . . **125** C1
College Rd
Ash GU12 . . . . **106** B3
Crawley RH10 . . . . **201** E6
Croydon CR0, CR9 . . . . . **61** D8
Dulwich SE19, SE21 . . . . **22** E6
Epsom KT17 . . . . **76** F5
Ewell KT17 . . . . **77** B5
Guildford GU1 . . . . **130** D8
Hounslow TW7 . . . . **5** F6

College Rd continued
Mitcham SW19 . . . . **20** D2
Sandhurst GU47 . . . . . . **64** E8
Woking GU22 . . . . **70** B3
College Rdbt 1 KT1 . . . **37** E6
College Ride
Bagshot GU19 . . . . **47** C2
Camberley GU15 . . . . . . **65** D7
COLLEGE TOWN **64** E8
College Town Inf Sch
GU47 . . . . **64** E8
College Town Jun Sch
GU47 . . . . **64** E8
College Way TW15 . . . . **13** F4
College Wlk 10 KT1 . . . . **37** E6
Collendean La RH6 . . . **159** F4
Collens Field GU24 . . . . **87** F4
Collette Ct SE25 . . . . . . **42** E4
Colley La RH2 . . . . **117** E3
Colley Manor Dr RH2 . . **117** D2
Colley Way RH2 . . . . . . **117** E4
Collier Cl
Farnborough GU14 . . . . . **84** D5
West Ewell KT19 . . . . . . **57** B4
Collier Ct 1 CR0 . . . . . . **61** D6
Collier Row RH10 . . . . **201** D4
Colliers CR3 . . . . **101** A2
Colliers Cl GU21 . . . . . . **69** B2
Colliers Water La CR7 . . **42** A4
COLLIER'S WOOD **20** C2
Colliers Wood U Sta
SW19 . . . . **20** D1
Collier Way GU4 . . . . . **110** D3
Collingdon GU6 . . . . . **174** F1
Collingsbourne KT15 . . . **52** B6
Collingtree SE26 . . . . . **23** C4
Collingwood GU14 . . . . **85** E2
Collingwood Ave KT5 . . **38** C1
Collingwood Cl
4 East Grinstead RH19 . . **205** F7
Horley RH6 . . . . **161** B4
Horsham RH12 . . . . . . **217** C4
3 Penge SE20 . . . . **43** B8
Twickenham TW2 . . . . . **16** A8
Collingwood Coll GU15 . . **66** A8
Collingwood Cres GU1 . . **110** A2
Collingwood Ct SM1 . . . **59** B6
Collingwood Grange Cl
GU15 . . . . **66** B8
Collingwood Mount GU15 . **66** A7
Collingwood Pl
Camberley GU15 . . . . . . **66** B8
Walton-on-Thames KT12 . . **54** B7
Collingwood Rd
Crawley RH10 . . . . **202** D5
Horsham RH12 . . . . . . **217** B4
Mitcham CR4 . . . . **40** E6
Sutton SM1 . . . . **59** A6
Collingwood Rise GU15 . . **66** A7
Collingwood Sch SM6 . . **60** B5
Collins Gdns GU12 . . . . **106** B2
Collins Rd RH11 . . . . . **200** E4
Collis Prim Sch TW11 . . **17** B2
Coll of Law The GU2 . . . **130** C5
Coll of Richard Collyer The
RH12 . . . . **217** D4
Coll of St Barnabas RH7 . **185** F8
Collyer Ave CR0 . . . . . . **60** E6
Collyer Rd CR0 . . . . **60** E6
Colman Cl KT18 . . . . . . **77** C2
Colman Ho RH1 . . . . . **118** F3
Colmans Hill GU5 . . . . **154** E7
Colman Way RH1 . . . . **118** E4
Colmer Rd SW16 . . . . . **21** E1
COLNBROOK **1** D7
Colnbrook By-Pass
Colnbrook SL3 . . . . **1** D7
Harmondsworth UB7 . . . . **2** C7
Colnbrook CE Prim Sch
SL3 . . . . **1** D7
Colnbrook Ct
Poyle SL3 . . . . **1** F6
Upper Tooting SW17 . . . . **20** D4
Colndale Rd SL3 . . . . **1** E5
Colnebridge Cl TW18 . . . **12** E3
Colne Ct KT19 . . . . **57** C6
Colne Dr KT12 . . . . **54** D7
Colne Ho 2 RH1 . . . . . . **118** F2
Colne Lodge KT12 . . . . . **54** D7
Colne Rd TW2 . . . . **16** E7
Colne Reach TW19 . . . . . **1** F2
Colne Way
Ash GU12 . . . . **106** A1
Wraysbury TW19 . . . . . . **12** B6
Coln Wlk RH11 . . . . . . **200** F4
Coln Trad Est SL3 . . . . . **1** F6
Coloma Convent Girls' Sch
CR9 . . . . **62** D7
Colonel's La KT16 . . . . . **33** A3
Colonial Ave TW2 . . . . . . **5** C1
Colonial Rd TW14 . . . . . **14** E8
Colonnades The CR0 . . . **61** A4
Colonsay Rd RH11 . . . . **201** B3
Colony Gate GU16 . . . . . **66** D2
Colson Rd CR0, CR9 . . . . **61** E8
Colson Way SW16 . . . . . **21** C4
Colston Ave SM5 . . . . . **59** E6
Colston Ct SM5 . . . . . . **59** F6
Colston Rd SW14 . . . . . . **7** C3
Coltash Rd RH10 . . . . . **202** A5
Coltsfoot Dr
Guildford GU1 . . . . **110** B4
Horsham RH12 . . . . . . **217** E5
Coltsfoot La RH8 . . . . . **123** A2
Columbia Ave KT4 . . . . **38** F2
Columbia Ct KT3 . . . . . **38** F2
Columbine Ave CR2 . . . . **61** B3

Columbus Dr GU14 84 C4
Colvill Ct CR2 61 B2
Colville Gdns GU18 67 C8
Colvin Cl SE26 23 C3
Colvin Rd CR7 42 A4
Colwood Gdns SW19 20 D1
Colworth Rd CR0 43 A1
Colwyn Cl
Crawley RH11 200 F4
Streatham SW16 21 C3
Colwyn Cres TW3 5 C6
Colyton Cl GU21 69 C1
Colyton La 2 SW16 22 A3
Combe Ho SW14 7 C5
Combe La
Bramley GU5 151 D2
Chiddingfold GU8 191 A7
Farnborough GU14 85 A6
Shere KT24, GU4 133 B8
Whiteley Village KT12 53 F2
Wormley GU8 170 F1
Combemartin Rd SW18 19 E7
Combe Rd GU7 150 E8
Combe Rise GU10 146 D5
Combermere Rd SM4 40 B4
Combe View GU8 191 A5
Comeragh Cl GU22 89 A7
Comet Cl GU12 105 F5
Comet Rd
Farnborough GU14 84 C1
Stanwell TW19 13 D8
Comforts Farm Ave RH8 123 A3
Comfrey Cl
Farnborough GU14 84 C5
Wokingham RG40 25 E8
Commerce Pk CR0 60 F8
Commerce Rd TW8 6 C7
Commerce Way CR0 60 F8
Commercial Rd
Aldershot GU12 126 C8
Guildford GU1 130 D8
Staines TW18 13 A2
Commercial Way GU21 69 F2
Commodore Ct GU14 105 B8
Common Cl GU21 69 D5
Commonfield Rd SM7 78 B6
Commonfields GU24 67 F6
Common La
Claygate KT10 56 A3
New Haw KT15 52 C2
Common Rd
Claygate KT10 56 A3
Redhill RH1 139 F7
Commonside
Great Bookham KT23 94 A5
Redhill RH1 139 F7
Common Side KT18 76 A4
Commonside Cl
Coulsdon CR5 100 B7
Sutton SM2 78 B8
Commonside Ct SW16 21 E2
Commonside E CR4 41 B6
Commonside W CR4 40 F6
Common The
Ashtead KT21 75 D3
Cranleigh GU6 174 C3
Wonersh GU5 152 B8
Commonwealth Dr RH10 202 C7
Commonwealth Rd CR3 101 A4
Community Cl TW5 4 B6
Como Rd SE23 23 E6
Compass Cl TW15 14 C1
Compasses Mobile Home Pk
GU6 193 F5
Compass Hill TW10 6 D1
Compassion Cl RH11 200 E5
Comper Cl RH11 200 E4
Comport Gn CR0 82 E7
COMPTON
Farnham 125 F1
Guildford 129 B3
Compton Cl
Bracknell RG12 26 E3
Esher KT10 55 D5
Sandhurst GU47 45 C1
Compton Cres
Chessington KT9 56 E4
Chiswick W4 7 C8
Compton Ct
7 Guildford GU1 130 F8
Sutton SM1 59 C6
9 West Norwood SE19 22 E3
Compton Gdns KT15 52 B5
Compton Hts GU3 129 D6
Compton Place Bsns Ctr
GU15 65 A4
Compton Rd
Croydon CR0 43 B1
Wimbledon SW19 19 F2
Comptons Brow La
RH13 218 A3
Comptons Ct 4 RH13 217 F3
Comptons La RH13 217 F3
Comptons The RH13 218 A3
Compton Way GU10 126 B1
Comsaye Wlk RG12 27 C4
Conal Ct SW16 21 D3
Conaways Cl KT17 58 A1
Concord Ct KT1 37 F6
Concorde Bsns Pk TN16 83 D4
Concorde Cl TW3 5 B5
Concorde Ho
Addlestone KT15 52 B6
Crawley RH6 182 B7
Concorde Rd GU14 84 C1
Concord Ho 4 KT3 38 E6
Condor Ct GU2 130 C7
Condor Rd TW18 33 C6
Conduit La CR0 62 A5
Conduit The RH1 120 D6
Coney Acre SE21 22 C7
Coneyberry RH2 139 D5
Coneybury RH1 120 E1
Coneybury Cl CR6 101 B8
Coney Cl RH11 201 B8
Coney Croft RH12 218 B5
CONEY HALL 63 F7
Coney Hall Par BR4 63 E7
Coney Hill Rd BR4 63 F8
Coneyhurst La GU6 175 D7
Conford Dr GU4 130 E2
Coniers Way GU4 110 B4
Conifer Cl RH2 118 A3
Conifer Ct
Ashford TW15 13 F3
23 Putney SW19 19 D7
Sutton SM2 59 D4
Conifer Dr GU15 66 A6
Conifer Gdns
Streatham SW16 21 F5
Sutton SM1 59 B8
Conifer La TW20 12 C3
Conifer Pk KT17 76 E8
Conifers KT13 53 F6
Conifers Cl
Horsham RH12 218 B6
Teddington TW11 17 C1
Conifers The RG45 45 A7
Coningsby RG12 27 C5
Coningsby Ct 4 CR4 41 A7
Coningsby Rd CR2 61 C2
Conisborough Cres SE6 24 C5
Conista Ct GU21 68 F3
Coniston Cl
Barnes SW13 7 F7
Chiswick W4 7 C7
Crawley RH11 200 D4
Farnborough GU14 84 E3
Frimley GU15 66 C3
Horsham RH12 218 B6
West Barnes SM4 39 D3
Coniston Ct
Ashford TW15 13 D5
Beckenham BR3 44 C8
Chessington KT9 56 E7
Lightwater GU18 48 B1
Penge SE26 23 B2
3 Wallington SM6 60 B6
Weybridge KT13 53 B4
Coniston Dr GU9 125 A6
Coniston Gdns SM2 59 D4
Coniston Rd
Catford BR1 24 E2
Coulsdon CR5 79 C3
Croydon CR0 43 A2
Old Woking GU22 90 B7
Twickenham TW2 5 B1
Coniston Way
Chessington KT9 56 E7
Redhill RH2 118 E2
2 Thorpe Lea TW20 12 B1
Connaught Ave
Ashford TW15 13 E4
Hounslow TW4 4 E3
Mortlake SW14 7 C3
Connaught Bsns Ctr
Mitcham CR4 40 F4
Wallington CR9 60 F4
Connaught Cl SM1 59 D8
Connaught Cres GU24 87 F7
Connaught Dr KT13 72 A8
Connaught Gdns
Crawley RH10 201 D8
Morden SM4 40 C5
Connaught Ho KT6 37 D4
Connaught Jun Sch GU19 47 E2
Connaught L Ctr GU12 126 E7
Connaught Rd
Aldershot GU12 105 D2
Bagshot GU19 47 C3
Brookwood GU24 87 F7
Camberley GU15 65 F5
Carshalton SM1 59 D8
New Malden KT3 38 E5
5 Richmond TW10 6 F2
Teddington TW11 16 D3
Connaught Sch The
GU12 126 E7
Connell Ho 6 SM6 60 C4
Connington 2 KT1 38 A7
Connolly Ct GU25 31 E5
Connolly Ho
Epsom KT19 57 B2
Wimbledon SW19 20 C2
Connop Way GU16 65 F3
Conquest Rd KT15 52 A5
Conrad Dr KT4 39 D1
Consero Ct 8 RH1 119 A3
Conservatory Ct SE19 22 E1
Consfield Ave KT3 39 A4
Consort Ct 1 GU22 69 E1
Consort Dr GU15 66 C7
Consort Mews TW7 5 D2
Consort Way RH6 161 A3
Consort Way E RH6 161 B2
Constable Gdns TW7 5 D2
Constable Rd RH10 201 F2
Constable Way GU47 64 E6
Constable Wlk SE21 22 E5
Constance Cres BR2 44 F1
Constance Rd
Sutton SM1 59 C6
Thornton Heath CR0 42 B2
Twickenham TW2 16 B8
Constantine Ho SW2 22 B7
Constant Rd GU14 84 A2
Constitution Hill GU22 89 E8
Control Tower Rd
Crawley RH6 181 D6
Harlington TW6 3 B4
Convent Cl BR3 24 C1
Convent Hill SE19 22 C2
Convent La KT11 72 F7
Convent Lodge TW15 14 B3
Convent Rd TW15 14 B3
Conway Cl GU16 65 F1
Conway Dr
Ashford TW15 14 C2
Farnborough GU14 84 D4
Sutton SM2 59 B4
Conway Gdns CR4 41 E5
Conway Ho
Reigate RH2 139 A4
6 Streatham SW2 21 E7
Conway Rd
Feltham TW13 15 D3
Harlington TW6 3 B4
Twickenham TW4 16 A8
Wimbledon SW20 39 C8
Conway Wlk TW12 15 F2
Conyers Cl KT12 54 D5
Conyer's Rd SW16 21 D3
Cookes La SM3 58 E4
Cookham Cl GU47 45 C1
Cookham Rd RG12 26 E7
Cook Rd
Crawley RH10 201 F4
Horsham RH12 217 D6
Cooks Hill RH12 214 A8
Cooks Mdw RH12 199 D7
Cooks Mead RH12 199 D7
Cook Way GU2 108 D2
Coolarne Rise GU15 66 A6
Coolgardie Rd TW15 14 C3
Coolham Ct RH11 200 F6
Coolhurst La RH13 218 A1
COOMBE 18 D1
Coombe Ave CR0 61 E6
Coombe Bank KT2, KT3 38 E8
Coombe Boys' Sch KT3 39 A4
Coombe Cl
Crawley RH11 181 D1
Frimley GU16 85 D8
Hounslow TW3 5 A3
Coombe Cotts RH3 116 D4
Coombe Cres TW12 15 E1
Coombe Ct
2 Beckenham BR3 43 F8
2 Croydon CR0 61 D6
Tadworth KT20 97 C4
Coombe Dene 8 BR2 44 F5
Coombe Dr KT15 51 F4
Coombe End KT2 18 D1
Coombefield Cl KT3 38 E4
Coombe Gdns
New Malden KT3 38 F5
Wimbledon SW20 39 A8
Coombe Girls Sch KT3 38 D7
Coombe Hall Pk RH19 205 D6
Coombe Hill Glade KT2 18 E1
Coombe Hill Inf Sch KT3 38 D8
Coombe Hill Jun Sch KT3 38 D8
Coombe Hill Rd
East Grinstead RH19 205 D6
Kingston upon Thames KT2 18 E1
Coombe Hill Stables KT2 18 E1
Coombe House Chase
KT3 38 D8
Coombehurst (Kingston
University) KT2 18 C3
Coombe La
Ascot SL5 29 C5
South Croydon CR0 62 B5
Wimbledon SW20 39 B7
Worplesdon GU3 108 D7
Coombelands La KT15 52 A4
Coombe Lane Flyover
SW20 38 F8
Coombe Lane Halt CR0 62 C5
Coombe Lane W KT2 18 E1
Coombe Manor GU24 68 B4
Coombe Neville KT2 18 D1
Coombe Pine RG12 27 D3
Coombe Pk KT2 18 D3
Coombe Pl KT2 18 C3
Coombe Rd
Croydon CR0 61 E6
Forest Hill SE26 23 B4
Hampton TW12 15 F2
Kingston upon Thames KT3 38 E6
Kingston upon Thames, Norbiton
KT2 38 A8
South Croydon CR0, CR2 61 E6
Coombe Ridings KT2 18 C3
Coombe Rise KT2 38 C8
Coomber Way CR0, CR4 41 D2
Coombes The GU5 152 A5
Coombe The RH3 116 D4
Coombe Way
Byfleet KT14 71 F7
Farnborough GU14 85 C4
Coombe Wlk SM1 59 B7
Coombe Wood Hill CR8 80 C6
Coombe Wood Nature
Reserve★ KT2 18 F1
Coombe Wood Rd KT2 18 C3
Cooper Cl RH6 162 A3
Cooper Cres SM5 59 F7
Cooper Ct GU14 85 C4
Cooper Ho
Upper Tooting SW17 20 D4
7 West Norwood SW27 22 B3
Cooper House TW4 4 F4
Cooper Lodge RH6 160 F2
Cooper Rd
Croydon CR0, CR9 61 B6
Guildford GU1 130 F8
Windlesham GU20 48 D4
Cooper Row RH10 201 D3
Coopers Cl TW18 12 E3
Coopers Hill Dr GU24 87 C7
Cooper's Hill La TW20 11 D4
Cooper's Hill Rd
Nutfield RH1 120 A1
South Nutfield RH1 141 B5
Coopers Mews BR3 44 A7
Coopers Place Bsns Pk
GU8 190 F8
Coopers Rise GU7 150 C3
Cooper's Terr GU9 125 C3
Cooper's Yd SE19 22 E2
Cootes Ave RH12 217 A3
Copeland Ho SW17 20 D4
Copelands BR3 23 F1
Copelands Cl GU15 66 D4
Copeman Cl SE26 23 C3
Copenhagen Way KT12 54 B7
Copenhagen Wlk RG45 45 B4
Copers Cope Rd BR3 23 F1
Copgate Path SW16 22 A2
Copleigh Dr KT20 97 E7
Copley Cl
Knaphill GU21 88 E8
Redhill RH1 118 E3
Copley Pk SW16 21 F2
Copley Way KT20 97 D7
Copnall Way 12 RH12 217 C2
Coppard Gdns KT9 56 C4
Coppedhall 2 SE21 22 D6
Copped Hall Dr GU15 66 C6
Copped Hall Way GU15 66 C6
Copper Beech RG42 28 A8
Copper Beech Cl GU22 89 B6
Copper Beeches TW7 5 D6
Copper Beech Ho 17
GU22 69 F2
Copper Cl SE19 22 F1
Copperfield Ave GU47 45 E2
Copperfield Cl CR2 80 C8
Copperfield Ct KT22 95 A6
Copperfield Pl RH12 217 B4
Copperfield Rise KT15 51 F4
Copperfields
Beckenham BR3 44 C8
Fetcham KT22 94 C5
Copper Mill Dr TW7 5 F5
Copper Mill La SW17 20 C4
Coppermill Rd TW19 1 B2
Coppice Cl
Beckenham BR3 44 B5
Guildford GU2 108 D2
Heath End GU9 125 E6
West Barnes SW20 39 C6
Coppice Dr TW19 11 D8
Coppice End GU22 70 E3
Coppice La RH2 117 F3
Coppice Pl GU8 190 F8
Coppice Rd RH12 218 A5
Coppice The
Ashford TW15 14 B2
Crawley Down RH10 204 B8
Coppice Wlk RH10 202 A7
Copping Cl CR0 61 E6
Coppin Ho SW2 22 B7
Coppins The CR0 63 B4
Coppsfield KT8 36 A6
Copse Ave
Heath End GU9 125 E8
West Wickham BR4 63 B7
Copse Cl
Camberley GU15 66 A6
Chilworth GU4 131 C3
Crawley Down RH10 204 B8
East Grinstead RH19 186 A3
Horsham RH12 217 F6
Copse Cres RH11 201 C7
Copse Dr RG41 25 A7
Copse Edge
Cranleigh GU6 174 F4
Elstead GU8 148 C3
Copse Edge Ave KT17 76 F6
Copse End GU15 66 A6
Copse Glade KT6 37 D1
COPSE HILL 19 B1
Copse Hill
Belmont SM2 59 B3
London SW19 19 C2
Purley CR8 79 E6
Wimbledon SW20 19 B1
Copse Ho RG41 25 A5
Copse La RH6 161 C4
Copsem Dr KT10 55 B4
Copsem La
Esher KT10 55 C3
Oxshott KT22 55 C1
Copsem Way KT10 55 C4
Copsen Wood KT22 74 C8
Copse Rd
Cobham KT11 73 B6
Haslemere GU27 207 D5
Knaphill GU21 68 F1
Reigate RH1 139 D7
Copse Side GU7 129 D1
Copse The
Caterham CR3 101 A1
Cranleigh GU6 175 A3
Crawley RH10 202 A6
Farnborough GU14 84 D3
Fetcham KT22 94 B4
Rowledge GU10 145 F4
South Nutfield RH1 140 E7
Westerham TN16 103 C7
Copse View CR2 62 E2
Copse Way GU10 145 F6
Copse Wood Ct RH1 118 E3
Copsleigh Ave RH1 140 A3
Copsleigh Cl RH1 140 A3
Copsleigh Way RH1 140 A3
Copthall Gdns TW1 16 F7
Copthall Way KT15 52 A1
Copt Hill La KT20 97 F7
COPTHORNE 183 C3
Copthorne Ave SW12 21 D8
Copthorne Bank RH10,
RH6 183 C4
Copthorne CE Jun Sch
RH10 183 B3
Copthorne Chase TW15 13 F4
Copthorne Cl TW17 34 C3
Copthorne Common Rd
RH10 183 C3
Copthorne Ct
Crawley RH10 182 A1
Sutton SM1 59 C7
Copthorne Dr GU18 48 B1
Copthorne Fairway Inf Sch
RH10 183 B3
Copthorne Ho KT20 97 E7
Copthorne Prep Sch
RH10 183 E3
Copthorne Rd
Copthorne RH10 182 F1
Crawley RH10 202 E8
Domewood RH19 184 D4
Leatherhead KT22 95 B7
Copthorne Rise CR8 80 D6
Copthorne Way RH10 182 F2
Copyhold Rd RH19 205 D8
Coral Reef - Bracknell's Wr
World★ RG12 27 D1
Corban Rd TW3 5 A4
Corbet Cl SM6 60 A8
Corbet Rd KT17 57 E1
Corbett Cl CR0 82 D7
Corbett Ct 3 SE6 23 F4
Corbett Dr GU18 66 F7
Corbiere Ct SW19 19 D2
Corby Cl
Crawley RH11 200 E3
Englefield Green TW20 11 C2
Corby Dr TW20 11 C2
Cordelia Croft RG42 27 E8
Cordelia Gdns
Ash Vale GU12 85 F1
Stanwell TW19 13 E8
Cordelia Rd TW19 13 E8
Corderoy Pl KT16 32 F3
Cordrey Gdns CR5 79 E4
Cordrey Ho KT15 52 B8
Cordwalles Cres GU15 65 F8
Cordwalles Jun Sch GU15 65 F8
Coresbrook Way GU21 88 B8
Corfe Cl
Ashtead KT21 75 C1
Feltham TW4 15 E7
Corfe Gdns GU16 65 F1
Corfe Lodge 15 SE21 22 D6
Corfe Way GU14 85 E1
Coriander Cl GU14 84 C4
Coriander Cres GU2 109 A6
Coriander Ct SL5 29 E3
Corium Ho GU7 150 F5
Cork Ho BR1 24 D3
Corkran Rd KT6 37 E2
Corkscrew Hill BR4 63 D7
Cork Tree Ho 3 SW27 22 B3
Cormongers La RH1 119 D2
Cormorant Ct 13 SE21 22 D6
Cormorant Pl
Cheam SM1 58 F5
Sandhurst GU47 64 E7
Cornbunting Cl GU47 64 D8
Cornelia Cl GU14 84 D3
Cornelia Ho 19 TW1 6 D1
Cornelian Cotts 1 SM6 60 B5
Cornercroft SM3 58 D5
Corner Farm Cl KT20 97 C5
Corner Fielde SW2 21 F7
Corner House Par 3
KT17 57 F1
Cornerside TW15 14 C1
Cornerstone Sch The
KT19 76 C6
Corney Rd W4 7 E8
Corney Reach Way W4 7 E7
Cornfield Rd RH2 139 C8
Cornfields GU7 151 A8
Cornfield Sch RH1 139 F4
Cornflower La CR0 43 D1
Cornford Gr SW12 21 B6
Cornhill Cl KT15 52 B8
Cornish Gr SE20 43 B8
Cornwall Ave
Byfleet KT14 71 F5
Claygate KT10 55 F3
Cornwall Cl GU15 65 F7
Cornwall Ct SW17 20 E4
Cornwall Gdns 6 RH19 205 F8
Cornwallis Cl CR3 100 C5
Cornwall Rd
Belmont SM2 59 A2
Thornton Heath CR0, CR9 61 B8
Twickenham TW1 17 A7
Cornwall Way TW18 12 E2
Coronation Cotts GU8 191 C5
Coronation Rd
Aldershot GU11 126 B7

Coronation Rd continued
Ascot SL5. . . . . 29 A2
East Grinstead RH19. . . . 205 E7
Coronation Sq RG40. . . . . 25 D7
Coronet Cl RH10. . . . . . 202 E7
Coronet The RH6. . . . . . 161 C1
Corporation Ave TW4. . . . 4 E3
Corpus Christi RC Prim Sch
KT3. . . . . 38 C6
Corrib Dr SM1. . . . . 59 E5
Corrie Gdns GU25. . . . . . 31 C2
Corrie Rd
Addlestone KT15. . . . . . . 52 D6
Old Woking GU22. . . . . . 90 C7
Corrigan Ave CR5. . . . . . . 79 A5
Corry Rd GU26. . . . . 188 C6
Corsair Cl TW19. . . . . 13 E8
Corsair Rd TW19. . . . . . . 13 E8
Corscombe Cl KT2. . . . . . 18 C3
Corsehill St SW16. . . . . . 21 C2
Corsell Ho ⑤ TW8. . . . . . . 6 C7
Corsham Way RG45. . . . . 45 B5
Corsletts Ave RH12. . . . . 216 D3
Corsten Hollow ⑦ RH1. . 139 E4
Cortayne Rd ④ TW2. . . . . 16 E6
Corunna Dr RH13. . . . . . 217 F2
Cosdach Ave SM6. . . . . . 60 D3
Cosedge Cres CR0, CR9 . . 61 B5
Cosford Rd GU8. . . . . . . 169 E4
Coteford St SW17. . . . . . 21 A4
Cotelands CR0. . . . . 61 E7
Cotford Rd CR7. . . . . 42 C5
Cotherstone KT19. . . . . . 57 D2
Cotherstone Rd SW2. . . . 21 F7
Cotland Acres RH1. . . . . 139 D7
COTMANDENE. 136 B7
Cotsford Ave KT3. . . . . . 38 D4
Cotswold Cl
Crawley RH11. . . . . 201 B6
Farnborough GU14. . . . . 84 B7
Hinchley Wood KT10. . . . 55 F8
Kingston upon Thames KT2 . 18 C2
Staines TW18. . . . . 13 A3
Cotswold Ct RH13. . . . . . 217 E2
Cotswold Rd
Belmont SM2. . . . . 59 B1
Hampton TW12. . . . . 16 A2
Cotswold St SE27. . . . . . 22 B4
Cotswold Way KT4. . . . . . 58 C8
Cottage Cl
Horsham RH12. . . . . . . 218 B6
Ottershaw KT16. . . . . . . 51 C4
Cottage Farm Way TW20 . 32 C6
Cottage Gdns GU14. . . . . 84 F4
Cottage Gr KT6. . . . . 37 D3
Cottage Pl RH10. . . . . . . 183 E3
Cottage Rd KT19. . . . . . . 57 D3
Cottage The KT15. . . . . . 52 D7
Cottenham Ct SW20. . . . . 39 B8
Cottenham Dr SW20. . . . . 19 B1
Cottenham Par SW20. . . . 39 B7
COTTENHAM PARK. 39 B8
Cottenham Park Rd
Wimbledon, Copse Hill
SW20. . . . . 19 C1
Wimbledon, Cottenham Park
SW20. . . . . 39 B8
Cottenham Pl SW20. . . . . 19 B1
Cottenhams RH7. . . . . . . 163 E8
Cotterill Rd KT6. . . . . 37 F1
Cottesbrooke Cl SL3. . . . . 1 D6
Cottesloe Cl GU24. . . . . . . 67 F3
Cottesmore RG12. . . . . . . 27 A2
Cottimore Ave KT12. . . . . 35 B1
Cottimore Cres KT12. . . . 35 B2
Cottimore La KT12. . . . . . 35 B2
Cottimore Terr KT12. . . . . 35 B2
Cottingham Ave RH12. . . 217 D4
Cottingham Rd SE20. . . . . 23 D1
Cottington Rd TW13. . . . . 15 D4
Cotton Cl GU11. . . . . 104 F1
Cottongrass Cl CR0. . . . . 43 D1
Cotton Hill BR1. . . . . 24 D4
Cotton Ho ⑰ SW12. . . . . . 21 E8
Cotton Row RH5. . . . . . . 176 C8
Cotton Wlk RH11. . . . . . 201 A1
Cottrell Flats GU14. . . . . 105 D8
Cotts Wood Dr GU4. . . . . 110 A6
Couchmore Ave KT10. . . . 55 E8
COULSDON. 79 C3
Coulsdon CE Prim Sch
CR5. . . . . 79 F1
Coulsdon Court Rd CR5 . . 79 F3
Coulsdon Ho ⑤ SW2. . . . . 21 E7
Coulsdon La CR5. . . . . . . 99 A8
Coulsdon Pl CR3. . . . . . . 100 D5
Coulsdon Rd CR3, CR5. . . 100 B7
Coulsdon Rise CR5. . . . . . 79 E2
Coulsdon Sixth Form Coll
CR5. . . . . 100 A8
Coulsdon South Sta CR5 . 79 D3
Coulthurst Ct SW16. . . . . 21 E1
Council Cotts
Betchworth RH3. . . . . . 116 D1
Loxwood RH14. . . . . . . 213 A4
Plaistow RH14. . . . . . . 211 D3
West End GU24. . . . . 67 F7
Countisbury Gdns KT15. . 52 B5
Countisbury Ho SE26. . . . 23 A5
Country Way TW16, TW15 . 15 C3
County Bsns Ctr RH11. . . 181 D2
County Mall RH10. . . . . . 201 E5
County Oak La RH11. . . . 181 D3
COUNTY OAK. 181 D2
County Oak Ind Est
RH10. . . . . 181 D2
County Oak Ret Pk RH11 181 D2
County Oak Way RH10,
RH11. . . . . 181 D2
County Par TW8. . . . . 6 D7
County Rd CR7. . . . . 42 B7
Courier Ho ⑰ SW2. . . . . . 22 A8
Courland Rd KT15. . . . . . 52 B7
Course Rd SL5. . . . . 29 A6
Court Ave CR5. . . . . 100 A8
Court Bushes Rd CR3. . . . 101 B7
Court Cl
East Grinstead RH19. . . . 185 F1
Twickenham TW2. . . . . . . 16 B5
Wallington SM6. . . . . 60 D3
Court Close Ave TW2. . . . 16 B5
Court Cres
Chessington KT9. . . . . . . 56 D4
East Grinstead RH19. . . . 185 F1
Court Downs Rd BR3. . . . . 44 B7
Court Dr
Carshalton SM1. . . . . . . 59 E6
Croydon CR0. . . . . 60 F6
Courtenay Ave SM2. . . . . 59 A2
Courtenay Dr BR3. . . . . . 44 D7
Courtenay Mews GU21. . . 70 A3
Courtenay Rd
Heath End GU9. . . . . . . 125 E7
North Cheam KT4, SM3. . . 58 C7
Penge BR3, SE20. . . . . . . 23 D2
Woking GU21. . . . . 70 A3
Court Farm Ave KT19. . . . 57 D5
Court Farm Gdns KT19 . . 76 C8
Court Farm Ind Est TW19. . 2 F1
Court Farm Pk CR6. . . . . . 81 A3
Court Farm Rd CR6. . . . . . 81 A2
Court Gdns GU15. . . . . . . 65 D5
Court Green Hts GU22. . . 89 C7
Court Haw SM7. . . . . 78 E4
Court Hill
Sanderstead CR2. . . . . . 80 E7
Woodmansterne CR5. . . . 78 F2
Courthope Rd SW19. . . . . 19 E3
Courthope Villas SW19. . . 19 E1
Court House Mansions
KT19. . . . . 76 D7
Court La
Dulwich SE21. . . . . 22 F8
Epsom KT19. . . . . 76 C6
Courtland Ave SW16. . . . . 21 F1
Courtlands
⑪ Beckenham BR3. . . . . 44 B7
⑩ Belmont SM2. . . . . . . 59 B3
Richmond TW10. . . . . 7 A2
② Walton-on-Thames KT12 35 A2
Courtlands Ave
Esher KT10. . . . . 55 A4
Hampton TW12. . . . . 15 F2
Richmond TW9. . . . . 7 B5
West Wickham BR2. . . . . 44 F1
Courtlands Cl CR2. . . . . . 62 A1
Courtlands Cres SM7. . . . 78 A3
Courtlands Dr KT19. . . . . 57 F4
Courtlands Rd KT5. . . . . . 38 A2
Courtleas KT11. . . . . 74 A6
Courtleigh Manor SL5. . . 30 A2
Court Lodge Rd RH6. . . . 160 F3
Courtney Cl SE19. . . . . . . 22 E2
Courtney Cres SM5. . . . . 59 F2
Courtney Pl
Cobham KT11. . . . . 73 F7
Croydon CR0. . . . . 61 A7
Dorking RH4. . . . . 115 D1
Courtney Rd
Croydon CR0, CR9. . . . . 61 A7
Mitcham SW19. . . . . 20 E1
Courtney Way TW6. . . . . . 3 A5
Courtoak La RH1. . . . . . . 162 C5
Court One TW15. . . . . 14 C5
Court Rd
⑩ Aldershot GU11. . . . . 105 A2
Banstead SM7. . . . . 78 A4
Caterham CR3. . . . . 100 E4
South Norwood SE25. . . . 42 F6
Tyler's Green RH9. . . . . 121 C4
Courts Hill Rd GU27. . . . 208 B6
Courtside SE23. . . . . 23 C7
Courts Mount Rd GU27. . 208 B6
Courts The SW16. . . . . . . 21 E1
Court The
Guildford GU2. . . . . 130 C7
Warlingham CR6. . . . . . . 81 E1
Court Three TW15. . . . . . 14 C5
Court Two TW15. . . . . . . 14 C5
Court Way TW2. . . . . 16 F8
Court Wood La CR0. . . . . 62 F1
Courtwood Prim Sch CR0 62 F1
Courtyard Apartments
TW11. . . . . 16 D3
Courtyard Bsns Ctr The
RH12. . . . . 217 B2
Courtyard The
Addlestone KT15. . . . . . . 52 C6
Cranleigh GU6. . . . . . . 153 E1
❶ Crawley RH10. . . . . . 201 D5
East Grinstead RH19. . . 186 B1
Faygate RH12. . . . . 218 E4
❶ Guildford GU1. . . . . 130 D8
Kingswood KT20. . . . . . . 98 C4
Oxted RH8. . . . . 122 E6
② Staines TW18. . . . . . . 12 F4
Thornton Heath CR0. . . . 41 F3
West Byfleet KT14. . . . . . 71 A7
Whyteleafe CR3. . . . . . . 80 F1
Coutts Ave KT9. . . . . 56 E5
Coval Gdns SW14. . . . . . . 7 B3
Coval La SW14. . . . . 7 B3
Coval Pas SW14. . . . . 7 C3
Coval Rd SW14. . . . . 7 C3
COVE. 84 D5
Coveham Cres KT11. . . . . 73 A6
Cove Inf Sch GU14. . . . . . 84 E6
Cove Jun Sch GU14. . . . . 84 E5
Coventry Hall SW16. . . . . 21 E3
Coventry Rd SE25. . . . . . 43 A5
Coverack Cl CR0. . . . . . . 43 E2
Cove Rd GU14. . . . . 84 F4
Coverdale Ct RH19. . . . . 185 C3
Coverdale Gdns CR0. . . . 61 F7
Covers La GU27. . . . . . . 207 C6
Covert Cl RH10. . . . . 201 E7
Coverton Rd SW17. . . . . . 20 E3
Coverts Cl GU9. . . . . 125 E4
Coverts Rd KT10. . . . . . . 55 F3
Covert The
Ascot SL5. . . . . 29 B2
Farnborough GU14. . . . . 84 E8
South Norwood SE19. . . . 22 F1
Covey Cl
Farnborough GU14. . . . . 85 A8
Merton SW19. . . . . 40 B7
Covey Rd KT4. . . . . 58 D8
Covey The RH10. . . . . . . 202 E8
Covington Gdns SW16. . . 22 B1
Covington Way
South Norwood SW16. . . . 22 A1
Streatham SW16. . . . . . . 21 F2
Cowbridge Mdw GU24. . . 87 C4
Cowden Cl GU9. . . . . 125 E3
Cowden St SE6. . . . . 24 A4
Cowdray Cl RH10. . . . . . 202 C5
Cowdrey Rd SW19. . . . . . 20 C3
Cowfold Cl RH11. . . . . . . 200 F3
Cowick Rd SW17. . . . . . . 20 F4
Cow La GU7. . . . . 150 D4
Cowleaze Rd KT2. . . . . . . 37 E8
Cowley Ave KT16. . . . . . . 32 F2
Cowley Cl CR2. . . . . 62 C2
Cowley Cres KT12. . . . . . 54 C6
Cowley La KT16. . . . . 32 F2
Cowley Rd SW14. . . . . 7 E4
Coworth Cl SL5. . . . . 30 B4
Coworth Flexlands Sch
GU24. . . . . 49 B6
Coworth Rd SL5. . . . . 30 A4
Cowper Ave SM1. . . . . . . 59 D6
Cowper Cl KT16. . . . . 32 F3
Cowper Gdns SM6. . . . . . 60 C4
Cowper Rd
Richmond TW10. . . . . . . 17 F3
Wimbledon SW19. . . . . . 20 C2
Cowshot Cres GU24. . . . . 87 D7
Cowslip La RH5. . . . . 115 B7
Coxbridge Bsns Pk GU10 145 E8
Coxbridge Mdws GU9. . . 124 F1
Coxbridge Rdbt GU9. . . . 145 F8
Cox Cnr RH5. . . . . 177 A7
Coxcombe La GU8. . . . . . 191 B4
Coxcomb Wlk RH11. . . . . 201 A4
Coxdean KT18. . . . . 97 C8
COX GREEN. 195 E2
Cox La
Chessington KT9. . . . . . . 56 F6
West Ewell KT19. . . . . . . 57 C5
Coxley Rise CR8. . . . . . . 80 C6
Coxs Ave TW17. . . . . 34 E6
Coxwell Rd SE19. . . . . . . 22 E2
Coxwold Path KT9. . . . . . 56 E3
Coydon Visitor Ctr ✦ ⑫
CR0. . . . . 61 D8
CR0, CR9 CR6. . . . . 82 F7
Crabbet Rd RH10. . . . . . 202 B7
Crab Hill BR3. . . . . 24 D1
Crab Hill La RH1. . . . . . . 140 F4
Crabtree Cl KT23. . . . . . . 94 C1
Crabtree Cnr TW20. . . . . 32 B8
Crabtree Dr KT22. . . . . . . 95 C2
Crabtree La
Churt GU10. . . . . 168 A2
Great Bookham KT23. . . . 94 C1
Headley KT18. . . . . 96 C1
Westhumble RH5. . . . . . 115 A5
Crabtree Office Village
TW20. . . . . 32 C7
Crabtree Rd
Camberley GU15. . . . . . . 65 B2
Crawley RH11. . . . . 201 C7
Thorpe TW20. . . . . 32 C7
Crabtree Wlk ⑧ CR0. . . . 43 A1
Crabwood RH8. . . . . 122 E7
Craddocks Ave
Ashtead KT21. . . . . 75 F3
Epsom KT18. . . . . 96 B6
Craddocks Cl KT21. . . . . . 76 A3
Craddocks Par KT21. . . . . 75 E2
Cradhurst Cl RH4. . . . . . 135 C6
Cradle La GU35. . . . . . . 166 C4
Crafnant Ct TW15. . . . . . 13 F3
Craigans RH11. . . . . 201 A5
Craigen Ave CR0. . . . . . . 43 B1
Craigmore Twr ⑪ GU22. . 89 E8
Craignair Rd SW2. . . . . . . 22 A8
Craignish Ave SW16. . . . . 41 F7
Craig Rd TW10. . . . . 17 C4
Craigside
Kingston upon Thames
KT2. . . . . 38 B8
Craigside continued
Purley CR8. . . . . 79 F5
Craigwell Ave TW13. . . . . 15 A5
Craigwell Cl TW18. . . . . . 32 E8
Crail Cl RG41. . . . . 25 A3
Crakell Rd RH2. . . . . 139 C8
Crake Pl GU47. . . . . 64 D8
Cramer Ct KT3. . . . . 38 C6
CRAMHURST. 170 E6
Cramhurst Ho ❸ SM1. . . . 59 D5
Cramhurst La GU8. . . . . . 170 E6
Cramond Ct TW14. . . . . . 14 E7
Crampshaw La KT21. . . . . 95 F7
Crampton Rd SE20. . . . . . 23 C2
Cranberry Wlk GU17. . . . . 64 F3
Cranborne Ave KT6. . . . . 57 A7
Cranborne Wlk RH10. . . . 201 F4
CRANBOURNE. 9 B6
Cranbourne Cl
Hersham KT12. . . . . 54 C4
Horley RH6. . . . . 161 B5
Thornton Heath SW16. . . 41 E6
Cranbourne Cotts SL4. . . . 9 B5
Cranbourne Ct KT12. . . . . 35 B2
Cranbourne Hall SL4. . . . . 9 B7
Cranbourne Prim Sch SL4. 9 A4
Cranbourne Twrs SL5. . . . 28 D8
Cranbrook Ct
⑩ Brentford TW8. . . . . . . 6 D8
Croydon CR2. . . . . 61 E5
Cranbrook Dr
Thames Ditton KT10. . . . 36 C1
Twickenham TW2. . . . . . . 16 B8
Cranbrook House SE19. . . 42 D8
Cranbrook Rd
Hounslow TW4. . . . . 4 F3
South Norwood CR7. . . . . 42 C7
Wimbledon SW19. . . . . . 19 E1
Cranbrook Terr GU6. . . . 174 F3
Crane Ave TW7. . . . . 6 A2
Cranebank TW4. . . . . 4 A4
Cranebank Mews TW7. . . . 6 A3
Cranebank Nature Reserve✦
TW14. . . . . 4 A5
Cranebrook TW2. . . . . . . 16 C6
Crane Ct
Sandhurst GU47. . . . . . . 64 D8
West Ewell KT19. . . . . . . 57 C6
Craneford Cl TW2. . . . . . 16 F8
Craneford Way TW2. . . . . 16 F8
Crane Ho
Catford BR1. . . . . 24 D3
Feltham TW13. . . . . 16 A5
Crane Lodge Rd TW5. . . . . 4 B8
Crane Mead Ct TW1. . . . . 16 F8
Crane Park Prim Sch
TW13. . . . . 15 F6
Crane Park Rd TW2. . . . . 16 B6
Crane Rd
Stanwell TW19. . . . . 3 A1
Twickenham TW2. . . . . . . 16 F7
Cranesbill Cl SW16. . . . . . 41 D7
Cranes Dr KT5. . . . . 37 F5
Cranes Park Ave KT5, KT6. 37 F5
Cranes Park Cres KT5. . . . 37 F5
Cranes Pk KT5, KT6. . . . . 37 E4
Craneswater TW6. . . . . . . 3 F7
Crane Way TW2. . . . . 16 C8
Cranfield Ct ⑥ GU21. . . . 68 F1
Cranfield Road E SM5. . . . 60 A2
Cranfield Road W SM5. . . 60 A2
CRANFORD. 4 C6
Cranford Ave TW19. . . . . 13 F8
Cranford Cl
Purley CR8. . . . . 80 C6
Stanwell TW19. . . . . 13 E8
Wimbledon SW20. . . . . . 19 B1
Cranford Com Coll TW5. . . 4 B8
Cranford Ct SM1. . . . . . . 59 C6
Cranford Jun & Inf Schs
TW4. . . . . 4 B5
Cranford La
Harlington TW6. . . . . 3 F6
Hatton TW6. . . . . 3 F4
Heston TW5. . . . . 4 F7
Cranford Lodge SW19. . . . 19 E6
Cranford Rise KT10. . . . . 55 C5
CRANLEIGH. 174 D2
Cranleigh CE Prim Sch
GU6. . . . . 174 D3
Cranleigh Cl
Penge SE20. . . . . 43 B7
Sanderstead CR2. . . . . . 81 A7
Cranleigh Ct
Farnborough GU14. . . . . 84 F4
Mitcham CR4. . . . . 40 D6
Richmond TW9. . . . . 7 A4
Cranleigh Gdns
Kingston upon Thames
KT2. . . . . 17 F2
Sanderstead CR2. . . . . . 81 A7
South Norwood SE25. . . . 42 E6
Sutton SM1. . . . . 59 B8
Cranleigh Ho SW20. . . . . 39 B7
Cranleigh L Ctr GU6. . . . 174 D2
Cranleigh Mead GU6. . . . 174 E3
Cranleigh Prep Sch GU6 174 D4
Cranleigh Rd
Ewhurst GU6. . . . . 175 D4
Feltham TW13. . . . . 14 F4
Merton SW19. . . . . 40 A6
Thames Ditton KT10. . . . 36 C1
Wonersh GU5. . . . . 152 C7
Cranleigh Sch GU6. . . . . 174 C5
Cranleigh Village Hospl
GU6. . . . . 174 D3
Cranley Cl GU1. . . . . 110 A1
Cranley Ct BR2. . . . . 44 D7
Cranley Dene GU1. . . . . . 110 A1
Cranley Gdns SM6. . . . . . 60 C3
Cranley Manor ④ GU1. . . 110 A1
Cranley Pl GU21. . . . . 68 D1
Cranley Rd
Guildford GU1. . . . . 109 F1
Hersham KT12. . . . . 53 F5
Cranmer Cl
Warlingham CR6. . . . . . . 81 E2
West Barnes SM4. . . . . . 39 E3
Weybridge KT13. . . . . . . 53 A3
Cranmer Ct
Hampton TW12. . . . . 16 B3
Kingston upon Thames KT2 . 17 D4
② Knaphill GU21. . . . . . 68 C1
Cranmere Prim Sch KT10. 36 C1
Cranmer Farm Cl CR4. . . . 40 F5
Cranmer Gdns CR6. . . . . . 81 E2
Cranmer Prim Sch CR4. . . 40 F5
Cranmer Rd
Croydon CR0, CR9. . . . . 61 C7
Hampton TW12. . . . . 16 B3
Kingston upon Thames KT2 . 17 E3
Mitcham CR4. . . . . 40 F5
Cranmer Terr SW17. . . . . 20 D3
Cranmer Wlk RH10. . . . . 202 C5
Cranmore Ave TW7. . . . . . 5 C7
Cranmore Cl GU11. . . . . . 104 E1
Cranmore Ct GU16. . . . . . 85 F4
Cranmore Gdns GU11. . . 104 E1
Cranmore La
Aldershot GU11. . . . . . . 104 E1
West Horsley KT24. . . . . 112 C6
Cranmore Prep Sch
KT24. . . . . 112 C6
Cranmore Rd
Catford BR1. . . . . 24 F5
Mytchett GU16. . . . . 86 A4
Cranston Cl
Hounslow TW3, TW4. . . . . 4 E5
Reigate RH2. . . . . 139 B8
Cranston Rd
East Grinstead RH19. . . . 185 F2
Forest Hill SE23. . . . . . . 23 E6
Cranston Way RH10. . . . . 204 C8
Cranstoun Cl GU3. . . . . . 108 F5
Crantock Rd SE6. . . . . . . 24 C6
Cranwell Ct CR0. . . . . 62 D8
Cranwell Gr
Lightwater GU18. . . . . . . 66 F8
Littleton TW17. . . . . 33 F5
Cranwell Rd TW6. . . . . 3 B5
Craster Rd SW2. . . . . 21 F8
Cravan Ave TW13. . . . . . . 15 A6
Craven Cl GU10. . . . . 146 C6
Craven Ct GU15. . . . . 64 F4
Craven Gdns SW19. . . . . . 20 B3
Craven Ho ② SW14. . . . . . 7 D4
Craven Rd
Crawley RH10. . . . . 202 B5
Croydon CR0. . . . . 62 F8
Kingston upon Thames KT2 . 37 F8
Cravens The RH6. . . . . . . 162 A3
Crawford Cl TW7. . . . . 5 E5
Crawford Gdns
Camberley GU15. . . . . . . 65 B5
Horsham RH13. . . . . . . 217 E4
Crawford Way RH19. . . . . 185 F3
CRAWLEY. 201 E5
Crawley Ave
Crawley, Ifield RH10,
RH11. . . . . 201 A6
Crawley RH10. . . . . 182 C1
Crawley Bsns Ctr RH10. . 181 E2
Crawley Bsns Quarter
RH10. . . . . 181 E1
Crawley Chase RG42. . . . . 8 B2
Crawley Coll RH11. . . . . . 201 C7
CRAWLEY DOWN. 204 C7
Crawley Down Rd RH10. . 184 F4
Crawley Down Village CE
Sch RH10. . . . . 204 B8
Crawley Dr GU15. . . . . . . 65 F6
Crawley Foyer The RH11 201 C6
CRAWLEY HILL. 65 E5
Crawley Hill GU15. . . . . . 65 F5
Crawley Hospl RH11. . . . 201 C6
Crawley La RH10. . . . . . . 202 C7
Crawley L Pk RH10. . . . . 201 D7
Crawley Mus Ctr✦ RH11 201 C5
Crawley Rd
Crawley RH11. . . . . 200 B1
Faygate RH12. . . . . 218 D7
Horsham RH12. . . . . . . 218 B5
Crawley Ridge GU15. . . . . 65 F6
Crawley Ridge Inf Sch
GU15. . . . . 65 F6
Crawley Ridge Jun Sch
GU15. . . . . 65 F7
Crawley Rise GU15. . . . . . 66 A7
Crawley Sta RH10. . . . . . 201 E5
Crawley Wood Cl GU15. . . 65 F5
Crawshaw Rd KT16. . . . . . 51 D4
Crawters Cl RH10. . . . . . 201 F7
Cray Ave KT21. . . . . 75 F2
Crayke Hill KT9. . . . . 56 E3
Crayonne Cl TW16. . . . . . 34 E8
Crealock St SW18. . . . . . . 20 B8
Creasys Dr RH11. . . . . . . 201 A1
Credenhill St SW16. . . . . 21 C2
Crediton Way KT10. . . . . . 56 A5
Credon Cl GU14. . . . . 84 F5
Creed Ct CR0. . . . . 61 F8
Creek Rd KT8. . . . . 36 E5
Creek The TW16. . . . . 35 A4
Creeland Gr SE6. . . . . . . 23 F7
Cree's Meadow GU20. . . . 48 D3
Creg Malin ⑦ TW10. . . . . . 6 E2

Cremorne Gdns KT19....57 D2
Crendon Ct TW13......15 B7
Crerar Cl GU14..........84 D3
Crescent Ct
　Beckenham BR3........44 B7
　Kingston upon Thames KT6..37 D4
Crescent Gdns SW19....20 A5
Crescent Gr CR4........40 E5
Crescent Ho 8 SW20....39 D8
Crescent La GU12......106 B5
Crescent Rd
　Beckenham BR3........44 B7
　Bletchingley RH1.....120 C2
　Caterham CR3.........101 A3
　East Grinstead RH19...185 D1
　Kingston upon Thames KT2..18 B1
　Reigate RH2..........139 A7
　Shepperton TW17.......34 C4
　Wimbledon SW20.......39 D8
　Wokingham RG40.......25 C5
Crescent Resource Ctr
　CR0..................63 C1
Crescent The
　Ashford TW15.........13 F3
　Barnes SW13...........7 F5
　Beckenham BR3........44 B8
　Belmont SM2..........78 A8
　Carshalton SM1.......59 D5
　Chertsey KT16.........33 A6
　East Molesey KT8......36 A5
　Egham TW20...........11 F2
　Epsom KT18...........76 A4
　Farnborough GU14.....85 C3
　Felcourt RH19........185 C8
　Guildford GU2........109 A3
　Harlington UB3........3 D7
　Heath End GU9........125 D8
　Horley RH6..........182 B8
　Horsham RH12........217 A2
　Kingston upon Thames KT6..37 E4
　Kingston upon Thames, Norbiton
　　KT3................38 C7
　Leatherhead KT22......95 B5
　Lower Halliford TW17..34 F2
　Reigate, Meadvale RH1..139 D6
　Reigate RH2..........118 B1
　Thornton Heath CR0, SE25..42 D3
　West Wickham BR4.....44 E3
　Weybridge KT13.......53 A7
　Wimbledon SW19.......20 A5
　Woking GU24...........88 A6
　Woldingham CR3......102 A4
Crescent Way
　Horley RH6..........161 A1
　South Norwood SW16...22 A1
Crescent Wood Rd SE21,
　SE26.................23 A5
Cressage Ho 9 TW8.....6 E8
Cressall Cl KT22.......95 B7
Cressall Mead KT22....95 B7
Cressingham Gr SM1....59 C6
Cressinghams The KT18..76 D6
Cresswell Ct TW19......2 D1
Cresswell Rd
　Croydon SE25.........43 A5
　Feltham TW13.........15 E4
　Twickenham TW1........6 D1
Cresta Dr KT15.........51 F1
Crest Hill GU5........133 E1
Creston Ave GU21......68 E3
Creston Way KT4.......39 D1
Crest Rd
　South Croydon CR2....62 B3
　West Wickham BR2.....44 F2
Crest The
　Surbiton KT5..........38 A4
　10 West Norwood SW27..22 B3
Crestwood Way TW4.....4 E2
Creswell GU21.........68 D2
Creswell Cnr GU21.....68 D2
Creswell Dr BR3.......44 B4
Crewdson Rd RH6.......161 B3
Crewe's Ave CR6.......81 D5
Crewe's Cl CR6........81 C2
Crewe's Farm La CR6...81 E2
Crewe's La CR6........81 D3
Crichton Ave SM6......60 D6
Crichton Rd SM5.......59 F3
Cricket Cl GU26.......188 D6
Cricket Ct RH19......185 E3
Cricketers Cl
　Chessington KT9......56 D6
　Ockley RH5..........177 C4
Cricketers La
　Englefield Green TW20..11 C4
　Windlesham GU20......48 A4
　Winkfield RG42........8 A3
Cricketers Terr 2 SM5..59 E7
Cricketers Wlk SE26...23 C3
Cricket Field Gr RG45..45 D4
Cricket Field Rd RH12..217 B1
Cricket Gn CR4........40 F5
Cricket Green Special Sch
　CR4..................40 E6
Cricket Hill RH1......140 F7
Cricket La
　Farnham GU10........146 D6
　Penge BR3............23 E3
Cricketts Hill GU5...133 A4
Cricket View KT13.....53 B5
Cricket Way KT13......53 E8
Cricklade Ave SW2.....21 F6
Crieff Ct 2 TW11......17 C1
Criffel Ave SW2.......21 E7
Crimea Rd GU11.......105 B2
Crimp Hill SL4, TW20..11 A6
Cripley Rd GU14........84 D6

Cripplecrutch Hill GU27..209 F5
Cripps Ho RH11.......201 B2
Crispen Rd TW13.......15 E4
Crispin Cl
　Ashtead KT21.........75 F1
　Wallington SM6.......60 E8
Crispin Cres CR0......60 D8
CRITCHMERE..........207 E7
Critchmere Hill GU27..207 E7
Critchmere La GU27....207 E6
Critchmere Vale GU27..207 E6
Criterion Bldgs KT7....37 B2
Crittenden Lodge BR4...44 A1
Critten La KT24, RH5..113 D2
Crocker Cl SL5........28 F8
Crockers La RH7......163 D4
Crockerton Rd GU7....20 F6
Crockford Cl KT15.....52 C6
Crockford Park Rd KT15..52 C5
Crockham Cl RH11....201 C4
Crocknorth Rd KT24...113 A2
CROOKED BILLET......19 C2
Crooked Billet SW19...19 C2
Crooksbury La GU10...147 E8
Crooksbury Rd
　Farnham GU10.......126 C2
　Tilford GU10........147 D8
Crocus Cl CR0.........43 D1
Croffets KT20..........97 D6
Croft Ave
　Dorking RH4.........115 B1
　West Wickham BR4.....44 C1
Croft Cl
　Harlington UB7........3 C7
　Wokingham RG41.......25 A2
Croft Ct SM1..........59 D8
Croft End Cl KT9.......56 F7
Crofters Cl
　Frimley GU16.........86 D8
　Isleworth TW7.........5 D2
　Redhill RH1.........140 B7
Crofter's Cl GU47.....64 A8
Crofters Mead CR0.....62 F2
Croftleigh Ave CR8....80 B3
Crofton
　Ashtead KT21.........75 E1
　Haslemere GU27......207 F7
Crofton Ave
　Chiswick W4..........7 D7
　Walton-on-Thames KT12..54 C7
Crofton Cl
　Bracknell RG12.......27 E4
　Ottershaw KT16.......51 C3
Crofton Terr TW9.......6 F3
Croft Rd
　Aldershot GU11......126 B8
　Carshalton SM1.......59 E5
　Godalming GU7.......150 E4
　Merton SW19.........20 C1
　South Norwood SW16...22 A1
　Witley GU8..........170 E6
　Wokingham RG40.......25 A1
　Woldingham CR3......102 A5
Crofts Cl GU8........191 B5
Croftside The SE25....43 A6
Crofts The TW17.......34 E5
Croft The
　Crawley RH11........201 A6
　Croydon CR9..........61 F7
　Elstead GU8.........148 E3
　Epsom KT17...........76 F5
　Heston TW5...........4 E7
　Leatherhead KT22.....94 E4
　New Malden KT3.......38 E4
　Wokingham RG40.......25 D5
Croft Way
　Frimley GU16.........65 F2
　Horsham RH12........217 A3
　Richmond TW10........17 B5
Croham Cl CR2........61 E4
Croham Manor Rd CR2..61 E4
Croham Mount CR2.....61 E3
Croham Park Ave CR0,
　CR2..................61 F5
Croham Rd
　Croydon CR0, CR2.....61 E5
　South Croydon CR2....61 E5
Croham Valley Rd CR2..62 B3
Croindene Rd SW16....41 E8
Cromar Ct GU21........69 C3
Cromer Ct SW16........21 E5
Cromer Mans 6 SM1....59 B5
Cromer Rd
　Croydon SE25.........43 B6
　Harlington TW6........3 A5
　Mitcham SW17........21 A2
Cromford Way KT3......38 D8
Crompton Fields RH10..181 E1
Crompton Way RH10...181 E1
Cromwell Ave KT3......38 E4
Cromwell Cl
　Staines TW18.........13 C2
　Walton-on-Thames KT12..35 B1
Cromwell Ct
　15 Kingston upon Thames
　KT2.................18 A1
　Knaphill GU21........88 C8
Cromwell Gr CR3......100 C6
Cromwell Ho 2 CR0.....61 B7
Cromwell Lodge TW13...14 F5
Cromwell Pl
　Cranleigh GU6.......174 F1
　1 East Grinstead RH19..205 F7
　Mortlake SW14.........7 A4
　16 Redhill RH1......118 F2
Cromwell Rd
　Ascot SL5............29 B4
　Beckenham BR3........44 A5
　Camberley GU15.......65 D7
　Caterham CR3........100 C6
　Feltham TW13.........15 B7
　Hounslow TW3..........5 A3
　Kingston upon Thames KT2..37 E8
　Redhill RH1.........118 F1

Cromwell Rd continued
　Teddington TW11......17 A2
　Thornton Heath CR0...42 D2
　Walton-on-Thames KT12..35 C1
　Wimbledon SW19.......20 B3
　Worcester Park KT4...57 E7
Cromwell St TW3........5 A3
Cromwell Way GU14....85 C7
Cromwell Wlk 3 RH1...118 F1
Crondall Ct GU15......65 B4
Crondall Ho SW15......19 A7
Crondall La GU9, GU10..124 D2
Crondall Rd GU10.....145 A6
Cronks Hill RH1, RH2..139 D7
Cronks Hill Cl RH1....139 D7
Cronks Hill Rd RH1....139 D7
CROOKED BILLET......19 C2
Crooksbury Rd
Crosby Cl TW13........15 E4
Crosby Hill Dr GU15...65 F7
Crosby Way
　Farnham GU10.......125 A1
　Streatham SW2........22 A8
Crosby Wlk SW2........22 A8
Crossacres GU22.......70 E4
Cross Deep TW1........17 A4
Cross Deep Gdns TW1...16 F6
Cross Farm Inf Sch GU16..85 E6
Cross Fell RG12........27 A5
Crossfield Pl KT13.....53 B3
Cross Gates Cl RG12...27 F6
Cross Gdns GU16.......85 F6
Cross Keys RH10......201 D6
Cross La
　Burstow RH6........162 C1
　Frimley GU16.........85 F6
　Ottershaw KT16.......51 C4
Cross Lances Rd TW3....5 B3
Crossland Rd
　Redhill RH1.........119 A1
　Thornton Heath CR7...42 B3
Crosslands KT16.......51 E6
Crosslands Rd KT19....57 D4
Cross Lanes GU1......130 F8
Crossleigh Ct SW16....21 C4
Crossley Cl TW16......83 D4
Crossman Ct RH11....201 B1
Crossman Hos 18 SW12..21 E8
Crossness Ho KT19.....57 A1
Cross Oak La RH1.....161 C7
Crosspath RH10......201 E7
Cross Rd
　Ash GU12...........106 B3
　Belmont SM2.........59 A1
　Carshalton SM1.......59 D5
　Croydon CR0..........42 D1
　Farnborough GU14.....84 E1
　Feltham TW13.........15 E4
　Kingston upon Thames KT2..17 F1
　Merton SW19.........20 A1
　Oatlands Park KT13....53 D7
　Purley CR8...........80 B6
　Tadworth KT20........97 C5
　Wentworth SL5.........30 A1
Crossroads The KT24..113 D7
Cross St
　6 Aldershot GU11....105 A2
　Farnborough GU14....105 C8
　Hampton TW12........16 C3
　Mortlake SW14.........7 A4
　Wokingham RG40.......25 C6
CROSSWATER.........167 E4
Crosswater La GU10...167 F4
Crossway
　Bracknell RG12.......27 C7
　Crawley RH6........181 F8
　West Barnes KT3, SW20..39 C5
CROSSWAYS..........170 F5
Crossways
　Aldershot GU12......105 C1
　Charlton TW16........14 F1
　Churt GU10.........167 F1
　Crawley RH10.......202 A7
　Effingham KT24......113 D8
　Egham TW20..........12 D2
　Guildford GU3.......107 C1
　South Croydon CR0, CR2..62 F3
　Sutton SM2...........59 D2
　Tatsfield TN16......103 C3
Crossways Ave RH19...185 C1
Crossways Cl
　Churt GU10.........167 F1
　Crawley RH10.......201 C7
Crossways Cotts GU6..194 A3
Crossways Ct TN16...103 C7
Crossways La RH2.....118 D7
Crossways Par CR0.....62 F3
Crossways Rd
　Beckenham BR3........44 A5
　Grayshott GU26......188 C3
　Mitcham CR4..........41 B6
Crossways The
　Abinger Hammer RH5..134 B3
　Coulsdon CR5........100 A8
　Guildford GU2.......129 F7
　Heston TW5...........4 F7
　Lower Kingswood RH2..118 C7
　Merstham RH1........119 C6
Crosswell Ct TW17.....34 C7
Crouch Cl BR3.........24 A2
Crouchfield RH4.......136 C4
Crouch Ind Est KT22...95 B8
Crouch La SL4..........8 F7

Crouchmans Cl SE21, SE26..23 A5
Crouch Oak La KT15....52 C6
Crowberry Cl 1 RH11..201 A2
Crowborough Cl CR6....81 C1
Crowborough Dr CR6....81 C1
Crowborough Rd SW17..21 A3
Crowcroft Cl GU2.....109 B5
Crowholt GU10.......145 F5
CROWHURST..........143 E3
Crowhurst SE25........43 A6
Crowhurst Cl RH10....202 E6
Crowhurst Keep RH10..202 E6
Crowhurst La RH7, RH8..143 D4
CROWHURST LANE
　END.................143 B5
Crowhurst Mead RH9..121 C5
Crowhurst Rd RH7.....164 D7
Crowhurst Village Rd
　RH7.................143 E2
Crowland Rd CR7.......42 D5
Crowland Wlk SM4......40 C3
Crowley Cres CR0......61 A5
Crowmarsh Gdns SE23..23 C8
Crown Arc KT1.........37 D7
Crownbourne Ct SM1...59 B6
Crown Cl
　Colnbrook SL3........1 C7
　Walton-on-Thames KT12..35 C2
Crown Cotts
　Bracknell SL5........28 C4
　Oxshott KT22........74 B5
Crown Ct
　Godalming GU7.......150 E4
　4 Twickenham TW1....17 B8
Crown Dale SE19, SE27..22 C3
Crown Dr GU9.........126 A5
Crown Hill Ct SL5.....29 B4
Crown Ho CR0..........61 C8
Crown Hts GU1........130 E6
Crown La
　Badshot Lea GU9.....126 A5
　Merton SM4, SW19.....40 A6
　South Norwood SW16...22 A2
　Virginia Water GU25...31 D3
Crown Lane Gdns SE27..22 A3
Crown Lane Prim Sch
　SW16................22 B3
Crown Mdw SL3..........1 B7
Crown Mill CR4.........40 E4
Crown Par SM4.........40 A5
Crown Pas KT1.........37 D7
Crownpits La GU7.....150 E3
Crown Pl GU47........45 E1
Crown Point Par SE19..22 B2
Crown Rd
　Kingston upon Thames
　KT3.................38 C8
　Morden SM4, SW19.....40 B5
　Sutton SM1...........59 B6
　Twickenham TW1........6 B1
　Virginia Water GU25...31 C3
Crown Rise RH1........32 F1
Crown Row RG12........27 D3
Crown St TW20.........12 A4
Crown Terr TW9.........6 F3
Crowntree Cl TW7......5 F8
CROWN WOOD..........27 D3
Crown Wood Prim Sch
　RG12................27 E3
Crown Yard TW3........5 C4
Crowther Rd SE25.....43 A5
CROWTHORNE.........45 D5
Crowthorne Bsns Est The
　RG45................45 D7
Crowthorne CE Prim Sch
　RG45................45 C5
Crowthorne Cl SW18...19 F7
Crowthorne Lodge RG12..27 B5
Crowthorne Rd
　Bracknell, Easthampstead
　RG12................27 A5
　Bracknell RG40, RG12..26 F2
　Sandhurst GU47.......45 B2
Crowthorne Road N RG12..27 B6
Croxall Ho KT12.......35 C3
Croxden Wlk SM4.......40 C3
Croxted Cl SE21.......22 C8
Croyde Cl GU14........85 A7
CROYDON.............61 D7
Croydon Airport Ind Est
　CR9.................60 F4
Croydon Coll Annexe CR0..42 D1
Croydon Flyover The CR0,
　CR9.................61 C7
Croydon Gr CR0........42 B1
Croydon Higher Education
　Coll CR9............61 D8
Croydon High Sch CR2..62 D1
Croydon Ho CR0........41 F3
Croydon La SM7........78 D6
Croydon Lane S SM7...78 B5
Croydon Rd
　Beckenham BR3........43 E6
　Caterham CR3........101 A5
　Coney Hall BR2, BR4...63 F7
　Croydon CR0, SM6.....60 D7
　Harlington TW6........3 B4
　Mitcham CR0, CR4, CR9..41 C4
　Penge SE20...........43 C8
　Reigate RH2.........118 C2
　Tatsfield TN16......103 F3
　Titsey CR6..........102 D5
Croydon Road Ind Est
　BR3.................43 D5
Croydon Tutorial Coll 11
　CR0.................61 C6

Cre-Cum 243

Croydon Valley Trad Pk
　CR0.................41 E2
Croylands Dr KT6......37 E2
Croysdale Ave TW16....35 A6
Crozier Dr CR2........62 B1
Cruikshank Lea GU47...64 E6
Crunden Rd CR2........61 D3
Crundwell Ct GU9.....125 D3
Crusader Gdns CR0.....61 E7
Crusoe Rd CR4.........20 F1
Crutchfield La
　Sidlow RH6.........160 B5
　Walton-on-Thames KT12..54 B8
Crutchley Rd
　Catford SE6..........24 E6
　Wokingham RG40.......25 D7
Crystal Ct SE19.......22 F3
CRYSTAL PALACE......23 A3
Crystal Palace Farm Park*
　SE19................23 A3
Crystal Palace Mus*
　SE19................22 F2
Crystal Palace National
　Sports Ctr SE19.....23 A2
Crystal Palace Par SE19..22 F3
Crystal Palace Park Rd SE19,
　SE26................23 B3
Crystal Palace Sta SE23..23 A2
Crystal Palace Station Rd
　SE19................23 A2
Crystal Terr SE19.....22 D2
Crystal View Ct BR1...24 D4
Cubitt Way GU21.......68 D1
Cuckfield Cl RH11....200 F3
Cuckmere Cres RH11..200 F5
Cuckoo La GU24.......67 D6
Cuckoo Vale GU24.....67 D6
Cuda's Cl KT19........57 F6
Cuddington Ave KT4....57 F6
Cuddington Cl KT20....97 D7
Cuddington Com Prim Sch
　KT4.................57 F7
Cuddington Croft Prim Sch
　SM2.................58 D2
Cuddington Glade KT19..76 A7
Cuddington Nature Reserve*
　SM2.................77 F7
Cuddington Park Cl SM7..77 F6
Cuddington Way SM2,
　SM7.................77 D8
Cudham Cl SM2........59 A1
Cudham Dr CR0........82 C8
Cudham Rd TN16......103 E8
Cudham St SE6........24 C8
CUDWORTH..........179 F8
Cudworth La
　Cudworth RH5.......179 E8
　Newdigate RH5......158 C1
Cudworth Pk RH5.....179 F8
Cuffs Hill RH10.....202 C2
Cullens Mews 5 GU11..105 A3
Cullerne Cl KT17......57 F1
Cullesden Rd CR8......80 B4
Cull's Rd GU3........107 C1
CULMER.............170 F3
Culmer Hill GU8......170 F2
Culmer La GU8........171 A2
Culmington Rd CR2....61 C2
Culsac Rd 1 KT6.......56 E8
Culverden Ct KT13.....53 D7
Culverden Rd SW12....21 C6
Culverden Terr 5 KT13..53 D7
Culver Dr RH8........122 E5
Culverhay KT21........75 E3
Culver Ho GU1........110 A1
Culverhouse Gdns SW16..21 F5
Culverlands Cres GU12..106 A3
Culverley Rd SE6......24 C7
Culver Rd GU47........45 D1
Culvers Ave SM5.......59 F8
Culvers House Prim Sch
　CR4.................41 A1
Culvers Retreat SM5...59 F8
Culverstone Cl BR2....44 F4
Culvers Way SM5.......59 F8
Culworth Ho GU1.....130 E8
Cumber Ho SW18.......20 A7
Cumberland Ave GU2,
　GU3................109 A6
Cumberland Cl
　Epsom KT19..........57 E1
　2 Twickenham TW1.....6 B1
　13 Wimbledon SW20....19 D1
Cumberland Ct
　4 Croydon CR0.......42 D1
　North Cheam KT4.....39 B1
Cumberland Dr
　Bracknell RG12.......27 E8
　Chessington KT9......56 F7
　Hinchley Wood KT10...56 A8
Cumberland Ho KT2....18 B1
Cumberland Lodge SL4..10 D3
Cumberland Pl
　Catford SE6..........24 F7
　Sunbury TW16........35 A5
Cumberland Rd
　Ashford TW15.........13 D5
　Barnes SW13..........7 F6
　Beckenham BR2.......44 F6
　Croydon SE25.........43 B3
　Frimley GU15.........66 C4
　Richmond TW9.........7 A7
Cumberlands CR8......80 D4
Cumberland St TW18...12 D3

244 Cum–Del

Cumberlow Ave SE25.... 43 A6
Cumbernauld Gdns TW16. 14 F3
Cumbernauld Wlk RH11 . 200 E2
Cumbrae Gdns KT6 .... 56 D8
Cumbria Ct
  Farnborough GU14 ...... 85 E1
  Reigate RH2................118 D2
Cumnor Gdns KT17 .... 58 A4
Cumnor House Sch CR2.. 61 B2
Cumnor Rd SM2 .... 59 C4
Cumnor Rise CR8 .... 80 C2
Cumnor Way RG12 ...... 27 E5
Cunard Mews GU6 ..... 193 C2
Cunliffe Cl KT18 .... 96 B3
Cunliffe Rd KT19 .... 57 F6
Cunliffe St SW16 .... 21 C2
Cunningham Ave GU1.. 110 B2
Cunningham Cl BR4.... 63 B8
Cunningham Rd SM7.... 78 D4
Cunnington Rd GU14.... 85 E2
Cunworth Ct RG12 ...... 26 F3
Curfew Bell Rd KT16 .... 32 F2
Curlew Cl CR2 .... 81 D8
Curlew Ct
  Aldershot GU11.........126 A7
  Tolworth KT6............. 57 A7
Curlew Gdns GU4........110 D3
Curley Hill Rd GU18 .... 66 F7
Curling Cl CR5............100 A1
Curling Vale GU2 ....130 A2
Curl Way RG41............ 25 A5
Curly Bridge Cl GU14.... 84 F8
Curnick's La SE27........ 22 C4
Curran Ave SM6 .... 60 A4
Currie Hill Cl SW19 .... 19 F4
Currie Ho [11] SW12.......... 21 D8
Curteys Wlk RH11........201 A3
Curtis Cl GU15............ 66 C7
Curtis Field Rd SW16.... 22 A4
Curtis Gdns [2] RH4........136 A8
Curtis Rd
  Dorking RH4............136 A8
  Twickenham TW4........ 15 F4
  West Ewell KT19 .... 57 C6
Curtis Road Ind Est RH4 135 C4
Curvan Cl KT17 .... 57 F1
Curzon Ave RH12 ....217 B3
Curzon Cl KT13 .... 53 A6
Curzon Ct BR2............ 44 D7
Curzon Rd
  Thornton Heath CR7 .... 42 A3
  Weybridge KT13 .... 53 A5
Cusack Cl TW1............ 16 F4
Cuthbert Gdns SE25.... 42 E6
Cuthbert Rd
  Ash GU12................106 B6
  Thornton Heath CR0, CR9.. 61 B8
Cuttinglye La RH10......184 A1
Cuttinglye Rd RH10......184 C2
Cutts Rd GU11............105 D7
Cyclamen Cl [4] TW12 ...... 16 A2
Cyclamen Way KT19.... 57 C5
Cygnet Ave TW14 ...... 15 D8
Cygnet Cl GU21.......... 69 B3
Cygnets Cl RH1............119 A3
Cygnets The
  Feltham TW13 .... 15 E4
  [6] Staines TW18 .... 12 F3
Cypress Ave TW2 ...... 16 C8
Cypress Ct
  Charlton TW16.......... 34 E8
  Sutton SM1 .... 59 A4
  Thorpe GU25............ 31 F5
  [8] West Norwood SW16... 22 A3
Cypress Gr GU21........105 F7
Cypress Hill Ct GU14.... 64 F1
Cypress Inf Sch SE25.... 42 E7
Cypress Jun Sch SE25.... 42 E7
Cypress Lodge SE25.... 42 E7
Cypress Rd
  Guildford GU1..........109 C4
  South Norwood SE25.... 42 E7
Cypress Way
  Banstead KT17 .... 77 D5
  Blackwater GU17...... 64 B5
  Grayshott GU26........188 D2
Cypress Wlk TW20 ...... 11 B2
Cyprians Ave GU24...... 88 B6
Cyprus Rd GU16.......... 86 D8
Cyrillian Ho [3] SM2........ 59 B4

D

D'abernon Cl KT10...... 55 A6
D'Abernon Dr KT11 .... 73 E3
Dacre Rd CR0............ 41 E2
Dacres Rd SE23.......... 23 D5
Daffodil Cl
  Croydon CR0 .... 43 D1
  [7] Hampton TW12.......... 16 A2
Daffodil Dr GU24........ 68 A3
Dafforne Rd SW17 ...... 21 A5
Dagden Rd GU4..........130 E3
Dagmar Rd
  [4] Kingston upon Thames
  KT2......................18 A1
  South Norwood SE25.... 42 E4
Dagnall Pk CR0, SE25.. 42 E4
Dagnall Rd SE25 .... 42 E3
Dagnan Rd SW12 ...... 21 C8
Dahlia Gdns CR4........ 41 D5
Dahomey Rd SW16...... 21 C2
Daimler Way SM6........ 60 E3
Dainford Cl BR1 .... 24 D3

Dairy Cl CR7..............42 C7
Dairyfields RH11..........201 A5
Dairy Gate Rd GU14....105 B8
Dairymans Wlk GU4....110 B6
Daisy Cl CR0.............. 43 D1
Daisy Mdw TW20........ 12 A3
Dakin Cl RH10............202 C2
Dakins The RH19........205 E8
Dakota SM6.............. 60 F3
Dalcross RG12 .... 27 E3
Dalcross Rd TW4, TW5..4 E5
Dale Ave TW4 ....4 E4
Dalebury Rd SW17 .... 20 F6
Dale Cl
  Addlestone KT15........ 52 B5
  Horsham RH12..........217 F5
  Leatherhead KT23......94 C2
  Sunningdale SL5........ 30 A4
  Wrecclesham GU10....145 F7
Dale Ct [3] KT2................17 F1
Daledene RH19..........205 B8
Dalegarth Gdns CR8.... 80 D6
Daleham Ave TW20 .... 12 A2
Dale Gdns GU47........ 64 A8
Dale Lodge Rd SL5...... 30 A4
Dale Park Ave SM5...... 59 F8
Dale Park Rd SE19...... 42 D8
Dale Rd
  Ashford TW16.......... 14 F1
  Cheam SM1.............. 58 F6
  Forest Row RH18........206 F1
  Purley CR8.............. 80 B7
  Walton-on-Thames KT12.. 34 F2
Daleside Rd
  Streatham SW17........ 21 B3
  West Ewell KT19........ 57 D4
Dale View
  Haslemere GU27.......207 F5
  Headley KT18............ 96 B4
  Woking GU21............ 69 B1
Dalewood Gdns
  Crawley RH10..........201 F8
  North Cheam KT4...... 58 B8
Dalkeith Rd SE21........ 22 C8
Dallas Ct SM3............ 58 E4
Dallas Rd
  Cheam SM3.............. 58 E4
  Forest Hill SE26........ 23 B5
Dallaway Gdns RH19....185 E1
Dalley Ct GU47.......... 64 D7
Dallington Cl KT12...... 54 C4
Dalmain Prim Sch SE23 .. 23 E7
Dalmain Rd SE23........ 23 D7
Dalmally Pas CR0........ 42 F2
Dalmally Rd CR0........ 43 A2
Dalmeny Ave
  North Cheam KT4...... 58 B7
  Wallington SM5........ 60 A3
Dalmeny Cres TW3...... 5 D3
Dalmeny Rd
  North Cheam KT4...... 58 B7
  Wallington SM5........ 60 A3
Dalmore Ave KT10 .... 55 F4
Dalmore Rd SE21........ 22 C6
Dalston Cl GU15........ 66 D3
Dalton Ave CR4.......... 40 E7
Dalton Cl
  Crawley RH11..........201 B1
  Purley CR8.............. 80 C7
Dalton Ct GU16.......... 86 D8
Dalton Ho
  [8] Balham SW12.......... 21 B8
  Merton SW19.......... 40 C8
Dalton St SE27.......... 22 B5
Damascene Wlk SE21 .. 22 C7
Damask Cl GU24........ 67 E6
Damask Ct SM1.......... 40 B1
Damer Ho [10] TW10..........6 F1
Damson Way SM5...... 59 F2
Danbrook Rd SW16...... 21 E1
Dan Bryant Ho [5] SW12.. 21 C8
Danbury Mews SM6.... 60 B6
Danby Ct RH6............161 B5
Dancer Rd TW9 ....7 A4
Danebury CR0............ 63 B4
Danebury Ave SW15.... 7 E1
Danebury Wlk GU16.... 85 F8
Daneby Rd SE6.......... 24 C6
Danecourt Gdns CR0.. 61 F7
Danecroft Rd SE24 .... 22 C2
Danefield Rd KT23...... 94 C5
Danehurst TW8 ....6 C7
Danehurst Cl TW20 .... 11 E2
Danehurst Cres RH13...217 F2
Danehurst Ct KT17...... 76 F6
Danemore La RH9......142 E2
Dane Rd
  Ashford TW15.......... 14 D2
  Merton SW19.......... 40 C8
  Warlingham CR6........ 81 D2
Danesbury Rd TW13.... 15 B7
Danes Cl KT22..........74 C5
Danescourt Cres SM1 .. 59 C8
Danesfield
  Send Marsh GU23...... 90 F4
  Wokingham RG40 ...... 25 D6
Danesfield Cl KT12...... 54 B8
Danesfield Manor Sch
  KT12......................54 C8
Daneshill RH1............118 E2
Danes Hill GU22........ 70 B1
Daneshill Cl RH1........118 E2
Danes Hill Pre-Prep Sch
  KT22......................74 C6
Danes Hill Sch KT22.... 74 C5
Danesmead KT11........ 74 A8
Danesrood GU1..........130 F8
Danes Way KT22........ 74 D5
Daneswood Ave SE6.... 24 C5

Daneswood Cl KT13......53 C5
Danetree Cl KT19........ 57 C3
Danetree Rd KT19........ 57 D3
Danetree Sch KT19...... 57 C4
Daniel Cl
  Mitcham SW17, SW19.. 20 E2
  Twickenham TW4........ 15 F8
Daniel Ct [3] BR3............ 24 A1
Daniell Way CR0, CR9.. 41 F1
Daniels La KT6............ 81 F4
Daniel Way SM7........ 78 B5
Danley La GU27..........207 A3
Danses Cl GU4..........110 D3
Danvers Way CR3........100 C4
Dapdune Ct GU1........109 C1
Dapdune Rd GU1........109 D1
Dapdune Wharf* GU1 .. 109 C1
Daphne Ct KT4.......... 57 E8
Daphne Jackson Rd GU2 129 E8
Daphne St SW18........ 20 C8
Darby Cl CR3............100 C5
Darby Cres TW16........ 35 C7
Darby Gdns TW16...... 35 C7
DARBY GREEN 64 B6
Darby Green La
  Blackwater GU17........ 64 B5
  Blackwater GU46...... 64 A5
Darby Green Rd GU17.. 64 B5
Darcy Ave SM6.......... 60 C6
Darcy Cl CR5............100 B8
Darcy Pl KT21.......... 75 F2
Darcy Rd
  Ashtead KT21.......... 75 F2
  Isleworth TW7..........6 A6
  Thornton Heath SW16.. 41 E7
D'arcy Rd SM3.......... 58 D6
Darell Prim Sch TW9.... 7 A4
Darell Rd TW9 ....7 A4
Darent Ho BR1............ 24 D3
Darenth Way RH6........160 F6
Darfield Rd GU4..........110 A4
Dargate Cl SE19........ 22 F1
Dark La GU3..............128 A4
Darlaston Rd SW19...... 19 E1
Darley Cl
  Addlestone KT15........ 52 C5
  Croydon CR0 .... 43 E3
Darleydale RH11..........201 C3
Darleydale Cl GU47 .... 45 D2
Darley Dene Ct KT15.... 52 C5
Darley Dene Inf Sch KT15 52 C5
Darley Dr KT3............ 38 D7
Darley Gdns SM4........ 40 B3
Darling Ho [24] TW1..........6 D1
Darlington Ct SE6...... 24 F7
Darlington Ho [2] KT6...... 37 D2
Darlington Rd SE27 .... 22 B3
Darmaine Cl CR2........ 61 C3
Darnley Pk KT13........ 53 B7
Darracott Cl GU15...... 66 B8
Darrell Ct BR2............ 44 E6
Darsena Ho [6] SM2........ 59 C3
Dart Cl SL3..............1 B8
Dart Ct RH10............186 A3
Dartmouth Ave GU21.. 70 D5
Dartmouth Cl RG12 .... 27 E6
Dartmouth Gn GU21.... 70 D5
Dartmouth Ho
  [17] Kingston upon Thames
  KT2......................37 E8
  Thornton Heath CR0.... 42 B1
Dartmouth Path GU21.. 70 D5
Dartmouth Pl
  Chiswick W4 ....7 E8
  Forest Hill SE23........ 23 C6
Dartmouth Rd SE23, SE26 .. 23 C5
Dartnell Ave KT14...... 71 B7
Dartnell Cl KT14........ 71 B7
Dartnell Cres KT14...... 71 B7
Dartnell Ct KT14........ 71 C7
DARTNELL PARK 71 C7
Dartnell Park Rd KT14.. 71 C8
Dartnell Pl KT14........ 71 B7
Dartnell Rd CR0........ 42 F2
Dart Rd GU14............ 84 D6
Darvel Cl GU21.......... 69 A3
Darvills La GU9..........125 C2
Darwall Dr SL5.......... 28 D7
Darwin Cl RH12..........217 F4
Darwin Ct
  Camberley GU15........ 65 B3
  Guildford GU1..........109 D5
Darwin Gr GU11..........105 C3
Darwin Pl RG12.......... 27 C5
Daryngton Dr GU1......110 B1
Dashwood Cl
  Bracknell RG12.......... 27 D8
  West Byfleet KT14...... 71 C7
Dashwood Ct TW3...... 5 C3
Dashwood Ho SE21.... 22 F5
Dashwood Lang Rd KT15. 52 E6
Dassett Rd SE27........ 22 B3
Datchet Rd SE6..........23 A6
Date Valley Sch CR4.... 40 F6
Daubeney Pl TW12...... 36 C8
Davenant Rd CR0, CR9.. 61 B6
Davenport Cl TW11 .... 17 A2
Davenport Lo TW5......4 E7
Davenport Lodge TW5... 4 E7
Davenport Rd RG12...... 27 E8
Daventry Cl SL3..........1 B6
Daventry Ct RG42...... 27 B8
Dave Porter Hts SW18.. 19 E8
David Cl UB3..............3 E7
David Ct [1] TW18.......... 13 A4

David Henry Waring Ct
  TW14..................14 C7
David Ho SE25............ 43 A6
David Livingstone Prim Sch
  CR7......................42 C8
David Rd SL3..............1 F5
Davids Ct SE6............ 24 A3
Davidson Lodge CR0.... 42 E2
Davidson Prim Sch CR0.. 42 E3
Davidson Rd CR0........ 42 F3
David's Rd SE23.......... 23 C7
David Twigg Cl [7] KT2.... 37 E8
Davies Cl
  Croydon CR0, SE25.... 43 A3
  Farncombe GU7........150 D7
Davies Walk TW7 ....5 D6
Davington Cl [16] SM2...... 59 A3
Davis Cl RH11............201 A1
Davis Gdns GU47...... 64 E7
Davison Cl KT19........ 76 B8
Davis Rd
  Chessington KT9...... 57 A6
  Weybridge KT13 ...... 52 F1
Davis Road Ind Pk KT9.. 57 A6
Davos GU22..............89 C8
Davy Cl RG40............ 25 C5
Dawell Dr TN16.......... 83 C2
Dawes Ave TW7 ....6 A3
Dawes Ct KT10.......... 55 B6
DAWESGREEN 137 F3
Dawes Green Cotts RH2.. 138 A3
Dawley Ride SL3..........1 E6
Dawlish Ave SW18...... 20 B6
Dawnay Cl SL5.......... 28 F8
Dawnay Cty Prim Sch
  KT23......................94 A1
Dawnay Gdns SW18.... 20 D6
Dawnay Rd
  Camberley GU15........ 65 B7
  Great Bookham KT23.. 94 C1
  Wandsworth SW17, SW18 .. 20 D6
Dawn Cl TW4..............4 E4
Dawn Ct GU15............ 65 F7
Dawney Hill GU24...... 87 F5
Dawneys Rd GU24...... 87 F5
Dawn Redwood Cl SL3.. 1 A4
Dawn Rise RH10..........183 A3
Dawn Wlk BR2............ 44 D7
Dawsmere Cl GU15...... 66 C5
Dawson Rd
  Byfleet KT14............ 71 E8
  Kingston upon Thames KT1.. 37 F6
Daws Pl RH1............119 C4
Dax Ct TW16............ 35 C6
Daybrook Rd SW19...... 40 B6
Day Ct GU6..............173 F2
Daymerslea Ridge KT22 .. 95 C6
Day's Acre CR2.......... 61 F1
Daysbrook Rd SW2...... 21 F7
Dayseys Hill RH1........162 A8
Dayspring GU2..........109 B5
Daytone Ho SW20...... 39 D8
Deacon Cl
  Downside KT11........ 93 B8
  Wallington CR8........ 60 E2
  Wokingham RG40 ...... 25 C8
Deacon Ct KT7.......... 164 C4
Deacon Field GU2...... 109 A2
Deacon Ho SM2........ 59 A1
Deacon Rd KT2........ 37 F8
Deacons Wlk TW12 .... 16 A4
Deadbrook La GU12....105 E3
Deal Rd SW17............ 21 A2
Dean City Farm* SW19 .. 40 C7
Dean Cl GU22............ 70 E3
Dean Ct
  [6] Chertsey KT16.......... 33 A3
  Farncombe GU7........150 D6
  [10] Kingston upon Thames
  KT2......................18 A1
Deanery Pl [1] GU7..........150 D4
Deanery Rd GU7........150 E6
Deanfield Gdns CR0.... 61 D6
Dean Gr RG40............ 25 C7
Deanhill Ct SW14........7 B3
Deanhill Rd SW14........7 B3
Dean La RH1..............99 C3
Deanoak La RH2........159 D8
Dean Par GU15.......... 65 F8
Dean Rd
  Croydon CR0............ 61 D6
  Farncombe GU7........150 D6
  Hampton TW12........ 16 A3
  Isleworth TW3..........5 B2
Deans Cl
  Chiswick W4 ....7 B8
  South Croydon CR0.... 61 F7
  Walton on the Hill KT20.. 97 B3
Deans Ct GU20.......... 48 D4
Deansfield CR3..........100 F4
Deansgate RG12........ 27 B2
Deans Gate Cl SE23.... 23 D5
Dean Shaw Cotts RH8.. 122 A4
Deanside GU15.......... 65 F8
Deans La
  Nutfield RH1............120 A2
  Walton on the Hill KT20.. 97 B2
Deans Rd
  Merstham RH1..........119 C5
  Sutton SM1 .... 59 B7
Deans Wlk CR5.......... 80 A1
Dean Wlk KT23.......... 94 B1
Dearmer Ho [2] SW2........ 22 A8
De'arn Gdns CR4........ 40 E6
Debden Cl KT2............ 17 D3
Deborah Cl TW7 ....5 E6
De Broome Rd TW13.... 15 C7
De Burgh Gdns KT20.. 97 D8

De Burgh Ho [10] SW19.... 20 C1
De Burgh Pk SM7...... 78 B4
Deburgh Rd SW19...... 20 C1
Decimus Cl [1] CR7.......... 42 D5
Decon Pl CR3..........100 C4
Dedham Ho SE6.......... 24 C4
Dedisham Cl RH10......202 A5
Dedswell Dr GU4........111 A6
Deedman Cl GU12......106 A2
DEEPCUT................86 C6
Deepcut Bridge Rd GU16.. 86 C7
Deepdale
  Bracknell RG12.......... 27 A5
  Horley RH6..............161 B2
  Wimbledon SW19 .... 19 D4
Deepdale Ave BR2...... 44 F5
Deepdale Cl CR0........ 61 D6
DEEPDENE................136 C8
Deepdene
  Farnham GU10..........146 D7
  Haslemere GU27........207 E6
Deepdene Ave
  Dorking RH4, RH5........136 C6
  South Croydon CR0.... 61 F7
Deepdene Avenue Rd
  RH4......................115 C1
Deepdene Ct BR2...... 44 E6
Deepdene Dr RH4........136 C6
Deepdene Gdns
  Dorking RH4............136 C8
  Streatham SW2........ 21 F8
Deepdene Lodge [8] SW2.. 21 F8
Deepdene Park Rd RH5.. 136 C8
Deepdene Point [9] SE26.. 23 D5
Deepdene Rdbt RH4.... 136 C8
Deepdene Vale RH4.... 115 C1
Deepdene Wood RH5.. 136 D7
Deepfield Rd RG12...... 27 D7
Deepfields RH6..........160 F5
Deepfield Way CR5.... 79 E3
Deep Pool La GU24...... 69 B6
Deepwell Cl TW7 ......6 A6
Deep Well Dr GU15...... 65 E5
Deerbarn Rd GU2........109 B2
Deerbrook Rd SE24.... 22 B7
Dee Rd TW9..............6 F3
Deerhurst
  Kingston upon Thames
  KT2......................38 B8
  Streatham SW16........ 21 E3
Deerhurst Cl TW13...... 15 B5
Deerhurst Cres TW12.. 16 C3
Deerhurst Ct CR0........ 42 B1
Deerhurst Rd SW16.... 21 F3
Deerings Rd RH2........118 C1
Deerleap GU35..........187 C4
Deer Leap GU18........ 67 A8
Deerleap Cotts RH5.... 134 C4
Deerleap Rd RH4........135 B6
Deer Park Cl KT2........ 18 B1
Deer Park Gdns CR4.... 40 D5
Deer Park Rd SW19.... 40 C7
Deer Park Way BR4.... 63 F8
Deer Rock Hill RG12.... 27 C3
Deer Rock Rd GU15.... 65 F8
Deers Farm Cl GU23.... 71 E3
Deerstead Ho GU22.... 89 B8
Deerswood Cl
  Caterham CR3..........101 A3
  Crawley RH11..........201 B7
Deerswood Rd RH11....201 A7
Deerswood Rd RH11....201 B7
Deer Way RH12..........217 A1
Deeside Rd SW17...... 20 D5
Dee Way KT19............ 57 E1
Defence Evaluation &
  Research Agency GU14.. 84 C1
Defiant Way SM6........ 60 E3
Defoe Ave TW9 ....7 A7
Defoe Cl SW17, SW19 .. 20 E2
Defoe Pl SW17..........20 F4
De Frene Rd SE23, SE26.. 23 E5
De Havilland Dr KT13.. 71 E8
De Havilland Rd TW5.. 4 C7
De Havilland Way TW19.. 2 E1
Delabole Rd RH1........119 E6
Delacy Ct SM2.......... 78 A8
Delamare Cres CR0.... 43 C3
Delamere Rd
  Reigate RH2.............139 C5
  Wimbledon SW20 .... 39 D8
Delancey Ct RH13......217 C4
Delaporte Cl KT17...... 76 E7
De Lara Way GU21...... 69 D1
De La Warr Rd RH19.. 185 F1
Delcombe Ave KT4...... 39 C1
Delderfield KT21.......... 95 D6
Delfont Cl RH10..........202 D4
Delft Ho KT2............37 F8
Delia St SW18............ 20 B8
Delius Gdns RH12......218 B4
Dellbow Rd TW14......4 B2
Dell Cl
  Fetcham KT22.......... 94 E4
  Haslemere GU27........208 A7
  Mickleham RH5........115 C8
  Wallington SM6........ 60 D6
Dell Close Cotts RH5.. 115 C8
Dellfield Cl BR3.......... 44 C8
Dell Gr GU16............ 65 F2
Dell Ho CR2..............61 C2
Della La GU11............ 58 A5
Dell Rd KT17............ 58 A4
Dells Cl TW11............ 16 F2
Dell The
  Brentford TW8..........6 C8
  Burgh Heath KT20...... 97 C6

Dell The *continued*
East Grinstead RH19 . . . . . . 186 B1
Englefield Green SL4 . . . . . **11** A5
Feltham TW14 . . . . **15** B8
Heath End GU9 . . . . 125 D7
Horley RH6 . . . . 161 B4
Reigate RH2 . . . . 118 A2
Sidlow RH6 . . . . 160 C5
South Norwood SE19 . . . . . 42 F8
Woking GU21 . . . . 69 C1
Dell Wlk KT3 . . . . 38 E7
Delmey Cl CR0 . . . . 61 F7
Delphian Ct 5 SW16 . . . . . 22 A4
Delrogue Rd RH11 . . . . . . 181 A1
Delta Bglws RH6 . . . . 161 A1
Delta Cl
Chobham GU24 . . . . 49 F1
Worcester Park KT4 . . . . . . 57 F7
Delta Dr RH6 . . . . 161 A1
Delta Ho RH6 . . . . 161 A1
Delta Rd
Chobham GU24 . . . . 49 F1
Woking GU21 . . . . 70 A3
Worcester Park KT4 . . . . . . 57 E7
Delta Way TW20 . . . . 32 C8
Delves RH4 . . . . 97 D6
Delville Cl GU14 . . . . 84 D3
De Mel Cl KT19 . . . . 76 B7
Demesne Rd SM6 . . . . 60 D6
De Montfort Par 1 SW16 . 21 E5
De Montfort Rd SW16 . . . . 21 E6
Dempsey Wlk RH11 . . . . . 201 A8
Dempster Cl KT6 . . . . 37 C1
Dempster Ho GU9 . . . . . . 125 D8
Denbies Wine Est★ RH5 . 115 B3
Denbigh Cl SM1 . . . . 58 F5
Denbigh Gdns TW10 . . . . . . 6 F2
Denbigh Rd
Haslemere GU27 . . . . 208 D5
Hounslow TW3 . . . . 5 B5
Denby Ct GU14 . . . . 85 C1
Denby Dene RG12 . . . . . . 106 B2
Denby Rd KT11 . . . . 73 C2
Denchers Plat RH11 . . . . . 181 D1
Den Cl BR3 . . . . 44 D6
Dencliffe 3 TW15 . . . . . . 14 A3
Dendy St SW12 . . . . 21 A7
Dene Ave TW3 . . . . 4 F4
Dene Cl
Ash GU12 . . . . 106 C3
Camberley GU15 . . . . 66 A8
Chipstead CR5 . . . . 98 E8
Farnham GU10 . . . . 146 E6
Haslemere GU27 . . . . 208 C6
Hayes BR2 . . . . 44 F1
Horley RH6 . . . . 160 E5
Worcester Park KT4 . . . . . . 57 F8
Dene Ct
12 Croydon CR2 . . . . 61 C5
Guildford GU1 . . . . 110 B3
Denefield Dr CR8 . . . . 80 D4
Dene Gdns KT7 . . . . 56 A8
Denehurst Gdns
Mortlake TW10 . . . . 7 A3
Twickenham TW2 . . . . 16 D8
Denehyrst Ct 2 GU1 . . . . 130 E8
Dene La GU10 . . . . 146 E6
Dene Lane W GU10 . . . . . 146 E5
Dene Pl GU9 . . . . 69 C1
Dene Rd
Ashtead KT21 . . . . 95 F8
Farnborough GU14 . . . . . . 84 F3
Guildford GU1 . . . . 130 E8
Dene St RH4 . . . . 136 B7
Dene Street Gdns RH4 . . 136 B7
Dene The
Abinger Hammer RH5 . . . . 134 B3
Belmont SM2 . . . . 77 F8
East Molesey KT12, KT8 . . 35 F4
South Croydon CR0 . . . . . . 62 D6
Dene Tye RH10 . . . . 202 D7
Dene Wlk GU10 . . . . 146 E6
Denewood 8 KT17 . . . . . . 76 E6
Denewood Ho 11 SM1 . . . . 59 C6
Denfield RH4 . . . . 136 C5
Denham Cres CR4 . . . . 40 F5
Denham Ct SE26 . . . . 23 B5
Denham Gr RG12 . . . . 27 C3
Denham Rd
Egham TW20 . . . . 12 A4
Ewell KT17 . . . . 76 F7
Feltham TW14 . . . . 15 C8
Denholm Gdns GU4 . . . . . 110 A4
Deniel Lodge TW1 . . . . 6 C2
Denison Rd
Feltham, Lower Feltham
TW13 . . . . 14 F4
Mitcham SW19 . . . . 20 D2
Denleigh Gdns KT7 . . . . . . 36 E3
Denly Way GU18 . . . . 48 C1
Denman Dr
Ashford TW15 . . . . 14 B2
Claygate KT10 . . . . 56 A5
Denmans Rd RH10 . . . . . . 202 D7
Denmark Ave SW19 . . . . . . 19 E1
Denmark Cl
Morden SM4 . . . . 40 A4
2 Weybridge KT13 . . . . . . 53 B7
Denmark Gdns SM5 . . . . . . 59 F7
Denmark Rd
Carshalton SM5 . . . . 59 F7
Croydon SE25 . . . . 43 B4
Guildford GU1 . . . . 130 E8
Kingston upon Thames KT1 . 37 E6
Twickenham TW2 . . . . 16 D5
Wimbledon SW19 . . . . 19 D2
Denmark Sq GU12 . . . . . . 105 E2

Denmark St
Aldershot GU12 . . . . 105 D2
Wokingham RG40 . . . . 25 C5
Denmead Ct RG12 . . . . 27 E3
Denmead Ho SW15 . . . . 7 F1
Denmead Rd CR0 . . . . 42 B1
Denmead Sch TW12 . . . . . 16 B1
Denmore Ct SM6 . . . . 60 B5
Dennan Rd KT6 . . . . 37 F1
Denne Par RH12, RH13 . . 217 C1
Denne Pl RH12 . . . . 217 C1
Denne Rd
Crawley RH11 . . . . 201 D5
Horsham RH12 . . . . 217 C1
Dennett Rd CR0 . . . . 42 A2
Denning Ave CR0 . . . . 61 A5
Denning Cl TW12 . . . . 15 F3
Denning Mews 5 SW12 . . 21 A8
Denningtons The KT4 . . . . 57 E8
Dennis Cl
Ashford TW15 . . . . 14 D1
Redhill RH1 . . . . 118 E3
Dennis Ho SM1 . . . . 59 A6
Dennis Park Cres SW20 . . 39 E8
Dennis Pilcher Ho RG12 . . 27 E6
Dennis Reeve Cl CR4 . . . . . 40 F8
Dennistoun Cl GU15 . . . . . 65 F5
DENNISVILLE 129 F8
Dennis Way GU1 . . . . 109 E6
Denny Ho 2 TW12 . . . . . . 36 B8
Den Rd BR2 . . . . 44 D6
Densham Dr CR8 . . . . 80 A5
Densole Cl BR3 . . . . 43 E8
Denton Cl RH1 . . . . 140 A4
Denton Gr KT12 . . . . 54 E8
Denton Rd
Twickenham TW1 . . . . 6 D1
Wokingham RG40 . . . . 25 C6
Denton Way
Frimley GU16 . . . . 65 D2
Woking GU21 . . . . 69 A2
Dents Gr KT20 . . . . 117 F7
Denvale Trad Pk
Crawley RH10 . . . . 201 E5
Mitcham CR4 . . . . 40 F5
Denwegan Ho 7 SM2 . . . . 59 C3
Denwood SE23 . . . . 23 D5
Denzil Rd GU2 . . . . 130 B8
Departures Rd RH6 . . . . . 181 F8
Depot Rd
Crawley RH11 . . . . 181 D1
Epsom KT17 . . . . 76 E6
Horsham RH13 . . . . 217 D2
Hounslow TW3, TW7 . . . . . 5 D4
Derby Arms Rd KT18 . . . . . 76 F7
Derby Cl KT18 . . . . 97 B8
Derby Ct SW14 . . . . 7 B3
Derby Hill SE23 . . . . 23 C6
Derby Hill Cres SE23 . . . . 23 C6
Derby Ho 4 SM6 . . . . 60 B5
Derby Rd
Cheam SM1 . . . . 58 F4
Guildford GU2 . . . . 108 F1
Haslemere GU27 . . . . 208 B7
Hounslow TW3 . . . . 5 B3
Merton SW19 . . . . 20 A1
Mortlake SW14 . . . . 7 B3
Surbiton KT5, KT6 . . . . . . 38 A1
Thornton Heath CR0 . . . . . 42 A1
Derby Road Ind Est 1 TW3 5 B3
Derby Sq The 10 KT19 . . . 76 D6
Derby Stables Rd KT18 . . 76 F7
Derek Ave
Hackbridge SM6 . . . . 60 B6
West Ewell KT19 . . . . 57 B5
Derek Cl KT19 . . . . 57 B5
Derek Horn Ct GU15 . . . . . 65 B6
Deri Dene Cl 2 TW19 . . . . 2 E1
Dering Pl CR0 . . . . 61 C6
Dering Rd CR0, CR9 . . . . . . 61 C6
Derinton Rd SW17 . . . . 21 A4
Derisley Cl KT14 . . . . 71 D7
Deronda Rd SE24, SW2 . . 22 B7
De Ros Pl TW20 . . . . 12 A2
Deroy Cl SM5 . . . . 59 F4
Derrick Ave CR2 . . . . 61 C1
Derrick Ho 13 SW2 . . . . . . 22 A7
Derrick Rd BR3 . . . . 43 F5
Derry Cl GU12 . . . . 105 F5
Derrydown GU22 . . . . 89 C6
Derry Rd
Farnborough GU14 . . . . . . 84 F8
Wallington CR0 . . . . 60 E7
Derryswood Ho GU5 . . . . . 152 E7
Derwent Ave
Ash Vale GU12 . . . . 105 F4
Kingston upon Thames
SW15 . . . . 18 E4
Derwent Cl
Addlestone KT15 . . . . 52 D5
Claygate KT10 . . . . 55 F4
Crawley RH11 . . . . 200 F5
East Bedfont TW14 . . . . . . 14 F7
Farnborough GU14 . . . . . . 84 E4
Hale GU9 . . . . 125 A6
Horsham RH12 . . . . 218 B6
Derwent Dr CR8 . . . . 80 E6
Derwent Ho
Penge SE20 . . . . 43 B7
Reigate RH2 . . . . 139 A7
Derwent Lodge KT4 . . . . . 58 B8
Derwent Rd
Lightwater GU18 . . . . 67 B8
Penge SE20 . . . . 43 B7
Thorpe Lea TW20 . . . . 12 B1
Twickenham TW2 . . . . 5 B1

Derwent Rd *continued*
West Barnes SM4 . . . . 39 D3
Wimbledon SW16 . . . . 60 B3
Desborough Cl TW17 . . . . . 34 A2
Desborough Ct SE25 . . . . . 43 B5
Deseret Ho 7 CR4 . . . . 40 F6
Desford Way TW15 . . . . . . 13 F6
Desmond Anderson Prim Sch
RH10 . . . . 201 D2
Desmond Tutu Dr SE23 . . 23 E7
Despard Ho SW2 . . . . 22 A6
de Stafford Coll CR3 . . . . 100 F6
de Stafford Sh Ctr CR3 . . 100 F6
Detherick Ct TW3 . . . . 5 C3
Detillens La RH8 . . . . 123 A6
Detling Rd RH11 . . . . 201 C1
Dettingen Cres GU16 . . . . . 86 D8
Dettingen Rd GU16 . . . . . . 86 E8
Devana End SM5 . . . . 59 F7
Devas Rd SW20 . . . . 39 C8
De Vere Cl SM6 . . . . 60 E3
Deveraux Cl BR3 . . . . 44 C4
Deverill Ct SE20 . . . . 43 C8
Devey Cl KT2 . . . . 18 D3
Devil's La TW20 . . . . 12 C2
De-Vitre Gn RG40 . . . . 25 F7
Devitt Cl KT21 . . . . 76 A3
Devoil Cl GU4 . . . . 110 B5
Devoke Way KT12 . . . . 54 D8
Devon Ave TW2 . . . . 16 C7
Devon Bank GU2 . . . . 130 C6
Devon Cl
Kenley CR8 . . . . 80 E3
Sandhurst GU47 . . . . 64 D7
Devon Cres RH1, RH2 . . . 118 D1
Devoncroft Gdns TW1 . . . . 17 A8
Devon Ct 2 TW12 . . . . . . 16 A1
Devon Ho
Caterham CR3 . . . . 100 F3
2 Knaphill GU21 . . . . 68 D2
Penge SE20 . . . . 23 B1
Devon Rd
Belmont SM2 . . . . 58 E2
Hersham KT12 . . . . 54 C6
Merstham M1 . . . . 119 C5
Devonshire Ave
Box Hill KT20 . . . . 116 C4
Sheerwater GU21 . . . . 70 D6
Sutton SM2 . . . . 59 C3
Devonshire Ct
16 Balham SW12 . . . . 21 B8
Croydon CR0 . . . . 44 A1
Feltham TW13 . . . . 15 B6
6 Richmond TW9 . . . . 6 F6
Devonshire Dr
Camberley GU15 . . . . 65 F7
Long Ditton KT6 . . . . 37 D1
Devonshire Gdns W4 . . . . . 7 C7
Devonshire Ho
Hounslow TW3 . . . . 5 C4
14 Sutton SM2 . . . . 59 C3
Devonshire Pl 11 W4 . . . 104 F1
Devonshire Prim Sch 22
SM2 . . . . 59 C3
Devonshire Rd
6 Chiswick W4 . . . . 7 E8
Feltham TW13 . . . . 15 E4
Forest Hill SE23 . . . . 23 C8
Hackbridge SM5, SM6 . . . . 60 A6
Horsham RH13 . . . . 217 D2
Mitcham SW17, SW19 . . . . 20 E1
Sutton SM2 . . . . 59 C3
Thornton Heath CR0 . . . . . 42 D2
Weybridge KT13 . . . . 53 A6
Devonshire St 1 W4 . . . . . 7 E8
Devonshires The K18 . . . . 76 F5
Devonshire Way CR0, CR9 . 62 F8
Devon Way
Chessington KT9 . . . . 56 C6
West Ewell KT19 . . . . 57 B5
Devon Waye TW5 . . . . 4 F7
Dewar Cl 2 RH11 . . . . . . 200 E5
Dewar Ho SW17 . . . . 20 E3
Dewey St SW17 . . . . 20 F3
Dewlands RH9 . . . . 121 C4
Dewlands Cl GU6 . . . . 174 E3
Dewlands La GU6 . . . . 174 E3
Dew Pond Cl RH13 . . . . . . 217 F3
Dewsbury Gdns KT4 . . . . . 58 A7
Dexter Dr RH19 . . . . 205 E8
Diamedes Ave TW19 . . . . . 13 D7
Diamond Cotts GU5 . . . . . 152 B7
Diamond Ct 4 RH1 . . . . . . 119 A2
Diamond Est SW17 . . . . . . 20 E5
Diamond Hill GU15 . . . . . . 65 E7
Diamond Pl RH2 . . . . 118 C2
Diamond Ridge GU15 . . . . 65 E7
Diana Ct SM5 . . . . 60 A3
Diana Gdns KT6 . . . . 56 F8
Diana Ho SW13 . . . . 7 F6
Dianthus Cl KT16 . . . . 32 C2
Dianthus Ct GU22 . . . . 69 D1
Dianthus Pl RG42 . . . . 8 B2
Dibdin Cl SM1 . . . . 59 A7
Dibdin Rd SM1 . . . . 59 A8
Diceland Lodge SM7 . . . . . 77 F3
Diceland Rd SM7 . . . . 77 F3
Dickens Cl
East Grinstead RH19 . . . . . 185 C1
Richmond TW10 . . . . 17 E6
Dickens Ct RG40 . . . . 25 B6
Dickens Dr KT15 . . . . 51 F4
Dickenson Rd TW13 . . . . . 15 D3
Dickenson's La SE25 . . . . 43 A3
Dickenson's Pl SE25 . . . . . 43 A3
Dickens Pl SL3 . . . . 1 E6

Dickens Rd RH10 . . . . 201 E3
Dickenswood Cl SE19 . . . . 22 B1
Dickerage Hill KT3 . . . . . . 38 C7
Dickerage La KT3 . . . . 38 C6
Dickerage Rd KT1, KT2,
KT3 . . . . 38 C7
Dickins Way
3 Horsham RH12 . . . . . . 217 F4
Horsham RH13 . . . . 217 F1
Dickson Ho 9 TW10 . . . . . . 6 F1
Dick Turpin Way TW14 . . . 3 F3
Digby Ct RH10 . . . . 61 F7
Digby Stuart Coll SW15 . . 7 F2
Digby KT14 . . . . 71 F7
Digdens Rise KT18 . . . . . . 76 C4
Dillwyn Cl SE26 . . . . 23 E4
Dilston Rd KT22 . . . . 95 A8
Dilton Gdns SW15 . . . . 19 B7
Dingle Cl RH11 . . . . 201 B7
Dingle Rd TW15 . . . . 14 B3
Dingle The RH11 . . . . 201 B6
Dingley La SW16 . . . . 21 D6
Dingley Way GU14 . . . . . . 105 A8
Dingwall Ave CR0, CR9 . . . 61 C8
Dingwall Rd
Croydon CR0, CR9 . . . . . . 61 D8
Wallington SM5 . . . . 59 F2
Wandsworth SW18 . . . . . . 20 C8
Dinorben 3 SM6 . . . . 60 C3
Dinsdale Cl GU22 . . . . 70 A1
Dinsdale Gdns SE25 . . . . . 42 E4
Dinsmore Rd SW12 . . . . . . 21 B8
Dinton Rd
Kingston upon Thames
KT2 . . . . 17 F1
Mitcham SW17, SW19 . . . . 20 D2
Dione Wlk RH11 . . . . 200 E4
Dippenhall Rd GU10 . . . . 124 C2
DIPPENHALL 124 D2
Dippenhall St GU10 . . . . . 124 A5
Diprose Lodge SW17 . . . . . 20 D4
Dirdene Cl KT17 . . . . 76 F7
Dirdene Gdns KT17 . . . . . . 76 F7
Dirdene Gr KT17 . . . . 76 F7
Dirtham La KT24 . . . . 113 B6
Dirty La RH19 . . . . 206 F2
Discovery Pk RH10 . . . . . . 182 A2
Disraeli Ct SL3 . . . . 1 B8
Distillery Wlk 14 TW8 . . . . 6 E8
Distin Ct 3 SM1 . . . . 59 B5
Ditches La CR3, CR5 . . . . . 99 E6
Ditchling RG12 . . . . 27 A2
Ditchling Hill RH11 . . . . . 201 C4
Ditton Cl KT7 . . . . 37 A2
Dittoncroft Cl CR0 . . . . . . 61 E6
Ditton Grange Cl KT6 . . . . 37 D1
Ditton Grange Dr KT6 . . . . 37 D1
Ditton Hill KT6 . . . . 56 D8
Ditton Hill Rd KT6 . . . . . . 37 C1
Ditton Lawn KT7 . . . . 37 A1
Ditton Pl 7 SE20 . . . . 43 B8
Ditton Rd KT6 . . . . 37 E1
Ditton Reach KT7 . . . . 37 B3
Dixon Dr KT13 . . . . 52 F1
Dixon Pl BR4 . . . . 44 B1
Dixon Rd SE25 . . . . 42 F6
Dobbins Pl RH11 . . . . 200 E5
Doble Ct CR2 . . . . 81 A8
Dobson Rd RH11 . . . . 181 D1
DOCKENFIELD 166 E6
Dockenfield St GU10 . . . . 166 C6
Dockett Eddy La TW17 . . . 33 F1
Dockett Moorings KT16 . . 33 F1
Dock Rd TW8 . . . . 6 D7
Dockwell Cl TW14 . . . . 4 A3
Dockwell's Ind Est TW14 . . 4 B2
Doctors Cl SE26 . . . . 23 C3
Doctors La CR3 . . . . 100 A3
Dodbrooke Rd SE27 . . . . . 22 A5
Dodds Cres KT14 . . . . 71 B5
Dodd's La KT14 . . . . 71 A5
Dodds Pk RH3 . . . . 137 B7
Doel Cl SW19 . . . . 20 C1
Dogflud Way GU9 . . . . . . 125 C3
Doggett Rd SE6 . . . . 24 A8
Doghurst Ave UB3 . . . . 3 B7
Doghurst Dr UB7 . . . . 3 B7
Doghurst La CR5 . . . . 98 F7
DOGKENNEL GREEN 113 D1
Doland Ct SW17 . . . . 20 F2
Dolby Terr RH6 . . . . 180 E6
Dolliffe Cl CR4 . . . . 40 E7
Dollis Cl RH10 . . . . 202 C5
Dollis Ct GU9 . . . . 125 D3
Dollis Dr GU9 . . . . 125 D3
Dolphin Cl
Haslemere GU27 . . . . 207 E6
Kingston upon Thames KT6 . 37 D4
Dolphin Court N TW19 . . . 13 A5
Dolphin Ct
Bracknell RG12 . . . . 27 C5
Merton SW19 . . . . 20 A1
Stanwell TW19 . . . . 13 A5
2 Wallington SM6 . . . . . . 60 B4
Dolphin Est The TW16 . . . 34 D8
Dolphin Rd TW16 . . . . 34 E8
Dolphin Road N TW16 . . . 34 E8
Dolphin Road S TW16 . . . 34 E8
Dolphin Road W TW16 . . . 34 E8
Dolphin Sq 2 W4 . . . . 7 E7
Dolphin St KT1 . . . . 37 E8
Doman Rd GU15 . . . . 65 A4
Dome Hill CR3 . . . . 120 E8
Dome Hill Peak CR3 . . . . . 100 E1
Dome Hill Pk SE26 . . . . . . 22 F4
Dome The RH1 . . . . 118 F2
Dome Way RH1 . . . . 118 F2
DOMEWOOD 184 A5

Del – Dor **245**

Dominion Cl TW3 . . . . 5 D5
Dominion Rd CR0 . . . . 42 F2
Donald Ct CR2 . . . . 61 E4
Donald Lynch Ho CR4 . . . . 40 F7
Donald Rd CR0, CR9 . . . . . 41 F2
Donald Woods Gdns KT5 . 57 C8
Doncaster Wlk RH10 . . . . 202 A4
Doncastle Rd RG12 . . . . . . 26 E6
**Donhead (Wimbledon Coll
Prep Sch)** SW19 . . . . 19 D1
Donkey La
Abinger Common RH5 . . . 155 D8
Crawley RH6 . . . . 182 D7
DONKEY TOWN 67 D6
Donnafields GU24 . . . . 68 A3
Donne Cl RH10 . . . . 202 B8
Donne Gdns GU22 . . . . 70 E4
Donne Pl CR4 . . . . 41 B5
Donnington Cl GU15 . . . . . 65 B4
Donnington Ct 2 RH11 . . 200 F4
Donnington Rd KT4 . . . . . . 58 A8
Donnybrook RG12 . . . . 27 A2
Donnybrook Rd SW16 . . . . 21 D1
Donovan Cl KT19 . . . . 57 D1
Donyngs Recn Ctr RH1 . . . 118 E2
Doods Park Rd RH2 . . . . . 118 C1
Doods Pl RH2 . . . . 118 D1
Doods Rd RH2 . . . . 118 C2
Doods Way RH2 . . . . 118 D2
Doomsday Gdn RH13 . . . . 218 A1
Doone Cl TW11 . . . . 17 A2
Doradus Ct 20 SW19 . . . . . 19 D7
Doral Way SM5 . . . . 59 F5
Doran Dr RH2 . . . . 118 D1
Doran Gdns RH2 . . . . 118 D1
Dora Rd SW19 . . . . 20 A4
DORA'S GREEN 124 C5
Dora's Green La GU10 . . . 124 C5
Dorcas Ct GU15 . . . . 65 B3
Dorchester Cl KT10 . . . . . . 55 F8
Dorchester Ct
Camberley GU15 . . . . 65 B6
Reigate RH2 . . . . 118 C2
Staines TW18 . . . . 13 A4
5 Streatham SW16 . . . . . 21 E6
Woking GU22 . . . . 70 A3
Dorchester Dr TW14 . . . . . . 3 E1
Dorchester Gr 8 W4 . . . . . 7 E8
Dorchester Ho
Richmond TW9 . . . . 7 B7
Wallington SM5 . . . . 59 F5
Dorchester Mews
New Malden KT3 . . . . 38 D5
Twickenham TW1 . . . . 6 C1
Dorchester Par SW16 . . . . 21 E6
Dorchester Prim Sch KT4 . 39 C1
Dorchester Rd
Morden CR4 . . . . 40 C2
North Cheam KT4 . . . . 39 C1
Weybridge KT13 . . . . 53 B7
Doreen Cl GU14 . . . . 84 E7
Dore Gdns SM4 . . . . 40 B2
Doresa Cl KT15 . . . . 52 A5
Dorey Ho 7 TW8 . . . . 6 C7
Dorian Dr SL5 . . . . 29 E8
Doric Dr KT20 . . . . 97 F7
Dorien Rd SW20 . . . . 39 D7
Dorin Ct
Pyrford GU22 . . . . 70 E4
Warlingham CR6 . . . . 101 B7
Doris Rd TW15 . . . . 14 D2
DORKING 136 C6
Dorking Adult Learning Ctr
RH4 . . . . 136 C7
Dorking Bsns Pk RH4 . . . . 136 A8
Dorking Cl KT4 . . . . 58 D8
Dorking (Deepdene) Sta
RH4 . . . . 115 C1
Dorking Hospl RH4 . . . . . 136 A6
Dorking L Ctr RH5 . . . . . . 136 C8
Dorking Rd
Chilworth GU4 . . . . 131 E3
Epsom KT18 . . . . 76 B4
Gomshall GU5 . . . . 133 D4
Great Bookham KT23 . . . . 114 C8
Kingsfold RH12, RH5 . . . . 198 B4
Leatherhead KT22 . . . . 95 B3
Lower Kingswood KT20 . . . 116 F7
Walton on the Hill KT20 . . 97 C3
Warnham RH12 . . . . 217 B6
Dorking Sta RH4 . . . . 115 C1
Dorking West Sta RH4 . . . 136 A8
Dorlcote Rd SW18 . . . . 20 E8
Dorlcote Way GU8 . . . . . . 170 E5
Dorling Dr KT17 . . . . 76 F7
Dorly Cl TW17 . . . . 34 E4
Dormans RH11 . . . . 201 A5
Dormans Ave RH7 . . . . . . 165 A2
Dorman's Cl RH7 . . . . 186 A8
Dormans Gdns RH19 . . . . 185 E6
Dormans High St RH7 . . . 186 A8
DORMANSLAND 165 B1
Dormansland Prim Sch
RH7 . . . . 165 B1
DORMANS PARK 185 E6
Dormans Park Rd
Dormans Park RH19 . . . . . 185 E6
East Grinstead RH19 . . . . . 185 D3
Dormans Rd RH7 . . . . 165 A2
Dormans Sta RH7 . . . . . . 185 E6
Dormans Station Rd
RH7 . . . . 185 F7
Dormer Cl RG45 . . . . 45 A5
Dormers Cl GU7 . . . . 150 D7
Dormy Ho The GU25 . . . . . 30 F3

Dorney Gr KT13 . . . . **53** B8
Dorney Way TW4 . . . .**4** E2
Dornford Gdns CR5 . . . . . **100** C8
Dornton Rd
  South Croydon CR2 . . . . . **61** D5
  Upper Tooting SW12, SW17 **21** C6
Dorothy Pettingel Ho 5
  SM1 . . . . **59** B7
Dorrien Wlk SW16 . . . . **21** D6
Dorrington Ct SE25 . . . . . . **42** E7
Dorrington Way BR3 . . . . . **44** C4
Dorrit Cres GU3 . . . . **108** E3
Dorryn Ct SE26 . . . . **23** D3
Dorset Ave RH19 . . . . **185** C3
Dorset Ct
  Camberley GU15 . . . . **65** F8
  Epsom KT17 . . . . **76** F7
  3 Horsham RH12 . . . . . . **217** D2
Dorset Dr GU22 . . . . **70** B2
Dorset Gdns
  East Grinstead RH19 . . . . **185** C3
  Thornton Heath SW16 . . . **41** F5
Dorset Hall SW19 . . . . **40** A8
Dorset Ho 2 SE20 . . . . **43** B8
Dorset Mews RH19 . . . . . . **185** C3
Dorset Rd
  Ashford TW15 . . . . **13** D5
  Ash GU12 . . . . **106** B5
  Belmont SM2 . . . . **59** A1
  Merton SW19 . . . . **40** A7
  Mitcham CR4 . . . . **40** E7
  Penge BR3 . . . . **43** D6
Dorset Sq KT19 . . . . **57** C7
Dorset Way
  Byfleet KT14 . . . . **52** D1
  Twickenham TW2 . . . . **16** D7
Dorset Waye TW5 . . . .**4** F7
Dorsten Sq RH11 . . . . **200** F3
Dorton Villas UB7 . . . .**3** A6
Dorton Way GU23 . . . . **91** B6
Douai Cl GU14 . . . . **85** C4
Douai Gr TW12 . . . . **36** C8
Douglas Ave KT3 . . . . **39** B5
Douglas Cl
  Guildford GU4 . . . . **109** D6
  Wallington SM6 . . . . **60** E4
Douglas Ct
  Biggin Hill TN16 . . . . **83** E2
  Caterham CR3 . . . . **100** D5
  1 Upper Tooting SW17 . . . **20** C1
Douglas Dr
  Croydon CR0 . . . . **63** A7
  Godalming GU7 . . . . **150** F5
Douglas Gr GU10 . . . . **146** C5
Douglas Gracey Ho SW18 . **19** E8
Douglas Ho
  Little Bookham KT23 . . . . . **94** A3
  Twickenham TW1 . . . .**6** B2
Douglas Houghton Ho 11
  RH1 . . . . **118** F2
Douglas Mews SM7 . . . . . . **77** F3
Douglas Pl GU14 . . . . **85** A5
Douglas Rd
  Addlestone KT15 . . . . **52** B7
  Hounslow TW3 . . . .**5** B4
  Kingston upon Thames KT1 . **38** B7
  Reigate RH2 . . . . **118** B2
  Stanwell TW19 . . . .**2** D1
  Surbiton KT6 . . . . **37** F1
  Thames Ditton KT10 . . . . . **55** B8
Douglas Robinson Ct
  SW16 . . . . **21** E1
Douglas Sq SM4 . . . . **40** A3
Doultons The TW18 . . . . . . **13** A1
Dounesforth Gdns SW18 . . **20** B7
Dove Cl
  Crawley RH11 . . . . **201** D8
  Selsdon CR2 . . . . **81** D8
  Wallington SM6 . . . . **60** F3
Dovecote Cl KT13 . . . . **53** B7
Dovecote Gdns 9 SW14 . . . .**7** D4
Dove Ct TW19 . . . . **13** E8
Dovedale Cl
  Guildford GU4 . . . . **110** A4
  Sandhurst GU47 . . . . **45** D2
Dovedale Cres RH11 . . . . . **201** B4
Dovedale Rise CR4 . . . . **20** F1
Dovehouse Gn 1 KT13 . . . . **53** D6
Dove Pl KT10 . . . . **56** A2
Dovercourt Ave CR7 . . . . . . **42** A5
Dovercourt La SM1 . . . . **59** C7
Dovercourt Rd SE21, SE22 . **22** E8
Dover Ct
  Carshalton SM1 . . . . **59** D6
  Cranleigh GU6 . . . . **175** A3
Doverfield Rd
  Guildford GU4 . . . . **110** A4
  Streatham SW2 . . . . **21** E8
Dover Gdns SM5 . . . . **59** F7
Dover Ho
  7 Beckenham BR3 . . . . . . **24** A1
  15 Penge SE20 . . . . **43** B8
Dover House Rd SW15 . . . . **19** B8
Dover Rd SE19 . . . . **22** D2
DOVERSGREEN **139** B5
Dovers Green Rd RH2 . . . . **139** B4
Dovers Green Sch RH2 . . . **139** C5
Doversmead GU21 . . . . **68** E3
Dover Terr TW9 . . . .**7** A5
Doveton Rd CR2 . . . . **61** D5
Dowanhill Rd SE6 . . . . **24** D7
Dowdeswell Cl SW15 . . . .**7** E3
Dowding Ct RG45 . . . . **45** C6
Dowding Rd TN16 . . . . **83** D4
Dowell Ho SE21 . . . . **22** F5

Dower Ave SM6 . . . . **60** B2
Dower Cotts GU8 . . . . **170** F8
Dower Ho The SL5 . . . . **29** C4
Dower House GU8 . . . . **170** F8
Dower Wlk RH11 . . . . **201** A5
Dowes Ho 13 SW16 . . . . . . **21** E5
Dowgate Ho KT13 . . . . **53** A7
Dowlands Cl KT23 . . . . **114** A8
Dowlands La RH10, RH6 . . **183** D7
Dowler Ct 2 KT2 . . . . **37** F8
Dowles Gn RG40 . . . . **25** E8
DOWLESGREEN **25** E8
Dowman Cl 2 SW19 . . . . . . **20** B1
Downderry Prim Sch BR1 . . **24** E4
Downderry Rd BR1 . . . . **24** E4
Downe Cl RH6 . . . . **160** E5
Downe Rd CR4 . . . . **40** F7
Downer Mdw GU7 . . . . **150** E8
Downes Cl TW1 . . . .**6** B1
Downes Ho CR0 . . . . **61** B6
Downey Lodge RH10 . . . . . **201** D4
Downfield 7 KT4 . . . . **39** A1
Downfield Cl KT3 . . . . **38** D1
Down Hall Rd KT2 . . . . **37** D8
DOWNHAM **24** F3
Downham Ent Ctr SE6 . . . . . **24** F6
Downham La BR1 . . . . **24** D3
Downham Way BR1 . . . . **24** E4
Downhurst Rd GU6 . . . . **175** E6
Downing Ave GU2 . . . . **129** F8
Downing Ho 9 SW19 . . . . . . **20** A1
Downing St GU9 . . . . **125** B2
Downland Cl
  Burgh Heath KT18 . . . . . . **77** B1
  Wallington CR5 . . . . **79** B5
Downland Ct RH11 . . . . **201** C4
Downland Dr RH11 . . . . **201** C3
Downland Gdns KT18 . . . . . **77** B1
Downland Pl RH11 . . . . **201** C4
Downlands Rd CR8 . . . . **79** F6
Downland Way KT18 . . . . . . **77** B1
Downmill Rd RG12 . . . . **26** F7
Down Rd
  Guildford GU1 . . . . **110** B1
  Teddington TW11 . . . . **17** B2
Downs Ave KT18 . . . . **76** F4
Downs Bridge Rd BR3 . . . . . **44** D8
Downs Court Rd CR8 . . . . . . **80** B6
Downs Ct
  Purley CR8 . . . . **61** B1
  3 Redhill RH1 . . . . **119** A4
  17 Wimbledon SW20 . . . . **19** D1
Downsend Sch KT22 . . . . . . **95** D7
Downsend Sch Ashtead
  Lodge 1 KT21 . . . . **75** E1
Downsend Sch (Epsom
  Lodge) KT17 . . . . **76** F7
Downsend Sch Leatherhead
  Lodge KT22 . . . . **95** C6
Downs Hill BR2, BR3 . . . . . . **44** D8
Downs Hill Rd KT18 . . . . **76** E5
Downshire Way
  Bracknell, Priestwood RG12,
   RG42 . . . . **27** A2
  Bracknell RG12 . . . . **27** B6
DOWNSIDE **93** B8
Downside
  Beacon Hill GU26 . . . . . . **188** D7
  Epsom KT18 . . . . **76** E5
  Twickenham TW1 . . . . **16** F4
Downside Bridge Rd KT11 . . **73** B4
Downside Cl SW19 . . . . **20** C2
Downside Common Rd
  KT11 . . . . **73** C1
Downside Ct RH1 . . . . **119** C6
Downside Orch GU22 . . . . . . **70** A2
Downside Rd
  Carshalton SM2 . . . . **59** E4
  Downside KT11 . . . . **73** B2
  Guildford GU4 . . . . **131** B8
Downside Wlk TW8 . . . .**6** C8
Downs La KT22 . . . . **95** B3
Downs Lodge Ct KT17 . . . . . **76** E5
Downsman Ct RH10 . . . . . . **201** D3
Downs Rd
  Ashtead KT18 . . . . **96** C7
  Beckenham BR3 . . . . **44** B7
  Coulsdon CR5 . . . . **79** D1
  Epsom KT17, KT18 . . . . . . **76** E3
  Mickleham RH5 . . . . **115** C7
  Purley CR8 . . . . **80** B8
  South Norwood CR7 . . . . . **42** C8
  Sutton SM2 . . . . **78** C8
Downs Side SM2 . . . . **77** F8
Down St KT8 . . . . **36** A4
Downs The
  Leatherhead KT22 . . . . . . **95** C2
  Wimbledon SW20 . . . . **19** D1
Downs View
  Dorking RH4 . . . . **115** D1
  Hounslow TW7 . . . .**6** A6
  Tadworth KT20 . . . . **97** B6
Downsview Ave GU22 . . . . . . **89** F6
Downsview Cl KT11 . . . . **93** B8
Downsview Ct GU1 . . . . **109** C5
Downsview Gdns
  Dorking RH4 . . . . **136** B6
  South Norwood SE19 . . . . **22** C1
Downs View Lodge 9
  KT6 . . . . **37** E3
Downsview Prim Sch
  SE19 . . . . **22** C1
Downsview Rd
  Headley Down GU35 . . . . **187** C5
  Horsham RH12 . . . . **218** B6

Downsview Rd continued
  South Norwood SE19 . . . . **22** C1
Downs View Rd KT23 . . . . . **114** C8
Downsway
  Guildford GU1 . . . . **110** E1
  South Croydon CR2 . . . . . **80** E8
  Whyteleafe CR3 . . . . **80** F2
Downs Way
  Epsom KT18 . . . . **76** F3
  Great Bookham KT23 . . . . **94** C1
  Oxted RH8 . . . . **122** E8
  Tadworth KT20 . . . . **97** B6
Downsway Cl KT20 . . . . **97** A6
Downs Way Cty Prim Sch
  RH8 . . . . **122** E7
Downsway The SM2 . . . . **59** C2
Downswood RH2 . . . . **118** D4
Downs Wood KT18 . . . . **77** B2
Downton Ave SW2 . . . . **21** F6
Downview Cl GU26 . . . . **188** D6
Down Yhonda GU8 . . . . **148** C3
Doyle Ct GU27 . . . . **208** A6
Doyle Rd SE25 . . . . **43** A5
Dragon La KT13 . . . . **53** A1
Dragoon Ct GU11 . . . . **104** E2
Drake Ave
  Caterham CR3 . . . . **100** C5
  Mytchett GU16 . . . . **86** A1
  Staines TW18 . . . . **12** F3
Drake Cl
  Bracknell RG12 . . . . **27** B4
  Horsham RH12 . . . . **217** E6
Drake Ct
  Dulwich SE19 . . . . **22** F3
  Kingston upon Thames KT5 . **37** F5
Drakefield Rd SW17 . . . . **21** A5
Drake Rd
  Chessington KT9 . . . . **57** A5
  Crawley RH10 . . . . **201** E3
  Horley RH6 . . . . **160** E3
  Mitcham CR4 . . . . **41** A3
  Thornton Heath CR0, CR9 . . **41** F2
Drakes Cl GU6 . . . . **174** E3
Drake's Cl KT10 . . . . **55** A6
Drakes Ct SE23 . . . . **23** C7
Drakes Way GU22 . . . . **89** D5
Drakewood Rd SW16 . . . . . . **21** D1
Draper Cl TW7 . . . .**5** D5
Drapers Cres KT12 . . . . **53** F1
Draven Cl BR2 . . . . **44** F2
Drax Ave SW20 . . . . **19** A1
Draxmont SW19 . . . . **19** E2
Draycot Rd KT6 . . . . **38** A1
Draycott RG12 . . . . **27** E4
Draycott Ct GU2 . . . . **130** B8
Dray Ct GU2 . . . . **130** B8
Drayhorse Dr GU19 . . . . **47** E2
Drayman Way TW7 . . . .**5** F4
Drayton Cl
  Bracknell RG12 . . . . **27** D7
  Fetcham KT22 . . . . **94** E3
  Hounslow TW4 . . . .**4** F2
Drayton Ct
  Tolworth KT5 . . . . **57** B8
  West Byfleet KT14 . . . . **71** A6
Drayton House Sch GU1 . . **130** F8
Drayton Rd CR0, CR9 . . . . . . **61** B8
Dreadnought Cl SW19 . . . . . **40** D7
Dresden Way KT13 . . . . **53** C5
Drew Ho 12 SW16 . . . . **21** E5
Drew Pl CR3 . . . . **100** D4
Drewstead La SW16 . . . . **21** D6
Drewstead Rd SW16 . . . . . . **21** D6
Dreycourt 4 KT4 . . . . **58** A8
Driftbridge The KT17 . . . . . . **77** C5
Drifters Dr GU16 . . . . **66** D1
Drift Rd SL4 . . . .**9** B8
Drift The KT24 . . . . **92** E3
Drift Way SL3 . . . .**1** C7
Driftway The
  Banstead SM7 . . . . **77** C4
  Mitcham CR4 . . . . **41** A8
Driftway (Worple Rd) The
  KT22 . . . . **95** B4
Driftwood Dr CR8 . . . . **80** C2
Drill Hall Rd
  Chertsey KT16 . . . . **33** A2
  Dorking RH4 . . . . **135** A7
Drive Ho CR4 . . . . **40** E5
Drive Mead CR5 . . . . **79** E5
Drive Rd CR5 . . . . **99** F7
Drivers Mead RH7 . . . . **164** D3
Drive Spur KT20 . . . . **98** B6
Drive The
  Artington GU3 . . . . **130** B5
  Ashford TW15 . . . . **14** D1
  Banstead SM7 . . . . **77** E3
  Beckenham BR3 . . . . **44** A8
  Belmont SM2 . . . . **77** F7
  Cobham KT11 . . . . **73** F5
  Copthorne RH10 . . . . **183** C3
  Coulsdon CR5, CR8 . . . . . . **79** E5
  Cranleigh GU6 . . . . **174** F2
  Farnham GU9 . . . . **146** B7
  Feltham TW14 . . . . **15** C8
  Fetcham KT22 . . . . **94** E5
  Godalming GU7 . . . . **150** F2
  Guildford GU2 . . . . **130** A7
  Guildford GU5 . . . . **173** C8
  Guildford, Park Barn GU2 . **108** F1
  Headley KT18, KT22 . . . . . **96** A3
  Horley RH6 . . . . **161** B1
  Hounslow TW3, TW7 . . . . . .**5** D5
  Ifold RH14 . . . . **212** D2
  Kingston upon Thames KT2 . **18** C1
  Leatherhead KT22, KT18 . . **95** F4
  Morden SM4 . . . . **40** D4
  Shackleford GU7, GU8 . . . **149** E4
  South Norwood CR7 . . . . . **42** D5

Drive The continued
  Surbiton KT6 . . . . **37** E2
  Thames Ditton KT10 . . . . . **36** C1
  Thorpe GU25 . . . . **31** F4
  Wallington CR8, SM6 . . . . . **60** D1
  West Ewell KT19 . . . . **57** F4
  West Wickham BR4 . . . . . . **44** D2
  Wimbledon SW19, SW20 . . **19** C1
  Woking GU22 . . . . **89** B7
  Wonersh GU5 . . . . **152** B6
Dr Johnson Ave SW17 . . . . . **21** B5
Dr Johnson Ho SW16 . . . . . . **21** D4
Drodges Cl GU5 . . . . **151** F8
Droitwich Cl
  Bracknell RG12 . . . . **27** E6
  Forest Hill SE26 . . . . **23** A5
Drove Rd GU4 . . . . **132** A7
Drovers Ct 3 KT1 . . . . **37** E7
Drovers Rd CR2 . . . . **61** D5
Drovers Way
  Ash GU12 . . . . **106** C1
  Bracknell RG12 . . . . **27** F6
  Hale GU9 . . . . **125** A6
Druce Wood SL5 . . . . **28** E8
Druid's Cl KT21 . . . . **95** F7
Druids Way BR2 . . . . **44** D5
Drumaline Ridge KT4 . . . . . . **57** E8
Drummond Cl RG12 . . . . **27** F8
Drummond Cl 4 GU1 . . . . . **109** D1
Drummond Gdns KT19 . . . . . **76** B8
Drummond Rd
  Crawley RH11 . . . . **200** E5
  Croydon CR0, CR9 . . . . . . **61** C8
  Guildford GU1 . . . . **109** D1
Drummonds Pl TW9 . . . .**6** E3
Drungewick La RH14 . . . . . **213** D3
Drury Cl RH10 . . . . **202** D4
Drury Cres CR0, CR9 . . . . . . **61** A8
Drury Lo 6 RH19 . . . . **185** F2
Dry Arch Rd SL5 . . . . **29** F3
Dryden RG12 . . . . **27** A2
Dryden 11 TW10 . . . . **17** D4
Dryden Rd
  Farnborough GU14 . . . . . . **84** F6
  Wimbledon SW19 . . . . **20** C2
Drynham Pk KT13 . . . . **53** E7
Du Cane Ct SW12 . . . . **21** A7
Ducavel Ho SW2 . . . . **21** F7
Duchess Cl
  Crowthorne RG45 . . . . **45** B7
  Sutton SM1 . . . . **59** C6
Duchess Ct KT13 . . . . **53** D7
Duchess of Kent Cl GU2 . . **109** B5
Duck's Wlk TW1 . . . .**6** C2
Dudley Cl KT15 . . . . **52** C7
Dudley Dr SM4 . . . . **39** E2
Dudley Gr KT18 . . . . **76** C5
Dudley Ho RG12 . . . . **27** C7
Dudley Rd
  Ashford TW15 . . . . **13** F4
  East Bedfont TW14 . . . . . . **14** D7
  Kingston upon Thames KT1 . **37** F6
  Richmond TW9 . . . .**7** A5
  Walton-on-Thames KT12 . . **35** A2
  Wimbledon SW19 . . . . **20** A2
Dudset La TW5 . . . .**4** A6
Duett Ct TW5 . . . .**4** E7
Duffield Rd KT20 . . . . **97** B3
Duffins Orch KT16 . . . . **51** C3
Duke Cl RH10 . . . . **202** C2
Duke of Cambridge Cl
  TW2 . . . .**5** D1
Duke of Connaughts Rd
  GU11 . . . . **105** D5
Duke of Cornwall Ave
  GU15 . . . . **46** D1
Duke of Edinburgh Rd
  SM1 . . . . **59** D8
Duke of Kent Sch GU6 . . . . **154** D2
Dukes Ave
  Hounslow TW4 . . . .**4** E3
  New Malden KT3 . . . . **38** F6
  Richmond KT2, TW10 . . . . . **17** D4
Duke's Ave W4 . . . .**7** D8
Dukes Cl
  Ashford TW15 . . . . **14** C4
  Cranleigh GU6 . . . . **175** A2
  Hale GU9 . . . . **125** A6
  Hampton TW12 . . . . **15** F3
Dukes Covert GU19 . . . . **47** E6
Dukes Ct
  Addlestone KT15 . . . . **52** C6
  Beckenham BR3 . . . . **43** E6
  Dulwich SE22 . . . . **23** A7
  4 Epsom KT19 . . . . **57** E2
  Farnborough GU14 . . . . . . **85** B3
Duke's Dr GU7 . . . . **150** B7
Dukes Green Ave TW14 . . . . .**4** A2
Dukes Hill CR3 . . . . **101** E7
Duke's Hill GU19 . . . . **47** E5
Dukeshill Rd RG42 . . . . **27** B8
Duke's La
  Cranbourne SL5 . . . .**9** F1
  Old Windsor SL4, SL5 . . . . **10** B3
Dukes Pk GU11 . . . . **105** D6
Dukes Rd KT12 . . . . **54** D5
Duke's Rd RH5 . . . . **179** D5
Dukes Ride RH5 . . . . **136** D4
Duke's Ride RG45 . . . . **45** B5
Dukes Sq RH12 . . . . **217** C1
Duke St
  Carshalton SM1 . . . . **59** D5
  Richmond TW10, TW9 . . . . . .**6** E2
  Woking GU21 . . . . **69** F2
Dukesthorpe Rd SE26 . . . . . **23** D4
Dukes Way BR4 . . . . **63** E7
Dukes Wlk GU9 . . . . **125** A6
Dukes Wood RG45 . . . . **45** B5

Dulcima Ho 13 RH12 . . . . . **217** C2
Dulshitt Gr KT18 . . . . **76** E6
Dulverton Ct 12 KT6 . . . . . . **37** E4
Dulverton Rd CR2 . . . . **62** C1
DULWICH **22** E5
Dulwich Bsns Ctr SE23 . . . . **23** D7
Dulwich Coll SE21 . . . . **22** E6
Dulwich Coll Inf Sch SE21 . . **22** F5
Dulwich Coll Prep Sch
  SE21 . . . . **22** E5
Dulwich Comm SE21 . . . . . . **22** E7
Dulwich Ct SE22 . . . . **23** B7
Dulwich Oaks The SE21 . . . **22** F5
Dulwich Picture Gall★
  SE21 . . . . **22** E8
DULWICH VILLAGE **22** E8
Dulwich Village SE21 . . . . . . **22** E8
Dulwich Wood Ave SE19 . . . **22** E3
Dulwich Wood Pk SE19,
  SE21 . . . . **22** E4
Dumbleton Cl KT2 . . . . **38** B8
Dumville Dr RH9 . . . . **121** B4
Dunally Pk TW17 . . . . **34** D2
Dunbar Ave
  Beckenham BR3 . . . . **43** E5
  Thornton Heath CR7, SW16 . **42** A7
Dunbar Ct
  3 Bromley BR2 . . . . **44** F5
  Carshalton SM1 . . . . **59** D5
  6 Walton-on-Thames KT12 . **35** C1
Dunbar Ho 1 RH1 . . . . **118** F1
Dunbar Rd
  Frimley GU16 . . . . **85** F7
  Kingston upon Thames KT3 . **38** C5
Dunbar St SE27 . . . . **22** C5
Dunboe Pl TW17 . . . . **34** C2
Dunbridge Ho SW15 . . . .**7** F1
Duncan Dr
  Guildford GU1 . . . . **110** A2
  Wokingham RG40 . . . . **25** F5
Duncan Gate 10 BR1 . . . . . . **24** F1
Duncan Gdns TW18 . . . . **13** A2
Duncan Rd
  Burgh Heath KT20 . . . . . . **97** E8
  Richmond TW9 . . . .**6** E3
Duncombe Ct TW18 . . . . **12** F1
Duncombe Hill SE23 . . . . . . **23** E8
Duncombe Ho 7 SW19 . . . . **19** D7
Duncombe Rd GU7 . . . . **150** D2
Duncroft Cl RH2 . . . . **117** F1
Duncroft Manor TW18 . . . . . **12** E4
Duncton Cl RH11 . . . . **201** B8
Dundaff Cl GU15 . . . . **66** A5
Dundas Cl RG12 . . . . **27** B5
Dundas Gdns KT8 . . . . **36** B6
Dundee Rd SE25 . . . . **43** B4
Dundela Gdns KT17, KT4 . . . **58** B6
Dundonald Prim Sch
  SW19 . . . . **19** F1
Dundonald Rd SW19 . . . . . . **19** F1
Dundonald Rd Halt SW19 . . **19** F1
Dundrey Cres RH1 . . . . **119** C6
Dundry Ho 8 SE26 . . . . **23** A5
Dunedin Dr CR3 . . . . **100** E2
Duneevan KT13 . . . . **53** E8
Dunelm Gr SE27 . . . . **22** C5
Dunfee Way KT14 . . . . **71** E7
Dunfield Gdns SE6 . . . . **24** B3
Dunfield Rd SE6 . . . . **24** B3
Dungates La RH3 . . . . **117** A2
Dunheved Cl CR7 . . . . **42** A3
Dunheved Ct 2 CR7 . . . . **42** A3
Dunheved Road N CR7 . . . . **42** A3
Dunheved Road S CR7 . . . . **42** A3
Dunheved Road W CR7 . . . . **42** A3
Dunhill Point 12 SW15 . . . . . **19** B7
Dunkeld Rd SE25 . . . . **42** D5
Dunkirk St 12 SE27 . . . . **22** C5
Dunleary Cl TW4 . . . . **15** F8
Dunley Dr CR0 . . . . **63** C4
Dunlin Cl RH1 . . . . **139** F4
Dunlin Ct 12 SE21 . . . . **22** D6
Dunlin Rise GU4 . . . . **110** D3
Dunmail Dr CR2, CR8 . . . . . . **80** E6
Dunmore GU2 . . . . **108** D2
Dunmore Rd SW20 . . . . **39** D8
Dunmow Cl TW13 . . . . **15** E4
Dunnets GU21 . . . . **68** E2
Dunnings Mill Sports Club
  RH19 . . . . **205** E6
Dunning's Rd RH19 . . . . . . **205** E7
Dunnock Ct 11 SE21 . . . . . . **22** D6
Dunnymans Rd SM7 . . . . **77** E4
Dunoon Gdns SE23 . . . . **23** D8
Dunoon Rd SE23 . . . . **23** C8
Dunottar Cl RH1 . . . . **139** D7
Dunottar Sch RH2 . . . . **139** D8
Dunraven Ave RH1 . . . . **140** D3
Dunraven Ho 12 TW9 . . . .**6** F6
Dunraven Sch SW16 . . . . . . **21** F5
Dunsborough Cotts GU23 . . **91** C7
Dunsbury Cl SM2 . . . . **59** B2
Dunsdon Ave GU2 . . . . **130** B8
DUNSFOLD **192** F5
Dunsfold Cl RH11 . . . . **201** A5
Dunsfold Common Rd
  GU8 . . . . **192** F5
DUNSFOLD GREEN **192** F6
Dunsfold Ho
  10 Kingston upon Thames
   KT2 . . . . **18** B2
  7 Streatham SW2 . . . . **21** F8
Dunsfold Rd
  Alfold GU6 . . . . **193** E3
  Bramley GU6 . . . . **173** C1
  Dunsfold GU8 . . . . **193** B8
  Plaistow GU8, RH14 . . . . **211** D4

Dunsfold Rise CR5 ..... 79 D6
Dunsfold Way CR0 ..... 63 C3
Dunsmore Rd KT12 .... 35 B3
Dunstall Pk CR5
  East Molesey KT8 ..... 35 F5
  Richmond TW10, TW9 ... 6 E3
Dunstall Pk GU14 ..... 85 A7
Dunstall Rd SW20 .... 19 C2
Dunstall Way KT8 .... 36 B6
Dunstan Ct
  Staines TW18 .... 13 A4
  1 Whyteleafe CR3 ...101 A8
Dunstan Rd CR5 ..... 79 D2
Dunstan's Rd SE22 ... 23 A8
Dunster Ave SM4 .... 39 D1
Dunster Ct 6 SW20 .. 39 D8
Dunster Ho SE6 ...... 24 B5
Dunster Way SM6 .... 41 A1
Dunton Cl KT6 ...... 37 E1
Dunton Ct SE26 ..... 23 B6
Dunton Ho 14 SW16 .. 21 E5
Duntshill Rd SW18 ... 20 B7
Dunvegan Cl KT8 .... 36 B5
Dunvegan Ho 14 RH1. 118 F1
Dupont Rd SW20 .... 39 D7
Duppas Ave CR0 ..... 61 B6
Duppas Cl TW17 ..... 34 D4
Duppas Ct CR0 ...... 61 B7
Duppas Hill La CR0 .. 61 B6
Duppas Hill Rd CR0 .. 61 B6
Duppas Hill Terr CR0, CR9. 61 B7
Duppas Jun Sch CR0. 61 B5
Duppas Rd CR0, CR9 . 61 B7
Dura Den Cl BR3 ..... 24 B1
Durand Cl SM5 ...... 40 F1
Durban Rd
  Beckenham BR3 ...... 43 F7
  West Norwood SE27 .. 22 D4
Durbin Rd KT9 ...... 56 F6
Durfold Dr RH2 ..... 118 C1
Durfold Rd RH12 .... 217 D7
Durfold Wood RH14 . 211 D5
Durfold Wood Woodlands
  Wlks* GU8 .... 211 C6
Durford Cres SW15 .. 19 B7
Durham Ave BR2 .... 44 F5
Durham Cl
  Crawley RH10 ...... 201 E2
  Guildford GU2 ...... 108 F3
  Wimbledon SW20 .... 39 B7
Durham Ct
  2 Leatherhead KT22 .. 95 A5
  Teddington TW11 .... 16 E4
Durham Dr GU16 .... 66 D1
Durham Hill BR1 .... 24 F4
Durham Ho BR2 ..... 44 E5
Durham Lodge SW20 . 39 B8
Durham Rd
  Beckenham BR2 ..... 44 F6
  Feltham TW14 ...... 15 C8
  Sandhurst GU47 .... 45 E2
  Wimbledon SW20 .... 39 B8
Durham Wharf Dr TW8 . 6 C7
Durkins Rd RH19 .... 185 D3
Durleston Park Dr KT23 . 94 C2
Durley Mead RG12 .. 27 F4
Durlston Rd KT2 .... 17 E2
Durnford Ho SE6 .... 24 B5
Durning Rd SE19 .... 22 D3
Durnsford Ave SW18,
  SW19 .... 20 A6
Durnsford Rd SW18, SW19 20 B5
Durnsford Way GU6.. 175 A2
Durnston Ct SM1 .... 59 B4
Durrell Way TW17.... 34 D3
Durrington Ave SW19 19 C1
Durrington Park Rd SW20 39 C8
Dutch Barn Cl TW19.. 2 D1
Dutchells Copse RH12. 217 E7
Dutch Gdns KT2 ..... 18 B2
Dutton Ho SW2 ..... 22 B7
Duval Pl GU19 ...... 47 E3
Duxford Ho 10 KT1 .. 38 A7
Duxhurst La RH2 .... 160 B7
Dwelly La
  Haxted TN8 ....165 D8
  Oxted TN8 .... 144 D3
Dyehouse Rd GU8.... 169 C4
Dyer House TW12 ... 36 B8
Dyer Rd RG40 ...... 25 E7
Dyers Almshouses RH10 201 D4
Dyer's Field RH6 .... 162 B3
Dykes Ct 11 SW2 ... 21 F7
Dykes Path GU22.... 70 C4
Dykes Way BR2 ..... 44 F6
Dymes Path SW19 ... 19 D6
Dymock Ho SM6 .... 60 C6
Dynevor Pl GU3 .... 108 C5
Dynevor Rd TW10 .... 6 E2
Dysart Ave KT2, TW10. 17 C4
Dysart Sch KT6 ..... 37 F2
Dyson Ct 7 RH4 .... 136 A7
Dyson Wlk RH11 .... 201 B1

E

Eady Cl RH13 .... 217 F2
Eagle Cl
  Crowthorne RG45 .... 45 A7
  Wallington SM6 ..... 60 E4
Eagle Ct 10 SE21 ... 22 D6
Eagle Hill SE19 ..... 22 D2
Eagle House Sch
  Mitcham CR4 .... 40 F7
  Sandhurst GU47 .... 45 B2
Eagle Rd GU1 ...... 109 D1
Eagles Dr TN16 ..... 83 D1

Eagles Nest GU47 ... 45 A1
Eagle Star Ho SM1 .. 59 B6
Eagle Trad Est CR4 .. 40 F3
Ealing Rd TW8 ...... 6 E8
Eardley Rd SW16 ... 21 C2
Eardley Sch SW16 ... 21 C2
Earle Gr RG12 ...... 27 B2
Earle Ho 2 RH19 ... 185 F2
Earleswood KT11 ... 73 E7
Earl of Chester Dr GU16. 86 D8
Earl Rd SW14 .... 7 C3
Earlsbrook Rd RH1 . 139 F7
EARLSFIELD 20 C7
Earlsfield Ho 13 KT2. 37 D8
Earlsfield Prim Sch SW18 20 C6
Earlsfield Rd SW18 .. 20 C8
Earlsfield Sta SW18 . 20 C7
Earls Gr GU15 ...... 65 C6
Earlsthorpe Rd SE26. 23 D4
EARLSWOOD 139 F7
Earlswood RG12 .... 27 B2
Earlswood Ave CR7 . 42 A4
Earlswood Cl RH13 . 218 A4
Earlswood Comm Nature
  Reserve* RH1 ..... 139 E6
Earlswood Ct RH1 .. 139 F7
Earlswood Ho 2 SW2. 21 F7
Earlswood Inf Sch 1
  RH1 ....140 A8
Earlswood Rd RH1 . 139 F7
Earlswood Sta RH1 . 139 F7
Early Commons RH10 201 E7
Easby Cres SM4 .... 40 B3
Easedale Ho TW7 .... 5 F2
Eashing La
  Godalming GU7, GU8 .150 A3
  Shackleford GU7, GU8. 149 F3
Eashing Point 9 SW15. 19 B7
Easington Pl GU1 ... 130 F8
East Ave
  Heath End GU9 .....125 D6
  Wallington SM6 ..... 60 F5
  Whiteley Village KT12 . 53 F1
Eastbank Rd TW12 .. 16 C3
EAST BEDFONT 14 E7
Eastbourne Gdns SW14. 7 C4
Eastbourne Rd
  Chiswick W4 .... 7 C8
  Felbridge RH7 ......184 C4
  Feltham TW13 ...... 15 D6
  Godstone RH9 ......121 D2
  Mitcham SW17 ..... 21 A2
  Newchapel RH7 .... 163 F5
  South Godstone RH9. 142 E4
Eastbrook Cl GU21 .. 70 A3
Eastbury Gr 7 W4 .... 7 E8
Eastbury La GU3 ... 129 A3
Eastbury Rd KT2 .... 17 E1
Eastchurch Rd TW6 .. 3 E4
Eastchurch Road Rdbt
  TW6 .... 3 E5
EAST CLANDON 111 E4
Eastcote Ave KT8 ... 36 A4
Eastcott Cl KT2 .... 18 C3
Eastcourt TW16 .... 35 C7
Eastcroft Ct GU1 ... 131 A8
Eastcroft Mews RH12. 216 F1
Eastcroft Rd KT19 .. 57 E3
East Croydon Sta/Halt
  CR0 .... 61 D8
Eastdean Ave KT18 .. 76 B6
East Dr
  Wallington SM5 .... 59 F2
  Wentworth GU25 ... 31 B3
Eastern Ave
  Brookwood GU24 ... 88 B6
  Chertsey KT16 ..... 33 A6
Eastern Bsns Pk TW6... 3 F5
Eastern Ind Area RG12. 27 D7
Eastern La RG45 .... 45 F4
Eastern Perimeter Rd
  TW14 .... 3 F5
Eastern Rd
  Aldershot GU12 .... 105 E2
  Bracknell RG12 .... 27 D7
Eastern View TN16 .. 83 C2
Easter Way RH9 .... 142 F5
EAST EWELL 58 D1
Eastfield Rd RH1 ... 140 C8
Eastfields GU8 ..... 170 F5
Eastfields Rd CR4 .. 41 A7
East Flexford La GU3. 128 F6
Eastgate
  Banstead SM7 ..... 77 F5
  12 Woking GU22 ... 69 F2
Eastgate Gdns GU1. 130 E8
Eastgate Ho 3 GU1. 130 E8
Eastgate Mews 4 RH13. 217 D1
East Gdns
  Mitcham SW17, SW19. 20 E2
  Woking GU22 ...... 70 C2
East Gn GU17 ...... 64 C4
EAST GRINSTEAD .. 185 E2
East Grinstead Mus*
  RH19 .... 185 F1
East Grinstead Rd RH7. 164 D3
East Grinstead Sta RH19 185 D1
EASTHAMPSTEAD .. 27 B5
East Hampstead Mobile
  Home Pk RG40 .... 45 C8
Easthampstead Park Sch
  RG12 .... 26 D3
Easthampstead Rd
  Bracknell RG12 .... 27 A7
  Wokingham RG40 .. 25 E4

EASTHEATH 25 B3
Eastheath Ave RG41. 25 A4
Eastheath Gdns RG41. 25 B3
East Hill
  Biggin Hill TN16 .... 83 B1
  Dormans Park RH19. 185 D1
  Oxted RH8 .... 122 F6
  South Croydon CR2 . 61 E1
  Woking GU22 ...... 70 C2
East Hill Ct RH8 .... 122 F5
East Hill La RH10 ... 183 D5
East Hill Rd RH8 ... 122 E6
East India Way CR0 . 42 F1
East La
  Kingston upon Thames
  KT1 .... 37 D6
  West Horsley KT24 .. 92 D1
Eastlands Cl RH8 ... 122 D8
Eastlands Way RH8 . 122 D8
Eastleigh Cl SM2 ... 59 B3
Eastleigh Rd TW6 .... 3 F4
Eastleigh Way TW14. 15 A7
Eastleigh Wlk 9 SW15. 19 A8
East Lodge 8 KT22 . 95 C6
Eastman Way KT19 . 57 B1
Eastmead
  Farnborough GU14 .. 85 B3
  Woking GU21 ...... 69 B2
East Meads GU2 ... 130 A8
Eastmearn Rd SE21, SE27. 22 C6
EAST MOLESEY 36 C4
Eastmont Rd KT10 .. 55 F8
Eastney Rd CR0 .... 42 B1
Eastnor Cl RH2 .... 138 F6
Eastnor Rd RH2 .... 139 A6
Easton Ho 4 SE27 .. 22 B5
East Park La RH7 ... 163 C1
East Parkside CR6 .. 82 B4
East Pk KT1 .... 37 D6
East Pl SE27 .... 22 C4
East Ramp TW6 ..... 3 B6
East Rd
  East Bedfont TW14 . 14 D8
  Kingston upon Thames KT2. 37 E8
  Merton SW19 ...... 20 C2
  Reigate RH2 .... 117 F2
  Weybridge KT13 .... 53 D3
East Ring GU10 .... 127 A7
Eastry Ave BR2 ..... 44 F3
EAST SHALFORD ... 131 A3
East Shalford La GU4. 131 A3
EAST SHEEN 7 D3
East Sheen Ave SW14. 7 D3
East Sheen Prim Sch SW14 7 E3
East St
  Brentford TW8 ...... 6 C7
  Ewell KT17 .... 76 E7
  Farnham GU9 ...... 125 C3
  Great Bookham KT23. 94 B2
  Horsham RH12 .... 217 C1
  Rusper RH12 ...... 199 E7
  Turners Hill RH10, RH19. 204 C4
East Station Rd GU12. 105 B1
East Stratton Cl RG12. 27 F4
East Surrey Coll RH1. 119 A5
East Surrey Hospl RH1. 140 A5
East Surrey Mus* CR3. 101 A3
East View Cotts GU6. 174 C3
East View La GU6 .. 174 C3
Eastway
  Crawley RH6 ...... 182 B7
  Epsom KT19 .... 76 D8
  Guildford GU2 ..... 108 F1
  Merton SM4, SW20. 39 E5
  Wallington SM6 .... 60 C6
East Way CR0 ..... 62 E7
Eastway E RH6 ..... 182 C7
Eastwell Cl BR3 .... 23 E1
East Whipley La GU5. 173 F7
Eastwick Ct 2 SW19. 19 D7
Eastwick Dr KT23 .. 94 B4
Eastwick Inf Sch KT23. 94 B3
Eastwick Jun Sch KT23. 94 B3
Eastwick Park Ave KT23. 94 B3
Eastwick Rd
  Great Bookham KT23. 94 B2
  Hersham KT12 ..... 54 B5
East Wlk RH2 ..... 118 B1
Eastwood
  Crawley RH10 ..... 201 F6
  3 Weybridge KT13. 53 D4
Eastwood Lodge GU5. 151 F7
Eastwood Rd GU5 .. 151 F7
Eastwood St SW16 . 21 C2
Eastworth Rd KT15, KT16. 33 A1
Eaton Ct
  Guildford GU1 ..... 110 A3
  Sutton SM2 .... 59 D4
  West Norwood SE27. 22 D4
Eaton Dr KT2 ...... 18 A1
Eaton Ho GU1 ..... 130 F7
Eaton Lodge SM2 .. 59 D4
Eaton Pk KT11 .... 73 F5
Eaton Pk KT11 .... 73 E5
Eaton Rd
  Camberley GU15 ... 65 B4
  Isleworth TW3, TW7 .. 5 D3
  Sutton SM2 .... 59 D4
Eatonville Rd SW17 . 20 F6
Eatonville Villas SW17. 20 F6
Eaves Cl KT15 ..... 52 C4
Ebba's Way KT18 ... 76 B4
Ebbisham Cl RH4 .. 136 A7
Ebbisham Ct
  Epsom KT18 ...... 76 C4
  Felbridge RH19 .... 185 A4
Ebbisham La KT20 .. 97 A4

Ebbisham Rd
  Epsom KT18 ...... 76 B5
  North Cheam KT4 .. 58 C8
Ebenezer Wlk CR4 .. 41 C8
Ebor Cotts SW15 ... 18 E5
Ebsworth St SE23 .. 23 D8
Ebury Mews SE27 .. 22 B5
Ecclesbourne Inf Sch CR7 42 C4
Ecclesbourne Jun Sch
  CR7 .... 42 C4
Ecclesbourne Rd CR7. 42 C4
Eccleshill 6 BR2 .... 44 F5
Eccles Hill RH5 .... 136 C3
Echelford Dr TW15 .. 14 A4
Echelford Prim Sch The
  TW15 .... 14 B3
Echo Barn La GU10 . 145 F5
Echo Pit Rd GU1, GU4. 130 E6
Eclipse Est KT19 .... 76 C6
Ecob Cl GU3 ...... 108 F5
Ecton Rd KT15 .... 52 B6
Ector Rd SE6 ...... 24 E6
Eddeys Cl GU35 ... 187 B6
Eddeys La GU35 ... 187 B6
Eddington Hill RH11. 201 B1
Eddington Rd RG12 . 26 E3
Eddinton Cl CR0 ... 63 C4
Eddisbury Ho 7 SE26. 23 A5
Eddy Rd GU12 ..... 105 C1
Eddystone Ct GU10. 167 F1
Eddystone Wlk TW19. 13 E8
Ede Cl TW4 .... 4 F4
Ede Ct KT17 .... 76 F7
Edenbrook RH7 .... 164 E4
Eden Cl KT15 ...... 52 B1
Edencourt Rd SW16 . 21 B2
Edencroft GU5 ..... 151 F7
Edenfield Gdns KT4 . 57 F7
Eden Grove Rd KT14. 71 E6
Edenhall 1 KT12 ... 35 A2
Edenham High Sch CR0. 43 F2
Eden Mews SW17 .. 20 C5
Eden Park Ave BR3.. 44 A4
Eden Park Sta BR3.. 44 A4
Eden Pl SL5 .... 30 A2
Eden Rd
  Crawley RH11 ..... 200 F4
  Croydon CR0 ...... 61 D6
  Penge BR3 .... 43 E8
  West Norwood SE27. 22 B3
Edenside Rd KT23 .. 93 F3
Edensor Gdns W4 .... 7 E7
Edensor Rd W4 ..... 7 E7
Eden St KT1, KT2 .. 37 E7
Eden Vale
  Dormans Park RH19. 185 F5
  East Grinstead RH19. 185 D4
Edenvale Cl CR4 ... 21 A1
Edenvale Rd CR4 .. 21 A1
Eden Way
  Beckenham BR3 ... 44 A3
  Warlingham CR6 ... 81 E1
Eden Wlk 5 KT1 ... 37 E7
Eden Wlk Sh Ctr KT1. 37 E7
Ederline Ave SW16 . 42 A7
Ede's Cotts KT21 ... 95 D8
Edgar Cl RH10 .... 202 E5
Edgar Ct KT3 ...... 38 E6
Edgar Rd
  South Croydon CR2. 61 D2
  Tatsfield TN16 .... 103 D6
  Twickenham TW4 .. 15 F8
Edgbarrowhill Star RG45. 45 A3
Edgbarrow Rise GU47. 45 A2
Edgbarrow Sch RG45. 45 C3
Edgbarrow Sp Ctr RG45. 45 C3
Edgbarrow Woods Nature
  Reserve* RG45 .... 45 B4
Edgcumbe Park Dr RG45. 45 A5
Edgeborough Ct 6 GU1. 130 F8
Edgeborough Sch GU10. 146 C3
Edge Cl KT13 ...... 53 A3
Edgecombe Ho SW19. 19 E8
Edgecombe CR2 .... 62 D2
Edgecoombe Cl KT2. 18 D1
Edgecumbe Ct
  2 Croydon CR0 .... 43 A1
  Egham TW18 ...... 12 F2
Edgedale Cl RG45 .. 45 B4
Edgefield Cl
  Cranleigh GU6 ..... 174 C4
  Redhill RH1 .... 140 A4
Edge Hill SW19 .... 19 D1
Edge Hill Ct 4 KT12. 35 C1
Edge Hill Ct SW19 . 19 D1
Edgehill Ho 4 RH1 . 118 F1
Edgehill Rd
  Mitcham CR4 ...... 41 B8
  Purley CR2, CR8 ... 61 B1
Edge L Ctr The GU27. 207 D7
Edgeley KT23 ...... 93 E3
Edgell Cl GU25 .... 31 F6
Edgell Rd TW18 .... 12 F3
Edgemoor Rd GU16. 66 C3
Edge Point Cl SE27. 22 B3
Edgewood Cl RG45 . 45 A7
Edgewood Gn CR0 . 43 D1
Edgeworth Cl CR3 . 81 A1
Edgington Rd SW16. 21 D2
Edinburgh Cl
  Catford SE6 .... 24 F7
  2 Kingston upon Thames
  KT1 .... 37 E6
  West Barnes SM4 .. 39 D4
Edinburgh Dr TW15, TW18. 13 D1
Edinburgh Ho SM1 . 59 D8
Edinburgh Rd SM1 . 59 D8

Edinburgh Way RH19. 205 F7
Edith Ct TW14 .... 3 D1
Edith Gdns KT5 .... 38 B2
Edith Rd
  Thornton Heath SE25. 42 D4
  Wimbledon SW19 .. 20 B2
Edmonds Ct RG12 .. 27 C8
Edmund Gr TW13 .. 15 F6
Edmund Rd CR4 ... 40 E6
Edmunds Gate 7 GU7. 150 D4
Edna Rd SW20 ..... 39 D7
Edolph's Copse Nature
  Reserve* RH6 .... 159 C2
Edrich Rd RH11 ... 201 A1
Edridge Ho 9 SE27. 22 B5
Edridge Rd CR0, CR9. 61 D7
Educare Small Sch KT2. 37 E8
Edward Alleyn Ho SE21. 22 D8
Edward Ave
  Camberley GU15 ... 65 A5
  Morden CR4, SM4 .. 40 D4
Edward Cl TW12 ... 16 C3
Edward Ct
  10 Aldershot GU11. 105 A1
  Farnborough GU14 . 85 B4
  Staines TW18 ...... 13 C2
Edward Ho
  East Molesey KT8 .. 36 A4
  Epsom KT19 .... 57 B1
  12 Guildford GU1 . 109 D1
  Redhill RH1 .... 140 A6
Edward II Ave KT14 . 71 F5
Edward Pauling Ho TW14. 14 F8
Edward Pauling Prim Sch
  TW13 .... 14 E6
Edward Pinner Ct 5 KT6. 56 E8
Edward Rd
  Biggin Hill TN16 .... 83 E1
  Coulsdon CR5 ..... 79 D4
  Croydon CR0 ...... 42 E2
  Farnham GU9 ..... 146 C7
  Hampton TW12 .... 16 C3
  Hatton TW14 .... 3 E2
  Penge SE20 ...... 23 D2
  Windlesham GU20 .. 48 D4
Edwards Cl KT4 .... 58 D8
Edwards Ct 5 CR2 . 61 E6
Edwards Ho 7 TW10. 17 C5
Edward St 2 GU11 . 105 A2
Edward Way TW15 . 13 F6
Edwina Ct SM1 .... 59 B6
Edwin Cl KT24 ..... 92 D2
Edwin Pl 9 CR0 .... 42 D1
Edwin Rd
  Twickenham TW2 .. 16 E7
  West Horsley KT24. 92 D2
Edwins Ct GU14 ... 85 C7
Edwin Stray Ho TW13. 16 A5
Eelmoor Plain Rd GU11. 104 D5
Eelmoor Rd
  Aldershot GU11 ... 104 D5
  Farnborough GU14 . 84 F2
Eelmoor Road Trad Est
  GU14 .... 84 F2
EFFINGHAM 113 E8
Effingham Cl SM2 .. 59 B3
Effingham Common Rd
  KT24 .... 93 C2
Effingham Ct
  Mitcham SW19 .... 20 E1
  13 Woking GU22 .. 89 E8
Effingham Ho 9 KT2. 18 B2
Effingham Junction Sta
  KT24 .... 93 A4
Effingham La RH10 . 183 E4
Effingham Lodge 1 KT6. 37 E4
Effingham Pl KT24 . 113 D8
Effingham Rd
  Copthorne RH10, RH6. 183 D6
  Reigate RH2 ...... 139 B8
  Thames Ditton KT6, KT7. 37 C2
  Thornton Heath CR0. 41 F2
Effort St SW17 .... 20 E3
Effra Cl SW19 ..... 20 B2
Effra Ct SE19 ..... 22 E1
Effra Rd SW19 .... 20 B2
Egan Cl CR3 ...... 100 D3
Egbury Ho SW15 .... 7 F1
Egerton Ct
  7 Guildford GU2 .. 108 E1
  5 Richmond TW10. 6 E2
Egerton Ho W4 ..... 7 C8
Egerton Pl KT13 ... 53 C4
Egerton Rd
  Guildford GU2 ..... 129 F8
  New Malden KT3 .. 38 F5
  Sandhurst GU15 ... 64 F7
  Sandhurst GU15 ... 65 A7
  South Norwood SE25. 42 E6
  Twickenham TW2 .. 16 E8
  Weybridge KT13 ... 53 C4
Egerton Way UB3 .... 3 B7
Eggar's Ct GU12 ... 105 B1
Eggar's Hill GU11 . 126 A8
EGHAM 12 A4
Egham Bsns Village
  TW20 .... 32 C7
Egham By-Pass TW20. 12 A4
Egham Cl
  Cheam SM3 .... 58 E8
  Putney SW19 ..... 19 E6
Egham Cres SM3 ... 58 D8
Egham Ct KT6 ..... 37 D4
Egham Hill TW20 ... 11 D2
Egham Hill Rdbt TW20. 11 F3

EGHAM HYTHE 12 E2
Egham L Ctr TW20 . . . . . . 12 B2
Egham Mus★ TW20 . . . . . 12 A3
Egham Sta TW20 . . . . 12 A3
EGHAM WICK 11 A1
Egleston Rd SM4 . . . . 40 B3
Egley Dr GU22 . . . . 89 D5
Egley Rd GU22 . . . . 89 D6
Eglinton Rd GU10 . . . . . . 168 B7
Eglise Rd CR6 . . . . 81 E2
Egmont Ave KT6 . . . . 37 F1
Egmont Ct KT12 . . . . 35 B2
Egmont Ho
  18 Sutton SM2 . . . . 59 C3
  Walton-on-Thames KT12 . . 35 B1
Egmont Mews KT19 . . . . . 57 D6
Egmont Park Rd KT20 . . . . 97 A2
Egmont Rd
  New Malden KT3 . . . . 38 F5
  Surbiton KT6 . . . . 38 A1
  Sutton SM2 . . . . 59 C3
  Walton-on-Thames KT12 . . 35 B2
Egmont Way KT20 . . . . 97 E8
Egremont Rd SE27 . . . . . . 22 A5
Egret Gdns GU11 . . . . . . 126 A7
Eight Acres GU26 . . . . . . 188 C7
Eighteenth Rd CR4 . . . . . . 41 E5
Eileen Rd SE25 . . . . 42 D4
Eindhoven Cl SM5 . . . . . . 41 A1
Eisenhower Ho KT8 . . . . . . 37 C8
Eland Pl CR9 . . . . 61 B7
Eland Rd
  Aldershot GU12 . . . . 105 D1
  Croydon CR0, CR9 . . . . . . 61 B7
Elberon Ave CR0 . . . . 41 C3
Elborough Rd SE25 . . . . . . 43 A4
Elborough St SW18 . . . . . . 20 A7
Elbourne Ho 3 RH6 . . . . 161 B3
Elbow Mdw SL3 . . . . 1 F6
Elcho Rd GU24 . . . . 87 D8
Elderberry Gr 10 SE27 . . . 22 C4
Elder Cl GU4 . . . . 110 A4
Elderfield Pl SW17 . . . . . . 21 B4
Elder Gdns 9 SE27 . . . . . 22 C4
Eldergrove GU14 . . . . 85 E2
Elder Oak Cl SE20 . . . . . . 43 B8
Elder Rd
  Bisley GU24 . . . . 68 A4
  West Norwood SE27 . . . . . 22 C3
Eldersley Cl RH1 . . . . 118 F3
Eldersley Gdns RH1 . . . . 118 F3
Elderslie Cl BR3 . . . . 44 B3
Elderton Rd SE26 . . . . 23 E4
Eldertree Pl CR4 . . . . 41 C8
Eldertree Way CR4 . . . . . . 41 C8
Elder Way RH5 . . . . 136 C3
Elderwood Pl SE27 . . . . . . 22 C3
Eldon Ave
  Croydon CR0 . . . . 62 C8
  Heston TW5 . . . . 5 A7
Eldon Ct KT13 . . . . 53 C5
Eldon Dr GU10 . . . . 146 D5
Eldon Pk SE25 . . . . 43 B5
Eldon Rd CR3 . . . . 100 D6
Eldrick Cl TW14 . . . . 14 D7
Eldridge Cl TW14 . . . . 15 A7
Eleanor Ave KT19 . . . . 57 D1
Eleanor Ct GU1 . . . . 130 D7
Eleanor Gr SW13, SW14 . . . 7 E4
Eleanor Ho
  Ewell KT17 . . . . 76 E1
  6 Merton SW19 . . . . 40 B8
Electric Par 4 KT6 . . . . . . 37 D3
Elenora Terr 5 SM1 . . . . . 59 C5
Elfin Gr TW11 . . . . 16 F3
Elfin Lodge 11 TW11 . . . . 16 F3
Elfrida Cres SE6 . . . . 24 A4
Elfrida Prim Sch SE6 . . . . 24 A4
Elgar Ho
  Crowthorne RG45 . . . . 45 B7
  Thornton Heath SW16 . . . . 41 E6
  Tolworth KT5, KT6 . . . . . . 38 B2
Elgar Ho
  Kenley CR8 . . . . 80 C5
  Twickenham TW2 . . . . 5 D1
Elgar Way RH13 . . . . 218 B4
Elger Way RH10 . . . . 183 A4
Elgin Ave TW15 . . . . 14 C2
Elgin Cl RH13 . . . . 217 F3
Elgin Cres
  Caterham CR3 . . . . 101 A5
  Harlington TW6 . . . . 3 E5
Elgin Ct
  6 Croydon CR0 . . . . 61 C6
  Purley CR8 . . . . 80 B8
Elgin Gdns GU1 . . . . 110 A2
Elgin Pl KT13 . . . . 53 C4
Elgin Rd
  Croydon CR0 . . . . 61 F8
  Sutton SM1 . . . . 59 C7
  Wallington SM6 . . . . 60 C4
  Weybridge KT13 . . . . 53 B5
Elgin Way GU1 . . . . 85 F8
Eliot Bank SE23, SE26 . . . 23 B6
Eliot Bank Prim Sch SE26 23 B6
Eliot Cl GU15 . . . . 66 B7
Eliot Dr GU27 . . . . 207 E6
Eliot Ho 11 TW10 . . . . 6 F1
Elis David Almshouses
  CR0 . . . . 61 B6
Elixwood Cotts RH5 . . . . 134 D1
Elizabethan Ct TW19 . . . . 13 D8
Elizabethan Way
  Crawley RH10 . . . . 202 C5
  Stanwell TW19 . . . . 13 D8

Elizabeth Ave
  Bagshot GU19 . . . . 47 F2
  Staines TW18 . . . . 13 D2
Elizabeth Cl
  Bracknell RG12 . . . . 27 C5
  Cheam SM1 . . . . 58 F6
Elizabeth Cotts 5 TW9 . . . . 7 A6
Elizabeth Cres RH19 . . . . 185 F3
Elizabeth Ct
  Croydon CR0 . . . . 61 E7
  Ewell KT17 . . . . 57 F2
  Farncombe GU7 . . . . 150 E7
  Horley RH6 . . . . 161 A3
  Kingston upon Thames KT2 . 37 E8
  2 Oatlands Park KT13 . . . 53 D6
  Streatham SW17 . . . . 21 A3
  Sunbury TW16 . . . . 35 C6
  3 Teddington TW11 . . . . . 16 E3
  West Barnes SM4 . . . . . . 39 E2
  Whyteleafe CR3 . . . . 80 F1
Elizabeth Gdns
  Ascot SL5 . . . . 29 B4
  Isleworth TW7 . . . . 6 A3
  Sunbury TW16 . . . . 35 C6
Elizabeth Hart Ct KT13 . . 52 F5
Elizabeth Ho
  1 Ashford TW15 . . . . 13 F4
  Caterham CR3 . . . . 101 A3
  Cheam SM3 . . . . 58 E4
Elizabeth Rd
  Farncombe GU7 . . . . 150 E7
  Wokingham RG40 . . . . 25 D6
Elizabeth Way
  Feltham TW13 . . . . 15 C4
  South Norwood SE19 . . . . 22 D1
Elkins Gdns GU4 . . . . . . 110 A4
Elkins Gr GU9 . . . . 124 F2
Ella Cl BR3 . . . . 44 A7
Ellacombe Ho 1 SW2 . . . 22 A8
Elland Rd KT12 . . . . 54 D8
Ellenborough Cl RG12 . . . 27 D8
Ellenbridge Way CR2 . . . . 61 E2
Ellens Ct BR4 . . . . 63 D8
ELLEN'S GREEN 196 A4
Elleray 2 GU22 . . . . 70 B2
Elleray Ct GU12 . . . . 106 A5
Ellerdine Rd TW3 . . . . 5 D3
Ellerker Gdns TW10 . . . . . . 6 E1
Ellerman Ave TW2 . . . . . . 15 F7
Ellerslie Ct 6 SM6 . . . . . . 60 B4
Ellerslie Ct RG40 . . . . 25 E5
Ellerton Rd
  Surbiton KT6 . . . . 37 F1
  Wandsworth SW17, SW18 . 20 D7
  Wimbledon SW20 . . . . 19 A1
Ellerton Way GU10 . . . . . 145 F2
Ellery Cl GU6 . . . . 174 E1
Ellery Rd SE19 . . . . 22 D1
Elles Ave GU1 . . . . 110 C1
Elles Cl GU14 . . . . 85 B3
Ellesfield Ave RG12 . . . . . 26 E5
Ellesmere Ave BR3 . . . . . . 44 B7
Ellesmere Ct
  Chiswick W4 . . . . 7 D8
  Penge SE20 . . . . 43 B7
  Weybridge KT12 . . . . 53 E4
Ellesmere Dr CR2 . . . . 81 B5
Ellesmere Pl KT12 . . . . . . 53 E5
Ellesmere Rd
  Twickenham TW1 . . . . 6 C1
  Weybridge KT13 . . . . 53 E4
Ellice Rd RH8 . . . . 122 F6
Ellies Mews TW15 . . . . . . 13 E6
Ellingham GU22 . . . . 89 E8
Ellingham Prim Sch KT9 . 56 D3
Ellingham Rd KT9 . . . . . . 56 D4
Ellington Rd
  Feltham TW13 . . . . 14 F4
  Hounslow TW3 . . . . 5 B4
Ellington Way KT18 . . . . . 77 B2
Elliot Cl RH10 . . . . 202 C4
Elliott Cl GU21 . . . . 70 A3
Elliott Gdns TW17 . . . . . . 34 A5
Elliott Ho 3 CR7 . . . . 42 B5
Elliott Park GU12 . . . . . . 105 E2
Elliott Rd CR7 . . . . 42 B5
Elliott Rise SL5 . . . . 28 E7
Ellis Ave GU2 . . . . 129 F7
Ellis Cl CR5 . . . . 99 F7
Ellis Farm Cl GU22 . . . . . 89 D5
Ellisfield Dr SW15 . . . . . . 19 A8
Ellison Rd
  Barnes SW13 . . . . 7 F5
  Streatham SW16 . . . . 21 E1
Ellison Way
  Tongham GU10 . . . . 126 F7
  Wokingham RG40 . . . . 25 B6
Ellis Rd
  Coulsdon CR5 . . . . 99 F7
  Crowthorne RG45 . . . . 45 B6
  Mitcham CR4 . . . . 40 F3
Ellora Rd SW16 . . . . 21 D3
Ellson Cl RH10 . . . . 202 C4
Ellswood Ct 18 KT6 . . . . . 37 D2
Elmbank Ave
  Englefield Green TW20 . . . 11 B2
  Guildford GU2 . . . . 130 A8
Elm Bank Gdns SW13 . . . . 7 E5
Elm Bank Mans SW13 . . . . 7 E5
Elmbourne Rd SW17 . . . . 21 B5
Elmbridge Ave KT5 . . . . . . 38 C3
Elmbridge Cotts GU6 . . . 174 B3
Elmbridge La GU22 . . . . . 89 F8
Elmbridge Mus★ KT13 . . 53 A6

Elmbridge Open Space
  Nature Reserve★ KT5 . . 38 C3
Elmbridge Rd GU6 . . . . . 173 F2
ELMBRIDGE VILLAGE . . . 173 F2
Elmbridge Xcel L Ctr
  KT12 . . . . 35 B4
Elmbrook Cl TW16 . . . . . . 35 B8
Elmbrook Rd SM1 . . . . 58 F6
Elm Cl
  Box Hill KT20 . . . . 116 C5
  Carshalton SM5 . . . . 40 F1
  Leatherhead KT22 . . . . . . 95 B5
  Send Marsh GU23 . . . . . . 91 A3
  South Croydon CR2 . . . . . 61 E4
  Stanwell TW19 . . . . 13 D7
  Tolworth KT6 . . . . 38 C2
  Twickenham TW2 . . . . 16 B6
  Warlingham CR6 . . . . 81 D2
  West Barnes SW20 . . . . . 39 C5
  Woking GU21 . . . . 69 D4
Elm Cres
  Heath End GU9 . . . . 125 D7
  Kingston upon Thames KT2 . 37 E8
Elmcroft
  2 Ashford TW15 . . . . 14 A3
  Little Bookham KT23 . . . . 94 A3
  12 Woking GU22 . . . . 69 E1
Elmcroft Cl
  Chessington KT9 . . . . 56 E7
  Feltham TW14 . . . . 3 F1
  Frimley GU16 . . . . 85 F7
Elm Croft Ct RH10 . . . . . 201 E6
Elmcroft Dr
  Ashford TW15 . . . . 14 A3
  Chessington KT9 . . . . 56 E7
Elm Ct
  Catford SE6 . . . . 24 B7
  5 Charlton TW16 . . . . . . 14 F1
  3 East Grinstead RH19 . 185 D2
  East Grinstead, Sunnyside
  RH19 . . . . 205 E8
  Knaphill GU21 . . . . 68 D2
  Mitcham CR4 . . . . 40 F7
  Sandhurst GU47 . . . . 45 E2
  Walton-on-Thames KT12 . . 54 C8
Elmdene KT5 . . . . 38 C1
Elmdene Cl BR3 . . . . 43 F4
Elmdene Ct 15 GU22 . . . . 89 E8
Elmdon Rd
  Hatton TW6 . . . . 3 F4
  Hounslow TW5 . . . . 4 E5
Elm Dr
  Chobham GU24 . . . . 49 F1
  Cranbourne SL4 . . . . 9 B7
  East Grinstead RH19 . . . 186 A1
  Leatherhead KT22 . . . . . . 95 B4
  Sunbury TW16 . . . . 35 C7
Elmer Cotts KT22 . . . . 95 A4
Elmer Gdns TW7 . . . . 5 D5
Elmer Mews KT22 . . . . 95 A5
Elmer Rd SE6 . . . . 24 C8
Elmer's Dr TW11 . . . . 17 B2
ELMERS END 43 D6
Elmers End Rd
  Beckenham BR3 . . . . 43 D5
  Penge BR3, SE20 . . . . . . 43 D5
Elmers End Sta/Halt BR3 43 D5
Elmerside Rd BR3 . . . . . . 43 E5
Elmers Rd
  Croydon CR0, SE25 . . . . . 43 A2
  Ockley RH5 . . . . 177 C4
Elmfield KT23 . . . . 94 A4
Elmfield Ave
  Mitcham CR4 . . . . 41 A8
  Teddington TW11 . . . . 16 F3
Elm Field Cotts GU3 . . . . 108 A2
Elmfield Ho GU4 . . . . 110 A4
Elmfield Mans 5 SW17 . . . 21 A6
Elmfield Rd SW17 . . . . . . 21 B6
Elmfield Way CR2 . . . . 61 F2
Elmgate Ave TW13 . . . . . . 15 C5
Elm Gdns
  Burgh Heath KT18 . . . . . . 97 C8
  Claygate KT10 . . . . 55 F6
  Mitcham CR4 . . . . 41 D5
Elm Gr
  Bisley GU24 . . . . 68 A3
  Caterham CR3 . . . . 100 E5
  Cranleigh GU6 . . . . 174 A3
  Epsom KT18 . . . . 76 C5
  Heath End GU9 . . . . 125 C7
  Horsham RH13 . . . . 217 E1
  Kingston upon Thames KT2 . 37 E8
  Sutton SM1 . . . . 59 B6
  Wimbledon SW19 . . . . . . 19 E1
Elmgreen Sch The SE27 . . 22 C4
Elmgrove Cl GU21 . . . . . . 88 D8
Elm Grove Par SM6 . . . . . 60 A4
Elmgrove Rd
  Croydon CR0 . . . . 43 B2
  Weybridge KT13 . . . . 53 A7
Elm Grove Rd
  Barnes SW13 . . . . 7 F5
  Cobham KT11 . . . . 73 D3
  Farnborough GU14 . . . . . . 85 B4
Elm Hill Bglws GU3 . . . . 106 E3
Elm Ho
  3 Kingston upon Thames
  KT2 . . . . 17 F1
  Teddington TW11 . . . . 17 C1
  Weybridge KT13 . . . . 53 B6
Elmhurst SM1 . . . . 59 D8
Elmhurst Ave CR4 . . . . . . 21 B1
Elmhurst Ct
  Camberley GU15 . . . . 65 D5

Elmhurst Ct continued
  Croydon CR0 . . . . 61 D5
  Guildford GU1 . . . . 130 F8
Elmhurst Dr RH4 . . . . 136 B5
Elmhurst Lodge 5 SM2 . . 59 C3
Elmhurst Sch for Boys
  CR2 . . . . 61 D5
Elm La
  Ash GU10 . . . . 126 F8
  Forest Hill SE6 . . . . 23 F6
  Ockham GU23 . . . . 92 A8
Elmore Rd CR5 . . . . 99 A6
Elmpark Gdns CR2 . . . . . . 62 C1
Elm Park Rd SE25 . . . . . . 42 F6
Elm Pk
  Streatham SW2 . . . . 21 F8
  Sunningdale SL5 . . . . 29 E1
Elm Pl GU11 . . . . 126 C8
Elm Rd
  Beckenham BR3 . . . . 43 F7
  Carshalton CR4, SM6 . . . . 41 A1
  Chessington KT9 . . . . 56 E6
  Claygate KT10 . . . . 55 F4
  East Bedfont TW14 . . . . . 14 D8
  Ewell KT17 . . . . 57 F4
  Farncombe GU7 . . . . 150 F8
  Heath End GU9 . . . . 125 D7
  Kingston upon Thames KT2 . 37 F8
  Leatherhead KT22 . . . . . . 95 B5
  Mortlake SW14 . . . . 7 C3
  New Malden KT3 . . . . 38 D6
  Purley CR8 . . . . 80 B6
  Redhill RH1 . . . . 118 E1
  South Norwood CR7 . . . . . 42 D5
  Warlingham CR6 . . . . 81 D2
  Woking GU21 . . . . 69 D1
  Woking, Horsell GU21 . . . . 69 D1
Elm Road W SM3, SM4 . . . 39 F2
Elmscott Rd BR1 . . . . 24 F3
Elms Cotts CR4 . . . . 40 F7
Elms Ct SW19 . . . . 20 B1
Elmshorn KT17 . . . . 77 C3
Elmside
  Guildford GU2 . . . . 130 A8
  Milford GU8 . . . . 149 F1
  New Addington CR0 . . . . . 63 B4
Elmsleigh Ct
  Farnborough GU14 . . . . . . 84 F4
  1 Sutton SM1 . . . . 59 B7
Elmsleigh Ho TW2 . . . . . . 16 D6
Elmsleigh Rd
  Farnborough GU14 . . . . . . 84 F4
  Staines TW18 . . . . 12 F3
  Twickenham TW2 . . . . 16 D6
Elmsleigh Sh Ctr TW18 . . 12 F4
Elmslie Cl KT18 . . . . 76 C5
Elms Rd
  Aldershot GU11 . . . . 105 A2
  Wokingham RG40 . . . . 25 B5
Elmstead RH19 . . . . 205 E8
Elmstead Cl KT19 . . . . 57 E5
Elmstead Gdns KT4 . . . . . 58 A7
Elmstead Rd KT14 . . . . . . 71 A5
Elms The
  7 Ashford TW15 . . . . 14 A3
  Ash GU10 . . . . 126 A6
  Blackwater GU17 . . . . 64 D4
  Claygate KT10 . . . . 55 F3
  Croydon CR0 . . . . 42 C1
  Farnham GU9 . . . . 125 C2
  Hamsey Green CR6 . . . . . 81 C4
  Mortlake SW13 . . . . 7 F4
  Newell Green RG42 . . . . . . 8 A2
  Twickenham TW1 . . . . 6 C2
  Wallington SM6 . . . . 60 C6
Elmsway TW15 . . . . 14 A3
Elmswood KT23 . . . . 93 F3
Elmsworth Ave TW3 . . . . . . 5 B5
Elm Tree Ave KT10 . . . . . . 36 E2
Elmtree Cl KT14 . . . . 71 E6
Elm Tree Cl
  Ashford TW15 . . . . 14 B3
  Chertsey KT16 . . . . 51 E8
Elmtree Rd TW11 . . . . 16 E3
Elm Tree Wlk GU14 . . . . . 84 F8
Elm View GU12 . . . . 106 B3
Elm Way
  North Cheam KT4 . . . . 58 C7
  West Ewell KT19 . . . . 57 D5
Elm Wlk SW20 . . . . 39 D5
Elmwood Ave TW13 . . . . . 15 B5
Elmwood Cl
  Ashtead KT21 . . . . 75 D2
  Hackbridge SM6 . . . . 60 B8
  Stoneleigh KT17 . . . . 58 A3
Elmwood Ct KT21 . . . . 75 D2
Elmwood Dr KT17 . . . . 58 A3
Elmwood Ho TW13 . . . . . . 15 B5
Elmwood Inf Sch CR0 . . . 42 B3
Elmwood Jun Sch CR0 . . 42 B3
Elm Wood Prim Sch SE27 22 D5
Elmwood Rd
  Chiswick W4 . . . . 7 C8
  Knaphill GU21 . . . . 88 D3
  Mitcham CR4 . . . . 40 F6
  Redhill RH1 . . . . 119 B5
  Thornton Heath CR0 . . . . . 42 B2
Elmworth Gr SE21 . . . . . . 22 D6
Elphinstone Cl
  Brookwood GU24 . . . . 88 A6
  Pirbright GU24 . . . . 87 F6
Elphinstone Ct SW16 . . . . 21 E2
Elsa Ct 6 BR3 . . . . 43 F8
Elsdon Rd GU21 . . . . 69 A1
Elsenham St SW18, SW19 . 19 F6
Elsenwood Cres GU15 . . . 66 A6
Elsenwood Dr GU15 . . . . . 66 A7
Elsinore Ave TW19 . . . . . . 13 E8

Elsinore Rd SE23 . . . . 23 E7
Elsinore Way TW9 . . . . 7 B4
Elsley Cl GU16 . . . . 85 F6
Elsrick Ave SM4 . . . . 40 A4
Elstan Way CR0 . . . . 43 E2
ELSTEAD 148 D3
Elstead Ct SM4 . . . . 39 E1
Elstead Gn GU8 . . . . 148 D4
Elstead Ho 12 SW2 . . . . . 21 F8
Elstead Rd
  Milford GU8 . . . . 149 C3
  Seale GU10 . . . . 127 B2
  Shackleford GU8 . . . . . . 149 E6
Elsted Cl RH11 . . . . 201 B8
Elston Pl GU12 . . . . 126 C8
Elston Rd GU12 . . . . 126 C8
Elstree Hill BR1 . . . . 24 E1
Elsworth Cl TW14 . . . . 14 E7
Elsworthy KT7 . . . . 36 E3
Elthorne Ct TW13 . . . . 15 C7
Elton Cl KT1 . . . . 17 C1
Elton Rd
  Kingston upon Thames
  KT2 . . . . 38 A8
  Purley CR8 . . . . 79 C7
Elveden Cl GU22 . . . . 71 B2
Elveden Ct 9 KT22 . . . . . . 95 C6
Elveden Rd KT11 . . . . 73 C8
Elvedon Rd TW13 . . . . 14 F5
Elvington Gn BR2 . . . . 44 F4
Elvington Lodge 5 RH2 . 118 A2
Elvino Rd SE26 . . . . 23 E3
Elwell Cl TW20 . . . . 12 A2
Elwill Way BR3 . . . . 44 D5
Ely Cl
  Crawley RH10 . . . . 201 F2
  Frimley GU16 . . . . 86 A7
Kingston upon Thames
  SW20 . . . . 38 F7
Ely Ho 9 RH1 . . . . 118 F1
Ely Rd
  Hatton TW6 . . . . 3 F5
  Hounslow TW4 . . . . 4 C4
  Thornton Heath CR0 . . . . . 42 D4
Elystan Cl SM6 . . . . 60 C2
Emanuel Dr TW12 . . . . . . 15 F3
Emarc Ho 3 GU11 . . . . . 105 B2
Embankment The
  Twickenham TW1 . . . . 17 A7
  Wraysbury TW19 . . . . 11 C7
Embassy Ct
  Kingston upon Thames
  KT6 . . . . 37 D4
  7 Wallington SM6 . . . . . . 60 B4
Embassy Gdns BR3 . . . . . 43 F8
Ember Cl KT15 . . . . 52 D5
Embercourt Rd KT10, KT7,
  KT8 . . . . 36 E3
Ember Ctr KT12 . . . . 54 E8
Ember Farm Ave KT8 . . . . 36 D3
Ember Farm Way KT8 . . . . 36 E2
Ember Gdns KT10, KT8 . . 36 E2
Ember Ho BR1 . . . . 24 D3
Ember La KT10, KT8 . . . . . 36 D2
Emberhurst Sch KT10 . . . 36 D2
Ember La KT10, KT8 . . . . . 36 D2
Emberwood RH11 . . . . . . 201 D8
Embleton Rd GU35 . . . . . 187 B6
Embleton Wlk TW12 . . . . . 15 F3
Emerald Ct CR5 . . . . 79 D4
Emerald Ho 9 CR0 . . . . . 61 D8
Emerson Ct
  Crowthorne RG45 . . . . 45 B5
  7 Wimbledon SW19 . . . . . 19 E2
Emerton Rd KT22 . . . . 94 C6
Emery Down Cl RG12 . . . . 28 A6
Emily Davison Dr
  Banstead KT18 . . . . 77 B1
  Burgh Heath KT18 . . . . . . 97 B8
Emley Rd KT15 . . . . 52 B6
Emlyn La KT22 . . . . 95 A5
Emlyn Rd
  Horley RH6 . . . . 160 E4
  Redhill RH1 . . . . 140 A7
Emmanuel Cl GU2 . . . . . 109 A4
Emmanuel Ho SE21 . . . . . 22 D5
Emmanuel Rd SW12 . . . . 21 C7
Emmbrook Rd RG41 . . . . . 25 A8
Emmbrook Sch The RG41 . 25 A8
Emmeline Ct 1 KT12 . . . . 35 C2
Emmetts Cl GU21 . . . . 69 D2
Emmott Ho RH2 . . . . 118 B1
Empire Villas RH1 . . . . . . 161 A7
Empress Ave GU14 . . . . . . 85 B5
Empress Ct 8 GU14 . . . . . 85 B4
Emsworth Cl RH10 . . . . . 202 C3
Emsworth Ct 4 SW12 . . . . 21 E5
Emsworth St SW2 . . . . 21 F6
Ena Rd SW16 . . . . 41 E6
Endale Cl SM5 . . . . 59 F8
Endeavour Pl GU10 . . . . . 145 E8
Endeavour Way
  Wallington CR0 . . . . 41 E2
  Wimbledon SW19 . . . . . . 20 B4
Enderley House SE19 . . . . 42 F8
Endlesham Ct 4 SW12 . . . 21 A8
Endlesham Rd SW12 . . . . 21 A8
Endsleigh Cl CR2 . . . . 62 C1
Endsleigh Gdns
  Hersham KT12 . . . . 54 C5
  Kingston upon Thames KT6 . 37 C3
Endsleigh Mans 4 SW16 . 21 E5
Endsleigh Rd RH1 . . . . . . 119 C6
Endway KT5 . . . . 38 B2
Enfield Rd
  Ash GU12 . . . . 106 C1
  Crawley RH11 . . . . 201 C2
  Harlington TW6 . . . . 3 E5
Enfield Road Rdbt TW6 . . . 3 E5

Engadine Cl CR0 . . . . 61 F7
Engadine St SW18 . . . . . 20 A7
Engalee RH19. . . . . .185 C2
England Way KT3 . . . . 38 B5
Englefield RH12. . . . . .216 F2
Englefield Cl
  Englefield Green TW20 . . . . 11 C2
  Thornton Heath CR0 . . . . . 42 C3
ENGLEFIELD GREEN . . . 11 B1
Englefield Green Inf Sch
  TW20 . . . . 11 C3
Englefield Rd GU21 . . . . . . 68 D2
Engleheart Dr TW14 . . . . . . .3 E1
Engleheart Rd SE6 . . . . . . 24 C8
Englehurst TW20 . . . . 11 C2
Englemere Pk
  Ascot SL5. . . . . 28 D5
  Oxshott KT22. . . . . 74 B6
Englemere Pond Nature
  Reserve★ SL5 . . . . 28 C6
Englesfield GU15 . . . . 66 D5
Engliff La GU22. . . . . 71 A3
English Cotts RH1. . . . . . .120 A6
Enid Wood Ho RG12. . . . . 27 C7
Enmore Ave SE25 . . . . . . 43 A4
Enmore Gdns SW14 . . . . . .7 D2
Enmore Rd SE25 . . . . 43 A4
Ennerdale RG12. . . . . 27 A5
Ennerdale Cl
  Cheam SM1 . . . . 58 F6
  Crawley RH11 . . . . .201 B4
  East Bedfont TW14 . . . . . . 14 F7
Ennerdale Gr GU9. . . . . . .125 A6
Ennerdale Rd TW9 . . . . . . .6 F5
Ennismore Ave GU1. . . . .109 F1
Ennismore Gdns KT7 . . . . 36 A5
Ennor Ct KT4 . . . . 58 C6
Ensign Cl
  Purley CR8 . . . . 61 A1
  Stanwell TW19 . . . . 13 D7
Ensign Way
  Stanwell TW19 . . . . 13 D7
  Wallington SM6 . . . . 60 E3
Enterdent Cotts RH9 . . . .121 D2
Enterdent Rd RH9. . . . . . .121 D2
Enterdent The RH9. . . . . .121 D2
Enterprise Cl CR0 . . . . 42 A1
Enterprise Ct RG12 . . . . . . 26 F7
Enterprise Ct RH10. . . . . .181 D2
Enterprise Ctr TW RH10. 181 F2
Enterprise Est GU1. . . . . .109 E5
Enterprise Ho
  2 Aldershot GU11 . . . . . .105 B2
  Walton-on-Thames KT12 . . . 35 B2
Enterprise Ind Est GU12. 105 E5
Enterprise Way TW11 . . . . 16 F2
ENTON GREEN 171 B5
Enton Hall GU8 . . . . .171 B5
Enton La GU8 . . . . .171 B3
Enton Pl TW3 . . . . .5 B3
Enversham Ct SE23 . . . . . 23 E5
Envis Way GU3. . . . . .108 C4
Eothen Cl CR3 . . . . .101 A3
Epping Way RG12 . . . . . . 27 F5
Epping Wlk RH10 . . . . . . .201 D4
EPSOM. 76 C5
Epsom Bsns Pk KT17. . . . 76 E8
Epsom Cl GU15 . . . . 65 C8
Epsom Coll KT17. . . . . . . 77 A5
Epsom Comm Nature
  Reserve★ KT18 . . . . 75 F5
Epsom Downs Metro Ctr
  KT20. . . . . 97 B7
Epsom Downs Sta KT17. . 77 B4
Epsom & Ewell High Sch
  KT19 . . . . 57 C5
Epsom General Hospl
  KT18 . . . . 76 C4
Epsom Ho SM1 . . . . 59 B6
Epsom Lane N KT18, KT20. 97 B7
Epsom Lane S KT20 . . . . 97 C5
Epsom Pl GU6 . . . . .174 F3
Epsom Prim Sch KT19. . . 76 D8
Epsom Rd
  Ashtead KT18, KT21 . . . . . 76 A2
  Crawley RH10 . . . . .202 A4
  Croydon CR0 . . . . 61 A6
  East Clandon GU4 . . . . . .111 D3
  Ewell KT17 . . . . 76 F8
  Guildford GU4 . . . . .110 F2
  Guildford, Merrow GU1,
    GU4. . . . . .110 C1
  Leatherhead KT22 . . . . . . 95 C6
  Morden SM3, SM4. . . . . . 39 F2
  West Horsley GU4, KT24. .112 C5
Epsom Sq TW6 . . . . .3 F5
Epsom Sta KT19 . . . . 76 D6
Epworth Rd TW7, TW8 . . .6 B7
Eresby Dr BR3 . . . . 44 A1
Erica Cl GU24 . . . . 67 E6
Erica Cotts GU26 . . . . . . .188 C6
Erica Ct GU22 . . . . 69 D1
Erica Dr RG40. . . . . 25 D5
Erica Gdns CR0 . . . . 63 B7
Erica Ho **6** SW19 . . . . . . 19 E1
Erica Way
  Copthorne RH10 . . . . . . .183 A2
  Horsham RH12 . . . . .217 D5
Eridge Cl RH10 . . . . .202 D6
Erin Cl BR1 . . . . 24 E1
Erindale Ct **1** BR3 . . . . . 44 A8
Erlswell Cres KT12 . . . . . . 53 F4
Erlswell Rd KT12. . . . . . . 53 F5
Erkenwald Cl KT16 . . . . . 32 E3
Ermine Cl TW4. . . . . .4 C5
Ermyn Cl KT21. . . . . 95 D6
Ermyn Cotts RH6. . . . . . .163 A6
Ermyn Way KT22 . . . . 95 D6

Erncroft Way TW1 . . . . . . .5 F1
Ernest Ave SE27 . . . . 22 B4
Ernest Bevin Coll SW17 . 20 E6
Ernest Cl
  Beckenham BR3. . . . . 44 A4
  Farnham GU10, GU9 . . . .146 B6
Ernest Cotts KT17. . . . . . 57 F3
Ernest Gdns W4 . . . . .7 B8
Ernest Gr BR3 . . . . 43 F4
Ernest Rd KT1 . . . . 38 B7
Ernest Sq KT1 . . . . 38 B7
Ernle Rd SW20 . . . . 19 C1
Ernst Chain Rd GU2 . . . .129 D8
Eros Ho SE6 . . . . 24 B8
Erridge Rd SW19 . . . . 40 A7
Errington Manor SM5 . . . 59 F7
Errol Gdns KT3 . . . . 39 A5
Erskine Cl
  Carshalton SM1 . . . . 59 E7
  Crawley RH11 . . . . .200 E2
Erskine Rd SM1. . . . . 59 D7
Esam Way SE27, SW16 . . 22 A3
Escombe Ct **5** CR3 . . . . .101 A8
Escombe Dr GU2, GU3 . . .109 B6
Escot Rd TW16 . . . . 14 C1
Escott Pl KT16 . . . . 51 D4
ESHER. 55 C6
Esher Ave
  Cheam SM3 . . . . 58 D7
  Walton-on-Thames KT12 . . 35 A1
Esher CE High Sch KT10. 55 A7
Esher CE Prim Sch KT10 55 C5
Esher Cl KT10. . . . . 55 B5
Esher Coll KT7. . . . . 36 E2
Esher Comm Nature
  Reserve★ KT10 . . . . 55 A1
Esher Cres TW6. . . . . .3 F5
Esher Gdns SW19 . . . . . . 19 D6
Esher Gn KT10. . . . . 55 B6
Esher Green Dr KT10 . . . . 55 B7
Esher Mews **3** CR4 . . . . 40 F6
Esher Park Ave KT10 . . . . 55 C5
Esher Place Ave KT10 . . . 55 B6
Esher Rd
  Camberley GU15 . . . . 47 A1
  East Molesey KT8 . . . . . . 36 D4
  Hersham KT10, KT12. . . . . 54 E6
Esher Sta KT10 . . . . 55 D8
Eskdale Gdns CR8. . . . . . 80 D5
Eskdale Way GU15 . . . . . 66 D4
Eskmont Ridge SE19 . . . . 22 E1
Esme Ho SW15. . . . . .7 F3
Esparto St SW18 . . . . 20 B8
Essame Cl RH19. . . . . 25 D6
Essendene Cl CR3. . . . . .100 E4
Essendene Lodge Sch
  CR3. . . . . .100 E4
Essendene Rd CR3. . . . . .100 E5
Essenden Rd CR2 . . . . . . 61 E3
Essex Ave TW7. . . . . .5 E4
Essex Cl
  Addlestone KT15 . . . . 52 C6
  Frimley GU16. . . . . 86 A7
  West Barnes SM4 . . . . . . 39 D2
Essex Ct
  Barnes SW13. . . . . .7 F5
  South Norwood SE19. . . . 22 D2
Essex Dr GU6 . . . . .173 F2
Essex Gr SE19 . . . . 22 D2
Essex Ho
  5 Croydon CR0. . . . . . . 61 D8
  Thames Ditton KT7 . . . . . 37 A2
Essex Tower **5** SE20 . . . 43 B8
Estcots Cty Prim Sch
  RH19. . . . . .186 A1
Estcots Dr RH19. . . . . . . .186 A1
Estcourt Rd CR0, SE25 . . . 43 B3
Estella Ave KT3 . . . . 39 B5
Estoria Cl SW2. . . . . 22 A8
Estreham Rd SW16. . . . . . 21 D2
Estridge Cl TW3 . . . . .5 A3
Eswyn Rd SW17 . . . . 20 F3
Ethel Bailey Cl RH19. . . . . 76 A7
Ethelbert Rd SW20. . . . . . 39 D8
Ethelbert St SW12 . . . . . . 21 B7
Ethel Rd TW15. . . . . 13 E3
Ethelred Ct **4** CR3 . . . . .101 A8
Ethelworth Ct **4** SW2 . . 22 A7
Etherley Hill RH5 . . . . . . .177 A7
Etherow St SE22 . . . . 23 A8
Etherstone Gn SW16 . . . . 22 A4
Etherstone Rd SW16 . . . . 22 A4
Eton Ave
  Heston TW5. . . . . .5 A8
  New Malden KT3 . . . . 38 D5
Eton Cl SW18 . . . . 20 B8
Eton Ct
  Staines TW18. . . . . 12 F3
  Teddington TW11 . . . . 16 D3
Eton Ho **7** TW20. . . . . . . 12 A3
Eton Pl GU9 . . . . .125 B7
Eton Rd UB3 . . . . .3 F7
Eton St TW10. . . . . .6 E2
Etps Rd GU14 . . . . .105 A8
Ettrick Ct GU14. . . . . . . .105 B8
Etwell Pl KT5 . . . . 37 F3
Eureka Rd KT1. . . . . 38 A7
Europa Park Rd GU1 . . . .109 C2
Eurythmy Sch RH19 . . . .205 D6
Eustace Cres RG40 . . . . . 25 D8
Eustace Rd GU4. . . . . . . .110 D3
Euston Rd CR0. . . . . 42 A1
Evans Cl RH10 . . . . .202 D5
Evans Gr TW13. . . . . 16 A6
Evans Rd SE6 . . . . 24 E6
Eve Ct CR4 . . . . 41 A7
Evedon RG12 . . . . 27 B2
Evelina Rd SE20. . . . . 23 D1

Eveline Day Sch **1** SW17. 20 F6
Eveline Rd CR4 . . . . 40 F8
Evelyn Ave
  Aldershot GU11 . . . . .126 B8
  Titsey RH8 . . . . .103 C3
Evelyn Cl
  Felbridge RH19 . . . . .184 F4
  Twickenham TW2. . . . . . . 16 B8
  Woking GU22. . . . . 89 D7
Evelyn Clark Ho RH18 . . .206 F2
Evelyn Cotts
  Abinger Common RH5 . . . .155 D8
  South Godstone RH9 . . . .142 E6
Evelyn Cres TW16. . . . . . . 34 F8
Evelyn Ct CR0. . . . . 43 A2
Evelyn Gdns
  Richmond TW9 . . . . .6 E3
  Tyler's Green RH9 . . . . . .121 C5
Evelyn Lancaster Ho
  RH12 . . . . .217 E6
Evelyn Rd
  Richmond, Ham TW10. . . . 17 C5
  Richmond TW9. . . . . .6 E4
  Wimbledon SW19 . . . . . . 20 B2
Evelyn Terr TW9 . . . . .6 E4
Evelyn Way
  Epsom KT19 . . . . 76 A8
  Stoke D'Abernon KT11. . . 73 F3
  Sunbury TW16 . . . . 34 F8
  Wallington SM6 . . . . 60 D6
Evelyn Wlk RH10. . . . . . .201 E3
Evelyn Woods Rd GU11. .105 C7
Evendon's Cl RG41 . . . . . 25 A3
Evendon's La RG41. . . . . 25 A3
Evening Hill BR3. . . . . 24 C1
Evenlode Way GU47 . . . . 64 D8
Everard La CR3 . . . . .101 B5
Eve Rd
  Isleworth TW7 . . . . .6 A3
  Sheerwater GU21 . . . . . . 70 B4
Everest Ct
  South Norwood SE19. . . . . 42 E8
  Woking GU21. . . . . 68 E3
Everest Rd
  Camberley GU15 . . . . 65 D8
  Crowthorne RG45 . . . . . . 45 B6
  Stanwell TW19 . . . . 13 E8
Everglade TN16. . . . . 83 D1
Everglades BR2. . . . . 44 E6
Evergreen Ct TW19 . . . . . 13 D8
Evergreen Rd GU16 . . . . . 66 A3
Evergreens The GU8 . . . .171 B1
Everglade Way GU19. . . . 13 D8
Everlands Cl **6** GU22. . . . 69 E1
Eversfield Ct **2** RH2 . . . .118 C1
Eversfield Rd
  Horsham RH13 . . . . .217 E1
  Reigate RH2. . . . . .118 B1
  Richmond TW9. . . . . .6 F5
Eversley Cres TW7 . . . . . .5 D6
Eversley Pk SW19 . . . . . . 19 B3
Eversley Rd
  Kingston upon Thames
    KT5. . . . . 37 F4
  South Norwood SE19 . . . . 22 D1
Eversley Way
  Croydon CR0 . . . . 63 A7
  Thorpe TW20 . . . . 32 C7
Everton Rd CR0 . . . . 43 A1
Evesham Cl
  Belmont SM2 . . . . 59 A3
  Reigate RH2. . . . . .117 F2
Evesham Ct GU1 . . . . . . .131 A8
Evesham Gn SM4 . . . . . . 40 B3
Evesham Rd
  Morden SM4 . . . . 40 B3
  Reigate RH2. . . . . .117 F2
Evesham Road N RH3 . . .117 F2
Evesham Wlk GU47 . . . . . 45 D1
Ewart Rd SE23 . . . . 23 D8
Ewelands RH6 . . . . .161 C4
EWELL. 58 A1
Ewell By-Pass KT17. . . . . 58 A2
Ewell Castle Jun Sch
  KT17. . . . . 58 A2
Ewell Castle Sch KT17. . . 58 A2
Ewell Court Ave KT19 . . . 57 E5
Ewell Downs Rd KT17 . . . 77 A7
Ewell East Sta KT17. . . . . 58 B1
Ewell Grove Ct **4** KT17. . 57 F2
Ewell Grove Inf Sch **5**
  KT17. . . . . 57 F1
Ewell House KT17 . . . . . . 57 F1
Ewell House Gr KT17 . . . . 57 F1
Ewell Park Gdns KT17. . . 58 A3
Ewell Park Way KT17. . . . 58 A3
Ewell Rd
  Cheam SM2, SM3 . . . . . . 58 D4
  Surbiton KT5, KT6 . . . . . . 37 F2
  Thames Ditton KT6, KT7 . . 37 B2
  Tolworth KT6. . . . . 38 A1
Ewell West Sta KT19 . . . . 57 E2
Ewelme Rd SE23 . . . . 23 C7
Ewen Cres SW2. . . . . 22 A8
EWHURST. 175 F5
Ewhurst Ave CR2. . . . . . . 61 F2
Ewhurst CE Inf Sch GU6. 175 E5
Ewhurst Cl
  Crawley RH11 . . . . .201 C6
  East Ewell SM2 . . . . 58 C2
Ewhurst Ct CR4. . . . . 40 D6
EWHURST GREEN 175 E4
Ewhurst Rd
  Cranleigh GU6 . . . . .174 E3
  Crawley RH11 . . . . .201 C7
  Peaslake GU6 . . . . .154 D5
Ewins Cl GU12 . . . . .106 A2

Ewood La RH5 . . . . .158 C6
EWSHOT 124 D8
Ewshot Hill Cross GU10 .124 D7
Exbury Rd SE6 . . . . 24 A6
Excalibur Cl RH11. . . . . . .200 E5
Excelsior Cl KT1 . . . . 38 A7
Exchange Rd
  Ascot SL5. . . . . 29 C4
  Crawley RH10 . . . . .201 E6
Exchange The
  8 Purley CR8 . . . . 80 A8
  14 Woking GU22 . . . . . . 69 F2
Exeforde Ave TW15 . . . . . 14 A4
Exeter Cl RH10 . . . . .201 E2
Exeter Ct
  Kingston upon Thames
    KT6. . . . . 37 E4
  Mitcham SW19 . . . . 20 E1
Exeter Ho
  Feltham TW13 . . . . 16 A6
  Woking GU21 . . . . 69 F3
Exeter Rd
  Ash GU12. . . . . .106 A3
  Croydon CR0 . . . . 42 F2
  Feltham TW13 . . . . 15 F5
  Harlington TW6 . . . . .3 E4
Exeter Way TW6 . . . . .3 E5
Explorer Ave TW19 . . . . . 13 E8
Eyebright Cl CR0. . . . . . . 43 D1
Eyhurst Cl KT20 . . . . 97 F3
Eyhurst Spur KT20 . . . . . 97 F3
Eyles Cl RH12. . . . . .217 B4
Eylewood Rd SE27 . . . . . 22 C3
Eyot Lodge **9** TW1 . . . . . 17 A7
Eyre Ct RG40 . . . . 25 B4
Eyston Dr KT13 . . . . 53 A1

F

Fabyc Ho TW9 . . . . .7 A7
Factory Cotts GU10 . . . . .124 D2
Factory La CR0, CR9 . . . . 61 B8
Fagg's Rd TW14 . . . . .4 A2
Fairacre
  Hounslow TW7. . . . . .5 D6
  Kingston upon Thames KT3. 38 E6
Fairacres
  Burgh Heath KT20 . . . . . . 97 C6
  Cobham KT11 . . . . 73 E7
  New Addington CR0. . . . . . 62 F2
  Salfords RH1. . . . . .140 C1
Fairbairn Cl CR8 . . . . 80 A6
Fairborne Way GU2 . . . . .109 A4
Fairbourne KT11. . . . . 73 D6
Fairbourne Cl GU21 . . . . . 69 A1
Fairbourne La CR3 . . . . . .100 C4
Fairbriar Ct **9** KT18. . . . . 76 E6
Fairchildes Ave CR0. . . . . 82 D7
Fairchildes Cotts CR6 . . . 82 F6
Fairchildes Prim Sch CR9 82 E7
Fairchildes Rd CR6. . . . . . 82 E7
Faircroft SE26 . . . . 23 C4
Faircross RG12 . . . . 27 B6
Fairdene Rd CR5. . . . . . . 79 D2
Fairfax RG42 . . . . 27 A8
Fairfax Ave
  Ewell KT17 . . . . 58 B2
  Redhill RH1 . . . . .118 F2
Fairfax Cl
  Oxted RH8 . . . . .122 E5
  Walton-on-Thames KT12 . . 35 B1
Fairfax Ind Est GU14 . . . .105 E2
Fairfax Mews GU14 . . . . . 85 D2
Fairfax Rd
  Farnborough GU14 . . . . . . 85 C7
  Old Woking GU22. . . . . . . 90 B7
  Teddington TW11 . . . . 17 B1
FAIRFIELD 95 B6
Fairfield App TW19 . . . . . 11 D8
Fairfield Ave
  Horley RH6 . . . . .161 A1
  Staines TW18 . . . . 12 F4
  Twickenham TW2. . . . . . . 16 B7
Fairfield Cl
  Dorking RH4. . . . . .115 C1
  Great Bookham KT23. . . . . 94 B1
  Guildford GU2 . . . . .109 A4
  Mitcham CR4 . . . . 20 E1
  West Ewell KT19 . . . . 57 E5
Fairfield Cotts GU8 . . . . .191 C3
Fairfield Ct
  Dorking RH4. . . . . .115 B1
  Leatherhead KT22 . . . . . . 95 B6
Fairfield Dr
  Dorking RH4. . . . . .136 B8
  Frimley GU16. . . . . 65 E3
Fairfield E KT1★ 37 E7
Fairfield Halls★ CR0 . . . . 61 D7
Fairfield Ind Est KT1 . . . . 37 F6
Fairfield La GU24 . . . . 68 A7
Fairfield Lodge GU2 . . . . .109 A2
Fairfield N KT1, KT2 . . . . . 37 E7
Fairfield Path CR0, CR9 . . 61 E7
Fairfield Pk KT11 . . . . 73 D5
Fairfield Pl KT1. . . . . 37 E6
Fairfield Rd
  Beckenham BR3. . . . . 44 A7
  East Grinstead RH19. . . . .205 F8
  Kingston upon Thames KT1. 37 E7
  Leatherhead KT22 . . . . . . 95 B6
  South Croydon CR0, CR9 . . 61 E7
Fairfield Rise GU2 . . . . . .108 F2
Fairfields
  Chertsey KT16. . . . . 33 B1
  Lewisham SE6 . . . . 24 B8
Fairfield S KT1. . . . . 37 F7
Fairfields Rd TW3. . . . . . . .5 C4

Fairfield The GU9 . . . . . .125 C2
Fairfield W KT1. . . . . 37 E7
Fairfield Way
  Coulsdon CR5 . . . . 79 D5
  West Ewell KT19 . . . . 57 E5
Fairfield Wlk KT22 . . . . . . 95 B6
Fairford SE6 . . . . 24 A7
Fairford Ave CR0. . . . . . . 43 D4
Fairford Cl
  Croydon CR0 . . . . 43 E4
  Pyrford KT14. . . . . 70 F5
  Reigate RH2. . . . . .118 C3
Fairford Ct SM2. . . . . 59 B3
Fairford Gdns KT4 . . . . . . 57 F7
Fair Green Ct **1** CR4 . . . . 40 F6
Fairgreen Rd CR7. . . . . . . 42 B4
Fairhall RH2 . . . . .117 C2
Fairhaven TW20 . . . . 11 F3
Fairhaven Ave CR0. . . . . . 43 D3
Fairhaven Ct
  7 Croydon CR2. . . . . . . 61 C5
  1 Egham TW20 . . . . . . 11 F3
Fairhaven Rd RH1. . . . . . .119 A5
Fairhill GU7 . . . . .150 D6
Fairholme TW14 . . . . 14 E8
Fairholme Cres KT21 . . . . 75 C2
Fairholme Gdns GU9 . . . .125 C1
Fairholme Ho **4** KT3. . . . . 38 E5
Fairholme Prim Sch
  TW14 . . . . 14 D7
Fairholme Rd
  Ashford TW15 . . . . 13 F3
  Cheam SM1 . . . . 58 F4
  Thornton Heath CR0 . . . . . 42 A2
Fairings The KT12. . . . . . . 54 B6
Fair La CR5, RH2. . . . . . . 98 D1
FAIRLANDS 108 C4
Fairlands GU35 . . . . .187 D5
Fairlands Ave
  Fairlands GU3 . . . . .108 C5
  Sutton SM1 . . . . 59 A8
  Thornton Heath CR7 . . . . . 42 A4
Fairlands Cl GU3. . . . . . . .108 C5
Fairlands Rd GU3 . . . . . .108 D5
Fairlawn
  Little Bookham KT23 . . . . . 93 F3
  Weybridge KT13 . . . . 53 E5
Fairlawn Cl
  Claygate KT10 . . . . 55 F4
  Feltham TW13 . . . . 15 F4
  Kingston upon Thames KT2 . 18 C2
Fairlawn Cres RH19 . . . . .185 B2
Fairlawn Ct **1** SE26 . . . . 23 E3
Fairlawn Dr
  East Grinstead RH19 . . . .185 B2
  Reigate RH1. . . . . .139 E7
Fairlawnes SM6. . . . . 60 B5
Fairlawn Gr SM7 . . . . 78 D6
Fairlawn Ho RH10. . . . . . .202 A6
Fairlawn Pk
  Forest Hill SE26. . . . . 23 E3
  Woking GU21. . . . . 69 C1
Fairlawn Prim Sch SE23. . 23 C8
Fairlawn Rd
  Merton SW19 . . . . 19 F1
  Sutton SM2, SM5. . . . . . . 78 C4
Fairlawns
  Addlestone KT15 . . . . 52 B5
  Guildford GU1 . . . . .110 C1
  Horley RH6 . . . . .161 B2
  Sunbury TW16 . . . . 35 A6
  Twickenham TW1 . . . . . . .6 C1
  Woodham KT15 . . . . 70 F8
Fairlawns Cl TW18 . . . . . . 13 B2
Fairleas **12** BR3 . . . . 44 B7
Fairlie Gdns SE23 . . . . . . 23 C8
Fairlight
  Hampton TW12 . . . . 16 B3
  Sheerwater GU21 . . . . . . 70 B7
Fairlight Cl KT4 . . . . 58 C6
Fairlight Rd SW17 . . . . . . 20 D4
Fairline Ct BR3 . . . . 44 C7
Fairlop Wlk GU6 . . . . . . .173 F2
Fairmead
  Tolworth KT5, KT6. . . . . . . 38 B1
  Woking GU21. . . . . 69 C1
Fairmead Cl
  Heston TW5. . . . . .4 D7
  Kingston upon Thames KT3. 38 D6
  Sandhurst GU47 . . . . 64 D7
Fairmead Ct
  Camberley GU15 . . . . 65 C4
  Richmond TW9 . . . . .7 B4
Fairmead Rd CR0 . . . . . . 42 A2
Fairmeads KT11 . . . . 73 F6
FAIRMILE. 73 F7
Fairmile Ave
  Cobham KT11 . . . . 73 F6
  Streatham SW16 . . . . 21 D3
Fairmile Ct KT11 . . . . 73 E7
Fairmile Ho TW11 . . . . . . 17 A4
Fairmile Hts KT11. . . . . . . 74 A6
Fairmile La
  Cobham KT11 . . . . 73 E6
  Stoke D'Abernon KT11. . . 73 E4
Fairmile Park Copse KT11 73 F6
Fairmile Park Rd KT11 . . . 73 F6
Fairoak Cl CR8. . . . . 80 B4
Fair Oak Cl KT22 . . . . 74 D7
Fairoak La
  Chessington KT9, KT22,
    KT10 . . . . 75 B8
  Oxshott KT22. . . . . 74 E8
Fairoaks Airport GU24. . . 50 E1
Fairoaks Ct KT15. . . . . . . 52 B5

Fairoaks Residential Pk
GU3 ....108 A6
Fairs Rd KT22........95 A8
Fair St TW3...........5 C4
Fairstone Ct 2 RH6...161 B4
Fairview
East Ewell KT17.......77 C8
Godstone RH9........121 C7
Fair View RH12.......217 A3
Fairview Ave GU22....69 F1
Fairview Cl
Forest Hill SE26......23 E3
Woking GU21.........69 F1
Fairview Cotts GU25...31 D3
Fairview Ct
Ashford TW15........14 A3
13 East Grinstead RH19..205 B4
Kingston upon Thames KT2. 38 B8
Fairview Dr TW17.....33 F4
Fairview Gdns GU9....125 D6
Fairview Ho 17 SW2...21 F8
Fairview Ind Est RH8..123 A2
Fairview Pl SW2......21 F8
Fairview Rd
Ash GU12...........106 B3
Carshalton SM1.......59 E5
Ewell KT17..........76 F8
Headley Down GU35...187 C5
Thornton Heath SW16..41 F8
Wokingham RG40......25 C5
Fairview Terr GU35...187 A6
Fairwater Dr KT15....52 D2
Fairwater Ho TW11....17 A4
Fairway
Chertsey KT16........33 B1
Copthorne RH10......183 B2
Crawley RH11........200 D4
Guildford GU1.......110 D1
Sutton SM5..........78 C8
West Barnes SW20....39 C6
Fairway Cl
Copthorne RH10......183 A2
Croydon BR3, CR0....43 E4
Heston TW4...........4 C2
Hounslow TW4.........4 C2
West Ewell KT19......57 C6
Woking GU23.........89 B7
Fairway Est TW4.......4 C2
Fairway Gdns BR3.....44 D3
Fairway Hts GU15.....66 B6
Fairways
Ashford TW15........14 B2
Beacon Hill GU26....188 B6
Hounslow TW7.........5 E6
Kenley CR8..........80 C2
Teddington TW11.....17 D1
Fairways The RH1.....139 D6
Fairway The
East Molesey KT8....36 B6
Farnborough GU14....84 A1
Farnborough GU14....104 B8
Frimley GU15........66 A3
Godalming GU7.......150 F2
Heath End GU9......125 D7
Kingston upon Thames KT3. 38 D8
Leatherhead KT22.....75 A1
Pirbright GU3........88 C3
Weybridge KT13......72 A8
Fairwell La KT24.....112 B7
Fairwood Ho KT13.....52 F6
Fairwyn Rd SE26.....23 E4
Fakenham Way GU47...45 D2
Falaise TW20.........11 F3
Falaise GU11........105 B3
Falcon Cl
Chiswick W4..........7 C8
Crawley RH11........201 D8
Lightwater GU18......66 F8
Falcon Ct
Frimley GU16........65 D1
Sheerwater GU21......70 C6
9 West Norwood SE21..22 D6
Falcon Dr TW19........2 E1
Falcon Ho 9 SW19....40 B8
Falconhurst
4 Kingston upon Thames KT6............37 E4
Oxshott KT22........74 D4
Falcon Rd
Guildford GU1.......109 D1
Hampton TW12........15 F1
Falconry Ct KT1......37 E6
Falcons Cl TN16......83 D2
Falcons Pre Prep Sch The
W4..................7 B8
Falcons Prep Sch for Boys
The TW9..............6 B1
Falcon Way
Feltham TW14.........4 B2
Sunbury TW16........34 E7
Falconwood
East Horsley KT24....92 F3
Englefield Green TW20..11 E3
Falcon Wood KT22.....94 F7
Falconwood Rd CR0....63 A3
Falcourt Cl SM1......59 B5
Falkland Ct GU14....105 E8
Falkland Gdns RH4...136 A6
Falkland Gr RH4.....136 A6
Falkland Ho SE6.....24 C4
Falkland Park Ave SE25..42 E7
Falkland Rd RH4.....136 A6
Falklands Dr RH13...218 B4
Falkner Ct GU9......125 C2
Falkner Rd GU9......125 B2

Fallow Deer Cl RH13..218 B4
Fallowfield Way 1 RH6..161 B4
Fallsbrook Rd SW16...21 C2
Falmer Cl RH11......201 D4
Falmouth Cl GU15.....66 A4
Falmouth Ho 12 KT2...37 D8
Falmouth Rd KT12....54 C6
Falstone GU21........69 B1
Fambridge Cl SE26....23 F4
Famet Ave CR8.......80 C6
Famet Cl CR8........80 C6
Famet Ct RH19.......185 C3
Famet Gdns CR8......80 C5
Famet Wlk CR8.......80 C6
Fanchford Rd RH2....117 E1
Fanes Cl RG42........26 F8
Fanfare The GU21.....70 C4
Fanshawe Rd TW10....17 C4
Faraday Ave RH19....205 F6
Faraday Cl
Crawley RH10.......181 F2
East Molesey KT8.....36 A5
Faraday Ctr The RH10..181 F1
Faraday Ho
7 Balham SW12......21 B8
5 Hampton TW12.....16 B2
Faraday Pl
Bracknell RG42.......26 F8
East Molesey KT8.....36 A5
Faraday Rd
Crawley RH10.......181 F2
East Molesey KT8.....36 A5
Farnborough GU14....85 C6
Guildford GU1.......109 C2
Wimbledon SW19.....20 B2
Farcrosse Cl GU47....64 C8
Farebrothers 2 RH8..216 F8
Fareham Ho 13 SW15..19 A7
Fareham Rd TW14.....15 C8
Farendon Ho 18 SM2..59 C4
Farewell Pl CR4......40 E8
Farhalls Cres RH12...217 F6
Faringdon Cl GU47....45 C1
Faringdon Dr RG12....27 D4
Farington Acres KT13..53 D7
Faris Barn Dr KT15...70 F8
Faris La KT15........70 F8
FARLEIGH............81 F5
Farleigh Ave BR2.....44 F2
Farleigh Court Rd CR6..82 B5
Farleigh Ct
Croydon CR2........61 C5
3 Guildford GU2....108 E1
Farleigh Dean Cres CR0..82 B8
Farleigh Ho 7 KT2...18 B2
Farleigh Rd
Warlingham CR6......81 E2
Woodham KT15.......71 A8
Farleton Cl KT13.....53 D4
Farley Copse RG42....26 E8
Farley Copse Nature
Reserve★ RG42..26 D8
Farleycroft 1 CR0....43 A1
Farley Croft BR2.....44 E7
Farley Ct GU14.......85 D2
FARLEY GREEN.......153 C6
Farley Heath Rd GU5..153 C6
Farley Ho SE26.......23 B5
Farley Mews SE6......24 C4
Farley Moor RG42.....26 D8
Farley Pl SE25.......43 A5
Farley The
Lewisham SE6.......24 C8
South Croydon CR2....62 B2
Farleys Cl KT24......92 C1
Farlington Pl SW15...19 B8
Farlington Sch RH12..216 B6
Farlton Rd SW18......20 B8
Farm App RH9........163 C5
Farm Ave
Horsham RH12.......217 B3
Streatham SW16......21 C4
Farm Cl
Ascot SL5...........29 C4
Bracknell RG42.......26 F8
Byfleet KT14........71 F7
Chertsey KT16........32 A3
Chipstead CR5.......98 F7
Coney Hall BR4.......63 F7
Crawley RH10.......202 A7
Crowthorne RG45.....45 C7
East Grinstead RH19..206 B8
East Horsley KT24...112 F7
Egham TW18.........12 C1
Fairlands GU3......108 C6
Fetcham KT22........94 E3
Guildford GU1......109 D4
Lower Halliford TW17..34 A2
Loxwood RH14.......213 A3
Sutton SM2.........59 D3
Wallington SM6......60 C1
Warnham RH12......216 F7
Farmdale Rd SM5......59 E3
Farm Dr
Croydon CR0........62 F8
Purley CR8..........79 D8
Farmer's Rd TW18....12 E3
Farmfield Dr RH6....181 B8
Farmfield Hospl (Private)
RH6................160 B1
Farmfield Rd BR1....24 E3
Farm Fields CR2......80 F8
Farmhouse Cl GU22...70 D4
Farmhouse Rd SW16...21 C1
Farmington Ave SM1...59 D7
Farm La
Addlestone KT15......52 A3

Farm La continued
Ashtead KT21, KT18...76 B2
Croydon CR0........62 F8
East Horsley KT24...112 F7
Godstone RH9.......121 B7
Purley CR8..........60 C1
Send GU23..........90 C3
Farmleigh Cl RH10...202 C8
Farmleigh Gr KT12....53 F5
Farm Rd
Aldershot GU12.....105 E3
Frimley GU16........65 F2
Morden SM4.........40 B4
Old Woking GU22.....90 B7
Staines TW18........13 B2
Sutton SM2..........59 D3
Thames Ditton KT10...55 B8
Twickenham TW4......15 E7
Warlingham CR6.....101 E8
Farm Way
North Cheam KT4.....58 C7
Stanwell TW19.........1 F1
Farm Wlk
Ash GU12...........127 C8
Guildford GU2.......129 F7
Farnaby Rd BR1......44 E8
Farnan Ho SW16......21 E3
Farnan Rd SW16......21 E3
FARNBOROUGH.......85 C3
Farnborough Airport
GU14...............84 E1
Farnborough Air Sciences
Trust & Mus★ GU14..85 C1
Farnborough Ave CR2..62 E3
Farnborough Bsns Ctr
GU14...............84 F2
Farnborough Bsns Pk
GU14...............85 B2
Farnborough Coll of Tech
GU14...............85 C2
Farnborough Cres
3 Coney Hall BR2....44 F1
South Croydon CR2...62 E2
Farnborough Gate Ret Pk
GU14...............85 C2
Farnborough Grange Inf Sch
GU14...............85 A8
FARNBOROUGH GREEN...85 C6
Farnborough Hill Sch
GU14...............85 C5
Farnborough Ind Est
GU14...............85 A3
Farnborough L Ctr GU14..85 B3
Farnborough North Sta
GU14...............85 D6
FARNBOROUGH PARK...85 D4
Farnborough Rd
Aldershot GU11.....104 E3
Farnborough GU14....85 C5
Heath End GU11, GU9..125 D7
Farnborough St GU14..85 D6
Farnborough Sta GU14..85 B5
FARNBOROUGH STREET...85 D5
FARNCOMBE.........150 E8
Farncombe CE Inf sch
GU7................150 E7
Farncombe Hill GU7...150 E7
Farncombe St GU7....150 E7
Farncombe Sta GU7...150 F7
Farnell Mews KT13....53 B7
Farnell Rd
Isleworth TW7........5 D4
Stanwell TW18.......13 A5
Farnell's Almshouses TW7..5 F5
FARNHAM...........125 B1
Farnham Adult Learning Ctr
23 GU9.............125 B2
Farnham Bsns Ctr GU9..125 C3
Farnham Bsns Pk GU9..146 A8
Farnham By-Pass GU9..125 C2
Farnham Castle★ GU9..125 B3
Farnham Cl RG12......27 D7
Farnham Cloisters GU9..146 A6
Farnham Com Hospl
GU9................125 E4
Farnham Ct SM3.......58 E4
Farnham Gdns SW20...39 B7
Farnham Heath End Sch
GU9................125 E6
Farnham La GU27.....208 A7
Farnham L Ctr GU9...125 C2
Farnham Park Cl GU9..125 B6
Farnham Park Dr GU9..125 B6
Farnham Rd
Churt GU10.........167 D3
Elstead GU8.........148 C4
Guildford, Guildford Park GU1,
GU2, GU3.........130 B7
Guildford, Onslow Village GU2,
GU3..............129 E6
Farnham Road Hospl
GU2................130 B7
Farnham Sixth Form Coll
GU9................125 C1
Farnham Sta GU9.....125 C1
Farnham Trad Est GU9..125 F4
Farnhurst La GU6....193 F4
Farningham RG12......27 E3
Farningham Cres CR3..101 A4
Farningham Ct SW16...21 D1
Farningham Ho RG12...27 E3
Farningham Rd CR3...101 A4

Farnley GU21.........68 F2
Farnley Rd CR7, SE25..42 D5
Farnsworth Ho 8 SW27..22 B3
Farquhar Rd
Dulwich SE19........22 F3
Wimbledon SW19......20 A5
Farquharson Rd CR0...42 C1
Farrell Cl GU15......65 C3
Farren Ho GU14......85 C1
Farren Rd SE23......23 E6
Farrer Ct TW1.......17 D8
Farrer's Pl CR0......62 D6
Farrier Cl TW16......35 A5
Farrier Pl
Sandhurst GU47......64 B7
Sutton SM1..........59 B8
Farriers KT18........96 C3
Farriers Cl KT17.....76 E7
Farriers The GU5....152 A5
Farriers Ct
Belmont SM2.........58 E3
Wimbledon SW19......19 E1
Farriers Rd KT17.....76 E8
Farriers The GU5....152 A5
Farthing Ct 3 SL5....30 B2
Farthingfield Ho GU9..125 C3
Farthingham La GU6..175 E6
Farthings GU21......68 E3
Farthings The 1 KT2..38 A8
Farthing Way CR5....79 C2
Farwig La BR1.......44 F8
Fassett Rd KT1.......37 E5
Fauconberg Ct W4.....7 C8
Fauconberg Rd W4.....7 C8
Faulkner Pl GU21.....47 F4
Faulkner's Rd KT12...54 C5
Faversham Ct SE6.....23 F7
Faversham Rd
Beckenham BR3......43 F7
Forest Hill SE6......23 F7
Morden SM4.........40 B3
Sandhurst GU47......45 D1
Fawcett Cl SW16......22 A4
Fawcett Rd CR0, CR9..61 C7
Fawcus Cl KT10.......55 C4
Fawler Mead RG12....27 F5
Fawley Cl GU6.......174 F2
Fawley Ct SE27.......22 B6
Fawn Dr GU12.......105 E3
Fawns Manor Cl TW14..14 C7
Fawns Manor Rd TW14..14 D7
Fawsley Cl SL3........1 E7
FAYGATE............199 F1
Faygate Bsns Ctr RH12..199 F1
Faygate Ct CR2.......61 B3
Faygate La
Blindley Heath RH9...142 E3
Faygate RH12.......199 F4
Faygate Rd SW2......21 F6
Faygate Sta RH12....199 F1
Fayland Ave SW16....21 C3
Fay Rd RH12.........217 C5
Fays Pas 12 GU1.....130 C8
Fearn Cl KT24.......112 E6
Fearnley Cres TW12...15 F2
Featherbed La CR0, CR6..82 C7
Feathercombe La GU8..171 E4
Feathers La TW19.....12 A6
Featherstone RH7....142 D1
Featherstone Ave SE23..23 C6
Federation of St Elphege's
RC Sch SM6.........60 E4
Fee Farm Rd KT10.....55 F3
FELBRIDGE.........184 F4
Felbridge Ave RH10..202 D7
Felbridge Cl
Belmont SM2.........59 B2
East Grinstead RH19..185 C3
Frimley GU16........65 F1
Streatham SW16......22 A4
Felbridge Ct
East Grinstead RH19..185 A4
Feltham TW13.........15 B7
Harlington UB3........3 D8
South Croydon CR2....61 C3
Felbridge Ctr The RH19..185 A3
Felbridge Prim Sch
RH19..............184 F4
Felbridge Rd RH19...184 D3
Felcote Ho RH2......138 F7
Felcot Rd RH19......184 C4
Felcott Cl KT12......54 C7
Felcott Rd KT12......54 C7
FELCOURT..........185 C8
Felcourt Cotts RH19..185 C8
Felcourt La RH19.....164 C1
Felcourt Rd RH19, RH7..185 C7
Felday Glade RH5....155 B5
Felday Hos RH5......155 C7
Felday Rd RH5.......133 F3
Feldemore Cotts RH5..155 C6
Feld The RH19.......185 A4
Felicia Ct GU7.......150 E4
Felix Dr GU4........111 A7
Felix La KT17........34 F3
Felix Rd KT12........35 A3
Felland Way RH2.....139 D5
Fellbrook TW10.......17 B5
Fellcott Way RH12...216 F1
Fellmongers Yd 4 CR0..61 C7
Fellowes Rd SM1, SM5..59 E8
Fellows Rd GU14......84 D8
Fellow Gn GU24......67 F6
Fellow Green Rd GU24..67 F6
Fell Rd CR0, CR9.....61 C7
Felmingham Rd SE20...43 C7
Felnex Trad Est SM6...60 A8

Felsberg Rd SW2......21 E8
Felside Ct KT13.......53 A5
Felstead Rd KT19.....76 D8
FELTHAM............15 B6
Feltham Airparcs L Ctr
TW13...............15 D6
Feltham Arenas TW14..15 A8
Feltham Ave KT8......36 E5
Felthambrook Ind Est
TW13...............15 B5
Felthambrook Way TW13..15 B3
Feltham Bsns Complex
TW13...............15 B6
Feltham Com Coll TW13..15 C6
Feltham Corporate Ctr
TW13...............15 B5
FELTHAMHILL.......14 F3
Feltham Hill Jun & Inf Schs
TW13...............14 F5
Feltham Hill Rd
Ashford TW15.......14 C2
Feltham TW13........15 C3
Feltham Rd
Ashford TW15........14 C4
Mitcham CR4.........41 A7
Redhill RH1........139 F4
Feltham Sta TW13.....15 B7
Feltham Wlk RH1.....139 F4
Feltonfleet Sch KT11...72 E6
Felwater Ct RH19....185 A3
Fenby Cl RH13.......218 C4
Fenchurch Rd RH10...202 B4
Fencote RG12.........27 D3
Fendall Rd KT19......57 C5
Fender Ho RH12......217 B2
Fenemore Rd CR3.....100 D7
Fengates Rd RH1.....118 E1
Fenhurst Cl RH12....216 F1
Fennel Cl
Ascot SL5...........29 A5
Croydon CR0........43 D1
Farnborough GU14....84 B4
Guildford GU1......110 B4
Fennel Cres RH11....201 B2
Fennells Mead KT17...57 F2
Fenner Ho KT12.......54 A6
Fenn Ho TW7..........6 B6
Fenning Ct CR4.......40 E5
Fennscombe Ct GU24...67 F6
Fenns La GU24........67 E5
Fenn's Way GU21......69 E4
Fenstanton Prim Sch
SW2................22 A7
Fenton Ave TW18......13 C3
Fenton Cl RH1.......119 A1
Fenton Ct TW5........4 E7
Fenton Ho TW5........5 A8
Fenton Lodge GU15....65 E6
Fenton Rd RH1.......119 A1
Fentum Rd GU2......109 A3
Fenwick Cl GU21......69 B1
Fenwick Pl CR2.......61 B3
Ferguson Ave KT5.....37 F4
Ferguson Cl BR2......44 D6
Fermandy La RH10....184 A1
Fermor Dr GU11......104 F3
Fermor Rd SE23......23 E7
Fern Ave CR4.........41 D5
Fernbank Ave KT12....35 E2
Fernbank Cl RH5.....176 E6
Fernbank Cres SL5....28 D8
Fernbank Pl SL5......28 D7
Fernbank Rd
Addlestone KT15......52 A5
North Ascot SL5......28 D8
Fernbrae Cl GU10....146 B3
Fern Cl
Crowthorne RG45.....45 A7
Frimley GU16........66 C3
Warlingham CR6......81 E1
Fern Cotts RH5......133 E4
Fern Ct GU12........105 F1
Ferndale GU3.......108 E3
Ferndale Ave
Chertsey KT16.......51 E7
Hounslow TW4.........4 E4
Ferndale Rd
Ashford TW15........13 E3
Banstead SM7........77 F3
Croydon SE25........43 B4
Woking GU21........69 F3
Ferndene Rd
Ashford TW15........13 E3
Ferndown
Crawley RH10.......182 D2
Horley RH6.........161 A5
5 Kingston upon Thames KT6............37 E4
Ferndown Cl
Guildford GU1......131 A8
Sutton SM2..........59 D4
Ferndown Ct GU10...146 D5
Ferndown Gdns
Cobham KT11........73 C6
Farnborough GU14....84 E4
Fernery The TW18.....12 E3
Ferney Ct KT14.......71 D7
Ferney Meade Way TW7..6 A5
Ferney Rd KT14.......71 D7
Fern Gr TW14........15 B8
Ferngrove Cl KT22....94 E4
Fernham Rd CR7......42 C6
Fernhead 18 SM1.....59 C6
FERNHILL..........182 E7
Fernhill KT22........74 D5
Fernhill Cl
Crawley Down RH10..184 B1

Fernhill Cl *continued*
Farnborough GU17 . . . . 64 F1
Hale GU9 . . . . 125 B6
Woking GU22 . . . . 89 D7
Fernhill Ct KT2 . . . . 17 D3
Fernhill Dr GU9 . . . . 125 B6
Fernhill Gdns KT2 . . . . 17 E3
Fernhill Ho GU14 . . . . 85 D2
Fernhill La
Farnborough GU17 . . . . 64 F1
Hale GU9 . . . . 125 B6
Woking GU22 . . . . 89 C7
Fernhill Pk GU22 . . . . 89 D7
Fernhill Prim Sch GU14 . . . 64 F1
Fern Hill Prim Sch KT2 . . . 17 E2
Fernhill Rd
Blackwater GU14, GU17 . . . 64 E2
Crawley RH6 . . . . 182 D7
Farnborough, West Heath GU14 . . . . 84 E6
Fernhill Sch GU14 . . . . 64 F1
Fernhill Wlk GU17 . . . . 64 F1
Fernhurst Cl RH11 . . . . . . 201 B8
Fernhurst Rd
Ashford TW15 . . . . 14 C4
Croydon CR0 . . . . 43 B1
Ferniehurst GU15 . . . . 65 F4
Fernihough Cl KT13 . . . . . . 72 A8
Fernlands Cl KT16 . . . . 51 E7
Fernlea KT23 . . . . 94 B3
Fern Lea GU9 . . . . 126 B6
Fernlea Pl KT11 . . . . 73 D7
Fernlea Rd
Balham SW12 . . . . 21 B7
Mitcham CR4 . . . . 41 A8
Fernleigh Cl
Croydon CR0 . . . . 61 A6
Walton-on-Thames KT12 . . . 54 B7
Fernleigh Ct GU14 . . . . 85 B4
Fernleigh Rise GU16 . . . . . . 86 C7
Fernley Ho GU7 . . . . 150 E8
Fern Lodge 14 SW16 . . . . . . 22 A3
Fern Pl GU14 . . . . 84 E5
Fern Rd GU7 . . . . 150 F6
Ferns Cl CR2 . . . . 62 B1
Fernside KT7 . . . . 37 B1
Fernside Ave TW13 . . . . 15 B4
Fernside Rd SW12 . . . . 21 A8
Ferns Mead GU9 . . . . 125 B1
Ferns The 4 GU14 . . . . . . 105 D8
Fernthorpe Rd SW16 . . . . . . 21 C2
Fern Twrs CR3 . . . . 101 A2
Fern Way RH12 . . . . 217 D5
Fern Wlk TW15 . . . . 13 D3
Fernwood
New Addington CR0, CR2 . . 62 E2
Putney SW19 . . . . 19 F7
Fernwood Ave SW16 . . . . . . 21 D4
Feroners Cl RH10 . . . . 202 A4
Feroners Ct RH10 . . . . 202 A4
Ferrard Cl SL5 . . . . 28 D8
Ferraro Cl TW5 . . . . 5 A8
Ferrers Ave SM6 . . . . 60 D6
Ferrers Rd SW16 . . . . 21 D3
Ferriby Ct RG12 . . . . 27 C7
Ferriers Ct RH12 . . . . 217 C2
Ferring Cl RH11 . . . . 201 B8
Ferrings SE21 . . . . 22 E5
Ferris Ave CR0 . . . . 62 F7
Ferry Ave TW18 . . . . 12 E1
Ferry La
Barnes SW13 . . . . 7 F8
Brentford TW8 . . . . 6 E8
Chertsey KT16 . . . . 33 A3
Guildford GU2, GU3 . . . . . 130 C5
Laleham TW18 . . . . 33 C6
Lower Halliford TW17 . . . . . 34 A1
Richmond TW9 . . . . 6 F8
Wraysbury TW19 . . . . 12 B5
Ferrymoor TW10 . . . . 17 B5
Ferry Quays Ctyd 15 TW8 . . 6 D8
Ferry Rd
East Molesey KT8 . . . . 36 A6
Richmond TW11 . . . . 17 B3
Thames Ditton KT7 . . . . 37 B3
Twickenham TW1 . . . . 17 B7
Ferry Sq
1 Brentford TW8 . . . . 6 E8
Lower Halliford TW17 . . . . . 34 B2
Ferry Wks TW17 . . . . 34 A1
Festival Cotts SL3 . . . . 1 C7
Festival Ct
Cheam SM1 . . . . 40 B1
Crawley RH10 . . . . 202 C4
FETCHAM 94 C4
Fetcham Common La KT22 . . . . 94 B6
Fetcham Grove Cotts KT22 . . . . 95 A5
Fetcham Lodge KT22 . . . . . . 94 D5
Fetcham Park Dr KT22 . . . . 94 E4
Fetcham Village Inf Sch KT22 . . . . 94 D5
Fettes Rd GU6 . . . . 175 A3
FICKLESHOLE 82 E5
Fiddicroft Ave SM7 . . . . 78 C5
Field Cl
Chessington KT9 . . . . 56 C5
Cranford TW4 . . . . 4 B6
East Molesey KT8 . . . . 36 B4
Guildford GU4 . . . . 110 D3
Hamsey Green CR2 . . . . 81 B5
Harlington UB7 . . . . 3 C7
Fieldcommon La KT12 . . . . . 35 F1
Field Ct
Oxted RH8 . . . . 122 E8
Wimbledon SW19 . . . . 20 A5
Fieldend
Horsham RH12 . . . . 218 B5
Teddington TW1 . . . . 16 F4
Field End
Coulsdon CR5 . . . . 79 D5
Farnham GU9 . . . . 125 F4
West End GU24 . . . . 67 F6
Fieldend Rd SW16 . . . . 41 C8
Fielden Pl RG12 . . . . 27 D7
Fielders Gn 3 GU1 . . . . . . 110 A1
Fieldfare Dr RG12 . . . . 26 D5
Fieldgate Ct KT11 . . . . 73 A5
Field Ho 8 TW10 . . . . 17 C5
Field House Cl SL5 . . . . 29 A1
Fieldhouse Rd SW12 . . . . . . 21 C7
Fieldhouse Villas SM7 . . . . . 78 E4
Fieldhurst Cl KT15 . . . . 52 B5
Fielding Ave TW2 . . . . 16 C5
Fielding Gdns RG45 . . . . . . 45 B4
Fielding Ho 3 W4 . . . . 7 E8
Fielding Rd GU47 . . . . 64 E6
Fieldings The
Banstead SM7 . . . . 77 F2
Forest Hill SE23 . . . . 23 C7
Horley RH6 . . . . 161 C4
Woking GU21 . . . . 68 F3
Field La
Brentford TW8 . . . . 6 C7
Camberley GU16 . . . . 66 A1
Farncombe GU7 . . . . 150 F7
Frimley GU16 . . . . 65 E1
Teddington TW11 . . . . 17 A3
Fieldoaks Way RH1 . . . . . . 119 C6
Fieldpark Gdns CR0 . . . . . . 43 E1
Field Path GU14 . . . . 64 F1
Field Pk RG12 . . . . 27 D8
Field Pl KT3 . . . . 38 F3
Field Rd
Farnborough GU14 . . . . 64 F1
Feltham TW14 . . . . 4 B1
Fieldsend Rd SM3 . . . . 58 E5
Fieldside Rd BR1 . . . . 24 D3
Field Stores App GU11 . . 105 C3
Fieldview
Horley RH6 . . . . 161 B4
Wandsworth SW17, SW18 . 20 D7
Field View
Egham TW20 . . . . 12 C3
Feltham TW13 . . . . 14 D5
Field View Cotts GU7 . . . . 150 B4
Fieldview Ct TW18 . . . . 13 A2
Fieldway GU27 . . . . 208 C7
Field Way
Aldershot GU12 . . . . 105 E3
New Addington CR0 . . . . 63 B4
Send Marsh GU23 . . . . 90 F2
Tongham GU10 . . . . 126 F7
Fieldway Halt CR0 . . . . 63 B3
Field Wlk RH6 . . . . 162 C4
Fiennes Ct RH12 . . . . 217 D6
Fifehead Cl TW15 . . . . 13 E2
Fife Rd
Kingston upon Thames KT2 . . . . 37 E7
Mortlake SW14 . . . . 7 C2
Fife Way KT23 . . . . 94 A2
Fifield La GU10 . . . . 146 C2
Fifield Path SE23 . . . . 23 D5
Fifth Cross Rd TW2 . . . . . . 16 D6
Figge's Rd CR4 . . . . 21 A1
Figgs Wood CR5 . . . . 99 C5
Filbert Cres RH11 . . . . 201 A6
Filby Rd KT9 . . . . 56 F4
Filey Cl
Biggin Hill TN16 . . . . 103 B8
Crawley RH11 . . . . 200 F4
Sutton SM2 . . . . 59 C3
Filmer Gr GU7 . . . . 150 E5
Finborough Rd SW17 . . . . . 20 F2
Finchampstead Rd RG41, RG40 . . . . 25 B3
Finch Ave SE27 . . . . 22 D4
Finch Cl GU21 . . . . 68 C2
Finch Cres RH10 . . . . 204 C5
Finchdean Ho SW15 . . . . . . 18 F8
Finch Dr TW14 . . . . 15 D8
Finches Rise GU1 . . . . 110 C3
Finch Rd 9 GU1 . . . . 109 D1
Finch's Cross RH8 . . . . . . 144 A8
Findhorn Cl GU47 . . . . 64 D7
Findings The GU14 . . . . 84 E8
Findlay Dr GU3 . . . . 108 F5
Findon Ct KT15 . . . . 51 F5
Findon Rd RH11 . . . . 201 B8
Findon Way RH12 . . . . 216 D3
Finlay Gdns KT15 . . . . 52 C6
Finlays Cl KT9 . . . . 57 A5
Finmere RG12 . . . . 27 C2
Finnart Cl KT13 . . . . 53 C6
Finney Dr GU20 . . . . 48 D4
Finney La TW7 . . . . 6 A6
Finsbury Cl RH11 . . . . 201 C2
Finstock Gn RG12 . . . . 27 F5
Finton House Sch SW17 . . 20 F6
Fintry Pl GU14 . . . . 84 E7
Fintry Wlk GU14 . . . . 84 E7
Finucane Ct TW9 . . . . 6 F4
Fiona Cl KT23 . . . . 94 A3
Fir Acre Rd GU12 . . . . 106 A6
Firbank 3 BR3 . . . . 43 F7
Firbank Ct BR2 . . . . 44 D6
Firbank Dr GU21 . . . . 89 B8
Firbank La GU21 . . . . 89 B8
Firbank Pl TW20 . . . . 11 B2
Firbank Way RH19 . . . . . . 185 D1
Fir Cl KT12 . . . . 35 A2
Fircroft 2 KT22 . . . . 95 C6
Fircroft Cl GU22 . . . . 69 F1
Fircroft Ct 10 GU22 . . . . . . 69 F1
Fircroft Prim Sch SW17 . . 20 F5
Fircroft Rd
Chessington KT9 . . . . 56 F6
Englefield Green TW20 . . . . 11 C1
Upper Tooting SW17 . . . . . . 20 F5
Firdene KT5 . . . . 38 C1
Fir Dr GU17 . . . . 64 D3
Fireball Hill SL5 . . . . 29 D2
Fire Bell Alley KT6 . . . . 37 E3
Fire Station Flats TW7 . . . . 5 E5
Fire Station Mews BR3 . . . 44 B8
Fire Station Rd GU11 . . . . 105 B3
Firfield Rd
Addlestone KT15 . . . . 52 A6
Farnham GU9 . . . . 146 A7
Firfields KT13 . . . . 53 B4
Fir Gr KT3 . . . . 38 F3
Fir Grange Ave KT13 . . . . . 53 B5
Firgrove GU21 . . . . 89 B8
Firgrove Ct
7 Farnborough GU14 . . . . . 85 B4
Farnham GU9 . . . . 125 C1
Firgrove Hill GU9 . . . . 125 C1
Firgrove Par 5 GU14 . . . . . 85 B4
Firgrove Rd 6 GU14 . . . . . . 85 B4
Firhill Rd SE6 . . . . 24 A5
Firlands
Bracknell RG12 . . . . 27 C4
Horley RH6 . . . . 161 B4
North Ascot SL5 . . . . 28 D6
Weybridge KT13 . . . . 53 E4
Firlands Ave GU15 . . . . 65 D5
Firle Cl RH10 . . . . 201 E8
Firmston Ho 10 SW14 . . . . . 7 D4
Fir Rd
Cheam SM3 . . . . 39 F1
Feltham TW13 . . . . 15 D3
Firs Ave
Bramley GU5 . . . . 152 A6
Mortlake SW14 . . . . 7 C3
Firsby Ave CR0 . . . . 43 E1
Firs Cl
Claygate KT10 . . . . 55 E4
Dorking RH4 . . . . 136 A5
Farnborough GU14 . . . . 85 C2
Forest Hill SE23 . . . . 23 E8
Mitcham CR4 . . . . 41 B8
Firsdene Cl KT16 . . . . 51 D4
Firs Dr TW5 . . . . 4 B7
Firs La GU5 . . . . 152 D4
Firs Rd CR8 . . . . 80 B4
First Ave
East Molesey KT8 . . . . 36 A5
Mortlake SW14 . . . . 7 E4
Walton-on-Thames KT12 . . . 35 B3
West Ewell KT19 . . . . 57 E2
Woodham KT15 . . . . 52 B2
First Cl KT8 . . . . 36 C6
First Cross Rd TW2 . . . . . . 16 E6
Firs The
Artington GU3 . . . . 130 B5
Belmont SM2 . . . . 59 B3
Bisley GU24 . . . . 68 A3
6 Bracknell RG12 . . . . 27 F5
2 Caterham CR3 . . . . 100 D5
Claygate KT10 . . . . 55 E4
East Molesey KT7 . . . . 36 E5
Ewell KT17 . . . . 77 A5
Forest Hill SE26 . . . . 23 C3
2 Forest Hill, Upper Sydenham SE26 . . . . 23 B3
Great Bookham KT23 . . . . . 94 C3
Lower Kingswood KT20 . . . . 97 F1
Wimbledon SW20 . . . . 19 A1
First Quarter Bsns Pk KT19 . . . . 76 E8
Firstway SW20 . . . . 39 C7
Firsway GU2 . . . . 109 A2
Firswood Ave KT19 . . . . 57 F5
Fir Tree Alley 14 GU11 . . . 105 A2
Firtree Ave CR4 . . . . 41 A7
Fir Tree Ave GU27 . . . . . . 207 D6
Fir Tree Cl
Ascot SL5 . . . . 29 A2
Banstead KT17 . . . . 77 C4
Crawley RH11 . . . . 181 B1
Esher KT10 . . . . 55 C5
Leatherhead KT22 . . . . 95 C4
Streatham SW16 . . . . 21 C3
Worcester Park KT19 . . . . . 57 F6
Firtree Ct BR2 . . . . 44 F6
Fir Tree Gdns CR0 . . . . 63 A6
Fir Tree Gr SM5 . . . . 59 F3
Firtree Ho SE13 . . . . 24 D8
Fir Tree Rd
Banstead KT17, SM7 . . . . . . 77 D5
Guildford GU1 . . . . 109 D4
Hounslow TW4 . . . . 4 E3
Leatherhead KT22 . . . . 95 C4
Fir Tree Wlk RH2 . . . . 118 D1
Firway GU26 . . . . 187 E5
Fir Wlk KT17, SM3 . . . . 58 D4
Firwood Cl GU21 . . . . 88 E8
Firwood Dr GU15 . . . . 65 C5
Firwood Rd GU25 . . . . 30 E3
Fisher Cl
Crawley RH10 . . . . 201 E4
Croydon CR0 . . . . 42 F1
Hersham KT12 . . . . 54 B6
Fisherdene KT10 . . . . 56 A3
Fisher La
Aldershot GU12 . . . . 126 C8
Chiddingfold GU8 . . . . 210 E7
Dunsfold GU8 . . . . 211 B7
Fisherman Cl TW10 . . . . . . 17 C4
Fisherman Ho KT16 . . . . . . 33 C1
Fishermen's Cl GU11 . . . . 105 E5
Fisher Rowe Cl GU5 . . . . . 152 A6
Fishers Cl SW16 . . . . 21 D5
Fishers Ct
Horsham RH12 . . . . 217 C4
7 Teddington TW11 . . . . 16 F3
FISHER'S HILL 88 F6
FISHERSTREET 209 F3
Fishers Wood SL5 . . . . 30 C1
Fishing Temple Park Homes TW18 . . . . 32 F8
Fishponds Cl RG41 . . . . 25 A4
Fishponds Est RG41 . . . . . . 25 A4
Fishponds Rd
Upper Tooting SW17 . . . . . . 20 F4
Wokingham RG41 . . . . 25 A4
Fishpond Wood & Beverley Meads Nature Reserve★ SW19 . . . . 18 F3
Fisk Cl TW16 . . . . 14 F2
Fiske Ct
1 Merton SW19 . . . . 20 C1
Sutton SM2 . . . . 59 C3
Fitch Ct 8 CR4 . . . . 41 A7
Fitchet Cl RH11 . . . . 201 B8
Fitzalan Rd
Claygate KT10 . . . . 55 E3
Horsham RH12, RH13 . . . . 218 A4
Fitzgeorge Ave KT2, KT3 . . 38 D8
Fitzgerald Ave SW14 . . . . . . 7 E4
Fitzgerald Rd
Mortlake SW14 . . . . 7 D4
Thames Ditton KT7 . . . . 37 A3
Fitzhardinge Ho BR3 . . . . . 44 B7
Fitzherbert Ho 12 TW10 . . . 6 F1
Fitzjames Ave CR0 . . . . 62 A8
Fitzjohn Cl GU4 . . . . 110 C4
Fitzrobert Pl TW20 . . . . 12 A2
Fitzroy Cl RG12 . . . . 27 A3
Fitzroy Cres W4 . . . . 7 D7
Fitzroy Gdns SE19 . . . . 22 E1
Fitzroy Pl RH2 . . . . 118 D1
Fitzwilliam Ave TW9 . . . . . . 6 F5
Fitzwilliam Ho TW9 . . . . 6 D3
Fitzwilliam Hts SE23 . . . . . 23 C6
Fitz Wygram Cl TW12 . . . . . 16 C3
Fiveacre Cl CR7 . . . . 42 A3
Five Acres RH10 . . . . 201 E8
Five Oaks Cl GU21 . . . . 88 E8
Five Oaks Rd RH12, RH13 . 216 B2
Five Ways Bsns Ctr TW13 . 15 B5
Flag Cl CR0 . . . . 43 D1
Flambard Way GU7 . . . . . . 150 E4
Flamborough Cl TN16 . . . . 103 B8
Flamsteed Hts RH11 . . . . . 201 B1
Flanchford Ho 2 RH2 . . . . 118 A2
Flanchford Rd RH2 . . . . . . 138 D5
Flanders Cotts GU5 . . . . . . 152 D5
Flanders Cres SW17, SW19 20 F2
Flanders Ct TW20 . . . . 12 C3
Flashes Nature Reserve The★ GU10 . . . . 168 A5
Flatford Ho SE6 . . . . 24 C4
Flather Cl 12 SW16 . . . . 21 C3
Flats The GU17 . . . . 64 C4
Flat The 3 GU7 . . . . 150 D4
Flaxley Rd SM4 . . . . 40 B2
Flaxmore Ct CR7 . . . . 42 D7
Fleece Rd KT6 . . . . 37 C1
Fleet Cl KT8 . . . . 35 F4
Fleet Rd
Aldershot GU11 . . . . 104 D6
Blackwater GU51 . . . . 84 A4
Farnborough GU14 . . . . 84 C4
Fleet GU11, GU14 . . . . 104 D6
Fleetside KT8 . . . . 36 A4
Fleet Terr SE6 . . . . 24 C8
Fleetway TW20 . . . . 32 C6
Fleetwood Cl
Chessington KT9 . . . . 56 D3
South Croydon CR0 . . . . 61 F7
Tadworth KT20 . . . . 97 D7
Fleetwood Ct
8 Stanwell TW19 . . . . 2 E1
3 West Byfleet KT14 . . . . . . 71 A6
Fleetwood Rd KT3 . . . . 38 B6
Fleetwood Sq KT3 . . . . 38 B6
Fleming Cl GU14 . . . . 85 D6
Fleming Ct CR0 . . . . 61 A5
Fleming Ctr The RH10 . . . . 181 E2
Fleming Mead CR4, SW19 . . 20 F1
Fleming Way
Crawley RH10, RH11 . . . . . 181 F2
Isleworth TW7 . . . . 5 F3
Fleming Wlk RH19 . . . . . . 205 F6
Flemish Fields KT16 . . . . . . 33 A2
Flemming Ho KT19 . . . . 57 B2
Fletcher Cl
Crawley RH10 . . . . 201 E4
Ottershaw KT16 . . . . 51 E4
Fletcher Gdns RG42 . . . . . . 26 D8
Fletcher Rd KT16 . . . . 51 D4
Fletchers Cl RH13 . . . . 217 E1
Fleur Gates 7 SW19 . . . . . . 19 D8
FLEXFORD 107 C1
Flexford Gn RG12 . . . . 26 E3
Flexford Rd GU3 . . . . 107 C1
Flimwell Cl BR1 . . . . 24 E3
Flint Cl
Banstead SM7 . . . . 78 B5
Crawley RH10 . . . . 202 B3
Great Bookham KT23 . . . . . 94 C1
Redhill RH1 . . . . 118 F2
Flint Ct CR0 . . . . 41 F3
Flintgrove RG12 . . . . 27 D8
Flint Hill RH4, RH5 . . . . . . 136 B5
Flint Hill Cl RH4 . . . . 136 B4
Flintlock Cl TW19 . . . . 2 A3
Flitwick Grange GU8 . . . . . 149 F1
Flock Mill Pl SW18 . . . . 20 B7
Flockton Ho KT13 . . . . 53 A8
Flood La 5 TW1 . . . . 17 A7
Flora Gdns CR0 . . . . 82 C8
Floral Ct KT21 . . . . 75 C1
Floral House KT16 . . . . 32 F1
Florence Ave
Morden SM4 . . . . 40 C4
Woodham KT15 . . . . 71 A8
Florence Cl KT12 . . . . 35 B2
Florence Cotts
Kingston upon Thames SW15 . . . . 18 E5
Winkfield SL4 . . . . 8 C7
Florence Ct
Knaphill GU21 . . . . 68 C1
5 Wimbledon SW19 . . . . 19 E2
Florence Gdns
Chiswick W4 . . . . 7 C8
Staines TW18 . . . . 13 B1
Florence Ho 5 KT2 . . . . 17 F1
Florence Rd
Feltham TW13 . . . . 15 B7
6 Kingston upon Thames KT2 . . . . 17 F1
Penge BR3 . . . . 43 E7
Sandhurst GU47 . . . . 64 E7
South Croydon CR2 . . . . 61 D2
Walton-on-Thames KT12 . . . 35 B2
Wimbledon SW19 . . . . 20 B2
Florence Terr SW15 . . . . 18 E5
Florence Villas GU18 . . . . . . 48 B1
Florence Way
Knaphill GU21 . . . . 68 C1
Upper Tooting SW12 . . . . . . 20 F7
Florian Ave SM1 . . . . 59 D6
Florida Ct
Beckenham BR2 . . . . 44 F5
Staines TW18 . . . . 13 A3
Florida Rd
Shalford GU4 . . . . 130 E3
South Norwood CR7 . . . . 42 B8
Florys Ct 7 SW19 . . . . 19 E7
Flower Cres KT16 . . . . 51 C4
Flower La RH9 . . . . 121 D6
Flowersmead SW17 . . . . 21 A6
Flower Wlk GU2 . . . . 130 C6
Floyd's La GU22 . . . . 71 A3
Foden Rd GU11 . . . . 105 A1
Foley Cotts KT10 . . . . 55 F4
Foley Mews KT10 . . . . 55 E4
Foley Rd
Biggin Hill TN16 . . . . 83 D1
Claygate KT10 . . . . 55 E3
Foley Wood KT10 . . . . 55 F3
Follyfield Rd SM7 . . . . 78 A5
Folly Hill GU9 . . . . 125 A5
Folly Hill Inf Sch GU9 . . . 125 A6
Folly La RH5 . . . . 157 B7
Folly Lane N GU9 . . . . 125 B6
Folly Lane S GU9 . . . . 125 A6
Follys End Christian Sch 9 CR2 . . . . 61 E6
Fontaine Ct 3 BR3 . . . . 43 F8
Fontaine Rd SW16 . . . . 21 F1
Fontana Cl RH10 . . . . 202 E5
Fontenoy Rd SW12, SW17 . . 21 C6
Fonthill Cl SE20 . . . . 43 A7
Fonthill Ct SE23 . . . . 23 C8
Fonthill Lodge Sch RH19 . . . . 205 C6
Fontigarry Farm Bsns Pk RH2 . . . . 160 C8
Fontley Way SW15 . . . . 19 A8
Fontmell Cl TW15 . . . . 14 A3
Fontmell Pk TW15 . . . . 14 A3
Fontwell Cl GU12 . . . . 105 D2
Fontwell Rd RH10 . . . . 202 A3
Forbench Cl GU23 . . . . 91 B5
Forbes Chase GU47 . . . . 64 D7
Forbes Cl RH10 . . . . 202 B2
Forbes Ct SE19 . . . . 22 E3
Forburys GU9 . . . . 146 B8
Fordbridge Cl KT16 . . . . 33 B1
Fordbridge Ct TW15 . . . . . . 13 E2
Fordbridge Rd
Ashford TW15 . . . . 13 F3
Sunbury TW16 . . . . 35 A5
Upper Halliford TW16, TW17 . . . . 34 F3
Ford Cl
Ashford TW15 . . . . 13 E2
Littleton TW17 . . . . 34 A4
Thornton Heath CR7 . . . . . . 42 B4
Fordel Rd SE6 . . . . 24 D7
Fordham Cl KT4 . . . . 39 B1
Ford Ho TW20 . . . . 11 C1
Fordingbridge Cl RH12 . . . 217 C1
Fordington Ho SE26 . . . . . . 23 B5
Ford La GU10 . . . . 146 B6
Ford Manor Cotts RH7 . . . 165 B1
Ford Manor Rd RH7 . . . . . . 165 B2
Fordmill Rd SE6 . . . . 24 A6
Ford Rd
Ashford TW15 . . . . 13 F4
Bisley GU24 . . . . 67 F4
Chertsey KT16 . . . . 33 B1
Chobham GU24 . . . . 49 C1
Old Woking GU22 . . . . 90 B7
Fordwater Rd KT15, KT16 . . 33 B1
Fordwater Trad Est KT16 . . 33 C1
Fordwells Dr RG12 . . . . 27 F5
Fordyce Ho 3 SW16 . . . . . . 21 C4
Foreman Pk GU12 . . . . 106 B2
Foreman Rd GU12 . . . . 106 B1

Forest Cl
Bracknell SL5 . . . 28 C6
Crawley Down RH10 . . . 204 B8
East Horsley KT24 . . . 92 F2
Horsham RH12 . . . 218 B4
Woking GU22 . . . 70 D4
Forest Cres KT21 . . . 76 A3
Forest Croft SE23 . . . 23 B6
Forest Ct RG41 . . . 25 A4
FORESTDALE . . . 62 F2
Forestdale GU26 . . . 188 E3
Forestdale Ctr The CR0 . . . 62 F3
Forestdale Prim Sch CR0 . 62 F2
Forest Dene Ct 10 SM2 . . . 59 C4
Forest Dr
Charlton TW16 . . . 14 F1
Farnham GU10 . . . 146 C4
Kingswood KT20 . . . 98 A6
Forest End GU47 . . . 45 A1
Forest End Rd GU47 . . . 64 A8
Forester Rd RH10 . . . 201 E4
Foresters Cl
Knaphill GU21 . . . 68 F1
Wallington SM6 . . . 60 D3
Foresters Dr CR8, SM6 . . . 60 D2
Foresters Prim Sch SM6 . . 60 D4
Foresters Rd The RH13 . . 217 F1
Foresters Sq RG12 . . . 27 E6
Foresters Way RG45 . . . 45 F1
FOREST ESTATE . . . 11 A2
Forestfield
Crawley RH10 . . . 202 B3
Horsham RH13 . . . 218 A3
Forest Gate RH11 . . . 201 D1
Forest Glade GU10 . . . 145 D3
Forest Gn RG12 . . . 27 D7
FOREST GREEN . . . 176 E7
FOREST HILL . . . 23 D7
Forest Hill Bsns Ctr SE23 . 23 B6
Forest Hill Ct SE26 . . . 23 B5
Forest Hill Ind Est 9
SE23 . . . 23 C6
Forest Hill Rd SE23 . . . 23 C8
Forest Hills GU15 . . . 65 B4
Forest Hill Sch SE23 . . . 23 D5
Forest Hill Sta SE23 . . . 23 C6
Forestholme Cl SE23 . . . 23 C6
Forest Ho The SE23 . . . 23 E7
Forest La KT24 . . . 92 F3
Forest Lodge
2 East Grinstead RH19 . . 205 F8
Forest Hill SE23 . . . 23 C5
Forest Mews RH12 . . . 218 B5
Forest Oaks RH13 . . . 218 B4
Forest Rd
Cheam SM3, SM4 . . . 40 A2
Crowthorne RG45 . . . 45 C5
East Horsley KT24 . . . 92 F2
Faygate RH12, RH13 . . . 218 D5
Feltham TW13 . . . 15 C5
Richmond TW9 . . . 7 A7
Windsor SL4 . . . 9 E7
Winkfield RG42, SL5 . . . 8 D2
Woking GU22 . . . 70 D4
Forest Ridge BR3 . . . 44 A6
FOREST ROW . . . 206 F3
Forest Row Bsns Pk
RH18 . . . 206 F3
Forest Row CE Prim Sch
RH18 . . . 206 F2
Forestry Rd The RH14 . . . 212 B4
Forest Sch The RH13 . . . 217 F1
Forest Side KT4 . . . 38 F1
Forest View
Crawley RH10 . . . 202 A3
Farnham GU10 . . . 166 B8
Forest View Rd RH19 . . . 205 E6
FOREST WALK . . . 27 E3
Forest Way
Ashtead KT21 . . . 76 A3
Newell Green RG42 . . . 8 A2
Forest Wlk GU6 . . . 173 F2
Forge Ave CR5 . . . 100 B7
Forge Bridge La CR5 . . . 99 B5
Forge Cl
Broadbridge Heath
RH12 . . . 216 D4
Farnham GU9 . . . 125 D3
Harlington UB3 . . . 3 D8
Forge Cotts KT23 . . . 93 F4
Forge Dr KT10 . . . 56 A3
Forge End GU21 . . . 69 E2
Forgefield TN16 . . . 83 D3
Forge La
Broadbridge Heath
RH12 . . . 216 D4
Cheam SM3 . . . 58 E3
Crawley RH10 . . . 202 A7
Farnborough GU11 . . . 105 A6
Feltham TW13 . . . 15 E3
Richmond TW10 . . . 17 E7
Sunbury TW16 . . . 35 A6
Forge Lane Prim Sch
TW13 . . . 15 E3
Forge Lodge 2 TW7 . . . 6 A4
Forge Mews
Addington CR0 . . . 63 A5
Sunbury TW16 . . . 35 A6
Forge Pl RH6 . . . 160 E1
Forge Rd
Crawley RH10 . . . 202 A7
Sleaford GU35 . . . 166 A1
Forge Steading SM7 . . . 78 B4
Forge The RH12 . . . 216 E7
Forge Wood RH10 . . . 182 D3
Forge Wood Ind Est
RH10 . . . 182 B2
Forman Ct TW1 . . . 16 F7
Forrester Path SE26 . . . 23 C4
Forrest Gdns SW16 . . . 41 F6
Forster Ho SE6 . . . 24 D5
Forster Park Prim Sch
SE6 . . . 24 E5
Forster Rd
Beckenham BR3 . . . 43 E6
Guildford GU2 . . . 109 A5
Streatham SW2 . . . 21 E8
Thornton Heath CR0 . . . 42 C2
Forsyte Cres SE19 . . . 42 E8
Forsyte Ct KT2 . . . 38 B8
Forsyth Ct KT3 . . . 38 E7
Forsythe Shades BR3 . . . 44 C8
Forsythia Pl GU1 . . . 109 C3
Forsyth Path GU21 . . . 70 D6
Forsyth Rd GU21 . . . 70 C5
Fortescue Ave TW2 . . . 16 C5
Fortescue Rd
Mitcham SW19 . . . 20 D1
Weybridge KT13 . . . 52 F6
Forth Cl GU14 . . . 84 D6
Fort La RH2 . . . 118 B5
Fort Narrien GU15 . . . 64 F7
Fort Rd
Box Hill KT20 . . . 116 B4
Guildford GU1 . . . 130 E6
Fortrose Cl GU47 . . . 64 D7
Fortrose Gdns SW12, SW2 . 21 E7
Fortune Dr GU6 . . . 174 E1
Forty Foot Rd KT22 . . . 95 C6
Forum The
Chertsey KT16 . . . 32 F1
East Molesey KT8 . . . 36 B5
3 Horsham RH12 . . . 217 C2
Forval Cl CR4 . . . 40 F4
Foss Ave CR0, CR9 . . . 61 A5
Fosseway RG45 . . . 45 A5
Fosse Way KT14 . . . 70 F6
Fossewood Dr GU15 . . . 65 D7
Foss Rd SW17 . . . 20 D4
Fosterdown RH9 . . . 121 B6
Fosters Gr GU20 . . . 48 B6
Fosters La GU21 . . . 68 C2
Foulser Rd SW17 . . . 21 A5
Foulsham Rd CR7 . . . 42 D6
Foundation Units GU1 . . . 109 E5
Founders Gdns SE19 . . . 22 C1
Foundry Cl RH13 . . . 217 E4
Foundry Ct KT16 . . . 33 A2
Foundry Ct RH13 . . . 217 E3
Foundry La
Haslemere GU27 . . . 208 A6
Horsham RH13 . . . 217 E3
Horton SL3 . . . 1 B4
Foundry Mews 1 KT16 . . . 33 A2
Foundry Pl SW18 . . . 20 B8
Fountain Ct
New Malden KT3 . . . 38 C5
Penge SE26 . . . 23 C2
Fountain Dr
Dulwich SE19 . . . 22 F4
Wallington SM5 . . . 59 F2
Fountain Ho 3 CR4 . . . 40 F7
Fountain Rd
Redhill RH1 . . . 139 E7
South Norwood CR7 . . . 42 C7
Upper Tooting SW17 . . . 20 D4
Fountains Ave TW13 . . . 15 F5
Fountains Cl
Crawley RH11 . . . 201 A4
Feltham TW13 . . . 15 F5
Fountains Garth RG12 . . . 27 A6
Four Acres
Cobham KT11 . . . 73 E6
Guildford GU1 . . . 110 C3
Four Seasons Cres SM3 . . . 58 F8
Four Square Ct TW4 . . . 5 A1
Fourth Cross Rd TW2 . . . 16 D6
Fourth Dr CR5 . . . 79 D3
Fourways 2 CR0 . . . 61 F8
Four Wents KT11 . . . 73 C5
Fowler Ave GU14 . . . 85 B2
Fowler Cl RH10 . . . 202 C4
Fowler Rd
Farnborough GU14 . . . 84 F3
Mitcham CR4 . . . 41 A7
Fowlerscroft GU3 . . . 129 B2
Fowlers La RG42 . . . 27 B8
Fowlers Mead GU24 . . . 49 E2
Fowler's Rd GU11 . . . 105 D6
Foxacre CR3 . . . 100 E5
FOXBORO PARK . . . 119 C4
Foxboro Rd RH1 . . . 119 B3
Foxborough Hill Rd GU5 151 D6
Foxbourne Rd SW17 . . . 21 A6
Foxbridge La RH14 . . . 212 C1
Foxburrow Hill GU5 . . . 151 D6
Foxburrows Ave GU2 . . . 108 F2
Foxburrows Ct GU2 . . . 108 F2
Fox Cl
Crawley RH11 . . . 181 B1
Weybridge KT13 . . . 53 D5
Woking GU22 . . . 70 D4
Foxcombe CR0 . . . 63 B4
Foxcombe Rd 6 SW15 . . . 19 A7
FOX CORNER . . . 88 C2
Fox Corner Nature Reserve★
GU3 . . . 88 C2
Fox Covert
Fetcham KT22 . . . 94 D3
Lightwater GU18 . . . 67 A8
Fox Covert Cl SL5 . . . 29 C4
Fox Ct
Aldershot GU12 . . . 105 E3
Fox Ct *continued*
Sandhurst GU47 . . . 64 C8
Fox Dene GU7 . . . 150 C2
Foxdown Cl GU15 . . . 65 C5
Foxearth Cl TN16 . . . 83 E1
Foxearth Rd CR2 . . . 62 C2
Foxearth Spur CR2 . . . 62 C2
Foxenden Rd GU1 . . . 109 E1
Foxes Dale BR2 . . . 44 D6
Foxes Path GU4 . . . 89 F1
Foxglove Ave RH12 . . . 217 E6
Foxglove Cl
Stanwell TW19 . . . 13 D7
Winkfield RG42 . . . 8 A2
Foxglove Gdns
Guildford GU4 . . . 110 C3
Purley CR8 . . . 79 F8
Foxglove La KT9 . . . 57 A6
Foxglove Way CR4 . . . 41 B1
Foxglove Wlk RH11 . . . 201 B3
Fox Gr KT12 . . . 35 B2
Foxgrove Ave BR3 . . . 24 B1
Foxgrove Dr GU21 . . . 70 A4
Foxgrove Rd BR3 . . . 24 C1
Foxhanger Gdns GU22 . . . 70 A3
Foxhaven Ct SL5 . . . 29 C4
Foxheath RG12 . . . 27 E4
Fox Heath GU14 . . . 84 C3
Fox Hill SE19 . . . 22 F1
Foxhill Cres GU15 . . . 66 B8
Fox Hill Gdns SE19 . . . 22 F1
Fox Hill Prim Sch RG12 . . . 27 B4
Foxhills GU21 . . . 69 C2
Foxhills Cl KT16 . . . 51 C4
Fox Hills La GU12 . . . 106 C3
Foxhills Mews KT16 . . . 51 B7
Fox Hills Rd KT16 . . . 51 B5
Fox Ho KT16 . . . 32 F1
Foxholes
Rudgwick RH12 . . . 214 D8
Weybridge KT13 . . . 53 D5
Fox Hollow KT12 . . . 54 D8
Foxhurst Rd GU12 . . . 106 A4
Fox La
Little Bookham KT23 . . . 93 F3
Reigate RH2 . . . 118 B4
Foxlake Rd KT14 . . . 71 F7
FOX LANE . . . 84 F8
Fox Lane N KT16 . . . 32 F1
Fox Lane S KT16 . . . 32 F1
Foxleigh Chase RH12 . . . 217 F5
Foxley Cl
Blackwater GU17 . . . 64 C5
Redhill RH1 . . . 140 A4
Foxley Ct SM2 . . . 59 C3
Foxley Gdns CR8 . . . 80 B6
Foxley Hall CR8 . . . 80 A6
Foxley Hill Rd CR8 . . . 80 A7
Foxley La CR8 . . . 60 E1
Foxley Lodge 5 CR8 . . . 80 A7
Foxley Rd
Purley CR8 . . . 80 B5
Thornton Heath CR7 . . . 42 B5
Foxley Wood Nature
Reserve★ CR8 . . . 80 A6
Foxoak Hill KT12 . . . 53 E1
Foxon Cl CR3 . . . 100 E6
Foxon La CR3 . . . 100 E6
Foxon Lane Gdns CR3 . . . 100 E6
Fox Path CR4 . . . 40 E7
Fox Rd
Farnham GU10 . . . 146 C7
Haslemere GU27 . . . 207 E6
Foxtail Ho TW3 . . . 5 C6
Foxton KT1 . . . 38 A6
Foxton Gr CR4 . . . 40 D7
Foxwarren KT10 . . . 55 F2
Fox Way GU10 . . . 124 D8
Foxwood RH12 . . . 198 B5
Fox Wood KT12 . . . 53 F3
Foxwood Cl
Feltham TW13 . . . 15 B5
Wormley GU8 . . . 190 F8
Fox Yd GU9 . . . 125 B2
Frailey Cl GU22 . . . 70 B3
Frailey Hill GU22 . . . 70 B3
Framfield Cl RH11 . . . 201 A8
Framfield Rd CR4 . . . 21 A1
Frampton Cl SM2 . . . 59 A3
Frampton Rd TW4 . . . 4 E2
France Hill Dr GU15 . . . 65 C5
Frances Ct
Ascot SL5 . . . 29 D5
South Norwood SE25 . . . 42 F7
Franche Court Rd SW17 . . . 20 C5
Francis Ave TW13 . . . 15 A5
Francis Barber Cl SW16 . . . 21 F4
Franciscan Prim Sch
SW17 . . . 21 A3
Franciscan Rd SW17 . . . 21 A4
Francis Chichester Cl SL5 29 B4
Francis Cl
Littleton TW17 . . . 34 A5
West Ewell KT19 . . . 57 D6
Francis Cnr KT24 . . . 133 B8
Francis Crick Rd GU2 . . . 129 D8
Francis Ct
Farnborough GU14 . . . 84 F4
Guildford GU2 . . . 109 B3
Kingston upon Thames KT5 . 37 E5
Francis Edwards Way
RH11 . . . 200 E2
Francis Gr SW19 . . . 19 F2
Francis Rd
Caterham CR3 . . . 100 D5
Hounslow TW4 . . . 4 D5
Thornton Heath CR0 . . . 42 B2
Wallington SM6 . . . 60 C4
Francis Way GU15 . . . 66 C4
Frangate KT24 . . . 112 E8
Frank Dixon Cl SE21 . . . 22 E7
Frank Dixon Way SE21 . . . 22 E7
Frankland Ho 4 SW12 . . . 21 B8
Franklands Dr KT15 . . . 51 F3
Franklin Cl
Kingston upon Thames
KT1 . . . 38 A6
West Norwood SE27 . . . 22 B5
Franklin Cres CR4 . . . 41 C5
Franklin Ct
Farnborough GU14 . . . 84 C4
2 Guildford GU2 . . . 108 F1
Wormley GU8 . . . 170 F1
Franklin Ho BR2 . . . 44 E7
Franklin Ind Est SE20 . . . 43 C8
Franklin Rd
Crawley RH10 . . . 202 C5
Penge SE20 . . . 43 C8
Walton-on-Thames KT12 . . . 35 A3
Franklin Way CR0, CR9 . . . 41 E2
Franklyn Rd
Godalming GU7 . . . 150 B3
Walton-on-Thames KT12 . . . 35 B3
Franks Ave KT3 . . . 38 C5
Franksfield GU5 . . . 154 E7
Franks Ho TW7 . . . 6 B3
Franks Rd GU2 . . . 109 A3
Frank Towell Ct TW14 . . . 15 A7
Fransfield Gr SE26 . . . 23 B5
Frant Cl SE20 . . . 23 C1
Franthorne Way SE6 . . . 24 B5
Frant Rd CR0, CR7 . . . 42 B4
Fraser Ct TW5 . . . 4 E7
Fraser Gdns RH4 . . . 136 A8
Fraser Mead GU47 . . . 64 E6
Fraser Rd RG42 . . . 27 B8
Frederick Cl SM1 . . . 58 F5
Frederick Gdns
Cheam SM1 . . . 58 F5
Thornton Heath CR0 . . . 42 B3
Frederick Ho TW15 . . . 13 E4
Frederick Pl RG41 . . . 25 A6
Frederick Rd SM1 . . . 58 F5
Frederick Sanger Rd
GU2 . . . 129 D8
Frederick St GU11 . . . 105 A2
Freeborn Way RG12 . . . 27 E7
Freedown La SM2 . . . 78 C6
Freehold Ind Ctr TW4 . . . 4 C2
Freelands Ave CR2 . . . 62 D2
Freelands Rd KT11 . . . 73 B5
Freeman Cl TW17 . . . 34 E5
Freeman Ct SW16 . . . 41 E7
Freeman Dr KT8 . . . 35 F5
Freeman Ho 13 SW2 . . . 21 E8
Freeman Rd
Morden CR4, SM4 . . . 40 D4
Warnham RH12 . . . 216 F8
Freemantle Rd GU19 . . . 47 F4
Freemantles Sch GU22 . . . 89 C5
Freemason's Rd CR0 . . . 42 E1
Free Prae Rd KT16 . . . 33 A1
Freesia Dr GU24 . . . 68 A3
Freethorpe Cl SE19 . . . 42 E8
French Apartments The
CR8 . . . 80 A7
Frenchaye KT15 . . . 52 C5
Frenches Ct 4 RH1 . . . 119 A3
Frenches Rd RH1 . . . 119 B4
Frenches The RH1 . . . 119 A3
French Gdns
Blackwater GU17 . . . 64 D4
Cobham KT11 . . . 73 C5
Walton-on-Thames KT12 . . . 35 F1
French La GU8 . . . 169 E3
Frenchlands Hatch KT24 112 E8
French St TW16 . . . 35 C7
FRENSHAM . . . 167 D7
Frensham RG12 . . . 27 D3
Frensham Ct
Mitcham CR4 . . . 40 D6
Rowledge GU10 . . . 146 B4
Frensham Ctry Pk★
GU10 . . . 167 E5
Frensham Dr
New Addington CR0 . . . 63 C3
Roehampton SW15 . . . 19 A6
Frensham Heights Rd
GU10 . . . 146 A2
Frensham Heights Sch
GU10 . . . 146 A2
Frensham Ho 7 KT6 . . . 37 E4
Frensham La GU35, GU10 . 166 F1
Frensham Rd
Crowthorne RG45 . . . 45 B7
Farnham GU10, GU9 . . . 146 D6
Purley CR8 . . . 80 B5
Frensham Vale GU10 . . . 146 C4
Frensham Way KT17 . . . 77 C3
Frere Cotts KT23 . . . 94 C1
Fresham Ho BR2 . . . 44 F6
Freshborough Ct 1 GU1 130 F8
Freshfield KT20 . . . 117 F8
Freshfield Bank RH18 . . . 206 E2
Freshfield Cl RH10 . . . 202 A5
Freshfields CR0 . . . 43 F1
Freshford Ct 16 BR2 . . . 44 F5
Freshford St SW17, SW18 . 20 C5
Freshmount Gdns KT19 . . . 76 B8
Freshwater Cl SW17 . . . 21 A2
Freshwater Rd SW17 . . . 21 A2
Freshwood Cl BR3 . . . 44 B8
Freshwoods RH12 . . . 214 D8
Freshwood Way SM6 . . . 60 C2
Frewin Rd SW18 . . . 20 D7
Friar Mews SE27 . . . 22 B5
Friars Ave SW15 . . . 18 F5
Friars Croft GU4 . . . 110 C4
Friars Ct
Farnham GU9 . . . 125 D7
5 Wallington SM6 . . . 60 B6
Friars Field GU9 . . . 125 B3
Friar's Gate GU2 . . . 130 A7
Friars Keep RG12 . . . 27 B5
Friars La TW9 . . . 6 D2
Friars Orch KT22 . . . 94 D6
Friars Rd GU25 . . . 31 D5
Friars Rise GU22 . . . 70 A1
Friars Rookery RH10 . . . 201 F6
Friars Stile Pl 10 TW10 . . . 6 E1
Friars Stile Rd TW10 . . . 6 E1
Friars Way KT16 . . . 33 A3
Friars Wood CR0 . . . 62 E2
Friary Bridge GU1 . . . 130 C7
Friary Ct GU21 . . . 68 F1
Friary Ho 4 GU1 . . . 130 C8
Friary Island SL4 . . . 11 C8
Friary Pas GU1 . . . 130 C7
Friary Rd
Ascot SL5 . . . 29 B3
Wraysbury TW19 . . . 11 C8
Friary Sh Ctr The GU1 . . . 220 C8
Friary The
5 Guildford GU1 . . . 130 C8
Windsor SL4 . . . 11 C8
Friary Way RH10 . . . 201 E5
Friday Grove Mews SW12 . 21 C8
Friday Rd CR4 . . . 20 F1
Friday St
Abinger Common RH5 . . . 155 F8
Faygate RH12 . . . 198 E6
Ockley RH5 . . . 177 E4
Warnham RH12 . . . 216 E7
Friend Ave GU12 . . . 105 D1
Friends Cl RH11 . . . 181 D1
Friendship Way RG12 . . . 27 B6
Friends Rd CR8 . . . 80 B7
Friends' Rd CR0, CR9 . . . 61 D7
Friends Wlk 1 TW18 . . . 12 F3
Friern Rd SE22 . . . 23 A8
FRIMLEY . . . 65 F2
Frimley Ave SM6 . . . 60 F5
Frimley Bsns Pk GU16 . . . 85 B8
Frimley CE Jun Sch GU16 85 E7
Frimley Cl
New Addington CR0 . . . 63 C3
Putney SW19 . . . 19 E6
Frimley Cres CR0 . . . 63 C3
Frimley Gdns CR4 . . . 40 E6
FRIMLEY GREEN . . . 85 F6
Frimley Green Rd GU16 . . 85 E7
Frimley Grove Gdns GU16 65 E1
Frimley Hall Dr GU15 . . . 65 F6
Frimley High St GU16 . . . 85 D8
Frimley Ho CR4 . . . 40 E6
Frimley Park Hospl GU16 . 65 D2
Frimley Rd
Ash Vale GU12 . . . 106 A8
Camberley GU15, GU16 . . . 65 B3
Chessington KT9 . . . 56 E5
FRIMLEY RIDGE . . . 66 B3
Frimley Sq GU16 . . . 65 E1
Frimley Sta GU16 . . . 85 C8
Frinton Rd SW17 . . . 21 A2
Friston Wlk RH11 . . . 201 A7
Fritham Cl KT3 . . . 38 E3
FRITHEND . . . 166 C4
Frith End Rd GU34, GU35 . 166 A6
FRITH HILL . . . 150 E6
Frith Hill Rd
Farncombe GU7 . . . 150 D6
Frimley GU16 . . . 66 B1
Frith Knowle
Cobham KT11 . . . 73 B6
Hersham KT12 . . . 54 B5
Frith Pk RH19 . . . 185 E3
Frith Rd CR0, CR9 . . . 61 C8
Friths Dr RH2 . . . 118 B4
Frithwald Rd KT16 . . . 32 F2
Frobisher RG12 . . . 27 C2
Frobisher Cl CR8 . . . 80 C2
Frobisher Cres TW19 . . . 13 E8
Frobisher Ct
Belmont SM2 . . . 58 F3
Forest Hill SE23 . . . 23 B6
Frobisher Gdns
Guildford GU1 . . . 110 A2
Stanwell TW19 . . . 13 E8
Frodsham Way GU47 . . . 45 E2
Froggetts La RH5 . . . 176 C1
Frog Grove La GU3 . . . 107 F4
Frog Hall RG40 . . . 25 F5
Frog Hall Dr RG40 . . . 25 E5
Frog La
Bracknell RG12 . . . 27 A6
Woking GU4 . . . 89 E2
FROGMORE . . . 64 C6
Frogmore Cl SM3 . . . 58 E7
Frogmore Comm Coll
GU46 . . . 64 A5
Frogmore Ct GU17 . . . 64 C4
Frogmore Gdns SM3 . . . 58 E6
Frogmore Gr GU17 . . . 64 C4
Frogmore Inf Sch GU17 . . 64 B5
Frogmore Jun Sch GU17 . 64 B5
Frogmore Park Dr GU17 . . 64 D4
Frogmore Rd GU17 . . . 64 C5
Frome Cl GU14 . . . 84 D6
Fromondes Rd SM3 . . . 58 E5
Fromow Gdns GU20 . . . 48 D4
Froxfield Down 6 RG12 . . 27 F4
Fruen Rd TW14 . . . 14 F8
Fry Cl RH11 . . . 201 B1
Fryern Wood CR3 . . . 100 C3

Fry La GU19 . . . . 47 D2
Frylands Ct CR0 . . . . . . 82 C8
Fry's Cross GU8 . . . . . 193 A2
Fryston Ave
  Croydon CR0 . . . . 62 A8
  Wallington CR5 . . . . . 79 B5
Fuchsia Way GU24 . . . 67 E6
Fuel Farm Rd
  Crawley RH6 . . . . . . 181 E8
  Hookwood RH6 . . . . 160 E1
Fulbourn 4 KT1 . . . . . . 38 A7
Fulbourne Cl RH1 . . . 118 E3
Fulbrook La GU8 . . . . 148 C5
Fulford Rd
  Caterham CR3 . . . . . 100 D6
  West Ewell KT19 . . . 57 D3
Fulham Cl RH11 . . . . . 201 B2
Fullbrook Ave KT15 . . 38 F1
Fullbrooks Ave KT4 . . 38 F1
Fullbrook Sch KT15 . . 71 A8
Fullers Ave KT6 . . . . . 56 F8
Fullers Farm Rd KT24 112 B1
Fullers Rd GU10 . . . . 145 D3
Fullers Vale GU35 . . . 187 A5
Fullers Way N KT6 . . . 56 F7
Fullers Way S KT9 . . . 56 F7
Fuller's Wood CR0 . . . 63 A6
Fullers Wood La RH1 . 119 C1
Fullerton Cl KT14 . . . . 71 F5
Fullerton Ct 9 TW11 . 17 A3
Fullerton Dr KT14 . . . 71 E5
Fullerton Rd
  Byfleet KT14 . . . . . . 71 F5
  Croydon CR0 . . . . . . 42 F2
  Wallington SM5 . . . . 59 E2
Fullerton Way KT14 . . 71 E5
Fullmer Way KT15 . . . 51 F1
Fulmar Cl 1 RH11 . . . 200 D5
Fulmar Ct
  Surbiton KT5 . . . . . . 37 F3
  6 West Norwood SE21 . . 22 D6
Fulmar Dr RH19 . . . . 186 B3
Fulmer Cl TW12 . . . . . 15 E3
Fulstone Cl TW4 . . . . . .4 F3
Fulvens GU5 . . . . 133 E1
Fulwell Ct TW11 . . . . . 16 E4
Fulwell Park Ave TW2 . 16 C6
Fulwell Rd TW11 . . . . . 16 D4
Fulwell Sta TW2 . . . . . 16 D4
Fulwood Ct TW19 . . . . .2 F1
Fulwood Gdns TW1 . . . 6 A1
Fulwood Wlk SW19 . . . 19 E7
Furlong Cl CR4 . . . . . . 41 B1
Furlong Rd RH4 . . . . 135 C6
Furlongs The KT10 . . . 55 B7
Furlough The GU22 . . . 70 A2
Furlong Way RH6 . . . 181 F8
Furmage St SW18 . . . . 20 B8
Furnace Dr RH10 . . . 201 F4
Furnace Farm Rd RH10 . 202 A4
FURNACE GREEN . . . 202 A5
Furnace Par RH10 . . . 202 A4
Furnace Pl RH10 . . . . 202 A4
Furnance Farm Rd RH19 184 C3
Furneaux Ave SE27 . . . 22 B3
Furness Lo SW14 . . . . . .7 B3
Furness Rd SM4 . . . . . 40 B3
Furniss Ct GU6 . . . . . 173 F2
Furnival Cl GU25 . . . . 31 D3
Furrows Pl CR3 . . . . . 100 F4
Furrows The KT12 . . . . 54 C8
Furse Cl GU15 . . . . . . 66 C4
Furtherfield GU6 . . . . 174 E4
Furtherfield Cl CR0 . . 42 A3
Further Green Rd SE6 . 24 E7
Furzebank SL5 . . . . . . 29 D5
Furze Cl
  Ash Vale GU12 . . . . 106 A7
  Horley RH6 . . . . 161 D3
  Redhill RH1 . . . . 118 F2
Furzecroft 4 TW15 . . . 14 A3
Furze Ct CR0 . . . . 62 A8
FURZEDOWN 21 B4
Furzedown Cl TW20 . . 11 E2
Furzedown Dr SW17 . . 21 B3
Furzedown Prim Sch
  SW17 . . . . 21 A2
Furzedown Rd
  Streatham SW17 . . . . 21 B3
  Sutton SM2 . . . . 78 C8
Furzefield RH11 . . . . 201 C7
Furze Field KT22 . . . . 74 E6
Furzefield Chase RH19 185 E6
Furzefield Cres RH2 . 139 C7
Furzefield Prim Sch
  RH1 . . . . 119 D7
Furzefield Rd
  East Grinstead RH19 . 185 D4
  Horsham RH12 . . . . 218 B5
  Reigate RH2 . . . . . . 139 C7
Furze Gr KT20 . . . . . . 97 F6
Furze Hall KT20 . . . . . 97 F6
Furzehill RH1 . . . . . . 118 E2
Furze Hill
  Kingswood KT20 . . . 97 F6
  Purley CR8 . . . . 79 F8
Furze Hill Cres RG45 . 45 C4
Furze Hill Rd GU35 . . 187 C4
Furze La
  East Grinstead RH19 . 185 B4
  Farncombe GU7, GU3 . 150 F8
  Purley CR8 . . . . 79 F8
Furzeland Ho 2 KT3 . 38 E2
Furzemoors RG12 . . . . 27 B4
Furzen Cotts RH1 . . . 196 A3
Furzen La RH12, RH5 . 196 A6
Furze Rd
  Addlestone KT15 . . . . 51 F4

Furze Rd continued
  Rudgwick RH12 . . . . 214 D8
  South Norwood CR7 . . 42 C6
Furze Vale Rd GU35 . 187 B4
Furzewood TW16 . . . . 35 A8
Fuscia Ct TW13 . . . . . 14 F5
Fusion Cl SW15 . . . . . 18 E5
Fydlers Cl SL4 . . . . . . .9 B2
Fyfield Cl
  Beckenham BR2 . . . . 44 D5
  Blackwater GU17 . . . 64 D5

G

Gable Ct
  Forest Hill SE26 . . . . 23 B4
  9 Redhill RH1 . . . . . 119 A2
Gable End
  6 Aldershot GU11 . . . 105 B2
  Farnborough GU14 . . 85 B4
Gable Lodge BR4 . . . . 44 C1
Gables Ave TW15 . . . . 13 F3
Gables Cl
  Ash Vale GU12 . . . . 106 A5
  Farnborough GU14 . . 85 A4
  Old Woking GU22 . . . 89 F7
Gables Ct
  Cheam SM3 . . . . 58 D6
  Old Woking GU22 . . . 89 F7
Gables The
  Banstead SM7 . . . . . 77 F2
  Copthorne RH10 . . . 183 B3
  Elstead GU8 . . . . . . 148 C3
  Grayshott GU26 . . . 188 D3
  Guildford GU2 . . . . . 109 B4
  Horsham RH12 . . . . 217 D4
  Hounslow TW5 . . . . . .5 A8
  Mitcham CR4 . . . . . . 41 B6
  Oxshott KT22 . . . . . . 74 C7
  Weybridge KT13 . . . . 53 C5
Gables Way SM7 . . . . . 77 F3
Gabriel Cl TW13 . . . . . 15 D4
Gabriel Dr GU15 . . . . . 66 B4
Gabriel Rd RH10 . . . . 202 C2
Gabriel St SE23 . . . . . 23 E8
Gadbridge La GU6 . . . 175 E4
Gadbrook Rd RH3 . . . 137 D4
Gadd Cl RG40 . . . . 25 F7
Gadesden Rd KT19 . . . 57 C4
Gage Cl RH10 . . . . . . 184 C1
Gaffney Cl GU11 . . . . 105 D7
Gage Ridge RH18 . . . 206 E2
Gainsborough RG12 . . 27 C3
Gainsborough Cl
  Beckenham BR3 . . . . 24 A1
  Camberley GU15 . . . . 65 F7
  Farnborough GU14 . . 85 D2
  Thames Ditton KT10 . . 36 E1
Gainsborough Ct
  Dulwich SE21 . . . . . . 22 E6
  Farnborough GU12 . . 105 C8
  Walton-on-Thames KT12 . 54 A6
  Worcester Park KT19 . . 57 F4
Gainsborough Dr
  North Ascot SL5 . . . . 28 D7
  Sanderstead CR2 . . . . 81 A6
Gainsborough Gdns TW7 . .5 D2
Gainsborough Ho RH10 . 201 D6
Gainsborough Mews SE26 23 B5
Gainsborough Pl RH11 . 73 E4
Gainsborough Rd
  Crawley RH10 . . . . . 201 F3
  Epsom KT19 . . . . 57 C1
  New Malden KT3 . . . . 38 D2
  Richmond TW9 . . . . . .6 F4
Galahad Rd RH11 . . . 200 E6
Galba Ct 1 TW8 . . . . . .6 D7
Gale Cl
  Hampton TW12 . . . . . 15 E2
  Mitcham CR4 . . . . . . 40 D6
Gale Cres SM7 . . . . . . 78 A2
Gale Dr GU18 . . . . 48 A1
Gale Ho SM5 . . . . 59 E5
Galen Ct KT19 . . . . . . 76 A8
Gales Cl
  Guildford GU4 . . . . 110 D3
  Haslemere GU27 . . . 207 E5
Gales Dr RH10 . . . . . . 201 F6
Gales Pl RH10 . . . . . . 201 F6
Galgate Cl 4 SW19 . . . 19 E7
Galileo Ct RG12 . . . . . 27 E7
Gallery Ct 14 TW20 . . 12 A3
Gallery Rd
  Dulwich SE21 . . . . . . 22 D7
  Pirbright GU24 . . . . . 87 D8
Galleymead Rd SL3 . . . .1 F6
Gallica Ct SM1 . . . . . . 40 B1
Gallops The KT10 . . . . 55 B7
Gallop The
  South Croydon CR2 . . 62 B3
  Sutton SM2 . . . . 59 D2
Galloway Path CR0 . . . 61 D6
Gallwey Rd GU11 . . . 105 C3
Galpin's Rd CR4, CR7 . 41 F4
Galsworthy Rd
  6 Chertsey KT16 . . . . 33 A2
  Kingston upon Thames KT2 38 B8
Galton Rd SL5 . . . . . . 29 F3
Galvani Way CR0, CR9 . 41 F1
Galvins Ct GU2 . . . . . 109 A4
Gambles La GU23 . . . . 91 C2
Gamble Rd SW17 . . . . 20 E4
Gamma Ct 8 CR0 . . . . 42 D1
Gander Green Cres TW12 . 36 A8
Gander Green La KT4, SM1,
  SM3 . . . . 58 F7

Gangers Hill RH9 . . . 121 F7
Ganghill GU1 . . . . . . 110 A3
Gannet Ct 5 SE21 . . . . 22 D6
Ganymede Ct RH11 . . 200 E3
Gapemouth Rd GU16,
  GU24 . . . . 86 E5
Gap Rd SW19 . . . . 20 B3
Garbetts Way GU10 . . 126 F6
Garbrand Wlk KT17 . . 57 F2
Garden Ave CR4 . . . . . 21 B1
Garden Cl
  Addlestone KT15 . . . . 52 D6
  Ashford TW15 . . . . . . 14 C2
  Banstead SM7 . . . . . 78 A4
  East Grinstead RH19 . 205 F7
  Farnborough GU14 . . 84 E3
  Hampton TW12 . . . . . 15 F3
  Leatherhead KT22 . . . 95 C3
  Putney SW15 . . . . . . 19 B8
  Shamley Green GU5 . 152 D4
  Wallington SM6 . . . . 60 E5
  West Barnes SM4 . . . 39 D2
Garden Cotts SL3 . . . . .1 D7
Garden Ct
  10 Belmont SM2 . . . . 59 A3
  Bromley BR1 . . . . . . 24 F1
  Hampton TW12 . . . . . 15 F3
  4 Richmond TW9 . . . .6 F6
  South Croydon CR0 . . 61 F7
  Wimbledon SW20 . . . 39 D8
Gardeners Cl RH12 . . 216 E8
Gardeners Ct 2 RH13 . 217 D1
Gardeners Gn RH12 . . 199 C6
GARDENERS GREEN . . 25 F2
Gardener's Hill Rd GU10. 146 B4
Gardeners Rd
  Thornton Heath CR0 . 42 B1
  Winkfield RG42 . . . . . 8 A2
Gardener's Wlk KT23 . 94 B1
Gardenfields KT20 . . . 97 E8
Garden Flats SW16 . . . 21 E5
Gardenia Ct 1 BR3 . . . 24 A1
Gardenia Dr GU24 . . . 67 F6
Garden La SW2 . . . . . . 21 F7
Garden Pl 2 RH12 . . . 217 D1
Garden Prim Sch CR4 . 41 D6
Garden Rd
  Mortlake TW9 . . . . . . .7 A4
  Penge SE20 . . . . 43 C8
  Walton-on-Thames KT12 . 35 B2
Gardens The
  Beckenham BR3 . . . . 44 D7
  Esher KT10 . . . . 55 A6
  Hatton TW14 . . . . . . .3 D1
  Pirbright GU24 . . . . . 87 F5
  Tongham GU10 . . . . 126 F7
Garden Wlk
  Beckenham BR3 . . . . 43 F8
  Crawley RH11 . . . . . 201 C6
  3 Horsham RH12 . . . 217 C4
Garden Wood Rd RH19 . 205 C8
Gardiner Ct CR2 . . . . . 61 D4
Gardner Ct TW3 . . . . . .5 A4
Gardner Ho TW13 . . . . 15 F6
Gardner Ind Est SE26 . 23 F3
Gardner La RH10 . . . . 204 A8
Gardner Pl TW14 . . . . . .4 B1
Gardner Rd GU1 . . . . 109 D1
Garendon Gdns SM4 . . 40 B2
Garendon Rd SM4 . . . . 40 B2
Gareth Cl KT4 . . . . 58 D8
Gareth Ct SW16 . . . . . 21 D5
Garfield Prim Sch SW19. 20 C2
Garfield Rd
  Addlestone KT15 . . . . 52 C6
  Camberley GU15 . . . . 65 C5
  3 Twickenham TW1 . . 17 A7
  Wimbledon SW19 . . . 20 C2
Garibaldi Rd RH1 . . . 139 F8
Garland Dr TW3 . . . . . .5 C5
Garland Ho 18 KT2 . . . 37 E8
Garland Rd RH19 . . . . 185 D2
Garlands Ct CR0 . . . . . 61 D6
Garlands Rd
  Leatherhead KT22 . . . 95 C4
  Redhill RH1 . . . . 118 F1
Garland Way CR3 . . . 100 D5
Garlichill Rd KT17, KT18. 77 B2
Garlies Rd SE23 . . . . . 23 E5
Garner Ct 13 TW19 . . . .2 E1
Garnet Ct TW13 . . . . . 14 E5
Garnet Ho KT4 . . . . . . 38 D1
Garnet Rd CR7 . . . . . . 42 D5
Garrad's Rd SW16 . . . 21 D4
Garrat La SW17, SW18 . 20 C5
Garratt Cl CR0 . . . . . . 60 E6
Garratt La SW17, SW18 . 20 C5
Garratt Park Sec Specl Sch
  SW18 . . . . 20 C5
Garratts La SM7 . . . . . 78 A4
Garratt Terr SW17 . . . 20 E4
Garraway Ho SE21 . . . 22 F5
Garrett Cl RH10 . . . . 202 D4
Garrett Mews 9 GU11 . 105 A1
Garrick Cl
  Hersham KT12 . . . . . 54 B6
  1 Richmond TW9 . . . .6 D2
  Staines TW18 . . . . . . 13 A1
Garrick Gdns KT8 . . . . 36 A6
Garrick Ho
  4 Chiswick W4 . . . . . .7 E8
  2 Kingston upon Thames
    KT1 . . . . 37 E5
  7 Streatham SW16 . . . 21 C3
Garrick Rd TW9 . . . . . .7 A5

Garrick's Ait KT8 . . . . 36 C7
Garricks Ho KT1 . . . . . 37 D7
Garrick's Villa TW12 . . 36 C7
Garrick Way GU16 . . . 85 E7
Garrick Wlk RH10 . . . 201 E3
Garrison Cl TW4 . . . . . .4 E1
Garrison La KT9 . . . . . 56 E3
Garrone Rd CR10 . . . . 54 F4
Garrones The RH10 . . 202 E2
Garside Cl
  Hampton TW12 . . . . . 16 B2
  Redhill RH1 . . . . 119 A2
Garson Ct GU10 . . . . . 54 F4
Garson La TW19 . . . . . 11 D8
Garson Rd KT10 . . . . . 54 F4
Garson's La SL4 . . . . . .8 A7
Garstons Cl CR8 . . . . . 80 D4
Garston Gdns CR8 . . . 80 D4
Garston La CR8 . . . . . 80 D4
Garstons The KT23 . . . 94 A2
Garswood RG12 . . . . . 27 D3
Garth Cl
  Farnham GU9 . . . . . 146 A7
  Kingston upon Thames KT2 17 F3
  West Barnes SM4 . . . 39 D2
Garth Ct W4 . . . . .7 D8
Garth Hill Coll RG12 . . 27 C8
Garthorne Rd SE23 . . . 23 D8
Garth Rd
  Chiswick W4 . . . . . . .7 D8
  Kingston upon Thames KT2 17 F3
  West Barnes SM4 . . . 39 D2
Garth Road Ind Ctr The
  SM4 . . . . 39 D1
Garthside TW10 . . . . . 17 E3
Garth The
  Ash GU12 . . . . 105 F1
  Cobham KT11 . . . . . . 73 E6
  Farnborough GU14 . . 85 D4
  Hampton TW12 . . . . . 16 B2
Gartmoor Gdns SW19 . 19 F7
Garton Cl RH11 . . . . . 200 E5
Garvens SE19 . . . . 22 E3
Gascoigne Rd
  New Addington CR0 . . 63 C2
  Weybridge KT13 . . . . 53 B7
Gasden Copse GU8 . . 170 D5
Gasden Dr GU8 . . . . . 170 D6
Gasden La GU8 . . . . . 170 D6
Gaskyns Cl RH12 . . . . 214 D7
Gassiot Rd SW17 . . . . 20 F4
Gassiot Way SM1 . . . . 59 D7
Gasson Wood Rd RH11 . 200 E4
Gaston Bell Cl TW9 . . . .6 F4
Gaston Bridge Rd
  Shepperton TW17 . . . 34 D3
  Upper Halliford TW17 . 34 D4
Gaston Rd CR4 . . . . . . 41 A6
Gaston Way TW17 . . . . 34 D4
Gatcombe Cres 2 SL5 . 28 F8
Gatcombe Ct BR3 . . . . 24 A1
Gate Ct 4 KT13 . . . . . 53 B7
Gateford Dr RH12 . . . 217 F6
Gate Ho 4 KT6 . . . . . . 37 E1
Gatehouse Cl KT2 . . . . 18 C1
Gatehouse Lodge RH1 . 140 A6
Gates Cl RH10 . . . . . . 202 C2
Gatesden Cl KT22 . . . . 94 C4
Gatesden Rd KT22 . . . 94 C4
Gates Green Rd BR4 . . 63 F7
Gateside Rd SW17 . . . 20 F5
Gatestone Ct 11 SE19 . 22 E2
Gatestone Rd SE19 . . . 22 E2
Gate Way 7 KT13 . . . . 53 B7
Gateway 3 K9 . . . . . . 57 A6
Gateway Ho
  11 Guildford GU1 . . . 130 C8
  3 Upper Tooting SW17 . 20 E8
Gateways
  Guildford GU1 . . . . . 131 B8
  Kingston upon Thames KT6 . 37 E4
Gateways Ct SM6 . . . . 60 B5
Gateways The TW9 . . . .6 D3
Gateway The GU21 . . . 70 C5
Gatfield Gr TW13 . . . . 16 A6
Gatfield Ho TW13 . . . . 16 A6
Gatley Ave KT19 . . . . . 57 B5
Gatley Dr GU1 . . . . . . 109 F4
GATTON 118 F7
Gatton Bottom
  Gatton RH2, RH1 . . . 118 E7
  Merstham RH1, RH2 . 119 B8
Gatton Cl
  Belmont SM2 . . . . . . 59 B2
  Reigate RH2 . . . . . . 118 C4
Gatton Park Bsns Ctr
  RH1 . . . . 119 B6
Gatton Park Ct RH1 . . 118 F4
Gatton Park Rd RH1, RH2 118 E4
Gatton Point RH1 . . . . 119 A5
Gatton Prim Sch SW17 . 20 E4
Gatton Rd
  Reigate RH2 . . . . . . 118 C4
  Upper Tooting SW17 . . 20 E4
Gatwick Airport Beehive
  Area RH6 . . . . 182 B5
Gatwick Airport-London
  RH6 . . . . 181 F7
Gatwick Airport Sta RH6 182 B7
Gatwick Aviation Mus★
  RH6 . . . . 180 F6
Gatwick Gate Est RH6 . 181 E5
Gatwick Ho RH6 . . . . 182 E7
Gatwick Metro Ctr RH6. 161 B3
Gatwick Park Hospl (Private)
  RH6 . . . . 160 E2
Gatwick Rd
  Crawley RH6, RH10 . . 182 A3
  Wandsworth SW18 . . . 19 F8
Gatwick Way RH6 . . . 181 F7
Gauntlet Rd SM1 . . . . 59 D5
Gavell Rd KT11 . . . . . . 73 A6

Gaveston Cl KT14 . . . . 71 F6
Gaveston Rd KT22 . . . 95 A7
Gavina Cl SM4 . . . . . . 40 E4
Gawton Cres CR5 . . . . 99 C5
Gayfere Rd KT17 . . . . . 58 A5
Gayhouse La RH1 . . . 162 E8
Gayler Cl RH1 . . . . . . 120 F2
Gaynesford Rd
  Forest Hill SE23 . . . . 23 D6
  Wallington SM5 . . . . 59 F3
Gays Cotts RH7 . . . . . 143 A2
Gayton Cl KT21 . . . . . 75 E1
Gayton Ct
  New Malden KT3 . . . . 38 F4
  Reigate RH2 . . . . . . 118 A2
Gaywood Cl SW2 . . . . 22 A7
Gaywood Rd KT21 . . . 75 F1
Gearing Cl SW17 . . . . 21 A4
Geary Cl RH6 . . . . 162 B1
Gedge Ct CR4 . . . . 40 E5
Geffers Ride SL5 . . . . . 28 E7
Gemima Ct SM1 . . . . . 59 A5
Gemini Cl RH11 . . . . 200 E4
Gemini Ct 11 CR8 . . . . 80 A8
Gemma Ct BR3 . . . . . . 43 F7
Gemmell Cl CR8 . . . . . 79 F5
Genesis Bsns Ctr RH13 . 217 E3
Genesis Bsns Pk GU21 . 70 C4
Genesis Cl TW19 . . . . . 13 E1
Genesis Ho KT6 . . . . . 37 D1
Geneva Cl TW17 . . . . . 34 E7
Geneva Rd
  Kingston upon Thames
    KT1 . . . . 37 E5
  Thornton Heath CR7 . 42 C4
Genoa Rd SE20 . . . . . . 43 C8
Gentles La GU30, GU35 . 187 A3
Genyn Rd GU2 . . . . . . 130 B8
Geoffrey Ct TW18 . . . . 13 A1
George Abbot Sch GU1. 110 A3
George Denyer Cl GU27 . 208 C7
George Eliot Cl GU8 . . 170 F4
George Gdns GU11 . . . 126 C4
George Groves Rd SE20 . 43 A8
Georgeham Rd GU47 . . 45 D2
George Ho
  8 Penge SE26 . . . . . 23 B3
  16 Richmond TW9 . . . .6 D2
George Horley Pl RH5 . 158 B1
Georgelands GU23 . . . 91 B6
George Pinion Ct RH12 . 217 B3
George Rd
  Farncombe GU7 . . . 150 F7
  Guildford GU1 . . . . 109 D1
  Kingston upon Thames KT2 . 18 C1
  Milford GU8 . . . . . . 149 F2
  New Malden KT3 . . . . 38 F4
George St Halt CR0 . . . 61 C8
George Sq SW19 . . . . . 40 A6
George's Rd TN16 . . . 103 D7
George St
  Croydon CR0, CR9 . . . 61 D8
  Hounslow TW3, TW5 . . .4 F5
  Pirbright GU24 . . . . . 87 A6
  Richmond TW10 . . . . .6 D2
  Staines TW18 . . . . . . 12 F4
Georges Terr CR3 . . . . 100 D5
Georgetown Cl 4 SE19 . 22 E3
George Wyver Cl SW18 . 19 E8
Georgian Cl
  Camberley GU15 . . . . 65 E7
  Crawley RH10 . . . . . 202 D6
  Staines TW18 . . . . . . 13 B4
Georgian Ct CR0, CR9 . 42 D1
Georgina Ct 5 TW1 . . . .6 C1
Gerald Ct RH13 . . . . . 217 E2
Geraldine Rd W4 . . . . . .7 A8
Gerald's Gr SM7 . . . . . 77 D5
Geranium Cl RG45 . . . 45 B8
Gerard Ave TW4 . . . . . 16 A8
Gerard Rd SW13 . . . . . .7 F6
Germander Dr GU24 . . 68 A4
German Sch The TW10 . 17 D7
Gerrards Mead SM7 . . 77 F3
Ghent St SE6 . . . . 24 A6
Ghyll Cres RH13 . . . . 217 F1
Gibbet La GU15 . . . . . 66 A7
Gibbon Rd KT2 . . . . . . 17 F1
Gibbons Cl
  Crawley RH10 . . . . . 202 C3
  Sandhurst GU47 . . . . 64 C8
Gibb's Acre GU24 . . . . 87 F4
Gibbs Ave SE19 . . . . . 22 D3
Gibbs Brook La RH8 . . 143 D6
Gibbs Cl SE19 . . . . . . 22 D3
Gibbs Ho
  6 Balham SW12 . . . . 21 B8
  2 Bromley BR1 . . . . . 44 F8
Gibbs Sq SE19 . . . . . . 22 D3
Giblets La RH12 . . . . . 217 F7
Giblets Way RH12 . . . 217 E7
Gibraltar Cres KT19 . . 57 E1
Gibson Cl
  Chessington KT9 . . . . 56 C5
  Isleworth TW7 . . . . . .5 D4
Gibson Ct KT10 . . . . . 55 F7
Gibson Dr RG12 . . . . . 27 D6
Gibson Ho
  South Croydon CR2 . . 61 C4
  Sutton SM1 . . . . 59 A6

254 Gib-Goo

Gibson Mews [14] TW1 .... 6 C1
Gibson Pl TW19............ 2 C1
Gibson Rd SM1 .... 59 B5
Gibson's Hill SW16....... 22 A1
Gidd Hill CR5 .... 79 A3
Giffard Dr GU14........ 84 F5
Giffards Cl RH19 ...... 185 F1
Giffards Mdw GU9 .... 125 E1
Giffard Way GU2....... 109 A4
Giggshill Gdns KT7.... 37 A1
Giggs Hill Rd KT7 ...... 37 A2
Gilbert Cl [1] SW19 .... 40 B8
Gilbert Ct CR5 .... 79 D3
Gilbert Rd
  Frimley GU16......... 65 C2
  Merton SW19.......... 20 C1
Gilbert Scott Prim Sch
  CR2...................62 E3
Gilberts Lodge KT17 ... 76 E8
Gilbert St TW3 .... 5 C4
Gilbey Rd SW17......... 20 E3
Gilders Rd KT9.......... 56 F4
Giles Coppice SE19 ...... 22 F4
Gilesmead KT18 .... 76 E5
Giles Travers Cl TW20... 32 C6
Gilham La RH18......... 206 E2
Gilham's Ave SM7........ 77 E7
Gill Ave GU2............ 129 E8
Gillespie Ho GU25....... 31 E5
Gillett Ct RH13.......... 218 B4
Gillette Cnr TW7........ 6 A7
Gillett Ho RH13........ 218 B4
Gillett Rd CR7 .... 42 D5
Gillham's La GU27 ..... 207 A5
Gilliam Gr CR8.......... 61 A1
Gilliams Ho [11] RH4 ... 136 A1
Gillian Ave GU11, GU1.. 126 D8
Gillian Cl GU12......... 126 D8
Gillian Park Rd SM3..... 39 F1
Gilliat Dr GU4......... 110 D3
Gilligan Cl RH12 ...... 217 B2
Gillman Lodge TN16 .... 83 C7
Gillray Ho [2] SM1...... 59 D5
Gilmais KT23 .... 94 C2
Gilmore Cres TW15 ...... 14 A2
Gilpin Ave SW14 .... 7 D3
Gilpin Cl CR4 .... 40 E7
Gilpin Cres TW2 .... 16 B8
Gilpin Ho KT3............ 38 E4
Gilpin Way UB3......... 3 D7
Gilsland Rd CR7........ 42 D5
Gilson Ct SL4 .... 11 C8
Gilton Rd SE6............ 24 E5
Gimcrack Hill KT22..... 95 B5
Gingell Ho TW20....... 11 D3
Gingers Cl GU6 .... 174 F2
Ginhams Rd RH11..... 201 B6
Gipsy Hill SE19......... 22 E3
Gipsy Hill Sta SE19...... 22 E3
Gipsy La
  Bracknell RG12........ 27 D7
  Wokingham RG40 ...... 25 C4
Gipsy Rd SE21, SE27... 22 D4
Gipsy Road Gdns SE27... 22 C4
Girdwood Rd SW18, SW19. 19 E8
Girling Way TW14....... 4 A4
Girtin Ho [12] SM2..... 59 B3
Girton Cl GU47......... 45 E1
Girton Gdns CR0........ 63 A7
Girton Rd SE26......... 23 D3
Gisbourne Cl SM6....... 60 D7
Gittens Cl BR1.......... 24 F4
GIVONS GROVE 95 C2
Gladebury Ct [2] SW19... 19 F2
Glade Cl KT6 .... 56 D8
Glade Gdns CR0 .... 43 E2
Glade Ho SL5............ 29 C4
Glade Mews GU1........130 F8
Gladeside CR0........... 43 D3
Gladeside Cl KT9........ 56 D3
Gladeside Ct CR6 ...... 101 B7
Glade Spur KT20........ 98 B6
Glades The RH19....... 186 B1
Glade The
  Ascot SL5............. 29 C4
  Belmont SM2.......... 58 E2
  Coulsdon CR5, CR8 .... 100 A8
  Crawley RH10 .... 202 A4
  Croydon CR0.......... 43 D3
  Fetcham KT22........ 94 B5
  Heath End GU9 .... 125 D7
  Horsham RH13........ 218 A3
  Kingswood KT20 ...... 98 B6
  Mytchett GU16........ 86 A2
  Rowledge GU10....... 145 B1
  Sheerwater KT14...... 70 E6
  Staines TW18......... 13 B2
  Stoneleigh KT17...... 58 A4
  West Wickham BR4.... 63 B7
Gladiator St SE23 ...... 23 E8
Gladiator Way GU14....105 A8
Gladioli Cl [2] TW12 ... 16 A2
Gladsmuir Cl KT12 .... 54 C8
Gladstone Ave
  Feltham TW14 .... 4 B1
  Twickenham TW2....... 16 D8
Gladstone Ct [12] SW19... 20 A1
Gladstone Gdns TW3 ... 5 C6
Gladstone Ho
  Epsom KT19............ 76 B8
  [2] Mitcham CR4..... 40 F7
Gladstone Mews [2] SE20. 23 C1
Gladstone Pl KT8 .... 36 E4
Gladstone Rd
  Ashtead KT21 .... 75 D1

Gladstone Rd continued
  Croydon CR0.......... 42 D2
  Horsham RH12....... 217 D3
  Kingston upon Thames KT1. 38 A6
  Merton SW19.......... 20 A1
  Surbiton KT6 .... 56 E8
Glamis Cl GU16........ 85 F7
Glamis Ho [12] RH2.... 118 F1
Glamorgan Cl CR4, SW16.. 41 E6
Glamorgan Rd KT1...... 17 C1
Glanfield Rd BR3...... 43 F5
Glanty The TW20....... 12 B4
Glanville Rd [4] SW12... 21 C8
Glanville Wlk [7] RH11.. 201 A3
Glasbrook Ave TW2..... 15 F7
Glasford St SW17....... 20 F2
Glassmill La BR2....... 44 F7
Glassonby Wlk GU15 ... 66 C5
Glastonbury Rd SM4.... 40 A2
Glayshers Hill GU35 ... 187 B6
Glazebrook Cl SE21..... 22 D6
Glazebrook Rd TW11.... 16 F1
Glaziers La GU3........ 107 C2
Gleave Cl RH19........ 186 A2
Glebe Ave CR4.......... 40 E7
Glebe Cl
  Aldershot GU11........126 A7
  Crawley RH10........ 201 E7
  Great Bookham KT23... 94 A1
  Lightwater GU18...... 48 C1
  Sanderstead CR2...... 80 F8
Glebe Cotts
  Feltham TW13 .... 16 A5
  Sutton SM1 .... 59 B6
  West Clandon GU4.... 111 B3
Glebe Ct
  Coulsdon CR5 .... 79 B4
  Guildford GU1........ 109 F1
  Mitcham CR4.......... 40 F6
Glebe Gdns
  Byfleet KT14........... 71 E5
  New Malden KT3...... 38 E2
Glebe Ho TW13 .... 16 A5
Glebehyrst [18] SE19.... 22 E4
Glebe Hyrst CR2....... 80 F7
Glebe La
  Abinger Common RH5. 155 D8
  Rushmoor GU10...... 168 C5
Glebeland Ctr [1] RH4.. 136 A7
Glebeland Gdns TW17... 34 C3
Glebeland Rd GU15 .... 64 F4
Glebelands
  Claygate KT10........ 55 F2
  Crawley Down RH10... 204 A7
  East Molesey KT8 .... 36 B5
  Loxwood RH14...... 212 F4
  Mitcham CR4.......... 40 E6
Glebelands Rd
  East Bedfont TW14 .... 15 A8
  Wokingham RG40 .... 25 C7
Glebelands Sch GU6.... 174 D3
Glebe Path CR4......... 40 F6
Glebe Rd
  Ashtead KT21 .... 75 D1
  Belmont SM2 .... 58 E2
  Cranleigh GU6....... 174 E4
  Dorking RH4......... 135 F7
  Egham TW20 .... 12 C2
  Farnborough GU14.... 84 F5
  Merstham CR5........ 99 B3
  Staines TW18......... 13 B3
  Wallington SM5...... 59 F4
  Warlingham CR6...... 81 D2
Glebe Sch BR4.......... 63 D8
Glebe Side TW1......... 5 F1
Glebe Sq CR4........... 40 F6
Glebe The
  Blackwater GU17...... 64 E4
  Copthorne RH10 ..... 183 B3
  Ewhurst GU6......... 175 E6
  Felbridge RH19...... 185 A4
  Horley RH6.......... 160 F3
  Leigh RH2........... 138 A2
  New Malden KT4...... 38 F1
  Streatham SW16...... 21 D4
Glebe Way
  Feltham TW13 .... 16 A5
  Sanderstead CR2..... 80 F8
  West Wickham BR4.... 63 D8
Glebewood RG12 .... 27 C4
Gledhow Wood KT20... 98 B5
Gleeson Mews KT15.... 52 F6
Glen Albyn Rd SW19 ... 19 D6
Glenalmond House TW15. 13 E5
Glena Mount SM1...... 59 C6
Glen Ave TW15 .... 14 A4
Glenavon Cl KT10..... 56 A4
Glenavon Ct KT4...... 58 B8
Glenbow Rd BR1....... 24 E3
Glenbuck Ct [6] KT6... 37 E3
Glenbuck Rd KT6...... 37 E3
Glenburnie Rd SW17... 20 F5
Glencairn Rd SW16.... 21 E1
Glen Cl
  Beacon Hill GU26..... 188 C6
  Kingswood KT20...... 97 E4
  Littleton TW17....... 34 A5
Glencoe Cl GU16...... 86 A8
Glencoe Rd KT13...... 53 A7
Glencroft Ct SM1...... 59 A5
Glen Ct
  Addlestone KT15 ..... 51 F5
  Beacon Hill GU26..... 188 C6
  [9] Bromley BR1...... 24 F1
  Glen Ct KT14 .... 71 D8
Glen Ct
  [10] Penge SE20...... 43 B8
  Staines TW18......... 12 F1

Glen Ct continued
  Woking GU21.......... 89 A8
Glendale Cl
  Horsham RH12....... 218 A6
  Woking GU21.......... 69 C1
  Wokingham RG41 ..... 25 A3
Glendale Dr
  Guildford GU4........110 C5
  Wimbledon SW19 ..... 19 F3
Glendale Ho [5] TW10....6 E1
Glen Dale Mews BR3... 44 B8
Glendale Rise CR8 ..... 80 B4
Glendene Ave KT24 .... 92 E1
Glendon Ho [9] RH10... 201 D5
Glendower Gdns [11] SW14. 7 C7
Glendower Rd SW14 .... 7 C7
Glendyne Cl RH19..... 206 A4
Glendyne Way RH19... 206 A4
Gleneagle Lodge BR3... 44 A8
Gleneagle Mews SW16.. 21 D3
Gleneagle Rd SW16.... 21 D3
Glen Eagles RH6....... 161 B2
Gleneagles Cl TW19.... 2 D1
Gleneagles Ct
  Crawley RH10........ 201 D5
  [3] Teddington TW11... 17 A3
Gleneagles Dr GU14.... 84 C3
Gleneagles Ho RG12 ... 26 E3
Gleneldon Mews SW16.. 21 E4
Gleneldon Rd SW16.... 21 E4
Glen Elgin Ho TW14.... 15 A8
Glenesk Rd SE24...... 92 D2
Glenfarg Rd SE6....... 24 D7
Glenfield Cl RH3...... 137 B5
Glenfield Cotts RH6... 180 D7
Glenfield Ho RG12 .... 27 C5
Glenfield Rd
  Ashford TW15........ 14 C2
  Banstead SM7........ 78 B4
  Brockham RH3...... 137 B6
  Streatham SW12..... 21 C8
Glengall Ct SE23 ...... 23 E8
Glen Gdns CR0, CR9... 61 A6
Glenhaven Dr TW19.... 2 A1
Glenheadon Cl KT22 ... 95 D4
Glenheadon Rise KT22.. 95 D4
Glen Ho SM6............ 60 C6
Glenhurst
  Beckenham BR3....... 44 C8
  Windlesham GU20..... 48 A6
Glenhurst Cl GU17..... 64 E4
Glenhurst Rd TW8..... 6 C8
Glenhurst Rise SE19.... 22 C1
Glen Innes GU47...... 45 E1
Glenister Park Rd SW16. 21 D1
Glenlea GU35........ 188 E1
Glenlea Hollow GU26.. 207 E8
Glenlee GU22.......... 89 D8
Glenlion Ct [2] KT13... 53 D7
Glenmill TW12......... 15 F3
Glenmore Cl KT15..... 52 B7
Glenmore Ho [4] 6 C1
Glenmount Rd GU16 ... 86 A2
Glenn Ave CR8......... 80 B8
Glennie Ct SE21....... 23 A7
Glennie Rd SE27, SW16.. 22 A5
Glen Rd
  Beacon Hill GU26..... 188 C6
  Chessington KT9..... 56 E7
  Grayshott GU26..... 188 D3
Glen Road End SM6.... 60 B2
Glenrose Ho [18] SM1... 59 C6
Glenside [1] RH19..... 185 E1
Glentanner Way SW17.. 20 D5
Glen The
  Addlestone KT15 ..... 51 F5
  Ascot SL5............. 29 D5
  Beckenham BR2....... 44 E7
  Croydon CR0......... 62 D7
  Heath End GU9 ...... 125 C6
  [8] Redhill RH1..... 139 F8
Glenthorne Ave CR0, CR9. 43 C1
Glenthorne Cl SM3.... 40 A1
Glenthorne Gdns SM3.. 40 A1
Glenthorne High Specialist
  Arts Coll SM3........ 40 A1
Glenthorne Rd KT1.... 37 F5
Glenthorpe Rd SM4.... 39 D4
Glenview CR0 RH10.... 201 F8
Glenville Gdns GU26... 188 F4
Glenville Mews SW18... 20 A8
Glenville Rd KT2....... 38 A8
Glen Vue RH19........ 185 E1
Glen Wlk TW7.......... 5 D2
Glenwood
  Bracknell RG12 ...... 27 D5
  Dorking RH5........ 136 C5
  Heath End GU9 ..... 125 C6
  Virginia Water GU25.. 31 C8
Glenwood Ct GU14.... 85 A4
Glenwood Rd
  Forest Hill SE6....... 24 A7
  Hounslow TW3........ 5 D4
  Stoneleigh KT17..... 58 A4
Glenwood Way CR0.... 43 D3
Globe Farm La GU17... 64 B5
Glorney Mead GU9..... 126 A6
Glory Mead RH4...... 136 C4
Glossop Ho TW7....... 6 A3
Glossop Rd CR2....... 61 D2
Gloster Rd GU12...... 105 F5
Gloster Ct GU21...... 69 F3
Gloster Rd
  New Malden KT3..... 38 E5
  Old Woking GU22.... 90 A7
Gloucester Cl
  East Grinstead RH19.. 206 A8
  Frimley GU16........ 85 E6

Gloucester Cl continued
  Thames Ditton KT7... 37 A1
Gloucester Cres TW18... 13 D2
Gloucester Ct
  Dulwich SE22......... 23 A7
  Richmond TW9........ 7 A7
  [8] Surbiton KT6 .... 37 D2
Gloucester Dr TW18,
  TW19 .... 12 D5
Gloucester Gdns
  Bagshot GU19........ 47 E3
  Sutton SM1 .... 59 B8
Gloucester Ho TW10.... 7 A2
Gloucester Lo CR0 ..... 61 F8
Gloucester Rd
  Aldershot GU11......126 C7
  Bagshot GU19........ 47 E3
  Crawley RH10....... 201 E2
  Croydon CR0......... 42 E2
  Feltham TW13 .... 15 C7
  Guildford GU2....... 108 F3
  Hampton TW12...... 16 B1
  Hounslow TW4........ 4 E3
  Kingston upon Thames KT1,
  KT2................. 38 B7
  Redhill RH1......... 118 F2
  Richmond TW9....... 7 A7
  Teddington TW11.... 16 E3
  Twickenham TW2..... 16 C7
Glovers Cl TN16....... 83 B3
Glovers Field GU27... 207 F6
Glovers Ho GU27..... 207 F6
Glovers Lodge [25] TW9.. 6 D2
Glover's Rd
  Charlwood RH6...... 180 D7
  Reigate RH2........ 139 B8
Gloxinia Wlk TW12.... 16 A2
Glyn Cl
  Ewell KT17........... 58 A2
  South Norwood SE19, SE25. 42 E8
Glyn Ct SE27.......... 22 A5
Glyndale Grange SM2.. 59 B4
Glynde Ho RH10...... 201 E8
Glynde Pl [8] RH12... 217 C2
Glyn Rd KT4, SM3..... 58 D8
Glynswood
  Frimley GU15........ 65 F3
  Rowledge GU10..... 146 A4
Glyn Tech Sch KT17... 76 F8
Glynwood Ct SE23.... 23 C6
Goaters Rd SL5....... 28 C7
Goat Rd CR4........... 40 F2
Goatsfield Rd TN16... 103 C7
Goat Wharf TW8....... 6 E8
GODALMING 150 F3
Godalming Ave SM6... 60 F5
Godalming Bsns Ctr GU7. 150 F4
Godalming Coll GU7... 150 D2
Godalming Jun Sch GU7. 150 F5
Godalming L Ctr GU7.. 151 A7
Godalming Mus ★ [10]
  GU7................ 150 D4
Godalming Rd
  Dunsfold GU8....... 193 A8
  Hascombe GU8...... 172 E3
Godalming Sta GU7.... 150 D4
Goddard Cl
  Crawley RH10....... 202 B3
  Guildford GU2....... 109 A5
  Littleton TW17....... 33 F6
Goddard Ho SW19..... 19 D6
Goddard Rd BR3...... 43 E5
Goddards Ho SM7..... 78 B5
Goddards La GU15.... 65 B3
Goddens The RH19.... 205 E7
Godfrey Ave TW2...... 16 D8
Godfrey Cl GU47...... 64 D7
Godfrey Way TW4..... 15 F8
Godley Rd
  Byfleet KT14........ 71 F6
  Wandsworth SW18.... 20 D7
Godolphin Cl SM2..... 77 F8
Godolphin Ct RH10... 201 D5
Godolphin Ho [7] SW2.. 22 A7
Godolphin Rd KT13... 53 D4
Godric Cres CR0...... 63 D1
Godson Rd CR0, CR9... 61 A7
GODSTONE 121 B3
Godstone Farm ★ [11] RH9. 121 C3
Godstone Green Rd RH9. 121 B4
Godstone Hill RH9.... 121 C5
Godstone Ho [1] KT2... 18 B2
Godstone Mount [3] CR8. 80 B7
Godstone Rd
  Bletchingley RH1..... 120 F2
  Caterham CR3....... 101 A3
  Lingfield RH7....... 164 C4
  Oxted RH8, RH9..... 122 C5
  Purley CR8........... 80 C4
  Sutton SM1 .... 59 C6
  Twickenham TW1..... 6 B1
Godstone Sta RH9.... 142 E5
Godstone Village Sch
  RH9................ 121 B3
Godstone Vineyards ★
  RH9................ 121 C7
Godwin Cl
  West Ewell KT19..... 57 C4
  Wokingham RG41 .... 25 B4
Godwin Ct
  [3] Horsham RH12... 217 A1
  South Croydon CR2.. 61 C4
Godwin Way RH13.... 218 A4
Goepel Ct RH10...... 202 B3
Goffs Cl RH11........ 201 C5
Goffs La RH11........ 201 B6
Goffs Park Rd RH11... 201 C4
Goffs Rd TW15........ 14 D2

Gogmore Farm Cl KT16. 32 F2
Gogmore La KT16....... 33 A2
Goidel Cl SM6.......... 60 D6
Goldcliff Cl SM4........ 40 A2
Goldcrest Cl RH6...... 160 E4
Goldcrest Way
  New Addington CR0.... 63 D3
  Wallington CR8....... 60 D1
Gold Cup La SL5....... 28 D8
Golden Ct
  Hounslow TW7........ 5 D5
  [9] Richmond TW9.... 6 D2
Golden Mews SE20.... 43 C8
Golden Orb Wood RG42. 26 D8
Goldfinch Cl
  Aldershot GU11......125 F8
  Crawley RH11....... 201 D8
  Horsham RH12...... 217 C2
Goldfinch Cres RG12... 26 D5
Goldfinch Gdns GU4... 110 D2
Goldfinch Rd CR0, CR2.. 62 E1
Goldfort Wlk GU21.... 68 E3
Goldhill GU10......... 146 C6
Golding Cl
  Chessington KT9 .... 56 C4
  Crawley RH10....... 202 C5
Goldings The GU21.... 68 F3
Gold La GU11......... 105 E4
Goldney Rd GU15..... 66 C4
Goldrings Rd KT22.... 74 C6
Goldsmiths Cl GU21... 69 C1
Goldsmith Way RG45.. 45 B4
Goldstone Farm View
  KT23............... 114 A8
Goldsworth Orch [6] GU21. 69 A1
GOLDSWORTH PARK.. 69 A3
Goldsworth Park Ctr
  GU21............... 69 A3
Goldsworth Park Trad Est
  GU21............... 69 B3
Goldsworth Prim Sch
  GU21............... 69 C1
Goldsworth Rd GU21.. 69 D2
Goldsworth Road Ind Est
  GU21............... 69 D2
Goldwell Rd CR7...... 41 F5
Gole Rd GU24......... 87 D6
Golf Cl
  Pyrford GU22........ 70 E5
  South Norwood SW16. 42 A8
Golf Club Dr KT2...... 18 C2
Golf Club Rd
  Weybridge KT13..... 53 C1
  Woking GU22........ 89 B7
Golf Course Cotts KT20. 98 A3
Golf Dr GU15.......... 65 F4
Golf Links Ave GU26.. 188 B6
Golf Rd CR8........... 80 D1
Golf Side
  Belmont SM2......... 77 E8
  Twickenham TW2..... 16 D5
Golf Side Cl KT3...... 38 E7
Gomer Gdns TW11.... 17 A2
Gomer Pl TW11....... 17 A2
GOMSHALL........... 133 D4
Gomshall Ave SM6.... 60 E5
Gomshall Gdns CR8... 80 E4
Gomshall La GU5..... 133 B4
Gomshall Rd KT17, SM2. 58 C1
Gomshall Sta GU5.... 133 D4
Gong Hill GU10...... 146 D2
Gong Hill Dr GU10... 146 D4
Gong Hill Frensham Rd
  GU10............... 146 D4
Gonston Ct SW19..... 19 E6
Gonville Prim Sch CR7. 41 F4
Gonville Rd CR7...... 41 F4
Goodbehere Ho [7] SE27. 22 C4
Goodcare Cl [7] KT13.. 53 C5
Goodchild Rd RG40 ... 25 D6
Gooden Cres GU14.... 84 F3
Goodenough Cl CR5... 100 A7
Goodenough Rd SW19.. 19 F1
Goodenough Way CR5.. 99 F7
Goodhart Way BR4.... 44 E3
Goodhew Rd CR0, SE25. 43 A3
Gooding Cl KT3....... 38 C4
Goodings Gn RG40 ... 25 F6
Goodland Ho [1] KT3.. 38 E2
Goodman Cres
  Croydon CR0......... 42 C3
  Streatham SW2...... 21 D6
Goodman Pl [1] TW18.. 12 F4
Good Shepherd RC Prim Sch
  Catford BR1......... 24 F4
  New Addington CR0.. 63 B3
Goodson Ho SM4..... 40 C2
Goodways Dr RG12... 27 D7
Goodwin Cl
  Crawley RH11....... 200 F3
  Mitcham CR4........ 40 D6
Goodwin Ct SW19..... 20 E1
Goodwin Gdns CR0, CR2. 61 A4
Goodwin Rd CR0...... 61 B5
Goodwins Cl RH19.... 185 D3
Goodwood Cl
  Camberley GU15..... 65 C8
  Crawley RH10....... 202 A3
  Morden SM4........ 40 A5
Goodwood Ct SE27... 22 C5
Goodwood Ho SE26.. 23 B3
Goodwood Lodge SM6. 60 D7
Goodwood Par BR3.. 43 E5
Goodwood Pl GU14.. 85 E3
Goodwood Rd RH1... 118 F3
Goodworth Rd RH1... 119 B3
Goodwyns Pl RH4.... 136 B5
Goodwyns Rd RH4... 136 C4

Goose Gn GU5 ... 133 C4
Goose Green Cl RH12 ... 217 D5
Goose La GU22 ... 89 B5
Goose Rye Rd
Woking GU3 ... 89 A2
Worplesdon GU3 ... 88 E1
Goossens Cl 1 SM1 ... 59 C5
Gordon Ave
Camberley GU15 ... 65 C4
Isleworth TW1 ... 6 B2
Mortlake SW14 ... 7 E3
South Croydon CR2, CR8 ... 61 C1
Gordon Cl
Chertsey KT16 ... 51 E7
Staines TW18 ... 13 B2
Gordon Clifford Ct 3
RG42 ... 27 B8
Gordon Cres
Camberley GU15 ... 65 C4
Croydon CR0 ... 42 F1
Gordon Ct
Chiswick W4 ... 7 B8
Hampton TW12 ... 16 C3
6 Wimbledon SW20 ... 19 D1
Gordondale Rd SW18,
SW19 ... 20 A6
Gordon Dr
Chertsey KT16 ... 51 E7
Shepperton TW17 ... 34 D2
Gordon Rd
Aldershot GU11 ... 105 A1
Ashford TW15 ... 13 E5
Beckenham BR3 ... 43 F6
Camberley GU15 ... 65 C5
Caterham CR3 ... 100 D6
Chiswick W4 ... 7 B8
Claygate KT10 ... 55 E3
Crowthorne RG45 ... 45 D3
Farnborough GU14 ... 105 D8
Horsham RH12 ... 217 D4
Hounslow TW3 ... 5 C3
Kingston upon Thames KT2 ... 37 F8
Redhill RH1 ... 119 A4
Richmond TW9 ... 6 F5
Shepperton TW17 ... 34 D3
Surbiton KT5 ... 37 F2
Wallington SM5 ... 59 F4
Gordon's Sch GU24 ... 67 E7
Gordons Way RH8 ... 122 D7
Gore Rd SW20 ... 39 C7
Goring Rd TW18 ... 12 E3
Goring's Mead RH13 ... 217 D1
Goring's Sq TW18 ... 12 E4
Gorling Cl RH11 ... 200 E5
Gorrick Sq RG41 ... 25 B3
Gorringe Park Ave CR4,
SW17 ... 21 A1
Gorringe Park Prim Sch
CR4 ... 41 A8
Gorringes Brook RH12 ... 217 D6
Gorse Bank GU18 ... 67 A8
Gorse Cl
Burgh Heath KT20 ... 97 B7
Copthorne RH10 ... 183 B2
Crawley RH11 ... 201 B1
Wrecclesham GU10 ... 146 B6
Gorse Cotts GU26 ... 207 C8
Gorse Ct GU4 ... 110 C3
Gorse Dr RH6 ... 162 C3
Gorse End RH12 ... 217 D5
Gorse Hill La GU25 ... 31 D5
Gorse Hill Rd GU25 ... 31 D5
Gorse La
Chobham GU24 ... 49 E3
Wrecclesham GU10 ... 146 B6
Gorselands GU9 ... 125 C7
Gorselands Cl
Ash GU12 ... 106 A5
Headley Down GU35 ... 187 C4
West Byfleet KT14 ... 71 C8
Gorse Pl RG42 ... 8 B1
Gorse Rd
Croydon CR0 ... 63 A7
Frimley GU16 ... 65 E2
Gorse Rise SW17 ... 21 A3
Gorsewood Rd GU21 ... 88 E7
Gort Cl GU11 ... 105 E7
Gosberton Rd SW12 ... 21 A7
Gosbury Hill KT9 ... 56 E6
Gosden Cl
Crawley RH10 ... 202 A5
Shalford GU5 ... 151 F8
GOSDEN COMMON ... 151 E8
Gosden Cotts GU5 ... 151 F7
Gosden Hill Rd GU4 ... 110 C5
Gosden Ho 17 GU22 ... 89 E8
Gosden House Sch GU5 ... 151 E8
Gosden Rd GU24 ... 67 F6
Gosfield Rd KT19 ... 76 D7
Gosnell Cl GU16 ... 66 D3
Gospatric Home Ho 3
SW14 ... 7 E4
GOSPEL GREEN ... 209 E4
Gosport Ho 9 SW15 ... 19 A7
Gossops Dr RH11 ... 201 A5
GOSSOPS GREEN ... 201 A5
Gossops Green Com Prim
Sch RH11 ... 201 A5
Gossops Green La RH11 ... 201 A5
Gossops Par RH11 ... 200 F5
Gostling Rd TW2 ... 16 A7
Goston Gdns CR7 ... 42 A6
Gostrode La GU8 ... 210 A6
Gothic Ct
Harlington UB3 ... 3 D8
Sandhurst GU47 ... 64 B7
Gothic Ho 2 KT12 ... 35 A1
Gothic Rd TW2 ... 16 D6
Goudhurst Cl RH10 ... 202 E6
Goudhurst Ho 9 SE20 ... 23 C1
Goudhurst Keep RH10 ... 202 E6
Goudhurst Rd BR1 ... 24 F3
Gough Ho 4 KT1 ... 37 E7
Gough's La RG12 ... 27 D8
Gough's Mdw GU47 ... 64 B7
Gould Ct
Dulwich SE19 ... 22 E3
Guildford GU4 ... 110 D3
Goulding Gdns CR7 ... 42 C7
Gould Rd
East Bedfont TW14 ... 14 E8
Twickenham TW2 ... 16 E7
Government House Rd GU11,
GU14 ... 105 B7
Government Rd GU11 ... 105 E4
Governor's Rd GU15 ... 64 F6
Govett Ave TW17 ... 34 C4
Govett Gr GU20 ... 48 D5
Gower Ho SW19 ... 20 D3
Gower Lodge KT13 ... 53 D4
Gower Pk GU47 ... 64 D7
Gower Rd
Horley RH6 ... 160 E3
Hounslow TW7 ... 5 F8
Weybridge KT13 ... 53 D4
Gower The TW20 ... 32 C6
Gowland Pl BR3 ... 43 F7
Gowlland Cl CR0 ... 43 A2
Gowrie Pl CR3 ... 100 C5
Graburn Way KT8 ... 36 D6
Grace Bennett Cl GU14 ... 85 A7
Grace Bsns Ctr CR4 ... 40 F3
Grace Ct
Belmont SM2 ... 59 B2
5 Croydon CR0 ... 61 B7
2 Twickenham TW2 ... 16 E6
Gracedale Rd SW16, SW17 21 B3
Gracefield Gdns SW16 ... 21 E5
Grace Ho SE26 ... 23 B3
Grace Mews BR3 ... 24 A2
Grace Path SE26 ... 23 C4
Grace Rd
Crawley RH11 ... 201 A1
Thornton Heath CR0 ... 42 C3
Wallington SM5 ... 59 F4
Gracious Pond Rd GU24 ... 50 B4
Gradient The SE26 ... 23 A4
Graemesdyke Ave SW14 ... 7 B3
Graffham Cl RH11 ... 201 B8
Grafham Grange Sch
GU5 ... 173 B8
Grafton Cl
Twickenham TW4 ... 15 F7
West Byfleet KT14 ... 70 F6
Worcester Park KT4 ... 57 E7
Grafton Ct TW14 ... 14 D7
Grafton Park Rd KT4 ... 57 E8
Grafton Rd
Kingston upon Thames
KT3 ... 38 E6
Thornton Heath CR0 ... 42 A1
Worcester Park KT4 ... 57 E7
Grafton Way KT8 ... 35 F5
Graham Ave CR4 ... 41 A8
Graham Cl CR0 ... 63 A8
Graham Gdns KT6 ... 37 E1
Graham Ho
5 Balham SW12 ... 21 B8
Little Bookham KT23 ... 94 A3
Redhill RH1 ... 118 E3
Graham Rd
Hampton TW12 ... 16 A4
Merton SW19 ... 19 F1
Mitcham CR4 ... 41 A8
Purley CR8 ... 80 A6
Windlesham GU20 ... 48 C4
Grainford Ct RG40 ... 25 C5
Grainger Rd TW7 ... 5 F5
Grampian Cl
Harlington UB3 ... 3 D7
Sutton SM2 ... 59 C3
Grampian Rd GU47 ... 45 A2
Gramsci Way SE6 ... 24 B5
Granada St SW17 ... 20 F3
Granard Rd SW11, SW12 ... 20 F8
Granary Cl
Horley RH6 ... 161 A5
Horsham RH12 ... 216 F1
Granary Way RH12 ... 217 A1
Grand Ave
Camberley GU15 ... 65 C6
Tolworth KT5 ... 38 B3
Grand Avenue Prim Sch
KT5 ... 38 C3
Grand Dr KT3, SM4, SW20 ... 39 C5
Granden Rd SW16 ... 41 E7
Grandfield Ct W4 ... 7 D8
Grandis Cotts GU23 ... 91 B5
Grandison Rd KT4 ... 58 C7
Grand Par
Crawley RH10 ... 201 D6
Mortlake SW14 ... 7 C3
Tolworth KT6 ... 38 A1
Grand Regency Hts SL5 ... 28 E6
Grand Stand Rd KT17,
KT18 ... 77 A2
Grand View Ave TN16 ... 83 C3
Grange Ave
Crowthorne RG45 ... 45 B6
South Norwood SE25 ... 42 E7
Twickenham TW2 ... 16 E6
Grange Cl
Ashtead KT22 ... 95 D7
Bletchingley RH1 ... 120 D2
Crawley RH10 ... 202 A8
East Molesey KT8 ... 36 B5
Godalming GU7 ... 151 A5
Grange Cl *continued*
Guildford GU2 ... 109 B5
Heston TW5 ... 4 F8
Merstham RH1 ... 119 B7
Grangecliffe Gdns SE25 ... 42 E7
Grange Com Inf Sch The
KT15 ... 52 A1
Grange Com Jun Sch
GU14 ... 85 A7
Grange Cres RH10 ... 204 B7
Grange Ct
Belmont SM2 ... 59 B3
Egham TW20 ... 11 F3
Hackbridge SM6 ... 60 B7
Littleton TW17 ... 34 A5
Merstham RH2 ... 119 B7
South Godstone RH9 ... 142 E5
5 Staines TW18 ... 13 A3
Walton-on-Thames KT12 ... 54 A8
Grange Dr
Merstham RH1 ... 119 B7
Woking GU21 ... 69 E4
Grange End RH6 ... 162 A3
Grange Farm Est TW17 ... 34 E6
Grange Farm Rd GU12 ... 106 A3
Grangefields Rd GU4 ... 109 D6
Grange Gdns
Banstead SM7 ... 78 B6
South Norwood SE25 ... 42 E7
Grange Hill SE25 ... 42 E7
Grange La SE21 ... 22 F6
Grange Lodge SW19 ... 19 D2
Grange Mansions KT17 ... 57 F3
Grange Mdw SM7 ... 78 B6
Grangemill Rd SE6 ... 24 A6
Grange Mills SW12 ... 21 C7
Grangemill Way SE6 ... 24 A6
Grangemount KT22 ... 95 D7
Grange Park Pl SW20 ... 19 B1
Grange Park Rd CR7 ... 42 D6
Grange Pk
Cranleigh GU6 ... 174 F3
Woking GU21 ... 69 F5
Grange Pl
Laleham TW18 ... 33 C7
Walton-on-Thames KT12 ... 54 A8
Grange Rd
Ash GU12 ... 106 B1
Ashtead KT21 ... 95 D7
Belmont SM2 ... 59 A3
Bracknell RG12 ... 27 C8
Camberley GU15 ... 65 E5
Caterham CR3 ... 101 A2
Chessington KT9 ... 56 E6
Crawley Down RH10 ... 204 A7
East Molesey KT8 ... 36 B5
Egham TW20 ... 11 F3
Farnborough GU14 ... 85 B7
Guildford GU2, GU3 ... 109 B5
Hersham KT12 ... 54 E6
Kingston upon Thames KT1 ... 37 E6
Pirbright GU24 ... 87 D5
Rushmoor GU10 ... 168 C7
South Croydon CR2 ... 61 C2
South Norwood SE19, SE25 ... 42 D7
Tongham GU10 ... 126 E6
Woking GU21 ... 69 E5
Woodham KT15 ... 52 B1
Grange The
Bletchingley RH1 ... 120 D2
Chobham GU24 ... 49 E1
Croydon CR0 ... 62 F8
Frensham GU10 ... 167 D7
Horley RH6 ... 161 A6
New Malden KT3 ... 39 A4
Virginia Water GU25 ... 31 E5
Walton-on-Thames KT12 ... 54 B8
Walton on the Hill KT20 ... 97 A2
Wimbledon SW19 ... 19 D2
Worcester Park KT4 ... 57 D6
Grange Vale SM2 ... 59 B3
Grangeway RH6 ... 162 A3
Grangewood La BR3 ... 23 F2
Gransden Cl GU6 ... 175 E5
Grantchester 3 KT1 ... 38 A7
Grant Cl TW17 ... 34 B3
Grantham Cl GU47 ... 45 E1
Grantham Ct KT2 ... 17 D3
Grantham Dr 2 GU14 ... 84 D5
Grantham Ho 5 TW16 ... 14 E1
Grantham Rd W4 ... 7 E7
Grantley Ave GU5 ... 152 B6
Grantley Cl GU4 ... 130 E2
Grantley Ct GU9 ... 145 F6
Grantley Gdns GU2 ... 109 A2
Grantley Ho SW19 ... 19 D7
Grantley Pl KT10 ... 55 C5
Grantley Rd
Cranford TW4, TW5 ... 4 C5
Guildford GU2 ... 109 A2
Granton Prim Sch SW16 ... 21 C1
Granton Rd SW16 ... 41 C8
Grant Pl 2 CR0 ... 42 F1
Grant Rd
Crowthorne RG45 ... 45 C3
Croydon CR0 ... 42 F1
Grants Cotts KT10 ... 55 D8
Grants La TN8, RH8 ... 144 C6
Grant Way TW7, TW8 ... 6 A8
Grant Wlk SL5 ... 29 E1
Grantwood Cl RH1 ... 140 B4
Granville Ave
Feltham TW13 ... 15 A6
Hounslow TW3, TW4 ... 5 A2
Granville Cl
Byfleet KT14 ... 71 F6
South Croydon CR0 ... 61 E8
Weybridge KT13 ... 53 C4
Granville Gdns SW16 ... 21 F1
Granville Rd
Limpsfield RH8 ... 123 A7
Merton SW19 ... 20 A1
Wandsworth SW18 ... 19 F8
Weybridge KT13 ... 53 C4
Woking GU22 ... 89 F7
Granwood Ct TW7 ... 5 E6
Grapsome Cl KT9 ... 56 C3
Grasmere GU15 ... 65 E7
Grasmere Ave
Kingston upon Thames
SW15 ... 18 E4
Merton SW19 ... 40 A6
Twickenham TW3 ... 5 B1
Grasmere Cl
East Bedfont TW14 ... 14 F7
Guildford GU1 ... 110 B2
5 Thorpe Lea TW20 ... 12 B1
Grasmere Ct
Forest Hill SE26 ... 23 A3
13 Sutton SM2 ... 59 C4
Grasmere Gdns RH12 ... 218 B6
Grasmere Rd
Bromley BR1 ... 24 F1
Croydon SE25 ... 43 B4
Farnborough GU14 ... 84 E4
Hale GU9 ... 125 A6
Lightwater GU18 ... 48 B1
Purley CR8 ... 80 B8
Streatham SW16 ... 21 F3
Grasmere Way KT14 ... 71 F7
Grassfield Cl CR5 ... 99 C8
Grasslands RH6 ... 162 A3
Grassmere RH6 ... 161 C4
Grassmount
Forest Hill SE23 ... 23 B6
Wallington CR8 ... 60 C1
Grassway SM6 ... 60 C6
Grateley Ho 10 SW15 ... 19 B7
Grattons Dr RH10 ... 182 C1
Grattons Park Nature
Reserve★ RH10 ... 182 B1
Grattons The RH13 ... 215 E3
Graveley 7 KT1 ... 38 A7
Gravel Hill
Leatherhead KT22 ... 95 B6
South Croydon CR0, CR2 ... 62 E4
Gravel Hill Halt CR0 ... 62 E4
Gravel Hill Rd GU10 ... 145 A3
Gravelly Hill CR3 ... 120 F7
Gravelpits Cotts GU5 ... 133 C4
Gravel Pits La GU5 ... 133 C4
Gravel Rd
Farnborough GU14 ... 105 D8
Hale GU9 ... 125 B7
Twickenham TW2 ... 16 E7
Gravenel Gdns SW17 ... 20 E3
Graveney Gr SE20 ... 23 C1
Graveney Rd
Crawley RH10 ... 202 C5
Upper Tooting SW17 ... 20 E4
Graveney Sch SW17 ... 21 B3
Gravetts La GU3 ... 108 E5
Gravetye Cl RH10 ... 202 A4
Gray Cl
Addlestone KT15 ... 52 B5
Lingfield RH7 ... 164 E4
Gray Ct 8 KT2 ... 17 D4
Grayham Cres KT3 ... 38 D5
Grayham Rd KT3 ... 38 D5
Graylands GU21 ... 69 E3
Graylands Cl GU21 ... 69 E3
Graylands Ct 5 GU1 ... 130 F8
Graylings Ho KT16 ... 33 C1
Gray Pl
Bracknell RG42 ... 26 E8
Ottershaw KT16 ... 51 D4
Grays Cl GU27 ... 208 E8
Grayscroft Rd SW16 ... 21 D1
Grayshot Dr GU17 ... 64 C5
GRAYSHOTT ... 188 C3
Grayshott CE Prim Sch
GU26 ... 188 B3
Grayshott Ct 15 SM2 ... 59 B3
Grayshott Rd GU26, GU35 ... 187 C5
Grays La TW15 ... 14 B4
Gray's La KT21 ... 95 F8
Grays Rd GU7 ... 150 F7
GRAYSWOOD ... 189 F1
Grays Wood RH6 ... 161 C3
Grayswood CE Inf Sch
GU27 ... 189 F2
Grayswood Dr GU16 ... 86 A2
Grayswood Gdns SW20 ... 39 B7
Grayswood Pl GU27 ... 208 E8
Grayswood Point 14
SW15 ... 19 A7
Grayswood Rd GU27 ... 189 F1
Grazeley Ct SE19 ... 22 E3
Great Austins GU9 ... 146 D8
Great Austins Ho GU9 ... 146 D8
GREAT BOOKHAM ... 94 B1
Great Brownings SE21 ... 22 F4
GREAT BURGH ... 77 C2
Great Chertsey Rd
Chiswick SW14, W4 ... 7 D6
Feltham TW13, TW2 ... 16 A5
Great Cockcrow Rly★
KT16 ... 32 D1
Great Ellshams SM7 ... 78 A3
GREAT ENTON ... 171 A4
Greatfield Cl GU14 ... 85 B8
Great Field Pl RH19 ... 186 B3
Greatfield Rd GU14 ... 85 B8
Greatford Dr GU1 ... 110 D1
Great Gatton Cl CR0 ... 43 E2
Great George St GU7 ... 150 E4
Great Goodwin Dr GU1 ... 110 B3
Greatham Rd RH10 ... 202 C3
Greatham Wlk 8 SW15 ... 19 A7
GREAT HOLLANDS ... 26 F3
Great Hollands Prim Sch
RG12 ... 26 E4
Great Hollands Rd RG12 ... 26 F3
Great Hollands Sq RG12 ... 26 F3
Great House Ct 4 RH19 ... 205 F8
Greathurst End KT23 ... 93 F3
Greatlake Ct RH6 ... 161 B4
Great Oaks Pk GU4 ... 110 C5
Great Quarry GU1 ... 130 D6
Great South-West Rd
East Bedfont TW14, TW6, TW4,
TW5 ... 3 D2
Hounslow TW5 ... 4 B4
Greatstone Ho 12 SE20 ... 23 C1
Great Tattenhams KT18 ... 77 C1
Great West Ho TW8 ... 6 C8
Great West Rd
Brentford TW8 ... 6 B8
Cranford, Heston TW5 ... 4 F6
Hounslow TW5, TW7 ... 5 C6
Great West Road Cedars Rd
W4 ... 7 C8
Great West Road Chiswick 1
W4 ... 7 F8
Great West Road Ellesmere
Rd W4 ... 7 D8
Great West Road Hogarth La
W4 ... 7 E8
Great West Trad Est TW8 ... 6 B8
Greatwood Cl KT16 ... 51 C2
Great Woodcote Dr CR8 ... 60 D1
Great Woodcote Pk CR8,
SM6 ... 60 E1
Greaves Pl SW17 ... 20 E4
Grebe Cres RH13 ... 218 A1
Grebe Ct
Cheam SM1 ... 58 F5
Staines TW18 ... 13 B4
Grebe Terr 4 KT1 ... 37 E6
Grecian Cres SE19 ... 22 B2
Greenacre
Knaphill GU21 ... 68 E3
Whyteleafe CR3 ... 101 B7
Green Acre GU11 ... 104 F1
Greenacre Ct TW20 ... 11 C2
Greenacre Pl SM6 ... 60 B8
Greenacres
Crawley RH10 ... 202 A5
Farnham GU10 ... 126 C2
Great Bookham KT23 ... 94 A3
Horsham RH12 ... 217 C4
Lower Kingswood KT20 ... 117 F7
Oxted RH8 ... 122 E8
Green Acres CR0 ... 61 F7
Greenacre Sch for Girls
SM7 ... 78 B6
Greenaway Terr TW19 ... 13 E7
Greenbank Way GU15 ... 65 D2
Green Bsns Ctr TW20 ... 12 C4
Greenbush La GU6 ... 174 F1
Green Cl
Beckenham BR2 ... 44 E6
Carshalton SM5 ... 59 F8
Feltham TW13 ... 15 E3
Green Cotts The GU6 ... 175 E4
Green Court Ave CR0 ... 62 B8
Green Court Gdns CR0 ... 62 B8
Greencroft
2 Farnborough GU14 ... 85 B4
Guildford GU1 ... 110 B1
Green Croft
Badshot Lea GU9 ... 126 B6
Wokingham RG40 ... 25 E8
Greencroft Rd TW5 ... 4 F6
GREEN CROSS ... 168 B1
Green Cross La GU10 ... 168 A1
Green Ct TW16 ... 14 F2
Green Curve SM7 ... 77 F4
Greendale Ct CR2 ... 61 C4
Green Dene KT24 ... 112 E3
Green Dr
Send Marsh GU23 ... 90 F4
Wokingham RG40 ... 25 E4
Green Dragon Prim Sch
TW8 ... 6 E8
Greene Fielde End TW18 ... 13 D1
Green End KT9 ... 56 E6
Greener Ct 10 SW20 ... 39 D8
Green Farm Rd GU19 ... 47 F3
Greenfield Ave KT5 ... 38 B3
Greenfield Ho
Englefield Green TW20 ... 11 B2
28 Putney SW19 ... 19 D7
Greenfield Link CR5 ... 79 E4
Greenfield Rd
Farnham GU9, GU10 ... 146 A7
Slinfold RH13 ... 215 D3
Wrecclesham GU9 ... 145 F7
Greenfield Sch 18 GU22 ... 89 E8
Greenfields Cl
Horley RH6 ... 160 E5
Horsham RH12 ... 218 A6
Greenfields Pl RH5 ... 157 D4
Greenfields Rd
Horley RH6 ... 160 F5
Horsham RH12 ... 218 A5
Greenfields Sch RH18 ... 206 C1
Greenfields Way RH12 ... 218 A6
Greenfield Way RG45 ... 45 A7
Greenfinch Cl GU47 ... 64 D8
Green Finch Cl RG45 ... 45 A6

Greenfinch Way RH12 . . . . . **217** D7
Greenford Rd SM1 . . . . **59** B6
Greenham Ho TW7 . . . . **5** D4
Greenham Lo CR2 . . . . **61** D1
Greenham Wlk GU21 . . . . . **69** C1
Greenham Wood RG12 . . **27** C3
Greenhanger GU10 . . . . **188** A8
Greenhayes Ave SM7 . . . . . **78** A4
Greenhayes Cl RH2 . . . . . **118** C1
Greenhayes Gdns SM7 . . . **78** A4
Green Hedges **8** TW1 . . . . **6** C1
Green Hedges Ave RH19 **185** D2
Green Hedges Cl RH19 . **185** D2
Greenheys Pl GU22 . . . . . **69** F1
Greenhill SM1 . . . . **59** C8
Green Hill BR6 . . . . **83** F7
Greenhill Ave CR3 . . . . . **101** B6
Greenhill Cl
  Godalming GU7 . . . . **150** D3
  Wrecclesham GU9 . . . . . . **146** A7
Green Hill Cl GU15 . . . . . **66** C6
Greenhill La CR6 . . . . . . **81** F2
Greenhill Rd GU9 . . . . . **146** D8
Green Hill Rd GU15 . . . . **66** C6
Greenhills GU9 . . . . **146** E8
Greenhill Way GU9 . . . . **146** A7
Greenholme GU15 . . . . . **66** D5
Green House The **5**
  SW19 . . . . **19** E7
Greenhow RG12 . . . . **27** A6
Greenhurst La RH8 . . . . **123** A3
Greenhurst Rd SE27 . . . . **22** A3
Green La
  Alfold Crossways GU6 . . . **193** F4
  Ascot SL5 . . . . **29** E8
  Ashford TW16 . . . . **14** F2
  Ashtead KT22 . . . . **95** D6
  Ashtead, Lower Ashtead
    KT21 . . . . **75** D1
  Bagshot GU19 . . . . **47** F2
  Blackwater GU17 . . . . . . **64** B4
  Blackwater, Hawley GU17 . . **64** E4
  Burstow RH6 . . . . **182** F6
  Byfleet KT14 . . . . **71** F7
  Caterham CR3 . . . . **100** C6
  Chertsey KT15, KT16 . . . . **51** E7
  Chessington KT9 . . . . . . **56** E3
  Chobham GU24 . . . . **49** F1
  Church GU10 . . . . **168** A1
  Cobham KT11 . . . . **73** E7
  Copthorne RH10 . . . . . . **183** C4
  Crawley, Northgate RH10 . **201** E8
  Crawley, Worth RH10 . . . **202** D6
  Cudworth RH5 . . . . **179** D8
  Dockenfield GU10 . . . . . **166** E6
  East Molesey KT8 . . . . . **36** B4
  Egham TW20 . . . . **12** B3
  Farncombe GU7 . . . . . . **150** E8
  Farnham GU9 . . . . **146** A7
  Farnham, Weybourne GU9 . **125** F7
  Faygate RH12 . . . . **198** F4
  Feltham TW13 . . . . **15** E3
  Guildford GU1 . . . . **110** B1
  Hersham KT12 . . . . **54** B5
  Hounslow TW4 . . . . **4** C3
  Kingsley Green GU27 . . . **208** B4
  Leigh RH2 . . . . **158** A3
  Lingfield RH7 . . . . **164** C4
  Lower Kingswood KT20 . . . **97** F1
  Milford GU8 . . . . **170** E8
  Morden SM4 . . . . **40** B3
  New Malden KT3 . . . . . . **38** C4
  North Cheam KT4 . . . . . . **39** A1
  Penge SE20 . . . . **23** D1
  Purley CR8 . . . . **60** D1
  Redhill RH1 . . . . **118** E3
  Redhill, Whitebushes RH1 . **140** A4
  Reigate RH2 . . . . **117** F1
  Sandhurst GU47 . . . . **64** C7
  Shamley Green GU5 . . . . **153** A7
  Shepperton TW17 . . . . . . **34** C4
  South Norwood CR7, SW16 . **42** B8
  South Nutfield RH1 . . . . **140** F1
  Streatham SW16 . . . . . . **21** F1
  Thorpe TW18 . . . . **32** E8
  Tilford GU10 . . . . **147** E6
  West Clandon GU4 . . . . . **111** B8
  West Horsley GU23 . . . . . **92** B3
Greenlake Terr TW18 . . . **13** A1
Greenlands
  Addlestone KT16 . . . . . . **51** C7
  Selsdon CR2 . . . . **62** C2
  West Ewell KT19 . . . . . . **57** B5
Greenlands Ct **6** TW18 . . **13** A4
Greenlands Rd
  Camberley GU15 . . . . . . **65** B1
  Staines TW18 . . . . **13** A4
  Weybridge KT13 . . . . . . **53** C7
Greenland Way CR0 . . . . **41** D2
Green Lane Ave KT12 . . . **54** C5
Green Lane Cl
  Byfleet KT14 . . . . **71** F7
  Camberley GU15 . . . . . . **65** C2
  Chertsey KT16 . . . . **51** E8
Green Lane Cotts GU10 . . **167** F1
Green Lane E
  Flexford GU3 . . . . **128** B8
  Normandy GU12 . . . . . . **127** F8
Green Lane Gdns CR7 . . . **42** C7
Green Lane Mews SM4 . . **40** B3
Green Lane Prim Sch KT4 **39** B2
Green Lane W
  Normandy GU12 . . . . . . **127** E8

Green Lane W *continued*
  West Horsley KT24 . . . . . **92** A2
Greenlaw Gdns KT3 . . . . . **38** F2
Green Leaf Ave SM6 . . . . **60** D6
Greenleaf Cl **6** SW2 . . . . **22** A8
Greenlea Pk SW19 . . . . . **40** E8
Greenleas GU16 . . . . **65** E2
Green Leas
  Ashford TW16 . . . . **14** F2
  Kingston upon Thames KT1 . **37** E6
Green Leas Cl TW16 . . . . **14** F2
Greenleaves Ct TW15 . . . **14** B2
Green Link Wlk TW9 . . . . . **7** B6
Green Man La TW14 . . . . . **4** A2
Green Mead KT10 . . . . . . **54** F4
Greenmead Cl SE25 . . . . **43** A4
Greenmeads GU22 . . . . . **89** E5
Green Oak CE Prim Sch
  GU7 . . . . **150** B3
Greenoak Rise TN16 . . . . **83** C1
Greenoak Way SW19 . . . . **19** D4
Greenock Rd SW16 . . . . . **41** D8
Greeno Cres TW17 . . . . . **34** A4
Green Pk TW18 . . . . **12** E5
Green Rd TW20 . . . . **32** B5
Greensand CE RH1 . . . . **119** D7
Green Sch The TW7 . . . . . . **6** A6
Greenshaw High Sch SM1 **59** D8
Greenside Cl
  Catford SE6 . . . . **24** D6
  Guildford GU4 . . . . **110** C3
Greenside Cotts GU23 . . . **91** C6
Greenside Dr KT21 . . . . . **75** B1
Greenside Rd CR0 . . . . . . **42** A2
Greenside Wlk TN16 . . . . **83** B1
Greensleeves Manor SM1 **59** B4
Green's School La GU14 . . **85** A4
Green St TW16 . . . . **35** A7
Greenstede Ave RH19 . . . **185** F2
Green The
  Badshot Lea GU9 . . . . . . **126** A6
  Bracknell RG12 . . . . **27** B5
  Burgh Heath KT20 . . . . . . **97** E8
  Carshalton SM6 . . . . **60** A8
  Chiddingfold GU8 . . . . . **191** C3
  Claygate KT10 . . . . **55** F4
  Copthorne RH10 . . . . . . **183** B3
  Crawley RH11 . . . . **201** C7
  Ewell KT17 . . . . **77** A7
  Ewhurst GU6 . . . . **175** A4
  Feltham TW13 . . . . **15** B6
  Fetcham KT22 . . . . **94** D3
  Frimley GU16 . . . . **85** F6
  Hale GU9 . . . . **125** C6
  Heston TW5 . . . . **5** A8
  Kingston upon Thames KT3 . **38** C7
  Merton SM4 . . . . **39** E6
  New Addington CR0 . . . . . **62** F2
  Richmond TW9 . . . . **6** D3
  Ripley GU23 . . . . **91** C6
  Staines TW18 . . . . **13** D3
  Sutton SM1 . . . . **59** B7
  The Sands GU10 . . . . . . **126** E1
  Twickenham TW2 . . . . . . **16** E6
  Tyler's Green RH9 . . . . . **121** C4
  Upper Halliford TW17 . . . . **34** E5
  Wallington SM5 . . . . **60** A6
  Warlingham CR6 . . . . **81** D1
  Whiteley Village KT12 . . . . **53** E1
  Wimbledon SW19 . . . . . . **19** D3
  Woldingham CR3 . . . . . . **102** A4
Greenvale Prim Sch CR2 . **81** D8
Greenvale Rd GU21 . . . . . **68** D1
Greenvale Sch
  Forest Hill SE23 . . . . **23** E5
  London SE6 . . . . **24** E5
Green View
  Chessington KT9 . . . . . . **56** F3
  Godstone RH9 . . . . **121** B4
Greenview Ave CR0 . . . . . **43** E3
Greenview Ct
  Ashford TW15 . . . . **13** F4
  Wandsworth SW18 . . . . . **20** E8
Greenway
  Great Bookham KT23 . . . . **94** B4
  Horsham RH12 . . . . **217** B3
  Tatsfield TN16 . . . . **103** C2
  Wallington SM6 . . . . **60** C6
  West Barnes SW20 . . . . . **39** C5
Green Way
  Aldershot GU12 . . . . **105** C3
  Redhill RH1 . . . . **118** E3
  Sunbury TW16 . . . . **35** A5
Greenway Cl KT14 . . . . . . **71** A6
Greenway Dr TW18 . . . . . **33** D8
Greenway Gdns CR0 . . . . **62** F7
Greenways
  Beckenham BR3 . . . . **44** A7
  Egham TW20 . . . . **11** E3
  Forest Hill SE26 . . . . **23** C4
  Hinchley Wood KT10 . . . . **55** E6
  Sandhurst GU47 . . . . **45** B1
  Walton on the Hill KT20 . . . **97** B2
Greenway Sch RH12 . . . . **217** B3
Greenways Dr SL5 . . . . . . **29** E1
Greenways The **1** TW1 . . . **6** A1
Greenways Wlk RH11 . . . **201** C1
Greenway The
  Epsom KT18 . . . . **76** A5
  Hounslow TW4 . . . . **4** F3
  Oxted RH8 . . . . **123** B2
Greenwell Cl RH9 . . . . . . **121** B5
Greenwich Cl RH11 . . . . **201** C2
Green Wlk
  Crawley RH10 . . . . **201** E8
  Hampton TW12 . . . . **15** F2
Greenwood
  4 Bracknell RG12 . . . . . **27** F5

Greenwood *continued*
  North Ascot SL5 . . . . **28** C8
  8 Putney SW19 . . . . **19** D8
Greenwood Cl
  Hinchley Wood KT7 . . . . . **37** A1
  Merton SM4 . . . . **39** E5
  Woodham KT15 . . . . **70** F8
Greenwood Cotts SL5 . . . **30** C3
Greenwood Ct
  2 Crawley RH11 . . . . . **201** B1
  10 Epsom KT18 . . . . **76** E6
Greenwood Dr RH1 . . . . **140** A4
Greenwood Flats RH6 . . **182** F6
Greenwood Gdns
  Caterham CR3 . . . . **101** A2
  Oxted RH8 . . . . **123** A1
Greenwood La TW12 . . . . **16** B3
Greenwood Pk KT2 . . . . . **18** E1
Greenwood Rd
  Crowthorne RG45 . . . . . . **45** B6
  Hinchley Wood KT7 . . . . . **56** A8
  Isleworth TW7 . . . . **5** F4
  Knaphill GU21 . . . . **88** E7
  Mitcham CR4 . . . . **41** D6
  Pirbright GU24 . . . . **87** C7
  Thornton Heath CR0, CR9 . . **42** C2
Greenwood The GU1 . . . . **110** A1
Green Wrythe Cres SM5 . . **40** E1
Green Wrythe La SM4,
  SM5 . . . . **40** E2
Green Wrythe Prim Sch
  SM5 . . . . **40** D3
Gregan Ct GU11 . . . . **104** F1
Gregory Cl
  Crawley RH10 . . . . **202** C2
  Woking GU21 . . . . **69** C2
Gregory Ct
  2 East Grinstead RH19 . . **185** E1
  Purley CR8 . . . . **80** B6
Gregsons RH12 . . . . **216** E8
Greig Ho **9** TW10 . . . . . . **17** C5
Grenaby Ave CR0 . . . . . . **42** D2
Grenaby Rd CR0 . . . . **42** D2
Grenadier Pl CR3 . . . . . **100** C5
Grenadier Rd GU12 . . . . **106** B4
Grenadiers Way GU14 . . . **84** C3
Grena Gdns TW9 . . . . **6** F3
Grena Rd TW10, TW9 . . . . . **6** F3
Grendon Cl RH6 . . . . . . **160** F5
Grenfell Rd CR4, SW17 . . . **20** F2
Grennell Cl SM1 . . . . **59** D8
Grennell Rd SM1 . . . . **59** C8
Grenside Rd KT13 . . . . . . **53** B7
Grenville Cl
  Cobham KT11 . . . . **73** E6
  Tolworth KT5 . . . . **38** C1
Grenville Ct SE19 . . . . . . **22** F3
Grenville Gdns GU16 . . . . **85** E6
Grenville Mews TW12 . . . **16** B3
Grenville Pl
  Ashtead KT21 . . . . **75** F1
  Bracknell RG12 . . . . **27** C7
Grenville Rd
  New Addington CR0 . . . . . **63** C2
  Shacklenord GU8 . . . . . . **149** D7
Gresham Ave CR6 . . . . . . **81** E1
Gresham Cl RH8 . . . . . . **122** F7
Gresham Ct
  Farnborough GU14 . . . . . **105** C8
  Frimley GU15 . . . . **65** F4
  Hounslow TW3 . . . . **5** C6
  3 Purley CR8 . . . . **80** A8
  8 Staines TW18 . . . . **13** A3
Gresham Ho
  5 Teddington TW11 . . . . **16** F3
  3 Thames Ditton KT7 . . . **37** A2
  West Barnes KT3 . . . . . . **39** B5
Gresham Ind Est GU12 . . **105** E2
Gresham Prim Sch CR2 . . **81** A7
Gresham Rd
  Croydon SE25 . . . . **43** A5
  Hampton TW12 . . . . **16** A2
  Hounslow TW3, TW5 . . . . . **5** C6
  Limpsfield RH8 . . . . **122** F6
  Penge BR3 . . . . **43** E7
  Staines TW18 . . . . **13** A3
Gresham Way
  Frimley GU16 . . . . **85** E6
  Wimbledon SW19 . . . . . . **20** A5
Gresham Way Est SW19 . . **20** B5
Gresham Wlk RH10 . . . . **201** E3
Gressenhall Rd SW18 . . . **19** F8
Greta Bank KT24 . . . . **92** C1
Greville Ave CR2 . . . . **62** D1
Greville Cl
  Aldershot GU11 . . . . **104** F3
  Ashtead KT21 . . . . **95** E8
  Twickenham TW1 . . . . . . **17** B8
Greville Ct
  Ashtead KT21 . . . . **75** E1
  Fetcham KT22 . . . . **94** C2
Greville Park Ave KT21 . . **75** E1
Greville Park Rd KT21 . . . **75** E1
Greville Prim Sch KT21 . . **75** F2
Greville Rd TW10 . . . . **6** F1
Grey Alders KT17 . . . . **77** C5
Greycot Rd BR3 . . . . **24** A3
Grey Court Sch TW10 . . . **17** C5
Greyfields Cl CR8 . . . . . . **80** B6
Greyfriars Dr
  Ascot SL5 . . . . **29** B3
  Bisley GU24 . . . . **68** A4
Greyfriars Rd GU23 . . . . . **91** A3
Greyfriars **16** SE26 . . . . **23** A5
Greyhound Cl GU12 . . . . **105** F1
Greyhound La SW16 . . . . **21** D2

Greyhound Rd SM1 . . . . . **59** C5
Greyhound Slip RH10 . . . **202** D7
Greyhound Terr SW16 . . . **41** C8
Greylees GU7 . . . . **150** E5
Greys Ct GU11 . . . . **104** E2
Greystead Pk GU10 . . . . **145** E5
Greystead Rd SE23 . . . . . **23** C8
Greystoke Ct RG45 . . . . . **45** A4
Greystone Cl CR2 . . . . . . **81** C8
Greystones Cl RH1 . . . . **139** D7
Greystones Ct TW2 . . . . . **16** C6
Greystones Dr RH2 . . . . **118** C3
Greyswood St SW16 . . . . **21** B2
Greythorne Rd GU21 . . . . **69** A1
Greytiles TW11 . . . . **16** F2
Greywaters GU5 . . . . **152** A6
Grice Ave TN16 . . . . **83** C6
Grier Cl RH11 . . . . **200** E5
Grierson Ho SW16 . . . . . **21** C4
Grierson Rd SE23 . . . . . . **23** D8
Grieve Cl GU10 . . . . **126** E7
Griffin Ct
  Ashtead KT21 . . . . **95** E8
  8 Brentford TW8 . . . . **6** E8
  Great Bookham KT23 . . . . **94** B1
Griffin Ctr TW14 . . . . **4** B1
Griffin Ctr The KT1 . . . . . **37** D7
Griffin Pk (Brentford FC)
  TW8 . . . . **6** D8
Griffin Way
  Great Bookham KT23 . . . . **94** A1
  Sunbury TW16 . . . . **35** A7
Griffiths Cl KT4 . . . . **58** B8
Griffiths Rd SW19 . . . . . . **20** B1
Griffon Cl GU14 . . . . **84** D3
Griggs Mdw GU8 . . . . . . **192** F7
Grimwade Ave CR0 . . . . . **62** A7
Grimwood Rd TW1 . . . . . . **16** F8
Grindall Cl CR0 . . . . **61** B6
Grindley Gdns CR0 . . . . . **42** F3
Grindstone Cres GU21 . . . **68** B1
Grindstone Handle Cnr
  GU21 . . . . **68** B1
Grinstead La RH19 . . . . . **205** B1
Grisedale Cl
  Crawley RH11 . . . . **201** C4
  Sanderstead CR8 . . . . . . **80** E5
Grisedale Gdns CR8 . . . . **80** E5
Grizedale Terr SE23 . . . . . **23** B6
Grobars Ave GU21 . . . . . . **69** C4
Grogan Cl TW12 . . . . **15** F2
Groombridge Cl KT12 . . . **54** B5
Groombridge Ho SE20 . . . **23** D1
Groombridge Way RH12 . **216** F1
Groom Cres SW18 . . . . . . **20** D8
Groomfield Cl SW17 . . . . **21** A4
Grooms The RH10 . . . . . **202** D8
Groom Wlk GU1 . . . . **109** E4
Grosslea SM4 . . . . **40** D4
Grosvenor Ave
  Carshalton SM5 . . . . **59** F4
  Mortlake SW14 . . . . **7** E4
  Richmond TW10 . . . . **6** E2
  Wallington SM5 . . . . **60** A4
Grosvenor Cl RH6 . . . . . **161** A1
Grosvenor Ct
  Blackwater GU17 . . . . . . **64** D3
  Guildford GU4 . . . . **110** B4
  11 Leatherhead KT22 . . . . **95** C6
  Morden SM4 . . . . **40** A5
  Penge SE19 . . . . **22** F2
  2 Richmond TW10 . . . . **6** F1
  7 Sutton SM2 . . . . **59** C4
  Teddington TW11 . . . . . . **17** A2
  2 Wimbledon SW19 . . . . **19** E2
Grosvenor Gdns
  Kingston upon Thames
    KT2 . . . . **17** D2
  Mortlake SW14 . . . . **7** E4
  Wallington SM6 . . . . **60** C3
Grosvenor Hill SW19 . . . . **19** E2
Grosvenor Ho RH19 . . . . **185** E3
Grosvenor Ho
  2 Farnborough GU14 . . . . **105** D8
  8 Guildford GU1 . . . . . . **130** F8
  5 Sutton SM1 . . . . **59** B5
Grosvenor Mews RH2 . . . **139** B6
Grosvenor Pl
  1 Oatlands Park KT13 . . . **53** D7
  1 Woking GU21 . . . . **69** F2
Grosvenor Rd
  Aldershot GU11 . . . . **105** A1
  Brentford TW8 . . . . **6** D8
  Castle Green GU24 . . . . . **68** D6
  Croydon SE25 . . . . **43** A5
  East Grinstead RH19 . . . . **185** D1
  Godalming GU7 . . . . **150** E3
  Hounslow TW3, TW4 . . . . . **4** F4
  Langley Vale KT18 . . . . . . **96** E8
  Richmond TW10 . . . . **6** E2
  Staines TW18 . . . . **13** A1
  Twickenham TW1 . . . . . . **17** A7
  Wallington SM6 . . . . **60** B5
  West Wickham BR4 . . . . . **63** B8
Groton Rd SW18 . . . . **20** B6
Grotto Rd
  Twickenham TW1 . . . . . . **16** F6
  Weybridge KT13 . . . . **53** B7
Grouse Mdws RG12 . . . . . **26** D5
Grove Ave
  Epsom KT17 . . . . **76** E6
  Sutton SM1 . . . . **59** A4
  Twickenham TW1 . . . . . . **17** A7
Grovebarns TW18 . . . . . . **13** A2
Grovebell Ind Est GU9 . . **145** F7
Grove Cl
  Cranleigh GU6 . . . . **174** F1
  Epsom KT19 . . . . **57** B1

Grove Cl *continued*
  Forest Hill SE23 . . . . **23** E7
  Kingston upon Thames KT1 . **37** F6
  Old Windsor SL4 . . . . **11** B8
Grove Cnr **1** KT23 . . . . . **94** B1
Grove Cres
  Feltham TW13 . . . . **15** E4
  Kingston upon Thames KT1 . **37** E6
  Walton-on-Thames KT12 . . **35** B2
Grove Cross Rd GU16 . . . . **65** D1
Grove Ct
  Dorking RH4 . . . . **136** A6
  East Molesey KT8 . . . . . **36** D4
  Egham TW20 . . . . **12** A3
  3 Forest Hill SE26 . . . . . **23** E4
  Hounslow TW3 . . . . **5** A3
  8 Kingston upon Thames
    KT1 . . . . **37** E6
  New Malden KT3 . . . . . . **38** E6
  Penge SE20 . . . . **23** B1
  1 Sutton SM1 . . . . **59** B4
Grove End GU19 . . . . **47** F5
Grove End La KT10 . . . . . **36** D1
Grove End Rd GU9 . . . . . **146** B8
Grove Farm Ct CR4 . . . . . **40** F4
Grove Farm Pk GU16 . . . . **85** F1
Grovefields Ave GU16 . . . **65** D1
Grove Gdns TW11 . . . . . . **17** A4
Grove Heath Ct GU23 . . . . **91** C3
Grove Heath La GU23 . . . . **91** D4
Grove Heath N GU23 . . . . **91** B5
Grove Heath Rd GU23 . . . . **91** B4
Grovehill Ct BR1 . . . . **24** F2
Grovehill Rd RH1 . . . . . . **118** F1
Grove Ho
  7 Epsom KT17 . . . . **76** E6
  Old Windsor SL4 . . . . **11** C8
  8 Redhill RH1 . . . . **118** F1
Grove La
  Kingston upon Thames
    KT1 . . . . **37** E5
  Wallington CR5 . . . . **79** B5
  Winkfield RG42 . . . . **8** B4
Groveland Ave SW16 . . . . **21** F1
Groveland Rd BR3 . . . . . . **43** F6
Grovelands
  East Molesey KT8 . . . . . **36** A5
  Farnham GU10 . . . . **146** E7
  Horley RH6 . . . . **161** B2
  Kingston upon Thames KT1 . **37** D5
Grovelands Rd CR8 . . . . . **79** F7
Grovelands Sch KT12 . . . . **35** B3
Groveland Way KT3 . . . . . **38** D4
Groveley Rd TW13, TW16 . . **14** F3
Grove Lodge **8** TW1 . . . . **17** A7
Grove Mill CR4 . . . . **40** E4
Grove Mill Pl SM5 . . . . . . **60** D4
GROVE PARK **7** C6
Grove Park Bridge W4 . . . . **7** C7
Grove Park Gdns W4 . . . . . **7** C7
Grove Park Prim Sch W4 . . **7** C8
Grove Park Rd W4 . . . . **7** B7
Grove Park Terr W4 . . . . . . **7** B8
Grove Pl KT13 . . . . **53** C5
Grove Prim Sch The GU16 **65** E2
Grove Rd
  Ash GU12 . . . . **106** A3
  Ashtead KT21 . . . . **95** F8
  Barnes SW13 . . . . **7** F5
  Beacon Hill GU26 . . . . . . **188** C6
  Camberley GU15 . . . . . . **65** F5
  Chertsey KT16 . . . . **32** F3
  Cranleigh GU6 . . . . **174** F1
  East Molesey KT8 . . . . . **36** D5
  Epsom KT17, KT18 . . . . . . **76** E6
  Godalming GU7 . . . . **150** C3
  Guildford GU1 . . . . **110** C1
  Horley RH6 . . . . **160** F4
  Hounslow, Spring Grove TW7 **5** E6
  Hounslow TW3 . . . . **5** B3
  Kingston upon Thames KT6 . **37** D4
  Lingfield RH7 . . . . **164** E5
  Merton SW19 . . . . **20** C1
  Mitcham CR4 . . . . **41** B7
  Richmond TW10 . . . . **6** F1
  Shepperton TW17 . . . . . . **34** C3
  Sutton SM1 . . . . **59** A4
  Tandridge RH8 . . . . **122** C2
  Tatsfield TN16 . . . . **103** C2
  Thornton Heath CR7 . . . . . **42** A5
  Twickenham TW2 . . . . . . **16** D5
  Woking GU21 . . . . **69** F3
Grove Rd Prim Sch TW3 . . . **5** A3
Grovers Manor GU26 . . . **188** D6
Grove Shaw KT20 . . . . **97** E3
Groveside KT23 . . . . **114** A8
Groveside Cl
  Carshalton SM5 . . . . **59** E8
  Great Bookham KT23 . . . **114** A8
Grovestile Waye TW14 . . . **14** D8
Grove Terr TW11 . . . . **17** A4
Grove The
  Addlestone KT15 . . . . . . **52** B5
  Aldershot GU11 . . . . **105** A1
  Biggin Hill TN16 . . . . **83** E1
  Caterham CR3 . . . . **100** C6
  Coulsdon CR5 . . . . **79** D5
  Crawley RH11 . . . . **201** C6
  Egham TW20 . . . . **12** A3
  Epsom KT17 . . . . **76** E6
  Farnborough GU14 . . . . . **85** D1
  Frimley GU16 . . . . **65** D1
  Horley RH6 . . . . **161** B2
  Hounslow TW7 . . . . **5** E6
  North Ascot SL5 . . . . **28** C8
  Teddington TW11 . . . . . . **17** A4
  1 Twickenham TW1 . . . . . **6** B1
  Walton-on-Thames KT12 . . **35** B2

Grove The continued
West Wickham BR4 . . . . 63 C7
Woking GU21 . . . . 69 F3
Grove Villas GU12 . . . . 106 A3
Grove Way KT10 . . . . . . 36 C1
Grovewood 9 TW9 . . . . . 7 A6
Grovewood Ct TW7 . . . . 5 E6
Grove Wood Hill CR5 . . . 79 D5
Grub St RH8 . . . . 123 C7
Guardian Ct GU8 . . . . . 148 C3
Guards Ave CR3 . . . . . 100 C3
Guards Ct SL5 . . . . 30 B2
Guerdon Pl RG12 . . . . . 27 D2
Guernsey Cl
  Crawley RH11 . . . . . . 201 A2
  Guildford GU4 . . . . . . 110 A6
  Heston TW5 . . . . 5 A7
Guernsey Farm Dr GU21. 69 D4
Guernsey Gr SE24 . . . . 22 C8
Guildables La TN8 . . . . 144 E7
Guildcroft GU1 . . . . . . 110 A1
Guildersfield Rd SW16 . . 21 E1
GUILDFORD 130 A7
Guildford Ave TW13 . . . . 15 A6
Guildford Business Park Rd
  GU2 . . . . 109 B2
Guildford Castle ★ GU1 . 130 D7
Guildford Cath ★ GU2 . . 109 B1
Guildford Coll Merrist Wood
  Campus GU3 . . . . . . 108 C7
Guildford Coll of FE & HE
  GU1 . . . . 109 E2
Guildford Cty Sch GU2 . . 130 B7
Guildford & Godalming By-
  Pass Rd
  Guildford GU2, GU3 . . 129 E6
  Shackleford GU7, GU8 . 149 F6
Guildford Grove Prim Sch
  GU2 . . . . 108 A1
Guildford High Sch GU1 . 109 E1
Guildford House Gall ★
  GU1 . . . . 220 D8
Guildford Ind Est GU2 . . 109 A2
Guildford La GU22 . . . . 89 E8
Guildford Lido GU1 . . . . 109 D2
Guildford Lodge Dr KT24 112 F6
Guildford Mus ★ GU1 . . 130 D7
Guildford Nuffield Hospl
  GU2 . . . . 108 E1
GUILDFORD PARK 130 B8
Guildford Park Ave GU2 . 130 B8
Guildford Park Rd GU2 . . 130 C8
Guildford Rd
  Aldershot GU11, GU12 . 126 C6
  Ash GU12, GU3 . . . . . 106 D3
  Bagshot GU19 . . . . . . 47 E3
  Broadbridge Heath RH12 216 B6
  Castle Green GU21, GU24 68 D6
  Chertsey KT16 . . . . . . 32 F1
  East Horsley KT24 . . . 112 F5
  Farncombe GU7 . . . . 151 B7
  Farnham GU10, GU9 . . 125 F4
  Fetcham KT22 . . . . . . 94 F3
  Frimley GU16 . . . . . . 85 F6
  Great Bookham KT23, KT22. 94 A1
  Horsham RH12 . . . . . 217 A2
  Lightwater GU18, GU19. 48 B1
  Loxwood RH14 . . . . . 212 F4
  Mytchett GU16 . . . . . 86 B5
  Normandy GU3 . . . . . 107 B4
  Ottershaw KT16 . . . . . 51 C5
  Pirbright GU3 . . . . . . 88 A2
  Pirbright GU24 . . . . . . 87 F4
  Rowhook RH12, RH13 . 215 C7
  Rowly GU6 . . . . 174 B6
  Rudgwick RH12 . . . . . 214 C6
  Runfold GU10 . . . . . . 126 B4
  Shamley Green GU5 . . 152 D5
  Thornton Heath CR0 . . 42 D3
  Westcott RH4 . . . . . . 135 C6
  West End GU24 . . . . . 67 F7
  Windlesham GU19 . . . 47 F2
  Woking, Westfield GU22,
    GU4 . . . . 89 C4
  Wotton RH5 . . . . 134 C3
Guildford Road E GU14 . 85 C1
Guildford Road Ind Est
  GU9 . . . . 125 D3
Guildford Road W GU14 . 85 C1
Guildford Spectrum L Ctr
  GU1 . . . . 109 E3
Guildford St
  Chertsey KT16 . . . . . . 33 A2
  Staines TW18 . . . . . . 13 A2
Guildford Sta GU1 . . . . 130 C8
Guildford Sta GU1 . . . . 130 D8
Guildford Way SM6 . . . . 60 E5
Guildown Ave GU2 . . . . 130 B6
Guildown Rd GU2 . . . . . 130 C6
Guildway Hos GU7 . . . . 150 D7
Guileshill La GU23 . . . . 91 F5
Guilford Ave KT5. . . . . . 37 F4
Guillemont Fields GU14 . 84 D5
Guillemont Jun Sch GU14 84 D6
Guillemont Pk GU14 . . . 84 C6
Guillemot Path 2 RH11 . 200 D5
Guinea Wlk RG12 . . . . . 26 D5
Guinevere Ct SE6 . . . . . 24 C4
Guinevere Ho 19 RH1 . . 119 A2
Guinevere Rd RH11 . . . 200 E6
Guinness Ct
  Crawley RH11 . . . . . . 201 C2
  6 Croydon CR0. . . . . . 61 E8
  4 Knaphill GU21. . . . . 68 F1
Gulliver Ct CR2 . . . . . . 61 B3
Gumbrells Cl GU3. . . . . 108 C5
Gumley Gdns TW7 . . . . . 6 A4

Gumley House Convent Sch
  12 TW7 . . . . 6 A4
Gun Hill GU11 . . . . . . 105 B3
Gunnell Cl
  Croydon SE25 . . . . . . 43 A3
  Penge SE26 . . . . 23 A3
Gunnell Ct 8 CR4. . . . . 40 E8
Gunners Rd SW18 . . . . 20 D6
Gunning Cl RH11 . . . . . 201 A3
Gun Pit Rd RH7 . . . . . . 164 D4
Gunters Mead KT22 . . . 74 C8
Gunton Rd SW17. . . . . . 21 A2
Gurdon's La GU8. . . . . 170 F2
Gurney Cres CR0. . . . . . 41 F1
Gurney Rd SM5 . . . . . . 60 A6
Gurney's Cl 4 RH1. . . . 139 F8
Guyatt Gdns CR4. . . . . . 41 A7
Guy Rd SM6 . . . . 60 D7
Gwendolen Ho TW19 . . . 13 E7
Gwendoline Ct TW15 . . . 13 E4
Gwydor Rd BR3 . . . . . . 43 D6
Gwydyr Rd BR2 . . . . . . 44 F6
Gwynne Ave CR0. . . . . . 43 D2
Gwynne Cl 4 W4 . . . . . . 7 F8
Gwynne Ct
  Guildford GU2 . . . . . 109 B5
  Wimbledon SW20 . . . . 39 C8
Gwynne Gdns RH19 . . . 185 C2
Gwynne Ho 6 SW2 . . . . 21 F7
Gwynne Rd CR3. . . . . . 100 D4

H

Habershon Dr GU16 . . . 66 D2
Haccombe Rd SW19 . . . 20 C2
HACKBRIDGE 60 B8
Hackbridge Park Gdns
  SM5 . . . . 59 F8
Hackbridge Prim Sch
  SM6 . . . . 41 A1
Hackbridge Rd SM6 . . . 60 A8
Hackbridge Sta SM6 . . . 60 B8
Hackenden Cl RH19 . . . 185 E3
Hackenden La RH19 . . . 185 E3
Hacketts La GU22 . . . . . 70 F4
Hackhurst Downs Nature
  Reserve ★ GU5. . . . . 133 E6
Hackhurst La RH5. . . . . 133 F4
Hackington Cres BR3 . . 24 A2
Haddenham Ct SW17. . . 20 D4
Haddington Rd BR1 . . . 24 D4
Haddon Cl
  New Malden KT3 . . . . 38 F4
  Oatlands Park KT13 . . . 53 D6
Haddon Rd SM1. . . . . . 59 B6
Hadfield Rd TW19 . . . . . 2 D1
Hadleigh Cl SW20 . . . . . 39 F7
Hadleigh Dr SM2. . . . . . 59 B2
Hadleigh Gdns GU16 . . . 85 E6
Hadley Ct SL3. . . . . 1 E6
Hadley Pl KT13 . . . . . . 53 A3
Hadley Rd CR4. . . . . . . 41 D5
Hadleys GU10. . . . . . . 145 E3
Hadley Wood Rise CR8 . 80 B5
Hadlow Pl SE19 . . . . . . 23 A1
Hadmans Cl RH12 . . . . 217 C1
Hadrian Cl TW19 . . . . . 13 E8
Hadrian Ct 1 SM2 . . . . 59 B3
Hadrians GU9. . . . . . . 125 E4
Hadrian Way TW19 . . . . 13 D8
Hafton Rd SE6 . . . . 24 E6
Haggard Rd TW1. . . . . . 17 B8
Haigh Cres RH1. . . . . . 140 B7
HAIG HOMES 40 A3
Haig Ho 7 SM4 . . . . . . 40 A3
Haig Rd
  Aldershot GU12 . . . . . 105 C1
  Biggin Hill TN16 . . . . . 83 E2
  Sandhurst GU15 . . . . . 64 F6
Hailes Cl SW19 . . . . . . 20 C2
Hailey Pl GU6. . . . . . . 174 F4
Hailsham Ave SW2. . . . . 21 F6
Hailsham Cl
  Sandhurst GU47 . . . . . 45 D1
  Surbiton KT6 . . . . 37 D2
Hailsham Rd SW17. . . . . 21 A2
Haines Ct KT13 . . . . . . 53 D5
Haines Wlk SM4 . . . . . . 40 B2
Haining Gdns GU16 . . . . 86 A3
Hainthorpe Rd SE27. . . . 22 B4
Halcroft Ct SM1. . . . . . 59 D6
Halcyon Cl KT22 . . . . . 74 D4
Halcyon Ct TW18. . . . . . 33 B7
Haldane Pl SW18 . . . . . 20 B7
HALE 125 C6
Halebourne La GU24 . . . 49 A2
Hale End RG12 . . . . 27 F5
Hale Ends GU22. . . . . . 89 B6
Hale House La GU10 . . . 168 B2
Hale Pit Rd KT23. . . . . . 94 C1
Hale Pl GU9 . . . . 125 E5
Hale Prim Sch GU9 . . . . 125 B7
Hale Rd GU9 . . . . 125 D5
Hale Rdbt GU9 . . . . . . 125 E5
Hale Reeds GU9 . . . . . 125 E6
Hales Ct 6 TW11 . . . . . 17 A3
Hales Field KT22. . . . . . 208 C6
Hales Ho 3 SW2 . . . . . . 21 B8
Hales Oak KT23 . . . . . . 94 C1
Halesowen Rd SM4 . . . . 40 B2
Haleswood KT11 . . . . . . 73 C5
Hale St TW18. . . . . 12 E4
Hale Way GU16 . . . . . . 85 D8
Halewood RG12. . . . . . . 26 F3
Half Acre TW8 . . . . 6 D8
Half Acre Mews TW8 . . . 6 D8
Halfacres RH10 . . . . . . 201 E7

Half Moon Hill GU27 . . . 208 C6
Half Moon St GU19. . . . . 47 E3
Halford Rd TW10. . . . . . 6 E3
Halford Rd TW10. . . . . . 56 E3
Halfpenny Cl GU4 . . . . 131 D3
Halfpenny Cross KT11. . . 73 A2
Halfpenny Ct 2 SL5. . . . 30 B2
Halfpenny La
  Guildford GU4 . . . . . 131 C5
  Sunningdale SL5 . . . . 30 A2
Half Way Cotts GU10 . . . 124 C3
Halfway Gn KT12. . . . . . 54 B7
Halfway La GU7. . . . . . 150 B4
Haliburton Rd TW1, TW7 . 6 A3
Halifax Cl
  Crawley RH10 . . . . . . 182 E1
  Farnborough GU14 . . . 84 F3
  Teddington TW11 . . . . 16 E2
Halifax Rd RG12 . . . . . . 27 C5
Halifax St SE26 . . . . . . 23 B5
Halimote Rd GU11 . . . . 105 A1
Haling Down Pas CR8 . . 61 C1
Haling Gr CR2 . . . . 61 C3
Haling Park Gdns CR2. . . 61 B4
Haling Park Rd CR2 . . . . 61 B4
Haling Rd CR2 . . . . 61 D4
Hallam Rd GU7 . . . . . . 150 F5
Halland Cl RH10 . . . . . . 202 A7
Hallane Ho SE27 . . . . . 22 C3
Hall Cl
  Camberley GU15 . . . . 65 E6
  Farncombe GU7 . . . . 150 E7
Hall Ct TW11 . . . . 16 F3
Hall Dene Cl GU1 . . . . 110 C3
Hall Dr SE26 . . . . 23 C3
Halley Cl RH11 . . . . . . 201 B1
Halley Dr SL5 . . . . 28 D7
Halley's App GU21 . . . . . 69 A1
Halley's Ct 1 GU21 . . . . 69 A1
Halley's Wlk KT15 . . . . . 52 C3
Hall Farm Dr TW2. . . . . 16 D8
Hallgrove Bottom GU19 . 47 F5
Hall Grove Farm Ind Est
  GU19. . . . . 47 F5
Hall Grove Sch GU19. . . 48 A3
Hall Hill RH8. . . . . 122 D4
Halliards The KT12. . . . . 35 A3
Halliford Cl TW17. . . . . . 34 E6
Halliford Rd
  Sunbury TW16 . . . . . . 35 A5
  Upper Halliford TW16,
    TW17 . . . . 34 F5
Halliford Sch TW17 . . . . 34 C2
Halliloo Valley Rd CR3 . . 101 E7
Hallington Cl GU21. . . . . 69 B2
Hall La UB3 . . . . 3 D7
Hallmark Cl GU47 . . . . . 64 E8
Hallmead Rd SM1. . . . . 59 B7
Hallowell Ave CR0. . . . . 60 E6
Hallowell Cl CR4 . . . . . . 41 A6
Hallowell Gdns 1 CR7. . . 42 C7
Hallowes Cl GU2. . . . . 109 B6
Hallowfield Way CR4. . . . 40 E6
Hallows Gr TW16 . . . . . 14 F3
Hall Pl
  Dunsfold GU6. . . . . . 193 D7
  Woking GU21. . . . . . . 70 A3
Hall Place Dr KT13 . . . . 53 E5
Hall Rd
  Bramley GU5 . . . . . . 151 F6
  Isleworth TW7. . . . . . . 5 D1
  Wallington SM6 . . . . . 60 B2
Hall Sch Wimbledon 11
  SW20 . . . . 39 D8
Hall Sch Wimbledon Jun
  Dept SW15 . . . . 19 A5
Halls Dr RH12 . . . . 199 F1
Halls Farm Cl GU21 . . . . 68 D2
Hallsland RH10 . . . . . . 204 C8
Hallsland Way RH8. . . . . 122 F3
Halnaker Wlk 8 RH11. . . 200 F3
Halsford Croft RH19. . . . 185 B3
Halsford Gn RH19 . . . . 185 B3
Halsford La RH19 . . . . . 185 C3
Halsford Park Prim Sch
  RH19. . . . . 185 C2
Halsford Park Rd RH19 . 185 C2
Halstead Cl CR0, CR9 . . 61 C7
Halstead Prep Sch GU21. 70 B4
Halters End GU26 . . . . 188 A3
Halton Rd CR3 . . . . . . 100 E7
HAM 17 C5
Hamble Ave GU17 . . . . . 64 D5
Hamble Cl GU21 . . . . . . 69 A2
Hamble Ct TW12 . . . . . . 17 D1
Hambledon Ct RG12 . . . 27 E5
HAMBLEDON 171 D2
Hambledon Ct 9 SM6. . . 60 B4
Hambledon Gdns SE25 . 42 F6
Hambledon Hill KT18. . . 76 C3
Hambledon Ho 2 KT2. . . 18 B2
Hambledon Pk GU8 . . . 171 B1
Hambledon Pl
  Dulwich SE21 . . . . . . 22 F7
  Little Bookham KT23 . . 94 A4
Hambledon Rd
  Caterham CR3 . . . . . 100 D4
  Hydestile GU8, GU7. . . 171 D5
  Wandsworth SW18 . . . 19 F8
Hambledon Vale KT18 . . 76 C3
Hambleton Cl
  Frimley GU16. . . . . . . 66 B3
  North Cheam KT4 . . . . 58 C8
Hambleton Ct RH11 . . . 201 C4
Hambleton Hill RH11 . . 201 C4
Hamble Wlk GU21 . . . . . 69 A2

Hambly Mans SW16 . . . . 21 E2
Hambridge Way SW2. . . . 22 A8
Hambrook Rd SE25 . . . . 43 B6
Hambro Rd SW16 . . . . . 21 D5
Ham Cl TW10 . . . . 17 C5
Ham Comm TW10 . . . . . 17 D5
Ham Comm Nature Reserve ★
  TW10 . . . . 17 E4
Ham Croft Cl TW13. . . . . 15 A5
Hamers Ho 19 SW2. . . . . 22 A8
Hamesmoor Rd GU16 . . 85 E4
Hamesmoor Way GU16. . 85 F4
Ham Farm Rd KT2, TW10. 17 E4
Hamfield Ct RH8. . . . . . 122 C8
Ham Gate Ave
  Richmond, Richmond Park
    TW10 . . . . 18 A4
  Richmond TW10. . . . . 17 E4
Hamhaugh Island TW17 . 53 A8
Hamilton Ave
  Cheam SM3 . . . . 58 E8
  Cobham KT11 . . . . . . 73 A6
  Pyrford GU22. . . . . . . 70 E3
  Tolworth KT6 . . . . 57 A8
Hamilton Cl
  Ashford TW13 . . . . . . 14 F3
  Bagshot GU19 . . . . . . 47 E3
  Chertsey KT16 . . . . . . 32 F1
  Epsom KT19 . . . . 76 C7
  Guildford GU2 . . . . . 109 A6
  Purley CR8 . . . . 80 B7
  Teddington TW11 . . . . 17 B2
Hamilton Cres TW3 . . . . 5 B2
Hamilton Ct
  Catford SE6 . . . . 24 F7
  Cobham KT11 . . . . . . 73 A6
  Croydon CR0 . . . . . . 43 A1
  Farnborough GU17 . . . 64 C1
  Great Bookham KT23. . 94 B2
Hamilton Dr
  Guildford GU2 . . . . . 109 A6
  Sunningdale SL5 . . . . 29 E2
Hamilton Gdns 1 GU14 . 84 D5
Hamilton Gordon Ct
  GU1 . . . . 109 C2
Hamilton Ho
  5 Chiswick W4. . . . . . . 7 B8
  10 Richmond TW9 . . . . . 7 A6
Hamilton Mews
  Wandsworth SW18 . . . 20 A7
  3 Weybridge KT13 . . . . 53 A6
Hamilton Par TW13 . . . . 15 A4
Hamilton Pl
  Aldershot GU11 . . . . . 104 F1
  Guildford GU2 . . . . . 109 A6
  Horley/Gatwick RH6. . . 161 A2
  Kingswood KT20 . . . . 97 F4
  Sunbury TW16 . . . . . . 15 B1
Hamilton Rd
  Brentford TW8 . . . . . . 6 D8
  Feltham TW13 . . . . . . 14 F4
  Horsham RH12 . . . . . 217 B3
  Merton SW19 . . . . . . 20 B1
  South Norwood CR7 . . 42 D6
  Twickenham TW2 . . . . 16 E7
  West Norwood SE27 . . 22 D4
Hamilton Road Ind Est
  SE27. . . . . 22 D4
Hamilton Road Mews 1
  SW19. . . . . 20 B1
Hamilton Way SM6. . . . . 60 D7
Ham La
  Elstead GU8. . . . . . . 148 E4
  Englefield Green TW20 . 11 B4
Ham Lands Nature Reserve ★
  TW10 . . . . 17 A5
Hamlash Cotts GU10 . . . 146 C2
Hamlash La GU10 . . . . 146 C1
Hamlet St RG42 . . . . . . 27 E8
Hamlyn Gdns SE19 . . . . 22 E1
Hamlyn Ho TW13 . . . . . 15 B7
Hamm Court Est KT13 . . 52 F8
Hammelton Ct 4 BR1. . . 44 F8
Hammelton Rd 5 BR1. . . 44 F8
HAMMER 207 D5
Hammerfield Dr RH5. . . . 133 F3
Hammer Hill GU27 . . . . 207 B6
Hammer La
  Grayshott GU10, GU26 . 187 E6
  Haslemere GU30. . . . . 207 A6
  Haslemere, Hammer GU27 207 C5
  Haslemere, Nutcombe GU26,
    GU27. . . . . 207 C8
Hammerpond Rd RH13. . 217 F1
Hammersley Rd GU11 . . 105 C2
Hammer Vale GU27 . . . 207 B6
Hammerwood Copse
  GU27 . . . . 207 D5
Hammerwood Rd RH19. . 206 E6
HAMM MOOR 52 E6
Hamm Moor La KT15 . . . 52 E6
Hammond Ave CR4 . . . . 41 B7
Hammond Cl
  Hampton TW12 . . . . . 36 A8
  Woking GU21. . . . . . . 69 C4
Hammond Jun Sch GU18. 48 A1
Hammond Rd GU21 . . . . 69 C4
Hammonds Ho TW19 . . . 13 F7
Hammond Way GU18. . . . 48 B1
Hamond Cl CR2 . . . . . . 61 B2
Hampden Ave BR3 . . . . 43 E7
Hampden Cl RH10. . . . . 182 C1
Hampden Rd
  Beckenham BR3. . . . . 43 E7
  Kingston upon Thames KT1. 38 A6
Hampers Ct 2 RH13 . . . 217 D2

Hamper's La RH13 . . . . 218 A2
Hampshire Cl GU12 . . . 126 D7
Hampshire Ct
  Addlestone KT15 . . . . 52 C5
  Barnes SW13. . . . . . . 7 F5
  6 Horsham RH12 . . . . 217 D2
Hampshire Rd GU15. . . . 65 F8
Hampstead La RH4. . . . 135 F6
Hampstead Rd RH4 . . . 136 A6
HAMPTON 36 A7
Hampton Cl
  1 Knaphill GU21 . . . . . 68 C1
  Wimbledon SW20 . . . . 19 C1
  4 Woking GU21 . . . . . 68 C1
Hampton Com Coll TW12. 16 A4
Hampton Court Ave KT8. . 36 D6
Hampton Court Cres KT8. 36 D6
Hampton Court Ho Sch
  KT8. . . . . 36 E7
Hampton Court Palace ★
  KT8. . . . . 36 F6
Hampton Court Par KT8. . 36 E5
Hampton Court Rd KT1,
  KT8. . . . . 37 B6
Hampton Court Sta KT8. . 36 E5
Hampton Court Way KT10, KT7,
  KT8. . . . . 36 E3
Hampton Farm Ind Est
  TW13 . . . . 15 E5
Hampton Gr KT17 . . . . . 76 F8
HAMPTON HILL 16 C3
Hampton Hill Bsns Pk
  TW12 . . . . 16 C3
Hampton Hill Jun Sch
  TW12 . . . . 16 C3
Hampton Inf Sch TW12 . . 16 A1
Hampton Jun Sch 12
  TW12 . . . . 36 A8
Hampton La TW13 . . . . . 15 E4
Hampton Lodge RH6 . . . 161 A2
Hampton Pool TW12 . . . 16 C1
Hampton Rd
  Hale GU9 . . . . 125 B6
  North Cheam KT4 . . . . 58 B8
  Redhill RH1 . . . . 139 F4
  Teddington TW11, TW12 . 16 D3
  Thornton Heath CR0 . . 42 C3
  Twickenham TW2. . . . . 16 D5
Hampton Road E TW13 . 15 F5
Hampton Road Ind Pk
  CR0. . . . . 42 C3
Hampton Road W TW13 . 15 E5
Hampton Sch TW12 . . . . 16 A3
Hampton Sta TW12 . . . . 36 A8
Hampton Terr GU26 . . . 188 C6
Hampton Way RH19 . . . 205 F7
HAMPTON WICK 37 D8
Hampton Wick Inf Sch
  KT1 . . . . 17 D1
Hampton Wick Sta KT1. . 37 C8
Ham Ridings TW10. . . . . 17 F3
HAMSEY GREEN 81 C4
Hamsey Green Gdns CR6 . 81 C3
Hamsey Green Inf Sch
  CR6. . . . . 81 B3
Hamsey Green Jun Sch
  CR6. . . . . 81 B3
Hamsey Way CR2 . . . . . 81 B4
Ham St TW10 . . . . 17 C5
Ham The TW8 . . . . 6 C7
Ham View CR0. . . . . . . 43 E3
Hanbury Ct GU23 . . . . . 71 E3
Hanbury Dr TN16 . . . . . 83 B6
Hanbury Path GU21. . . . 70 D5
Hanbury Rd RH11 . . . . 200 E5
Hanbury Way GU15 . . . . 65 C3
Hancock Rd SE19 . . . . . 22 D2
Hancocks Mount SL5 . . . 29 B3
Hancombe Rd GU47. . . . 45 A1
Handcroft Rd CR0. . . . . 42 B1
Handel Ho TW2. . . . . . . 5 D1
Handley Page Rd SM6. . . 60 F3
Handpost Cnr RG40 . . . . 25 A1
Handside Cl KT4 . . . . . . 39 D1
Handsworth Ho 8 RH10 . 201 D5
Hanford Cl SW18. . . . . . 20 A7
Hanford Row SW19 . . . . 19 C2
Hanger Ct GU21. . . . . . 68 E2
Hanger Hill KT13. . . . . . 53 B5
Hanley Pl BR3 . . . . 24 A1
Hannah Cl BR3. . . . . . . 44 C6
Hannah Ct
  14 Sutton SM1. . . . . . 59 B4
  Wimbledon SW19 . . . . 19 D1
  4 Woking GU21. . . . . . 70 A3
Hannah Mews SM6 . . . . 60 C3
Hannah Peschar Sculpture
  Gdn ★ RH5. . . . . . . 177 A2
Hannay Wlk SW16. . . . . 21 D6
Hannen Rd SE27. . . . . . 22 B5
Hannibal Rd TW19 . . . . 13 E8
Hannibal Way CR0. . . . . 60 F4
Hanning Lodge TW3 . . . . 5 C3
Hanno Cl SM6 . . . . 60 D3
Hanover Ave
  Feltham TW13 . . . . . . 15 A6
Hanover Cl
  Cheam SM3 . . . . 58 F6
  Crawley RH10 . . . . . . 201 F3
  Englefield Green TW20 . 11 B2
  Frimley GU16 . . . . . . 65 E1
  Merstham RH1. . . . . . 119 C7
  Richmond TW9. . . . . . 7 A7
Hanover Ct
  Dorking RH4 . . . . 135 F7
  Guildford GU1 . . . . . 109 D3

Hanover Ct *continued*
1 Horsham RH13 . . . . 217 F3
1 Penge SE19 . . . . 23 A1
2 Teddington TW11 . . . . . . 16 F3
4 Woking GU22 . . . . 89 E8
Hanover Gdns
Bracknell RG12 . . . . 26 F2
Farnborough GU14 . . . . 84 E6
Hanover Ho
9 New Malden KT3 . . . . . . 38 E5
Tolworth KT6 . . . . 38 A1
Hanover Pk 1 SL5 . . . . 28 F8
Hanover Rd SW19 . . . . 20 C1
Hanover St CR0, CR9 . . . . . . 61 B7
Hanover Terr TW7 . . . . 6 A6
Hanover Wlk KT13 . . . . 53 E7
Hansard KT18 . . . . 97 D8
Hansler Ct 14 SW19 . . . . . . 19 E7
Hansler Gr KT8 . . . . 36 D5
Hanson Cl
Balham SW12 . . . . 21 B8
Beckenham BR3 . . . . 24 B2
Camberley GU15 . . . . 66 B7
Guildford GU1 . . . . 109 F4
Mortlake SW14 . . . . 7 C4
HANWORTH
Bracknell 27 A2
Feltham 15 D4
Hanworth Cl RG12 . . . . 27 C3
Hanworth La KT16 . . . . 32 F1
Hanworth Park Ct TW13 . . 15 C7
Hanworth Rd
Bracknell RG12 . . . . 27 A2
Feltham TW13 . . . . 15 B7
Hampton TW12 . . . . 16 A3
Hounslow TW3, TW4 . . . . 5 A2
Redhill RH1 . . . . 139 F4
Sunbury TW16 . . . . 15 A1
Twickenham TW4 . . . . 15 F8
Hanworth Terr TW3 . . . . 5 B3
Hanworth Trad Est
Chertsey KT16 . . . . 32 F1
Feltham TW13 . . . . 15 E5
Harberson Rd SW12 . . . . . . 21 B7
Harbie Brow KT4 . . . . 57 E7
Harbin Ho 5 SW2 . . . . 22 A7
Harbledown Rd CR2 . . . . . . 81 A8
Harborough Rd SW16 . . . . . 21 F4
Harbour Cl
Farnborough GU14 . . . . 85 A8
1 Mitcham CR4 . . . . 41 A8
Harbourfield Rd SM7 . . . . . 78 B4
Harbridge Ave SW15 . . . . . . 19 A8
Harbury Rd SM5 . . . . 59 E3
Harcourt Ave SM6 . . . . 60 B6
Harcourt Cl
Egham TW20 . . . . 12 C2
Isleworth TW7 . . . . 6 A4
Harcourt Field SM6 . . . . . . 60 B6
Harcourt Lodge 2 SM6 . . 60 B6
Harcourt Rd
Bracknell RG12 . . . . 27 B4
Camberley GU15 . . . . 65 B5
Merton SW19 . . . . 20 A1
Thornton Heath CR7 . . . . . . 42 A3
Wallington SM6 . . . . 60 B6
Harcourt Way RH9 . . . . . . 142 E6
Hardcastle Cl SE25 . . . . 43 A3
Hardcourts Cl BR4 . . . . 63 B7
Hardell Cl TW20 . . . . 12 A3
Hardel Rise SW2 . . . . 22 B7
Hardel Wlk SW2 . . . . 22 A8
Harden Farm Cl CR5 . . . . . 99 C6
Hardham Cl RH11 . . . . 201 A8
Hardie Ho TW13 . . . . 15 E4
Harding Cl
Kingston upon Thames
KT2 . . . . 37 F8
South Croydon CR0 . . . . 61 F7
Harding Ct SE25 . . . . 42 F7
Harding Ho SM6 . . . . 60 C2
Harding Pl
Forest Hill SE23 . . . . 23 E8
Wokingham RG40 . . . . 25 C7
Harding Rd KT18 . . . . 96 E8
Hardings La SE20 . . . . 23 D2
Hardman Rd KT2 . . . . 37 E7
Hardwell Way RG12 . . . . . . 27 E5
Hardwick Cl KT22 . . . . 74 C4
Hardwicke Ave TW5 . . . . 5 A6
Hardwicke Rd
Reigate RH2 . . . . 118 A2
Richmond TW10 . . . . 17 C4
Hardwick La KT16 . . . . 32 D1
Hardwick Rd RH1 . . . . 139 D7
Hardy Cl
Crawley RH10 . . . . 202 C7
Dorking RH5 . . . . 136 B3
Horley RH6 . . . . 160 E3
Horsham RH12 . . . . 217 B4
Hardy Gn RG45 . . . . 45 B4
Hardy Ho KT19 . . . . 57 B1
Hardy Rd SW19 . . . . 20 B1
Hardys Mews KT8 . . . . 36 E5
Harebell Hill KT11 . . . . 73 E5
Harecroft
Dorking RH4 . . . . 136 C4
Fetcham KT23 . . . . 94 C3
Haredon Cl SE23 . . . . 23 D8
Harefield KT10 . . . . 55 E7
Harefield Ave SM2 . . . . 58 E2
Harefield Ct 4 SW19 . . . . . 20 A1
Harefield Rd SW16 . . . . 21 F1
Hare Hill KT15 . . . . 51 F4
Hare Hill Cl GU22 . . . . 71 A4
Hare La
Claygate KT10 . . . . 55 E4
Crawley RH11 . . . . 201 B8
Farncombe GU7 . . . . 150 F6
Horne RH7 . . . . 163 D5
Harelands Cl GU21 . . . . . . 69 C2
Harelands La GU21 . . . . . . 69 C2
Harendon KT20 . . . . 97 D6
Harepit Cl CR2 . . . . 61 B3
Hares Bank CR0 . . . . 63 D1
Harestone Ct CR2 . . . . 61 E4
Harestone Dr CR3 . . . . . . 100 F2
Harestone Hill CR3 . . . . . . 100 F2
Harestone La CR3 . . . . . . 100 E2
Harestone Valley Rd
CR3 . . . . 100 F2
Hareward Rd GU4 . . . . 110 C4
Harewood SW15 . . . . 18 D4
Harewood Cl
Crawley RH10 . . . . 182 A1
Reigate RH2 . . . . 118 C4
Harewood Gdns CR2 . . . . . . 81 C4
Harewood Rd
Hounslow TW7 . . . . 5 F6
Mitcham SW19 . . . . 20 E2
South Croydon CR2 . . . . 61 E4
Harfield Rd TW16 . . . . 35 D7
Harkness Cl KT17 . . . . 77 C3
Harkness Ct SM1 . . . . 40 B1
Harland Ave CR0 . . . . 62 A7
Harland Cl SW19 . . . . 40 B6
Harlech Ct 1 SE23 . . . . 23 C7
Harlech Gdns TW5 . . . . 4 C7
Harlech Rd GU17 . . . . 64 D4
Harlequin Ave TW8 . . . . 6 A8
Harlequin Cl TW7 . . . . 5 E2
Harlequin Ct CR2 . . . . 61 C3
Harlequin Rd TW11 . . . . 17 B1
Harlequins RFC TW2 . . . . . . 16 E8
Harlequin The★ 18 RH1 . 118 F2
HARLINGTON 3 C8
Harlington Cl UB7 . . . . 3 C7
Harlington Cnr UB3 . . . . . . 3 D6
Harlington Road E TW13,
TW14 . . . . 15 C7
Harlington Road W TW14 . . 4 B1
Harlow Ct 4 RH2 . . . . 118 D1
Harman Pl CR8 . . . . 80 B8
Harmans Dr RH19 . . . . . . 186 B1
Harmans Mead RH19 . . . . 186 B1
HARMANS WATER 27 D5
Harmans Water Prim Sch
RG12 . . . . 27 E4
Harmans Water Rd RG12 . 27 D4
Harmar Cl RG40 . . . . 25 E6
Harmes Way GU14 . . . . . . 105 D7
HARMONDSWORTH 2 E8
Harmondsworth La UB7 . . . 2 E8
**Harmondsworth Moor Ctry
Pk**★ UB7 . . . . 2 B7
Harmondsworth Prim Sch
UB7 . . . . 2 D8
Harmony Cl
Crawley RH11 . . . . 200 E4
Wallington SM6 . . . . 60 E2
Harms Gr GU4 . . . . 110 C4
Harold Ct 6 TW11 . . . . 16 E3
Harold Rd
Carshalton SM1 . . . . 59 D6
Crawley RH10 . . . . 202 E5
South Norwood SE19 . . . . . . 22 D1
Haroldslea RH6 . . . . 161 E2
Haroldslea Cl RH6 . . . . . . 161 C1
Haroldslea Dr RH6 . . . . . . 161 D1
Harpenden Rd SE27 . . . . . . 22 B6
Harper Dr RH10 . . . . 202 C2
Harper Mews SW17 . . . . . . 20 C5
Harper's Rd GU12 . . . . . . 106 D2
HARPESFORD 31 C3
Harpesford Ave GU25 . . . . . 31 C4
Harps Oak La RH1 . . . . 99 A2
Harpswood Cl CR5 . . . . 99 C5
Harpurs KT20 . . . . 97 D5
Harrier Cl GU6 . . . . 174 E4
Harrier Ct RH10 . . . . 182 D1
Harrier Ho 10 KT2 . . . . 37 E8
Harrier Way RG12 . . . . 26 D5
Harriet Ct 7 GU11, GU12 . 105 B1
Harriet Gdns CR0 . . . . 62 A8
Harriet Tubman Cl SW2 . . 22 A8
Harrington Cl
Leigh RH2 . . . . 138 A2
Wallington CR0 . . . . 60 E8
Harrington Ct 7 CR0 . . . . . 61 D8
Harrington Rd SE25 . . . . . . 43 B5
Harrington Rd Halt SE25 . 43 C6
Harriotts Cl KT22 . . . . 95 C7
Harriotts La KT21, KT22 . . . 95 C8
Harris Acad CR2 . . . . 61 B3
Harris Acad Merton CR4 . 41 D6
Harris Acad South Norwood
1 SE25 . . . . 42 F6
Harris Boys Acad SE21 . . . 22 E5
**Harris City Acad Crystal
Palace** SE19 . . . . 42 F8
Harris Cl
Crawley RH11 . . . . 201 B3
Hounslow TW5 . . . . 5 A6
Harris Lodge SE6 . . . . 24 C7
Harrison Cl RH2 . . . . 139 B8
Harrison's Rise CR0, CR9 . . 61 B7
Harrison Way TW17 . . . . . . 34 B4
Harris Path RH11 . . . . 201 B3
Harris Way TW16 . . . . 34 E8
Harrodian Sch The SW13 . . 7 F7
Harrogate Ct 2 SE26 . . . . . 23 A5
Harrow Bottom Rd GU25 . 31 F3
Harrow Cl
Chertsey KT15 . . . . 52 B8
Chessington KT9 . . . . 56 D3
Dorking RH4 . . . . 136 A6
Harrowdene GU6 . . . . 174 E4
Harrowdene Ct SW19 . . . . . 19 E3
Harrowdene Gdns TW11 . . 17 A1
Harrow Gate Gdns RH4 . . 136 A5
Harrow Gdns CR6 . . . . 81 F3
Harrow La GU7 . . . . 150 E7
Harrowlands Pk RH4 . . . . 136 B6
Harrow Lodge SM2 . . . . . . 59 D4
Harrow Rd
Ashford TW15 . . . . 14 A6
Carshalton SM5 . . . . 59 E4
Warlingham CR6 . . . . 81 F3
Harrow Road E RH4 . . . . . 136 B6
Harrow Road W RH4 . . . . 136 A6
Harrowsley Ct 3 RH6 . . . . 161 B4
Harrow Way TW17 . . . . 34 C7
Harry Cl CR7 . . . . 42 C3
Hart Cl
Bletchingley RH1 . . . . 120 E2
Farnborough GU14 . . . . 84 E8
Hart Dene Ct GU19 . . . . . . 47 E3
Hart Dyke Cl RG40, RG41 . . 25 B2
Harte Rd TW3 . . . . 4 F5
Hartfield Cres SW19 . . . . . . 19 F1
Hartfield Ct CR2 . . . . 61 B3
Hartfield Gr SE20 . . . . 43 C8
Hartfield Rd
Chessington KT9 . . . . 56 D5
Forest Row RH18 . . . . 206 F2
Merton SW19 . . . . 20 A1
Hartford Rd KT19 . . . . 57 B4
Hartford Rise GU15 . . . . . . 65 D6
Hart Gdns RH4 . . . . 136 B8
Hartham Cl TW7 . . . . 6 A6
Hartham Rd TW7 . . . . 6 A6
Hart Ho SW2 . . . . 22 A7
Harting Ct RH11 . . . . 200 F3
Hartington Cl RH2 . . . . . . 118 A3
Hartington Ct W4 . . . . 7 B7
Hartington Rd
Chiswick W4 . . . . 7 C6
Twickenham TW1 . . . . 6 B1
Hartland Cl KT15 . . . . 52 C2
Hartland Pl GU14 . . . . 85 A7
Hartland Rd
Addlestone KT15 . . . . 52 A3
Cheam SM4 . . . . 40 B2
Hampton TW12 . . . . 16 B4
Isleworth TW7 . . . . 6 A4
Hartlands The TW5 . . . . 4 B8
Hartland Way
Croydon CR0 . . . . 62 E8
Morden SM4 . . . . 39 F2
Hartley Cl GU17 . . . . 64 B5
Hartley Ct 2 CR4 . . . . 40 E8
Hartley Down CR8 . . . . 79 F5
Hartley Farm CR8 . . . . 79 F4
Hartley Hill CR8 . . . . 79 F4
Hartley Old Rd CR8 . . . . . . 79 F5
Hartley Rd CR0 . . . . 42 C2
Hartley Way CR8 . . . . 79 F4
Hart Rd
Byfleet KT14 . . . . 71 E6
Dorking RH4 . . . . 136 B8
Hartscroft CR0 . . . . 62 E2
Harts Gdns GU2 . . . . 109 B4
Harts Grove GU8 . . . . 191 B5
Hartshill GU2 . . . . 108 D2
Hartshill Wlk GU21 . . . . . . 69 B3
Hart's La RH9 . . . . 142 D7
Harts Leap Cl GU47 . . . . . . 45 B1
Harts Leap Rd GU47 . . . . . . 64 A8
Hartspiece Rd RH1 . . . . . . 140 B7
Hart Sq SM4 . . . . 40 A3
Hartswood RH5 . . . . 136 D4
Hartswood Ave RH2 . . . . . 139 A5
Hartswood Ho 10 SW2 . . . . 21 E7
Harts Yd
15 Farnham GU9 . . . . 125 B2
Godalming GU7 . . . . 150 E4
Hart The GU9 . . . . 125 B2
Harvard Hill W4 . . . . 7 B8
Harvard Rd
Hounslow TW7 . . . . 5 E6
Sandhurst GU47 . . . . 45 E1
Harven Sch GU22 . . . . 70 A2
Harvest Bank Rd BR4 . . . . 63 F7
Harvest Ct
Beckenham BR3 . . . . 24 A1
Hamsey Green CR2 . . . . 81 B5
Littleton TW17 . . . . 34 A5
Thames Ditton KT10 . . . . . . 55 A8
Harvester Rd KT19 . . . . 57 D1
Harvesters RH12 . . . . 217 D5
Harvesters Cl TW7 . . . . 5 D2
Harvest Hill
East Grinstead RH19 . . . . . 205 E8
Godalming GU7 . . . . 150 D4
Harvest La KT7 . . . . 37 A3
Harvest Lea RG42 . . . . 28 A8
Harvest Rd
Crawley RH10 . . . . 202 C4
Englefield Green TW20 . . . . 11 D2
Feltham TW13 . . . . 15 A5
Harvest Ride RG12, RG42,
SL5 . . . . 28 A8
Harvestside RH6 . . . . 161 C4
Harvey Cl RH11 . . . . 201 A1
Harvey Ct KT19 . . . . 57 B2
Harvey Dr TW12 . . . . 36 A8
Harvey Lodge 8 GU1 . . . . 130 E8
Harvey Rd
Farnborough GU14 . . . . 84 C5
Guildford GU1 . . . . 130 E8
Harvey Rd *continued*
Twickenham TW4 . . . . 15 F8
Walton-on-Thames KT12 . . . 35 A2
Harwarden Cl RH10 . . . . . 204 C8
Harwood Ave CR4 . . . . 40 E6
Harwood Ct SE24 . . . . 22 B7
Harwood Gdns SL4 . . . . 11 B8
Harwood Pk RH1 . . . . 161 A8
Harwood Rd RH12, RH13 . 218 A3
Harwoods Cl 3 RH19 . . . 205 F7
Harwoods La RH19 . . . . . . 205 F7
HASCOMBE 172 D4
Hascombe Ct RH11 . . . . . . 201 A5
Hascombe Ho 11 SW15 . . . 19 B7
Hascombe Rd GU8 . . . . . . 151 A1
Haseley End SE23 . . . . 23 C8
Haseltine Prim Sch SE6 . . 23 F4
Haseltine Rd SE26 . . . . 23 F4
Haskins Dr GU14 . . . . 84 D5
Haslam Ave SM3, SM4 . . . . 39 E1
Hasle Dr GU27 . . . . 208 B6
HASLEMERE 208 D6
Haslemere Ave
Cranford TW5 . . . . 4 C5
Mitcham CR4, SW19 . . . . . . 40 D7
Wimbledon SW18 . . . . 20 B6
Haslemere Cl
Frimley GU16 . . . . 66 C3
Hampton TW12 . . . . 15 F3
Wallington SM6 . . . . 60 E5
**Haslemere Educational
Mus**★ GU27 . . . . 208 D7
**Haslemere & Heathrow Est
The** TW4 . . . . 4 B5
Haslemere Hospl GU27 . . 208 D7
Haslemere Ind Est
Feltham TW14 . . . . 4 A2
Haslemere GU27 . . . . 208 C7
Wimbledon SW18 . . . . 20 B6
Haslemere Prep Sch
GU27 . . . . 208 D5
Haslemere Prim Sch CR4 . 40 D7
Haslemere Rd
Brook GU8 . . . . 170 C5
Kingsley Green GU27 . . . . . 208 B1
Thornton Heath CR7 . . . . . . 42 B4
Haslemere Sta GU27 . . . . 208 B6
Haslett Ave E RH10 . . . . . 202 A6
Haslett Ave W RH10 . . . . . 201 D5
Haslett Rd TW17 . . . . 34 E7
Hassall Ct GU22 . . . . 90 A6
Hassocks Cl SE23, SE26 . . . 23 B5
Hassocks Ct 3 RH11 . . . . 200 F3
Hassocks Rd SW16 . . . . 41 D8
Haste Hill GU27 . . . . 208 D5
Hastings Cl GU16 . . . . 86 A7
Hastings Ct
Carshalton SM1 . . . . 59 D6
Teddington TW11 . . . . 16 D3
Hastings Dr KT6 . . . . 37 C3
Hastings Pl 1 CR0 . . . . 42 F1
Hastings Rd
Crawley RH10 . . . . 202 C6
Croydon CR0 . . . . 42 F1
Hastings View RG12 . . . . . . 27 D5
Hasty Cl CR4 . . . . 41 A8
Hatch Cl
Addlestone KT15 . . . . 52 B7
Alfold Crossways GU6 . . . . 194 A3
Hatch End
Forest Row RH18 . . . . 206 F2
Windlesham GU20 . . . . 48 C4
Hatches The
Farnham GU9 . . . . 145 F8
Frimley GU16 . . . . 85 F6
Hatchet La SL4, SL5 . . . . 9 B5
Hatchett Rd TW14 . . . . 14 C7
Hatchetts Dr GU27 . . . . . . 207 D7
Hatch Farm Mews KT15 . . 52 C7
HATCHFORD END 92 C8
Hatchford Manor KT11 . . . 72 E1
Hatchgate RH6 . . . . 160 F2
Hatchgate Copse RG12 . . . 26 E3
Hatch Gdns KT20 . . . . 97 D7
Hatch Ho 14 TW10 . . . . . . 17 C5
Hatchingtan The GU3 . . . . 89 C1
Hatch La
Banstead SM7 . . . . 79 A4
Harmondsworth UB7 . . . . 2 D7
Kingsley Green GU27 . . . . . 208 B2
Ockham GU23 . . . . 72 B1
Ockham GU23 . . . . 92 B7
South Nutfield RH1 . . . . . . 140 F3
Wormley GU8 . . . . 190 D8
Hatchlands
Capel RH5 . . . . 178 C5
Horsham RH12 . . . . 218 A7
Hatchlands Pk★ GU4 . . . . 111 F5
Hatchlands Rd RH1 . . . . . 118 E1
Hatch Pl TW10 . . . . 17 F3
Hatch Rd SW16 . . . . 41 E7
Hatch Ride RG45 . . . . 45 B7
Hatch Ride Prim Sch
RG45 . . . . 45 B7
Hatfield Cl
Belmont SM2 . . . . 59 B2
Mitcham CR4 . . . . 40 D5
West Byfleet KT14 . . . . 71 B7
Hatfield Ct GU15 . . . . 65 B5
Hatfield Gdns GU14 . . . . . . 85 E3
Hatfield Ho
4 Ash Vale GU12 . . . . 105 F5
16 Kingston upon Thames
KT6 . . . . 37 E4
Hatfield Mead SM4 . . . . 40 A4
Hatfield Prim Sch SM4 . . . 39 E3
Hatfield Rd KT21 . . . . 95 F8
Hatfield Wlk RH11 . . . . . . 200 E2
Hathaway Ct 10 RH1 . . . . . 119 A2
Hathaway Rd CR0 . . . . 42 B2
Hatherleigh Cl
Chessington KT9 . . . . 56 D5
Morden SM4 . . . . 40 A5
Hatherleigh Ho SM4 . . . . . . 40 A5
Hatherley Rd TW9 . . . . 6 F6
Hatherop Rd TW12 . . . . 15 F1
Hathersham Cl RH6 . . . . . 162 A4
Hathersham La RH1, RH6 . 161 F6
Hatherwood KT21 . . . . 95 E6
HATTON 3 F2
Hatton Cross Rdbt TW6 . . . . 3 F4
Hatton Cross U Sta TW6 . . . . 3 F3
Hatton Gdns CR4 . . . . 40 F4
Hatton Gn TW14 . . . . 4 A3
HATTON HILL 48 C5
Hatton Hill GU20 . . . . 48 C5
Hatton Rd
East Bedfont TW14 . . . . 14 D8
Hatton TW14, TW6 . . . . 3 E2
Thornton Heath CR0 . . . . . . 42 A1
Hatton Rd N TW6 . . . . 3 D6
Haughton Ho GU27 . . . . . . 208 B6
Havana Rd SW18, SW19 . . . 20 A6
Havelock Cotts GU22 . . . . . 89 D5
Havelock Hall 8 CR0 . . . . . 42 F1
Havelock Ho
4 Croydon CR0 . . . . 42 F1
Farnborough GU14 . . . . . . 105 C8
Forest Hill SE23 . . . . 23 C7
Havelock Rd
Croydon CR0 . . . . 61 F8
Wimbledon SW19 . . . . 20 C3
Wokingham RG41 . . . . 25 A6
Havelock St RG41 . . . . 25 A6
Havelock Wlk SE23 . . . . 23 C6
Havenbury Ind Est 1
RH4 . . . . 136 A8
Haven Cl
Hinchley Wood KT10 . . . . . . 55 E8
Wimbledon SW19 . . . . 19 D5
Haven Ct
Beckenham BR3 . . . . 44 C7
Hinchley Wood KT10 . . . . . . 55 E8
Havengate RH12 . . . . 217 F5
Haven Gdns RH10 . . . . 184 B1
Haven Pl KT10 . . . . 55 E8
Haven Rd
Ashford TW15 . . . . 14 B5
Rudgwick RH12, RH14 . . . . 214 D3
Havenswood Ct KT2 . . . . . . 18 B2
HAVEN THE 214 D2
Haven The
Ashford TW16 . . . . 15 A1
Richmond TW9 . . . . 7 A4
Thornton Heath CR7 . . . . . . 42 A6
Haven Way GU9 . . . . 125 D4
Haverfield Gdns TW9 . . . . . . 7 A7
Haverhill Rd SW12 . . . . 21 C7
Haverley 19 SW19 . . . . 19 D1
Havers Ave KT12 . . . . 54 D5
Haversham Cl
Crawley RH10 . . . . 201 F6
Twickenham TW1 . . . . 6 D1
Haversham Dr RG12 . . . . . . 27 B3
Haversham Ho RH6 . . . . . . 161 B5
Havisham Pl SW16 . . . . 22 B1
Hawarden Gr SE24 . . . . 22 C8
Hawarden Rd CR3 . . . . 100 C6
Hawes Down Jun & Inf Schs
BR4 . . . . 44 D1
Hawes La BR4 . . . . 44 D1
Hawes Rd KT20 . . . . 97 D7
Haweswater Ho TW1 . . . . . . 5 F2
Hawkedale Fst Sch TW16 . 34 F6
Hawker Ct 14 KT2 . . . . 18 A1
Hawke Rd SE19 . . . . 22 E2
Hawker Rd GU12 . . . . 105 F5
Hawkesbourne Rd RH12 . 217 F5
Hawkes Cl RG41 . . . . 25 A7
Hawkesfield Rd SE23, SE6 . 23 F6
Hawkes Leap GU20 . . . . . . 48 B6
Hawkesley Cl TW1 . . . . 17 A4
Hawkesmoor Rd RH11 . . . 200 E4
Hawkes Rd
East Bedfont TW14 . . . . 15 A8
Mitcham CR4 . . . . 40 F8
Hawkesworth Dr GU19 . . . . 47 E1
Hawkewood Rd TW16 . . . . . 35 A6
Hawkfield Ct TW7 . . . . 5 E5
Hawkhirst Rd CR8 . . . . 80 E3
Hawk Ho TW13 . . . . 15 A6
Hawkhurst KT11 . . . . 74 A5
Hawkhurst Gdns KT9 . . . . . 56 E6
Hawkhurst Rd SW16 . . . . . . 41 D8
Hawkhurst Way
New Malden KT3 . . . . 38 D4
West Wickham BR4 . . . . 63 B8
Hawkhurst Wlk RH10 . . . . 202 B4
Hawkins Cl RG12 . . . . 28 A7
Hawkins Ho 10 TW10 . . . . . 17 C5
Hawkins Rd
Crawley RH10 . . . . 201 E4
Teddington TW11 . . . . 17 B2
Hawkins Way
Catford SE6 . . . . 24 A3
Wokingham RG40 . . . . 25 E6
Hawk La RG12 . . . . 27 C5
Hawkley Gdns SE27 . . . . . . 22 B6
Hawkridge RH12 . . . . 195 E1
Hawkridge Ct RG12 . . . . . . 27 E6
Hawksbrook La BR3 . . . . . . 44 C3
Hawkshead Cl BR1 . . . . 24 E1
HAWK'S HILL 94 F4
Hawk's Hill KT22 . . . . 94 F4
Hawkshill Cl KT10 . . . . 55 A4
Hawks Hill Cl KT22 . . . . 94 F4

Hawks Hill Ct KT22 . . . . . . 95 A4
Hawks Hill Ho KT22 . . . . . . 94 F3
Hawkshill Way KT10 . . . . . . 55 A4
Hawksmoor Dr RH5 . . . . . 157 C4
Hawks Rd KT1 . . . . 37 F7
Hawksview KT11 . . . . 73 F6
Hawksway TW18 . . . . 12 F5
Hawkswell Cl GU21 . . . . . . 68 F2
Hawkswell Wlk GU21 . . . . . 68 F3
Hawkswood Ave GU16 . . . . 65 F2
Hawkswood Ho RG42 . . . . . 26 E8
Hawkwood Dell KT23 . . . . . 94 A1
Hawkwood Ho 3 KT23 . . . . 94 A1
Hawkwood Rise KT23 . . . . 94 A1
HAWLEY 64 E3
Hawley Cl TW12 . . . . 15 F2
Hawley Ct GU14 . . . . 84 E8
Hawley Garden Cotts
GU17 . . . . 64 D4
Hawley Gn GU17 . . . . 64 E3
Hawley Gr GU17 . . . . 64 E2
Hawley La GU14 . . . . 85 B8
HAWLEY LANE 85 B7
Hawley Lodge GU14 . . . . . . 64 F2
Hawley Place Sch GU17 . . 64 E1
Hawley Prim Sch GU17 . . . 64 E3
Hawley Rd GU14, GU17 . . . 64 F3
Hawley Way TW15 . . . . 14 B3
Hawmead RH10 . . . . 204 C8
Haworth Rd RH10 . . . . 202 C5
Hawth Ave RH10 . . . . 201 F4
Hawth Cl RH10 . . . . 201 E4
Hawthorn Ave CR7 . . . . 42 B8
Hawthorn Cl
Banstead SM7 . . . . 77 E5
Bracknell RG42 . . . . 27 A8
Cranford TW5 . . . . 4 B7
Crawley RH11 . . . . 181 C1
Hampton TW12 . . . . 16 A3
Horsham RH12 . . . . 217 C4
Redhill RH1 . . . . 140 A4
Woking GU22 . . . . 89 E7
Hawthorn Cotts CR2 . . . . . 61 C6
Hawthorn Cres
Selsdon CR2 . . . . 81 C8
Upper Tooting SW17 . . . . . 21 A3
Hawthorn Ct
1 Farnborough GU14 . . . . 105 C8
Littleton Common TW15 . . 14 C1
Richmond TW9 . . . . 7 B6
Sutton SM1 . . . . 59 A6
9 West Norwood SW16 . . . 22 A3
Hawthorndene Cl 3 BR2 . 63 F8
Hawthorndene Rd 4 BR2 63 F8
Hawthorn Dr BR4 . . . . 63 E6
Hawthorne Ave
Biggin Hill TN16 . . . . 83 D4
Cranbourne SL4 . . . . 9 B6
Mitcham CR4 . . . . 40 D7
Wallington SM5 . . . . 60 A3
Hawthorne Cl
Aldershot GU12 . . . . 126 E7
Sutton SM1 . . . . 59 C8
Hawthorne Cres GU17 . . . . 64 E4
Hawthorne Ct TW19 . . . . . 13 D8
Hawthorne Pl KT17 . . . . . . 76 E7
Hawthorne Rd TW20 . . . . . 12 C4
Hawthorne Way
Cranbourne SL4 . . . . 9 B7
Guildford GU4 . . . . 110 B5
Stanwell TW19 . . . . 13 D8
Hawthorn Gr SE20 . . . . 43 B8
Hawthorn Hatch TW8 . . . . . . 6 B7
Hawthorn La
Newell Green SL4 . . . . 8 A7
Rowledge GU10 . . . . 145 F3
Hawthorn Lodge 4 KT12 . 35 A1
Hawthorn Pl GU4 . . . . 110 D3
Hawthorn Rd
Brentford TW8 . . . . 6 B7
Carshalton SM1 . . . . 59 E4
9 Farnborough GU14 . . . . 85 B4
Feltham TW13 . . . . 15 A7
Frimley GU16 . . . . 65 F2
Godalming GU7 . . . . 150 B2
Send Marsh GU23 . . . . 91 A3
Wallington SM5, SM6 . . . . 60 B3
Woking GU22 . . . . 89 D7
Hawthorns Sch The RH1 . 120 B4
Hawthorns The
1 Belmont SM2 . . . . 59 A4
Ewell KT17 . . . . 58 A3
Oxted RH8 . . . . 123 A2
Poyle SL3 . . . . 1 F6
Hawthorn Trad Est RH13 . 217 E4
Hawthorn Way
Bisley GU24 . . . . 68 A3
Redhill RH1 . . . . 140 B8
Upper Halliford TW17 . . . . 34 D5
Woodham KT15 . . . . 52 C1
Hawth The RH10 . . . . 201 F5
HAXTED 165 F8
Haxted Rd RH7, TN8 . . . . 165 C7
Haxted Watermill Mus*
TN8 . . . . 165 D8
Haybarn Dr RH12 . . . . 217 E7
Haycroft Cl CR8 . . . . 80 B1
Haycroft Rd KT6 . . . . 56 E7
Hayden Ct KT15 . . . . 71 B8
Haydn Ave CR8 . . . . 80 A4
Haydock Lodge SM6 . . . . . 60 D7
Haydon Ct
3 Leatherhead KT22 . . . . . 95 A5
West Barnes SM4 . . . . 39 D1
Haydon Park Rd SW19 . . . 20 B3
Haydon Pl
Farnborough GU14 . . . . . . 85 A8
Guildford GU1 . . . . 130 D8
Haydon's Rd SW19 . . . . . . 20 C2
Haydons Road Sta SW19 . 20 C3
HAYES 44 F3
Hayes Barton GU22 . . . . . . 70 D3
Hayes Chase BR4 . . . . 44 E3
Hayes Cres SM3 . . . . 58 D6
Hayes Ct
Streatham SW12 . . . . 21 E7
Wimbledon SW19 . . . . 19 E2
Hayesend Ho SW17 . . . . . . 20 C4
Hayesford Park Dr BR2 . . . 44 F4
Hayes Hill BR2 . . . . 44 E1
Hayes Hill Rd BR2 . . . . 44 F1
Hayes La
Beckenham BR2, BR3 . . . . 44 D5
Purley CR8 . . . . 80 B3
Slinfold RH13 . . . . 215 D2
Hayes Mead Rd BR2 . . . . . 44 E1
Hayes Prim Sch The CR8 . 80 B3
Hayes Sta BR2 . . . . 44 F1
Hayes The KT18 . . . . 96 E8
Hayes Way BR3 . . . . 44 D5
Hayes Wlk RH6 . . . . 162 A4
Hayfields RH6 . . . . 161 C4
Haygarth Pl SW19 . . . . 19 D3
Haygreen Cl KT2 . . . . 18 B2
Haylett Gdns KT1 . . . . 37 D5
Hayling Ave TW13 . . . . 15 A5
Hayling Ct
Cheam SM3 . . . . 58 C6
Crawley RH11 . . . . 201 C3
Haymeads Dr KT10 . . . . . . 55 C4
Haymer Gdns KT4 . . . . 58 A7
Hayne Rd BR3 . . . . 43 F8
Haynes Cl GU23 . . . . 91 B5
Haynes La SE19 . . . . 22 E2
Haynt Wlk SW20 . . . . 39 E6
Hays Bridge Bsns Ctr
RH9 . . . . 163 C6
Haysbridge Cotts RH9 . . . 163 C7
Haysleigh Gdns SE20 . . . . 43 A7
Haysleigh Ho SE20 . . . . . . 43 B7
Hays Wlk SM2 . . . . 58 D1
Haywain RH8 . . . . 122 D5
Hayward Cl SW19 . . . . 40 B8
Hayward Ct CR4 . . . . 40 D7
Haywardens RH7 . . . . 164 D5
Hayward Rd KT7 . . . . 36 F1
Haywards RH10 . . . . 182 D1
Haywood RG12 . . . . 27 C2
Hazel Ave
Farnborough GU14 . . . . . . 84 F3
Guildford GU1 . . . . 109 C5
Hazelbank KT5 . . . . 38 C1
Hazel Bank SE25 . . . . 42 E7
Hazel Bank Cotts GU6 . . . 175 E5
Hazelbank Ct
Chertsey KT16 . . . . 33 C1
Chessington KT9 . . . . 56 F4
Hazelbank Rd
Catford SE6 . . . . 24 E6
Chertsey KT16 . . . . 33 C2
Hazelbury Cl SW19 . . . . . . 40 A7
Hazel Cl
Brentford TW8 . . . . 6 B7
Crawley Down RH10 . . . . 204 C8
Crawley RH11 . . . . 181 C1
Croydon CR0 . . . . 43 D1
Englefield Green TW20 . . . 11 B2
Mitcham CR4 . . . . 41 D5
Reigate RH2 . . . . 139 C7
Twickenham TW2 . . . . 16 C8
Hazel Ct
Cobham KT11 . . . . 73 A6
Guildford GU1 . . . . 109 D5
4 Horsham RH12 . . . . . . 217 F4
Warlingham CR6 . . . . 81 E1
10 West Norwood SW16 . . 22 A3
Hazeldene KT15 . . . . 52 C5
Hazeldene Ct
Kenley CR8 . . . . 80 D4
Woking GU21 . . . . 69 C4
Hazel Dr GU23 . . . . 90 F2
Hazel Gr
Feltham TW13 . . . . 15 A7
Forest Hill SE26 . . . . 23 D4
Haslemere GU26 . . . . 188 E2
Staines TW18 . . . . 13 C2
Hazelhurst
Beckenham BR3 . . . . 44 D8
Horley RH6 . . . . 161 C4
Hazelhurst Cl GU4 . . . . . 110 B6
Hazelhurst Cres RH12 . . . 216 F1
Hazelhurst Ct SE6 . . . . 24 C3
Hazelhurst Dr RH10 . . . . 202 E6
Hazelhurst Rd SW17 . . . . . 20 D4
Hazell Hill RG12 . . . . 27 C6
Hazel Lodge TW20 . . . . . . 12 A4
Hazell Rd GU9 . . . . 124 F1
Hazel Mead KT17 . . . . 58 A1
Hazelmere Cl
Hatton TW14 . . . . 3 E1
Leatherhead KT22 . . . . 95 B8
Hazelmere Ct 10 SW2 . . . 21 F7
Hazel Par KT22 . . . . 94 C5
Hazel Rd
Ash GU12 . . . . 127 C8
Mytchett GU16 . . . . 86 A2
Reigate RH2 . . . . 139 C7
West Byfleet KT14 . . . . 71 A5
Hazel Way
Chipstead CR5 . . . . 78 F1
Crawley Down RH10 . . . . 204 C8
Fetcham KT22 . . . . 94 C4
Hazelway Cl KT22 . . . . 94 C4
Hazelwick Ave RH10 . . . . 202 B8
Hazelwick Mews RH10 . . 202 A8
Hazelwick Mill La RH10 . 202 A8
Hazelwick Rd RH10 . . . . . 202 A7
Hazelwick Sch RH10 . . . . 202 A8
Hazel Wlk RH5 . . . . 136 C4
Hazelwood RH11 . . . . 201 A5
Hazelwood Ave SM4 . . . . . 40 B5
Hazelwood Cl RH10 . . . . . 203 F8
Hazelwood Cotts
Cranleigh GU6 . . . . 194 D4
8 Godalming GU7 . . . . . . 150 D4
Hazelwood Ct
Farnborough GU14 . . . . . . 84 E8
Surbiton KT6 . . . . 37 E3
Hazelwood Gr CR2 . . . . . . 81 B6
Hazelwood Ho
Beckenham BR2 . . . . 44 E6
9 Sutton SM1 . . . . 59 C6
Hazelwood Hts RH8 . . . . . 123 A4
Hazelwood La CR5 . . . . . . 98 F8
Hazelwood Lodge BR4 . . . 44 C2
Hazelwood Rd
Knaphill GU21 . . . . 68 E1
Oxted RH8 . . . . 123 B3
Hazelwood Sch RH8 . . . . 123 A4
Hazledean Rd CR0, CR9 . . . 61 D8
Hazleden Cross RH19 . . . 205 B6
Hazledene Rd W4 . . . . 7 C8
Hazlemere KT12 . . . . 54 C8
Hazlemere Gdns KT4 . . . . 39 A1
Hazlewood GU8 . . . . 148 E4
Hazlitt Cl TW13 . . . . 15 E4
Hazon Way KT19 . . . . 76 C7
Headcorn Pl CR7 . . . . 41 F5
Headcorn Rd
Bromley BR1 . . . . 24 F3
Thornton Heath CR7 . . . . . 41 F5
Headingley Dr BR3 . . . . . . 24 A2
Headington Cl RG40 . . . . . 25 D8
Headington Dr RG40 . . . . . 25 D8
Headington Rd SW18 . . . . 20 C6
Headlam Rd SW4 . . . . 21 D8
Headland Way RH7 . . . . . 164 D4
HEADLEY 96 C2
Headley Ave SM6 . . . . 60 F5
Headley Cl
Chessington KT19 . . . . 57 A4
Crawley RH10 . . . . 182 D1
Headley Common Rd KT18,
KT20 . . . . 116 D7
Headley Ct SE26 . . . . 23 C3
HEADLEY DOWN 187 B4
Headley Dr
Burgh Heath KT18 . . . . 97 B8
New Addington CR0 . . . . . 63 C3
Headley Gr
Burgh Heath KT20 . . . . 97 C7
Headley KT20 . . . . 116 D7
Headley Heath App KT20 116 B4
Headley Hill Rd GU35 . . . 187 A5
Headley Rd
Ashtead KT18 . . . . 96 C6
Grayshott GU26 . . . . 188 C3
Headley KT18, KT22 . . . . . 96 A4
Leatherhead KT18, KT22 . . 95 E4
Mickleham RH5 . . . . 115 E7
Headon Ct GU9 . . . . 125 D1
Headway Cl TW10 . . . . 17 C4
Headway The KT17 . . . . . . 57 F2
HEARN 187 B7
Hearne Rd W4 . . . . 7 A8
Hearn Vale GU35 . . . . 187 A7
Hearnville Rd SW12 . . . . . 21 A7
Hearn Wlk RG12 . . . . 27 E8
Hearsey Gdns GU17 . . . . . 64 C6
Heart Sh Ctr The KT12 . . . 34 F1
Heathacre SL3 . . . . 1 E6
Heatham Pk TW2 . . . . 16 F8
Heathbridge KT13 . . . . 53 A4
Heath Bsns Ctr RH1 . . . . 161 B8
Heath Bsns Ctr The TW3 . . . 5 C3
Heath Cl
Aldershot GU12 . . . . 105 D1
Banstead SM7 . . . . 78 B5
Beacon Hill GU26 . . . . . . 188 C7
Broadbridge Heath RH12 . 216 E3
Croydon CR2 . . . . 61 B4
Harlington UB3 . . . . 3 D7
Heath End GU9 . . . . 125 C7
Stanwell TW19 . . . . 2 C1
Virginia Water GU25 . . . . . 31 D5
Wokingham RG41 . . . . 25 B4
Heath Cnr GU15 . . . . 66 A3
Heathcote KT20 . . . . 97 D5
Heathcote Cl GU12 . . . . . 106 A3
Heathcote Dr RH19 . . . . . 185 C2
Heathcote Rd
Ash GU12 . . . . 106 B3
Camberley GU15 . . . . 65 D5
Epsom KT18 . . . . 76 E6
Twickenham TW1 . . . . 6 B2
Heathcotes RH10 . . . . 202 D4
Heath Cotts GU26 . . . . . . 188 C6
Heathcroft Ave TW16 . . . . 14 F1
Heath Ct
Carshalton SM1 . . . . 59 D8
4 Croydon CR0 . . . . 61 D6
Heathdale Ave TW4 . . . . . . 4 E4
Heathdene
Burgh Heath KT20 . . . . 77 E1
Weybridge KT13 . . . . 53 A5
Heathdene Rd
Streatham SW16 . . . . 21 F1
Wallington SM5, SM6 . . . . 60 B3
Heathdown Rd GU22 . . . . 70 D4
Heath Dr
Brookwood GU24 . . . . 88 A7
Send GU23 . . . . 90 B5
Sutton SM2 . . . . 59 C2
Walton on the Hill KT18 . . . 97 A2
Heath Dr continued
West Barnes SW20 . . . . 39 C5
Heathedge SE23, SE26 . . . . 23 B6
HEATH END 125 D6
Heath End Cotts GU8 . . . . 170 E7
Heatherbank GU26 . . . . . 188 E4
Heatherbank Cl KT11 . . . . 73 D8
Heather Cl
Aldershot GU11 . . . . 104 E1
Ash GU12 . . . . 106 B5
Copthorne RH10 . . . . 183 B2
Guildford GU2 . . . . 109 B3
Hampton TW12 . . . . 35 F8
Horsham RH12 . . . . 217 D5
Isleworth TW7 . . . . 5 D2
Kingswood KT20 . . . . 97 E5
2 Lewisham SE13 . . . . 24 D8
Redhill RH1 . . . . 119 B5
Woking GU21 . . . . 69 C4
Woodham KT15 . . . . 52 B1
Wrecclesham GU9 . . . . . . 145 F6
Heather Cotts GU12 . . . . 106 A8
Heather Ct
12 Aldershot GU11 . . . . . 105 A1
Hindhead GU26 . . . . 188 F4
West Norwood SW16 . . . . . 22 A4
Heatherdale Cl KT2 . . . . . . 18 B1
Heatherdale Rd GU15 . . . . 65 D4
Heatherdene KT24 . . . . 92 D2
Heatherdene Cl CR4 . . . . . 40 E5
Heatherdene Ct CR4 . . . . . 40 D5
Heatherdene Mans 5 TW1 6 D1
Heather Dr SL5 . . . . 30 B2
Heatherfield La KT13 . . . . . 53 E5
Heatherfields KT15 . . . . . . 52 B1
Heather Gdns
Belmont SM2 . . . . 59 A4
Farnborough GU14 . . . . . . 84 E2
Heatherlands
Ashford TW16 . . . . 15 A2
8 Horley RH6 . . . . 161 B4
Heatherlea Gr KT4 . . . . . . 39 B1
Heatherleigh Ct RH12 . . . 217 C4
Heatherley Cl GU15 . . . . . 65 B5
Heatherley Rd GU15 . . . . . 65 B5
Heather Mead GU16 . . . . . 65 F2
Heather Mead Ct GU16 . . . 65 F2
Heathermount RG12 . . . . . 27 E5
Heather Mount GU3 . . . . . 108 E3
Heathermount Dr RG45 . . . 45 A6
Heathermount, The Learning
Ctr SL5 . . . . 29 D3
Heather Pl KT10 . . . . 55 B6
Heather Ridge Arc GU15 . . 66 C4
Heather Ridge Inf Sch
GU15 . . . . 66 D4
Heatherset Cl KT10 . . . . . . 55 C5
Heatherset Gdns SW16 . . . 21 F1
HEATHERSIDE 66 B4
Heatherside Cl KT23 . . . . . 93 F2
Heatherside Cnr GU15 . . . . 66 D6
Heatherside Dr GU25 . . . . 31 A3
Heatherside Rd KT19 . . . . . 57 D3
Heathers Land RH4 . . . . . 136 C4
Heathers The TW19 . . . . . . 13 F8
Heathervale Rd KT15 . . . . . 52 B1
Heathervale Way
West Byfleet KT15 . . . . 71 C8
Weybridge KT15 . . . . 52 C1
Heatherway
Crowthorne RG45 . . . . 45 A5
Felbridge RH19 . . . . 184 F7
Heather Way
Chobham GU24 . . . . 49 E3
Hindhead GU26 . . . . 188 F4
South Croydon CR2 . . . . . . 62 D2
Heather Wlk
Crawley RH11 . . . . 201 B3
Pirbright GU24 . . . . 87 D7
Smallfield RH6 . . . . 162 C3
5 Twickenham TW2 . . . . . 16 A8
Whiteley Village KT12 . . . . 53 F1
Heatherwood Hospl SL5 . . 28 E6
HEATHFIELD 62 D4
Heathfield
Cobham KT11 . . . . 74 A5
Crawley RH10 . . . . 202 D8
Reigate RH2 . . . . 138 D8
Heathfield Ave
Ascot SL5 . . . . 29 E4
Wandsworth SW18 . . . . . . 20 D8
Heathfield Cl
Ashtead KT21 . . . . 95 C8
Godalming GU7 . . . . 150 E2
Woking GU22 . . . . 70 A1
Heathfield Ct
Ashford TW15 . . . . 13 E5
Penge SE20 . . . . 23 C1
Wandsworth SW18 . . . . . . 20 D8
Heathfield Dr
Mitcham CR4 . . . . 20 E1
Redhill RH1 . . . . 139 E4
Heathfield Gdns CR0 . . . . . 61 D6
Heathfield Inf Sch TW2 . . . 16 A7
Heathfield Jun Sch TW2 . . 16 A7
Heathfield N TW2 . . . . 16 F8
Heathfield Rd
Bromley BR1 . . . . 24 F1
Croydon CR0 . . . . 61 D6
Hersham KT12 . . . . 54 E6
Wandsworth SW18 . . . . . . 20 D8
Woking GU22 . . . . 70 A1
Heathfield S TW2 . . . . 16 F8
Heathfield St Mary's Sch
SL5 . . . . 28 B7
Heathfield Sq SW18 . . . . . . 20 D8
Heathfield Vale CR2 . . . . . 62 E2
Heath Gdns TW1 . . . . 16 F6
Heath Gr
Ashford TW16 . . . . 14 F1
Penge SE20 . . . . 23 C1
Heath Hill
Dockenfield GU10 . . . . . . 166 E3
Dorking RH4 . . . . 136 B7
Heath Hill Road N RG45 . . 45 B5
Heath Hill Road S RG45 . . 45 B4
Heath Ho
Frimley GU16 . . . . 85 F6
Thornton Heath CR7 . . . . . 42 A4
1 Weybridge KT13 . . . . . . 53 A6
Heath House Rd GU22 . . . . 88 D5
Heathhurst Rd CR2 . . . . . . 61 E2
Heath La
Albury GU5 . . . . 132 E2
Crondall GU10 . . . . 124 B7
Godalming GU7 . . . . 151 A2
Heath End GU9 . . . . 125 C7
Heathlands
Chobham GU24 . . . . 49 E1
Tadworth KT20 . . . . 97 D5
Weybridge KT13 . . . . 53 C5
Heathland Sch The TW4 . . . . 4 F1
Heathlands Cl
Sunbury TW16 . . . . 35 A7
Twickenham TW1 . . . . 16 F7
Woking GU21 . . . . 69 E5
Heathlands Ct
Hounslow TW4 . . . . 4 E2
Mitcham CR4 . . . . 41 A6
Heathlands Rd RG40 . . . . . 25 E2
Heathland St GU11 . . . . . 105 A2
Heathlands Way TW4 . . . . . 4 E2
Heath Mead SW19 . . . . 19 D5
Heathmere Prim Sch
SW15 . . . . 19 A7
Heath Mews GU23 . . . . 91 B4
Heath Mill La GU3 . . . . 88 C2
Heathmoors RG12 . . . . 27 C4
Heathpark Dr GU20 . . . . . . 48 E4
Heath Rd
Bagshot GU19 . . . . 47 E3
Caterham CR3 . . . . 100 D3
Haslemere GU27 . . . . 207 D5
Isleworth TW3, TW7 . . . . . . 5 C3
Oxshott KT22 . . . . 74 C7
South Norwood CR7 . . . . . . 42 C6
Twickenham TW1 . . . . 16 F7
Weybridge KT13 . . . . 53 A5
Woking GU21 . . . . 69 F4
Heath Ridge Gn KT11 . . . . . 74 A6
Heathrise GU23 . . . . 91 B4
Heath Rise
Camberley GU15 . . . . 65 D5
Hayes BR2 . . . . 44 F3
Virginia Water GU25 . . . . . 31 D5
Westcott RH4 . . . . 135 C5
Heathrow GU5 . . . . 133 C4
Heathrow Airport London
TW6 . . . . 3 A5
Heathrow Airport T4 Sta
TW6 . . . . 3 C1
Heathrow Airport T5 Sta
TW6 . . . . 2 C4
Heathrow Airport T123 Sta
TW6 . . . . 3 B4
Heathrow Airport Visitor
Ctr* TW6 . . . . 3 C6
Heathrow Bvd UB7 . . . . 2 F7
Heathrow Causeway Est
TW4 . . . . 4 B4
Heathrow Cl TW6 . . . . 2 B6
Heathrow International Trad
Est TW4 . . . . 4 B4
Heathrow Prim Sch UB7 . . . 2 F8
Heathshott 9 TW10 . . . . . . 6 E1
Heathside
Hinchley Wood KT10 . . . . . 55 E7
Twickenham TW4 . . . . 15 F8
Weybridge KT13 . . . . 53 B5
Heathside Cl KT10 . . . . 55 E7
Heathside Cres GU22 . . . . . 69 F2
Heathside Ct KT20 . . . . 97 C4
Heathside Gdns GU22 . . . . 70 A2
Heathside La GU26 . . . . . 188 D6
Heathside Park Rd GU22 . . 70 A1
Heathside Pk GU15 . . . . . . 66 C7
Heathside Pl KT18 . . . . 77 D1
Heathside Rd GU22 . . . . . . 69 F1
Heathside Sch KT13 . . . . . . 52 F4
Heath The CR3 . . . . 100 C3
Heathvale Bridge Rd
GU12 . . . . 106 A6
Heathview GU21 . . . . 69 E3
Heath View KT24 . . . . 92 F2
Heathview Ct SW19 . . . . . . 19 D6
Heathview Gdns SW15 . . . . 19 C8
Heathview Rd
Thornton Heath CR7 . . . . . 42 A5
Witley GU8 . . . . 170 E7
Heathway
Camberley GU15 . . . . 65 D5
Caterham CR3 . . . . 100 D2
Croydon CR0 . . . . 62 F7
East Horsley KT24 . . . . 93 A3
North Ascot SL5 . . . . 28 E8
Heath Way RH12 . . . . 217 D5
Heathway Cl GU15 . . . . . . 65 D5
Heathwood KT20 . . . . 97 C4
Heathwood Ct
Hounslow TW3 . . . . 5 B3
Streatham SW12 . . . . 21 C7
Heathwood Point 7 SE23 23 D5
Heathyfields Rd GU9 . . . . 125 A6

Heaton Rd CR4 21 A1
Heavers Farm Prim Sch SE25 42 F4
Hebdon Rd SW17 20 F5
Hebe Ct SM1 59 C6
Hectors La RH19 206 C7
Heddon Cl TW7 6 A3
Heddon Wlk 1 GU14 85 A7
Hedge Cnr KT20 97 C4
Hedgecourt Pl RH19 184 E4
Hedge Croft Cotts GU23 91 B6
Hedgehog La GU27 208 B5
Hedgerley Ct GU21 69 C2
Hedgers Almshouses GU1 110 D2
Hedgeside RH11 201 C1
Hedgeway GU2 130 A7
Hedge Wlk SE6 24 B4
Hedingham Cl RH6 161 C4
Hedingham Ho 13 KT2 37 E8
Hedley Rd TW2 16 A8
Heelas Rd RG41 25 A5
Heenan Cl GU16 85 E7
Heighton Gdns CR0 61 B5
Heights Cl
Banstead SM7 77 E3
Wimbledon SW20 19 B1
Heights The
Beckenham BR3 24 C1
Forest Hill SE23 23 C8
Helder Gr SE12 24 F8
Helder St CR2 61 D4
Heldmann Cl TW7 5 D3
Helena Ho RH1 140 A6
Helen Ave TW14 15 B8
Helen Cl KT8 36 B5
Helen Ct GU14 85 B4
Helford Wlk 3 GU21 69 A1
Helgiford Gdns TW16 14 E1
Helicon Ho RH11 201 C5
Helios Rd SM6 41 A1
Helix Bsns Pk GU15 65 B3
Helix Ho TW7 6 B5
Helix The SW19 19 D6
Helm Cl KT19 76 A7
Helme Cl SW19 19 F3
Helmsdale
Bracknell RG12 27 E4
3 Woking GU21 69 B1
Helmsdale Rd SW16 21 D1
Helston Cl GU16 86 A7
Helvellyn Cl TW20 12 C1
Helvetia St SE6 23 F6
Hemingford Rd SM3 58 C6
Hemlock Cl
Kingswood KT20 97 E4
London SW16 41 D7
Hemming Cl 9 TW12 36 A8
Hemmings Mead KT19 57 C4
Hempshaw Ave SM7 78 F3
Hemsby Rd KT9 56 F4
Hemsby Wlk RH10 202 B4
Henage Cnr GU24 49 E2
Henage La GU22 90 C7
Henbane Ct 2 RH11 201 B2
Henbit Cl KT20 97 B8
Henchley Dene GU4 110 D4
Henderson Ave GU2 109 B5
Henderson Ct SW18 20 E8
Henderson Dr TN16 83 C7
Henderson Hospl SM2 59 B2
Henderson Rd
Crawley RH11 201 B1
Thornton Heath CR0 42 D3
Wandsworth SW18 20 E8
Henderson Way RH12 216 F1
Hendfield Ct 5 SM6 60 B4
Hendham Rd SW17 20 F6
Hendon Gr KT19 57 A2
Hendon Terr TW15 14 D2
Hendon Way TW19 2 D1
Hendrick Ave SW12 20 F8
Heneage Cres CR0 63 C1
Henfield Rd SW19 39 F8
Henfold Cotts RH5 158 A2
Henfold Dr RH5 157 E3
Henfold La RH5 157 F5
Hengelo Gdns CR4 40 D5
Hengist Cl RH12 217 A1
Hengist Way
Beckenham BR2 44 E5
Wallington SM6 60 D3
Hengrave Rd SE23 23 D8
Hengrove Cres TW15 13 D5
Henhurst Cross La RH5 157 A2
Henley Ave SM3 58 E7
Henley Bank GU2 130 A7
Henley Cl
Crawley RH10 202 D3
Farnborough GU14 84 E8
Hounslow TW7 5 F6
Henley Ct
11 Egham TW20 12 A3
Kingston upon Thames KT3 38 D6
Mitcham CR4 41 A6
Old Woking GU22 90 A7
Henley Dr
Frimley GU16 85 E7
Kingston upon Thames KT2 18 F1
Henley Gate GU24 107 C8
Henley Lodge SE25 42 F5
Henley Way TW13 15 D3
Henley Wood CR6 82 A2
Henlow Pl TW10 17 D6
Hennel Cl SE23 23 C5
Hennessy Ct GU21 70 C6
Henrietta Ct TW1 17 C8
Henry Cavendish Prim Sch SW12 21 C7
Henry Ct GU12 86 A1
Henry Doulton Dr SW17 21 B4
Henry Hatch Ct SM2 59 C3
Henry Macaulay Ave 11 KT2 37 D8
Henry Marshall Ho 5 GU7 150 D4
Henry Peters Dr TW11 16 E3
Henry Randell's Almshouses GU17 64 E3
Henry Tate Mews SW16 22 A3
Henry Tyndale Sch GU14 85 D6
Henshaw Cl RH11 200 F4
Henslow Way GU21 70 D5
Henson Rd RH10 202 B7
Hensworth Rd TW15 13 D3
Henty Cl RH11 200 E3
Hepburn Gdns BR2 44 F1
Hepple Cl TW7 6 B5
Hepplewhite Cl RH11 201 B1
Hepworth Croft GU47 64 E6
Hepworth Ct SM3 40 A1
Hepworth Rd SW16 21 E1
Hepworth Way KT12 34 F1
Herald Ct
5 Aldershot GU12 105 B1
South Norwood SE19 22 B2
Herald Gdns SM6 60 B7
Herbert Cl RG12 27 B4
Herbert Cres GU21 68 E1
Herbert Ct KT5 37 F3
Herbert Gdns W4 7 B8
Herbert Pl TW7 5 D5
Herbert Rd
Kingston upon Thames KT1 37 F6
Merton SW19 19 F1
Herbs End GU14 84 C5
Hercules Way GU14 104 F8
Hereford Cl
Crawley RH10 201 E2
Epsom KT18 76 D6
Guildford GU2 108 F3
Staines TW18 33 B8
Hereford Copse GU22 89 B8
Hereford Ct
Belmont SM2 59 A3
6 Croydon CR0 42 F1
Hereford Gdns TW2 16 C7
Hereford Ho 11 GU11 105 A1
Hereford La GU9 125 B7
Hereford Rd TW13 15 C7
Hereford Way KT9 56 D5
Hereward Ave CR8 61 A1
Hereward Rd SW17 20 F4
Heriot Ct KT16 32 F2
Heriot Rd KT16 33 A2
Heritage Cl TW16 35 A8
Heritage Cotts GU3 107 B4
Heritage Ct 2 TW20 12 A3
Heritage Ho
22 Putney SW19 19 D7
4 Twickenham TW1 17 A8
Heritage Lawn RH6 161 C4
Herlwyn Gdns SW17 20 F4
Herm Cl
Crawley RH11 201 A2
Hounslow TW7 5 C7
Hermes Ho BR3 43 E8
Hermitage Cl
Claygate KT10 56 A4
Farnborough GU14 85 D1
Frimley GU16 65 F1
Littleton TW17 34 A5
Hermitage Ct TW18 12 F3
Hermitage Dr SL5 28 E7
Hermitage Gdns SE19 22 C1
Hermitage La
Croydon CR0 43 A3
East Grinstead RH19 205 F8
Streatham SW16 21 F1
Hermitage Par SL5 29 A6
Hermitage Rd
East Grinstead RH19 185 D3
Kenley CR8 80 C3
Knaphill GU21 88 D8
South Norwood SE19 22 D2
Hermitage Rdbt GU21 88 D8
Hermitage Sch The GU21 88 E8
Hermitage The
Barnes SW13 7 F6
Feltham TW13 14 F5
Forest Hill SE23 23 C7
Kingston upon Thames KT1 37 D5
Richmond TW10 6 E2
Hermitage Woods Cres GU21 88 E7
Hermitage Woods Est GU21 88 E8
Hermits Rd RH10 201 F7
Hermonger La RH12 195 F2
Herndon Cl TW20 12 A4
Herne Rd KT6 56 E8
Hernes Cl TW18 33 B8
Heron Cl
Cheam SM1 58 F5
Crawley RH11 201 C8
Farnham GU9 145 F8
Guildford GU2 109 B4
Mytchett GU16 85 F4
North Ascot SL5 28 D8
Heron Ct
8 Dorking RH4 136 A8
6 Hampton TW12 36 B8
Heron Ct *continued*
5 Kingston upon Thames KT1 37 E6
Merton SW20 39 E7
3 Mitcham CR4 40 E8
Sandhurst GU47 64 C7
Staines TW18 13 B4
Stanwell TW19 13 E7
7 West Norwood SE21 22 D6
Herondale
Bracknell RG12 27 C2
Haslemere GU27 207 E6
Selsdon CR2 62 D2
Heron Dale KT15 52 D5
Herondale Ave SW18 20 E7
Heronfield TW20 11 C2
Heron Ho KT1 37 C8
Heron Pl RH19 205 F8
Heron Rd
Croydon CR0 61 E8
Isleworth TW1 6 B3
Heronry The KT12 54 A4
Heronsbrook SL5 29 F7
Herons Cl RH10 184 B5
Heronscourt GU18 67 C8
Herons Crest GU1 109 F1
Herons Croft KT13 53 D4
Heron Shaw GU6 174 E1
Herons L Ctr GU27 207 F6
Herons Lea RH10 184 A4
Herons Pl TW7 6 B4
Heron Sq 28 TW10 6 D2
Herons Way GU24 87 D6
Heron's Way RG40 25 E7
Heronswood Ct RH6 161 B4
Herontye Dr RH19 206 A8
Herontye Ho RH19 205 F7
Heron Way
Hatton TW14 4 A3
Horsham RH13 218 A1
Wallington SM6 60 D3
Heron Way Prim Sch RH13 218 A1
Heron Wlk GU21 70 C5
Heron Wood Rd GU12 126 D7
Herretts Gdns GU12 105 D1
Herrett St GU12 126 D8
Herrick Cl
Crawley RH10 202 C8
Frimley GU16 66 C3
Herrick Ct 4 TW10 17 D4
Herrings La
Chertsey KT16 33 A3
Windlesham GU20 48 D4
Herron Ct 15 BR2 44 F5
Herschell Rd SE23 23 E8
Herschel Wlk 9 RH11 201 B1
HERSHAM 54 D5
Hersham Cl SW15 19 A8
Hersham Ctr KT12 54 D5
Hersham Gdns KT12 54 C6
Hersham Rd
Hersham KT12 54 D6
Walton-on-Thames KT12 54 B7
Hersham Sta KT12 54 E7
Hersham Trad Est KT12 54 E8
Hershell Ct SW14 7 B3
Hertford Ave SW14 7 E3
Hertford Lodge 10 SW19 19 E7
Hertford Way CR4 41 E5
Hesiers Hill CR6 82 E2
Hesiers Rd CR6 82 F3
Hesketh Cl GU6 174 E3
Heslop Ct 1 SW12 21 A7
Heslop Rd SW12 20 F7
Hessle Gr KT17 76 F8
Hester Ct SW16 21 C3
Hesterman Way CR0, CR9 41 F1
Hester Terr TW9 7 A4
HESTON 4 F7
Heston Ave TW5 4 E7
Heston Com Sch TW5 5 A7
Heston Grange TW5 4 F8
Heston Grange La TW5 4 F8
Heston Ind Mall TW5 4 F7
Heston Inf Sch TW5 5 A7
Heston Jun Sch TW5 5 A7
Heston Phoenix Distribution Pk TW5 4 C8
Heston Pool TW5 5 F8
Heston Rd
Heston TW5 5 A7
Redhill RH1 139 F4
Heston Wlk RH1 139 F4
Hetherington Rd TW17 34 C7
Hethersett Cl RH2 118 C4
Hetley Gdns 1 SE19 22 F1
Heverfield Ct CR4 20 F1
Hevers Ave RH6 161 A4
Hevers Cnr RH6 160 F4
Hewells Ct 4 RH12 217 C2
Hewers Way KT20 97 C7
Hewitt Cl CR0 63 A7
Hewitts Ind Est GU6 174 B3
Hewlett Pl GU19 47 F3
Hewshott La GU30 207 A5
Hexal Rd SE6 24 E5
Hexham Cl
Crawley RH10 202 E6
Sandhurst GU47 45 D2
Hexham Gdns TW7 6 A7
Hexham Rd
Cheam SM4 40 B1
West Norwood SE27 22 C6
Hextalls La RH1 120 E6
Heybridge Ave SW16 21 F2
Heydon Ct BR4 63 E8
Heyford Ave SW20 39 F6
Heyford Rd CR4 40 E7
Heymede KT22 95 C4
Hey The CR2 61 E1
Heythorp Cl GU21 68 F2
Heythorp St SW18 19 F6
Heyward Ct SM2 59 A4
Heywood Dr GU19 47 D3
HG Wells Ctr★ GU21 69 F2
Hibernia Gdns TW3 5 A2
Hibernia Rd TW3 5 A3
Hickey's Almshouses 10 TW9 6 F3
Hickling Wlk RH10 202 B4
Hickmans Cl RH9 121 C3
Hicks La GU17 64 B5
Hidaburn Ct 7 SW16 21 C4
Hidcote Cl GU22 70 B3
Hidcote Gdns SW20 39 B6
Hidcote Ho 15 SM2 59 C3
Hidden Cl KT8 36 C5
Hieover SE21 22 C6
Higgins Wlk TW12 15 E2
Higgs La GU19 47 D3
Highacre RH4 136 B4
Highams Hill RH11 200 F5
Highams La GU20, GU24 49 A5
High Ashton 11 KT2 18 B1
High Barn Rd KT24, RH5 113 E3
Highbarrow Cl CR8 60 F1
Highbarrow Rd CR0 43 A1
High Beech
Bracknell RG12 27 F5
South Croydon CR2 61 E3
High Beeches
Banstead KT17, SM7 77 D5
Frimley GU16 65 D2
Weybridge KT13 53 E4
High Beeches Cl CR8 60 D1
Highbirch Cl RH12 218 B5
High Broom Cres BR4 44 B2
Highbury Ave CR7 42 B7
Highbury Cl
New Malden KT3 38 C4
West Wickham BR4 63 B8
Highbury Cres GU15 66 A8
Highbury Dr KT22 95 A6
Highbury Gr GU27 208 C8
Highbury Rd SW19 19 E3
High Cedar Dr SW20 19 B1
Highclere
Ascot SL5 29 D4
Guildford GU1 110 A4
Highclere Cl
Bracknell RG12 27 E7
Kenley CR8 80 C4
Highclere Ct GU21 68 C2
Highclere Dr GU15 66 A7
Highclere Gdns GU21 68 D2
Highclere Rd
Aldershot GU12 126 D8
Kingston upon Thames KT3 38 D6
Knaphill GU21 68 C2
Highclere St SE26 23 E4
Highcliffe BR3 44 B8
Highcliffe Dr SW15 7 F1
High Close Sch RG40 25 C7
Highcombe Edge Sch GU26 188 F5
High Coombe Pl KT2 18 D1
High Copse GU9 125 A6
Highcotts La GU4, GU23 91 A1
Highcroft
Beacon Hill GU26 188 D6
Milford GU8 170 F8
Purley CR8 79 F5
2 Surbiton KT5 37 F4
High Croft GU5 152 E4
Highcroft Ct KT23 94 A4
Highcroft Dr RH12 195 E1
Highcross Way 4 SW15 19 A7
Highdaun Dr SW16 41 F5
Highdene
Guildford GU1 131 A8
6 Woking GU22 69 F1
Highdown KT4 57 F8
Highdown Cl SM7 77 F3
Highdown Ct RH10 202 B3
High Down Rd SM2 78 B8
Highdown Way RH12 217 F6
High Dr
Kingston upon Thames KT2, KT3 38 C7
Oxshott KT22 74 D5
Woldingham CR3 102 A5
Higher Alham RG12 27 E2
Highercombe Rd GU27 208 E8
Higher Dr
Belmont KT17, SM7 77 D6
East Horsley KT24 112 E8
Kenley CR8 80 B5
Purley CR8 80 A6
Higher Gn KT17 77 A6
Highfield
Bracknell RG12 26 F3
Shalford GU4 130 F1
Woodmansterne SM7 78 E2
Highfield Ave GU11 126 A8
Highfield Cl
Aldershot GU11 126 B8
Englefield Green TW20 11 C2
Farnborough GU14 84 F4
Farnham GU9 146 B7
Long Ditton KT6 37 C1
Oxshott KT22 74 D8
West Byfleet KT14 71 A6
Wokingham RG40 25 B6
Highfield Cres GU26 188 F4
Highfield Ct
Englefield Green TW20 11 D2
Mitcham CR4 40 E5
Highfield Dr
Beckenham BR2 44 F5
West Ewell KT19 57 F4
West Wickham BR4 63 C7
Highfield Gdns GU11 126 B8
Highfield Hill SE19 22 E1
Highfield Ho RH11 201 D7
Highfield Inf Sch BR2 44 E5
Highfield Jun Sch BR2 44 E5
Highfield La
Puttenham GU3 128 A3
Thursley GU8 169 B2
Highfield Path GU14 84 F4
Highfield Rd
Biggin Hill TN16 83 C3
Carshalton SM1 59 E5
Caterham CR3 101 A5
Chertsey KT16 33 A1
East Grinstead RH19 185 D3
Farnborough GU14 84 F4
Feltham TW13 15 A6
Hounslow TW7 5 F6
Purley CR8 61 A1
Tolworth KT5 38 C2
Upper Halliford TW16 34 F4
Walton-on-Thames KT12 35 A1
West Byfleet KT14 71 A6
Highfields
Ashtead KT21 95 D8
East Horsley KT24 112 F7
Fetcham KT22 94 D3
Forest Row RH18 206 F2
Sutton SM1 59 A8
High Fields SL5 29 F4
High Foleys KT10 56 B3
High Gables BR2 44 E7
High Garth KT10 55 C4
HIGHGATE 206 F1
Highgate Ct
Crawley RH11 201 C2
Farnborough GU14 85 C5
Highgate Ho 11 SE26 23 A5
Highgate La GU14 85 C5
Highgate Rd RH18 206 F1
Highgate Wlk SE23 23 C6
High Gdns GU22 89 B8
Highgrove 2 GU14 85 B7
Highgrove Ave SL5 28 F8
Highgrove Ct BR3 24 A1
Highgrove Ho GU4 110 C3
Highgrove Mews SM5 59 E7
High Hill Rd CR6 82 C5
High La
Haslemere GU27 208 C8
Warlingham CR3, CR6 101 F8
Highland Cotts SM6 60 C6
Highland Croft BR3 24 B2
Highland Lodge 2 SE19 22 F1
Highland Pk TW13 14 F4
Highland Rd
Aldershot GU12 105 D2
Beare Green RH5 157 D3
Bromley BR1 44 F8
Camberley GU15 65 E8
Purley CR8 80 A5
West Norwood SE19 22 E2
Highlands KT21 95 C8
Highlands Ave
Horsham RH13 217 E2
Leatherhead KT22 95 C5
Highlands Cl
Farnham GU9 146 B7
Hounslow TW3 5 B6
Leatherhead KT22 95 B5
Highlands Cres RH13 217 E2
Highlands Ct SE19 22 E2
Highlands Heath SW15 19 C8
Highlands La GU22 89 E5
Highlands Pk KT22 95 D4
Highlands Rd
Heath End GU9 125 C7
Horsham RH13 217 F2
Leatherhead KT22 95 C5
Reigate RH2 118 D2
Highlands The KT24 92 E2
Highland View GU6 174 C7
High Level Dr SE26 23 A4
High Limes 2 SE19 22 E2
High Loxley Rd GU8 193 B7
Highmead GU7 150 F6
High Mead
Farncombe GU7 150 F6
West Wickham BR4 63 E8
High Meadow Cl RH4 136 B6
High Meadow Ho RH4 136 B6
High Meadow Pl KT16 32 F3
High Oaks RH11 201 B4
High Park Ave
East Horsley KT24 92 F1
Richmond TW9 7 A6
High Park Rd
Farnham GU9 125 C3
Richmond TW9 7 A6
High Par The SW16 21 E5
High Path SW19 40 C8
High Path Rd GU1 110 C1
High Pewley GU1 130 E7
High Pine Cl KT13 53 C5
High Pines CR6 101 C8
High Pines The RG42 8 B5
High Pitfold GU26 188 D1
Highpoint KT13 53 A5
High Range SW20 19 C1
High Rd
Byfleet KT14 71 E6

High Rd *continued*
Chipstead CR5, RH2 98 F4
High Ridge GU7 150 D2
Highridge Cl KT18 76 E5
Highridge Ct KT18 76 E5
High St Mews SW19 19 E3
High St
Addlestone KT15 52 B6
Aldershot GU11 105 A2
Aldershot GU11, GU12 105 B1
Ascot SL5 29 A6
Ascot, Sunninghill SL5 29 D4
Bagshot GU19 47 E3
Banstead SM7 78 B4
Beckenham BR3 44 A7
Bletchingley RH1 120 D2
Bracknell RG12 27 B7
Bracknell RG12 27 C7
Bramley GU5 151 F6
Brentford TW8 6 D8
Camberley GU15 65 D6
Carshalton SM5 60 A6
Caterham CR3 100 E4
Cheam SM1, KT17 58 E4
Chobham GU24 68 E8
Claygate KT10 55 F4
Cobham KT11 73 B4
Colnbrook SL3 1 C7
Cranford, Heston TW5 4 B7
Cranleigh GU6 174 D3
Crawley RH10 201 D6
Crawley RH10 201 D6
Crowthorne RG45 45 C4
Croydon CR0, CR9 61 C7
Croydon, Woodside SE25 43 A5
Dorking RH4 136 B8
East Grinstead RH19 205 F8
East Molesey KT8 36 A5
4 Egham TW20 11 F3
Epsom KT17, KT18 76 D6
Esher KT10 55 B6
Ewell KT17 58 A2
Farnborough GU14 105 D8
Feltham TW13 15 A6
Godalming GU7 150 D4
Godstone RH9 121 C4
Great Bookham KT23 94 B2
Guildford GU1, GU2 130 D7
Harlington UB3 3 D8
Harmondsworth UB7 2 D8
Haslemere GU27 208 D7
Horley RH6 161 B3
Hounslow TW3 5 B4
Kingston upon Thames KT1 37 D6
Knaphill GU21 68 C2
Leatherhead KT22 95 B5
Limpsfield RH8 123 B7
Lingfield RH7 164 D4
Loxwood RH14 212 F3
Merstham RH1 119 B7
New Malden KT3 38 E5
Nutfield RH1 119 F2
Old Woking GU22 90 B6
Oxshott KT22 74 D5
Oxted RH8 122 D5
Penge SE19, SE20, BR3 23 C1
Purley CR8 80 B8
Redhill RH1 118 F2
Reigate RH2 118 A1
Ripley GU23 91 C6
Rowledge GU10 145 E4
Rusper RH12 199 D7
Sandhurst GU47 64 A8
Sandhurst, Little Sandhurst GU47 45 A1
Shepperton TW17 34 C3
South Norwood CR7, SE25 42 D5
Staines TW18 12 F4
Stanwell TW19 2 D1
Sunningdale SL5 30 A4
Sutton SM1 59 B5
Tadworth KT20 97 C4
Teddington, Hampton Hill TW12 16 C2
Teddington, Hampton Wick KT1 37 D8
Teddington TW11 17 A3
Thames Ditton KT7 37 A3
Twickenham TW2 16 C8
Walton-on-Thames KT12 35 A1
West End GU24 67 F7
West Wickham BR4 44 B1
Weybridge KT13 53 A6
Wimbledon SW19 19 D3
Woking GU21 69 F2
Woking, Horsell GU21 69 C3
High Standing CR3 100 C2
High Street Collier's Wood SW17, SW19 20 D2
High Street Gn GU8 191 F2
HIGHSTREET GREEN 192 A3
High Street Harlington TW6 3 D7
High Thicket Rd GU10 166 D5
High Tree Cl KT15 52 A5
High Trees
Cheam SM3 39 F2
Croydon CR0 43 E1
Streatham SW2 22 A7
High Trees Cl CR3 100 F5
High Trees Ct
Caterham CR3 100 F4
Sidlow RH6 160 A4
High Trees Rd RH2 139 D8
Highview CR3 100 E2
High View
Belmont SM2 77 F8
Godalming GU7 150 E4
High View *continued*
Gomshall GU5 133 C4
Knaphill GU21 68 E2
5 Penge SE19 22 F1
High View Ave SM6 60 F5
High View Cl
Farnborough GU14 85 A4
South Norwood SE19, SE25 42 F7
Highview Cres GU15 46 F1
Highview Ct
2 Putney SW19 19 E7
2 Reigate RH2 118 D1
High View Ct SW16 22 A5
High View Lodge 18 GU11 105 A2
High View Prim Sch SM6 60 E5
High View Rd
Farnborough GU14 85 A4
Guildford GU2 129 E6
Lightwater GU18 66 F8
South Norwood SE19 22 D2
Highway RG45 45 A5
Highwayman's Ridge GU20 48 B6
Highway The SM2 59 C2
Highwold CR5 79 A1
Highwood BR2 44 D6
Highwood Cl
Dulwich SE22 23 A7
Kenley CR8 80 C2
Highwood Pk RH11 201 C2
Highwoods
Caterham CR3 100 E2
Leatherhead KT22 95 C6
Highwoods Ct RH12 216 D3
Hilary Ave CR4 41 A6
Hilbert Rd SM3 58 D7
Hilborough Cl SW19 20 C1
Hilda Duke's Way RH19 185 E3
Hildenborough Gdns BR1 24 F2
Hildenbrough Ho BR3 23 F1
Hildenlea Pl BR2 44 E7
Hildenley Cl RH1 119 D7
Hildens The RH4 135 C5
Hilder Gdns GU14 85 D3
Hilders La TN8 144 F4
Hilders The KT21 76 B2
Hilditch Ho 7 TW10 6 F1
Hildreth St SW12 21 B7
Hildreth Street Mews 3 SW12 21 B7
Hilgay GU1 109 F1
Hilgay Cl GU1 109 F1
Hilgay Ct GU1 109 F1
Hillacre CR3 100 E2
Hillars Heath Rd CR5 79 E4
Hillary Cl
East Grinstead RH19 186 A3
Farnham GU9 146 B7
Hillary Cres KT12 35 C1
Hillary Ct TW19 13 E7
Hillary Dr
Crowthorne RG45 45 B6
Isleworth TW7 5 F2
Hillary Ho 10 RH1 118 F2
Hillary Rd GU9 146 B7
Hillbarn CR2 80 E8
Hillberry RG12 27 C2
Hillbrook Gdns KT13 53 A3
Hillbrook Prim Sch SW17 21 A4
Hillbrook Rd SW17 21 A4
Hillbrook Rise GU9 125 B6
Hillbrow
New Malden KT3 38 F6
3 Reigate RH2 118 C1
Richmond TW10 6 E1
Hillbrow Cl GU3 108 B2
Hillbrow Cotts RH9 121 C3
Hillbrow Ct
Esher KT10 55 C6
Godstone RH9 121 C3
Hillbrow Rd
Catford BR1 24 E2
Esher KT10 55 C6
Hillbury Cl CR6 81 C1
Hillbury Gdns CR6 81 C1
Hillbury Rd
Upper Tooting SW17 21 B5
Warlingham CR3, CR6 81 B1
Hill Cl
Cobham KT11 74 A7
Purley CR8 80 C6
Woking GU21 69 D3
Wonersh GU5 152 B6
Hill Copse View RG12 27 E8
Hill Corner Farm Est GU14 84 D7
Hillcote Ave SW16 22 A1
Hill Cres
Kingston upon Thames KT5 37 F4
North Cheam KT4 58 C8
Hillcrest
Heath End GU9 125 D8
Oxted RH8 122 E6
Weybridge KT13 53 B6
Hill Crest
Dormans Park RH19 185 E6
Elstead GU8 148 D4
Hillcrest Ave KT16 51 E6
Hillcrest Cl
Beckenham BR3 43 F3
Crawley RH10 202 D6
Epsom KT18 76 F4
Forest Hill SE26 23 A4
Hillcrest Ct
3 Lewisham SE6 24 D8
Sutton SM2 59 D4
Hillcrest Ct *continued*
4 Weybridge KT13 53 B6
Hillcrest Gdns KT10 55 F7
Hillcrest Ho GU4 110 C3
Hill Crest London Sch 9 CR0 42 F1
Hillcrest (Mobile Home Pk) KT20 116 B4
Hillcrest Par CR5 79 B5
Hillcrest Rd
Biggin Hill TN16 83 D3
Camberley GU15 66 B7
Guildford GU2 108 F2
Kenley CR3 80 F2
Wallington CR8 60 F1
Hillcrest Sch RH13 215 C4
Hillcrest View BR3 43 F3
Hillcroft GU27 208 C6
Hillcroft Ave CR5, CR8 79 D6
Hillcroft Coll KT6 37 E3
Hillcroft Ct CR3 100 E4
Hillcroft Prim Sch CR3 100 E4
Hillcroome Rd SM2 59 D4
Hillcross Ave SM4 39 E4
Hillcross Prim Sch SM4 39 F5
Hill Ct
Farncombe GU7 150 E6
Haslemere GU27 208 B6
8 Kingston upon Thames KT2 18 B1
14 Surbiton KT6 37 E4
8 Wimbledon SW19 19 E2
Hilldale Rd SM1 58 F6
Hilldeane Rd CR8 61 A1
Hilldown Ct SW16 21 E1
Hilldown Rd
Streatham SW16 21 F1
West Wickham BR2 44 F1
Hill Dr SW16 41 F6
Hillers KT20 97 B6
Hilley Field La KT22 94 C6
Hill Farm Cl GU27 207 F5
Hillfield Ave SM4 40 E4
Hillfield Cl
Guildford GU1 110 C3
Redhill RH1 119 A1
Hillfield Ct KT10 55 B5
Hillfield Lo SW17 20 F3
Hillfield Par SM4 40 D3
Hillfield Rd RH1 119 A1
Hill Field Rd TW12 35 F8
Hillford Pl RH1 140 A3
Hillgarth GU26 188 D5
Hillgate Pl SW12 21 B8
Hill Gr TW13 15 F6
Hillground Gdns CR2 61 B1
Hillhampton SL5 29 F2
Hill Ho
Beacon Hill GU26 188 C6
Bromley BR2 44 F7
Hill House Cl RH10 204 A5
Hill House Dr
Hampton TW12 36 A8
Reigate RH2 139 B7
Weybridge KT13 72 A8
Hillhouse La RH12 194 F1
Hill House Rd SW16 21 F3
Hillhurst Gdns CR3 100 E7
Hilliard Ct SM6 60 D4
Hilliards View GU6 174 E4
Hillier Gdns CR0 61 A5
Hillier Ho
Guildford GU1 110 A1
Guildford, Guildford Park GU2 130 B7
Hillier Lodge TW11 16 D3
Hillier Mews GU1 110 A1
Hillier Pl KT9 56 C4
Hillier Rd GU1 110 A1
Hillier's La CR0, SM6 60 E7
Hillingdale
Biggin Hill TN16 83 B1
Crawley RH11 201 C1
Hillingdon Ave TW19 13 E7
Hill La KT20 97 E6
Hillmead RH11 200 F6
Hill Mead RH12 217 B3
Hillmont Rd KT10 55 E7
Hillmore Gr SE26 23 E3
Hillmount 13 GU22 69 E1
Hill Park Dr KT22 94 F8
Hill Pl RH11 201 C5
Hill Rd
Beacon Hill GU26 188 C6
Carshalton SM5 59 E4
Fetcham KT23 94 B5
Grayshott GU26 188 C3
Haslemere GU27 208 C6
Heath End GU9 125 D7
Mitcham CR4 21 B1
Purley CR8 79 F7
Sutton SM1 59 B5
Hillrise
Brands Hill SL3 1 A8
Walton-on-Thames KT12 34 F2
Hill Rise
Dorking RH4 115 A1
Forest Hill SE23 23 B7
Hinchley Wood KT10 56 B8
Richmond TW10 6 D2
Hill Rise Ct KT22 95 B6
Hillsborough Ct GU14 84 E8
Hillsborough Pk GU15 66 C5
Hills Farm La RH12 216 F1
Hillside
Ascot SL5 29 C4
Banstead SM7 77 E4
10 Carshalton SM1 59 D5
Hillside *continued*
Crawley Down RH10 204 B8
Esher KT10 55 B5
Forest Row RH18 206 F3
Horsham RH12 217 A2
Sandhurst GU15 64 F7
Wentworth GU25 31 C3
Wimbledon SW19 19 D2
Woking GU22 89 D7
Hillside Ave CR8 80 B6
Hillside Cl
Banstead SM7 77 E3
Brockham RH3 137 A8
Crawley RH11 201 B4
East Grinstead RH19 185 E3
Headley Down GU35 187 A6
Knaphill GU21 68 D2
Merton SM4 39 E5
Hillside Cres GU16 85 F7
Hillside Ct
6 Guildford GU1 130 E8
7 Kingston upon Thames KT2 18 B1
Hillside Flats GU26 188 D6
Hillside Gdns
Addlestone KT15 51 F5
Brockham RH3 116 A1
Streatham SW2 22 A6
Wallington SM6 60 C3
Hillside Glen CR0 61 B6
Hillside Ho CR0 61 B6
Hillside La
Coney Hall BR2 63 F8
Heath End GU9 125 D8
Hillside Pk SL5 29 F1
Hillside Rd
Aldershot GU11 126 A8
Ash GU12 106 B3
Ashtead KT21 75 F2
Beckenham BR2 44 F6
Belmont SM2 58 F3
Coulsdon CR5 79 F1
Croydon CR0 61 B6
East Ewell KT17 58 C1
Farnham GU10 146 C3
Haslemere GU27 207 F5
Heath End GU9 125 E7
Kingston upon Thames KT5 38 A4
Streatham SW2 22 A6
Tatsfield TN16 103 E8
Whyteleafe CR3 81 A1
Hillside Way GU7 150 D7
Hills Manor RH12 217 A2
Hillsmead Way CR2 81 B6
Hills Pl RH12 217 A2
Hillspur Cl GU2 108 F2
Hillspur Rd GU2 108 F2
Hill St TW10 6 D2
Hillswood Dr KT16 51 C6
Hill The CR3 100 F3
Hillthorpe Cl CR8 60 F1
Hill Top SM3 39 F2
Hilltop Cl
Ascot SL5 29 E7
Guildford GU3 108 F5
Leatherhead KT22 95 C4
Hilltop Cotts RH6 160 D2
Hilltop Ct SE19 42 D8
Hilltop La CR3, RH1 100 A1
Hilltop Prim Sch RH11 201 C4
Hilltop Rd
Kenley CR3 80 F2
Reigate RH2 139 B7
Hilltop Rise KT23 94 C1
Hilltop Wlk CR3 101 E6
Hillview
Whyteleafe CR3 80 F2
Wimbledon SW20 19 B1
Hill View
Dorking RH4 136 C8
Mitcham CR4 41 E5
Hill View Cl
Purley CR8 80 B8
Tadworth KT20 97 C6
Hill View Cres GU2 108 F3
Hillview Ct SE19 22 E4
Hill View Ct 15 GU22 69 E1
Hillview Dr RH1 140 A8
Hill View Pl KT11 73 F6
Hillview Rd SM1 59 D7
Hill View Rd
Claygate KT10 56 A3
Farnham GU9 124 F2
Twickenham TW1 6 A1
Woking GU22 69 F1
Hillworth 7 BR3 44 B7
Hillworth Rd SW2 22 A8
Hillybarn Rd RH11 180 C1
Hilly Mead SW19 19 E1
Hilsea Point 7 SW15 19 B7
Hilton Ct RH6 161 C4
Hilton Way CR2 81 B4
Himley Rd SW17 20 F2
Hinchley Cl KT10 55 F7
Hinchley Dr KT10 55 F7
Hinchley Manor KT10 55 F7
Hinchley Way KT10 56 A7
HINCHLEY WOOD 55 F8
Hinchley Wood Prim Sch KT10 56 A8
Hinchley Wood Sch & Sixth Form Ctr KT10 56 A8
Hinchley Wood Sta KT10 55 F7
Hindell Cl GU14 85 A8
HINDHEAD 188 F4
Hindhead Cl RH11 201 C4
Hindhead Common★ GU8 189 A5
Hindhead Ho GU26 188 F4
Hindhead Point 6 SW15 19 B7
Hindhead Rd GU26, GU27 188 F2
Hindhead Way SM6 60 E5
Hindsley's Pl SE23 23 C6
Hine Cl
Epsom KT19 76 B8
Hooley CR5 99 C5
Hinstock Cl GU14 85 A3
Hinton Ave TW4 4 D3
Hinton Cl RG45 45 B7
Hinton Dr RG45 45 B7
Hinton Rd SM6 60 C4
Hipley Ct GU1 131 A8
Hipley St GU22 90 B7
Hippisley Ct TW7 5 F4
Hitchcock Cl TW17 33 F6
Hitchings Way RH2 139 A5
Hitherbury Cl GU2 130 C6
Hitherfield Prim Sch SW2 22 A6
Hitherfield Rd SE27, SW16 22 A5
Hither Green La SE13 24 E8
Hitherhooks Hill RG42 26 E8
Hitherlands SW12 21 B6
Hithermoor Rd TW19 2 A2
Hitherwood GU6 174 E2
Hitherwood Cl RH2 118 E3
Hitherwood Ct SE19 22 F4
Hitherwood Dr SE19 22 F4
H Jones Cres GU11 105 C3
Hoadly Rd SW16 21 D6
Hobart Ct CR2 61 D5
Hobart Gdns CR7 42 D6
Hobart Ho 25 KT6 37 E4
Hobart Pl 15 TW10 6 F1
Hobart Rd KT4 58 B7
Hobbs Cl KT14 71 B6
Hobbs Ind Est RH7 184 D7
Hobbs Rd
Crawley RH11 201 A2
5 West Norwood SE27 22 C4
Hobill Wlk KT5 37 F3
Hocken Mead RH10 202 D8
HOCKERING ESTATE 70 B1
Hockering Gdns GU22 70 B1
Hockering Rd GU22 70 B1
Hockford Cl GU24 88 B1
Hockley Ind Ctr RH1 139 F8
Hodge La SL4 9 A3
Hodges Cl GU19 47 E1
Hodgkin Cl RH10 202 C5
Hodgson Gdns GU4 110 A4
HOE 154 E8
Hoe Bridge Sch GU22 90 B8
Hoebrook Cl GU22 89 E6
Hoe Cotts GU5 154 E8
Hoe La
Hascombe GU8 172 D4
Peaslake GU5, RH5 154 F8
Hoffmann Gdns CR2 62 B3
Hogarth Ave TW15 14 C2
Hogarth Bsns Pk W4 7 E8
Hogarth Cl GU47 64 E6
Hogarth Cres
Mitcham CR4, SW19 40 D8
Thornton Heath CR0 42 C2
Hogarth Ct
Dulwich SE19 22 F4
Heston TW5 4 E7
Hogarth Gdns TW5 5 A7
Hogarth Ho
1 Carshalton SM1 59 D5
6 West Norwood SE27 22 C4
Hogarth La W4 7 E8
Hogarth Rd RH10 201 F3
Hogarth Rdbt 9 W4 7 E8
Hogarth's Ho★ W4 7 E8
Hogarth Way TW12 36 C8
Hogden La RH5 113 E3
HOG HATCH 125 A6
Hoghatch La GU9 125 A6
Hogoak La SL4 8 A8
Hogscross La CR5 98 F5
Hogshill La KT11 73 C5
Hogsmill Way KT19 57 C6
Hogspudding La RH5 158 C2
Hogtrough La
Nutfield RH1 140 D8
Oxted RH8 122 B6
Hogwood Rd RH14 212 C3
Holbeach Mews 2 SW12 21 B7
Holbeach Prim Sch SE6 24 A8
Holbeach Rd SE6 24 B8
Holbeck RG12 26 F3
Holbein Rd RH10 201 F3
Holberry Ho 5 SE21 22 E4
Holborn Way CR4 40 F7
Holbreck Pl GU22 69 F1
HOLBROOK 217 E8
Holbrook Cl
Heath End GU9 125 F8
Shalford GU4 130 E2
Holbrook Ct TW20 12 C3
Holbrooke Pl 26 TW9 6 D2
Holbrook Ho 5 SW2 21 F7
Holbrook Meadow TW20 12 C2
Holbrook Pk RH12 217 E8
Holbrook Prim Sch RH12 217 E7
Holbrook School La RH12 217 E7
Holbrook Way GU11 126 B7
Holcon Ct RH1 119 A4
Holden Pl KT11 73 B5

Holdernesse Rd
Isleworth TW7 . . . . . 6 A6
7 Upper Tooting SW17 . . . 21 A6
Holderness Way SE27 . . . . 22 B3
Holder Rd
Aldershot GU12 . . . . . 105 E1
Crawley RH10 . . . . . 202 B3
Holdfast La GU27 . . . . . 208 F7
Holdsworth Ho 4 SW2 . . . 22 A8
Hole Hill RH4 . . . . . 135 B7
Hole La TN8 . . . . . 144 F7
Holford Rd GU1 . . . . . 110 C1
HOLLAND 123 A1
Holland Ave
Belmont SM2 . . . . . 59 A2
Wimbledon SW20 . . . . . 38 F8
Holland Cl
Coney Hall BR2 . . . . . 63 F8
Epsom KT19 . . . . . 76 C8
Farnham GU9 . . . . . 146 E8
Redhill RH1 . . . . . 118 F1
Holland Cres RH8 . . . . . 123 A2
Holland Ct TW15 . . . . . 13 F2
Holland Dr SE23 . . . . . 23 E5
Holland Gdns
Brentford TW8 . . . . . 6 E8
Egham TW20 . . . . . 32 F7
Holland Jun Sch RH8 . . . 123 A1
Holland La RH8 . . . . . 123 A2
Holland Pines RG12 . . . . . 26 F2
Holland Rd
Croydon SE25 . . . . . 43 A4
Oxted RH8 . . . . . 123 A1
Hollands Field RH13 . . . . 216 E4
Hollands The
Feltham TW13 . . . . . 15 D4
New Malden KT4 . . . . . 38 F1
3 Woking GU22 . . . . . 69 E1
Hollands Way
East Grinstead RH19 . . . . . 186 A4
Warnham RH12 . . . . . 216 F8
Holland Way BR2 . . . . . 63 F8
Hollerith Rise RG12 . . . . . 27 B3
Holles Cl TW12 . . . . . 16 A3
Hollie Cl RH6 . . . . . 162 B2
Hollies Ave KT14 . . . . . 70 F6
Hollies Cl
South Norwood SW16 . . . . . 22 A2
Twickenham TW1 . . . . . 16 F6
Hollies Ct KT15 . . . . . 52 C5
Hollies The
Oxted RH8 . . . . . 123 B2
14 Redhill RH1 . . . . . 118 F2
Streatham SW12 . . . . . 21 C6
Hollies Way 3 SW12 . . . . 21 A8
Hollin Ct RH10 . . . . . 181 E1
Hollingbourne Cres
RH11 . . . . . 201 C1
Hollingsworth Ct 7 KT6 . . 37 D2
Hollingsworth Rd CR0,
CR2 . . . . . 62 B4
Hollington Cres KT3 . . . . . 39 A3
Hollingworth Cl KT8 . . . . . 35 F5
Hollis Row RH1 . . . . . 139 F7
Hollis Wood Dr GU10 . . . . 145 E5
Hollman Gdns SW16 . . . . . 22 B2
Holloway Dr GU25 . . . . . 31 E5
HOLLOWAY HILL 150 E2
Holloway Hill
Godalming GU7 . . . . . 150 D4
Lyne KT16 . . . . . 51 D8
Holloway La UB7 . . . . . 2 E8
Holloway St TW3 . . . . . 5 B4
Hollow Cl GU2 . . . . . 130 B8
Hollow Combe SE26 . . . . . 23 B4
Hollow La
Dormansland RH19, RH7 . . 186 D6
Virginia Water GU25 . . . . . 31 C6
Wotton RH5 . . . . . 134 D2
Hollow The
Crawley RH11 . . . . . 200 F5
Shackleford GU7 . . . . . 149 F4
Holly Acre GU22 . . . . . 89 C4
Holly Ave
Frimley GU16 . . . . . 66 B3
Walton-on-Thames KT12 . . . 35 D1
Woodham KT15 . . . . . 52 A1
Hollybank GU24 . . . . . 67 F6
Hollybank Cl TW12 . . . . . 16 A3
Hollybank Rd KT14 . . . . . 71 A5
Holly Bank Rd GU22 . . . . . 89 B7
Hollybush Bsns Ctr RH6 . 182 F4
Hollybush Cl RH10 . . . . . 201 E8
Holly Bush Ind Pk GU11 . 105 E5
Hollybush La GU11 . . . . . 105 E6
Holly Bush La TW12 . . . . . 15 F1
Hollybush Rd
Crawley RH10 . . . . . 201 E8
Kingston upon Thames KT2 . 17 E2
Hollybush Tk GU19, GU20 . 47 F6
Holly Cl
Aldershot GU12 . . . . . 105 C2
Beckenham BR3 . . . . . 44 C5
Crawley RH10 . . . . . 202 A8
Englefield Green TW20 . . . . 11 B2
Farnborough GU14 . . . . . 85 A4
Feltham TW13 . . . . . 15 E3
Headley Down GU35 . . . . . 187 C5
Horsham RH12 . . . . . 218 B5
Longcross KT16 . . . . . 50 A7
Wallington SM6 . . . . . 60 B3
Woking GU21 . . . . . 89 B8
Hollycombe TW20 . . . . . 11 C4
Holly Cott KT7 . . . . . 37 A1
Holly Cres BR3 . . . . . 43 F4
Hollycroft Cl
Harmondsworth UB7 . . . . . 3 A8
South Croydon CR2 . . . . . 61 E5
Hollycroft Gdns UB7 . . . . . 3 A8
Holly Ct
4 Belmont SM2 . . . . . 59 A3
Catford SE6 . . . . . 24 C5
Leatherhead KT22 . . . . . 95 A5
Hollydene BR1 . . . . . 44 F8
Hollyfield Rd KT5 . . . . . 37 F2
Hollyfield Sch The KT6 . . . 37 E4
Hollyfields Cl GU15 . . . . . 65 B5
Holly Gate KT15 . . . . . 52 B6
Holly Gn KT13 . . . . . 53 D6
Holly Grove Cl TW3 . . . . . 4 F3
Holly Hedge Cl GU16 . . . . 65 E2
Hollyhedge Rd KT11 . . . . . 73 B5
Holly Hedge Rd GU16 . . . . 65 E2
Hollyhill Dr SM7 . . . . . 78 A3
Hollyhill Pk SM7 . . . . . 78 A2
Holly Ho
Bracknell RG12 . . . . . 27 B3
Brentford TW8 . . . . . 6 C8
Dorking RH4 . . . . . 136 B7
Whyteleafe CR3 . . . . . 80 F2
Hollyhock Dr GU24 . . . . . 68 A4
Hollyhock Cl RG45 . . . . . 45 A6
Holly Hough KT20 . . . . . 116 B5
Holly La
Banstead SM7 . . . . . 78 C2
Godalming GU7 . . . . . 150 C4
Worplesdon GU3 . . . . . 108 D7
Holly Lane E SM7 . . . . . 78 B3
Holly Lane W SM7 . . . . . 78 B2
Holly Lea GU4 . . . . . 109 D7
Holly Lo SW20 . . . . . 39 B7
Holly Lodge
Oatlands Park KT13 . . . . . 53 E7
4 Wimbledon SW19 . . . . . 19 E2
16 Woking GU22 . . . . . 69 F2
Holly Lodge (Mobile Home Pk) KT20 . . . . . 97 E1
Holly Lodge Prim Sch
GU12 . . . . . 105 F8
Hollymead SM5 . . . . . 59 F7
Hollymead Rd CR5 . . . . . 79 A1
Hollymeoak Rd CR5 . . . . . 79 B1
Hollymoor La KT19 . . . . . 57 D1
Hollymount Sch SW20 . . . . 39 C8
Holly Rd
Aldershot GU12 . . . . . 105 D1
Farnborough GU14 . . . . . 85 A4
Hampton TW12 . . . . . 16 C2
Hounslow TW3 . . . . . 5 B3
Reigate RH2 . . . . . 139 B7
Twickenham TW1 . . . . . 17 A7
Hollyridge GU27 . . . . . 208 B6
Holly Ridge GU24 . . . . . 67 E6
Holly Spring Inf Sch RG12 27 E7
Holly Spring Jun Sch
RG12 . . . . . 27 E7
Holly Spring La RG12 . . . . 27 D8
Hollytree Cl SW19 . . . . . 19 D7
Hollytree Gdns GU16 . . . . 85 D8
Holly Tree Rd CR3 . . . . . 100 E5
Holly Way
Blackwater GU17 . . . . . 64 D4
Mitcham CR4 . . . . . 41 D6
Holly Wlk SL4 . . . . . 9 E4
Hollywoods CR0 . . . . . 62 F2
Holman Ct KT17 . . . . . 58 A2
Holman Rd KT19 . . . . . 57 C5
Holmbank Dr TW17 . . . . . 34 E5
Holmbrook Cl GU14 . . . . . 84 C4
Holmbrook Gdns GU14 . . . . 84 C4
Holmbury Ave RG45 . . . . . 45 A7
Holmbury Cl RH11 . . . . . 201 C4
Holmbury Ct
6 Croydon CR0 . . . . . 61 E5
Mitcham SW19 . . . . . 20 E1
Upper Tooting SW17 . . . . . 20 F5
Holmbury Dr RH5 . . . . . 136 C4
Holmbury Gr CR0 . . . . . 62 F3
Holmbury Hill Rd RH5 . . . . 155 B3
Holmbury Keep RH6 . . . . . 161 C4
Holmbury Rd RH5 . . . . . 155 D1
HOLMBURY ST MARY 155 B5
Holmbush Cl RH12 . . . . . 217 D6
Holmbush Farm World★
RH12 . . . . . 200 B1
Holm Cl KT15 . . . . . 70 E7
Holmcroft
Crawley RH10 . . . . . 201 E5
Walton on the Hill KT20 . . . . 97 B2
Holm Ct
6 Caterham CR3 . . . . . 100 D5
Dorking RH4 . . . . . 136 B4
Farncombe GU7 . . . . . 150 D7
Holmdene Cl BR3 . . . . . 44 C7
Holme Chase KT13 . . . . . 53 C4
Holme Cl RG45 . . . . . 45 A7
Holme Ct 10 TW7 . . . . . 6 A4
Holmefield Pl KT15 . . . . . 52 B1
Holme Grange Craft Village
RG40 . . . . . 25 E2
Holme Grange Sch RG40 . 25 F3
HOLME GREEN 25 F3
Holme Lodge GU7 . . . . . 150 E6
Holmes Cl
Ascot SL5 . . . . . 29 C3
Purley CR8 . . . . . 79 F6
Woking GU23 . . . . . 89 F6
Wokingham RG41 . . . . . 25 A4
Holmes Cres RG41 . . . . . 25 A4
Holmes Ct GU26 . . . . . 188 D3
Holmesdale 2 KT13 . . . . . 53 D4
Holmesdale Ave
Mortlake SW14 . . . . . 7 B3
Holmesdale Ave *continued*
Redhill RH1 . . . . . 119 C4
Holmesdale Cl
Guildford GU1 . . . . . 110 B2
South Norwood SE25 . . . . . 42 F6
Holmesdale Pk RH1 . . . . . 119 F1
Holmesdale Rd
Dorking RH5 . . . . . 136 C3
Reigate RH2 . . . . . 118 B2
Richmond TW9 . . . . . 6 F6
South Norwood SE25 . . . . . 42 E5
South Nutfield RH1 . . . . . 140 F7
Teddington TW11 . . . . . 17 C2
Thornton Heath CR0 . . . . . 42 D4
Holmesdale Sch RH2 . . . . . 118 B3
Holmesdale Villas RH5 . . 136 B1
Holmes Rd
Merton SW19 . . . . . 20 C1
Twickenham TW1 . . . . . 16 F6
Holmeswood 18 SM2 . . . . . 59 B3
HOLMETHORPE 119 B4
Holmethorpe Ave RH1 . . . 119 B4
Holmethorpe Ind Est
RH1 . . . . . 119 B4
Holmewood Cl RG41 . . . . . 25 A2
Holmewood Gdns SW2 . . . 21 F8
Holmewood Ho SM7 . . . . . 77 F2
Holmewood Rd
South Norwood SE25 . . . . . 42 E6
Streatham SW2 . . . . . 21 F8
Holmgrove Ho CR8 . . . . . 80 A7
Holmhurst SW20 . . . . . 19 C1
Holming End RH12 . . . . . 218 B5
Holmlea Ct CR0 . . . . . 61 D6
Holmoak Cl CR8 . . . . . 60 F1
Holmoaks House BR3 . . . . 44 C7
Holmshaw Cl SE26, SE6 . . . 23 E4
Holmsley Cl KT3 . . . . . 38 F2
Holmsley Ho SW15 . . . . . 18 F8
Holmstead Ct CR2 . . . . . 61 D5
Holmstoun KT15 . . . . . 70 E7
Holmwood 2 KT5 . . . . . 37 F3
Holmwood Ave CR2 . . . . . 80 F6
Holmwood Cl
Addlestone KT15 . . . . . 52 A5
Cheam SM2 . . . . . 58 D3
East Horsley KT24 . . . . . 112 E6
HOLMWOOD CORNER 157 D5
Holmwood Ct KT3 . . . . . 38 D6
Holmwood Gdns SM6 . . . . 60 B4
Holmwood Rd
Chessington KT9 . . . . . 56 E5
East Ewell KT17, SM2 . . . . . 58 C2
Holmwood Sta RH5 . . . . . 157 C4
Holmwood View Rd RH5 . 136 B1
Holne Chase SM4 . . . . . 40 A3
Holroyd Rd KT10 . . . . . 55 F2
Holsart Cl KT20 . . . . . 97 B5
Holstein Ave KT13 . . . . . 53 A6
Holsworthy Way KT9 . . . . . 56 C5
Holt Barns GU35 . . . . . 166 A5
Holt Cl GU14 . . . . . 85 C7
Holt Copse & Joel Pk Nature
Reserve★ RG40 . . . . . 25 A7
Holt La RG41 . . . . . 25 B7
Holton Heath 8 RG12 . . . . 27 F5
HOLT POUND 145 D4
Holt Pound La GU10 . . . . . 145 C5
Holt Sch The RG41 . . . . . 25 B7
Holt The
Morden SM4 . . . . . 40 A5
Wallington SM6 . . . . . 60 C6
Holt Wood CR6 . . . . . 82 A3
Holtwood Rd KT22 . . . . . 74 C6
Holtye Ave RH19 . . . . . 186 A3
Holtye Pl RH19 . . . . . 186 B3
Holtye Rd RH19 . . . . . 186 B3
Holtye Wlk RH10 . . . . . 202 A4
Holwood Cl KT12 . . . . . 54 C8
Holybourne Ave SW15 . . . . 19 A8
Holy Cross Girls Sch The 4
KT3 . . . . . 38 E4
Holy Cross Hospl GU27 . . 207 F7
Holy Cross Prep Sch KT2 . 18 C1
Holy Cross RC Prim Sch
SE6 . . . . . 24 C7
Holy Family RC Prim Sch The
KT15 . . . . . 52 A5
Holy Ghost RC Prim Sch
SW12 . . . . . 21 A8
Holyhead Ct KT1 . . . . . 37 D5
Holyoake Ave GU21 . . . . . 69 C2
Holyoake Cres GU21 . . . . . 69 C2
Holyrood RH19 . . . . . 206 A8
Holy Trinity CE Jun Sch
Guildford GU1 . . . . . 130 F7
Wallington SM6 . . . . . 60 C6
Holy Trinity CE Prim Sch
8 Forest Hill SE26 . . . . . 23 C6
Mortlake TW10 . . . . . 7 A3
Streatham SW2 . . . . . 21 F8
Sunningdale SL5 . . . . . 30 A3
West End GU24 . . . . . 68 A7
Holy Trinity CE Sch The
RH11 . . . . . 201 A4
Holy Trinity Prim Sch
SW19 . . . . . 20 B2
Holywell GU22 . . . . . 89 B6
Holywell Cl
Farnborough GU14 . . . . . 85 A7
Stanwell TW19 . . . . . 13 E7
Holywell Way TW19 . . . . . 13 E7
Homan Ho 4 SW4 . . . . . 21 D8
Hombrook Dr RG42 . . . . . 26 E8
Hombrook Ho RG42 . . . . . 26 E8
Homebeech Ho 7 GU22 . . 69 E1
Home Cl
Carshalton SM5 . . . . . 59 F8
Home Cl *continued*
Crawley RH10 . . . . . 202 C8
Fetcham KT22 . . . . . 94 D6
Virginia Water GU25 . . . . . 31 D3
Homecoppice Ho 1 BR1 . . 24 F1
Homecroft Rd SE26 . . . . . 23 C3
Home Ct KT6 . . . . . 37 D4
Homedale Ho SM1 . . . . . 59 B6
Home Farm RH2 . . . . . 118 F6
Home Farm Cl
Betchworth RH3 . . . . . 137 E8
Burgh Heath KT18 . . . . . 77 D2
Esher KT10 . . . . . 55 B4
Farnborough GU14 . . . . . 85 D6
Ottershaw KT16 . . . . . 51 A3
Thames Ditton KT7 . . . . . 36 F2
Upper Halliford TW17 . . . . . 34 E5
Home Farm Cotts GU8 . . 149 C5
Home Farm Gdns KT12 . . . 54 C8
Home Farm Ho 1 RH12 . 217 C2
Home Farm Rd GU7 . . . . . 150 F2
Homefield
Hersham KT12 . . . . . 54 D6
Leatherhead KT22 . . . . . 95 C6
Morden SM4 . . . . . 40 A5
Thursley GU8 . . . . . 169 C3
Homefield Cl
Horley RH6 . . . . . 161 B4
Leatherhead KT22 . . . . . 95 C6
Woodham KT15 . . . . . 70 E7
Homefield Gdns
Burgh Heath KT20 . . . . . 97 C7
Mitcham CR4, SW19 . . . . . 40 D7
Homefield Ho SE23 . . . . . 23 D5
Homefield Pk SM1 . . . . . 59 B4
Homefield Pl SW19 . . . . . 19 D3
Homefield Prep Sch SM1 . 59 A5
Homefield Rd
Coulsdon CR5 . . . . . 100 B7
Walton-on-Thames KT12 . . . 35 E2
Warlingham CR6 . . . . . 101 C8
Wimbledon SW19 . . . . . 19 E3
Homegreen Ho GU27 . . . . 208 A6
Homeland Dr SM2 . . . . . 59 B2
Homelands
Kingsley Green GU27 . . . . . 208 B1
Leatherhead KT22 . . . . . 95 C6
Homelands Dr SE19 . . . . . 22 E1
Homelea Cl GU14 . . . . . 85 B8
Homeleigh Cres GU12 . . . 106 A8
Homeleigh Ct 8 SW16 . . . 21 E5
Home Mdw SM7 . . . . . 78 A3
Homemead SW12 . . . . . 21 B6
Homemead Rd CR0 . . . . . 41 C3
Home Park Cl GU5 . . . . . 151 F6
Homepark Ho GU9 . . . . . 125 C2
Home Park Rd SW19 . . . . . 19 F4
Home Park Wlk KT1 . . . . . 37 D5
Home Pk RH8 . . . . . 123 A4
Homer Rd CR0 . . . . . 43 D3
Homersham Rd KT1 . . . . . 38 B7
Homesdale Rd CR3 . . . . . 100 D4
Homestall GU2 . . . . . 108 D2
Homestall Rd RH19 . . . . . 206 E8
Homestead GU6 . . . . . 174 F4
Homestead Dr GU3 . . . . . 107 D4
Homestead Gdns KT10 . . . 55 E5
Homestead Rd
Caterham CR3 . . . . . 100 D4
Staines TW18 . . . . . 13 B2
Homesteads The BR3 . . . . 24 B2
Homestead The GU1 . . . . . 130 F7
Homestead Way CR0 . . . . . 82 D7
Homestream Ho RH12 . . . 217 B1
Homethorne Ho RH11 . . . 201 C5
Homewalk Ho SE26 . . . . . 23 C4
Homewater Ho 1 KT17 . . . 76 E6
Homewaters Ave TW16 . . . 34 F8
Homewood GU6 . . . . . 175 A3
Homewood Cl TW12 . . . . . 15 F2
Homewood Gdns SE25 . . . 42 E4
Homewoods 2 SW12 . . . . . 21 C8
Homeworth 8 GU22 . . . . . 69 E1
Homildon Ho 10 SE26 . . . . 23 A5
Homington Ct KT2 . . . . . 17 E1
Hone Hill GU47 . . . . . 64 B8
Hones Yard Bsns Pk
GU9 . . . . . 125 D2
Honeybrook Rd SW12,
SW4 . . . . . 21 C8
Honeycrock Ct RH1 . . . . . 140 A2
Honeycrock La RH1 . . . . . 140 B2
Honeyfield Mews 15 SE23 . 23 D5
Honey Hill RG40 . . . . . 26 A1
Honeyhill Rd RG42 . . . . . 27 A8
Honeypot La TN8 . . . . . 144 D4
Honeypots Rd GU22 . . . . . 89 D5
Honeysuckle Bottom
KT24 . . . . . 112 E2
Honeysuckle Cl
Crowthorne RG45 . . . . . 45 A7
Horley RH6 . . . . . 161 C4
Honeysuckle Ct
Colnbrook SL3 . . . . . 1 C7
15 Sutton SM1 . . . . . 59 B4
Honeysuckle Gdns CR0 . . . 43 D1
Honeysuckle La
Crawley RH11 . . . . . 181 C1
Dorking RH5 . . . . . 136 C4
Headley Down GU35 . . . . . 187 B5
Honeysuckle Wlk RH12 . . 218 A5
Honeywood La RH5 . . . . . 196 F5
Honeywood Mus★ SM5 . . . 59 F6
Honeywood Rd
Horsham RH13 . . . . . 218 A4
Isleworth TW7 . . . . . 6 A3
Honeywood Wlk SM5 . . . . . 59 F6
Honister Hts CR8 . . . . . 80 E5
Honister Wlk GU15 . . . . . 66 D4
Honley Rd SE6 . . . . . 24 B8
Honnor Gdns TW7 . . . . . 5 D5
Honnor Rd TW18 . . . . . 13 D1
Honor Oak Rd SE23 . . . . . 23 C8
Hood Ave SW14 . . . . . 7 C2
Hood Cl CR0, CR9 . . . . . 42 B1
Hood Rd SW20 . . . . . 18 F1
HOOK 56 E6
Hooke Rd KT24 . . . . . 92 F2
Hookfield KT18, KT19 . . . . 76 C6
Hookfield Mews KT19 . . . . 76 C6
HOOK HEATH 89 B7
Hook Heath Ave GU22 . . . . 89 C8
Hook Heath Farm GU22 . . 89 A7
Hook Heath Gdns GU22 . . . 88 F6
Hook Heath Rd GU22 . . . . 89 B6
Hook Hill CR2 . . . . . 61 E1
Hook Hill La GU22 . . . . . 89 C6
Hook Hill Pk GU22 . . . . . 89 B6
Hook Ho 9 SW27 . . . . . 22 B3
Hook House La GU8 . . . . . 192 C6
Hookhouse Rd GU8 . . . . . 192 D6
Hook La
Gomshall GU5 . . . . . 133 C2
Puttenham GU3 . . . . . 128 D3
West End GU24 . . . . . 67 C6
Hookley Cl GU8 . . . . . 148 E3
Hookley La GU8 . . . . . 148 E3
Hook Mill La GU18 . . . . . 48 D2
Hook Rd
Chessington KT6 . . . . . 56 E7
Epsom KT19, KT17 . . . . . 57 C2
Ewell KT19 . . . . . 76 D8
Surbiton KT6, KT9 . . . . . 56 E7
Hook Rise N
Surbiton KT6 . . . . . 56 E7
Tolworth KT6 . . . . . 57 B8
Hook Rise S
Chessington KT6 . . . . . 56 E7
Tolworth KT5, KT6 . . . . . 57 B8
Hook Rise South Ind Pk
KT6 . . . . . 57 A7
Hookstile La GU9 . . . . . 125 C1
Hookstone La GU24 . . . . . 67 F8
Hook Underpass KT6 . . . . . 56 E7
HOOKWOOD 160 D2
Hookwood Bglws RH8 . . . 123 B7
Hookwood Cnr RH8 . . . . . 123 B7
Hookwood Cotts KT18 . . . . 96 C3
HOOLEY 99 B5
Hooley La RH1 . . . . . 139 F8
Hoover Ho SE6 . . . . . 24 C4
Hope Ave RG12 . . . . . 27 E2
Hope Cl SM1 . . . . . 59 C5
Hope Ct RH11 . . . . . 201 B1
Hope Fountain GU15 . . . . . 65 F4
Hope Grant's Rd GU11 . . . 105 A4
Hope La GU9 . . . . . 125 B6
Hopeman Cl GU47 . . . . . 64 D7
Hope Pk BR1 . . . . . 24 F1
Hopes Cl TW5 . . . . . 5 A8
Hope St GU8 . . . . . 148 D4
Hope Way GU11 . . . . . 104 F3
Hopfield GU21 . . . . . 69 E3
Hopfield Ave KT14 . . . . . 71 E6
Hophurst Cl RH10 . . . . . 204 B8
Hophurst Dr
Crawley Down RH10 . . . . . 204 B8
Crawley RH10 . . . . . 202 E7
Hophurst Hill RH19 . . . . . 184 D2
Hophurst La RH10 . . . . . 184 B1
Hop Kiln The GU9 . . . . . 146 B8
Hop Kiln Villas GU12 . . . . 105 C1
Hopkin Cl GU2 . . . . . 109 B5
Hopkins Ct RH11 . . . . . 201 B1
Hopper Vale RG12 . . . . . 27 A3
Hoppety The KT20 . . . . . 97 D5
Hoppingwood Ave KT3 . . . 38 E6
Hopton Ct 1 GU2 . . . . . 108 E1
Hopton Gdns KT3 . . . . . 39 A3
Hopton Par SW16 . . . . . 21 E3
Hopton Rd SW16 . . . . . 21 E3
Hopwood Cl SW17 . . . . . 20 C5
Horace Rd KT1 . . . . . 37 F6
Horatio Ave RG42 . . . . . 27 E8
Horatio Ho 4 SW19 . . . . . 20 B1
Horatio Pl SW19 . . . . . 40 A8
Horatius Way CR0 . . . . . 60 F4
Horbury Lodge TW12 . . . . . 16 A1
Hordern Ct RH12 . . . . . 217 A1
Horewood Rd RG12 . . . . . 27 B3
Horizon Bsns Village
KT13 . . . . . 72 A7
HORLEY 161 C3
Horley Anderson Ctr
RH6 . . . . . 160 E3
Horley Inf Sch RH6 . . . . . 161 A3
Horley Lodge La RH1 . . . . 161 A8
Horley Rd
Hookwood RH6 . . . . . 181 B7
Redhill RH1 . . . . . 139 F5
Horley Row RH6 . . . . . 161 A4
Horley Sta RH6 . . . . . 161 B2
Hormer Cl GU47 . . . . . 45 D1
Hornbeam Cl
Farnborough GU14 . . . . . 84 C5
Horsham RH13 . . . . . 217 F1
Sandhurst GU47 . . . . . 45 D1
Hornbeam Copse RG42 . . . 28 A8
Hornbeam Cres TW8 . . . . . 6 B7
Hornbeam Gdns KT3 . . . . . 39 A3
Hornbeam Ho SE26 . . . . . 23 D1
Hornbeam Rd
Guildford GU1 . . . . . 109 C3
Reigate RH2 . . . . . 139 C6
Hornbeam Terr SM5 . . . . . 40 E1
Hornbeam Wlk KT12 . . . . . 53 F2

Hornby Ave RG12 . . . . 27 D2
Hornby Ho 13 TW10 . . . . . . 17 C5
Hornchurch Cl KT2. . . . . . . 17 D3
Hornchurch Hill CR3 . . . . . 80 F1
Horndean Cl
  Crawley RH10 . . . . .182 D2
  3 Roehampton SW15 . . . . 19 A7
Horndean Rd RG12 . . . . 27 F3
HORNE. 162 F5
Hornecourt Hill RH6 . . . .162 F7
Horne Rd TW17 . . . . 34 A5
Horner La CR4 . . . . 40 D7
Hornhatch GU4 . . . . .131 B3
Hornhatch Cl GU4 . . . . . . .131 B3
Hornhatch La GU4 . . . . . . .131 B3
Horniman Dr SE23 . . . . 23 C8
Horniman Grange 7
  SE23. . . . . 23 C7
Horniman Mus & Gdns★
  SE23. . . . . 23 B7
Horniman Prim Sch SE23. 23 B7
Horn Rd GU14 . . . . 84 E5
Hornsby House Sch 5
  SW12 . . . . 21 A7
Hornshill La RH12. . . . . . .213 F7
Horsebrass Dr GU19. . . . . . 47 E2
Horsecroft SM7. . . . . 77 F2
Horsecroft Mdws SM7. . . . 77 F3
Horse Fair KT1. . . . . 37 D7
Horse Gate Ride SL5 . . . . . 29 A3
Horse Hill RH6. . . . . .160 B4
HORSELL. 69 D3
Horsell Birch GU21 . . . . . . 69 A4
Horsell CE Jun Sch GU21. 69 C3
HORSELL COMMON. 69 E6
Horsell Common Rd
  GU21 . . . . 69 C5
Horsell Cl KT16 . . . . 33 B2
Horsell Moor GU21. . . . . . . 69 D2
Horsell Park Cl GU21. . . . . 69 D3
Horsell Pk GU21 . . . . 69 E3
Horsell Rise GU21. . . . . 69 E4
Horsell Rise Cl GU21. . . . . . 69 D4
Horsell Vale GU21. . . . . 69 E3
Horsell Village Sch GU21 . 69 D3
Horsell Way GU21. . . . . 69 C3
Horseshoe Bend GU26 . . . .188 B3
Horseshoe Cl
  Camberley GU15 . . . . 65 F8
  Crawley RH10 . . . . .202 D7
Horseshoe Cres GU15 . . . . 65 F8
Horse Shoe Gn SM1. . . . . . 59 B8
Horseshoe La
  Ash Vale GU12. . . . . .106 A7
  Cranleigh GU6 . . . . .174 D4
Horseshoe Lane E GU1. . . .110 C2
Horseshoe Lane W GU1. . .110 B1
Horseshoe Ridge KT13 . . . 72 C8
Horseshoe The
  Banstead SM7. . . . . 77 F4
  Coulsdon CR5, CR8 . . . . . . 79 D6
  Godalming GU7 . . . . .150 C4
HORSHAM. 217 C3
Horsham Comm Hospl
  RH12. . . . . .217 C3
Horsham Mus★ RH12 . . . .217 C1
Horsham Rd
  Alfold Crossways GU6,
    RH12. . . . . .194 C1
  Alfold GU6 . . . . .193 F8
  Bramley GU5 . . . . .151 E2
  Capel RH5 . . . . .178 D8
  Cranleigh GU6 . . . . .174 E1
  Crawley RH11 . . . . .201 B4
  Dorking, Mid Holmwood
    RH5. . . . . .136 B2
  Dorking RH4 . . . . .136 A6
  East Bedfont TW14 . . . . . . 3 C1
  Ellen's Green RH12, RH5. .196 F3
  Ewhurst GU6 . . . . .175 F3
  Holmbury St M RH5. . . . .155 C6
  Kingsfold RH5 . . . . .178 C2
  Palmers Cross GU5, GU6. .173 D5
  Rusper RH12 . . . . .199 B5
  Sandhurst GU47 . . . . 45 D1
  Shalford GU4 . . . . .130 E3
  South Holmwood RH5. . . .157 C6
  Wallis Wood RH5, GU6. . .176 E4
Horsham Sta RH13. . . . . . .217 D2
Horsham Trad Est RH13 . .217 E4
Horsley Cl KT19 . . . . 76 D6
Horsley Ct KT24. . . . . 92 E1
Horsley Dr
  Kingston upon Thames
    KT2. . . . . 17 D3
  New Addington CR0. . . . . . 63 C3
Horsley Rd KT11, KT24 . . . 93 B7
Horsley Sta KT24. . . . . 92 E2
Horsneile La RG42 . . . . 27 B8
HORTON. 1 B4
Horton Country Pk★
  KT19. . . . . 57 A3
Horton Country Pk Nature
  Reserve★ KT19 . . . . 75 F8
Horton Cres KT19 . . . . 57 B1
Horton Gdns KT19 . . . . 76 C8
Horton Hill KT19. . . . . 76 C8
Horton La KT19, KT18 . . . . 57 B2
Horton Park Children's
  Farm★ KT19. . . . . 57 A1
Horton Rd
  Horton SL3. . . . . 1 A6
  Poyle SL3, TW19 . . . . 1 E4
  Stanwell TW19. . . . . 2 A2
Horton Trad Est SL3. . . . . . . 1 B6
Horton Way CR0 . . . . 43 D4
Horvath Cl KT13 . . . . 53 D6
Hosack Rd SW12, SW17 . . 21 A6

Hoskins Pl RH19 . . . . .186 A4
Hoskins Place Ind Est
  GU15. . . . . 65 B3
Hoskins Rd RH8. . . . . .122 E6
Hoskins The RH8. . . . . . . .122 E6
Hoskins Wlk RH8 . . . . . . .122 E6
Hospital Bridge Rd TW2. . 16 B7
Hospital Hill GU11 . . . . . .105 A3
Hospital of the Holy Trinity
  (Almshouses) 5 CR9 . . . 61 C8
Hospital Rd
  Aldershot GU11 . . . . .105 B3
  Hounslow TW3. . . . . 5 A4
Hospital Way 1 SE13 . . . . 24 D8
Hot Bridge Pre Prep Sch
  GU22. . . . . 90 C8
Hotham Cl KT8 . . . . 36 A6
Hotham Rd SW19 . . . . 20 C1
Hotham Road Mews 12
  SW19 . . . . 20 C1
Houblon Almshouses 15
  TW10. . . . . 6 E2
Houblon Rd TW10. . . . . 6 E2
Houghton Cl TW12 . . . . . . 15 E2
Houghton Rd RH10. . . . . .202 C3
Houlder Cres CR0. . . . . 61 B4
Houlton Ct GU19. . . . . 47 F2
Hound House Rd GU5 . . . .154 A5
Houndown La GU8 . . . . . .169 A5
HOUNSLOW 5 A5
Hounslow Ave TW3 . . . . . . .5 B2
Hounslow Bsns Pk TW3 . . .5 B3
Hounslow Central U Sta
  TW3 . . . . .5 B2
Hounslow Ctr The TW3 . . . .5 B2
Hounslow East U Sta TW3 . 5 C1
Hounslow Gdns TW3. . . . . .5 B2
Hounslow Heath Jun & Inf
  Schs TW4 . . . . .4 D4
Hounslow Heath Nature
  Reserve★ TW4, TW14. . . . 4 E1
Hounslow Manor Sch TW3 5 C4
Hounslow Rd
  Feltham, Hanworth TW13 . 15 D4
  Feltham, North Feltham
    TW14 . . . . 4 B1
  Twickenham TW2, TW3 . . . 5 C1
Hounslow Sta TW3. . . . . . . .5 B2
Hounslow Town Prim Sch
  TW3 . . . . 5 D4
Hounslow Urban Farm★
  TW14 . . . . 4 A2
HOUNSLOW WEST. 4 D4
Hounslow West U Sta TW3 .4 E5
Houseman Rd GU14 . . . . . 84 F6
Housman Rd RH19. . . . . . .184 F4
Houston Ct 3 CR0 . . . . . . 42 E1
Houston Pl KT10 . . . . 36 E1
Houston Rd
  Forest Hill SE23, SE6. . . . 23 E5
  Thames Ditton KT7 . . . . . . 37 B3
Houstoun Ct TW5. . . . . .4 F7
Hove Gdns SM1. . . . . 40 B1
Hovenden Ho 6 SE21 . . . . 22 E4
Howard Ave KT17 . . . . 58 A4
Howard Bldgs GU4. . . . . . .110 A5
Howard Cl
  Ashford TW16 . . . . 14 F2
  Ashtead KT21 . . . . 75 F1
  Bracknell RG12 . . . . 27 A4
  Hampton TW12 . . . . 16 C2
  Leatherhead KT22 . . . . 95 C4
  Walton on the Hill KT20. . . 97 A2
  West Horsley KT24 . . . . . . 92 D2
Howard Cole Way GU11 . .104 E2
Howard Ct
  Beckenham BR3. . . . . 44 C7
  2 Knaphill GU21. . . . . . . 88 C8
  Reigate RH2. . . . . .118 B2
Howard Dr GU4. . . . . 84 B4
Howard Gdns GU1 . . . . . . .110 A2
Howard Ho
  Penge SE20 . . . . 43 C8
  Reigate RH2. . . . . .118 B2
Howard Pl RH2 . . . . .118 A3
Howard Prim Sch CR0. . . . 61 C6
Howard Rd
  Coulsdon CR5 . . . . 79 D5
  Crawley RH11 . . . . .200 D2
  Croydon SE25 . . . . 43 A3
  Dorking, North Holmwood
    RH5. . . . . .136 C3
  Dorking RH4 . . . . .136 A7
  East Horsley KT24. . . . . . . 93 A4
  Great Bookham KT23. . . . .114 C8
  Horsham RH13 . . . . .218 A4
  Isleworth TW7. . . . . .5 F4
  New Malden KT3. . . . . 38 F5
  Penge SE20 . . . . 43 C8
  Reigate RH2. . . . . .139 C8
  Surbiton KT5 . . . . 37 F3
  Wokingham RG40 . . . . 25 C5
Howard Ridge GU4. . . . . . .110 A3
Howards Cl GU22 . . . . 90 A7
Howards Crest Cl BR3. . . . 44 C7
Howards La KT15 . . . . 51 F3
Howards Rd GU22 . . . . 89 F7
Howard St KT7. . . . . 37 B3
Howberry Chase GU27 . . .208 B6
Howberry Rd CR7 . . . . 42 D7
Howden Ct SE25 . . . . 42 F7
Howden Rd SE25. . . . . 42 F7
Howe Dr CR3 . . . . .100 D5
Howell Hill Cl KT17. . . . . . 77 C8
Howell Hill Gr KT17. . . . . . 58 C1
Howe Lo TW1. . . . . 17 A8

Howf The GU14. . . . . 84 B1
Howgate Rd SW14 . . . . 7 D4
Howitts Cl KT10. . . . . 55 A5
How La CR5 . . . . 79 A1
Howland Ho 9 SW16 . . . . 21 E5
Howley Rd CR0, CR9 . . . . . 61 C7
Howmic Ct 1 TW1. . . . . . . 6 C1
Howorth Ct RG12 . . . . 27 E5
Howson Terr TW10. . . . . . . .6 E1
Hoylake Ct RH11. . . . . . . .200 D5
Hoyle Hill RH5. . . . . .157 D1
Hoyle Rd SW17 . . . . 20 E3
Hubbard Dr KT9 . . . . 56 C4
Hubbard Rd SE27 . . . . 22 C4
Hubberholme RG12 . . . . . . 27 A6
Hub Bldgs The 1 SW2 . . . 21 B7
Huddleston Cres RH1. . . . .119 D7
Hudson Ct
  Croydon SE25 . . . . 43 A5
  Guildford GU2 . . . . .108 F1
  4 Merton SW19 . . . . 40 B8
Hudson Rd
  Crawley RH10 . . . . .201 E4
  Harlington UB7 . . . . 3 D8
Hudsons RH10 . . . . 97 D6
Huggins Pl SW2 . . . . 21 F7
Hughenden Rd KT4 . . . . . . 39 A2
Hughes Ct CR0. . . . . 42 A1
Hughes Rd
  Ashford TW15 . . . . 14 C2
  Wokingham RG40 . . . . 25 E7
Hughes Wlk CR0 . . . . 42 C2
Hugh Herland KT1. . . . . . . 37 E6
Hulbert Gate RG40 . . . . . . 25 B6
Hullbrook La GU5. . . . . . .152 E4
Hullmead GU5 . . . . .152 E4
Hulton Cl KT22. . . . . 95 C4
Hulverston Cl SM2. . . . . . . 59 B2
Humberstone Ct 1 GU22. 70 B3
Humber Way GU47. . . . . . . 64 D8
Humbolt Cl GU2 . . . . .108 F1
Hummer Rd TW20 . . . . 12 A4
Humphrey Cl KT22. . . . . . . 94 C5
Humphries Ind Est RG12 . 27 C5
Humphries Yd RG12. . . . . . 27 C5
Hungerford Cl GU47. . . . . . 64 C8
Hungerford Sq 4 KT13. . . 53 D6
Hungry Hill La GU23. . . . . 91 D3
Hunstanton Cl
  Colnbrook SL3 . . . . 1 C7
  8 Crawley RH11. . . . . . . .200 D5
Hunston Rd SM4 . . . . 40 B1
Hunter Cl
  Upper Tooting SW12 . . . . . 21 A7
  Wallington SM6 . . . . 60 E3
Huntercombe-Roehampton
  Hospl The SW15 . . . . 19 A8
Hunter Ct KT19 . . . . 57 A1
Hunter Ho
  Crawley RH10 . . . . .201 D3
  Feltham TW13 . . . . 15 A7
Hunter Rd
  Crawley RH10 . . . . .201 D4
  Farnborough GU14 . . . . . . 84 F3
  Guildford GU1 . . . . .130 E8
  South Norwood CR7 . . . . . 42 D6
  Wimbledon SW20 . . . . 39 C8
Hunters Chase RH9 . . . . .142 F6
Hunters Cl KT19 . . . . 76 C6
Hunters Ct 5 TW9 . . . . 6 E2
Huntersfield Cl RH2. . . . . .118 B4
Hunters Gate RH1. . . . . . .119 F2
Hunters Lodge 8 RH1. . . .200 E5
Hunters Mews GU1 . . . . . .104 F2
Hunters Rd KT9 . . . . 56 E6
Hunters The BR3. . . . . 44 C8
Hunters Way CR0 . . . . 61 E6
Hunting Cl KT10 . . . . 55 A6
Huntingdon Cl CR4, SW16. 41 E5
Huntingdon Ct SW14. . . . . . 7 C4
Huntingdon Gdns
  Chiswick W4. . . . . 7 C7
  North Cheam KT4. . . . . 58 C7
Huntingdon House Dr
  GU26 . . . . .188 E3
Huntingdon Rd
  Redhill RH1. . . . . .118 F1
  Woking GU21 . . . . 68 F2
Huntingfield CR0 . . . . 62 F3
Huntingfield Way TW20 . . 12 D2
Huntingford Cl GU26 . . . .188 D2
Hunting Gate Dr KT9. . . . . 56 E3
Hunting Gate Mews
  Sutton SM1 . . . . 59 B7
  Twickenham TW2. . . . . 16 E7
Huntley Cl TW19 . . . . 13 E8
Huntley Ho
  7 Dulwich SE21. . . . . 22 E4
  Whiteley Village KT12 . . . . 53 F2
Huntley Way SW20 . . . . . . 39 A7
Huntly Rd SE25. . . . . 42 E5
Hunts Cl GU2 . . . . .108 C2
Huntsgreen Ct RG12 . . . . . 27 C7
Hunts Hill Rd GU3. . . . . . .107 A4
Huntsmans Cl
  Feltham TW13 . . . . 15 B4
  Fetcham KT22 . . . . 94 D3
  Warlingham CR6 . . . . .101 C8
Huntsmans Ct 2 CR3 . . . .100 C6
Huntsmans Mdw SL5. . . . . 28 F8
Huntsman's Mews GU16. . 85 F3
Huntsmoor Rd KT19. . . . . . 57 D5
Huntspill St SW17 . . . . 20 D5
Hunts Slip Rd SE21. . . . . . 22 E6
Huntsworth Ct SE6. . . . . . 24 A7
Hurland La GU30, GU35 . .187 A3

Hurlands Bsns Ctr GU9. . .125 F4
Hurlands Cl GU9. . . . . . . .125 F4
Hurlands La GU8. . . . . . . .192 F2
Hurlands Pl GU9. . . . . . . .125 F4
Hurley Cl KT12. . . . . 54 B8
Hurley Ct RG12 . . . . 27 E5
Hurley Gdns GU4 . . . . . . .110 A4
Hurlford GU21 . . . . 69 A2
Hurlstone Rd SE25 . . . . . . 42 E4
Hurn Court Rd TW5 . . . . . . 4 D5
Hurn Ct TW5. . . . . 4 D5
Hurnford Cl CR2 . . . . 61 E1
Huron Rd SW17 . . . . 21 A5
Hurricane Rd SM6 . . . . 60 E3
Hursley Ct 11 KT6. . . . . . . 37 D2
Hurst Ave RH12 . . . . .217 D3
Hurst Cl
  Chessington KT9 . . . . 57 A5
  Crawley RH11 . . . . .200 F4
  Hayes BR2. . . . . 44 F1
  Headley KT18 . . . . 96 C3
  Woking GU22 . . . . 89 C7
Hurstcourt Rd SM1. . . . . . . 59 B8
Hurst Croft GU1 . . . . .130 E6
Hurst Dr KT20 . . . . 97 A1
Hurst Farm Cl GU8. . . . . .149 F2
Hurst Farm Rd RH19. . . . .205 D2
Hurstfield Rd KT8. . . . . . . 36 A6
Hurstleigh Cl RH1. . . . . . .118 F3
Hurstleigh Dr RH1 . . . . . .118 F3
Hurst Gr GU1. . . . . 34 F1
HURST GREEN. 123 B3
Hurst Green Cl RH8 . . . . .123 A3
Hurst Green Inf Sch RH8 123 A3
Hurst Green Rd RH8. . . . .122 F3
Hurst Green Sta RH8. . . . .122 F3
Hurst Hill Cotts GU5. . . . .152 A4
Hurst Ho 7 SE26. . . . . 23 B3
Hurst La
  East Molesey KT8. . . . . . . 36 C6
  Headley KT18 . . . . 96 D4
  Thorpe TW20 . . . . 32 A7
Hurstlands RH8. . . . . .123 A3
Hurstleigh RH8 . . . . .123 A3
Hurstmere Cl GU26 . . . . . .188 D3
Hurstmere Ho GU26. . . . . .188 D3
HURST PARK 36 B6
Hurst Park Prim Sch KT8. 36 A6
Hurst Pk RH12 . . . . .217 D3
Hurst Rd
  Aldershot GU11 . . . . .105 C4
  Croydon CR0 . . . . 61 E1
  East Molesey KT8, KT12 . . 36 C6
  Epsom KT18 . . . . 76 D8
  Farnborough GU14 . . . . . . 85 B8
  Headley KT18, KT20 . . . . . 96 E4
  Horley RH6 . . . . .160 E4
  Horsham RH12 . . . . .217 D3
  Walton-on-Thames KT8,
    KT12. . . . . 35 D5
Hurst View Grange CR2 . . 61 E3
Hurst View Rd CR2. . . . . . . 61 E3
Hurst Way
  Pyrford GU22. . . . . 70 E5
  South Croydon CR2 . . . . . . 61 E4
Hurstwood SL5 . . . . 29 A3
Hurtbank Cotts RH5. . . . . .155 C6
HURTMORE. 150 A7
Hurtmore Chase GU7. . . . .150 B7
Hurtmore Rd GU7 . . . . . . .150 B7
Hurtwood House Sch
  RH5. . . . . .155 A2
Hurtwood Rd KT12. . . . . . . 35 F2
Hussar Ct GU11 . . . . .104 E2
Hussars Cl TW4. . . . . .4 E4
Hutchingson's Rd CR0. . . . 82 C8
Hutchins Ho 6 SW4 . . . . . 21 D8
Hutchinson's Bank Nature
  Reserve★ CR0. . . . . 83 C7
Hutchins Way RH6 . . . . . .160 F5
Hutsons Cl RG40 . . . . 25 D8
Hutton Cl
  Hersham KT12. . . . . 54 B5
  Windlesham GU20 . . . . 48 D3
Hutton Rd GU12. . . . . .106 A6
Huxley Cl GU7 . . . . .150 D7
Huxley Rd GU2 . . . . .129 D8
Hyacinth Cl 3 TW12 . . . . 16 A2
Hyacinth Rd SW15 . . . . . . 19 A7
Hyde Cl TW16. . . . . 14 E2
Hyde Ct
  Forest Hill SE23. . . . . 23 E6
  Hounslow TW3. . . . . 5 A2
Hyde Dr RH11. . . . . .200 D5
Hyde Farm Mews SW12 . . 21 D7
Hyde Heath Ct RH10. . . . .202 D8
Hyde Ho 8 SM7 . . . . 77 F5
Hyde La
  Beacon Hill GU10, GU8 . . .168 E1
  Thursley GU8. . . . . .169 A2
Hyde Rd
  Richmond TW10. . . . . 6 F2
  Sanderstead CR2. . . . . 80 E6
HYDESTILE 171 E6
Hydestile Cotts GU8. . . . .171 D5
Hyde Terr TW15, TW16 . . 14 E2

Hydethorpe Rd SW12. . . . 21 C7
Hyde Wlk SM4 . . . . 40 A2
Hydons The GU8 . . . . .171 E5
Hydro KT16. . . . . 33 C1
Hylands Cl
  Crawley RH10 . . . . .202 A5
  Epsom KT18 . . . . 76 C4
Hylands Mews KT18. . . . . . 76 C4
Hylands Rd KT18. . . . . 76 C4
Hylton Lodge KT12 . . . . . . 54 C5
Hylton Pl RH1 . . . . .119 C4
Hyndewood 14 SE23. . . . . 23 D5
Hyperion Ct RH11 . . . . . . .200 E4
Hyperion Ho 9 SW2 . . . . . 21 F8
Hyperion Pl KT19 . . . . 57 D2
Hyperion Wlk RH6 . . . . . .161 B1
Hyrstdene CR0. . . . . 61 B6
Hyrst The CR0 . . . . 43 E1
Hythe Cl RG12 . . . . 27 E4
Hythe Comm Prim Sch The
  TW18 . . . . 12 D3
HYTHE END. 12 B6
Hythe End Rd TW19 . . . . . 12 A5
Hythe Field Ave TW20 . . . 12 D2
Hythe Park Rd TW20 . . . . 12 D2
Hythe Rd
  Egham TW18 . . . . 12 D3
  South Norwood CR7, SE25 . 42 D7
Hythe The TW18 . . . . 12 E3

I

Ian Ct SE23 . . . . 23 C6
Iberian Ave SM6 . . . . 60 E6
Iberian Way GU15 . . . . 66 B6
Ibis La W4. . . . . 7 C6
Ibotson Ct SL3 . . . . .1 E6
Ibsley Gdns SW15 . . . . 19 A7
Ibstock Place Sch SW15. . .7 E1
Icehouse Wood RH8 . . . . .122 F4
Icklesham Ho 9 RH10. . . .200 F3
Icklingham Gate KT11. . . . 73 C7
Icklingham Rd KT11. . . . . . 73 D6
Iden Cl BR2. . . . . 44 E5
Idlecombe Rd SW17. . . . . . 21 A2
Idmiston Ho KT4. . . . . 38 F2
Idmiston Rd
  New Malden KT4. . . . . 38 F2
  West Norwood SE21, SE27 . 22 C4
Idmiston Sq KT4. . . . . 38 F2
IFIELD 201 A7
Ifield Ave RH11 . . . . .201 C7
Ifield Cl RH1. . . . . .139 E7
Ifield Com Coll RH11. . . . .201 A6
Ifield Dr RH11. . . . . .201 A7
Ifield Gn RH11 . . . . .181 A1
IFIELD GREEN. 181 A1
Ifield Rd
  Charlwood RH6 . . . . .180 E5
  Crawley, West Green
    RH11. . . . . .201 C6
  Ifield St RH11 . . . . .200 F8
  Ifield Sta RH11. . . . . .201 A6
Ifield Watermill★ RH11. . .200 E5
IFIELDWOOD 180 D1
Ifield Wood RH11 . . . . . . .180 E1
IFOLD. 212 D3
Ifold Bridge La RH14 . . . .212 D4
Ifoldhurst RH14 . . . . .212 C2
Ifold Rd RH1 . . . . .140 A7
Ightham Ho BR3. . . . . 23 F1
Ikea Ampere Way Halt
  CR0. . . . . 41 F1
Ikona Ct KT13. . . . . 53 C5
Ildersly Gr SE21. . . . . 22 C4
Ilex Cl
  Englefield Green TW20 . . . 11 B1
  Sunbury TW16 . . . . 35 C7
Ilex Ho KT15. . . . . 52 A1
Ilex Way SW16 . . . . 22 A3
Ilford Ct GU6 . . . . .173 F2
Ilfracombe Rd BR1. . . . . . . 24 F5
Ilkley Cl SE19 . . . . 22 D2
Illingworth Cl CR4 . . . . . . 40 D6
Illingworth Gr RG12. . . . . . 27 F8
Imber Cl KT7 . . . . 36 F3
Imber Court Trad Est KT8. 36 D3
Imber Cross KT7 . . . . 36 F3
Imber Gr KT10 . . . . 36 D2
Imberhorne Bsns Ctr
  RH19. . . . . .185 B3
Imberhorne La RH19 . . . .185 B2
Imberhorne Lower Sch
  RH19. . . . . .185 D3
Imberhorne Sch RH19 . . .185 B3
Imberhorne Way RH19 . . .185 B3
Imber Park Rd KT10. . . . . . 35 D3
Imjin Cl GU11. . . . . .105 B3
Immanuel CE Prim Sch
  SW16 . . . . 21 E2
Impact Ct SE20. . . . . 43 B7
Imperial Ctr RH10. . . . . . .182 A3
Imperial Gdns CR4. . . . . . . 41 B6
Imperial House GU25. . . . . 31 E4
Imperial Pk KT22. . . . . 95 A7
Imperial Rd TW14. . . . . 14 E8
Imperial Way CR0, CR9. . . 61 A4
Impington 8 KT1. . . . . 38 A7
Imran Ct GU12. . . . . .126 C8
Ince Rd KT12. . . . . 53 E4
Inchmery Rd SE6. . . . . 24 C7
Inchwood
  Bracknell RG12 . . . . 27 C1
  Croydon BR4, CR0. . . . . . . 63 B6

Independence Ho 4
SW19 . . . . 40 D8
Independent Bsns Pk
RH19 . . . . 185 A3
Indigo Ct TW13 . . . . 14 F5
Ingatestone Rd SE25 . . . . 43 B5
Ingham Cl CR2 . . . . 62 D2
Ingham Rd CR2 . . . . 62 D2
Ingleboro Dr CR8 . . . . . . 80 D6
Ingleby Way SM6 . . . . 60 D3
Ingle Dell GU15 . . . . 65 D4
Ingle Rd SW12 . . . . 21 D7
Inglehurst KT15 . . . . 52 B1
Inglemere Ct CR4, SW17 . . 20 F1
Inglemere Rd
Forest Hill SE23 . . . . 23 D5
Mitcham CR4, SW17 . . . . 20 F1
Inglenook Yd RH5 . . . . . . 158 B1
Ingleside
Poyle SL3 . . . . .1 F6
Surbiton KT6 . . . . 37 E2
Ingleside Cl BR3 . . . . 24 A1
Ingleside Ct CR2 . . . . 61 C4
Ingleton RG12 . . . . 27 A6
Ingleton Rd SM5 . . . . 59 E2
Inglewood
Chertsey KT16 . . . . 51 F7
New Addington CR0 . . . . 62 E2
Woking GU21 . . . . 69 B1
Inglewood Ave GU15 . . . . 66 D5
Inglewood Ct 5 BR1 . . . . . 24 F1
Inglewood Mews KT6 . . . . 38 A1
Inglis Rd CR0 . . . . 42 F1
Ingram Cl RH12 . . . . 217 A2
Ingram Ho KT8 . . . . 37 C8
Ingram Rd CR7 . . . . 42 C8
Ingrams Cl KT12 . . . . 54 C5
Ingrebourne Ho BR1 . . . . 24 D3
Inholmes Clay Pit Nature
Reserve★ RH5 . . . . . . 136 C3
Inholms La RH5 . . . . 136 C3
Inkerman Rd GU21 . . . . . . 68 E1
Inkerman Way GU21 . . . . 68 E1
Inkpen La RH18 . . . . 206 F1
Inman Rd SW18 . . . . 20 C8
Inner Park Rd SW19 . . . . 19 D6
Inner Ring E TW6 . . . . .3 B4
Inner Ring W TW6 . . . . 3 A4
Innes Cl SW20 . . . . 39 E7
Innes Lodge SE23 . . . . . . 23 D5
Innes Rd RH12 . . . . 217 F4
Innes Yd CR0, CR9 . . . . . 61 C7
Innings La RG12 . . . . 27 E8
Innisfail Gdns GU11 . . . . 125 F8
Institute Rd
Aldershot GU12 . . . . 105 D1
Westcott RH4 . . . . 135 C6
Institute Wlk 6 RH19 . . . . 185 E1
Instow Gdns GU14 . . . . . . 85 A7
Int Coll of Accountancy The
SW17 . . . . 20 F5
Interchange The 1 CR0 . . 42 B2
International Way TW16 . . 34 E8
Inval Hill GU27 . . . . 208 C8
Inveresk Gdns KT4 . . . . . . 58 A7
Inverness Ct SE6 . . . . 24 F7
Inverness Rd
Hounslow TW3 . . . . 5 A3
North Cheam KT4 . . . . . . 39 D1
Inverness Way GU47 . . . . 64 D7
Invicta Cl TW14 . . . . 14 F7
Invicta Ct KT9 . . . . 56 F5
Invincible Rd GU14 . . . . . 85 A3
Inwood Ave
Coulsdon CR5 . . . . 100 A7
Hounslow TW3 . . . . 5 C4
Inwood Bsns Pk TW3 . . . . .5 B3
Inwood Cl CR0 . . . . 62 E8
Inwood Ct 1 KT12 . . . . . . 54 C8
Inwood Rd TW3 . . . . 5 C3
Iona Cl
Crawley RH11 . . . . 201 B3
Forest Hill SE13, SE4, SE6 . . 24 A8
Morden SM4 . . . . 40 B2
Iona Ho 20 GU11 . . . . . . 105 A2
Ipsley Lodge GU10 . . . . 126 E5
Ipswich Rd SW17 . . . . . . 21 A2
IQ Farnborough Bsns Pk
GU14 . . . . 85 B2
Irene Rd KT11 . . . . 74 B5
Ireton Ave KT13 . . . . 53 F8
Iris Cl
Croydon CR0 . . . . 43 D1
Surbiton KT6 . . . . 37 F2
Iris Rd
Bisley GU24 . . . . 68 A4
West Ewell KT19 . . . . . . 57 B5
Iron La GU5 . . . . 151 D5
IRONS BOTTOM 139 A1
Ironsbottom RH2 . . . . . . 159 F8
Irvine Ct CR7 . . . . 42 A3
Irvine Dr GU14 . . . . 84 E8
Irvine Pl GU25 . . . . 31 E4
Irving Wlk RH10 . . . . 201 E3
Irwin Ct TW15 . . . . 13 D5
Irwin Dr RH12 . . . . 217 A2
Irwin Rd GU2 . . . . 130 A7
Isabel Cotts KT18 . . . . . . 76 B5
Isabel Hill Cl 3 TW12 . . . 36 B8
Isabella Ct 8 TW10 . . . . . .6 F1
Isabella Pl KT2 . . . . 17 F3
Isbells Dr RH2 . . . . 139 B7
Isham Rd SW16 . . . . 41 E7
Isis Ct W4 . . . . .7 B7
Isis Ho KT16 . . . . 33 C2

Isis St SW18 . . . . 20 C6
Isis Way GU47 . . . . 64 D8
Island Cl TW18 . . . . 12 E4
Island Cotts GU23 . . . . . . 91 D6
Island Farm Ave KT8 . . . . 35 F4
Island Farm Rd KT8 . . . . . 36 A4
Island Ho SW19 . . . . 40 C5
Island Rd CR4, SW19 . . . . 20 F1
Island The
Downside KT11 . . . . 73 B1
Weybridge KT13 . . . . . . 52 E4
Wraysbury TW19 . . . . . . 12 A3
Islay Gdns TW4 . . . . 4 D2
ISLEWORTH 6 B4
Isleworth Ait Nature
Reserve★ TW7 . . . . 6 B4
Isleworth Bsns Complex
TW7 . . . . .5 F5
Isleworth Sta TW7 . . . . . . .5 F5
Isleworth & Syon Sch for
Boys TW7 . . . . 5 E7
Isleworth Town Prim Sch
TW7 . . . . 6 A5
Islington Ho 7 RH11 . . . . 201 B2
Issa Rd 9 TW3 . . . . .4 F3
Itchingwood Common Rd
RH8 . . . . 123 E2
Ivanhoe Cl RH11 . . . . . . 181 D1
Ivanhoe Ho 12 SW12 . . . . 21 B8
Ivanhoe Rd TW4 . . . . 4 D4
Iveagh Cl RH11 . . . . 201 C1
Iveagh Ct
Beckenham BR3 . . . . 44 B6
Bracknell RG12 . . . . 27 C4
Iveagh Rd GU2 . . . . 130 B7
Ively Rd GU14 . . . . 84 D1
Ively Rdbt GU14 . . . . 84 E2
Iverna Gdns TW14 . . . . . . 3 D2
Ivers Way CR0 . . . . 63 B3
Ivestor Terr SE23 . . . . . . 23 C8
Ivies The 2 RH1 . . . . . . 139 F8
Ivor Cl GU1 . . . . 131 A8
Ivory Ct TW13 . . . . 15 A7
Ivory Wlk RH11 . . . . 200 E3
Ivybank GU7 . . . . 150 E6
Ivybridge Cl 3 TW1 . . . . . 17 A8
Ivybridge Prim Sch TW1 . .5 F6
Ivychurch Cl SE20 . . . . . . 23 C1
Ivy Cl TW16 . . . . 35 C7
Ivydale Rd SM5 . . . . 59 F8
Ivyday Gr SW16 . . . . 21 F5
Ivydene
East Molesey KT12, KT8 . . 35 F4
Knaphill GU21 . . . . 68 B1
Ivydene Cl
Redhill RH1 . . . . 140 B4
Sutton SM1 . . . . 59 C6
Ivydene Ind Est RH19 . . . 206 D7
Ivy Dene La RH19 . . . . . . 206 D6
Ivy Dr GU18 . . . . 67 A7
Ivy Gdns CR4 . . . . 41 D6
Ivy Hall Bglw GU6 . . . . . 174 D3
Ivy Hatch Ct 3 BR3 . . . . . 24 F1
Ivy Ho CR0 . . . . 43 D1
Ivy La
Farnham GU9 . . . . 125 B2
Hounslow TW4 . . . . .4 F3
Woking GU22 . . . . 70 B1
Ivy Lodge KT15 . . . . 52 B6
Ivy Mill Cl RH9 . . . . 121 B3
Ivy Mill La RH1, RH9 . . . 121 B3
Ivymount Rd SE27 . . . . . . 22 A5
Ivy Rd
Aldershot GU12 . . . . 105 E2
Hounslow TW3 . . . . .5 B3
Tolworth KT6 . . . . 38 A1
Upper Tooting SW17 . . . . 20 E3

J

Jacaranda Cl KT3 . . . . . . 38 E6
Jacaranda Ho KT15 . . . . . 52 D8
Jackass La RH9 . . . . 121 F4
Jack Ct GU17 . . . . 64 E4
Jackdaw Cl RH11 . . . . . . 201 C8
Jackdaw La RH12 . . . . . . 217 E6
Jack Goodchild Way KT1 . 38 B6
Jack & Jill Sch
Hampton TW12 . . . . 16 A2
8 Twickenham TW2 . . . 16 E6
Jackman's La GU21 . . . . . 89 B8
Jackson Cl
Bracknell RG12 . . . . 27 B4
Elmbridge Village GU6 . . 173 F2
Epsom KT18 . . . . 76 D5
Jackson's Pl CR0 . . . . . . 42 E1
Jackson's Way CR0 . . . . . 63 B7
Jackson Way KT19 . . . . . 57 A2
Jacob Cl RG42 . . . . 26 D7
Jacobean Cl RH10 . . . . . 202 C5
Jacob Rd GU15 . . . . 65 A7
Jacobs Ct RH10 . . . . 202 C7
JACOBSWELL 109 D7
Jacobs Well Rd GU4 . . . . 109 D6
Jaggard Way SW12 . . . . . 20 F8
Jail La TN16 . . . . 83 E3
Jamaica Rd CR7 . . . . 42 B3
James Black Rd GU2 . . . 129 D8
James Boswell 1 SW16 . . 22 A4
James Dixon Prim Sch 13
SE20 . . . . 23 B1
James Est CR4 . . . . 40 F7
James Pl RH10 . . . . 201 D5
James Rd
Camberley GU15 . . . . . . 65 B2
Shalford GU3 . . . . 130 C1
James's Cotts TW9 . . . . . 7 A7

James Searle Ind Est
RH12 . . . . 217 E4
James St TW3 . . . . 5 D4
Jameston RG12 . . . . 27 C1
James Watt Way RH10 . . 182 A4
James Way GU15 . . . . . . 65 B2
Jamieson Ho TW4 . . . . . . .4 F1
Jamnagar GU18 . . . . 12 F2
Janoway Hill GU21 . . . . . 89 C8
Japonica Cl GU21 . . . . . . 69 C1
Japonica Ct GU12 . . . . . 105 F1
Japonica Rd RH15 . . . . . . 52 D8
Jarman Ct 6 GU21 . . . . . 70 A3
Jarrett Cl SW2 . . . . 22 B7
Jarrow Rd SM4 . . . . 40 B4
Jarvis Rd CR2 . . . . 61 D4
Jasmine Cl
Redhill RH1 . . . . 140 A4
Woking GU21 . . . . 68 F3
Jasmine Ct
Horsham RH12 . . . . 217 C2
11 Wallington SM6 . . . . 60 B4
Wimbledon SW19 . . . . . 20 A3
Jasmine Gdns CR0 . . . . . 63 B7
Jasmine Gr SE20 . . . . . . 43 B8
Jasmine Ho KT15 . . . . . . 52 D8
Jasmine Way KT7 . . . . . . 36 E5
Jasmin Rd KT19 . . . . 57 B5
Jason Cl
Redhill RH1 . . . . 139 E4
Weybridge KT13 . . . . . . 53 C5
Jasons Dr GU4 . . . . 110 C4
Jasper Ho KT4 . . . . 38 D1
Jasper Rd SE19 . . . . 22 F2
Javelin Ct RH10 . . . . 182 D1
Jawahar Bagh SW16 . . . . 22 B2
Jay Ave KT15 . . . . 52 E7
Jays Ct SL5 . . . . 29 D5
Jay's La GU27 . . . . 209 C3
Jays Nest Cl GU17 . . . . . 64 D4
Jayson Ct 7 GU21 . . . . . . 43 A1
Jay Wlk RH10 . . . . 204 C5
Jeal Oakwood Ct KT18 . . 76 E5
Jean Batten Cl SM6 . . . . 60 F3
Jeanette Ct 5 TW15 . . . . 13 F4
Jean Ho SW17 . . . . 20 E3
Jean Humbert Ho 2
SE27 . . . . 22 D4
Jeans Ct 10 RH11 . . . . . 201 B1
Jeddere Cotts RH7 . . . . . 165 A2
Jefferson Rd GU24 . . . . . 87 C7
Jeffery Cl RG40 . . . . 25 D6
Jeffries Pas GU1 . . . . . . 130 D8
Jeffries Rd KT24 . . . . . . 112 C5
Jeffs Cl TW12 . . . . 16 B2
Jeffs Rd SM1 . . . . 58 F6
Jefton Ct SM6 . . . . 60 C4
Jemma Cl 16 SW2 . . . . . 22 A7
Jemmett Cl KT2 . . . . 38 B8
Jengar Cl SM1 . . . . 59 B6
Jenkins Cl GU14 . . . . 47 D2
Jenkins' Hill GU19 . . . . . 47 D2
Jenkins Pl GU11 . . . . . . 105 D8
Jenner Dr GU24 . . . . 68 A6
Jenner Rd
Crawley RH10 . . . . 181 F3
Guildford GU1 . . . . 130 E8
Jenners Cl RH7 . . . . 164 D4
Jenner Way KT19 . . . . . . 57 A2
Jennett Rd CR0, CR9 . . . . 61 A7
JENNETTS PARK 26 D6
Jennifer Rd BR1 . . . . 24 F5
Jennings
Long Ditton KT6 . . . . 37 C2
New Haw KT15 . . . . 52 C2
Jennings Way RH6 . . . . . 161 D3
Jenny La KT7 . . . . 164 C4
Jennys Way CR5 . . . . 99 C5
Jenson Way SE19 . . . . . . 22 F1
Jeppo's Ct 4 . . . . 40 F5
Jeremiah Ct RH1 . . . . . . 119 C4
Jerome Cnr RG45 . . . . . . 45 C3
Jerome Ho KT1 . . . . 37 D7
Jersey Cl
Chertsey KT16 . . . . 51 F7
Guildford GU4 . . . . 110 B6
Jersey Pl SL5 . . . . 29 D3
Jersey Rd
Crawley RH11 . . . . 201 A2
Hounslow TW5, TW7 . . . . 5 D7
Mitcham SW17 . . . . 21 B2
Jerviston Gdns SW16 . . . 22 A2
Jesmond Cl CR4 . . . . 41 B6
Jesmond Rd CR0 . . . . . . 42 F2
Jessamy Rd KT13 . . . . . . 53 B8
Jesses La GU5 . . . . 154 C8
Jessie's Hollow GU5 . . . 133 C1
Jessiman Terr TW17 . . . . 34 A4
Jessop Ho GU27 . . . . . . 208 A6
Jessop Pl CR4 . . . . 40 E5
Jessops Way CR0, CR4 . . 41 C3
Jessops Wharf 4 TW8 . . . 6 C7
Jeston Ho 10 SE27 . . . . . 22 B5
Jetty Ho KT16 . . . . 33 C2
Jevington RG12 . . . . 27 C1
Jewell Ho 1 SW12 . . . . . 21 C8
Jewels Hill TN16, CR6 . . . 83 A6
Jewel Wlk RH11 . . . . 201 A3
Jews Wlk SE26 . . . . 23 B4
Jeypore Rd SW18 . . . . . . 20 C8
Jigsaw Sch GU6 . . . . 193 E6
Jig's La S RG42 . . . . 27 E8
Jillian St TW12 . . . . 16 A1
Joanne Ct 4 TW1 . . . . 6 A1
Jobson's La GU27 . . . . . 209 D2
Jocelyn Rd TW9 . . . . .6 E4
Jockey Mead RH12 . . . . 217 A1
Jock's La RG42 . . . . 26 E8

Jodie Ct BR3 . . . . 24 A2
Jodrell Cl TW7 . . . . .6 A6
Joe Hunte Ct 2 SW27 . . . 22 B3
John Ades Cl GU12 . . . . 106 B3
John Arthur Gall★ RH4 . 136 A7
John Austin Cl KT2 . . . . . 37 F8
John Baird Ct SE26 . . . . . 23 D4
John Baird Ho 13 SE20 . . 23 C1
John Barter House TW3 . . .4 F5
John Burns Cotts RH8 . . 123 E5
John Cl GU11 . . . . 125 E8
John Cobb Rd KT13 . . . . 53 A3
John Day Ho TW7 . . . . . . .6 B4
John Dee Ho 3 SW14 . . . .7 D4
John Fisher Sch The CR8 . 60 E1
John F Kennedy Meml★
TW20 . . . . 11 D6
John Gale Ct KT17 . . . . . 57 F2
John Kaye Ct TW17 . . . . . 34 A4
John Kirk Ho
Kenley CR8 . . . . 80 B5
5 Streatham SW16 . . . . 21 E5
John Nike Leisuresport
Complex RG12 . . . . . . 26 C7
John Nike Way RG12 . . . . 26 C7
John Paul II RC Sch
SW19 . . . . 19 D8
John Pounds Ho RH11 . . 201 D4
John Ruskin Coll CR2 . . . 62 E3
John Russell Cl GU2 . . . 109 A4
John's Ct 2 SM2 . . . . 59 B4
Johnsdale RH8 . . . . 122 F6
Johns La SM4 . . . . 40 C4
Johnson Rd
Heston TW5 . . . . 4 C7
Thornton Heath CR0 . . . . 42 D2
Johnson's Cl SM1 . . . . . . 59 F7
Johnson Terr TW2 . . . . . . 36 C8
Johnson Wlk GU2 . . . . . 109 A5
John's Rd TN16 . . . . 103 D7
John St
Croydon SE25 . . . . 43 A5
Hounslow TW3, TW5 . . . . 4 E5
John's Terr CR0 . . . . 42 E1
Johnstone Ct CR0 . . . . . . 61 D7
Johnston Gn GU2 . . . . . 109 A5
Johnston Wlk GU2 . . . . . 109 A5
Johns Wlk CR3 . . . . 101 A8
John Watkin Cl 1 KT17 . . 57 B2
John Wesley Ct 6 TW1 . . 17 A7
John William Cl 10 KT2 . . 37 D8
John Wiskar Dr GU6 . . . . 174 D2
Joinville Pl KT15 . . . . 52 D6
Jolesfield Ct RH11 . . . . . 200 F3
Jolliffe Rd RH1 . . . . 99 C1
Jones Cnr SL5 . . . . 28 E8
Jones Wlk 6 TW10 . . . . . .6 F1
Jonquil Gdns 5 TW12 . . . 16 A2
Jonson Ct CR4 . . . . 41 B6
Jordan Cl CR2 . . . . 80 F8
Jordan Lo SW17 . . . . 20 E3
Jordans Cl
Crawley RH11 . . . . 201 D8
Guildford GU1 . . . . 110 A2
Redhill RH1 . . . . 140 A4
Stanwell TW19 . . . . 13 C8
Jordans Cres RH11 . . . . 181 D1
Jordans Mews 6 TW2 . . . 16 E6
Jordans The RH19 . . . . . 205 E8
Josef Perrin Ho 1 SE27 . . 22 D4
Joseph Hood Prim Sch
SW20 . . . . 39 E6
Josephine Ave KT20 . . . 117 F8
Josephine Cl KT20 . . . . . 117 F8
Joseph Locke Way KT10 . 55 A8
Joseph's Rd GU1 . . . . . . 109 D2
Joshua Cl CR2 . . . . 61 B3
Joshua Oldfield Ho SW17 . 20 F3
Joviel Ho TW18 . . . . 13 A1
Jubilee Ave
North Ascot SL5 . . . . 28 E8
Twickenham TW2 . . . . . . 16 C7
Wokingham RG41 . . . . . 25 B7
Jubilee Cl
Farnborough GU14 . . . . . 84 D4
North Ascot SL5 . . . . 28 E8
Stanwell TW19 . . . . 13 C8
Teddington KT1 . . . . 37 C8
Jubilee Cres KT15 . . . . . . 52 D5
Jubilee Ct
Bracknell RG12 . . . . 27 C6
Hounslow TW3 . . . . .5 B4
Staines TW18 . . . . 13 A4
20 Sutton SM2 . . . . 59 C4
Thornton Heath CR7 . . . . 42 A5
Jubilee Dr GU12 . . . . . . 106 A6
Jubilee Hall Rd GU14 . . . 85 C4
Jubilee High Sch KT15 . . 52 A5
Jubilee House 5 TW12 . . 36 A8
Jubilee La
Grayshott GU26 . . . . . . 188 C3
Rowledge GU10 . . . . . . 146 A5
Jubilee Rd
Aldershot GU11 . . . . . . 126 B7
Cheam SM3 . . . . 58 D3
Mytchett GU16 . . . . 86 A2
Rudgwick RH12 . . . . . . 214 D8
Jubilee Terr RH3 . . . . . . 137 C5
Jubilee Villas KT10 . . . . . 36 E1
Jubilee Way
East Bedfont TW14 . . . . . 15 A7
Merton SW19 . . . . 40 B8
Tolworth KT5, KT6, KT9 . . 57 B7
Jubilee Wks SW19 . . . . . 40 C7
Jubilee Wlk
Crawley RH10 2 . . . . . 202 A6

Jubilee Wlk continued
14 Horsham RH12 . . . . 217 C2
Jubilee Wood Nature
Reserve★ KT9 . . . . 75 B8
Judges Cl RH19 . . . . 205 E8
Judge's Terr RH19 . . . . . 205 E8
Judge Wlk KT10 . . . . 55 E4
Julian Cl GU21 . . . . 69 C1
Julian Hill KT13 . . . . 53 B3
Julian Ho
Dulwich SE21 . . . . 22 E4
Wallington SM6 . . . . 60 C5
Julian's Prim Sch SW16 . . 22 A4
Julian Taylor Path SE23 . . 23 B6
Julien Rd CR5 . . . . 79 D4
Juliet Gdns RG42 . . . . . . 27 F8
Julius Ct TW8 . . . . .6 E7
Julius Hill RG42 . . . . 27 F8
Jumps Rd GU10 . . . . 168 B3
Junction Pl GU27 . . . . . . 207 F6
Junction Rd
Ashford TW15 . . . . 14 D3
Croydon CR2 . . . . 61 D5
Dorking RH4 . . . . 136 A7
Lightwater GU18 . . . . . . 48 B1
June Cl CR5 . . . . 79 B5
June La RH1 . . . . 140 B2
Junewood Cl KT15 . . . . . 70 F8
Juniper RG12 . . . . 27 C1
Juniper Cl
Biggin Hill TN16 . . . . 83 E2
Chessington KT9 . . . . . . 56 F5
Guildford GU1 . . . . 109 C6
Oxted RH8 . . . . 123 B2
Reigate RH2 . . . . 139 C7
Juniper Ct
East Molesey KT8 . . . . . . 36 B5
Hounslow TW3 . . . . .5 B3
6 Thornton Heath CR0 . . 42 A3
Juniper Dr GU24 . . . . 68 A4
Juniper Gdns
Ashford TW16 . . . . 14 F2
Mitcham CR4 . . . . 41 C8
Juniper Hall (Field Study
Ctr) RH5 . . . . 115 C6
Juniper Ho 9 TW9 . . . . . .7 B6
Juniper Pl GU4 . . . . 130 D2
Juniper Rd
Crawley RH11 . . . . 181 C1
Farnborough GU14 . . . . . 84 C5
Reigate RH2 . . . . 139 C7
Juniper Terr GU4 . . . . . . 130 D2
Juniper Wlk RH3 . . . . . . 137 C7
Jura Cl RH11 . . . . 201 B3
Justin Cl TW8 . . . . .6 D7
Justin Ct 3 CR7 . . . . 42 A4
Justin Plaza CR4 . . . . . . 40 E5
Jutland Gdns CR5 . . . . . . 99 F7
Jutland Pl TW20 . . . . 12 C3
Jutland Rd SE6 . . . . 24 C8
Juxon Cl RH11 . . . . 200 F4

K

K2 L Ctr RH10 . . . . 201 D2
Kaine Pl CR0 . . . . 43 E2
Kaithewood Ho RH12 . . . 218 B5
Kangley Bridge Ctr SE26 . 23 F3
Kangley Bridge Rd SE26 . . 23 F3
Karen Ct BR1 . . . . 44 F8
Kashmir Cl KT15 . . . . 52 D2
Kashmir Ct 3 GU14 . . . . . 85 C1
Katana 8 GU22 . . . . 89 E8
Katharine Rd 1 TW1 . . . . 17 A7
Katharine St CR0, CR9 . . . 61 C7
Katherine Cl KT15 . . . . . . 52 A4
Katherine Ct
2 Camberley GU15 . . . . 65 D5
Forest Hill SE23 . . . . 23 C7
3 Knaphill GU21 . . . . . . 88 C8
Katherine Ho
3 Croydon CR0 . . . . 61 C7
West Norwood SE19 . . . . 22 E2
Katherine Mews CR3 . . . . 80 F2
Kathleen Godfree Ct
SW19 . . . . 20 A3
Kathleen Moore Ct BR4 . . 63 C8
Kavanagh Ct 1 KT3 . . . . . 38 E6
Kay Ave KT15 . . . . 52 E7
Kay Cres GU35 . . . . 187 B6
Kaye Ct GU1 . . . . 109 C5
Kaye Don Way KT13 . . . . 53 A1
Kayemoor Rd SM2 . . . . . 59 E4
Kaynes Pk SL5 . . . . 28 E8
Keable Rd GU10 . . . . . . 145 E7
Kean Ho 14 TW1 . . . . 6 D1
Kearton Cl CR8 . . . . 80 C2
Kearton Pl CR3 . . . . 101 A5
Keates Gn RG42 . . . . 27 B8
Keats Ave RH1 . . . . 119 B3
Keats Cl
Horsham RH12 . . . . 217 C7
Mitcham SW17, SW19 . . . 20 D2
Keats Ho BR3 . . . . 24 B2
Keats Pl RH19 . . . . 185 D1
Keats Way
Crowthorne RG45 . . . . . . 45 B6
Croydon CR0 . . . . 43 C3
Keble Cl
Crawley RH10 . . . . 182 D1
New Malden KT4 . . . . . . 38 F1
Keble Ct 7 SW19 . . . . . . 20 A2
Keble St SW17 . . . . 20 C4
Keble Way GU47 . . . . 45 E2
Kedeston Ct SM3 . . . . . . 40 B1
Keeble Ho RG41 . . . . 25 A6
Keedonwood Rd BR1 . . . . 24 F3

Keel KT16 . . . . 33 C2
Keeley Rd CR0, CR9 . . . . . . 61 C8
Keeling 2 TW1 . . . . 16 E3
Keeling Ct TW0 . . . . 61 B6
Keens Cl SW16 . . . . 21 D3
Keens La GU2, GU3 . . . . . . 108 F5
Keens Park Rd GU3 . . . . . . 108 F5
Keen's Rd CR0 . . . . 61 C6
Keepers Cl GU4 . . . . 110 D4
Keepers Combe RG12 . . . . . 27 D3
Keepers Ct 4 CR2 . . . . 61 C5
Keepers Mews TW11 . . . . . . 17 C2
Keepers Terr GU25 . . . . 31 B4
Keepers Wlk GU25 . . . . 31 D4
Keephatch Ho RG40 . . . . . . 25 F7
Keep Hatch Prim Sch
  RG40 . . . . 25 D7
Keephatch Rd RG40 . . . . . . 25 E7
Keep The
  Catford SE6 . . . . 24 B7
  Kingston upon Thames KT2. 17 F1
Keevil Dr SW19 . . . . 19 E8
Keir Hardie Ho 7 RH11 . 201 B1
Keir The SW19 . . . . 19 E8
Keith Lucas Rd GU14 . . . . 84 F2
Keith Park Cres TN16 . . . . 83 C7
Keldholme RG12 . . . . 27 A6
Kellie Ho SL5 . . . . 30 A1
Kelling Gdns CR0 . . . . 42 B2
Kellino St SW17 . . . . 20 F4
Kelly Cl TW17 . . . . 34 E7
Kelmscott 5 SE23 . . . . 23 D5
Kelmscott Pl KT21 . . . . 75 C2
Kelsall Mews TW9 . . . . 7 B6
Kelsey Cl RH6 . . . . 160 F3
Kelsey Ct BR3 . . . . 44 B6
Kelsey Gate 8 BR3 . . . . . . 44 B7
Kelsey La BR3 . . . . 44 A6
Kelsey Park Ave BR3 . . . . . 44 B7
Kelsey Park Mans BR3 . . . . 44 B6
Kelsey Park Rd BR3 . . . . . . 44 A7
Kelsey Park Sports Coll
  BR3. . . . . 44 A6
Kelsey Sq BR3 . . . . 44 A7
Kelsey Way BR3. . . . . 44 A6
Kelso Cl RH10 . . . . 202 E7
Kelso Ct SE20. . . . . 23 B1
Kelso Rd SM5. . . . . 40 C2
Kelvedon Ave KT12. . . . . . . 53 F3
Kelvedon Cl KT2 . . . . 18 A2
Kelvin Ave KT22 . . . . 94 F8
Kelvinbrook KT8 . . . . 36 B6
Kelvin Bsns Ctr RH10 . . . . 181 F1
Kelvin Cl KT19 . . . . 57 A4
Kelvin Ct
  Chiswick W4 . . . . 7 C7
  Isleworth TW7. . . . . 5 E5
  8 Penge SE20 . . . . 43 B8
  8 Twickenham TW1 . . . . . . 6 B1
Kelvin Dr TW1 . . . . 6 B1
Kelvin Gate RG12 . . . . 27 D7
Kelvin Gdns CR0 . . . . 41 E2
Kelvin Gr
  Chessington KT6 . . . . 56 E7
  Forest Hill SE26. . . . . 23 B5
Kelvin Grove Prim Sch
  SE26 . . . . 23 B5
Kelvington Cl CR0. . . . . 43 E2
Kelvin Ho RH10 . . . . 181 F1
Kelvin La RH10. . . . . 181 F2
Kelvin Way RH10. . . . . 181 F2
Kelway Ho 20 SW2 . . . . . . 22 A8
Kemble Cl KT13 . . . . 53 D6
Kemble Cotts KT15 . . . . . . 52 A4
Kemble Rd
  Croydon CR0, CR9 . . . . . 61 B7
  Forest Hill SE23. . . . . 23 D7
Kembleside Rd TN16 . . . . . 83 C1
Kemerton Rd
  Beckenham BR3. . . . . 43 C8
  Croydon CR0 . . . . 42 F2
Kemishford GU22 . . . . 89 A4
Kemnal Pk GU27 . . . . 208 D7
Kemp Ct GU19 . . . . 47 F2
Kemp Gdns CR0 . . . . 42 C3
Kempshott Rd
  Horsham RH12 . . . . 217 B4
  Streatham SW16 . . . . 21 C1
Kempston Ho SM2 . . . . 59 B2
Kempton Ave TW16 . . . . . . 35 B8
Kempton Ct
  Farnborough GU14 . . . . . 84 F2
  Sunbury TW16 . . . . 35 B8
Kempton Gate Bsns Ctr
  TW12 . . . . 35 F8
Kempton Ho KT20. . . . . 97 C4
Kempton Lodge SM4 . . . . . 60 D7
Kempton Park Nature
  Reserve★ TW13. . . . . . . 15 D2
Kempton Park Race Course
  TW16 . . . . 15 C1
Kempton Park Sta TW16. . . 15 B1
Kempton Wlk CR0 . . . . 43 E3
Kemsing Cl
  1 Coney Hall BR2. . . . . . 63 F8
  Thornton Heath CR7 . . . . 42 C5
Kemsley Rd TN16 . . . . 103 D8
Kendal Cl
  East Bedfont TW14 . . . . . 14 F7
  Farnborough GU14 . . . . . 84 E4
  Redhill RH2 . . . . 118 D2
Kendal Ct
  7 Croydon CR0. . . . . 42 E1
  Kenley CR8. . . . . 80 D5
Kendale Rd RH10 . . . . 202 C2
Kendale Rd BR1 . . . . 24 E3
Kendal Gdns SM1 . . . . 59 C8
Kendal Gr GU15. . . . . 66 D4

Kendal Ho
  5 Croydon CR0. . . . . 42 E1
  Forest Hill SE23. . . . . 23 D7
  Penge SE20 . . . . 43 B7
Kendall Ave
  Penge BR3. . . . . 43 E7
  South Croydon CR2 . . . . . 61 D2
Kendall Ave S CR2 . . . . . . 61 D1
Kendall Ct
  Mitcham SW17 . . . . 20 D2
  4 Penge SE19 . . . . 22 F1
Kendall Ho 3 SE12 . . . . . . 24 F8
Kendall Rd
  Isleworth TW7. . . . . 6 A5
  Penge BR3. . . . . 43 E7
Kendor Ave KT19 . . . . 76 C8
Kendra Ct CR2 . . . . 61 B3
Kendra Rd CR2 . . . . 61 B3
Kendrey Gdns TW2. . . . . . . 16 E8
Kendrick Cl RG40 . . . . 25 C5
Kenilford Rd SW12 . . . . . . 21 B8
Kenilworth Ave
  Bracknell RG12 . . . . 27 D8
  Oxshott KT11 . . . . 74 B5
  Wimbledon SW19 . . . . . . 20 A4
Kenilworth Cl
  Banstead SM7 . . . . 78 B3
  Crawley RH11. . . . . 201 B2
Kenilworth Ct TW2. . . . . . . 16 E6
Kenilworth Dr KT12 . . . . . . 54 D7
Kenilworth Gdns TW18 . . . 13 C3
Kenilworth Rd
  Ashford TW15, TW19. . . . . 13 D5
  Farnborough GU14 . . . . . 84 C5
  Penge SE20 . . . . 43 D8
  Stoneleigh KT17. . . . . 58 A5
Kenilworth Terr 5 SM2 . . 59 A3
KENLEY 80 D3
Kenley Gdns CR7. . . . . 42 B5
Kenley Ho 5 CR0 . . . . 43 A1
Kenley La
  Kenley CR8. . . . . 80 D3
  Purley/Kenley CR8 . . . . . 80 D2
Kenley Prim Sch CR3. . . . . 80 E3
Kenley Rd
  Headley Down GU35 . . . 187 C5
  Kingston upon Thames KT1,
    KT3 . . . . 38 B7
  Merton SW19. . . . . 40 A6
  Twickenham TW1 . . . . 6 B1
Kenley Sta TW8 . . . . 80 C5
Kenley Wlk SM3 . . . . 58 D6
Kenlor Rd SW17 . . . . 20 D3
Kenmara Cl RH10 . . . . 182 A1
Kenmara Ct RH10 . . . . 182 A2
Kenmare Dr CR4 . . . . 20 F1
Kenmare Rd CR7. . . . . 42 A3
Kenmore Cl
  Frimley GU16. . . . . 85 D8
  Richmond TW9. . . . . 7 A7
Kenmore Ct CR8. . . . . 80 B5
Kennard Ct RH18. . . . . . . 206 E3
Kennedy Ave RH19 . . . . . 185 D3
Kennedy Cl 1 CR4 . . . . . . 41 A7
Kennedy Ct TW15 . . . . 14 C3
Kennedy Rd RH13 . . . . . . 217 D1
Kennel Ave SL5 . . . . 28 F8
Kennel Cl
  Fetcham KT22 . . . . 94 C3
  North Ascot SL5. . . . . 8 C7
Kennel Gn SL5. . . . . 28 E8
Kennel La
  Fetcham KT22 . . . . 94 C4
  Frensham GU10. . . . . . . 146 C2
  Hookwood RH6 . . . . 160 D2
  Windlesham GU20. . . . . . 48 C5
Kennel Ride SL5 . . . . 8 F1
Kennels La GU14 . . . . 84 C2
Kennel Wood SL5 . . . . 28 F8
Kennel Wood Cres CR0. . . 82 D8
Kennet Cl
  Ash GU12. . . . . 106 A1
  Crawley RH11. . . . . 200 F5
  Farnborough GU14 . . . . . 84 E6
Kennet Ct GU21. . . . . 69 F3
Kennet Ho 6 RH1 . . . . . . 118 F2
Kenneth Rd SM7 . . . . 78 D4
Kennet Rd TW7 . . . . 5 F4
Kennet Sq CR4. . . . . 40 E8
Kennett Ct W4. . . . . 7 B7
Kennoldes SE21. . . . . 22 D6
Kenrick Sq RH1. . . . . 120 E1
Kensington Ave CR7 . . . . . 42 A8
Kensington Avenue Prim Sch
  CR7. . . . . 42 A8
Kensington Gdns KT1. . . . . 37 D6
Kensington Rd RH11 . . . . . 201 C2
Kensington Terr CR2 . . . . . 61 D3
Kent Cl
  Mitcham CR4, SW16 . . . . 41 E5
  Staines TW18. . . . . 13 D2
Kent Ct 4 RH12 . . . . 217 D2
Kent Dr TW11. . . . . 16 E3
Kent Gate Way
  Addington CR0. . . . . 63 B5
  New Addington CR0. . . . . 62 F4
Kent Hatch Rd RH8, TN8 . .123 D4
Kent Ho TW10. . . . . 7 A2
Kent House La BR3. . . . . . . 23 E3
Kent House Rd SE26, BR3. . 23 E2
Kent House Sta BR3 . . . . . 43 E8
Kent House Station App
  BR3. . . . . 23 E3
Kentigern Dr RG45 . . . . . . 45 E5
Kent Lodge 9 SW19 . . . . . 19 D7
Kenton Ave TW16 . . . . 35 E7

Kenton Cl
  Bracknell RG12 . . . . 27 D7
  Frimley RG12 . . . . 65 F1
Kenton Ct
  2 Forest Hill SE26 . . . . . 23 E4
  8 Twickenham TW1 . . . . . 6 D1
Kenton Way GU21. . . . . 68 F2
Kent Rd
  East Molesey KT8 . . . . . . 36 C5
  Kingston upon Thames KT1. 37 D6
  Richmond TW9. . . . . 7 A7
  West Wickham BR4 . . . . . 44 B1
  Windlesham GU20. . . . . . 48 D5
  Woking GU22 . . . . 70 C3
Kent Way KT6 . . . . 56 F8
Kentwood Farm RG40. . . . . 25 D8
Kidworth CR8 . . . . 160 F5
Kentwyns Rise RH1 . . . . . 140 F8
Kenward Ct RH3. . . . . 137 C5
Kenwood Cl UB7. . . . . 3 A8
Kenwood Dr
  Beckenham BR3. . . . . 44 C6
  Hersham KT12. . . . . 54 B5
Kenwood Pk KT13. . . . . 53 D4
Kenwood Ridge CR8 . . . . . 80 B2
Kenworth Gr GU18 . . . . 48 A1
Kenwyn Rd SW20 . . . . 39 C8
Kenya Ct RH6. . . . . 160 F4
Kenyngton Dr TW16 . . . . . . 15 A3
Kenyngton Manor Prim Sch
  TW16 . . . . 15 A2
Kenyons KT24 . . . . 112 B7
Keogh Barracks GU16 . . . . 86 B1
Keogh Cl GU12. . . . . 86 B2
Keppel Rd RH4 . . . . 115 B1
Keppel Spur SL4 . . . . 11 B8
Kepple Pl GU19 . . . . 47 F3
Kernal Ct GU1. . . . . 109 C1
Kerria Way GU24. . . . . 67 F6
Kerrill Ave CR5 . . . . 100 A8
Kerrsland Cotts GU7 . . . . 149 F7
Kerry Terr GU21 . . . . 70 B3
Kersey Dr CR2 . . . . 81 D7
Kershaw Ho 7 SE27 . . . . . 22 B5
Keston Ave
  Coulsdon CR5, CR8 . . . . 100 B8
  Woodham KT15 . . . . 71 A8
Keston Prim Sch CR5 . . . . 100 A8
Keston Rd CR7. . . . . 42 A3
Kestral Ct SM6. . . . . 60 C5
Kestrel Ave TW18 . . . . 12 F5
Kestrel Cl
  Ash Vale GU12. . . . . 106 A7
  Crawley RH11. . . . . 201 C8
  Crondall GU10 . . . . 124 D7
  Epsom KT19. . . . . 76 B8
  Guildford GU4 . . . . 110 D3
  Horsham RH12 . . . . 217 E5
  Kingston upon Thames KT2. 17 D4
Kestrel Ct 2 CR2 . . . . 61 C4
Kestrel Ho GU9 . . . . 146 A8
Kestrel Rd GU14 . . . . 85 B2
Kestrel Way
  New Addington CR0. . . . . 63 D2
  Woking GU21. . . . . 69 B3
Kestrel Wlk RH10 . . . . 204 C5
Keswick Ave
  Kingston upon Thames
    SW15 . . . . 18 E3
  Merton SW19. . . . . 40 A7
  Upper Halliford TW17 . . . . 34 E6
Keswick Cl
  Crawley RH11. . . . . 200 D4
  Frimley GU15. . . . . 66 D4
  Sutton SM1 . . . . 59 C6
Keswick Ct
  17 Bromley BR2 . . . . 44 F5
  Catford SE6 . . . . 24 F7
Keswick Dr GU18 . . . . 67 B8
Keswick Rd
  Fetcham KT22, KT23 . . . . 94 C2
  Thorpe Lea TW20. . . . . . . 12 B1
  Twickenham TW2. . . . . 5 C1
  West Wickham BR4 . . . . . 63 E8
  Witley GU8. . . . . 170 D6
Kettering Ct CR7. . . . . 42 C5
Kettering St SW16 . . . . 21 C2
Kettlewell Cl GU21 . . . . 69 E4
Kettlewell Dr GU21. . . . . . . 69 E5
Kettlewell Hill GU21. . . . . . 69 E4
Ketton Gn RH1. . . . . 119 D7
Kevan Dr GU23. . . . . 90 E2
Kevin Cl TW4 . . . . 4 D5
KEW 7 A8
Kew Bridge Rd TW8. . . . . . . 6 F8
Kew Coll TW9 . . . . 7 A7
Kew Cres SM3 . . . . 58 F7
Kew Ct KT2 . . . . 37 E8
Kew Foot Rd TW9. . . . . 6 E4
Kew Gardens Rd TW9 . . . . . 7 A6
Kew Gardens Sta/U Sta
  TW9 . . . . 7 A6
Kew Gn TW9. . . . . 6 F8
Kew Green Prep Sch TW8 . .6 F8
Kew Lodge 11 TW9. . . . . . . 6 F6
Kew Montessori Sch TW9 . 7 A6
Kew Observatory★ TW9 . . 6 C4
Kew Palace★ TW9 . . . . 6 E7
Kew Rd TW9, W4. . . . . 6 F5
Kew Ret Pk TW9. . . . . 7 B6
Kew Riverside Prim Sch
  TW9 . . . . 7 B5
Key Cross GU10. . . . . 147 D5
Keymer Cl TN16. . . . . 83 D8
Keymer Rd
  Crawley RH11. . . . . 201 D4
  Streatham SW2 . . . . 21 F6
Keynsham Rd SM4 . . . . 40 B1
Keynsham Way GU47. . . . . 45 D2

Keynsham Wlk SM4 . . . . . . 40 B1
Keys Ct CR0 . . . . 61 D7
Keysham Ave TW5 . . . . 4 A4
Keywood Dr TW16 . . . . 15 A2
Khama Rd SW17 . . . . 20 E4
Khartoum Rd
  Upper Tooting SW17 . . . . 20 D4
  Witley GU8. . . . . 170 E6
Kibble Gn RG12 . . . . 27 C3
Kidborough Down KT23 . . .114 A8
Kidborough Rd RH11 . . . . 200 F5
Kidbrooke Rise RH18. . . . . 206 E2
Kidderminster Pl CR0 . . . . 42 B1
Kidderminster Rd CR0. . . . 42 C2
Kidmans Cl RH12 . . . . 217 F5
Kielder Wlk GU15 . . . . 66 C4
Kier Pk SL5 . . . . 29 C6
Kilberry Cl TW7. . . . . 5 D6
Kilcorral Cl KT17. . . . . 77 A5
Killasser Ct KT20. . . . . 97 C4
Killburns Mill Cl SM6. . . . . 60 B8
Killearn Rd SE6 . . . . 24 D7
Killester Gdns KT17, KT4 . . 58 B6
Killick Ho SM1 . . . . 59 B6
Killick Mews SM3 . . . . 58 E4
Killieser Ave SW2 . . . . 21 E6
Killigrew Ho 4 TW16 . . . . 14 E1
Killinghurst La GU27,
  GU8 . . . . 209 D8
Killowen Cl KT20. . . . . 97 D5
Killy Hill GU24 . . . . 49 E3
Kilmarnock Pk RH2 . . . . . 118 B2
Kilmartin Ave SW16 . . . . . . 42 A6
Kilmartin Gdns GU16. . . . . 65 F1
Kilmington Cl RG12 . . . . . . 27 E2
Kilmiston Ave TW17 . . . . . . 34 C3
Kilmiston House TW17 . . . . 34 C3
Kilmore Dr GU15. . . . . 66 B4
Kilmorey Gdns TW1. . . . . . . 6 B3
Kilmorey Rd TW1 . . . . 6 B3
Kilmorie Prim Sch SE23 . . 23 E6
Kilmorie Rd SE23 . . . . 23 E6
Kilmuir Cl GU47. . . . . 64 D7
Kiln Ave GU27 . . . . 208 C8
Kilnbridge Ho GU21. . . . . . 88 F8
Kiln Cl
  Crawley Down RH10 . . . . 204 B7
  Harlington UB3 . . . . 3 D8
Kiln Copse GU6 . . . . 174 E4
Kilnfield Rd RH12 . . . . 214 D8
Kiln La
  Bracknell RG12 . . . . 27 A7
  Brockham RH3. . . . . 116 C1
  Cranbourne SL4. . . . . 9 B2
  Ewell KT17 . . . . 76 E8
  Farnham GU10, GU9 . . . 146 C6
  Horley RH6 . . . . 161 A5
  Ripley GU23. . . . . 91 B3
  Sunningdale SL5 . . . . 30 A4
Kiln Mdws GU3 . . . . 108 C5
Kilnmead RH10 . . . . 201 E7
Kilnmead Cl RH10. . . . . . . 201 E7
Kiln Mews SW17 . . . . 20 D3
Kiln Rd RH10 . . . . 204 B7
Kilnside KT10. . . . . 56 A3
Kilns The
  Farnham GU10. . . . . 125 F3
  Frithend GU35 . . . . 166 A5
Kiln Way
  Aldershot GU11. . . . . 126 B7
  Grayshott GU26 . . . . 187 E5
Kiln Wlk RH1 . . . . 140 A4
Kilnwood La
  Crawley RH12 . . . . 200 B3
  Faygate RH12 . . . . 199 F3
Kilravock Ho SE25 . . . . 42 D6
Kilross Rd TW14 . . . . 14 E7
Kilrue La KT12 . . . . 53 F6
Kilrush Terr GU21 . . . . 70 A3
Kilsha Rd KT12. . . . . 35 C3
Kimber Ct GU4. . . . . 110 D3
Kimberley Cl
  Harlington UB3 . . . . 3 D8
  Redhill RH1 . . . . 139 E7
Kimberley Ho 4 TW16 . . . 14 D4
Kimberley Pl 7 CR8 . . . . . 80 A8
Kimberley Rd
  Crawley RH10. . . . . 202 B7
  Penge BR3. . . . . 43 D7
  Thornton Heath CR0, CR7. . 42 B3
Kimberley Ride KT11 . . . . . 74 B6
Kimberley Wlk KT12. . . . . . 35 B2
Kimber Pl 6 TW4. . . . . 16 A8
Kimber Rd SW18 . . . . 20 B8
Kimbers La GU9 . . . . 125 D3
Kimble Rd SW19 . . . . 20 D2
Kimbolton Cl 1 SE12 . . . . 24 F8
Kimmeridge RG12 . . . . 27 E3
Kimpton Ho SW15 . . . . 19 A8
Kimpton Link Bsns Ctr
  SM3 . . . . 58 F8
Kimpton Park Way SM3 . . . 58 F8
Kimpton Rd SM3. . . . . 58 F8
Kimpton Trad & Bsns Ctr
  SM3 . . . . 58 F8
Kinburn Dr TW20 . . . . 11 E3
Kindell Ho 4 SW14 . . . . . . 7 D4
Kindersley Cl RH19 . . . . . 186 B3
Kinfauns Rd SW2 . . . . 22 A6
King Acre Ct TW18 . . . . . . 12 E5
King Alfred Ave SE6. . . . . . 24 A4
Kingates Ct BR3 . . . . 44 B6
King Athelstan Prim Sch 1
  KT1. . . . . 37 F6
King Charles Cres KT5 . . . . 37 F2
King Charles' Rd KT5, KT6. . 37 F3

King Charles Wlk 6
  SW19 . . . . 19 E7
Kingcup Cl CR0. . . . . 43 D1
Kingcup Dr GU24 . . . . 68 A4
Kingdom Ho 5 GU14. . . . 105 D1
King Edward Dr KT6 . . . . . 56 E7
King Edwards Cl SL5. . . . . 28 E8
King Edward's Gr TW11 . . . 17 C2
King Edwards Rd SL5 . . . . 28 E8
King Edwards Rise SL5. . . 28 E8
King Edward's Sch GU8 . . 170 F1
KINGFIELD 89 F7
Kingfield Cl GU22. . . . . 89 F7
Kingfield Dr GU22. . . . . 89 F7
Kingfield Gdns GU22 . . . . . 89 F7
Kingfield Rd GU22 . . . . 89 F7
Kingfield Sch GU22 . . . . . . 90 A7
Kingfisher Cl
  Crawley RH10. . . . . 182 A1
  Farnborough GU14 . . . . . 84 D6
  Hersham KT12. . . . . 54 E5
Kingfisher Ct
  Cheam SM1 . . . . 58 F5
  4 Dorking RH4. . . . . 136 A8
  East Molesey KT8 . . . . . . 36 E5
  Guildford GU4 . . . . 110 D3
  Hounslow TW7. . . . . 5 D5
  Isleworth TW3 . . . . 5 B2
  Putney SW19 . . . . 19 E6
  Sheerwater GU21 . . . . . . 70 C5
  Woking GU21. . . . . 69 E2
Kingfisher Dr
  Guildford GU4 . . . . 110 C3
  Redhill RH1 . . . . 119 A3
  Staines TW18. . . . . 12 F4
  Teddington TW10 . . . . . . 17 B4
Kingfisher Gdns CR2 . . . . . 62 D1
Kingfisher La RH10. . . . . . 204 C5
Kingfisher Lodge TW11 . . . 17 A4
Kingfisher Rd GU9 . . . . . . 145 F3
Kingfisher Rise RH19 . . . . 205 F8
Kingfisher Way
  Beckenham CR0. . . . . 43 D4
  Horsham RH12 . . . . 217 C5
Kingfisher Wlk GU12. . . . . 105 F2
King Garth Mews SE23 . . . 23 C6
King Gdns CR0. . . . . 61 B5
King George Ave
  East Grinstead RH19 . . . 185 C3
  Walton-on-Thames KT12. . 35 D1
King George Cl
  Ashford TW16 . . . . 14 E3
  Farnborough GU14 . . . . . 85 D2
King George's Cotts GU8 192 F6
King George's Dr KT15 . . . 52 A1
King George's Lodge
  GU2 . . . . 109 A4
King George Sq TW10 . . . . . 6 F1
King George's Trad Est
  KT9 . . . . 57 A6
King George VI Ave
  Biggin Hill TN16 . . . . 83 D3
  Mitcham CR4. . . . . 40 F5
Kingham Cl SW18 . . . . 20 C8
Kingham Pl GU9 . . . . 125 B2
King Henry's Dr CR0 . . . . . 82 E8
King Henry's Dr Halt CR0. 63 B2
King Henry's Rd KT1, KT3 . . 38 B6
Kinglake Ct 2 GU21. . . . . . 68 E1
Kings Acre RH1 . . . . 140 F6
Kings Apartments GU15 . . 65 C4
Kings Ave
  Ash GU10. . . . . 126 F8
  Bromley BR1 . . . . 24 F2
  Byfleet KT14 . . . . 71 D7
  New Malden KT3 . . . . 38 F5
  Redhill RH1 . . . . 139 E7
  Streatham SW12, SW4 . . . 21 D8
  Wallington SM5 . . . . 59 F3
King's Ave
  Ashford TW16 . . . . 14 F2
  Hounslow TW3, TW5 . . . . . 5 B6
Kingsbridge Ho 11 SE20 . . 43 B8
Kingsbridge Rd
  Walton-on-Thames KT12. . 35 B2
  West Barnes SM4 . . . . . . 39 D2
Kingsbrook KT22. . . . . 75 A1
Kingsbury Cres TW18 . . . . 12 D4
Kingsbury Dr SL4 . . . . 11 B8
Kings Chase KT8 . . . . 36 C6
Kings Cl KT12 . . . . 35 B1
King's Cl
  Staines TW18. . . . . 13 D1
  Thames Ditton KT7 . . . . . 37 A2
Kingsclear Pk GU15. . . . . . 65 D4
Kingsclere Cl SW15 . . . . . . 19 A8
Kingscliffe Gdns SW19 . . . 19 F7
Kings' Coll for the Arts &
  Technology GU2. . . . . . . 108 C3
Kings Coll Jun Sch SW19. 19 C2
King's Coll Sch SW19 . . . . 19 D2
Kings Copse 9 RH19. . . . . 205 F8
Kingscote Hill RH11. . . . . . 201 B4
Kingscote Rd
  Croydon CR0, CR9 . . . . . 43 B2
  Kingston upon Thames KT3. 38 D6
Kingscote Sta★ RH19 . . . . 204 F4
Kings Court Bsns Ctr 5
  GU15. . . . . 65 D5
King's Court Fst Sch SL4 . . 11 B8
Kings Court Mews KT8 . . . 36 D4
Kingscourt Rd SW16 . . . . . 21 D5
Kings Cres GU15 . . . . 65 C8
Kingscroft Cty Jun Sch
  TW18 . . . . 13 A2

Kingscroft La RG42........8 A6
Kingscroft Rd
  Leatherhead KT22........95 B7
  Woodmansterne SM7 ....78 E4
Kings Cross La RH1..140 E6
Kings Ct
  Horsham RH13........217 E3
  16 Kingston upon Thames
    KT2........18 A1
  Leatherhead KT22........95 A6
  11 Roehampton SW15....19 A8
  Tadworth KT20........97 C5
  3 Wallington SM6........60 B4
King's Ct
  Aldershot GU10, GU12...126 E8
  Beckenham BR3........44 B6
  Wimbledon SW19........20 A2
Kingsdale Rd SE20.......23 D1
Kingsdale Sch SE21......22 E5
Kingsdene KT20........97 B5
Kingsdown SW19........19 D1
Kingsdown Ave CR2, CR8..61 C2
Kingsdowne Rd KT6.....37 F2
Kingsdown Rd
  Cheam SM3........58 E5
  Ewell KT17........77 A6
Kings Dr KT5........38 A3
King's Dr KT7........37 B2
Kings Dr The KT12......53 F2
Kings Farm Ave TW10......7 A3
Kingsfield GU5........153 E7
Kingsfield Bsns Pk RH1..140 A8
Kingsfield Ct GU12......106 A3
Kingsfield Way RH1....140 A8
KINGSFOLD........198 B5
Kingsfold Ct RH12......198 B5
Kings Gate
  Addlestone KT15........52 B6
  Farncombe GU7........150 F6
  Horsham RH12........217 E2
  8 Knaphill GU21........68 D2
  Woking GU21........69 D1
Kingsgate Rd KT2........37 E8
Kingsgrove Ind Est GU14..85 A3
Kings Hall Rd BR3........43 E8
King's Head La KT14....71 D8
Kingshill Ave KT4........39 B2
Kings Ho 12 KT2........37 E8
King's House Sch TW10....6 F2
Kings International Coll for
  Bsns & the Arts GU15..65 C2
Kings Keep KT6........37 E5
King's Keep
  Beckenham BR2........44 E6
  Sandhurst GU47........45 B1
Kings La
  Englefield Green TW20.....11 A2
  Windlesham GU20........48 E5
  Wrecclesham GU10....145 F6
King's La SM1........59 D5
Kingsland RH5........158 A3
Kingsland Ct RH10......202 A6
Kingslea
  Horsham RH13........217 E3
  Leatherhead KT22........95 A7
Kingslea Prim Sch RH13.217 E3
Kingslee Ct 13 SM2......59 B3
Kingsleigh Cl TW8........6 D8
Kingsleigh Pl CR4........40 F6
Kingsleigh Wlk BR2......44 F5
Kingsley Ave
  Banstead SM7........78 A4
  Camberley GU15........65 D3
  Carshalton SM1........59 D6
  Englefield Green TW20.....11 B2
  Hounslow TW3........5 C5
Kingsley Cl
  Crowthorne RG45........45 B3
  Horley RH6........160 F5
Kingsley Ct
  Aldershot GU11........105 B2
  Walton-on-Thames KT12....54 A7
  Worcester Park KT4......57 F8
Kingsley Dr KT4........57 F8
Kingsley Gdns KT16......51 D4
Kingsley Gr RH2........139 B5
KINGSLEY GREEN........208 B4
Kingsley Ho 8 KT6......37 E4
Kingsley Prim Sch CR0...42 A1
Kingsley Rd
  Crawley RH11........201 A3
  Farnborough GU14 ......84 F6
  Horley RH6........160 F5
  Hounslow TW3........5 C5
  Thornton Heath CR0......42 A1
  Wimbledon SW19........20 B3
Kingslyn Cres SE19......42 E8
Kingsmead
  Biggin Hill TN16........83 D3
  Cranleigh GU6........174 E3
  Farnborough GU14 ......85 B4
  Frimley GU16........85 E7
  Richmond TW10........6 F1
  Weybridge KT13........53 D4
  11 Woking GU21........70 A3
Kings Mead
  Smallfield RH6........162 B3
  South Nutfield RH1.....140 E7
Kingsmead Ave
  Mitcham CR4........41 C6
  North Cheam KT4........58 B7
  Sunbury TW16........35 C7
  Tolworth KT6........57 A8
Kingsmead Cl
  Horsham RH12........218 B6

Kingsmead Cl continued
  Teddington TW11........17 B2
  West Ewell KT19........57 D3
Kingsmead Ct BR1........24 F1
Kingsmead Lodge SM2...59 D4
Kingsmeadow Stadium
  (Kingstonian FC) KT1...38 A6
  (Kings Mead Pk) KT10....55 E3
Kingsmead Pl RH12.....216 C3
Kingsmead Rd
  Broadbridge Heath
    RH12........216 D3
  Streatham SW2........22 A4
Kingsmead Sh Ctr GU14..85 B3
Kingsmere SE6........24 B7
Kingsmere Rd
  Bracknell RG42........26 F8
  Putney SW19........19 D6
Kings Mews
  Frimley GU16........85 F6
  Horsham RH12........217 E2
Kingsmill Bsns Pk KT1....37 F6
Kings Mill La RH1......140 D5
Kingsmount Ct SM1......59 B6
Kingsnympton Pk KT2....18 B2
Kingsoak Ho 2 GU21....70 A3
King's Paddock TW12....36 C8
Kings Par 3 SM5........59 E7
Kingspark Bsns Ctr KT3..38 C6
Kings Peace The GU26..188 C3
Kings Penny Ho 4 KT2...17 E1
Kings Pl RH13........217 E3
Kings Rd
  Belmont SM2........59 A1
  Biggin Hill TN16........83 C2
  Feltham TW13........15 C7
  Horley RH6........161 A3
  Mitcham CR4........41 A6
  Richmond TW10, TW9.....6 F2
  Rudgwick RH12........214 D7
  Shalford GU4........130 C2
  Walton-on-Thames KT12...35 B1
  West End GU24........68 A6
  Woking GU21........70 A3
  Wonersh GU5........152 B8
  Woodham KT15........71 B8
King's Rd
  Aldershot GU11........104 F1
  Ascot SL5........29 D4
  Cranleigh GU6........174 F2
  Crowthorne RG45........45 C5
  Croydon SE25........43 A6
  Egham TW20........12 A6
  Farncombe GU7........150 F6
  Haslemere GU27........208 A6
  Horsham RH13........217 E3
  Long Ditton KT6........37 C1
  Mortlake SW14........7 A4
  Teddington TW11........16 D3
  Twickenham TW1........6 B1
  Wimbledon SW19........20 A2
King's Ride
  Bracknell SL5........28 D5
  Camberley GU15........65 D7
Kings Ride Gate TW10....7 A3
King's Ride Ho SL5........28 E5
Kingsridge SW19........19 E6
Kings Road Ind Est
  GU27........208 A6
King's Shade Wlk 1 KT18 76 D6
Kings's Rd 2 GU21.....109 D1
King St
  Chertsey KT16........33 A1
  East Grinstead RH19.....185 E1
  Richmond TW10, TW9 ....6 D2
  Twickenham TW1........17 A7
King's Terr
  Brands Hill SL3........1 B8
  9 Isleworth TW7........6 A4
Kingsthorpe Rd SE26....23 D4
Kingston Ave
  Cheam SM3........58 E7
  East Horsley KT24........92 E1
  Feltham TW14........3 F1
  Leatherhead KT22........95 B6
Kingston Bsns Ctr KT9...56 F7
Kingston By-Pass KT6, KT7,
  KT9........56 C7
Kingston Cl TW11........17 B2
Kingston Coll
  Kingston upon Thames
    KT1........37 D6
  Kingston upon Thames KT2..37 E8
Kingston Cres
  Beckenham BR3........43 F8
  Staines TW15........13 D2
Kingston Gdns CR0......60 E7
Kingston Gram Sch KT2..37 F7
Kingston Hall Rd KT1....37 D6
Kingston Hill KT2........18 C2
Kingston Hill Pl KT2......18 C4
Kingston Hospl KT2......38 B8
Kingston House Est KT6..37 B3
Kingston House Gdns
  KT22........95 B6
Kingston La
  Teddington TW11........17 B2
  West Horsley KT24......112 A8
Kingston Lodge 2 KT3....38 E5
Kingston Mus* KT1........37 E7
Kingston Par KT19........57 F4
Kingston Rd
  Ashtead KT15, TW17.....13 F2
  Ashtead KT22, KT9........75 A3
  Camberley GU15........47 A1
  Kingston upon Thames KT1,
    KT3........38 C5
  Leatherhead KT22........75 A1

Kingston Rd continued
  Merton SW19, SW20......39 E7
  Putney SW15, SW19......19 B7
  Staines TW15, TW18......13 B2
  Teddington TW11........17 B2
  Worcester Park KT17, KT19, KT4,
    KT5, KT6........57 D6
Kingston Rise KT15......52 A1
Kingstons Ind Est GU12.105 E2
Kingston Sq
  Leatherhead KT22........95 A8
  West Norwood SE19......22 D3
Kingston Sta KT2........37 E8
Kingston Univ
  Kingston upon Thames,
    Kingston Vale KT1........18 D3
  Kingston upon Thames KT1..37 D6
  Kingston upon Thames KT1..37 E6
Kingston Univ Roehampton
  Vale Ctr SW15........18 F5
KINGSTON UPON
  THAMES........37 C6
KINGSTON UPON
  THAMES........18 D4
Kingston Vale SW15......18 E5
King Street Par 1 TW1...17 A7
Kings View Ct 1 SW20...19 D1
Kings Warren KT22........74 D8
Kings Way CR0........60 F5
King's Way GU24........87 D8
Kingsway Ave
  Selsdon CR2........62 D2
  Woking GU21........69 D1
Kingsway Bsns Pk
  Hampton TW12........35 F8
  Sheerwater GU21........70 C5
Kingsway Rd SM3........58 E3
Kingsway Terr KT13......53 A2
Kingsway The KT17......57 F1
Kingswear Ho SE23......23 C6
Kingswick Cl SL5........29 D5
Kingswick Dr SL5........29 D5
Kings Wlk CR2........81 B5
King's Wlk GU15........64 F6
KINGSWOOD........97 F6
Kingswood GU26........188 D2
Kingswood Ave
  Beckenham BR2........44 E5
  Hampton TW12........16 B2
  Hamsey Green CR2........81 C4
  Hounslow TW3, TW5........4 F5
  Thornton Heath CR7......42 A4
Kingswood Cl
  Ashford TW15........14 D3
  Camberley GU15........66 A8
  Englefield Green TW20....11 D4
  Guildford GU1........110 C2
  New Malden KT3........38 F3
  Surbiton KT6........37 E2
  Weybridge KT13........53 B3
Kingswood Ct
  7 Richmond TW10........6 F2
  Woking GU21........69 E3
Kingswood Dr
  Belmont SM2........59 B2
  Carshalton SM5........40 F1
  Dulwich SE19, SE21......22 F4
Kingswood Firs GU26...188 C2
Kingswood Grange KT20 118 A8
Kingswood Hall of Residence
  TW20........11 A4
Kingswood Ho 3 KT2.....18 B2
Kingswood House Sch
  KT19........76 C6
Kingswood La
  Grayshott GU26........188 C2
  Warlingham CR6........81 C4
Kingswood Mans 8 SM2..59 A4
Kingswood Pk GU20......97 E6
Kingswood Pl CR3......101 A4
Kingswood Prim Sch
  Lower Kingswood KT20...117 F7
  West Norwood SE27......22 D3
Kingswood Rd
  Beckenham BR2........44 E6
  Merton SW19........39 F8
  Penge SE20........23 C2
  Streatham SW2........21 E8
  Tadworth KT20........97 B6
Kingswood Rise TW20....11 D4
Kingswood Sta KT20......97 F6
Kingsway
  Hamsey Green CR2........81 C6
  Selsdon CR2........81 D7
  Wallington SM6........60 E5
Kingsworth Cl BR3........43 E4
Kingsworthy Cl KT1......37 F6
King's Yd SL5........28 E5
King William IV Gdns
  SE20........23 C2
Kinloss Rd SM5........40 C2
Kinnaird Ave
  Bromley BR1........24 F2
  Chiswick W4........7 C7
Kinnaird Cl BR1........24 F2
Kinnear Ct 7 SW20......39 D8
Kinnersley Wlk RH2.....139 B4
Kinnibrugh Dr RH7......165 A1
Kinross Ave
  Ascot SL5........28 F4
  Worcester Park KT4........58 A8

Kinross Cl TW16........14 F3
Kinross Ct
  Ascot SL5........28 F4
  Catford SE6........24 F6
Kinross Dr TW16........14 F3
Kinsella Gdns SW19......19 B3
Kinsey Ho SE21........22 E4
Kintyre Cl SW16........41 F6
Kintyre Ct 16 SW2........21 E8
Kinver Rd SE26........23 C4
Kipings KT20........97 D5
Kipling Cl RH10........202 C8
Kipling Ct RH13........218 A4
Kipling Dr SW17........20 D2
Kipling Hall RG45........45 B5
Kipling Way RH19......185 C1
Kirby Cl KT19........57 F5
Kirby Rd GU21........69 D2
Kirby Way KT12........35 C3
Kirdford Cl RH11.......201 A8
Kirkby Ct GU16........65 E1
Kirkdale SE26........23 B5
Kirkefields GU2........109 A4
Kirkgate The 2 KT7......76 E6
Kirkham Cl GU47........45 D2
Kirkland Ave GU21........68 F3
Kirkland Terr BR3........24 A2
Kirkleas Rd KT6........37 E1
Kirkley Rd SW19........40 A8
Kirkly Cl CR2........61 E2
Kirk Rise SM1........59 B7
Kirkstall RH4........136 A6
Kirkstall Gdns SW2......21 E7
Kirkstall Rd SW2........21 E7
Kirksted Rd SM4........40 B1
Kirkstone Cl GU15......66 D4
Kirkstone Way BR1......24 E1
Kirrane Cl KT3........38 F4
Kirriemuir Gdns GU12..106 D3
Kirsty Cl RH5........136 C5
Kirtley Rd SE26........23 E4
Kisimul Sch KT6........56 C8
Kitchener Rd CR7........42 D6
Kitchenride Cnr KT16....51 A6
Kites Cl RH11........201 C6
Kithurst Cl RH11.......201 D4
Kitley Gdns SE19........42 F8
Kitsbridge Ho RH10.....183 A2
Kitsmead RH10........183 A2
Kitsmead La KT16........50 D8
Kittiwake Cl
  Crawley RH11........200 D4
  Selsdon CR0, CR2........62 E1
Kittiwake Pl SM1........58 F5
Klondyke Villas GU27...190 A1
Knaggs Ho 1 TW11......16 E3
Knap Ct 5 GU21........68 D2
Knapdale Cl SE23........23 B6
Knapmill Rd SE6........24 B6
Knapmill Way SE6........24 B6
Knapp Rd TW15........13 F4
Knapton Mews SW17....21 A2
Knaresborough Dr SW18..20 B7
Kneller Gdns TW7........5 D1
Kneller Rd
  New Malden KT3........38 E2
  Twickenham TW2........5 D1
Knepp Cl RH10........202 C6
Knevett Terr TW3........5 A3
Knight Ho KT4........58 A8
Knighton Cl
  Crawley RH10........182 D2
  Croydon CR2........61 B2
Knighton Lodge KT12....54 C8
Knighton Park Rd SE26..23 D3
Knighton Rd RH1.......140 A7
Knightons La GU8.......193 A2
Knightsbridge Terr TW18 13 B2
Knightsbridge Ho 10
  GU1........130 F8
Knightsbridge Rd GU15..65 E7
Knights Cl
  East Molesey KT8........35 F4
  Egham TW20........12 D2
Knights Ct
  Kingston upon Thames
    KT1........37 E6
  Penge BR3........43 E8
  Reigate RH2........118 C1
  South Croydon CR2........61 D4
Knight's Ct BR1........24 F5
KNIGHT'S HILL........22 C7
Knight's Hill SE27........22 B4
Knight's Hill Sq SE27....22 B4
Knights Mead RH7......164 D6
Knight's Pk KT1........37 E6
Knights Pl 21 RH1......119 A2
Knight's Pl TW2........16 E7
Knights Rd GU9........125 E7
Knight's Pl TW2........16 E7
Knights Way GU15........66 C4
Knightswood
  Bracknell RG12........27 B1
  Woking GU21........68 F1
Knightwood Cl
  Farnborough GU14........85 E2
  Reigate RH2........139 A7
Knightwood Cres KT3....38 E3
Knipp Hill KT11........73 F6
Knobfield RH5........154 F8
Knob Hill RH12........198 A1
Knockholt Cl SM2........59 B1
Knockhundred La GU26.207 C8
Knock The GU47........64 D7

Knole Cl
  Crawley RH10........202 D7
  Croydon CR0........43 C3
Knole Gr RH19........185 C3
Knole Wood SL5........29 E1
Knoll Ct SE19........22 F3
Knoll Ho BR3........44 B8
Knollmead KT4, KT5......38 C1
Knollmead Prim Sch KT5.57 C8
Knoll Park Rd KT16......32 F1
Knoll Quarry GU7......150 E6
Knoll Rd
  Camberley GU15........65 D6
  Dorking RH4........136 A5
  Farncombe GU7........150 E6
Knolls Cl KT4........58 B7
Knolls The KT17........77 C3
Knoll The
  Beckenham BR3........44 B8
  Chertsey KT16........32 F1
  Cobham KT11........74 A6
  Leatherhead KT22........95 C6
Knoll Wood GU7........150 D6
Knolly's Cl SW16........22 A5
Knolly's Rd SW16........22 A5
Knotley Way BR4........63 B8
Knott Park Ho KT22......74 C4
Knowle Cl RH10........183 C3
Knowle Dr RH10........183 B3
Knowle Gdns KT14......70 F6
Knowle Gn TW18........13 A3
Knowle Gr GU25........31 C2
KNOWLE GREEN........13 A3
Knowle Grove Cl GU25..31 C2
KNOWLE HILL........31 C2
Knowle Hill GU25........31 C2
Knowle La GU6, RH12...194 D4
Knowle Lodge CR3......101 A4
Knowle Park Ave TW18..13 B3
Knowle Park Inf Sch
  TW18........13 A3
Knowle Pk KT11........73 E4
Knowle Rd TW2........16 E7
Knowle The GU35......187 B5
Knowl Hill GU22........70 B1
Knowl Hill Sch The GU24 87 F5
Knowlton Gn 2 BR2......44 F4
Knox Rd GU2........109 A6
Kohat Ct GU11........104 F2
Kohat Rd SW19........20 B3
Kohima Cl GU11........105 B3
Koonowla Cl TN16........83 D4
Kooringa CR6........101 B8
Korda Cl TW17........33 F6
Korea Cotts KT11........73 D3
Kreisel Wlk TW9........6 F8
Kristina Ct 4 SM2........59 A4
Krooner Rd GU15........65 B3
Kuala Gdns SW16........41 F8
Kurnool Mortar Cross Roads
  GU15........65 A6
Kyle Cl RG12........27 B6
Kyle Ho TW12........36 C8
Kynaston Ave CR7........42 C4
Kynaston Cres CR0, CR7...42 C4
Kynaston Ct CR3........100 E2
Kynaston Ho 7 SW2......21 F7
Kynaston Rd CR0, CR7....42 C4
Kynersley Cl SM5........59 F7
Kyngeshene Gdns GU1..131 B8

L

Laburnam Ct 13 SW16....22 A3
Laburnham Ct SM1........59 A5
Laburnum Ave 6 SM1....59 E7
Laburnum Cl
  1 Aldershot GU11.......105 A1
  Guildford GU1........109 C4
Laburnum Cres TW16....35 B8
Laburnum Ct
  Chertsey KT16........33 A1
  5 Mitcham CR4........41 A7
  3 Twickenham TW1........6 A1
Laburnum Gdns CR0......43 D1
Laburnum Gr
  Brands Hill SL3........1 B8
  Hounslow TW3........4 F3
  Kingston upon Thames KT3..38 D7
Laburnum Pas 2 GU11...105 A1
Laburnum Pl TW20........11 B2
Laburnum Rd
  Aldershot GU11........105 A2
  Chertsey KT16........33 A1
  Epsom KT18........76 E6
  Heath End GU9........125 E7
  Merton SW19........20 C1
  Mitcham CR4........41 A7
  Woking GU22........89 D7
Laburnums The GU17....64 B5
Laburnum Villas RH1......76 E6
Laburnum Way TW19......13 F7
Lace Tutorial Coll SW17..20 F5
Lacey Ave CR5........100 A7
Lacey Cl TW20........12 D1
Lacey Dr
  Coulsdon CR5........100 B7
  Hampton TW12........35 F8
Lackford Rd CR5........78 F1
Lacock Cl SW19........20 C2
Lacrosse Way SW16......41 D8
Lacy Gn CR5........100 A7
Ladas Rd SE27........22 C4
Ladbroke Cotts 2 RH1...119 A2
Ladbroke Ct 7 RH1......119 A3
Ladbroke Gr RH1........119 A2

Ladbroke Hurst RH7 . . . . .165 A1
Ladbroke Rd
  Epsom KT18. . . . . .76 D5
  Horley RH6 . . . . .161 B5
  Redhill RH1 . . . . .119 A3
Ladbrook Rd SE25 . . . . .42 D5
Ladderstile Ride KT2 . . . . . .18 B3
Ladlands SE22 . . . . .23 A8
Ladybank RG12 . . . . .27 B1
Lady Booth Rd 7 KT1 . . . . .37 E7
Ladycross GU8. . . . . .170 E8
Ladyegate Cl RH5 . . . . . . .136 D8
Ladyegate Rd RH5 . . . . . .136 D8
Lady Eleanor Holles Sch The
  (Jun Girls) TW12 . . . . . .16 B3
Lady Eleanor Holles Sch The
  (Senior Girls) TW12 . . . .16 B3
Lady Elizabeth Ho SW14 . . . .7 C4
Lady Forsdyke Way KT19 . .57 A2
Ladygate Dr GU26 . . . . . . .188 A3
Ladygrove CR2 . . . . .62 D2
Ladygrove Dr GU4 . . . . . .110 B6
Lady Harewood Way KT19 .57 A2
Lady Hay KT4 . . . . .57 F8
Lady Jane Ct 1 KT2. . . . . .37 F7
Lady Margaret Rd
  Crawley RH11 . . . . .201 A7
  Sunningdale SL5 . . . . .29 F2
Lady Margaret Wlk
  RH11 . . . . .201 A7
Ladymead GU1 . . . . .109 C2
Ladymead Cl RH10 . . . . . .202 C3
Ladymead Ret Ctr GU1 . .109 C2
Ladymere Pl GU7 . . . . . . .150 D4
Ladythorpe Cl KT15 . . . . . .52 B6
Ladywood Ave GU14 . . . . .84 C4
Ladywood Grange SL5 . . . .29 F1
Ladywood Rd KT6. . . . . . . .57 A8
Laffan's Rd GU11 . . . . . . .104 E6
Laffan Tk GU11 . . . . .104 E6
Lafone Ave TW13 . . . . .15 C6
Lafone Ho 11 SW2 . . . . . . .21 E8
Lagham Pk RH9. . . . . .142 E6
Lagham Rd RH9. . . . . .142 F5
Laglands Cl RH2 . . . . .118 C3
Laings Ave CR4 . . . . .40 F7
Laings Cnr CR4 . . . . .40 F8
Lainlock Pl TW3 . . . . .5 B6
Lainson St SW18 . . . . .20 A8
Lairdale Cl SE21 . . . . .22 C8
Laird Ct GU19. . . . . .47 E1
Lait Ho BR3. . . . . .44 B8
Laitwood Rd SW12 . . . . . . .21 B7
Lake Cl
  Byfleet KT14 . . . . .71 D7
  6 Wimbledon SW19 . . . . .19 F3
Lake Cotts GU8 . . . . .169 F4
Lake End Way RG45 . . . . . .45 A4
Lakefield Cl SE20 . . . . .23 B1
Lake Gdns
  Hackbridge SM6 . . . . .60 B7
  Richmond TW10. . . . . .17 B6
Lakehall Gdns CR7 . . . . . . .42 B4
Lakehall Rd CR7 . . . . .42 B4
Lake Ho 4 SW27 . . . . .22 B3
Lakehurst Rd KT19 . . . . . . .57 E5
Lake La
  Dockenfield GU10 . . . . . .166 E6
  Horley RH1, RH6. . . . . . .161 C6
Lakeland Dr GU16. . . . . . . .65 E1
Lakeman Ct CR7 . . . . .42 C7
Laker Ct RH10 . . . . .202 A6
Lake Rd
  Croydon CR0 . . . . .62 F8
  Frimley GU16. . . . . .86 B6
  Ockley RH5 . . . . .177 D6
  Virginia Water GU25 . . . . .31 B5
  Wimbledon SW19 . . . . . . .19 F3
Laker Ind Est SE26 . . . . . . .23 F3
Lakers Lea RH14 . . . . .212 F1
Lakers Rise SM7 . . . . .78 E3
Lakes Cl GU4 . . . . .131 B3
Lakeside
  Beckenham BR3. . . . . .44 B6
  Hackbridge SM6 . . . . .60 B6
  Horsham RH12 . . . . .217 C5
  10 Kingston upon Thames
    KT2. . . . . .18 B1
  Knaphill GU21 . . . . .88 E8
  Oatlands Park KT13. . . . . .53 E8
  Redhill RH1 . . . . .119 A3
  West Ewell KT19 . . . . .57 E4
Lakeside Bsns Pk GU47. . .64 A7
Lakeside Cl
  Ash Vale GU12. . . . . .105 F4
  Knaphill GU21 . . . . .88 E8
  South Norwood SE25. . . . .43 A7
Lakeside Dr
  Esher KT10 . . . . .55 C4
  Woking GU24. . . . . .68 E6
Lakeside Est SL3 . . . . .2 A8
Lakeside Gdns GU14 . . . . .84 C7
Lakeside Grange KT13. . . . .53 C7
Lakeside Pk KT16 . . . . .33 C1
Lakeside Pk Nature
  Reserve* GU12. . . . . . . .105 F4
Lakeside Prim Sch GU16 . .65 F1
Lakeside Rd
  Ash Vale GU11, GU12 . . .105 F4
  Colnbrook SL3 . . . . .1 F7
  Farnborough GU14 . . . . . .105 A4
Lake Side The GU17. . . . . .64 D4
Lakeview SL5. . . . . .28 D6
Lake View RH5. . . . . .136 C4
Lake View Cotts RH4 . . . . .135 A6
Lakeview Rd SE27. . . . . . . .22 B3
Lake View Rd
  Copthorne RH19 . . . . . . .184 C4

Lake View Rd continued
  Dormans Park RH19 . . . . .185 F5
LALEHAM 33 C6
Laleham Abbey TW18 . . . .33 C5
Laleham CE Prim Sch
  TW18 . . . . .33 C7
Laleham Cl TW18 . . . . .33 B8
Laleham Ct GU21 . . . . .69 E3
Laleham Lea Prep Sch
  CR8. . . . . .60 E1
Laleham Rd
  Catford SE6. . . . . .24 C8
  Littleton SW17 . . . . .34 A4
  Staines TW18. . . . . .12 F2
Laleham Reach KT16 . . . . .33 B6
Lamberhurst Rd SE27 . . . .22 A3
Lamberhurst Wlk RH10. . .202 A5
Lambert Ave TW9 . . . . .7 B4
Lambert Cl TN16 . . . . .83 D3
Lambert Cotts RH1. . . . . . .120 E2
Lambert Cres GU17 . . . . . . .64 C4
Lambert Ho SM7 . . . . .78 B5
Lambert Rd SM7 . . . . .78 B5
Lambert's Pl CR0 . . . . .42 D1
Lambert's Rd KT6. . . . . .37 F4
Lambeth Cl RH11 . . . . .201 B2
Lambeth Prospect SE19 . . .22 D2
Lambeth Rd CR0 . . . . .42 B1
Lambeth Wlk RH11 . . . . . .201 B2
Lambly Hill GU25 . . . . .31 E6
Lamborne Cl GU47. . . . . . . .45 A1
Lambourn Cl
  Croydon CR2 . . . . .61 B2
  East Grinstead RH19 . . . .185 E3
Lambourne Ave SW19 . . . .19 F4
Lambourne Cl RH10 . . . . . .201 F4
Lambourne Cres GU21 . . . .70 D6
Lambourne Dr
  Bagshot GU19 . . . . .47 D2
  Cobham KT11. . . . . .73 D4
Lambourne Gr
  Bracknell RG12 . . . . .27 E7
  Kingston upon Thames KT1 . .38 B7
Lambourne Way GU10. . . .126 F7
Lambrook Haileybury Sch
  RG42. . . . . .8 A3
Lamb's Bsns Pk RH9 . . . . .142 C5
Lambs Cres RH12 . . . . . . .217 F5
Lambs Farm Cl RH12 . . . . .218 A5
Lambs Farm Rd RH12 . . . .218 A6
LAMBS GREEN 199 F6
Lambs Green Rd RH12 . . .199 F6
Lambton Rd SW20 . . . . . . .39 C8
Lambyn Croft RH6 . . . . . . .161 C4
Lamerock Rd BR1. . . . . .24 F4
Lamerton Lodge 10 TW9 . . .6 F6
Lammas Ave CR4 . . . . .41 A7
Lammas Cl
  Godalming GU7 . . . . .151 A6
  Staines TW18. . . . . .12 E5
Lammas Ct
  Farncombe GU7. . . . . . . .150 E5
  Stanwell TW19. . . . . .12 D5
Lammas Dr TW18 . . . . .12 D4
Lammas Gate GU7 . . . . . .150 F6
Lammas Gn SE26 . . . . .23 B5
Lammas Hill KT10. . . . . . . .55 A5
Lammas La KT10 . . . . .55 A6
Lammas Rd
  Godalming GU7 . . . . .151 A5
  Richmond TW10. . . . . .17 C4
Lammermoor Rd SW12. . . .21 B8
Lampard La GU10 . . . . . . .167 E2
Lampeter Cl GU22. . . . . . . .69 E1
Lampeter Ho 4 GU22. . . . .69 E1
Lampson Ct RH10 . . . . . . .183 B3
Lampton Ave TW5 . . . . .5 B6
Lampton Ct TW5 . . . . .5 B6
Lampton House Ave TW3 .19 D4
Lampton Park Rd TW3 . . . . .5 B5
Lampton Rd TW3, TW5. . . . .5 B5
Lampton Sch TW3 . . . . .5 A6
Lanadron Cl 4 TW7. . . . . . .5 F5
Lanain Ct SE12 . . . . .24 F8
Lanark Cl
  Frimley GU16. . . . . .65 E2
  Horsham RH13 . . . . .217 E2
Lancaster Ave
  Farnham GU9. . . . . .146 D8
  Guildford GU1 . . . . .130 F7
  Mitcham CR4. . . . . .41 E4
  West Norwood SE21, SE27 .22 C6
  Wimbledon SW19 . . . . . . .19 D3
Lancaster Cl
  Ashford TW15 . . . . .13 E4
  Ash Vale GU12. . . . . .105 F5
  Beckenham BR2. . . . . .44 F5
  Crawley RH10 . . . . .182 D1
  Englefield Green TW20 . . . .11 D3
  Kingston upon Thames KT2 . .17 E3
  New Malden KT4 . . . . .39 B2
  Stanwell TW19. . . . . .2 E1
  Woking GU21. . . . . .70 A3
Lancaster Cotts 1 TW10 . . .6 E1
Lancaster Dr
  Camberley GU15 . . . . .65 D6
  East Grinstead RH19 . . . .186 A3

Lancaster Gdns
  Blindley Heath RH7 . . . . .163 E8
  Kingston upon Thames KT2 . .17 D3
  Wimbledon SW19 . . . . . . .19 E3
Lancaster Ho
  Bracknell RG12 . . . . .27 B4
  Redhill RH1 . . . . .139 E6
  Wandsworth SW18 . . . . . .20 B8
Lancaster Mews 2 TW10 . .6 E1
Lancaster Pk TW10. . . . . . . .6 E2
Lancaster Pl
  Hounslow TW5. . . . . .4 D5
  Twickenham TW1. . . . . . . .17 A8
  Wimbledon SW19 . . . . . . .19 D3
Lancaster Rd
  Farnborough GU14 . . . . . .85 B1
  South Norwood SE25. . . . .43 A6
  Wimbledon SW19 . . . . . . .19 E3
Lancaster Way GU14 . . . . .85 C7
Lancastrian Rd SM6 . . . . . .60 F3
Lancelot Cl RH11. . . . . . . .200 E6
Lancelot Ho
  Carshalton SM5 . . . . .40 E1
  18 Redhill RH1 . . . . .119 A2
Lancer Ct GU11 . . . . .104 E2
Lanchester Dr RG45. . . . . .45 C7
Lancing Cl RH11 . . . . .201 A8
Lancing Ct RH12 . . . . .218 A4
Lancing Ho 7 CR0 . . . . . . .61 D6
Lancing Rd
  Feltham TW13 . . . . .14 F6
  Thornton Heath CR0 . . . . .41 F2
Landau Ct 11 CR2 . . . . .61 C5
Landen Ct RG40 . . . . .25 B4
Landen Pk RH6 . . . . .160 E5
Landgrove Rd SW19 . . . . . .20 A3
Landon Way TW15 . . . . . . .14 B2
Landscape Rd CR6 . . . . . . .101 B8
Landseer Cl
  8 Mitcham SW19 . . . . . . .40 D8
  Sandhurst GU47 . . . . .64 E6
Landseer Rd
  Cheam SM1 . . . . .59 A4
  New Malden KT3 . . . . .38 D2
Lane Cl KT15 . . . . .52 B5
Lane Ct SW11 . . . . .20 F8
LANE END 167 D8
Lane End
  Dormansland RH7 . . . . . .165 B1
  Epsom KT18. . . . . .76 B5
  Hambledon GU8 . . . . .191 B8
Lane End Dr GU21. . . . . . . .68 C2
Lane Gdns KT10. . . . . .55 F3
Lane Ho 1 RH13 . . . . .217 D2
Lanehurst Gdns RH10 . . . .202 C8
Lanercost Cl SW2 . . . . .22 A6
Lanercost Rd
  Crawley RH11 . . . . .201 C5
  Streatham SW2 . . . . .22 A6
Lanesborough Sch GU1 . .109 F1
Laneside Cotts KT22 . . . . .74 B5
Lane The
  Chertsey KT16. . . . . .33 A6
  Ifold RH14. . . . . .212 C4
  Thursley GU8. . . . . .169 C4
  Virginia Water GU25 . . . . .31 E6
Langaller La KT10 . . . . .94 B6
Langborough Rd RG40 . . . .25 C5
Langbourne Prim Sch
  SE21 . . . . .22 E5
Langbourne Way KT10 . . . .56 A4
Lang Cl KT23 . . . . .94 B4
Langcroft Cl SM5 . . . . .59 F2
Langdale Ave CR4. . . . . . . .40 F6
Langdale Cl
  Farnborough GU14 . . . . . .84 E4
  Mortlake SW14 . . . . .7 B3
  Woking GU21. . . . . .69 C3
Langdale Dr SL5 . . . . .28 E7
Langdale Par 9 CR4 . . . . .40 F6
Langdale Rd
  Crawley RH11 . . . . .200 D4
  Thornton Heath CR7 . . . . .42 A5
Langdon Cl GU15 . . . . .66 C4
Langdon Pk TW11 . . . . .17 C1
Langdon Pl SW14 . . . . .7 C4
Langdon Rd SM4 . . . . .40 C4
Langdon Wlk SM4. . . . . . . .40 C4
Langham Cl GU7 . . . . .150 F4
Langham Ct
  Farnham GU9. . . . . .146 C7
  Merton SW20. . . . . .39 C7
  12 Twickenham TW1 . . . . . .6 C1
Langham Dene CR8 . . . . . .80 B4
Langham Gdns TW10. . . . . .17 C4
Langham Ho KT4 . . . . .38 F2
Langham House Cl TW10 . .17 D4
Langham Park Pl BR2. . . . .44 F5
Langham Pk GU7 . . . . .150 F4
Langham Pl
  Chiswick W4 . . . . .7 E8
  Egham TW20 . . . . .11 F3
Langham Rd
  Teddington TW11. . . . . . . .17 B2
  Wimbledon SW20 . . . . . . .39 C8
Lang Ho TW19 . . . . .13 E7
Langholm Cl SW12 . . . . . . .21 D8
Langhorn Dr TW2 . . . . .16 E8
LANGHURST 144 E7
Langhurst Cl RH12 . . . . . .198 E4
Langhurst La RH12, RH11. .200 A4
Langhurstwood Rd
  RH12 . . . . .198 D3
Langland Gdns CR0 . . . . . .62 F8
Langland Ho SW19 . . . . . . .20 D3
Langlands Rise KT19 . . . . .76 C6

Langley Ave
  North Cheam KT4, SM3. . . .58 D8
  Surbiton KT6 . . . . .37 E1
Langley Cl
  Guildford GU1 . . . . .109 D2
  Langley Vale KT18 . . . . . . .96 D8
Langley Cres UB3 . . . . .3 F7
Langley Ct
  Crawley RH10 . . . . .202 A6
  Reigate RH2. . . . . .118 B2
  21 Sutton SM2. . . . . .59 C4
Langley Dr
  Aldershot GU11 . . . . .126 A8
  Camberley GU15 . . . . .65 D6
  Crawley RH11 . . . . .201 B6
Langley Gr KT3 . . . . .38 E7
LANGLEY GREEN 181 C2
Langley Green Prim Sch
  RH11. . . . . .201 C8
Langley Ho GU21 . . . . .89 A8
Langley La RH11 . . . . .201 A8
Langley Lawns SM2 . . . . . .59 D3
Langley Manor BR3 . . . . . .44 C4
Langley Oaks Ave CR2. . . .62 A1
Langley Par RH11 . . . . . . .181 C1
Langley Park Rd SM1,
  SM2 . . . . .59 C3
Langley Park Sch for Boys
  BR3. . . . . .44 B3
Langley Park Sch for Girls
  BR3. . . . . .44 C3
Langley Pl
  Crawley RH11 . . . . .181 C1
  North Cheam KT4 . . . . . . .58 D8
Langley Rd
  Beckenham BR3. . . . . .43 E5
  Isleworth TW7 . . . . .5 F5
  Merton SW19. . . . . .40 A8
  Selsdon CR2. . . . . .62 D2
  Staines TW18. . . . . .12 F2
  Surbiton KT6 . . . . .37 E2
LANGLEY VALE 96 D8
Langley Vale Rd KT18,
  KT21. . . . . .76 E1
Langley Way BR4 . . . . .44 E2
Langley Wlk
  Crawley RH11 . . . . .181 B1
  Woking GU22. . . . . .89 B8
Langmans Way GU21 . . . . .68 E3
Langmead St SE27 . . . . . . .22 C4
Langport Ct KT12 . . . . .35 C1
Langridge Dr RH19 . . . . . .205 E8
Langridge Ho 2 RH12. . . .217 B2
Langridge Mews TW12 . . . .15 F2
Langroyd Rd SW17 . . . . . . .20 F6
Langshott RH6 . . . . .161 C5
Langshott Cl KT15 . . . . . . .70 F8
Langshott Cty Inf Sch
  RH6. . . . . .161 C3
Langshott La RH6 . . . . . . .161 C4
Langsmead RH7 . . . . .163 E8
Langstone Cl RH10 . . . . . .202 C3
Langthorne Ct SE6 . . . . . . .24 C4
Langton Ave KT17. . . . . . . .76 F8
Langton Cl
  Addlestone KT15 . . . . .52 B7
  Woking GU21. . . . . .68 F2
Langton Dr GU35. . . . . . . .187 A7
Langton Ho 5 SW16 . . . . .21 C4
Langton Pl SW18 . . . . .20 A7
Langton Rise SE22, SE23. . .23 B8
Langton Way
  Egham TW20 . . . . .12 C2
  South Croydon CR0 . . . . . .61 E6
Langwood Chase TW11 . . .17 C2
Langwood Cl KT21 . . . . . . .76 A2
Lanherne Ho 11 SW20 . . . .19 D1
Lanigan Dr TW3 . . . . .5 B2
Lankester Sq RH8. . . . . . . .122 D7
Lankton Cl BR3 . . . . .44 C8
Lannock Ct 2 SW17 . . . . .20 E2
Lansbury Ave TW14 . . . . . . .4 B1
Lansbury Est GU21 . . . . . . .68 D1
Lansbury Rd RH11 . . . . . . .201 B1
Lansdell Rd CR4 . . . . .41 A7
Lansdown GU1. . . . . .110 A1
Lansdown Cl
  Horsham RH12 . . . . .218 B6
  Knaphill GU21 . . . . .88 F8
  Walton-on-Thames KT12 . . .35 C1
Lansdowne Cl
  Twickenham TW1. . . . . . . .16 F7
  Wimbledon SW20 . . . . . . .19 D1
Lansdowne Copse 1 KT4. .58 A8
Lansdowne Ct
  Purley CR8 . . . . .61 B1
  2 Worcester Park KT4. . . .58 A8
Lansdowne Hill SE27 . . . . .22 B5
Lansdowne Ho 18 SM2 . . .59 B3
Lansdowne Pl SE19 . . . . . .22 F1
Lansdowne Rd
  Aldershot GU11 . . . . .105 A1
  Croydon CR0 . . . . .42 D1
  Frimley GU16. . . . . .86 A8
  Hounslow TW3. . . . . .5 B4
  Purley CR8. . . . . .80 A7
  Staines TW18. . . . . .13 B1
  West Ewell KT19 . . . . .57 D3
  Wimbledon SW19, SW20. . .19 C1
Lansdowne Wood Cl 11
  SE27. . . . . .22 B5
Lantern Ct 5 SW20 . . . . . .39 D8
Lanyon Cl RH12 . . . . .218 A6
Lanyon Mews RH12 . . . . .218 A6
Lapse Wood Wlk SE22. . . .23 B7
Lapwing Cl
  Horsham RH13 . . . . .217 F3

Lapwing Cl continued
  Selsdon CR0, CR2 . . . . . . .62 E1
Lapwing Ct KT6 . . . . .57 A7
Lapwing Gr GU4 . . . . .110 D3
Lara Cl KT9 . . . . .56 E3
Lara Lo SM1 . . . . .59 A5
Larbert Rd SW16. . . . . .21 C1
Larby Pl KT17. . . . . .57 E1
Larch Ave
  Ascot SL5. . . . . .29 E4
  Guildford GU1 . . . . .109 C4
  Wokingham RG41 . . . . .25 A7
Larch Cl
  Camberley GU15 . . . . .65 E8
  Kingswood KT20 . . . . .98 C6
  Reigate RH2 . . . . .139 C7
  Upper Tooting SW12 . . . . .21 B6
  Warlingham CR6 . . . . . . .101 E8
Larch Cres KT19 . . . . .57 B4
Larch End RH12 . . . . .217 B4
Larches Ave SW14 . . . . .7 D3
Larches Ho RH19. . . . . . . .186 B4
Larches The
  East Grinstead RH19 . . . .186 B4
  Horsham RH12 . . . . .218 C6
  Newell Green RG42 . . . . . . .8 A1
  Woking GU21. . . . . .69 E3
Larches Way
  Blackwater GU17. . . . . . . .64 B5
  Crawley Down RH10 . . . . .204 C8
Larch Rd GU35. . . . . .187 B6
Larch Tree Way CR0 . . . . . .63 A7
Larchvale Ct SM2 . . . . .59 B3
Larch Way GU14 . . . . .84 C3
Larchwood 5 RG12 . . . . . .27 F5
Larchwood Cl SM7 . . . . . . .77 E4
Larchwood Dr TW20 . . . . . .11 B2
Larchwood Glade GU15 . . .66 A7
Larchwood Rd GU21 . . . . . .88 D8
Larcombe Cl CR0 . . . . .61 F6
La Retraite RC Girls Sch
  SW12 . . . . .21 C8
Larges Bridge Dr RG12. . . .27 D6
Larges La RG12 . . . . .27 C7
Largewood Ave KT6. . . . . . .57 A8
Lark Ave TW18. . . . . .12 F5
Larkbere Rd SE26 . . . . .23 E4
Larkfield
  Cobham KT11. . . . . .73 A6
  Ewhurst GU6 . . . . .175 E4
Larkfield Cl
  2 Coney Hall BR2. . . . . . .63 F8
  Farnham GU9. . . . . .124 F2
Larkfield Ct RH6 . . . . .162 A3
Larkfield Rd
  Farnham GU9. . . . . .124 F2
  Richmond TW9. . . . . .6 E3
Larkhall Cl KT12 . . . . .54 C4
Larkham Cl TW13 . . . . .14 E5
Larkin Cl CR5. . . . . .79 F2
Larkins Rd RH6 . . . . .181 D7
Lark Rise
  Crawley RH11 . . . . .201 C8
  East Horsley KT24 . . . . . .112 E4
  Turners Hill RH10 . . . . . .204 C5
Larksfield
  Englefield Green TW20 . . . .11 C1
  Horley RH6 . . . . .161 B4
Larkspur Cl GU11 . . . . . . .126 A7
Larkspur Ct SM6 . . . . .60 B3
Larkspur Way
  Dorking RH5 . . . . .136 D4
  West Ewell KT19 . . . . .57 C5
Larks Way GU21 . . . . .68 C3
Larkswood Cl GU47 . . . . . .45 A1
Larkswood Dr RG45 . . . . . .45 B5
Lark Way SM5 . . . . .40 E2
Lascombe La GU3. . . . . . . .128 B4
Lashmere
  Copthorne RH10 . . . . . . .183 D3
  Cranleigh GU6 . . . . .174 B3
Laski Ct RH11. . . . . .201 B1
Lasswade Ct KT16. . . . . . . .32 F2
Lasswade Rd KT16 . . . . . . .32 F2
Lastingham Ct TW18 . . . . .13 A2
Latchmere Cl KT2, TW10 . .17 E3
Latchmere La KT2, TW10 . .17 F3
Latchmere Prim Schs KT2 .17 F2
Latchmere Rd KT2 . . . . .17 F2
Latchwood La GU10 . . . . .146 D5
Lateward Rd TW8 . . . . .6 D8
Latham Ave GU16. . . . . . . .65 E2
Latham Cl
  Biggin Hill TN16 . . . . .83 C3
  6 Twickenham TW1 . . . . . .17 A8
Latham Ct GU21 . . . . .68 C2
Latham Rd TW1 . . . . .16 F8
Latham's Way CR0 . . . . . . .60 F8
Lathkill Ct 5 BR3. . . . . .43 F8
Lathwood Ho 6 SE26 . . . .23 B3
Latimer RG12 . . . . .27 B1
Latimer Cl
  Crawley RH11 . . . . .181 C1
  North Cheam KT4 . . . . . . .58 B6
  Woking GU22. . . . . .70 B3
Latimer Ct
  4 Bromley BR2. . . . . .44 F5
  Redhill RH1 . . . . .139 F7
Latimer Ho GU7. . . . . .150 E3
Latimer Rd
  1 Croydon CR0, CR9 . . . . .61 B7
  Godalming GU7 . . . . .150 E4
  Teddington TW11. . . . . . . .16 F3
  Wimbledon SW19 . . . . . . .20 B2
  Wokingham RG41 . . . . .25 B5

Latitude KT16.........33 C1
Lattimer Pl W4♦.........7 E7
Latton Cl
  Esher KT10.........55 B6
  Walton-on-Thames KT12.........35 E2
Latymer Cl KT13.........53 C6
Laubin Cl TW1.........6 B3
Laud Dr RH10.........202 D5
Lauder Cl GU16.........65 E2
Lauderdale GU14.........84 D3
Lauderdale Dr TW10.........17 D5
Lauderdale Ho 4 TW18.........12 F1
Laud St CR0, CR9.........61 C7
Laud Way RG40.........25 E6
Laughton Rd RH12.........217 F5
Launceston Ct CR7.........42 A3
Laundry La GU47.........64 E5
Laundry Mews SE23.........23 E8
Laundry Rd GU1.........130 C8
Laundry Way RH5.........178 C5
Lauradale RG12.........27 A5
Laurel Ave
  Englefield Green TW20.........11 B3
  Twickenham TW1.........16 F7
Laurel Cl
  Camberley GU15.........65 D4
  Crawley RH10.........202 A3
  Farnborough GU14.........84 C3
  Poyle SL3.........1 E7
  Upper Tooting SW17.........20 E3
Laurel Cres
  Croydon CR0.........63 A7
  Sheerwater GU21.........70 D6
Laurel Ct
  2 Croydon CR2.........61 E6
  South Norwood SE25.........42 E4
Laureldene GU3.........107 B1
Laurel Dene RH19.........185 F1
Laurel Dr RH8.........122 F4
Laurel Gdns
  Aldershot GU11.........126 A7
  Hounslow TW4.........4 E3
  Woodham KT15.........52 B1
Laurel Gr
  Forest Hill SE26.........23 E4
  Penge SE20.........23 C1
  Rowledge GU10.........145 F5
Laurel Grange KT14.........71 E7
Laurel Ho SM4.........40 B4
Laurel Manor SM2.........59 C3
Laurel Rd
  Teddington TW12.........16 D3
  Wimbledon SW20.........39 B8
Laurels The
  Banstead SM7.........77 F2
  Beckenham BR3.........44 C7
  Camberley GU15.........66 A7
  Crawley RH10.........182 A1
  Effingham KT24.........113 D8
  Heath End GU9.........125 F7
  6 Oatlands Park KT13.........53 D7
  Penge BR3.........23 F1
  Stoke D'Abernon KT11.........73 E4
Laurel Wlk RH13.........217 F1
Laurier Rd CR0.........42 F2
Lauriston Cl GU21.........68 D2
Lauriston Ho 19 SW19.........19 D2
Lauser Rd TW19.........13 C8
Laustan Cl GU1.........110 C2
Lavant Cl RH11.........200 F5
Lavender Ave
  Mitcham CR4.........40 F8
  North Cheam KT4, SM3.........58 C7
Lavender Cl
  Caterham CR3.........100 C2
  Coulsdon CR5.........99 C8
  Leatherhead KT22.........95 C5
  Redhill RH1.........140 B4
  Wallington SM5.........60 B6
Lavender Cotts KT22.........95 C5
Lavender Ct
  East Molesey KT8.........36 B6
  Feltham TW14.........4 B1
  Leatherhead KT22.........95 C5
  Sutton SM2.........59 C3
Lavender Gate KT22.........74 B5
Lavender Gr CR4.........40 E8
Lavender Ho TW9.........7 B6
Lavender La GU10.........145 F4
Lavender Lodge 1 KT17.........57 F2
Lavender Park Rd 5
  KT14.........71 A6
Lavender Pk SL5.........28 C6
Lavender Rd
  Carshalton SM1.........59 D6
  Thornton Heath CR0.........41 F3
  Wallington SM5.........60 A6
  West Ewell KT19.........57 B4
  Woking GU22.........70 B3
Lavender Vale SM6.........60 D4
Lavender Way CR0.........43 D3
Lavengro Rd SE27.........22 C6
Laverock Sch RH8.........122 E7
Laverstoke Gdns SW15.........19 A8
Lavington Cl RH11.........201 A4
Lavington Rd CR0.........60 F6
Lavinia Ct BR1.........24 E1
Lawbrook La GU5.........154 C7
Lawday Link GU9.........125 A7
Lawday Pl GU9.........125 A7
Lawday Place La GU9.........125 A7
Lawdons Gdns CR0.........61 B6
Lawford Gdns CR8.........80 C3
Lawford Rd W4.........7 C7
Lawford's Hill Cl GU3.........88 C3

Lawford's Hill Rd GU3.........88 C3
Lawley Ho 2 TW1.........6 D1
Lawman Ct 2 TW9.........6 F6
Lawn Cl KT3.........38 E7
Lawn Cres TW9.........7 A5
Lawn Ho BR3.........23 F1
Lawn Rd
  Beckenham BR3.........23 F1
  Guildford GU2.........130 C6
Lawns Cotts RH12.........195 A3
Lawnsmead GU5.........152 B7
Lawns Rd RH12.........195 A3
Lawns The
  Belmont SM2.........58 E3
  Farnborough GU14.........84 E3
  Milford GU8.........149 F1
  North Ascot SL5.........28 D6
  Purley CR8.........61 B1
  South Norwood SE19.........42 D8
  1 Wimbledon SW19.........19 F3
Lawnwood Ct GU7.........151 A5
Lawrence Ave
  New Malden KT3.........38 E2
Lawrence Cl
  Crawley RH10.........202 D4
  Guildford GU4.........110 B6
  Wokingham RG40.........25 D6
Lawrence Cres GU20.........48 D4
Lawrence Ctr RG41.........25 A4
Lawrence Est TW4.........4 C3
Lawrence Gr RG42.........26 D8
Lawrence La RH3.........117 B3
Lawrence Lodge GU15.........65 D7
Lawrence Rd
  Hampton TW12.........15 F1
  Hounslow TW4.........4 C3
  Richmond TW10.........17 C4
  South Norwood SE25.........42 F5
Lawrence Way GU15.........64 F4
Lawrence Weaver Cl SM4.........40 A3
Lawrie Park Ave SE26.........23 B3
Lawrie Park Cres SE26.........23 B3
Lawrie Park Gdns SE26.........23 B3
Lawrie Park Rd SE19, SE26 23 C3
Laws Cl
  Crawley RH11.........200 E5
  South Norwood SE25.........42 D5
Lawson Cl SW19.........19 D5
Lawson Ct 13 KT6.........37 D2
Lawson Hunt Ind Pk
  RH12.........216 D4
Lawson Way SL5.........30 B3
Lawson Wlk SM5.........60 A2
Laws Terr GU11.........105 C3
Laxton Ct 2 CR2.........42 C5
Laxton Gdns RH1.........119 D7
Layard Rd CR7.........42 D7
Layburn Cres SL3.........1 B8
Layhams Rd
  Coney Hall BR2, BR4.........63 F5
  West Wickham BR2.........63 F1
Layton Cres CR0.........61 B5
Layton Ct KT13.........53 B6
Layton Pl TW9.........7 A6
Layton Rd TW3.........5 B3
Layton's La TW16.........34 F7
Lazare Ct 2 TW18.........12 F1
Lazell Gdns RH3.........137 C3
Leach Gr KT22.........95 C5
Lea Cl
  Ash GU11.........106 A1
  Badshot Lea GU9.........126 A6
  Crawley RH11.........200 F5
  Twickenham TW2.........15 F8
Lea Cotts CR4.........41 A7
Leacroft
  East Grinstead RH19.........185 D2
  Staines TW18.........13 B4
  Sunningdale SL5.........30 A4
Lea Croft RG45.........45 B6
Leacroft Ave SW12.........20 F8
Leacroft Cl
  Kenley CR8.........80 C3
  Staines TW18.........13 B4
Lea Ct GU9.........125 F7
Leaf Cl KT7, KT8.........36 E4
Leaf Gr SE27.........22 A3
Leafield Cl
  South Norwood SW16.........22 B2
  Woking GU21.........69 B1
Leafield Copse RG12.........27 F5
Leafield Rd
  Merton SW19, SW20.........39 F6
  Sutton SM1.........59 A8
Leafy Way CR0.........62 F8
Leamington Ave SM4.........39 F5
Leamington Cl TW3.........5 C2
Leamington Ct 4 SE26.........23 A5
Leander Ct 5 KT6.........37 D2
Leander Rd
  4 Streatham SW2.........21 F8
  Thornton Heath CR7.........41 F5
Leapale La GU1.........130 D8
Leapale Rd GU1.........130 D8
Lea Rd
  Beckenham BR3.........44 A7
  Camberley GU15.........65 B2
Leas Cl KT9.........56 F3
Leaside KT23.........94 A4
Leas La CR6.........81 D1
Leas Rd
  Guildford GU1.........130 C8
  Warlingham CR6.........81 D1
Lea The TW20.........12 C1
Leather Cl CR4.........41 A7
LEATHERHEAD.........95 D5
Leatherhead Bsns Pk
  KT22.........94 F8

Leatherhead By-Pass Rd
  KT22.........95 D5
Leatherhead Comm Hospl
  ....95 C5
Leatherhead Ind Est KT22 95 A6
Leatherhead L Ctr KT22.........95 A4
Leatherhead Mus of Local
  History★ KT22.........95 B5
Leatherhead Rd
  Ashtead KT21, KT22.........95 E7
  Chessington KT9.........75 C6
  Great Bookham KT23.........94 C2
  Oxshott KT22.........74 D4
Leatherhead Sta KT22.........95 A6
Leatherhead Trinity Sch
  Leatherhead KT22.........95 A8
  Leatherhead KT22.........95 B6
Leather La GU5.........133 C4
Leaveland Cl BR3.........44 A5
Leavesden Rd KT13.........53 B5
Leaves Gn RG12.........27 D3
LEAVES GREEN.........83 D8
Leaves Green Cres BR2.........83 C8
Leaves Green Rd BR2.........83 D8
Lea Way RG12.........105 F3
Leazes Ave CR3.........100 A4
Lebanon Ave TW13.........15 D3
Lebanon Ct 11 TW1.........17 B8
Lebanon Dr KT11.........74 A6
Lebanon Gdns TN16.........83 D7
Lebanon Park Mans 12
  TW1.........17 B8
Lebanon Pk TW1.........17 B8
Lebanon Rd CR0.........42 E1
Lebanon Rd Halt CR0.........61 E8
Le Chateau CR0.........61 D7
Lechford Rd RH6.........161 A1
Leckford Rd SW18.........20 C7
Leckhampton Pl 2 SW2.........22 A8
Leconfield Ave SW13, SW15 .7 F4
Ledbury Pl CR0.........61 C6
Ledbury Rd
  Croydon CR0, CR9.........61 D6
  Reigate RH2.........118 A2
Ledger Cl GU1.........110 B3
Ledger Dr KT15.........51 F4
Ledgers Rd CR6.........82 B2
Ledrington Rd SE19.........23 A2
Leechcroft Rd SM6.........60 A7
Leech La KT18.........96 C1
Leechpool La RH12, RH13 218 A4
Leechpool & Owlbeech
  Woods★ RH13.........218 C4
Leechpool Prim Sch
  RH13.........218 A4
Lee Ct GU11.........126 C8
Leeds Ct
  Carshalton SM5.........59 F7
  Catford SE6.........24 B5
Leegate Cl GU21.........69 B3
Lee Ho TW9.........20 B2
Lee Hollow GU5.........133 C1
Leehurst GU8.........149 E1
Lee Mews BR3.........43 E6
Lee Rd
  Aldershot GU11.........104 E2
  Merton SW19.........40 B8
Lee's Ct GU20.........48 D4
Lees Farm Barn GU22.........71 B4
Leeside RH1.........199 C6
Leeson Ho 8 TW1.........17 B8
Lee St RH6.........160 E4
Lees The CR0.........62 F8
Leeward Gdns SW19.........19 F2
Leewood Way KT24.........113 D8
Legge Cres GU11.........104 E1
Leggyfield Ct RH12.........217 B5
Legion Ct SM4.........40 A3
Legion Ho BR1.........24 D3
Legrace Ave TW4, TW5.........4 D5
Legsheath La RH19.........205 D1
Leicester RG12.........27 E2
Leicester Ave CR4.........41 E5
Leicester Cl KT4.........58 C6
Leicester Ct
  6 Bromley BR1.........24 F1
  Crawley RH10.........202 D6
  10 Twickenham TW1.........6 D1
Leicester Ho
  7 Carshalton SM1.........59 E7
  2 Thames Ditton KT7.........37 A2
Leicester Rd CR0.........42 E2
LEIGH.........138 B2
Leigham Ave SW16.........21 E5
Leigham Court Rd SE27, SW16,
  SW21.........22 A4
Leigham Ct 9 SM6.........60 C4
Leigham Dr TW7.........5 E7
Leigham Hall 3 SW16.........21 E5
Leigham Hall Par 2
  SW16.........21 E5
Leigham Vale SW2, SW16 22 A6
Leigh Cl
  Addlestone KT15.........51 F3
  New Malden KT3.........38 D5
Leigh Close Ind Est KT3.........38 D5
Leigh Court Cl KT11.........73 D5
Leigh Cres CR0.........63 C3
Leigh Ct CR0.........82 E8
Leigh Hill Rd KT11.........73 D5
Leigh Ho 4 KT2.........18 B2
Leigh Jenkins Way RH6 .182 B7
Leighlands RH10.........202 C8
Leigh Orchard Cl SW16.........21 F5
Leigh Pl
  Cobham KT11.........73 C5
  Feltham TW13.........15 C7

Leigh Place La RH9.........121 E3
Leigh Rd
  Betchworth RH3.........137 C2
  Cobham KT11.........73 B5
  Isleworth TW3.........5 D3
Leigh The KT2.........18 E1
Leighton Gdns
  Sanderstead CR2.........81 B6
  Thornton Heath CR0.........42 B1
Leighton Ho 7 KT6.........37 E3
Leighton St CR0.........42 B1
Leighton Way KT18.........76 D5
Leinster Ave SW14.........7 C3
Leisure La KT13.........71 B7
Leith Cl RG45.........45 A7
Leithcote Gdns SW16.........21 F4
Leithcote Path SW16.........21 F5
Leith Dr GU11.........104 F3
Leith Gr RH5.........157 D4
Leith Hill Rd
  Abinger Common RH5.........155 F5
  Wotton RH5.........156 A3
Leith Hill Tower★ RH5.........156 B3
Leith Ho
  Leatherhead KT22.........95 A6
  Reigate RH2.........139 A6
  16 Streatham SW2.........21 F8
Leith Lea RH5.........157 D4
Leith Rd
  Beare Green RH5.........157 D4
  Ewell KT17.........76 E7
Leith Twrs SM2.........59 B3
Leith Vale Cotts RH5.........177 A2
Leith View RH5.........136 C3
Leith View Cotts RH11.........198 B6
Leith View Rd RH12.........218 A3
Lela Ave TW4, TW5.........4 C5
Le Marchant Rd GU15,
  GU16.........65 F3
Le May Cl RH6.........161 A4
Lemington Gr RG12.........27 B3
Lemmington Way RH12.........218 A2
Lemon Gr TW13.........15 A7
Lemon's Farm Rd RH5.........155 F6
Lendore Rd GU16.........85 D8
Lenelby Rd KT6.........38 A1
Leney Cl RG40.........25 D8
Lenham Rd
  South Norwood CR7.........42 D7
  Sutton SM1.........59 C5
Lennard Ave BR4.........63 E8
Lennard Cl BR4.........63 E8
Lennard Rd
  Penge BR3, SE20, SE26.........23 E2
  Thornton Heath CR0.........42 C1
Lennox Ct 13 RH1.........119 A2
Lennox Gdns CR0.........61 B6
Lennox Ho 1 TW1.........6 D1
Lenten Cl GU5.........133 D1
Lentmead Rd BR1.........24 F5
Lenton Rise TW9.........6 E4
Leo Ct 4 TW8.........6 D7
Leof Cres SE6.........24 B3
Leominster Rd SM4.........40 C3
Leominster Wlk SM4.........40 C3
Leonard Ave SM4.........40 C4
Leonard Cl GU16.........85 D8
Leonard Rd CR4, SW16.........41 C8
Leonardslee Ct RH10.........202 B3
Leonard Way RH13.........217 F2
Leopardstown Ho RH7.........142 E1
Leopold Ave
  Farnborough GU14.........85 B5
  Wimbledon SW19.........19 F3
Leopold Ct 18 SW19.........19 F3
Leopold Rd
  Crawley RH11.........201 C6
  Wimbledon SW19.........19 F4
Leopold Terr SW19.........20 A4
Le Personne Homes 1
  CR3.........100 D5
Leppington RG12.........27 B2
Leret Way KT22.........95 B6
Lesbourne Rd RH2.........139 B8
Lescombe Cl SE23.........23 E5
Lescombe Rd SE23, SE6.........23 E5
Lesley Ct 8 SM6.........60 B6
Lesley Gdns SM2.........59 A3
Leslie Gr CR0.........42 E1
Leslie Grove Pl CR0.........42 E1
Leslie Park Rd CR0.........42 E1
Leslie Rd
  Chobham GU24.........49 E1
  Dorking RH4.........115 D1
Lessingham Ave SW17.........21 A4
Lessing St SE23.........23 E8
Lessness Rd SM4.........40 C4
Lestock Cl 2 SE25.........43 A6
Lestor Ct TW7.........5 F4
Letchworth Ave TW14.........14 F8
Letchworth Ct RH11.........200 E3
Letchworth St SW17.........20 F4
Letcombe Sq RG12.........27 F5
Levana Cl SW19.........19 E7
Levehurst Ho SE27.........22 C3
Levendale Rd SE23, SE6.........23 F6
Leveret Cl CR0.........82 D8
Leveret La RH11.........201 B8
Leverette Cl GU12.........105 D3
Leverkusen Rd RG12.........27 B6
Levern Dr GU9.........125 C6
Leverson St SW16.........21 C2
Levett Ho 8 SW16.........21 C3
Levett Rd KT22.........95 B7
Levylsdene GU1.........110 D1
Levylsdene Ct GU1.........110 D1
Lewes Cl RH10.........202 C6
Lewes Ct 5 CR4.........40 F6

Lewesdon Cl 13 SW19.........19 D7
Lewes Ho RH2.........139 B5
Lewes Rd
  Ashurst Wood RH19.........206 C6
  Forest Row RH18.........206 E2
Lewin Ct SW16.........21 E2
Lewin Rd
  Mortlake SW14.........7 D4
  Streatham SW16.........21 D2
Lewins Rd KT18.........76 D5
Lewin Terr TW14.........14 D8
Lewis Cl KT15.........52 C6
LEWISHAM.........24 C8
Lewisham Cl RH11.........201 C2
Lewisham Way GU47.........45 D2
Lewis Rd
  Mitcham CR4.........40 E7
  20 Richmond TW10.........6 D2
  Sutton SM1.........59 B6
Lewiston Cl KT4.........39 B2
Lexden Rd CR4.........41 D5
Lexington Ct CR8.........80 C8
Lexington Pl KT1.........37 D8
Lexton Gdns SW12.........21 D7
Leyborne Pk TW9.........7 A6
Leybourne Ave KT14.........71 E6
Leybourne Cl
  Byfleet KT14.........71 F6
  Crawley RH11.........201 C1
Leybourne Ct 1 SE25.........43 A6
Leybourne Pl RH19.........184 F4
Leyburn Gdns CR0.........61 E8
Leycester Cl GU20.........48 B6
Leyfield KT4.........38 F1
Leyland Ho 12 TW10.........17 C5
Leylands La TW19.........2 A2
Ley Rd GU14.........85 A8
Leyside RG45.........45 A5
Leys Rd KT22.........74 D7
Leys The KT12.........54 E6
Leyton Rd SW19.........20 C1
Liberty Cl 4 KT4.........39 C1
Liberty Ct RH2.........139 B8
Liberty Hall Rd KT15.........52 A5
Liberty Ho KT16.........32 F1
Liberty La KT15.........52 B5
Liberty Rise KT15.........52 A4
Liberty Sch CR4.........40 E7
Library Way TW2.........16 C8
Licensed Victuallers Sch
  SL5.........28 C7
Lichfield Ct
  Kingston upon Thames
  KT6.........37 E4
  Richmond TW9.........6 F6
Lichfield Gdns TW10, TW9..6 E2
Lichfield Rd
  Hounslow TW4.........4 C4
  Richmond TW9.........6 F6
Lichfields RG12.........27 E7
Lichfield Terr 1 TW9.........6 E2
Lichfield Way CR2.........62 D2
Lickfolds Rd GU10.........145 E3
Liddell Ct 2 CR8.........80 A7
Liddell Way SL5.........29 A4
Liddesdale Ho E KT2.........38 B8
Liddesdale Ho W KT2.........38 B8
Liddington Hall Dr GU3.........108 E4
Liddington Hall Est GU3.........108 E4
Liddington New Rd GU3.........108 E4
Lidiard Rd SW18.........20 C6
Lido Rd GU1.........109 D2
Lidsey Cl RH10.........202 C4
Lidstone Cl GU21.........69 B2
Lightbox The (Gall & Mus)★
  GU22.........221 D3
LIGHTWATER.........66 F8
Lightwater Ctry Pk★
  GU18.........47 F1
Lightwater L Ctr GU18.........47 F1
Lightwater Mdw GU18.........67 B8
Lightwater Rd GU18.........67 C8
Lightwater Village Sch
  GU18.........48 A1
Lightwood RG12.........27 D3
Lilac Ave GU22.........89 D7
Lilac Cl GU1.........109 C5
Lilac Ct TW11.........16 F4
Lilac Gdns CR0.........63 A7
Lilah Mews BR2.........44 F7
Lilian Rd CR4, SW16.........41 C8
Lilian Rolfe Ho 5 SE27.........22 D4
Lilleshall Rd SM4.........40 D3
Lilley Dr KT20.........98 B5
Lilley Mead RH1.........119 C4
Lillie Rd TN16.........83 D1
Lilycourt RG41.........25 A6
Lilyfields Chase GU6.........175 E4
Lily Hill Dr RG12.........27 E7
Lily Hill Rd RG12.........27 F7
Lime Ave
  Camberley GU15.........66 A6
  Cranbourne SL4.........9 F5
  Horsham RH12.........218 A4
Limebush Cl KT15.........52 C2
Lime Cl
  Carshalton SM5.........59 F8
  Copthorne RH10.........183 B3
  Crawley RH11.........181 C1
  Reigate RH2.........139 B6
  West Clandon GU4.........111 B7
Lime Cres
  Ash GU12.........106 B2
  Sunbury TW16.........35 C7

Lime Ct
Chipstead CR5 78 F1
3 Kingston upon Thames KT3 38 E6
Kingston upon Thames, Norbiton KT1 38 B6
Mitcham CR4 40 D7
Lime Gr
Addlestone KT15 52 A6
Guildford GU1 109 B5
Kingston upon Thames KT3 38 E6
Twickenham TW1 6 A1
Warlingham CR6 81 E1
West Clandon GU4 111 B7
Woking GU22 89 E6
Lime Ho 7 TW9 7 B6
Limekiln Pl SE19 22 F1
Lime Lodge 3 TW16 14 F1
Lime Meadow Ave CR2 81 B6
Lime Mews TW20 11 F3
Limerick Cl
Bracknell RG42 27 A8
Streatham SW12 21 C8
Limerick Ct 1 SW12 21 C8
Limerick Ho GU22 70 A1
Lime St Rdbt GU11 104 F2
Limes Ave
Barnes SW13 7 F5
Carshalton SM5 40 F1
Croydon CR0, CR9 61 A7
Horley RH6 161 B1
Penge SE20 23 B1
Limes Cl TW15 14 A3
Limes Ct BR3 44 B7
Limes Field Rd SW14 7 E4
Limes Rd
Beckenham BR3 44 B7
Egham TW20 11 F3
Farnborough GU14 84 C5
Thornton Heath CR0 42 D2
Weybridge KT13 53 A6
Lime St GU11 104 F2
Limes The
2 Belmont SM2 59 A4
Dormans Park RH19 185 A5
East Molesey KT8 36 B5
Epsom KT19 57 B1
Haslemere GU27 208 A6
Leatherhead KT22 95 B4
9 Woking GU21 70 A3
Woking, Horsell GU21 69 D4
Lime Tree Ave KT10, KT7 36 E1
Limetree Cl SW2 21 F7
Lime Tree Cl KT23 94 A3
Lime Tree Copse RG42 8 A1
Lime Tree Ct
Ashtead KT21 75 E1
Old Windsor SL4 11 C8
South Croydon CR2 61 C4
Lime Tree Gr CR0 62 F7
Limetree Mews TN16 103 D7
Limetree Pl CR4 41 B8
Lime Tree Rd TW5 5 B6
Limetree Wlk
2 Upper Tooting SW17 21 A3
Virginia Water GU25 31 E5
Lime Tree Wlk
Coney Hall BR4 63 F6
Farnborough GU14 105 E8
Lime Villas KT3 38 E6
Limeway Terr RH4 115 A1
Lime Wlk RG12 27 C5
Limewood Cl
Beckenham BR3 44 C4
Knaphill GU21 88 D7
LIMPSFIELD 123 A6
Limpsfield Ave
Putney SW19 19 D6
Thornton Heath CR7 41 F4
Limpsfield CE Inf Sch RH8 123 C6
Limpsfield Grange Sch RH8 123 A8
Limpsfield Rd
Chelsham CR6 102 B8
Hamsey Green CR2, CR6 81 C3
Linacre Dr GU6, RH12 195 C4
Lince La RH4 135 D6
LINCHMERE 207 B2
Linchmere Comm Nature Reserve* GU27 207 B3
Linchmere Pl RH11 201 A7
Linchmere Rd
Haslemere GU27 207 D5
Lewisham SE12 24 F8
Linchmere GU27 207 C4
Lincoln Ave
Twickenham TW2 16 C6
Wimbledon SW19 19 D5
Lincoln Cl
Ash Vale GU12 105 F5
Crawley RH10 201 E3
Croydon SE25 43 B3
Frimley GU15 66 B4
Horley RH6 161 A2
Lincoln Ct
5 Croydon CR2 61 C5
Hampton TW12 15 F3
Mitcham CR4 41 E4
Weybridge KT13 53 D4
Lincoln Dr GU22 70 E3
Lincoln Hall KT4 39 B2
Lincoln Lodge 10 BR3 44 B7
Lincoln Rd
Croydon SE25 43 B6
Dorking RH4 115 C1
Farnborough GU14 105 B8
Feltham TW13 15 F5

Lincoln Rd *continued*
Guildford GU2 108 F3
Kingston upon Thames KT3 38 C6
Mitcham CR4 41 E4
North Cheam KT4 39 B1
Lincolns Mead RH7 164 C3
Lincoln Terr 6 SM2 59 A3
Lincoln Way TW16 34 E8
Lincoln Wlk KT19 57 D1
Lincombe Ct KT15 52 B5
Lincombe Rd BR1 24 F5
Linda Ct KT9 56 D6
Lindale SW19 19 E6
Lindale Cl GU25 30 F5
Lindbergh Rd SM6 60 E3
Linden 3 RG12 27 F4
Linden Ave
Coulsdon CR5 79 B3
East Grinstead RH19 185 C2
Hounslow TW3 5 B2
Thornton Heath CR7 42 B5
Linden Bridge Sch KT4 57 E7
Linden Cl
Crawley RH10 202 A3
Horsham RH12 217 E4
Tadworth KT20 97 D7
Thames Ditton KT7 37 A2
Woodham KT15 71 A8
Linden Cotts 6 SW19 19 E2
Linden Cres KT1 37 F7
Linden Ct
Beckenham BR3 44 B6
2 Bromley BR1 24 F1
Camberley GU15 65 F7
Englefield Green TW20 11 B2
Leatherhead KT22 95 B6
Penge SE20 23 B1
Linden Dr CR3 100 C3
Linden Gate SW20 39 C6
Linden Gdns KT22 95 C6
Linden Gr
Kingston upon Thames KT3 38 E6
Penge SE20 23 C2
Teddington TW11 16 F3
Walton-on-Thames KT12 53 F8
Warlingham CR6 81 E1
Lindenhill Rd RG42 26 F8
Linden Ho TW12 16 B2
Linden Lea RH4 136 C5
Linden Leas BR4 63 D8
Linden Lodge Sch SW19 19 E7
Linden Pit Path KT22 95 B6
Linden Pl
Ewell KT17 76 E7
Mitcham CR4 40 E5
Staines TW18 13 A4
Linden Rd
Guildford GU1 109 D1
Hampton TW12 36 A8
Headley Down GU35 187 C5
Leatherhead KT22 95 B6
Weybridge KT13 53 C2
Lindens Cl KT24 113 E7
Lindens The
Camberley GU16 85 F3
Chiswick W4 7 D6
Copthorne RH10 183 B3
Farnham GU9 125 D1
New Addington CR0 63 C4
Linden Way
Send Marsh GU23 90 F3
Shepperton TW17 34 C4
Wallington CR8 60 C1
Woking GU22 89 F6
Lindfield Gdns GU1 109 F2
Lindfield Rd CR0 42 F3
Lindgren Wlk RH11 201 B1
Lindisfarne Rd SW20 19 A1
Lindley Ct KT1 37 C8
Lindley Ho KT14 71 B7
Lindley Pl TW9 7 A6
Lindley Rd
Tyler's Green RH9 121 C5
Walton-on-Thames KT12 54 D7
Lindon-Bennett Sch The TW13 15 D3
Lindon Ct SL5 28 E6
Lindores Rd SM5 40 C1
Lind Rd SM1 59 C5
Lindsay Cl
Chessington KT9 56 E3
Epsom KT18 76 C6
Stanwell TW19 2 D2
Lindsay Ct
6 Croydon CR0 61 D6
Sutton SM1 59 A5
Lindsay Dr TW17 34 D3
Lindsay Rd
Hampton TW12 16 B4
North Cheam KT4 58 B8
Woodham KT15 71 B8
Lindsey Cl CR4, SW16 41 E5
Lindsey Gdns TW14 14 D8
Lindum Cl GU11 105 A1
Lindum Dene GU11 105 A1
Lindum Rd TW11 17 C1
Lindums The BR3 23 F2
Lindvale GU21 69 E4
Lindway SE27 22 B3
Linersh Dr GU5 152 A6
Linersh Wood Cl GU5 152 B5
Linershwood Rd GU5 152 A6
Linfield Cl KT12 54 B5
Linford Ct 6 CR4 40 E8
Ling Cres GU35 187 B6
Ling Dr GU18 66 F7
LINGFIELD 164 D5

LINGFIELD COMMON 164 D6
Lingfield Common Rd RH7 164 C6
Lingfield Ct
Croydon CR0 61 F8
Wimbledon SW19 19 D2
Lingfield Dr RH10 202 E7
Lingfield Gdns CR5 100 B8
Lingfield Ho
Kingston upon Thames KT1 37 E5
Penge SE26 23 B2
Tadworth KT20 97 B4
Lingfield Notre Dame Sch RH7 164 F3
Lingfield Park Race Course RH7 164 E2
Lingfield Pl 1 RH1 118 E2
Lingfield Prim Sch RH7 164 D4
Lingfield Rd
East Grinstead RH19 185 D3
Edenbridge TN8 165 F8
Haxted TN8 165 F8
North Cheam KT4 58 C7
Wimbledon SW19 19 D2
Lingfield Sta RH7 164 E4
Lingfield Wildlife Area Nature Reserve* RH7 164 D5
Ling's Coppice SE21 22 D6
Lingwell Rd SW17 20 E5
Lingwood RG12 27 C3
Lingwood Gdns TW7 5 E7
Link Day Prim Sch The CR0 60 E6
Linkfield KT8 36 B6
Linkfield Cnr RH1 118 E2
Linkfield Gdns RH1 118 E1
Linkfield La RH1 118 F3
Linkfield Rd TW7 5 F5
Linkfield St RH1 118 E1
Link La SM6 60 E4
Linklater's Cotts GU14 84 B6
Link Rd
Addlestone KT15 52 E6
Carshalton CR4, SM6 41 A1
East Bedfont TW14 14 F8
Farnborough GU14 84 D1
Links Ave SM4 40 A5
Links Brow KT22 94 E4
Links Bsns Ctr GU22 90 C8
Links Cl
Ashtead KT21 75 C2
Ewhurst GU6 175 E6
Linkscroft Ave TW15 14 B2
Link Sec Sch The CR0 60 F6
Links Gdns SW16 22 A1
Links Green Way KT11 74 A5
LINKSIDE 188 B6
Linkside KT3 38 E7
Linkside E GU26 188 C7
Linkside N GU26 188 B7
Linkside S GU26 188 C6
Linkside W GU26 188 B6
Links Ind Est TW13 15 E5
Links Pl KT21 75 D2
Links Prim Sch SW17 21 A2
Links Rd
Ashford TW15 13 E3
Ashtead KT21 75 C2
Bramley GU5 151 E7
Mitcham SW16, SW17 21 A2
West Wickham BR4 44 C1
Link's Rd KT17 77 A5
Links The
North Ascot SL5 28 E7
Walton-on-Thames KT12 54 A8
Links View Ave RH3 116 A1
Links View Rd
Croydon CR0 63 A7
Hampton TW12 16 C4
Links Way
Beckenham BR3 44 A3
Effingham KT24 113 E7
Farnborough GU14 84 C3
Mitcham SW17 21 A2
Link The
Crawley RH11 201 D6
Teddington TW11 16 F2
Linkway
Camberley GU15 65 C4
Crawley RH6 182 C7
Crowthorne RG45 45 A5
Guildford GU2 108 F2
West Barnes SW20 39 B5
Woking GU22 70 C2
Link Way
Richmond TW10 17 B6
Staines TW18 13 B2
Linkway The SM2 59 C2
Linley Ct
1 Dulwich SE21 22 E4
Sutton SM1 59 C6
Linley House Sch KT5 37 F3
Linnell Rd RH1 140 B8
Linnet Cl
Bracknell RG12 26 D5
Selsdon CR2 62 D1
Turners Hill RH10 204 C6
Linnet Ct
1 Croydon CR0 61 E7
5 Mitcham CR4 40 E8
Linnet Gr GU4 110 D3
Linnet Mews SW12 21 A8
Linsford Bsns Pk GU16 85 F3
Linsford La GU16 85 F3
Linslade Cl TW4 4 E2
Linstead Rd GU14 84 E8
Linstead Way SW18, SW19 19 E8

Linton Cl CR4, SM5 40 F2
Linton Glade CR0 62 E1
Linton Gr SE27 22 C3
Linton's La KT17 76 E7
Lintott Ct TW19 2 D1
Lintott Gdns RH13 217 E3
Lion and Lamb Way 12 GU9 125 B2
Lion and Lamb Yd 14 GU9 125 B2
Lion Ave TW1 16 F7
Lion Cl
Haslemere GU27 207 F7
Littleton TW17 33 E6
Lion Ctr The TW13 15 E5
Lion Gate Gdns TW9 6 F4
Lion Gate Mews SW18 20 A8
Lion Gn GU27 207 F6
Lion Green Rd CR5 79 D3
Lion Ho 18 TW10 6 D2
Lion La
Haslemere GU27 207 F7
Turners Hill RH10 204 A4
Lion Mead GU27 207 F6
Lion Park Ave KT9 57 A6
Lion Rd
Thornton Heath CR0 42 C4
Twickenham TW1 16 F7
Lion Ret Pk GU22 70 B3
Lion Way TW8 6 D7
Lion Wharf Rd TW7 6 B4
Liphook Cres SE23 23 C8
Liphook Rd
Haslemere GU27 207 F6
Linchmere GU27 207 B4
Lipsham Cl SM7 78 D6
Lisbon Ave TW2 16 C6
Liscombe RG12 27 B2
Liscombe Ho RG12 27 B2
Liskeard Dr 2 GU14 85 A6
Liskeard Lodge CR3 101 A1
Lisle Cl SW17 21 B4
Lismore 9 SW19 19 F3
Lismore Cl TW7 6 A5
Lismore Cres RH11 201 B3
Lismore Rd CR2 61 E4
Lissant Cl KT6 37 D2
Lissoms Rd CR5 79 A1
Lister Ave RH19 205 F6
Lister Cl SW19 40 E8
Lister Ct 1 CR8 80 B7
Litchfield Ave SM4 39 F2
Litchfield Gdns KT11 73 B5
Litchfield Rd SM1 59 C6
Litchfield Way GU2 129 F7
Lithgow's Rd TW14, TW6 3 F3
Little Acre
Beckenham BR3 44 A6
Little Bookham KT23 93 F3
Little Austins Rd GU9 146 D8
Little Birch Cl KT15 52 D2
LITTLE BIRKETTS 155 D1
LITTLE BOOKHAM 93 E3
Little Bookham St KT23 93 F2
Little Bornes SE21 22 E4
Little Borough RH3 137 A8
Littlebourne 2 SE13 24 E8
Littlebrook Cl CR0 43 D3
Little Brownings SE23 23 B6
Little Browns La TN8 144 F4
Little Collins RH1 162 B7
Little Common La RH1 120 C3
Little Comptons RH13 217 F2
Littlecote Cl SW19 19 E8
Little Crabtree RH11 201 C7
Little Cranmore La KT24 112 C6
Littlecroft Rd 2 TW20 11 F3
Little Ct BR4 63 E8
Littledale Cl RG12 27 E6
Little Davids Sch CR0 63 B4
Little Dimocks SW12 21 B6
Little East Field CR5 99 D6
Little Elms UB3 3 D7
Little Ferry Rd TW1 17 B7
Littlefield Cl
Ash GU12 106 A1
Fairlands GU3 108 D5
9 Kingston upon Thames KT1 37 E7
Littlefield Cotts GU3 108 B6
Littlefield Ct UB7 2 D7
Littlefield Gdns GU12 106 A1
Littlefield Way GU3 108 D5
Littleford La GU4, GU5 152 F7
Little Gn
Elstead GU8 148 D4
Richmond TW9 6 D3
Little Grebe RH12 217 C5
Little Green La
Addlestone KT16 51 E7
Wrecclesham GU9 146 A6
Little Halliards KT12 35 A3
Little Hatch RH12 217 F5
LITTLE HAVEN 217 E4
Littlehaven Inf Sch RH12 217 F5
Littlehaven La RH12 217 F5
Littlehaven Sta RH12 217 F5
Little Heath La KT11 74 A5
Littleheath Rd CR2 62 B2
Little Heath Rd GU24 49 E2
Little Hide GU1 110 B3
Little Kiln GU7 150 E8
Little King St RH19 185 E1
Little Lascombe Cotts GU3 128 A4
LITTLE LONDON 132 F2
Little London
Shere GU5 132 F2

Little London *continued*
Witley GU8 170 E5
Little Lullenden RH7 164 E5
Little Manor Gdns GU6 174 E2
Littlemead KT10 55 D6
Little Mead GU21 68 F3
Little Mead Ind Est GU6 174 B3
Little Moor GU47 45 C1
Little Moreton Cl KT14 71 B7
Little Oak Cl TW17 33 F5
Little Orch
Woking GU21 70 A5
Woodham KT15 71 A8
Little Orchard Cl KT10 55 C7
Little Orchards KT18 76 E5
Little Orchard Way GU4 130 E1
Little Paddock GU15 66 A8
Little Park Dr TW13 15 E6
Little Park Enterprises RH6 180 E3
Little Platt GU2 108 D2
Little Queens Rd TW11 16 F2
Littleriding GU22 70 B3
Little Ringdale RG12 27 E5
Little Roke Ave CR8 80 B5
Little Roke Rd CR8 80 C5
Littlers Cl SW19 40 D8
Little St Leonards SW14 7 C4
LITTLE SANDHURST 45 B1
Little St GU2 109 B5
Little Stanford Cl RH7 164 D4
Littlestone Cl BR3 24 A2
Little Tangley Flats GU5 131 C1
Little Thatch GU7 150 F6
Little Thurbans Cl GU9 146 A6
LITTLETON
Chertsey 34 A6
Guildford 130 A3
Littleton CE Inf Sch TW17 34 A6
LITTLETON COMMON 14 D1
Littleton Cross GU3 130 A4
Littleton Grange RH2 138 C7
Littleton Ho
Littleton Common TW15 14 C1
4 Reigate RH2 118 A2
Littleton La
Artington GU3 130 A3
Littleton TW17, TW18 33 E4
Reigate RH2 138 E7
Littleton Rd TW15, TW17 14 C1
Littleton St SW18 20 C6
Little Tumners Ct GU7 150 E6
Little Warren Cl GU4 131 B7
Little Wellington St 9 GU11 105 A2
Littlewick Cotts GU21 68 F4
Littlewick Rd GU21 68 E3
Littlewood GU6 174 F3
Little Woodcote Est SM5 79 A8
Little Woodcote La CR8, SM5, SM6 79 B8
Littlewood Ho CR2 81 B5
Littleworth Ave KT10 55 D5
Littleworth Common Rd KT10 55 D7
Littleworth La KT10 55 D6
Littleworth Pl KT10 55 D6
Littleworth Rd
Hinchley Wood KT10 55 E6
Puttenham GU10 148 C8
The Sands GU10 126 F1
Liverpool Rd
Kingston upon Thames KT2 18 A1
South Norwood CR7 42 C6
Livesey Cl KT1 37 F6
Livingstone Cl GU6 174 F1
Livingstone Ct TW19 13 E7
Livingstone Rd
Caterham CR3 100 D5
Crawley RH10 201 E4
Horsham RH13 217 D1
Hounslow TW3 5 C3
South Norwood CR7 42 D7
Llanaway Cl GU7 150 F6
Llanaway Ho GU7 150 F6
Llanaway Rd GU7 150 F6
Llangar Gr RG45 45 A5
Llanthony Rd SM4 40 D4
Llanvair Cl SL5 29 A3
Llanvair Dr SL5 28 F3
Llewellyn Ct SE20 43 C8
Lloyd Ave
Thornton Heath SW16 41 E8
Wallington CR5 79 B5
Lloyd Ct 6 SE27 22 B5
Lloyd Ho BR3 24 B2
Lloyd Park Ave CR0 61 F6
Lloyd Pk Halt CR0 61 F6
Lloyd Rd KT4, SM3 58 D7
Lloyds Ct RH10 181 E1
Lloyds Way BR3 43 F4
Lobelia Rd GU24 68 A4
Locarno Ct 15 SW16 21 C3
Lochinvar St SW12 21 B8
Lochinver RG12 27 B2
Lock Cl KT15 70 E7
Locke King Cl KT13 53 A3
Locke King Rd KT13 53 A3
Lockesley Sq KT6 37 D3
Lockestone KT13 52 F4
Lockestone Cl KT13 52 F4
Locke Way GU21 69 F2
Lockfield Cotts GU21 69 A1
Lockfield Dr GU21 68 F2

Lockhart Rd KT11 . . . . 73 C6
Lockhursthatch La GU5 . 153 E6
Lock La GU22, GU23 . . . . . . 71 C3
Lock Rd
  Farnborough GU11 . . . . . 105 D5
  Guildford GU1 . . . . 109 D4
  Richmond TW10 . . . . 17 C4
Lock's La CR4 . . . . 41 A7
Locksley Dr GU21 . . . . 68 F2
Locks Mdw RH7 . . . . 165 A1
Locksmeade Rd TW10 . . 17 A1
Locks Ride SL5 . . . . 8 C2
Lockswood GU24 . . . . 88 B7
Lockton Chase SL5 . . . . . . 28 D6
Lockton Ho RG40 . . . . 25 C6
Lockwood Cl
  Farnborough GU14 . . . . . . 84 E8
  Forest Hill SE26 . . . . 23 D4
  Horsham RH12 . . . . 218 A5
Lockwood Ct
  Crawley RH10 . . . . 201 F8
  Kingston upon Thames KT3 . 38 C5
Lockwood Path GU21 . . . . 70 E6
Lockwood Way KT9 . . . . . . 57 A5
Locomotive Dr TW14 . . . . 15 A7
Lodden Lodge [17] SM2 . . . 59 C3
Loddon Cl GU15 . . . . 66 A6
Loddon Rd GU14 . . . . 84 D6
Loddon Way GU12 . . . . . 106 A1
Loder Cl GU21 . . . . 70 D6
Lodge Ave
  Croydon CR0, CR9 . . . . 61 A7
  Mortlake SW14 . . . . 7 E4
Lodgebottom Rd KT18,
  RH5 . . . . 116 A8
Lodge Cl
  Aldershot GU11 . . . . 126 C8
  Brentford TW7 . . . . 6 B6
  Carshalton CR4 . . . . 41 A1
  Crawley RH11 . . . . 201 C6
  Dorking RH5 . . . . 136 C3
  East Ewell KT17 . . . . 58 C1
  East Grinstead RH19 . . . . 185 D1
  Englefield Green TW20 . . . 11 D3
  Fetcham KT22 . . . . 94 D5
  Stoke D'Abernon KT11 . . . 73 F3
Lodge Gdns BR3 . . . . 43 F4
Lodge Hill CR8 . . . . 80 A4
Lodge Hill Cl GU10 . . . . . 146 D6
Lodge Hill Rd GU10 . . . . 146 E7
Lodge La
  New Addington CR0 . . . . . 63 B3
  Salfords RH1 . . . . 139 F1
  South Croydon CR0 . . . . . . 63 A4
  South Holmwood RH5 . . . 157 F8
Lodge Pl SM1 . . . . 59 B5
Lodge Rd
  Fetcham KT22 . . . . 94 D5
  Sutton SM1 . . . . 59 B5
  Thornton Heath CR0 . . . . . 42 B2
  Wallington SM6 . . . . 60 B5
Lodge Sch CR8 . . . . 79 D7
Lodge The
  Englefield Green TW20 . . . 11 C3
  Farnham GU9 . . . . 125 E4
  Guildford GU1 . . . . 130 F8
  Newchapel RH7 . . . . 163 E1
  [8] Sutton SM1 . . . . 59 C6
Lodge Way
  Ashford TW15 . . . . 13 E6
  Charlton TW17 . . . . 34 C7
Lodge Wlk CR6 . . . . 82 A3
Lodsworth GU14 . . . . 84 D3
Lofthouse Pl KT9 . . . . 56 C4
Lofts The GU8 . . . . 190 F8
Logan Cl TW4 . . . . 4 F4
Loggetts SE21 . . . . 22 E5
LOGMORE GREEN 135 C2
Logmore La RH4 . . . . 135 D3
Lois Dr TW17 . . . . 34 B4
Lollesworth La KT24 . . . . 112 C4
Loman Rd GU16 . . . . 86 A4
Lomas Cl CR0 . . . . 63 C3
Lombard Bsns Pk
  Merton SW19 . . . . 40 B7
  Thornton Heath CR0 . . . . . 41 F2
Lombard Rd SW19 . . . . . . 40 B7
Lombard St GU8 . . . . 149 B7
Lombardy Cl GU21 . . . . . . 68 F2
Lomond Gdns CR2 . . . . . . 62 E3
Loncin Mead Ave KT5 . . . 52 C2
Lond Meadow Villas
  RH6 . . . . 180 E5
London Acad The [11] CR0 . 61 D8
London Aerial Photo Liby
  GU24 . . . . 50 E1
London Cross KT24 . . . . 112 F4
London Fields Ho RH11 . 201 C2
London Ho [5] GU11 . . . . 105 B2
London Ho TW9 . . . . 6 F4
London Inst The SW17 . . . 21 B3
London La
  Bromley BR1 . . . . 24 F1
  Shere GU5 . . . . 133 A5
London Rd
  Ascot SL5 . . . . 29 D5
  Ashford TW15, TW18, TW19,
    TW14 . . . . 13 D5
  Bagshot GU15, GU19 . . . . 47 D2
  Bagshot GU19 . . . . 47 D2
  Blackwater GU15, GU17 . . 64 E4
  Bracknell RG12, SL5 . . . . . 28 C6
  Brands Hill SL3 . . . . 1 B8
  Brentford TW7, TW8 . . . . . . 6 B6
  Bromley BR1 . . . . 24 F1

London Rd continued
  Camberley GU15 . . . . 65 C6
  Caterham CR3 . . . . 100 A5
  Crawley RH10 . . . . 181 E3
  Dorking RH4 . . . . 115 C3
  East Grinstead RH19 . . . . 185 D3
  Englefield Green TW20 . . . 11 C1
  Forest Hill SE22, SE23 . . . . 23 C7
  Forest Row RH18 . . . . . . 206 E4
  Guildford, Burpham GU1,
    GU4 . . . . 110 B4
  Guildford GU1 . . . . 109 F1
  Hackbridge SM6 . . . . 60 B7
  Hindhead GU26 . . . . 188 F4
  Horsham RH12 . . . . 217 C2
  Hounslow TW3, TW7, TW1,
    TW8 . . . . 5 D5
  Kingston upon Thames KT1,
    KT2 . . . . 37 F7
  Mitcham CR4, SW17 . . . . . 40 F6
  Morden SM4 . . . . 40 A5
  Redhill RH1 . . . . 119 A3
  Reigate RH2 . . . . 118 A2
  Send Marsh GU23 . . . . 90 E1
  Stoneleigh KT17, KT4, SM3 . 58 B5
  Sunningdale, Blacknest SL5 . 30 B6
  Thornton Heath CR0, CR7,
    SW16 . . . . 42 A3
  Twickenham TW1 . . . . 17 A7
  Virginia Water GU25, TW20 . 31 B7
  Wentworth SL5, GU25 . . . . 30 C4
  Windlesham GU19, GU20,
    SL5 . . . . 48 C7
  Wokingham RG40 . . . . 25 E6
London Rd N RH1 . . . . 99 B2
London Rd S
  Merstham RH1 . . . . 119 B6
  Redhill RH1 . . . . 119 B6
London Road Sta (Guildford)
  GU1 . . . . 109 F1
London Sq GU1 . . . . 109 E1
London St KT16 . . . . 33 A2
Loneacre GU20 . . . . 48 E4
Lone Oak RH6 . . . . 162 B1
Lonesome Fst Sch CR4 . . . 41 B7
Lonesome La RH1, RH2 . . 139 D3
Lonesome Way CR4 . . . . . 41 C8
Longacre GU12 . . . . 106 A2
Long Acre RH10 . . . . 204 A8
Longacre Pl SM5 . . . . 60 A4
Longacre Sch GU5 . . . . . 152 D4
Long Ave GU24 . . . . 88 A6
Long Beech Dr GU14 . . . . 84 C3
Longbourne Gn GU7 . . . . 150 E8
Longbourne Way KT16 . . . 32 F3
Longboyds KT11 . . . . 73 B4
Long Bridge GU9 . . . . 125 C2
Longbridge Gate RH6 . . 181 E8
Longbridge Rd
  Crawley RH6 . . . . 181 F8
  Horley RH6 . . . . 160 F1
Longbridge Rdbt RH6 . . 160 E2
Longbridge Wlk RH6 . . . 160 F1
Longbrook Ct GU20 . . . . . 48 D4
Longchamp Cl RH6 . . . . . 161 C3
Long Cl RH10 . . . . 202 D6
Long Copse Cl KT23 . . . . . 94 B4
Longcroft Ave SM7 . . . . . . 78 C5
LONGCROSS 50 A7
Longcross Rd
  Addlestone KT16 . . . . 51 B7
  Longcross KT16 . . . . 50 D2
Longcross Sta GU25 . . . . . 30 F1
Longdale Mans SW12 . . . . 21 D7
Longdene Rd GU27 . . . . . 208 B6
LONG DITTON 37 C1
Long Ditton Inf Sch KT6 . . 37 C1
Longdown GU10 . . . . 146 C6
Longdown La N KT17 . . . . 77 A6
Longdown La S KT17,
  KT18 . . . . 77 A4
Longdown Lodge GU47 . . 64 B8
Longdown Rd
  Catford SE6 . . . . 24 A4
  Ewell KT17 . . . . 77 A6
  Farnham GU10 . . . . 146 C5
  Guildford GU1 . . . . 131 B6
  Sandhurst GU47 . . . . 45 B1
Long Dyke GU1 . . . . 110 B3
Longfellow Cl RH12 . . . . 217 E7
Longfellow Rd KT4 . . . . . . 39 B1
Longfield [3] BR1 . . . . 44 F8
Longfield Ave CR4, SM6 . . 41 A1
Longfield Cl GU14 . . . . 85 B8
Longfield Cres
  Burgh Heath KT20 . . . . 97 C7
  Forest Hill SE23, SE26 . . . . 23 C5
Longfield Dr
  Mitcham SW19 . . . . 40 E8
  Mortlake SW14 . . . . 7 B2
Longfield Ho SW14 . . . . 7 B2
Longfield Rd
  Ash GU12 . . . . 106 A2
  Dorking RH4 . . . . 135 F6
  Horsham RH12 . . . . 217 A1
Longfield St SW18 . . . . . . 20 A8
LONGFORD 2 C6
Longford Ave
  Feltham TW14 . . . . 3 F1
  Stanwell TW19 . . . . 13 E7
Longford Cl
  Camberley GU15 . . . . 65 D4
  Feltham TW13 . . . . 15 E5
  Hampton TW12 . . . . 16 A4
Longford Com Sch TW14 . 14 F8
Longford Ct
  Hampton TW12 . . . . 16 B2
  West Ewell KT19 . . . . 57 C6

Longford Gdns SM1 . . . . . 59 C8
Longford Ho
  Catford BR1 . . . . 24 D3
  Hampton TW12 . . . . 16 A4
Longford Ind Est TW12 . . 16 B2
Longford Rd TW2 . . . . 16 B7
Longford Rdbt UB7 . . . . 2 B6
Longford Way TW19 . . . . . 13 E7
Longford Wlk [10] SW2 . . . 22 A8
Long Garden Mews [3]
  GU9 . . . . 125 B2
Long Garden Way GU9 . 125 B2
Long Garden Wlk [4]
  GU9 . . . . 125 B2
Long Garden Wlk E [2]
  GU9 . . . . 125 B2
Long Garden Wlk W [1]
  GU9 . . . . 125 B2
Long Gdn Pl GU9 . . . . 125 B3
Long Gore GU7 . . . . 150 E8
Longheath Dr KT23 . . . . . . 93 E3
Longheath Gdns CR0 . . . . 43 C4
Longhedge Ho SE26 . . . . . 23 A4
Long Hill
  The Sands GU10 . . . . 126 E1
  Woldingham CR3 . . . . 101 F6
Longhill Rd SE6 . . . . 24 D5
Long Hill Rd RG12, SL5 . . . 28 A7
Long Ho SM5 . . . . 59 E8
Longhope Dr GU10 . . . . . 146 A6
Long Houses GU24 . . . . . . 87 D3
Longhurst Rd
  Crawley RH11 . . . . 201 A1
  Croydon RH0 . . . . 43 B3
  East Horsley KT24 . . . . . . 112 E6
Long La
  Croydon CR0 . . . . 43 C3
  Stanwell TW15, TW19 . . . . 13 F7
Longlands Ave CR5 . . . . . . 79 A5
Longlands Ct CR4 . . . . 41 A8
Longlands Way GU15 . . . . 66 D5
Longleat Sq GU14 . . . . 85 E3
Longleat Way TW14 . . . . . 14 D8
Longley Rd
  Farnham GU9 . . . . 125 D1
  Thornton Heath CR0 . . . . . 42 B2
  Upper Tooting SW17 . . . . . 20 F2
Long Lodge Dr KT12 . . . . . 54 C7
Longmead Cl CR3 . . . . . . 100 E5
Longmead Ho SE27 . . . . . 22 C3
Longmeadow
  Frimley GU15, GU16 . . . . . 65 F3
  Little Bookham KT23 . . . . . 93 F2
Long Meadow Cl BR4 . . 44 C2
Longmead Rd
  Epsom KT19 . . . . 57 E1
  Thames Ditton KT7 . . . . . . 36 F2
  Upper Tooting SW17 . . . . . 20 F3
Longmere Gdns KT20 . . . . 97 C8
Longmere Rd RH10 . . . . . 201 D8
Long Mickle GU47 . . . . 45 B1
Longmoors RG42 . . . . 26 E8
Longmore Rd KT12 . . . . . . 54 E6
Long Orchards KT20 . . . . . 97 E7
Longpoles Rd GU6 . . . . . . 174 F2
Long Rd The GU10 . . . . . 146 A2
Long Reach GU23, KT24 . . 92 B3
Longridge Gr GU22 . . . . . . 70 E5
Longs Cl GU22 . . . . 71 A3
Longs Ct [2] TW9 . . . . 6 F3
Longsdon Way CR3 . . . . . 101 A3
Longshaw KT22 . . . . 95 A7
Longshot Est RG12 . . . . . . 26 E7
Longshot La RG12 . . . . 26 E7
Longside Cl TW20 . . . . 32 C8
Longstaff Cres SW18 . . . . 20 A8
Longstaff Rd SW18 . . . . . . 20 A8
Longstone Rd SW17 . . . . . 21 B3
Long's Way RG40 . . . . 25 E7
Longthorne Lodge [7]
  SW2 . . . . 22 A8
Longthornton Rd SW16 . . 41 D7
Longton Ave SE26 . . . . 23 A4
Longton Gr SE26 . . . . 23 B4
Longwater Rd RG12 . . . . . 27 C3
Long Wlk
  Burgh Heath KT18 . . . . 97 D8
  Kingston upon Thames KT3 . 38 C6
Long Wlk The SL4 . . . . 10 D7
Longwood Dr SW15 . . . . . 19 B8
Longwood Rd CR8 . . . . . . 80 D3
Longwood View RH10 . . . 202 A3
Longyard Ho RH6 . . . . 161 B5
Lonsdale Gdns CR7, SW16 . 41 F5
Lonsdale Mews [4] TW9 . . 7 A6
Lonsdale Pl [1] RH4 . . . . . 136 B8
Lonsdale Rd
  Barnes SW13 . . . . 7 F7
  Croydon SE25 . . . . 43 B5
  Dorking RH4 . . . . 136 B8
  Weybridge KT13 . . . . 53 A3
Look Out Discovery Ctr The★
  RG12 . . . . 27 D1
Loop Rd
  Epsom KT18 . . . . 76 C3
  Old Woking GU22 . . . . 89 F7
Loppets Rd RH10 . . . . 201 F3
Lorac Ct SM2 . . . . 59 A3
Loraine Gdns KT21 . . . . . . 75 E2
Loraine Ho [1] SM5 . . . . . . 60 B6
Loraine Rd W4 . . . . 7 B8
Lord Chancellor Wlk KT2 . 38 C8

Lordell Pl SW19 . . . . 19 C2
Lord Knyvett Cl TW19 . . . . . 2 D1
Lord Knyvetts Ct [3] TW19 . . 2 D1
Lordsbury Field SM6 . . . . . 60 C1
Lords Cl
  Feltham TW13 . . . . 15 E6
  West Norwood SE21 . . . . . 22 C6
Lordsgrove Cl KT20 . . . . . . 97 B7
Lords Hill Cotts GU5 . . . . 152 C4
Lordshill Rd GU5 . . . . 152 C5
Lordship La SE21, SE22 . . 23 A8
Lords Wood Ho CR5 . . . . . 99 D5
Loretto Cl GU6 . . . . 175 A3
Lorian Dr RH2 . . . . 118 C2
Loriners RH10 . . . . 201 D3
Loriners Cl KT11 . . . . 73 A5
Loring Rd TW7 . . . . 5 F5
Lorne Ave CR0 . . . . 43 D2
Lorne Gdns
  Croydon CR0 . . . . 43 D2
  Knaphill GU21 . . . . 88 D8
Lorne Rd [3] TW10 . . . . 6 F2
Lorne The KT19 . . . . 94 A1
Lorraine Ct BR3 . . . . 44 C8
Lorraine Sch GU15 . . . . . . 65 E8
Lory Ridge GU19 . . . . 47 E4
Loseberry Rd KT10 . . . . . . 55 D5
Loseley Fields Prim Sch
  GU7 . . . . 129 E1
Loseley Ho★ GU3 . . . . . . 129 E3
Loseley Rd GU7 . . . . 150 E3
Lothian Rd GU24 . . . . 87 A6
Lothian Wood GU24 . . . . . 87 B5
Lotus Bsns Pk TW18 . . . . . 12 D4
Lotus Rd TN16 . . . . 83 F1
Loubet St SW17 . . . . 20 F2
Loudwater Cl TW16 . . . . . . 35 A5
Loudwater Rd TW16 . . . . . 35 A5
Loughborough RG12 . . . . . 27 E3
Louie Black Ho [4] SW19 . . 19 E1
Louisa Ct TW2 . . . . 16 E6
Louisa Ho SW15 . . . . 7 F3
Louise Margaret Rd
  GU11 . . . . 105 C3
Louis Fields GU3 . . . . 108 C5
Louisville Rd SW17 . . . . . . 21 A5
Lovatt Ct SW12 . . . . 21 B7
Lovat Wlk TW5 . . . . 4 E7
Loveday Ho [2] SW2 . . . . . 22 A7
Lovedean Ct RG12 . . . . . . 27 A3
Lovekyn Cl KT2 . . . . 37 F7
Love La
  Cheam SM3 . . . . 58 E4
  Croydon SE25 . . . . 43 B6
  Godstone RH9 . . . . 121 C3
  Long Ditton KT6 . . . . 56 D8
  Mitcham CR4 . . . . 40 E6
  Morden SM4 . . . . 40 B2
  Walton on the Hill KT20 . . . 97 A1
Lovelace Cl KT24 . . . . 93 A4
Lovelace Ct GU23 . . . . 91 B6
Lovelace Dr GU22 . . . . 70 F3
Lovelace Gdns
  Hersham KT12 . . . . 54 C5
  Surbiton KT6 . . . . 37 D2
Lovelace Prim Sch KT9 . . 56 C5
Lovelace Rd
  Bracknell RG12 . . . . 26 E5
  Surbiton KT6 . . . . 37 D2
  West Norwood SE21 . . . . . 22 C7
Lovelands La
  Castle Green GU24 . . . . . . 68 C6
  Lower Kingswood KT20 . . 118 B8
Lovoletts RH11 . . . . 201 A5
Lovel La SL4 . . . . 9 B3
Lovell Ho [4] SW19 . . . . . . 40 C8
Lovell Path [1] RH11 . . . . . 200 E5
Lovell Rd TW10 . . . . 17 C5
Lovells Cl GU18 . . . . 48 B1
Lovelock Ct CR8 . . . . 80 C2
Lovel Rd SL4 . . . . 9 A4
Lovers La GU10 . . . . 167 C7
Lovett Dr SM5 . . . . 40 D2
Lovett Ho [3] GU9 . . . . . . 125 B2
Lovett Rd TW20 . . . . 12 C4
Lowbury RG12 . . . . 27 E5
Lowburys RH4 . . . . 136 B4
Lowdells Cl RH19 . . . . 185 C4
Lowdells Dr RH19 . . . . . . 185 D4
Lowdells La RH19 . . . . . . 185 C3
Lowe Cl GU11 . . . . 104 F3
Lower Addiscombe Rd
  CR0 . . . . 42 C6
LOWER ASHTEAD 75 D1
Lower Barn Cl RH12 . . . . . 217 F5
Lower Barn Rd CR8 . . . . . . 80 D6
LOWER BOURNE 146 D5
Lower Breache Rd GU6 . . 176 B4
Lower Bridge Rd RH1 . . . 118 F1
Lower Broadmoor Rd
  RG45 . . . . 45 D4
Lower Charles St GU15 . . 65 C6
Lower Church La GU9 . . . 125 B2
Lower Church St CR0, CR9 . 61 B8
Lower Coombe St CR0,
  CR9 . . . . 61 C6
Lower Court Rd KT19 . . . . 76 C8
Lower Ct SM1 . . . . 59 C6
Lower Ct Rd KT19 . . . . 76 C8
Lower Dene
  East Grinstead RH19 . . . . 186 A1
  East Grinstead RH19 . . . . 206 A8
Lower Downs Rd SW20 . . . 39 D8
Lower Dunnymans [4]
  SM7 . . . . 77 F5
LOWER EASHING 149 E4
Lower Eashing GU7 . . . . . 149 F4

Lower Edgeborough Rd
  GU1 . . . . 130 F8
Lower Farm Rd KT24 . . . . 93 C3
Lower Farnham Rd GU11,
  GU12 . . . . 126 C7
LOWER FELTHAM 14 F5
Lower Forecourt RH6 . . . 182 B7
Lower George St [12] TW10 . 6 D2
Lower Gn KT12 . . . . 54 D5
Lower Gn W CR4 . . . . 40 E6
LOWER GREEN 55 A8
Lower Green Gdns [8]
  KT4 . . . . 39 A1
Lower Green Rd KT10 . . . . 55 C8
Lower Grove Rd TW10 . . . . 6 F2
Lower Guildford Rd GU21 . 68 D1
LOWER HALLIFORD 34 D2
Lower Ham La GU8 . . . . . 148 E4
Lower Hampton Rd TW12,
  TW16 . . . . 35 D7
Lower Ham Rd KT2 . . . . . . 17 D2
Lower Hanger GU27 . . . . . 207 D6
Lower Hill Rd KT19 . . . . . . 76 B7
Lower House Rd GU8 . . . . 169 F2
Lower Kings Rd KT2 . . . . . 17 E1
LOWER KINGSWOOD . . . 117 F8
Lower Manor Rd
  Farncombe GU7 . . . . 150 F6
  Milford GU8 . . . . 149 E1
Lower Marsh La KT1, KT5 . 38 A5
Lowermead RH1 . . . . 118 F3
Lower Mere RH19 . . . . 205 F8
Lower Mill Field GU19 . . . . 47 D2
Lower Morden La SM4 . . . . 39 E3
Lower Mortlake Rd TW9 . . . 6 F4
Lower Moushill La GU8 . . 149 D1
Lower Nelson St [4]
  GU11 . . . . 105 A2
Lower Northfield [5] SM7 . 77 F5
Lower Nursery SL5 . . . . . . 30 A4
Lower Park Rd CR5 . . . . . . 78 E1
Lower Peryers KT24 . . . . . 112 E7
Lower Pillory Down SM5 . . 79 B7
Lower Rd
  Effingham KT24 . . . . 113 D8
  Forest Row RH18 . . . . 206 F3
  Grayswood GU27 . . . . 189 F2
  Great Bookham KT22, KT23 . 94 C3
  Purley CR8 . . . . 80 B6
  Reigate RH1 . . . . 139 D7
  Sutton SM1 . . . . 59 C6
Lower Richmond Rd SW14,
  TW9 . . . . 7 B4
Lower Sandfields GU23 . . . 90 D3
Lower Sand Hills KT6 . . . . 37 C2
Lower Sawleywood [2]
  SM7 . . . . 77 F5
Lower Shott KT23 . . . . 94 B1
LOWER SOUTH PARK . . . 142 B3
Lower South St [4] GU7 . . 150 D4
Lower South View GU9 . . . 125 C3
Lower Sq
  Forest Row RH18 . . . . 206 F3
  Isleworth TW7 . . . . 6 B4
Lower St
  Haslemere GU27 . . . . 208 C6
  Shere GU5 . . . . 133 A4
Lower Sunbury Rd TW12 . . 36 A7
LOWER SYDENHAM 23 E4
Lower Sydenham Sta
  SE26 . . . . 23 F3
Lower Tanbridge Way [11]
  RH12 . . . . 217 B2
Lower Teddington Rd
  KT1 . . . . 37 D8
Lower Village Rd SL5 . . . . 29 C4
Lower Weybourne La
  Badshot Lea GU9 . . . . 126 A6
  Heath End GU9 . . . . 125 F6
Lower Wood Rd KT10 . . . . 56 B4
Loweswater Wlk GU15 . . . 66 D4
Lowfield Cl GU18 . . . . 67 A8
LOWFIELD HEATH 181 E4
Lowfield Heath Ind Est
  RH6 . . . . 181 E5
Lowfield Heath Rd RH6 . . 180 F5
Lowfield Heath Windmill★
  RH6 . . . . 180 C6
Lowfield Rd RH13 . . . . . . 215 D3
Lowfield Way RH6 . . . . . . 181 E5
Lowicks Rd GU10 . . . . 168 C6
Low La GU9 . . . . 126 B6
Lowlands Dr TW19 . . . . 2 D2
Lowlands Rd GU17 . . . . . . 64 C4
Lowndes Bldgs GU9 . . . . 125 B3
Lowndes Mews SW16 . . . . 21 E6
Lowood Ct SE19 . . . . 22 F3
Lowry Cl GU47 . . . . 64 D6
Lowry Cres CR4 . . . . 40 E7
Lowry Ct [3] W4 . . . . 7 E7
Lowther Hill SE23 . . . . 23 E8
Lowther Rd
  Barnes SW13 . . . . 7 F6
  Kingston upon Thames KT2 . 37 F8
Lowthorpe [2] GU21 . . . . . 69 A1
Loxford Ct GU6 . . . . 173 F2
Loxford Rd CR3 . . . . 100 F2
Loxford Way CR3 . . . . 100 F2
LOXHILL 172 E1
Loxley Cl SE26 . . . . 23 D3
Loxley Rd
  Hampton TW12 . . . . 15 F4
  Wandsworth SW18 . . . . . . 20 D7
Loxmeadows RH14 . . . . . 212 D3
Loxton Rd SE23 . . . . 23 D7
LOXWOOD 212 F4
Loxwood Cl TW14 . . . . 14 E7

Loxwood Ct CR0 .... 60 E7
Loxwood Place Farm
RH14 .... 212 F3
Loxwood Prim Sch RH14 213 A4
Loxwood Rd
Alfold GU6 .... 193 F2
Loxwood, Alfold Bars GU6,
RH14 .... 212 F8
Loxwood RH12, RH14 .... 213 D4
Plaistow RH14 .... 212 A2
Rudgwick RH12 .... 214 A6
Loxwood Wlk RH11 ..... 201 A8
Lucan Dr TW18 .... 13 D1
Lucas Cl
Crawley RH10 .... 202 C3
East Grinstead RH19 .... 186 A1
Lucas Ct SE26 .... 23 E3
Lucas Field GU27 .... 207 E6
LUCAS GREEN 67 E6
Lucas Green Rd GU24 .... 67 E5
Lucas Rd
Penge SE20 .... 23 C2
Warnham RH12 .... 216 F8
Lucerne Cl GU22 .... 89 E8
Lucerne Ct 8 BR3 .... 24 A1
Lucerne Dr RH10 .... 202 D4
Lucerne Rd CR7 .... 42 C5
Lucie Ave TW15 .... 14 B2
Lucien Rd
Upper Tooting SW17 ...... 21 A4
Wimbledon SW18 .... 20 B6
Lucille Ho SE26 .... 23 B2
Luckley Oakfield Sch
RG40 .... 25 B3
Luckley Path RG40 .... 25 C6
Luckley Rd RG41 .... 25 B3
Luckley Wood RG41 .... 25 B3
Lucraft Ho 12 SW2 .... 21 E8
Luddington Ave GU25 .... 31 F7
Ludford Cl CR0 .... 61 B6
Ludgrove Sch RG40 .... 25 D3
Lud Lodge TW15 .... 13 E6
Ludlow RG12 .... 27 B2
Ludlow Cl GU16 .... 86 A7
Ludlow Rd
Feltham TW13 .... 15 A4
Guildford GU2 .... 130 B8
Ludovick Wlk SW15 .... 7 E3
Ludshott Gr GU35 .... 187 B5
Ludshott Manor GU30 ... 187 C1
Luke Rd GU11 .... 125 E8
Luke Rd E GU11 .... 125 F8
Lukes Ct SE6 .... 24 A3
Lullarook Cl TN16 .... 83 C3
Lullington Garth 2 BR1 .. 24 E1
Lullington Rd SE20 ...... 23 A1
Lulworth Ave TW5, TW7 .... 5 C7
Lulworth Cl
Crawley RH11 .... 201 B3
Farnborough GU14 .... 85 A7
Lulworth Cres CR4 .... 40 E7
Lumiere Ct 6 SW17 .... 21 A6
Lumley Ct RH6 .... 161 A4
Lumley Gdns SM3 .... 58 E5
Lumley Ho KT3 .... 38 D1
Lumley Rd
Cheam SM3 .... 58 E5
Horley RH6 .... 161 A3
Lunar Cl TN16 .... 83 D3
Luna Rd CR7 .... 42 C6
Lundy Cl RH11 .... 201 C3
Lunghurst Rd CR3 .... 102 A5
Lunham Rd SE19 .... 22 E2
Lunn Cotts GU26 .... 188 F4
Lupin Cl
Bagshot GU19 .... 47 C1
Croydon CR0 .... 43 D1
Streatham SW2 .... 22 B6
Lupin Ride RG45 .... 45 B7
Lupus Ct SE19 .... 42 D8
Luscombe Ct BR2 .... 44 E7
Lushington Dr KT11 ...... 73 B5
Lushington Ho KT12 ...... 35 C3
Lushington Rd SE6 .... 24 B3
Lusted Hall La TN16 .... 103 C7
Lusteds Cl RH4 .... 136 C4
Lutchens Cl KT24 .... 113 D8
Lutea Ho SM2 .... 59 C3
Luther Mews 3 TW11 ...... 16 F3
Luther Rd TW11 .... 16 F3
Lutwyche Rd SE23, SE6 ... 23 F6
Lutyens Cl RH11 .... 200 E4
Luxford Cl RH12 .... 217 F5
Luxford's La RH19 ...... 206 B6
Lyall Ave SE21 .... 22 F4
Lyall Pl GU9 .... 125 B7
Lycett Ho 10 SW2 .... 21 E8
Lych Way GU21 .... 69 D3
Lyconby Gdns CR0 .... 43 E2
Lydbury RG12 .... 27 F6
Lydden Gr SW18 .... 20 B8
Lydden Rd SW18 .... 20 B8
Lydele Cl GU21 .... 69 F4
Lydford Cl
2 Farnborough GU14 ...... 85 A7
Frimley GU16 .... 86 A7
Lydger Cl GU22 .... 90 C7
Lydhurst Ave SW2 .... 21 F6
Lydney RG12 .... 27 B2
Lydney Cl SW19 .... 19 E6
Lydon Ho RH11 .... 181 D1
Lye Copse Ave GU14 ..... 85 B8
Lyefield La GU6, RH5 ... 176 C5
Lye The KT20 .... 97 C5
Lye View Cotts GU21 .... 89 A8
Lyfield KT22 .... 74 B5
Lyford Rd SW18 .... 20 E7
Lygarth Cl KT23 .... 94 C2
Lygon Ct SW19 .... 19 F1
Lyham Rd SW2 .... 21 E8
Lyle Cl CR4 .... 41 A2
Lyle Ct SM4 .... 40 D3
Lymbourne Cl SM2 .... 59 A1
Lymden Gdns RH2 .... 139 B7
Lymer Ave SE19 .... 22 F3
Lyme Regis Ct SM7 .... 77 F2
Lyme Regis Rd SM7 .... 77 F2
Lymescote Gdns SM1 ..... 59 A8
Lyminge Gdns SW17,
SW18 .... 20 E7
Lymington Cl SW16 ...... 41 D7
Lymington Ct SM1 .... 59 C7
Lymington Gdns KT19 .... 57 F5
Lynchen Cl TW5 .... 4 B6
Lynchford La GU11, GU14 105 E8
Lynchford Rd GU14 ..... 105 D8
Lynchmere Pl GU2 ...... 109 A4
Lynch Rd GU9 .... 125 E2
Lyncroft Gdns
Ewell KT17 .... 57 F2
Isleworth TW3 .... 5 C2
Lyn Ct GU1 .... 131 A8
Lyndale Ct
3 Redhill RH1 .... 119 A4
6 West Byfleet KT14 ..... 71 A6
Lyndale Rd RH1 .... 119 A4
Lynde Ho KT12 .... 35 C3
Lynden Gate SW15 .... 19 B8
Lynden Hurst CR0 .... 61 F8
Lyndhurst Ave
Aldershot GU11 .... 126 C6
Blackwater GU17 .... 64 C6
Mitcham SW16 .... 41 D7
Sunbury TW16 .... 35 A6
Tolworth KT5 .... 38 B1
Twickenham TW2 .... 16 A7
Lyndhurst Cl
Bracknell RG12 .... 28 A6
Crawley RH11 .... 201 D5
South Croydon CR0 .... 61 F7
Woking GU21 .... 69 D4
Lyndhurst Ct 12 SM2 ..... 59 A3
Lyndhurst Dr KT3 .... 38 F2
Lyndhurst Farm Cl RH19 184 D4
Lyndhurst Ho 2 SW15 ..... 19 A8
Lyndhurst Rd
Ascot SL5 .... 29 A5
Coulsdon CR5 .... 79 A3
Reigate RH2 .... 139 A6
Thornton Heath CR7 ...... 42 A5
Lyndhurst Sch GU15 ..... 65 B5
Lyndhurst Way
Belmont SM2 .... 59 A2
Chertsey KT16 .... 51 E8
Lyndon Ave SM6 .... 60 A7
Lyndon Yd SW17 .... 20 B4
Lyndsey Cl GU14 .... 84 B4
LYNE 32 B1
Lyne Cl GU25 .... 31 F3
Lyne Crossing Rd KT16,
GU25 .... 32 B3
Lyne Ct GU25 .... 31 F2
Lynegrove Ave TW15 ...... 14 C3
Lyneham Rd RG45 .... 45 B5
Lyne Ho RH5 .... 179 A1
Lyne La
Chertsey KT16, TW20,
GU25 .... 32 A3
Lyne KT16 .... 32 A2
Lyne & Longcross CE Inf Sch
KT16 .... 51 B8
Lyne Place Manor GU25 .. 31 F2
Lyne Rd GU25 .... 31 E3
Lynfield Ct SE23 .... 23 D8
Lynford Ct 5 CR2 .... 61 E6
Lynmouth Ave SM4 .... 39 D2
Lynmouth Gdns TW5 .... 4 D6
Lynn Cl TW15 .... 14 D3
Lynn Ct
Streatham SW16 .... 21 D3
Whyteleafe CR3 .... 80 F1
Lynne Cl CR2 .... 81 C8
Lynne Ct
Forest Hill SE23 .... 23 F8
13 Guildford GU1 .... 130 F8
South Croydon CR2 .... 61 E6
Wimbledon SW20 .... 39 B8
Lynne Wlk KT10 .... 55 C5
Lynn Rd SW12 .... 21 B8
Lynn Way GU14 .... 84 F7
Lynn Wlk RH2 .... 139 B6
Lynscott Way CR2 .... 61 B2
Lynsted Ct BR3 .... 43 E7
Lynton KT7 .... 37 A2
Lynton Cl
Chessington KT9 .... 56 E6
East Grinstead RH19 .... 186 A2
Farnham GU9 .... 146 A7
Isleworth TW7 .... 5 F3
Lynton Ct
Ewell KT17 .... 76 F8
Sutton SM2 .... 59 C4
Lynton Park Ave RH19 .. 186 A2
Lynton Rd
New Malden KT3 .... 38 D4
Thornton Heath CR0, CR7 .. 42 A3
Lynwick St
Rudgwick, Cox Green
RH12 .... 195 D1
Rudgwick RH12 .... 214 C8
Lynwood GU2 .... 130 B8
Lynwood Ave
Egham TW20 .... 11 E2
Epsom KT17 .... 76 F5
Wallington CR5 .... 79 B4
Lynwood Cl GU21 .... 70 D6
Lynwood Cres SL5 .... 29 E3
Lynwood Ct
Ashford TW15 .... 13 F3
Horsham RH12 .... 217 C3
Kingston upon Thames KT1 . 38 B7
Lynwood Dr
Mytchett GU16 .... 86 A3
North Cheam KT4 .... 58 A8
Lynwood Flats SL5 .... 29 E4
Lynwood Gdns CR0 .... 60 F6
Lynwood Rd
Epsom KT17 .... 76 F5
Hinchley Wood KT7 .... 55 F8
Redhill RH1 .... 119 A3
Thames Ditton KT7 .... 36 F1
Upper Tooting SW17 ...... 20 F4
Lynx Hill KT24 .... 112 F8
Lynx Terr SW17 .... 20 A5
Lyon Cl RH10 .... 202 C2
Lyon Ct RH13 .... 217 E2
Lyon Rd
Crowthorne RG45 .... 45 C6
Merton SW19 .... 40 C8
Walton-on-Thames KT12 ... 54 E8
Lyons Cl RH13 .... 215 D3
Lyons Ct RH4 .... 136 B7
Lyonsdene KT20 .... 117 F8
Lyons Dr GU2 .... 109 A6
Lyons Rd RH13 .... 215 E3
Lyon Way GU16 .... 65 C1
Lyon Way Ind Est GU16 .. 65 C1
Lyric Cl RH10 .... 202 D4
Lyric Mews SE26 .... 23 D4
Lyric Rd SW13 .... 7 F6
Lysander Rd CR0 .... 60 F4
Lysias Rd SW12 .... 21 B8
Lysons Ave GU12 .... 105 F8
Lysons Rd GU11 .... 105 A1
Lysons Way GU12 .... 106 A7
Lyster Mews KT11 .... 73 C6
Lytchet Minster Cl 4
RG12 .... 27 F4
Lytchgate Cl CR2 .... 61 E3
Lytcott Dr KT8 .... 35 F6
Lytham
Bracknell RG12 .... 26 E3
Horley RH6 .... 161 B2
Lytham Ct SL5 .... 29 C4
Lytton Dr RH10 .... 202 D7
Lytton Gdns SM6 .... 60 D6
Lytton Ho 3 TW12 .... 16 B2
Lytton Pk KT11 .... 73 F7
Lytton Rd GU22 .... 70 B3
Lyveden Rd SW17, SW19 .. 20 F2
Lywood Cl KT20 .... 97 C5

M

Mabbotts KT20 .... 97 D6
Mabel St GU21 .... 69 D2
Maberley Cres SE19 ..... 23 A1
Maberley Ct SE19 .... 23 A1
Maberley Rd
Penge, Elmers End BR3 .... 43 D6
Penge SE19 .... 23 A1
Mabley Ct RG12 .... 27 A3
MacAdam Ave RG45 ...... 45 C7
McAlmont Ridge GU7 ... 150 D7
McArdle Way SL3 .... 1 D7
Mac Arthur Ho 4 SW2 ... 21 E8
MacAulay Ave KT10 ..... 55 E8
MacAulay Ct CR3 ...... 100 E6
MacAulay Rd CR3 ...... 100 F6
Macbeth Ct RG42 .... 27 E8
McCarthy Rd TW13 ...... 15 D3
McClaren Tech Ctr GU21 .. 70 A8
Macclesfield Rd CR0, SE25 43 C4
McCormick Ho 9 SW2 .... 22 A7
MacDonald Ct TW3 .... 5 C3
McDonald Ho 1 KT2 ..... 17 F1
MacDonald Rd
Heath End GU9 .... 125 B7
Lightwater GU18 .... 67 A8
McDonald's Almshouses
GU9 .... 125 A1
McDonough Cl KT9 ...... 56 E6
McDougall Ct TW9 .... 7 A5
MacDowall Rd GU2 ..... 109 B5
Macfarlane La TW7 ...... 6 A8
McGechie Ho RH19 ..... 185 D3
MacGregor Ho SW12 ..... 21 D7
McIndoe Rd RH19 ...... 185 D3
McIntosh Cl SM6 .... 60 E3
McIver Cl RH19 .... 184 F4
McKay Cl GU11 .... 105 C3
McKay Rd SW20 .... 19 C2
McKay Trad Est SL3 ..... 1 E5
Mackenzie Ho RH19 .... 185 A4
Mackenzie Rd BR3 ...... 43 D7
McKenzie Way KT19 ..... 57 A1
Mackie Ho 18 SW2 ...... 22 A8
Mackie Rd SW2 .... 22 A8
Mackies Hill GU5 ..... 154 D7
McKinlay Ct BR3 .... 43 F7
Macklin Ho SE23 .... 23 B6
Mackrells RH1 .... 139 C6
MacLaren Dr
Bracknell RG42 .... 27 F8
Newell Green RG42 ...... 8 A1
Winkfield RG42 .... 28 A8
McLeod Ct SE21 .... 23 A7
McLeod Ho SE23 .... 23 C6
MacLeod Rd RH13 ...... 217 F1
Macmahon Cl GU24 ...... 49 E1
McMillan Ct
Catford SE6 .... 24 F7
Whyteleafe CR3 .... 80 F1
Macmillan House SM7 ... 77 F4
Macmillan Way SW17 .... 21 B4
Macnaghten Woods GU15 65 E6
McNaughton Cl GU14 .... 84 D3
MacPhail Cl RG40 ...... 25 E8
McRae La CR4 .... 40 F2
Madans Wlk KT18 .... 76 D5
Maddison Cl TW11 ...... 16 F2
Maddox Dr RH10 ...... 202 E5
Maddox La KT23 .... 93 E3
Maddox Pk KT23 .... 93 E4
Madehurst Ct RH11 .... 200 F3
Madeira Ave
Bromley BR1 .... 24 E1
Horsham RH12 .... 217 C2
Madeira Cl KT14 .... 71 A6
Madeira Cres KT14 ..... 70 F6
Madeira Rd
Mitcham CR4 .... 40 F5
Streatham SW16 .... 21 E3
West Byfleet KT14 ..... 71 A6
Madeira Wlk RH2 ..... 118 D2
Madeline Rd SE20 ...... 23 A1
Maderia Ct GU14 .... 84 E5
Madgehole La GU5 .... 153 B3
Madingley RG12 .... 27 B1
Madingley Ct TW1 .... 6 C2
Madison Gdns BR2 ...... 44 F6
Madox Brown End GU47 .. 64 E6
Madrid Rd GU2 .... 130 B8
Maesmaur Rd TN16 .... 103 D6
Mafeking Ave TW8 .... 6 E8
Mafeking Rd TW19 ...... 12 B6
Magazine Cotts GU4 ... 131 C3
Magazine Pl KT22 ...... 95 B5
Magazine Rd
Caterham CR3 .... 100 B5
Farnborough GU14 ..... 104 D8
Magdala Rd
Isleworth TW7 .... 6 A4
South Croydon CR2 ..... 61 D3
Magdalen Cl KT14 ...... 71 E5
Magdalen Cres KT14 .... 71 E5
Magdalen Ct SE25 ...... 43 A4
Magdalene Cl RH10 ... 182 C1
Magdalene Rd
Littleton TW17 .... 33 F6
Sandhurst GU47 .... 45 F2
Magdalen Rd SW18 ...... 20 D7
Magellan Terr RH10 ... 182 A2
Magna Carta La TW19 ... 11 E7
Magna Carta Sch The
Egham TW18 .... 12 D2
Egham TW20 .... 12 E2
Magna Rd TW20 .... 11 B2
Magnolia Cl
Kingston upon Thames
KT2 .... 18 B2
Sandhurst GU47 .... 45 D1
Winkfield RG42 .... 28 A8
Magnolia Ct
3 Belmont SM2 .... 59 B3
Feltham TW13 .... 15 A7
Horley RH6 .... 161 A3
Penge SE26 .... 23 C3
Richmond TW9 .... 7 B6
Wallington SM6 .... 60 B5
Magnolia Dr
Banstead SM7 .... 77 F3
Biggin Hill TN16 .... 83 E3
Magnolia Pl GU1 ...... 109 C4
Magnolia Rd W4 .... 7 B8
Magnolia Way
Dorking RH5 .... 136 D4
West Ewell KT19 .... 57 C5
Magnolia Wharf W4 ...... 7 B8
Magpie Cl
Coulsdon CR5 .... 79 C1
Crondall GU10 .... 124 D8
Magpie Wlk RH10 ..... 201 F8
Maguire Dr
Frimley GU16 .... 66 C3
Richmond TW10 .... 17 C4
Mahonia Cl GU24 .... 67 F6
Maida Rd GU11 .... 105 B4
MAIDENBOWER 202 C4
Maidenbower Bsns Pk
RH10 .... 202 E4
Maidenbower Dr RH10 .. 202 D4
Maidenbower Jun & Inf Schs
RH10 .... 202 C4
Maidenbower La RH10 .. 202 C4
Maidenbower Pl RH10 .. 202 C4
Maidenbower Sq RH10 .. 202 C4
Maiden La RH11 ...... 201 C8
Maiden's Gn SL4 .... 8 B6
MAIDEN'S GREEN 8 C6
Maidenshaw Rd KT19 .... 76 D7
Maids of Honour Row 4
TW9 .... 6 D2
Main Dr
Newell Green, Chavey Down
RG42, SL5 .... 28 B8
Newell Green RG42 ...... 8 A1
Main Gate Lodges SL4 .. 10 F5
Mainprize Rd RG12 ..... 27 E7
Main Rd TN16 .... 83 C5
Main St
Chertsey KT15 .... 52 E7
Feltham TW13 .... 15 D3
Mainstone Cl GU16 ..... 86 C7
Mainstone Cres GU24 ... 87 D6
Mainstone Rd GU24 ..... 67 F3
Mainwaring Ct 3 CR4 ... 41 A7
Mais Ho SE26 .... 23 B6
Maisie Webster Cl TW19 . 13 D8
Maisonettes The SM1 ... 58 F5
Maitland Cl
Hounslow TW4 .... 4 F4
Walton-on-Thames KT12 .. 54 E8
West Byfleet KT14 ..... 71 A6
Maitland Rd
Farnborough GU14 ..... 105 B8
Penge SE26 .... 23 D2
Maitlands Cl GU10 .... 126 F6
Maizecroft RH6 ...... 161 C4
Majestic Way CR4 ...... 40 F7
Major's Farm Rd SL3 .... 1 A8
Major's Hill RH10 .... 203 C5
Malacca Farm GU4 .... 111 B7
Malan Cl TN16 .... 83 E2
Malatia CR2 .... 61 C4
Malcolm Cl SE20 .... 23 C1
Malcolm Dr KT6 .... 37 E1
Malcolm Gdns RH6 .... 160 D1
Malcolm Prim Sch SE20 .. 23 C1
Malcolm Rd
Coulsdon CR5 .... 79 D4
Croydon CR0, SE25 ..... 43 A3
Penge SE20 .... 23 C1
Wimbledon SW19 .... 19 E2
Malden Ave SE25 .... 43 B6
Malden Ct KT3 .... 39 B6
Malden Ctr The KT3 .... 38 F5
Malden Green Ave KT4 .. 39 A1
Malden Hill KT3 .... 38 F6
Malden Hill Gdns KT3 .. 38 F6
Malden Manor Prim Sch
KT3 .... 38 E2
Malden Manor Sta KT3 .. 38 E2
Malden Parochial Prim Sch
KT4 .... 38 E1
Malden Pk KT3 .... 38 F3
Malden Rd
Cheam KT4, SM3 .... 58 D5
New Malden KT3, KT4 ... 38 F2
MALDEN RUSHETT 75 C7
Malden Way KT3 .... 39 A5
Malden Way (Kingston By
Pass) KT3, KT5 .... 38 E4
Maldon Ct SM6 .... 60 C5
Maldon Rd SM6 .... 60 B5
Malet Cl TW20 .... 12 D2
Maley Ave SE27 .... 22 B6
Malham Cl RH10 ...... 202 C3
Malham Fell RG12 ...... 27 A5
Malham Rd SE23 .... 23 D7
Malham Road Ind Est
SE23 .... 23 D7
Mallard Cl
Ash GU12 .... 105 F2
Haslemere GU27 ...... 207 E6
Horley RH6 .... 161 A5
Horsham RH12 .... 217 C5
Redhill RH1 .... 119 A4
2 Twickenham TW2 ...... 16 A8
Mallard Ct
Aldershot GU11 ...... 126 A7
7 Dorking RH4 .... 136 A8
28 Richmond TW10 .... 6 D1
Mallard Pl
East Grinstead RH19 .. 205 F8
Farnborough GU14 ...... 65 A1
Twickenham TW1 .... 17 A5
Mallard Rd CR2 .... 62 D1
Mallard's Reach KT13 .. 53 D8
Mallards The
Frimley GU16 .... 65 F2
Laleham TW18 .... 33 B7
Mallards Way GU18 ..... 67 A8
Mallard Way SM6 .... 60 C2
Mallard Wlk BR3, CR0 .. 43 D4
Mall Camberley The (Sh Ctr)
GU15 .... 65 C6
Malling Cl CR0 .... 43 C3
Malling Gdns SM4 ...... 40 C3
Malling Ho 9 BR3 ...... 24 A1
Malling Way BR2 .... 44 F2
Mallinson Rd CR0 ...... 60 D7
Mallow Cl
Burgh Heath KT20 ...... 97 B8
Croydon CR0 .... 43 D1
Horsham RH12 .... 217 E6
Mallow Cres GU4 ..... 110 C4
Mallowdale Rd RG12 ... 27 E2
Mall Sch The TW2 ...... 16 D5
Mall The
Brentford TW8 .... 6 D8
6 Guildford GU1 ...... 130 C8
Hersham KT12 .... 54 D5
Kingston upon Thames KT6 . 37 D4
Mortlake SW14 .... 7 C2
Malmains Cl BR3 .... 44 D5
Malmains Way BR3 ..... 44 D5
Malmesbury Prim Sch
SM4 .... 40 C3
Malmesbury Rd SM4 ..... 40 C3
Malmstone Ave RH1 ... 119 D6
Malory Cl BR3 .... 43 E7
Malta Rd GU16 .... 86 E8
Maltby Rd KT9 .... 57 A4
Malt Hill TW20 .... 11 E3
Malt House SL4 .... 11 B8
Malt House Cl SL4 ..... 11 B8
Malthouse Ct GU4 .... 130 E4
Malthouse Dr
Chiswick W4 .... 7 F8
Feltham TW13 .... 15 D3
Malthouse La
Hambledon GU8 .... 171 C1
Pirbright GU3 .... 88 C2
West End GU24 .... 67 F7

Malthouse Mead GU8 ... **170** F5
Malthouse Rd RH10 ... **201** D4
Malthouses The GU6 ... **174** E3
Maltings SW13 ... **.7** E5
Maltings Lodge 5 W4 ... **.7** F3
Maltings Sh Ctr The
GU9 ... **125** B2
Maltings The
Byfleet KT14 ... **71** F6
Oxted RH8 ... **122** F4
Staines TW18 ... **12** E4
Malting Way TW7 ... **.5** F4
Malton House SE25 ... **42** E5
Malus Cl KT15 ... **51** F3
Malus Dr KT15 ... **51** F3
Malvern Cl
Mitcham CR4 ... **41** C6
Ottershaw KT16 ... **51** C4
Penge SE20 ... **43** A7
Surbiton KT6 ... **37** E1
Malvern Ct
Belmont SM2 ... **59** A3
Brands Hill SL3 ... **.1** A8
Epsom KT18 ... **76** D5
3 Surbiton KT6 ... **37** E1
Malvern Dr TW13 ... **15** D3
Malvern Rd
Crawley RH11 ... **201** C5
Farnborough GU14 ... **84** D7
Hampton TW12 ... **16** A1
Harlington UB3 ... **.3** E7
Surbiton KT6 ... **37** E1
Thornton Heath CR7 ... **42** A5
Malyons The TW1 ... **34** D3
Manatee Pl SM6 ... **60** D7
Manby Lodge Inf Sch
KT13 ... **53** C5
Manchester Rd CR7 ... **42** C6
Mandeville Cl
Guildford GU2 ... **109** A4
Merton SW19 ... **39** E8
Mandeville Ct TW20 ... **12** A4
Mandeville Dr KT6 ... **37** D1
Mandeville Rd
Isleworth TW7 ... **.6** A5
Littleton TW17 ... **34** A4
Mandora Rd GU11 ... **105** B4
Mandrake Rd SW17 ... **20** F5
Manfield Pk GU6 ... **174** B5
Manfield Rd GU12 ... **106** A2
Mangles Ct 1 GU1 ... **130** C8
Mangles Rd GU1 ... **109** D3
Manley Bridge Rd GU10 ... **145** E4
Mannamead KT18 ... **96** E8
Mannamead Cl KT18 ... **96** E8
Mann Cl CR0, CR9 ... **61** C7
Manning Gdns CR0 ... **43** B2
Manning Cl RH19 ... **185** D2
Manning Pl TW10 ... **.6** F1
Mannings Cl RH10 ... **182** D1
Manningtree Cl SW19 ... **19** E7
Mann's Cl TW7 ... **.5** F4
Manoel Rd TW2 ... **16** C6
Manor Ave
Caterham CR3 ... **100** E3
Hounslow TW4 ... **.4** D5
Manor Chase KT13 ... **53** B5
Manor Cl
East Horsley KT24 ... **112** E7
Haslemere GU27 ... **207** E6
Horley RH6 ... **160** F3
New Malden KT4 ... **38** E1
Pyrford GU22 ... **70** F3
South Godstone RH9 ... **142** F5
Tongham GU10 ... **126** F7
Warlingham CR6 ... **81** E2
Manor Cotts GU21 ... **68** E5
Manor Cres
Byfleet KT14 ... **71** F6
Epsom KT19 ... **76** A7
Guildford GU2 ... **109** B3
Haslemere GU27 ... **207** E6
Pirbright GU24 ... **87** D7
Surbiton KT5 ... **38** A3
Manorcroft Prim Sch
TW20 ... **12** A2
Manorcrofts Rd TW20 ... **12** A2
Manor Ct
Horsham RH12 ... **218** A5
Kingston upon Thames KT2 . **38** A8
Streatham SW16 ... **21** E5
14 Sutton SM1 ... **59** C6
Twickenham TW2 ... **16** C6
Wallington SM6 ... **60** A7
Weybridge KT13 ... **53** B6
Manordene Ct KT7 ... **37** A1
Manor Dr
Feltham TW13 ... **15** D3
Hinchley Wood KT10 ... **56** A7
Horley RH6 ... **160** F3
Sunbury TW16 ... **35** A7
Surbiton KT5 ... **38** A3
West Ewell KT19 ... **57** E4
Woodham KT15 ... **52** A1
Manor Dr N KT3, KT4 ... **38** D2
Manor Dr The KT4 ... **38** F1
Manor Farm
9 Egham TW20 ... **12** A3
Wanborough GU3 ... **128** C6
Manor Farm Ave TW17 ... **34** B3
Manor Farm Bsns Ctr
GU10 ... **126** F5
Manor Farm Cl
Ash GU12 ... **105** F1
New Malden KT4 ... **38** E1

Manor Farm Cl continued
Normandy GU3 ... **107** B3
Manor Farm Cotts GU3 . **128** C6
Manor Farm Ct TW20 ... **12** A3
Manor Farm La TW20 ... **12** A3
Manor Farm Rd CR7,
SW16 ... **42** A7
Manorfield Prim Sch
RH6 ... **160** F3
Manorfields RH11 ... **200** D2
Manor Fields
Horsham RH12, RH13 ... **218** A4
Milford GU8 ... **149** E2
Seale GU10 ... **127** B4
Manorgate Rd KT2 ... **38** A8
Manor Gdns
Effingham KT24 ... **113** D7
Farncombe GU7 ... **150** E7
Farnham GU10 ... **146** D5
Guildford GU2 ... **109** B3
Hampton TW12 ... **16** C1
Merton SW19, SW20 ... **39** F7
Richmond TW10, TW9 ... **.6** F3
South Croydon CR2 ... **61** F4
Sunbury TW16 ... **35** A7
Manor Gn GU8 ... **149** E1
Manor Gr
Beckenham BR3 ... **44** B7
Richmond TW9 ... **.7** A4
Manor Green Coll RG11 . **201** A4
Manor Green Prim Sch
RH11 ... **201** A4
Manor Green Rd KT19 ... **76** C7
Manor Hill SM7 ... **78** F4
Manor Ho
Horsham RH12 ... **217** C1
5 Twickenham TW2 ... **16** E6
Wallington SM6 ... **60** B5
Manor Ho The
Kingswood KT20 ... **98** C4
Limpsfield RH8 ... **123** B7
Manor House Ct
Epsom KT18 ... **76** C6
Lower Halliford TW17 ... **34** B2
Manor House Dr
Ascot SL5 ... **.9** A1
Hersham KT13 ... **53** F5
Manor House Flats GU10 **126** F6
Manorhouse La KT23 ... **113** E8
Manor House Sch KT23 . **113** E8
Manor House The GU15 . **.65** D6
Manor House Way TW7 ... **.6** B4
Manor Inf Sch GU14 ... **84** E6
Manor Jun Sch GU14 ... **84** F6
Manor La
Feltham TW13 ... **15** A6
Harlington UB3 ... **.3** D8
Lewisham SE12 ... **24** F8
Lower Kingswood KT20 ... **118** A6
Shamley Green GU5 ... **152** E3
Sunbury TW16 ... **35** B7
Sutton SM1 ... **59** C5
Manor Lea GU27 ... **207** E6
Manor Lea Cl GU8 ... **149** E2
Manor Lea Rd GU8 ... **149** E2
Manor Leaze TW20 ... **12** B3
Manor Lodge GU2 ... **109** B3
Manor Mead Sch TW17 ... **34** B4
Manor Mews GU22 ... **90** B6
Manor Mount SE23 ... **23** C7
Manor Park Cl BR4 ... **44** B1
Manor Park Ind Est 2
GU2 ... **105** C1
Manor Park Prim Sch 9
SM1 ... **59** C5
Manor Park Rd
Sutton SM1 ... **59** C5
West Wickham BR4 ... **44** B1
Manor Pk
Richmond TW9 ... **.6** F3
Staines TW18 ... **12** D5
Manor Pl
East Bedfont TW14 ... **15** A7
Great Bookham KT23 ... **94** A1
Mitcham CR4 ... **41** C6
Staines TW18 ... **13** B3
Sutton SM1 ... **59** B6
4 Walton-on-Thames KT12 **35** A2
Manor Rd
Aldershot GU11, GU12 ... **126** A8
Ashford TW15 ... **14** A3
Ash GU10, GU12 ... **126** F8
Beckenham BR3 ... **44** B7
Belmont SM2 ... **58** F2
Croydon SE25 ... **43** A6
East Grinstead RH19 ... **185** C2
East Molesey KT8 ... **36** D5
Farnborough GU14 ... **85** D3
Farnham GU9 ... **125** E4
Guildford GU2 ... **109** B3
Horsham RH12 ... **218** A5
Merstham RH1 ... **119** C6
Merton SW20 ... **39** F7
Mitcham CR4, SW16 ... **41** C6
Reigate RH2 ... **117** F3
Richmond TW10, TW9 ... **.6** F3
Send Marsh GU23 ... **90** F4
Tatsfield TN16 ... **103** E7
Teddington TW11 ... **17** B3
Twickenham TW2 ... **16** D6
Wallington SM5, SM6 ... **60** B5
Walton-on-Thames KT12 ... **34** F2
West Wickham BR4 ... **63** B8
Woking GU21 ... **69** D3
Wokingham RG41 ... **25** A4
Manor Rd N
Hackbridge SM6 ... **60** B6
Hinchley Wood KT7 ... **56** A8

Manor Rd S KT10 ... **55** E6
MANOR ROYAL ... **181** F2
Manor Royal RH10 ... **181** E1
Manor Royal Ind Est
RH10 ... **181** E2
Manor The
Forest Hill SE23 ... **23** C8
Milford GU8 ... **149** F1
Manor Way
Bagshot GU19 ... **47** F3
Beckenham BR3 ... **44** A6
Egham TW20 ... **11** F2
Guildford GU2 ... **129** F6
Mitcham CR4, SW16 ... **41** C6
New Malden KT4 ... **38** F1
Old Woking GU22 ... **90** B6
Oxshott KT22 ... **74** C3
Purley CR8 ... **79** E7
South Croydon CR2 ... **61** F4
Woodmansterne SM7 ... **78** F3
Manor Way The SM6 ... **60** B6
Manor Wlk
1 Aldershot GU12 ... **105** B1
Weybridge KT13 ... **53** B5
Manor Wood Rd CR8 ... **79** E6
Mansard Beeches SW17 . **21** A3
Mansard Manor 8 SM2 ... **59** C3
Manse Cl UB3 ... **.3** D8
Mansel Cl GU2 ... **109** B6
Mansell Way CR3 ... **100** D5
Mansel Rd SW19 ... **19** F2
Mansfield Cl SL5 ... **28** D7
Mansfield Cres RG12 ... **27** B3
Mansfield Dr RH1 ... **119** D6
Mansfield Ho GU4 ... **110** A4
Mansfield Pl SL5 ... **28** D8
Mansfield Rd
Chessington KT9 ... **56** D5
South Croydon CR2 ... **61** D4
Wokingham RG41 ... **25** A5
Manship Rd CR4 ... **41** A8
Mansion Apartments The
BR3 ... **44** C5
Manston Cl SE20 ... **43** C8
Manston Dr RG12 ... **27** C3
Manston Gr KT2 ... **17** D3
Manston Rd GU4 ... **110** A5
Mantelmas Cotts RH1 ... **204** A4
Mantilla Rd SW17 ... **21** A4
Mantlet Cl SW16 ... **21** C1
Manton Ct SW20 ... **39** B8
Manville Ct 4 SW17 ... **20** F5
Manville Gdns SW17 ... **21** B5
Manville Rd SW17 ... **21** B5
Manygate La TW17 ... **34** C3
Many Gates SW12 ... **21** B6
Maori Rd GU1 ... **130** F8
Mapel Ct 3 RG12 ... **27** F5
Maple Ave GU14 ... **84** D5
Maple Cl
Ash Vale GU12 ... **106** A7
Blackwater GU17 ... **64** C5
Crawley RH11 ... **181** C1
Hampton TW12 ... **15** F2
Horsham RH12 ... **218** A5
Mitcham CR4 ... **41** B8
Whyteleafe CR3 ... **80** F2
Maple Ct
Ashford TW15 ... **14** D1
Carshalton SM1 ... **59** D6
Catford SE6 ... **24** B7
2 Croydon CR0 ... **61** C6
Englefield Green TW20 ... **11** B2
Kingston upon Thames KT3 . **38** D6
12 West Norwood SW16 ... **22** A3
Woking GU21 ... **69** C3
Mapledale Ave CR0 ... **62** B7
Maple Dr
Crowthorne RG45 ... **45** C7
East Grinstead RH19 ... **186** A1
Great Bookham KT23 ... **94** B3
Lightwater GU18 ... **66** F8
Mapledrakes Cl GU6 ... **175** E5
Mapledrakes Rd GU6 ... **175** E5
Maple Gdns
Epsom KT17 ... **76** E6
Stanwell TW15, TW19 ... **13** C6
Maple Gr
Brentford TW8 ... **.6** B7
Guildford GU1 ... **109** D3
Woking GU22 ... **89** E6
Maple Gr Bsns Ctr TW4 ... **.4** C3
Maplegreen RH11 ... **201** C5
Maplehatch Cl GU7 ... **150** E2
Maple Ho
2 Kingston upon Thames
KT6 ... **37** E4
10 Reigate RH2 ... **118** F1
4 Richmond TW9 ... **.7** B6
Teddington KT1 ... **17** C1
Maple House Ind Montessori
Sch CR7 ... **42** C6
Maplehurst
2 Beckenham BR2 ... **44** E7
Fetcham KT22 ... **94** D4
Maplehurst Cl KT1 ... **37** E5
Maple Ind Est TW13 ... **15** A5
Maple Inf Sch KT6 ... **37** D4
Mapleleaf Cl CR2 ... **81** D8
Maple Leaf Cl
Biggin Hill TN16 ... **83** D3
Farnborough GU14 ... **84** F3
Maple Mews SW16 ... **21** F3
Maple Pl KT17 ... **77** D5

Maple Rd continued
Redhill RH1 ... **139** F5
Send Marsh GU23 ... **91** A3
Whyteleafe CR3 ... **80** F2
Maplestead Rd SW2 ... **21** F8
Maples The
Banstead SM7 ... **78** B5
Ottershaw KT16 ... **51** C4
3 Teddington KT1 ... **17** C1
Maplethorpe Rd CR7 ... **42** B5
Maple Way
Feltham TW13 ... **15** B5
Headley Down GU35 ... **187** B6
Hooley CR5 ... **99** B6
Maple Wlk
Aldershot GU12 ... **126** D8
Belmont SM2 ... **59** B1
Marble Hill Cl TW1 ... **17** B8
Marble Hill Gdns TW1 ... **17** B8
Marble Hill Ho★ TW1 ... **17** C8
Marbles Way KT20 ... **97** D8
Marcheria Cl RG12 ... **27** B3
Marches Rd RH12 ... **197** E4
Marches The RH12 ... **198** B5
Marchmont Ho 10 SW16 . **21** C3
Marchmont Rd
Richmond TW10 ... **.6** F2
Wallington SM6 ... **60** C3
March Rd
9 Twickenham TW1 ... **17** A8
Weybridge KT13 ... **53** A5
Marchside Cl TW5 ... **.4** D6
Marcus Ct
Brentford TW8 ... **.6** E7
Woking GU21 ... **69** F1
Marcuse Rd CR3 ... **100** D4
Mardale GU15 ... **66** C4
Mardell Rd CR0 ... **43** D4
Marden Ave BR2 ... **44** F3
Marden Cres CR0 ... **41** F3
Marden Lodge Cty Prim Sch
CR3 ... **101** B6
Marden Rd CR0 ... **41** F3
Mardens The RH11 ... **201** B7
Mare Hill GU8 ... **170** E5
Mare La GU8 ... **172** C4
Marenello Rd KT24 ... **92** E1
Mareschal Rd GU2 ... **130** C7
Maresfield CR0 ... **61** E7
Maresfield Ho GU4 ... **110** D2
Mareth Cl GU11 ... **105** B2
Marfleet Cl SM5 ... **59** E8
Margaret Cl TW18 ... **13** D2
Margaret Ho 6 SM1 ... **59** B7
Margaret Lockwood Cl
KT1 ... **37** F5
Margaret Rd GU1 ... **130** C8
Margaret Roper RC Prim Sch
CR8 ... **61** A1
Margaret Rutherford Pl
SW12 ... **21** C7
Margaret Way CR8 ... **100** B8
MARGERY ... **118** A6
Margery Gr KT20 ... **117** E6
Margery Hall RH2 ... **118** B5
Margery La KT20, RH2 ... **118** A6
Margin Dr SW19 ... **19** D4
Marham Gdns
Morden SM4 ... **40** C3
Wandsworth SW17, SW18 . **20** E7
Marian Ct 1 SM1 ... **59** B5
Marian Lodge 9 SW20 ... **19** D1
Marian Rd CR4, SW16 ... **41** C8
Marian Vian Prim Sch
BR3 ... **43** E4
Maria Theresa Cl KT3 ... **38** D4
Marie Carlile 2 GU2 ... **70** A2
Mariette Way SM6 ... **60** E2
Marigold Cl RG45 ... **45** A6
Marigold Ct GU1 ... **109** E4
Marigold Dr GU24 ... **68** A4
Marigold Way CR0 ... **43** D1
Marina Ave KT3 ... **39** B4
Marina Cl KT16 ... **33** C1
Marina Pl 9 KT1 ... **37** D8
Marina Way TW11 ... **17** D1
Mariner Gdns TW10 ... **17** C5
Mariners Dr
Farnborough GU14 ... **85** C6
Normandy GU3 ... **107** A2
Marion Ave TW17 ... **34** B4
Marion Ct SW17 ... **20** E3
Marion Rd
Crawley RH10 ... **202** B3
Thornton Heath CR0 ... **42** D4
Marist RC Prim Sch The
KT14 ... **70** F6
Marist Schs The SL5 ... **29** D5
Maritime Ct KT19 ... **76** D8
Marius Mans 3 SW17 ... **21** A6
Marius Rd SW17 ... **21** A6
Marjoram Cl
Farnborough GU14 ... **84** B4
Guildford GU2 ... **109** A5
Marjory Kinnon Sch TW14 . **.3** E2
Marjory Pease Cotts
RH8 ... **123** E5
Markedge La CR5, RH1,
RH2 ... **98** F2
Markenfield Rd GU1 ... **109** D1
Markenhorn GU7 ... **150** D7
Market Field Rd 16 RH2 . **118** F1
Marketfield Way RH1 ... **119** A1
Market House & Visitor Ctr★
KT2 ... **37** D7
Market Par
Croydon SE25 ... **43** A5
3 Ewell KT17 ... **57** F2

Market Par continued
Feltham TW13 ... **15** E6
Market Pl
Bracknell RG12 ... **27** B7
Brentford TW8 ... **.6** C7
Kingston upon Thames KT1 . **37** D7
Wokingham RG40 ... **25** C5
Market Rd TW9 ... **.7** A4
Market Sq
9 Horsham RH12 ... **217** C2
Reigate RH2 ... **118** A1
Staines TW18 ... **12** E4
Market St
Bracknell RG12 ... **27** B7
Guildford GU1 ... **130** D8
Market The SM1, SM5 ... **40** C1
Markfield CR0 ... **81** F8
Markfield Rd CR3 ... **101** B2
Markham Ct
Beckenham BR3 ... **44** B6
Camberley GU15 ... **65** D6
Markham Ho 9 SE21 ... **22** E4
Markham Rd RH5 ... **178** C5
Markhole Cl TW12 ... **15** F1
Mark Oak La KT22 ... **94** A6
Marksbury Ave TW9 ... **.7** A4
Marks Ct SE6 ... **24** A3
Marks Rd
Warlingham CR6 ... **81** E1
Wokingham RG41 ... **25** A8
Mark St RH2 ... **118** B2
Markville Gdns CR3 ... **101** A2
Mark Way GU7 ... **150** B8
Markway The TW16 ... **35** C7
Markwell Cl SE26 ... **23** B4
Markwick La GU8 ... **172** C2
Marlang Ct BR3 ... **44** D8
Marlborough Rd TW7, TW8 . **.6** B7
Marlborough 11 SW19 ... **19** D7
Marlborough Cl
Crawley RH11 ... **201** C2
Hersham KT12 ... **54** D7
4 Horsham RH12 ... **217** D5
Mitcham SW19 ... **20** E2
Marlborough Cres UB3 ... **.3** D7
Marlborough Ct
Ashtead KT21 ... **75** F1
6 Beckenham BR3 ... **44** A8
7 Bromley BR1 ... **24** F1
3 Croydon CR2 ... **61** E6
Dorking RH4 ... **136** B7
1 Wallington SM6 ... **60** C3
Wokingham RG40 ... **25** D7
Marlborough Dr KT13 ... **53** C7
Marlborough Gdns KT6 ... **37** D2
Marlborough Hill RH4 ... **136** B7
Marlborough Ho
Richmond TW10 ... **.7** A2
Wimbledon SW19 ... **19** D5
Marlborough Inf Sch
GU11 ... **105** C2
Marlborough Mews SM7 . **78** A4
Marlborough Pl RH12 ... **217** C3
Marlborough Prim Sch
TW7 ... **.6** A6
Marlborough Rd
Ashford TW15 ... **13** E3
Dorking RH4 ... **136** B7
Feltham TW13 ... **15** D6
Hampton TW12 ... **16** A2
Mitcham SW19 ... **20** E2
Richmond TW10 ... **.6** F1
South Croydon CR2 ... **61** C3
Sutton SM1 ... **59** A8
Woking GU21 ... **70** A3
Marlborough Rise GU15 . **65** E6
Marlborough Trad Est TW9 . **.7** B6
Marlborough View GU14 . **84** C5
Marld The KT21 ... **75** F1
Marler Rd SE23 ... **23** F7
Marlesford Ct SM6 ... **60** C6
Marles La RH14 ... **214** C1
Marley Cl KT15 ... **51** F4
Marley Combe Rd GU27 . **207** F4
Marley Croft TW18 ... **12** E5
Marley Hanger GU27 ... **208** A3
MARLEY HEIGHTS ... **208** A1
Marley La GU27 ... **207** E4
Marley Rise RH4 ... **136** A4
Marlfield Cl KT4 ... **39** A1
Marlfield Ct KT3 ... **38** F2
Marlin Cl TW16 ... **14** E2
Marling Ct TW12 ... **15** F2
Marlingdene Cl TW12 ... **16** A2
Marlings Cl CR3 ... **80** E2
Marlins Cl 3 SM1 ... **59** C5
Marlow Cl SE20 ... **43** B6
Marlow Cres TW1 ... **.5** F1
Marlow Ct RH10 ... **201** D7
Marlow Dr SM3 ... **58** D7
Marlowe Ct
Dulwich SE19 ... **22** F3
6 Kingston upon Thames
KT2 ... **17** D4
Marlowe Ho
Kingston upon Thames
KT1 ... **37** D5
Wimbledon SW20 ... **39** B8
Marlowe Lodge CR0 ... **62** E8
Marlowe Sq CR4 ... **41** C5
Marlowe Way CR0 ... **60** E8
Marlow Ho
Teddington TW11 ... **17** A4
Wallington SM6 ... **60** E7
Marlow Rd SE20, SE25 ... **43** B7
Marlpit Ave CR5 ... **79** E2
Marlpit Cl RH19 ... **185** E4
Marlpit La CR5 ... **79** E2

Marlyns Cl GU4 . . . . 110 A4
Marlyns Dr GU4 . . . . 110 A5
Marmion Ho 14 SW12 . . 21 B8
Marmot Rd TW4 . . . . 4 D4
Marncrest Ct
  Hersham KT12 . . . . 54 B5
  Surbiton KT5 . . . . 37 F4
Marnell Way TW4 . . . . . . 4 D4
Marneys Cl KT18 . . . . . . 76 A4
Marnfield Cres SW2 . . . . 21 F7
Marnham Pl KT15 . . . . . . 52 C6
Maroons Way SE6 . . . . . . 24 B8
Marqueen Towers SW16 . 21 F1
Marquis Ct
  1 Kingston upon Thames
    KT1 . . . . 37 E5
  Stanwell TW19 . . . . . . 13 E7
Marriott Cl TW14 . . . . . . 3 D1
Marriott Ho SE6 . . . . . . 24 C4
Marriott Lodge Cl KT15 . . 52 C6
Marrowbrook Cl GU14 . . . 85 A4
Marrowbrook La GU14 . . 85 A3
Marrowells KT13 . . . . . . 53 F7
Marryat Ct 8 TW3 . . . . 4 F3
Marryat Pl SW19 . . . . . . 19 E4
Marryat Rd SW19 . . . . . . 19 E3
Marryfields Way 4 SE6 . 24 B8
Marsault Ct 2 TW9 . . . . 6 E3
Marshall Cl
  Farnborough GU14 . . . . 84 F1
  Frimley GU16 . . . . 66 D2
  Hounslow TW4 . . . . 4 F2
  Sandhurst GU47 . . . . . 81 A6
Marshall Ho 5 KT3 . . . . 38 E5
Marshall Par GU22 . . . . . 70 F4
Marshall Pl KT15 . . . . . . 52 C2
Marshall Rd
  Crawley RH10 . . . . 202 C4
  Farncombe GU7 . . . . . . 150 E6
  Sandhurst GU47 . . . . . 64 D6
Marshalls GU9 . . . . 146 B8
Marshalls Cl KT19 . . . . . 76 C6
Marshall's Rd SM1 . . . . 59 B6
Marsham Ct 19 SW19 . . 19 D7
Marsh Ave
  Epsom KT19 . . . . 57 E1
  Mitcham CR4 . . . . 41 A7
Marsh Ct
  Crawley RH11 . . . . 201 B1
  3 Merton SW19 . . . . . 40 C8
Marsh Farm Rd TW2 . . . 16 F7
Marshgate Sch TW10 . . . 6 F2
Marsh La KT15 . . . . 52 B6
Marsh View RH5 . . . . . . 133 F4
Marshwood Rd GU18 . . . 67 D8
Marston KT19 . . . . 76 C8
Marston Ave KT9 . . . . . . 56 E4
Marston Ct KT12 . . . . . . 35 C1
Marston Dr
  Farnborough GU14 . . . . 85 B7
  Warlingham CR6 . . . . . 81 E1
Marston Ho 2 RH1 . . . . 118 F1
Marston Rd
  Farnham GU9 . . . . 124 F2
  Richmond TW11 . . . . . 17 B3
  Woking GU21 . . . . 69 B2
Marston Way
  North Ascot SL5 . . . . . 28 E7
  South Norwood SE19 . . 22 C1
Martel Cl GU15 . . . . 66 C7
Martell Rd SE21 . . . . . . 22 D5
Martens Pl GU7 . . . . 150 E6
Martin Cl
  Crawley RH11 . . . . 201 D8
  Selsdon CR2 . . . . 62 D1
  Warlingham CR6 . . . . . 81 B3
Martin Cres CR0 . . . . . . 42 A1
Martin Ct
  Croydon CR0 . . . . 61 E5
  Lewisham SE12 . . . . . 24 F8
  Merton SW19 . . . . 20 A1
Martindale SW14 . . . . . . 7 C2
Martindale Ave GU15 . . . 66 C4
Martindale Cl GU4 . . . . . 110 D3
Martindale Rd
  Balham SW12 . . . . 21 B8
  Hounslow TW4 . . . . 4 E4
  Woking GU21 . . . . 69 A1
Martineau Cl KT10 . . . . . 55 D6
Martineau Dr
  Dorking RH4 . . . . 136 B5
  Isleworth TW1 . . . . . . 6 B3
Martingale Cl TW16 . . . . 35 A5
Martingale Ct GU11 . . . . 104 E2
Martingales Cl TW10 . . . 17 D5
Martin Gr SM4, SW19 . . . 40 A6
Martin Ho 7 KT3 . . . . . 38 E5
Martin Rd GU1 . . . . 109 A3
Martins Cl
  Blackwater GU17 . . . . . 64 D4
  Guildford GU1 . . . . . . 110 C2
  West Wickham BR4 . . . 63 D8
Martins Dr RG41 . . . . . . 25 B7
MARTIN'S HERON 27 F6
Martin's Heron Sta RG12 . 27 F5
Martins La RG12 . . . . . . 27 E6
Martins Pk GU14 . . . . . . 84 D7
Martin's Rd BR2 . . . . . . 44 F7
Martins The
  Crawley Down RH10 . . . 204 C8
  Forest Hill SE26 . . . . . 23 B3
Martins Wood GU8 . . . . . 170 E7
Martinsyde GU22 . . . . . . 70 C2
Martin Way
  Frimley GU16 . . . . 65 E2
  Merton SW19, SW20, SM4 . 39 E6
  Woking GU21 . . . . 69 A1
Martlands Ind Est GU22 . 89 A4

Martlet Cnr RH12 . . . . . . 214 D7
Martlets Cl RH12 . . . . . . 217 C5
Martlets The RH10 . . . . . 201 E6
Marton Cl SE6 . . . . 24 A5
Marts The RH12 . . . . 214 D7
Martyns Pl RH19 . . . . . . 206 A8
MARTYR'S GREEN 92 E7
Martyrs La GU21 . . . . . . 70 B7
Marvell Cl RH10 . . . . . . 202 C8
Marwell Cl BR4 . . . . 63 F8
Mary Adelaide Cl SW15 . 18 E5
Mary Ct 20 SM2 . . . . . . 59 C3
Marydene Ct RG12 . . . . . 26 C7
Mary Drew Almshouses The
  TW20 . . . . 11 D2
Marygold Ho TW3 . . . . . 5 C6
Maryhill Cl CR8 . . . . 80 C2
Maryland Cl KT1 . . . . . . 38 B7
Maryland Rd CR7 . . . . . . 42 B8
Marylake Way TW16 . . . . 35 A7
Marylebone Ho 16 RH1 . 118 F2
Marymount International Sch
  KT2 . . . . 18 C1
Mary Rd GU1 . . . . 130 C8
Mary Rose Cl TW12 . . . . 36 A8
Mary's Terr TW1 . . . . . . 17 A8
Mary Tates Cotts CR4 . . . 40 F5
Mary Vale GU7 . . . . 150 D2
Marzena Ct TW3 . . . . . . 5 C2
Masefield Ct 19 KT6 . . . 37 D2
Masefield Gdns RG45 . . . 45 B3
Masefield Rd
  Crawley RH11 . . . . 200 E3
  Hampton TW13 . . . . . . 15 F4
Masefield Way TW19 . . . 13 F7
Maskall Cl SW2 . . . . 22 A7
Maskani Wlk 2 SW16 . . . 21 C1
Maskell Rd SW17 . . . . . . 20 C5
Maskell Way GU14 . . . . . 84 D3
Mason Cl
  East Grinstead RH19 . . . 185 E2
  Hampton TW12 . . . . . . 35 F8
  Wimbledon SW20 . . . . 39 D8
Mason Ct 3 SE19 . . . . . 22 F1
Masonic Hall Rd KT16 . . . 32 F3
Mason Rd
  Crawley RH10 . . . . 201 E4
  Farnborough GU14 . . . . 84 E6
  Sutton SM1 . . . . 59 B5
Mason's Ave CR0, CR9 . . . 61 C7
Mason's Bridge Rd RH1 . 140 C3
Masons Paddock RH4 . . . 115 A1
Mason's Pl CR4 . . . . 40 F8
Mason's Yd SW19 . . . . . 19 D3
Mason Way GU11 . . . . . . 126 B7
Massetts Rd RH6 . . . . . . 161 A2
Massingberd Way SW17 . 21 B4
Master Cl RH8 . . . . 122 E6
Masters Cl SW16 . . . . . . 21 C2
Mastin Ho SW18 . . . . . . 20 A7
Maswell Park Cres TW3 . 5 C2
Maswell Park Rd TW3 . . 5 C3
Matcham Ct 16 TW1 . . . 6 D1
Matham Rd KT8 . . . . . . 36 D4
Mathews Cl GU14 . . . . . 105 E8
Mathias Cl KT18 . . . . . . 76 C6
Mathisen Way SL3 . . . . . 1 E5
Mathon Ct GU1 . . . . 109 F1
Matilda Cl SE19 . . . . . . 22 D1
Matlock Cres SM3 . . . . . 58 E6
Matlock Gdns SM3 . . . . . 58 E6
Matlock Pl SM3 . . . . 58 E6
Matlock Rd CR3 . . . . . . 100 E6
Matlock Way KT3 . . . . . . 38 D8
Matthew Arnold Cl
  Cobham KT11 . . . . 73 A5
  Staines TW18 . . . . 13 C2
Matthew Arnold Sch The
  TW18 . . . . 13 C2
Matthew Ct CR4 . . . . . . 41 D4
Matthew Rd GU11 . . . . . 125 E8
Matthews Cl SL5 . . . . . . 29 D5
Matthews Dr RH10 . . . . . 202 C3
Matthew's Gdns CR0 . . . 82 D8
MATTHEWSGREEN 25 A8
Matthewsgreen Rd RG41 . 25 A8
Matthews La TW18 . . . . . 12 F4
Matthews Rd GU15 . . . . . 65 C8
Matthew's St RH2 . . . . . 139 A5
Matthew Terr GU11 . . . . 105 C2
Matthey Pl RH10 . . . . . . 182 D1
Matthias Ct 13 TW10 . . . 6 E1
Maultway Cl GU15 . . . . . 66 B8
Maultway Cres GU15 . . . 66 B8
Maultway Ct GU15 . . . . . 57 D5
Maultway N GU15 . . . . . 47 B1
Maultway The GU15, GU16 . 66 D6
Maunsell Pk RH10 . . . . . 202 B6
Maureen Campbell Ct
  TW17 . . . . 34 B4
Maurice Ave CR3 . . . . . . 100 D5
Maurice Ct 3 TW8 . . . . 6 D7
Mauveine Gdns TW3 . . . 5 A3
Mavery Ct 8 BR1 . . . . . 24 F1
Mavins Rd GU9 . . . . 146 D8
Mavis Ave KT19 . . . . . . 57 E5
Mavis Cl KT19 . . . . 57 E5
Mawbey Rd KT16 . . . . . . 51 D4
Mawson Cl SW20 . . . . . . 39 E7
Mawson La W4 . . . . 7 E1
Maxine Cl GU47 . . . . . . 45 E1
Maxton Wlk RH11 . . . . . 201 B2
Maxwell Cl CR0 . . . . 41 E1
Maxwell Ct SE21 . . . . . . 23 A7
Maxwell Dr KT14 . . . . . . 71 C3
Maxwell Rd TW15 . . . . . 14 C2

Maxwell Way RH10 . . . . . 182 A1
May Bate Ave KT2 . . . . . 37 D8
Maybelle Cl RH5 . . . . . . 157 D3
Mayberry Pl KT5 . . . . . . 37 F2
Maybourne Cl SE26 . . . . 23 B3
Maybourne Grange CR0 . 61 E8
Maybourne Rise GU22 . . 89 D3
MAYBURY 70 C2
Maybury Cl
  Burgh Heath KT20 . . . . 97 E8
  Frimley GU16 . . . . 85 D8
Maybury Ct
  Beckenham BR3 . . . . . . 23 F1
  South Croydon CR2 . . . 61 B5
  Woking GU22 . . . . 70 B2
MAYBURY ESTATE 70 C3
Maybury Hill GU21, GU22 . 70 B2
Maybury Ho GU21 . . . . . 70 B2
Maybury Rd GU21 . . . . . 70 A3
Maybury Rough GU22 . . . 70 B2
Maybury St SW17 . . . . . 20 E3
May Cl
  Chessington KT9 . . . . . 56 F4
  Godalming GU7 . . . . . . 150 B2
  2 Sandhurst GU47 . . . . 64 D8
May Cotts CR5 . . . . 98 B2
May Cres GU12 . . . . 105 E1
Maycroft
  2 Coney Hall BR2 . . . . 44 F1
  Reigate RH2 . . . . 139 C7
Maycross Ave SM4 . . . . 40 A5
May Ct 2 SW19 . . . . . . 40 C8
Mayday Rd CR0, CR7 . . . 42 B3
Mayday University Hospl
  CR7 . . . . 42 B3
Maydwell Ave RH13 . . . . 215 C2
Mayefield Rd CR7 . . . . . 41 F4
Mayell Cl KT22 . . . . 95 C4
Mayes Cl
  Crawley RH10 . . . . 202 C5
  Warlingham CR6 . . . . . 81 D1
MAYES GREEN 176 E3
Mayes La RH12 . . . . 197 F3
Mayfair Ave
  New Malden KT4 . . . . . 39 A1
  Twickenham TW2 . . . . . 16 C8
Mayfair Cl
  Beckenham BR3 . . . . . . 44 B8
  Surbiton KT6 . . . . 37 E1
Mayfair Ct
  Beckenham BR3 . . . . . . 44 B8
Mayfield
  Crawley RH10 . . . . 202 D6
  Dormansland RH7 . . . . 165 A1
  Hersham KT12 . . . . . . 54 C6
  6 Leatherhead KT22 . . . 95 C6
  Rowledge GU10 . . . . . 145 F3
Mayfield Ave KT15 . . . . . 52 C1
Mayfield Cl
  Ashford TW15 . . . . 14 B2
  Badshot Lea GU9 . . . . . 126 B6
  Hersham KT12 . . . . . . 54 A6
  Hinchley Wood KT7 . . . 37 B1
  Penge SE20 . . . . 43 B8
  Redhill RH1 . . . . 140 A3
  Weybridge KT15 . . . . . 52 C1
Mayfield Cres CR7 . . . . . 41 F5
Mayfield Ct
  11 Bromley BR2 . . . . . 44 F5
  Redhill RH1 . . . . 139 F4
  Sutton SM2 . . . . 59 C3
Mayfield Gdns
  Egham TW18 . . . . 12 F2
  New Haw KT15 . . . . . . 52 B1
  Walton-on-Thames KT12 . 54 A6
Mayfield Ho KT13 . . . . . 53 A5
Mayfield Light Ind Est SL4 . 9 B5
Mayfield Rd
  Camberley GU15 . . . . . 65 B1
  Farnborough GU14 . . . . 84 F7
  Hersham KT12 . . . . . . 54 A6
  Merton SW19 . . . . 39 F8
  South Croydon CR2 . . . 61 D2
  Sutton SM2 . . . . 59 D4
  Weybridge KT13 . . . . . 52 F5
MAYFORD 89 D5
Mayford Cl
  Balham SW12 . . . . 20 F8
  Penge BR3 . . . . 43 D6
  Woking GU22 . . . . 89 D5
Mayford Ctr The GU22 . . 89 C5
Mayford Gn GU22 . . . . . 89 C5
Mayford Nature
  Reserve★ GU22 . . . . . 89 D6
Mayford Rd SW12 . . . . . 21 A8
Mayhurst Ave GU22 . . . . 70 C3
Mayhurst Cl GU22 . . . . . 70 C3
Mayhurst Cres GU22 . . . 70 C3
Mayhurst Mews GU22 . . 70 C3
Maynard Cl RH10 . . . . . 183 C4
Maynard Ct TW18 . . . . . 13 A4
Maynooth Gdns CR4 . . . 40 F2
Mayo Rd
  Thornton Heath CR0 . . . 42 D4
  Walton-on-Thames KT12 . 35 A2
Mayow Rd SE23, SE26 . . 23 D4
Maypole Rd
  Ashurst Wood RH19 . . . 206 E6
  East Grinstead RH19 . . . 185 D2
May Rd TW2 . . . . 16 E7
Mayroyd Ave KT6 . . . . . 57 A8
Mays Cl KT13 . . . . 52 F1
Mays Cnr GU23 . . . . 90 D3
Maysfield Rd GU23 . . . . . 90 D4

Mays Gr GU23 . . . . 90 D4
MAY'S GREEN 92 F7
May's Hill Rd BR2 . . . . . 44 E6
Mays Rd
  Teddington TW11 . . . . . 16 D3
  Wokingham RG40 . . . . . 25 E6
Maytree Cl GU1 . . . . 109 C5
Maytree Ct CR4 . . . . 41 A6
Maytrees GU21 . . . . 68 C2
Maytree Wlk SW2 . . . . . 22 A6
Maywater Cl CR2 . . . . . . 80 D8
Maywood Cl BR3 . . . . . . 24 B1
Maywood Dr GU15 . . . . . 66 A7
Maze Rd TW9 . . . . 7 A7
Meachen Ct RG40 . . . . . 25 C6
Mead Ave RH1 . . . . 140 A1
Mead Cl
  Cranleigh GU6 . . . . . . 174 E2
  Egham TW20 . . . . 12 B2
  Redhill RH1 . . . . 119 A4
Mead Cotts GU7 . . . . . . 151 A6
Mead Cres
  Carshalton SM1 . . . . . . 59 E6
  Little Bookham KT23 . . . 94 A2
Meadcroft Ho 5 KT3 . . . 38 E2
Meade Cl
  Addlestone KT15 . . . . . 52 D7
  Egham TW20 . . . . 12 C2
  Woking GU21 . . . . 68 E3
Meade Ct
  Bagshot GU19 . . . . 47 F3
  Walton on the Hill KT20 . 97 A3
Mead End KT21 . . . . 75 F3
Meades Cl RH7 . . . . 165 B1
Meades The RH7 . . . . . . 165 A1
Meadfoot Rd SW16 . . . . 41 C8
Mead Ho TN16 . . . . 83 D3
Meadhurst Club TW16 . . 14 E3
Meadhurst Pk TW16 . . . . 14 E2
Meadhurst Rd KT16 . . . . 33 B1
Mead Inf Sch The KT19 . . 57 F6
Mead La
  Chertsey KT16 . . . . . . 33 C1
  Farnham GU9 . . . . 125 B2
Meadlands Dr TW10 . . . . 17 D6
Meadlands Prim Sch
  TW10 . . . . 17 C4
Meadow App RH10 . . . . . 183 A3
Meadow Ave CR0 . . . . . . 43 D3
Meadowbank KT5 . . . . . 37 F3
Meadow Bank
  East Horsley KT24 . . . . 112 E8
  Farnham GU9 . . . . 125 B1
Meadowbank Cl TW7 . . . 5 E6
Meadowbank Gdns TW4,
  TW5 . . . . 4 B6
Meadowbank Rd GU18 . . 48 C1
Meadow Bglws GU4 . . . . 131 B3
Meadowbrook RH8 . . . . . 122 D5
Meadowbrook Cl SL3 . . . 1 F6
Meadowbrook Ct TW7 . . 5 F3
Meadow Brook Ind Ctr
  RH10 . . . . 182 A1
Meadowbrook Rd RH4 . . 136 A7
Meadow Cl
  Ash Vale GU12 . . . . . . 85 F1
  Blackwater GU17 . . . . . 64 D4
  Catford SE6 . . . . 24 A3
  Copthorne RH10 . . . . . 183 A3
  Farncombe GU7 . . . . . . 150 E7
  Hinchley Wood KT10 . . . 55 F7
  Horsham RH12 . . . . . . 218 A5
  Milford GU8 . . . . 150 A1
  Purley CR8 . . . . 79 D6
  Richmond TW10 . . . . . 17 E7
  Sutton SM1 . . . . 59 C8
  1 Twickenham TW4 . . . 16 A8
  West Barnes SW20 . . . 39 C5
Meadow Cotts GU24 . . . . 67 F7
Meadowcroft Cl
  Crawley RH11 . . . . 200 F5
  East Grinstead RH19 . . . 185 C2
Meadow Croft Cl RH6 . . 182 C8
Meadowcroft Cty Inf Sch
  KT16 . . . . 51 F7
Meadow Ct
  East Grinstead RH19 . . . 185 E2
  Epsom KT18 . . . . 76 C6
  Farnborough GU14 . . . . 84 F4
  Staines TW18 . . . . 12 E5
Meadow Dr GU23 . . . . . . 90 F4
Meadow Farm La RH12 . . 217 F7
Meadow Gate KT21 . . . . 75 E2
Meadow Gate Ave GU14 . 84 F1
Meadow Gdns TW18 . . . . 12 D3
Meadow Hill
  New Malden KT3 . . . . . 38 E3
  Purley CR5, CR8 . . . . . 79 C6
Meadow Ho
  Blackwater GU17 . . . . . 64 E4
  Guildford GU4 . . . . . . 110 D2
Meadow La KT22 . . . . . . 94 C5
Meadowlands
  Cobham KT11 . . . . 73 A6
  Crawley RH11 . . . . 201 C6
  Oxted RH8 . . . . 123 A1
  West Clandon GU4 . . . . 111 B5
Meadowlea Cl UB7 . . . . . 2 D8
Meadow Pl 1 W4 . . . . . 7 E7
Meadow Prim Sch KT17 . 58 B6
Meadow Rd
  Ashford TW15 . . . . 14 D3
  Ashtead KT21 . . . . 75 E2
  Beckenham BR2 . . . . . . 44 E7
  Carshalton SM1 . . . . . . 59 E5

Meadow Rd continued
  Claygate KT10 . . . . . . 55 E4
  Farnborough GU14 . . . . 85 B7
  Feltham TW13 . . . . 15 E6
  Guildford GU4 . . . . . . 110 A5
  Merton SW19 . . . . 20 C1
  Wentworth GU25 . . . . . 30 E4
  Wokingham RG41 . . . . . 25 A5
Meadow Rise
  Coulsdon CR5 . . . . 79 D6
  Knaphill GU21 . . . . . . 68 C2
Meadows Bsns Pk GU17 . 64 E4
Meadows End TW16 . . . . 35 A8
Meadowside
  Great Bookham KT23 . . . 94 A4
  7 Horley RH6 . . . . 161 B4
  Twickenham TW1 . . . . . 17 D8
  Walton-on-Thames KT12 . 54 C8
Meadowside Pk (Mobile
  Homes) RH7 . . . . 164 C6
Meadowside Rd SM2 . . . 58 E2
Meadows Leigh Cl KT13 . 53 C7
Meadows The
  Ash GU12 . . . . 106 A2
  Churt GU10 . . . . 167 F1
  Guildford GU2 . . . . . . 130 C6
Meadows The GU47 . . . . 64 E5
Meadows The CR6 . . . . . 81 E2
Meadow Stile CR0, CR9 . . 61 C7
Meadowsweet Cl KT3 . . . 39 C5
Meadow The RH10 . . . . . 183 A3
Meadow Vale GU27 . . . . 208 A6
Meadow Vale Prim Sch
  RG42 . . . . 26 F8
Meadowview
  Shepperton TW17 . . . . 34 C2
  Stanwell TW19 . . . . . . 1 F2
Meadow View
  Chertsey KT16 . . . . . . 33 C1
  Smallfield RH6 . . . . . . 162 C3
  Woking GU22 . . . . 89 F5
Meadow View Cotts TW17 34 B3
Meadowview Rd
  Catford SE6 . . . . 24 A3
  West Ewell KT19 . . . . . 57 E2
Meadow View Rd CR7 . . 42 B4
Meadow Way
  Addlestone KT15 . . . . . 52 B6
  Aldershot GU12 . . . . . . 105 F3
  Blackwater GU17 . . . . . 64 C5
  Bracknell RG42 . . . . . . 27 A8
  Burgh Heath KT20 . . . . 77 E2
  Chessington KT9 . . . . . 56 E5
  Great Bookham KT23 . . . 94 B4
  Horley/Gatwick RH6 . . . 161 C5
  Reigate RH2 . . . . 139 B5
  Rowledge GU10 . . . . . 145 F3
  West End GU24 . . . . . . 67 F6
  West Horsley KT24 . . . 92 D2
  Wokingham RG41 . . . . . 25 A5
Meadow Waye TW5 . . . . 4 E7
Meadow Wlk
  Hackbridge SM6 . . . . . 60 B7
  Walton on the Hill KT20 . 97 B3
  West Ewell KT17, KT19 . 57 F3
  Wokingham RG41 . . . . . 25 A6
Mead Pl
  Smallfield RH6 . . . . . . 162 C3
  Thornton Heath CR0 . . . 42 C1
Mead Rd
  Caterham CR3 . . . . . . 100 F4
  Cranleigh GU6 . . . . . . 174 E3
  Crawley RH10 . . . . 201 F7
  Hersham KT12 . . . . . . 54 E6
  Hindhead GU26 . . . . . . 188 F4
  Richmond TW10 . . . . . 17 C5
Meadrow GU7 . . . . 150 F6
Meadrow Ct GU7 . . . . . . 151 A6
Meadside
  4 Epsom KT18 . . . . . . 76 D6
  7 Woking GU22 . . . . . . 69 F1
Meadside Cl BR3 . . . . . . 43 E8
Meads Prim Sch The
  RH19 . . . . 205 E7
Meads Rd GU1 . . . . 110 B1
Meads The
  Cheam SM3 . . . . 58 E7
  East Grinstead RH19 . . . 205 E7
  Haslemere GU27 . . . . . 207 F6
  Weybridge KT13 . . . . . 53 D4
Meadsview Ct 3 GU14 . . 85 B4
Mead The
  Ashtead KT21 . . . . 95 E8
  Beckenham BR3 . . . . . . 44 C8
  Dorking RH4 . . . . 136 C4
  Farnborough GU14 . . . . 85 B3
  Wallington SM6 . . . . . . 60 D4
  West Wickham BR4 . . . 44 D1
MEAD VALE 139 D6
Meadvale RH12 . . . . 216 E2
Meadvale Hts RH1 . . . . . 139 D7
Meadvale Rd CR0 . . . . . 43 C4
Meadway
  Ashford TW15 . . . . 14 A4
  Beckenham BR3 . . . . . . 44 C8
  Effingham KT24 . . . . . . 113 E7
  Epsom KT19 . . . . 76 C7
  Esher KT10 . . . . 55 B2
  Frimley GU16 . . . . 65 F2
  Haslemere GU27 . . . . . 207 F6
  Oxshott KT22 . . . . 74 E5
  Staines TW18 . . . . 13 A1
  Tolworth KT5 . . . . 38 C1
  Twickenham TW2 . . . . . 16 D7
  Warlingham CR6 . . . . . 81 C3

Meadway continued
West Barnes SW20 .... 39 C5
Mead Way
Coulsdon CR5 .... 79 F1
Croydon CR0 .... 62 E8
Guildford GU4 .... 110 C6
Hayes BR2 .... 44 F3
Meadway Cl TW18 ..... 13 A1
Meadway Dr
New Haw KT15 .... 52 C3
Woking GU21 .... 69 D4
Meadway The RH6 ..... 161 C4
Meaford Way SE20 .... 23 B1
Meare Cl KT20 .... 97 D4
MEATH GREEN 160 F5
Meath Green Ave RH6.. 160 F5
Meath Green Inf Sch
RH6 .... 160 F5
Meath Green Jun Sch
RH6 .... 160 F5
Meath Green La RH1,
RH6 .... 160 E6
Meath Sch KT21 ...... 51 D3
Medawar Rd GU2 ..... 129 D8
Medcroft Gdns SW14... 7 C2
Mede Cl TW19 .... 11 D7
Mede Ct TW18 .... 12 E5
Medefield KT22 ...... 94 D3
Medfield St SW15 .... 19 B8
Medhurst Cl GU24 .... 49 F2
Medhurst Dr BR1 ..... 24 E3
Medina Ave KT10 ..... 55 E7
Medina Sq KT19 ...... 57 A2
Medlake Rd TW20 ..... 12 C2
Medlar Cl
Crawley RH11 .... 181 C1
Guildford GU1 .... 109 C3
Medlar Dr GU17 ...... 64 F3
Medlars Ct RH5 ..... 158 B1
Medora Rd SW2 .... 21 F8
Medway RH10 .... 204 A5
Medway Cl CR0 .... 43 C2
Medway Ct
Horsham RH13 .... 218 B5
South Norwood SE25.... 42 E4
Medway Dr
East Grinstead RH19... 205 D6
Farnborough GU14 ...... 84 E7
Medway Ho 6 KT2 ..... 37 D8
Medway Rd RH11 ..... 200 F5
Medwin Wlk 5 RH12... 217 C2
Meers Ct SW20 .... 39 C8
Melbourne Cl SM6 .... 60 C5
Melbourne Ct
Penge SE20 .... 23 A1
Twickenham TW2 .... 16 D7
Melbourne Ho 5 SE25.. 42 F5
Melbourne Mews SE6... 24 C8
Melbourne Rd
Merton SW19 .... 40 A8
Teddington TW11 ...... 17 C2
Wallington SM6 .... 60 C5
Melbourne Way RH12... 217 F5
Melbury Cl
Chertsey KT16 .... 33 A2
Claygate KT10 .... 56 B4
West Byfleet KT14 .... 71 A5
Melbury Gdns SW20 .... 39 B8
Melbury Ho TW2 ...... 16 D6
Meldone KT3 .... 38 D1
Meldone Cl KT5 ...... 38 B3
Meldrum Cl RH8 ..... 123 A3
Melfield Gdns SE6 .... 24 C3
Melford Cl KT9 ...... 56 F5
Melford Ct
Dulwich SE22 .... 23 A8
2 Sutton SM2 .... 59 C3
Melford Rd SE21, SE22.. 23 A7
Melfort Ave CR7 ..... 42 B6
Melfort Rd CR7, SW16... 42 B6
Meliot Rd SE6 .... 24 D6
Melksham Cl
Horsham RH13 .... 217 E1
Sandhurst GU47 .... 45 D1
Mellersh Hill Rd GU5... 152 C6
Mellifont Cl SM5 .... 40 D2
Mellish Ct KT6 ...... 37 E3
Mellison Rd SW17 .... 20 E3
Melliss Ave TW9 ...... 7 B6
Mellor Cl KT12 ...... 35 F2
Mellor Ct 2 SW19 .... 20 C1
Mellor Ho 2 SE21 .... 22 E4
Mellow Cl SM7 .... 78 C5
Mellows Rd SM6 ...... 60 D5
Melody Rd TN16 ...... 83 C1
Melrose RG12 .... 27 B1
Melrose Ave
Farnborough GU14 ...... 84 C5
Mitcham CR4 .... 21 B1
Thornton Heath SW16... 42 A6
Twickenham TW2 .... 16 B8
Wimbledon SW19 .... 20 A5
Melrose Cl GU14 ..... 84 C5
Melrose Gdns
Hersham KT12 .... 54 C5
Kingston upon Thames KT3.. 38 D6
Melrose Mews KT3 .... 38 D6
Melrose Rd
Barnes SW13 .... 7 F5
Biggin Hill TN16 ..... 83 C3
Coulsdon CR5 .... 79 B4
Merton SW19 .... 40 A8
Weybridge KT13 .... 53 A5
Melrose Special Sch CR4. 40 E6

Melrose Tudor SM6 .... 60 E5
Melsa Rd SM4 .... 40 C3
Melton Ct
11 Croydon CR0 .... 61 F8
Sutton SM2 .... 59 C3
2 Twickenham TW1 ..... 17 B8
Melton Fields KT19 ... 57 D2
Melton Pl KT19 ...... 57 D2
Melton Rd RH1 ...... 119 C5
Melville Ave
Frimley GU16 .... 65 F1
South Croydon CR0, CR2.. 61 F1
Wimbledon SW20 .... 19 A1
Melville Ct
Guildford GU2 .... 130 C6
West Byfleet KT14 .... 71 E7
Melvin Ct 11 TW9 ..... 7 A6
Melvin Rd SE20 ...... 43 C8
Melvinshaw KT22 ..... 95 C6
Membury Cl GU16 ..... 86 A7
Membury Wlk RG12 .... 27 F5
Memorial Cl
Heston TW5 .... 4 F8
Oxted RH8 .... 122 D8
Memory Cotts KT20 .... 97 E8
Mendip Cl
Forest Hill SE26 ..... 23 C4
Harlington UB3 .... 3 D7
North Cheam KT4 ...... 58 C8
Mendip Ct CR0 .... 61 C5
Mendip Rd
Bracknell RG12 .... 27 E4
Farnborough GU14 ...... 84 E7
Mendip Wlk RH11 .... 201 B6
Menin Way GU9 ...... 125 D1
Menin Wks CR4 .... 40 F7
Menlo Gdns SE19 ..... 22 D1
Mennis Ho SM5 .... 59 E8
Meon Cl
Farnborough GU14 ...... 84 D6
Tadworth KT20 .... 97 B5
Meon Ct TW7 .... 5 E5
Meopham Rd CR4, SW16.. 41 C8
Merantun Way SW19 .... 40 C8
Mercer Cl
Crawley RH10 .... 202 C3
Thames Ditton KT7 .... 36 F2
Mercer Rd RH12 ..... 217 C8
Mercers Park Ctry Pk★
RH1 .... 119 E4
Merchants Cl
Croydon CR0 .... 43 A5
Knaphill GU21 .... 68 C2
Merchiston Rd SE6 .... 24 D6
Mercia Ho TW15 ...... 34 C8
Mercia Wlk 8 GU21 ... 69 F2
Meredith Ct KT1 ..... 37 F7
Mere End CR0 .... 43 D2
Merefield KT18 ...... 97 D8
Merefield Gdns KT20 .. 97 D8
Mere Rd
Oatlands Park KT13 ... 53 D7
Shepperton TW17 ...... 34 B3
Walton on the Hill KT20.. 97 B4
Mereside Pk TW15 .... 14 C4
Meretune Ct SM4 ..... 39 F6
Merevale Cres SM4 .... 40 C3
Mereway Industry TW2.. 16 E7
Mereway Rd TW2 ...... 16 E7
Merewood Gdns CR0 .... 43 D2
Mereworth Cl BR2 .... 44 F4
Mereworth Dr RH10 ... 202 D8
Meridian Cl
Catford SE6 .... 24 F7
Croydon CR0 .... 61 A6
Sunningdale SL5 ...... 29 B1
Meridian Ctr CR0 .... 63 E1
Meridian Rd RH6 .... 161 C4
Meridian Way RH19 ... 185 F3
Merland Cl KT20 ..... 97 C7
Merland Gn KT20 ..... 97 C7
Merland Rise KT18, KT20.. 97 C7
Merle Common Rd RH8.. 144 B7
Merlewood RG12 ...... 27 D4
Merlewood Cl CR3 ... 100 D7
Merlin Cl
Brands Hill SL3 .... 1 B8
Crawley RH11 .... 200 E6
Mitcham CR4 .... 40 E6
South Croydon CR0 .... 61 E6
Wallington SM6 .... 60 F4
Merlin Clove RG42 .... 8 B2
Merlin Ct
Beckenham BR2 .... 44 F5
Frimley GU16 .... 65 D1
4 Mitcham CR4 .... 40 E8
Sheerwater GU21 ...... 70 C5
Merlin Ctr RH11 .... 181 D2
Merling Cl KT9 ...... 56 D5
Merlin Gr BR3 .... 44 A4
Merlin Rd GU14 ...... 85 B2
Merlins Cl GU9 ..... 125 C1
Merlin Way
Bracknell RG12 .... 26 D5
East Grinstead RH19 .. 186 A3
Farnborough GU14 ...... 84 D3
Merrick Ho RH2 ..... 118 C1
Merricks Ct SW14 ..... 7 B3
Merrilands Rd KT4 .... 39 C1
Merrilyn Cl KT10 .... 56 A4
Merrin Hill CR2 ..... 80 E8

Merritt Gdns KT9 .... 56 C4
Merrivale Gdns GU21 .. 69 C2
MERROW 110 C2
Merrow Bsns Pk GU4 .. 110 D4
Merrow CE Inf Sch GU4.. 110 D3
Merrow Chase GU1 ... 110 D1
Merrow Common Rd
GU4 .... 110 D4
Merrow Copse GU1 ... 110 B2
Merrow Croft GU1 ... 110 C2
Merrow Ct
Guildford GU1 .... 110 D1
Mitcham CR4 .... 40 D7
Merrow Grange GU1 .. 110 C1
Merrow Ho GU4 ...... 110 D4
Merrow La GU4 ...... 110 C5
Merrow Pl GU4 ...... 110 D3
Merrow St SM2 .... 58 D2
Merrow St GU4 ...... 110 D2
Merrow Way CR0 ...... 63 C4
Merrow Woods GU1 ... 110 B3
Merryacres GU8 ..... 170 E6
Merryfield Dr RH12 .. 217 A3
Merryhill Rd RG42 ... 27 B8
Merryhills Cl TN16 .. 83 D3
Merry Hills La RH14 . 213 A5
Merrylands KT16 ..... 51 E7
Merrylands Ct KT23 .. 93 F4
Merrylands Farm
Great Bookham KT23 ... 94 A3
Little Bookham KT23 .. 93 F3
Merrylands Rd KT23 .. 93 F3
Merryman Dr RG45 .... 45 A7
Merrymeet SM7 .... 78 F5
Merryweather Ct 1 KT3.. 38 E4
Merrywood 7 KT20 .... 95 C6
Merrywood Gr KT20 .. 117 E5
Merrywood Pk
Frimley GU15 .... 65 F4
Reigate RH2 .... 118 B3
Merrywood Pk (Mobile Home Pk) KT20 .... 116 B5
Merryworth Cl GU12 . 105 F1
Mersham Pl
Penge SE20 .... 43 B8
South Norwood CR7 .... 42 D7
Mersham Rd CR7 ...... 42 D7
MERSTHAM 119 D7
Merstham Prim Sch
RH1 .... 119 C6
Merstham Rd RH1 .... 120 A5
Merstham Sta RH1 ... 119 C7
MERTON 40 B8
Merton Cl GU47 ...... 45 F2
Merton Coll SM4 ..... 39 F4
Mertonford RG40 ..... 25 D5
Merton Gdns KT20 .... 97 D8
Merton Hall Gdns SW20.. 39 E8
Merton Hall Rd SW19,
SW20 .... 39 E8
Merton High St SW19 . 20 C1
Merton Ho
2 New Malden KT3 ..... 38 F4
Wandsworth SW18 ...... 20 A7
Merton Ind Pk SW19 .. 40 C8
Merton Lodge SW16 ... 21 E3
Merton Mans SW20 .... 39 D7
Merton Park Prim Sch
SW19 .... 40 A7
Merton Pk Halt SW19 . 40 A8
Merton Pl 9 SW19 .... 20 C1
Merton Rd
Croydon SE25 .... 43 A4
1 London CR0 .... 42 F3
Merton SW19 .... 20 B1
Wandsworth SW18 ...... 20 A7
Merton Road Ind Est
SW18 .... 20 A8
Merton Way
East Molesey KT8 ..... 36 C6
Leatherhead KT22 ..... 95 A8
Merton Wlk KT22 ..... 75 A1
Mervyn Rd TW17 ...... 34 C2
Messenger Ct RH11 .. 201 A8
Messer Ct CR0 .... 61 B6
Metana Ho RH10 ..... 182 A3
Metcalfe Wlk TW13 ... 15 E4
Metcalf Rd TW15 ..... 14 B3
Metcalf Way RH11 ... 181 D2
Meteor Way SM6 ...... 60 E3
Metro Bsns Ctr SE26 . 23 F3
Metro Ind Ctr TW7 .... 5 E5
Metropolis Apartments 6
SW12 .... 21 B7
Metro The 4 SW21 .... 69 E2
Meudon Ave GU14 ..... 85 B3
Meudon Ct KT6 .... 37 D4
Mews Ct RH19 .... 205 F6
Mewsend TN16 .... 83 D1
Mews The
Banstead SM7 .... 78 B4
11 Beckenham BR3 ..... 44 A8
Broadbridge Heath RH12.. 216 D4
Dunsfold GU8 .... 192 F5
6 Farnham GU9 .... 125 B2
Guildford GU1 .... 130 C8
Hampton TW12 .... 16 C2
Meyer Ho 2 SW12 ..... 21 B8
Meyrick Cl GU21 ..... 68 E3
Meyrick Ct 4 CR7 .... 42 A3
Mezel Hill Cotts SL4.. 10 C3
Miall Wlk SE26 ...... 23 E4

Michael Cres RH6 ... 161 A1
Michael Fields RH18 . 206 E2
Michael Hall Sch RH18.. 206 D1
Michael La GU1 ..... 109 B6
Michaelmas Cl SW20 .. 39 C6
Michael Rd SE25 ..... 42 E6
Michaelson Ho 4 SE21.. 22 E4
Micheldever Way RG12.. 27 F4
Michelet Cl GU18 .... 48 B1
Michelham Gdns
Burgh Heath KT20 ..... 97 C7
Twickenham TW1 .... 16 F5
Michell Cl RH12 .... 217 A2
Michels Almshouses 9
TW10 .... 6 E2
Michelsdale Dr 4 TW9.. 6 E3
Michel's Row 3 TW9 ... 6 E3
Micklefield Ct 2 CR0 . 42 B3
Micklefield Prep Sch
RH2 .... 118 A2
MICKLEHAM 115 C7
Mickleham Downs RH5.. 95 D1
Mickleham Dr KT22 ... 95 C1
Mickleham Gdns SM3 .. 58 E4
Mickleham Hall RH5 . 115 C7
Mickleham Way CR0 ... 63 D3
Mickle Hill GU47 .... 45 A1
Midas Metro Ctr SM4 . 39 D2
Middle Ave GU9 ..... 146 D8
MIDDLE BOURNE 146 C7
Middle Bourne La GU10.. 146 C7
Middle Church La 20
GU9 .... 125 B2
Middle Cl
Coulsdon CR5 .... 100 A7
Ewell KT17 .... 76 E7
Frimley GU15 .... 66 C6
Middle Farm Cl KT24 . 113 D8
Middle Farm Pl KT24 . 113 D8
Middlefield
Farnham GU9 .... 146 A7
Horley RH6 .... 161 C4
Middlefield Cl GU9 . 146 A8
Middlefields CR0 .... 62 E2
Middle Gn
Brockham RH3 .... 137 B7
Staines TW18 .... 13 C1
Middle Gordon Rd GU15.. 65 D5
Middle Green Cl 3 KT5.. 37 F3
Middle Hill
Aldershot GU11 ...... 105 A3
Englefield Green TW20 . 11 D3
Middle La
Ewell KT17 .... 76 E7
Teddington TW11 ...... 16 F2
Middlemarch GU8 .... 170 E5
Middlemead Cl KT23 .. 94 A3
Middlemead Rd KT23 .. 93 F2
Middle Mill KT5 ..... 37 F6
Middlemoor Rd GU16 .. 85 E3
Middle Old Pk GU9 .. 124 F4
Middle Rd
Leatherhead KT22 ..... 95 B6
Mitcham SW16 .... 41 C8
Middle Row 1 RH19 .. 205 F8
Middlesex Ct KT15 ... 52 C6
Middlesex Ho 4 SE20 . 23 C1
Middlesex Rd CR4 .... 41 E4
Middle St
Brockham RH3 .... 137 C5
Croydon CR0, CR9 ..... 61 C7
7 Horsham RH12 ...... 217 C2
Horsham RH12 .... 217 C2
Shere GU5 .... 133 A4
Middleton Gdns GU14 . 84 E6
Middleton Rd
Camberley GU15 ...... 65 F7
Downside KT11 .... 93 C8
Epsom KT19 .... 57 D1
Horsham RH12 .... 217 A2
Morden SM4, SM5 ...... 40 D2
Middleton Way RH10 . 200 E5
Middleview Dr GU3 .. 107 C4
Middle Way SW16 ..... 41 D7
Midgarth Cl KT22 .... 74 D6
Midgley Rd RH10 .... 201 F8
Midholm Rd CR0 ...... 62 E8
Midhope Cl GU22 ..... 89 E8
Midhope Gdns 5 GU22.. 89 E8
Midhope Rd GU22 ..... 89 E8
Midhurst SE26 .... 23 C2
Midhurst Ave CR0 .... 42 A2
Midhurst Cl RH11 ... 201 A7
Midhurst Rd GU27 ... 208 B5
Midleton Cl GU8 .... 149 F2
Midleton Ind Est GU2 ... 109 B1
Midleton Industrial Estate Rd
GU2 .... 109 B2
Midleton Rd
Guildford GU2 .... 109 A2
Guildford GU2 .... 109 B2
Kingston upon Thames KT3.. 38 C7
Midmoor Rd
Streatham SW12 .... 21 C7
Wimbledon SW19 .... 39 E8
Mid St
Nutfield RH1 .... 119 F1
South Nutfield RH1 .. 140 F7
Midsummer Apartments 14
SM2 .... 59 A3
Midsummer Ave TW4 .... 4 F3
Midsummer Wlk GU21 .. 69 D3
Midway
Cheam SM3 .... 39 F2
Walton-on-Thames KT12.. 54 B8

Midway Ave
Chertsey KT16 .... 33 A6
Thorpe TW20 .... 32 B6
Midway Cl TW19 ...... 13 B5
Miena Way KT21 ...... 75 D2
Mike Hawthorn Dr GU9.. 125 C3
Milbanke Ct RG12 .... 26 F7
Milbanke Way RG12 ... 26 F7
Milborne Rd RH10 ... 202 C2
Milborough Cres SE12.. 24 E8
Milbourne La KT10 ... 55 C5
Milbourne Lodge Sch
KT10 .... 55 D4
Milbrook KT10 .... 55 C4
Milburn Ho SW20 ..... 39 B7
Milburn Wlk KT18 .... 76 E4
Milcombe Ct 5 GU21 . 69 B1
Milden Cl GU16 ...... 86 A6
Milden Gdns GU16 .... 85 F6
Mile Path GU22 ...... 89 B7
Mile Rd
Carshalton CR4, SM6 .. 41 A1
Wallington CR0, CR4, CR9,
SM6 .... 41 C1
MILES GREEN 68 A2
Miles La
Cobham KT11 .... 73 E6
South Godstone RH9 .. 142 F7
Tandridge RH8 .... 143 A7
Miles Pl GU18 .... 66 F7
Miles Rd
Ash GU12 .... 106 B3
Epsom KT19 .... 76 D7
Mitcham CR4 .... 40 E6
Miles's Hill RH5 ... 155 C3
Milestone Cl
Ripley GU23 .... 91 B5
Sutton SM2 .... 59 D3
Milestone Ct TW7 ..... 6 A6
Milestone Dr CR8 .... 79 F5
Milestone Rd SE19 ... 22 F2
MILFORD 149 E1
Milford By Pass Rd GU8. 149 D2
Milford Ct RH5 ..... 157 C6
Milford Gdns CR0 .... 43 D4
Milford Gr SM1 ...... 59 C6
Milford Heath Rd GU8.. 170 E8
Milford Ho
Milford GU8 .... 150 A1
1 Woking GU22 .... 70 B2
Milford Hospl GU7 .. 171 C8
Milford Lodge GU8 .. 170 F8
Milford Mews SW16 ... 21 F5
Milford Rd GU8 ..... 148 E4
Milford Sta GU8 .... 171 A7
Milkhouse Gate 2 GU1. 130 D7
Milking La
Biggin Hill BR6 ...... 83 E7
Biggin Hill, Leaves Green
BR2 .... 83 D8
Millais RH13 .... 218 A3
Millais Cl RH11 .... 200 F2
Millais Cres KT19 ... 57 E5
Millais Ct RH13 .... 218 A4
Millais Rd KT3 ...... 38 E2
Millais Sch RH13 ... 217 F2
Millais Way KT19 .... 57 C6
Millan Cl KT15 ...... 52 B1
Milland Ho 11 SW15 .. 19 A7
Millbank SM6 .... 60 D5
Millbank The RH11 .. 200 F6
Mill Bay La RH12 ... 217 B1
Millbottom La RH5 .. 157 D7
Millbourne Rd TW13 .. 15 E4
MILLBRIDGE 146 D1
Millbrook
Guildford GU1 .... 130 D7
Oatlands Park KT13 .. 53 E6
Millbrook Way SL3 .... 1 E5
Mill Cl
Bagshot GU19 .... 47 D3
Carshalton SM5 .... 60 A8
East Grinstead RH19 . 205 E7
Great Bookham KT23 ... 94 A3
Haslemere GU27 ...... 207 F6
Horley RH6 .... 160 E4
Mill Cleave 1 KT14 .. 71 A7
Mill Copse Rd GU27 . 208 B4
Mill Cotts
East Grinstead RH19 . 205 E7
Rudgwick RH12 .... 214 D5
Millcroft Ho SE6 .... 24 B4
Mill Ct SE19 .... 22 E1
Millennium Cotts GU5.. 132 C4
Millennium Ctr GU21 . 125 A1
Millennium Ho RH11 . 200 F3
Millennium Tutorial Coll
SE27 .... 22 B4
Millennium Way RG12 . 27 C8
Miller Cl CR4 .... 40 F7
Miller Ho
5 Penge SE20 .... 23 A1
3 Streatham SW2 ..... 21 E8
Miller Rd
Guildford GU4 .... 110 C4
Mitcham SW19 .... 20 D2
Thornton Heath CR0 .. 42 A1
Millers Bsns Ctr RG41 . 25 A5
Millers Cl TW18 ..... 13 B3
Millers Copse
Langley Vale KT18 ... 96 D8
Outwood RH1 .... 162 B7
Miller's Ct TW20 .... 12 D2
Millers Gate RH12 .. 217 D6
Miller's La RH1 .... 162 C7
Millers Mead Ct SW19.. 20 D1
Millers Thumb RG12 .. 27 E8

Mill Farm Ave TW16...... 14 E1
Millfarm Bsns Pk TW4.... 15 E8
Mill Farm Cres TW4...... 15 E7
Mill Farm Rd RH13......218 A4
Millfield
 Charlton TW16...........34 D8
 Kingston upon Thames KT1. 37 F6
 Worcester Park KT4 ..... 57 F8
Mill Field GU19 .... 47 D3
Millfield La KT20........98 A2
Millfield Rd TW4........ 15 F7
Millfields Cres RH6 .....180 D6
Millford GU21............ 69 B2
Millford Sch GU8 ...... 149 F1
Millgate Ct GU9........125 D3
Mill Gdns SE26.......... 23 B5
Mill Gn CR4 .... 41 A2
Mill Green Bsns Pk CR4.. 41 A2
Mill Green Rd CR4 ...... 41 A2
Millhedge Cl KT11 ...... 73 E3
Mill Hill RH3............137 B8
Mill Hill La RH3........116 B1
Mill Ho SW19 ....40 C5
Millholme Wlk GU15 .... 66 C4
Mill House La KT16...... 32 B5
Millhouse Pl SE27....... 22 B4
Milligan Ho SE23........ 23 F7
Millins Cl GU47......... 45 E1
Mill La
 Ascot SL5...............30 A7
 Bracknell RG12 .... 26 F5
 Bramley GU5...........151 F6
 Byfleet KT14 .... 71 F6
 Carshalton SM5.........60 A7
 Chiddingfold GU8......191 B3
 Chilworth GU4, GU5...131 F4
 Copthorne RH10 ....183 A3
 Crawley RH11 ....201 A8
 Croydon CR0............61 A7
 Dorking RH4 ....136 B8
 Dunsfold GU8..........192 F4
 Ewell KT17 .... 57 F2
 Felbridge RH19 ....184 E5
 Felcourt RH7 ....164 F2
 Fetcham KT22 .... 95 A5
 Forest Green RH5 .....176 D7
 Frensham GU10........167 B7
 Godalming GU7 ....150 D4
 Guildford GU1 ....130 D3
 Hookwood RH6 ....160 D3
 Horton SL3............... 1 C4
 Kingsley Green GU27...208 C3
 Merstham RH1.........119 D4
 Ockham GU23 .... 91 D8
 Oxted RH8 ....122 F2
 Parkgate RH5 ....158 D5
 Pirbright GU24..........87 E3
 Shalford GU3 ....130 C1
 The Chart RH8.........123 F4
 Thorpe TW20 ....32 C5
 Witley GU8............170 F5
Mill Lane Trad Est CR0... 60 F7
Millmead
 Byfleet KT14 .... 71 F7
 Guildford GU2 ....130 C2
 Wokingham RG41 ...... 25 A7
Mill Mead TW18 .... 12 F4
Millmead Terr GU2......130 C2
Mill Pl KT1 .... 37 F6
Mill Plat TW7 .... 6 A5
Mill Plat Ave TW7 .... 6 A5
Millpond Cotts GU8 ....172 D4
Millpond Ct KT15 .... 52 E5
Millpond Pl SM6 .... 60 A7
Mill Pond Rd GU20...... 48 B6
Mill Pool Ho GU7 ......150 D4
Mill Prim Sch The RH11 .201 A6
Mill Rd
 Cobham KT11 .... 73 C4
 Crawley RH10 ....202 B7
 Epsom KT18 .... 76 F7
 Kingswood KT20 .... 97 D4
 Merton SW19...........20 C1
 South Holmwood RH5...157 D7
 Thames Ditton KT10 .... 55 A8
 Twickenham TW2....... 16 C6
Mill Reach GU4 ....131 F5
Mill Ride SL5 .... 28 D8
Mills Cl RH13 ....217 F1
Mill Shaw RH4 ....122 F3
Mills Ho GU12 ....105 D3
Millside SM5 ....59 F8
Millside Ct KT23 .... 94 A2
Millside Pl TW7........... 6 B5
Mills Rd KT12 .... 54 C5
Mills Spur SL4 .... 11 B8
Mill St
 Colnbrook SL3 .... 1 D7
 Kingston upon Thames KT1. 37 E6
 Redhill RH1 ....139 F8
Millstead Cl KT20 ...... 97 B5
Mill Stream GU9 ....125 E6
Millstream The GU27...207 E6
Mill The RH13........... 53 A7
Millthorpe Rd RH12 ....217 F4
Mill Vale BR2............ 44 F7
Millview Cl RH2.........118 D3
Mill View Cl KT17 ...... 57 F3
Mill View Gdns CR0 .... 62 D7
Millway RH2 ....118 D1
Mill Way
 East Grinstead RH19 ...205 E7
 Feltham TW14 .... 4 B2
 Headley KT18......... 96 A2
Millwood RH10 ....204 C5
Millwood Rd TW3, TW7... 5 C2
Milman Cl RG12......... 28 A7
Milne Cl RH11 ....200 E3

Milne Pk E CR0 .... 82 D8
Milne Pk W CR0 .... 82 D8
Milner App CR3.........101 A6
Milner Cl CR3...........101 A5
Milner Dr
 Cobham KT11........... 73 F7
 Twickenham TW2....... 16 D8
Milner Rd
 Caterham CR3 ....101 A6
 Kingston upon Thames KT1. 37 D6
 Merton SW19...........40 B8
 Morden CR4, SM4 ..... 40 D4
 South Norwood CR7 .... 42 D6
Milnthorpe Rd W4 ...... 7 D8
Milnwood Rd RH12......217 C3
Milton Ave
 Carshalton SM1.........59 E6
 Croydon CR0 .... 42 D2
 Westcott RH4 ....135 D6
Milton Cl
 Bracknell RG12 .... 27 B3
 Carshalton SM1.........59 D7
 Horton SL3.............. 1 A4
 Normandy GU3 ....107 B3
Milton Cres RH19 ....205 C8
Milton Ct
 Richmond KT2 .... 17 E4
 Twickenham TW2....... 16 E5
 Wokingham RG40 ...... 25 B7
Milton Dr
 Littleton TW17......... 33 E5
 Wokingham RG40 ...... 25 B7
Milton Gdns
 Epsom KT18............ 76 E5
 Stanwell TW19......... 13 F7
 Wokingham RG40 ...... 25 B6
Milton Grange GU12 ...106 A5
Milton Ho
 [12] Beckenham BR3... 24 A1
 [5] Kingston upon Thames
  KT2..................18 B2
 Sutton SM1............. 59 A7
Milton Lodge TW1 ..... 16 F8
Milton Mount RH10 ....182 D1
Milton Mount Ave RH10.202 D8
Milton Mount Prim Sch
 RH10.................202 C8
Milton Rd
 Addlestone KT15 .... 52 A4
 Caterham CR3 ....100 D6
 Crawley RH10 ....202 C7
 Croydon CR0 .... 42 D2
 Egham TW20 .... 11 F3
 Hampton TW12 .... 36 B8
 Horsham RH12 ....217 C3
 Mitcham CR4 .... 21 A1
 Mortlake SW14 .... 7 D4
 Sutton SM1............. 59 A6
 Wallington SM6 .... 60 B4
 Walton-on-Thames KT12... 54 D7
 Wimbledon SW19 ...... 20 C2
 Wokingham RG40, RG41.. 25 B6
Miltons Cotts GU8 .....170 F5
Miltons Cres GU7 .....150 B2
Milton St RH4...........135 D6
Milton Way KT23 ...... 94 C2
Milverton Ho SE23..... 23 E5
Milward Gdns RG12 ... 26 C7
MIMBRIDGE 69 A7
Mina Rd SW19 .... 40 A8
Minard Rd SE6......... 24 E7
Minchin Cl KT22 .... 95 A5
Mincing La GU24....... 49 F2
Mindelheim Ave RH19..186 B2
Minden Rd
 Cheam SM3............. 58 F8
 Penge SE20............ 43 B8
Minehead Rd SW16 .... 21 F3
Minehurst Rd GU16 .... 85 F4
Minerva Cl TW19....... 2 A2
Minerva Rd KT1......... 37 F7
Minimax Cl TW14 ...... 4 A1
Mink Ct TW4............ 4 C5
Minley Cl GU14 .... 84 E4
Minley Ct RH2 ....118 A2
Minley Rd
 Blackwater GU17, GU14 .. 84 A7
 Farnborough GU14 .....84 D5
Minniedale KT5......... 37 F4
Minorca Ave GU16 ..... 66 E2
Minorca Rd
 Frimley GU16........... 66 E1
 Weybridge KT13 .... 53 A6
Minshull Pl [24] BR3 ... 24 A1
Minstead Cl RG12 ...... 27 F6
Minstead Gdns SW15... 18 E8
Minstead Way KT3 ..... 38 E3
Minster Ave SM1...... 59 A8
Minster Cl GU14 ...... 85 D1
Minster Ct
 Camberley GU15 .... 65 D7
 Camberley, York Town GU15 64 F4
Minster Dr CR0 .... 61 E6
Minster Gdns KT8....... 35 F5
Minsterley Ave TW16,
 TW17.................34 E5
Minster Rd GU7.........150 E1
Minstrel Gdns KT5 ..... 37 F5
Mint Gdns RH4 ....136 A8
Mint La KT20 ....118 A6
Mint Rd
 Wallington SM6 .... 60 B6
 Woodmansterne SM7 ... 78 C3
Mint St GU7 ....150 D4
Mint The GU7...........150 D4
Mintwater Cl KT17 ..... 58 A1

Mint Wlk
 Croydon CR0, CR9 ..... 61 C7
 Knaphill GU21 .... 68 E2
 Warlingham CR6 ...... 81 D2
Miranda Wlk RH11 ....200 E4
Mirfield Ct SE20 .... 43 A7
Misbrooks Green Rd
 RH5..................178 E8
Missenden Cl TW14 .... 14 F7
Missenden Gdns SM4 .. 40 C3
Mission Sq [13] TW8..... 6 E8
Mistletoe Cl CR0 ...... 43 D1
Mistley Ct [6] KT18 .... 76 D6
Mistley Gdns RH6 .....160 D2
Misty's Field KT12 ..... 35 C1
MITCHAM 40 F5
Mitcham Ct SW16 ...... 47 B1
Mitcham Eastfields Sta
 CR4..................41 A7
Mitcham Garden Village
 CR4..................41 A4
Mitcham Halt CR4 ...... 40 E5
Mitcham Ind Est
 Mitcham CR4 .... 21 B1
 Mitcham CR4 .... 41 A8
Mitcham Junc Sta/Halt
 CR4..................41 A4
Mitcham La SW16 ...... 21 C3
Mitcham Pk CR4 .... 40 F5
Mitcham Rd
 Camberley GU15 .... 47 A1
 Thornton Heath CR0, CR9.. 41 A1
 Upper Tooting SW17 ... 20 F3
Mitchell Ct
 Horley RH6 ....161 A2
 Mortlake SW14 .... 7 E3
Mitchell Gdns RH13 ...215 B5
Mitchells Cl GU4.......130 E3
Mitchells Cotts GU4...131 E1
Mitchell's Pl SE21...... 22 E8
Mitchells Rd RH10 .....201 F6
Mitchell's Row GU4....130 E3
Mitchley Ave CR2, CR8.. 80 E6
Mitchley Hill CR2 ...... 80 F6
Mitchley Gr CR2........ 81 A6
Mitchley View CR2...... 81 A6
Mitford Cl KT9 .... 56 C4
Mitford Wlk [10] RH11 ..201 A3
Mitre Cl
 Shepperton TW17 ...... 34 D3
 Sutton SM2............ 59 D3
Mitre Ct
 [10] Horsham RH12 ....217 B2
 Weybridge KT13 .... 53 A5
Mixbury Gr KT13....... 53 D4
Mixnams La KT16 ...... 33 A6
Mizen Cl KT11 .... 73 D5
Mizen Way KT11 .... 73 D4
Moat Ct
 Ashtead KT21 .... 75 E2
 Ottershaw KT16........ 51 C4
Moated Farm Dr KT15... 52 C3
Moat Lo GU6 ....174 D3
Moat Rd RH19 ....185 E2
Moat Side TW13........ 15 C4
Moat The KT3 .... 38 E8
Moat Wlk RH10 ....202 C7
Moats La RH1 ....140 F3
Moberly Rd SW4........ 21 D8
Moberly Way CR8......100 D7
Mocatta Mews RH1....119 C4
Mockford Mews RH1...119 C4
Model Cotts
 Mortlake SW14 .... 7 C4
 Pirbright GU24..........87 D6
Moffat Ct
 Upper Tooting SW17 ... 20 E4
 Wimbledon SW19 ...... 20 A3
Moffat Rd
 South Norwood CR7 .... 42 D7
 Upper Tooting SW17 ... 20 F4
Moffatts Cl GU47....... 64 A8
MOGADOR 117 D6
Mogador Cotts KT20 ..117 D7
Mogador Rd KT20 .....117 E7
Mogden La TW7 .... 5 F2
Moira Ct SW17 .... 21 A6
Moir Cl CR2 .... 62 A2
Mole Abbey Gdns KT8.. 36 B6
Mole Bsns Pk KT22 .... 95 A6
Mole Cl
 Crawley RH11 ....201 B8
 Farnborough GU14 .....84 D6
Mole Ct KT19 .... 57 C6
Mole Ho KT12........... 54 E5
Molember Ct KT7....... 36 E5
Molember Rd KT8....... 36 E4
Mole Rd
 Fetcham KT22 .... 94 D6
 Hersham KT12.......... 54 D5
Moles Cl RG40 .... 25 D5
Molesey Ave KT12, KT8.. 35 F4
Molesey Bsns Ctr KT8... 35 F4
Molesey Cl KT12 .... 54 E6
Molesey Dr SM3 .... 58 E7
Molesey Hospl KT8..... 36 A4
Molesey Park Ave KT8.. 36 B4
Molesey Park Cl KT8 ... 36 B4
Molesey Park Rd KT8 .. 36 C4
Molesey Rd
 East Molesey KT12 .... 35 E2
 Hersham KT12.......... 54 D5
Molesham Cl KT8....... 36 B6
Molesham Way KT8 .... 36 B6
Moles Hill KT22 .... 74 D8
Molesey Rd (cont)
 Hersham KT12.......... 54 E8
 Walton-on-Thames KT12.. 54 E8

Mole St RH5 ....177 B5
Molesworth Rd KT11 ... 73 A6
Mole Valley Pl KT21.... 95 D8
Moliner Ct [4] BR3...... 24 A1
Molins Ct [4] RH11 ....201 A3
Mollie Davis Ct SE19 ... 22 F2
Mollison Dr SM6........ 60 E3
Mollison Sq SM6........ 60 E3
Molloy Ct GU21 .... 70 A3
Molly Huggins Cl SW12.. 21 C8
Molly Millar Bridge RG41.. 25 B4
Molly Millars Cl RG41 .. 25 B4
Molly Millar's La RG41 .. 25 A4
Molvic Ct [2] BR3....... 43 F7
Molyneux Dr SW17 .... 21 B4
Molyneux Rd
 Farncombe GU7........150 F7
 Weybridge KT13 .... 53 A5
 Windlesham GU20 ..... 48 D4
Monahan Ave CR8 ..... 79 F8
Monarch Cl
 Coney Hall BR4 .... 63 F6
 Crawley RH11 ....201 A3
 East Bedfont TW14 .... 14 E8
Monarch Mews SW16 .. 22 A3
Monarch Par CR4....... 40 F7
Monarch Pl SM1........ 59 D5
Monaveen Gdns KT8 ... 36 B6
Mondial Way UB7....... 3 C7
Monet Ho [4] W4........ 7 C7
Money Ave CR3 ....100 E5
Money Rd CR3 ....100 D5
Mongers La [1] KT17... 57 F1
Monica Ct SW16 .... 21 D2
Monivea Rd BR3........ 23 F1
Monkey Puzzle Rdbt
 GU14.................84 E3
Monkleigh Rd SM4, SW20.. 39 E5
Monks Ave KT8 .... 35 F4
Monks Cl
 Ascot SL5...............29 B3
 Farnborough GU14 .....85 C4
Monks Cres
 Addlestone KT15 ...... 52 B5
 Walton-on-Thames KT12.. 35 B1
Monks Ct RH2 ....118 B1
Monksdene Gdns SM1.. 59 B7
Monks Dr SL5 .... 29 B3
Monksfield RH10.......201 F7
Monks Gn KT22 .... 94 D6
Monkshanger GU9 .....125 E2
Monks Hill Sp Ctr CR2.. 62 D3
Monkshood Cl RG40.... 25 E7
Monks La
 Oxted TN8 ....144 E6
 Rowhook RH5 ....196 F5
Monks Manor RH5 .....196 F5
MONKS ORCHARD ... 43 E2
Monks Orchard Prim Sch
 CR0..................43 D4
Monks Orchard Rd BR3,
 CR0..................44 A2
Monks Pl CR3...........101 B5
Monks Rd
 Banstead SM7 .... 78 A3
 Virginia Water GU25 ... 31 D5
Monks Way
 Beckenham BR3......... 44 A3
 Harmondsworth UB7.... 2 E8
 Staines TW18........... 13 D1
Monks' Well GU10 ....147 C8
Monkswell La CR5...... 98 D3
Monks Wlk SL5 .... 29 B3
Monk's Wlk
 Farnham GU10, GU9.. 146 F8
 Reigate RH2...........118 B1
Monk Terr SE23......... 23 F6
Monkton La GU9........125 E5
Monkton Pk GU9........125 F4
Monmouth Ave KT1..... 17 C1
Monmouth Cl CR4, SW16.. 41 E5
Mono La TW13.......... 15 B6
Monro Dr GU2 ....109 B4
Monro Pl KT19 .... 57 A2
Mons Cl GU11 ....105 E7
Monsell Gdns TW18.... 12 E3
Monson Rd RH1 ....118 F4
Mons Wlk TW20 .... 12 C3
Montacute Cl GU14 .... 85 D4
Montacute Rd
 Forest Hill SE23, SE6... 23 F8
 Morden SM4 .... 40 D3
 New Addington CR0.... 63 C2
Montague Ave CR2..... 80 E7
Montague Cl
 Camberley GU15 .... 65 B5
 Lightwater GU18 .... 48 A1
 Walton-on-Thames KT12.. 35 A2
 Wokingham RG40 ...... 25 E7
Montague Dr CR3 ....100 C5
Montague Rd
 Hounslow TW3.......... 5 B4
 Merton SW19........... 20 B1
 Richmond TW10........ 6 E1
 Thornton Heath CR0 ... 42 B1
Montague Terr [7] BR2.. 44 F5
Montagu Gdns SM6 .... 60 C6
Montana Cl CR2 .... 61 D1
Montana Gdns
 [2] Beckenham SE6 ... 23 F3
 [7] Sutton SM1........ 59 C5
Montana Rd
 Upper Tooting SW17 ... 21 A5
 Wimbledon SW20 ...... 39 C8
Montem Rd
 Forest Hill SE23....... 23 F8
 New Malden KT3....... 38 E5

Mil–Moo 275

Montford Rd TW16..... 35 A5
Montford Pl SW19 ..... 19 D7
Montfort Rise RH1 .....139 F1
Montgomerie Ct [2] BR3.. 44 A8
Montgomerie Dr GU2 ..109 A4
Montgomery Ave KT10.. 55 E8
Montgomery Cl
 Mitcham CR4 .... 41 E5
 Sandhurst GU47 .... 64 B8
Montgomery Ct
 Chiswick W4 .... 7 C8
 Leatherhead KT22..... 95 C7
Montgomery Gdns SM2.. 59 D3
Montgomery Ho [5] SW14.. 7 A4
Montgomery Of Alamein Ct
 RG12.................27 D8
Montgomery Rd
 Farnborough GU14 .....84 F3
 [2] Woking GU22 ...... 69 E1
Montpelier Ct [10] BR2.. 44 F5
Montpelier Rd
 Purley CR2, CR8.........61 B1
 Sutton SM1............ 59 C6
Montpelier Row TW1.... 17 C8
Montpellier Ct KT12.... 35 B3
Montrave Rd SE20 ..... 23 C1
Montreal Ho SE6........ 24 B7
Montrell Rd SW2........ 21 E7
Montreux Ct RH11 .....201 B6
Montrose Ave TW2..... 16 B8
Montrose Cl
 Ashford TW15 ....14 C3
 Frimley GU16........... 65 E2
Montrose Ct SE6........ 24 F6
Montrose Gdns
 Mitcham CR4 .... 40 F7
 Oxshott KT22 .... 74 D7
 Sutton SM1............ 59 B8
Montrose Rd TW14..... 3 D1
Montrose Way SE23 .... 23 D7
Montrose Wlk KT13 .... 53 B7
Montrouge Cres KT17... 77 C3
Montserrat Cl SE19 .... 22 D3
Montway Hts SW19 .... 20 B1
Monument Bridge Ind Est E
 GU21.................70 B4
Monument Bridge Ind Est W
 GU21.................70 A4
Monument Bsns Ctr GU21.70 B4
Monument Gn KT13 .... 53 B6
Monument Hill KT13 ... 53 B6
Monument Rd
 Sheerwater GU21...... 70 B4
 Weybridge KT13 .... 53 B7
Monument Way E GU21.. 70 B4
Monument Way W GU21.. 70 A4
Moon Ct KT22 .... 94 D6
Moon Hall Coll & Burys Court
 RH2..................138 C3
Moon Hall Rd GU6 ....154 C1
Moon Hall Sch RH5 ...155 D6
Moonsgate RH13.......217 E1
Moons Hill GU10......146 C2
Moons La RH13 ....217 E1
Moon's La RH7 ....186 E8
Moor Cl GU47........... 45 E1
Moorcroft RH9..........121 C3
Moorcroft Ct [1] BR1...201 B7
Moorcroft Rd SW16 .... 21 E5
Moordale Ave RG42 ... 26 E8
Moorcic Cl
 Addlestone KT15 ...... 52 B5
 Ash GU10.............126 F8
 Mitcham CR4........... 41 B7
 Mortlake SW14 .... 7 C4
Moore Ct RH12 ....217 A1
Moore Grove Cres TW20.. 11 F1
Moore Ho
 Wandsworth SW17..... 20 D5
 [1] West Norwood SE27.. 22 C4
Mooreland Rd [19] BR1.. 24 F1
Moore Rd
 Pirbright GU24..........87 B6
 South Norwood SE19... 22 C2
Moores Gn RG40....... 25 E8
Moore's Rd RH4, RH5.. 136 B8
Moore Way SM2........ 59 A2
Moorfield
 Haslemere GU27.......207 F5
 South Holmwood RH5...157 D7
Moorfield Ctr The GU1.. 109 D5
Moorfield Point GU1 ...109 E5
Moorfield Rd
 Chessington KT9 ...... 56 E5
 Guildford GU1 ....109 E5
Moorfields Cl TW18.... 32 E8
Moorfields Ct [6] SW16.. 21 C4
Moorhayes Dr TW18.... 33 C6
Moorhead Rd RH12 ....218 B5
Moorholme GU22 ...... 89 E8
Moorhouse Rd RH8 ...123 F5
Moor House Sch RH8 ..122 F3
Moorhurst La RH5 .....157 B4
Moorings Ho [3] TW8... 6 C7
Moorings The
 East Grinstead RH19...185 A3
 Great Bookham KT23... 94 A2
 Hindhead GU26 ....188 E3
 Old Windsor SL4 ...... 11 C8
 West Byfleet KT14..... 71 C7
Moor La
 Bracknell RG12 .... 26 C6
 Chessington KT9 ...... 56 E5
 Harmondsworth UB7.... 2 C8
 Lingfield RH7, TN8....165 D3

Moor La continued
Staines TW18............12 D6
Woking GU22............89 F5
Moorland Cl TW2........16 A8
Moorland Ct KT4........58 A6
Moorland Rd
Crawley RH10..........202 C3
Harmondsworth UB7......2 C8
Moorlands
18 Wallington SM6......60 B4
Walton-on-Thames KT12...54 A7
Moorlands Cl GU26......188 E4
Moorlands Pl GU15......65 B5
Moorlands Rd GU15......65 B4
Moorlands The GU22......89 F6
Moormead Dr KT19........57 E5
Moor Mead Rd TW1........6 A1
Moormede Cres TW18......12 F4
Moor Park Cres RH11......200 D5
Moor Park Gdns KT2......18 E1
Moor Park Ho RG12........26 E3
Moor Park La GU10, GU9..126 A2
Moor Park Way GU9......125 F2
Moor Pk RH6............161 B2
Moor Pk La GU9........125 E4
Moor Pl
East Grinstead RH19......185 D2
Windlesham GU20........48 B5
Moor Rd
Farnborough GU14........85 A8
Frimley GU16............85 F8
Haslemere GU27........207 C5
Moorside Cl GU14........65 A1
Moorside Rd BR1........24 F4
Moors La GU8............148 C3
Moorsom Way CR5........79 D2
Moors The
Redhill RH1............119 B4
Tongham GU10..........126 F7
Moray Ave GU47........64 D7
Moray Ho 11 KT6........37 E4
Mordaunt Dr RG45........45 B3
MORDEN............40 B3
Morden BR2............44 D7
Morden Cl
Bracknell RG12..........27 F5
Burgh Heath KT20........97 D7
Morden Court Par SM4...40 A5
Morden Ct SM4..........40 B5
Morden Gdns CR4........40 D5
Morden Hall Park★ SW19 40 C6
Morden Hall Rd SM4,
SW19..............40 C5
Morden Ho SM4..........40 A5
MORDEN PARK............39 E3
Morden Park Nature
Reserve★ SM4..........39 E4
Morden Park Pools SM4.. 39 F4
Morden Prim Sch SM4....40 A4
Morden Rd
Merton SW19............40 B7
Mitcham CR4, SM4, SW19..40 D5
Morden Rd Halt SW19.....40 B7
Morden South Sta SM4....40 A4
Morden U Sta SW19.......40 B6
Morden Way SM3........40 A2
Mordred Rd SE6..........24 E6
Morecambe Cl RH11......200 F4
More Circ GU7..........150 E7
More Cl CR8............80 A8
Morecoombe Cl KT2......18 B1
Morecote Cl GU4........130 E2
Morecroft TW2..........16 B6
More House Sch GU10....146 C2
More La KT10............55 B7
Moreland Ave SL3........1 C7
Moreland Cl SL3..........1 C7
Morella Cl GU25..........31 E5
Morella Rd SW11, SW12...20 F8
Moremead Rd SE6........24 A4
Morena St SE6..........24 B8
More Rd GU7............150 E7
Moresby Ave KT5........38 E2
Moretaine Rd TW15......13 D5
Moreton Cl GU10........167 E1
Moreton Ho SW17........20 D4
Moreton Rd
North Cheam KT4........58 B8
South Croydon CR2......61 D5
Morey Ct 10 CR2........61 C5
Morgan Ct
Ashford TW15..........14 B3
Carshalton SM5..........59 F6
Farnborough GU14........84 C4
Moring Rd SW17........21 A4
Morkyns Wlk SE21........22 E5
Morland Ave CR0........42 E1
Morland Cl
Hampton TW12..........15 F3
Mitcham CR4............40 E6
Morland Rd
Aldershot GU11........126 C6
Croydon CR0............42 F2
Penge SE20............23 D2
Sutton SM1............59 C5
Morland's Rd GU11......105 D5
Morley Ct
Bromley BR3............44 D8
Fetcham KT22..........94 D6
Hayes BR2............44 F5
Sunningdale SL5..........29 F3
Morley Ho SW2..........21 E8
Morley Rd
Cheam SM3............39 F1

Morley Rd continued
Farnham GU9..........125 D1
South Croydon CR2......61 F1
Twickenham TW1..........6 D1
Morningside Rd KT4......58 C8
Mornington Cl TN16......83 D2
Mornington Cres TW5......4 B6
Mornington Rd TW15......14 C3
Mornington Wlk TW10......17 C4
Morrell Ave RH12........217 F6
Morris Cl BR3, CR0........43 E4
Morris Ct CR0............61 B6
Morris Gdns SW18........20 A8
Morrish Rd SW2..........21 F8
Morrison Ct 5 RH11......201 B1
Morrison Ho
Feltham TW13..........15 A5
Streatham SW2..........22 A7
Morris Rd
Farnborough GU14......105 D8
Isleworth TW7............5 F4
South Nutfield RH1......140 E7
Morriss Ct 5 RH2........118 F1
Morris Stephany Ho 4
SE27................22 B4
Morston Cl KT20..........97 B7
Morth Gdns 3 RH12......217 C1
Mortimer Cl SW16........21 D6
Mortimer Cres KT4........57 D7
Mortimer Dr TN16........83 C7
Mortimer Lodge 11 SW19. 19 E7
Mortimer Rd
Capel RH5............178 D6
Mitcham CR4............40 F8
MORTLAKE............7 C4
Mortlake Cl CR0..........60 E7
Mortlake Dr CR4..........40 E8
Mortlake High St SW14....7 D4
Mortlake Rd TW9, TW9....7 A6
Mortlake Sta SW14........7 C4
Mortlake Terr TW9........7 A7
Mortlake Rd TW20........97 D6
Morton Cl
Frimley GU16............85 F7
Wallington SM6..........60 F3
Woking GU21............69 D4
Morton Gdns SM6........60 C5
Morton Ho SE27..........22 D3
Morton Rd
East Grinstead RH19......205 D7
Morden CR4, SM4........40 D4
Woking GU21............69 D4
Morval Cl GU14..........84 E4
Morven Rd SW17..........20 F5
Moseley Heath Nature
Reserve★ KT8..........36 A3
Moselle Cl GU14..........84 D5
Moselle Rd TN16..........83 F1
Mosford Cl RH6..........160 F5
Mospey Cres KT17........76 F4
Mosquito Cl SM6..........60 E3
Mosquito Way GU14......84 F2
Mossfield KT11..........73 A6
Moss Gdns
Feltham TW13..........15 A6
South Croydon CR2......62 D3
Moss La GU7............150 D4
Moss Lane Sch GU7......150 D4
Mosslea Rd
Kenley CR3............80 F2
Penge SE20............23 C2
Mossville Gdns SM4, SW20. 39 F5
Mostyn Rd SW19..........39 F7
Mostyn Terr RH1........140 A8
Moth Cl SM6............60 E3
MOTSPUR PARK..........39 A3
Motspur Park Sta KT3....39 B4
Motspur Pk KT3..........39 A3
Mott Ho KT19............57 B1
Motts Hill La KT20........97 A4
Mouchotte Cl TN16........83 C7
Moulton Ave TW3, TW5....4 F5
Mountacre Cl SE26........23 A4
Mount Adon Pk SE21,
SE22................23 A8
Mountain Ash Ct 1
RH12................217 F4
Mount Alvernia Hospl
(Private) GU1..........130 E7
Mount Angelus Rd SW15..18 F8
Mount Ararat Rd TW10....6 E2
Mount Arlington 3 BR2.. 44 E7
Mount Ash Rd SE26........23 B5
Mount Ave CR3..........100 C3
Mount Cl
Crawley RH10..........202 D7
Ewhurst GU6............175 E5
Fetcham KT22..........94 F4
Kenley CR8............80 D3
Wallington SM5..........60 A2
Woking GU22............89 C6
Mount Cl The GU25........31 D3
Mountcombe Cl KT6........37 E2
Mountcombe Ho SW19.....20 D3
Mount Ct
Guildford GU1..........130 C7
6 Kingston upon Thames
KT2................18 B1
West Norwood SE27......22 B5

Mount Ct continued
West Wickham BR4......63 E8
Mount Dr The RH2........118 D3
Mountearl Gdns SW16,
SW2................21 F5
Mount Ephraim La SW16..21 D5
Mount Ephraim Rd SW16.. 21 D5
Mount Felix KT12........34 F2
Mountfield Cl SE6........24 D8
Mount Gdns SE26........23 B5
MOUNT HERMON..........89 D8
Mount Hermon Cl GU22.. 69 E1
Mount Hermon Rd GU22.. 69 E1
Mount Holme KT7..........37 B2
Mounthurst Rd BR2........44 F2
Mount La
Bracknell RG12..........27 C7
Turners Hill RH10......204 A4
Mount Lee TW20..........11 F3
Mount Mews TW12........36 B8
Mount Noddy RH10......203 C2
Mount Nod Rd SW16, SW2 21 F5
Mount Park Ave CR2......61 B2
Mount Pk SM5............60 A2
Mount Pl GU1............130 C7
Mount Pleasant
Biggin Hill TN16........83 D2
Bracknell RG12..........27 C6
Effingham KT24........113 E7
Ewell KT17..............57 F1
Farnham GU9..........125 A1
Guildford GU2..........130 C7
Sandhurst GU47........45 A1
West Horsley KT24......112 B6
West Norwood SE27......22 C4
Weybridge KT13..........53 A7
Wokingham RG41........25 A6
Mount Pleasant Cl GU18.. 48 A1
Mount Pleasant Cotts
TW20................11 D2
Mount Pleasant Rd
Aldershot GU12........105 C2
Caterham CR3..........101 A4
Kingston upon Thames KT3. 38 C6
Lingfield RH7..........164 C4
Mount Prim Sch The KT3. 38 C6
Mount Rd
Chessington KT9........56 F5
Chobham GU24..........69 B7
Cranleigh GU6..........174 E2
Feltham TW13..........15 E5
Kingston upon Thames KT3. 38 D6
Mitcham CR4............40 E7
South Norwood SE19......22 D2
Wimbledon SW18, SW19.. 20 B6
Woking GU22............89 B6
Mount Rise
Forest Hill SE23........23 C6
Reigate RH1............139 D7
Mountsfield Cl TW19......2 A2
Mounts Hill SL4..........9 C3
Mountside
Caterham CR3..........100 F3
Guildford GU2..........130 B7
Mountside Pl 1 GU22.....69 F1
Mount St RH4............136 A7
Mount The
Belmont SM1............59 A4
Cranleigh GU6..........174 E4
6 Croydon CR2..........61 C5
Esher KT10..............55 A4
Ewell KT17..............57 F1
Ewhurst GU6............175 E5
Fetcham KT22..........94 E4
Grayswood GU27........189 F1
Guildford GU2..........130 C7
Headley Down GU35......187 A6
Lower Kingswood KT20....97 F1
New Malden KT3........38 F6
North Cheam KT4........58 B6
Oatlands Park KT13......53 E8
Rusper RH1, RH12......180 B1
Rusper RH12............200 B8
Virginia Water GU25......31 D3
Wallington SM6..........79 B5
Warlingham CR6........101 A8
Witley GU8............170 F3
Woking GU21, GU22......69 D1
Mountview 5 SW16........21 F5
Mount View GU11........105 A1
Mountview Dr RH1........139 E7
Mount View Rd KT10......56 B3
Mount Villas SE27........22 B5
Mount Way SM5..........60 A2
Mountwood KT8..........36 B6
Mountwood Cl CR2........62 B1
MOUSEHILL............170 E8
Moushill La GU8........170 E8
Mowat Ct KT4............57 F8
Mowatt Rd GU26........188 D2
Mowbray Ave KT14........71 E6
Mowbray Cres TW20......12 A3
Mowbray Ct SE19........42 F8
Mowbray Dr RH11........200 F4
Mowbray Gdns RH4......115 B1
Mowbray Rd
Richmond TW10..........17 C5
South Norwood SE19......42 F8
Mower Cl RG40..........25 F7
Mower Pl GU6..........174 E4
Moyne Ct 3 GU21........68 F1
Moyne Rd RH11........201 C2
Moys Cl CR0............41 E3
Moyser Rd SW16, SW17.. 21 B3
Moys Ho RH1............118 F3
Muchelney Rd SM4........40 C3
Muckhatch La TW20......32 B7
Mudie Ho 8 SW2..........21 E8

Muggeridge Cl CR2........61 D5
Muggeridge's Hill RH12,
RH5................198 B8
MUGSWELL............98 B2
Muirdown Ave SW14........7 D3
Muirfield Cl RH11........200 D5
Muirfield Ho
Bracknell RG12..........26 E3
Sunningdale SL5..........30 A1
Muirfield Rd GU21........69 A1
Muirkirk Rd SE6..........24 C7
Mulberries The GU9......125 F4
Mulberry Ave SW19......13 E7
Mulberry Bsns Pk RG41.. 25 A4
Mulberry Cl
Ash GU12............106 A4
Crowthorne RG45........45 C4
Horsham RH12..........217 C5
1 Sandhurst GU47......64 D8
Streatham SW16........21 C4
Weybridge KT13..........53 B7
Woking GU21............69 E5
Mulberry Cres TW8........6 C7
Mulberry Ct
Ashtead KT21..........75 D1
1 Bracknell RG12......27 F4
Guildford GU4..........110 D3
4 Surbiton KT6..........37 D2
Twickenham TW1..........16 F5
Wokingham RG40........25 C6
Mulberry Gate SM7........77 F3
Mulberry La CR0..........42 F1
Mulberry Mews 2 SM6....60 C4
Mulberry Rd RH11........181 B1
Mulberry The CR3..........80 F2
Mulberry Trees TW17......34 D2
Mulberry Way 3 GU14....84 D5
Mulgrave Ct 2 SM2........59 B4
Mulgrave Hall 8 SM2......59 B4
Mulgrave Manor SM2......59 B4
Mulgrave Rd
Croydon CR0, CR9......61 D7
Frimley GU16............65 D7
Sutton SM2............59 B4
Mulgrave Way GU21......68 E1
Mulholland Cl CR4........41 B7
Mullards Cl CR4..........41 F1
Mullberry Pl RH5........158 C2
Mullein Wlk RH11........201 A2
Mullens Rd TW20..........12 C3
Mullins Path SW14........7 D4
Mulroy Dr GU15..........66 A6
Multon Rd SW18..........20 D8
Muncaster Cl TW15........14 A4
Muncaster Rd TW15........14 B3
Muncies Mews SE6........24 C6
Munday's Boro GU3......128 A4
Munday's Boro Rd GU3...128 B4
Munnings Dr GU47........64 E6
Munnings Gdns TW7........5 D2
Munroe Ho RH2..........139 A6
Munro Way GU14........105 D8
Munslow Gdns SM1......59 D6
Munstead Ct 16 SM2......59 C3
Munstead Heath Rd GU8.. 151 C3
Munstead Pk GU8........151 C2
Munstead View GU3......130 C4
Munstead View Rd GU5.. 151 D5
Munster Ave TW4..........4 E2
Munster Ct TW11..........17 C2
Munster Rd TW11..........17 C2
Murdoch Cl TW18........13 A3
Murdoch Rd RG40........25 D5
Murdock Cl RG40........25 D5
Murfett Cl SW19..........19 E6
Murray Ave TW3..........5 B2
Murray Ct
Ascot SL5..............29 C3
Crawley RH11..........201 A1
Horsham RH13..........218 B4
Twickenham TW2........16 D6
Murray Gn GU21..........70 C3
Murray Ho
Ottershaw KT16..........51 D4
Wokingham RG41........25 A6
Murray Rd
Farnborough GU14........84 F3
Ottershaw KT15, KT16..51 D5
Richmond TW10..........17 C6
Wimbledon SW19..........19 D2
Wokingham RG41........25 A6
Murray's La KT14..........71 E5
Murrays Rd GU11........105 D6
Murrellhill La RG42........26 C8
Murrell Rd GU12........106 A3
Murrells La GU15........65 B3
Murrells Wlk KT23........94 A3
Murreys The KT21........75 D1
Murthead La KT4..........57 F8
Muschamp Prim Sch SM5. 59 E8
Muschamp Rd SM1, SM5.. 59 E8
Museum Hill GU27........208 D6
Museum of Croydon★
CR0................61 C7
Museum of Richmond★
TW10................6 D2
Musgrave Ave RH19......205 D8
Musgrave Rd TW7..........5 F6
Mushroom Castle La RG42..8 D2
Musical Museum The★
TW8................6 E8
Musquash Way TW4........4 C5
Mustard Mill Rd TW18....12 F4
Mutton Hill RH7..........186 B7
Mutton Oaks RG12........26 D8
Muybridge Rd KT3........38 C7
Mychell Ho 8 SW19......20 C1
Mychett Prim Sch GU16.. 85 F4

Myers Way GU16..........66 D2
Myherin Ct SE23..........23 F6
Mylis Cl SE26............23 B4
Mylne Sq RG40..........25 D6
Mylor Cl GU21............69 E5
Mynn's Cl KT18..........76 B5
Mynterne Ct 16 SW19.....19 D7
Mynthurst Farm Cotts
RH2................159 B7
Myrna Cl SW19..........20 E1
Myrtle Ave TW14..........3 E2
Myrtle Cl
Lightwater GU18..........67 B8
Poyle SL3..............1 E6
Myrtle Dr GU17..........64 D5
Myrtle Gr KT3............38 C7
Myrtle Rd
Croydon CR0............63 A7
Dorking RH4..........136 A8
Hampton TW12..........16 C2
Hounslow TW3..........5 C5
Sutton SM1............59 C5
MYTCHETT............85 F3
Mytchett Heath GU16......86 A3
Mytchett Lake Rd GU16...86 A1
Mytchett Place Rd GU12,
GU16................86 C1
Mytchett Rd GU12, GU16.. 85 F3
Myton Rd SE21..........22 D5

N

Naafi Rdbt GU11........105 B2
Nadine Ct SM6..........60 C2
Nailsworth Cres RH1......119 D6
Nairn Cl GU16............65 E2
Nairn Ct
3 Wallington SM6......60 C4
Wimbledon SW19........20 B2
Naish Ho SW19..........40 B6
NALDERSWOOD..........159 C7
Naldrett Cl RH12........217 F4
Naldretts La RH12........214 D5
Nallhead Rd TW13........15 C3
Namba Roy Cl SW16......21 F4
Namton Dr CR7, SW16....41 F5
Nanhurst Park Ho GU6.. 173 D2
Naomi Watts Ho 11 SW19. 19 E1
Napier Cl
Crowthorne RG45........45 D5
Farnborough GU11......105 E7
Napier Ct
Caterham CR3..........100 E5
18 Croydon CR0........61 C5
1 Surbiton KT6..........37 D2
12 Wallington SM6......60 B4
Woking GU21............69 E3
Napier Dr GU15..........66 A8
Napier Gdns GU1........110 B2
Napier La GU12..........106 A4
Napier Lodge TW15........14 D2
Napier Rd
Ashford TW15..........14 D1
Crowthorne RG45........45 C4
Croydon SE25............43 B5
Isleworth TW7............6 A3
South Croydon CR2......61 D3
Napier Way RH10........182 A1
Napier Wlk TW15........14 D1
Napoleon Ave GU14......85 B6
Napoleon Rd TW1........17 B8
Napper Cl SL5............28 D7
Napper Pl GU6..........174 E1
Narrow La CR6..........101 B8
Naseby RG12............27 B1
Naseby Cl TW7............5 E6
Naseby Ct KT12..........54 C8
Naseby Rd SE19..........22 D2
Nash Cl
Carshalton SM1..........59 D7
Farnborough GU14........84 F4
Nash Coll of Further Ed
BR2................63 F8
Nash Dr 6 RH1..........119 A3
Nash Gdns
North Ascot SL5..........28 E7
Redhill RH1............118 F3
Nash Rd RH10..........201 E3
Nassau Rd SW13..........7 F6
Nasturtium Dr GU24......68 A4
Natalie Cl TW14..........14 D8
Natalie Mews TW2........16 D5
Natal Rd
South Norwood CR7......42 D6
Streatham SW16........21 D2
National Archives The★ TW9 .7 B7
National Physical Laboratory
TW11................16 E2
National Wks TW4..........4 F4
Nayland Ho SE6..........24 C4
Neald Ct 6 SW19........20 A2
Neale Cl RH19..........185 B3
Neath Gdns SM4..........40 C3
Neb La RH8............122 D4
Needles Bank RH9........121 B4
Needles Cl RH12........217 B1
Neelem Ct 4 GU14........85 C1
Neil Cl TW15............14 C3
Neil Wates Cres 18 SW2.. 22 A7
Nelgarde Rd SE6..........24 A8
Nell Ball RH14..........211 E2
Nell Gwynn Ave TW17....34 D3
Nell Gwynne Ave SL5......29 D5
Nell Gwynne Cl
Ascot SL5..............29 D5
Epsom KT19............76 A8
Nello James Gdns SE27.. 22 D4

Nelson Cl
Aldershot GU12 . . . . 105 D1
Biggin Hill TN16 . . . . 83 E2
Bracknell RG12 . . . . 27 E7
Crawley RH10 . . . . 202 C5
East Bedfont TW14 . . . . . . 14 E7
Heath End GU9 . . . . 125 D8
Thornton Heath CR0 . . . . . 42 B1
Walton-on-Thames KT12 . . 35 B1
Nelson Ct
Carshalton SM5 . . . . 59 F7
Chertsey KT16 . . . . 33 A1
Nelson Gdns
Guildford GU1 . . . . 110 A2
Twickenham TW3, TW4 . . . . 5 A1
Nelson Grove Rd SW19 . . 40 C8
Nelson Ho
19 Aldershot GU11 . . . . . 105 A2
Epsom KT19 . . . . 57 B1
Nelson Hospl SW20 . . . . . 39 F7
Nelson Prim Sch TW2 . . . 16 B8
Nelson Rd
Ashford TW15 . . . . 13 E3
Caterham CR3 . . . . 100 D4
Harmondsworth TW6 . . . . . . 2 F6
Heath End GU9 . . . . 125 D8
Horsham RH12 . . . . 217 C3
Merton SW19 . . . . 20 C1
New Malden KT3 . . . . 38 D4
Twickenham TW2 . . . . 16 B8
Nelson St **3** GU11 . . . . . 105 A2
Nelson Trad Est SW19 . . . 40 B8
Nelson Way GU15 . . . . 64 F4
Nelson Wlk KT19 . . . . 57 A2
Nene Gdns TW13 . . . . 15 F6
Nene Rd TW6, UB7 . . . . 3 B6
Nepean Cl **4** SW15 . . . . . 19 A8
Neptune Cl RH11 . . . . 200 E4
Neptune Ct RH12 . . . . 217 B4
Neptune Rd TW6 . . . . 3 C6
Nero Ct TW8 . . . . 6 D7
Nesbit Cl RH11 . . . . 200 E3
Nesbitt Sq SE19 . . . . 22 E1
Netheravon Rd S **2** W4 . . . 7 F8
Netherby Pk KT13 . . . . 53 E5
Netherby Rd SE23 . . . . 23 C8
Nethercote Ave GU21 . . . . 68 F2
Netherfield BR2 . . . . 44 D6
Netherfield Rd SW17 . . . . 21 A5
Netherlands Ct **14** SM2 . . 59 C4
Netherlands The CR5 . . . . 99 C8
Netherleigh Pk RH1 . . . . 140 E6
Nether Mount GU2 . . . . . . 130 B7
Nethern Court Rd CR3 . . . 102 A4
Netherne Dr CR5 . . . . 99 C5
Netherne La
Netherne-on-t-H CR5 . . . . 99 C6
Netherne-on-t-H CR5, RH1 . 99 C4
**NETHERNE-ON-THE-
HILL** 99 D5
Netherton RG12 . . . . 27 A5
Netherton Rd TW1 . . . . 6 B2
Netherwood RH11 . . . . . . 201 B4
Netherwood Ct GU7 . . . . . 150 E5
Netley Cl
Cheam SM3 . . . . 58 D5
Gomshall GU5 . . . . 133 C6
New Addington CR0 . . . . . . 63 C3
Netley Dr KT12 . . . . 35 F2
Netley Gdns SM4 . . . . 40 C2
Netley Rd
Brentford TW8 . . . . 6 E8
Morden SM4 . . . . 40 C2
Netley St GU14 . . . . 105 C8
Nettlecombe RG12 . . . . . . 27 D3
Nettlecombe Cl SM2 . . . . . 59 B2
Nettlefold Pl SE27 . . . . . . 22 B5
Nettlestead Cl BR3 . . . . . . 23 F1
Nettles Terr **3** GU1 . . . . . 109 D1
Nettleton Rd TW6 . . . . 3 B6
Nettlewood Rd SW16 . . . . 21 D1
Neuchatel Rd SE6 . . . . 23 F6
Neuman Cres RG12 . . . . . . 27 A3
Nevada Cl
Farnborough GU14 . . . . . . 84 D3
Kingston upon Thames KT3 . 38 C5
Nevelle Cl RG42 . . . . 26 D8
Neville Ave KT3 . . . . 38 D8
Neville Cl
Banstead SM7 . . . . 78 B5
Esher KT10 . . . . 54 F4
Hounslow TW3 . . . . 5 B5
Neville Cl **10** SW12 . . . . . 21 C8
Neville Duke Rd GU14 . . . 84 F8
Neville Ho **8** TW1 . . . . . . 17 A8
Neville Rd
Croydon CR0 . . . . 42 D2
Kingston upon Thames KT1 . 38 A7
Richmond TW10 . . . . 17 C6
Neville Wlk SM5 . . . . 40 E2
Nevis Rd SW17 . . . . 21 A6
NEW ADDINGTON 63 D3
New Addington Halt CR0 . 63 C1
Newall Rd TW6 . . . . 3 C6
Newark Cl
Guildford GU4 . . . . 110 B6
Ripley GU23 . . . . 91 A6
Newark Ct KT12 . . . . 35 C1
Newark La
Ripley GU23 . . . . 91 B6
Woking GU22 . . . . 90 F8
Newark Rd
Crawley RH10 . . . . 201 F8
South Croydon CR2 . . . . . . 61 D4
Windlesham GU20 . . . . 48 B6
New Barn Cl SM6 . . . . 60 F4

New Barn La
Kenley CR3 . . . . 80 E3
Wallis Wood RH5 . . . . 177 A3
New Barns Ave CR4 . . . . . 41 E5
New Battlebridge La
RH1 . . . . 119 B5
NEW BECKENHAM 23 F2
New Beckenham Sta BR3 . 23 F1
New Belmont Ho **4** SE23 . 23 C7
New Berry La KT12 . . . . . . 54 D5
Newbolt Ave SM3 . . . . 58 D5
Newborough Ct KT3 . . . . . 38 D5
Newborough Ho SW19 . . . 20 D1
Newbridge Cl RH12 . . . . . 216 C3
Newbridge Ct
Cranleigh GU6 . . . . 174 B3
Upper Tooting SW17 . . . . . 20 C4
Newbridge Point **3** SE23 . 23 D5
Newbury Gdns KT19 . . . . . 57 F6
Newbury Rd
Crawley RH10 . . . . 202 D6
Harmondsworth TW6 . . . . . . 2 F6
NEWCHAPEL 163 F1
Newchapel Rd
Lingfield RH7 . . . . 164 B3
Newchapel RH7 . . . . 163 F2
New Chapel Sq TW13 . . . . 15 B7
New Church Ct **4** SE19 . . . 23 A1
New Cl
Feltham TW13 . . . . 15 E3
Mitcham SW19 . . . . 40 C6
New Colebrooke Ct SM5 . . 60 A3
Newcombe Gdns **7** SW3 . . 4 F3
Newcombe Rd GU9 . . . . . 125 C6
Newcome Gdns SW16 . . . . 21 E4
Newcome Pl GU12 . . . . . . 126 D7
New Coppice GU21 . . . . . . 88 E8
New Cotts
Betchworth RH3 . . . . 116 D4
Pirbright GU24 . . . . 87 D5
Sidlow RH2 . . . . 138 F1
Turners Hill RH10 . . . . 204 A4
New Cross Rd GU2 . . . . . . 109 B3
New Cswy RH2 . . . . 139 C6
New Dawn Cl GU14 . . . . . . 84 D3
NEWDIGATE 158 B1
Newdigate CE Inf Sch
RH5 . . . . 158 B1
Newdigate Ho
6 Kingston upon Thames
KT2 . . . . 18 B2
West Norwood SW16 . . . . . 22 A4
Newdigate Rd
Beare Green RH5 . . . . 157 E2
Leigh RH2 . . . . 137 F2
Rusper RH12 . . . . 199 C8
NEWELL GREEN 8 A1
NEW ENGLAND 67 D7
New England Trad Est
RH8 . . . . 123 A2
Newenham Rd KT23 . . . . . 94 A1
Newent Cl SM5 . . . . 40 F1
**New Epsom & Ewell Cottage
Hospl The** KT19 . . . . 75 E8
New Farm La TW18 . . . . . . 33 C8
New Farthingdale RH7 . . . 186 B8
Newfield Ave GU14 . . . . . . 84 E6
Newfield Cl TW12 . . . . 36 A8
Newfield Rd GU12 . . . . . . 106 A6
New Forest Cotts GU22 . . . 89 F7
New Forest Ride RG12 . . . . 27 F4
Newfoundland Rd
Frimley GU16 . . . . 86 D8
Woking GU24 . . . . 87 C5
Newgate CR0 . . . . 42 C1
Newgate Cl TW13 . . . . 15 E5
New Green Pl SE19 . . . . . . 22 E2
Newhache RH7 . . . . 165 A1
Newhall Gdns KT12 . . . . . . 54 C8
Newhaven Cres TW15 . . . . 14 D3
Newhaven Rd SE25 . . . . . . 42 D4
NEW HAW 52 C3
New Haw Com Jun Sch
KT15 . . . . 52 A1
New Haw Rd KT15 . . . . 52 C4
New Heston Rd TW5 . . . . . . 4 F7
Newholme Ct **2** KT13 . . . . 53 E7
New Horizons Ct TW8 . . . . 6 A8
New Horton Manor SL3 . . . 1 A4
Newhouse **6** KT3 . . . . 38 E2
Newhouse Bsns Ctr
RH12 . . . . 218 C7
Newhouse Cl KT3 . . . . 38 E2
New House Farm La
GU3 . . . . 108 C2
New House La RH1 . . . . . . 161 B8
Newhouse Wlk SM4 . . . . . . 40 C2
New Inn Ct The KT8 . . . . . 36 D4
New Inn La GU4 . . . . 110 B4
New Kelvin Ave TW11 . . . . 16 E2
New La GU22, GU4 . . . . 89 F3
Newland House Sch TW1 . 16 F4
Newland House Sch Annex
TW1 . . . . 16 F4
Newlands Ave
Thames Ditton KT7 . . . . . . 36 E1
Woking GU22 . . . . 89 F6
Newlands Cl
Hersham KT12 . . . . 54 E6
Horley RH6 . . . . 160 F5
**Newlands Corner Visitor
Ctr** ★ GU4 . . . . 132 A7
Newlands Cres
East Grinstead RH19 . . . . 185 D2
Guildford GU1 . . . . 130 F7
Newlands Croft SE20 . . . . . 23 D2

Newlands Ct
Addlestone KT15 . . . . 52 B5
1 Caterham CR3 . . . . . . 100 C6
Penge SE26 . . . . 23 C2
Streatham SW16 . . . . 21 E3
Newlands Dr
Ash GU12 . . . . 106 B4
Poyle SL3 . . . . 1 E4
Newlands Estate GU8 . . . 170 F5
Newlands Flats GU1 . . . . 109 F2
Newlands Pk
Copthorne RH10 . . . . 183 E3
Penge SE26 . . . . 23 D3
Newlands Pl RH18 . . . . . . 206 F3
Newlands Rd
Camberley GU15 . . . . 65 B1
Crawley RH11 . . . . 201 C5
Horsham RH12 . . . . 217 C4
Thornton Heath SW16 . . . . 41 E7
Newlands The
Thames Ditton KT7 . . . . . . 36 E1
Wallington SM6 . . . . 60 D3
Newlands Way KT9 . . . . . . 56 C5
Newlands Woods CR0 . . . . 62 F2
New Lodge Dr RH8 . . . . . . 122 F7
Newlyn KT13 . . . . 53 F6
Newlyn Ho **12** SM1 . . . . . . 59 C6
NEW MALDEN 38 F5
New Malden Sta KT3 . . . . . 38 E6
Newman Cl RH10 . . . . 202 C4
Newman Ho **11** TW10 . . . . 17 C5
Newman Rd CR0 . . . . 41 F1
Newmans Ct **9** SW3 . . . . . . 4 F3
Newmans La **1** KT6 . . . . . 37 D3
Newmans Pl SL5 . . . . 30 B2
Newman Terr **11** CR4 . . . . 40 F6
Newmarket Rd RH10 . . . . 202 A4
New Mdw SL5 . . . . 28 D8
New Mile Rd SL5 . . . . 29 C7
Newminster Rd SM4 . . . . . 40 C3
New Monument Sch
GU22 . . . . 70 C4
New Moorhead Dr RH12 . 218 C6
Newnham Cl CR7 . . . . 42 C7
Newnham Ho SE6 . . . . 24 C5
New North Rd RH2 . . . . . . 138 F6
New Par TW15 . . . . 14 C3
New Park Ct **25** SW2 . . . . . 21 E8
New Park Par **14** SW2 . . . . 21 E8
New Park Rd
Ashford TW15 . . . . 14 C3
Cranleigh GU6 . . . . 174 F2
Streatham, Streatham Hill SW12,
SW2 . . . . 21 E7
New Pl CR0 . . . . 63 A4
New Place Gdns RH7 . . . . 164 E4
New Pond Rd GU3, GU7 . . 129 E1
New Poplars Ct GU12 . . . 106 A1
Newport Jun Sch GU12 . . 105 D1
Newport Rd
Aldershot GU11 . . . . 105 D1
Harmondsworth TW6 . . . . . . 3 A6
Newquay Rd SE6 . . . . 24 C6
New Rd
Albury GU5 . . . . 132 D3
Bagshot GU19 . . . . 47 F3
Blackwater GU17 . . . . 64 E4
Brentford TW8 . . . . 6 D8
Carshalton CR4 . . . . 41 A1
Chilworth GU4 . . . . 131 B3
Crowthorne RG45 . . . . 45 C5
East Bedfont TW14 . . . . 3 D1
East Clandon GU4 . . . . . . 111 E4
East Molesey KT8 . . . . 36 A6
Egham TW18 . . . . 12 C3
Esher KT10 . . . . 55 C6
Feltham, Hanworth TW13 . . 15 E3
Feltham TW14 . . . . 15 B7
Forest Green RH5 . . . . 176 E6
Gomshall GU5 . . . . 133 C4
Harlington TW6, UB7 . . . . . . 3 C7
Haslemere GU27 . . . . 207 F5
Hounslow TW3 . . . . 5 B3
Hydestile GU8 . . . . 171 F5
Kingston upon Thames KT2 . 18 A1
Limpsfield RH8 . . . . 123 B5
Littleton TW17 . . . . 34 B6
Milford GU8 . . . . 170 E8
North Ascot SL5 . . . . 8 F1
Oxshott KT22 . . . . 74 F8
Richmond TW10 . . . . 17 C4
Sandhurst GU47 . . . . 64 A8
Smallfield RH6 . . . . 162 B3
Tadworth KT20 . . . . 97 C4
Tandridge RH8 . . . . 143 A7
Tongham GU10 . . . . 126 F6
Weybridge KT13 . . . . 53 C5
Windlesham GU19, GU20 . . 48 A4
Wonersh GU5 . . . . 152 B8
Wormley GU8 . . . . 191 A8
New Rd Units TW3 . . . . 5 B3
New Residences KT16 . . . . 51 C7
Newry Rd TW1 . . . . 6 A2
New Scotland Hill Prim Sch
GU47 . . . . 45 A2
Newsham Rd **1** GU21 . . . . 68 F2
New Site KT15 . . . . 52 E7
New Sq TW14 . . . . 14 C7
New St
Crawley RH10 . . . . 202 A7
Horsham RH13 . . . . 217 D2
Staines TW18 . . . . 13 A4
Newstead Cl GU7 . . . . 150 D6
Newstead Hall RH6 . . . . . 161 D4
Newstead Ho
Caterham CR3 . . . . 101 B1
Thames Ditton KT8 . . . . . . 36 D3

Newstead Rd SE12 . . . . . . 24 F8
Newstead Rise CR3 . . . . . 101 B1
Newstead Way SW19 . . . . . 19 E4
Newtimber RH12 . . . . 199 F1
Newton Ave RH19 . . . . . . 205 F6
Newton Ct **2** KT19 . . . . . . 57 E2
Newton Rd
Crawley RH10 . . . . 181 F2
Farnborough GU14 . . . . . . 85 D6
Isleworth TW7 . . . . 5 F5
Merton SW19 . . . . 19 E1
Purley CR8 . . . . 79 C7
Newton Way GU10 . . . . . . 124 B5
Newton Wood Rd KT21 . . . 75 F3
New Town RH10 . . . . 183 B3
Newtown Ct RH13 . . . . . . 217 E1
Newtown Rd GU47 . . . . . . 64 B8
New Victoria Hospl KT3 . . 38 E8
New Way GU7 . . . . 150 C4
New Wickham La TW20 . . . 12 B1
New Wokingham Rd
RG45 . . . . 45 A6
New Woodlands Sch BR1 . 24 E4
New Zealand Ave KT12 . . . 34 F1
Nexus Pk GU12 . . . . 105 F8
Nicholas Ct **7** W4 . . . . 7 E7
Nicholas Gdns GU22 . . . . . 70 F3
Nicholas Ho SE26 . . . . 23 B2
Nicholas Lodge KT10 . . . . 55 A8
Nicholas Rd CR0 . . . . 60 E6
Nicholass Ct **2** CR8 . . . . . 80 B7
Nicholes Rd TW3 . . . . 5 A3
Nicholls Cl CR3 . . . . 100 C5
Nichols Cl KT9 . . . . 56 C4
Nicholsfield RH14 . . . . . . 212 F4
Nicholson Mews **4** KT1 . . . 37 E5
Nicholson Rd CR0 . . . . 42 F1
Nicholson Wlk **3** TW20 . . . 12 A3
Nicola Cl CR2 . . . . 61 C4
Nicola Ct GU12 . . . . 105 D2
Nicol Cl **6** TW1 . . . . 6 B1
Nicosia Rd SW18 . . . . 20 E8
Niederwald Rd SE26 . . . . . 23 E4
Nigel Fisher Way KT9 . . . . 56 D3
Nightingale Ave KT24 . . . . 92 D2
Nightingale Cl
Biggin Hill TN16 . . . . 83 C3
Carshalton SM5 . . . . 60 A8
Chiswick W4 . . . . 7 C8
Cobham KT11 . . . . 73 D8
Crawley RH11 . . . . 201 C8
East Grinstead RH19 . . . . 205 D7
Epsom KT19 . . . . 76 A8
Farnborough GU14 . . . . . . 84 C6
Nightingale Cres
Bracknell RG12 . . . . 27 D4
West Horsley KT24 . . . . 92 C2
Nightingale Ct
2 Knaphill GU21 . . . . 68 F1
Penge SE19 . . . . 22 F2
8 Redhill RH1 . . . . 119 A2
Sutton SM1 . . . . 59 C5
Nightingale Dr
Mytchett GU16 . . . . 86 A3
West Ewell KT19 . . . . 57 C3
Nightingale Gdns GU47 . . 64 B8
Nightingale Ind Est
RH12 . . . . 217 D3
Nightingale La
Balham SW11, SW12 . . . . . 20 F8
Richmond TW10 . . . . 17 E8
Turners Hill RH10 . . . . 204 C5
Nightingale Pl GU27 . . . . 208 D7
Nightingale Rd
Ash GU12 . . . . 106 C3
Carshalton SM5 . . . . 60 A8
East Horsley KT24 . . . . 92 F2
East Molesey KT8 . . . . 36 B4
Esher KT10 . . . . 54 F4
Farncombe GU7 . . . . 150 E6
Guildford GU1 . . . . 109 E1
Hampton TW12 . . . . 16 A2
Horsham RH12 . . . . 217 D3
Selsdon CR2 . . . . 62 D1
Walton-on-Thames KT12 . . 35 B2
Nightingales GU6 . . . . 174 E1
Nightingales Cl RH13 . . . . 217 F2
Nightingale Sch SW17 . . . 20 E6
Nightingale Shott TW20 . . 11 F2
Nightingale Sq SW12 . . . . 21 A8
Nightingales The TW19 . . . 13 F7
Nightingale Way RH1 . . . . 120 C2
Nightjar GU10 . . . . 124 D8
Nimbus Rd KT19 . . . . 57 D1
Nimrod Ct RH10 . . . . 182 D1
Nimrod Rd SW16, SW17 . . 21 B3
Nineacres Way CR5 . . . . . . 79 E3
Nine Elms Cl TW14 . . . . . . 14 F7
Ninehams Cl CR3 . . . . 100 D7
Ninehams Gdns CR3 . . . . 100 D7
Ninehams Rd
Caterham CR3 . . . . 100 D6
Tatsfield TN16 . . . . 103 D6
Nine Mile Ride RG12, RG40 26 F1
Nineteenth Rd CR4 . . . . . . 41 E5
Ninfield Ct RH11 . . . . 200 E4
Niton Rd TW9 . . . . 7 A4
Niven Cl RH10 . . . . 202 D5
Noahs Ct RH10 . . . . 204 A4
Nobel Dr UB3 . . . . 3 E7
Noble Cnr TW5 . . . . 5 A6
Noble Ct CR4 . . . . 40 D7
Noble St KT12 . . . . 54 C7
Nobles Way TW20 . . . . 11 E2
Noel Ct TW4 . . . . 4 F4
Noel Terr SE23 . . . . 23 C6
Noke Dr RH1 . . . . 119 A2

Nonsuch Court Ave KT17 . 58 B1
Nonsuch Cl SM3 . . . . 58 E4
Nonsuch High Sch for Girls
SM3 . . . . 58 D3
Nonsuch Ho **5** SW19 . . . . . 40 D8
Nonsuch Ind Est KT17 . . . 76 E8
Nonsuch Prim Sch KT17 . . 58 B5
Nonsuch Wlk SM2 . . . . 58 D1
Nook The SW19 . . . . 40 A7
Noons Corner Rd RH5 . . . 156 D3
NORBITON 38 A7
Norbiton Ave KT1, SW19 . . 38 A7
Norbiton Common Rd KT1,
KT3 . . . . 38 B6
Norbiton Hall KT2 . . . . 37 F7
Norbiton Sta KT1 . . . . 38 A8
Norbury Ave
Isleworth TW3 . . . . 5 D3
South Norwood CR7, SW16 . 42 B7
Norbury Cl SW16 . . . . 42 B8
Norbury Court Rd SW16 . . 41 E7
Norbury Cres SW16 . . . . . . 42 A7
Norbury Cross SW16 . . . . . 41 E6
Norbury Hill SW16 . . . . . . 22 B1
**Norbury Manor Bsns & Ent
Coll for Girls** CR7 . . . . . . 42 A8
Norbury Manor Prim Sch
SW16 . . . . 41 E8
Norbury Rd
Feltham TW13 . . . . 14 F5
Reigate RH2 . . . . 117 F1
South Norwood CR7 . . . . . . 42 C6
Norbury Rise SW16 . . . . . . 41 E6
Norbury Sta SW16 . . . . 41 F8
Norbury Trad Est SW16 . . . 41 F7
Norbury Way KT23 . . . . 94 C2
Norcroft Gdns SE22 . . . . . 23 A8
**Nore Hill Pinnacle Nature
Reserve** ★ CR6 . . . . 102 B8
Norfolk Ave CR2 . . . . 62 A1
Norfolk Cl
Crawley RH11 . . . . 200 E2
Horley RH6 . . . . 161 A2
5 Twickenham TW1 . . . . . 6 B1
Norfolk Cotts RH1 . . . . . . 140 E7
Norfolk Ct
Dorking RH5 . . . . 136 D3
Horsham RH12 . . . . 218 A5
Surbiton KT5 . . . . 37 F3
Norfolk Farm Cl GU22 . . . . 70 D3
Norfolk Farm Rd GU22 . . . 70 D3
Norfolk Gdns GU21 . . . . . . 88 F8
Norfolk Ho
13 Bromley BR2 . . . . 44 F5
2 Croydon CR0 . . . . 61 D8
11 Merton SW19 . . . . 20 C1
Penge SE20 . . . . 43 C8
Richmond TW10 . . . . 7 A2
Norfolk House Rd SW16 . . 21 D5
Norfolk La RH5 . . . . 136 B1
Norfolk Mews **8** RH4 . . . . 136 A7
Norfolk Rd
Claygate KT10 . . . . 55 E5
Dorking RH4 . . . . 136 A7
Feltham TW13 . . . . 15 C7
Horsham RH12 . . . . 217 D2
Mitcham SW19 . . . . 20 E2
South Holmwood RH5 . . . . 157 C6
South Norwood CR7 . . . . . . 42 C6
Norfolk Terr **7** RH12 . . . . 217 D2
Norgrove St SW12 . . . . 21 A8
Norheads La TN16 . . . . 83 B2
Norhyrst Ave SE25 . . . . 42 F6
NORK 77 D4
Nork Gdns SM7 . . . . 77 E5
Nork Rise SM7 . . . . 77 D3
Nork Way KT17, SM7 . . . . . 77 D4
Norlands La TW18, TW20 . . 32 E7
Norley Vale SW15 . . . . 19 A7
Norman Ave
Ewell KT17 . . . . 76 F7
Feltham TW13 . . . . 15 F6
South Croydon CR2, CR8 . . 61 C1
Twickenham TW1 . . . . 17 C8
Norman Cl KT18 . . . . 97 B8
Norman Colyer Ct KT19 . . 57 D1
Norman Cres TW5 . . . . 4 D7
Norman Ct
Dulwich SE22 . . . . 23 A8
Farnham GU9 . . . . 125 C1
11 Hampton TW12 . . . . . . 36 A8
4 Staines TW18 . . . . 13 A4
Streatham SW16 . . . . 22 A3
Normande Ct SE21 . . . . . . 22 D7
NORMANDY 107 A3
Normandy RH12 . . . . 217 C1
Normandy Cl
Crawley RH10 . . . . 202 C4
7 East Grinstead RH19 . . 205 F8
Forest Hill SE26 . . . . 23 E5
Frimley GU16 . . . . 86 E8
Normandy Common La
GU3 . . . . 107 B4
Normandy Gdns **4**
RH12 . . . . 217 C1
Normandy Wlk TW20 . . . . . 12 C3
Norman Ho
Belmont SM1 . . . . 59 A4
Feltham TW13 . . . . 15 F6
Reigate RH2 . . . . 138 F6
Norman House Rd TW17 . . 34 A2
Normanhurst TW15 . . . . . . 14 A3
Normanhurst Cl RH10 . . . 201 F6
Normanhurst Dr TW1 . . . . . 6 B2

Normanhurst Rd
  Streatham SW2 ...... 21 F6
  Walton-on-Thames KT12 ... 54 D8
Norman Keep RG42 .... 27 F8
Norman Rd
  Ashford TW15 ...... 14 D2
  Merton SW19 ...... 20 C1
  Sutton SM1 ...... 59 A5
  Thornton Heath CR7 .... 42 B4
Normansfield Ave KT1, TW11 ...... 17 C1
Normans La TN8 ...... 165 E7
Norman's Rd RH1, RH6. .. 162 C5
Normanton RH2 ...... 117 D2
Normanton Ave SW18, SW19 ...... 20 A6
Normanton Ct 4 CR0 .... 61 E5
Normanton Rd CR2 ...... 61 E4
Normanton St SE23 ...... 23 D6
Normington Cl SW16 ...... 22 A3
NORNEY 149 E6
Norrels Dr KT24 ...... 92 F1
Norrels Ride KT24 ...... 92 F2
Norreys Ave RG40 ...... 25 D7
Norris Cl KT19 ...... 76 B8
Norris Hill Rd GU14 .... 104 A8
Norris Rd TW18 ...... 12 F4
Norstead Pl SW15 ...... 19 A6
North Acre SM7 ...... 77 F3
Northampton Cl RG12 .... 27 E6
Northampton Rd CR0, CR9 62 A8
Northanger Rd SW16 ...... 21 E2
NORTH ASCOT 28 F8
North Ash 1 RH12 ...... 217 C4
North Ave
  Heath End GU9 ...... 125 D7
  8 Richmond TW9 ...... 7 A6
  Wallington SM5 ...... 60 A3
  Whiteley Village KT12 .. 53 E2
Northborough Rd SW16 .. 41 E7
Northbourne GU7 ...... 150 F8
North Breache Rd GU6 .. 176 A5
Northbrook Copse RG12.. 27 F3
Northbrook Rd
  Aldershot GU11 ...... 126 B8
  Thornton Heath CR0 .... 42 D4
Northbury Ho 1 GU22 .. 70 A2
NORTH CAMP 105 C7
North Camp Sta GU12 .. 105 B8
NORTH CHEAM 58 C8
North Cl
  Ash GU12 ...... 105 E1
  Crawley RH10 ...... 201 F7
  Dorking RH5 ...... 136 C3
  East Bedfont TW14 ...... 3 D1
  Farnborough GU14 ...... 85 A8
  Merton SM4 ...... 39 E5
Northcliffe Cl KT4. ...... 57 E7
North Comm KT13 ...... 53 C6
Northcote KT15 ...... 52 D6
Northcote Ave
  Isleworth TW7 ...... 6 A2
  Tolworth KT5 ...... 38 B2
Northcote Cl KT24 ...... 92 C2
Northcote Cres KT24 .... 92 C2
Northcote La GU5 ...... 152 E6
Northcote Pk KT22 ...... 74 C4
Northcote Rd
  Ash Vale GU12 ...... 106 A7
  Farnborough GU14 ...... 84 F6
  Isleworth TW1, TW7 .... 6 A2
  Kingston upon Thames KT3. 38 D6
  Thornton Heath CR0 .... 42 D3
  West Horsley KT24 ...... 92 C2
Northcott RG12 ...... 27 A1
Northcott Gdns GU14 .... 84 D5
Northcroft Cl KT4 ...... 11 B3
Northcroft Gdns TW20 .. 11 B3
Northcroft Rd
  Englefield Green TW20 .. 11 B3
  West Ewell KT19 ...... 57 E3
North Crofts SE21 ...... 23 B7
Northcroft Villas TW20 .. 11 B3
North Ct
  Camberley GU15 ...... 65 C6
  6 Twickenham TW1 .... 6 D1
North Dene TW5 ...... 5 B6
North Down CR2 ...... 80 F7
Northdown Cl RH12 .... 217 F4
Northdown Ct RH9 ...... 121 C5
Northdown La GU1 ...... 130 E6
Northdown Rd
  Belmont SM2 ...... 59 A1
  Woldingham CR3 ...... 102 A2
Northdowns GU6 ...... 174 E1
North Downs Cres CR0 .. 63 B1
North Downs Hospl (Private)
  CR3 ...... 100 F2
North Downs Rd CR0 .... 63 C1
Northdown Terr RH19 .. 185 D3
North Dr
  Beckenham BR3 ...... 44 B5
  Dormansland RH19 .... 186 B6
  Hounslow TW3, TW7 .... 5 C5
  Pirbright GU24 ...... 87 C6
  Streatham SW16 ...... 21 C4
  Wentworth GU25 ...... 30 E4
North East Surrey Coll of Tech KT17 ...... 77 A8
NORTH END 185 B3
North End CR0, CR9 ...... 61 C8
Northend Ct KT23 ...... 94 C1
North End La SL5 ...... 30 B2
Northernhay Wlk SM4 .... 39 E5

Northern Perimeter Rd TW6 ...... 3 E6
Northern Perimeter Rd W TW6 ...... 2 E6
Northey Ave SM2 ...... 58 E1
North Farm Cl GU14 .... 84 F8
North Farm Rd GU14 .... 84 F8
North Farnborough Inf Sch GU14 ...... 85 D5
NORTH FELTHAM 4 B2
North Feltham Trad Est TW14 ...... 4 B3
Northfield
  Lightwater GU18 ...... 67 B8
  Shalford GU4 ...... 130 E1
  Witley GU8. ...... 170 F4
Northfield Cl GU12 ...... 105 D1
Northfield Cres SM3 .... 58 E6
Northfield Ct TW18 ...... 33 B8
Northfield Farm Mews KT11 ...... 73 A5
Northfield Pl KT13 ...... 53 B3
Northfield Rd
  Cobham KT11 ...... 73 B6
  Heston TW5 ...... 4 D7
  Staines TW18 ...... 33 B8
Northfields
  Ashtead KT21 ...... 95 E8
  Ewell KT17 ...... 76 E8
Northfleet Lodge 16 GU22 89 B8
NORTHGATE 201 F7
Northgate Ave RH10 .... 201 F7
Northgate Dr GU15 ...... 66 A7
Northgate Pl RH10 ...... 201 F7
Northgate Prim Sch RH10 ...... 201 E7
North Gate Rd GU14 .... 85 B2
North Gdns SW19 ...... 20 D1
North Gn RG12 ...... 27 D8
North Gr KT16 ...... 32 F3
North Heath Cl RH12 .... 217 D5
North Heath La RH12 .... 217 E6
North Heath Lane Ind Est RH12 ...... 217 D6
North Heath Prim Sch RH12 ...... 217 D5
North Holmes Cl RH12 .. 218 B5
NORTH HOLMWOOD 136 A3
North Hyde La TW5 ...... 4 F8
Northington Cl RG12 .... 27 F3
North La
  Aldershot GU11, GU12... 105 D2
  Teddington TW11 ...... 16 F2
Northlands Bglws RH5 .. 158 B1
Northlands Bsns Pk RH12 ...... 197 C4
Northlands Cotts RH12 .. 197 D4
Northlands Rd
  Horsham RH12 ...... 217 E7
  Warnham RH12 ...... 197 D2
North Lodge Dr SL5 ...... 28 C7
NORTH LOOE 77 C6
Northmead GU14 ...... 85 B4
North Mead
  Crawley RH10 ...... 201 E8
  Redhill RH1 ...... 118 F4
Northmead Jun Sch GU2 109 B4
North Minden Ho GU16.. 86 D7
Northmoor 4 SE23 ...... 23 D5
North Moors GU1 ...... 109 E6
North Munstead La GU8. 151 A1
Northolmes Jun Sch RH12 ...... 218 A4
Northolt Rd UB7 ...... 2 D6
Northover BR1 ...... 24 F5
North Par
  Chessington KT9 ...... 56 F5
  Horsham RH12 ...... 217 C3
North Park La RH9 ...... 121 A5
North Pl
  Mitcham SW19 ...... 20 F1
  Teddington TW11 ...... 16 F2
Northpoint Cl SM1 ...... 59 C7
North Pole La BR2 ...... 63 F4
North Rd
  Ash Vale GU12 ...... 105 F4
  Brentford TW8 ...... 6 E8
  Crawley RH10 ...... 202 A7
  East Bedfont TW14 ...... 3 D1
  Guildford GU2 ...... 109 B4
  Hersham KT12 ...... 54 C5
  Heston TW5 ...... 4 C8
  Kingston upon Thames KT6. 37 D3
  Mitcham SW17, SW19 ... 20 C2
  Reigate RH2 ...... 138 F6
  Richmond TW9 ...... 7 A5
  1 West Wickham BR4 .. 44 B1
  Winkfield SL5 ...... 28 B8
  Woking GU21 ...... 70 A3
Northrop Rd TW6 ...... 3 E6
NORTH SHEEN 7 A5
North Sheen Sta TW10 .. 7 A3
North Side GU10 ...... 126 F7
Northspur Rd SM1 ...... 59 A7
North St
  Carshalton SM5 ...... 59 F6
  Cranbourne SL4 ...... 9 A6
  Dorking RH4 ...... 136 A7
  Egham TW20 ...... 11 F2
  Farncombe GU7 ...... 150 E7
  Guildford GU1 ...... 130 D8
  Horsham RH12, RH13 .. 217 D3
  Isleworth TW7 ...... 6 A4
  Leatherhead KT22 ...... 95 A6

North St continued
  Redhill RH1 ...... 118 F2
  Turners Hill RH10 ...... 204 A4
  Westcott RH4 ...... 135 C6
North Station App RH1 .. 140 F7
Northstead Rd SW2 ...... 22 A6
North Terminal App RH6 181 F8
NORTH TOWN 105 D2
Northtown Trad Est GU12 ...... 105 E1
Northumberland Ave
  1 Hounslow TW7 ...... 5 F6
  Hounslow TW7 ...... 6 A7
Northumberland Cl TW19 ..2 E1
Northumberland Cres TW14 ...... 3 E1
Northumberland Ct 1 CR0 ...... 61 E5
Northumberland Gdns
  Hounslow TW7 ...... 6 A7
  Mitcham CR4 ...... 41 D4
Northumberland Pl 27 TW10 ...... 6 D2
Northumbria Ct 12 TW9 ..6 E3
North View
  Bracknell RG12 ...... 26 C6
  Wimbledon SW19 ...... 19 C3
North View Cres KT18 .... 77 C2
Northway
  Crawley RH10 ...... 181 F8
  Farncombe GU7 ...... 150 F7
  Guildford GU2 ...... 109 A3
  Merton SM4, SW20 ...... 39 E5
  Wallington SM6 ...... 60 C6
Northway Rd CR0 ...... 42 F2
North Weald La KT2 ...... 17 D3
North Weylands Ind Est KT12 ...... 54 E8
North Wlk CR0 ...... 63 C5
Northwood Ave
  Knaphill GU21 ...... 68 D1
  Purley CR8 ...... 80 B6
Northwood Pk RH10 .... 182 A2
Northwood Rd
  Forest Hill SE23 ...... 23 F7
  Harmondsworth TW6 .... 2 D6
  South Norwood CR7 .... 42 C7
  Wallington SM5 ...... 60 A4
Northwood Way 1 SE19.. 22 E2
North Worple Way SW14 .. 7 D4
Norton Ave KT5 ...... 38 B2
Norton Cl GU3 ...... 88 D1
Norton Ct BR3 ...... 43 F8
Norton Gdns SW16 ...... 41 E7
Norton Ho 6 KT3 ...... 38 E5
Norton La KT11 ...... 92 F8
Norton Pk SL5 ...... 29 C4
Norton Rd
  Frimley GU15 ...... 66 C4
  Wokingham RG40 ...... 25 C5
Norwegian Sch in London The SW20 ...... 19 C1
Norwich Ave GU15 ...... 65 E3
Norwich Rd
  Crawley RH10 ...... 202 B5
  South Norwood CR7 .... 42 C6
Norwood Cl
  Effingham KT24 ...... 113 E7
  Twickenham TW2 ...... 16 D6
Norwood Cres TW6 ...... 3 C6
Norwood Farm La KT11 .. 73 B8
Norwood Heights Sh Ctr SE19 ...... 22 E2
Norwood High St SE27 .. 22 E4
NORWOOD HILL 159 E3
Norwood Hill RH6. ...... 159 F2
Norwoodhill Rd RH6 .... 159 F2
Norwood Junction Sta SE25 ...... 43 A5
Norwood Lodge 6 KT13.. 53 C5
NORWOOD NEW TOWN .. 22 C2
Norwood Park Rd SE27.. 22 C3
Norwood Rd
  Effingham KT24 ...... 113 E7
  Streatham SE24, SE27... 22 B7
Norwood Sch SE27 ...... 22 C3
Notley End TW20 ...... 11 C1
Notre Dame Prep & Senior Sch KT11 ...... 72 F8
Notson Rd SE25 ...... 43 B5
Nottingham Cl GU21 .... 68 F1
Nottingham Ct 5 GU21.. 68 F1
Nottingham Rd
  Croydon CR2 ...... 61 C5
  Isleworth TW7 ...... 5 F5
  Upper Tooting SW17 .... 20 F7
Nova Mews SM4 ...... 39 E2
Nova Rd CR0. ...... 42 C2
Nower Close E RH4 .... 135 F6
Nower Close W RH4. .... 135 F6
Nower Rd RH4 ...... 136 A6
Nowhurst La RH12 ...... 216 A5
Noyna Rd SW17 ...... 20 F5
Nubia Way SE6 ...... 24 F5
Nuffield Ct TW5. ...... 4 F7
Nuffield Dr GU47. ...... 45 F1
Nugee Ct RG45 ...... 45 B5
Nugent Cl GU8. ...... 192 F6
Nugent Ct
  Guildford GU2 ...... 109 B4
  Streatham SW16 ...... 21 C4
Nugent Rd
  Guildford GU2 ...... 129 D8
  South Norwood SE25 .... 42 F6
Numa Ct TW8. ...... 6 D7
Nunappleton Way RH8 .. 123 A4
Nuneaton RG12 ...... 27 E3
Nuneham SW16 ...... 21 D4

Nunns Field RH5 ...... 178 D6
Nuns Wlk GU25 ...... 31 D4
Nuptown La SL4 ...... 8 A4
Nursery Ave CR0 ...... 62 D8
Nursery Cl
  Capel RH5 ...... 178 C5
  Croydon CR0 ...... 62 D8
  Ewell KT17 ...... 57 F1
  Feltham TW14 ...... 15 B8
  Frimley GU16 ...... 85 F7
  Walton on the Hill KT20.. 97 B2
  Woking GU21 ...... 69 C3
  Woodham KT15 ...... 51 F1
Nursery Cotts GU21 .... 88 F8
Nursery Gdns
  Chilworth GU4 ...... 131 B3
  Feltham TW12 ...... 15 F4
  Hounslow TW4 ...... 4 F2
  Staines TW18 ...... 13 B1
  Sunbury TW16 ...... 34 F7
  Sutton SM1 ...... 59 C6
Nursery Gdns GU5 ...... 152 D5
Nursery La
  Hookwood RH6 ...... 160 D2
  North Ascot SL5 ...... 28 E8
Nurserylands RH11 ...... 201 A6
Nursery Rd
  Farncombe GU7 ...... 150 F7
  Knaphill GU21 ...... 68 D2
  Merton SW19 ...... 40 B7
  Mitcham CR4 ...... 40 E6
  South Norwood CR7, SE25 .. 42 C6
  Sunbury TW16 ...... 34 F7
  Sutton SM1 ...... 59 C6
  Walton on the Hill KT20.. 97 B2
  Wimbledon SW19 ...... 19 E1
Nutborn Ho SW19 ...... 19 D2
Nutbourne GU9 ...... 125 E2
Nutbourne Cotts GU8 .. 191 E2
Nutbourne Ct
  2 Horsham RH12 ...... 217 D5
  Staines TW18 ...... 12 F1
NUTCOMBE 188 E1
Nutcombe Height GU26 . 188 F4
Nutcombe La
  Dorking RH4 ...... 135 C4
  Haslemere GU26, GU27.. 188 E1
Nutcroft Gr KT22. ...... 94 E6
NUTFIELD 119 F2
Nutfield Church CE Prim Sch RH1. ...... 140 F4
Nutfield Cl SM5 ...... 59 E7
Nutfield Ct
  Camberley GU15 ...... 65 D7
  Nutfield RH1 ...... 119 F2
Nutfield Marsh Rd RH1.. 119 E4
Nutfield Pl 1 CR7 ...... 42 B5
Nutfield Rd
  Coulsdon CR5 ...... 79 A3
  Merstham RH1 ...... 119 C5
  Redhill RH1 ...... 119 C1
  Thornton Heath CR7 .... 42 B5
Nutfield Sta RH1 ...... 140 F7
Nuthatch Cl GU10 ...... 124 D7
Nuthatch Gdns RH2 .... 139 C5
Nuthatch Way
  Horsham RH12 ...... 217 D7
  Turners Hill RH10 ...... 204 C5
Nuthurst RG12 ...... 27 E4
Nuthurst Ave
  Cranleigh GU6 ...... 174 E3
  Streatham SW2 ...... 21 F6
Nuthurst Cl RH11 ...... 201 A7
Nutley RG12 ...... 27 A1
Nutley Ct 1 RH2 ...... 118 A1
Nutley Dean Bsns Pk RH6 ...... 159 E6
Nutley La RH2 ...... 117 F2
Nutmeg Ct 1 GU14 ...... 84 C5
Nutshell La GU9 ...... 125 C6
Nuttall Gdns GU6 ...... 174 E4
Nutty La TW17 ...... 34 C6
Nutwell St SW17 ...... 20 E3
Nutwood GU7 ...... 150 E5
Nutwood Ave RH3. ...... 137 C8
Nutwood Cl RH3. ...... 137 C8
Nyefield Pk KT20. ...... 97 A1
Nylands Ave TW9 ...... 7 A5
Nymans Cl RH12 ...... 218 A7
Nymans Ct RH10 ...... 202 B3
Nymans Gdns SW20 ...... 39 B6
Nyon Gr SE23, SE6 ...... 23 F6

O

Oakapple Cl
  Crawley RH11 ...... 201 B1
  Hamsey Green CR2 ...... 81 B5
Oak Ave
  Brookwood GU24 ...... 88 A6
  Croydon CR0 ...... 63 B8
  Egham TW20 ...... 12 D1
  Hampton TW12 ...... 15 E2
  Heston TW5 ...... 4 E7
  Sandhurst GU47 ...... 45 D1
Oakbank
  Fetcham KT22 ...... 94 D4
  Woking GU22 ...... 89 E8
Oak Bank CR0 ...... 63 C4
Oakbank Ave KT12 ...... 35 F2
Oakbark Ho 10 TW8 ...... 6 C7
Oakbraes GU7 ...... 150 D6
Oakbrook 3 BR3 ...... 44 B7
Oak Cl
  Box Hill KT20 ...... 116 B5
  Chiddingfold GU8. ...... 191 A4

Oak Cl continued
  Copthorne RH10 ...... 183 A3
  Ewhurst GU6 ...... 175 E6
  Farncombe GU7 ...... 150 E8
  Sutton SM1 ...... 59 C8
Oak Cnr RH5. ...... 157 C4
Oakcombe Cl KT3 ...... 38 E8
Oak Cottage Cl
  Catford SE6 ...... 24 F7
  Wood St V GU3 ...... 108 C2
Oak Cotts
  Compton GU3. ...... 129 C2
  Haslemere GU27 ...... 207 E6
Oak Croft RH19 ...... 206 A8
Oakcroft Bsns Ctr KT9 .. 56 F6
Oakcroft Cl KT14. ...... 70 F5
Oakcroft Ho 4 KT3 ...... 38 E2
Oakcroft Rd
  Chessington KT9 ...... 56 F6
  Pyrford KT14 ...... 70 F5
Oakcroft Villas KT9 ...... 56 F6
Oak Ct CR5 ...... 78 F1
Oak Ct RH10 ...... 181 D2
Oak Ct
  Farnborough GU14 ...... 85 E1
  Farnham GU9 ...... 125 B1
Oakdale
  Beckenham BR3 ...... 44 C7
  Bracknell RG12 ...... 27 D3
  Windlesham GU20 ...... 48 D4
Oakdale Rd
  Epsom KT19 ...... 57 D2
  Streatham SW16 ...... 21 E3
  Weybridge KT13 ...... 53 A7
Oakdale Way CR4 ...... 41 A2
Oak Dell RH10 ...... 202 C7
Oakdene
  Beckenham BR3 ...... 44 C7
  Chobham GU24 ...... 49 F1
  Kingswood KT20 ...... 97 E7
  Sunningdale SL5 ...... 29 F3
  1 West Norwood SE19... 22 E3
Oakdene Ave KT7 ...... 37 A1
Oakdene Cl
  Brockham RH3 ...... 137 C7
  Great Bookham KT23 .... 114 C8
Oakdene Ct
  Hampton TW12 ...... 15 F4
  Streatham SW16 ...... 21 E3
  Walton-on-Thames KT12 .. 54 B7
  6 Weybridge KT13 .... 53 A6
Oakdene Dr KT5 ...... 38 C1
Oakdene Ho KT15 ...... 52 C5
Oakdene Lodge SE20 .... 23 B1
Oakdene Mews SM3. .... 39 F1
Oakdene Par KT11 ...... 73 B5
Oakdene Pl
  Billingshurst RH14 ...... 212 D3
  Shalford GU3 ...... 130 C1
Oakdene Rd
  Brockham RH3 ...... 137 C8
  Cobham KT11 ...... 73 B5
  Godalming GU7 ...... 150 D3
  Little Bookham KT23 .... 93 F3
  Redhill RH1 ...... 118 F1
  Shalford GU3 ...... 130 C1
Oak Dr KT20 ...... 116 B5
Oaken Coppice KT21 .... 96 A8
Oaken Copse GU15 ...... 66 C7
Oaken Copse Cres GU14.. 85 B7
Oak End RH5 ...... 157 C4
Oaken Dr KT10. ...... 55 F4
Oak End Way KT15 ...... 70 F7
Oakengates RG12 ...... 27 A1
Oaken La KT10. ...... 55 E5
Oakenshaw Cl KT6 ...... 37 E2
Oakey Dr RG40. ...... 25 B5
Oak Farm Cl GU17 ...... 64 C5
Oak Farm Com Sch GU14. 84 F6
Oak Farm Pl RH19 ...... 184 F3
Oakfield
  Plaistow RH14 ...... 211 E2
  Woking GU21 ...... 68 D3
Oakfield Cl
  New Malden KT3 ...... 38 F4
  Weybridge KT13 ...... 53 C6
Oakfield Ct
  Croydon CR2 ...... 61 C4
  5 Weybridge KT13 .... 53 C5
  Wokingham RG41 ...... 25 A5
Oakfield Dr RH2 ...... 118 B3
Oakfield Gdns
  Beckenham BR3. ...... 44 A4
  Carshalton SM5. ...... 40 F1
  3 Dulwich SE19 ...... 22 C6
Oakfield Glade KT13 .... 53 C6
Oakfield Jun Sch KT22 .. 94 D4
Oakfield Pl GU14. ...... 84 C4
Oakfield Prep Sch SE21 .. 22 D7
Oakfield Rd
  Ashford TW15 ...... 14 B3
  Ashtead KT21 ...... 75 E1
  Blackwater GU17. ...... 64 F3
  Cobham KT11. ...... 73 B5
  Penge SE20 ...... 23 B1
  Thornton Heath CR0 .... 42 C1
  Wimbledon SW19 ...... 19 D5
Oakfield Road Ind Est SE20 ...... 23 B1
Oakfields
  Camberley GU15 ...... 65 B5
  Crawley RH10 ...... 202 D7
  Guildford GU3 ...... 108 F3
  Wallis Wood RH5 ...... 196 D8
  Walton-on-Thames KT12 .. 35 A1
  West Byfleet KT14 ...... 71 B5
Oakfield Sch GU22 ...... 70 F4
Oakfield Way RH19 ...... 185 F3

Oak Gdns CR0 . . . . 63 A8
Oak Glade KT19 . . . . . . 76 A7
Oak Gr
  Cranleigh GU6 . . . . 174 F1
  Loxwood RH14 . . . . 213 A4
  Sunbury TW16 . . . . . 15 B1
  West Wickham BR4 . . 44 C1
Oak Grange Rd GU4 . . . 111 B6
Oak Grove Cres GU15 . . . 64 F6
Oak Grove Rd SE20 . . . . 43 C7
Oakhall Ct TW16 . . . . . . 14 F3
Oakhall Dr TW16 . . . . . . 14 F3
Oakham Cl SE6 . . . . 23 F6
Oakham Dr BR2 . . . . 44 F5
Oakham & Wisley Nature
  Reserve★ GU23 . . . . 72 C2
Oakhaven RH10 . . . . . . 201 D4
Oak Heights Independent
  Sch ◫ TW3 . . . . 5 D4
OAKHILL 217 B1
Oakhill KT10 . . . . 56 A4
Oak Hill
  Epsom KT18 . . . . 76 D3
  Guildford GU4 . . . . . 110 C6
  Surbiton KT6 . . . . . . 37 E2
  Wood St V GU3 . . . . 108 B3
Oakhill Chase RH10 . . . 202 D7
Oakhill Cl KT21 . . . . 75 C1
Oak Hill Cres KT6 . . . . . 37 E2
Oakhill Ct
  ◫ Surbiton KT6 . . . . 37 E3
  Wimbledon SW19 . . . 19 D1
Oakhill Gdns KT13 . . . . . 53 E8
Oak Hill Gr KT6 . . . . 37 E2
Oakhill Lodge
  Purley CR8 . . . . 80 A6
  ◫ Sutton SM1 . . . . . 59 B7
Oakhill Rd
  Addlestone KT15 . . . . 51 F4
  Ashtead KT21 . . . . . . 75 C1
  Beckenham BR3 . . . . 44 C7
  Headley Down GU35 . 187 B5
  Horsham RH13 . . . . 217 E2
  Reigate RH2 . . . . . . 139 B8
  Sutton SM1 . . . . 59 C7
  Thornton Heath SW16 . 41 F8
Oak Hill Rd KT6 . . . . 37 E3
Oak Ho
  Enton Green GU8 . . . 171 B3
  Farnborough GU14 . . . 85 A7
  Grayshott GU26 . . . . 188 D3
  Penge SE20 . . . . 43 B7
  ◪ Richmond TW9 . . . . 7 B6
  Teddington TW11 . . . . 17 C2
  ◫ Woking GU22 . . . . 69 F2
Oakhurst
  Chobham GU24 . . . . 49 E2
  Grayshott GU26 . . . 188 D3
  Kenley CR8 . . . . 80 C5
  Woking GU21 . . . . . . 69 D3
Oakhurst Cl ◪ TW11 . . . 16 E3
Oakhurst Cottage★ GU8 191 C8
Oakhurst Gdns RH19 . . 185 C2
Oakhurst Grange Sch
  CR3 . . . . 100 D1
Oakhurst La RH14 . . . . 212 F7
Oakhurst Mews RH12 . . 218 A4
Oakhurst Rd KT19 . . . . . 57 D4
Oakhurst Rise SM5 . . . . 59 E1
Oakies Ho GU26 . . . . . . 188 D3
Oakington ◪ KT1 . . . . . 38 A7
Oakington Cl TW16 . . . . 35 C7
Oakington Dr TW16 . . . . 35 C7
Oak La
  Broadbridge Heath RH12 216 E3
  Englefield Green TW20 . 11 C5
  Godalming GU8 . . . . 210 F4
  Isleworth TW7 . . . . . . 5 E3
  Twickenham TW1 . . . . 17 A8
  Woking GU22 . . . . . . 70 B3
Oakland Ave GU9 . . . . . 125 E7
Oaklands
  Croydon CR0 . . . . . . 61 B5
  Fetcham KT22 . . . . . . 94 D3
  Haslemere GU27 . . . 208 C4
  Horley RH6 . . . . 161 C3
  Horsham RH13 . . . . 217 E2
  Purley CR8 . . . . 80 C5
  South Godstone RH9 . 142 E5
  Twickenham TW2 . . . . 16 C8
Oaklands Ave
  Hounslow TW7 . . . . . . 5 F8
  Thames Ditton KT10 . . 36 D1
  Thornton Heath CR7 . . 42 A5
  West Wickham BR4 . . 63 B7
Oaklands Cl
  Chessington KT9 . . . . 56 C6
  North Ascot SL5 . . . . . 8 F1
  Shalford GU4 . . . . . . 130 E1
Oaklands Ct
  Addlestone KT15 . . . . 52 B7
  Beckenham BR3 . . . . 44 C7
Oaklands Dr
  North Ascot SL5 . . . . . 8 F1
  Redhill RH1 . . . . 140 B7
  Twickenham TW2 . . . . 16 C8
  Wokingham RG41 . . . 25 A4
Oaklands Gdns CR8 . . . . 80 C5
Oaklands Inf Sch RG45 . 45 A6
Oaklands Jun Sch RG45 . 45 A6
Oaklands La
  Biggin Hill TN16 . . . . 83 C5
  Crowthorne RG45 . . . 45 B7
Oaklands Pk RG41 . . . . . 25 A4
Oaklands Prim Sch TN16 . 83 C3
Oaklands Rd
  Bromley BR1 . . . . 24 E1
  Mortlake SW14 . . . . . . 7 D4

Oaklands Sch TW3 . . . . . . 5 D4
Oaklands Way
  Tadworth KT20 . . . . . . 97 C5
  Wallington SM6 . . . . . 60 D3
Oakland Way KT19 . . . . . 57 E4
Oaklawn GU21 . . . . 70 A4
Oaklawn Rd KT22 . . . . . . 74 E2
Oaklea GU12 . . . . 106 A5
Oaklea Ct CR2 . . . . 61 D2
Oak Leaf Cl
  Epsom KT19 . . . . 76 C1
  Guildford GU2 . . . . . 108 D2
Oak Leaf Ct SL5 . . . . 28 D8
Oakleigh
  Epsom KT18 . . . . 76 E5
  Lightwater GU18 . . . . 67 C8
Oakleigh Ave KT6 . . . . . . 57 B8
Oakleigh Ct
  Oxted RH8 . . . . 122 E6
  Penge SE20 . . . . 23 B1
Oakleigh Rd RH12 . . . . . 217 F4
Oakleigh Way
  Mitcham CR4 . . . . . . 41 B8
  ◪ Tolworth KT6 . . . . 38 B1
Oakley Ave CR0 . . . . 60 E6
Oakley Cl
  Addlestone KT15 . . . . 52 D6
  East Grinstead RH19 . 206 B7
  Hounslow TW7 . . . . . . 5 D6
Oakley Cotts RH19 . . . . 206 C7
Oakley Ct
  Carshalton CR4 . . . . . 41 A2
  Harlington UB3 . . . . . . 3 C7
  ◪ Redhill RH1 . . . . . 119 A2
Oakley Dell GU4 . . . . . . 110 C3
Oakley Gdns
  Banstead SM7 . . . . . . 78 B4
  Brockham RH3 . . . . . 137 C3
Oakley Ho GU7 . . . . 150 E8
Oakley Rd
  Camberley GU15 . . . . 65 B4
  Croydon SE25 . . . . . . 43 B4
  Whyteleafe CR6 . . . . . 81 A1
Oak Lodge
  ◪ Charlton TW16 . . . 14 F1
  Cobham KT11 . . . . . . 73 C4
  Crowthorne RG45 . . . 45 C5
  ◪ Sutton SM1 . . . . . 59 C6
  ◪ West Norwood SE21 . 22 D6
Oak Lodge Cl KT12 . . . . . 54 C5
Oak Lodge Dr
  Salfords RH1 . . . . . . 140 A1
  West Wickham BR4 . . 44 B2
Oak Lodge Prim Sch BR4 . 44 B2
Oak Lodge Sch SW12 . . . 21 A8
Oakman Ho ◪ SW19 . . . 19 D7
Oak Mead GU7 . . . . 150 E8
Oakmead Gn KT18 . . . . . 76 C4
Oakmead Pl CR4 . . . . . . 40 E8
Oakmead Rd
  Upper Tooting SW12 . . 21 B7
  Wallington CR0 . . . . . 41 D3
Oakmere Ave
  Beckenham BR3 . . . . 44 C7
  Chessington KT9 . . . . 56 F4
  Epsom KT18 . . . . 57 B2
  Mitcham CR4 . . . . . . 40 C7
  Purley CR8 . . . . 80 C7
Oak Rd
  Caterham CR3 . . . . . 100 E5
  Crawley RH11 . . . . . 201 C5
  Farnborough GU14 . . . 85 C3
  Kingston upon Thames KT3 . 38 D7
  Leatherhead KT22 . . . 95 A8
  Reigate RH2 . . . . . . 118 B2
  Stoke D'Abernon KT11 . 73 E4
Oakridge GU4 . . . . 67 F6
Oak Ridge RH4 . . . . 136 B4
Oakridge La BR1 . . . . 24 D3
Oakridge Rd BR1 . . . . . . 24 E3
Oak Row CR4 . . . . 41 C7
Oaks Ave
  Feltham TW13 . . . . . . 15 E6
  North Cheam KT4 . . . . 58 B6
  West Norwood SE19, SE27 . 22 E3
Oaks Cl
  Horsham RH12 . . . . 218 B6
  Leatherhead KT22 . . . 95 A6
Oaks Ct KT22 . . . . 95 A6
Oaksend Cl KT22 . . . . . . 74 E2
Oaksford Ave SE26 . . . . . 23 B5
Oaks Golf Centre The
  SM5 . . . . 78 E8
Oakshade Rd
  Catford BR1 . . . . 24 D4
  Oxshott KT22 . . . . . . 74 C5
Oakshaw RH8 . . . . 122 D8
Oakshaw Rd SW18 . . . . . 20 B8
Oakside Ct RH6 . . . . 161 C4
Oakside La RH6 . . . . . . 161 C4
Oaks La
  South Croydon CR0 . . 62 C7
  South Holmwood RH5 . 157 B8
Oaks Prim Sch The RH10 201 F3
Oaks Rd
  Purley CR8 . . . . 80 B5
  Reigate RH2 . . . . . . 118 D2
  South Croydon CR0 . . 62 C6
  Stanwell TW19 . . . . . . 2 D1
Oak's Rd GU21 . . . . 69 E2
Oaks Sq The ◪ KT19 . . . 76 E6
Oaks The
  Bracknell RG12 . . . . . 27 D7
  Chiddingfold GU8 . . . 191 B4
  Claygate KT9 . . . . 56 C7
  Dorking RH4 . . . . . . 136 B4
  East Grinstead RH19 . 206 B8
  Epsom KT18 . . . . 76 F5
  Farnborough GU14 . . . 84 D3
  Smallfield RH6 . . . . . 162 B3
  Staines TW18 . . . . . . 12 F4
  Sutton SM1 . . . . 59 A5

Oaks The continued
  Tadworth KT20 . . . . . . 97 C4
  Wallington SM6 . . . . . 60 C6
  West Byfleet KT14 . . . 71 A5
  Wimbledon SW19 . . . 19 E2
Oaks Track SM5, SM6 . . . 60 B1
Oaks Way
  Burgh Heath KT18 . . . 97 B8
  Long Ditton KT6 . . . . 37 D1
  Purley CR8 . . . . 80 C5
  Send Marsh GU23 . . . 91 A3
  Wallington SM5 . . . . . 59 F3
Oak Tree Cl
  Aldershot GU12 . . . . 126 E8
  Ash Vale GU12 . . . . . 85 F1
  East Grinstead RH19 . 185 C3
  Guildford, Burpham GU4 . 110 B6
  Guildford, Jacobswell GU4 109 D6
  Knaphill GU21 . . . . . . 68 B1
  Virginia Water GU25 . . 31 D3
Oak Tree Dr
  Englefield Green TW20 . 11 C3
  Guildford GU1 . . . . . 109 C5
Oak Tree La
  Dunsfold GU8 . . . . . 192 F5
  Haslemere GU27 . . . 207 D6
Oak Tree Rd
  Knaphill GU21 . . . . . . 68 B1
  Milford GU8 . . . . 149 F1
Oaktrees
  Ash GU12 . . . . 105 F1
  Hale GU9 . . . . 125 B6
Oaktree Sch The GU22 . . 88 E8
Oaktrees Ct ◪ GU12 . . . 105 F1
Oak Tree View GU9 . . . . 125 E6
Oaktree Way GU47 . . . . . 45 A1
Oak Tree Way RH13 . . . . 217 F4
Oakview RG40 . . . . 25 B4
Oakview Bsns Pk GU8 . . 190 F7
Oakview Gr CR0 . . . . 43 E1
Oakview Rd SE6 . . . . 24 B3
Oakway
  Aldershot GU12 . . . . 126 E8
  Beckenham BR2 . . . . 44 D7
  Knaphill GU21 . . . . . . 88 E8
  West Barnes SW20 . . . 39 C5
Oak Way
  Ashtead KT21 . . . . . . 76 A3
  Crawley RH10 . . . . . 201 E8
  Croydon CR0 . . . . . . 43 D3
  East Bedfont TW14 . . . 14 E7
  Ifold RH14 . . . . 212 D2
  Reigate RH2 . . . . . . 139 D8
Oakway Dr GU16 . . . . . . 65 E1
Oak Wlk SM6 . . . . 41 A1
Oakwood
  Epsom KT18 . . . . 76 E5
  Guildford GU2 . . . . . 109 A6
  Wallington SM6 . . . . . 60 B2
Oakwood Ave
  Beckenham BR3 . . . . 44 C7
  Chessington KT9 . . . . 56 F4
  Mitcham CR4 . . . . . . 40 D7
  Purley CR8 . . . . 80 C7
Oakwood Cl
  East Horsley KT24 . . . 112 E6
  Redhill RH1 . . . . 119 A1
  South Nutfield RH1 . . 140 F7
Oakwood Ct
  Beckenham BR3 . . . . 44 C7
  Bisley GU24 . . . . 68 A3
  ◪ Sutton SM1 . . . . . 59 C6
Oakwood Dr
  East Horsley KT24 . . . 112 E6
  West Norwood SE19 . . 22 E2
Oakwood Gdns
  Knaphill GU21 . . . . . . 68 B1
  Sutton SM1 . . . . 59 A8
Oakwood Grange KT13 . . 53 E7
Oakwood Hall KT20 . . . . 98 C4
OAKWOOD HILL 197 A7
Oakwood Ho GU23 . . . . . 71 E3
Oakwood Ind Pk RH10 . . 182 A2
Oakwood Ind Sch CR8 . . 80 B6
Oakwood Pk RH18 . . . . 206 F2
Oakwood Pl
  Crowthorne RG45 . . . 45 A4
  Thornton Heath CR0 . . 42 A3
Oakwood Rd
  Bletchingley RH1 . . . 120 A6
  Bracknell RG12 . . . . . 27 E7
  Horley RH6 . . . . 161 B4
  Knaphill GU21 . . . . . . 88 E8
  Thornton Heath CR0, CR7 . 42 A3
  Thorpe GU25 . . . . . . 31 C4
  Wimbledon SW20 . . . 39 A8
  Windlesham GU20 . . . 48 E4
Oakwood Rise CR3 . . . . 100 C5
Oakwood Sch RH6 . . . . 161 C3
Oakwood Sp Ctr RH6 . . 161 B3
Oareborough RG12 . . . . . 27 E4
Oarsman Pl KT8 . . . . 36 E5
Oasis Acad Coulsdon
  CR5 . . . . 100 B7
Oasis Acad Shirley Park
  CR0 . . . . 43 B2
Oast House Cl TW19 . . . . 11 E8
Oast House Cres GU9 . . 125 D6
Oast House La GU9 . . . . 125 D6
Oast La GU11 . . . . 126 B7
Oast Lodge ◪ W4 . . . . . . 7 E7
Oast Rd RH8 . . . . 122 F4
Oates Ct BR2 . . . . 44 D6
Oates Wlk RH10 . . . . . . 201 D3
Oatfield Rd KT20 . . . . . . 97 B6

Oatlands
  Crawley RH11 . . . . . 201 A5
  Horley RH6 . . . . 161 C1
  Horley RH6 . . . . 161 C1
Oatlands Ave KT13 . . . . . 53 E6
Oatlands Chase KT12,
  KT13 . . . . 53 E7
Oatlands Cl KT13 . . . . . . 53 D6
Oatlands Ct ◪ SW19 . . . 19 D7
Oatlands Dr KT13, KT12 . . 53 D7
Oatlands Gn KT13 . . . . . 53 D7
Oatlands Mere KT13 . . . . 53 D7
OATLANDS PARK 53 E6
Oatlands Rd KT20 . . . . . 97 E8
Oatlands Sch KT13 . . . . . 53 D6
Oban Rd SE25 . . . . 42 D5
Obelisk Way GU15 . . . . . 65 C6
Oberon Way
  Crawley RH11 . . . . . 200 E3
  Littleton TW17 . . . . . . 33 E6
Oberursel Way GU11 . . . 104 F2
Observatory Rd SW14 . . . 7 C3
Observatory Wlk ◪ RH1 . 118 F1
Observer Ct RH12 . . . . . 217 C1
Occam Rd GU2 . . . . 129 D8
Ochre Ct TW13 . . . . 14 F5
Ockenden Cl ◪ GU22 . . . 69 F1
Ockenden Gdns GU22 . . 69 F1
Ockenden Rd GU22 . . . . 69 F1
Ockfields GU8 . . . . 149 F1
Ockford Ct GU7 . . . . 150 D4
Ockford Dr GU7 . . . . 150 D3
Ockford Rd GU7 . . . . . . 150 D4
OCKFORD RIDGE 150 B3
Ockford Ridge GU7 . . . . 150 B2
OCKHAM 92 B6
Ockham Dr KT24 . . . . . . 92 B3
Ockham La GU23, KT11 . . 92 D7
Ockham Road N GU23,
  KT24 . . . . 92 C3
Ockham Road S KT24 . . 112 E2
OCKLEY 177 D5
Ockley Ct
  Guildford GU4 . . . . . 110 B6
  ◪ Sutton SM1 . . . . . 59 C6
Ockley Ho ◪ KT2 . . . . . . 18 B2
Ockley Rd
  Beare Green RH5 . . . 157 C2
  Ewhurst GU6 . . . . . . 175 F6
  Forest Green GU6, RH5 . 176 C2
  Ockley RH5 . . . . 177 B7
  Streatham SW16 . . . . 21 C4
  Thornton Heath CR0, CR9 . 41 F2
Ockleys Mead RH9 . . . . 121 C5
Ockley Sta RH5 . . . . . . 178 A5
O'Connor Rd GU11 . . . . 105 E7
Octagon Rd KT12 . . . . . . 53 E1
Octavia RG12 . . . . 27 A1
Octavia Cl CR4 . . . . 40 E4
Octavia Ho SE6 . . . . 24 B8
Octavia Rd TW7 . . . . 5 F4
Octavia Way TW18 . . . . . 13 A2
October Ct BR2 . . . . 44 F6
Odard Rd KT8 . . . . 36 A5
Odette Ho ◪ SE27 . . . . . 22 B4
Odiham Rd GU9, GU10 . . 124 D7
Offley Pl TW7 . . . . 5 D5
Off Upper Manor Rd
  GU7 . . . . 150 E7
Ogden Ho TW13 . . . . 15 E4
Ogden Pk RG12 . . . . 27 E6
O'gorman Ave GU14 . . . . 85 B2
Okeburn Rd SW17 . . . . . 21 A3
Okehurst Rd RH14 . . . . 214 C1
Okingham Cl GU47 . . . . . 45 D1
Olaf Palme Ho TW13 . . . . 15 B5
Oldacre GU24 . . . . 67 F7
Old Acre KT14 . . . . 71 A5
Old Ave
  Sheerwater KT14 . . . . 70 E6
  Weybridge KT13 . . . . 53 C3
Old Avenue Cl KT14 . . . . 70 E6
Old Bakehouse Ct RG45 . 45 B4
Old Bake House Mews
  GU27 . . . . 208 D6
Old Bakery Ct GU6 . . . . 175 E5
Old Bakery Mews GU5 . . 132 B4
Old Bakery The ◪ TW20 . 12 A3
Old Barn Cl SM2 . . . . . . 58 E3
Old Barn Dr RH5 . . . . . . 178 D6
Old Barn La
  Churt GU10 . . . . 168 B1
  Kenley CR3 . . . . 80 F3
Old Barn Rd KT18 . . . . . 76 C2
Old Barn View GU7 . . . . 150 C2
Old Bisley Rd GU16 . . . . 66 C3
Old Bracknell Cl RG12 . . 27 B6
Old Bracknell Lane E
  RG12 . . . . 27 B6
Old Bracknell Lane W
  RG12 . . . . 27 B6
Old Brewery Ct RH4 . . . 136 B7
Old Brickfield Rd GU11 . 126 B7
Old Bridge Rd GU10 . . . 126 B4
Old Bridge St KT1 . . . . . . 37 D7
Old Brighton Road S
  RH6 . . . . 181 E5
Old Bromley Rd BR1 . . . . 24 D3
Oldbury RG12 . . . . 26 F6
Oldbury Cl
  Frimley GU16 . . . . . . 85 F8
  Horsham RH12 . . . . 218 A7
Oldbury Rd KT16 . . . . . . 32 E2
Old Chapel La GU12 . . . 106 A1
Old Charlton Rd TW17 . . 34 C4
Old Char Wharf RH4 . . . 135 F8
Old Chertsey Rd GU24 . . 50 C1

Oak–Old 279

Old Chestnut Ave KT10 . . 55 B4
Old Chiswick Yd ◪ W4 . . . 7 E8
Old Church La GU9 . . . . 146 D7
Old Church Path KT10 . . . 55 B6
Old Claygate La KT10 . . . 56 A5
Old Coalyard The TW20 . . 11 F2
Old Comm Nature Reserve★
  KT11 . . . . 73 B7
Old Common Rd KT11 . . . 73 B7
Old Compton La GU9 . . . 125 F2
Old Convent The
  Dockenfield GU10 . . . 166 D3
  East Grinstead RH19 . . 185 E2
Old Corn Mews GU7 . . . 150 F6
Old Cote Dr TW5 . . . . 5 A8
Old Cotts GU3 . . . . 130 C2
OLD COULSDON 100 B7
Old Court Rd GU2 . . . . . 130 A8
Old Crawley Rd RH12 . . 218 C7
Old Cross Tree Way
  GU12 . . . . 127 C8
Old Dairy Mews SW12 . . . 21 A7
Old Dairy The
  ◪ Dorking RH4 . . . . 136 B8
  Woking GU21 . . . . . . 69 D2
Old Dean Rd GU15 . . . . . 65 D7
Old Deer Park Gdns TW9 . . 6 E4
Old Denne Gdns ◪
  RH12 . . . . 217 C1
Old Devonshire Rd SW12 . 21 B8
Old Dock Cl TW9 . . . . 7 A8
Old Dr GU5 . . . . 133 C5
Olde Farm Dr GU17 . . . . 64 B5
Old Elstead Rd GU8 . . . . 149 E2
Olden La CR8 . . . . 80 A7
Old Esher Cl KT12 . . . . . 54 D5
Old Esher Rd KT12 . . . . . 54 E5
Old Farleigh Rd CR6, CR22 81 E6
Old Farm Cl TW4 . . . . 4 F3
Old Farm Ct KT10 . . . . . 55 B4
Old Farmhouse Dr KT22 . 74 D4
Old Farm Pl GU14 . . . . . 105 F5
Old Farm Rd
  Guildford GU1 . . . . . 109 D4
  Hampton TW12 . . . . . 15 F2
Old Farnham La
  Bentley GU10 . . . . . . 124 A1
  Farnham GU9 . . . . . . 146 C8
Oldfield Cl RH6 . . . . 160 F1
Oldfield Gdns KT21 . . . . . 95 D8
Oldfield Ho SW16 . . . . . . 21 B4
Oldfield House Specl Sch
  TW12 . . . . 35 F8
Oldfield Rd
  Hampton TW12 . . . . . 35 F8
  Horley RH6 . . . . 160 F1
  Wimbledon SW19 . . . 19 E2
Oldfields Rd SM1, SM3 . . 59 A8
Oldfields Trad Est SM1 . . 59 A7
Oldfieldwood GU22 . . . . . 70 B2
Old Ford Ho CR0 . . . . . . 60 E7
Old Forge Cl RH12 . . . . 199 F1
Old Forge Cres TW17 . . . 34 B3
Old Forge End GU47 . . . . 64 B7
Old Fox Cl CR3 . . . . 100 B6
Old Frensham Rd GU10 . 146 E4
Old Green La GU15 . . . . . 65 C7
Old Guildford Rd
  Mytchett GU16 . . . . . 86 C4
  Warnham RH12 . . . . 216 A4
Old Hall Cotts GU3 . . . . 107 B4
Oldham Ho ◪ SE21 . . . . 22 E4
Old Haslemere Rd GU27 208 C5
Old Heath Way GU9 . . . . 125 C7
Old Hill GU22 . . . . 89 D7
Old Hollow RH10 . . . . . . 202 F7
Old Horsham Rd
  Beare Green RH5 . . . 157 C4
  Crawley RH11 . . . . . 201 B4
Old Hospital Cl SW12,
  SW17 . . . . 20 F7
Old House Cl
  Ewell KT17 . . . . 57 F1
  Wimbledon SW19 . . . 19 E3
Old House Gdns ◪ TW1 . . 6 C1
Oldhouse La
  Bisley GU24 . . . . 68 A5
  Windlesham GU18, GU20 . 48 C2
Olding Ho ◪ SW12 . . . . . 21 C8
Old Ively Rd GU14 . . . . . 104 B8
Old Kiln GU9 . . . . 125 A2
Old Kiln Cl GU10 . . . . . . 167 F2
Old Kiln Courtyard ◪
  GU9 . . . . 125 B2
Old Kiln La
  Brockham RH3 . . . . . 137 C8
  Churt GU10 . . . . 167 F2
Old Kingston Rd KT4 . . . . 57 C7
Old La
  Aldershot GU11 . . . . 126 A7
  Aldershot, North Town
  GU12 . . . . 105 E3
  Dockenfield GU10 . . . 166 A4
  East Horsley KT11 . . . 93 A5
  Martyr's Green GU23 . . 92 E7
  Ockham GU23, KT11 . . 72 B1
  Oxted RH8 . . . . 122 F5
  Tatsfield TN16 . . . . . 103 D6
Old Lands Hill RG12 . . . . 27 D8
Old Lane Gdns KT11 . . . . 93 A5
Old Lane The GU10 . . . . 187 F8
Old Lodge Cl GU7 . . . . . 150 D5
Old Lodge La CR8 . . . . . 80 A3
Old Lodge Pl ◪ TW1 . . . . 6 B1

Old London Rd
Epsom KT17, KT18......**77** A2
Kingston upon Thames KT2 . **37** E7
Mickleham RH5..........**115** C8
OLD MALDEN...........**38** E1
Old Malden La KT4......**57** E8
Old Malt Way GU21......**69** D2
Old Manor Cl RH11......**201** A8
Old Manor Ct RH11......**201** A8
Old Manor Dr TW7......**5** C1
Old Manor Gdns GU4....**131** C3
Old Manor House Mews
TW17..................**34** A6
Old Market Ct SM1......**59** B6
Old Martyrs RH11......**181** D1
Oldmeadow Ho RH11....**201** D6
Old Merrow St GU4....**110** D3
Old Mill La RH1.........**119** B7
Old Millmeads RH12....**217** C5
Old Mill Pl
Haslemere GU27......**207** F7
Horton TW19............**1** B1
Old Museum Ct GU27....**208** D6
Old Nursery Pl TW15....**14** B3
Old Oak Ave CR5.........**98** E8
Old Oak Cl
Chessington KT9......**56** F6
Cobham KT11.........**73** B6
Old Orch
Byfleet KT14...........**71** F7
Sunbury TW16.........**35** C7
Old Orchards RH10......**202** E6
Old Orchard The GU9 ..**146** A7
Old Palace La TW9........**6** C2
Old Palace of John Whitgift
Sch
[8] Croydon CR0.........**61** B7
South Croydon CR2 ......**61** F5
Old Palace Rd
Croydon CR0, CR9 ......**61** C7
Guildford GU2.........**130** A8
Weybridge KT13.........**53** B7
Old Palace Terr [7] TW9 . **6** D2
Old Palace Yd [2] TW9....**6** D2
Old Park Cl GU9 ....**125** A6
Old Park La
Farnham GU9...........**125** A4
Hale GU9..............**124** F6
Old Park Mews TW5.......**4** F7
Old Parvis Rd KT14......**71** C7
Old Pasture Rd GU16,
GU15................**65** F3
Old Pharmacy Ct RG45 . **45** C4
Old Pond Cl GU15........**65** C1
Old Portsmouth Rd
Artington GU2, GU3,
GU7................**130** C3
Frimley GU16.........**66** A5
Thursley GU8.........**169** D4
Old Pottery Cl RH2.......**139** B7
Old Pound Cl TW7........**6** A6
Old Quarry The GU27....**207** F4
Old Rd
Addlestone KT15........**51** F3
Buckland RH3.........**116** F1
East Grinstead RH19....**185** F1
Old Rectory Cl
Bramley GU5.........**151** F6
Walton on the Hill KT20..**97** A3
Old Rectory Dr GU12....**106** B2
Old Rectory Gdns
Farnborough GU14......**85** D4
Godalming GU7.........**150** F2
Old Rectory La KT24......**92** E1
Old Rectory The KT23....**113** F8
Old Redstone Dr RH1....**140** A8
Old Reigate Rd
Brockham RH3.........**116** C1
Dorking RH4...........**115** F2
Oldridge Rd SW12........**21** B8
Old St Mary's KT24......**112** B6
Old Sawmill La RG45 ....**45** C6
Old School Cl
Ash GU12.............**106** A3
[10] Guildford GU1.........**109** D1
Merton SW19.........**40** A7
Penge BR3.............**43** E7
Old School Ct
Leatherhead KT22......**95** B5
Wraysbury TW19......**11** E8
Old School Ho CR4......**40** E6
Old School La RH3......**137** A7
Old School Mews
Egham TW20.........**12** D3
Oatlands Park KT13......**53** D6
Old School Pl
Croydon CR0..........**61** A6
Lingfield RH7.........**164** D4
Woking GU22.........**89** F6
Old Schools La KT17....**57** F2
Old School Sq KT7......**36** F3
Old School Terr SM3....**58** D3
Old School The SW19....**40** A7
Old Stables The GU1....**110** D2
Old Station App KT22....**95** A6
Old Station Cl RH10....**204** B7
Old Station Rd GU7....**150** E6
Old Station Way GU7....**150** E5
Old Station Works TW9 . **7** A5
Oldstead RG12............**27** D4
Oldstead Rd BR1.........**24** D4
Old Stede Cl KT21.......**75** F2
Old Studio Cl CR0........**42** D2
Old Surgery The [4]
RH19................**185** F2

Old Surrey Mews The
RH9..................**121** C5
Old Swan Yd SM5......**59** F6
Old Tilburstow Rd RH9 . **142** C8
Old Town CR0, CR9 ......**61** B7
Old Tye Ave TN16........**83** E3
Old Vicarage Sch TW10....**6** E1
Old Vicarage The
Mitcham CR4..........**40** E6
Wrecclesham GU10....**145** F7
Old Village Stores The
GU23..................**71** E3
Old Water Yd RH4......**136** A8
Old Westhall Cl CR6....**101** C8
Old Wharf Way KT13....**52** F6
Old Wickhurst La RH12 . **216** D2
OLD WINDSOR.........**11** A8
OLD WOKING...........**90** A7
Old Wokingham Rd RG45 . **45** C7
Old Woking Rd
Pyrford GU22, KT14....**70** D3
West Byfleet KT14......**71** A6
Woking GU22.........**90** C8
Oldwood Chase GU14....**84** C3
Old Yd The RH1........**120** C2
Oleander Cl RG45........**45** A7
Oliver Ave SE25.........**42** F6
Oliver Cl
Addlestone KT15......**52** B6
Brentford W4...........**7** B8
Oliver Ct
Isleworth TW7...........**5** F4
Penge SE26...........**23** C2
Olive Rd [3] SW19........**20** C1
Oliver Gr SE25.........**42** F5
Oliver Ho GU22.........**69** E1
Oliver Rd
Ascot SL5.............**29** B5
Carshalton SM1........**59** D6
Horsham RH12.......**217** A1
Kingston upon Thames KT3 . **38** C7
Olivier Cres RH4.......**136** C5
Olivier Rd RH10........**202** D5
Ollerton RG12............**27** A1
Olley Cl SM6.............**60** E4
Olveston Wlk SM4, SM5 . **40** D3
Olyffe Dr BR3...........**44** C8
Olympos L Ctr RH19....**185** E2
Omega Rd GU21.........**70** A3
Omega Way TW20........**32** C8
One Bens Ctr RG42......**27** A7
One Tree Cnr GU1......**131** B8
One Tree Hill Rd GU4....**131** B7
Ongar Cl KT15...........**51** F4
Ongar Hill KT15.........**52** A4
Ongar Par KT15.........**52** A4
Ongar Pl KT15...........**52** A4
Ongar Place Inf Sch KT15 **52** A4
Ongar Rd KT15..........**52** A5
Onslow Ave
Belmont SM2..........**77** F8
Richmond TW10.........**6** E2
Onslow Avenue Mans [13]
TW10..................**6** E2
Onslow Cl
Thames Ditton KT7......**36** E1
Woking GU22.........**70** A2
Onslow Cres GU22......**70** A2
Onslow Ct RH10........**182** A1
Onslow Dr SL5...........**9** A1
Onslow Gdns
Sanderstead CR2......**81** A7
Thames Ditton KT7......**36** E1
Wallington SM6.........**60** C3
Onslow Ho [1] KT2......**37** F8
Onslow Inf Sch GU2....**129** F7
Onslow Lodge
Staines TW18.........**12** F1
Streatham SW2........**22** A8
Onslow Mews [1] KT16....**33** A3
Onslow Rd
Guildford GU1.........**109** D1
Hersham KT12.........**54** A5
New Malden KT3........**39** A5
Richmond TW10.........**6** E1
Sunningdale SL5........**30** B2
Thornton Heath CR0....**42** A1
Onslow St GU1.........**130** C8
ONSLOW VILLAGE......**129** E7
Onslow Way
Pyrford GU22..........**70** F4
Thames Ditton KT7......**36** E1
Ontario Cl RH6.........**162** A2
Onyx Cl KT4.............**38** D1
Onyz The RG12...........**27** E6
Opal Ho SW17...........**20** D6
Openview SW17, SW18 ....**20** D6
Opladen Way RG12......**27** C4
Opossum Dr TW4.........**4** C4
Opus Pk GU4...........**109** D6
Orangery The TW10......**17** C6
Orchard Ave
Ashford TW15.........**14** C2
Carshalton CR4........**41** A1
Croydon CR0..........**43** E1
Hatton TW14............**3** D2
Heston TW5.............**4** E7
Hinchley Wood KT7......**56** A8
Kingston upon Thames KT3 . **38** E6
Woodham KT15.........**70** F8
Orchard Bsns Ctr SE26 . **23** F3
Orchard Bsns Ctr The
RH1..................**161** A8
Orchard Cl
Ashford TW15.........**14** C2
Ash Vale GU12.........**106** A5
Badshot Lea GU9......**126** A6
Banstead SM7.........**78** B5

Orchard Cl continued
East Horsley KT24......**92** F3
Egham TW20...........**12** B3
Elstead GU8..........**148** E4
Farnborough GU17......**64** F1
Fetcham KT22.........**94** D5
Flexford GU3.........**107** B1
Guildford GU1.........**110** B1
Haslemere GU27......**207** F5
Horley RH6...........**161** A3
Leatherhead KT22......**94** F8
Thames Ditton KT6......**37** B2
Walton-on-Thames KT12 . **35** B2
West Barnes SW20......**39** C5
West End GU24.........**67** D6
West Ewell KT19........**57** B4
Woking GU22..........**70** B3
Wokingham RG40......**25** D6
Orchard Cotts
Charlwood RH6.......**180** F7
Lingfield RH7.........**165** B3
Woking GU21..........**69** A1
Orchard Ct
Barnes SW13............**7** F4
Beckenham BR2........**44** E6
Bracknell RG12.........**27** C7
Camberley GU15........**65** B2
Caterham CR3.........**100** F3
Croydon CR0..........**44** A1
Forest Hill SE26........**23** E3
Harmondsworth UB7......**2** C7
Hounslow TW7...........**5** D7
[9] New Malden KT4......**39** A1
Penge SE26...........**23** D3
Wallington SM6.........**60** B5
Walton-on-Thames KT12 . **34** F1
Orchard Dene [4] KT14....**71** A6
Orchard Dr
Ashtead KT21.........**95** D7
Horley/Gatwick RH6....**161** B6
Upper Halliford TW17....**34** E6
Woking GU21..........**69** F4
Orchard End
Caterham CR3.........**100** E5
Fetcham KT22.........**94** C3
Oatlands Park KT13......**53** E8
Rowledge GU10.......**145** F3
Orchard Farm Pk RH1 . **161** F8
Orchardfield Rd GU7....**150** F7
Orchard Gate
Sandhurst GU47........**64** B8
Thames Ditton KT10......**36** D1
Orchard Gdns
Aldershot GU11.......**126** C8
Chessington KT9......**56** E6
Cranleigh GU6.......**174** F2
Effingham KT24.......**113** E7
Epsom KT18...........**76** C4
Sutton SM1...........**59** A5
Orchard Gr
Croydon CR0..........**43** E2
Penge SE20...........**23** A1
Orchard Hill
Rudgwick RH12.......**214** C7
Wallington SM5.........**59** F5
Windlesham GU20......**48** D3
Orchard Hill Coll [19] SM6 . **60** B4
Orchard Ho
Crawley RH10........**181** D1
Guildford GU1.........**110** D2
Tongham GU10.......**126** F5
Orchard La
Thames Ditton KT8......**36** D3
Wimbledon SW20......**39** B8
Orchard Lea Cl GU22....**70** E4
Orchardleigh KT22......**95** B5
Orchard Mains GU22....**89** C8
Orchard Mew GU21......**68** B1
Orchard (Mobile Home Pk)
The KT20...........**116** B5
Orchard Pl RG40.........**25** C6
Orchard Prim Sch The
TW3...................**5** A3
Orchard Rd
Badshot Lea GU9......**126** A6
Brentford TW8...........**6** C8
Chessington KT9......**56** E6
Dorking RH4..........**136** B6
Farnborough GU14......**85** A4
Feltham TW13.........**15** A7
Guildford, Burpham GU4 . **110** B5
Guildford, Onslow Village
GU2................**129** F7
Hampton TW12.........**15** F1
Hamsey Green CR2......**81** B5
Horsham RH12.......**217** E2
Hounslow TW4...........**5** A2
Kingston upon Thames KT1 . **37** E7
Mortlake TW9...........**7** A4
Reigate RH2..........**118** B1
Shalford GU4.........**130** E3
Shere GU5...........**133** A4
Smallfield RH6........**162** C3
Sunbury TW16.........**15** B1
Sutton SM1...........**59** A6
Twickenham TW1.........**6** B2
Orchard Rise
Croydon CR0..........**43** F1
Kingston upon Thames KT2 . **38** C8
Mortlake TW9...........**7** B3
Orchard Sch The
East Molesey KT8......**36** D5
[20] Streatham SW2......**21** F8
Orchards Cl KT14.........**71** A5
Orchards The
[4] Crawley RH11......**200** D5
Horsham RH12.......**217** F5

Orchards The continued
[14] Woking GU22........**69** F1
Orchard The
Banstead SM7.........**78** A4
Dorking RH5.........**136** C3
Ewell KT17...........**57** F1
Horley RH6...........**161** A3
Hounslow TW3...........**5** C5
Lightwater GU18........**67** B8
Virginia Water GU25......**31** E4
West Ewell KT17........**57** F3
Weybridge KT13........**53** B6
Woking, Horsell GU21....**69** B3
Woking, Westfield GU22 . **89** E5
Orchard View KT16......**33** A3
Orchard Way
Addlestone KT15........**52** B4
Aldershot GU11, GU12...**126** C8
Ashford TW15.........**13** F6
Beckenham BR3, CR0....**43** E3
Camberley GU15........**65** B2
Carshalton SM1........**59** D6
Croydon BR3, CR0......**43** E3
Dorking RH4..........**136** B6
East Grinstead RH19....**185** E1
Esher KT10...........**55** C4
Flexford GU3.........**107** B1
Lower Kingswood KT20....**97** F1
Oxted RH8...........**123** A2
Reigate RH2..........**139** B6
Send GU23............**90** C2
Orchard Way Prim Sch
CR0..................**43** E2
Orchid Cl KT9............**56** C3
Orchid Ct BR1...........**24** D5
Orchid Dr GU24.........**68** A4
Orchid Gdns TW4.........**4** F3
Orchid Mead SM7........**78** B5
Orde Cl RH10...........**182** D1
Ordnance Cl TW13........**15** A6
Ordnance Rd GU11......**105** C3
Ordnance Rdbt GU11....**105** B2
Oregano Way GU2......**109** A6
Oregon Cl KT3............**38** C5
Orestan La KT24.......**113** C8
Orewell Gdns RH2......**139** B7
Orford Ct
Wallington SM6.........**60** C5
West Norwood SE27......**22** B6
Orford Gdns TW1........**16** F6
Orford Rd SE6...........**24** B5
Organ Crossroads KT17 . **58** A3
Oriana Ct CR2............**61** D3
Oriel Cl
Crawley RH10........**182** C1
Mitcham CR4..........**41** D6
Oriel Ct [6] CR0.........**42** D1
Oriel High Sch RH10....**202** C4
Oriel Hill GU15..........**65** D4
Oriel Prim Sch TW13....**15** E5
Oriental Cl GU22........**70** A2
Oriental Rd
Ascot SL5.............**29** D5
Woking GU22..........**70** A3
Orion RG12...............**27** A1
Orion Ct
Crawley RH11........**200** D4
Horsham RH12.......**217** B3
Orion Ctr The CR0......**60** E8
Orion Mews SM4..........**40** A5
Orlando Gdns KT19......**57** D1
Orleans Cl KT10.........**55** D8
Orleans Ct [10] TW1......**17** B8
Orleans House Gallery★
TW1..................**17** B7
Orleans Inf Sch TW1......**17** B8
Orleans Park Sch TW1....**17** B8
Orleans Rd
South Norwood SE19......**22** D2
Twickenham TW1.........**17** C8
Orltons La RH12.......**179** F2
Ormanton Rd SE26......**23** A4
Orme Ho RH9...........**142** D8
Orme Rd SW12............**21** B7
Ormeley Rd SW12........**21** B7
Orme Rd
Kingston upon Thames KT1,
KT3................**38** B7
Sutton SM1...........**59** B4
Ormerod Gdns CR4......**41** A8
Ormesby Wlk RH10......**202** B4
Ormond Ave
Hampton TW12.........**36** B8
[24] Richmond TW10.......**6** D2
Ormond Cres TW12......**36** B8
Ormond Dr TW12........**16** B1
Ormonde Ave KT19......**57** D1
Ormonde Pl KT13........**53** D4
Ormonde Rd
Farncombe GU7........**150** E6
Mortlake SW14...........**7** C4
Woking GU21..........**69** C3
Wokingham RG41......**25** A5
Ormond Rd TW10..........**6** D2
Ormsby SM2.............**59** B3
Ormside Way RH1......**119** B5
Ormuz Cotts RH7......**164** C4
Orpin Rd RH1..........**119** C5
Orpwood Cl TW12........**15** F2
Orwell Cl GU14..........**84** E6
Orwell Ho [7] RH1......**118** F2
Osborne Ave TW19......**13** F7
Osborne Cl
Beckenham BR3.........**43** E5
Feltham TW13.........**15** D3
Frimley GU16.........**85** F8
Osborne Ct
Crawley RH11........**201** B2

Osborne Ct continued
Farnborough GU14......**105** C8
[10] Surbiton KT6.........**37** E3
Osborne Dr GU18........**67** A8
Osborne Gdns CR7......**42** C7
Osborne Pl SM1..........**59** D5
Osborne Rd
Egham TW20...........**11** F2
Farnborough GU14......**105** C8
Hounslow TW3, TW4......**4** F4
Kingston upon Thames KT2 . **17** E1
Redhill RH1...........**119** A4
South Norwood CR7......**42** C7
Walton-on-Thames KT12 . **35** A1
Wokingham RG40......**25** C6
Osborne Way KT9.........**56** F5
Osborn La SE23.........**23** E8
Osborn Rd GU9.........**125** D4
Osbourne Ho
Richmond TW10.........**7** A2
Twickenham TW2........**16** D6
Osbourne Terr [1] SW17....**21** A3
Oscar Cl CR8.............**80** A8
Osgood Cl GU10........**126** E8
Osier Pl TW20............**12** C2
Osier Way
Banstead KT17, SM7......**77** E5
Mitcham CR4..........**40** F4
Oslac Rd SE6.............**24** B3
Oslo Ct SW19............**20** D1
Osman's Cl RG42...........**8** B1
Osmond Gdns SM6......**60** C5
Osmunda Bank RH19....**185** E6
Osmund Cl RH10........**202** E6
Osnaburgh Hill GU15....**65** B5
Osney Cl RH11.........**201** C5
Osney Wlk SM4, SM5....**40** D3
Osprey Ave RG12........**26** D5
Osprey Cl
Cheam SM1...........**58** F5
Fetcham KT22.........**94** C5
Osprey Ct SW16.........**41** F7
Osprey Dr KT18.........**77** B2
Osprey Gdns
Aldershot GU11.......**126** A7
Selsdon CR0, CR2......**62** E1
Osprey Ho TW7...........**6** B4
Ospringe Cl [8] SE20......**23** C1
Ossier Mews [6] W4......**7** F8
Ostade Rd SW2...........**21** F8
OSTERLEY...............**5** D7
Osterley Ave TW7........**5** D7
Osterley Cl RG40........**25** F5
Osterley Cres TW7.........**5** F6
Osterley Ct TW7..........**5** D6
Osterley Lodge TW7.......**5** E6
Osterley Rd TW7..........**5** E6
Osterley U Sta TW7........**5** D7
Osterly Gdns CR7........**42** C7
Ostlers Dr TW15.........**14** C3
Oswald Cl KT22..........**94** C5
Oswald Rd KT22..........**94** C5
Osward CR0.............**62** F1
Osward Rd SW12, SW17....**20** F6
Otford Cl SE20..........**43** C8
Othello Gr RG42.........**27** E8
Otho Ct [5] TW8...........**6** D7
Otterbourne Pl RH19....**185** B1
Otterbourne Rd [1] CR0,
CR9..................**61** C8
Otterburn Gdns TW7......**6** A7
Otterburn St SW17......**20** F2
Otter Cl
Aldershot GU12.......**105** D3
Crowthorne RG45......**45** A7
Ottershaw KT16.........**51** B4
Otterden St SE6.........**24** A4
Otter Mdw KT22.........**94** F8
Ottermead La KT16......**51** C4
OTTERSHAW............**51** D5
Ottershaw CE Inf Sch
KT16................**51** E4
Ottershaw CE Jun Sch
KT16................**51** D4
Ottershaw Pk KT16......**51** A3
Otto Cl SE26.............**23** B5
Ottways Ave KT21........**95** D8
Ottways La KT22.........**95** D8
Otway Cl RH11.........**200** F4
Oulton Wlk RH10.......**202** B4
Our Lady Immaculate RC
Prim Sch KT6..........**38** B1
Our Lady of the Rosary RC
Sch TW18............**13** A2
Our Lady Queen of Heaven
RC Prim Sch SW19......**19** D8
Our Lady Queen of Heaven
RC Sch RH11.........**201** B8
Our Lady & St Philip Neri RC
Infants Sch [16] SE23....**23** D5
Our Lady & St Philip Neri RC
Jun Sch [6] SE26........**23** A4
Our Lady's Prep Sch RG45 **45** B5
Ouseley Rd
Upper Tooting SW12......**20** F7
Wraysbury TW19.........**11** D8
Outdowns KT24.........**113** B5
Outram Pl KT13.........**53** C5
Outram Rd CR0..........**61** F8
OUTWOOD.............**162** B7
Outwood Ct CR2.........**61** C3
Outwood Ho [6] SW2....**21** F8
Outwood La
Bletchingley RH1.......**141** D7
Chipstead CR5, KT20....**98** C6
Outwood RH1.........**141** D1
Outwood Post Windmill★
RH1..................**162** D8

Oval Ct 9 TW11 16 F3
Oval Prim Sch CR0 42 E1
Oval Rd CR0 42 E1
Oval The
Banstead SM7 78 A5
Farncombe GU7 150 F7
Guildford GU2 130 A8
Wood St V GU3 108 B2
Overbrae BR3 24 A3
Overbrook
Godalming GU7 151 A5
West Horsley KT24 112 B6
Overbury BR3 44 C6
Overbury Ave BR3 44 C6
Overbury Cres CR0 63 C1
Overdale
Ashtead KT21 75 E3
Bletchingley RH1 120 C2
Dorking RH5 136 D8
Overdale Ave KT3 38 D7
Overdale Rise GU16 65 E3
Overdene Dr RH11 201 A6
Overdown Rd SE6 24 B4
Overford Cl GU6 174 E2
Overford Dr GU6 174 E2
Overhill CR6 101 C8
Overhill Rd
Dulwich SE21, SE22 23 A8
Wallington CR8 61 A1
Overhill Way BR3 44 D4
Overlord Cl GU15 65 C8
Overlord Ct KT22 94 D6
Overslea Lodge 10 KT22 95 C6
Overstand Cl BR3 44 A4
Overstone Gdns CR0 43 F2
Overthorpe Cl GU21 68 E2
Overton Cl
Aldershot GU11 126 C6
1 Hounslow TW7 5 F5
Overton Ct
Belmont SM2 59 A3
4 East Grinstead RH19 185 E1
Overton Grange Sch SM2 59 B2
Overton Ho SW15 18 F8
Overton Rd SM2 59 A3
Overton Shaw RH19 185 E4
Overton's Yd CR0, CR9 61 C7
Overton Toft SM2 59 A4
Oveton Way KT23 94 B1
Ovett Cl SE19 22 E2
Ovington Ct GU21 68 F3
Owen Cl CR0 42 D3
Owen Ho
Feltham TW14 15 A8
6 Twickenham TW1 17 B8
Owen Pl KT22 95 B5
Owen Rd
Farncombe GU7 150 F6
Windlesham GU20 48 D5
Owens Way SE23 23 E8
Owen Wlk 10 SE20 23 A1
Owers Cl RH13 217 E2
Owlbeech Ct RH13 218 B4
Owlbeech Lodge RH13 218 B4
Owlbeech Pl RH13 218 B4
Owlbeech Way RH13 218 B4
Owl Cl CR2 62 D1
Owletts RH10 202 D7
Owlscastle Cl RH12 217 D5
OWLSMOOR 45 E1
Owlsmoor Prim Sch GU47 45 E1
Owlsmoor Rd GU47 45 D1
Ownstead Gdns CR2 80 F8
Ownsted Hill CR0 63 D1
Oxdowne Cl KT11 74 B5
Oxenden Ct GU10 126 E8
Oxenden Rd GU10, GU12 126 F8
Oxenhope RG12 27 A5
Oxford Ave
Harlington TW6 3 F7
Merton SW20 39 E7
Oxford Cl
Littleton Common TW15, TW17 14 C1
Mitcham CR4 41 C6
Oxford Cres KT3 38 D3
Oxford Ct
Epsom KT18 76 E5
17 Kingston upon Thames KT6 37 E4
Oxford Gdns W4 7 A8
Oxford Ho
3 New Malden KT3 38 F4
Wokingham RG41 25 A6
Oxford Rd
Carshalton SM5 59 E5
Crawley RH10 201 F2
Farnborough GU14 85 C1
Guildford GU1 130 D7
Horsham RH13 217 E2
Redhill RH1 118 E2
Sandhurst GU47 45 E2
South Norwood SE19 22 D2
Teddington TW11 16 D3
Wallington SM6 60 C5
Wokingham RG41 25 A6
Oxford Terr GU1 130 D7
Oxford Way TW13 15 D4
Oxleigh Cl KT3 38 E4
Oxlip Cl CR0 43 D1
OXSHOTT 74 C6
Oxshott Rd
Ashtead KT22 74 F3
Leatherhead KT22 75 A2
Oxshott Rise KT11 73 E5
Oxshott Sta KT22 74 C6
Oxshott Way KT11 73 E4
OXTED 122 E5
Oxted Cl CR4 40 D6
Oxted Gn GU8 170 E7
Oxted Rd RH9 121 D4
Oxted Sch RH8 122 F7
Oxted Sta RH8 122 E6
Oxtoby Way SW16 41 D8
Oyster La KT14 71 E7

P

Pacific Cl TW14 14 F7
Pacific Hts BR3 24 A1
Packer Cl RH19 186 A3
Packham Ct KT4 58 C7
Packway GU9 146 E7
Padbrook RH8 123 A6
Padbrook Cl RH8 123 B6
Padbury Cl TW14 14 D7
Padbury Oaks UB7 2 B6
Paddock Cl
Beare Green RH5 157 D4
Camberley GU15 66 A6
Forest Hill SE26 23 D4
Hambledon GU8 171 C1
Lingfield RH7 164 C4
New Malden KT4 38 E1
Oxted RH8 122 F4
Paddock Ct SW20 39 C5
Paddock Gdns
East Grinstead RH19 205 E7
South Norwood SE19 22 E2
Paddock Gr RH5 157 D4
Paddock Ho
Ascot SL5 28 E6
Guildford GU4 110 D2
Paddockhurst Rd
Crawley, Gossops Green RH11 201 A5
Crawley RH10 203 C2
Paddock Sch SW15 7 F3
Paddocks Cl
Ashtead KT21 75 E1
Cobham KT11 73 C5
Paddocks Mead GU21 68 F3
Paddocks Rd GU4 110 A5
Paddocks The
Addington CR0 63 A4
Flexford GU3 107 C1
Great Bookham KT23 94 B1
Oatlands Park KT13 53 E7
Virginia Water GU25 31 E3
Woodham KT15 52 B1
Paddocks Way
Ashtead KT21 75 E1
Chertsey KT16 33 B1
Paddock The
Cranleigh GU6 174 D3
Crawley RH10 202 D7
Crowthorne RG45 45 A6
Ewhurst GU6 175 E4
Godalming GU7 150 F3
Grayshott GU26 188 A4
Guildford GU1 110 D2
Haslemere GU27 208 A8
Westcott RH4 135 C6
Paddock Way
Grayswood GU27 190 A2
Oxted RH8 122 F4
Putney SW15 19 C8
Sheerwater GU21 70 B5
Paddock Wlk CR6 101 B8
Padley Cl KT9 56 F6
Padstow Wlk
Crawley RH11 200 F4
East Bedfont TW14 14 F7
Padua Rd SE20 43 C8
Padwick Rd RH13 218 A2
Pageant Wlk CR0 61 E7
Page Cl TW12 15 E2
Page Cres CR0 61 B5
Page Croft KT15 52 B8
Page Ct RH13 217 D1
Pagehurst Rd CR0 43 B2
Page Rd TW14 3 D1
Page's Croft RG40 25 D5
Page's Yd 11 W4 7 E8
Paget Ave SM1 59 D7
Paget Cl
Camberley GU15 66 B7
Hampton TW12 16 D4
Paget La TW7 5 E4
Paget Pl
Kingston upon Thames KT2 18 C2
Thames Ditton KT7 36 F1
PAGEWOOD 180 D7
Pagewood Cl RH10 202 D4
Pagoda Ave TW9 6 F4
Pagoda Gr SE21, SE27 22 C6
Paice Gn RG40 25 D7
Painesfield Dr KT16 33 A1
Pain's Cl CR4 41 B7
Pains Hill RH8 123 C4
Pain's Hill Ho KT11 72 F5
Painshill Pk* KT11 72 E5
Paisley Rd SM5 40 D1
Paisley Terr SM5 40 D2
Pakenham Cl SW12 21 A7
Pakenham Dr GU11 104 F3
Pakenham Rd RG12 27 D2
Palace Ct
2 South Norwood CR7 42 D5
Streatham SW2 22 A6
8 Woking GU21 70 A3
Palace Dr KT13 53 B7
Palace Gate KT8 36 E6
Palace Gn CR0 62 F3
Palace Gr SE19 22 F1
Palace Rd
East Molesey KT8 36 D6
Kingston upon Thames KT1 37 D5
Penge SE19 22 F1
Streatham SW2 22 A6
Woodham KT15 52 B2
Palace Sq SE19 22 F1
Palace View CR0 62 F6
Palace Way
Old Woking GU22 90 B7
6 Weybridge KT13 53 B7
Palestine Gr SW19 40 D8
Palewell Common Dr
SW14 7 D2
Palewell Pk SW14 7 D3
Palgrave Ho TW2 16 C8
Palisade Ct 5 BR1 24 E1
Palladino Ho SW17 20 E3
Pallingham Dr RH10 202 C3
Palliser Ct GU26 188 C6
Palm Ct BR3 43 F6
Palmer Ave KT4, SM3 58 C6
Palmer Cl
Crowthorne RG40 45 A8
Heston TW5 5 A6
Horley RH6 160 F5
Redhill RH1 140 A8
West Wickham BR4 63 D8
Palmer Cres
Kingston upon Thames KT1 37 E6
Ottershaw KT16 51 D4
Palmer Rd RH10 202 C3
Palmer School Rd RG40 25 C6
PALMERS CROSS 173 C6
Palmersfield Rd SM7 78 B5
Palmers Gr KT8 36 A5
Palmer's Lodge GU2 130 B8
Palmers Rd
Mortlake SW14 7 C4
Thornton Heath SW16 41 F7
Palmerston Cl
Farnborough GU14 84 D3
Redhill RH1 140 A6
Woking GU21 70 A5
Palmerston Ct
8 Richmond TW10 6 E1
9 Surbiton KT6 37 D2
8 Sutton SM1 59 C5
Palmerstone Ct GU25 31 E4
Palmerston Gr 11 SW19 20 A1
Palmerston House SM7 77 F4
Palmerston Rd
Carshalton SM5 60 A6
Hounslow TW3 5 C6
Merton SW19 20 A1
Mortlake SW14 7 C3
Sutton SM1 59 C5
Thornton Heath CR0 42 D4
Twickenham TW2 5 E1
Palm Gr GU1 109 C5
Pamela Ct 13 BR1 24 F1
Pamir Ct 10 SM2 59 B4
Pampisford Rd
Croydon CR2, CR8 61 B2
Purley CR2, CR8 61 B2
Pams Way KT19 57 D5
Pandora Ct 4 KT6 37 E3
Pangbourne Ct SW17 20 C4
Pankhurst Cl TW7 5 F4
Pankhurst Ct 11 RH11 201 B1
Pankhurst Dr RG12 27 D4
Pankhurst Farm GU24 68 A8
Pankhurst Ho SW16 21 D3
Pankhurst Rd KT12 35 C2
Panmuir Rd SW20 39 B8
Panmure Rd SE26 23 B5
Pannell Cl RH19 185 D1
Pannells GU10 146 D5
Pannells Ash RH14 212 C3
Pannells Cl KT16 32 F1
Pannells Ct
Guildford GU1 130 D8
Hounslow TW5 5 A8
Pan's Gdns GU15 65 F4
Pantile Rd KT13 53 D6
Pantiles Cl GU21 69 B1
Panton Cl CR0 42 B1
Papercourt La GU23 90 F6
Paper Mews RH4 136 B8
Papermill Cl SM5 60 A6
Papillon House Sch
KT20 116 E6
Papplewick Sch SL5 29 A8
Papworth Way SW2 22 A8
Parade Mews SE27, SW2 22 B6
Parade The
Ashford TW16 14 F1
Ash GU12 106 A4
Burgh Heath, Great Burgh KT20 77 E2
Burgh Heath KT20 97 E8
Claygate KT10 55 E4
Coulsdon CR5 80 A1
Crawley RH10 201 E7
Epsom KT18 76 D6
Epsom, The Wells KT18 76 A5
Leatherhead KT22 95 B7
Loxwood RH14 212 F4
Thornton Heath CR0 41 E3
Thornton Heath, Norbury CR7 42 A6
Virginia Water GU25 31 D3
Wallington CR0 60 F5
Worcester Park KT4 57 F6
Paradise Rd TW10 6 E2
Paragon Gr KT5 37 F3
Parbury Rise KT9 56 E4
Parchmore Rd CR7 42 C6
Parchmore Way CR7 42 B7
Parc Ho 11 KT2 37 E8
Pares Cl GU21 69 D3
Parfew Ct SE22 23 B6
Parfitts Cl GU9 125 A2
Parfour Dr CR8 80 C3
Parham Rd RH11 200 F7
Parish Church CE Inf & Jun Schs 7 CR0 61 B7
Parish Cl
Ash GU12 106 B1
Hale GU9 125 A6
Parish Ct KT6 37 E3
Parish Ho 6 RH11 201 D5
Parish La SE20, SE26 23 D1
Parish Rd GU14 105 B8
Park Ave
Bromley BR1 24 F2
Camberley GU15 65 D4
Caterham CR3 100 E3
Egham TW20 12 C1
Isleworth TW3 5 B1
Mitcham CR4 21 B1
Mortlake SW14 7 D3
Peper Harow GU8 149 C5
Salfords RH1 139 F1
Staines TW18 13 A2
Upper Halliford TW17 34 E6
Wallington SM5 60 A4
West Wickham BR4 63 C8
Wokingham RG40 25 B6
Park Avenue E KT17 58 A4
Park Avenue Mews CR4 21 B1
Park Avenue W KT17 58 A4
PARK BARN 108 E2
Park Barn Dr GU2 108 E2
Park Barn E GU2 108 F2
Park Chase
Godalming GU7 150 E2
Guildford GU1 109 E1
Park Cl
Brockham RH3 137 B4
Esher KT10 55 A4
Fetcham KT22 94 D3
Grayswood GU27 190 A1
Hampton TW12 36 C8
Isleworth TW3, TW7 5 C2
Kingston upon Thames KT2 38 A8
Limpsfield RH8 122 F7
Oatlands Park KT13 53 F8
Rowledge GU10 145 A2
Wallington SM5 59 F4
Woodham KT15 52 C1
Park Close Cotts TW20 10 F3
Park Copse RH5 136 D7
Park Corner Dr KT24 112 E7
Park Cotts 10 TW1 6 B1
Park Cres
Sunningdale SL5 29 F3
Twickenham TW2 16 D7
Parkcroft Rd SE12 24 F8
Park Ct
Beckenham BR3 44 B6
16 Croydon CR2 61 C5
Farnham GU9 125 D3
Great Bookham KT23 94 A2
Hounslow TW3 5 B2
New Malden KT3 38 D5
Teddington KT1 37 C8
Upper Tooting SW12 21 A7
Wallington SM6 60 E5
West Norwood SE21 22 D5
Woking GU22 69 F1
Parkdale Cres KT4 57 D7
Park Dr
Bramley GU5 151 F6
Cranleigh GU6 174 F3
Mortlake SW14 7 D3
Sunningdale SL5 29 F3
Weybridge KT13 53 B5
Woking GU22 69 F1
Park End BR1 44 F8
Parker Cl
Crawley RH10 202 D5
Wallington SM5 59 F4
Parker Ct SW19 19 E1
Parke Rd TW16 35 A5
Parker Rd CR0, CR9 61 C6
Parker's Cl KT21 95 E8
Parkers Ct GU19 47 E3
Parker's Hill KT21 95 E8
Parker's La
Ashtead KT21 95 F8
Winkfield RG42 8 B5
Park Farm GU9 126 A5
Park Farm Cl RH12 217 D7
Park Farm Ct BR3 44 B6
Park Farm Ind Est GU15 65 C1
Park Farm Rd
Horsham RH12 217 D7
Kingston upon Thames KT2 17 E1
Parkfield
Godalming GU7 150 F2
Horsham RH12 217 C3
Hounslow TW7 5 E6
13 Wimbledon SW19 19 D1
Parkfield Ave
Feltham TW13 15 A5
Mortlake SW14 7 E3
Parkfield Cl RH11 200 F6
Parkfield Cres TW13 15 A5
Parkfield Ho RG45 45 C4
Parkfield Par TW13 15 A5
Parkfield Rd TW13 15 A5
Parkfields
Croydon CR0 43 F1
Parkfields *continued*
Oxshott KT22 74 D8
Parkfields Ave SW20 39 B7
Parkfields Cl SM5 60 A6
Parkfields Rd TW10 17 F3
PARKGATE 158 D4
Parkgate Cl KT2 18 B2
Park Gate Cotts GU6 174 C3
Park Gate Ct
Teddington TW12 16 C3
11 Woking GU22 69 E1
Parkgate Gdns SW14 7 D2
Parkgate Rd
Newdigate RH5 158 C3
Reigate RH2 139 B8
Wallington SM5, SM6 60 B5
Park Gdns KT2 17 F3
Park Gn KT23 94 A3
Park Hall Rd
Reigate RH2 118 A3
West Norwood SE21 22 D5
Park Hall Road Trad Est
SE21 22 D5
Parkham Ct BR2 44 E7
Park Hill
Forest Hill SE23 23 C7
Richmond TW10 6 F1
Wallington SM5 59 F4
Parkhill Cl GU17 64 D4
Park Hill Cl SM5 59 E5
Park Hill Ct
South Croydon CR0 61 E8
Upper Tooting SW17 20 F5
Parkhill Ho SW16 22 A3
Park Hill Inf Sch CR0 61 E7
Park Hill Jun Sch CR0 61 E7
Park Hill Mans 1 CR0 61 E8
Parkhill Rd GU17 64 D4
Park Hill Rd
Beckenham BR2 44 E7
Ewell KT17 76 F8
South Croydon CR0, CR2 61 E7
Wallington SM6 60 B3
Park Hill Rise CR0 61 F7
Park Hill Sch 19 KT2 18 A1
Park Ho
3 Aldershot GU11 105 A1
Penge SE26 23 A3
Reigate RH2 138 F7
Richmond TW10 6 E1
Park Horsley KT24 113 A6
Park House Cotts GU6 174 F3
Park House Dr RH2 138 F7
Park House Gdns TW1 6 C2
Park Hts
Epsom KT18 76 D5
17 Woking GU22 69 E1
Parkhurst KT19 57 C1
Parkhurst Cotts GU10 187 F8
Parkhurst Fields GU10 167 F1
Parkhurst Gr RH6 160 F4
Parkhurst Rd
Carshalton SM1 59 D6
Guildford GU2 109 B2
Horley RH6 160 E4
Parkin Ho SE20 23 D1
Park La
Ashtead KT21 96 A8
Ashurst Wood RH19 206 D6
Brook GU8 190 A8
Camberley GU15 65 C5
Cheam SM3 58 E4
Cranbourne SL4 9 B7
Cranford TW5 4 A7
Croydon CR0, CR9 61 D7
Guildford GU4 110 D3
Hooley CR5 99 D6
Horton SL3 1 A4
Lingfield RH7 164 F5
Ockley RH5 177 F7
Reigate RH2 138 E8
Richmond TW9 6 D3
Teddington TW11 16 F2
Wallington SM5, SM6 60 A5
Park La E RH2 139 A7
Parkland Dr RG12 27 E8
Parkland Gdns 12 SW19 19 D7
Parkland Gr
Ashford TW15 14 A4
Heath End GU9 125 F8
Hounslow TW7 5 F6
Parkland Rd TW15 14 A4
Parklands
Addlestone KT15 52 C5
Dorking RH5 136 B3
Gomshall GU5 133 A2
Great Bookham KT23 94 A4
Guildford GU2 109 A5
Haslemere GU27 188 E1
Kingston upon Thames KT5 37 F4
Oxted RH8 122 E4
Redhill RH1 119 A3
Parklands Cl SW14 7 C2
Parklands Ct TW5 4 D5
Parklands Par TW5 4 D5
Parklands Pl GU1 110 B1
Parklands Rd SW16, SW17 21 B3
Parklands Way KT4 57 E8
Park Lane Mans CR0 61 D7
PARK LANGLEY 44 D4
Park Lawn CR7 42 C7
Parklawn Ave
Epsom KT18 76 B6
Horley RH6 160 F5
Park Lawn Rd KT13 53 C6

Parkleigh Ct SW19 . . . . . . 40 B7
Parkleigh Rd SW19. . . . . . 40 B7
Park Ley Rd CR3 . . . . . . 101 D6
Parkleys KT2, TW10. . . . . 17 D4
Park Lodge KT23. . . . . . 94 A2
Park Manor 3 SM2 . . . . . 59 C3
Park Mans
　Forest Hill SE26. . . . . . . 23 C5
　Hampton TW12 . . . . 16 B3
Park Mead Prim Sch
　GU6. . . . . 175 A3
Park Mews
　East Molesey KT8 . . . . . 36 C5
　Stanwell TW19. . . . . . . 13 F8
Parkpale La RH3 . . . . . 137 A4
Park Pl
　Blackwater GU17. . . . . . 64 F3
　Hampton TW12 . . . . . . 16 C2
　1 Horsham RH12. . . . . 217 C1
　4 Woking GU22. . . . . . 69 F1
Park Prim Sch GU11 . . . 126 C7
Park Rd
　Albury GU5 . . . . 132 E2
　Aldershot GU11. . . . . . 126 B8
　Ashford TW15 . . . . 14 B3
　Ashtead KT21 . . . . 75 E1
　Banstead SM7 . . . . 78 C3
　Beckenham BR3. . . . . . 23 F1
　Bracknell RG12 . . . . . . 27 D8
　Burstow RH6. . . . . . . 162 C1
　Camberley GU15 . . . . . 65 C4
　Caterham CR3 . . . . . . 100 E4
　Cheam SM3 . . . . 58 E4
　Chiswick W4 . . . . 7 D8
　Crowhurst RH7 . . . . . 143 E2
　Dormans Park RH19 . . 185 F6
　East Grinstead RH19. . 185 D1
　East Molesey KT8 . . . . 36 C5
　Egham TW20 . . . . 12 A4
　Esher KT10 . . . . 55 B6
　Farnborough GU14 . . . 105 E8
　Farnham GU9. . . . . . . 125 D4
　Faygate RH12 . . . . . . 199 F1
　Feltham TW13 . . . . . . 15 D4
　Fickleshole CR6 . . . . . 82 E5
　Forest Row RH18. . . . 206 F2
　Godalming GU7 . . . . . 150 E2
　Guildford GU1 . . . . . . 109 D1
　Hackbridge SM6 . . . . . 60 B8
　Hampton TW12 . . . . . 16 C3
　Haslemere GU27 . . . . 208 C6
　Hounslow TW3, TW7 . . . 5 C2
　Isleworth TW7. . . . . . . 6 B5
　Kenley CR8. . . . . 80 C4
　Kingston upon Thames KT2. 18 A1
　Limpsfield RH8. . . . . . 122 F7
　Lower Halliford TW17 . . 34 A1
　Mitcham SW19 . . . . . . 20 E2
　New Malden KT3 . . . . . 38 D5
　Redhill RH1 . . . . 118 F3
　Richmond TW10. . . . . . 6 F1
　Sandhurst GU47 . . . . . 64 C8
　Slinfold RH13 . . . . . . 215 D3
　South Norwood SE25. . 42 E5
　Stanwell TW19 . . . . . . 2 C1
　Sunbury TW16 . . . . . . 15 B1
　Surbiton KT5 . . . . 37 C8
　Teddington, Hampton Wick
　　KT1 . . . . 37 C8
　Teddington TW11. . . . . 16 F2
　Twickenham TW1. . . . . 6 C1
　Wallington SM6 . . . . . 60 B5
　Woking GU22. . . . . . . 70 A2
　Wokingham RG40 . . . . 25 B6
Park Rise
　Forest Hill SE23. . . . . . 23 E7
　Horsham RH12 . . . . . 217 B4
　Leatherhead KT22 . . . . 95 B6
Parkrise KT22 . . . . 95 B6
Park Rise Rd SE23 . . . . . 23 E7
Park Road Ho 3 KT2. . . . 18 A1
Park Row GU9 . . . . . . 125 B3
Park Sch The GU22. . . . . 70 A2
Park Sheen SW14. . . . . . 7 B3
Parkshot TW9 . . . . 6 E3
Parkside
　1 Beckenham BR3. . . . 44 B7
　Cheam SM3 . . . . 58 E4
　Crawley RH10 . . . . . . 201 E6
　East Grinstead RH19. . 185 D1
　Hale GU9 . . . . 125 C6
　Teddington TW12. . . . . 16 D3
　Wimbledon SW19 . . . . 19 D4
　Woodham KT15 . . . . . 52 C1
Parkside Cl
　East Horsley KT24 . . . . 92 F2
　Penge SE20 . . . . 23 C1
Parkside Cotts
　Tatsfield TN16 . . . . . . 103 E6
　West Clandon GU4. . . 111 A3
Parkside Cres KT5. . . . . 38 C3
Parkside Ct
　Epsom KT17 . . . . 76 F6
　Redhill RH1 . . . . 119 A5
　Weybridge KT13 . . . . . 53 A6
Parkside Gdns
　Coulsdon CR5 . . . . . . 79 B2
　Wimbledon SW19 . . . . 19 D4
Parkside Ho
　Guildford GU4 . . . . . . 110 A5
　2 West Byfleet KT14 . . 71 A7
　Wimbledon SW19 . . . . 19 D3
Parkside Hospl (Private)
　SW19 . . . . 19 D5

Parkside Mews
　Chelsham CR6 . . . . . . 82 A3
　Horsham RH12. . . . . . 217 D2
Parkside Pl
　East Horsley KT24 . . . . 92 F2
　Staines TW18. . . . . . . 13 A2
Parkside Rd
　Hounslow TW3. . . . . . . 5 B2
　Sunningdale SL5 . . . . . 30 A4
Parkside Sch KT11 . . . . 74 A1
Park Sq KT10 . . . . 55 B6
Park St
　Bagshot GU19 . . . . . . 47 E3
　Camberley GU15 . . . . . 65 C5
　4 Camberley GU15 . . 65 C6
　10 Croydon CR0. . . . . 61 D8
　Croydon CR0, CR9 . . . . 61 C8
　Guildford GU1, GU2. . . 130 C7
　Horsham RH12 . . . . . 217 D2
　Poyle SL3 . . . . 1 D6
　Slinfold RH13. . . . . . . 215 C3
　Teddington TW11. . . . . 16 E2
Parkstone Dr GU15. . . . . 65 C4
PARK STREET 215 C4
Park Terr
　1 Carshalton SM5 . . . 59 E7
　New Malden KT4 . . . . . 39 A1
Park Terr E RH13 . . . . . 217 D1
Park Terr W RH13 . . . . . 217 D1
Park The
　Forest Hill SE23. . . . . . 23 C7
　Great Bookham KT23. . 94 A3
　Wallington SM5 . . . . . 59 F5
Park View
　Addlestone KT15 . . . . . 52 C5
　Ascot SL5. . . . . 29 E8
　Bagshot GU19 . . . . . . 47 D3
　Banstead SM7 . . . . . . 78 B4
　Caterham CR3 . . . . . . 101 A2
　Crawley RH11 . . . . . . 201 C5
　Great Bookham KT23. . 94 A2
　Horley RH6 . . . . 161 A3
　Morden SM4 . . . . 40 D4
　New Malden KT3 . . . . . 38 F6
　Purley CR8. . . . . 80 B8
　Tandridge RH8. . . . . . 143 B5
Park View Cl SM5 . . . . . 60 A3
Parkview Cres 2 KT4. . . . 39 C1
Parkview Ct
　Sunbury TW16 . . . . . . 35 A6
　Twickenham TW1. . . . . 17 C8
Park View Ct
　Croydon SE20 . . . . 43 B8
　Woking GU22. . . . . . . 89 F8
Park View Dr CR4 . . . . . 40 D7
Park View Ho TW12 . . . . 16 C3
Parkview Lodge BR3 . . . . 44 B6
Parkview Rd CR0, CR9 . . 43 A1
Park View Rd
　Leatherhead KT22 . . . . 94 F7
　Salfords RH1 . . . . 140 A1
　Woldingham CR3 . . . . 101 F5
Parkview Vale GU4. . . . . 110 C3
Parkway
　Camberley GU15 . . . . . 65 C3
　Crawley RH10 . . . . . . 202 C7
　Crowthorne RG45 . . . . 45 A5
　Dorking RH4 . . . . 136 A8
　Guildford GU1 . . . . . . 109 E2
　Horley RH6 . . . . 161 A3
　New Addington CR0. . . 63 C1
　Oatlands Park KT13. . . 53 D6
　West Barnes SW20 . . . 39 D5
Park Way
　East Molesey KT8 . . . . 36 B6
　Feltham TW14 . . . . . . 15 B8
　Great Bookham KT23. . 94 A4
　Horsham RH12 . . . . . 217 C2
Parkway Ho
　2 Horsham RH12. . . . 217 C1
　Mortlake SW14 . . . . . . 7 D3
Parkway The TW5. . . . . . 4 B7
Parkway Trad Est TW5. . . . 4 A7
Park Wlk KT21 . . . . 95 F8
Parkwood BR3. . . . . . . 24 A1
Parkwood Ave KT10. . . . 36 C1
Park Wood Cl SM7 . . . . . 77 D4
Parkwood Gr TW16 . . . . 35 A6
Parkwood Rd
　Biggin Hill TN16. . . . . 103 F6
　Hounslow TW7. . . . . . . 5 F6
　Nutfield RH1 . . . . 119 E2
　Wimbledon SW19 . . . . 19 F3
Park Wood Rd SM7 . . . . 77 D4
Park Wood View SM7 . . . 77 D4
Park Works Rd RH1 . . . . 119 E2
Parley Dr GU21 . . . . . . 69 C1
Parliamentary Rd GU24 . . 87 A6
Parliament Mews SW14 . . 7 C5
Parnall Ho 11 SE19. . . . . 22 E4
Parnell Cl RH10. . . . . . 202 D4
Parnell Gdns KT13 . . . . 72 A8
Parnham Ave GU18 . . . . 67 D8
Parr Ave KT17 . . . . 58 B2
Parr Cl KT22 . . . . 94 F7
Parr Ct
　1 Epsom KT19 . . . . . . 57 E2
　Feltham TW13 . . . . . . 15 C4
　1 Knaphill GU21. . . . . 88 C8
Parris Croft RH4 . . . . . 136 C4
Parritt Rd RH1 . . . . . . 119 B3
Parr's Pl TW12. . . . . . . 16 A1
Parry Cl
　Horsham RH13 . . . . . 218 C4
　Stoneleigh KT17. . . . . 58 A3
Parry Dr KT13. . . . . . . 53 A1

Parry Rd SE25 . . . . 42 E6
Parsley Gdns CR0 . . . . . 43 D1
Parsonage Bsns Pk
　RH12. . . . . 217 E4
Parsonage Cl
　Warlingham CR6 . . . . . 81 F3
　Westcott RH4 . . . . . . 135 C5
Parsonage Farm Inf Sch
　GU14. . . . . 84 C5
Parsonage La RH4 . . . . 135 C6
Parsonage Rd
　Cranleigh GU6. . . . . . 174 D3
　Englefield Green TW20 . 11 D3
　Horsham RH13 . . . . . 217 D1
Parsonage Sq 3 RH4 . . . 136 A7
Parsonage Way
　Frimley GU16. . . . . . . 65 E1
　Horsham RH12 . . . . . 217 E4
Parsons Cl
　Aldershot GU11 . . . . . 105 B2
　Haslemere GU27 . . . . 208 C8
　Horley RH6 . . . . 160 E4
　Sutton SM1 . . . . 59 B7
Parsons Field GU47 . . . . 64 B8
Parsonsfield Cl SM7. . . . 77 D4
Parsonsfield Rd SM7 . . . 77 D4
Parsons Gn
　Guildford GU1 . . . . . . 109 D3
　Haslemere GU27 . . . . 208 C8
Parsons Ho 20 SW12 . . . 21 E8
Parsons La GU26. . . . . . 188 D6
Parsons Mead KT8 . . . . . 36 C6
Parson's Mead CR0 . . . . 42 B1
Parson's Pightle CR5. . . 100 A7
Parthia Cl KT20 . . . . 97 B8
Partridge Cl
　Bracknell RG12 . . . . . . 26 E5
　Crondall GU10 . . . . . . 124 D8
　Frimley GU16. . . . . . . 65 E1
Partridge Knoll CR8. . . . 80 B6
Partridge La
　Newdigate RH5, RH12. . 179 F3
　Parkgate RH5 . . . . . . 158 E2
Partridge Mead SM7 . . . 77 C4
Partridge Pl RH10. . . . . 204 C6
Partridge Rd 8 TW12 . . . 16 A2
Partridge Way GU4 . . . . 110 D3
Parvis Rd KT14. . . . . . . 71 D7
Pascals Coll BR3. . . . . . 44 A7
Paschal Rd GU15. . . . . . 65 F8
Passfield Lodge GU18 . . . 48 C1
Passfields SE6 . . . . 24 C5
Passingham Ho TW5 . . . . 5 A8
Pastens Rd RH8. . . . . . 123 C4
Paston Cl SM6 . . . . 60 C7
Pasture Rd SE6. . . . . . . 24 F7
Pasture The RH10. . . . . 202 C6
Pasturewood Rd RH5 . . . 155 D6
Patcham Ct SM2 . . . . . . 59 C2
Patching Cl RH11 . . . . . 200 F7
Patchings RH13. . . . . . 217 F3
Paterson Cl GU16. . . . . . 66 C3
Pates Manor Dr TW14 . . . 14 D8
Pathfield GU8 . . . . 191 B4
Pathfield Cl
　Chiddingfold GU8. . . . 191 B4
　Rudgwick RH12 . . . . . 214 D7
Pathfield Rd
　Rudgwick RH12 . . . . . 214 D7
　Streatham SW16 . . . . . 21 D2
Pathfields
　Haslemere GU27 . . . . 208 C7
　Shere GU5. . . . . 133 A4
Pathfields Cl GU27 . . . . 208 D7
Pathfinders The GU14. . . 84 C3
Path Link RH10. . . . . . . 201 E7
Path The SW19 . . . . 40 B8
Pathway Ho SW17. . . . . . 20 F2
Pathway Lo CR4 . . . . . . 40 F8
Pathway The GU23. . . . . 90 F2
Patmore La KT12. . . . . . 53 F4
Patricia Gdns SM2 . . . . . 78 A8
Patrington Cl RH11 . . . . 201 A3
Patten Ash Dr RG40 . . . . 25 E7
Pattenden Rd SE23, SE6. . 23 F7
Patten Rd SW18 . . . . . . 20 E8
Patterdale Cl
　Catford BR1. . . . . 24 E2
　Crawley RH10 . . . . . . 201 C4
Patterson Ct SE19 . . . . . 22 F2
Patterson Rd SE19 . . . . . 22 F2
Pat Williams Ho SE27 . . . 22 C5
Paul Cl GU11 . . . . 125 E8
Paul Gdns CR0 . . . . 61 F8
Pauline Cres TW2. . . . . . 16 C7
Pauls Mead RH7 . . . . . 164 E5
Paul's Pl KT21 . . . . 96 B8
Paul Vanson Ct KT12 . . . 54 D4
Paved Ct 8 TW9. . . . . . . 6 D2
Pavement Sq CR0. . . . . . 43 A1
Pavement The
　Crawley RH10 . . . . . . 201 E6
　11 Isleworth SW7. . . . . 6 A4
　11 West Norwood SE27. . . 22 C4
Pavilion Cl
　3 Merton SW19 . . . . . 19 E1
　Streatham SW16 . . . . . 21 F1
Pavilion Gdns TW18. . . . 13 B1
Pavilion Rd GU11 . . . . . 104 C1
Pavilions End The GU15 . . 65 D3
Pavilions in the Park (L Ctr)
　RH12. . . . . 217 D2
Pavilion Sq SW17 . . . . . 20 F5
Pavilions The BR3 . . . . . 24 A2
Pavilion The RH20. . . . . 98 C4
Pavilion Way RH19. . . . . 205 E8
Pavilion Ct GU6 . . . . . . 174 C3
Paviors GU9 . . . . 125 C3

Pawley Cl GU10 . . . . . . 126 F7
Pawleyne Cl SE20 . . . . . 23 C1
Pawson's Rd CR0 . . . . . 42 C4
Pax Cl RH11 . . . . 200 E4
Paxton Cl
　Richmond TW9. . . . . . . 6 F5
　Walton-on-Thames KT12 . 35 C2
Paxton Ct
　1 Forest Hill SE26. . . . 23 E4
　Mitcham CR4 . . . . 40 F7
Paxton Gdns GU21 . . . . . 70 E7
Paxton Pl SE27 . . . . 22 E4
Paxton Prim Sch SE19 . . . 22 E2
Paxton Rd
　Chiswick W4 . . . . 7 E8
　Forest Hill SE23. . . . . . 23 E5
Payley Dr RG40 . . . . . . 25 E8
Payne Cl RH10 . . . . . . 202 D8
Paynesfield Ave SW14. . . . 7 D4
Paynesfield Rd
　Tatsfield TN16 . . . . . . 103 D7
　Tatsfield TN16 . . . . . . 103 D7
PAYNES GREEN 197 D8
Paynetts Ct KT13. . . . . . 53 D5
Peabody Cl CR0. . . . . . . 43 C1
Peabody Est SE24 . . . . . 22 C8
Peabody Hill SE21 . . . . . 22 C7
Peabody Rd GU14 . . . . . 105 D8
Peacemaker Cl RH11. . . . 200 E4
Peaches Cl SM2. . . . . . . 58 E3
Peaches Ct SM2 . . . . . . 58 E3
Peach Rd TW13 . . . . 15 A7
Peach St SE20. . . . . 25 C6
Peach Tree Cl GU14. . . . . 85 A7
Peacock Ave TW14. . . . . 14 C7
Peacock Cotts RG40. . . . . 26 C5
Peacock Gdns CR0, CR2. . 62 E1
Peacock La RG12 . . . . . . 26 D6
Peacocks Sh Ctr The
　1 Woking GU21 . . . . . 69 E2
　Woking GU21. . . . . . . 221 C2
Peacock Wlk 8 RH11 . . . 201 A3
Peakfield GU10 . . . . . . 167 C7
Peak Hill SE26. . . . . 23 C4
Peak Hill Ave SE26. . . . . 23 C4
Peak Hill Gdns SE26. . . . 23 C4
Peak Rd GU2 . . . . 109 A4
Peaks Hill CR8. . . . . 60 E1
Peaks Hill Rise CR8 . . . . 60 E1
Peak The SE26. . . . . 23 C5
Peall Rd CR0 . . . . 41 F3
Peall Rd Ind Est CR0 . . . 41 F3
Pearce Cl 2 CR4 . . . . . . 41 A7
Pearcefield Ave 5 SE23. . 23 C7
Pearce Ho 7 SW2 . . . . . 21 E8
Pearfield Rd SE23. . . . . . 23 E5
Pearing Cl KT4 . . . . 58 D8
Pearl Ct GU21. . . . . 68 E3
Pearmain Cl TW17 . . . . . 34 B4
Pears Ave TW17 . . . . . . 34 E6
Pearson Ct SE8 . . . . 80 B8
Pearson Ct SM4. . . . . . . 40 B4
Pearson Rd RH10 . . . . . 202 C6
Pearson Way CR4 . . . . . 41 A8
Pears Rd TW3 . . . . 5 C4
Pear Tree Cl
　Addlestone KT15 . . . . . 52 A5
　Chessington KT9 . . . . . 57 A5
　Mitcham CR4 . . . . 40 E7
Pear Tree Ct GU15 . . . . . 66 B8
PEARTREE GREEN 192 D7
Pear Tree Hill RH1 . . . . . 161 A8
Pear Tree Ho 4 SE19 . . . 22 E2
Pear Tree La GU10 . . . . . 145 F3
Pear Tree Rd
　Addlestone KT15 . . . . . 52 A5
　Ashford TW15 . . . . . . 14 C3
Peary Cl RH11 . . . . 201 A3
Pease Pottage Hill RH11 201 D1
PEASLAKE 154 D6
Peaslake Ct SM2 . . . . . . 59 C3
Peaslake La GU5. . . . . . 154 D6
Peaslake Rd GU6 . . . . . 154 D2
Peaslake Sch GU5 . . . . . 154 E7
PEASMARSH 130 C1
Peat Comm GU8 . . . . . . 148 C2
Peatmore Ave GU22. . . . . 71 A3
Peatmore Cl GU22 . . . . . 71 A3
Peatmore Dr GU24 . . . . . 87 C6
Pebble Cl KT20 . . . . 116 E6
Pebble Hill KT24 . . . . . . 112 C2
Pebble Hill Cotts RH8 . . . 123 B6
Pebblehill Rd KT20, RH3. . 116 E5
Pebble La KT18, KT22 . . . 96 A5
Pebworth Ct 10 RH1. . . . 119 A3
Pebworth Lo SE26 . . . . . 59 B3
Pebworth Lodge SE25. . . 42 F5
Peckarmans Wood SE21,
　SE26. . . . . 23 A5
Peek Cres SW19 . . . . . . 19 D3
Peeks Brook La
　Crawley RH6 . . . . 182 E7
　Horley RH6 . . . . 161 F2
Peel Ave GU16 . . . . 86 A7
Peel Ct GU14 . . . . 105 C8
Peel Ho TW20 . . . . 12 A3
Peel Ret Ctr The RG12. . . 27 B7
Pegasus Ave GU12 . . . . . 105 E2
Pegasus Cl GU12 . . . . . 105 E1
Pegasus Ct
　Banstead SM7 . . . . . . 78 A4
　Caterham CR3 . . . . . . 101 A4
　Crawley RH11 . . . . . . 200 E4
　Farnborough GU14 . . . 85 E1
　Kingston upon Thames KT1 . 37 D6

Pegasus Ct continued
　12 Leatherhead KT22 . . 95 C6
　Sutton SM1 . . . . 59 B8
Pegasus Pl RH10. . . . . . 182 A1
Pegasus Rd
　Croydon CR0, CR9 . . . . 61 A4
　Farnborough GU14 . . . 84 F7
Pegasus Way RH19. . . . . 186 B3
Peggotty Pl GU47 . . . . . . 45 E2
Pegg Rd TW5. . . . . 4 D7
Pegler Way RH11. . . . . . 201 D6
Pegwell Cl RH11. . . . . . 200 F4
Peket Cl TW18. . . . . 32 E8
Pelabon Ho 20 TW1. . . . . 6 D1
Peldon Ct CR3. . . . . 6 F2
Pelham Cl
　Crawley RH11 . . . . . . 201 B2
　Great Bookham KT23. . 94 C1
　5 Horsham RH12. . . . 217 B2
　Staines TW18. . . . . . . 13 B3
Pelham Ct Bsns Ctr
　RH11. . . . . 201 B2
Pelham Dr RH11 . . . . . . 201 A2
Pelham Ho CR3 . . . . . . 100 F3
Pelham Pl
　Crawley RH11 . . . . . . 201 B2
　Rowledge GU10 . . . . . 146 A4
Pelham Prim Sch 14
　SW19 . . . . 20 A1
Pelham Rd
　Merton SW19 . . . . 20 A1
　Penge BR3, SE20. . . . . 43 C7
Pelhams Cl KT10. . . . . . 55 A6
Pelhams Wlk KT10 . . . . . 55 A6
Pelham Way KT23. . . . . . 94 C1
Pelinore Rd SE6 . . . . . . 24 E6
Pelling Hill SL4 . . . . 11 B7
Pellings Cl BR2. . . . . . . 44 E6
Pelman Way KT19. . . . . . 57 B1
Pelton Ave SM2. . . . . . . 59 B1
Pelton Ct CR2. . . . . 61 C4
Pemberley Chase KT19. . 57 B5
Pemberley Cl KT19. . . . . 57 B5
Pemberton Cl TW19. . . . 13 E7
Pemberton Ho SE26. . . . 23 A4
Pemberton Pl KT10. . . . . 55 C7
Pemberton Rd KT8. . . . . 36 C5
Pemberton Terr KT8 . . . . 36 C5
Pembley Gn RH10. . . . . 183 E3
Pembridge Ave TW4 . . . . 15 F7
Pembroke RG12 . . . . . . 27 A1
Pembroke Ave
　Hersham KT12 . . . . . . 54 D6
　Surbiton KT5 . . . . 38 B4
Pembroke Broadway
　GU15 . . . . 65 C5
Pembroke Cl
　Ascot SL5. . . . . 29 C4
　Banstead SM7 . . . . . . 78 B2
Pembroke Ct
　Beckenham BR3 . . . . . 44 B6
　Woking GU22. . . . . . . 70 B3
Pembroke Gdns GU22 . . . 70 A1
Pembroke Ho SW19 . . . . 20 D3
Pembroke Mews SL5. . . . 29 D4
Pembroke Pl TW7. . . . . . . 5 E5
Pembroke Rd
　Crawley RH10 . . . . . . 182 C1
　Mitcham CR4 . . . . 41 A7
　South Norwood SE25. . 42 E5
　Woking GU22. . . . . . . 70 A2
Pembroke Villas TW9 . . . 6 D3
Pembrook Lodge 2
　SW16 . . . . 21 F5
Pembury Ave KT4 . . . . . 39 A2
Pembury Cl
　Hayes BR2. . . . . 44 F2
　Wallington CR5 . . . . . 79 A5
Pembury Ct UB3 . . . . 3 D8
Pembury Pl 5 GU12 . . . 105 C1
Pembury Rd SE25 . . . . . 43 A5
Pemdevon Rd CR0 . . . . . 42 A2
Penarth Ct SM2. . . . . . . 59 C3
Penates KT10. . . . . 55 D6
Penberth Rd SE6 . . . . . . 24 C7
Penceat Ct SE20 . . . . . . 43 C7
Pendarves Rd SW20 . . . . 39 C8
Pendell Ave UB3 . . . . 3 F7
Pendell Ct RH1 . . . . . . 120 B4
Pendell Rd RH1 . . . . . . 120 B4
Pendennis Cl KT14. . . . . 71 A5
Pendennis Rd SW16 . . . . 21 E4
Pendenza KT11 . . . . 73 E3
Penderel Rd TW3 . . . . . . 5 A2
Penderry Rise SE6 . . . . . 24 D6
Pendine Pl RG12 . . . . . . 27 B4
Pendlebury RG12 . . . . . . 27 A2
Pendle Ho 18 SE26. . . . . 23 A5
Pendle Rd SW16 . . . . . . 21 B3
Pendleton Cl RH1 . . . . . 139 F7
Pendleton Rd RH1 . . . . . 139 E6
Pendragon Rd BR1. . . . . 24 F5
Pendragon Way GU15 . . . 66 D3
Penerley Rd SE6 . . . . . . 24 B7
Penfold Cl CR0, CR9 . . . . 61 A7
Penfold Croft GU9 . . . . . 125 F4
Penfold Ct 7 CR4. . . . . . 41 A7
Penfold Manor GU27 . . . 208 D6
Penfold Rd RH10. . . . . . 202 B2
PENGE 23 D2
Penge East Sta SE20 . . . 23 C2
Penge La SE20. . . . . 23 D1
Penge Rd SE20, SE25. . . . 43 A6
Penge West Sta SE20 . . . 23 B2
Pengilly Ho GU1 . . . . . . 110 C1
Pengilly Rd GU9 . . . . . . 125 B1
Penhurst GU21. . . . . . . 69 F5
Peninsula Pl RG45 . . . . . 45 C4

Peninsular Cl
Camberley GU15 . . . . 66 B7
Feltham TW13 . . . . 3 E1
Penistone Rd SW16 . . . . . . 21 E1
Penlee Ho [10] GU22 . . . . . . 89 E8
Pennards The TW16 . . . . . 35 C6
Penn Cl 181 D1
Pennefather's Rd GU11. . 104 F3
Penner Cl SW19 . . . . 19 E6
Penners Gdns KT6 . . . . . . 37 E2
Pennine Cl RH11. . . . . 201 B6
Pennine Way
Farnborough GU14 . . . . . 84 E7
Harlington UB7 . . . . 3 D7
Pennings Ave GU3 . . . . . . 108 F3
Pennington Cl [10] SE27 . . 22 D4
Pennington Dr KT13. . . . . 53 E7
Pennington Lodge [18] KT5 37 E4
Penns Wood GU14 . . . . . . 85 D1
Pennthorpe Sch RH12. . . 214 D7
Pennycroft CR0 . . . . 62 E2
Penny Dr GU3 . . . . 108 B2
Pennyfield KT11 . . . . 73 A6
Penny La TW17 . . . . 34 E2
Pennymead Dr KT24 . . . . 112 F8
Pennymead Rise KT24. . . 112 F8
Penny Mews SW12 . . . . . . 21 B8
PENNY POT. 68 C7
Pennypot La GU24 . . . . . . 68 C7
Penny Royal SM6 . . . . 60 D4
Penrhyn Cl
Aldershot GU11. . . . . 105 B1
Caterham CR3 . . . . 100 D7
Penrhyn Cres SW14 . . . . . 7 C3
Penrhyn Gdns KT1 . . . . . . 37 D5
Penrhyn Rd KT1 . . . . 37 E6
Penrith Cl
Beckenham BR3. . . . . 44 B8
Redhill RH2. . . . . 118 E2
Penrith Pl SE27 . . . . 22 B6
Penrith Rd
New Malden KT3 . . . . 38 D5
South Norwood CR7 . . . . 42 C7
Penrith St SW16 . . . . 21 C2
Penrose Ct TW20 . . . . 11 C2
Penrose Dr KT19. . . . . 76 A8
Penrose Gdns GU12. . . . . 106 A6
Penrose Rd KT22. . . . . 94 C5
Penryn Dr GU35. . . . . 187 C5
Penryn Ho [5] RH1. . . . . . 119 A3
Pensfold La RH12. . . . . . . 214 A5
Pensford Ave TW9 . . . . . . 7 A5
Pensford Cl RG45. . . . . . . 45 B7
Penshurst Ave TW10 . . . . 202 D7
Penshurst Ct CR2 . . . . . . 61 B3
Penshurst Gn BR2. . . . . . . 44 F4
Penshurst Rd CR7. . . . . . . 42 B4
Penshurst Rise GU16. . . . 85 F8
Penshurst Way SM2. . . . . 59 A3
Penshurst Wlk [6] BR2. . . 44 F4
Penstock Mews [7] SW11. 151 A5
Pentelow Gdns TW14 . . . . 4 A1
Pentire Cl GU21. . . . . 69 E5
Pentland Ave TW17 . . . . . 34 A4
Pentland Pl GU14 . . . . 84 E7
Pentlands BR3. . . . . 44 C8
Pentlands Cl CR4 . . . . 41 B6
Pentney Rd
Streatham SW12 . . . . 21 C7
Wimbledon SW19, SW20. . 39 E8
Penton Ave TW18 . . . . . . 32 F8
Penton Ct TW18 . . . . 12 F2
Penton Hall TW18. . . . . . . 33 A8
Penton Hall Dr TW18. . . . 33 A8
Penton Ho SM2. . . . . 59 C3
Penton Hook Marina
KT16 . . . . 33 A6
Penton Hook Rd TW18 . . 33 A8
Penton Rd TW18 . . . . 12 F1
Pentreath Ave GU2 . . . . . 129 F8
Penwerris Ave TW5, TW7. 5 C7
Penwerris Ct TW7 . . . . . . 5 C7
Penwith Dr GU27 . . . . 207 E5
Penwith Rd SW18 . . . . . . 20 B6
Penwith Wlk GU22 . . . . . . 89 D8
Penwood End GU22 . . . . . 89 B6
Penwood Gdns RG12 . . . . 26 D3
Penwood Ho SW15. . . . . . 7 F1
Penwortham Prim Sch
SW17 . . . . 21 B2
Penwortham Rd
South Croydon CR2 . . . . . 61 D1
Streatham SW16 . . . . 21 C2
Peperham Cotts GU27. . . 208 C7
Peperham Ho GU27 . . . . . 208 C7
Peperham Rd GU27 . . . . . 208 C8
PEPER HAROW. 149 C5
Peper Harow Ho GU8 . . . 149 D4
Peper Harow La GU8. . . . 149 C6
Peperharow Rd GU7 . . . . 150 C6
Peppard Rd RH10 . . . . . . 202 D3
Pepperbox La GU5. . . . . . 173 E4
Pepper Cl CR3. . . . . 100 E2
Peppercorn Cl CR7. . . . . . 42 D7
Peppermint Cl CR0. . . . . . 41 E2
Peppin Ct [2] KT12 . . . . . 35 C1
Pepys Cl
Ashtead KT21 . . . . 76 A2
Brands Hill SL3. . . . . 1 B8
Pepys Ct SW20. . . . . 39 C7
Pepys Rd SW20 . . . . 39 C8
Perak Ct KT5 . . . . 38 C2
Peralta Terr CR4 . . . . 41 E5
Percheron Cl TW7. . . . . . 5 F4
Percheron Dr GU21 . . . . . 88 C8
Percival Cl KT22. . . . . 74 B8
Percival Rd
Feltham TW13 . . . . 14 F6

Percival Rd *continued*
Mortlake SW14 . . . . 7 C3
Percival Way KT19 . . . . . . 57 D6
Percy Ave TW15 . . . . 14 A3
Percy Bilton Ct TW5. . . . . 5 B6
Percy Bryant Rd TW16. . . 14 E1
Percy Ct [1] KT5. . . . . . . 37 F3
Percy Gdns
[4] Isleworth TW7 . . . . . . 6 A4
New Malden KT4 . . . . 38 E1
Percy Ho [4] SW16 . . . . . 21 C4
Percy Rd
Carshalton CR4 . . . . 41 A2
Croydon SE25 . . . . 43 A4
Guildford GU2 . . . . 109 B3
Hampton TW12 . . . . 16 A1
Horsham RH12 . . . . 217 B3
Isleworth TW7 . . . . 6 A3
Penge SE20 . . . . 43 D8
Twickenham TW2 . . . . . . 16 C7
Percy Way TW2 . . . . 16 C7
Peregrine Cl
Bracknell RG12. . . . . 27 B4
Cranleigh GU6 . . . . 174 E4
Peregrine Ct SW16. . . . . . 21 F4
Peregrine Gdns CR0 . . . . 62 E8
Peregrine Rd TW16 . . . . . 34 F7
Peregrine Way SW19,
SW20 . . . . 19 C1
Perifield SE21 . . . . 22 C7
Perimeter Rd E RH6. . . . . 182 B6
Perimeter Rd N RH6. . . . . 181 D8
Perimeter Rd S RH6. . . . . 181 E5
Perkin Cl TW3 . . . . 5 B3
Perkins Ct TW15 . . . . 13 F3
Perkins Way RG41 . . . . . . 25 A5
Perkstead Ct [6] RH11. . . 201 A3
Perleybrooke La GU21. . . 69 A2
Perowne St GU11. . . . . . . 104 F2
Perram Works GU4 . . . . . 110 C4
Perran Rd SE24, SW2. . . . 22 B6
Perran Wlk [16] TW8 . . . . 6 E8
Perrin Cl TW15 . . . . 13 F3
Perrin Ct
[2] Kingston upon Thames
KT2 . . . . 37 E7
Sutton SM1 . . . . 59 A5
Perryfield Ho [7] RH10. . . 201 D5
Perryfield Rd RH11. . . . . . 201 D5
Perryfield Way TW10. . . . 17 B6
Perry Hill SE6. . . . . 23 F5
Perry Ho [23] SW2. . . . . . 21 E8
Perry How KT4 . . . . 38 F1
Perrylands RH6 . . . . 180 F7
Perrylands La RH6 . . . . . . 162 A2
Perrymount Prim Sch [6]
SE23 . . . . 23 D6
Perryn Ct [2] TW1 . . . . . . 17 A8
Perry Oaks RG12. . . . . . . 27 E7
Perry Rise SE23, SE6. . . . 23 E5
Perry Vale SE23. . . . . 23 D6
Perry Way
Bracknell RG12. . . . . 27 E7
Farnham GU9. . . . . 125 B7
Lightwater GU18 . . . . . . 66 F7
Perrywood Bsns Pk RH1. 140 B1
Persant Rd SE6 . . . . 24 C6
Perseverance Cotts GU23. 91 C6
Persfield Cl KT17. . . . . . . 58 A1
Persfield Mews [2] KT17. 57 F1
Pershore Gr SM5 . . . . 40 D3
Perth Cl
Crawley RH11 . . . . 181 D1
Wimbledon SW20 . . . . . . 39 A7
Perth Rd BR3 . . . . 44 C7
Perth Way RH12 . . . . 217 B4
Perystreete SE23 . . . . . . 23 C6
Petavel Rd TW11 . . . . . . 16 E2
Peter Ave RH8 . . . . 122 D6
Peterborough Rd
Carshalton CR4, SM4,
SM5. . . . . 40 E3
Crawley RH10 . . . . 201 D4
Guildford GU2 . . . . 108 F3
Peterhouse Cl GU47. . . . . 45 F2
Peterhouse Par RH10 . . . 182 C1
Peter Kennedy Ct CR0. . . 43 F3
Peterlee Wlk RH11. . . . . . 200 E2
Peters Ct KT18. . . . . 76 E5
Petersfield Ave TW15,
TW18 . . . . 13 C2
Petersfield Cres CR5. . . . 79 E4
Petersfield Rd TW18 . . . . 13 C3
Petersfield Rise SW15. . . 19 B7
PETERSHAM 17 E7
Petersham Ave KT14 . . . . 71 E7
Petersham Cl
Byfleet KT14. . . . . 71 E7
Cheam SM1 . . . . 59 A5
Richmond TW10. . . . . . . 17 D6
Petersham Rd TW10 . . . . 17 E7
Petersham Terr CR0 . . . . 60 E7
Peters Ho SM3. . . . . 58 D5
Petersmead Cl KT20 . . . . 97 B4
Peter's Path SE26. . . . . . 23 B4
Peterstow Cl SW19. . . . . 19 E6
Peters Wood RH8 . . . . . . 178 C5
Peterwood Pk CR9. . . . . . 60 F8
Peterwood Way CR0 . . . . 60 F8
Petrel Ct [8] SE21 . . . . . . 22 D6

Petridge Rd RH1. . . . . 139 F4
Petters Rd KT21 . . . . 75 F3
Petts La TW17 . . . . 34 A5
Petworth Cl
Coulsdon CR5 . . . . 99 C8
Frimley GU16. . . . . 85 F8
Petworth Ct
Crawley RH11 . . . . 200 F3
Frimley GU15 . . . . 65 F4
Haslemere GU27 . . . . . . 208 D6
[2] Woking GU22 . . . . . . 70 B3
Petworth Dr RH12 . . . . . . 217 F7
Petworth Gdns SW20. . . . 39 B6
Petworth Rd
Chiddingfold, Ansteadbrook
GU27. . . . . 209 B6
Chiddingfold GU8. . . . . . 191 C4
Witley GU8. . . . . 170 F5
Wormley GU8. . . . . 171 A1
Pevensey Cl
Crawley RH10 . . . . 202 C5
Hounslow TW7. . . . . 5 C7
Pevensey Ct SW16 . . . . . 22 A5
Pevensey Ho RH2 . . . . . . 139 B5
Pevensey Rd
Feltham TW13 . . . . 15 E7
Upper Tooting SW17 . . . . 20 D4
Pevensey Road Nature
Reserve★ TW4. . . . . 15 E7
Pevensey Way GU16. . . . . 86 A8
Peverel Rd RH11. . . . . 200 E5
Peveril Dr TW11 . . . . 16 D3
Pewley Bank GU1. . . . . . . 130 E7
Pewley Down Inf Sch
GU1. . . . . 130 E7
Pewley Down Nature
Reserve★ GU10. . . . . . . 130 F6
Pewley Hill GU1. . . . . 130 E7
Pewley Point GU1. . . . . . . 130 E7
Pewley Way GU1. . . . . . . 130 F7
Pewsey Vale RG12 . . . . . . 27 F4
Peyton's Cotts RH1 . . . . . 119 F3
Pharaoh Cl CR4. . . . . 40 F2
Pheasant Cl CR8 . . . . 80 B6
Pheasant Way GU6. . . . . . 26 D5
Philanthropic Rd RH1. . . . 140 B8
Philip Gdns CR0 . . . . 62 F8
Philip Morris Ho TW13 . . 15 B7
Philip Rd TW18 . . . . 13 D2
Philips Ho GU26 . . . . 188 B3
Philip Southcote Sch
KT15 . . . . 52 C8
Phillip Copse RG12. . . . . . 27 D2
Phillips Cl
Aldershot GU10 . . . . 126 E8
Crawley RH10 . . . . 202 C2
Godalming GU7 . . . . 150 D2
Phillips Cotts GU7 . . . . . . 150 B4
Phillips Hatch GU5. . . . . . 152 C8
Philpot La GU24 . . . . 69 C7
Phipps Bridge Halt CR4. . 40 D6
Phipp's Bridge Rd CR4,
SW19 . . . . 40 D6
Phoenix Bsns Pk RG12 . . 26 C7
Phoenix Cl
Epsom KT19 . . . . 76 A7
West Wickham BR4 . . . . . 63 E8
Phoenix Ct
[13] Aldershot GU11 . . . . 105 A2
Croydon SE25 . . . . 43 A4
[3] Epsom KT17 . . . . 76 E6
Feltham TW13 . . . . 14 E4
Guildford GU1 . . . . 130 D7
South Croydon CR2 . . . . 61 F5
Phoenix Ctr TW20 . . . . . . 60 E3
Phoenix Ctr The KT20 . . . 97 C7
Phoenix Ho KT3. . . . . 38 F6
Phoenix La RH19 . . . . 206 E6
Phoenix Pl TW18 . . . . 13 A3
Phoenix Rd SE20 . . . . . . 23 C2
Phoenix Terr RH19 . . . . . 206 E6
Phoenix Way TW5. . . . . . 4 D8
Phyllis Ave KT3 . . . . 39 B4
Phyllis Ho CR0. . . . . 61 B6
Piccards The GU2. . . . . . 130 C5
Pickering RG12. . . . . 27 A5
Pickering Gdns CR0. . . . . 42 F3
Pickering Pl GU2 . . . . 109 A3
Picket Post Cl RG12 . . . . 27 F6
Pickets St SW12 . . . . 21 B8
Picketts Hill GU35. . . . . . 166 C1
Picketts La RH1. . . . . 161 C8
Pickford St GU11 . . . . . . 105 B2
Pickhurst Inf Sch BR4. . . 44 F3
Pickhurst Jun Sch BR4. . . 44 F3
Pickhurst La BR2, BR3, BR4 44 E2
Pickhurst Mead BR2 . . . . 44 F2
Pickhurst Pk BR2 . . . . . . 44 F4
Pickhurst Rd GU8. . . . . . . 191 D2
Pickhurst Rise BR4. . . . . . 44 D1
Pickins Piece SL3. . . . . . . 1 A5
Pickwick Cl TW4. . . . . . . 4 E2
Pickwick Gdns GU15 . . . . 66 B4
Pickwick Rd SE21. . . . . . 22 E8
Picquets Way KT20, SM7. 77 F2
Picton Cl GU15 . . . . 66 B7
Picton Ho [1] SW4. . . . . . 21 E8
Picton Mount CR3 . . . . . . 101 A8
Picton Pl KT6. . . . . 38 A1
Pierpoint SE25. . . . . 42 E6
Pierrefondes Ave GU14. . 85 B5
Pierson Ho [12] SE19 . . . 22 E4
Pigbush La RH14. . . . . . . 213 A7

Pigeon Gr RG12. . . . . 26 D5
Pigeonhouse La
Lower Kingswood CR5. . . 98 C3
Winkfield SL5. . . . . 8 E4
Pigeon La TW12. . . . . 16 A4
Pigeon Pass RH10. . . . . . 204 C5
Pigott Ct RG40 . . . . 25 D6
Pigott Rd RG40 . . . . 25 E8
Pike Cl GU11 . . . . 105 C2
Pikes Hill KT17 . . . . 76 E6
Pikes La RH7. . . . . 143 E2
Pikethorne SE23 . . . . 23 D6
Pilgrim Cl SM4 . . . . 40 B2
Pilgrim Ct GU8 . . . . 170 F8
Pilgrim Hill SE27 . . . . 22 C4
Pilgrim Ho GU1 . . . . 130 D7
Pilgrims Cl
Farnham GU9. . . . . 146 A8
Shere GU5 . . . . 133 A4
Westhumble RH5. . . . . . 115 B4
Pilgrims La
Caterham CR3 . . . . 100 B1
Titsey RH8, TN16. . . . . . 103 D3
Pilgrims Pl RH2. . . . . 118 A3
Pilgrims View GU12. . . . . 127 C8
Pilgrims Way
Bisley GU24 . . . . 68 A3
Shere GU5 . . . . 133 A4
Westhumble RH5. . . . . . 115 B4
Pilgrims' Way
Guildford GU4 . . . . 130 E5
Reigate RH2. . . . . 118 A3
Pilgrim's Way CR2 . . . . . . 61 F5
Pilgrims Way Cotts RH3. 116 C2
Pilgrims Way Prim Sch The
GU9. . . . . 146 B8
Pilsden Cl SW19 . . . . 19 D7
Pilton Est The CR0 . . . . . 61 B8
Pimms Cl GU4 . . . . 110 A5
Pinckards GU8. . . . . 191 B5
Pincott La KT24. . . . . 112 B6
Pincott Rd SW19 . . . . . . 40 C8
Pineacre Ct GU22. . . . . . . 70 B2
Pine Ave
Brookwood GU24. . . . . . . 88 A6
Camberley GU15 . . . . . . 65 D3
West Wickham BR4 . . . . . 44 B1
Pine Bank GU26. . . . . 188 E4
Pine Cl
Ash Vale GU12. . . . . 106 A6
Kenley CR8. . . . . 80 D2
Penge SE20 . . . . 43 C8
Sandhurst GU15 . . . . . . 64 E7
Woking GU21. . . . . 69 C3
Woodham KT15 . . . . 71 B8
Pine Coombe CR0. . . . . . 62 D6
Pinecote Dr SL5 . . . . 29 F2
Pine Cres SM5 . . . . 78 D8
Pinecrest GU17 . . . . 64 E1
Pine Croft KT13. . . . . 53 D4
Pine Croft Rd RG41 . . . . . 25 A2
Pine Ct
Bracknell RG12. . . . . 27 E5
Farnborough GU14 . . . . . 85 C1
[1] Guildford GU1 . . . . . . 110 A1
[3] Weybridge KT13 . . . . 53 C5
Pine Dean KT23. . . . . 94 B2
Pine Dr GU17 . . . . 64 E3
Pinefields KT15 . . . . 52 B6
Pinefields Cl RG45 . . . . . . 45 B4
Pine Gdns
Horley RH6 . . . . 161 A2
Surbiton KT5 . . . . 38 A5
Pine Gr
East Grinstead RH19. . . . 185 B3
Farnham GU10. . . . . 146 E6
Weybridge KT13 . . . . 53 C5
Wimbledon SW19 . . . . . . 19 F3
Windlesham GU20. . . . . . 48 D4
Pine Grove Mews [2] KT13 53 C5
Pine Hill KT18 . . . . 76 D4
Pinehill Rd RG45. . . . . . . 45 C3
Pinehill Rise GU47. . . . . . 64 C8
Pinehurst
Ascot SL5. . . . . 29 D4
Egham TW20 . . . . 11 C1
Horsham RH12 . . . . 217 C4
[8] Woking GU22 . . . . . . 69 F1
Pinehurst Ave GU14 . . . . 85 B2
Pinehurst Cl KT20 . . . . . . 98 A5
Pinehurst Cotts GU14 . . . 85 B2
Pinehurst Gdns KT14 . . . 71 C7
Pinehurst Rd GU14 . . . . . 85 A2
Pinel Cl GU25. . . . . 31 E5
Pine Lodge KT11 . . . . . . 73 C4
Pine Mount Rd GU15 . . . . 65 D4
Pine Pk GU3 . . . . 108 A6
Pine Pl KT17 . . . . 77 D5
Pine Rd GU22 . . . . 89 C7
Pine Ridge SM5. . . . . 60 A2
Pineridge Ct KT13. . . . . . 53 C5
Pine Ridge Dr GU10 . . . . 146 C5
Pine Ridge Prim Sch
GU15. . . . . 47 A1
Pines Ct [14] SW19 . . . . . 19 D7
Pine Shaw RH10 . . . . 202 D7
Pines Prim Sch The RG12. 27 A2
Pines The
Camberley GU15 . . . . . . 65 F7
Chessington KT9 . . . . . . 56 E7
Crawley RH10 . . . . 202 D6
Dorking RH4 . . . . 136 B6
Horsham RH12 . . . . 218 C5
Purley CR8 . . . . 80 C6
South Norwood SE19. . . . 22 B2
Sunbury TW16 . . . . 35 A6
Woking GU21. . . . . 69 F5

Pines Trad Est The GU3. . 108 E3
Pinetops RH12 . . . . 218 C5
Pine Tree Cl TW5 . . . . . . 4 B6
Pine Tree Hill GU22 . . . . . 70 D3
Pine Tree Lodge BR2. . . . 44 F5
Pine Trees Bsns Pk TW18. 12 E3
Pinetrees Cl RH10. . . . . . 183 B3
Pineview GU14. . . . . 85 A4
Pine View GU35. . . . . 187 C6
Pine View Cl
Badshot Lea GU9. . . . . . 126 A5
Chilworth GU4 . . . . 131 F3
Haslemere GU27 . . . . . . 208 C8
Pine Way TW20 . . . . 11 B2
Pine Way Cl RH19 . . . . . . 205 D7
Pine Wlk
Caterham CR3 . . . . 100 F5
Cobham KT11 . . . . 73 D5
East Horsley KT24. . . . . . 112 F7
Great Bookham KT23. . . . 94 B2
Surbiton KT5 . . . . 38 A3
Sutton SM5, SM2. . . . . . 59 D1
Woodmansterne CR5, SM7 78 F2
Pinewood [3] BR1. . . . . . . 24 E1
Pine Wood TW16 . . . . . . 35 A8
Pinewood Ave
Crowthorne RG45 . . . . . . 45 C6
Woodham KT15 . . . . 52 C1
Pinewood Cl
Broadbridge Heath
RH12. . . . . 216 D3
South Croydon CR0 . . . . 62 E7
Woking GU21. . . . . 70 A4
Pinewood Cotts GU21. . . 70 B7
Pinewood Cres GU14. . . . 84 C5
Pinewood Ct
Addlestone KT15 . . . . . . 52 D6
Wimbledon SW19 . . . . . . 20 B1
[1] Woking GU21 . . . . . . 70 A3
Pinewood Dr
Addlestone KT15 . . . . . . 52 C1
Staines TW18. . . . . 13 A3
Pinewood Gdns GU19 . . . 47 C3
Pinewood Gr KT15 . . . . . . 52 B1
Pinewood Inf Sch GU14 . 84 D7
Pinewood Mews TW19 . . . 2 D1
Pinewood Pk
Bracknell RG40 . . . . 45 C8
Farnborough GU14 . . . . . 84 C7
Woodham KT15 . . . . 71 B8
Pinewood Pl KT19 . . . . . . 57 D6
Pinewood Rd
Feltham TW13 . . . . 15 B5
Normandy GU12 . . . . 106 D3
Wentworth GU25 . . . . . . 31 A5
Pinfold Rd SW16. . . . . . . 21 E4
Pinglestone Cl UB7 . . . . . 2 E7
Pinkcoat Cl TW13 . . . . . . 15 B5
Pinkerton Pl SW16. . . . . . 21 D4
Pinkhurst La RH13 . . . . . 216 A2
Pinks Mews GU8. . . . . . . 170 F8
Pinova Cl RH11. . . . . 181 A1
Pioneer Pl CR0 . . . . 63 A2
Pioneers Ind Pk CR0 . . . . 41 E1
Piper Rd KT1 . . . . 38 A6
Pipers Cl KT11 . . . . 73 C5
Pipers End RH13 . . . . 215 E3
Piper's End GU25 . . . . . . 31 D6
Pipers Gdns CR0 . . . . 43 E2
Pipers Patch [1] GU14 . . . 85 B4
Pipewell Rd SM5. . . . . . . 40 E3
Pippbrook Gdns RH4 . . . . 136 B8
Pippin Cl CR0. . . . . 43 F1
Pippin Link RH11. . . . . . . 181 A1
Pippins Ct TW15 . . . . 14 B2
Pippins Sch SL3 . . . . 1 C6
Piquet Rd BR3, SE20. . . . 43 C7
PIRBRIGHT 87 F4
Pirbright Cres CR0. . . . . . 63 C4
Pirbright Ho [11] KT2 . . . 18 B2
Pirbright Prim Sch GU24 . 87 E5
Pirbright Rd
Farnborough GU14 . . . . . 85 C3
Normandy GU3 . . . . 107 B6
Wandsworth SW18 . . . . . 20 A7
Pirbright Terr GU24 . . . . . 87 F4
Piries Pl RH12 . . . . 217 C2
Pisley La RH5. . . . . 177 A4
Pitcairn Ct CR4. . . . . 20 F1
Pitcairn Rd CR4. . . . . 20 F1
Pitchfont La CR6, RH8 . . . 102 F2
PITCH PLACE
Beacon Hill 169 A3
Guildford 108 F6
Pit Farm Rd GU1. . . . . . . 110 A3
Pitfold Ave GU27. . . . . . . 207 D6
Pitfold Cl GU27 . . . . 207 E6
Pitlake CR0, CR9. . . . . . . 61 B8
Pitland St RH5. . . . . 155 C5
Pitson Cl KT15 . . . . 52 D6
Pitt Cres SW19. . . . . 20 B4
Pitt La GU10 . . . . 167 A6
Pitt Pl KT17. . . . . 76 E5
Pitt Rd
Epsom KT17. . . . . 76 E5
Thornton Heath CR0, CR7. 42 C4
Pitts Rd GU11. . . . . 105 B4
Pittville Gdns SE25. . . . . . 43 A6
Pitt Way GU14 . . . . 84 F5
Pit Wood Gn KT20. . . . . . 97 C7
Pitwood Park Ind Est
KT20 . . . . 97 B7
Pixfield Ct BR2. . . . . 44 F7
PIXHAM 115 D1
Pixham Ct [14] SW19 . . . 19 F3

Pixham Firs RH4 . . . . . . .115 C2
Pixham La RH4 . . . . .115 C2
Pixholme Ct RH4 . . . . . . .115 C2
Pixholme Gr RH4 . . . . . . .115 C1
Pixton Way CR0, CR2. . . . . .62 E2
Place Ct GU11 . . . . .126 C7
Place Farm Rd RH1 . . . . . .120 D4
Placehouse La CR5. . . . . . .80 A1
PLAISTOW. 211 F2
Plaistow & Kirdford Prim Sch
RH14. . . . . .211 F3
Plaistow Rd
Chiddingfold GU8. . . . . . .210 D6
Dunsfold GU8. . . . . .192 D2
Ifold RH14. . . . . .212 D1
Plaistow St RH7 . . . . . . .164 D4
Plane St SE26. . . . . .23 B5
Planes The RH16. . . . . . . .33 C2
Plane Tree Cres TW13. . . . .15 B5
Plane Tree Wlk SE19 . . . . .22 E2
Plantagenet Cl KT4 . . . . . .57 D6
Plantagenet Pk RG42. . . . . .27 F8
Plantain Cres RH11 . . . . . .201 A2
Plantation La GU6. . . . . . .101 E8
Plantation Row GU15. . . . . .65 B5
Plantation The RH7 . . . . . .184 C7
Plassy Rd SE6 . . . . .24 B8
Plateau The
Newell Green RG42. . . . . . .8 A1
Winkfield RG42. . . . . .28 A8
Plat The RH12 . . . . .217 A3
Platt Mdw GU4 . . . . .110 D3
Platt's Eyot TW12 . . . . . . .36 A7
Platt The RH7. . . . . .186 A8
Plaws Hill GU5. . . . . .154 D6
Playden Ct [3] RH11 . . . . . .201 A3
Playgreen Way SE6 . . . . . .24 A4
Playground Cl BR3. . . . . . .43 D7
Playing Field Cl GU27 . . . .208 C8
Pleasant Gr CR0. . . . . . . .62 F7
Pleasant Pl KT12. . . . . . . .54 D4
Pleasure Pit Rd KT21. . . . . .76 B1
Plesman Way SM6. . . . . . .60 E2
Plevna Rd TW12 . . . . .36 B8
Pleydell Ave SE19 . . . . . . .22 F1
Plough Cl RH11 . . . . .200 F8
Plough Ind Est KT22 . . . . . .95 A7
Plough La
Downside KT11 . . . . .73 A2
Horsham RH12 . . . . .217 E5
Purley CR8. . . . . .60 F1
[7] Teddington TW11. . . . . .17 A3
Wallington, Bandonhill SM6. .60 E5
Wimbledon SW17, SW19. . . .20 C4
Wokingham RG40 . . . . . . .25 F6
Ploughlands RG42 . . . . . . .26 F8
Plough Lane Cl SM6. . . . . .60 E5
Ploughmans End TW7 . . . . . .5 D2
Plough Rd
Dormansland RH7 . . . . . .165 A2
Smallfield RH6. . . . . . . .162 C3
West Ewell KT19 . . . . . . .57 D3
Plover Cl
Crawley RH11 . . . . .201 C8
Staines TW18. . . . . .12 F5
Plovers Rd RH13 . . . . . . .217 F3
Plovers Rise GU24 . . . . . . .87 E7
Plowman Ho SW19. . . . . . .19 D6
Plum Cl TW13 . . . . .15 A7
Plummer La CR4. . . . . . . .40 F7
Plummer Rd SW4. . . . . . . .21 D8
Plumpton Ct SE23. . . . . . .23 E8
Plumpton Way SM5 . . . . . .59 E7
Plumtree Cl SM6. . . . . . . .60 D3
Plymen Ho KT8 . . . . .36 A4
Plynlimmon Cotts GU6. . . .174 A3
Pocket Cl RG42 . . . . .26 D7
Pockford Rd GU8. . . . . . .191 D4
Pocklington Ct SW15. . . . . .19 A7
Poels Ct RH19 . . . . .185 E2
Pointers Cotts KT10 . . . . . .17 C6
Pointers Hill RH4. . . . . . .135 C4
Pointers Rd KT11 . . . . . . .72 E2
Pointers The KT21 . . . . . . .95 E7
Point Royal RG12 . . . . . . .27 B4
Point The RG22 . . . . .27 B7
Point Wharf La TW8. . . . . . .6 E1
Polden Cl GU14 . . . . .84 E7
Polecat Hill GU26 . . . . . .188 F1
Polecat Valley GU26. . . . . .188 F1
Polecroft La SE6. . . . . . . .23 F6
Polesden Gdns SW20. . . . . .39 B7
Polesden La
Ripley GU23. . . . . .91 A6
Send Marsh GU23. . . . . . .90 F5
Polesden Lacey★ KT23 . . . .114 C8
Polesden Lacey Inf Sch
KT23 . . . . .114 C8
Polesden Rd KT23, RH5. . . .114 B6
Polesden View KT23 . . . . .114 B8
Poles La RH11. . . . . .181 C3
Polesteeple Hill TN16 . . . . .83 D2
Police Station Rd KT12. . . . .54 C4
Pollard Ct SM4. . . . . .40 E4
Pollard Gr GU15 . . . . .66 C4
Pollard Ho KT4 . . . . .58 C6
Pollard Rd
Morden SM4. . . . . .40 D4
Woking GU22. . . . . .70 B3
Pollardrow Ave RG42. . . . . .26 F8
Pollards RH11. . . . . .201 A5
Pollards Cres SW16 . . . . . .41 E6
Pollards Dr RH13 . . . . . . .217 F2
Pollards Hill E SW16 . . . . .41 F6
Pollards Hill N SW16. . . . . .41 F6

Pollards Hill S SW16 . . . . .41 F6
Pollards Hill W SW16. . . . . .41 F6
Pollards Oak Cres RH8. . . .123 A3
Pollards Oak Rd RH8. . . . .123 A3
Pollards Wood Hill RH8. . . .123 B5
Pollards Wood Rd
Limpsfield RH8. . . . . . . .123 B4
Thornton Heath SW16. . . . .41 E6
POLLINGFOLD. 195 F5
Polo Ctr The SL5. . . . . . . .30 C5
Polsted La
Compton GU3. . . . . .129 C3
Guildford GU3. . . . . . . .129 F2
Polsted Rd SE6 . . . . .23 F8
Poltimore Rd GU2. . . . . . .130 B7
Polworth Rd SW16 . . . . . . .21 E3
Polyanthus Way RG45 . . . . .45 B8
Polygon Bsns Ctr SL3. . . . . .1 F5
Pomeroy Cl TW1. . . . . .6 B3
Pond Cl
Hersham KT12. . . . . .54 A4
Loxwood RH14. . . . . . . .212 F4
Pond Copse La RH14 . . . . .212 F5
Pond Cottage La BR3, BR4 . .44 A1
Pond Cotts SE21 . . . . .22 E7
Pond Farm Cl KT20. . . . . . .97 B3
Pondfield Ho SE27 . . . . . . .22 C3
Pondfield Rd
Farncombe GU7. . . . . . . .150 F7
Kenley CR8. . . . . .80 B3
Rudgwick RH12. . . . . . . .214 E8
West Wickham BR2. . . . . .44 E1
Pond Head La
Forest Green RH5. . . . . . .176 E5
Wallis Wood RH5. . . . . . .176 D3
Pond Hill Gdns SM3. . . . . .58 E4
Pond Ho
Chertsey KT16. . . . . .33 B2
Guildford GU4. . . . . . . .110 D2
Pond La
Frensham GU10. . . . . . . .167 C5
Peaslake GU5. . . . . .154 D7
Pond Mdw GU2. . . . . . . .108 E2
Pond Mdw Sch GU1 . . . . .109 C4
Pond Moor Rd RG12. . . . . .27 B4
Pondpenny La GU14. . . . . .84 A1
Pond Piece KT22. . . . . . . .74 B6
Pond Rd
Egham TW20 . . . . .12 C2
Headley Down GU35 . . . . .187 B4
Woking GU22. . . . . .89 B7
Pondside Ave [3] KT4. . . . . .39 C1
Pondside Cl UB3. . . . . .3 D7
Ponds La
Farley Green GU5 . . . . . .153 F7
Guildford GU5. . . . . . . .132 F1
Ponds The KT13 . . . . .53 E4
Pondtail Cl RH12. . . . . . . .217 D6
Pondtail Copse RH12. . . . .217 D6
Pondtail Dr RH12. . . . . . . .217 D7
Pondtail Pk RH12. . . . . . . .217 D6
Pondtail Rd RH12. . . . . . . .217 D6
Pond Way
East Grinstead RH19 . . . . .186 B1
Teddington TW11. . . . . . .17 C2
Pond Wood Rd RH10 . . . . .202 A8
Ponsonby Rd SW15 . . . . . .19 B8
Pontefract Rd BR1. . . . . . .24 F3
Ponton Ho SW2. . . . . .22 A7
Pony Chase KT11 . . . . . . .73 F6
Pook Hill GU8 . . . . .190 F3
Pool Cl
Beckenham BR3. . . . . . . .24 A3
East Molesey KT8 . . . . . . .35 F4
Pool Ct SE6. . . . . .24 A6
Poole Court Rd TW5 . . . . . . .4 E5
Poole Ct TW5. . . . . .4 E5
Pool End Cl TW17 . . . . . . .34 A4
Poole Rd
West Ewell KT19 . . . . . . .57 D4
Woking GU21. . . . . .69 E1
Pooley Ave TW20 . . . . . . .12 B3
POOLEY GREEN 12 C2
Pooley Green Cl TW20 . . . . .12 C3
Pooley Green Rd TW20 . . . . .12 C3
Pool Rd
Aldershot GU11 . . . . .126 C7
East Molesey KT12, KT8 . . .35 F4
Pope Cl
East Bedfont TW14 . . . . . .14 F7
Mitcham SW17, SW19. . . . .20 D2
Pope Ct [10] KT2 . . . . .17 D4
Pope's Ave TW2 . . . . .16 E6
Popes Cl SL3 . . . . .1 C7
Popes Ct [3] TW2. . . . . . . .16 E6
Popes Gr CR0. . . . . .62 F6
Pope's Gr TW1, TW2. . . . . .16 F6
Popes La RH8. . . . . .143 F8
Popes Mead GU27 . . . . . .208 C7
POPESWOOD 26 D8
Popeswood Rd RG42 . . . . . .26 D8
Popham Cl
Bracknell RG12 . . . . .27 F4
Feltham TW13 . . . . .15 F5
Popham Gdns TW9. . . . . . . .7 B4
Poplar Ave
Leatherhead KT22. . . . . . .95 C5
Mitcham CR4. . . . . .40 F8
Windlesham GU20. . . . . . .48 B6
Poplar Cl
Bracknell RG12 . . . . .27 D6
Crawley RH11 . . . . .181 C1
Epsom KT17. . . . . .76 F7
Mytchett GU16. . . . . .86 A3
Poyle SL3. . . . . .1 E6
Poplar Cotts GU16 . . . . . . .85 F6
Poplar Cres KT19 . . . . . . .57 C4

Poplar Ct
[4] Streatham SW16 . . . . . .21 F5
[13] Twickenham TW1. . . . . . .6 C1
Wimbledon SW19 . . . . . . .20 A3
Poplar Dr KT17, SM7 . . . . .77 D5
Poplar Farm Cl KT19 . . . . .57 C4
Poplar Gdns KT3. . . . . . . .38 D7
Poplar Gr
Kingston upon Thames
KT3. . . . . .38 D6
Woking GU22. . . . . .89 E8
Poplar La BR3 . . . . .44 B4
Poplar Prim Sch SW19 . . . . .40 A6
Poplar Rd
Ashford TW15 . . . . .14 C3
Cheam SM3 . . . . .39 F1
Leatherhead KT22 . . . . . . .95 C5
Merton SW19. . . . . .40 A7
Shalford GU4 . . . . .130 E2
Poplar Rd S SM4, SW19 . . . .40 A6
Poplars Cl GU14. . . . . . . .84 C5
Poplars The
Ascot SL5 . . . . .29 A4
Cudworth RH5 . . . . .179 B6
Horsham RH13. . . . . . . .217 E3
Poplar Way TW13 . . . . . . .15 B5
Poplar Wlk
Caterham CR3 . . . . .100 E4
Croydon CR0. . . . . .42 C1
Heath End GU9 . . . . . . .125 D7
Poppy Cl SM6 . . . . .41 A1
Poppyhills Rd GU15 . . . . . .65 F8
Poppy La CR0, CR9. . . . . . .43 C1
Poppy Pl RG40 . . . . .25 B6
Porchester SL5 . . . . .29 A5
Porchester Mead BR3. . . . . .24 B2
Porchester Rd KT1. . . . . . .38 B7
Porchfield Cl SM2 . . . . . . .59 B1
Porlock Ho [5] SE26 . . . . . .23 A5
Porridge Pot Alley GU2. . . .130 C7
Portal Cl SE27 . . . . .22 A5
Porteridges RH4 . . . . .136 C4
Portesbery Hill Dr GU15. . . .65 E6
Portesbery Rd GU15. . . . . .65 E6
Portesbery Sch GU15. . . . . .65 D6
Porthcawe Rd SE26 . . . . . .23 F4
Portia Gr RG42. . . . . .27 E8
Portland Ave KT3. . . . . . . .38 F2
Portland Cl KT4. . . . . .39 A8
Portland Cotts
[11] Dorking RH4. . . . . . . .136 A8
Feltham TW13 . . . . .15 E3
Wallington CR0 . . . . .41 D2
Portland Cres TW13,
TW15. . . . . .14 D4
Portland Ct SM1 . . . . .59 B4
Portland Dr RH1. . . . . . . .119 D6
Portland Ho
[5] East Grinstead RH19 . . .205 F8
Merstham RH1. . . . . . . .119 D6
[20] Streatham SW2 . . . . . . .22 A7
Portland House Mews
KT18. . . . . .76 D5
Portland Pl
Croydon SE25 . . . . .43 A5
Ewell KT17. . . . . .76 E7
Portland Rd
Ashford TW15 . . . . .13 E5
Croydon SE25 . . . . .43 B4
Dorking RH4 . . . . .136 A8
East Grinstead RH19 . . . . .205 F8
Kingston upon Thames KT1,
KT5. . . . . .37 F5
Mitcham CR4. . . . . .40 E7
Portland Terr TW9. . . . . . . .6 D3
Portley La CR3. . . . . .100 E6
Portley Wood Rd CR3 . . . .101 A7
Portman Ave SW14. . . . . . . .7 D4
Portman Cl [5] RG42. . . . . . .27 A8
Portman Rd KT1. . . . . .37 F7
Portmore Park Rd KT13 . . . .53 A7
Portmore Pl [7] KT13 . . . . . .53 D7
Portmore Quays KT13. . . . . .52 F6
Portmore Way KT13. . . . . . .53 A7
Portnall Dr GU25. . . . . . . .30 F4
Portnall Rd GU25 . . . . .30 F4
Portnall Rise GU25. . . . . . .30 F3
Portnalls Cl CR5. . . . . .79 B3
Portnalls Rd CR5. . . . . . . .79 B2
Portnalls Rise CR5. . . . . . .79 C3
Portobello Ho [6] SW27. . . . .22 B3
Porton Ct KT6. . . . . .37 C3
Portsea Ho [3] SW15. . . . . .19 B7
Portsmouth Ave KT7 . . . . . .37 A2
Portsmouth Rd
Camberley GU15 . . . . . . .66 A7
Cobham KT10, KT11. . . . . .73 C7
Downside KT11 . . . . .72 F6
Esher KT10 . . . . .55 D7
Godalming GU7, GU8. . . . .150 B2
Guildford GU2 . . . . .130 C6
Hindhead GU26 . . . . . . .188 E2
Milford GU8 . . . . .149 E1
Putney SW15 . . . . .19 C8
Ripley GU23 . . . . .91 A4
Thames Ditton KT1, KT6,
KT7. . . . . .37 C3
Thursley GU8. . . . . .169 D3
Wisley GU23, KT11. . . . . .72 C3
Witley GU8. . . . . .170 B6
Portswood Pl SW15. . . . . . . .7 F1
Portugal Gdns TW2 . . . . . .16 C6
Portugal Rd GU21. . . . . . . .69 F3
Portway KT17. . . . . .58 A2
Port Way GU24 . . . . .68 A3
Portway Cres KT17. . . . . . .58 A2
Post Boys Row KT11 . . . . . .73 A5
Postford Mill Cotts GU4 . . .131 F5

Post House La KT23 . . . . . .94 A2
Post La TW2 . . . . .16 D7
Postmill Cl CR0, CR9. . . . . .62 D7
Post Office Row RH8. . . . .123 E4
Potbury Cl SL4. . . . . .9 B2
POT COMMON 148 C2
Potley Hill Prim Sch
GU46. . . . . .64 A5
Potley Hill Rd GU46 . . . . . .64 A5
Potter Cl CR4. . . . . .41 B7
Potterhill Ct TW11 . . . . . . .17 B1
Potteries La GU16. . . . . . . .85 F4
Potteries The
Farnborough GU14 . . . . . .84 D6
Ottershaw KT16. . . . . . . .51 E4
Potterne Cl [5] SW15,
SW19. . . . . .19 D8
Potters Cl
Croydon CR0. . . . . .43 E1
Milford GU8. . . . . .149 F2
Potters Cres GU12 . . . . . . .106 B2
Potters Croft RH13. . . . . . .217 C2
Pottersfield RH10 . . . . . . .201 D7
Potters Gate GU9 . . . . . . .125 B2
Potters Gate CE Prim Sch
GU9. . . . . .125 A2
Potters Gr KT3. . . . . .38 C5
Potters Hill GU16 . . . . . . .171 D4
Potters La GU23 . . . . .90 B2
Potter's La SW16 . . . . .21 D2
Potters Pl RH12. . . . . .217 C2
Potters Way RH2. . . . . . . .139 C5
Pottery Ct GU10 . . . . .145 F6
Pottery La GU10 . . . . .145 F6
Pottery Rd TW8. . . . . .6 E8
Poulett Gdns TW1 . . . . . . .17 A7
Poullett Ho SW2 . . . . .22 B7
Poulton Ave SM1 . . . . .59 D7
Pound Cl
Epsom KT19. . . . . .76 D8
Godalming GU7 . . . . . . .150 E4
Long Ditton KT6. . . . . . . .37 C1
Loxwood RH14. . . . . . . .212 F5
Pound Cres KT22 . . . . .94 D6
Pound Ct
Ashtead KT21. . . . . .75 F1
Wood St V GU3 . . . . . . .108 B2
Pound Farm Cl KT10 . . . . . .36 D1
Pound Farm La GU12. . . . .106 D1
Pound Field GU1. . . . . . . .109 D1
Poundfield Ct GU22 . . . . . .90 C7
Poundfield Gdns GU22. . . . .90 C7
Poundfield La RH14 . . . . . .212 B3
POUND HILL 202 C8
Pound Hill GU3 . . . . .108 B2
Pound Hill Jun & Inf Schs
RH10. . . . . .202 C7
Pound Hill Par RH10 . . . . .202 C7
Pound Hill Pl RH10 . . . . . .202 C6
Pound La
Epsom KT19. . . . . .76 D8
Godalming GU7 . . . . . . .150 E4
Windlesham GU20. . . . . . .48 C4
Wood St V GU3 . . . . . . .108 B2
Pound Pl GU4 . . . . .130 F3
Pound Place Cl GU4. . . . . .130 F3
Pound Rd
Aldershot GU12 . . . . . . .105 C1
Banstead SM7 . . . . .78 A2
Chertsey KT16. . . . . .33 B2
Pound St V SM5 . . . . .59 F5
POVEY CROSS 160 D1
Povey Cross Rd RH6 . . . . .160 E1
Powderham Ct GU21. . . . . .68 D1
Powder Mill La TW2 . . . . . .16 A7
Powell Cl
Chessington KT9 . . . . . . .56 D5
Guildford GU2 . . . . .129 F7
Horley RH6 . . . . .160 E4
Wallington SM6. . . . . . . .60 E3
Powell Corderoy Prim Sch
RH4. . . . . .135 F6
Powell Ct CR0. . . . . .61 C6
Powell Gdns RH1 . . . . . . .119 B3
Powell Ho SW19 . . . . .19 E2
Powells Cl RH4 . . . . .136 C4
Powell's Wlk W4 . . . . .7 F8
Powell Terr CR4 . . . . .41 E5
Power Cl GU1. . . . . .109 C2
Power Ho [13] TW9. . . . . .7 A6
Powers Ct TW1 . . . . .17 D8
Pownall Gdns TW3. . . . . . . .5 B3
Pownall Rd TW3 . . . . .5 B3
POYLE. 1 E6
Poyle 14 Trad Est SL3 . . . . . .1 F7
Poyle Gdns RG12. . . . . . . .27 D8
Poyle Ho GU4. . . . . .110 D2
Poyle New Cotts SL3 . . . . . . .1 F5
Poyle Pk SL3. . . . . .1 E4
Poyle Rd
Guildford GU1 . . . . .130 E7
Poyle SL3. . . . . .1 E5
Tongham GU10 . . . . .127 D2
Poyle Tech Ctr The SL3 . . . . .1 E5
Poynder Lodge TW7 . . . . . . .6 A6
Poynders Gdns SW12. . . . . .21 C8
Poynders Rd SW12, SW4 . . .21 D8
Poynes Rd RH6. . . . . .160 E5
Poynings Rd RH11 . . . . . . .200 E5
Prairie Cl KT15 . . . . .52 B7
Prairie Rd KT15. . . . . .52 B7
Pratts Cnr GU8. . . . . .193 A8
Pratts La KT12 . . . . .54 D6
Precincts The SM4. . . . . . .40 A3
Precinct The
Cranleigh GU6 . . . . .174 E4
Egham TW20 . . . . .12 A3

Prendergast Ho [5] SW4 . . . .21 D8
Prentice Cl GU14. . . . . . . .85 B8
Prentice Ct [2] SW19 . . . . . .19 F3
Prentis Rd SW16 . . . . .21 D4
Presburg Rd KT3. . . . . . . .38 E4
Prescott RG12 . . . . .26 F2
Prescott Ho CR0 . . . . .61 A7
Prescott Rd SL3 . . . . .1 E5
Presentation Mews SW2 . . . .21 F7
Preshaw Cres CR4 . . . . . . .40 E6
Prestbury Cres SM7 . . . . . .78 E5
Prestbury Ct GU21 . . . . . . .69 A1
Preston Cl TW2 . . . . .16 E5
Preston Cross KT23 . . . . . .93 F1
Preston Ct KT12 . . . . .35 C1
Preston Dr KT19. . . . . .57 F4
Preston Gr KT21 . . . . .75 C2
Preston La KT20 . . . . .97 C7
Preston Pl TW10 . . . . .6 E2
Preston Rd
Littleton TW17. . . . . .34 A4
South Norwood SE19. . . . . .22 B2
Wimbledon SW20 . . . . . . .18 F1
Prestwick Cl RH11 . . . . . . .200 D5
Prestwick La GU8, GU27. . . .190 C3
Prestwood Cl RH11 . . . . . .181 B1
Prestwood Gdns CR0. . . . . .42 C2
Prestwood La RH11 . . . . . .180 C3
Pretoria Rd
Chertsey KT16 . . . . .32 F1
Streatham SW16 . . . . .21 C3
Pretty La CR5. . . . . .99 C6
Prey Heath Cl GU22 . . . . . .89 C3
Prey Heath Rd GU22 . . . . . .89 B3
Preymead Ind Est GU9 . . . .126 B7
Price Cl SW17. . . . . .20 F5
Price Rd CR0 . . . . .61 B5
Prices La RH2 . . . . .139 B6
Price Way TW12 . . . . .15 E2
Prickley Wood BR2. . . . . . .44 F1
Priddy Pl RH1 . . . . .119 C4
Priddy's Yd [4] CR0 . . . . . . .61 C8
Prideaux Gdns RH5 . . . . . .177 D4
Prides Crossing SL5. . . . . . .9 A1
Pridham Rd CR7 . . . . .42 D5
Priest Ave RG40 . . . . .25 F5
Priest Croft Cl RH11. . . . . .201 A6
Priestfield Rd SE23 . . . . . .23 E5
PRIEST HILL 77 B8
Priest Hill
Englefield Green TW19,
TW20. . . . . .11 C6
Limpsfield RH8. . . . . . . .123 B6
Priest La GU24. . . . . .67 C5
Priestlands Cl RH6 . . . . . . .160 F4
Priestley Gdns GU22 . . . . . .90 A7
Priestley Rd
Guildford GU2 . . . . .129 D8
Mitcham CR4. . . . . .41 A7
Priestley Way RH10 . . . . . .182 A3
Priests Bridge SW14, SW15. . .7 E4
PRIESTWOOD 27 A8
Priestwood Ave RG42 . . . . .26 F8
Priestwood Court Rd
RG42 . . . . .27 A8
Priestwood Sq [1] RG42. . . . .27 A8
Primrose Ave RH6 . . . . . . .161 B1
Primrose Cl
Carshalton CR4 . . . . .41 B1
Catford SE6 . . . . .24 C3
Crawley RH11 . . . . .201 B3
Primrose Copse RH12 . . . . .217 E7
Primrose Ct
Guildford GU4 . . . . .110 C4
New Malden KT4 . . . . . . .39 A2
[9] Streatham SW12 . . . . . .21 D8
Primrose Dr GU24. . . . . . . .68 A4
Primrose Gdns GU14 . . . . . .84 E3
Primrose Ho [1] TW9 . . . . . . .6 F6
Primrose La CR0. . . . . .43 D1
Primrose Pl [3] TW7 . . . . . . .5 F5
Primrose Rd KT12. . . . . . . .54 C5
Primrose Ridge GU7 . . . . . .150 B2
Primrose Way
Bramley GU5. . . . . .151 D5
Sandhurst GU47 . . . . .45 B1
Primrose Wlk
Bracknell RG12 . . . . .27 C4
Ewell KT17. . . . . .57 F3
Prince Albert Ct [6] TW16. . . .14 E1
Prince Albert Dr SL5 . . . . . .28 D5
Prince Albert Sq RH1 . . . . .140 A4
Prince Andrew Way SL5 . . . .28 D7
Prince Charles Cres GU14 . . .85 C8
Prince Charles Way SM6 . . . .60 B7
Prince Consort Dr SL5 . . . . .28 D5
Prince Consort's Dr SL4. . . . .10 A6
Prince Dr GU47 . . . . .45 A1
Prince George's Ave
SW20. . . . . .39 C7
Prince Georges Rd SW19 . . . .40 D8
Prince of Wales Rd RH1. . . .141 A2
Prince of Wales' Rd SM1 . . . .59 D8
Prince of Wales Wlk [1]
GU15. . . . . .65 C6
Prince Rd SE25 . . . . .42 E4
Prince Regent Pl [10] GU14 . . .85 C1
Prince Regent Rd TW3 . . . . .5 C4
Princes Ave
Hamsey Green CR2 . . . . . .81 B4
Tolworth KT6. . . . . .57 A8
Wallington SM5. . . . . . . .59 F2
Prince's Ave
Farnborough GU11 . . . . . .105 C5
Farncombe GU7 . . . . .150 C7
Princes Cl
Bagshot GU19 . . . . .47 E1
Hamsey Green CR2 . . . . . .81 B4

Prince's CI TW11 . . . . 16 D4
Princes Ct
  Englefield Green TW20 . . . . 11 C3
  11 Guildford GU1 . . . . .109 D1
  New Malden KT3 . . . . 38 F6
  Weybridge KT13 . . . . 53 B5
Prince's Dr KT22 . . . . 74 E7
Princes Gdns GU3 . . . . .108 E8
Princes Hall Theatre★ **22**
  GU11 . . . . .105 A2
Princes Mead GU14 . . . . 85 B4
Princes Mead Sh Ctr
  GU14 . . . . 85 B3
Princes Mews TW3 . . . . 5 A3
Princes Rd
  Ashford TW15 . . . . 13 F3
  Egham TW20 . . . . 11 F2
  Feltham TW13 . . . . 14 F5
  Kingston upon Thames KT2 . 18 A1
  Penge SE20 . . . . 23 D2
  Richmond, Kew TW9 . . . . . . .6 F6
  Richmond TW10 . . . . .6 F2
Prince's Rd
  Mortlake SW14 . . . . 7 A4
  Redhill RH1 . . . . .139 F7
  Teddington TW11 . . . . 16 D4
  Weybridge KT13 . . . . 53 C5
  Wimbledon SW19 . . . . 20 A2
Princess Anne Rd RH12 . .214 D6
Princess Ct
  Beckenham BR3 . . . . 44 B7
  3 Croydon CR0 . . . . 61 F8
  3 Farnborough GU14 . . . .105 C8
  Hounslow TW4 . . . . 4 C4
  7 Wimbledon SW20 . . . . 19 D1
Princess Gdns GU22 . . . . . . 70 B3
Princess Ho **1** RH1 . . . . . .119 A2
Princess Margaret Rd
  RH12 . . . . .214 D7
Princess Mary CI GU2 . . . .109 A5
Princess Mary's Rd KT15 . 52 C6
Princess of Wales
  Conservatory★ TW9 . . . . . .6 F7
Princess Rd
  Crawley RH11 . . . . .201 C6
  Thornton Heath CR0 . . . . . 42 C3
  Woking GU22 . . . . 70 C3
Princess Sq Sh Ctr RG12 . 27 B7
Princes St SM1 . . . . 59 D6
Prince's St TW10, TW9 . . . . .6 E2
Princess Way
  Camberley GU15 . . . . 65 C5
  Redhill RH1 . . . . .119 A2
Princes Way
  Aldershot GU11 . . . . .105 A2
  Coney Hall BR4 . . . . 63 F7
  Croydon CR0 . . . . 60 F5
  Putney SW15, SW19 . . . . . 19 E7
Princethorpe Rd SE26 . . . . 23 D4
Princeton Mews **3** KT2 . . 38 A8
Prince William Ct TW15 . . 13 F3
Pringle Gdns
  Purley CR8 . . . . 60 F1
  Streatham SW16 . . . . 21 C4
Prins Willem-Alexander Sch
  GU22 . . . . 70 C2
Prior Ave SM2 . . . . 59 E3
Prior Croft CI GU15 . . . . . . 66 A4
Prior End GU15 . . . . 66 A5
Prioress Rd SE27 . . . . 22 B5
Prior Heath Inf Sch GU15 . 66 A5
Prior Place Cross Roads
  GU15 . . . . 66 B4
Prior Rd GU15 . . . . 66 A5
Priors CI
  Compton GU7 . . . . .129 A1
  Farnborough GU14 . . . . . . 85 B8
Priors Croft GU22 . . . . 90 A7
Priors Ct
  Ash GU12 . . . . .105 E1
  Woking GU21 . . . . 69 A1
Priorsfield Rd GU7 . . . . . . .129 A1
Priors Field Sch GU7 . . . . .129 A1
Priors Hatch La GU7 . . . . .128 F1
Prior's La GU17 . . . . 64 A5
Priors Lodge **3** TW10 . . . . .6 E2
Priors Mead KT23 . . . . 94 C2
Priors The KT21 . . . . 95 D8
Priors Wlk RH10 . . . . .201 F6
Priorswood GU3 . . . . .128 F2
Priors Wood
  Haslemere GU27 . . . . .207 F6
  Hinchley Wood KT10 . . . . . 55 F8
  Kingsfold RH12 . . . . .198 B6
Priory Ave SM3 . . . . 58 D6
Priory CE Prim Sch SW19 20 B3
Priory CE Sch The RH4 . .135 F6
Priory CI
  Beckenham BR3 . . . . 43 E6
  Dorking RH4 . . . . .136 A5
  Hampton TW12 . . . . 35 F8
  Horley RH6 . . . . .160 F4
  3 Merton SW19 . . . . 40 B8
  Sheerwater GU21 . . . . 70 D6
  Sunbury TW16 . . . . 15 A1
  Sunningdale SL5 . . . . 30 A2
  Walton-on-Thames KT12 . . 54 A7
Priory Cres
  Cheam SM3 . . . . 58 D6
  South Norwood SE19 . . . . . 22 C1
Priory Ct
  Camberley GU15 . . . . 64 F5
  Cheam SM3 . . . . 58 E6
  Dorking RH4 . . . . .136 B5
  Egham TW20 . . . . 12 C2
  Farnham GU9 . . . . .146 C8
  3 Hampton TW12 . . . . . 16 A1
  Hounslow TW3 . . . . 5 B4

Priory Ct continued
  Reigate RH2 . . . . .117 F1
  Roehampton SW15 . . . . .7 F3
Priory Dr RH2 . . . . .139 A7
Priory Gdns
  Ashford TW15 . . . . 14 D3
  Hampton TW12 . . . . 35 F8
  Mortlake SW13 . . . . 7 F4
  South Norwood SE25 . . . . . 42 F5
Priory Gn TW18 . . . . 13 B3
Priory Grange The SW15 . . .7 F3
Priory Ho Ct SE6 . . . . 24 B7
Priory Hospl The GU21 . . . 68 C3
Priory La
  East Molesey KT8 . . . . 36 B5
  Frensham GU10 . . . . .167 E8
  Roehampton SW15 . . . . .7 F2
Priory Lodge BR4 . . . . 63 E7
Priory Mews TW18 . . . . 13 B3
Priory PI KT12 . . . . 54 A7
Priory Prep Sch SM7 . . . . . 78 A4
Priory Rd
  Cheam SM3 . . . . 58 D6
  Chessington KT9 . . . . 56 E7
  Forest Row RH18 . . . . . . .206 D2
  Hampton TW12 . . . . 16 A1
  Isleworth TW3 . . . . 5 C2
  Mitcham SW19 . . . . 20 D1
  Reigate RH2 . . . . .139 A6
  Richmond TW9 . . . . 7 A7
  Sunningdale SL5 . . . . 30 A2
  Thornton Heath CR0 . . . . . 42 A2
  Winkfield SL5 . . . . 28 B7
Priory Ret Pk SW19 . . . . . . 20 D1
Priory Specl Sch SE25 . . . . 42 F5
Priory St GU14 . . . . 85 D4
Priory The
  Croydon CR0 . . . . 61 A7
  Godstone RH9 . . . . .121 B3
  21 Kingston upon Thames
  KT6 . . . . 37 E4
Priory Way UB7 . . . . .2 E8
Priory Wlk
  Bracknell RG12 . . . . 27 F5
  Sunbury TW16 . . . . 15 A1
Priscilla Ho **8** TW14 . . . . 14 F1
Probyn Rd SW2 . . . . 22 B6
Proctor CI
  Crawley RH10 . . . . .202 C4
  Mitcham SW4 . . . . 41 A8
Proctor Gdns KT23 . . . . 94 B2
Proctors CI TW14 . . . . 15 A7
Proctors Rd RG40 . . . . 25 F6
Proffits Cotts KT20 . . . . 97 D5
Profumo Rd KT12 . . . . 54 D5
Progress Bsns Pk CR9 . . . . 60 F8
Progress Way CR0 . . . . 60 F8
Prologis Pk
  Hounslow TW4 . . . . 4 C4
  Wallington SM6 . . . . 41 D2
Promenade Approach Rd
  W4 . . . . .7 E7
Promenade De Verdun
  CR8 . . . . 79 D8
Promenade The W4 . . . . .7 E6
Prospect Ave GU14 . . . . 85 B6
Prospect CI
  Forest Hill SE26 . . . . 23 B4
  Hounslow TW5 . . . . 4 F6
Prospect Cott GU12 . . . . . .106 A4
Prospect Cotts RG42 . . . . . 26 D8
Prospect Cres TW2 . . . . 5 C1
Prospect Ct **4** GU1 . . . . .130 E8
Prospect Ho
  Epsom KT19 . . . . 57 B1
  3 Mitcham SW19 . . . . . . 40 D8
  Old Woking GU22 . . . . 90 B7
Prospect House Sch **9**
  SW15 . . . . 19 D8
Prospect La TW20 . . . . 11 A3
Prospect PI
  Crawley RH11 . . . . .201 C6
  Ewell KT17 . . . . 76 E6
  Staines TW18 . . . . 12 F3
  Wimbledon SW20 . . . . 19 B1
Prospect Rd
  Ash GU12 . . . . .106 A5
  Farnborough GU14 . . . . . . 85 A5
  Rowledge GU10 . . . . .145 B3
  Thames Ditton KT6 . . . . . . 37 C3
Prossers KT20 . . . . 97 D6
Providence Cotts RH3 . . .137 B8
Providence Ct UB3 . . . . 3 D7
Providence Ho GU19 . . . . . 47 E3
Providence La UB3 . . . . 3 D7
Providence PI
  Ewell KT17 . . . . 76 E7
  Farnham GU9 . . . . .125 C2
  West Byfleet GU22 . . . . . . 71 A5
Provincial Terr SE20 . . . . . 23 D1
Prune Hill TW20 . . . . 11 E1
Prunus CI GU24 . . . . 67 E6
Ptarmigan Hts RG12 . . . . . 26 D5
Puccinia Ct TW19 . . . . 13 E7
Puckeridge Gate Rd GU11 104 E6
Puckshill GU21 . . . . 68 D2
Puckshott Way GU22 . . . .208 D8
Puddenhole Cotts RH4 . .116 A2
Pudding La RH6 . . . . .180 E7
Puffin CI BR3, CR0 . . . . 43 D4
Puffin Hill RH10 . . . . .204 C5
Puffin Rd RH11 . . . . .200 D5
Pulborough Rd SW18 . . . . 19 F4
Pulborough Way TW4 . . . . . 4 C3
Pullman Ct SW2 . . . . 21 F7
Pullman La GU7 . . . . .150 C2
Pullman PI RH1 . . . . .119 C7
Pullmans PI **4** TW18 . . . 13 A3

Pulteney CI TW7 . . . . 6 A4
Puma Trade Pk CR4 . . . . . . 40 D5
Pump Alley **7** TW8 . . . . . . 6 D7
Pump House CI BR2 . . . . . . 44 F7
Pump La SL5 . . . . 29 E8
Pump Pail N CR0, CR9 . . . . 61 C7
Pump Pail S CR0, CR9 . . . . 61 C7
Punchbowl La RH4, RH5 .136 D6
Punch Copse Rd RH10 . . .201 F7
Punnetts Ct RH11 . . . . . . .200 F2
Purbeck Ave KT3 . . . . 38 F3
Purbeck CI RH1 . . . . .119 D7
Purbeck Ct **6** GU2 . . . . .108 E1
Purbeck Dr GU21 . . . . 69 F5
Purberry Gr KT17 . . . . 57 F1
Purberry Shot KT17 . . . . . . 57 F1
Purbrook RH4 . . . . .115 C2
Purbrook Ct RG12 . . . . 27 E3
Purbrook Ho **2** SW15 . . . 19 B7
Purcell CI
  Kenley CR8 . . . . 80 C5
  Teddington TW2 . . . . 5 D1
Purcell Rd
  Crawley RH11 . . . . .200 F3
  Crowthorne RG45 . . . . 45 B7
Purcell's CI KT21 . . . . 75 F1
Purdey Ct **8** KT4 . . . . 39 A1
PURLEY 80 B7
Purley Bury Ave CR8 . . . . . 80 C8
Purley Bury CI CR8 . . . . 80 C8
Purley CI RH10 . . . . .202 D3
Purley Ct CR8 . . . . 61 B1
Purley Downs Rd CR2 . . . . 80 E8
Purley Grange CR2 . . . . 61 C1
Purley Hill CR8 . . . . 80 B7
Purley Knoll CR8 . . . . 80 A8
Purley Oaks Prim Sch
  CR2 . . . . 61 D3
Purley Oaks Rd CR2 . . . . . . 61 D1
Purley Oaks Sta CR2 . . . . . 61 D2
Purley Par **9** CR8 . . . . . . 80 A8
Purley Park Rd CR8 . . . . . . 61 B1
Purley Rd
  Purley CR8 . . . . 80 A8
  South Croydon CR2 . . . . . . 61 D3
Purley Rise CR8 . . . . 79 F7
Purley Sta CR8 . . . . 80 A7
Purley Vale CR8 . . . . 80 B6
Purley View Terr CR2 . . . . 61 D3
Purley War Memorial Hospl
  13 CR8 . . . . 80 A8
Purley Way
  Croydon CR0, CR9 . . . . . . 61 A4
  Frimley GU16 . . . . 85 E8
  Purley CR8 . . . . 80 A8
  Thornton Heath CR0, CR9 . 41 F1
Purley Way Cres CR0 . . . . 41 F2
Purmerend CI GU14 . . . . . . 84 C5
Pursers Hollow GU5 . . . . .154 D8
Pursers La GU5 . . . . .154 D8
Pursers Lea GU5 . . . . .154 D7
Purslane RG40 . . . . 25 D5
Purton Rd RH12 . . . . .217 B4
Purvis Ho CR0 . . . . 42 D2
PUTNEY 19 C7
PUTNEY HEATH 19 C8
Putney Heath SW15 . . . . . . 19 B8
Putney Hill
  London SW15 . . . . 19 C8
  Putney SW15 . . . . 19 D8
PUTNEY VALE 19 A5
PUTTENHAM 128 C4
Puttenham CE Inf Sch
  GU3 . . . . .128 C4
Puttenham Common Nature
  Trails★ GU3 . . . . .148 E3
Puttenham Heath Rd
  GU3 . . . . .128 E3
Puttenham Hill GU3 . . . . .128 C5
Puttenham La GU3, GU8 . .128 C1
Puttenham Rd GU10 . . . . .127 C4
Puttocks CI GU27 . . . . .207 D5
Pye CI CR3 . . . . .100 D4
Pyecombe Ct **4** RH11 . .200 F3
Pyegrove Chase RG12 . . . . 27 E2
PYESTOCK 84 B2
Pyestock Cres GU14 . . . . . 84 C4
Pyke CI RG40 . . . . 25 D6
Pylbrook Rd SM1 . . . . 59 B7
Pyle Hill GU22 . . . . 89 D3
Pylon Way CR0 . . . . 41 E1
Pymers Mead SE21 . . . . . . 22 C7
Pyne Rd KT6 . . . . 38 A1
Pyrcroft Ct KT16 . . . . 32 F2
Pyrcroft Grange Prim Sch
  KT16 . . . . 32 E2
Pyrcroft La KT13 . . . . 53 B5
Pyrcroft Rd KT16 . . . . 32 E2
PYRFORD 70 E4
Pyrford CE Prim Sch
  GU22 . . . . 71 A3
Pyrford Common Rd
  GU22 . . . . 70 E2
PYRFORD GREEN 71 B2
Pyrford Heath GU22 . . . . . . 70 F3
Pyrford Place GU22 . . . . . . 71 C1
PYRFORD VILLAGE 71 A1
Pyrford Woods CI GU22 . . 70 F4
PYRFORD WOODS
  ESTATE 70 F3
Pyrford Woods Rd GU22 . . 70 F4
Pyrian CI GU22 . . . . 70 D2
Pyrland Rd TW10 . . . . 6 F1
Pyrmont Gr SE27 . . . . 22 B5
Pyrmont Rd W4 . . . . 7 A8
Pytchley Cres SE19 . . . . . . 22 C2

Q

Quadrangle Lodge SW19 . 20 A2
Quadrangle The
  Guildford GU2 . . . . .130 A8
  2 Horley RH6 . . . . .161 B3
Quadrant Ct RG12 . . . . 27 E6
Quadrant Ctyd **4** KT13 . . 53 A6
Quadrant Rd
  Richmond TW9 . . . . 6 D3
  Thornton Heath CR7 . . . . . 42 B5
Quadrant The
  Addlestone KT15 . . . . 52 C5
  Ash Vale GU12 . . . . .106 A4
  Merton SW20 . . . . 39 E8
  Richmond TW9 . . . . 6 E3
  Sutton SM2 . . . . 59 C4
Quadrant Way KT13 . . . . . . 53 A6
Quadrum Pk GU3 . . . . .130 B2
Quail CI RH12 . . . . .217 D7
Quail Cnr RG12 . . . . 26 E5
Quail Gdns CR0 . . . . 62 E1
Quakers La CR7 . . . . 6 A6
QUAKER'S PLATT 186 A8
Quakers Way GU3 . . . . . . .108 C5
Qualitas RG12 . . . . 26 F1
Quality St RH1 . . . . .119 B7
Quantock CI
  Crawley RH11 . . . . .201 B6
  Harlington UB3 . . . . 3 D7
Quantock Dr KT4 . . . . 58 C6
Quarr Rd SM5 . . . . 40 E3
Quarry Bank GU18 . . . . 67 A8
Quarry CI
  Horsham RH12 . . . . .217 F6
  Oxted RH8 . . . . .122 E5
Quarry Cotts RH1 . . . . 99 C1
Quarry Gdns KT22 . . . . 95 D6
Quarry Hill GU7 . . . . .150 B3
Quarry Hill Pk RH2 . . . . . .118 C4
Quarry Park Rd SM1 . . . . . 58 F4
Quarry Rd
  Leatherhead KT22 . . . . . . 95 D6
  Oxted RH8 . . . . .122 E5
  Shackleford GU7 . . . . . . .150 A3
  Woldingham RH9 . . . . . . .121 C7
Quarry Rise
  Cheam SM1 . . . . 58 F4
  East Grinstead RH19 . . . .186 A3
Quarryside Bsns Pk RH1 119 B5
Quarry St GU1 . . . . .130 D7
Quarry The RH3 . . . . .116 D3
Quarterbrass Farm Rd
  RH12 . . . . .217 D7
Quartermaine Ave GU22 . . 89 F5
Quartermaine Ho GU22 . . 89 F5
Quartermain Ho SM4 . . . . 40 C4
Quarter Mile Rd GU7 . . . .150 E2
Quayside Wlk KT1 . . . . 37 D7
Quay West TW11 . . . . 17 B3
Quebec CI RH6 . . . . .162 A3
Quebec Gdns GU17 . . . . . . 64 D4
Queen Adelaide Ct SE20 . 23 C2
Queen Adelaide Rd SE20 . 23 C1
Queen Alexandra's Ct **5**
  SW19 . . . . 19 F3
Queen Alexandra's Way
  KT19 . . . . 76 A7
Queen Anne Ave BR2 . . . . 44 F6
Queen Anne Dr KT10 . . . . . 55 E3
Queen Annes CI TW2 . . . . . 16 D5
Queen Anne's CI SL4 . . . . . 10 B5
Queen Annes Ct KT22 . . . . 95 B6
Queen Anne's Gate GU9 . .125 D7
Queen Anne's Gdns
  Leatherhead KT22 . . . . . . 95 B6
  4 Mitcham CR4 . . . . 40 F6
Queen Anne's Terr KT22 . . 95 B6
Queenborough Ho N **3**
  KT13 . . . . 53 E7
Queenborough Ho S **4**
  KT13 . . . . 53 E7
Queendale Ct GU21 . . . . . . 68 F3
Queen Eleanor's CE Jun Sch
  GU2 . . . . .130 A8
Queen Eleanor's Rd GU2 .129 F8
Queen Elizabeth CI
  GU12 . . . . .106 A2
Queen Elizabeth Dr
  GU11 . . . . .104 F2
Queen Elizabeth Gdns
  SM4 . . . . 40 A5
Queen Elizabeth Ho
  2 Balham SW12 . . . . 21 A8
  Weybridge KT13 . . . . 53 D5
Queen Elizabeth II Silver
  Jubilee Sch RH13 . . . . .217 F1
Queen Elizabeth Rd
  Camberley GU15 . . . . 46 D1
  Kingston upon Thames KT2 . 37 F7
  Rudgwick RH12 . . . . .214 D7
Queen Elizabeth's Dr CR0 63 D1
Queen Elizabeth's
  Foundation Training Coll
  KT22 . . . . 74 D2
Queen Elizabeth's Gdns
  CR0 . . . . 63 D1
Queen Elizabeth's Wlk
  SM6 . . . . 60 D6
Queen Elizabeth Way
  GU22 . . . . 90 A8
Queenhill Rd CR2 . . . . 62 B1
Queenhythe Cres GU4 . . .109 D7
Queenhythe Rd GU4 . . . . .109 D7
Queen Mary Ave
  Camberley GU15 . . . . 65 A5

Queen Mary Ave continued
  West Barnes SM4, SW20 . . 39 D4
Queen Mary CI
  Tolworth KT9 . . . . 57 A8
  Woking GU22 . . . . 70 C3
Queen Mary Ct TW19 . . . . 13 E7
Queen Mary Rd
  Charlton TW17 . . . . 34 C7
  South Norwood SE19 . . . . . 22 B2
Queen Mary's Ave SM5 . . . 59 F3
Queen Mary's Dr KT15 . . . 52 A1
Queen Mary's Hospital Sch
  SM5 . . . . 59 F2
Queens Acre SM3 . . . . 58 E3
Queens Ave
  Byfleet KT14 . . . . 71 D7
  Feltham TW13 . . . . 15 C4
Queen's Ave GU11 . . . . . . .105 B5
Queensberry Ho **6** TW9 . .6 D2
Queensberry PI **33** TW10 . .6 D2
Queensbridge Pk TW7 . . . . .5 E2
Queensbury Ct **2** CR7 . . 42 C7
Queensbury PI GU17 . . . . . 64 C3
Queen's CE Prim Sch The
  TW9 . . . . 7 A7
Queens CI
  Bisley GU24 . . . . 68 A3
  Walton on the Hill KT20 . . . 97 A3
Queen's CI
  Esher KT10 . . . . 55 B6
  Farnborough GU14 . . . . . .105 B8
  North Ascot SL5 . . . . 28 E8
  Wallington SM6 . . . . 60 B5
Queens Court Ride KT11 . . 73 A6
Queens Cres TW10 . . . . .6 F2
Queen's Cres RH4 . . . . . . .136 A6
Queens Ct
  Beckenham BR3 . . . . 24 B1
  Belmont SM2 . . . . 78 A8
  Epsom KT19 . . . . 57 E1
  Hale GU9 . . . . .125 C6
  Horsham RH13 . . . . .217 D1
  3 Redhill RH1 . . . . .119 A2
  Weybridge KT13 . . . . 53 E4
  9 Woking GU22 . . . . 69 F1
Queen's Ct
  Beckenham BR3 . . . . 44 A8
  Croydon CR2 . . . . 61 C5
  Farnborough GU14 . . . . . .105 C8
  Horley RH6 . . . . .161 A3
  1 Kingston upon Thames
  KT2 . . . . 18 A1
  3 Richmond TW10 . . . . . .6 F1
  Staines TW18 . . . . 13 D2
  Thornton Heath CR7 . . . . . 42 A4
Queens Ct Ride KT11 . . . . . 73 A6
Queens Dr
  Oxshott KT22 . . . . 74 C8
  Surbiton KT5 . . . . 38 A3
Queen's Dr
  Farncombe GU7 . . . . .150 C7
  Guildford GU2 . . . . .109 A4
  Thames Ditton KT7 . . . . . . 37 A3
Queensgate Ct SM3 . . . . . . 58 C6
Queensgate KT11 . . . . 73 D7
Queens Gate RH6 . . . . . . .182 C3
Queen's Gate Rd GU14 . . .105 B8
Queen's Gdns TW5 . . . . .4 E6
Queenshill Lodge SL5 . . . . 29 B6
Queen's Hill Rise SL5 . . . . 29 C6
Queen's Ho TW11 . . . . 16 F2
Queens Keep
  Camberley GU15 . . . . 65 D5
  10 Twickenham TW1 . . . . 6 C1
Queens La GU9 . . . . .125 B7
Queensland Ave SW19 . . . 40 B8
Queensmead
  Ashford TW15 . . . . 13 F3
  Farnborough GU14 . . . . . . 85 B8
Queen's Mead GU8 . . . . . .191 B4
Queensmead Ave KT17 . . . 58 B1
Queen's Mead Rd BR2 . . . . 44 F7
Queensmere **4** SM1 . . . . 59 B5
Queensmere CI SW19 . . . . 19 D6
Queensmere Rd SW19 . . . . 19 D6
Queens Park Gdns TW13 . 14 F5
Queen's Park Rd CR3 . . . .100 E4
Queens Pine RG12 . . . . 27 E3
Queens PI KT12 . . . . 53 F5
Queen's PI
  Ascot SL5 . . . . 29 A6
  Morden SM4 . . . . 40 A5
Queens Rd
  Aldershot GU11 . . . . .104 F2
  Belmont SM2 . . . . 78 A8
  Bisley GU24 . . . . 67 F1
  Camberley GU15 . . . . 65 B4
  Farnborough GU14 . . . . . .105 D8
  Hale GU9 . . . . .125 C6
  Hersham KT12 . . . . 54 A6
  Morden SM4 . . . . 40 A5
  Twickenham TW1 . . . . 17 A7
  Weybridge KT13 . . . . 53 C5
Queen's Rd
  Ascot SL5 . . . . 29 A4
  Beckenham BR3 . . . . 43 E7
  East Grinstead RH19 . . . .185 E1
  Egham TW20 . . . . 11 F2
  Feltham TW13 . . . . 15 B7
  Guildford GU1 . . . . .130 D8
  Hampton TW12 . . . . 16 B4
  Horley RH6 . . . . .161 A3
  Hounslow TW3 . . . . 5 B4
  Kingston upon Thames KT2 . 18 A1

Queen's Rd *continued*
Knaphill GU21 68 D1
Mitcham CR4 40 D6
Mortlake SW14 7 D4
New Malden KT3 38 F4
Richmond, Petersham KT2, TW10 17 E7
Richmond TW10 6 F1
Teddington TW11 16 F2
Thames Ditton KT7 36 F4
Thornton Heath CR0 42 C3
Wallington SM6 60 B5
Wimbledon SW19 20 A2
Queen's Rdbt GU11 105 B7
Queens Reach KT8 36 E5
Queens Ride RG45 45 B7
Queen's Rise TW10 6 F1
Queens Sq RH10 201 D6
Queens St 3 TW15 13 F4
Queen St
Aldershot GU12 105 D2
Chertsey KT16 33 A1
Croydon CR0, CR9 61 C6
Godalming GU7 150 E4
Gomshall GU5 133 C4
Horsham RH13 217 D1
Queen's Terr TW7 6 A3
Queensthorpe Rd SE26 23 D4
Queensville Rd SW12, SW4 21 D8
Queensway
Coney Hall BR4 63 F6
Cranleigh GU6 174 F2
Crawley RH10 201 E6
East Grinstead RH19 185 E1
Frimley GU16 86 A7
Hersham KT12 54 C6
Horsham RH13 217 C1
Redhill RH1 118 F2
Sunbury TW16 35 B7
Queens Way
Croydon CR0 60 F5
Feltham TW13 15 C4
Queen's Way GU24 87 D8
Queensway N KT12 54 C5
Queensway S KT12 54 C5
Queens Wlk TW15 13 D4
Queen's Wlk RH19 185 E1
Queenswood Ave
Hampton TW12 16 B2
Hounslow TW3, TW5 4 F5
Thornton Heath CR7 42 A4
Wallington CR0, SM6 60 D6
Queenswood Ct 11 SE27 22 D4
Queenswood Rd
Forest Hill SE23 23 E5
Knaphill GU21 88 D8
Queen Victoria Cross Roads GU15 65 A6
Queen Victoria Ct GU14 85 B5
Queen Victoria Ho RG40 25 D6
Queen Victoria Hospl The RH19 185 F3
Queen Victoria Way GU24 87 D8
Quennel Ho 7 SW12 21 C8
Quennell Cl KT21 95 F8
Quennells Hill GU10 145 E6
Quentin Way GU25 31 B5
Quicks Rd SW19 20 B1
Quiet Cl KT15 52 A6
Quillot The KT12 53 F5
Quince Cl SL5 29 D5
Quince Dr GU24 68 B4
Quince Ho TW13 15 A7
Quincy Rd TW20 12 A3
Quinnettes GU10 167 F1
Quinneys GU14 85 C1
Quintet The KT12 35 A1
Quintilis RG12 26 F1
Quintin Ave SW20 39 F8
Quintin Ct W4 7 C7
Quintock Ho 2 TW9 7 A6
Quinton Cl
Beckenham BR3 44 C6
Hackbridge SM6 60 B6
Heston TW5 4 B7
Quinton Rd KT7 37 A1
Quinton St SW18 20 C6
Quintrell Cl GU21 69 B2

R

Rabbit La KT12 54 B3
Rabies Heath Rd
Bletchingley RH1 120 F2
Godstone RH1, RH9 121 B1
Raby Rd KT3 38 D5
Raccoon Way TW4 4 C5
Racecourse Rd
Crawley RH6 182 A8
Dormansland RH7 165 A2
Lingfield RH7 164 F3
Racecourse Way RH6 181 F8
Rachel Ct SM2 59 D3
Rackfield GU27 207 D7
Rackham Cl RH11 201 D4
Rackham Mews SW16 21 C2
Racks Ct GU1 130 D7
Rackstraw Rd GU47 45 D2
Racquets Court Hill GU7 150 C6
Radar Rd GU14 84 D1
Radbourne Rd SW12 21 D7
Radcliffe Cl GU16 86 A7
Radcliffe Gdns SM5 59 E3
Radcliffe Rd CR0 61 F7
Radcliffe Way RG42 26 E8
Radcliff Mews TW12 16 C3
Radcot Point 2 SE23 23 D5
Radford Cl GU9 125 E5
Radford Rd RH6, RH10 182 C4
Radius Pk TW6 3 F3
Rad La GU5 133 D1
Radlet Ave SE23 23 B6
Radley Cl TW14 14 F7
Radley Ct BR1 24 C4
Radley Lodge 30 SW19 19 D7
Radnor Cl CR4 41 E5
Radnor Ct
6 Forest Hill SE23 23 D5
Redhill RH1 118 E1
Radnor Gdns TW1 16 F6
Radnor Ho
East Molesey KT8 36 D5
4 New Malden KT3 38 F4
Thornton Heath SW16 41 F7
Radnor La
Abinger Common RH5 155 B7
Ewhurst RH5 155 A2
Radnor Rd
Bracknell RG12 27 F6
Peaslake GU5, GU6 154 E4
Twickenham TW1 16 F6
Weybridge KT13 53 A7
Radnor Wlk CR0 43 E3
Radolphs KT20 97 D5
Radstock Way RH1 119 E7
Radstone Ct 11 GU22 69 F1
Raebarn Ct 6 SW16 21 E5
Raeburn Ave KT5 38 B3
Raeburn Cl KT1 17 D1
Raeburn Gr GU21 89 A8
Raeburn Ho 11 SM2 59 B3
Raeburn Open Space Nature Reserve* KT5 38 B4
Raeburn Way GU47 64 D6
Rae Rd GU14 85 B1
RAFBOROUGH 84 F3
Rafdene Copse GU22 89 C8
RAG HILL 103 E6
Rag Hill TN16 103 E6
Rag Hill Cl TN16 103 E6
Rag Hill Rd TN16 103 E6
Raglan Cl
Aldershot GU12 105 C1
Frimley GU16 86 A8
Hounslow TW4 4 F2
Reigate RH2 118 D3
Raglan Ct CR0, CR2 61 B5
Raglan Prec The CR3 100 E5
Raglan Rd
Knaphill GU21 68 E1
Reigate RH2 118 C3
Raglans Bglws RH2 118 B4
Ragwort Ct 1 SE26 23 B3
Raikes La RH5 134 B2
Railey Rd RH10 201 E7
Railshead Rd TW1, TW7 6 B3
Railton Rd GU2 109 B5
Railway App
East Grinstead RH19 185 E1
13 Twickenham TW1 17 A8
Wallington SM6 60 B5
Railway Cotts
East Grinstead RH19 204 F3
Purley CR8 79 F6
Railway Rd TW11 16 F4
Railway Side SW13, SW14 7 E4
Railway Terr
Egham TW18 12 D3
Feltham TW13 15 A7
Rainbow Ct GU21 68 E3
Rainbow Ind Est SW20 39 B7
Rainbow L Ctr KT17 76 E7
Rainbow Sch for Autistic Children SW17 20 C6
Rainforest Wlk RG12 27 B4
Rake La
Milford GU8 171 A7
Witley GU8 170 F7
Rakers Ridge RH12 217 D5
Raleigh Ave SM6 60 D6
Raleigh Ct BR3 44 B8
Raleigh Ct RH10 182 A3
Raleigh Ct
Dulwich SE19 22 F3
Staines TW18 13 A4
Wallington SM6 60 B4
Raleigh Dr
Esher KT10 55 D5
Smallfield RH6 162 A3
Tolworth KT5 38 C1
Raleigh Gdns CR4 40 F6
Raleigh Ho 1 KT7 37 A2
Raleigh Rd
Feltham TW13 14 F6
Penge SE20 23 D1
Richmond TW9 6 F4
Raleigh Sch The KT24 92 C2
Raleigh Way
Feltham TW13 15 C3
Frimley GU16 65 F3
Raleigh Wlk RH10 201 E4
Ralliwood Rd KT21 96 A8
Ralph Perring Ct BR3 44 A5
Ralphs Ride RG12 27 E6
Rama Cl SW16 21 E1
Rama La
London SE19 22 F1
Penge SE19 22 F1
Rambler Cl SW16 21 C4
Ramblers Ct RH12 216 E3
Ramblers Way 12 RH11 201 B1
Rame Cl SW17 21 A3
Ramillies Cl GU11 105 E7
Ramillies Rd GU11 105 D5
Ramin Ct GU1 109 C4
Ramornie Cl KT12 54 F6
Ramsay Cl GU15 66 B8
Ramsay Rd GU20 48 E5
Ramsbury Cl RG12 26 E3
Ramsdale Rd SW17 21 A3
Ramsdean Ho 1 SW15 19 B7
Ramsden Rd
Balham SW12 21 A8
Godalming GU7 150 D3
Ramsey Cl
Horley RH6 160 F3
Horsham RH12 217 D5
Ramsey Ct 18 RH11 201 B1
Ramsey Ho 7 SW19 40 B8
Ramsey Pl CR3 100 C5
Ramsey Rd CR7 41 F3
Rams La GU8 193 B3
Ramslade Cotts RG12 27 C6
RAMSNEST COMMON 210 A6
Rances La RG40 25 E5
Randal Cres RH2 139 A7
Randalls Bsns Pk KT22 95 A7
Randall Scofield Ct RH10 202 A7
Randalls Cotts KT11 73 B7
Randalls Cres KT22 95 A7
Randalls Park Ave KT22 95 A7
Randalls Park Dr KT22 95 A6
Randalls Rd KT22 94 E7
Randalls Way KT22 95 A7
Randell Cl GU17 64 E1
Randisbourne Gdns SE6 24 B5
Randle Rd TW10 17 C4
Randlesdown Rd SE6 24 B5
Randmore Ct 6 BR3 24 A1
Randolph Cl
Kingston upon Thames KT2 18 C3
Knaphill GU21 68 E2
Oxshott KT11 74 A4
Randolph Dr GU14 84 C3
Randolph Rd KT17 76 F5
Ranelagh Cres SL5 28 D8
Ranelagh Dr
Bracknell RG12 27 C6
Isleworth TW1 6 B2
Ranelagh Gdns W4 7 C7
Ranelagh Pl KT3 38 E4
Ranelagh Rd RH1 118 E1
Ranelagh Sch RG12 27 C6
Ranfurly Rd SM1 59 A8
Rangefield Prim Sch BR1 24 E3
Rangefield Rd BR1 24 F3
Range Rd
Farnborough GU14 84 C1
Farnborough GU14 84 D1
Range Ride GU15 64 F7
Ranger Mans SE19 22 F2
Ranger Wlk KT15 52 B5
Range The GU5 152 A4
Range View GU47 64 E8
Range Villas TW17 33 E2
Range Way TW17 34 A2
Rankine Cl GU9 126 A6
Ranmere St SW12 21 B7
Ranmore Ave CR0 61 F7
Ranmore Cl RH1 119 A4
Ranmore Common Rd RH5 114 D2
Ranmore Ct
Kingston upon Thames KT6 37 D4
5 Wimbledon SW20 39 D8
Ranmore Pl KT13 53 C5
Ranmore Rd
Dorking RH4, RH5 114 E1
East Ewell SM2 58 D2
Ranmore View 9 RH4 136 A7
Rann Ho 1 SW14 7 D4
Rannoch Ct 9 KT6 37 E4
Ransford Ho 16 SE21 22 E4
Ransome Cl RH11 200 E3
Ranyard Cl KT9 56 F7
Rapallo Cl GU14 85 C4
Raphael Cl KT1 37 D5
Raphael Dr KT7 36 F1
Raphel Dr KT7 37 A2
Rapley Cl GU15 65 F8
Rapley Gn RG12 27 C3
Rapley's Field GU24 87 E4
Rapsley La GU21 68 B1
Rastell Ave SW12 21 D7
Ratcliffe Rd GU14 85 A8
Rathbone Ho
Crawley RH11 201 B1
4 Wimbledon SW20 19 D1
Rathbone Sq CR0 61 C6
Rathfern Prim Sch SE6 23 F7
Rathfern Rd SE23, SE6 23 F7
Rathgar Cl RH1 140 A4
Rathlin Rd RH11 201 B3
Rattray Ct SE6 24 F6
Raven Cl
Horsham RH12 217 E6
Turners Hill RH10 204 C5
Ravendale Rd TW16 34 F7
Ravendene Ct 3 RH10 201 D5
Ravenfield Rd SW17 20 F5
Raven La RH11 201 C8
Ravensbourne Ave
Bromley BR2 44 E8
Catford BR2 24 D1
Stanwell TW19 13 E7
Ravensbourne Ct SE6 24 A8
Ravensbourne Ho
Catford BR1 24 D3
3 Twickenham TW1 6 C1
Ravensbourne Park Cres SE6 23 F8
Ravensbourne Pk SE4, SE6 24 A8
Ravensbourne Rd
Forest Hill SE23 23 F7
Twickenham TW1 6 C1
Ravensbourne Sta BR3 24 D1
Ravensbury Ave SM4 40 C4
Ravensbury Ct
5 Carshalton SM1 59 D5
Mitcham CR4 40 D5
Ravensbury Gr CR4 40 D5
Ravensbury La CR4 40 D5
Ravensbury Park Nature Reserve* CR4 40 D5
Ravensbury Rd SW18 20 B6
Ravensbury Terr SW18 20 B6
Ravenscar Lodge 18 SW20 19 D1
Ravenscar Rd
Catford BR1 24 E4
Surbiton KT6 56 F8
Ravens Cl
Bromley BR2 44 F7
Kingston upon Thames KT6 37 D3
Knaphill GU21 68 C3
Redhill RH1 118 F2
Ravenscote Jun Sch GU16 66 A3
Ravenscourt TW16 34 F8
Ravenscroft Cl GU12 106 C3
Ravenscroft Ct RH12 217 C3
Ravenscroft Rd
Penge BR3 43 D7
Weybridge KT13 72 C8
Ravensdale Gdns
Hounslow TW4 4 E4
South Norwood SE19 22 D1
Ravensdale Mews TW18 13 B2
Ravensdale Rd
Ascot SL5 29 A4
Hounslow TW4 4 E4
Ravensfield TW20 11 C2
Ravensfield Gdns KT19 57 E6
Ravenshead Cl CR2 81 C8
Ravens Ho KT1 37 D7
Ravenside KT6 37 D4
Ravenslea Rd SW11, SW12 20 F8
Ravensmead Rd BR2 24 D1
Ravensroost SE19 42 D8
Ravenstone Prim Sch SW12 21 A6
Ravenstone Rd GU15 66 D5
Ravenstone St SW12 21 A7
Ravensview Ct KT6 37 D4
Ravenswold CR8 80 C4
Ravenswood Ave
Tolworth KT6 57 A8
West Wickham BR4 44 C1
Ravenswood Cl KT11 73 D4
Ravenswood Cres BR4 44 C1
Ravenswood Ct
Dorking RH4 136 B6
Kingston upon Thames KT2 18 B2
Woking GU22 69 F1
Ravenswood Dr GU15 66 A5
Ravenswood Gdns TW7 5 E6
Ravenswood Rd
Balham SW12 21 B8
Croydon CR0, CR9 61 B7
Rawdon Rise GU15 66 B5
Rawlings Cl BR3 44 C4
Rawlins Cl CR2 62 F3
Rawlinson Rd
Crawley RH10 202 D4
Farnborough GU11 105 C5
Sandhurst GU15 64 F6
Rawnsley Ave CR4 40 E4
Raworth Cl RH10 202 C4
Rayat London Coll TW5 4 F7
Raybell Ct TW7 5 F5
Ray Cl
Chessington KT9 56 C4
Lingfield RH7 164 C5
Ray Cnr RH7 164 B6
Rayford Ave SE12 24 F8
Ray La
Blindley Heath RH7 163 F7
Lingfield RH7 164 B6
Rayleigh Ave TW11 16 E2
Rayleigh Ct 3 KT1 37 F7
Rayleigh Rd SW19 39 F8
Rayleigh Rise CR2 61 E4
Raymead Ave CR7 42 A4
Raymead Cl KT22 94 F5
Raymead Way KT22 94 F5
Raymer Wlk RH6 161 C4
Raymond Cl
Forest Hill SE26 23 C3
Poyle SL3 1 E6
Raymond Cres GU2 129 F8
Raymond Ct SM2 59 B4
Raymond Rd
Beckenham BR3 43 E5
Wimbledon SW19 19 E2
Raymond Way KT10 56 A4
Raynald Ho 16 SW16 21 E5
Rayners Cl SL3 1 C7
Raynesfield SW20 39 C6
RAYNES PARK 39 C6
Raynes Park High Sch SW20 39 B6
Raynes Park Sta SW20 39 C7
Ray Rd KT8 36 B4
Rays Rd BR4 44 C2
Raywood Cl UB7 3 C7
Read Cl KT7 37 A2
Readens The SM7 78 F3
Reading Arch Rd RH1 118 F1
Reading Rd
Blackwater GU17 64 B4
Farnborough GU14 85 D1
Sutton SM1 59 C5
Wokingham RG41 25 A7
Readman Ct 9 SE20 43 B8
Read Rd KT21 75 D2
Reads Rest La KT20 98 A7
Reapers Cl RH12 217 D5
Reapers Way TW7 5 D2
Rebecca Ct 3 BR3 44 A8
Recovery St SW17 20 E3
Recreation Cl GU14 64 F1
Recreation Rd
Bromley BR2 44 F7
Forest Hill SE26 23 D4
Guildford GU1 109 D1
Rowledge GU10 145 E3
Recreation Way CR4, SW16 41 E6
Rectory Cl
Ashtead KT21 95 F8
Bracknell RG12 27 C5
Byfleet KT14 71 E6
Ewhurst GU6 175 E5
Godalming GU7 150 F2
Guildford GU4 110 D3
Littleton TW17 34 A6
Long Ditton KT6 37 C1
Ockley RH5 177 C3
West Barnes SW20 39 C6
Wokingham RG40 25 C6
Rectory Ct
1 Beckenham BR3 43 F7
Cranford TW5 4 C5
Feltham TW13 15 C4
8 Guildford GU1 130 C8
Sanderstead CR2 80 F7
Wallington SM6 60 C6
Rectory Gdns BR3 44 A8
Rectory Gn BR3 43 F8
Rectory Gr
Croydon CR0, CR9 61 B8
Hampton TW12 15 F4
Rectory La
Ashtead KT21 95 F8
Bracknell RG12 27 B5
Buckland RH3 116 F3
Byfleet KT14 71 E6
Charlwood RH6 180 D7
Crawley RH11 200 F8
Great Bookham KT23 113 F8
Long Ditton KT6 37 C1
Shere GU5 133 A4
Streatham SW17 21 A3
Surbiton KT6 56 C8
Titsey TN16 103 E4
Wallington SM6 60 C6
Windlesham GU20 48 C4
Woodmansterne CR5, SM7 78 F3
Rectory Orch SW19 19 E4
Rectory Pk CR2 80 F7
Rectory Rd
Beckenham BR3 44 A8
Cranford TW5 4 C5
Farnborough GU14 85 D4
Lower Kingswood CR5 98 C2
Sutton SM1 59 B7
Wokingham RG40 25 C6
Rectory Row RG12 27 B5
Red Admiral St RH12 217 E5
Redan Gdns GU12 105 C2
Redan Hill Est GU12 105 C2
Redan Rd GU12 105 C2
Redbarn Cl CR8 80 B8
Redberry Gr SE23, SE26 23 C5
Redcar Ho SE26 23 B2
Redcliffe Gdns W4 7 B7
Redclose Ave SM4 40 A4
Redclyffe Terr 2 SM2 59 A3
Redcote Pl RH4 115 D1
Redcourt
Pyrford GU22 70 E4
Woking GU22 70 D4
Redcrest Gdns GU15 65 F5
Redcroft Wlk GU6 174 E2
Red Deer Cl RH13 218 B4
Reddington Cl CR2 61 D2
Redding Way GU21 68 C1
Redditch RG12 27 D2
Redditch Cl RH11 200 E2
Reddons Rd BR3 23 E1
Reddown Rd CR5 79 D2
Rede Ct
Farnborough GU14 85 C1
Weybridge KT13 53 B7
Redehall Ind Pk RH6 183 C7
Redehall Prep Sch RH6 162 B2
Redehall Rd
Burstow RH6 183 C8
Smallfield RH6 162 B2
Redesdale Gdns TW7 6 A7
Redfern Ave TW4 16 A8
Redfern Rd SE6 24 C8
Redford Ave
Horsham RH12 217 B4
Thornton Heath CR7 41 F5
Wallington, Clock House CR5 79 B4
Wallington, Roundshaw SM6 60 E4
Redford Cl TW13 14 F6
Redgarth Ct RH19 185 B3

Red–Rie 287

Red Gates Sch CR0 . . . . . . 61 A5
Redgrave Cl CR0 . . . . 42 F3
Redgrave Ct GU12 . . . . 105 F2
Redgrave Dr RH10 . . . . . . 202 D5
Redhall Ct CR3 . . . . 100 D4
Redhearne Fields GU10 . 167 E2
REDHILL 118 E2
Redhill Aerodrome RH1 . 140 D4
Redhill Ct SW2 . . . . 22 A6
Redhill Distribution Ctr
RH1 . . . . 161 A8
Redhill Rd KT11 . . . . 72 B5
Redhill Sta RH1 . . . . 119 A2
Red Ho The RH8 . . . . 123 C5
Red House La
Elstead GU8 . . . . 148 C2
Walton-on-Thames KT12 . . . 54 A8
Redhouse Rd TN16 . . . . . . 103 C6
Red House Rd CR0, CR9 . . . 41 D3
Redkiln Cl RH13 . . . . 217 F4
Redkiln Close Trad Est
RH13 . . . . 217 F3
Redkiln Way RH13 . . . . . . 217 F3
Redknap Ho TW10 . . . . 17 C5
Red La
Claygate KT10 . . . . 56 A4
Headley Down GU35 . . . . . 187 B7
Oxted RH8 . . . . 144 B7
South Holmwood RH5, RH3 136 F1
Redlake La RG40 . . . . 25 F2
Redland Gdns KT8 . . . . 35 F5
Redlands
Coulsdon CR5 . . . . 79 E3
Teddington TW11 . . . . 17 A2
Redlands Cotts RH5 . . . . . 136 B1
Redlands Ct BR1 . . . . 24 F1
Redlands Ctr CR5 . . . . 79 E4
Redlands La
Crondall GU10 . . . . 124 B7
Dorking RH5 . . . . 136 A1
Redlands The 5 BR3 . . . . . 44 B7
Redlands Way SW2 . . . . 21 F8
Redlane Cotts RH8 . . . . . . 123 B2
Redleaf Cl KT22 . . . . 94 E3
Redleaves Ave TW15 . . . . . . 14 B2
Redlees Cl TW7 . . . . 6 A3
Redlin Ct RH1 . . . . 118 F3
Red Lion Bsns Pk KT6 . . . . . 56 F7
Red Lion Cotts GU5 . . . . . 152 E4
Red Lion Ct TW3 . . . . 5 B4
Red Lion La
Chobham GU24 . . . . 49 E2
Farnham GU9 . . . . 125 B1
Red Lion Rd
Chobham GU24 . . . . 49 E2
Surbiton KT6 . . . . 57 A8
Red Lion St TW10 . . . . 6 D2
Red Lodge BR4 . . . . 44 C2
Red Lodge Rd BR3, BR4 . . . 44 D2
Redmayne GU15 . . . . 66 C4
Red Rd GU18, GU24, GU15 . . 67 C7
Red River Ct RH12 . . . . . . 217 B5
Redroofs Cl BR3 . . . . 44 B8
Redruth Gdns KT10 . . . . . . 55 F3
Redruth Ho SM2 . . . . 59 B3
Redshank Ct 5 RH11 . . . . 200 D5
Redstart Cl CR0 . . . . 63 D1
Redstone Hill RH1 . . . . . . 119 A1
Redstone Hollow RH1 . . . 140 A8
Redstone Manor RH1 . . . 119 A1
Redstone Pk RH1 . . . . 119 B1
Redstone Rd RH1 . . . . 140 A8
Redtiles Gdns CR8 . . . . 80 B4
Redvers Buller Rd GU11 105 D7
Redvers Ct CR6 . . . . 81 C1
Redvers Rd
Bracknell RG12 . . . . 27 B4
Warlingham CR6 . . . . 81 D1
Redway Cotts GU21 . . . . . . 88 F8
Redway Dr TW2 . . . . 16 C8
Redwing Ave GU7 . . . . 150 E8
Redwing Cl
Horsham RH13 . . . . 217 F3
Selsdon CR2 . . . . 81 D8
Redwing Ct 4 CR8 . . . . 80 B7
Redwing Gdns KT14 . . . . . . 71 B7
Redwing Rd SM6 . . . . 60 E3
Redwing Rise GU4 . . . . . . 110 D3
Redwood TW20 . . . . 32 E7
Redwood Cl
Crawley RH10 . . . . 201 E8
Kenley CR8 . . . . 80 C5
Redwood Ct
Ewell KT17 . . . . 76 F8
10 Surbiton KT6 . . . . 37 D2
Redwood Dr
Crawley RH11 . . . . 181 A1
Frimley GU15 . . . . 66 D4
Sunningdale SL5 . . . . 30 B3
Redwood Est TW5 . . . . 4 B8
Redwood Gr GU4 . . . . 131 C3
Redwood Lodge RH2 . . . . 118 C2
Redwood Manor GU27 . . . 208 C7
Redwood Mews TW15 . . . . . 14 D1
Redwood Mount RH2 . . . . 118 A4
Redwoods
Addlestone KT15 . . . . 52 A4
Roehampton SW15 . . . . 19 A7
Redwood Wlk KT6 . . . . 37 D1
Reed Cl GU11 . . . . 105 D5
Reed Dr RH1 . . . . 140 A6
Reedham Dr CR8 . . . . 80 A6
Reedham Park Ave CR8 . . 80 A3
Reedham Park Sch Ltd
CR8 . . . . 80 A5
Reedham Sta CR8 . . . . 79 F6
Reedings RH11 . . . . 200 D4
Reed Pl
Lower Halliford TW17 . . . . . 33 F1
Sheerwater GU21, KT14 . . . 70 E6
Reedsfield Cl TW15 . . . . . . 14 B5
Reedsfield Rd TW15 . . . . . . 14 B4
Reed's Hill RG12 . . . . 27 B4
Reeds Rd The
Frensham GU10 . . . . 146 E2
Tilford GU10 . . . . 147 A3
Reeds Sch KT11 . . . . 74 A7
Reeds The GU10 . . . . 147 A3
Rees Gdns CR0 . . . . 42 F3
Reeve Ct GU2 . . . . 109 A5
Reeve Rd RH2 . . . . 139 C5
Reeves Cnr CR0, CR9 . . . . . . 61 B8
Reeves Cnr Halt CR0 . . . . . 61 B8
Reeves Rd GU12 . . . . 105 C1
Reeves Way RG41 . . . . 25 A4
Regal Cres SM6 . . . . 60 B7
Regal Ct
1 Guildford GU1 . . . . 109 D1
2 Mitcham CR4 . . . . 40 F6
Regal Dr 10 RH19 . . . . 205 F8
Regalfield Cl GU2 . . . . . . 109 A5
Regan Cl GU2 . . . . 109 B6
Regatta Ho TW11 . . . . 17 A4
Regatta Point TW8 . . . . 6 F8
Regency Cl TW12 . . . . 15 F3
Regency Ct
6 Penge SE19 . . . . 23 A1
4 Surbiton KT5 . . . . 37 F4
Sutton SM1 . . . . 59 B6
Wimbledon SW19 . . . . 19 F1
Regency Dr KT14 . . . . 70 F6
Regency Gdns KT12 . . . . 35 D1
Regency Ho KT16 . . . . 32 F1
Regency Lodge KT13 . . . . . . 53 E7
Regency Mews
Beckenham BR3 . . . . 44 C8
Isleworth TW7 . . . . 5 E2
Regency Pl KT16 . . . . 33 A1
Regency Wlk
Croydon CR0 . . . . 43 F3
11 Richmond TW10 . . . . 6 E2
Regent Cl
Cranford TW5 . . . . 4 B6
New Haw KT15 . . . . 52 D2
Redhill RH1 . . . . 119 C6
Regent Cres RH1 . . . . 118 F3
Regent Ct
Bagshot GU19 . . . . 47 F2
Guildford GU2 . . . . 109 B3
South Norwood SE19 . . . . . . 22 B2
Regent Ho 1 SM7 . . . . 77 F5
Regent Lodge 9 SW2 . . . . . 21 F7
Regent Par 8 SM2 . . . . 59 C4
Regent Pk KT22 . . . . 75 A1
Regent Pl
Croydon CR0 . . . . 42 F1
Wimbledon SW19 . . . . 20 C3
Regent Rd KT5 . . . . 38 A4
Regents Cl
Crawley RH11 . . . . 201 C2
South Croydon CR2 . . . . 61 E4
Whyteleafe CR3 . . . . 80 F1
Regents Ct
23 Beckenham BR3 . . . . 24 A1
Bromley BR1 . . . . 24 F1
1 Kingston upon Thames
KT2 . . . . 37 E8
Staines TW18 . . . . 13 B2
Weybridge KT13 . . . . 53 B4
Woking GU21 . . . . 69 F3
Regents Ho 4 TW20 . . . . . . 12 A3
Regents Mews RH6 . . . . . . 161 A3
Regents Pl GU47 . . . . 64 C8
Regent St W4 . . . . 7 A8
Regents Wlk SL5 . . . . 29 C2
Regent Way GU16 . . . . 66 A1
Regiment Cl GU14 . . . . 84 C3
Regina Coeli RC Prim Sch
CR2 . . . . 61 B3
Regina Ct TW11 . . . . 16 E3
Reginald Ct BR3 . . . . 44 C8
Regina Rd SE25 . . . . 43 A6
Regis Ct
East Bedfont TW14 . . . . 3 D1
Mitcham SW19 . . . . 40 E8
Regnolruf Ct KT12 . . . . 35 A2
Reid Ave CR3 . . . . 100 D6
Reid Cl CR5 . . . . 79 B3
Reid Ct SW14 . . . . 7 C5
Reidonhill Cotts GU21 . . . . 68 B1
REIGATE 118 B2
Reigate Ave SM3, SM4 . . . . 40 B1
Reigate Cl RH10 . . . . 182 D1
Reigate Coll RH2 . . . . 118 B1
Reigate Gram Sch RH2 . . 118 C1
Reigate Heath Cotts
RH2 . . . . 117 E1
**Reigate Heath Nature
Reserve**★ RH2 . . . . 117 D1
Reigate Hill RH2 . . . . 118 B4
Reigate Hill Cl RH2 . . . . . 118 B4
**Reigate Parish Church Inf
Sch** RH2 . . . . 118 C1
Reigate Priory Jun Sch
RH2 . . . . 118 A1
Reigate Rd
Banstead KT17, KT18 . . . . . 77 C4
Betchworth RH3 . . . . 116 D2
Catford BR1 . . . . 24 F5
Dorking RH4 . . . . 115 E1
Hookwood RH2, RH6 . . . . . 160 C4
Leatherhead KT22 . . . . 95 D4
Reigate RH2 . . . . 118 C1
**Reigate St Mary's Prep &
Choir Sch** RH2 . . . . 118 B1
Reigate Sch RH1 . . . . 139 C6
Reigate Sta RH2 . . . . 118 A2
Reigate Way SM6 . . . . 60 E5
Reindorp Cl GU2 . . . . 130 A8
Relko Ct KT19 . . . . 76 D8
Relko Gdns SM1 . . . . 59 D5
Rembrandt Ct KT19 . . . . . . 57 F4
Rembrandt Way KT12 . . . . 54 B8
Renaissance Ct SM1 . . . . . 40 C1
Rendle Cl CR0, SE25 . . . . . . 43 A4
Renfree Way TW17 . . . . 34 A2
Renfrew Ct TW5 . . . . 4 E5
Renfrew Rd
Hounslow TW5 . . . . 4 E5
Kingston upon Thames KT2 . 18 C1
Renmans The KT21 . . . . 75 F3
Renmuir St SW17 . . . . 20 F2
Rennie Cl TW15 . . . . 13 D5
Rennie Terr RH1 . . . . 140 A8
Renown Cl CR0 . . . . 42 B1
Renshaw Cnr CR4 . . . . 41 A8
Renshaw Ct SW19 . . . . 19 E4
Renshaw Ho 11 SW27 . . . . . 22 B3
Replingham Rd SW18 . . . . . 20 A7
Repton Cl SM5 . . . . 59 E5
Repton Ct BR3 . . . . 44 B8
Reris Grange Cl GU8 . . . . 149 F2
Reservoir Cl CR7 . . . . 42 D6
Reservoir Rd GU14 . . . . 84 D1
Restmor Way SM5, SM6 . . . 60 A8
Restormel Cl TW3 . . . . 5 A2
Restwell Ave GU6 . . . . 174 B6
Retreat Rd TW9 . . . . 6 D2
Retreat The
Englefield Green TW20 . . . . 11 E3
Loxwood RH14 . . . . 212 F5
5 Mortlake SW14 . . . . 7 E4
North Cheam KT4 . . . . 58 B8
South Norwood CR7 . . . . . . 42 D5
Surbiton KT5 . . . . 37 F3
Revell Cl KT22 . . . . 94 B5
Revell Dr KT22 . . . . 94 B5
Revell Rd
Cheam SM1 . . . . 58 F4
Kingston upon Thames KT1 . 38 B8
Revelstoke Ave GU14 . . . . . 85 B6
Revelstoke Rd SW18,
SW19 . . . . 20 A6
Revere Way KT19 . . . . 57 E2
Revesby Cl GU24 . . . . 67 D6
Revesby Rd SM5 . . . . 40 E3
Rewley Rd SM4 . . . . 40 D3
Rex Ave TW15 . . . . 14 A3
Rex Ct GU27 . . . . 207 F6
Rex Ho TW13 . . . . 15 E5
Reynard Cl RH12 . . . . 218 B5
Reynard Ct 12 CR8 . . . . 80 A8
Reynard Dr SE19 . . . . 22 F1
Reynolds Ave KT9 . . . . 56 E3
Reynolds Cl
Carshalton CR4, SM5 . . . . . . 40 F1
Mitcham CR4, SW19 . . . . . . 40 D8
Reynolds Gn GU47 . . . . 64 D6
Reynolds Pl
Crawley RH11 . . . . 201 C7
13 Richmond TW10 . . . . 6 F1
Reynolds Rd
Crawley RH11 . . . . 201 C7
Farnborough GU14 . . . . . . 104 B8
New Malden KT3 . . . . 38 D2
Reynolds Way CR0 . . . . 61 E6
Rheingold Way SM6 . . . . . . 60 E2
Rhine Banks GU14 . . . . 84 D5
**Rhizotron & Xstrata Treetop
Walkway**★ TW9 . . . . 6 E6
Rhodes Cl TW20 . . . . 12 B3
Rhodes Ct TW20 . . . . 12 C3
Rhodes-Moorhouse Ct
SM4 . . . . 40 A3
Rhodes Way RH10 . . . . 201 F3
Rhododendron Cl SL5 . . . . . . 8 E1
Rhododendron Rd GU16 . . . 86 B8
Rhododendron Ride
TW20 . . . . 10 F2
Rhododendron Wlk SL5 . . . . 8 E1
Rhodrons Ave KT9 . . . . 56 E5
Rhyll Gdns GU11 . . . . 104 F1
Rialto Rd CR4 . . . . 41 A7
Ribble Pl GU14 . . . . 84 E7
Ribblesdale RH4 . . . . 136 B5
Ribblesdale Rd SW16 . . . . . 21 B3
Ricardo Ct GU5 . . . . 151 F5
Ricards Lodge High Sch
SW19 . . . . 19 F3
Ricards Rd SW19 . . . . 19 F3
Rice's Cnr GU4 . . . . 131 A2
Rices Hill RH19 . . . . 185 E1
Richard Atkins Prim Sch
SW2 . . . . 21 E8
Richard Challoner Sch
KT3 . . . . 38 D2
Richard Ct TW15 . . . . 13 F3
Richard Meyjes Rd GU2 . 129 E8
Richards Cl
Ash GU12 . . . . 106 A5
Harlington UB3 . . . . 3 D8
Richards Ct BR3 . . . . 43 D8
Richards Field KT19 . . . . . . 57 D2
Richard Sharples Ct 21
SM2 . . . . 59 C3
Richardson Ct 17 RH11 . . 201 B1
Richardson Ho TW7 . . . . 5 F4
Richardson's Lawn Cotts
SL4 . . . . 10 B5
Richards Rd KT11 . . . . 74 B5
Richbell Cl KT21 . . . . 75 D1
Richborough Ct RH11 . . . 201 C6
Richens Cl TW3 . . . . 5 D5
Richfield Ct 4 BR3 . . . . 43 F8
Richill Lodge TW2 . . . . 5 A1
Richland Ave CR5 . . . . 79 A5
Richlands Ave KT17 . . . . . . 58 A6
RICHMOND 6 D2
Richmond Adult Com Coll
TW9 . . . . 6 D3
**Richmond American Int Univ
in London** TW10 . . . . 17 E8
Richmond Ave
Feltham TW14 . . . . 3 E1
Merton SW20 . . . . 39 E8
Richmond Bridge TW1 . . . . . 6 D1
Richmond Bridge Mans 1
TW1 . . . . 6 D1
Richmond Cl
Biggin Hill TN16 . . . . 103 B8
Epsom KT18 . . . . 76 E5
Farnborough GU14 . . . . 84 D3
Fetcham KT23 . . . . 94 C3
Frimley GU16 . . . . 65 F1
Richmond Cres TW18 . . . . . 12 F3
Richmond Ct
Crawley RH10 . . . . 201 E5
12 Kingston upon Thames
KT2 . . . . 18 A1
Mitcham CR4 . . . . 40 D6
Wimbledon SW20 . . . . 39 B7
Richmond Dr TW17 . . . . 34 D3
Richmond Gate TW10 . . . . . 17 F8
Richmond Gn CR0 . . . . 60 E7
Richmond Healthcare Hamlet
TW9 . . . . 6 E4
RICHMOND HILL 6 E1
Richmond Hill TW10 . . . . 6 E1
Richmond Hill Ct TW10 . . . . . 6 E1
Richmond Ho
Caterham CR3 . . . . 100 F3
12 Forest Hill SE26 . . . . 23 A5
Sandhurst GU47 . . . . 64 E7
**Richmond House Sch
(Hampton Com Coll)**
TW12 . . . . 15 F3
Richmond Intnl Bsns Ctr 6
TW9 . . . . 6 F3
Richmond Mans 25 TW1 . . . 6 D1
Richmond Park Rd
Kingston upon Thames
KT2 . . . . 17 E1
Mortlake SW14 . . . . 7 D3
Richmond Rd
Coulsdon CR5 . . . . 79 B4
Farncombe GU7 . . . . 150 E6
Horsham RH12 . . . . 217 D4
Isleworth TW7 . . . . 6 A4
Kingston upon Thames KT2 . 17 E2
Sandhurst GU47 . . . . 64 E8
Staines TW18 . . . . 12 F3
Thornton Heath CR7 . . . . . . 42 B5
Twickenham TW1 . . . . 17 B8
Wallington CR0 . . . . 60 E7
Wimbledon SW20 . . . . 39 B8
Richmond Sq RH19 . . . . . . 185 D2
Richmond Sta/U Sta TW9 . . 6 E3
Richmond Upon Thames Coll
TW2 . . . . 16 E8
Richmond Way
East Grinstead RH19 . . . . . 205 F8
Fetcham KT23 . . . . 94 C3
Richmondwood SL5 . . . . 30 B1
Rickard Cl SW2 . . . . 22 A7
Rickards Cl KT6 . . . . 56 E8
Ricketts Hill Rd TN16 . . . . 103 E7
Rickfield RH11 . . . . 201 A5
Rickford Hill GU3 . . . . 88 D1
Rickman Cl RG12 . . . . 27 C3
Rickman Cres KT15 . . . . 52 B7
Rickman Ct KT15 . . . . 52 B7
Rickman Hill CR5 . . . . 79 B2
Rickman Hill Rd CR5 . . . . . 79 B1
Rickman's La RH14 . . . . . . 211 F2
Ricksons La KT24 . . . . 112 B8
Rickwood RH6 . . . . 161 B4
Rickyard GU2 . . . . 108 D1
Riddens The RH12 . . . . 214 A6
Riddings The CR3 . . . . 100 F2
RIDDLESDOWN 80 C5
Riddlesdown Ave CR8 . . . . 80 C7
Riddlesdown High Sch
CR2 . . . . 80 E5
Riddlesdown Rd CR8 . . . . . 80 C7
Riddlesdown Sta CR8 . . . . 80 C6
Ride La GU5 . . . . 153 D7
Riders Way RH9 . . . . 121 C4
Ride The RH14 . . . . 212 C2
Ride Way GU6 . . . . 154 C1
Rideway Cl GU15 . . . . 65 B4
Ridge Cl
Brockham RH3 . . . . 137 B5
Woking GU22 . . . . 89 B6
Ridge Ct CR6 . . . . 81 A1
Ridgedale RH10 . . . . 204 B8
Ridgegate Cl RH2 . . . . 118 D3
Ridge Gn RH1 . . . . 140 E6
RIDGE GREEN 140 E6
Ridge Green Cl RH1 . . . . . 140 E6
Ridge Ho 4 KT2 . . . . 18 B1
Ridgehurst Dr RH12 . . . . . 216 F1
Ridgelands KT22 . . . . 94 D3
Ridge Langley CR2 . . . . 62 A2
Ridgemead Rd TW20 . . . . . 11 B5
Ridge Moor Cl GU26 . . . . . 188 E5
Ridgemount
Guildford GU2 . . . . 130 B8
Oatlands Park KT13 . . . . 53 E8
Ridgemount Ave
Coulsdon CR5 . . . . 79 B2
Croydon CR0 . . . . 62 D8
Ridgemount Cl SE20 . . . . . 23 B1
Ridgemount Est GU16 . . . . 86 C7
Ridge Mount Rd SL5 . . . . . 30 A1
Ridgemount Way RH1 . . . 139 D7
Ridge Pk SM6 . . . . 60 D1
Ridge Rd
Cheam SM3, SM4 . . . . 39 F1
Mitcham CR4 . . . . 21 B1
Ridgeside RH10 . . . . 201 F6
Ridges The GU3 . . . . 130 C4
Ridge's Yd 6 CR0 . . . . 61 B7
Ridge The
Coulsdon CR5 . . . . 79 E5
Epsom KT18, KT21 . . . . 76 C1
Fetcham KT22 . . . . 94 D3
Rudgwick RH12 . . . . 214 E8
Sunningdale SL5 . . . . 30 A2
Surbiton KT5 . . . . 38 A4
Twickenham TW2 . . . . 16 D8
Wallington CR8 . . . . 60 D1
Woking GU22 . . . . 70 B2
Woldingham CR3, CR6 . . . . 102 D2
Ridge View Cotts GU7 . . . 150 F4
Ridgeway
East Grinstead RH19 . . . . . 205 E7
Epsom KT19 . . . . 76 C7
12 Richmond TW10 . . . . 6 E1
Walton-on-Thames KT12 . . . 34 F1
Woking GU21 . . . . 69 D4
Ridge Way
Feltham TW13 . . . . 15 E5
Virginia Water GU25 . . . . . . 31 E4
8 West Norwood SE19 . . . . . 22 E2
Ridgeway Cl
Cranleigh GU6 . . . . 175 A3
Dorking RH4 . . . . 136 A5
Fetcham KT22 . . . . 94 E3
Lightwater GU18 . . . . 67 A8
Oxshott KT22 . . . . 74 C5
Woking GU21 . . . . 69 D4
Ridgeway Com Sch The
GU9 . . . . 146 C7
Ridgeway Ct RH1 . . . . 118 F1
Ridgeway Dr RH4 . . . . 136 A4
Ridgeway Gdns GU21 . . . . . 69 D4
Ridgeway Hill Rd GU9 . . . 146 C8
Ridgeway Ho RH6 . . . . 161 A1
Ridge Way Ho 3 GU22 . . . . 70 B2
Ridgeway Prim Sch CR2 . . 61 E1
Ridgeway Rd
Dorking RH4 . . . . 136 A5
Hounslow TW7 . . . . 5 E6
Redhill RH1 . . . . 118 F1
Ridgeway Rd N TW7 . . . . . . 5 E7
Ridgeway The
Bracknell RG12 . . . . 27 C6
Brookwood GU24 . . . . 88 A7
Cranleigh GU6 . . . . 174 F3
Croydon CR0 . . . . 60 F7
Fetcham KT22 . . . . 94 D3
Guildford GU1 . . . . 131 A8
Horley RH6 . . . . 161 A1
Horsham RH12 . . . . 217 B4
Lightwater GU18 . . . . 48 B1
Oxshott KT22 . . . . 74 C5
Ridge Way The CR2 . . . . . . 61 E1
Ridgewell Cl SE26 . . . . 23 F4
Ridgewood Ctr (Hospl)
GU16 . . . . 66 C3
Ridgewood Dr GU16 . . . . . . 66 D3
Ridgley Rd GU8 . . . . 191 B4
Ridgway
Pyrford GU22 . . . . 71 A4
Wimbledon SW19, SW20 . . . 19 D2
Ridgway Ct SW19 . . . . 19 D2
Ridgway Gdns SW19 . . . . . . 19 D1
Ridgway Pl SW19 . . . . 19 E2
Ridgway Rd
Farnham GU9 . . . . 146 C8
Pyrford GU22 . . . . 70 F4
Ridgway The SM2 . . . . 59 D4
Riding Hill CR2 . . . . 81 A6
Ridings The
Addlestone KT15 . . . . 51 E4
Ashtead KT21 . . . . 75 D2
Biggin Hill TN16 . . . . 83 E2
Cobham KT11 . . . . 74 A7
Crawley RH10 . . . . 202 D7
East Horsley KT24 . . . . 92 F2
Epsom KT18 . . . . 76 F4
Ewell KT17 . . . . 57 F2
Frimley GU16 . . . . 66 B3
Kingswood KT20 . . . . 97 F7
Redhill RH2 . . . . 118 D3
Send Marsh GU23 . . . . 91 A4
Sunbury TW16 . . . . 35 A8
Surbiton KT5 . . . . 38 A4
Riding The
Cranleigh GU6 . . . . 174 E4
Sheerwater GU21 . . . . 70 B5
Ridlands Gr RH8 . . . . 123 E5
Ridlands La RH8 . . . . 123 E5
Ridlands Rise RH8 . . . . . . 123 E4
Ridleigh Ct TW15 . . . . 14 B4
Ridley Ct
Crawley RH10 . . . . 202 D8
Streatham SW16 . . . . 21 E2
Ridley Rd
Bromley BR2 . . . . 44 F6
Merton SW19 . . . . 20 B1
Warlingham CR6 . . . . 81 D1
Ridsdale Rd
Penge SE20 . . . . 43 B8
Woking GU21 . . . . 69 B2
Riesco Dr CR0 . . . . 62 C4

Rifle Way GU14 . . . . 84 C3
Rigby Cl CR0, CR9 . . . . 61 A7
Rigg Ho 2 SW4. . . . . 21 E8
Riggindale Rd SW16 . . . . . 21 D4
Rikkyo Sch-in-England
RH14. . . . . 213 D8
Riley Cl KT19 . . . . 76 B8
Riley Ho 1 SW4 . . . . 21 D8
Rillside RH10 . . . . 202 A3
Rill Wlk RH19. . . . . 186 B1
Rimbault Cl GU11 . . . . 105 E7
Rimini Ct SW12 . . . . 20 F7
Rinaldo Rd SW12 . . . . 21 B8
Rindle Cl GU14. . . . . 84 C4
Ringley Ave RH6 . . . . 161 A2
Ringley Oak RH12. . . . . 217 F4
Ringley Park Ave RH2 . . . 139 D8
Ringley Park Rd RH2. . . . . 118 C1
Ringley Rd RH12. . . . . 217 E4
Ringmead
Bracknell, Great Hollands
RG12. . . . . 26 E4
Bracknell, Hanworth RG12 . 27 B2
Ringmore Dr GU4. . . . . . . 110 C4
Ringmore Rd KT12 . . . . 54 C7
Ringmore Rise SE23. . . . . . . 23 B8
Ring Rd N RH6. . . . . 182 C8
Ring Rd S RH6. . . . . 182 C7
Ringstead Bldgs SE6 . . . . . . 24 B8
Ringstead Ct 4 SM1 . . . . . 59 D5
Ringstead Rd
Carshalton SM1. . . . . 59 D5
Lewisham SE6 . . . . 24 B8
Ring The RG12. . . . . 27 C7
Ringwold Cl BR3. . . . . 23 E1
Ringwood RG12. . . . . 26 F2
Ringwood Ave
Redhill RH1 . . . . 118 F4
Thornton Heath CR0, CR9 . . 41 E2
Ringwood Cl
Ascot SL5. . . . . 29 B5
Crawley RH10 . . . . 201 E4
Ringwood Gdns SW15. . . . 19 A7
Ringwood Lodge 1 RH1 119 A4
Ringwood Rd
Blackwater GU17. . . . . 64 C6
Farnborough GU14 . . . . 85 C7
Ringwood Way TW12. . . . . . 16 A4
RIPLEY. 91 C6
Ripley Ave TW20. . . . . 11 E2
Ripley By-Pass GU23. . . . . 91 C4
Ripley CE Inf Sch GU23. . . 91 B6
Ripley Cl CR0. . . . . 63 C4
Ripley Court Sch GU23 . . . 91 C6
Ripley Ct CR4. . . . . 40 D7
Ripley Gdns
Mortlake SW14 . . . . 7 D4
Sutton SM1 . . . . 59 C6
Ripley Ho
13 Kingston upon Thames
KT2. . . . . 18 B2
2 Mortlake SW14 . . . . 7 E4
5 Penge SE26 . . . . 23 B3
Ripley La
Ripley GU23. . . . . 91 F3
West Horsley KT24, GU23 112 A7
Ripley Rd
East Clandon GU23, GU4. . 111 D7
Hampton TW12 . . . . 16 A1
RIPLEY SPRINGS 11 E2
Ripley Way KT19. . . . . 76 A8
Riplington Ct SW15 . . . . . . 19 B8
Ripon Cl
Frimley GU15. . . . . 66 D3
Guildford GU2 . . . . 108 F3
Ripon Gdns KT9. . . . . 56 D5
Ripon Rd GU14. . . . . 84 A7
Ripplesmere RG12 . . . . 27 D5
Ripplesmore Cl GU47. . . . . . 64 B8
Ripston Rd TW15 . . . . 14 D3
Risborough Dr KT4. . . . . 39 A2
Rise Rd SL5. . . . . 29 F3
Rise The
Crawley RH10 . . . . 202 D6
Crowthorne RG45 . . . . 45 A5
East Grinstead RH19. . . . . 205 F8
East Horsley KT24. . . . . 92 E1
Ewell KT17. . . . . 57 F1
South Croydon CR2 . . . . 62 C2
Tadworth KT20. . . . . 97 C6
Winkfield RG42 . . . . 28 A8
Woking GU21. . . . . 69 D1
Wokingham RG41 . . . . 25 A7
Ritchie Cl RH10 . . . . 202 C2
Ritchie Rd CR0. . . . . 43 B3
Ritherdon Rd SW17 . . . . . . 21 B6
River Ave KT7. . . . . 37 A2
Riverbank
East Molesey KT8 . . . . 36 E5
Staines TW18. . . . . 12 F2
Westcott RH4 . . . . 135 B7
River Bank KT7 . . . . 36 F4
Riverbank Way TW8. . . . . . . 6 C8
River Cl GU1. . . . . 109 C3
River Crane Way TW13 . . . 15 F6
River Ct
Kingston upon Thames
KT6. . . . . 37 D4
Sheerwater GU21 . . . . 70 C5
Shepperton TW17 . . . . 34 C2
Riverdale
Dorking RH4 . . . . 115 C3
Wrecclesham GU10. . . . . . 145 E7
Riverdale Dr
Wandsworth SW18 . . . . 20 B7
Riverdale Dr *continued*
Woking GU22. . . . . 89 F6
Riverdale Gdns TW1 . . . . . . 6 C2
Riverdale Rd
Feltham TW13 . . . . 15 F4
Twickenham TW1. . . . . 6 C1
Riverdene Ct KT6 . . . . 37 D4
Riverdene Ind Est KT12. . . 54 D5
Riverfield Rd TW18 . . . . . . 12 F2
River Gdns
Carshalton SM5. . . . . 60 A7
Feltham TW14 . . . . 4 B2
River Gdns Bsns Ctr TW14. . 4 B3
River Grove Pk BR3 . . . . . . 43 F8
Riverhead Dr SM2. . . . . 59 B1
River Hill KT11. . . . . 73 B4
River Ho
Forest Hill SE26. . . . . 23 B5
Mortlake SW13 . . . . 7 E5
Riverholme KT8. . . . . 36 E6
Riverholme Dr KT19. . . . . . 57 E2
River Island Cl KT22. . . . . . 94 D7
River La
Cobham KT11. . . . . 73 E3
Fetcham KT22 . . . . 94 D6
Leatherhead KT22 . . . . 94 E7
Richmond TW10. . . . . 17 D7
Wrecclesham GU10, GU9 . 145 E7
Rivermead
Byfleet KT14 . . . . 71 F6
East Molesey KT8 . . . . 36 C6
Kingston upon Thames KT6 . 37 D4
River Mead
Crawley RH11 . . . . 181 A1
Horsham RH12 . . . . 217 B1
Rivermead Cl
New Haw KT15 . . . . 52 C3
Richmond TW11. . . . . 17 B3
Rivermead Ho TW16 . . . . . 35 C6
Rivermead Rd GU15. . . . . . 65 B2
River Meads Ave TW2. . . . . 16 B5
River Mole Bsns Pk KT10. 55 A8
River Mole Nature Reserve★
KT22. . . . . 95 A3
Rivermount TW16. . . . . 35 C6
River Mount KT12. . . . . 34 F2
River Mount Gdns GU2 . . 130 C6
Rivernook Cl KT12 . . . . 35 C4
River Park Ave TW18. . . . . . 12 D4
River Park Gdns BR2. . . . . . 24 D1
River Rd TW18. . . . . 32 F8
River Reach TW11 . . . . 17 C3
River Row Cotts GU9. . . . . 145 F8
Rivers Cl GU14. . . . . 85 E1
Riversdale Prim Sch
SW18 . . . . 20 A7
Riversdale Rd KT7 . . . . 37 A3
Riversdell Cl
Chertsey KT16 . . . . 32 F2
2 Chertsey KT16 . . . . 33 A2
Riverside
4 Catford SE6 . . . . 23 F4
Egham TW20 . . . . 12 A5
Forest Row RH18. . . . . 206 E3
Guildford, Bellfields GU1. . 109 D3
Guildford GU1 . . . . 130 D7
Horley RH6 . . . . 161 A1
Horsham RH12 . . . . 217 A2
Oatlands Park TW17 . . . . . . 34 E2
34 Richmond TW9. . . . . 6 D2
Sunbury TW16 . . . . 35 D7
Twickenham TW1. . . . . 17 B7
Wraysbury TW19. . . . . 11 C8
Riverside Ave
East Molesey KT8 . . . . 36 D4
Lightwater GU18. . . . . 67 C8
Riverside Bsns Ctr SW18 . 20 B7
Riverside Bsns Ctr The
GU1. . . . . 109 C1
Riverside Bsns Pk
Farnham GU9. . . . . 125 D3
Merton SW19. . . . . 40 C8
Riverside Cl
Brookwood GU24. . . . . 87 F7
Farnborough GU14 . . . . 84 F5
Hackbridge SM6 . . . . 60 B7
Kingston upon Thames KT1 . 37 D5
Staines TW18. . . . . 32 F8
Riverside Ct
Dorking RH4 . . . . 115 D1
Farnham GU9. . . . . 125 D3
Teddington TW11. . . . . 17 C3
Riverside Dr
Bramley GU5 . . . . 152 A7
Chiswick W4 . . . . 7 E6
Egham TW18 . . . . 12 E3
Esher KT10 . . . . 55 A6
Mitcham CR4. . . . . 40 E4
Richmond TW10. . . . . 17 B5
Staines TW18. . . . . 32 F8
Riverside Gdns
Cobham KT11. . . . . 73 A6
Old Woking GU22. . . . . 90 B6
Riverside Health & Racquets
Club The W4. . . . . 7 E6
Riverside Ho
Morden SW19 . . . . 40 C5
31 Richmond TW9 . . . . 6 D2
Riverside Ind Pk GU9 . . . 125 D3
Riverside Park Nature
Reserve★ GU4. . . . . 109 F4
Riverside Pk KT13. . . . . 52 E5
Riverside Pk SL3. . . . . 1 E5
Riverside Pl TW19 . . . . 2 D1
Riverside Rd
Hersham KT12. . . . . 54 E6
Staines TW18. . . . . 12 F1
Stanwell TW19. . . . . 2 E1
Riverside Rd *continued*
Wandsworth SW17, SW19 . 20 C5
Riverside The KT8 . . . . 36 D6
Riverside Way GU15. . . . . . 65 A3
Riverside Wlk
Isleworth TW7. . . . . 5 E4
8 West Wickham BR4 . . . . 44 B1
Riversmeet GU10 . . . . 147 D4
Riverstone Ct KT2. . . . . 37 F8
Riverview
Guildford GU1 . . . . 109 C1
Shepperton TW17 . . . . 34 D2
River View KT15 . . . . 52 C5
Riverview CE Prim Sch
KT19. . . . . 57 D6
Riverview Gdns KT11. . . . . 72 F6
River View Gdns TW1 . . . . 16 F6
Riverview Gr W4. . . . . 7 B8
Riverview Mans 4 TW1 . . . 6 D1
Riverview Pk SE6 . . . . 24 A6
Riverview Rd
Chiswick W4 . . . . 7 B7
West Ewell KT19 . . . . 57 D6
Riverway TW18 . . . . 33 B8
River Way
Twickenham TW2. . . . . 16 B6
West Ewell KT19 . . . . 57 E5
Riverway Est GU3 . . . . 151 C8
River Wlk KT12 . . . . 35 A3
Riverwood Ct GU1 . . . . . . 109 C3
Rivett Drake Cl GU2. . . . . 109 B5
Rivey Cl KT14. . . . . 70 F5
Rix Ho RH8 . . . . 122 F2
Road House Est GU22 . . . . 90 A7
Roakes Ave KT15. . . . . 52 B8
Robert Cl KT12. . . . . 54 B5
Robert Gerard Ho 7
SE27. . . . . 22 D4
Robertsbridge Rd SM5 . . . 40 D2
Roberts Cl
Cheam SM3 . . . . 58 D3
South Norwood CR7 . . . . . . 42 D6
Stanwell TW19. . . . . 2 C1
Roberts Ct
Chessington KT9 . . . . 56 D5
Penge SE20. . . . . 43 C8
Roberts Ho 5 SE27 . . . . . . 22 B5
Robertson Ct 5 GU21 . . . . 68 E1
Robertson Ho SW17. . . . . . 20 E3
Robertson Way GU12. . . . 105 F1
Roberts Rd
Aldershot GU12 . . . . 105 D1
Sandhurst GU15 . . . . 65 A6
Robert St CR0, CR9 . . . . . . 61 C7
Roberts Way
Cranleigh GU6 . . . . 174 E4
Englefield Green TW20 . . . . 11 C1
Robert Way
Horsham RH12 . . . . 217 F7
Mytchett GU16. . . . . 85 F3
Robina Ho RG42 . . . . 26 F8
Robin Cl
Addlestone KT15. . . . . 52 D5
Ash Vale GU12. . . . . 106 A6
Crawley RH11 . . . . 201 C8
1 East Grinstead RH19 . . 185 F2
Hampton TW12 . . . . 15 E3
Robin Ct SM6. . . . . 60 C4
Robin Gdns RH1 . . . . 119 A3
Robin Gr TW8 . . . . 6 C8
Robin Hill GU7. . . . . 150 D7
Robin Hill Dr GU15. . . . . . . 66 A3
Robinhood Cl CR4 . . . . 41 C6
Robin Hood Cl
Farnborough GU14 . . . . 85 A7
Knaphill GU21 . . . . 68 F1
Robin Hood Cres GU21 . . . 68 E2
Robin Hood Ct 2 SM1 . . . 59 B5
Robin Hood Inf Sch SM1 . 59 A5
Robin Hood Jun Sch 9
SM1 . . . . 59 B5
Robinhood La CR4 . . . . 41 C6
Robin Hood La
Kingston upon Thames
SW15 . . . . 18 E4
Sutton SM1 . . . . 59 B5
Warnham RH12 . . . . 216 F5
Woking GU4. . . . . 89 F3
Robin Hood Prim Sch
SW15 . . . . 18 E3
Robin Hood Rd GU21. . . . . 68 F1
Robin Hood Rdbt SW15. . . 18 E5
Robin Hood Way (Kingston
By Pass) KT2, SW15,
SW20. . . . . 18 E3
Robin Hood Works GU21 . 68 E2
Robinia Cl SE20. . . . . 43 A8
Robin La GU47. . . . . 45 C1
Robin Row RH10. . . . . 204 C5
Robin's Bow GU15 . . . . 65 B4
Robins Ct
Croydon CR2 . . . . 61 E6
Richmond TW10. . . . . 6 E1
Robin's Ct BR3. . . . . 44 D7
Robins Dale GU21. . . . . 68 C2
Robinson Cl GU22. . . . . 90 C7
Robinson Ct
7 Richmond TW9 . . . . 6 F3
1 Thornton Heath CR0. . . . 42 B3
Robinson Ho RH10 . . . . . . 201 D5
Robinson Rd SW19. . . . . . . 20 E2
Robinsway KT12 . . . . 54 C6
Robinswood Ct RH12. . . . 217 F4
Robin Way
Godalming GU8 . . . . 170 F1
Guildford GU2 . . . . 109 B5
Staines TW18. . . . . 12 F5
Wormley GU8. . . . . 190 F8
Robinwood Pl SW15. . . . . . 18 D4
Robson Rd SE21, SE27 . . . . 22 C5
Roby Dr RG12. . . . . 27 D2
Rochdale 9 SE19 . . . . 22 E2
Rochelle Ct BR3 . . . . 24 B1
Roche Rd SW16. . . . . 41 F8
Rochester Ave TW13 . . . . . 14 F6
Rochester Cl SW16. . . . . . . 21 E1
Rochester Ct SE25 . . . . 43 A7
Rochester Gdns
Caterham CR3 . . . . 100 E5
South Croydon CR0 . . . . 61 E7
Rochester Par TW13 . . . . . 15 A5
Rochester Rd
Carshalton SM5. . . . . 59 F6
Egham TW20 . . . . 12 D2
Rochester Wlk RH2 . . . . . 139 B5
Roche Wlk SM4, SM5 . . . . . 40 D3
Rochford Way CR0 . . . . 41 E3
Rock Ave 14 SW14 . . . . 7 D4
Rockbourne Rd SE23. . . . . 23 D7
Rock Cl CR4 . . . . 40 D7
Rockdale Dr GU26 . . . . . . 188 D3
Rockdene Cl RH19 . . . . . . 186 A1
Rockery The GU14 . . . . 84 E3
Rockfield Cl RH8. . . . . 122 F4
Rockfield Rd RH8 . . . . 122 F5
Rockfield Way 7 GU47. . . 64 D8
Rock Gdns GU11 . . . . 104 F1
Rockhampton Cl 4 SE27 . 22 A4
Rockhampton Rd
South Croydon CR2 . . . . 61 E4
West Norwood SE27, SW16 22 A4
Rock Hill SE26. . . . . 22 F4
Rockingham Cl SW15 . . . . . 7 F3
Rockingham Ct 20 BR3 . . . 24 A1
Rock La GU10. . . . . 146 A5
Rockmount Prim Sch
SE19 . . . . 22 D2
Rockmount Rd SE19. . . . . . 22 D2
Rockshaw Rd RH1 . . . . 119 E8
Rocks The RH19 . . . . 206 D6
Rockwell Gdns SE19 . . . . . 22 E4
Rockwood Pl RH1. . . . . 119 B6
Rocky La RH1, RH2 . . . . . . 119 A6
Rocombe Cres SE23. . . . . . 23 C8
Rodborough Tech Coll
GU8. . . . . 170 F7
Rodd Est TW17. . . . . 34 D4
Roden Gdns CR0, SE25 . . . . 42 E3
Rodenhurst Rd SW4. . . . . . . 21 C8
Rodgate La GU27 . . . . 209 E5
Rodgers Ho 3 SW4. . . . . . . 21 D8
Roding Cl GU6. . . . . 173 F2
Rodmel Ct GU14 . . . . 85 E1
Rodney Cl
New Malden KT3 . . . . 38 E4
Thornton Heath CR0 . . . . . . 42 B1
3 Walton-on-Thames KT12 35 C1
Rodney Gn 3 KT12 . . . . . . 54 C8
Rodney Pl SW19. . . . . 40 C8
Rodney Rd
Mitcham CR4. . . . . 40 E6
New Malden KT3 . . . . 38 E4
Twickenham TW2. . . . . 16 A8
Walton-on-Thames KT12 . . . 54 C8
Rodney Way
Guildford GU1 . . . . 110 A2
Poyle SL3. . . . . 1 E6
Rodona Rd KT13. . . . . 72 D8
Rodway Rd SW15 . . . . 19 A8
Rodwell Ct
Addlestone KT15. . . . . 52 C6
Walton-on-Thames KT12. . . 54 B7
Roebuck Cl
Ashtead KT21 . . . . 95 E7
Feltham TW13 . . . . 15 B4
Horsham RH13 . . . . 218 B4
Reigate RH2. . . . . 118 A1
Roebuck Ct 2 KT3. . . . . 38 E4
Roebuck Rd KT9. . . . . 57 A5
Roedean Cres SW15. . . . . . . 7 E2
Roedeer Copse GU27. . . . 207 E6
ROEHAMPTON 7 F2
Roehampton Church Sch
SW15 . . . . 19 B8
Roehampton Gate SW15. . . 7 E1
Roehampton High St
SW15. . . . . 19 A8
Roehampton La SW15,
SW19. . . . . 19 A8
Roehampton Univ Froebel
Coll SW15 . . . . 7 F1
Roehampton Univ
(Whitelands Coll) SW15. 19 A8
Roehampton Vale SW15. . 18 F5
Roe Way SM6. . . . . 60 E4
Roffe's La CR3. . . . . 100 D2
ROFFEY 218 A5
Roffey Cl
Horley RH6 . . . . 160 F3
Purley CR8. . . . . 80 B3
Roffey Cnr RH12 . . . . 218 B4
Roffey's Cl RH10 . . . . 183 A4
Roffords GU21 . . . . 69 B2
Roffye Ct RH12 . . . . 218 A4
Rogers Cl
Caterham CR3 . . . . 101 B5
Coulsdon CR5 . . . . 80 B1
Roger Simmons Ct KT23. . 94 A3
Rogers La CR6. . . . . 81 F1
Rogers Mead RH9. . . . . . . 121 B3
Rogers Rd SW17 . . . . 20 E4
Rojack Rd SE23 . . . . 23 D7
Rokeby Cl RG12. . . . . 27 D8
Rokeby Ct GU21. . . . . 68 F2
Rokeby Ho 10 SW12 . . . . . . 21 B8
Rokeby Pl SW20 . . . . 19 B1
Rokeby Sch KT2 . . . . 18 C1
Roke Cl
Purley CR8. . . . . 80 C5
Witley GU8. . . . . 170 E5
Rokefield Ho RH4. . . . . . . 135 B7
Roke Ho GU1 . . . . 110 C1
Roke La GU8. . . . . 170 F5
Roke Lane Cotts GU8. . . . 170 F5
Rokell Ho BR3 . . . . 24 B3
Roke Lodge Rd CR8 . . . . . . 80 B6
Roke Prim Sch CR8 . . . . . . 80 C5
Roke Rd CR8 . . . . 80 C5
Rokers La GU8. . . . . 149 D7
Roland Ct SE19 . . . . 42 F8
Roland Way KT4 . . . . 57 F8
Rollesby Rd KT9 . . . . 57 A4
Rolleston Rd CR2 . . . . 61 D3
Rollit Cres TW3. . . . . 5 A2
Rolls Royce Cl SM6 . . . . . . 60 E3
Rolston Ho GU27. . . . . 207 F6
Romana Ct TW18 . . . . 13 A4
Romanby Ct 1 RH1 . . . . . 139 F8
Roman Cl TW14. . . . . 4 C2
Roman Farm Rd GU2. . . . 108 D2
Roman Farm Way GU2 . . 108 D2
Romanfield Rd SW2. . . . . . 21 F8
Roman Ho RH2 . . . . 138 F7
Romanhurst Ave BR2. . . . . 44 E5
Romanhurst Gdns BR2 . . . 44 E5
Roman Ind Est CR0 . . . . . . 42 E2
Roman Rd RH4 . . . . 136 B5
Roman Rise SE19 . . . . 22 D2
Romans Bsns Pk GU9 . . . 125 D3
Romans Ind Pk GU9. . . . . 125 D3
Romans Way GU22. . . . . . . 71 A4
Roman Way
Croydon CR9 . . . . 61 B8
Farnham GU9. . . . . 125 E4
Thornton Heath CR9 . . . . . . 61 B8
Wallington SM5 . . . . 59 F2
Winkfield RG42 . . . . 27 F8
Romany Gdns SM3 . . . . 40 A2
Romany Prospect SE19. . . 22 D2
Romany The GU14 . . . . 84 A1
Roma Read Cl SW15 . . . . . 19 B8
Romayne Cl GU14 . . . . 85 A5
Romberg Rd SW17 . . . . 21 A5
Romeo Hill RG42. . . . . 27 F8
Romeyn Rd SW16. . . . . 21 F5
Romley Ct GU9 . . . . 125 D1
Rommany Ct SE27 . . . . 22 D4
Rommany Rd SE27 . . . . 22 D4
Romney Cl
Ashford TW15 . . . . 14 C3
Chessington KT9 . . . . 56 E6
Romney Ho
Bracknell RG12 . . . . 27 E5
Sutton SM2 . . . . 59 B4
Romney Rd
Farnborough GU14 . . . . 84 E1
New Malden KT3. . . . . 38 D3
Romola Rd SE24 . . . . 22 B7
Romsey Cl
Aldershot GU11 . . . . 126 C6
Blackwater GU17. . . . . 64 C6
Romulus Ct 6 TW8 . . . . 6 D7
Rona Cl RH11. . . . . 201 B3
Ronald Cl BR3 . . . . 43 F4
Ronald Ho 8 SM1 . . . . 59 D5
Ronald Ross Prim Sch
SW19 . . . . 19 E8
Ronelean Rd KT6 . . . . 56 F7
Ronneby Cl KT13. . . . . 53 E7
Ronson Way KT22. . . . . 95 A6
Ronver Rd SE12. . . . . 24 F7
Roof of the World (Park
Homes Est) KT20 . . . . . . 116 B3
Rookeries Cl TW13. . . . . . . 15 C5
Rookery Cl KT22 . . . . 94 E3
Rookery Dr RH4 . . . . 135 A5
Rookery Hill
Ashtead KT21 . . . . 76 A1
Outwood RH1, RH6 . . . . . . 162 B6
Rookery Mead CR5. . . . . . . 99 D5
Rookery Rd TW18 . . . . 13 B3
Rookery The RH4 . . . . 135 A5
Rookery Way KT20. . . . . . . 117 F8
Rook La CR3. . . . . 100 B3
Rookley Cl SM2. . . . . 59 B2
Rooks Hill GU5 . . . . 152 C2
Rooksmead Rd TW16. . . . . 35 A7
Rookstone Rd SW17. . . . . . 20 F3
Rook Way RH12. . . . . 217 F6
Rookwood Ave
Sandhurst GU47 . . . . 45 E2
Wallington SM6. . . . . 60 D6
West Barnes KT3. . . . . 39 A5
Rookwood Cl RH1. . . . . . . 119 B6
Rookwood Ct GU2 . . . . . . 130 C6
Rookwood Pk RH12 . . . . . 216 F3
Roosevelt Ct 15 SW19 . . . . 19 E7
Roothill La RH3. . . . . 137 A3
Ropeland Way RH12. . . . . 217 E7
Roper Ho 13 SE21. . . . . 22 E4
Ropers Wlk 13 SE24. . . . . . 22 A8
Roper Way CR4 . . . . 41 A7
Rorkes Drift GU16. . . . . . . 86 A4
Rosa Ave TW15 . . . . 14 A4
Rosalind Franklin Cl
GU2 . . . . 129 E8
Rosamond St SE26. . . . . . . 23 B5
Rosamund Cl CR2. . . . . 61 D6
Rosamund Rd RH10 . . . . . 202 B3
Rosary Cl TW3, TW5 . . . . 4 E5
Rosary Gdns TW15 . . . . 14 B4
Rosary RC Inf Sch TW5. . . . 5 A8
Rosary RC Jun Sch TW5. . . 5 A8
Roseacre RH8 . . . . 123 A1

Roseacre Cl TW17 34 A4
Roseacre Gdns GU4 131 F3
Rose Ave
Mitcham CR4 40 F8
Morden SM4 40 C4
Rosebank
Epsom KT18 76 C5
Penge SE20 23 B1
Rosebank Cl TW11 17 A2
Rose Bank Cotts GU22 89 E5
Rosebay RG40 25 E8
Rosebery Ave
Epsom KT17 76 E5
Kingston upon Thames KT3 38 F6
South Norwood CR7 42 C7
Rosebery Cl SM4 39 D3
Rosebery Cres GU22 89 F7
Rosebery Ct KT9 56 F4
Rosebery Gdns SM1 59 B6
Rosebery Par KT17 57 F3
Rosebery Rd
Cheam SM1 58 F4
Isleworth TW3, TW7 5 C2
Kingston upon Thames KT1 38 B7
Langley Vale KT18 96 E8
Rosebery Sch KT18 76 C5
Rosebery Sq KT1 38 B7
Rosebine Ave TW2 16 D8
Rosebriar Cl GU22 71 A3
Rosebriars
Caterham CR3 100 E7
Esher KT10 55 C5
Rosebury Ct SW16 41 F7
Rosebury Dr GU24 68 A4
Rose Bushes KT17 77 C3
Rose Cotts
Enton Green GU8 171 A2
Esher KT10 55 D5
Forest Row RH18 206 E3
Horsham RH12 218 D7
Rosecourt Rd CR0 41 F3
Rosecroft Cl TN16 83 F1
Rosecroft Gdns TW2 16 D7
Rose Ct
10 Wimbledon SW19 19 F3
Wokingham RG40 25 C6
Rosedale
Aldershot GU12 105 C2
Ashtead KT21 75 C1
Caterham CR3 100 E4
Rosedale Cl RH11 201 A4
Rosedale Gdns RG12 27 A4
Rosedale Ho 6 TW9 6 E3
Rosedale Pl CR0 43 D2
Rosedale Rd
Richmond TW9 6 E3
Stoneleigh KT17 58 A5
Rosedene Ave
Morden SM4 40 A4
Streatham SW16 21 F5
Thornton Heath CR0 41 E2
Rosedene La GU47 64 D7
Rose End KT4 39 D1
Rosefield Cl SM5 59 E5
Rosefield Gdns KT16 51 D4
Rosefield Rd TW18 13 A4
Rose Gdns
Farnborough GU14 84 E3
Feltham TW13 15 A6
Stanwell TW19 13 D8
Roseheath Rd TW4 4 F2
ROSEHILL 40 C1
ROSE HILL 136 B7
Rosehill
Claygate KT10 56 A4
Hampton TW12 36 A8
Reigate RH2 118 D2
Rose Hill
Dorking RH4 136 B7
Sutton SM1, SM4 40 B1
Rosehill Ave
Carshalton SM1, SM5 40 C1
Woking GU21 69 C3
Rosehill Ct SM4 40 C2
Rosehill Farm Mdw SM7 78 B4
Rosehill Gdns SM1 59 C8
Rose Hill Pk W SM1 59 C8
Rosehill Rd TN16 83 C2
Rose La GU23 91 D5
Roseleigh Cl 27 TW1 6 D1
Rose Lodge TW20 12 A4
Rosemary Alley GU1 130 D7
Rosemary Ave
Ash Vale GU12 106 A8
East Molesey KT8 36 A5
Hounslow TW4 4 D5
Rosemary Cl
Farnborough GU14 84 D4
Oxted RH8 123 A2
Thornton Heath CR0 41 E3
Rosemary Cotts SW19 19 C1
Rosemary Cres GU2 109 A5
Rosemary Ct
Haslemere GU27 208 C7
Horley RH6 160 E4
Rosemary Gdns
Blackwater GU17 64 D5
Chessington KT9 56 E6
Mortlake SW14 7 C4
Rosemary Ho RH10 182 A1
Rosemary La
Alfold GU6 212 E8
Blackwater GU17 64 D5
Charlwood RH6 180 E7
Horley RH6 161 B3
Mortlake SW14 7 C4
Rowledge GU10 145 E4
Thorpe TW20 32 B6
Rosemary Rd SW17 20 C5
Rose Mdw GU24 68 A6
Rosemead KT16 33 B2
Rosemead Ave
Feltham TW13 14 F6
Mitcham CR4, SW16 41 C7
Rosemead Cl RH1 139 D7
Rosemead Gdns RH10 201 E5
Rosemead Prep Sch
London SE27 22 B6
West Norwood SE27 22 C6
Rosemont Rd
Kingston upon Thames KT3 38 C6
Richmond TW10 6 E1
Rosemount Ave KT14 71 A6
Rosemount Ct SE25 42 D6
Rosemount Ho 7 KT14 71 A6
Rosemount Par KT14 71 A6
Rosemount Point 10 SE23 23 D5
Rosemount Twrs 5 SM6 60 C4
Rosendale Prim Sch SE21 22 C8
Rosendale Rd SE21, SE24 22 C7
Roseneath Ct CR3 101 A2
Roseneath Dr GU8 191 B4
Roseneath Pl SW16 21 F4
Rose Pk KT16 51 E2
Rosery The CR0 43 D3
Roses Cotts RH4 136 A7
Rose St RG40 25 C6
Rose Theatre★ KT2 37 D7
Rosethorn Cl SW12 21 D8
Rosetree Pl TW12 16 A2
Rosetrees GU1 131 A8
Rosetta Ct SE19 22 E1
Rose View KT15 52 C5
Roseville Ave TW3, TW4 5 A2
Rosevine Rd SW20 39 C8
Rose Walk Nature Reserve★ KT5 38 B5
Rosewall Ct SW19 20 B3
Rosewarne Cl GU21 69 A1
Rosewell Cl SE20 23 B1
Rose Wlk
Purley CR8 79 D8
Surbiton KT5 38 B4
West Wickham BR4 63 D8
Rosewood
Haslemere GU27 208 C5
Mytchett GU16 86 A4
Rose Wood GU22 90 A8
Rosewood Ct
Byfleet KT14 71 E7
Kingston upon Thames KT2 18 A1
7 Woking GU21 70 A3
Rosewood Dr TW17 33 F4
Rosewood Gr SM1 59 C8
Rosewood Lodge CR0 62 D8
Rosewood Way GU24 67 E6
Roshni Ho SW17 20 E2
Rosina Ct SW17 20 E3
Roskeen Ct SW19 19 C1
Roslan Ct RH6 161 B2
Roslyn Cl CR4 40 D7
Roslyn Ct 8 GU21 69 A1
Rossal Ct SE20 23 B1
Ross Cl RH10 201 F3
Ross Ct
Croydon CR2 61 C4
5 Horley RH6 161 B3
4 Putney SW15 19 D8
Rossdale SM1 59 E5
Rossendon Ct 1 SM6 60 C4
Rossenhallas RH1 119 B1
Rosset Cl RG12 27 B5
Rossetti Gdns CR5 79 F1
Ross Ho TW2 16 B6
Rossignol Gdns SM5 60 A8
Rossindel Rd TW3 5 A2
Rossiter Cl SE19 22 C1
Rossiter Lodge GU1 131 A8
Rossiter Rd SW12 21 B7
Rosslea GU20 48 A6
Rosslyn Ave
Feltham TW14 4 A1
Mortlake SW13, SW14 7 F4
Rosslyn Cl
Ashford TW16 14 E2
Coney Hall BR4 63 F7
Rosslyn Ho 8 TW9 6 F6
Rosslyn Pk KT13 53 D6
Rosslyn Rd TW1 6 C1
Rossmore Cl RH10 182 D2
Rossmore Gdns GU11 104 F1
Ross Par SM6 60 B4
Ross Rd
Cobham KT11 73 C6
South Norwood SE25 42 E6
Twickenham TW2 16 C7
Wallington SM6 60 C5
Rosswood Gdns SM6 60 C4
Rosswood Ho 13 SM6 60 B4
Rostella Rd SW17 20 D4
Rostrevor Rd SW19 20 A3
Rotary Ct KT8 36 E6
Rotary Lodge SE27 22 B5
Rothbury Gdns TW7 6 A7
Rothbury Wlk GU15 66 C4
Rother Cl GU47 64 C8
Rother Cres RH11 200 F5
Rotherfield Ave RG41 25 A7
Rotherfield Rd SM5 60 A5
Rotherhill Ave SW16 21 D2
Rother Ho 4 RH1 118 F2
Rother Rd GU14 84 E8
Rothervale RH6 160 F5
Rotherwick Ct GU14 105 C8
Rotherwood Cl SW19, SW20 39 E8
Rothesay Ave
Merton SW20 39 E7
Mortlake SW14, TW10 7 B3
Rothesay Ct SE6 24 F6
Rothesay Rd SE25 42 E5
Rothes Rd RH4 136 B8
Rothsay Ct KT13 53 D4
Rothschild St SE27 22 C4
Rothwell Ho
Crowthorne RG45 45 C4
Heston TW5 5 A8
Rotunda Est The GU11 105 B2
Rotunda The★ KT2 37 E7
Rougemont Ave SM4 40 A3
Roughets La RH1 120 E6
Rough Field RH19 185 D4
Roughlands GU22 70 E4
Rough Rd GU22 88 C5
Rough Rew RH4 136 B4
Rough Way RH12 217 F5
Rounce La GU24 67 D6
Roundabout Cotts RH12 214 C5
Roundacre SW19 19 D6
Roundals La GU8 191 E8
Roundell Ho 14 SE21 22 E4
Round Gr CR0 43 D2
Roundhay Cl SE23 23 D6
Roundhill GU22 90 B8
Round Hill SE23 23 C5
Roundhill Dr GU22 70 B1
Roundhill Way
Guildford GU2 108 F1
Oxshott KT11 74 B7
Round Oak Rd KT13 52 F6
ROUNDSHAW 60 F3
Roundshaw Downs Nature Reserve★ SM6 60 F2
Roundshead Dr RG42 27 D8
Roundtable Rd BR1 24 F5
Roundthorn Way GU21 68 F3
Roundway
Biggin Hill TN16 83 D4
Egham TW20 12 C3
Frimley GU15 66 C6
Roundway Cl GU15 66 C6
Roundway Ct RH10 201 D8
Roundway The KT10 55 F4
Roundwood View SM7 77 D4
Roundwood Way SM7 77 D4
Roupell Ho 7 KT2 17 F1
Roupell Rd SW2 21 F7
Rouse Gdns SE21 22 E4
Routh Ct TW14 14 D7
Routh Rd SW18 20 E8
Rowallan Ct SE6 24 F7
Rowan 2 RG12 27 F4
Rowan Ave TW20 12 C3
Rowan Chase GU10 146 A5
Rowan Cl
Ashford TW15 13 D4
Camberley GU15 65 F8
Crawley RH10 201 F6
Guildford GU1 109 C4
Horsham RH12 218 B5
Kingston upon Thames KT3 38 E7
Mitcham SW16 41 C8
Reigate RH2 139 C7
Rowan Cres SW16 41 C8
Rowan Ct
Forest Hill SE26 23 C4
Hounslow TW3 5 B2
11 Kingston upon Thames KT2 18 A1
Wimbledon SW20 39 B7
Rowan Dr RG45 45 C6
Rowan Gdns CR0 61 F7
Rowan Gn KT13 53 D6
Rowan Gr CR5 99 B6
Rowan Mead KT20 97 B8
Rowan Pre Prep Sch KT10 55 E3
Rowan Prep Sch KT10 55 F3
Rowan Rd
Brentford TW8 6 B7
Mitcham SW16 41 C7
Rowans Cl GU14 64 E1
Rowanside Cl GU35 187 C4
Rowans Sch The SW20 19 A1
Rowans The
Ashford TW16 14 F3
Grayshott GU26 188 D2
12 Sutton SM2 59 B4
Woking GU22 69 E1
Rowan Way RH12 218 C5
Rowan Wlk RH10 204 C8
Rowbarns Way KT24 112 F5
Rowbury GU7 151 A7
Rowcliffe Springs GU8 172 E4
Rowcroft Cl GU12 106 A6
Rowden Rd
Penge BR3 43 F8
West Ewell KT19 57 C6
Rowdown Cres CR0 63 E2
Rowdown Prim Sch CR0 63 D1
Rowe La GU24 88 A3
Rowena Ct 4 RH12 217 A1
Rowfant Bsns Ctr RH10 203 E6
Rowfant Cl RH10 202 E6
Rowfant Rd SW12, SW17 21 A6
Row Hill KT15 51 F4
Rowhill Ave GU11 125 F8
Rowhill Cl GU14 84 C4
Rowhill Copse Nature Reserve★ GU9 125 D8
Rowhill Cres GU11 125 F8
Rowhills GU9 125 E8
Rowhills Cl GU9 125 F7
ROWHOOK 196 E1
Rowhook Hill RH12 215 F8
Rowhook Rd
Rowhook RH12 196 E1
Slinfold RH12 216 A8
Rowhurst Ave KT15 52 B4
Row La GU5 153 E5
Rowland Cl RH10 183 E5
Rowland Ct CR0 61 E8
Rowland Gr SE26 23 B5
Rowland Hill Almshouses 9 TW15 14 A3
Rowland Ho GU6 174 D3
Rowland Pl
Purley/Kenley CR8 80 A3
Wokingham RG41 25 A2
Rowland Rd GU6 174 D3
Rowlands Rd RH12 218 A6
Rowland Way
Littleton Common TW15 14 D1
Merton SW19 40 B8
ROWLEDGE 145 F3
Rowledge CE Prim Sch GU10 145 E3
Rowley Cl
Bracknell RG12 27 E6
Pyrford GU22 71 B3
Rowley Ct CR3 100 C5
Rowlls Rd KT1 37 F6
ROWLY 174 B6
Rowly Dr GU6 174 A6
Rowly Edge GU6 174 A6
Rowntree Rd TW2 16 E7
Rowplatt Cl RH19 184 E4
Rowplatt La RH19 184 E4
Row The RH7 164 D4
ROW TOWN 51 F4
Row Town KT15 51 F3
Roxbee Cox Rd GU14, GU51 84 A1
Roxborough Ave TW7 5 F7
Roxburgh Cl GU15 66 C4
Roxburgh Rd SE27 22 B3
Roxeth Ct 8 TW15 14 A3
Roxford Cl TW17 34 E4
Roxton Gdns CR0 63 A5
Roxywood Ct CR2 61 C2
Royal Alexandra & Albert Sch The RH2 118 E6
Royal Ave KT4 57 E8
Royal Ballet Sch The TW10 18 D7
Royal Botanic Gardens★ TW9 6 E6
Royal Cir SE27 22 B5
Royal Cl
Putney SW19 19 D6
Worcester Park KT4 57 E8
Royal Crest Ho SM2 58 E3
Royal Ct
9 Kingston upon Thames KT2 18 B1
Knaphill GU21 68 C1
Royal Dr KT18 97 B8
Royal Duchess Mews 15 SW12 21 B8
Royal Earlswood Pk RH1 140 A6
Royale Cl GU11 126 C8
Royal Fst Sch The SL4 10 C4
Royal Grammar Sch GU1 130 D8
Royal Holloway Univ of London TW20 11 E1
Royal Horticultural Society Cotts GU23 71 E3
Royal Horticultural Society Garden Wisley★ GU23 71 E1
Royal Hosp The SW19 19 E8
Royal Hunt Ho SL5 28 D8
Royal Huts Ave GU26 188 F4
Royal Jun Sch The GU26 188 D1
Royal Kent CE Prim Sch The KT22 74 C5
Royal Logistic Corps Mus★ GU16 86 D8
Royal Marsden Hospl (Surrey Site) SM2 59 C1
Royal Mews KT8 36 E6
Royal Military Acad Sandhurst GU15 64 F6
Royal Military Sch of Music (Kneller Hall) TW2 5 D1
Royal Oak Ctr The CR2 61 C1
Royal Oak Dr RG45 45 B8
Royal Oak Ho RH10 204 B7
Royal Oak Mews 10 TW11 17 A3
Royal Oak Rd GU21 69 D1
Royal Orchard Cl SW18 19 E8
Royal Par
Hindhead GU26 188 F4
12 Richmond TW9 7 A6
Royal Rd TW11 16 D3
Royal Russell Sch CR9 62 B5
Royal Sch The GU27 189 A2
Royals The GU1 130 E8
Royal Surrey County Hospl GU2 108 E1
Royal Victoria Gdns SL5 29 A4
Royal Way The GU16 86 D7
Royal Wlk SM6 60 B7
Royce Rd RH10 182 A3
Roycroft Cl SW2 22 A7
Roydon Ct
Egham TW20 12 D2
Hersham KT12 54 A6
Roydon Lodge KT15 52 D7
Roy Gr TW12 16 B2
Roy Ho TW12 16 B2
Roylon Ct BR3 43 E5
Roymount Ct TW2 16 E5
Royston Ave
Byfleet KT14 71 E7
Carshalton SM1 59 D7
Wallington SM6 60 D6
Royston Cl
Cranford TW5 4 B6
Crawley RH10 182 A2
Walton-on-Thames KT12 35 A1
Royston Ct
Hinchley Wood KT10 55 F8
3 Richmond TW9 6 F6
Tolworth KT6 57 A8
Royston Lo SW19 20 C2
Royston Prim Sch 1 SE20 43 D8
Royston Rd
Byfleet KT14 71 E7
Penge BR3, SE20 43 D8
Richmond TW10 6 E2
Roystons The KT5 38 B4
Rozeldene GU26 188 E3
Rozelle Ct 1 CR7 42 A3
Rozel Terr CR0 61 C7
Rubens Gdns SE22 23 A8
Rubens St SE6 23 F6
Rubus Cl GU24 67 E6
Ruby Ct TW13 14 F5
Ruckmans La RH5 197 B7
Rudd Hall Rise GU15 65 E4
Ruden Way KT17 77 B4
Rudge Ho 2 RH19 185 F1
Rudge Rise KT15 51 F5
RUDGWICK 214 C7
Rudgwick Keep RH6 161 C4
Rudgwick Prim Sch RH12 214 D7
Rudgwick Rd RH11 200 F7
Rudloe Rd SW12 21 C8
Rudolph Ct SE22 23 B8
Rudsworth Cl SL3 1 D7
Ruffett & Big Woods Nature Reserve★ CR5 79 A5
Ruffetts Cl CR2 62 B3
Ruffetts The CR2 62 B3
Ruffetts Way KT20 77 E1
Rufus Bsns Ctr SW18 20 B6
Rufwood RH10 204 A8
Rugby Cl GU47 45 E1
Rugby Ct TW9 6 E3
Rugby La SM2 58 D2
Rugby Rd TW1, TW2, TW7 5 E1
Ruggles-Brise Rd TW15 13 D3
Rugosa Rd GU24 67 E6
Ruislip St SW17 20 F4
Rumsey Cl TW12 15 F2
Runcorn Cl RH11 200 E2
Runes Cl CR4 40 E5
RUNFOLD 126 C4
Runfold - St George GU10 126 B5
Runnemede Rd TW20 12 A4
Running Horse Yd 12 TW8 6 E8
Runnymede★ TW20 11 F5
Runnymede SW19 40 D8
Runnymede Cl TW2 16 B8
Runnymede Cotts TW19 12 D7
Runnymede Cres SW16 41 E8
Runnymede Ct
14 Croydon CR0 61 F8
Egham TW20 12 A4
Farnborough GU14 85 A7
Roehampton SW15 19 A7
1 Wallington SM6 60 B4
Runnymede Gdns TW2 16 B8
Runnymede Ho TW10 7 A2
Runnymede Hospl (Private) The KT16 51 D7
Runnymede Rd TW2 5 B1
Runnymede Rdbt TW20 12 B4
Runshooke Ct 9 RH11 201 A3
Runtley Wood La GU4 89 F2
Runwick La GU10 124 C1
Rupert Rd GU2 130 C8
Rural Cl GU9 145 F6
Rural Life Ctr★ GU10 146 F3
Rural Way
Mitcham SW16 21 B1
Redhill RH1 119 A1
Ruscoe Dr GU22 70 A2
Ruscoe Ho 12 SW27 22 B3
Ruscombe Way TW14 14 F8
Rusham Park Ave TW20 12 A2
Rusham Rd
Balham SW12 20 F8
Egham TW20 11 F2
Rushams Rd RH12 217 B3
Rusham Terr TW20 12 A2
Rushbridge Cl CR0 42 C3
Rushbury Ct 6 TW12 36 A8
Rush Common Mews SW2 21 F8
Rush Croft GU7 151 A8
Rushden Cl SE19 22 D1
Rushdene Wlk TN16 83 D2
Rushden Way GU9 125 D7
Rushen Wlk SM5 40 D1
Rushett Cl KT7 37 B1
Rushett Dr RH4 136 C4
Rushett La KT9, KT18 75 D7
Rushett Rd KT7 37 B2
RUSHETTS FARM 139 C6
Rushetts Pl RH11 181 C1

Rushetts Rd
  Crawley RH11 .... 181 B1
  Reigate RH2 .... 139 C5
Rushey Cl KT3 .... 38 D5
Rushey Gn SE6 .... 24 B8
Rushey Green Prim Sch
  SE6 .... 24 B7
Rushfords RH7 .... 164 E5
Rushmead TW10 .... 17 F6
Rushmead Cl CR0 .... 61 F6
Rushmere Ct KT4 .... 58 A8
Rushmere Ho 2 SW15 .... 19 A7
Rushmere Pl
  Englefield Green TW20 ..... 11 E3
  Wimbledon SW19 .... 19 D3
Rushmon Ct KT16 .... 32 F2
Rushmon Gdns KT12 .... 54 B7
Rushmon Pl SM3 .... 58 E4
Rushmon Villas KT3 .... 38 F5
RUSHMOOR 168 C5
Rushmoor Cl GU2 .... 108 F5
Rushmoor Ct GU14 .... 105 C8
Rushmoor Rd GU11 .... 104 E4
Rusholme Gr SE19 .... 22 E3
Rush The SW20 .... 39 F8
Rushton Ave RH9 .... 142 D5
Rushworth Rd RH2 .... 118 B2
Rushy Ho RG12 .... 27 E5
Rushy Meadow La SM5 ...... 59 E7
Rushy Meadow Prim Sch
  SM5 .... 59 E7
Ruskin Ave
  Feltham TW14 .... 3 F1
  Richmond TW9 .... 7 A7
Ruskin Cl RH10 .... 182 C1
Ruskin Dr KT4 .... 58 C8
Ruskin Ho CR2 .... 61 D5
Ruskin Par CR0 .... 61 D5
Ruskin Rd
  Croydon CR0, CR9 .... 61 B8
  Isleworth TW7 .... 5 F4
  Staines TW18 .... 12 F2
  Wallington SM5 .... 60 A5
Ruskin Way SW19 .... 40 D8
RUSPER 199 D7
Rusper Ct CR5 .... 79 D3
Rusper Prim Sch RH12 ..... 199 C5
Rusper Rd
  Capel RH5 .... 178 D2
  Crawley RH11 .... 200 D7
  Faygate RH12 .... 199 A1
  Horsham RH12 .... 217 F6
  Newdigate RH12, RH5 ...... 179 C4
Ruspers Keep RH11 .... 200 F7
Russel Cl BR3 .... 44 C6
Russell Cl
  Bracknell RG12 .... 27 D2
  5 Chiswick W4 .... 7 F8
  Walton on the Hill KT20 .. 97 A2
  Woking GU21 .... 69 C4
Russell Ct
  Blackwater GU17 .... 64 D5
  Bromley BR1 .... 24 F1
  3 Croydon SE25 .... 42 F5
  Guildford GU1 .... 109 C4
  Hindhead GU26 .... 188 F4
  Leatherhead KT22 .... 95 B5
  Streatham SW16 .... 21 F3
  1 Surbiton KT6 .... 37 E2
  Wallington SM6 .... 60 C5
Russell Dr TW19 .... 2 D1
Russell Gdns
  Harmondsworth UB7 .... 3 A8
  Richmond TW10 .... 17 C6
Russell Green Cl CR8 ..... 61 A1
RUSSELL HILL 60 F1
Russell Hill CR8 .... 60 F1
Russell Hill Par 6 CR8 ... 80 A8
Russell Hill Pl CR8 ...... 80 A8
Russell Hill Rd CR8 ...... 80 A8
Russell Kerr Cl W4 .... 7 C7
Russell Par 5 CR8 .... 80 A8
Russell Prim Sch The
  TW10 .... 17 D7
Russell Rd
  Lower Halliford TW17 ..... 34 C2
  Merton SW19 .... 20 A1
  Mitcham CR4 .... 40 E6
  Twickenham TW1, TW2 ...... 5 F1
  Walton-on-Thames KT12 ... 35 A3
  Woking GU21 .... 69 C4
Russells KT20 .... 97 D5
Russells Cres RH6 .... 161 A2
Russell's Yd GU22 .... 89 F7
Russell Way
  Crawley RH10 .... 202 A5
  Sutton SM1 .... 59 B5
Russell Wlk 4 TW10 .... 6 F1
Russet Ave TW17 .... 34 E6
Russet Cl
  Hersham KT12 .... 54 E7
  Horley RH6 .... 161 C3
  Stanwell TW19 .... 1 F1
  Tongham GU10 .... 126 F2
Russet Ct TW13 .... 14 E5
Russet Dr CR0 .... 43 E1
Russet Gdns GU15 .... 65 D3
Russet Glade GU11 .... 125 E8
Russet Ho 4 TW3 .... 4 F3
Russets KT20 .... 97 C4
Russett Ct
  Caterham CR3 .... 101 A2
  Horsham RH12 .... 218 A4
Russetts Cl GU21 .... 69 F4
Russet Way RH5 .... 136 D4

Russ Hill RH6 .... 180 C5
Russ Hill Cotts RH6 ...... 180 C6
Russ Hill Rd RH6 .... 180 D6
Russington Rd TW17 .... 34 D3
Russley Gn RG40 .... 25 A1
Rusthall Cl CR0 .... 43 C3
Rustic Ave SW16 .... 21 B1
Rustic Villas RH9 .... 121 B5
Rustington Wlk SM4 .... 39 F2
Ruston Ave KT5 .... 38 B2
Ruston Cl RH10 .... 202 C3
Ruston Way SL5 .... 28 E7
Rutford Rd SW16 .... 21 E3
Ruth Cl GU14 .... 84 C5
Ruthen Cl KT18 .... 76 B5
Rutherford Cl SM2 .... 59 D4
Rutherford Ct TW20 .... 20 D1
Rutherford Ho 14 TW11 .... 16 F3
Rutherford Sch CR2 .... 61 F5
Rutherford Way RH10 ...... 182 A3
Rutherford Way Ind Est
  RH10 .... 182 A3
Rutherwick Cl RH6 .... 160 F3
Rutherwick Rise CR5 ...... 79 E3
Rutherwyke Cl KT17 .... 58 A4
Rutherwyke Rd KT16 .... 32 E2
Rutland Cl
  Aldershot GU11 .... 105 A3
  Ashtead KT21 .... 75 E2
  Chessington KT9 .... 56 F4
  Epsom KT19 .... 57 D1
  Mitcham SW19 .... 20 E1
  Mortlake SW14 .... 7 C4
  Redhill RH1 .... 118 F2
Rutland Ct TW2 .... 16 E5
Rutland Dr
  Morden SM4 .... 40 A2
  Richmond TW10 .... 17 E7
Rutland Gate BR2 .... 44 F5
Rutland Gdns CR0 .... 61 E6
Rutland Lodge
  Forest Hill SE6 .... 23 F6
  Teddington TW11 .... 16 E3
  Wimbledon SW19 .... 19 D2
Rutland Pk SE6 .... 23 F6
Rutland Rd
  Mitcham SW19 .... 20 E1
  Twickenham TW2 .... 16 D6
Rutland Terr GU11 .... 105 A3
Rutland Wlk SE6 .... 23 F6
Rutlish Rd SW19 .... 40 A8
Rutlish Sch SW20 .... 39 F7
Rutson Rd KT14 .... 71 F5
Rutter Gdns CR4, SW19 .... 40 D5
Rutton Hill Rd GU8 .... 189 E8
Ruxbury Ct TW15 .... 13 E5
Ruxbury Rd KT16 .... 32 D3
Ruxley Cl KT19 .... 57 B5
Ruxley Cres KT10 .... 56 B3
Ruxley Ct
  West Ewell KT19 .... 57 C5
  Woking GU22 .... 89 D8
Ruxley Gdns SW17 .... 34 C4
Ruxley La KT19 .... 57 C5
Ruxley Mews KT19 .... 57 B5
Ruxley Ridge KT10 .... 56 A3
Ruxton Cl CR5 .... 79 C4
Ryan Ct SW16 .... 21 E1
Ryan Dr TW8 .... 6 A8
Ryan Mount GU47 .... 64 A8
Rybrook Dr SE6 .... 54 C8
Rycott Path SE22 .... 23 A8
Rydal Cl
  Crawley RH11 .... 200 D4
  Farnborough GU14 .... 84 D3
  Frimley GU15 .... 66 D5
  Sanderstead CR8 .... 80 D6
Rydal Ct 1 SW20 .... 39 D8
Rydal Dr BR4 .... 63 E8
Rydal Gdns
  Kingston upon Thames
  SW15 .... 18 E3
  Twickenham TW2, TW3 ...... 5 B1
Rydal Mount 9 BR2 .... 44 F5
Rydal Pl GU18 .... 67 B8
Rydal Rd SW16 .... 21 D4
Rydal Way TW20 .... 12 B1
Ryde Cl GU23 .... 91 C6
Ryde Ct GU12 .... 105 C1
Ryde Heron GU21 .... 68 E2
Ryde Lands GU6 .... 174 F4
RYDENS 54 B8
Rydens Ave KT12 .... 54 C8
Rydens Cl KT12 .... 54 C8
Rydens Ct KT12 .... 54 C7
Rydens Gr KT12 .... 54 D6
Rydens Pk KT12 .... 54 D8
Rydens Rd KT12 .... 54 C8
Rydens Sch KT12 .... 54 D6
Rydens Way GU22 .... 90 A7
Ryde Pl TW1 .... 6 D1
Ryder Ho 5 SW19 .... 40 B8
Ryders Way RH12 .... 217 F7
Rydes Ave GU2 .... 108 F4
Rydes Cl GU22 .... 90 C7
RYDESHILL 108 E4
Ryde's Hill Cres GU2 ..... 108 F5
Rydeshill Prep Sch GU2 ... 108 F3
Ryde's Hill Rd GU2 .... 108 F4
Ryde The TW18 .... 33 B8
Ryde Vale Rd SW12 .... 21 C6
Rydon Bsns Ctr KT22 ...... 95 B8
Rydon Mews SW19 .... 19 C1
Rydon's La CR5 .... 100 C3
Rydons Way RH1 .... 140 A8
Rydon's Wood Cl CR5 ...... 100 C2
Rye Ash RH10 .... 202 A7
Ryebridge Cl KT22 .... 75 A1

Ryebrook Bsns Pk KT22 .... 95 A7
Rye Brook Rd KT22 .... 75 A1
Rye Cl
  Farnborough GU14 .... 84 E7
  Guildford GU2 .... 108 E3
  Winkfield RG12 .... 27 D8
Ryecotes Mead SE21 .... 22 E7
Ryecroft Ave TW2 .... 16 B7
Ryecroft Dr RH12 .... 217 A3
Ryecroft Gdns GU17 .... 64 E4
Ryecroft Ho SW19 .... 20 B1
Ryecroft Rd SW16 .... 22 A2
Rye Ct BR3 .... 43 F8
Ryedale SE22 .... 23 B1
Rye Field KT21 .... 75 D3
Ryefield Path 7 SW15 ..... 19 A7
Ryefield Rd SE19 .... 22 C2
Rye Gr
  Cranleigh GU6 .... 174 A3
  Windlesham GU20, GU18 ... 48 F7
Ryehill Ct KT3 .... 38 F2
Ryelands
  Crawley RH11 .... 201 A5
  Horley RH6 .... 161 C4
Ryelands Ct CR3 .... 100 E6
Ryelands Ct KT22 .... 75 A1
Ryelands Pl KT13 .... 53 E7
Ryelands Prim Sch SE25 ... 43 B4
Ryemead La SL4 .... 8 C5
Ryersh La RH5 .... 178 C8
Ryfold Rd SW19 .... 20 A5
Rykens La RH3 .... 137 C4
Ryland Cl TW13 .... 14 F4
Rylandes Rd CR2 .... 62 B1
Ryland Ho 11 SW16 .... 21 C3
Ryle Rd GU9 .... 146 B8
Rylston Ho 3 KT12 .... 35 A1
Rymer Rd CR0 .... 42 E2
Rythe Cl
  Chessington KT9 .... 56 C3
Rythe Ct KT7 .... 37 A2
Rythe Ho BR1 .... 24 D3
Rythe Rd KT10 .... 55 E5
Rythe The KT22 .... 55 C1

S

Sabah Ct TW15 .... 14 A4
Sabin Gates RG12 .... 27 B6
Sable Cl TW4 .... 4 C4
Sable Ct 3 KT3 .... 38 E4
Sabre Ct GU11 .... 104 E2
Sachel Court Dr GU6 ...... 193 F2
Sachel Court Rd GU6 ...... 193 D3
Sackville Coll RH19 ...... 185 C3
Sackville Coll* RH19 ..... 185 F1
Sackville Com Coll RH19 .. 186 A1
Sackville Cotts RH1 ...... 120 D1
Sackville Ct 3 RH19 ...... 205 F8
Sackville Gdns RH19 ...... 185 C3
Sackville Ho 16 SW16 ..... 21 E5
Sackville La RH19 .... 185 C3
Sackville Rd SM2 .... 59 A3
Saco Ct 5 GU14 .... 85 C1
Sacred Heart RC Prim Sch
  Teddington TW11 .... 17 B1
  West Barnes SW20 .... 39 A5
Saddleback Rd GU15 .... 65 E8
Saddlebrook Pk TW16 ...... 14 E1
Saddler Cnr GU47 .... 64 B7
Saddler Row RH10 .... 201 D3
Saddlers Ct KT19 .... 76 D6
Saddlers Mews KT1 .... 37 C8
Saddlers Scarp GU26 ...... 188 A4
Saddlers Way KT18 .... 96 D8
Saddlewood GU15 .... 65 C4
Sadler Cl CR4 .... 40 F7
Sadlers Cl GU4 .... 110 D2
Sadlers Ride KT8 .... 36 C7
Saffron Cl
  Crawley RH11 .... 201 A3
  Thornton Heath CR0 ...... 41 E3
Saffron Ct
  East Bedfont TW14 .... 14 C8
  Farnborough GU14 .... 84 C4
Saffron Ho 6 TW9 .... 7 B6
Saffron Platt GU2 .... 109 A5
Saffron Rd RG12 .... 27 B5
Saffron Way KT6 .... 37 D1
Sage Ho RH10 .... 182 A1
Sage Yd 8 KT6 .... 37 F1
Sailors La GU8 .... 169 A2
Sainfoin Rd SW17 .... 21 A6
Sainsbury Ctr The KT16 ... 33 A2
Sainsbury Rd SE19 .... 22 E3
St Agatha's Dr KT2 .... 17 F2
St Agatha's Gr CR4, SM5 .. 40 F1
St Agatha's RC Prim Sch
  KT2 .... 17 F2
St Agnes Rd RH19 .... 185 E2
St Aidan's RC Prim Sch
  CR5 .... 79 C3
St Albans Ave
  Feltham TW13 .... 15 D3
  Weybridge KT13 .... 53 A7
St Albans Cl GU3 .... 108 B2
St Alban's Gdns TW11 ..... 17 A3
St Alban's Gr SM5 .... 40 F1
St Albans Ho 2 SW16 ...... 22 A4
St Alban's RC Aided Prim Sch
  KT8 .... 36 C4
St Alban's Rd
  Cheam SM1 .... 58 F6
  Kingston upon Thames KT2 .. 17 E2
St Alban's Rd RH2 .... 118 A3

St Alban's Rdbt GU14 ..... 105 C7
St Amunds Cl SE6 .... 24 A4
St Andrews
  Bracknell RG12 .... 26 E3
  Cranleigh GU6 .... 174 B4
  Horley RH6 .... 161 B2
St Andrew's CE Inf Sch
  GU9 .... 125 B2
St Andrew's CE Prim Sch
  RH10 .... 202 A4
St Andrew's CE VA High Sch
  CR0 .... 61 B6
St Andrews Cl
  Hinchley Wood KT7 .... 37 B1
  Wimbledon SW19 .... 20 B2
  Woking GU21 .... 69 C2
St Andrew's Cl
  Hounslow TW7 .... 5 E6
  Reigate RH2 .... 139 B8
  Upper Halliford TW17 .... 34 D5
  Wraysbury TW19 .... 11 E8
St Andrews Ct
  Ascot SL5 .... 29 C4
  4 Bromley BR1 .... 24 E1
  Chiswick W4 .... 7 C6
St Andrews Gate 2 GU22 ... 69 F1
St Andrews Gdns KT11 ..... 73 C6
St Andrews Mews SW12 ..... 21 D7
St Andrew's Prim Sch
  KT11 .... 73 C6
St Andrew's RC Prim Sch
  SW16 .... 21 E3
St Andrew's RC Sch KT22 .. 95 D7
St Andrews Rd
  Carshalton SM5 .... 59 E7
St Andrew's Rd
  Coulsdon CR5 .... 79 B4
  3 Croydon CR0, CR9 ..... 61 C6
  Kingston upon Thames KT6 .. 37 D4
St Andrew's & St Mark's CE
  Jun Sch KT6 .... 37 D4
St Andrew's Sch GU21 ..... 69 D3
St Andrew's Sch, The Grange
  KT22 .... 95 D7
St Andrews Sq KT6 .... 37 D3
St Andrews Way RH8 .... 123 F4
St Andrew's Way GU16 ..... 85 F7
St Andrew's Wlk KT11 ..... 73 B4
St Annes 13 SM2 .... 59 B4
St Anne's Ave TW19 .... 13 D8
St Annes Bvd RH1 .... 119 B3
St Annes Dr RG40 .... 26 A6
St Anne's Dr RH1 .... 119 A2
St Anne's Dr N RH1 .... 119 A3
St Annes Glade GU19 ...... 47 D3
St Annes Ind Sch CR0 ..... 42 D3
St Annes Mount 7 RH1 ..... 119 A3
St Anne's RC Prim Sch
  Banstead SM7 .... 78 A3
  Chertsey KT16 .... 33 A1
St Anne's Rd
  Crawley RH10 .... 182 C2
  Godalming GU7 .... 151 A5
St Annes Rise RH1 .... 119 A3
St Annes Way RH1 .... 119 A2
St Ann's Cl KT16 .... 32 F3
ST ANN'S HEATH 31 F5
St Ann's Heath Jun Sch
  GU25 .... 31 E4
St Ann's Hill SW18 .... 20 C8
St Ann's Hill Rd KT16 .... 32 D3
St Anns Rd SW13 .... 7 F6
St Ann's Rd KT16 .... 32 F3
St Ann's Specl Sch SM4 ... 40 B4
St Ann's Way CR2 .... 61 B4
St Anselm's Cl SW16 ...... 21 E3
St Anselm's RC Prim Sch
  SW17 .... 21 A5
St Anthonys Cl
  Bracknell RG42 .... 27 A8
  Upper Tooting SW17 ...... 20 E6
St Anthony's Ct
  1 Balham SW12 .... 21 A8
  Upper Tooting SW17 ...... 21 A8
St Anthony's Hospl KT4 ... 39 D1
St Anthony's RC Prim Sch 17
  SE20 .... 43 B8
St Anthony's Way TW14 .... 3 F3
St Arvans Cl CR0 .... 61 E7
St Aubin Cl RH11 .... 200 F2
St Aubyn's Ave
  Hounslow TW3, TW4 .... 5 A2
  Wimbledon SW19 .... 19 F3
St Aubyn's Ct SW19 .... 19 E2
St Aubyn's Rd SE19 .... 22 F2
St Augustine's Ave
  Croydon CR2 .... 61 C3
  South Croydon CR2 .... 61 C3
St Augustine's Cl GU12 ... 105 D1
St Augustines Ct BR3 ..... 43 E7
St Augustine's Ho 4 ...... 20 F4
St Augustine's Prim Sch
  GU16 .... 85 F7
St Augustines's RC Prim Sch
  SE6 .... 24 C3
St Austells Pl RH5 .... 157 C7
St Austins GU26 .... 188 D3
St Barnabas BR3 .... 44 C7
St Barnabas Ct RH10 ...... 202 C3
St Barnabas' Gdns KT8 .... 36 A4
St Barnabas Ho CR4 .... 21 A1
St Barnabas Rd
  Carshalton SM1 .... 59 D5

St Barnabas Rd *continued*
  Mitcham CR4 .... 21 A1
St Bartholomew's CE Prim
  Sch 8 SE26 .... 23 C4
St Bartholomew's Cl SE26 .. 23 C4
St Bartholomew's Ct
  GU1 .... 130 F7
St Bartholomew's Prim Sch
  GU27 .... 208 C7
St Bede's CE Jun Sch
  GU23 .... 90 D3
St Bede's RC Inf Sch
  SW12 .... 21 D7
St Bede's Sch RH1 .... 118 E4
St Benedict's Cl
  Aldershot GU11 .... 105 A1
  Upper Tooting SW17 ...... 21 A3
St Benets Cl SW17 .... 20 E6
St Benet's Gr SM4, SM5 ... 40 C2
St Bernadette RC Jun Sch
  SW12 .... 21 C8
St Bernadettes RC Prim Sch
  GU14 .... 85 A5
St Bernards CR0 .... 61 E7
St Bernards Cl 8 SE27 .... 22 D4
St Bernards Ho 7 KT6 ..... 56 E8
St Boniface RC Prim Sch
  SW17 .... 20 F3
St Brelades Cl RH4 .... 136 A5
St Brelades Rd RH11 ...... 200 F2
St Catherines
  Weybridge KT13 .... 53 B7
  Woking GU22 .... 89 C8
St Catherines Cl
  Chessington KT9 .... 56 D4
  Upper Tooting SW17 ...... 20 E6
St Catherine's Cross
  RH1 .... 120 E2
St Catherines Ct
  Feltham TW13 .... 15 A7
  2 Staines TW18 .... 13 A4
St Catherine's Ct 4
  RH19 .... 185 D2
St Catherine's Dr GU2 .... 130 B5
St Catherine's Hill GU2 .. 130 C5
St Catherine's Jun Sch
  GU5 .... 151 F6
St Catherines Pk GU1 ..... 130 F7
St Catherines Pl TW20 .... 12 A3
St Catherine's Prim Sch
  RH1 .... 120 E2
St Catherine's Rd
  Crawley RH10 .... 182 D1
  Frimley GU16 .... 86 A8
St Catherine's Sch
  Bramley GU5 .... 151 F7
  Twickenham TW1 .... 17 A6
St Catherines Wood GU15 .. 65 C4
St Cecilia's CE Sch SW18 .. 19 F8
St Cecilias Cl SM3 .... 39 E1
St Cecilia's RC Prim Sch
  SM3 .... 58 D8
St Chads Cl KT6 .... 37 C2
St Chad's RC Prim Sch
  SE25 .... 42 E4
St Charles Borromeo RC
  Prim Sch KT13 .... 53 A7
St Charles Cl KT13 .... 53 A5
St Charles Pl KT13 .... 53 A5
St Christopher's RC 7 RH7 .. 164 D4
St Christophers Cl
  Aldershot GU12 .... 105 D2
  5 Horsham RH12 .... 217 C4
St Christopher's Cl
  Haslemere GU27 .... 208 A6
  Hounslow TW7 .... 5 E6
St Christophers Gdns
  North Ascot SL5 .... 28 D8
  Thornton Heath CR7 ...... 42 A6
St Christopher's Gn
  GU27 .... 208 A6
St Christopher's Hospice
  SE26 .... 23 C3
St Christopher's Mews
  SM6 .... 60 C5
St Christophers Pl 1
  GU14 .... 85 A3
St Christopher's Rd
  2 Farnborough GU14 ..... 85 A3
  Haslemere GU27 .... 208 A6
St Christopher's Sch
  Beckenham BR3 .... 44 C7
  Epsom KT18 .... 76 E5
St Clair Cl
  Oxted RH8 .... 122 D5
  Reigate RH2 .... 118 C1
St Clair Cotts RH7 .... 165 B1
St Clair Dr KT4 .... 58 B6
St Clair's Rd CR0 .... 61 E8
St Clare Bsns Pk TW12 .... 16 C2
St Clare St BR3 .... 24 B1
St Clement Rd RH11 .... 200 F2
St Clements Ct GU14 ...... 85 B7
St Clements Ho 3 KT12 .... 35 A2
St Clements RC Prim Sch
  KT17 .... 57 F2
St Cloud Rd SE27 .... 22 D4
St Crispin Ho CR0 .... 61 D7
St Crispin's Sch RG40 .... 25 E6
St Crispins Way KT16 ..... 51 C2
St Cross Rd
  Farnham GU9 .... 125 C3
  Frimley GU16 .... 86 B7
St Cuthbert Mayne RC Prim
  Sch GU6 .... 174 C3
St Cuthbert's Cl TW20 .... 11 D2
St Cuthbert's RC Prim Sch
  TW20 .... 11 C1

St Cyprian's Greek Orthodox
Prim Sch CR7 ...... 42 C8
St Cyprian's St SW17 .... 20 F4
St David's CR5 .... 79 F2
St David's Cl
  Farnborough GU14 ..... 84 F8
  Heath End GU9 .... 125 E7
  Reigate RH2 .... 118 C2
  West Wickham BR4 .... 44 B2
St David's Coll BR4 ..... 44 B2
St Davids Ct
  4 Aldershot GU12 ...... 105 B1
  Ashford TW15 .... 13 F6
St Davids Dr TW20 ..... 11 C1
St Davids Sch TW8 ..... 79 F8
St David's Sch TW15 .... 13 F5
St Denis Rd SE27 .... 22 D4
St Denys Cl CR8 .... 61 B1
St Deny's Cl GU21 ...... 68 D1
St Dominic Cl GU14 .... 85 A8
St Dominic's Sch GU8 .. 171 C1
St Dunstan's CE Prim Sch
  SM3 .... 58 E3
St Dunstan's Coll SE6 ... 24 A7
St Dunstan's Hill SM1,
  SM3 .... 58 E5
St Dunstan's La BR3 .... 44 C4
St Dunstan's RC Prim Sch
  GU2 .... 70 A2
St Dunstan's Rd
  Cranford TW5 .... 4 B5
  Feltham TW13 .... 14 F5
  South Norwood SE25 ... 42 F5
St Edith Cl KT18 .... 76 C5
St Edmunds Cl
  Crawley RH11 .... 181 D1
  Upper Tooting SW17 ... 20 E6
St Edmund's La TW2 .... 16 B8
St Edmund's RC Prim Sch
  Godalming GU7 .... 150 F2
  Twickenham TW2 ..... 16 B8
St Edmunds Sch GU26 .. 188 D3
St Edwards Cl CR0 ..... 82 D8
St Edward's Cl RH19 ... 185 C1
St Elizabeth Dr KT18 ... 76 C5
St Elizabeth's RC Prim Sch
  TW10 .... 6 F1
St Faith's Rd SE24 ..... 22 B7
St Fillans GU22 .... 70 B3
St Fillans Rd SE6 ...... 24 C8
St Francis Gdns RH10 .. 183 C4
St Francis of Assisi Prim Sch
  RH10 .... 201 E4
St Francis RC Prim Sch
  Ascot SL5 .... 29 A3
  Whyteleafe CR3 ...... 100 F6
St Francis Wlk RH11 ... 200 E4
St Georges RH6 .... 161 B2
St George's Ave KT13 .. 53 C4
St George's Bsns Ctr
  KT13 .... 53 A2
St Georges Cl RH6 ..... 161 B3
St George's Cl
  Badshot Lea GU9 ...... 126 B6
  Weybridge KT13 ...... 53 C5
St George's Coll KT15 .. 52 D7
St George's Coll Jun Sch
  KT13 .... 53 B7
St Georges Cotts KT13 . 53 C5
St George's Cotts RH7 . 143 E4
St Georges Ct
  Addlestone KT15 ...... 52 C6
  Crawley RH10 .... 201 D8
  East Grinstead RH19 .. 185 C3
  Penge SE20 .... 43 B8
  Weybridge KT13 ...... 53 C4
St George's Ct GU47 ... 45 E2
St George's Gate KT15 . 52 D7
St George's Gdns
  Epsom KT17 .... 76 F5
  Horsham RH13 .... 217 E4
  Tolworth KT6 .... 57 B8
St George's Gr SW17 ... 20 D5
ST GEORGE'S HILL 53 C1
St George's Hospl SW17 . 20 D3
St Georges Ind Est GU15 . 65 B3
St George's Ind Est KT2 . 17 D3
St George's La SL5 ..... 29 B6
St George's Lodge KT13 . 53 D5
St Georges Mews GU9 . 125 C3
St Georges Rd
  Addlestone KT15 ...... 52 C6
  Badshot Lea GU9 ...... 126 B5
St George's Rd
  Beckenham BR3 .... 44 B8
  Camberley GU15 ...... 65 D6
  Farnham GU9 .... 125 D1
  Feltham TW13 .... 15 D4
  Isleworth TW1 .... 6 B2
  2 Kingston upon Thames
    KT2 .... 18 A1
  Mitcham CR4 .... 41 B6
  Richmond TW9 .... 6 F4
  South Nutfield RH1 ... 140 E1
  Wallington SM6 ...... 60 B5
  Weybridge KT13 ...... 53 D4
  Wimbledon SW19 ..... 19 F2
St George's Rd E 6
  GU12 .... 105 B1
St George's Sch SL5 .... 29 B6
St George's Sq KT3 .... 38 E6
St George's Wlk CR0, CR9 . 61 C7
St Georges Wood SE20 . 208 D8
St Georges Yd 5 GU9 .. 125 B2
St German's Rd SE23 .. 23 E7
St Giles CE Inf Sch 1
  KT21 .... 75 F1
St Giles Cl TW5 .... 4 E7

St Giles Specl Sch CR2 .. 61 B4
St Gothard Rd SE27 .... 22 D4
St Helena Terr 32 TW9 .. 6 D2
St Helens KT7 .... 36 F2
St Helens Cres GU47 ... 64 B8
St Helen's Cres SW16 .. 41 F8
St Helen's Rd SW16 .... 41 F8
ST HELIER 40 D2
St Helier Ave SM4 ..... 40 C3
St Helier Cl
  Crawley RH11 .... 201 A2
  Wokingham RG41 ..... 25 B3
St Helier Hospl SM5 .... 40 C1
St Heliers Ave TW3, TW4 . 5 A2
St Helier Sta SM4 ...... 40 A3
St Hilary's Sch GU7 .... 150 D1
St Hilda's Ave TW15 ... 13 E3
St Hildas Cl SW17 ..... 20 E6
St Hilda's Cl
  Crawley RH10 .... 182 C1
  Horley RH6 .... 161 B3
  Knaphill GU21 .... 68 D2
Saint Hill Gn RH19 ..... 205 D4
Saint Hill Manor★ RH19 205 C4
Saint Hill Rd RH19 ..... 205 C5
St Hughes Cl SW17 .... 20 E6
St Hugh of Lincoln RC Prim
  Sch GU21 .... 88 D8
St Hugh's Cl RH10 ..... 182 C1
St Hugh's Rd SE20 ..... 23 B1
St Ignatius RC Prim Sch
  TW16 .... 35 A8
St Ives Rd TW10 .... 202 C7
St Ives Sch GU27 ...... 208 E8
St James Ave
  Ewell KT17 .... 77 A8
  Sutton SM1 .... 59 A5
St James' Ave GU9 .... 125 D3
St James CE Prim Sch
  Elstead GU8 .... 148 C3
  Weybridge KT13 ...... 53 C7
St James Cl
  Epsom KT18 .... 76 E5
  Woking GU21 .... 69 A1
St James' Cl KT3 ...... 38 F4
St James Ct
  Ashtead KT21 .... 75 D2
  East Grinstead RH19 .. 185 E1
  Farnham GU9 .... 125 C3
  Forest Hill SE23 ..... 23 E7
  Thornton Heath CR0 .. 42 B2
St James' Ct
  7 Kingston upon Thames
    KT1 .... 37 E6
  12 Surbiton KT6 ...... 37 E3
St James Gate SL5 ..... 30 A2
St James Ho
  7 Banstead SM7 ...... 77 F5
  Woking GU21 .... 69 B1
St James Ind Sch for Senior
  Boys TW1 .... 17 A6
St James Mews KT13 .. 53 B6
St James Rd
  Carshalton SM5 ...... 59 E7
  East Grinstead RH19 .. 185 D1
  Sutton SM1 .... 59 A5
St James' Rd
  Kingston upon Thames
    KT6 .... 37 D3
  Mitcham CR4 .... 21 A1
  Purley CR8 .... 80 C6
St James's Ave
  Beckenham BR3 ...... 43 E6
  Hampton TW12 ...... 16 C3
St James's Cl SW17 ... 20 F6
St James's Cotts 13 TW10 . 6 D2
St James's Dr
  Balham SW12, SW17 .. 20 F8
  Upper Tooting SW17 .. 20 F7
St James's Lodge 4 CR0 . 42 E1
St James's Pk CR0 ..... 42 C2
St James's Pl GU6 ..... 174 E3
St James's RC Prim Sch
  TW2 .... 16 E5
St James's Rd
  Hampton TW12 ...... 16 B3
  Kingston upon Thames KT1 . 37 D7
  Thornton Heath CR0 .. 42 D2
St James's Terr 2 SW12 . 21 A7
St James' Terr GU9 .... 125 C3
St James The Great RC Prim
  Sch CR7 .... 42 B7
St James Wlk RH11 ... 201 C2
St Joan Cl RH11 .... 181 D1
St John Baptist CE Prim Sch
  BR1 .... 24 C4
St John Cl RH13 .... 217 E1
St John Fisher RC Prim Sch
  SW20 .... 39 D4
ST JOHNS 139 E7
ST JOHN'S 89 B8
St John's RH5 .... 136 C3
St Johns Ave KT17 .... 77 A7
St John's Ave KT12 .... 95 B6
St John's Beaumont Sch
  SL4 .... 11 B6
St John's CE Com Prim Sch
  RH4 .... 136 B4
St John's CE Fst Sch
  GU10 .... 167 E1
St John's CE Prim Sch
  Caterham CR3 .... 101 A2
  Croydon CR0 .... 62 D7
  16 Kingston upon Thames
    KT1 .... 37 E6
  14 Penge SE20 .... 23 C1
St Johns Church Rd RH5 134 F4

St John's Cl
  East Grinstead RH19 .. 185 E2
  Guildford GU2 .... 130 A8
  Leatherhead KT22 .... 95 C7
St John's Cotts
  2 Penge SE20 .... 23 C1
  Richmond TW9 .... 6 E4
St John's Cres RH12 ... 216 E3
St Johns Ct
  Egham TW20 .... 12 A3
  South Godstone RH9 .. 142 F5
  Woking GU21 .... 89 A8
St John's Ct
  Brookwood GU24 ..... 87 F7
  Farnborough GU14 ... 84 D5
  Isleworth TW7 .... 5 F5
  Westcott RH4 .... 135 C6
St John's Cty Prim Sch 7
  GU21 .... 68 E1
St John's Dr KT12 ..... 35 C1
St John's Dr SW18 .... 20 B7
St Johns Gdns GU21 ... 69 A1
St John's Gr GU9 ...... 146 B8
St John's Gr
  Barnes SW13 .... 7 F5
  1 Richmond TW9 ..... 6 E3
St John's Hill CR8 ..... 80 A2
St John's Hill Rd GU21 . 89 B8
St John's Ho SW16 .... 21 C6
St Johns Lodge GU21 .. 89 A8
St John's Lye
  Woking GU21 .... 88 F8
  Woking GU21 .... 88 F8
St John's Mdw RH7 ... 163 E8
St Johns Mews GU21 .. 89 A8
St John's Prim Sch RH1 . 139 E7
St John's RC Prim Sch
  RH12 .... 217 A1
St Johns Rd KT3 ...... 38 C6
St John's Rd
  Carshalton SM5 ...... 59 E7
  Crawley RH11 .... 201 C6
  East Grinstead RH19 .. 185 E2
  East Molesey KT8 .... 36 D5
  Farnborough GU14 ... 84 E5
  Farnham GU9 .... 146 B8
  Feltham TW13 .... 15 F4
  Guildford GU2 .... 130 A8
  Isleworth TW7 .... 5 F5
  Leatherhead KT22 .... 95 C6
  North Ascot SL5 ..... 8 F1
  Penge SE20 .... 23 C2
  Redhill RH1 .... 139 F7
  Richmond TW9 .... 6 E3
  Sandhurst GU47 ..... 64 C7
  Sutton SM1 .... 59 B8
  Teddington KT1 ...... 37 C7
  Westcott RH4 .... 135 C6
  Wimbledon SW19 .... 19 E2
  Woking GU21 .... 69 B2
St John's Rise GU21 ... 89 B8
St Johns Sch RG45 .... 45 B5
St John's St GU7 ...... 150 F6
St John's Terrace Rd
  RH1 .... 139 F7
St Johns Waterside 7
  GU21 .... 68 F1
St Johns Way KT16 .... 33 A1
St John the Baptist CE Jun
  Sch KT1 .... 17 D1
St John the Baptist Sch
  GU22 .... 90 A8
St Joseph's Coll SE19 .. 22 B2
St Joseph's RC Inf Sch
  SE19 .... 22 C2
St Joseph's RC Jun Sch
  SE19 .... 22 C2
St Josephs RC Prim Sch
  GU11 .... 126 A8
St Joseph's RC Prim Sch
  Bracknell RG12 ...... 27 D7
  Dorking RH4 .... 136 A7
  Epsom KT18 .... 76 C5
  Guildford GU2 .... 108 F3
  Kingston upon Thames KT1 . 37 F7
  Redhill RH1 .... 118 C2
St Joseph's RC Sch GU12 . 105 A1
St Joseph's Sch GU6 .. 174 F6
St Jude's CE Jun Sch
  TW20 .... 11 C2
St Jude's Cl TW20 .... 11 C3
St Jude's Cotts TW20 .. 11 C3
St Jude's Rd TW20 .... 11 C3
St Julian 5 RH12 ...... 185 F2
St Julian's Cl SW16 ... 22 A4
St Julian's Farm Rd SE27,
  SW16 .... 22 B4
St Katharines Rd CR3 .. 101 A2
St Kitts Terr SE19 ..... 22 E3
St Lawrence Bsns Ctr
  TW13 .... 15 B6
St Lawrence Ct GU24 .. 68 E8
St Lawrence Jun Sch KT8 36 D5
St Lawrence Prim Sch
  KT24 .... 113 D8
St Lawrence RC Prim Sch
  TW13 .... 15 B6
St Lawrences Ct SW14 . 7 D4
St Lawrence Way RH2 . 118 A1
St Lawrence Way CR3 . 100 D4
St Leonards RH12 ..... 217 F4
St Leonard's CE Prim Sch
  SW16 .... 21 D3
St Leonards Ct SW14 .. 7 D4
St Leonards Dr RH10 .. 202 A4
St Leonard's Gdns TW5 . 4 E6

St Leonard's Park Ho
  RH13 .... 218 C3
St Leonards Pk RH19 .. 185 E1
St Leonards Rd
  Burgh Heath KT18 .... 97 C8
  Horsham RH13 .... 218 A1
  Mortlake SW14 ...... 7 C4
St Leonard's Rd
  Claygate KT10 .... 55 F4
  Croydon CR0, CR9 .... 61 B7
  Kingston upon Thames KT6 . 37 D4
  Thames Ditton KT7 ... 37 A2
  Windsor SL4 .... 9 D8
St Leonard's Sq KT6 ... 37 D4
St Leonard's Wlk SW16 . 21 F1
St Louis Ct SE27 ...... 22 D6
St Louis Rd SE27 ..... 22 D6
St Luke's CE Prim Sch
  3 Kingston upon Thames
    KT2 .... 37 F8
  West Norwood SE27 .. 22 C3
St Luke's Cl SE25 ..... 43 B3
St Lukes Ct GU21 ..... 70 C5
St Lukes Mews CR3 ... 80 F1
St Luke's Rd CR3 ..... 80 F1
St Luke's Sq 4 GU1 .. 130 F8
St Margaret Clitherow RC
  Prim Sch RG12 ...... 26 F2
St Margaret Dr KT18 .. 76 C5
ST MARGARETS 6 B1
St Margaret's GU1 .... 109 F1
St Margarets Ave TW15 . 14 B3
St Margaret's Ave
  Cheam SM3 .... 58 E7
  Dormans Park RH19 .. 185 F6
St Margarets Bsns Ctr 11
  TW1 .... 6 B1
St Margaret's CE Prim Sch
  RH11 .... 201 B7
St Margarets Ct RH12 . 216 F7
St Margaret's Ct 9 TW1 . 6 B1
St Margaret's Dr TW1 . 6 B2
St Margaret's Gr TW1 . 6 A1
St Margaret's Rd
  East Grinstead RH19 .. 185 F3
  Hooley CR5 .... 99 B6
  Isleworth TW1 .... 6 B2
St Margaret's Sch CR0 . 97 D6
St Margaret's Sta TW1 . 6 B1
St Mark's CE Acad CR4 . 41 B7
St Mark's CE Prim Sch
  Bromley BR2 .... 44 F6
  1 Croydon SE25 ..... 43 A5
  Farnborough GU14 .. 105 D8
St Marks Cl GU14 ..... 85 C1
St Mark's Ct 9 GU22 .. 89 E8
St Mark's Hill KT6 .... 37 E4
St Mark's Hts 26 KT6 . 37 E4
St Mark's La RH12 .... 217 E6
St Marks Pl GU9 ...... 125 B7
St Mark's Pl SW19 .... 19 F2
St Mark's Prim Sch CR4 . 40 F7
St Mark's RC Sch TW3 . 5 A4
St Marks Rd KT18, KT20 . 77 C1
St Mark's Rd
  Bracknell RG42 ...... 26 C8
  Croydon SE25 .... 43 A5
  Teddington TW11 .... 17 B1
St Martha's Ave GU22 . 89 F6
St Martha's Cotts GU5 . 154 E8
St Martha's Ct GU4 ... 131 B3
St Martin in the Fields High
  Sch SW2 .... 22 A7
St Martin's Ave KT18 .. 76 E5
St Martin's CE Inf Sch
  KT18 .... 76 D4
St Martin's CE Jun Sch
  KT18 .... 76 D4
St Martin's CE Prim Sch
  RH4 .... 136 A8
St Martin's CE Prim Sch
  (Pixham) RH4 .... 115 C1
St Martins Cl KT18 .... 112 E6
St Martins Cl KT17 .... 76 E6
St Martins Ct KT24 .... 112 E6
St Martin's Ct
  Staines TW15 .... 13 C3
  West Norwood SE27 .. 22 B6
St Martins Dr KT12 ... 54 C7
St Martin's La BR3 .... 44 B4
St Martins Mews 4 RH4 . 136 A7
St Martin's Mews GU22 . 71 A3
St Martin's Sq RH4 .... 136 A7
St Martin's Way SW17 . 20 C5
St Martin's Wlk 4 RH4 . 136 B8
St Martin's Wlk Sh Ctr
  RH5 .... 219 B8
St Mary Ave SM6 ..... 60 B7
St Mary Magdalen's RC Prim
  Sch SW14 .... 7 D4
St Mary's 4 KT13 ..... 53 D7
St Mary's Abbey GU27 . 207 D7
St Mary's Ave
  Beckenham BR2 ...... 44 E6
  Stanwell TW19 ...... 13 D8
  Teddington TW11 .... 16 F2
St Mary's CE Fst Sch
  GU8 .... 149 E6
St Mary's CE Inf Sch
  GU10 .... 167 D7
St Mary's CE Jun Sch
  RH8 .... 122 E7
St Marys CE Prim Sch
  GU8 .... 191 C4
St Mary's CE Prim Sch
  Byfleet KT14 .... 71 E6
  Chessington KT9 ..... 56 F4
  5 East Grinstead RH19 . 185 D2

St Mary's CE Prim Sch
continued
  Horsham RH12 .... 217 C1
  Long Ditton KT7 ..... 37 B1
  14 Twickenham TW1 .. 17 A8
  Winkfield RG42 ...... 8 B3
St Mary's CE Prim Sch (Jun)
  TW1 .... 17 B8
St Marys Cl GU47 ..... 64 C8
St Mary's Cl
  Chessington KT9 ..... 56 F3
  Ewell KT17 .... 57 F2
  Fetcham KT22 .... 94 D4
  Oxted RH8 .... 122 E6
  Stanwell TW19 ...... 13 D8
  Sunbury TW16 ...... 35 A5
St Mary's Coll TW1 .... 16 F5
St Marys Cotts GU10 .. 167 C7
St Mary's Cres
  Hounslow TW7 .... 5 E7
  Stanwell TW19 ...... 13 D8
St Mary's Ct
  Kingston upon Thames
    KT3 .... 38 E6
  Wallington SM6 ...... 60 C6
  West Byfleet KT14 ... 71 E7
St Mary's Dr
  Crawley RH10 .... 202 B8
  East Bedfont TW14 .. 14 C4
St Mary's Gdns
  Bagshot GU19 .... 47 E3
  Horsham RH12 ...... 217 C1
St Mary's Gn TN16 .... 83 C1
St Mary's Gr
  Biggin Hill TN16 ..... 83 C1
  Chiswick W4 .... 7 B8
  Richmond TW10, TW9 . 6 F3
St Mary's High Sch CR0 . 42 C1
St Mary's Hill SL5 .... 29 C4
St Mary's Ho 6 RH12 . 217 C1
St Marys Homes RH9 . 121 D3
St Marys La SL4 ...... 8 D5
St Mary's Mews TW10 . 17 C6
St Mary's Mill GU8 ... 191 C3
St Mary's Mt CR3 .... 100 F3
St Mary's Pl GU9 ..... 125 C3
St Mary's RC Inf Sch
  Carshalton SM5 ...... 59 F6
  Croydon CR0 .... 42 D1
St Mary's RC Jun Sch
  Croydon CR0 .... 42 D1
  Wallington SM5 ..... 59 F5
St Mary's RC Prim Sch
  Beckenham BR3 ...... 24 C1
  Chiswick W4 .... 7 E8
  13 Isleworth TW7 .... 6 A4
  Merton SW19 .... 20 A1
St Marys Rd KT22 .... 95 B4
St Mary's Rd
  Ascot SL5 .... 29 B3
  Ash Vale GU12 ...... 106 A3
  East Molesey KT8 .... 36 D4
  Kingston upon Thames KT6 . 37 D3
  Long Ditton KT6 ..... 37 C1
  Oatlands Park KT13 .. 53 D6
  Reigate RH2 .... 139 B8
  South Croydon CR2 .. 61 D2
  South Norwood SE25 . 42 E6
  Wimbledon SW19 .... 19 F3
  Woking GU21 .... 69 C2
  Worcester Park KT4 .. 57 E8
St Mary's & St Peter's CE
  Prim Sch 15 TW1 ... 16 F3
St Mary's Sch Ascot SL5 . 29 B2
St Marys Way GU12 ... 108 E3
St Marys Wlk RH1 .... 120 D2
St Matthew's Ave KT6 . 37 F1
St Matthew's CE (Aided) Inf
  Sch KT11 .... 73 E1
St Matthew's CE Prim Sch
  Redhill RH1 .... 118 F3
  3 Surbiton KT6 ...... 37 E2
  Wimbledon SW20 .... 39 A8
St Matthew's Ct 1 TW15 . 14 A3
St Matthew's Rd RH1 . 118 F2
St Merryn Ct BR3 ..... 24 A1
St Michael RC Prim Sch 10
  TW15 .... 14 A3
St Michaels RH8 ...... 123 A5
St Michael's Ave GU3 . 108 C6
St Michael's CE Fst Sch
  RH5 .... 115 C8
St Michaels CE Inf Sch
  GU11 .... 126 B8
St Michaels CE Jun Sch
  GU11 .... 126 C8
St Michael's CE Prim Sch
  Bracknell RG12 ...... 27 A4
  1 Wandsworth SW18 . 19 F8
St Michaels Cl KT4 .... 57 F8
St Michael's Cl KT12 .. 54 C8
St Michaels Cotts RG40 . 45 C8
St Michaels Ct 4 KT13 . 53 C5
St Michael's Hall GU11 . 126 B8
St Michaels Ho 1 SE26 . 23 F4
St Michael's Pl GU15 .. 65 B5
St Michaels Rd
  Camberley GU15 ..... 65 B5
  Caterham CR3 .... 100 D5
  East Grinstead RH19 . 185 E2
St Michael's Rd
  Aldershot GU11, GU12 . 105 B1
  Ashford TW15 .... 14 A3
  Croydon CR0 .... 42 C1
  Farnborough GU14 .. 85 B6

St Michael's Rd continued
Sheerwater GU21 . . . . 70 D5
Wallington SM6 . . . . 60 C4
St Michael's & St Martin's RC
Prim Sch 1 TW4 . . . . .4 F4
St Michael's Sydenham CE
Prim Sch 5 SE26 . . . . . . 23 E4
St Michael's CE Prim Sch
SL5 . . . . 29 D4
St Mildreds Rd SE12, SE6. . 24 F8
St Mildred's Rd GU1 . . . . . . 109 F2
St Monica's Rd KT20 . . . . . . 97 F6
St Nazaire Cl TW20. . . . . . . 12 C3
St Nicholas Ave KT23. . . . . . 94 B2
St Nicholas CE Prim Sch
TW17 . . . . 34 B3
St Nicholas Cres GU22 . . . . 71 A3
St Nicholas Cl RH10. . . . . . 202 C7
St Nicholas Ctr 7 SM1. . . . 59 B5
St Nicholas Dr TW17 . . . . . . 34 A2
St Nicholas Glebe SW17. . . 21 A3
St Nicholas Hill KT22 . . . . . 95 B5
St Nicholas Ho 2 CR0. . . . . 61 E8
St Nicholas Mans SW17 . . . 20 F6
St Nicholas Rd
Sutton SM1 . . . . 59 B5
Thames Ditton KT7 . . . . . . 36 F3
St Nicholas Sch
Merstham RH1. . . . . 119 D6
Purley CR8. . . . . 80 A6
St Nicholas Way SM1. . . . . 59 B5
St Nicolas Ave GU6 . . . . . 174 E3
St Nicolas CE Inf Sch
GU2. . . . . 130 C7
St Nicolas Cl GU6 . . . . 174 E3
St Normans Way KT17 . . . . 58 A1
St Olave's Cl TW18. . . . . . . 12 F1
St Olave's Wlk SW16 . . . . . 41 D7
St Omer Rd GU1 . . . . 131 A8
St Omer Ridge GU1 . . . . . . 131 A8
St Osmund's RC Prim Sch
SW13 . . . . .7 F6
St Oswald's Rd SW16. . . . . 42 B8
St Patrick's RC Prim Sch
GU14. . . . . 85 D4
St Paul's CE Inf Sch
GU10. . . . . 127 A7
St Paul's CE Jun Sch
18 Kingston upon Thames
KT2 . . . . 18 A1
Wokingham RG41 . . . . 25 A6
St Paul's CE Prim Sch
Addlestone KT15 . . . . 52 A6
Brentford TW8. . . . . 6 D8
Chessington KT9 . . . . 56 E6
Dorking RH4 . . . . 136 B6
St Pauls Cl GU10 . . . . 126 F7
St Paul's Cl
Addlestone KT15 . . . . 52 A5
Ashford TW15 . . . . 14 C3
Carshalton SM5 . . . . 40 E1
Chessington KT9 . . . . 56 D6
Hounslow TW3, TW4 . . . . . . 4 E5
St Paul's Conversion
SE23. . . . . 23 C6
St Paul's Ct TW4. . . . . 4 E4
St Paul's Gate RG41 . . . . . . 25 A6
St Pauls Mews RH4 . . . . . 136 B6
St Paul's RC Coll TW16. . . . 35 A8
St Paul's RC Prim Sch
KT7 . . . . 36 E2
St Pauls Rd
Richmond TW9. . . . . 6 F4
Woking GU22. . . . . 70 B2
St Paul's Rd
Brentford TW8. . . . . 6 D8
Egham TW18 . . . . 12 D2
South Norwood CR7 . . . . . 42 C6
St Paul's Road E RH4,
RH5 . . . . 136 B7
St Paul's Road W RH4. . . . 136 B6
St Peter & Paul RC Prim Sch
CR4. . . . . 40 F5
St Peter & St Paul CE Inf Sch
CR3. . . . . 100 C4
St Peter's CE Jun Sch
GU14. . . . . 85 C4
St Peters CE Prim Sch
GU9. . . . . 146 A6
St Peter's CE Sch RH8 . . 122 A1
St Peters Cl SW17. . . . . . . 20 E6
St Peter's Cl
Old Woking GU22. . . . . . . 90 C7
Staines TW18. . . . . 12 F7
St Peters Ct
East Molesey KT8 . . . . 36 A5
5 Hampton TW12. . . . . . 36 B8
St Peter's Gdns
West Norwood SE27 . . . . . 22 A5
Wrecclesham GU10. . . . . 145 F6
St Peters Mead GU12. . . . 106 B2
St Peters Pk GU11 . . . . . . 125 E8
St Peter's Prim Sch CR2 . . 61 E5
St Peter's RC Comp Sch
GU1. . . . . 110 C2
St Peter's RC Prim Sch
Ashtead KT22 . . . . 95 C7
East Grinstead RH19. . . . 185 C1
St Peters Rd KT1. . . . . 38 A7
St Peter's Rd
Crawley RH11 . . . . 201 C6
Croydon CR0, CR2 . . . . . . 61 D6
East Molesey KT8 . . . . 36 A5
Isleworth TW1. . . . . 6 B2

St Peter's Rd continued
Old Woking GU22. . . . . . . 90 B7
St Peter's St CR0, CR2 . . . . 61 D5
St Peters Way UB3. . . . . 3 D8
St Peter's Way
Addlestone KT15, KT16 . . . 51 F6
Chertsey KT15 . . . . 52 B8
Frimley GU16. . . . . 85 F7
St Philip's Ave KT4. . . . . . . 58 B8
St Philips Gate KT4 . . . . . . 58 B8
St Philip's Rd KT6. . . . . 37 D3
St Philips Sch KT9 . . . . 56 D4
St Philomena's RC High Sch
for Girls SM5 . . . . 59 E5
St Pier's La RH7, TN8 . . . . 165 E5
St Piers Sch, The National
Ctr for Young People with
Epilepsy RH7. . . . . 165 A4
St Pinnock Ave TW18 . . . . . 33 A8
St Polycarp's RC Prim Sch
GU9. . . . . 125 D1
St Richards Ct TW10. . . . . . 17 B5
St Richard's with St Andrew's
CE Prim Sch TW10 . . . . . 17 B5
St Robert Southwell RC Prim
Sch RH12. . . . . 218 A6
St Sampson Rd RH11. . . . . 200 F2
St Saviour's Coll SE27 . . . . 22 D4
St Saviour's Pl GU1 . . . . . . 109 C1
St Saviour's Rd CR0 . . . . . . 42 C3
Saints Cl SE27 . . . . 22 B4
Saints Mews CR4 . . . . 40 E6
St Stephen Cl RH11 . . . . . . 181 D1
St Stephens Ave KT21 . . . . 75 E3
St Stephen's CE Jun Sch
TW1 . . . . .6 B1
St Stephen's CE Prim Sch
RH9. . . . . 142 F4
St Stephen's Cl GU27. . . . . 207 F6
St Stephen's Cres CR7 . . . . 42 A6
St Stephens Ct RH9 . . . . . . 142 E5
St Stephens Gdns TW1 . . . . 6 C1
St Stephen's Rd TW3, TW4. . 5 A2
St Swithun's Cl RH19 . . . . . 185 F1
St Teresa's Prep Sch
KT24 . . . . 113 D3
St Teresa's RC Prim Sch
SM4 . . . . 40 D3
St Theresa Cl KT18. . . . . . . 76 C5
St Theresa's RC Prim Sch
RG40. . . . . 25 D5
St Theresa's Rd TW14 . . . . . 3 F3
St Thomas Becket Prim Sch
1 SE25. . . . . 43 A3
St Thomas Cl
Chilworth GU4 . . . . 131 C3
Woking GU21. . . . . 69 C2
St Thomas' Cl KT6 . . . . 37 F1
St Thomas of Canterbury RC
Prim Sch
1 Guildford GU1 . . . . . . 110 B1
Mitcham CR4. . . . . 41 A6
St Thomas's Rd W4 . . . . 7 C8
St Thomas's Dr GU4. . . . . . 111 E4
St Thomas's Mews GU1 . 130 F7
St Thomas Wlk SL3 . . . . 1 D7
St Vincent Cl
Crawley RH10 . . . . 202 D5
West Norwood SE27 . . . . . 22 B3
St Vincent Rd
Twickenham TW2. . . . . 5 C1
Walton-on-Thames KT12. . . 54 B7
St Wilfrid's RC Sch RH11 201 B5
St William of York Prim Sch
1 SE23 . . . . 23 E7
St Winifreds CR8. . . . . 80 C4
St Winifred's RC Jun Sch 4
SE12. . . . . 24 F8
St Winifred's Rd
Biggin Hill TN16. . . . . 83 F1
Teddington TW11. . . . . . . 17 B2
Salamander Cl KT2. . . . . . . 17 C3
Salamander Quay KT1. . . . . 37 D8
Salbrook Rd RH1. . . . . 140 A1
Salcombe Dr SM4. . . . . 39 D1
Salcombe Ho SE23 . . . . 23 C6
Salcombe Rd TW15 . . . . . . 13 E5
Salcombe Villas 10 TW10. . . 6 F2
Salcot Cres CR0 . . . . 63 C1
Salcott Rd CR0. . . . . 60 F6
Saleem Ct CR2. . . . . 61 D5
Sale Garden Cotts RG40 . . 25 C5
Salem Pl CR0, CR9. . . . . . . 61 C7
Salerno Cl GU11 . . . . 105 A2
Sales Ct 6 GU11 . . . . 105 A1
Salesian Coll Farnborough
GU14. . . . . 85 D1
Salesian Gdns KT16 . . . . . . 33 A1
Salesian Sch
Addlestone KT16 . . . . 51 E8
Chertsey KT16 . . . . 33 A1
Salesian View GU14 . . . . . 105 E8
Salford Rd SW12, SW2 . . . . 21 D7
SALFORDS. 140 B1
Salfords Ind Est RH1. . . . . 161 A8
Salfords Prim Sch RH1. . . . 140 A3
Salfords Sta RH1. . . . . 140 B1
Salisbury Ave SM1. . . . . . . 58 F4
Salisbury Cl
Wokingham RG41 . . . . 25 A2
Worcester Park KT4 . . . . . 57 F7
Salisbury Gdns SW19. . . . . 19 E1
Salisbury Gr GU16 . . . . 86 A3
Salisbury Ho
5 Wallington SM6. . . . . . 60 B5
Wimbledon SW19 . . . . 19 D5
Salisbury Pl KT14 . . . . 71 C8

Salisbury Rd
Ash GU12. . . . . 106 A3
Banstead SM7 . . . . 78 B5
Blackwater GU17. . . . . 64 C5
Crawley RH10 . . . . 201 F2
Croydon CR0, SE25 . . . . . 43 A3
Farnborough GU14. . . . . . 85 C3
Feltham TW13 . . . . 15 C7
Harlington TW6. . . . . 3 C1
Hounslow TW4. . . . . 4 C4
Kingston upon Thames KT3 . 38 D6
Richmond TW9. . . . . 6 E3
Tyler's Green RH9. . . . . . . 121 C4
Wallington SM5. . . . . 59 F4
Wimbledon SW19 . . . . 19 E1
Woking GU22. . . . . 89 E8
Worcester Park KT4 . . . . . 57 E7
Salisbury Terr GU16. . . . . . 86 A3
Salix Cl
Fetcham KT22 . . . . 94 B4
Sunbury TW16 . . . . 15 B1
Salliesfield TW2 . . . . 5 D1
Salmon Rd GU11. . . . . 105 D5
Salmons La CR3 . . . . 100 F7
Salmons La W CR3. . . . . . . 100 E7
Salmons Rd
Chessington KT9 . . . . 56 E4
Effingham KT24 . . . . 113 C6
Saltash Cl SM1. . . . . 58 F6
Saltbox Hill TN16 . . . . 83 B6
Salt Box Rd GU3, GU4. . . . 109 B6
Saltdean Cl RH10. . . . . 201 D3
Salterford Rd SW17 . . . . . . 21 A2
Salterns Rd RH10. . . . . . . 202 C3
Salter Ho 8 SW16 . . . . . . 21 C4
Salter's Hill SE19, SE27. . . . 22 D3
Saltire Gdns 2 RG42 . . . . . 27 A8
Salt La GU8. . . . . 171 E5
Saltram Rd GU14. . . . . 85 E2
Salvador SW17 . . . . 20 F3
Salvation Pl KT22 . . . . 95 A3
Salvia Ct GU24 . . . . 68 A4
Salvington Rd RH11. . . . . . 200 F3
Salwey Cl RG12. . . . . 27 B3
Samaritan Cl RH11. . . . . . . 200 E4
Samarkand Cl GU15. . . . . . 66 B4
Sambrook Mews SE6. . . . . 24 B7
Samos Rd SE20 . . . . 43 B7
Samphire Cl RH11. . . . . . . 201 A3
Sampleoak La GU4. . . . . . . 131 E2
Sampson Bsns Pk GU15 . . 65 B3
Sampson Ct TW17 . . . . 34 C4
Sampson Pk RG42 . . . . 26 D8
Sampson's Almshouses
GU9. . . . . 125 A1
Samual Ho 3 SE27. . . . . . 22 B4
Samuel Cody Ho GU12 . . . 105 F7
Samuel Cody Sch GU14 . . 105 B7
Samuel Ct BR3. . . . . 44 B6
Samuel Gray Gdns KT2 . . . 37 D8
Samuel Johnson Cl SW16 . 21 F4
San Carlos App GU11. . . . . 105 C2
Sanctuary Rd TW19, TW6. . . 3 A1
Sanctuary The SM4 . . . . . . 40 A3
Sandal Rd KT3. . . . . 38 E5
Sandalwood GU2 . . . . 130 B8
Sandalwood Ave KT16. . . . . 51 E7
Sandbourne Ave SW19 . . . . 40 B7
Sandcross La RH2. . . . . . . 139 A5
Sandcross Prim Sch RH2 . 139 A6
Sandcross Sch RH2. . . . . . 138 F6
Sanders Cl TW12. . . . . 16 C3
Sandersfield Gdns SM7. . . . 78 A4
Sandersfield Rd SM7. . . . . . 78 B5
Sanders Ho SW16 . . . . 21 C2
SANDERSTEAD. 80 F6
Sanderstead Cl SW12 . . . . . 21 C8
Sanderstead Court Ave
CR2 . . . . 81 A6
Sanderstead Ct CR2. . . . . . 81 A7
Sanderstead Hill CR2 . . . . . 80 F8
Sanderstead Hts CR2 . . . . . 81 A8
Sanderstead Rd CR2 . . . . . 61 D2
Sanderstead Sta CR2. . . . . 61 D2
Sandes Pl KT22 . . . . 75 A1
Sandfield Ct GU1 . . . . 130 D8
Sandfield Cty Prim Sch
GU1. . . . . 130 D8
Sandfield Gdns CR7. . . . . . 42 B6
Sandfield Pl CR7. . . . . 42 C6
Sandfield Rd CR7 . . . . 42 B6
Sandfields GU23 . . . . 90 D3
Sandfield Terr GU1 . . . . . . 130 D8
Sandford Ct GU11. . . . . . . 104 F1
Sandford Down RG12. . . . . 27 F4
Sandford Rd
Aldershot GU11. . . . . 104 F1
Heath End GU9 . . . . 125 B7
Sandgate Ho 14 BR3. . . . . 24 A1
Sandgate La SW17, SW18 . 20 E7
Sandgates KT16. . . . . 32 E1
Sandhawes Hill RH19. . . . 186 A4
Sandheath Rd GU26. . . . . 188 C7
Sand Hill GU14. . . . . 85 B7
Sand Hill Ct GU14. . . . . 85 B7
Sandhill La RH10. . . . . 204 B7
SANDHILLS. 170 D1
Sandhills
Wallington CR0, SM6. . . . . 60 D6
Walton on the Hill KT20. . . 97 A3
Sandhills Ct GU25. . . . . 31 E4
Sandhills La GU25, TW20 . . 31 E4
Sandhills Mdw TW17. . . . . . 34 C2
Sandhills Rd RH2 . . . . 139 A7
SANDHURST. 64 C7
Sandhurst GU10. . . . . 126 C4
Sandhurst Ave KT5. . . . . . . 38 B2

Sandhurst Cl CR2 . . . . 61 E2
Sandhurst Jun & Inf Schs
SE6. . . . . 24 E7
Sandhurst La GU17. . . . . . . 64 B6
Sandhurst L Ctr GU47 . . . . 64 D8
Sandhurst Mkt SE6. . . . . . . 24 C7
Sandhurst Rd
Catford SE6 . . . . 24 D7
Crowthorne RG45 . . . . 45 B3
Wokingham RG40 . . . . 25 A6
Sandhurst Sch GU47. . . . . . 45 D1
Sandhurst Sta GU47. . . . . . 64 A8
Sandhurst Way CR2 . . . . . . 61 E3
Sandiford Ho CR3. . . . . . . 100 E3
Sandiford Rd SM3. . . . . 58 F8
Sandiland Cres BR2. . . . . . 63 F8
Sandilands CR0. . . . . 62 A7
Sandilands Halt CR0. . . . . . 61 F8
Sandlands Gr KT20. . . . . . . 97 A4
Sandlands Rd KT20. . . . . . . 97 A3
Sandmartin Way SM6 . . . . . 41 A1
Sandmore GU23. . . . . 90 D3
Sandon Cl KT10. . . . . 36 D1
Sandon Ho 5 SW2. . . . . . . 21 E8
Sandown Ave KT10. . . . . . . 55 C5
Sandown Ct
2 Belmont SM2. . . . . . . 59 B3
Crawley RH10 . . . . 202 D6
3 Redhill RH1 . . . . 118 E2
Sandown Dr
Frimley GU16. . . . . 65 E2
Wallington SM5. . . . . 60 A2
Sandown Gate KT10. . . . . . 55 D7
Sandown Ho
Esher KT10 . . . . 55 C6
Penge SE26 . . . . 23 B2
Sandown Ind Pk KT10. . . . . 55 A8
Sandown Lodge KT18 . . . . . 76 D5
Sandown Park KT10. . . . . . . 55 C6
Sandown Rd
Coulsdon CR5 . . . . 79 A3
Croydon SE25 . . . . 43 B4
Esher KT10 . . . . 55 C6
Sandpiper Cl RH11. . . . . . . 200 D4
Sandpiper Rd
Cheam SM1 . . . . 58 F5
Selsdon CR2. . . . . 81 D8
Sandpit Hall Rd GU24 . . . . . 69 A7
Sandpit Heath GU3. . . . . . 108 D5
Sandpit Rd
Catford BR1. . . . . 24 E3
Redhill RH1. . . . . 139 F8
Sandpits Rd
Richmond TW10. . . . . 17 D6
South Croydon CR0 . . . . . 62 D6
Sandra Cl TW3. . . . . .5 B2
Sandra House KT8 . . . . 36 D4
Sandringham Ave SW20 . . . 39 E7
Sandringham Cl
East Grinstead RH19. . . . 206 A8
1 Putney SW19 . . . . 19 D7
Pyrford GU22. . . . . 71 A3
Sandringham Ct
Beckenham BR3. . . . . 44 C8
Belmont SM2. . . . . 59 A2
Kingston upon Thames KT2 . 37 E8
2 Twickenham TW1 . . . . 17 A7
Sandringham Dr
3 Ascot SL5 . . . . 28 F8
Ashford TW15 . . . . 13 D4
Sandringham Gdns
Cranford TW5 . . . . 4 A6
East Molesey KT8 . . . . 36 A5
Sandringham Ho TW10. . . . . 7 A2
Sandringham Inf Sch
GU16. . . . . 85 F7
Sandringham Mews TW12 35 F8
Sandringham Pk KT11. . . . . 74 A7
Sandringham Rd
Crawley RH11 . . . . 201 B2
North Cheam KT4 . . . . 58 A7
Stanwell TW6. . . . . 2 E2
Thornton Heath CR0 . . . . . 42 C4
Sandringham Way GU16. . . 85 F8
Sandrock GU27 . . . . 208 C6
Sandrock Hill Rd GU10 . . . 146 A5
Sandrock Ho GU7. . . . . 150 D6
Sandrock Pl CR0. . . . . 62 D6
Sandrock Rd RH4 . . . . 135 B5
Sandroyd Way KT11. . . . . . . 74 A6
Sands Cl GU10. . . . . 126 D2
Sands Rd GU10. . . . . 126 D2
SANDS THE. 126 E2
Sandstone TW9. . . . . 7 A7
Sandways 6 TW9. . . . . 7 A6
Sandy Cl GU22. . . . . 70 C2
Sandycombe Ctr TW9 . . . . . 7 A4
Sandycombe Rd TW1 . . . . . 6 C1
Sandy Cotts RH10. . . . . . . 204 A8
Sandy Croft KT17 . . . . 58 C1
Sandy Cross GU10 . . . . . . 126 F4
Sandy Ct KT11. . . . . 73 F6
Sandy Dr
Cobham KT11. . . . . 74 A8
East Bedfont TW14 . . . . . . 14 E7
Sandy Hill Rd
Heath End GU9 . . . . 125 B7
Wallington SM6. . . . . 60 C2
Sandy Holt KT11. . . . . 73 F6
Sandy La
Albury GU5 . . . . 132 D2

Sandy La continued
Artington GU2, GU3. . . . . . 130 B5
Belmont SM2. . . . . 58 E2
Betchworth RH3. . . . . 116 E1
Bletchingley RH1 . . . . 120 C3
Bracknell RG12. . . . . 27 C8
Camberley GU15 . . . . 65 E6
Chobham GU24 . . . . 49 E2
Cobham KT11, KT22. . . . . 74 B7
Crawley Down RH10 . . . . . 204 A8
East Grinstead RH19. . . . 185 F1
Farnborough GU14 . . . . . . 84 D7
Farncombe GU7. . . . . 150 D6
Frensham GU10. . . . . 146 C1
Grayswood GU27. . . . . . . 189 E1
Guildford GU3 . . . . 107 D4
Haslemere GU26, GU27. . . 207 C7
Kingswood KT20 . . . . 98 A4
Limpsfield RH8. . . . . 123 B7
Milford GU8. . . . . 170 E8
Mitcham CR4. . . . . 41 A8
North Ascot SL5. . . . . 28 C8
Nutfield RH1 . . . . 119 E1
Oxted RH8 . . . . 122 C6
Pyrford GU22. . . . . 71 A3
Reigate RH2. . . . . 138 B8
Richmond TW10. . . . . 17 D6
Rushmoor GU10. . . . . 168 B5
Sandhurst GU47. . . . . 45 A2
Send GU23. . . . . 90 C4
Shere GU5. . . . . 133 A3
Sunningdale SL5 . . . . 30 A4
Teddington KT8, TW11. . . . 17 B1
Virginia Water GU25 . . . . . 31 E5
Walton-on-Thames KT12. . . 35 C3
Woking GU22. . . . . 70 C2
Sandy Lane N SM6. . . . . . . 60 D5
Sandy Lane Prim Sch
RG12. . . . . 27 C8
Sandy Lane S SM6 . . . . 60 C3
Sandy Mead KT19. . . . . 57 A2
Sandy Rd KT15. . . . . 52 A4
Sandy Ride SL5 . . . . 29 E5
Sandy Way
Cobham KT11. . . . . 74 A7
Croydon CR0. . . . . 62 F7
Walton-on-Thames KT12. . . 34 F1
Woking GU22. . . . . 70 C2
San Feliu Ct RH19. . . . . . . 186 B2
Sanger Ave KT9. . . . . 56 F6
Sanger Dr GU23. . . . . 90 C4
Sangers Dr RH6. . . . . 160 F3
Sangley Rd
Catford SE6 . . . . 24 C7
South Norwood SE25. . . . . 42 C7
Santina Cl GU9 . . . . 125 D6
Sanway Cl KT14. . . . . 71 E5
Sanway Rd KT14. . . . . 71 E5
Sappho Cl GU21 . . . . 68 E3
Sapte Cl GU6 . . . . 175 A3
Saracen Cl CR0 . . . . 42 D3
Sarah Ho SW15 . . . . .7 F3
Sarah Way GU14 . . . . 85 B4
Sardeson Ho 13 SW27. . . . . 22 B3
Sarel Way RH6. . . . . 161 B5
Sargent Cl RH10 . . . . 201 F2
Sarjant Path SW19 . . . . 19 D6
Sark Cl
Crawley RH11 . . . . 201 A2
Heston TW5. . . . . 5 A7
Sarsby Dr TW19. . . . . 12 A6
Sarsen Ave TW3. . . . . 5 A5
Sarsfeld Rd SW12, SW17 . . . 20 F7
Sarum RG12 . . . . 26 F1
Sarum Cres RG40 . . . . 25 D7
Sarum Gn KT13 . . . . 53 E7
Sarwin L Ctr TN16. . . . . 83 F3
Sassoons Cotts KT12 . . . . . 35 B2
Satellite Bsns Village
RH10. . . . . 181 E2
Satis Ct KT17 . . . . 76 F8
Saturn Cl RH11 . . . . 200 E4
Saturn Croft RG42 . . . . .8 B2
Saunders Cl RH10. . . . . . . 202 B7
Saunders Copse GU22 . . . . 89 B5
Saundersfield Ho SM7 . . . . 78 B5
Saunders Ho 11 SW2. . . . . . 22 A7
Saunders La GU22 . . . . 89 B5
Saunton Ave UB3 . . . . .3 F7
Saunton Gdns 1 GU14 . . . . 85 A6
Savernake Ct SE22 . . . . 23 A7
Savernake Way RG12. . . . . . 27 F4
Savernake Wlk RH10. . . . . 201 F3
Savery Dr KT6 . . . . 37 C2
Savile Cl
New Malden KT3. . . . . 38 E4
Thames Ditton KT7 . . . . . . 37 A1
Savile Gdns CR0. . . . . 61 F8
Saville Cl KT19. . . . . 76 B8
Saville Cres TW15. . . . . 14 D2
Saville Gdns GU15 . . . . 66 B5
Saville Ho 6 TW20. . . . . . . 12 A3
Saville Rd TW1 . . . . 16 F7
Saville Row BR2 . . . . 44 F1
Savill Garden The ★ TW20. . 10 E2
Savill Gdns SW20 . . . . 39 A6
Savill Mews TW20. . . . . 11 D2
Savin Lodge 11 SM2. . . . . . 59 C3
Savona Cl SW19 . . . . 19 D1
Savona Ct 2 SW20. . . . . . . 39 D8
Savoy Gr GU17. . . . . 64 D3
Sawkins Cl SW19 . . . . 19 E6
Sawtry Cl SM5 . . . . 40 E2
Sawyer Ho 15 SE21. . . . . . . 22 E4
Sawyer's Hill TW10 . . . . 17 F8
Saxby Rd SW2 . . . . 21 E8
Saxby's La RH7, GU3. . . . . . 164 D5
Saxley RH6. . . . . 161 C4

Saxon Ave TW13 . . . . 15 F6
Saxon Bsns Ctr SW19 . . . 40 F8
Saxonbury Ave TW16 . . . . 35 B7
Saxonbury Cl CR4 . . . . 40 D6
Saxonbury Gdns KT6 . . . . 37 C1
Saxon Cl KT6 . . . . 37 D3
Saxon Cres RH12 . . . . 217 B4
Saxon Croft GU9 . . . . 125 C1
Saxoncroft Ho SW16 . . . . . 21 D5
Saxon Ct 2 CR3 . . . . 101 A8
Saxon Dr RG42 . . . . 27 F8
Saxonfield Cl SW2 . . . . 21 F8
Saxon Ho
  Feltham TW13 . . . . 15 F6
  Reigate RH2 . . . . 138 F6
Saxon Prim Sch TW17 . . . 34 A4
Saxon Rd
  Ashford TW15 . . . . 14 D2
  Bromley BR1 . . . . 24 F1
  Crawley RH10 . . . . 202 E5
  Kingston upon Thames KT2 . 37 E8
  Thornton Heath CR0, SE25 . 42 C4
  Walton-on-Thames KT12 . . 54 D7
Saxons KT20 . . . . 97 D6
Saxon Terr SE6 . . . . 23 F6
Saxon Way
  Harmondsworth UB7 . . . . . 2 C8
  Reigate RH2 . . . . 117 F2
Sayers Cl
  Fetcham KT22 . . . . 94 C4
  Frimley GU16 . . . . 85 E7
  Horsham RH13 . . . . 217 E2
Sayers Croft Nature
  Reserve ★ GU6 . . . . 175 D5
Sayers The 5 RH19 . . . . 185 C1
Sayer's Wlk TW10 . . . . 17 F8
Sayes Court Farm Dr
  KT15 . . . . 52 B5
Sayes Court Sch KT15 . . . 52 B5
Sayes Ct KT15 . . . . 52 C5
Scallows Cl RH10 . . . . . . 202 A7
Scallows Rd RH10 . . . . . . 202 A7
Scania Wlk RG42 . . . . 8 B2
Scarborough Cl
  Belmont SM2 . . . . 77 F8
  Biggin Hill TN16 . . . . 83 C1
Scarborough Rd TW6 . . . . . 3 C1
Scarbrook Rd CR0, CR9 . . . 61 C7
Scarlet Oaks GU15 . . . . . . 65 E3
Scarlet Rd SE6 . . . . 24 E5
Scarlett Manor Wlk SW2 . 22 A8
Scarlett's Rd GU11 . . . . . 105 A4
Scarth Rd SW13 . . . . 7 F4
Scawen Cl SM5 . . . . 60 A6
Schaffer Ho RH10 . . . . . . 202 C4
Scholars Ct RH10 . . . . . . 204 B8
Scholars Rd SW12 . . . . . . 21 C7
Scholars Wlk
  Farnborough GU14 . . . . . . 85 B6
  Guildford GU2 . . . . 130 B8
School Cl
  Bisley GU24 . . . . 68 A4
  Guildford GU1 . . . . 109 D3
  Horsham RH12 . . . . 218 A6
School Cotts
  New Malden KT4 . . . . 38 E1
  Woking GU22 . . . . 89 C5
School Hill
  Crowthorne RG45 . . . . . . 45 D4
  Merstham RH1 . . . . 119 C7
  Sandhurst GU47 . . . . 45 A1
  Seale GU10 . . . . 127 B4
  Warnham RH12 . . . . 216 F8
  Wrecclesham GU10 . . . . 145 F6
School House La TW11 . . . 17 C1
School Houses GU8 . . . . . 172 E4
School La
  Addlestone KT15 . . . . 52 A6
  Ascot SL5 . . . . 28 D8
  Ashurst Wood RH19 . . . . 206 E6
  Bagshot GU19 . . . . 47 E2
  Caterham CR3 . . . . 100 F1
  Chiddingfold GU8 . . . . . . 191 C4
  Crondall GU10 . . . . 124 D8
  East Clandon GU4 . . . . . 111 A4
  Egham TW20 . . . . 12 A3
  Farnham GU10 . . . . 146 D6
  Fetcham KT22 . . . . 94 D5
  Forest Row RH18 . . . . . . 206 F2
  Lower Halliford TW17 . . . 34 B3
  Mickleham RH5 . . . . 115 C8
  Normandy GU3 . . . . 106 F4
  Ockham GU23 . . . . 92 B5
  Pirbright GU24 . . . . 87 E5
  Puttenham GU3 . . . . 128 C4
  Shackleford GU8 . . . . . . 149 E6
  Surbiton KT6 . . . . 38 A1
  Teddington KT1 . . . . 37 C8
  Walton on the Hill KT20 . . 97 A2
  Westcott RH4 . . . . 135 D6
  West Horsley KT24 . . . . . 112 B6
  Windlesham GU20 . . . . . . 48 D4
School Mdw GU2 . . . . 108 E2
School Pas 4 KT1 . . . . 37 F7
School Rd
  Ascot SL5 . . . . 29 D4
  Ashford TW15 . . . . 14 B2
  East Molesey KT8 . . . . . . 36 D5
  Grayshott GU26 . . . . 188 B4
  Hampton TW12 . . . . 16 C2
  Harmondsworth UB7 . . . . . 2 D8
  Haslemere GU27 . . . . . . 207 F5
  Hounslow TW3 . . . . 5 C4
  Rowledge GU10 . . . . 145 E3
  Teddington KT1 . . . . 37 C8
  Windlesham GU20 . . . . . . 48 B5
  Wokingham RG40 . . . . . . 25 D6

School Road Ave TW12 . . 16 C2
School Wlk TW16 . . . . 35 A6
Schroder Ct TW20 . . . . 11 B3
Scillonian Rd GU2 . . . . . 130 A7
Scilly Isles KT10 . . . . 55 E8
Scizdons Climb GU7 . . . 150 F4
Scoles Cres SW2 . . . . 22 A7
Scope Way 3 KT1 . . . . . . 37 E5
Scoresdale SE19 . . . . 42 E8
Scory Cl RH11 . . . . 201 A3
Scotia Rd SW2 . . . . 22 A8
Scotland Bridge Rd KT15 . 71 A8
Scotland Cl GU12 . . . . . . 106 A5
Scotland Farm Rd GU12 . 106 A5
Scotland Hill GU47 . . . . . . 64 A8
Scotland La GU27 . . . . . . 208 C5
Scotlands Cl GU27 . . . . . 208 B5
Scotlands Dr GU27 . . . . . 208 C5
Scotney Ho RH1 . . . . 139 F4
Scotsdale Cl SM2 . . . . 58 E3
Scotshall La CR6 . . . . 82 C4
Scott-Broadwood CE Inf Sch
  (Capel Base) RH5 . . . . 178 D6
Scott-Broadwood CE Inf Sch
  (Ockley Base) RH5 . . . 177 D4
Scott Cl
  Guildford GU2 . . . . 109 A3
  Thornton Heath SW16 . . . 41 F8
  West Ewell KT19 . . . . 57 C5
Scott Farm Cl KT7 . . . . . . 37 B1
Scott Gdns TW5 . . . . 4 D7
Scott Ho TW10 . . . . 17 C6
Scott Rd RH10 . . . . 201 F3
Scott's Ave
  Ashford TW16 . . . . 14 E1
  Beckenham BR2 . . . . 44 D7
Scotts Cl TW19 . . . . 13 D7
Scott's Ct GU14 . . . . 85 B7
Scotts Dr TW12 . . . . 16 B1
Scotts Farm Rd KT19 . . . . 57 C4
Scott's Grove Cl GU24 . . . 68 D6
Scott's Grove Rd GU24 . . 68 C6
Scott's Hill RH1, RH6. . . . 162 C5
Scott's La BR2 . . . . 44 D7
Scotts Mews SW5 . . . . 28 B8
Scott's Way TW16 . . . . 14 E1
Scott Terr RG12 . . . . 27 E8
Scott Trimmer Way TW3 . . 4 E5
Scrooby St 3 SE6 . . . . . . 24 B8
Scrutton Cl SW12 . . . . 21 D8
Sculpture Pk The ★
  GU10. . . . . 168 B3
Scutley La GU20 . . . . 48 E3
Scylla Cres TW6, TW14. . . 14 B8
Scylla Pl GU21 . . . . 89 A8
Scylla Rd TW14, TW6 . . . . . 3 B1
Seabrook Dr BR4 . . . . 63 E8
Seafire Way GU11. . . . . . 104 E7
Seaford Rd
  Crawley RH11 . . . . 201 A2
  Stanwell TW6. . . . . 2 D2
  Wokingham RG40 . . . . . . 25 D6
Seaforth Ave KT3 . . . . 39 B5
Seaforth Gdns KT19 . . . . . 57 F5
Seaforth Lodge SW13 . . . . 7 F5
Sealand Rd TW6 . . . . 3 A1
SEALE 127 B4
Seale La
  Puttenham GU3, GU10 . . 127 F4
  The Sands GU10, GU3 . . 126 E4
Seale Rd GU8, GU10 . . . . 148 B7
Seaman's Gn RH5 . . . . . . 178 D8
Searchwood Hts CR6 . . . . 81 B1
Searchwood Rd CR6 . . . . . 81 B1
Searle Ct 7 CR4 . . . . 40 E8
Searle Hill RH2 . . . . 139 F4
Searle Rd GU9 . . . . 146 C5
Searle's View RH12 . . . . . 217 E5
Searlewood Ct GU24 . . . . . 67 F5
Seath Ho 4 SE26 . . . . 23 B3
Seaton Cl
  Putney SW15 . . . . 19 B8
  Twickenham TW2 . . . . 5 D1
Seaton Dr TW15 . . . . 13 E6
Seaton House Sch SM2 . . 59 D1
Seaton Rd
  Camberley GU15 . . . . 65 B5
  Mitcham CR4 . . . . 40 E7
  Twickenham TW2 . . . . 5 C1
Sebastopol Rd GU11 . . . 105 B2
Second Ave
  Mortlake SW14 . . . . 7 E4
  Walton-on-Thames KT12 . . 35 B3
  Woodham KT15 . . . . 52 B2
Second Cl KT8 . . . . 36 C5
Second Cross Rd TW2 . . . 16 E6
Secrett Ho 6 TW10 . . . . . 17 C5
Seddon Ho SW8 . . . . 40 D4
Seddon Rd SM4. . . . . 40 D4
Sedgefield Cl RH10 . . . . 202 E7
Sedgehill Rd SE6 . . . . 24 B3
Sedgehill Sch SE6 . . . . . . 24 B3
Sedgemoor GU14 . . . . 85 B7
Sedgeway SE6 . . . . 24 F7
Sedgewick Rd RH10 . . . . 202 C6
Sedgwick Ho SW19 . . . . . 19 D6
Sedgwood Cl BR2. . . . . . . 44 F2
Sedley Cl SE26. . . . . 23 B6
Seebys Oak GU47 . . . . . . 64 E6
Seeley Dr SE21 . . . . 22 E4
Seely Rd SW17 . . . . 21 A2
SEETHING WELLS 37 C3
Seething Wells Halls Of
  Residence KT6 . . . . 37 C3
Seething Wells La KT6 . . 37 C3
Sefton Cl GU24 . . . . 67 F6
Sefton Ct TW5 . . . . 5 B6
Sefton Ho 16 GU11 . . . . . 105 A2

Sefton Lodge
  Kingston upon Thames
    KT2. . . . . 17 E2
  2 Twickenham TW1 . . . . . 6 C1
Sefton Rd
  Croydon CR0 . . . . 43 A1
  Epsom KT19. . . . . 57 D1
Sefton Villas RH5 . . . . . . 136 B3
Segal Cl SE23. . . . . 23 E8
Segrave Cl KT13 . . . . 53 A3
Sekhon Terr TW13 . . . . . . 16 A5
Selbar Rd GU12 . . . . 106 C6
Selborne RG12. . . . . 27 B6
Selborne Ave GU11 . . . . 126 C6
Selborne Cl GU17 . . . . 64 C6
Selborne Gdns GU9 . . . . 146 A7
Selborne Rd
  Kingston upon Thames
    KT3. . . . . 38 E7
  South Croydon CR0 . . . . . 61 F7
Selbourne Ave KT15. . . . . 52 B1
Selbourne Cl
  Crawley RH10 . . . . 182 D2
  Woodham KT15 . . . . 52 B1
Selbourne Rd GU4 . . . . . 110 A4
Selbourne Sq RH9 . . . . . 121 C5
Selby Cl KT9. . . . . 56 E3
Selby Ct TW2 . . . . 16 D6
Selby Gn SM5. . . . . 40 E2
Selbys RH1 . . . . 164 E5
Selby Wlk 1 GU21 . . . . . 69 B1
Selcroft Rd CR8. . . . . 80 B7
Selham Cl RH11. . . . . 201 A7
Selhurst Cl
  Putney SW19 . . . . 19 D7
  Woking GU21. . . . . 69 F4
Selhurst New Ct SE25 . . . 42 E3
Selhurst New Rd SE25 . . . 42 E3
Selhurst Park (Crystal Palace
  FC) SE25 . . . . 42 E5
Selhurst Pl CR0, SE25 . . . 42 E5
Selhurst Rd CR0, SE25 . . . 42 E4
Selhurst Sta SE25. . . . . . . 42 E4
Selkirk Rd
  Twickenham TW2 . . . . . . 16 C7
  Upper Tooting SW17 . . . . 20 E4
Sellar's Ghyll ★ SW17 . . 150 D7
Sellincourt Prim Sch
  SW17 . . . . 20 E2
Sellincourt Rd SW17 . . . . 20 E2
Sellindge Cl BR3. . . . . 23 F1
Sells Cl GU1 . . . . 130 F7
Selsdon Ave CR2 . . . . 61 D4
SELSDON. 62 D1
Selsdon Cl KT6 . . . . 37 E4
Selsdon Cres CR2 . . . . . . 62 C1
Selsdon High Sch CR2 . . . 62 D3
Selsdon Park Rd CR0, CR2. 62 E2
Selsdon Prim Sch CR2 . . . 62 C2
Selsdon Rd
  Croydon CR2 . . . . 61 D4
  West Norwood SE27 . . . . 22 B4
  Woodham KT15 . . . . 71 A8
Selsdon Road Ind Est
  CR2. . . . . 61 D4
Selsdon Wood Bird
  Sanctuary & Nature
  Reserve ★ CR2. . . . . . . 81 E8
Selsey Ct 3 RH11. . . . . . 201 B2
Selsey Rd RH11. . . . . 201 A2
SELSFIELD COMMON . . . 204 B1
Selsfield Rd RH10, RH19. . 204 A2
Seltops Cl GU6. . . . . 174 F2
Selwood Cl TW19 . . . . 2 C1
Selwood Gdns TW19 . . . . . 2 C1
Selwood Rd
  Cheam SM3 . . . . 39 F1
  Chessington KT9 . . . . . . 56 D6
  Croydon CR0 . . . . 43 B1
  Old Woking GU22. . . . . . . 90 B7
Selworthy Rd SE6 . . . . 23 F5
Selwyn Ave TW9 . . . . 6 F4
Selwyn Cl
  Crawley RH10 . . . . 182 C1
  Hounslow TW4. . . . . 4 E3
Selwyn Ct 8 TW10 . . . . . . 6 F2
Selwyn Rd KT3. . . . . 38 D4
Semaphore Rd GU1 . . . . 130 E7
Semley Pl SW16 . . . . 41 F7
Semley Rd SW16 . . . . 41 E7
Semper Cl GU21 . . . . 68 E2
SEND. 90 C4
Send Barns La GU23. . . . . 90 E2
Send CE Fst Sch GU23 . . . 90 E3
Send Cl GU23 . . . . 90 C4
Send Hill GU23. . . . . 90 C3
SEND MARSH 90 F3
Send Marsh Rd GU23. . . . 90 F4
Send Parade Cl GU23 . . . . 90 C4
Send Rd GU23 . . . . 90 C4
Seneca Rd CR7 . . . . 42 C5
Senga Rd CR4 . . . . 41 A1
Senhouse Rd SM3. . . . . . . 58 D7
Sequoia Pk RH11 . . . . . . 201 D4
Sergeants Pl CR3. . . . . . . 100 C5
Serpentine Gn RH1 . . . . . 119 D6
Serrin Way RH12. . . . . . . 217 E5
Service Rd RH6. . . . . 181 F8
Servite Ho
  Beckenham BR3. . . . . . . 43 F8
  Knaphill GU21 . . . . 68 D2
  Worcester Park KT4 . . . . . 57 F8

Servite House RH4 . . . . . 136 A5
Servius Ct 2 TW8 . . . . 6 D7
Sessions Terr CR4 . . . . . . 40 F8
Setley Way RG12. . . . . 27 F6
Seven Acres SM5 . . . . 59 E8
Seven Arches App KT13 . . 53 A3
Seven Hills Cl KT12, KT13 . 53 E2
Seven Hills Rd
  Weybridge KT12, KT13 . . 53 E3
  Whiteley Village KT11 . . . 72 E6
Seven Hills Road S KT11. . 72 E6
Seven Ho CR3 . . . . 100 E5
Seven Kings Way KT2 . . . . 37 E8
Sevenoaks Cl SM2 . . . . . . 59 B1
Seven Seas Rd TW6 . . . . . . 3 C1
Severn Cl GU47 . . . . 64 C8
Severn Cres SL3 . . . . 1 B8
Severn Dr
  Hinchley Wood KT10 . . . . 56 A8
  Walton-on-Thames KT12 . . 54 D8
Severn Rd
  Crawley RH10 . . . . 202 C5
  Farnborough GU14 . . . . . 84 E6
Seward Rd BR3. . . . . 43 D7
Sewell Ave RG41 . . . . 25 A8
Sewer's Farm Rd RH5 . . . 155 F6
Sewill Cl RH6 . . . . 180 F7
Seychelle Ct BR3 . . . . 24 B1
Seymour Ave
  Caterham CR3 . . . . 100 C1
  Ewell KT17 . . . . 58 C1
  West Barnes SM4 . . . . . . 39 D2
Seymour Cl KT8. . . . . 36 C4
Seymour Ct 3 KT19. . . . . . 57 E2
Seymour Dr GU15 . . . . 66 B7
Seymour Fst & Mid Sch
  RH1. . . . . 201 B2
Seymour Gdns
  Feltham TW13 . . . . 15 C4
  Kingston upon Thames KT5. 37 F4
  Twickenham TW1 . . . . 17 B8
Seymour Ho 6 SM2. . . . . . 59 B4
Seymour Mews KT17 . . . . 58 A1
Seymour Pl
  Croydon SE25 . . . . 43 B5
  Woking GU23 . . . . 89 B7
Seymour Rd
  Carshalton CR4 . . . . 41 A2
  Crawley RH11 . . . . 201 B2
  East Molesey KT8 . . . . . . 36 C4
  Godalming GU7 . . . . 150 B3
  Hampton TW12 . . . . 16 C3
  Headley Down GU35. . . . 187 C4
  Teddington KT1 . . . . 37 D8
  Wallington SM5 . . . . 60 A5
  Wandsworth SW18 . . . . . 19 F8
  Wimbledon SW19 . . . . . . 19 D5
Seymour Terr SE20 . . . . . 43 B8
Seymour Villas SE20 . . . . 43 A8
Seymour Way TW16 . . . . . 14 E1
Shabden Cotts CR5 . . . . . 98 F6
Shabden Park CR5 . . . . . . 98 E5
SHACKLEFORD. 149 D7
Shackleford Rd
  Elstead GU8. . . . . 148 F3
  Old Woking GU22. . . . . . . 90 A7
  Shackleford GU8 . . . . . . 149 E6
Shacklegate La TW11 . . . . 16 E4
Shackleton Cl
  Ash Vale GU12. . . . . 105 F6
  Forest Hill SE23. . . . . 23 B6
Shackleton Ct
  3 Dulwich SE21 . . . . . . 22 D6
  7 Stanwell TW19 . . . . 2 E1
Shackleton Lodge SW16. . 21 D3
Shackleton Rd RH10 . . . . 201 F3
Shackleton Wlk 4 GU2 . . 108 E1
Shackstead La GU7 . . . . . 150 C3
Shackster La GU7 . . . . . . 150 C3
Shadbolt Cl KT4 . . . . 57 F8
Shadyhanger GU7 . . . . . . 150 E6
Shady Nook GU9 . . . . 125 B6
Shaef Way TW11. . . . . 17 A1
Shaftesbury Ave TW14 . . . 4 A1
Shaftesbury Cl RG12 . . . . 27 D4
Shaftesbury Cres TW18. . . 13 D1
Shaftesbury Ct
  2 Farnborough GU14. . . 105 C8
  Wokingham RG40 . . . . . . 25 D7
Shaftesbury Ho
  Croydon SE25 . . . . 43 A3
  Upper Tooting SW17 . . . . 20 D4
Shaftesbury Mount GU17 . 64 D3
Shaftesbury Rd
  Beckenham BR3. . . . . . . 43 F7
  Bisley GU24. . . . . 67 F3
  Carshalton SM5 . . . . 40 E2
  Crawley RH10 . . . . 202 D4
  Richmond TW9. . . . . 6 E4
  Woking GU22. . . . . 70 B2
Shaftesbury Way TW2 . . . 16 D5
Shafteswood Ct SW17 . . . 20 F5
Shagbrook RH1 . . . . 117 C2
Shakespeare Ave TW14 . . . 4 A1
Shakespeare Gdns GU14 . 84 D5
Shakespeare Rd KT15 . . . 52 D6
Shakespeare Way
  Feltham TW13 . . . . 15 C4
  Winkfield RG42 . . . . 27 E8
Shalbourne Rise GU15 . . . 65 D5
Shalden Ho SW15. . . . . 7 F1
Shalden Rd GU12 . . . . . . 126 D8
Shaldon Dr SM4 . . . . 39 E4
Shaldon Way KT12 . . . . . . 54 C7
Shale Gn RH1. . . . . 119 D6
Shalesbrook La RH18. . . . 206 F1
SHALFORD. 130 E2

Shalford Inf Sch GU4. . . . 130 E3
Shalford La GU4 . . . . 130 E4
Shalford Mill ★ GU4. . . . . 130 E4
Shalford Rd GU1, GU4. . . 130 D5
Shalford Sta GU4 . . . . . . 130 E3
Shalstone Rd SW14, TW9. . 7 A4
Shalstone Villas KT5, KT6 . 37 F3
Shambles The GU1. . . . . . 130 D7
SHAMLEY GREEN. 152 E5
Shamrock Cl
  Fetcham KT22 . . . . 94 D6
  Frimley GU16 . . . . 85 D8
Shamrock Ho SE26 . . . . . 23 A4
Shamrock Rd CR0. . . . . . . 41 F3
Shandys Cl RH12 . . . . . . 217 A1
Shanklin Ct GU12 . . . . . . 105 C1
Shannon Cnr KT3 . . . . 39 A5
Shannon Cnr Ret Pk KT3. . 39 A5
Shannon Commercial Ctr
  KT3 . . . . 39 A5
Shannon Ct CR0 . . . . 42 C1
Shannon Way BR3 . . . . . . 24 B2
Shanti Ct SW18 . . . . 20 A7
Sharland Cl CR7 . . . . 42 A3
Sharon Cl
  Crawley RH10 . . . . 202 A4
  Epsom KT19. . . . . 76 C6
  Great Bookham KT23 . . . . 94 A3
  Long Ditton KT6 . . . . 37 C1
Sharon Ct 15 CR2 . . . . . . 61 C5
Sharonelle Ct RG40 . . . . . 25 B6
Sharp Ho 17 TW1 . . . . 6 D1
Sharpthorne Cl RH11 . . . 200 F6
Shaw Cl
  Ewell KT17 . . . . 76 F8
  Ottershaw KT16 . . . . 51 C4
  Sanderstead CR2. . . . . . . 80 F7
Shaw Cotts SE23, SE6 . . . 23 E5
Shaw Cres CR2 . . . . 80 F7
Shaw Ct
  Caterham CR3 . . . . 100 D6
  Morden SM4 . . . . 40 C2
Shaw Dr KT12 . . . . 35 C2
Shawfield La GU12 . . . . . 105 F2
Shawfield Prim Sch
  GU12. . . . . 106 A3
Shawfield Rd GU12. . . . . 106 A3
Shawfields 2 GU1 . . . . . 110 A1
Shawford Ct 9 SW15 . . . . 19 A8
Shawford Rd KT19 . . . . . . 57 D4
Shaw Ho CR3 . . . . 101 B6
Shawley Cres KT18. . . . . . 77 D1
Shawley Prim Sch KT18 . . 77 C1
Shawley Way KT18 . . . . . . 77 C1
Shaw Path BR1 . . . . 24 F5
Shaw Pk RG45 . . . . 45 B3
Shaw Rd
  Catford BR1. . . . . 24 F5
  Tatsfield TN16 . . . . 103 C7
Shaws Cotts GU3 . . . . . . 108 F6
Shaws Rd RH10 . . . . 201 F7
Shaw Way SM6 . . . . 60 E3
Shaxton Cres CR0 . . . . 63 C2
Shearing Dr SM4. . . . . 40 C2
Shears Ct TW16 . . . . 14 E1
Shears Way TW16 . . . . 34 E8
Shearwater Ct 6 RH11 . . 200 D5
Shearwater Rd SM1. . . . . . 58 F5
Sheath La KT22 . . . . 74 C6
Sheeling Cl GU12 . . . . . . 105 D3
Sheen Common Dr SW14,
  TW10. . . . . 7 A2
Sheen Court Rd TW10. . . . . 7 A3
Sheen Ct TW10 . . . . 7 A2
Sheendale Rd TW9. . . . . . . 6 F3
Sheenewood SE26 . . . . . . 23 B4
Sheen Gate Gdns SW14 . . 7 C3
Sheengate Mans SW14 . . . 7 D3
Sheen La SW14 . . . . 7 C3
Sheen Mount Prim Sch
  SW14 . . . . 7 B2
Sheen Pk TW10, TW9 . . . . . 6 E3
Sheen Rd TW10, TW9 . . . . 6 F3
Sheen Way SM6 . . . . 60 F5
Sheen Wood SW14. . . . . . . 7 C2
Sheepcote Cl TW5 . . . . 4 A7
Sheepfold Rd GU2 . . . . . 108 F4
Sheephatch La GU10 . . . . 147 C6
Sheephouse GU9 . . . . . . 146 C8
Sheephouse Gn RH5 . . . . 134 F3
Sheephouse La
  Wotton RH5 . . . . 135 A2
  Wotton RH5 . . . . 156 A6
Sheephouse Way KT3 . . . . 38 E2
Sheeplands Ave GU1 . . . 110 C3
Sheep Leas (Forest Walk)★
  KT24 . . . . 112 E2
Sheepwalk
  Littleton TW17 . . . . 34 A3
  Shepperton TW17 . . . . . . 33 F3
Sheepwalk La RH5 . . . . . 113 A1
Sheep Walk Mews SW19 . 19 E2
Sheep Wlk
  Langley Vale KT18. . . . . . 96 D5
  Reigate RH2. . . . . 117 E4
SHEERWATER. 70 D6
Sheerwater Ave KT15 . . . . 70 F7
Sheerwater Bsns Ctr
  GU21. . . . . 70 D6
Sheerwater Cotts KT14. . . 70 F6
Sheerwater Rd KT14, KT15 70 F6
Sheet's Heath La GU24. . . 88 A7
Sheet Street Rd SL4. . . . . 10 A7

Sheffield Cl
Crawley RH10 . . . . **202** B4
Farnborough GU14 . . . . **84** F4
Sheffield Rd TW14, TW6 . . . **3** C2
Sheffield Way TW14, TW6 . . . **3** D2
Shefford Cres RG40 . . . . . . **25** D8
Shelburne Dr TW4 . . . . **5** A1
Shelburne Ho **9** SW16 . . . . **21** C3
Shelby Ct BR1 . . . . **44** F8
Sheldon Cl
Crawley RH10 . . . . **202** D5
Penge SE20 . . . . **43** B8
Reigate RH2 . . . . **139** B8
Sheldon Ct **3** GU1 . . . . **130** F8
Sheldon Ho TW11 . . . . **17** A2
Sheldon St CR0, CR9 . . . . . . **61** C7
Sheldrick Cl CR4 . . . . **40** D7
Shelford **9** KT1 . . . . **38** A7
Shelford Rise SE19 . . . . **22** F1
Shelley Ave RG12 . . . . **27** E7
Shelley Cl
Banstead SM7 . . . . **77** E4
Coulsdon CR5 . . . . **79** F2
Crawley RH10 . . . . **202** C8
Shelley Cres TW5 . . . . **4** D6
Shelley Dr
Camberley GU15 . . . . **65** C5
Horsham RH12 . . . . **217** C11
9 Kingston upon Thames
 KT2 . . . . **17** D4
1 Walton-on-Thames KT12 **35** C1
West Barnes KT3 . . . . **39** A4
Shelley Dr RH12 . . . . **216** C3
Shelley Ho **7** RH12 . . . . . . **217** B2
Shelley Prim Sch RH12 . . . **216** A3
Shelley Rd
East Grinstead RH19 . . . . . **185** D1
Horsham RH12 . . . . **217** B3
Shelley Rise GU14 . . . . **84** F6
Shelley Way SW17 . . . . **20** D2
Shellfield Cl TW19 . . . . **2** A2
SHELLWOOD CROSS **158** D2
Shellwood Dr RH5 . . . . **136** C3
Shellwood Rd RH2 . . . . **137** D1
Shellys Ct RH13 . . . . **218** A3
Shelson Ave TW13 . . . . **14** F4
Shelton Ave CR6 . . . . **81** C2
Shelton Cl
Guildford GU2 . . . . **109** A6
Warlingham CR6 . . . . **81** C2
Shelton Rd SW19 . . . . **40** A8
Shelvers Gn KT20 . . . . **97** C6
Shelvers Hill KT20 . . . . **97** B6
Shelvers Spur KT20 . . . . . . **97** C6
Shelvers Way KT20 . . . . **97** D6
Shene Sch SW14 . . . . **7** E3
Shenfield Cl CR5 . . . . **99** C8
Shenley Cl CR2 . . . . **61** F1
Shenley Ho SW16 . . . . **21** C3
Shenley Rd TW5 . . . . **4** E6
Shenstone Ho SW16 . . . . . . **21** C3
Shenstone Pk SL5 . . . . **29** E5
Shepherd and Flock Rdbt
 GU9 . . . . **125** E3
Shepherd Cl
Crawley RH10 . . . . **201** E3
Feltham TW13 . . . . **15** E4
Shepherds Chase GU19 . . . **47** E2
Shepherds Cl TW17 . . . . **34** B3
Shepherds Cl GU9 . . . . **146** C8
Shepherdsgrove La
 RH19 . . . . **186** F5
SHEPHERD'S HILL **208** C6
Shepherds Hill RG12 . . . . . **27** C8
Shepherd's Hill
Guildford GU1 . . . . **109** A3
Haslemere GU27 . . . . **208** C6
Merstham RH1 . . . . **99** C1
Shepherd's Hill Bglws
 GU27 . . . . **208** C6
Shepherds La GU20 . . . . . . **49** A6
Shepherd's La GU2 . . . . **108** F4
Shepherds Way
Horsham RH12 . . . . **218** A5
South Croydon CR2 . . . . . . **62** D3
Tilford GU10 . . . . **147** D4
Shepherd's Way GU4 . . . . . **130** E4
Shepherds Wlk GU14 . . . . . **84** E7
Shepherds' Wlk KT18 . . . . . **96** A6
Shepley Cl SM5 . . . . **60** A7
Shepley Ct SW16 . . . . **21** C4
Shepley Dr SL5 . . . . **30** D3
Shepley End SL5 . . . . **30** D4
Sheppard Ct KT6 . . . . **37** E5
Sheppard Ho **8** SW2 . . . . . **22** A7
SHEPPERTON **34** C3
Shepperton Bsns Park
 TW17 . . . . **34** C4
Shepperton Court Dr
 TW17 . . . . **34** B4
Shepperton Ct TW17 . . . . . . **34** B3
SHEPPERTON GREEN **34** B5
Shepperton Ho TW17 . . . . . **34** C3
Shepperton Rd TW17,
 TW18 . . . . **33** D5
Shepperton Sta TW17 . . . . . **34** C4
Shepperton Studios TW17 **33** F6
Sheppey Cl RH11 . . . . **201** C3
Sheraton Cl GU17 . . . . **64** E4
Sheraton Dr KT19 . . . . **76** C6
Sheraton The **22** KT6 . . . . . **37** E4
Sheraton Wlk **13** RH11 . . . **201** B1
Sherborne Cl
Burgh Heath KT18 . . . . **77** C2
Poyle SL3 . . . . **1** E6

Sherborne Cres SM5 . . . . . . **40** E2
Sherborne Ct
Guildford GU2 . . . . **130** C7
Penge SE20 . . . . **43** C7
Sherborne Rd
Cheam SM3 . . . . **40** A1
Chessington KT9 . . . . **56** E5
East Bedfont TW14 . . . . . . **14** D7
Farnborough GU14 . . . . . . **85** D1
Sherborne Wlk **1** KT22 . . . **95** C6
Sherbourne GU5 . . . . **132** D5
Sherbourne Ct
2 Hampton TW12 . . . . . . **36** A8
17 Sutton SM2 . . . . **59** C4
Sherbourne Dr SL5 . . . . **30** D4
Sherbourne Farm* GU5 . . **132** E6
Sherbourne Gdns TW17 . . . **34** C3
Sherbrooke Way KT4 . . . . . **39** B2
SHERE **133** B4
Shere Ave KT17, SM2 . . . . . **58** C1
Shere CE Inf Sch GU5 . . . . **133** A4
Shere Cl
Chessington KT9 . . . . **56** D5
Dorking RH5 . . . . **136** C3
Shere Ct GU5 . . . . **133** B2
Shere La GU5 . . . . **133** A4
Shere Mus* GU5 . . . . **133** A4
Shere Rd
Albury GU4, GU5 . . . . **132** C6
Ewhurst GU6 . . . . **175** D7
Shere GU5 . . . . **133** B5
West Clandon GU4, KT24 . **111** B1
West Horsley KT24 . . . . . . **112** C4
Sherfield Cl KT3 . . . . **38** B5
Sherfield Gdns SW15 . . . . . . **7** F1
Sheridan Cl GU11 . . . . **126** A8
Sheridan Ct
7 Croydon CR0 . . . . **61** E6
Hounslow TW4 . . . . **4** E2
Sheridan Dr RH2 . . . . **118** B3
Sheridan Grange SL5 . . . . . **30** A3
Sheridan Pl
East Grinstead RH19 . . . . . **185** C1
Hampton TW12 . . . . **36** C8
Mortlake SW13 . . . . **7** F4
Sheridan Rd
Frimley GU16 . . . . **85** D8
Merton SW19 . . . . **39** F8
Richmond TW10 . . . . **17** C5
Sheridans Rd KT23 . . . . **94** C1
Sheridan Way BR3 . . . . **43** F8
Sheridan Wlk SM5 . . . . **59** F5
Sheringdale Prim Sch
 SW18 . . . . **19** F7
Sheringham Ave
Feltham TW13 . . . . **15** A5
Twickenham TW2 . . . . **16** A7
Sheringham St SW18 . . . . . . **20** C6
Sheringham Rd SE20 . . . . . . **43** C6
Sheriton Ct SM1 . . . . **59** A7
Sherland Rd TW1 . . . . **16** F7
Shermanbury Ct RH12 . . . **217** D4
Sherrdard Way GU16 . . . . . **85** E3
Sherriff Cl KT10 . . . . **55** B8
Sherrydon GU6 . . . . **174** F4
Sherwin Cres GU14 . . . . **85** C7
Sherwood
Long Ditton KT6 . . . . **56** D8
Surbiton KT6 . . . . **56** D8
Sherwood Ave SW16 . . . . . . **41** D8
Sherwood Cl
Colnbrook SL3 . . . . **1** D7
2 Croydon CR2 . . . . **61** C5
Sutton SM1 . . . . **59** A5
5 West Wickham BR4 . . . **44** B1
Sherwood Cres RH2 . . . . . **139** B5
Sherwood Park Rd
Mitcham CR4 . . . . **41** D5
Sutton SM1 . . . . **59** A4
Sherwood Park Sch SM6 . . **60** D7
Sherwood Rd
Coulsdon CR5 . . . . **79** C3
Croydon CR0, CR9 . . . . . . **43** B1
Hampton TW12 . . . . **16** C3
Knaphill GU21 . . . . **68** E2
Merton SW19 . . . . **19** F1
Sherwood Sch CR4 . . . . **41** C5
Sherwood Way BR4 . . . . **63** C8
Sherwood Wlk RH10 . . . . . **201** F3
Shetland Cl
Crawley RH10 . . . . **202** E7
Guildford GU4 . . . . **110** B6
Shetland Rd TW6 . . . . **3** C1
Shewens Rd KT13 . . . . **53** D6
Shey Copse GU22 . . . . **70** C2
Shield Dr TW8 . . . . **6** A8
Shield Rd TW15 . . . . **14** D4
Shifford Path SE23 . . . . **23** D5
Shilburn Way GU21 . . . . **69** A1
Shildon Cl GU15 . . . . **66** D3
Shillinglee Rd RH14 . . . . . . **211** B4
Shimmings The GU1 . . . . . **110** A2
Shinners Cl SE25 . . . . **43** A4
Shinwell Wlk **3** RH11 . . . . **201** B1
Ship Alley GU14 . . . . **85** C6
Shipbourne Ho BR3 . . . . . . **23** F1
Ship Field Cl TN16 . . . . **103** D6
Ship Hill TN16 . . . . **103** D6
Shipka Rd SW12 . . . . **21** B7
Ship La
Farnborough GU14 . . . . . . **85** C6
Mortlake SW14 . . . . **7** C5
Shiplake Ct SW17 . . . . **20** D4
Shiplake Ho RG12 . . . . **27** F5

SHIPLEY BRIDGE **182** F6
Shipley Bridge La
Burstow RH6, RH10. . . . . . **182** F4
Copthorne RH10 . . . . **183** A3
Shipley Ct SE20 . . . . **43** A7
Shipley Rd RH11 . . . . **201** A6
Shipman Rd SE23 . . . . **23** D6
Ship St RH19 . . . . **205** E8
Ship Yd KT13 . . . . **53** B7
Shirburn Cl SE23 . . . . **23** C8
Shire Cl GU19 . . . . **47** E2
Shire Ct
Aldershot GU11 . . . . **104** E2
Ewell KT17 . . . . **57** F3
Shire Horse Way TW7 . . . . . . **5** F4
Shire Mews TW2 . . . . **5** C1
Shire Par RH10 . . . . **202** D7
Shire Pl
12 Brentford TW8 . . . . **6** C7
Crawley RH10 . . . . **202** D7
Redhill RH1 . . . . **140** A7
Wandsworth SW18 . . . . . . **20** B8
Shires Cl KT21 . . . . **95** D8
Shires Ho KT14 . . . . **71** E6
Shires The TW10 . . . . **17** E4
SHIRLEY **62** C7
Shirley Ave
Belmont SM2 . . . . **58** F1
Carshalton SM1 . . . . **59** E6
Coulsdon CR5 . . . . **100** B8
Croydon CR0, CR9 . . . . . . **43** C1
Redhill RH1 . . . . **139** F4
Shirley Church Rd CR0 . . . . **62** E7
Shirley Cl
Crawley RH11 . . . . **200** E2
Isleworth TW3 . . . . **5** C2
Shirley Cott GU27 . . . . **207** F6
Shirley Cres BR3 . . . . **43** E5
Shirley Ct
Guildford GU1 . . . . **130** D8
Streatham SW16 . . . . **21** E1
Thornton Heath SW16 . . . . **41** F6
Shirley Dr TW3 . . . . **5** C2
Shirley High Sch CR0 . . . . . **62** D7
Shirley Hills Rd CR0 . . . . . . **62** D5
Shirley Hts SM6 . . . . **60** C2
Shirley Hyrst KT13 . . . . **53** D4
Shirley Lodge **4** SE26 . . . . **23** E4
SHIRLEY OAKS **43** E1
Shirley Oaks Hospl CR0 . . . **43** C2
Shirley Oaks Rd CR0, CR9 . **62** D8
Shirley Park Rd CR0 . . . . . . **43** C1
Shirley Pl GU21 . . . . **68** C2
Shirley Rd
Croydon CR0, CR9 . . . . **43** B1
Wallington SM6 . . . . **60** C2
Shirley Way CR0 . . . . **62** F7
Shoe La GU11 . . . . **105** A6
Shophouse La GU5 . . . . **153** C1
Shord Hill CR8 . . . . **80** D3
Shore Cl
Feltham TW14 . . . . **15** A8
Hampton TW12 . . . . **15** E3
Shore Gr TW13 . . . . **16** A6
Shoreham Cl CR0 . . . . **43** C3
Shoreham Rd RH10 . . . . . . **202** C3
Shoreham Rd E TW6 . . . . **2** E2
Shoreham Rd W TW6 . . . . . . **2** E2
Shore's Rd GU21 . . . . **69** F5
Shorndean St SE6 . . . . **24** C7
Shortacres RH1 . . . . **119** F2
Short Cl RH11 . . . . **201** D8
Shortcroft Rd KT17 . . . . **57** F3
Shortdale Rd GU11 . . . . . . **126** C6
SHORTFIELD COMMON . . . **146** C1
Shortfield Rd GU10 . . . . . . **146** C1
Short Gallop RH10 . . . . . . **202** D7
SHORTHEATH **146** A6
Shortheath Crest GU9 . . . . **145** F6
Shortheath Rd GU9,
 GU10 . . . . **146** A7
Short La
Limpsfield RH8 . . . . **123** B3
Stanwell TW15, TW19 . . . . **13** F7
SHORTLANDS **44** E6
Shortlands UB3 . . . . **3** D8
Shortlands Gdns BR2 . . . . . **44** E7
Shortlands Gr BR2 . . . . **44** D6
Shortlands Rd
Beckenham BR2 . . . . **44** E6
Kingston upon Thames KT2 . **17** F1
Shortlands Sta BR2 . . . . **44** E7
Short Rd W4 . . . . **7** E8
Shortsfield Cl RH12 . . . . . . **217** C5
Short St SM1 . . . . **105** A2
Short Way TW2 . . . . **16** C8
Shortwood GU22 . . . . **89** D8
Shortwood Ave TW18 . . . . . **13** B5
Shortwood Comm TW18 . . **13** B4
Shortwood Inf Sch TW18 . . **13** B5
Shotfield SM6 . . . . **60** B4
Shott Cl **4** SM1 . . . . **59** C5
SHOTTERMILL **207** F6
Shottermill RH11 . . . . **218** A7
Shottermill Cty Jun sch
 GU27 . . . . **207** F7
Shottermill Inf Sch GU27 **207** F7
Shottermill Pk GU27 . . . . . **207** E7
Shottermill Rd GU27 . . . . . **207** E5
Shottfield Ave SW14 . . . . **7** E3
Shovelstrode La RH19 . . . . **206** D8
Shrewsbury Ave SW14 . . . . . **7** D3
Shrewsbury Cl KT6 . . . . **56** E8
Shrewsbury House Sch
 KT6 . . . . **56** E8
Shrewsbury Lodge Sch
 KT10 . . . . **55** C4

Shrewsbury Rd
Beckenham BR3 . . . . **43** E6
Carshalton SM5 . . . . **40** E2
Harlington TW14, TW6 . . . . . **3** D1
Redhill RH1 . . . . **118** E1
Shrewsbury Wlk **8** TW7 . . . **6** A4
Shrewton Rd SW17 . . . . **20** F1
Shrivenham Cl **3** GU47 . . . **64** D8
Shroffold Rd BR1 . . . . **24** E4
Shropshire Cl CR4 . . . . **41** E5
Shrubbery Rd SW16 . . . . . . **21** E4
Shrubbery The
Farnborough GU14 . . . . . . **84** D3
2 Surbiton KT6 . . . . **37** E1
Shrubs Hill GU24 . . . . **49** C2
Shrubs Hill La SL5 . . . . **30** C3
Shrubs La GU10 . . . . **145** A4
Shrubland Ct SM7 . . . . **77** F3
Shrubland Gr KT4 . . . . **58** C7
Shrubland Rd SM7 . . . . **78** A3
Shrublands Ave CR0 . . . . . . **63** A6
Shrublands Cl SE26 . . . . . . **23** C5
Shrublands Dr GU18 . . . . . . **67** B8
SHRUBS HILL **30** C3
Shuna Wlk N1 . . . . **70** E7
Shute End RG40, RG41 . . . . **25** B6
Sibford Ct **6** CR4 . . . . **40** F6
Sibley Ct BR2 . . . . **44** E7
Sibthorp Rd **4** CR4 . . . . **40** F7
Sibton Rd SM5 . . . . **40** E2
Sickle Mill Ct GU27 . . . . . . **207** F6
Sickle Rd GU27 . . . . **208** A5
Sidbury Cl SL5 . . . . **30** A4
Siddeley Dr TW4 . . . . **4** E5
Siddons Rd
Croydon CR0, CR9 . . . . **61** B7
Forest Hill SE23 . . . . **23** E6
Sideways La RH6 . . . . **160** D2
Sidings The
Aldershot GU11 . . . . **105** C3
Rudgwick RH12 . . . . **214** D7
Staines TW18 . . . . **13** B4
Sidlaws Rd GU14 . . . . **84** D6
SIDLOW **139** B2
Sidmouth Ave TW7 . . . . **5** E5
Sidmouth Ct SM3 . . . . **58** C6
Sidney Gdns TW8 . . . . **6** D8
Sidney Rd
Croydon SE25 . . . . **43** A4
Penge BR3 . . . . **43** E7
Staines TW18 . . . . **13** A4
Twickenham TW1 . . . . **6** B1
Walton-on-Thames KT12 . . **35** B1
Sidney Wood Forest Wlks*
 GU6 . . . . **193** D2
Siebel Ct TW20 . . . . **12** B4
Siena Dr RH10 . . . . **182** C2
Sienna Cl KT9 . . . . **56** D4
Sienna Ct TW13 . . . . **14** F5
Signal Ct RH7 . . . . **164** E5
Sigrist Sq **4** KT2 . . . . **37** E8
Silbury Ave CR4 . . . . **40** E8
Silbury Ho **9** SE26 . . . . . . **23** A5
Silchester Ct
Ashford TW15 . . . . **13** E6
Thornton Heath CR7 . . . . . . **42** A5
Silchester Dr RH11 . . . . . . **201** B4
Silistria Cl GU21 . . . . **68** C1
Silkham Rd RH8 . . . . **122** E8
Silkin Wlk **8** RH11 . . . . . . **201** B1
Silkmore La
West Horsley KT24 . . . . **92** A2
West Horsley KT24 . . . . . . **112** B7
Silk Pl RG40 . . . . **25** D7
Silo Cl GU7 . . . . **150** F8
Silo Dr GU7 . . . . **150** F8
Silo Rd GU7 . . . . **150** F8
Silver Birch Cl
Forest Hill SE6 . . . . **23** F5
Woodham KT15 . . . . **70** E7
Silver Birch Cotts GU10 . . **168** E1
Silver Birches Way GU8 . . **148** E3
Silver Birch Ho RH11 . . . . **201** C1
Silver Birch Way GU14 . . . . **84** D5
Silver Cl KT20 . . . . **97** E3
Silver Ct
East Grinstead RH19 . . . . . **185** B2
Leatherhead KT22 . . . . **95** B7
Silverdale SE23, SE26 . . . . . **23** C4
Silverdale Ave
Oxshott KT22 . . . . **74** C5
Walton-on-Thames KT12,
 KT13 . . . . **53** F7
Silverdale Cl
Brockham RH3 . . . . **137** B5
Cheam SM1 . . . . **58** F6
Silverdale Ct TW18 . . . . **13** B3
Silverdale Dr TW16 . . . . **35** B7
Silver Dr GU16 . . . . **66** C3
Silvergate KT19 . . . . **57** C5
Silverglade KT9 . . . . **75** C7
Silverglade Bsns Pk KT9 . . **75** C7
Silverhall St TW7 . . . . **6** A4
Silver Hill GU47 . . . . **64** E8
Silver Jubilee Way TW4 . . . . **4** B5
Silver La
Purley CR8 . . . . **79** E7
West Wickham BR4 . . . . . . **63** D8
Silverlands Cl KT16 . . . . **51** D7
Silverlea Gdns RH6 . . . . . . **161** C2
Silverleigh Rd CR7 . . . . **42** A4
Silvermere Ct
Caterham CR3 . . . . **100** F3
1 Purley CR8 . . . . **80** A7
Silvermere Rd **1** SE6 . . . . . **24** B8
Silversmiths Way GU21 . . . **69** C1
Silverstone Cl RH1 . . . . **118** F3
Silverton Lodge SE19 . . . . . **22** E1

Silver Tree Cl KT12 . . . . **54** A6
Silver Wood Ind Est CR0 . . **60** F4
Silverwood Cl
Beckenham BR3 . . . . **24** A1
New Addington CR0 . . . . . . **63** A2
Silverwood Dr GU15 . . . . . . **66** A7
Silverwood Grange SL5 . . . **29** F2
Silwood RG12 . . . . **26** E1
Silwood Cl SL5 . . . . **29** D7
Silwood Park (Imperial Coll)
 SL5 . . . . **29** F6
Silwood Rd SL5 . . . . **29** F5
Simkins Cl RG42 . . . . **8** B2
Simmil Rd KT10 . . . . **55** E5
Simmonds Cl RG42 . . . . **26** E8
Simmonds Cotts GU7 . . . . **150** B4
Simmonds Ct KT9 . . . . **125** C2
Simmons Cl KT9 . . . . **56** C4
Simmons Ct GU1 . . . . **109** C5
Simmons Gate KT10 . . . . . . **55** C5
Simmons Pl TW18 . . . . **12** E3
Simms Cl SM5 . . . . **59** E8
Simone Dr CR8 . . . . **80** C3
Simon Lodge **31** SW19 . . . **19** D7
Simons Cl KT16 . . . . **51** C4
Simons Wlk TW20 . . . . **11** C1
Simplemarsh Ct KT15 . . . . . **52** B6
Simplemarsh Rd KT15 . . . . **52** B6
Simpson Cl CR0 . . . . **42** C3
Simpson Ho **1** KT12 . . . . . **35** A1
Simpson Rd
Richmond TW10 . . . . **17** C4
Twickenham TW4 . . . . **4** F1
Simpson Way KT6 . . . . **37** C3
Sim's Cotts KT10 . . . . **55** F4
Sinclair Cl RH10 . . . . **202** C4
Sinclair Ct
22 Beckenham BR3 . . . . . **24** A1
5 Croydon CR0 . . . . **61** F8
Sinclair Dr SM2 . . . . **59** B2
Sinclair Ho
Streatham, Streatham Hill
 SW12 . . . . **21** D7
Streatham SW16 . . . . **21** F1
Sincots Rd RH1 . . . . **118** F1
Sine Cl GU14 . . . . **85** B8
Singlegate Prim Sch
 SW19 . . . . **20** D1
Singleton Cl
Mitcham SW17, SW19 . . . . **20** F1
Thornton Heath CR0 . . . . . . **42** C2
Singleton Rd RH12 . . . . **216** D3
Sinhurst Rd GU15 . . . . **65** B4
Sion Ct TW1 . . . . **17** B7
Sion Rd TW1 . . . . **17** B7
SIPSON **3** A8
Sipson Cl UB7 . . . . **3** A8
Sipson La UB7 . . . . **3** B8
Sipson Rd UB7 . . . . **3** A7
Sipson Way UB7 . . . . **3** A7
Sir Arthur Bliss Ct **6** CR4 **40** F7
Sir Cyril Black Way **2**
 SW19 . . . . **20** A1
Sirdar Rd CR4 . . . . **21** A2
Sirl Cotts SL5 . . . . **29** C5
Sir William Perkin's Sch
 KT16 . . . . **32** F1
Sisken Ct **2** CR0 . . . . **61** E7
Siskin Ave RH10 . . . . **204** C5
Siskin Cl RH12 . . . . **217** E5
Siskin Gate RG12 . . . . **26** D5
Sissinghurst Cl
Catford BR1 . . . . **24** E3
Crawley RH10 . . . . **202** D7
Sissinghurst Rd CR0 . . . . . . **43** A2
Sistova Rd SW12 . . . . **21** B7
Siward Rd SW17 . . . . **20** C5
Six Acres RH13 . . . . **215** D2
Six Cross-Roads GU21 . . . . **70** A5
Sixth Cross Rd TW2 . . . . . . **16** C5
Sixth Form Coll Farnborough
 The GU14 . . . . **85** B6
Skeat Ho KT22 . . . . **95** B5
Skeena Hill SW18, SW19 . . **19** E8
Skelbrook St SW18 . . . . **20** C6
Skelmersdale Wlk RH11 . . **200** E2
Skerne Rd KT2 . . . . **37** D8
Skerne Wlk KT2 . . . . **37** D8
Skid Hill La CR6 . . . . **82** F5
Skiffington Cl SW2 . . . . **22** A7
Skiff La RH14 . . . . **213** A1
SKIMMINGTON **138** D8
Skimmington Cotts RH2 **138** D8
Skimpedhill La RG12 . . . . . . **27** B7
Skinners La
Ashtead KT21 . . . . **75** D1
Chiddingfold GU8 . . . . **191** D5
Heston TW5 . . . . **5** B6
Skipton Ct SE24 . . . . **22** B7
Skipton Way RH6 . . . . **161** B5
Sky Bsns Pk TW20 . . . . **32** C7
Skylark View RH12 . . . . **217** D7
Skyline Ct CR0 . . . . **61** D7
Skyport Dr UB7 . . . . **2** D7
Skyview Appartments **8**
 CR0 . . . . **61** D8
Skyway 14 Trad Est SL3 . . . . **1** F4
Slade Ct KT16 . . . . **51** D4
Slade House TW4 . . . . **4** F1
Slade Rd
Ottershaw KT16 . . . . **51** D4
Pirbright GU24 . . . . **87** D2
Slade Way CR4 . . . . **41** A8
Slaidburn Gn RG12 . . . . **27** E2
Slattery Rd TW13 . . . . **15** C7
Slaugham Ct RH11 . . . . **200** F3
SLEAFORD **166** A1
Sledmere Ct TW14 . . . . **14** E7

Sleets Rd RH12 216 E3
Slim Cl GU11 105 E7
Slim Rd GU15 65 C7
Slines New Rd CR3, CR6 101 E7
Slines Oak Rd CR3, CR6 102 B6
SLINFOLD 215 D3
Slinfold CE Prim Sch RH13 215 D4
Slinfold Wlk RH11 201 A6
Slip Of Wood GU6 174 F4
Slipshatch Rd RH2 138 E5
Slipshoe St 2 RH2 118 A1
Sloane Hospl BR3 44 D8
Sloane Wlk CR0 43 F3
Slocock Hill GU21 69 C2
Sloughbrook Cl RH12 217 F6
Slough La
Buckland RH3 117 A3
Headley KT18 96 C2
SLYFIELD 109 D5
Slyfield Ct GU1 109 E4
Slyfield Gn GU1 109 E5
Slyfield Ind Est GU1 109 E5
Smallberry Ave TW7 5 F5
Smallberry Green Prim Sch TW7 6 A5
SMALLFIELD 162 B2
Smallfield Rd
Horley RH6 161 D3
Horne RH6 162 E3
Smallmead RH6 161 B3
Smalls Hill Rd RH2, RH6 159 C6
Small's La RH11 201 C6
Smalls Mead RH11 201 C6
Smallwood Prim Sch SW17 20 D4
Smallwood Rd SW17 20 D4
Smart's Heath La GU22 89 A4
Smart's Heath Rd GU22 89 B5
Smeaton Cl KT9 56 D4
Smeaton Rd SW18 20 A8
Smeeds Cl RH19 186 A3
Smitham Bottom La CR5, CR8 79 D7
Smitham Downs Rd CR5, CR8 79 E6
Smitham Prim Sch CR5 79 C3
Smitham Sta CR5 79 E4
Smithbarn RH13 218 A2
Smithbarn Cl RH6 161 B4
Smithbrook Cotts GU6 173 D3
Smithbrook Gate GU6 173 D3
Smith Cl RH10 201 D3
Smith Ct GU21 70 D6
Smithers Cotts RH12 214 F7
Smithers Ho SE20 23 D1
Smithers The RH3 137 B7
Smithfield La GU35, GU10 167 A1
Smith Rd RH2 138 F6
Smith Sq RG12 27 D7
Smith St KT5 37 F3
Smith's Yd
6 Croydon CR0 61 C7
Wandsworth SW18 20 E6
Smithwood Ave GU6 174 B7
Smithwood Cl SW19 19 E6
Smithwood Common Rd GU6 174 B7
Smithy Cl KT20 97 F1
Smithy La
Lower Kingswood KT20 97 F1
Sleaford GU10 166 E2
Smithy's Gn GU20 48 D4
Smock Wlk CR0 42 C3
Smokejack Hill RH5 196 D7
Smoke La RH2 139 B7
Smolletts RH19 205 C8
Smoothfield TW3 5 A3
Smugglers' La RH5 197 E7
Smugglers' Way GU10 126 E1
Snailslynch GU9 125 D2
Snakey La TW13 15 B4
Snatts Hill RH8 122 F6
Snelgate Cotts GU4 111 D4
Snell Hatch RH11 201 B6
Snellings Rd KT12 54 C5
Snera Lodge SW19 20 E1
Snipe La GU27 208 A1
Snowdenham Hall GU5 151 D5
Snowdenham La GU5 151 E5
Snowdenham Links Rd GU5 151 D6
Snowdon Rd
Farnborough GU14 84 E7
Harlington TW6 3 C1
Snowdown Cl SE20 43 D8
Snowdrop Cl
Crawley RH11 201 A2
2 Hampton TW12 16 A2
Snowdrop Way GU24 68 A2
Snowe Ho SE27 22 B5
Snowerhill Rd RH3 137 F6
SNOW HILL 184 A4
Snow Hill
Copthorne RH10 183 F3
Crawley RH10 204 A3
Domewood RH10 183 E5
Snow Hill Bsns Ctr RH10 184 A4
Snowhill La RH10 183 F5
Snows Paddock GU20 48 B7
Snows Ride GU20 48 B6
Snowy Fielder Waye TW7 6 B5
Snoxhall Field GU6 174 D2
Soames Wlk KT3 38 E8
Soane Cl RH11 200 E4
Soaphouse La TW8 6 E7
Sohomills Ind Est SM6 41 B1
Sola Ct 7 CR0 42 D1
Solartron Rd GU14 85 B3
Solartron Ret Pk GU14 85 A3
Solecote KT23 94 A2
Sole Farm Ave KT23 93 F2
Sole Farm Cl KT23 93 F3
Sole Farm Rd KT23 93 F2
Solent Ct SW16 41 F7
Soloms Court Rd CR5, SM7 78 E2
Solway Cl TW4 4 E4
Sol-y-vista GU7 150 D6
Somborne Ho 12 SW15 19 A8
Somerfield Cl KT20 97 E8
Somergate RH12 216 F2
Somersbury La GU6, RH12 195 F7
Somersby Est SE20 23 C1
Somers Cl RH2 118 A2
Somerset Ave
Chessington KT9 56 D6
Wimbledon SW20 39 B7
Somerset Cl
Epsom KT19 57 D2
Hersham KT12 54 B5
New Malden KT3 38 E3
Sutton SM3 58 C7
Somerset Ct
Farnborough GU14 85 C1
8 Hampton TW12 36 A8
Somerset Gdns
Teddington TW11 16 E3
Thornton Heath SW16 41 F6
Somerset Ho
Wimbledon SW19 19 E5
15 Woking GU22 69 F2
Somerset Lodge 11 TW8 6 D8
Somerset Rd
Brentford TW8 6 C8
Farnborough GU14 85 C1
Kingston upon Thames KT1 37 F7
Reigate RH1 139 D7
Teddington TW11 16 E3
Wimbledon SW19 19 D5
Somerset Waye TW5 4 E7
Somers Pl
1 Reigate RH2 118 A2
Streatham SW2 21 F8
Somers Rd
Reigate RH2 118 A2
2 Streatham SW2 21 F8
Somerswey GU4 130 E1
Somerton Ave TW9 7 B4
Somerton Cl CR8 80 A3
Somertons Cl GU2 109 A4
Somerville Ct SW16 21 D2
Somerville Dr RH10 182 C1
Somerville Rd
Cobham KT11 74 A5
Penge BR3, SE20 23 D1
Somerville Rise RG12 27 B4
Sondes Farm RH4 135 F7
Sondes Place Dr RH4 135 F7
Songhurst Cl CR0 41 F3
Sonia Gdns TW5 5 A7
Sonic Ct GU1 109 C2
Sonnet Wlk TN16 83 C1
Sonning Ct CR0 62 A8
Sonninge Cl GU47 64 D8
Sonning Gdns TW12 15 E2
Sonning Rd CR0 43 A3
Soper Cl SE23 23 D6
Soper Dr CR3 100 D4
Sopwith Ave KT9 56 E5
Sopwith Cl
Biggin Hill TN16 83 D3
Richmond TW10 17 F3
Sopwith Dr KT13 71 E8
Sopwith Rd TW5 4 C7
Sopwith Way KT2 37 E8
Sorbie Cl KT13 53 D4
Sorrel Bank CR0 62 E1
Sorrel Cl
Crawley RH11 201 A2
Farnborough GU14 84 C5
Wokingham RG40 25 E8
Sorrel Dr GU18 66 F7
Sorrel Ho TW3 5 C6
Sorrel Rd RH12 217 E5
Sorrento Rd SM1 59 B7
South Albert Rd RH2 117 F2
Southall La TW5 4 B8
Southam Ho KT15 52 B5
Southampton Cl GU17 64 C6
Southampton Gdns CR4 41 E4
Southampton Road E TW6 2 F1
Southampton Road W TW6 2 E1
Southampton St GU14 105 B8
South Ascot Village Sch SL5 29 A4
South Atlantic Dr GU11 105 C3
South Ave
Egham TW20 12 C2
Heath End GU9 125 D6
Richmond TW9 7 A5
Wallington SM5 60 A3
Whiteley Village KT12 53 E1
Southbank KT7 37 B2
South Bank KT6 37 E3
South Bank Lodge 2 KT6 37 E3
South Bank Terr KT6 37 E3
SOUTH BEDDINGTON 60 C3
South Border The CR8 79 E8
SOUTHBOROUGH 37 D1
Southborough Cl KT6 37 D1
Southborough Rd KT6 37 E1
Southborough Sch KT6 56 E7
Southbridge Pl CR0, CR9 61 C6
Southbridge Rd CR0, CR9 61 C6
Southbrook RH11 201 C1
Southbrook Rd SW16 41 E8
Southbury GU2 130 C7
South Cl
Crawley RH10 201 F7
Morden SM4 40 A3
Twickenham TW2 16 A5
Woking GU21 69 C3
Wokingham RG40 25 D4
South Close Gn RH1 119 B6
Southcote GU21 69 D3
Southcote Ave
Feltham TW13 15 A6
Tolworth KT5 38 B2
Southcote Dr GU15 66 A5
Southcote Ho KT15 52 D8
Southcote Rd
Croydon SE25 43 B3
Merstham RH1 119 C6
South Croydon CR2 61 F1
Southcourt TW16 35 C6
Southcroft
Carshalton SM1 59 E5
Englefield Green TW20 11 B3
Southcroft Ave BR4 63 C8
Southcroft Rd SW17 21 A2
South Croxted Rd SE21 22 D4
SOUTH CROYDON 61 D3
South Croydon Sta CR2 61 D5
Southdean Gdns SW19 19 F6
Southdown Cl RH12 218 A5
Southdown Dr SW20 19 D1
Southdown Rd
Hersham KT12 54 E6
Wallington SM5 60 A2
Wimbledon SW20 39 D8
Woldingham CR3 101 F5
South Dr
Banstead SM7 78 E6
Belmont SM2 58 E2
Coulsdon CR5 79 D4
Dorking RH4 136 C7
Pirbright GU24 87 C6
Wentworth GU25 31 A2
Wokingham RG40 25 C5
SOUTH EARLSWOOD 139 F4
South Eden Park Rd
Beckenham BR3 44 B4
West Wickham BR3 44 B2
SOUTHEND 24 D4
South End
Croydon CR0, CR9 61 C6
Great Bookham KT23 94 B1
Southend La
Catford SE6 24 B4
Forest Hill SE26, SE6 23 F4
Southend Rd BR3 44 A8
Southerland Cl KT13 53 C6
Southern Ave
East Bedfont TW14 15 A7
Salfords RH1 140 A1
South Norwood SE25 42 F6
Southern Bglws GU4 131 B2
Southern Cotts TW19 2 A2
Southern Ind Area RG12 26 F6
Southern Perimeter Rd
East Bedfont TW6 3 B1
Harlington TW14, TW6 3 D2
Stanwell TW19, TW6 2 D2
Southern Rd GU15 65 C6
Southerns La CR5 98 C3
Southern Way
Farnborough GU14 84 E3
Farnham GU9 125 C1
Southey Ct KT23 94 B3
Southey Rd SW19 20 A1
Southey St SE20 23 D1
South Farm La GU19 48 A2
SOUTH FARNBOROUGH 85 D1
South Farnborough Inf Sch GU14 105 D8
South Farnborough Jun Sch GU14 85 D2
South Farnham Sch GU9 125 D1
Southfield Gdns TW1 16 F4
Southfield Park Prim Sch KT19 76 C8
Southfield Pl KT13 53 B3
SOUTHFIELDS 20 A7
Southfields KT8 36 E3
Southfields Ave TW15 14 B2
Southfield Sch RG40 25 D5
Southfields Com Coll SW18 20 A7
Southfields Ct SM3 59 A8
Southfields Rd CR3 102 B3
Southfields U Sta SW18 19 F7
SOUTHGATE 201 C4
Southgate Ave RH10 201 E4
South Gate Ave TW13 14 D4
Southgate Dr RH10 201 E4
Southgate Par RH10 201 D4
Southgate Prim Sch RH10 201 D4
Southgate Rd RH10 201 D4
South Gdns SW19 20 D1
SOUTH GODSTONE 142 F5
South Gr
Chertsey KT16 32 F3
Horsham RH13 217 D1
South Hill
Godalming GU7 150 F4
Guildford GU1 130 D7
South Hill Pk & Wilde Theatre RG12 27 C2
South Hill Rd
Beckenham BR2 44 E5
Bracknell RG12 27 B3
Southholme Cl SE19 42 E8
South Holmes Rd RH13 218 B4
SOUTH HOLMWOOD 157 C7
South La
Ash GU12 106 B1
Kingston upon Thames KT1 37 D6
New Malden KT3 38 D4
New Malden, Old Malden KT3 38 E2
Southlands
East Grinstead RH19 205 E7
Horley RH6 160 F3
Tandridge RH8 122 C2
Southlands Ave RH6 161 A4
Southlands Cl
Ash GU12 106 A1
Coulsdon CR5 79 F2
Wokingham RG40 25 D5
Southlands Dr SW19 19 D6
Southlands La RH8 122 C1
Southlands Rd
Ash GU12 106 A1
Wokingham RG40 25 D4
Southland Way TW7 5 D2
South La W KT3 38 D5
South Lawn Ct GU7 150 D6
South Lodge TW2 5 C1
South Lodge Ave CR4, CR7, SW16 41 E5
South Lodge Ct RH2 159 F7
South Lodge Rd KT12 54 B2
South Lynn Cres RG12 27 B4
South Mdw RG45 45 D3
South Mead
Redhill RH1 118 F4
West Ewell KT19 57 F3
Southmead Prim Sch SW19 19 E7
Southmead Rd
Aldershot GU11 126 B8
Putney SW19 19 E7
SOUTH MERSTHAM 119 D5
South Merton Sta SW20 39 F6
Southmont Rd KT10 55 E7
South Munstead La GU8 172 B7
SOUTH NORWOOD 42 E5
South Norwood Country Park★ SE25 43 C5
South Norwood Country Pk Nature Reserve★ SE25 43 C5
South Norwood Hill SE19, SE25 42 F7
South Norwood Prim Sch SE25 43 A5
SOUTH NUTFIELD 140 E7
South Oak Rd SW16 21 F4
South Par
Horley RH6 160 F4
Wallington SM6 60 C4
SOUTH PARK
Reigate 138 F6
South Godstone 142 A6
South Park Cres SE6 24 F7
Southpark Ct 4 SW19 20 A2
South Park Ct 25 BR3 24 A1
South Park Gr KT3 38 C5
South Park Hill Rd CR2 61 D6
South Park La RH1 142 A7
South Park Rd SW19 20 B2
South Pier Rd RH6 182 B7
South Pl
Surbiton KT5 37 F2
Wokingham RG40 25 C6
South Rd
Ash Vale GU12 106 A4
Bisley GU24 67 F3
Bracknell RG40, RG12 26 E1
Cranford TW5 4 D8
Crowthorne RG45 45 E3
Englefield Green TW20 11 D2
Feltham TW13 15 D3
Forest Hill SE23 23 D6
Guildford GU2 109 B3
Hampton TW12 15 F2
Mitcham SW19 20 D2
Reigate RH2 139 B8
Twickenham TW2 16 D5
Weybridge KT13 53 B2
Weybridge, St George's Hill KT13 53 C5
Woking GU21 69 C4
South Ridge KT13 72 B8
Southridge Pl SW20 19 D1
South Rise SM5 59 E2
Southsea Rd KT1 37 E5
South Side GU10 126 F7
Southside Comm SW19 19 D2
South St
Dorking RH4 136 A7
Epsom KT18 76 D5
Farnborough GU14 85 E1
Farnham GU9 125 C2
Godalming GU7 150 D4
Horsham RH12 217 C2
Isleworth TW7 6 A4
Staines TW18 12 F3
South Station App RH1 140 F7
South Terr
Dorking RH4 136 B6
Surbiton KT6 37 E3
South Thames Coll (Tooting Ctr) SW17 20 E3
South Vale SE19 22 E2
South View
Bracknell RG12 26 C6
South View *continued*
Epsom KT19 57 A1
Oxted RH8 123 A2
Wimbledon SW19 19 D2
Southview Cl SW17 21 A3
South View Cl RH10 183 E3
Southview Cotts GU10 146 D1
South View Cotts GU5 152 D4
Southview Ct 14 GU22 69 E1
South View Ct SE19 22 C1
Southview Gdns SM6 60 C3
Southview Rd
Catford BR1 24 D4
Headley Down GU35 187 B5
Woldingham CR3 102 B3
South View Rd KT21 95 D8
Southviews CR2 62 D2
Southville Cl
East Bedfont TW14 14 E7
West Ewell KT19 57 D2
Southville Cres TW14 14 E7
Southville Jun & Inf Schs TW14 14 F7
Southville Rd
East Bedfont TW14 14 E8
Thames Ditton KT7 37 B2
Southwark KT18 97 D8
Southwark Cl RH11 201 B2
Southwater Cl
Beckenham BR3 24 B1
Crawley RH11 201 A6
Southway
Camberley GU15 65 B4
Guildford GU2 108 F1
Wallington SM6 60 C6
West Barnes SW20 39 D5
South Way
Croydon CR0 62 E7
Sutton SM5 59 D1
Southway Ct GU2 108 E1
Southway Pk GU2 109 A2
Southways Pk RH10 181 D3
Southwell Park Rd GU15 65 C5
Southwell Rd CR0, CR7 42 A3
South Western Rd TW1 6 B1
Southwick GU19 47 E1
Southwick Cl RH19 185 D2
Southwick Ct RG12 27 E3
Southwick Ho RH19 185 D2
SOUTH WIMBLEDON 20 B2
South Wimbledon U Sta SW19 20 B1
South Wlk
Aldershot GU12 105 D2
Coney Hall BR4 63 E7
Southwold RG12 26 E1
SOUTHWOOD 84 D3
Southwood RG40 25 D4
Southwood Ave
Coulsdon CR5 79 C4
Kingston upon Thames KT2, KT3 38 C8
Knaphill GU21 68 D1
Ottershaw KT16 51 C3
Southwood Chase GU6 174 F1
Southwood Cl KT4 39 D1
Southwood Cres GU14 84 E4
Southwood Ct
Knaphill GU21 68 D1
Weybridge KT13 53 B5
Southwood Dr KT5 38 C1
Southwood Gdns KT10 56 A7
Southwood Inf Sch GU14 84 D3
Southwood La
Farnborough GU51 84 A3
Farnborough, Southwood GU14 84 D3
Southwood Open Space Nature Reserve★ KT4 38 D2
Southwood Rd GU14 84 E4
South Worple Way SW14 7 D4
Sovereign Cl CR8 60 F1
Sovereign Ct
14 Croydon CR2 61 C5
East Molesey KT8 35 F5
Harlington UB3 3 B7
8 Richmond TW9 6 F3
4 Sunningdale SL5 30 B2
Sovereign Dr GU15 66 B7
Sovereign Ho 3 SW19 19 E2
Sovereign House TW15 13 E4
Sovereign Hts SL3 1 A8
Soyer Ct 4 GU21 68 E1
Spa Central SW16 21 E1
Space Waye TW14 4 B2
Spa Cl SE19 42 E8
Spa Ct SW16 21 F4
Spa Dr KT18 76 A5
Spa Hill CR7, SE19 42 D8
Spalding Rd SW17 21 B3
Sparks Cl TW12 15 E2
Sparrow Cl TW12 15 E2
Sparrow Farm Dr TW14 15 D8
Sparrow Farm Inf Sch TW14 15 C8
Sparrow Farm Jun Sch TW14 15 C8
Sparrow Farm Rd KT17, KT4 58 B6
Sparrowhawk Cl GU10 124 D8
Sparrowhawk Way RG12 26 D5
Sparrow Row GU24 49 B4
Sparrows Mead RH1 119 A4
Spartan Cl SM6 60 E3
Spartan Way RH11 181 A1

Sparvell Rd GU21 ... 88 B8
Sparvell Way GU15 ... 65 C6
Spats La GU35 ... 187 A8
Spa View [6] SW16 ... 21 F5
Speaker's Ct [3] CR0 ... 42 D1
Spean Ho GU14 ... 85 D2
Speart La TW5 ... 4 E7
Speedbird Way UB7 ... 2 C7
Speedwell Cl GU4 ... 110 C4
Speedwell Ho [5] RH1 ... 119 A4
Speedwell Way RH12 ... 217 E5
Speer Rd KT7 ... 36 F3
Speirs Cl KT3 ... 38 F3
Speke Rd CR7 ... 42 D7
Speldhurst Cl [4] BR2 ... 44 F4
Spelthorne Gr TW16 ... 14 F1
Spelthorne Inf Sch TW15 ... 14 E2
Spelthorne Jun Sch TW15 ... 14 D2
Spelthorne La TW15, TW17 ... 34 C8
Spelthorne L Ctr TW18 ... 13 A3
Spelthorne Mus★ [7] TW18 ... 12 F3
Spence Ave KT14 ... 71 F5
Spencer Cl
  Frimley GU16 ... 85 E6
  Langley Vale KT18 ... 96 C6
  Sheerwater GU21 ... 70 D6
Spencer Ct
  Leatherhead KT22 ... 95 C4
  Wimbledon SW20 ... 39 B8
Spencer Gdns
  Englefield Green TW20 ... 11 D3
  Mortlake SW14 ... 7 C2
Spencer Hill SW19 ... 19 E1
Spencer Hill Rd SW19 ... 19 E1
Spencer Ho
  [24] Putney SW19 ... 19 D7
  Wimbledon SW19 ... 19 D5
Spencer Pk KT8 ... 36 C4
Spencer Pl CR0 ... 42 D2
Spencer Rd
  Bracknell RG42 ... 26 F8
  Bromley BR1 ... 24 F1
  Carshalton CR4 ... 41 A2
  Caterham CR3 ... 100 D6
  Chiswick W4 ... 7 C7
  Cobham KT11 ... 73 B4
  East Molesey KT8 ... 36 C4
  Hounslow TW3, TW5, TW7 ... 5 C6
  Mitcham CR4 ... 41 A6
  South Croydon CR2 ... 61 E5
  Twickenham TW2 ... 16 E6
  Wimbledon SW20 ... 39 B8
Spencers La RH6 ... 159 F2
Spencers Pl RH12 ... 217 B4
Spencers Rd RH11 ... 201 D5
Spencer's Rd RH12 ... 217 B3
Spencer Way RH1 ... 140 A4
Spenser Ave KT13 ... 53 A2
Spenser Ct [5] TW10 ... 17 D4
Spenser Mews SE21 ... 22 D7
Spiceall GU3 ... 129 B3
Spicer Cl KT12 ... 35 C3
Spicers Field KT22 ... 74 E6
Spices Yd CR0 ... 61 C6
Spiers Way RH6 ... 161 B1
Spindle Way RH10 ... 201 F5
Spindlewood Gdns CR0, CR2 ... 61 E6
Spindlewoods KT20 ... 97 B4
Spinis RG12 ... 26 F1
Spinnaker Ct [2] KT1 ... 37 D8
Spinner Gn RG12 ... 27 B4
Spinney Cl
  Ascot SL5 ... 29 C7
  Beckenham BR3 ... 44 B5
  Cobham KT11 ... 74 A8
  Crawley Down RH10 ... 204 C8
  Horsham RH12 ... 218 B6
  New Malden KT3 ... 38 E4
  Worcester Park KT4 ... 57 F8
Spinneycroft KT22 ... 74 D4
Spinney Dr TW14 ... 14 C8
Spinney Gdns SE19 ... 22 F3
Spinney Hill KT15 ... 51 F5
Spinney La SL4 ... 9 B7
Spinney Oak KT16 ... 51 D4
Spinney The
  Ascot SL5 ... 29 E4
  Burgh Heath KT18 ... 97 B8
  Cheam SM3 ... 58 C6
  Crawley RH11 ... 201 B4
  Frimley GU15 ... 66 C6
  Grayshott GU26 ... 188 A4
  Great Bookham KT23 ... 94 B3
  Haslemere GU27 ... 208 C8
  Headley KT18 ... 96 C1
  Horley RH6 ... 161 A5
  Oxshott KT22 ... 74 C7
  Purley CR8 ... 80 B8
  Ripley GU23 ... 111 C8
  Streatham SW16 ... 21 D5
  Sunbury TW16 ... 35 A8
Spinning Wlk The GU5 ... 133 A4
Spire Ct [11] TW10 ... 6 E1
Spire Pl CR6 ... 81 E1
Spires Ct [7] KT16 ... 33 A3
Spital Heath RH4 ... 136 C8
Spitfire Bsns Pk CR0 ... 61 A4
Spitfire Rd SM6 ... 60 E3
Spitfire Way GU14 ... 104 E7
Spoil La GU10 ... 126 F7
Spokane Cl GU11 ... 125 F8

Spook Hill RH5 ... 136 B3
Spooner Ho TW5 ... 5 A8
Spooners Rd RH12 ... 218 A4
Sportsbank St SE6 ... 24 C8
Spout Hill CR0 ... 63 A5
Spout La TW19 ... 2 A3
Spout La N TW19 ... 2 B3
Spratts La KT16 ... 51 E4
Spread Eagle Wlk [2] KT18 ... 76 D6
SPREAKLEY ... 167 B8
Spreighton Rd KT8 ... 36 B5
Spring Ave TW20 ... 11 F2
Springbank Rd SE13 ... 24 E8
Springbok Farm RH12 ... 193 E1
Spring Bottom La RH1 ... 120 C8
Springbourne Ct BR3 ... 44 C6
Spring Cl [11] RH11 ... 201 D5
Springclose La SM3 ... 58 E4
Spring Cnr TW13 ... 14 F5
Spring Copse
  Copthorne RH10 ... 183 C3
  East Grinstead RH19 ... 185 D3
Spring Copse Bsns Pk RH13 ... 215 C3
Springcopse Rd RH2 ... 139 C7
Spring Cotts
  Kingston upon Thames KT6 ... 37 D4
  South Holmwood RH5 ... 157 C6
Springcross Ave GU17 ... 64 D4
Spring Ct
  Ewell KT17 ... 57 F2
  Guildford GU2 ... 109 B5
Springfarm Rd GU27 ... 207 E5
Springfield
  East Grinstead RH19 ... 185 D4
  Elstead GU8 ... 148 D3
  Lightwater GU18 ... 67 D8
  Oxted RH8 ... 122 D5
  South Norwood SE25 ... 43 A6
Springfield Ave
  Hampton TW12 ... 16 B2
  Merton SW20 ... 39 F6
Springfield Christian Sch SE6 ... 23 F5
Springfield Cl GU21 ... 68 E1
Springfield Cres RH12 ... 217 B2
Springfield Ct
  Crawley RH11 ... 201 D5
  [2] Horsham RH12 ... 217 C2
  [9] Kingston upon Thames KT1 ... 37 E6
  Wallington SM6 ... 60 B5
Springfield Drive KT22 ... 94 F8
Springfield Gdns
  East Grinstead RH19 ... 184 F4
  West Wickham BR4 ... 63 B8
Springfield Gr TW16 ... 35 A8
Springfield La KT13 ... 53 B6
Springfield Mdws KT13 ... 53 B6
Springfield Park Ho RH12 ... 217 C3
Springfield Park Rd RH12 ... 217 B2
Springfield Pl KT3 ... 38 C5
Springfield Prim Sch TW16 ... 34 F7
Springfield Rd
  Ashford TW15 ... 13 F3
  Ash GU12 ... 106 A5
  Bracknell RG12 ... 26 C8
  Brands Hill SL3 ... 1 B7
  Crawley RH11 ... 201 D5
  East Ewell KT17 ... 58 C1
  Frimley GU15 ... 66 B5
  Guildford GU1 ... 109 E1
  Horsham RH12 ... 217 C2
  Kingston upon Thames KT1 ... 37 E6
  Penge SE26 ... 23 B3
  South Norwood CR7 ... 42 C8
  [8] Teddington TW11 ... 17 A3
  Twickenham TW2 ... 16 A7
  Wallington SM6 ... 60 B5
  Westcott RH4 ... 135 C6
  Wimbledon SW19 ... 20 A3
Springfield Rise SE26 ... 23 B5
Springfields Cl
  Billingshurst RH14 ... 212 D3
  Chertsey KT16 ... 33 B1
Springfield Terr GU5 ... 151 F6
Springfield University Hospl SW17 ... 20 E5
Spring Gdns
  Ascot SL5 ... 29 B5
  Biggin Hill TN16 ... 83 C1
  Copthorne RH10 ... 183 C3
  Crawley RH4 ... 183 C3
  Dorking RH4 ... 136 A8
  East Molesey KT8 ... 36 C5
  Farnborough GU14 ... 85 A7
  Frimley GU15 ... 66 A5
  Horsham RH12 ... 217 C3
  Wallington SM6 ... 60 C5
Spring Gr
  Brentford W4 ... 7 A8
  Farncombe GU7 ... 150 E8
  Fetcham KT22 ... 94 B4
  Hampton TW12 ... 36 B8
  Mitcham CR4 ... 41 A8
SPRING GROVE ... 5 E5
Spring Grove Cres TW3, TW5 ... 5 C6
Spring Grove Prim Sch TW7 ... 5 D5

Spring Grove Rd
  Hounslow TW3, TW5, TW7 ... 5 C6
  Richmond TW10 ... 6 F2
Springhaven GU8 ... 148 E3
Springhaven Cl GU1 ... 110 A1
SPRINGHEAD ... 207 E5
Springhill GU8 ... 148 E3
Spring Hill SE26 ... 23 C4
Springhill Ct RG12 ... 27 B5
Spring Ho SW19 ... 39 F8
Springholm Cl
  Badshot Lea GU9 ... 126 B6
  Biggin Hill TN16 ... 83 C1
Springhurst Cl CR0 ... 62 F6
Spring La
  Croydon CR0, SE25 ... 43 B3
  Hale GU9 ... 125 A7
  Oxted RH8 ... 122 D4
  Slinfold RH13 ... 215 C3
Springlakes Est GU12 ... 105 E3
Spring La W GU9 ... 125 A6
Spring Mdw RH18 ... 206 F1
Springmead Ct
  Haslemere GU27 ... 207 D5
  Sandhurst GU47 ... 45 E1
Spring Meadow RG12 ... 27 D8
SPRING PARK ... 62 F7
Spring Park Ave CR0 ... 62 D8
Springpark Dr BR3 ... 44 C6
Spring Park Prim Sch CR0 ... 63 A7
Spring Park Rd CR0 ... 62 D8
Spring Plat RH10 ... 202 C6
Spring Plat RH10 ... 202 C6
Spring Rd TW13 ... 14 F5
Spring Rise TW20 ... 11 E2
Springside GU1 ... 109 C2
Spring St KT17 ... 57 F2
Spring Terr TW10 ... 6 E2
Springvale Cl KT23 ... 94 B1
Spring Way RH19 ... 186 A4
Springwell Cl SW16 ... 21 F4
Springwell Ct TW5 ... 4 D5
Springwell Jun & Inf Schs TW5 ... 4 E7
Springwell Rd
  Beare Green RH5 ... 157 D3
  Heston TW5 ... 4 D6
  Streatham SW16 ... 22 A3
Springwood GU8 ... 150 A1
Springwood Ct CR2 ... 61 E6
Springwood Pl KT13 ... 53 B3
Spring Woods
  Sandhurst GU47 ... 45 C1
  Virginia Water GU25 ... 31 B5
Sprint Ind Est KT14 ... 71 D8
Sproggit Ind Est TW6 ... 2 F1
Spruce Cl RH11 ... 118 F2
Sprucedale Gdns
  South Croydon CR0 ... 62 D6
  Wallington SM6 ... 60 E2
Spruce Dr GU18 ... 67 A7
Sprucefield Ct RH11 ... 201 B6
Spruce Ho [2] TW8 ... 6 C7
Spruce Pk BR2 ... 44 F5
Spruce Pl RH19 ... 186 A3
Spruce Rd TN16 ... 83 D3
Spurfield KT8 ... 36 B6
Spurgeon Ave SE19 ... 42 D8
Spurgeon Cl RH11 ... 201 C7
Spurgeon Rd SE19 ... 22 D1
Spurgeon's Coll SE25 ... 42 E1
Spur Ho [10] SW19 ... 40 B8
Spur Rd
  Brentford TW7 ... 6 B7
  Feltham TW14 ... 4 B3
Spurs Ct GU11 ... 104 E2
Spur The
  Knaphill GU21 ... 68 B1
  Walton-on-Thames KT12 ... 54 C8
Spy La RH14 ... 213 A4
Sq The GU26 ... 188 D3
Square Dr GU27 ... 208 B1
Square The
  Bagshot GU19 ... 47 E3
  Bracknell RG12 ... 27 E5
  Caterham CR3 ... 101 A3
  Crawley RH10 ... 201 D6
  Elstead GU8 ... 148 D4
  Guildford GU2 ... 129 F7
  Harmondsworth TW6 ... 2 B6
  Lightwater GU18 ... 48 C1
  Lingfield RH7 ... 164 C4
  [11] Richmond TW10 ... 6 D2
  Rowledge GU10 ... 145 E3
  Shere GU5 ... 133 A4
  Tatsfield TN16 ... 103 C7
  Wallington SM5 ... 60 A5
  Weybridge KT13 ... 53 C5
  Wisley GU23 ... 71 E3
Squarey St SW17 ... 20 C5
Squire Ct [2] CR0 ... 42 E1
Squire's Bridge Rd KT17 ... 33 F5
Squire's Bridge Rd TW17 ... 34 A5
Squires Cl RH10 ... 204 A8
Squires Ct
  Camberley GU15 ... 65 C3
  Chertsey KT16 ... 33 B1
  Wimbledon SW19 ... 20 A4
Squires Hill La GU10 ... 147 C4
Squire's Rd TW17 ... 34 A5
Squires Wlk TW15 ... 14 D1
Squirrel Cl
  Crawley RH11 ... 181 B1
  Hounslow TW4 ... 4 C4
  Sandhurst GU47 ... 64 B8
Squirrel Ct GU12 ... 105 E3

Squirrel Dr SL4 ... 9 B7
Squirrel La
  Farnborough GU14 ... 85 A5
  Windsor SL4 ... 9 B7
Squirrels Cl GU7 ... 129 D1
Squirrels Ct KT4 ... 57 F8
Squirrels Gn
  Great Bookham KT23 ... 94 A4
  [12] Redhill RH1 ... 118 F2
  Worcester Park KT4 ... 58 A8
Squirrel's Way KT18 ... 76 D4
Squirrel Wood KT14 ... 71 B7
Stable Cl
  Crawley RH10 ... 202 D3
  Kingston upon Thames KT2 ... 17 F2
  Langley Vale KT18 ... 96 E8
Stable Croft GU19 ... 47 D2
Stable Ct
  Caterham CR3 ... 101 A5
  Wallington SM6 ... 60 A7
Stable Mews
  Reigate RH2 ... 118 A1
  Twickenham TW1 ... 16 F7
  West Norwood SE27 ... 22 C3
Stables The
  Bletchingley RH1 ... 120 D4
  Cobham KT11 ... 73 F5
  Sunningdale SL5 ... 30 B1
Stace Way RH10 ... 202 E8
Stacey Ct RH1 ... 119 C6
Stacey's Farm Rd GU8 ... 148 D4
Stacey's Mdw GU8 ... 148 D4
Stackfield Rd RH11 ... 200 E5
Stack Ho RH8 ... 122 E5
Staddon Cl BR3 ... 43 E5
Stadium House Bsns Ctr [5] GU21 ... 70 B4
Staff College Rd GU15 ... 65 B6
Staffhurst Wood Nature Reserve★ RH8 ... 144 C6
Staffhurst Wood Rd TN8, RH8 ... 144 C6
Stafford Cl
  Caterham CR3 ... 100 F4
  Cheam SM3 ... 58 E4
Stafford Cross SM6 ... 60 F5
Stafford Ct CR0 ... 61 A6
Stafford Gdns CR0 ... 60 F5
Stafford Lake GU21 ... 68 A1
Stafford Pl TW10 ... 17 F8
Stafford Rd
  Caterham CR3 ... 101 A6
  Crawley RH11 ... 181 B1
  Croydon CR0 ... 61 A6
  Kingston upon Thames KT3 ... 38 B8
  Wallington CR0, SM6 ... 60 E4
Staffords Pl RH6 ... 161 B2
Stafford Sq [3] KT13 ... 53 D6
Staff Rd GU12 ... 105 C2
Stagbury Ave CR5 ... 78 E1
Stagbury Cl CR5 ... 98 E8
Stagbury Ho CR5 ... 98 E8
Stag Ct [15] SM6 ... 60 B4
Stagelands RH11 ... 201 C8
Stagelands Ct RH11 ... 201 C8
Stag Hill GU2 ... 130 A8
Stag Hill Ct GU2 ... 109 B1
Stag La SW15 ... 18 F5
Stag Leys KT18 ... 95 E7
Stag Leys Cl SM7 ... 78 E4
Stags Way TW7 ... 5 F8
Stainash Cres TW18 ... 13 B3
Stainash Par TW18 ... 13 B3
Stainbank Rd CR4 ... 41 B6
STAINES ... 12 E6
Staines Ave SM3 ... 58 D8
Staines By-Pass TW15, TW18 ... 13 C3
Staines La KT16 ... 33 A3
Staines Lane Cl KT16 ... 32 F4
Staines Prep Sch TW18 ... 13 A3
Staines Rd
  Chertsey TW18 ... 33 A5
  East Bedfont TW14 ... 14 D8
  Feltham, Hounslow TW14, TW3, TW4 ... 4 D2
  Laleham TW18 ... 33 B7
  Twickenham TW2 ... 16 C6
  Wraysbury TW19 ... 11 F7
Staines Road E TW12, TW16 ... 35 C8
Staines Road W TW15 ... 14 D1
Staines Sta TW18 ... 13 A3
Stainford Cl TW15 ... 14 D3
Stainton Rd SE13 ... 24 D8
Stainton Wlk GU21 ... 69 C1
Staiths Way KT20 ... 97 B7
Stake La GU14 ... 85 A4
Stakescorner Rd GU3 ... 130 A2
Stambourne Way
  South Norwood SE19 ... 22 F1
  West Wickham BR4 ... 63 C7
Stambourne Woodland Wlk SE19 ... 22 E1
Stamford Ave GU16 ... 65 F1
Stamford Dr BR2 ... 44 F5
Stamford Green Cty Prim Sch KT19 ... 76 B7
Stamford Green Rd KT18 ... 76 B6
Stamford Ho SW19 ... 19 C3
Stamford Rd KT12 ... 54 D7
Stammerham Bsns Ctr RH12 ... 198 E8
Stanacre Ct KT20 ... 97 F6
Stanborough Cl TW12 ... 15 F2
Stanborough Rd TW3, TW7 ... 5 D4
Stanbridge Cl RH11 ... 200 E6

Stancliffe Ho [10] SM1 ... 59 C6
Standard Rd TW4 ... 4 E4
Standen Cl RH19 ... 185 A4
Standen House★ RH19 ... 205 D4
Standen Pl RH12 ... 218 A7
Standen Rd SW18 ... 20 A8
Standinghall La RH10 ... 203 A3
Standlake Point [1] SE23 ... 23 D5
Standon La RH5 ... 176 F2
Standor Ho [8] CR4 ... 40 F6
Stane Cl SW19 ... 20 B1
Stanedge Ct SW16 ... 21 E3
Stane St
  Ockley RH5 ... 177 D4
  Slinfold RH13 ... 215 C4
Stane Way KT17 ... 58 A1
Stanford Cl TW12 ... 15 F2
Stanford Cotts GU24 ... 87 E1
Stanford Ct RH10 ... 202 C4
Stanford Orch RH12 ... 216 F8
Stanford Prim Sch SW16 ... 41 D8
Stanford Rd SW16 ... 41 E7
Stanfords Pl RH7 ... 164 D3
Stanfords The KT17 ... 76 F7
Stanford Way
  Broadbridge Heath RH12 ... 216 D3
  Mitcham SW16 ... 41 D7
Stangate Mans TW1 ... 16 F5
Stanger Rd SE25 ... 43 A5
Stangrave Hall RH9 ... 121 B3
Stan Hill RH6 ... 180 D8
Stanhope Ave BR2 ... 44 F1
Stanhope Cotts RH7 ... 164 F3
Stanhope Gate GU15 ... 65 A5
Stanhope Gr BR3 ... 43 F5
Stanhope Heath TW19 ... 2 C1
Stanhope Rd
  Camberley GU15 ... 64 F4
  South Croydon CR0 ... 61 E7
  Wallington SM5 ... 60 A3
Stanhopes RH8 ... 123 B7
Stanhope Way TW19 ... 2 C1
Stanier Cl RH10 ... 202 B5
Staniland Dr KT13 ... 52 F1
Stanley Ave
  Beckenham BR2, BR3 ... 44 C6
  West Barnes KT3 ... 39 A4
Stanley Cl
  Coulsdon CR5 ... 79 F2
  Crawley RH10 ... 201 E4
Stanley Cotts [1] GU21 ... 68 D2
Stanleycroft Cl TW7 ... 5 E6
Stanley Ct
  Belmont SM2 ... 59 B3
  Wallington SM5 ... 60 A3
  [3] Wimbledon SW19 ... 20 A2
Stanley Ctr RH10 ... 181 F2
Stanley Dr GU14 ... 84 C3
Stanley Gardens Rd TW11 ... 16 E3
Stanley Gdns
  Hersham KT12 ... 54 C4
  Mitcham CR4 ... 21 A2
  Sanderstead CR2 ... 81 A7
  Wallington SM6 ... 60 C4
Stanley Gr CR0, CR7 ... 42 A3
Stanley Hill GU24 ... 87 C5
Stanley Inf Sch TW11 ... 16 E4
Stanley Jun Sch TW11 ... 16 E4
Stanley Mans SW17 ... 20 F6
Stanley Park High Sch SM5 ... 59 F3
Stanley Park Inf Sch SM5 ... 59 F3
Stanley Park Jun Sch SM5 ... 59 F3
Stanley Park Rd SM5, SM6 ... 60 A3
Stanley Rd
  Ashford TW15 ... 13 E3
  Belmont SM2 ... 59 B3
  Hounslow TW3 ... 5 C3
  Mitcham CR4 ... 21 A1
  Morden SM4 ... 40 A5
  Mortlake SW14 ... 7 B3
  Teddington TW11 ... 16 E4
  Thornton Heath CR0, CR7 ... 42 A3
  Twickenham TW2 ... 16 D5
  Wallington SM5 ... 60 A3
  Wimbledon SW19 ... 20 A2
  Woking GU21 ... 69 F2
  Wokingham RG40 ... 25 E6
Stanley Sq SM5 ... 59 F2
Stanley St CR3 ... 100 C5
Stanley Wlk
  Bracknell RG12 ... 27 C7
  [8] Horsham RH13 ... 217 D2
Stanmore Cl SL5 ... 29 A5
Stanmore Gdns
  Richmond TW9 ... 6 F4
  Sutton SM1 ... 59 C7
Stanmore Rd TW9 ... 6 F4
Stanmore Terr BR3 ... 44 A7
Stannard Ct SE6 ... 24 B7
Stannet Way SM6 ... 60 C6
Stansfield Rd TW4, TW5 ... 4 B5
Stanstead Cl
  Hayes BR2 ... 44 F3
  Whyteleafe/Caterham CR3 ... 100 E3
Stanstead Gr SE23 ... 23 F7
Stanstead Manor SM1 ... 59 A4
Stanstead Rd
  Caterham CR3, RH1 ... 100 E3
  Forest Hill SE23, SE6 ... 23 E7
Stansted Rd TW6 ... 2 F1
Stan's Way [10] RH12 ... 217 C2
Stanthorpe Cl SW16 ... 21 E3
Stanthorpe Rd SW16 ... 21 E3
Stanton Ave TW11 ... 16 E2

Stanton Cl
Cranleigh GU6 . . . . 174 A3
North Cheam KT4 . . . . . 39 D1
West Ewell KT19 . . . . . 57 B5
Stanton Ct CR0 . . . . . . 61 E5
Stanton Rd
Barnes SW13 . . . . 7 F5
Thornton Heath CR0 . . . 42 C2
Wimbledon SW20 . . . . . 39 D8
Stanton Sq 2 SE6 . . . . 23 F4
Stantons Wharf GU5 . . 152 A2
Stanton Way SE26, SE6 . 23 F4
Stanway Pl KT16 . . . . . 32 F2
Stanway Sch RH4 . . . . 115 B2
STANWELL 13 C7
Stanwell Cl TW19 . . . . . 2 D1
Stanwell Fields CE Prim Sch
TW19 . . . . 13 E8
Stanwell Gdns TW19 . . . 2 D1
STANWELL MOOR 2 A1
Stanwell Moor Rd
Harmondsworth TW19, TW6, UB7 . . . . . 2 B4
Stanwell TW19 . . . . 2 B4
Stanwell New Rd TW18, TW19 . . . . . 13 B5
STANWELL PLACE 2 C1
Stanwell Rd
Ashford TW15 . . . . 13 E4
East Bedfont TW14, TW19, TW6 . . . . . 14 B8
Horton SL3, TW19 . . . . . 1 C4
Stanworth Cl TW5 . . . . . 5 A7
Stanyhurst SE23 . . . . . 23 E7
Staplecross Ct 1 RH11 . 201 A3
Staplefield Cl 3 SW2 . . . 21 E7
Stapleford Cl
Kingston upon Thames KT1 . . . . . 38 A6
Putney SW19 . . . . 19 E8
Staple Hill GU24, KT16 . . 49 E6
Staplehurst RG12 . . . . . 26 E2
Staplehurst Cl RH2 . . . 139 C5
Staplehurst Rd
Reigate RH2 . . . . 139 C5
Sutton SM5 . . . . 59 E3
Staple La
East Clandon GU4, GU5 . 111 E2
Shere GU4 . . . . 132 F8
Stapleton Gdns CR0 . . . 61 A5
Stapleton Rd SW17 . . . . 21 A5
Star and Garter Hill TW10 . 17 E8
Starborough Cotts RH7 . 185 F1
Starborough Rd TN8 . . . 165 E5
Star Cl RH13 . . . . 218 A4
Star Hill GU10 . . . . . . 167 D2
Star Hill Dr GU10 . . . . 167 D2
Starhurst Sch RH5 . . . . 136 C5
Star La
Ash GU12 . . . . 105 F2
Hooley CR5 . . . . 99 A6
Woking GU22 . . . . 89 C8
Starling Cl CR0 . . . . . . 43 E3
Starling Roost RG12 . . . 26 D5
Starling Wlk TW12 . . . . 15 E3
Starmead Dr RG40 . . . . 25 E5
Star Post Rd GU15 . . . . 65 F8
Star Rd TW7 . . . . 5 D5
Starrett Ct KT12 . . . . . 54 C8
Starrock La CR5 . . . . . 99 A7
Starrock Rd CR5 . . . . . 99 C8
Starwood Cl KT14 . . . . 71 C6
Staten Gdns TW1 . . . . . 16 F7
Statham Ct RG42 . . . . . 26 E8
Station App
Ashford TW15 . . . . 13 F4
Ash Vale GU12 . . . . . . 106 A7
Beckenham, Lower Sydenham SE6 . . . . . 23 F3
Belmont SM2 . . . . 59 B1
Blackwater GU17 . . . . . 64 E4
Cheam SM2 . . . . 58 E3
Chipstead CR5 . . . . . . 78 F1
Coulsdon CR5 . . . . 79 D4
3 Croydon CR0 . . . . . . 61 D8
Dorking RH4 . . . . 115 C1
East Horsley KT24 . . . . 92 E1
Epsom KT17, KT19 . . . . 76 D6
Ewell KT17 . . . . 58 B1
Faygate RH12 . . . . . . 199 F1
Godalming GU7 . . . . . . 150 D4
Guildford GU1 . . . . . . 130 E8
Hampton TW12 . . . . . . 36 A8
Haslemere GU27 . . . . . 208 B6
Hinchley Wood KT10 . . . 55 F7
Horley RH6 . . . . 161 B2
4 Kingston upon Thames KT1, KT2 . . . . . 38 A8
Leatherhead KT22 . . . . 95 A6
6 New Malden KT4 . . . . 39 A1
Ockley RH5 . . . . 178 B5
Oxted RH8 . . . . 122 E6
Purley CR8 . . . . 80 A8
Richmond TW9 . . . . 7 A6
Shalford GU4 . . . . . . 130 E3
Shepperton TW17 . . . . . 34 C4
South Croydon CR2 . . . . 61 D2
Staines TW18 . . . . 13 A3
Streatham SW16 . . . . . 21 D3
Sunbury TW16 . . . . . . 35 A8
1 Surbiton KT6 . . . . . . 37 E3
Tadworth KT20 . . . . . . 97 C5
Virginia Water GU25 . . . 31 D5
West Byfleet KT14 . . . . 71 A7
Weybridge KT13 . . . . . . 53 A4
Whyteleafe CR3 . . . . . . 81 A1
Woking GU22 . . . . 69 F2
Worcester Park KT19 . . . 58 A5

Station Approach E RH1 . 139 F7
Station Approach Rd
Chiswick W4 . . . . 7 C7
Coulsdon CR5 . . . . 79 D4
Crawley RH6 . . . . 182 B7
Station Approach W RH1 . 139 F7
Station Ave
Caterham CR3 . . . . . . 101 A3
Kingston upon Thames KT3 . 38 E6
14 Richmond TW9 . . . . . 7 A6
Walton-on-Thames KT12 . 54 A6
West Ewell KT19 . . . . . 57 E2
Station Bldgs
Catford SE6 . . . . 24 A8
Merton SW20 . . . . 39 C7
Station Cl
Hampton TW12 . . . . . . 36 B8
Horsham RH13 . . . . . . 217 D2
Station Cotts CR8 . . . . 80 C5
Station Cres TW15 . . . . 13 E4
Station Ct CR4 . . . . . . 40 E5
Station Est BR3 . . . . . . 43 D5
Station Estate Rd TW14 . 15 B7
Station Gdns W4 . . . . . . 7 C7
Station Hill
Ascot SL5 . . . . 29 A5
Crawley RH10 . . . . . . 202 B7
Farnham GU9 . . . . 125 C2
Station Ind Est RG40 . . . 25 B6
Station La
Enton Green GU8 . . . . 171 A7
Wormley GU8 . . . . 170 F1
Station Par
2 Ashford TW15 . . . . . 13 F4
East Horsley KT24 . . . . 92 E1
Feltham TW14 . . . . . . 15 B8
Richmond TW9 . . . . 7 A6
South Croydon CR2 . . . . 61 D2
Sunningdale SL5 . . . . . 30 A2
6 Sutton SM2 . . . . 59 C4
4 Upper Tooting SW17 . . 21 A7
Virginia Water GU25 . . . 31 E4
Station Path TW18 . . . . 12 F4
Station Rd
Addlestone KT15 . . . . . 52 D6
Aldershot GU11 . . . . . 105 B2
Ashford TW15 . . . . 13 F4
Bagshot GU19 . . . . 47 E4
Barnes SW13 . . . . 7 F5
Beckenham BR2 . . . . . . 44 E7
Belmont SM2 . . . . 59 A1
Betchworth RH3 . . . . . 116 B3
Bracknell RG12 . . . . . . 27 B7
Bramley GU5 . . . . 152 A7
Carshalton SM5 . . . . . . 59 F6
Chertsey KT16 . . . . 33 A1
Chessington KT9 . . . . . 56 E5
Chobham GU24 . . . . . . 69 B6
Claygate KT10 . . . . . . 55 E5
Cranleigh RH11 . . . . . 195 C3
Crawley Down RH10 . . . 204 B8
Crawley RH10, RH11 . . . 201 D5
Croydon CR0 . . . . 42 C1
Dorking RH4 . . . . 136 A8
East Grinstead RH19 . . . 185 D1
Egham TW20 . . . . 12 A3
Farnborough GU14 . . . . 85 B4
Farncombe GU7 . . . . . 150 F7
Forest Row RH18 . . . . . 206 F3
Godalming GU7 . . . . . . 150 D4
Gomshall GU5 . . . . . . 133 D4
Hampton TW12 . . . . . . 36 B8
Horley RH6 . . . . 161 B3
Horsham RH13 . . . . . . 217 D2
Hounslow TW3 . . . . 5 B3
Hydestile GU8 . . . . . . 171 D6
Kenley CR8 . . . . 80 C5
Kingston upon Thames KT2 . 38 A8
Leatherhead KT22 . . . . 95 A6
Lingfield RH7 . . . . . . 164 E4
Loxwood RH14 . . . . . . 213 A3
Merstham RH1 . . . . . . 119 C7
Merton SW19 . . . . 40 C8
Oxted RH8 . . . . 122 E7
Penge SE20 . . . . 23 C2
Redhill RH1 . . . . 118 F2
Rudgwick RH12 . . . . . . 214 D7
Shalford GU4 . . . . . . 130 E3
Shepperton TW17 . . . . . 34 C4
South Godstone RH9 . . . 142 E5
South Norwood SE25 . . . 42 F5
Stoke D'Abernon KT11 . . 73 E3
Sunbury TW16 . . . . . . 15 A1
Sunningdale SL5 . . . . . 30 A4
Teddington, Hampton Wick KT1 . . . . . 37 D8
Teddington TW11 . . . . . 17 A2
Thames Ditton KT10 . . . 55 D8
Thames Ditton, Weston Green KT7 . . . . . 36 F2
Twickenham TW1 . . . . . 16 F8
Warnham RH12 . . . . . . 217 B8
West Barnes KT3 . . . . . 39 B4
West Byfleet KT14 . . . . 71 A7
West Wickham BR4 . . . . 44 C1
Whyteleafe CR3 . . . . . . 80 F1
Wokingham RG40 . . . . . 25 B6
Woldingham CR3 . . . . . 101 F5
Wraysbury TW19 . . . . . . 1 A1
Station Rd E
Ash Vale GU12 . . . . . . 106 A7
Oxted RH8 . . . . 122 E6
Station Rd N
5 Egham TW20 . . . . . . 11 F3
Merstham RH1 . . . . . . 119 C7
Station Rd S RH1 . . . . 119 C7

Station Rd W
Ash Vale GU12 . . . . . . 105 F8
Oxted RH8 . . . . 122 E6
Station Rise SE27 . . . . 22 B6
Station Row GU4 . . . . . 130 E3
Station Terr RH4 . . . . . 136 A8
Station View
Ash Vale GU12 . . . . . . 106 A8
Guildford GU1 . . . . . . 130 C8
Station Way
Bracknell RG12 . . . . . . 27 C7
Cheam SM2, SM3 . . . . . 58 E3
Claygate KT10 . . . . . . 55 E4
Crawley RH10, RH11 . . . 201 D5
11 Epsom KT19 . . . . . . 76 D6
Station Yd TW1 . . . . . . 17 A8
Staunton Rd KT2 . . . . . 17 F1
Staveley Gdns W4 . . . . . 7 D6
Staveley Rd
Ashford TW15 . . . . 14 D2
Chiswick W4 . . . . 7 D7
Staveley Way GU21 . . . . 68 E2
Staverton Cl RG40 . . . . 25 F6
Stavordale Rd SM4, SM5 . 40 C2
Stayne End GU25 . . . . . 31 A5
Stayton Rd SM1 . . . . . . 59 A7
Steadfast Rd KT1 . . . . . 37 D8
Steam Farm La TW14 . . . 3 F3
Steele Rd TW7 . . . . 6 A3
Steele's Rd GU11 . . . . . 105 B4
Steel's La KT11, KT22 . . 74 C5
Steep Hill
Chobham GU24 . . . . . . 49 C3
South Croydon CR0 . . . . 61 E6
Streatham SW16 . . . . . 21 D5
Steeple Cl SW19 . . . . . 19 E4
Steeple Ct
17 Egham TW20 . . . . . 12 A3
Wimbledon SW19 . . . . . 19 E3
Steeple Gdns SW15 . . . . 52 B5
Steeple Heights Dr TN16 . 83 D2
Steeple Point SL5 . . . . 29 B6
Steepways GU26 . . . . . 188 B6
Steeres Hill RH12 . . . . 199 C6
Steerforth Copse GU47 . . 45 E2
Steerforth St SW18 . . . 20 C6
Steers La CR4 . . . . 40 F8
Steers Mead CR4 . . . . . 40 F8
Steetley Ct 19 SM2 . . . . 59 C3
Steinman Ct TW7 . . . . . . 5 F4
Stella Rd SW17 . . . . . . 20 F2
Stembridge Rd SE20 . . . 43 B7
Stenning Ct KT22 . . . . . 95 B5
Stennings The RH19 . . . 185 C3
Stepgates KT16 . . . . . . 33 B2
Stepgates Cl KT16 . . . . 33 B2
Stepgates Com Sch KT16 . 33 B2
Stephanie Chase Ct RG40 . 25 D7
Stephen Cl TW20 . . . . . 12 C2
Stephen Ct 18 SW19 . . . 19 D7
Stephendale Rd GU9 . . . 125 D4
Stephen Gould Ho GU14 . 105 B8
Stephens Field GU8 . . . 191 A4
Stephenson Ct
Belmont SM2 . . . . 58 F3
Farnham GU9 . . . . 146 A8
Stephenson Dr RH19 . . . 205 F7
Stephenson Pl
Crawley RH10 . . . . . . 202 B6
Merstham RH1 . . . . . . 119 C7
Stephenson Rd
Guildford GU2 . . . . . . 108 D1
Twickenham TW2 . . . . . 16 A8
Stephenson Way RH10 . . 202 B6
Stepney Cl RH10 . . . . . 202 C4
Stepney Way CR4 . . . . . 41 A8
Stepping Stone Sch The GU26 . 188 F4
Sterling Bldgs 6 RH12 . 217 C2
Sterling Ctr The RG12 . . 27 D6
Sterling Pk RH10 . . . . 182 B3
Sterling Pl KT13 . . . . . 53 E6
Sternhold Ave SW12, SW2 . 21 D6
Sterry Dr
Thames Ditton KT7 . . . . 36 E3
Worcester Park KT19 . . . 57 E6
Steucers La SE23 . . . . . 23 E7
Steve Biko La SE6 . . . . 24 A4
Steve Biko Way TW3 . . . . 5 A4
Stevenage Rd RH11 . . . 200 E3
Stevens Cl
Beckenham BR3 . . . . . . 24 A2
Epsom KT17 . . . . 76 E6
Hampton TW12 . . . . . . 15 F2
Stevens Ct BR3 . . . . . . 24 A2
Stevens Ho KT1 . . . . . . 37 D7
Stevens' La KT10 . . . . . 56 A4
Stevens Pl CR8 . . . . . . 80 B6
Stewards Rise GU10 . . . 145 F7
Stewart KT20 . . . . 97 D6
Stewart Ave TW17 . . . . 34 A5
Stewart Cl
Hampton TW12 . . . . . . 15 E2
Woking KT21 . . . . 70 E6
Stewart Fleming Prim Sch SE20 . 43 C6
Steyning Cl
Crawley RH10 . . . . . . 201 E8
Purley CR8 . . . . 80 B3
Steyning Way TW4 . . . . . 4 C3
Sthrathbrook Rd SW16 . . 21 F1
Stickle Down GU16 . . . . 86 D8
Stildon Mews RH19 . . . 185 C3
Stile Gdns GU27 . . . . . 207 F6
Stile Ho GU4 . . . . 110 D2
Stile Path TW16 . . . . . 35 A6
Stillers GU8 . . . . 191 B4

Stirling Ave
Upper Halliford TW17 . . 34 E6
Wallington SM6 . . . . . . 60 E3
Stirling Cl
1 Ash Vale GU12 . . . . . 105 F5
Banstead SM7 . . . . . . 77 F2
Crawley RH10 . . . . . . 202 C5
Farnborough GU14 . . . . 85 A3
Frimley GU16 . . . . 65 F2
Mitcham SW16 . . . . . . 41 C8
Stirling Dr CR3 . . . . . 100 C6
Stirling Gr TW3 . . . . . . 5 C5
Stirling Ho 15 RH1 . . . 118 F1
Stirling Rd
Guildford GU2 . . . . . . 108 E1
Stanwell TW6 . . . . 2 F1
Twickenham TW2 . . . . . 16 B8
Stirling Way
East Grinstead RH19 . . . 186 B3
Farnborough GU11 . . . . 104 F3
Horsham RH13 . . . . . . 217 A3
Thornton Heath CR0 . . . 41 E2
Stirrup Way RH10 . . . . 202 D7
Stites Hill Rd CR3, CR5 . 100 F7
Stoatley Ho 10 SW15 . . . 19 A7
Stoatley Hollow GU27 . . 208 A8
Stoatley Rise GU27 . . . 208 A8
Stoats Nest Rd CR5 . . . 79 E5
Stoats Nest Village CR5 . 79 E4
Stockbridge Dr GU11 . . 126 C6
Stockbury Rd CR0 . . . . . 43 C3
Stockfield RH6 . . . . . . 161 B4
Stockfield Rd
Claygate KT10 . . . . . . 55 E5
Streatham SW16 . . . . . 21 F5
Stockhams Cl CR2 . . . . 61 D1
Stockhill Cl GU15 . . . . 65 F5
Stocklund Sq SW16 . . . . 41 D8
Stocklund Sq GU6 . . . . 174 D3
Stocklund Sq Maisonettes GU6 . 174 D3
Stockport Rd SW16 . . . . 41 D8
Stocks Cl RH6 . . . . . . 161 B2
Stockton Ho RH2 . . . . . 139 A6
Stockton Rd RH2 . . . . . 139 A6
Stockwell Ctr RH10 . . . 202 A6
Stockwell Rd RH19 . . . 205 E6
Stockwood Rise GU15 . . 65 F5
Stockwood Way GU9 . . . 125 F7
Stocton Cl GU1 . . . . . . 109 C2
Stocton Rd GU1 . . . . . . 109 D2
Stodart Rd SE20 . . . . . 43 C8
Stoford Cl SW19 . . . . . 19 E8
Stoke Cl KT11 . . . . 73 F3
Stoke Ct SE22 . . . . 23 A7
STOKE D'ABERNON . . . 73 F3
Stoke Fields 8 GU1 . . . 109 D1
Stokeford Cl 5 RG12 . . . 27 F4
Stoke Gr GU1 . . . . 109 D1
Stoke Hills GU1 . . . . . 109 D1
Stoke Hosp (Almshouses) 6 GU1 . 109 D1
Stoke Mews GU1 . . . . . 130 D8
Stoke Mill Cl GU1 . . . . 109 D3
Stoke Park Ct 5 GU1 . . . 109 D1
Stoke Rd
Guildford GU1 . . . . . . 109 D1
Kingston upon Thames KT2 . 18 C1
Stoke D'Abernon KT11 . . 73 E3
Walton-on-Thames KT12 . 54 C7
Stoke Rd Cotts KT22 . . . 94 D6
Stokers Cl RH6 . . . . . . 181 E7
Stokesby Rd KT9 . . . . . 56 F4
Stokesheath Rd KT22 . . . 74 C8
Stokes Rd CR0 . . . . 43 D3
Stokes Rd CR0 . . . . 97 D4
Stompond La KT12 . . . . 54 A8
Stoms Path SE6 . . . . . . 24 A3
Stonards Brow GU5 . . . 152 D4
Stondon Pk SE23 . . . . . 23 E8
Stonebanks KT12 . . . . . 35 A2
STONEBRIDGE 136 D4
Stonebridge Ct
Crawley RH11 . . . . . . 201 C2
Horsham RH12 . . . . . . 217 A2
Stonebridge Fields GU4 . 130 D2
Stonebridge Mews SE19 . 22 D1
Stonebridge Wharf GU4 . 130 D2
Stonecot Cl SM3, SM4 . . 39 E1
Stonecot Hill SM4 . . . . 39 E1
Stone Cotts RH10 . . . . 203 B1
Stonecourt Cl RH6 . . . . 161 C3
Stone Cres TW14 . . . . . 14 F8
Stonecroft Way CR0 . . . 41 E2
Stonecrop Cl RH11 . . . . 201 B3
Stonecrop Rd GU4 . . . . 110 C3
Stone Ct RH10 . . . . . . 202 D5
Stonedene GU35 . . . . . 187 B4
Stonefield Cl RH10, RH11 201 D5
Stonegate GU15 . . . . . . 66 C6
Stone Hatch GU6 . . . . . 194 A3
Stonehaven BR3 . . . . . . 44 B7
Stonehill Cl
Little Bookham KT23 . . . 94 A2
Mortlake SW14 . . . . 7 D2
Stonehill Cres KT16 . . . 50 E4
Stonehill Pk GU35 . . . . 187 C4
Stonehill Rd
Chobham GU24, KT16 . . . 50 D3
Headley Down GU35 . . . 187 C4
Lightwater GU18 . . . . . 48 A1
Mortlake SW14 . . . . 7 D2
Stonehills Ct SE21 . . . . 22 E5
Stonehill's Mans 3 SW16 . 21 E6
Stone House Gdns CR3 . . 100 E2
Stonehouse Rise GU16 . . 65 E1

STONELEIGH 58 A5
Stoneleigh Ave KT17, KT4 . 58 A7
Stoneleigh Broadway KT17 . 58 A5
Stoneleigh Cl RH19 . . . 185 F1
Stoneleigh Cres KT19 . . 57 F5
Stoneleigh Ct
5 Croydon CR0 . . . . . . 61 C4
Frimley GU16 . . . . 65 F1
Kingston upon Thames KT3 . 38 D6
Stoneleigh Lodge 13 TW9 . 6 F6
Stoneleigh Park Ave CR0 . 43 D3
Stoneleigh Park Rd KT19, KT4 . 58 A5
Stoneleigh Pk
Weybridge KT13 . . . . . . 53 C4
Worcester Park KT19 . . . 57 F4
Stoneleigh Rd
Carshalton SM5 . . . . . . 40 E2
The Chart RH8 . . . . . . 123 E5
Stoneleigh Sta KT19 . . . 58 A5
Stone Park Ave BR3 . . . . 44 B5
Stonepit Cl GU7 . . . . . 150 C4
Stone Pl KT4 . . . . 58 A4
STONEQUARRY 186 A3
Stone Rd BR2 . . . . 44 F4
Stones La RH4 . . . . . . 135 C6
Stone's Rd KT17 . . . . . 76 E7
Stone St GU12 . . . . . . 126 D8
Stoneswood Rd RH8 . . . 123 B5
Stoneworth Ct SE25 . . . 43 A3
Stoney Bottom GU26 . . . 188 C3
Stoneybrook RH12 . . . . 216 F1
Stoney Brook GU2 . . . . 108 E2
Stoneycroft GU11 . . . . 104 F1
Stoneycroft Cl SE12 . . . 24 F8
Stoneycroft Wlk 3 RH11 . 200 D5
Stoney Deep TW11 . . . . 17 A4
Stoneyfield Rd CR5 . . . 79 F2
Stoneyfields GU9 . . . . 125 E1
Stoney La SE19 . . . . . . 22 F2
Stoneyland Ct 6 TW20 . . 11 F3
Stoneylands Rd TW20 . . 11 F3
Stoney Rd RG42 . . . . . . 27 A8
Stonny Croft KT21 . . . . 75 F2
Stony Hill KT10 . . . . . 54 F3
Stoop Ct KT14 . . . . 71 B7
Stopham Rd RH10 . . . . 202 C3
Storer Ho KT19 . . . . . . 57 B1
Stormont Way KT9 . . . . 56 C5
Storrington Ct RH11 . . . 201 A7
Storrington Rd CR0 . . . 42 F1
Storr's La GU3 . . . . . . 88 C3
STOUGHTON 109 A4
Stoughton Ave SM3 . . . . 58 A5
Stoughton Cl SW15 . . . . 19 A7
Stoughton Inf Sch GU2 . 109 B4
Stoughton Rd GU1, GU2 . 109 B3
Stourhead Cl
Farnborough GU14 . . . . 85 D4
6 Putney SW19 . . . . . . 19 D8
Stourhead Gdns SW20 . . 39 A6
Stourton Ave TW13 . . . . 15 F4
Stovolds Hill GU6, GU8 . 193 D7
Stovold's Way GU11 . . . 125 F8
Stowell Ave CR0 . . . . . 63 D2
Stowford Coll 23 SM2 . . 59 C3
Strachan Pl SW19 . . . . 19 C2
Strachey Ct 1 RH11 . . . 201 B1
Strafford Rd
Hounslow TW3 . . . . 4 F4
Twickenham TW1 . . . . . 17 A8
Straight Rd SL4 . . . . . 11 C8
Strand Cl
Crawley RH10 . . . . . . 202 D4
Langley Vale KT18 . . . . 96 D3
Strand Dr TW9 . . . . 7 B7
STRAND ON THE GREEN . 7 A8
Strand on the Green W4 . 7 A8
Strand on the Green Inf Sch W4 . 7 A8
Strand on the Green Jun Sch W4 . 7 A8
Stranraer Way 1 TW6 . . . 2 E1
Stratfield RG12 . . . . . 26 E1
Stratfield Ho 12 GU11 . 105 A2
Stratford Ct
Farnborough GU14 . . . . 85 C4
Farnham GU9 . . . . 125 C1
New Malden KT3 . . . . . 38 D5
Woking GU21 . . . . 69 F3
Stratford Rd
Ash Vale GU12 . . . . . . 85 F1
Harlington TW6 . . . . 3 C2
Thornton Heath CR7 . . . 42 B6
Strathavon Cl GU6 . . . . 174 B7
Strathcona Ave KT24 . . 113 E7
Strathcona Gdns
Knaphill GU21 . . . . . . 68 C3
Knaphill GU21 . . . . . . 88 C8
Strathdale SW16 . . . . . 21 F3
Strathdon Dr SW17 . . . . 20 D5
Strathearn Ave
Harlington UB3 . . . . 3 F7
Twickenham TW2 . . . . . 16 C7
Strathearn Rd
Sutton SM1 . . . . 59 A5
Wimbledon SW19 . . . . . 20 A4
Strathmore Cl CR3 . . . . 100 E6
Strathmore Ct 3 GU15 . . 65 D5
Strathmore Rd
Crawley RH11 . . . . . . 181 A1
Teddington TW11 . . . . . 16 E4

Strathmore Rd *continued*
Thornton Heath CR0 . . . . . . 42 D2
Wimbledon SW19 . . . . 20 A5
Strathmore Sch TW10 . . . . 17 D6
Strathville Rd SW18 . . . . . 20 B6
Strathyre Ave CR7, SW16 . . 42 A6
Stratton Ave SM6 . . . . 60 D2
Stratton Cl
Heston TW5 . . . . 5 A6
Merton SW19 . . . . 40 A7
Walton-on-Thames KT12 . . . 35 C1
Stratton Ct
Guildford GU2 . . . . 109 A3
10 Kingston upon Thames KT6 . . . . 37 E4
Stratton Rd
Merton SW19 . . . . 40 A7
Sunbury TW16 . . . . 34 F7
Stratton Wlk GU14 . . . . 85 A7
Strawberry Cl GU24 . . . . . . 87 D7
Strawberry Ct GU16 . . . . . . 86 D8
Strawberry Fields GU24 . . 68 A4
STRAWBERRY HILL 16 F5
Strawberry Hill Cl TW1 . . . 16 F5
Strawberry Hill Rd TW1 . . 16 F5
Strawberry Hill Sta TW2 . . 16 F5
Strawberry La SM5 . . . . . . 60 A7
Strawberry Rise GU24 . . . . 68 A4
Strawberry Vale TW1 . . . . 17 A5
Straw Cl CR3 . . . . 100 C4
Strawson Ct RH6 . . . . 160 F4
Stream Banks GU3 . . . . 108 B2
Stream Cl KT14 . . . . 71 E7
Stream Farm Cl GU10 . . . 146 D7
Streamline Ct SE22 . . . . . . 23 A7
Streamline Mews SE22 . . . 23 A7
Stream Pk RH19 . . . . 185 A3
Stream Valley Rd GU10 . . 146 C6
STREATHAM 21 E2
Streatham Cl SW16 . . . . . . 21 E6
Streatham & Clapham High Sch SW2 . . . . 21 F7
Streatham & Clapham High Sch (Senior Sch) SW16 . 21 D5
Streatham Comm N SW16 21 F3
Streatham Common Sta SW16 . . . . 21 D1
Streatham Comm S SW16 21 F2
Streatham Ct SW16 . . . . . . 21 E5
Streatham High Rd SW16, SW2 . . . . 21 E3
STREATHAM HILL 21 E7
Streatham Hill SW2 . . . . . . 21 E7
Streatham Hill Sta SW2 . . 21 E6
Streatham L Ctr & Ice Arena SW16 . . . . 21 D3
STREATHAM PARK 21 C4
Streatham Pl SW2 . . . . 21 E8
Streatham Rd CR4 . . . . 41 A8
Streatham Sta SW16 . . . . . 21 D3
STREATHAM VALE 21 D1
Streatham Vale SW16 . . . . 21 D1
Streatham Wells Prim Sch SW2 . . . . 22 A6
Streathbourne Rd SW17 . . 21 A5
Streatleigh Par 4 SW16 . . 21 E6
Streeters Cl GU7 . . . . 151 A6
Streeters La SM6 . . . . 60 D7
Streetfield GU8 . . . . 169 C4
Streetfield Rd RH13 . . . . . 215 E3
Street Hill RH10 . . . . 202 E5
Streets Heath GU24 . . . . . . 67 F7
Street The
Albury GU5 . . . . 132 C4
Ashtead KT21 . . . . 75 F1
Betchworth RH3 . . . . 116 E1
Capel RH5 . . . . 178 D6
Charlwood RH6 . . . . 180 E7
Compton GU3 . . . . 129 B2
Dockenfield GU10 . . . . 166 E6
East Clandon GU4 . . . . 111 E4
Effingham KT24 . . . . 113 D8
Ewhurst GU6 . . . . 175 E5
Fetcham KT22 . . . . 94 D5
Frensham GU10 . . . . 167 C7
Godalming GU8 . . . . 172 D5
Plaistow RH14 . . . . 211 E2
Puttenham GU3 . . . . 128 C4
Shackleford GU8 . . . . 149 C8
Shalford GU4 . . . . 130 E3
Slinfold RH13 . . . . 215 D4
Thursley GU8 . . . . 169 C4
Tongham GU10 . . . . 126 F6
West Clandon GU4 . . . . 111 B5
West Horsley KT24 . . . . 112 B7
Wonersh GU5 . . . . 152 A7
Wrecclesham GU10 . . . . . . 145 F6
Stretford Ct 1 SW19 . . . . . 19 E1
Stretton Ct KT13 . . . . 52 F6
Stretton Rd
Croydon CR0 . . . . 42 E2
Richmond TW10 . . . . 17 C6
Strickland Cl 4 RH11 . . . . 200 E5
Strickland Row SW18 . . . . 20 D8
Strides Ct KT16 . . . . 51 C4
Stringer's Ave GU4 . . . . . . 109 D7
Stringhams Copse GU23 . . 91 A3
Strode Ho 3 SW2 . . . . 22 A7
Strode's Coll TW20 . . . . 11 F3
Strodes College La TW20 . 11 F3
Strode's Cres TW18 . . . . . . 13 C3
Strode St TW20 . . . . 12 A4
Stronsay Cl GU26 . . . . 188 E5
STROOD GREEN
Dorking 137 C6
STROOD GREEN *continued*
Horsham 216 A6
Strood Ho 11 SE20 . . . . 23 C1
Strood La
Cranbourne SL4, SL5 . . . . 9 C2
Warnham RH12 . . . . 216 C7
Stroud Cres SW15 . . . . 19 A5
STROUDE 31 F7
Stroude Rd
Egham TW20 . . . . 12 A1
Virginia Water GU25, TW20 . 31 E6
Stroudes Cl KT4 . . . . 38 F2
Stroud Green Gdns CR0 . . 43 C2
Stroud Green Way CR0 . . . 43 C3
Stroud La
Shamley Green GU5 . . . . . . 153 A3
Yateley GU17 . . . . 64 A4
Stroudley Cl RH10 . . . . . . 202 B5
Stroud Rd
Croydon SE25 . . . . 43 A3
Wimbledon SW19 . . . . 20 A5
Stroudwater Pk KT13 . . . . . 53 C4
Stroud Way TW15 . . . . 14 B2
Struan Gdns GU21 . . . . 69 E4
Strudgate Cl RH10 . . . . . . 202 B4
Strudwicks Field GU6 . . . 174 F4
Stuart Ave KT12 . . . . 35 C1
Stuart Cl
Crawley RH10 . . . . 202 D5
Farnborough GU14 . . . . 85 A5
Stuart Cres
Croydon CR0 . . . . 62 F7
Reigate RH2 . . . . 139 A6
Stuart Ct
4 Croydon CR0 . . . . 61 B7
Godalming GU7 . . . . 150 E4
16 Redhill RH1 . . . . 119 A2
Stuart Gr TW11 . . . . 16 E3
Stuart Ho
Bracknell RG42 . . . . 26 F8
5 Horsham RH13 . . . . 217 F3
Stuart Lodge
7 Epsom KT18 . . . . 76 D6
South Norwood SE25 . . . . . . 42 E7
Stuart Pl CR4 . . . . 40 F8
Stuart Rd
Reigate RH2 . . . . 139 A6
Richmond TW10 . . . . 17 B5
South Norwood CR7 . . . . . . 42 C5
Warlingham CR3, CR6 . . . . 101 C7
Wimbledon SW19 . . . . 20 A5
Stuart Way
East Grinstead RH19 . . . . . 205 F7
Staines TW18 . . . . 13 B2
Virginia Water GU25 . . . . . . 31 A5
Stubbs Folly GU47 . . . . 64 D7
Stubbs Ho SE19 . . . . 22 D1
Stubbs La KT20 . . . . 118 A7
Stubbs Moor Rd GU14 . . . . 84 F5
Stubbs Way 9 SW19 . . . . . . 40 D8
Stubfield RH12 . . . . 217 A3
Stubpond La RH7 . . . . 184 C8
Stubs Cl RH4 . . . . 136 C5
Stubs Hill RH4 . . . . 136 C4
Stubs Ind Site GU11 . . . . . 105 E5
Stucley Rd TW5, TW7 . . . . . . 5 C7
Studios Rd TW17 . . . . 33 F6
Studland Rd
Byfleet KT14 . . . . 71 F6
Kingston upon Thames KT2 . 17 E2
Penge SE26 . . . . 23 D3
Study Prep Sch The
London SW19 . . . . 19 D3
Wimbledon SW19 . . . . 19 C3
Study Sch The KT3 . . . . 38 E4
Stumblets RH10 . . . . 202 C7
Stumps Hill La BR3 . . . . . . 24 A2
Sturdee Cl GU16 . . . . 65 E1
Sturges Ct RG40 . . . . 25 D5
Sturges Rd RG40 . . . . 25 D5
Sturt Ave GU27 . . . . 207 F5
Sturt Ct GU4 . . . . 110 B3
Sturt Rd
Frimley GU16 . . . . 85 F5
Haslemere GU27 . . . . 207 F5
Heath End GU9 . . . . 125 B7
Sturt's La KT20 . . . . 117 A8
Stychens Cl RH1 . . . . 120 C2
Stychens La RH1 . . . . 120 C2
Styles End KT23 . . . . 114 B8
Styles Way BR3 . . . . 44 C5
Styventon Pl KT16 . . . . 32 F2
Subrosa Dr RH1 . . . . 119 B5
Succomb's Hill CR3, CR6 . 101 B7
Succombs Pl CR6 . . . . 101 B8
Sudbrook Gdns TW10 . . . . 17 E5
Sudbrook La TW10 . . . . 17 E6
Sudbury Gdns CR0 . . . . 61 E6
Sudell Ho KT6 . . . . 37 E2
Suffah Prim Sch TW4 . . . . . . 4 F3
Suffield Cl CR2 . . . . 81 D7
Suffield La GU3 . . . . 128 B2
Suffield Rd SE20 . . . . 43 C7
Suffolk Cl
Bagshot GU19 . . . . 47 E2
Horley RH6 . . . . 161 A2
Suffolk Ct
Frimley GU16 . . . . 86 D8
3 West Norwood SW16 . . . 22 A4
Suffolk Dr GU4 . . . . 110 B6
Suffolk Ho
12 Bromley BR2 . . . . 44 F5
4 Croydon CR0 . . . . 61 D8
Penge SE20 . . . . 43 C8
Suffolk Rd
Barnes SW13 . . . . 7 F7
South Norwood SE25 . . . . . . 42 F5
Worcester Park KT4 . . . . . . 57 F8
Sugden Rd KT7 . . . . 37 B1
Sulina Rd SW2 . . . . 21 E8
Sullington Hill RH11 . . . . 201 D4
Sullington Mead RH12 . . . 216 E3
Sullivan Cl GU14 . . . . 85 A4
Sullivan Ct 4 CR0 . . . . 43 A1
Sullivan Dr RH11 . . . . 200 E3
Sullivan Ho
Kenley CR8 . . . . 80 C5
Twickenham TW2 . . . . 5 D1
Sullivan Rd GU15 . . . . 65 A5
Sullivans Reach KT12 . . . . . 35 A2
Sultan St BR3 . . . . 43 D7
Sulzers Rdbt GU14 . . . . 85 B3
Summer Ave KT8 . . . . 36 E4
Summer Cl KT14 . . . . 71 F5
Summer Crossing KT7 . . . . 36 F4
Summerene Cl 3 SW16 . . . 21 C1
Summerfield KT21 . . . . 95 D8
Summerfield La
Long Ditton KT6 . . . . 56 D8
Rowledge GU10 . . . . 146 B2
Summerfield Pl KT16 . . . . . 51 D4
Summerfields Cl KT15 . . . . 51 F5
Summerfield St SE12 . . . . . 24 F8
Summerfold RH12 . . . . 214 E8
Summer Gdns
Frimley GU15 . . . . 66 C5
Thames Ditton KT8 . . . . 36 E4
Summerhayes Cl GU21 . . . . 69 E5
Summerhays KT11 . . . . 73 D6
Summerhill GU7 . . . . 150 D6
Summerhill Way CR4 . . . . . . 41 A8
Summer Ho RH11 . . . . 201 C5
Summerhouse Ave TW5 . . . . 4 E6
Summerhouse Cl GU7 . . . 150 D4
Summerhouse Ct GU26 . . 188 D3
Summerhouse La UB7 . . . . . . 2 D8
Summerhouse Rd GU7 . . . 150 D3
Summer La GU7 . . . . 150 A8
Summerlands GU6 . . . . 174 E4
Summerlay Cl KT20 . . . . 97 E7
Summerleigh 5 KT13 . . . . . 53 D4
Summerley St SW18 . . . . . . 20 B6
Summerly Ave RH2 . . . . . . 118 A2
Summer Pl RG12, RG42 . . . . 27 A7
Summer Rd
East Molesey KT8 . . . . 36 D4
Thames Ditton KT7, KT8 . . . 36 F4
Summersbury Dr GU4 . . . . 130 E1
Summersbury Hall GU4 . . 130 E1
Summersby Cl GU7 . . . . . . 150 F7
Summers Cl
Belmont SM2 . . . . 59 A3
Weybridge KT13 . . . . 72 A8
Summersell Ho SE27 . . . . . . 22 D3
Summer's Rd GU7 . . . . 151 A8
SUMMERSTOWN 20 C5
Summerstown SW17 . . . . . . 20 C4
Summersvere Cl RH10 . . . 182 A1
Summerswood Cl CR8 . . . . 80 D3
Summer Trees TW16 . . . . . . 35 B8
Summerville Gdns SM1 . . . 58 F4
Summerwood Rd TW1, TW7 5 F1
Summit Ave GU14 . . . . 84 C3
Summit Bsns Pk TW16 . . . . 15 A1
Summit Ctr
Farnborough GU14 . . . . 84 D4
Harmondsworth UB7 . . . . 2 D7
Summit Pl KT13 . . . . 53 A3
Summit Way SE19 . . . . 22 E1
Sumner Cl KT22 . . . . 94 D3
Sumner Ct GU9 . . . . 125 C3
Sumner Gdns CR0 . . . . 42 A1
Sumner Pl KT15 . . . . 52 A5
Sumner Rd
Farnham GU9 . . . . 125 C3
Thornton Heath CR0 . . . . . . 42 B1
Sumner Road S CR0 . . . . . . 42 A1
Sun Alley 10 TW9 . . . . 6 E3
Sun Brow GU27 . . . . 208 A5
SUNBURY 35 B6
Sunbury Ave SW14 . . . . 7 D3
Sunbury Cl KT12 . . . . 35 A3
SUNBURY COMMON 14 E1
Sunbury Court Island TW16 . . . . 35 D6
Sunbury Court Mews TW16 . . . . 35 D7
Sunbury Court Rd TW16 . . 35 C7
Sunbury Cres TW13 . . . . . . 14 F4
Sunbury Cross Ctr 9 TW16 . . . . 14 F1
Sunbury Ct TW16 . . . . 35 D7
Sunbury Ct (Conference Ctr) TW16 . . . . 35 D7
Sunbury Int Bsns Ctr TW16 . . . . 34 E8
Sunbury La KT12 . . . . 35 A3
Sunbury L Ctr TW16 . . . . . . 34 F8
Sunbury Manor Sch TW16 34 F8
Sunbury Rd
Cheam SM3 . . . . 58 E7
Feltham TW13 . . . . 14 F4
Sunbury Sta TW16 . . . . 35 A8
Sunbury Walled Gdn★ TW16 . . . . 35 B6
Sunbury Way TW13 . . . . . . 15 C3
Suncroft Pl SE26 . . . . 23 C5
Sundale Ave CR2 . . . . 62 C1
Sundeala Cl TW16 . . . . 15 A1
Sunderland Ct
Dulwich SE22 . . . . 23 A8
12 Stanwell TW19 . . . . 2 E1
Sunderland Mount SE23 . . 23 D6
Sunderland Rd SE23 . . . . . 23 D6
Sundew Cl
Crawley RH11 . . . . 201 A2
Sundew Cl *continued*
Lightwater GU18 . . . . 67 D8
Wokingham RG40 . . . . 25 E7
Sundial Ave SE25 . . . . 42 F6
Sundial Ct KT5 . . . . 57 B8
Sundon Cres GU25 . . . . 31 C4
Sundown Ave CR2 . . . . 80 F8
Sundown Rd TW15 . . . . 14 C3
Sundridge Pl 9 CR0 . . . . . . 43 A1
Sundridge Rd
Croydon CR0, CR9 . . . . 43 A1
Old Woking GU22 . . . . 90 A7
Sun Hill
Woking GU21 . . . . 69 A2
Woking GU22 . . . . 89 A6
Sunhill Ho RH9 . . . . 142 E2
Sun Inn Rd GU8 . . . . 192 F5
Sunken Rd CR0 . . . . 62 C5
Sunkist Way SM6 . . . . 60 E2
Sun Life Trad Est TW14 . . . . 4 A4
Sunlight Cl SW19 . . . . 20 C2
Sunmead Cl KT22 . . . . 94 F5
Sunmead Rd TW16 . . . . 35 A6
Sunna Gdns TW16 . . . . 35 B7
Sunna Lodge TW16 . . . . 14 F1
Sunniholme Ct CR2 . . . . . . 61 C5
Sunning Ave SL5 . . . . 29 E2
SUNNINGDALE 30 B4
Sunningdale RH6 . . . . 161 B2
Sunningdale Ave TW13 . . . 15 E6
Sunningdale Cl 2 KT6 . . . . 56 E8
Sunningdale Ct
Crawley RH10 . . . . 201 D4
13 Kingston upon Thames KT2 . . . . 18 A1
Sunningdale Park (National Coll of Government) SL5 . . . . 29 F4
Sunningdale Rd SM1 . . . . . 58 F6
Sunningdale Sch SL5 . . . . . 29 F3
Sunningdale Sta SL5 . . . . . 30 A2
SUNNINGHILL 29 C4
Sunninghill KT18 . . . . 76 E4
Sunninghill Cl SL5 . . . . 29 D5
Sunninghill Ct SL5 . . . . 29 D5
Sunninghill Lodge
Ascot SL5 . . . . 29 C7
Sunninghill SL5 . . . . 29 D5
Sunninghill Rd
Ascot SL5 . . . . 29 D5
Cranbourne SL4, SL5 . . . . 9 E2
Windlesham GU20 . . . . 48 A7
Sunning Ho
Ascot SL5 . . . . 29 C5
Windlesham SL5 . . . . 48 F8
Sunningvale Ave TN16 . . . 83 D3
Sunningvale Cl TN16 . . . . . 83 D3
Sunny Ave RH10 . . . . 204 A8
Sunnybank SL5 . . . . 29 A5
Sunny Bank
Croydon SE25 . . . . 43 A6
Epsom KT18 . . . . 76 C3
Warlingham CR6 . . . . 81 E2
Sunnybank Mews GU12 . . 106 B3
Sunnybank Rd GU14 . . . . . . 84 D6
Sunnybank Villas RH1 . . . 120 F3
Sunnycroft Rd
Croydon SE25 . . . . 43 A6
Hounslow TW3 . . . . 5 B5
Sunnydell La GU10 . . . . . . 146 A6
Sunnydene Rd CR8 . . . . 80 B6
Sunnydene St SE26 . . . . . . 23 E4
Sunny Down GU8 . . . . 170 E5
Sunnydown Sch CR3 . . . . 100 F6
Sunnyhill GU8 . . . . 170 E6
Sunnyhill Cl RH10 . . . . 204 A8
Sunnyhill Prim Sch SW16 21 F4
Sunnyhill Rd SW16 . . . . 21 E4
Sunny Hill Rd GU11 . . . . . 104 D2
Sunnyhurst Cl SM1 . . . . 59 A7
Sunnymead RH11 . . . . 201 D6
Sunnymead Ave CR4, SW16 . . . . 41 D6
Sunnymede Ave
Sutton SM5 . . . . 78 D8
West Ewell KT19 . . . . 57 E3
Sunny Nook Gdns CR2 . . . . 61 D4
Sunny Rise CR3 . . . . 100 D3
SUNNYSIDE 205 E7
Sunnyside
Knaphill GU21 . . . . 88 B8
Walton-on-Thames KT12 . . . 35 C4
Wimbledon SW19 . . . . 19 E2
Sunnyside Pl SW19 . . . . . . 19 E2
Sunnyside Rd
Headley Down GU35 . . . . . 187 C4
Teddington TW11 . . . . 16 D4
Sunny View Cl GU12 . . . . 105 C1
Sunray Ave KT5 . . . . 57 B8
Sun Ray Est GU47 . . . . 64 A8
Sunrise Cl TW13 . . . . 15 F5
Sunset Gdns SE25 . . . . 42 F7
Sunset Rd SW19 . . . . 19 B3
Sunshine Way CR4 . . . . 40 F7
Sunstone Gr RH1 . . . . 119 E6
Sunvale Ave GU27 . . . . . . 207 D6
Sunvale Cl GU27 . . . . 207 D6
SURBITON 37 E2
Surbiton Cres KT1, KT6 . . . 37 E5
Surbiton Ct KT6 . . . . 37 D3
Surbiton Ct Mews 5 KT6 . 37 D3
Surbiton Hall Cl KT1 . . . . . 37 E5
Surbiton High Jun Girls Sch KT1 . . . . 37 E5
Surbiton High Senior Sch KT1 . . . . 37 E5
Surbiton Hill Pk KT5 . . . . . . 38 A4
Surbiton Hill Rd KT6 . . . . . 37 E4
Surbiton Hospl KT6 . . . . . . 37 E3
Surbiton Par KT6 . . . . 37 E3
Surbiton Prep Sch KT6 . . . 37 E4
Surbiton Rd
Camberley GU15 . . . . 47 A1
Kingston upon Thames KT1 . 37 E5
Surbiton Sta KT6 . . . . 37 E3
Surrey Ave GU15 . . . . 65 A4
Surrey Bsns Pk KT17 . . . . . 76 E8
Surrey Cloisters GU7 . . . . 150 F6
Surrey Ct
Guildford GU2 . . . . 109 B1
5 Horsham RH12 . . . . 217 D2
Wallington SM6 . . . . 60 C4
Surrey Gdns KT24 . . . . 93 A4
Surrey Gr SM1 . . . . 59 D7
Surrey Heath Mus★ GU15 65 D6
Surrey Hills Ave KT20 . . . . 116 C4
Surrey Hills Bsns Pk RH5 . . . . 134 F4
Surrey Hills Pk GU3 . . . . . 107 E4
Surrey Hills Residential Pk KT20 . . . . 116 C5
Surrey Hills Sch SM5 . . . . . 79 B8
Surrey Hills Way KT20 . . . 116 C5
Surrey Ho GU4 . . . . 131 C3
Surrey Lodge
Claygate KT10 . . . . 55 E4
Hersham KT12 . . . . 54 B5
Merton SW20 . . . . 39 C7
Surrey Mews SE27 . . . . 22 E4
Surrey Mount SE23 . . . . 23 B7
Surrey Rd BR4 . . . . 44 B1
Surrey Research Pk The GU2 . . . . 129 D8
Surrey St CR0, CR9 . . . . 61 C7
Surrey Tech Ctr GU2 . . . . 129 D8
Surrey Twrs KT15 . . . . 52 C5
Surrey Way GU2 . . . . 109 B2
Surridge Ct GU19 . . . . 47 E2
Surridge Gdns SE19 . . . . . . 22 D2
Sury Basin KT2 . . . . 37 E8
Sussex Ave TW7 . . . . 5 E4
Sussex Cl
Knaphill GU21 . . . . 68 C1
New Malden KT3 . . . . 38 E5
Reigate RH2 . . . . 139 D8
4 Twickenham TW1 . . . . 6 B1
Sussex Ct
Addlestone KT15 . . . . 52 C5
Barnes SW13 . . . . 7 F5
Horsham RH13 . . . . 217 E1
Knaphill GU21 . . . . 68 C2
Mitcham CR4 . . . . 41 E4
Sussex Gdns KT9 . . . . 56 D4
Sussex Ho TW9 . . . . 6 F5
Sussex Manor Bsns Pk RH10 . . . . 182 A2
Sussex Mews SE6 . . . . 24 A7
Sussex Pl
Knaphill GU21 . . . . 68 C1
New Malden KT3 . . . . 38 E5
Sussex Rd
Croydon CR2 . . . . 61 D4
Knaphill GU21 . . . . 68 C1
Mitcham CR4 . . . . 41 E4
New Malden KT3 . . . . 38 E5
South Croydon CR2 . . . . 61 D4
Wallington SM5 . . . . 59 F4
2 West Wickham BR4 . . . . . 44 B1
Sussex Terr 3 SE20 . . . . 23 C1
Sutherland Ave
Biggin Hill TN16 . . . . 83 E1
Guildford GU4 . . . . 109 E7
Sunbury TW16 . . . . 34 F7
Sutherland Chase SL5 . . . . 28 E7
Sutherland Dr
Guildford GU4 . . . . 110 A4
Mitcham SW19 . . . . 40 D8
Sutherland Gdns
Mortlake SW14 . . . . 7 E4
North Cheam KT4 . . . . 39 B1
Sunbury TW16 . . . . 34 F7
Sutherland Gr
Putney SW18, SW19 . . . . . . 19 F8
Teddington TW11 . . . . 16 E3
Sutherland Ho
Guildford GU4 . . . . 110 A5
Richmond TW10 . . . . 17 C6
9 Sutton SM2 . . . . 59 C4
Sutherland Rd
Chiswick W4 . . . . 7 E8
Thornton Heath CR0 . . . . . . 42 A2
SUTTON 59 C5
SUTTON ABINGER 155 B8
Sutton Arena L Ctr SM5 . . 40 D2
Sutton Ave GU21 . . . . 88 E8
Sutton Cl BR3 . . . . 44 B8
Sutton Coll of Liberal Arts 8 SM1 . . . . 59 B5
Sutton Common Rd
Cheam SM3 . . . . 40 A1
Sutton SM1, SM3 . . . . 59 B8
Sutton Common Sta SM1 . 59 B8
Sutton Courtenay Ho SW17 . . . . 20 D4
Sutton Court Mans W4 . . . . 7 C8
Sutton Court Rd
Chiswick W4 . . . . 7 C8
Sutton SM1 . . . . 59 C4
Sutton Ct
Chiswick W4 . . . . 7 C8
East Molesey KT8 . . . . 35 F4
Penge SE19 . . . . 22 F1
Sutton SM2 . . . . 59 C4
Sutton Dene TW3 . . . . 5 B6
Sutton Gdns
Croydon CR0, SE25 . . . . 42 F4

Sutton Gdns *continued*
Merstham RH1 . . . 119 D6
Sutton Gr SM1 . . . 59 D5
Sutton Gram Sch for Boys SM1 . . . 59 C5
SUTTON GREEN . . . 89 F2
Sutton Green Rd GU4 . . . 89 F1
Sutton Hall TW5 . . . 5 A7
Sutton High Jun Sch SM1 59 B4
Sutton High Sch SM1 . . . 59 B4
Sutton Hill GU4 . . . 110 C6
Sutton Hospl SM2 . . . 59 B1
Sutton Hts SM2 . . . 59 D3
Sutton La
Abinger Common RH5 . . . 155 C8
Banstead SM2, SM7 . . . 78 B6
Brands Hill SL3 . . . 1 B8
Hounslow TW3, TW4, TW5 . . . 4 F5
Sutton La S W4 . . . 7 C8
Sutton Lodge GU1 . . . 109 E1
Sutton Park Rd SM1 . . . 59 B4
Sutton Pl
Brands Hill SL3 . . . 1 B8
Peaslake RH5 . . . 154 F8
Sutton Rd
Camberley GU15 . . . 47 A1
Heston TW5 . . . 5 A6
Sutton Sq TW5 . . . 4 F6
Sutton Sta SM2 . . . 59 C4
Sutton Way TW5 . . . 4 F6
Suva Ct RH19 . . . 185 C3
Swaby Rd SW17, SW18 . . . 20 C6
Swaffield Prim Sch 1 SW18 . . . 20 C8
Swaffield Rd SW18 . . . 20 C8
Swail Ho 8 KT18 . . . 76 D6
Swain Cl SW16, SW17 . . . 21 B2
Swain Ho CR4 . . . 20 F1
Swain Rd CR7 . . . 42 C4
Swains Rd CR4, SW17, SW19 . . . 20 F1
Swaledale RG12 . . . 27 A4
Swaledale Cl RH11 . . . 201 C3
Swale Ho 2 RH1 . . . 119 A3
Swale Rd GU14 . . . 84 E6
Swallands Rd SE6 . . . 24 A5
Swallow Cl
Staines TW18 . . . 12 F4
Witley GU8 . . . 170 E7
Swallow Ct KT4 . . . 58 B8
Swallowdale CR2 . . . 62 D2
Swallowfield
Dormansland RH7 . . . 165 A2
Englefield Green TW20 . . . 11 B2
Swallow Gdns SW16 . . . 21 D3
Swallow La RH5 . . . 136 B1
Swallow Pk KT6 . . . 56 F7
Swallow Rd RH11 . . . 201 C8
Swallow Rise GU21 . . . 68 C2
Swallows Ct SE20 . . . 23 D1
Swallow St RH10 . . . 204 C5
Swallowtail Rd RH12 . . . 217 E6
Swan Barn Rd GU27 . . . 208 D6
Swan Cl
Croydon CR0 . . . 42 E2
Feltham TW13 . . . 15 E4
Swancote Gn RG12 . . . 27 B4
Swan Ct
Blackwater GU17 . . . 64 E4
Feltham TW13 . . . 15 E4
Guildford GU1 . . . 109 D3
Leatherhead KT22 . . . 95 B6
Swan Ctr SW17 . . . 20 C5
Swandrift TW18 . . . 12 F1
Swan Ho GU47 . . . 64 B7
Swan La
Charlwood RH6 . . . 180 F7
Guildford GU1 . . . 130 D7
Sandhurst GU47 . . . 64 B7
Swan Mill Gdns RH4 . . . 115 D1
Swann Ct 7 TW7 . . . 6 A4
Swanns Mdw KT23 . . . 94 A1
Swann Way RH12 . . . 216 E3
Swan Pl SW13 . . . 7 F5
Swan Rd TW13 . . . 15 E4
Swansea Rd TW14, TW6 . . . 3 D1
Swans Ghyll RH18 . . . 206 E3
Swan Sh Ctr KT22 . . . 221 B6
Swan Sq RH12 . . . 217 C2
Swan St TW7 . . . 6 B4
Swanton Gdns SW19 . . . 19 D7
Swanwick Cl SW15 . . . 18 F8
Swan Wlk TW17 . . . 34 E2
Swan Wlk Sh Ctr RH12 . . . 217 C2
Swanworth La RH5 . . . 115 B7
Swayne's La GU1 . . . 110 E1
Swaynesland Rd RH8 . . . 123 F1
Swaythling Ho SW15 . . . 7 F1
Swedish Sch The SW13 . . . 7 F8
Sweeps Ditch Cl TW18 . . . 13 B1
Sweeps La TW20 . . . 11 F3
Sweetbriar RG45 . . . 45 A7
Sweet La GU5 . . . 154 E8
Sweetwater Cl GU5 . . . 152 D4
Sweetwater La
Enton Green GU8 . . . 171 B2
Shamley Green GU5 . . . 152 D4
Swievelands Rd TN16 . . . 83 C1
Swift Ct SM2 . . . 59 B3
Swift Ctr CR0 . . . 60 F3
Swift La
Crawley RH11 . . . 201 C8
Windlesham GU19 . . . 47 F3
Swift Rd
Feltham TW13 . . . 15 E4
Heath End GU9 . . . 125 C7
Swift's Cl GU10 . . . 126 B1
Swiftsden Way BR1 . . . 24 E2
Swinburn Ct 3 SW20 . . . 39 D8
Swinburne Cres CR0 . . . 43 C3
Swindon Rd
Harlington TW6 . . . 3 C2
Horsham RH12 . . . 217 B4
Swinfield Cl TW13 . . . 15 E4
Swingate Rd GU9 . . . 146 D8
Swinley Rd SL5 . . . 28 C4
Swiss Cl GU10 . . . 146 A4
Swissland Hill RH19, RH7 . 185 E7
Switchback La
Rowledge GU10 . . . 145 F4
Rowledge GU10 . . . 146 A3
Swordsman's Rd GU16 . . . 86 D8
Sycamore Ave RH12 . . . 218 C6
Sycamore Cl
Carshalton SM5 . . . 59 F6
Crawley RH11 . . . 181 C1
3 Croydon CR0 . . . 61 E5
Feltham TW13 . . . 15 A5
Fetcham KT22 . . . 94 F5
Frimley GU16 . . . 65 E1
Sandhurst GU47 . . . 64 B8
Sycamore Ct
4 Beckenham BR3 . . . 44 A8
Farncombe GU7 . . . 150 E8
Forest Hill SE26 . . . 23 C4
7 Guildford GU1 . . . 130 E8
Hounslow TW4 . . . 4 E3
Kingston upon Thames KT3 . 38 E6
Ottershaw KT16 . . . 51 C5
Oxted RH8 . . . 122 E6
Walton-on-Thames KT13 . . . 53 F7
11 West Norwood SW16 . . . 22 A3
Sycamore Dr
Ash Vale GU12 . . . 106 A7
East Grinstead RH19 . . . 186 A1
Frimley GU16 . . . 65 E1
Wrecclesham GU10 . . . 146 A6
Sycamore Gdns CR4 . . . 40 D7
Sycamore Gr
Kingston upon Thames KT3 . . . 38 E6
Penge SE20 . . . 43 A8
Sycamore Ho
Chelsham CR6 . . . 82 B4
Teddington TW11 . . . 17 C1
Twickenham TW2 . . . 16 F6
Sycamore Lodge 7 TW16 14 F1
Sycamore Manor SM6 . . . 60 C3
Sycamore Rd
Farnborough GU14 . . . 85 D2
Guildford GU1 . . . 109 D1
Wimbledon SW19 . . . 19 C2
Sycamore Rise
Banstead KT17, SM7 . . . 77 D5
Bracknell RG12 . . . 27 D6
Sycamores The
Blackwater GU17 . . . 64 B5
Farnborough GU14 . . . 85 D3
Great Bookham KT23 . . . 94 C3
Hooley CR5 . . . 99 B5
Sycamore Way TW11 . . . 17 C2
Sycamore Wlk
Englefield Green TW20 . . . 11 B2
Reigate RH2 . . . 139 C6
Sydcote SE21 . . . 22 C7
Sydenham Ave SE26 . . . 23 B3
Sydenham Girls Sch SE26 23 B5
Sydenham High Junior Sch 6 SE26 . . . 23 B4
Sydenham High Sch 13 SE26 . . . 23 B3
Sydenham Hill SE21, SE22, SE23, SE26, SE19 . . . 23 B5
Sydenham Hill Sta SE21 . . . 22 F5
Sydenham Ho 16 KT6 . . . 37 D2
Sydenham Ind Est SE26 . . . 23 F3
Sydenham Park Mans SE26 . . . 23 C5
Sydenham Park Rd SE23, SE26 . . . 23 C5
Sydenham Pk SE26 . . . 23 C5
Sydenham Rd
Forest Hill SE26, SE6 . . . 23 D3
Guildford GU1 . . . 130 E8
Thornton Heath CR0 . . . 42 D2
Sydenham Rise SE23 . . . 23 B6
Sydenham Sta SE26 . . . 23 C4
Sydenham Station App SE26 . . . 23 C4
Sydmons Ct SE23 . . . 23 C8
Sydney Ave CR8 . . . 79 F7
Sydney Cl RG45 . . . 45 C7
Sydney Cotts KT10 . . . 55 F4
Sydney Cres TW15 . . . 14 B2
Sydney Ct KT6 . . . 56 E8
Sydney Loader Pl GU46 . . . 64 A5
Sydney Pl GU1 . . . 130 F8
Sydney Rd
East Bedfont TW14 . . . 15 A7
Guildford GU1 . . . 130 F8
Merton SW20 . . . 39 D7
Richmond TW10, TW9 . . . 6 E3
Sutton SM1 . . . 59 A6
Teddington TW11 . . . 16 F3
Sydney Terr KT10 . . . 55 F4
Sydney Villas GU12 . . . 106 A8
Sykes Dr TW18 . . . 13 B3
Sylva Ct 3 SW15 . . . 19 D8
Sylvan Cl
Limpsfield RH8 . . . 123 B6
South Croydon CR2 . . . 62 B1
Woking GU22 . . . 70 B2
Sylvan Ct
1 Farnborough GU14 . . . 105 D8
South Croydon CR2 . . . 61 C4
Sylvan Gdns KT6 . . . 37 D2
Sylvan Hill SE19 . . . 42 E8
Sylvan Rd
Crawley RH10 . . . 202 A4
South Norwood SE19 . . . 42 F8
Sylvan Ridge GU47 . . . 45 A1
Sylvanus RG12 . . . 26 F2
Sylvan Way
Coney Hall BR4 . . . 63 E6
Redhill RH1 . . . 140 A8
Sylvaways Cl GU6 . . . 175 A3
Sylverdale Rd
Croydon CR0, CR9 . . . 61 B7
Purley CR8 . . . 80 B6
Syon Gate Way TW7, TW8 . . . 6 A7
Syon House & Pk★ TW8 . . . 6 C6
Syon La
Brentford TW7 . . . 5 F8
Hounslow TW7 . . . 6 A7
Syon Lane Sta TW7 . . . 6 A7
Syon Park Cotts TW8 . . . 6 C6
Syon Park Gdns TW7 . . . 5 F7
Syon Pl GU14 . . . 85 D4
Sythwood GU21 . . . 69 B2
Sythwood Prim Sch GU21 69 B3
Szabo Cres GU3 . . . 107 B1

T

Tabard Ho KT1 . . . 37 C8
Tabarin Way KT17 . . . 77 C3
Tabor Ct SM3 . . . 58 E4
Tabor Gdns SM3 . . . 58 F3
Tabor Gr SW19 . . . 19 F1
Tachbrook Rd TW14 . . . 14 F8
Tadcaster Ct 8 TW9 . . . 6 E3
Tadlow KT1 . . . 38 A6
Tadmor Cl TW16 . . . 34 F5
Tadorne Rd KT20 . . . 97 C5
TADWORTH . . . 97 C5
Tadworth Ave KT3 . . . 38 F4
Tadworth Cl KT20 . . . 97 D5
Tadworth Prim Sch KT20 . 97 D5
Tadworth St KT20 . . . 97 C5
Tadworth Sta KT20 . . . 97 C5
Taffy's How CR4 . . . 40 E6
Taggs Ho KT1 . . . 37 D7
Tailors Ct 9 SW16 . . . 21 C4
Tait Rd CR0, SE25 . . . 42 E2
Tait Rd Ind Est CR0 . . . 42 E2
Talavera Inf Sch GU11 . . . 105 B3
Talavera Jun Sch GU11 . . 105 A2
Talbot Cl
Mytchett GU16 . . . 86 A4
Reigate RH2 . . . 139 B8
Talbot La RH12 . . . 217 C1
Talbot Lodge KT10 . . . 55 A5
Talbot Pl GU19 . . . 47 E4
Talbot Rd
Ashford TW15 . . . 13 E3
Farnham GU9 . . . 146 B8
Isleworth TW1, TW7 . . . 6 A3
Lingfield RH7 . . . 164 D4
South Norwood CR7 . . . 42 D5
Twickenham TW2 . . . 16 F7
Wallington SM5 . . . 60 A5
Talcott Path 12 SW2 . . . 22 A7
Taleworth Cl KT21 . . . 95 D7
Taleworth Pk KT21 . . . 95 D7
Taleworth Rd KT21 . . . 95 E7
Talfourd Way RH1 . . . 140 A6
Talgarth Dr GU14 . . . 85 D2
Taliesin Hts GU7 . . . 150 D6
Talisman Sq SE26 . . . 23 A4
Talisman Way KT17 . . . 77 C3
Tall Elms Cl BR2 . . . 44 F4
Tallis Cl RH11 . . . 200 F3
Tallow Rd TW8 . . . 6 C7
Tall Trees
Poyle SL3 . . . 1 E6
Thornton Heath SW16 . . . 41 F6
Tally Rd RH8 . . . 123 E4
Talma Gdns TW2 . . . 16 E8
Talmage Cl SE23 . . . 23 C8
Talman Cl RH11 . . . 200 E5
Tamar Cl RH10 . . . 202 C5
Tamarind Cl GU2 . . . 109 A6
Tamarind Ct 3 TW20 . . . 11 F3
Tamarisk Rise RG40 . . . 25 C7
Tamerton Sq 1 GU22 . . . 89 E8
Tamesa House TW17 . . . 34 A2
Tamesis Gdns KT4 . . . 57 E8
Tamian Ind Est TW4 . . . 4 C3
Tamian Way TW4 . . . 4 C3
Tamil Ho SE6 . . . 24 A6
Tamworth RG12 . . . 27 D2
Tamworth La CR4 . . . 41 B6
Tamworth Pk CR4 . . . 41 B6
Tamworth Pl 3 CR0, CR9 . 61 C8
Tamworth Rd CR0, CR9 . . . 61 C8
Tanbridge Ho RH12 . . . 217 B1
Tanbridge House Sch RH12 . . . 216 F2
Tanbridge Pk RH12 . . . 217 B1
Tanbridge Pl RH12 . . . 217 B1
Tanbridge Ret Pk RH12 . . 217 B1
Tandem Ctr SW19 . . . 40 D8
TANDRIDGE . . . 122 A2
Tandridge Ct
Caterham CR3 . . . 101 A5
Sutton SM2 . . . 59 B4
Tandridge Gdns CR2 . . . 81 A6
Tandridgehill La RH9 . . . 121 F6
Tandridge La RH7, RH8 . . 143 B4
Tandridge L Ctr RH8 . . . 122 E6
Tandridge Rd CR6 . . . 101 D8
Tanfield Ct 4 RH12 . . . 217 B2
Tanfield Rd CR0, CR9 . . . 61 C6
Tangier Ct GU11 . . . 104 F2
Tangier Rd
Guildford GU1 . . . 131 A8
Mortlake TW10 . . . 7 B4
Tangier Way KT20 . . . 77 E1
Tangier Wood KT20 . . . 77 E1
Tangle Oak RH19 . . . 184 E4
Tanglewood Cl
Longcross KT16 . . . 50 B7
South Croydon CR0 . . . 62 C7
Woking GU22 . . . 70 D3
Tanglewood Ride GU24 . . . 67 D7
Tanglewood Way TW13 . . . 15 B5
Tangley Dr RG41 . . . 25 B4
Tangley Gr SW15 . . . 18 F8
Tangley La GU3 . . . 108 F6
Tangley Park Rd TW12 . . . 15 F3
Tanglyn Ave TW17 . . . 34 B4
Tangmere Gr KT2 . . . 17 D3
Tangmere Rd RH11 . . . 200 F6
Tanhouse La RG41 . . . 25 A5
Tanhouse Rd RH8 . . . 122 E3
Tanhurst Ho 28 SW2 . . . 21 E8
Tanhurst La RH5 . . . 155 E2
Tanker Rd GU14 . . . 85 B1
Tankerton Rd KT6 . . . 56 F8
Tankerton Terr CR0 . . . 41 F3
Tankerville Rd SW16 . . . 21 E1
Tank Rd GU15 . . . 64 F5
Tanner Ho 1 SW19 . . . 40 C8
Tanners Cl KT12 . . . 35 B3
Tanners Ct GU27 . . . 208 C7
Tanner's Ct RH3 . . . 137 C5
Tanners Dean KT22 . . . 95 D5
Tannersfield GU4 . . . 130 E1
Tanner's Hill RH3 . . . 137 B8
Tanners La GU27 . . . 208 C7
Tanners Mdw RH3 . . . 137 B5
Tanners Row RG41 . . . 25 A3
Tanners Yd GU19 . . . 47 E3
Tannery Cl
Beckenham BR3, CR0 . . . 43 D4
Slinfold RH13 . . . 215 D3
Tannery Ho GU23 . . . 90 D5
Tannery La
Send GU23 . . . 90 E5
Shalford GU5 . . . 151 F8
Tannery The RH1 . . . 118 F1
Tannsfeld Rd SE26 . . . 23 D3
Tansy Cl GU4 . . . 110 C3
Tantallon Rd SW12 . . . 21 A7
Tanyard Ave RH19 . . . 206 A8
Tanyard Cl
Crawley RH10 . . . 202 C3
Horsham RH13 . . . 217 E1
Tanyard Ho 8 TW8 . . . 6 C7
Tanyard Way RH6 . . . 161 B4
Tapestry Cl SM2 . . . 59 B3
Taplow Ct CR4 . . . 40 E5
Tapner's Rd RH2 . . . 137 F3
Tapping Cl 5 KT2 . . . 18 A1
Tara Ct 4 BR3 . . . 44 B7
Tarbat Ct 6 GU47 . . . 64 D8
Target Cl TW14 . . . 3 E1
Target Hill Pk Nature Reserve★ RH11 . . . 200 F2
Tarham Cl RH6 . . . 160 E5
Tarleton Gdns SE23 . . . 23 B7
Tarmac Way UB7 . . . 2 B7
Tarnbrook Way RG12 . . . 27 E2
Tarn Cl GU14 . . . 84 E2
Tarn Rd GU26 . . . 188 E3
Tarquin Ho SE26 . . . 23 A4
Tarragon Cl GU14 . . . 84 C4
Tarragon Ct GU2 . . . 109 A5
Tarragon Dr GU2 . . . 109 A5
Tarragon Gr SE26 . . . 23 D2
Tarrington Cl SW16 . . . 21 D5
Tartar Hill KT11 . . . 73 B6
Tartar Rd KT11 . . . 73 C6
Tasis The American Sch in England TW20 . . . 32 C6
Tasker Cl UB7 . . . 3 C7
Tasman Ct TW16 . . . 14 E1
Tatchbury Ho SW15 . . . 7 F1
Tate Cl KT22 . . . 95 C4
Tate Rd SM1 . . . 59 A5
Tate's Way RH12 . . . 214 D7
Tatham Ct RH11 . . . 201 B1
TATSFIELD . . . 103 D7
TATSFIELD GREEN . . . 103 E4
Tatsfield La TN16 . . . 103 F6
Tatsfield Prim Sch TN16 103 D6
Tattenham Corner Rd KT18 . . . 77 A1
Tattenham Corner Sta KT18 . . . 77 B1
Tattenham Cres KT18 . . . 77 B1
Tattenham Gr KT18 . . . 97 B8
Tattenham Way KT18, KT20 . . . 77 E2
Tattersall Cl RG40 . . . 25 E5
Tatton Cl SM6 . . . 41 A1
Taunton Ave
Caterham CR3 . . . 100 F4
Hounslow TW3 . . . 5 C5
Wimbledon SW20 . . . 39 B7
Taunton Cl
Cheam SM3 . . . 40 A1
Crawley RH10 . . . 202 E6
Taunton La CR5 . . . 100 B8
Tavern Cl SM5 . . . 40 E2
Tavistock Cl TW18 . . . 13 D1
Tavistock Cres CR4 . . . 41 E5
Tavistock Ct 1 CR0 . . . 42 D1
Tavistock Gdns GU14 . . . 85 B7
Tavistock Gr CR0 . . . 42 D2
Tavistock Rd
Carshalton SM5 . . . 40 D1
Croydon CR0 . . . 42 D1
Tavistock Wlk SM5 . . . 40 D1
Tavy Ho 3 RH1 . . . 118 F2
Tawfield RG12 . . . 26 E2
Tawny Cl TW13 . . . 15 A5
Tayben Ave TW2 . . . 5 E1
Tay Cl GU14 . . . 84 E6
Tayles Hill Dr KT17 . . . 57 F1
Tayles Hill Ho KT17 . . . 57 F1
Taylor Ave TW9 . . . 7 B5
Taylor Cl
Epsom KT19 . . . 76 A8
Hampton TW12 . . . 16 C3
Hounslow TW3 . . . 5 C6
Taylor Ct SE20 . . . 43 C7
Taylor Ho
Carshalton SM5 . . . 59 E8
10 Streatham SW2 . . . 22 A7
Taylor Rd
Ashtead KT21 . . . 75 D2
Farnborough GU11 . . . 105 D7
Mitcham CR4 . . . 20 E1
Wallington SM6 . . . 60 B5
Taylors Cres GU6 . . . 174 F3
Taylors Ct TW13 . . . 15 A6
Taylor's La SE26 . . . 23 B4
Taylor Wlk RH11 . . . 201 C6
Taymount Grange SE23 . . 23 C6
Taymount Rise SE23 . . . 23 C6
Taynton Dr RH1 . . . 119 D6
Teal Cl
Horsham RH12 . . . 217 C5
Selsdon CR2 . . . 81 D8
Teal Ct
5 Dorking RH4 . . . 136 A8
Wallington SM6 . . . 60 C5
Teale Cl GU7 . . . 150 F6
Tealing Dr KT19 . . . 57 D6
Teal Pl SM1 . . . 58 F5
Teasel Cl
Crawley RH11 . . . 201 B3
Croydon CR0 . . . 43 D1
Teazlewood Pk KT22 . . . 75 A1
Tebbit Cl RG12 . . . 27 D7
Tebbs Ho 14 SW2 . . . 22 A8
Teck Cl TW7 . . . 6 A5
Ted Adams Ho GU2 . . . 129 E8
Tedder Cl KT9 . . . 56 C5
Tedder Rd CR2 . . . 62 D2
Tedding Bsns Pk TW11 . . . 16 F2
TEDDINGTON . . . 17 B3
Teddington Cl KT19 . . . 57 D1
Teddington Memorial Hospl TW11 . . . 16 E2
Teddington Park Rd TW11 . . . 16 F4
Teddington Pk TW11 . . . 16 F3
Teddington Sch TW11 . . . 17 C2
Teddington Sta TW11 . . . 17 A2
Tedham La RH9 . . . 163 B7
Tees Cl GU14 . . . 84 E6
Teesdale RH11 . . . 201 C3
Teesdale Ave TW7 . . . 6 A6
Teesdale Ct TW7 . . . 6 A6
Teesdale Gdns
Isleworth TW7 . . . 6 A6
South Norwood SE25 . . . 42 E7
Teevan Cl CR0 . . . 43 A2
Teevan Rd CR0, CR9 . . . 43 A2
Tegg's La GU22 . . . 70 F3
Tekels Ave GU15 . . . 65 D4
Tekels Ct GU15 . . . 65 E4
Tekels Way GU15 . . . 65 F3
Telconia Cl GU35 . . . 187 C4
Telegraph La KT10 . . . 55 F5
Telegraph Rd SW15 . . . 19 C8
Telegraph Track SM5, SM6 . . . 60 A1
Telfer Ho 8 SE21 . . . 22 E4
Telferscot Prim Sch SW12 . . . 21 D7
Telferscot Rd SW12 . . . 21 D7
Telford Ave
Crowthorne RG45 . . . 45 C8
Streatham SW12, SW2 . . . 21 E7
Telford Ave Mans 7 SW2 21 E7
Telford Cl SE19 . . . 22 F2
Telford Ct 2 GU1 . . . 130 F8
Telford Dr KT12 . . . 35 C2
Telford Par Mans 8 SW2 . 21 E7
Telford Pl RH10 . . . 201 E5
Telford Rd TW2 . . . 16 A8
Telham Ct 5 RH11 . . . 200 F3
Tellisford KT10 . . . 55 B6
Temperley Rd SW12 . . . 21 A8
Tempest Ho 9 KT2 . . . 37 E8
Tempest Rd TW20 . . . 12 C2
Templar Ave GU9 . . . 146 B8
Templar Cl GU47 . . . 64 A8
Templar Ct CR0 . . . 62 E2
Templar Pl TW12 . . . 16 A1
Templars Lo RG12 . . . 27 D3
Temple Ave CR0 . . . 62 F7
Temple Bar Rd GU21 . . . 88 F8
Temple Cl
Crawley RH10 . . . 202 D5
Epsom KT19 . . . 76 D7
Templecombe Mews GU22 . . . 70 B3
Templecombe Way SM4 . . 39 E4
Templecroft TW15 . . . 14 D2
Temple Ct 6 KT13 . . . 53 B6
Templedene BR2 . . . 44 D7

Templedene Ave TW18 . . . . . 13 C2
Temple Field Cl KT15 . . . 52 B4
Temple Gdns TW18 . . . . . 32 F8
Temple La RH5 . . . . 178 F5
Templeman Cl CR8 . . . . . 80 B3
Templemere KT13 . . . . . . 53 D7
Temple Mkt KT13 . . . . . . 53 B6
Templer Ave GU14 . . . . . . 85 A2
Temple Rd
  Biggin Hill TN16 . . . . 83 D2
  Croydon CR0 . . . . 61 D6
  Epsom KT19 . . . . 76 D7
  Hounslow TW3 . . . . 5 C3
  Richmond TW9 . . . . 6 F4
Temple's Cl GU10 . . . . . 126 C1
Temple Sheen SW14 . . . . . 7 C2
Temple Sheen Rd SW14 . . . 7 C3
Templeton Ho CR7, SE19 . . 42 D8
Temple Way
  Bracknell RG42 . . . . 26 E8
  Carshalton SM1 . . . . 59 D7
Temple Wood Dr RH1 . . . 118 F4
Templewood Ho RH1 . . . 118 F4
Tenacre GU21 . . . . 69 A1
Ten Acre La TW20 . . . . . 32 C7
Ten Acres KT22 . . . . 94 D3
Ten Acres Cl KT22 . . . . . 94 D3
Tenbury Ct SW12 . . . . . . 21 D7
Tenby Dr SL5 . . . . 29 D4
Tenby Rd GU16 . . . . 86 A8
Tenchley's La
  Limpsfield RH8 . . . . 123 D4
  The Chart RH8 . . . . 123 D3
Tenham Ave SW2 . . . . . . 21 D6
Tenniel Cl GU2 . . . . 109 B3
Tennison Cl CR5 . . . . . . 100 B7
Tennison Rd SE25 . . . . . . 42 F4
Tennyson Ave
  Twickenham TW1 . . . . . . 16 F7
  West Barnes KT3 . . . . . . 39 B4
Tennyson Cl
  Crawley RH10 . . . . 202 B8
  Feltham TW14 . . . . 4 A1
  Horsham RH12 . . . . 217 E6
Tennyson Ct **3** TW10 . . . 17 D4
Tennyson Ho KT3 . . . . . . 39 A4
Tennyson Rd
  Addlestone KT15 . . . . . . 52 E6
  Ashford TW15 . . . . 13 E3
  Hounslow TW3 . . . . 5 C5
  Penge SE20 . . . . 23 D1
  Wimbledon SW19 . . . . . . 20 C2
Tennyson Rise RH19 . . . . 205 C8
Tennyson's La
  Haslemere GU27 . . . . . . 208 E4
  Lurgashall GU27 . . . . . . 209 A2
Tennysons Ridge GU27 . . 208 E5
Tensing Ct TW19 . . . . . . 13 E7
Tenterden Gdns CR0 . . . . 43 A2
Tenterden Rd CR0 . . . . . . 43 A2
Tern Rd RH11 . . . . 200 D5
Terrace Gdns SW13 . . . . . 7 F5
Terrace La TW10 . . . . 6 E1
Terrace Rd KT12 . . . . 35 B3
Terraces The **12** SW20 . . . 19 D1
Terrace The
  Addlestone KT15 . . . . . . 52 E5
  Ascot SL5 . . . . 29 D4
  Barnes SW13, SW14 . . . . . 7 E5
  Camberley GU15 . . . . . . 65 A5
  Crowthorne RG45 . . . . . . 45 D5
  Old Woking GU22 . . . . . . 90 A6
  Wokingham RG40 . . . . . . 25 B6
Terracotta Rd RH9 . . . . . 142 C5
Terrano Ho **1** TW9 . . . . . .7 B6
Terrapin Ct SW17 . . . . . . 21 B5
Terrapin Rd SW17 . . . . . . 21 B5
Terrapins KT6 . . . . 37 D2
Terry Ct **8** SM6 . . . . . . 60 C4
Terry Ho SW2 . . . . 22 A7
Terry Lodge **2** CR7 . . . . 42 A4
Terry Rd RH11 . . . . 201 B1
Tersha St TW9 . . . . .6 E3
Testard Rd GU2 . . . . 130 C7
Testers Cl RH8 . . . . 123 B8
Test House Gate Rd GU14 85 B2
Teviot Cl GU2 . . . . 109 A4
Tewkesbury Ave SE23 . . . 23 B8
Tewkesbury Cl KT14 . . . . 71 D8
Tewkesbury Rd SM5 . . . . 40 D1
Teynham Ct BR3 . . . . 44 B6
Thackeray Cl
  Isleworth TW7 . . . . 6 A5
  Wimbledon SW19 . . . . . . 19 D1
Thackeray Manor SM1 . . . 59 C5
Thackery Lodge TW14 . . . . 3 D1
Thakeham Cl SE26 . . . . . 23 B3
Thames Ave
  Chertsey KT16 . . . . 33 A6
  1 Worcester Park KT4 . . 39 C1
Thames Bank SW14 . . . . . 7 C5
Thames Cl
  Chertsey KT16 . . . . 33 C2
  East Molesey TW12 . . . . . 36 B7
  Farnborough GU14 . . . . . 84 E6
Thames Cnr TW16 . . . . . . 35 C6
Thames Cotts KT7 . . . . . . 37 B3
Thames Cres W4 . . . . .7 E7
Thames Ct KT8 . . . . 36 B7
THAMES DITTON 36 F3
Thames Ditton Inf Sch
  KT7 . . . . 36 F3
Thames Ditton Island KT7 37 A3
Thames Ditton Jun Sch
  KT7 . . . . 36 F2

Thames Ditton Sta KT7 . . . 36 F2
Thames Edge Ct TW18 . . . 12 E4
Thames Eyot **10** TW1 . . . 17 A7
Thamesfield Ct TW17 . . . . 34 C2
Thamesfield Ho TW17 . . . . 34 C2
Thamesfield Mews TW17 . . 34 C2
Thamesgate TW18 . . . . . . 33 B8
Thamesgate Cl TW10 . . . . 17 B4
Thames Haven KT6 . . . . . 37 D4
Thameside TW11 . . . . 17 D1
Thameside Ctr TW8 . . . . . .6 F8
Thameside Ho **11** KT1 . . . 37 D8
Thames Link Ho **11** TW9 . . .6 E3
Thames Mdw
  East Molesey TW8 . . . . . 36 A6
  Lower Halliford KT12, TW17 34 E1
Thamesmead KT12 . . . . . 35 A2
Thamesmead Sch TW17 . . 34 D3
Thamesmead Sp Ctr
  TW17 . . . . 34 D3
Thamespoint TW11 . . . . . 17 D1
Thames Rd W4 . . . . .7 B8
Thames Row TW8 . . . . . . .6 F8
Thames Side
  Kingston upon Thames
    KT1 . . . . 37 D8
  Laleham KT16, TW18 . . . . 33 C4
  Staines TW18 . . . . 12 F2
  Thames Ditton KT7 . . . . . 37 B3
Thames St
  East Molesey TW12 . . . . . 36 B7
  Kingston upon Thames KT1,
    KT2 . . . . 37 D7
  Staines TW18 . . . . 12 F3
  Sunbury TW16 . . . . 35 B6
  Walton-on-Thames KT12 . . 34 F2
  Weybridge KT13 . . . . 53 B7
Thamesvale Cl TW3 . . . . . .5 A5
Thames View Ho TW12 . . . 35 A3
Thames Village W4 . . . . . .7 C6
Thanescroft Ct CR0 . . . . . 61 F7
Thanescroft Gdns CR0 . . . 61 E7
Thanet Ho
  10 Croydon CR0 . . . . . . 61 C6
  1 West Norwood SE27 . . 22 B5
Thanet Pl CR0 . . . . 61 C6
Tharp Rd SM6 . . . . 60 D5
Thatcher Rd RH10 . . . . . 201 D3
Thatchers Cl
  Horley RH6 . . . . 161 B5
  Horsham RH12 . . . . 217 E4
Thatchers La GU3 . . . . . . 108 E8
Thatchers Way TW7 . . . . . .5 D2
Thaxted Pl **14** SW20 . . . . 19 D1
Thayers Farm Rd BR3 . . . 43 E8
Theal Cl GU47 . . . . 64 D8
Theatre Rd GU14 . . . . . . 105 B8
Thelma Gr TW11 . . . . 17 A2
Thelton Ave RH12 . . . . . 216 D3
Theobald Rd CR0, CR9 . . . 61 B8
Theobalds Way GU16 . . . . 66 C3
Thepps Cl RH1 . . . . 140 F6
Therapia La
  Thornton Heath CR0 . . . . 41 E3
  Wallington CR0 . . . . 41 D2
  Wallington CR0 . . . . 41 E2
Therapia La Halt CR0 . . . . 41 E2
Theresa's Wlk CR2 . . . . . 61 D2
Therfield Sch KT22 . . . . . 95 A8
Thesiger Rd BR3, SE20 . . . 23 D1
Thetford Ct
  Dulwich SE21 . . . . 23 B6
  New Malden KT3 . . . . . . 38 E4
Thetford Rd
  Ashford TW15 . . . . 13 E5
  New Malden KT3 . . . . . . 38 E4
Thetford Wlk RH11 . . . . . 200 E2
Thetis Terr TW9 . . . . .7 A8
Theydon Cl RH10 . . . . . . 202 A4
Theydon Ct GU6 . . . . . . 174 A2
Thibet Rd GU47 . . . . 64 C8
Thicket Cres SM1 . . . . . . 59 C6
Thicket Ct **5** SM1 . . . . . 59 C6
Thicket Gr SE20 . . . . 23 A1
Thicket Rd
  Penge SE19, SE20 . . . . . 23 B1
  Sutton SM1 . . . . 59 C6
Thickthorne La TW18 . . . . 13 C1
Third Cl KT8 . . . . 36 C5
Third Cross Rd TW2 . . . . . 16 D6
Thirlestane Ct GU26 . . . . 188 F5
Thirlmere Cl
  Farnborough GU14 . . . . . 84 E4
  Thorpe Lea TW20 . . . . . . 12 B1
Thirlmere Ho TW1 . . . . . . .5 F2
Thirlmere Rd
  Crawley RH11 . . . . 200 D4
  Streatham SW16 . . . . . . 21 D4
Thirlmere Rise BR1 . . . . . 24 F2
Thirlmere Wlk GU15 . . . . 66 D4
Thirsk Cl GU12 . . . . 105 D2
Thirsk Rd
  Mitcham CR4 . . . . 21 A1
  South Norwood SE25 . . . . 42 D5
Thisledown Ct SE25 . . . . . 42 D6
Thistlecroft Rd KT12 . . . . 54 C6
Thistledene
  Thames Ditton KT7 . . . . . 36 E3
  West Byfleet KT14 . . . . . . 70 F6
Thistledown Vale RH14 . . 212 D3
Thistles The KT22 . . . . . . 95 C5
Thistle Way RH6 . . . . . . 162 C3
Thistlewood Cres CR0 . . . 82 D7
Thistleworth Cl TW7 . . . . .5 D7
Thistley Cl CR5 . . . . 99 D5
Thistley La GU6 . . . . 174 E4
Thomas Ave CR3 . . . . . . 100 C6

Thomas Bennett Com Coll
  RH10 . . . . 201 D2
Thomas Dean Rd SE26 . . . 23 F4
Thomas Ho **14** SM2 . . . . 59 B3
Thomas Knyvett Coll
  TW15 . . . . 13 E5
Thomas' La SE6 . . . . 24 A8
Thomas Moore Ho RH2 . . 118 C1
Thomas More Sch CR8 . . . 61 A1
Thomas Pooley Ct **2** KT6 37 E2
Thomas Wall Cl SM1 . . . . 59 B5
Thompson Ave TW9 . . . . . .7 A4
Thompson Cl SM3 . . . . . . 40 A1
Thompson Rd TW3 . . . . . .5 B3
Thompsons Cl GU24 . . . . 87 D4
Thompson's La GU24 . . . . 49 D2
Thomson Cres CR0 . . . . . 42 A1
Thorburn Chase GU47 . . . 64 E6
Thorburn Way **7** SW19 . . 40 C8
Thorfield GU8 . . . . 169 C4
Thorkhill Gdns KT7 . . . . . 37 B2
Thorkhill Rd KT7 . . . . 37 B2
Thorlands RH5 . . . . 208 A7
Thorley Cl KT14 . . . . 71 A5
Thorley Gdns KT14 . . . . . 71 A5
Thornash Cl GU21 . . . . . . 69 C4
Thornash Rd GU21 . . . . . 69 C4
Thornash Way GU21 . . . . 69 C4
Thorn Bank GU2 . . . . . . 130 A7
Thornbank Cl TW19 . . . . . .2 A2
Thornberry Way GU1 . . . 109 F5
Thornbury Ave TW7 . . . . . .5 D7
Thornbury Cl **2** RG45 . . . 45 B5
Thornbury Ct
  Croydon CR2 . . . . 61 D5
  Hounslow TW7 . . . . .5 E7
  Whyteleafe CR3 . . . . . . 100 F7
Thornbury Rd TW7 . . . . . .5 D6
Thorn Cl GU10 . . . . 145 F4
Thorncombe St GU5 . . . . 151 E2
THORNCOMBE STREET . . 151 E1
Thorncroft
  Englefield Green TW20 . . . 11 C1
  4 Leatherhead KT22 . . . 95 A5
Thorncroft Cl CR5 . . . . . 100 A8
Thorncroft Rd SM1 . . . . . 59 B6
Thorndean St SW18 . . . . . 20 C6
Thorndon Gdns KT19 . . . . 57 E6
Thorndown La GU20 . . . . 48 D3
Thorndyke Cl RH10 . . . . . 202 D5
Thorne Cl
  Claygate KT10 . . . . 56 A3
  Crowthorne RG45 . . . . . . 45 A7
  Littleton Common TW15 . . 14 C1
Thorneloe Gdns CR0, CR9 . 61 B5
Thorne's Cl BR3 . . . . 44 C6
Thorne St SW13, SW14 . . . .7 E4
Thorneycroft Cl KT12 . . . . 35 C3
Thornfield Gn GU17 . . . . . 64 F3
Thornfield Rd SM7 . . . . . 78 A2
Thornhill
  Bracknell RG12 . . . . 27 E5
  Crawley RH11 . . . . 201 B4
Thornhill Ave KT6 . . . . . . 56 E8
Thornhill Cres GU11 . . . . 105 C3
Thornhill Rd
  Aldershot GU11 . . . . . . 105 D4
  Surbiton KT6 . . . . 56 F8
  Thornton Heath CR0 . . . . 42 C2
Thornhill Way TW17 . . . . . 34 A4
Thornlaw Rd SE27 . . . . . . 22 B4
Thornleas Pl KT24 . . . . . . 92 E1
Thorn Rd GU10 . . . . 146 A5
Thornsbeach Rd SE6 . . . . 24 C6
Thornsett Pl SE20 . . . . . . 43 B7
Thornsett Rd
  Penge SE20 . . . . 43 B7
  Wandsworth SW18 . . . . . 20 B7
Thornsett Terr SE20 . . . . . 43 B7
Thornton Ave
  Streatham SW2 . . . . 21 D7
  Thornton Heath CR0 . . . . 41 F3
Thornton Cl
  Guildford GU2 . . . . 109 A4
  Horley RH6 . . . . 160 E3
Thornton Cres CR5 . . . . . 100 A8
Thornton Ct SW20 . . . . . . 39 D4
Thornton Dene BR3 . . . . . 44 A7
Thornton Gdns SW12 . . . . 21 D7
Thornton Health L Ctr
  CR7 . . . . 42 C5
THORNTON HEATH 42 B3
Thornton Heath Coll CR7 . 42 A4
Thornton Heath Sta CR7 . 42 C5
Thornton Hill SW19 . . . . . 19 E1
Thornton Lo **8** SW19 . . . 19 E1
Thornton Pl RH6 . . . . . . 160 F3
Thornton Rd
  Carshalton SM5 . . . . 40 D1
  Mortlake SW14 . . . . .7 D4
  Streatham SW12, SW2 . . . 21 D7
  Thornton Heath CR0, CR7,
    CR9 . . . . 41 F3
  Wimbledon SW19 . . . . . . 19 D1
Thornton Road E SW19 . . . 19 D2
Thornton Road Ind Est
  CR0 . . . . 41 F3
Thornton Row CR7 . . . . . . 42 A4
Thornton Side RH1 . . . . . 119 B4
Thornville Gr CR4 . . . . . . 40 D7
Thornycroft Ct TW9 . . . . . .6 F5
Thornyhurst Rd GU16 . . . . 86 A4
Thorold Cl CR0, CR2 . . . . 62 D1
Thorold Ho **6** SW2 . . . . . 21 E8
Thorold Rd GU9 . . . . 125 C3
Thoroughfare The KT20 . . 97 A3
THORPE 32 C6

Thorpe By-Pass TW20 . . . . 32 B6
Thorpe CE Inf Sch TW20 . . 32 B6
Thorpe Cl
  Forest Hill SE26 . . . . 23 D4
  New Addington CR0 . . . . . 82 C8
  Wokingham RG41 . . . . . . 25 A3
Thorpe Ct SW17 . . . . 20 E4
Thorpe Ind Est TW20 . . . . 32 C7
Thorpe Ind Pk TW20 . . . . 32 C8
THORPE LEA 12 B1
Thorpe Lea Prim Sch
  TW20 . . . . 12 D2
Thorpe Lea Rd TW20 . . . . 12 C2
Thorpe Park★ TW20,
  TW16 . . . . 32 E5
Thorpe Rd
  Chertsey KT16 . . . . 32 D4
  Egham TW18, TW20 . . . . . 12 D3
  Kingston upon Thames KT2 . 17 E1
Thorpes Cl GU2 . . . . 109 A4
Thorpeside Cl TW18, TW20 32 E7
Thorpewood Ave SE23,
  SE26 . . . . 23 B6
Thorsden Cl GU22 . . . . . . 89 E8
Thorsden Ct **10** GU22 . . . 69 E1
Thorsden Way **2** SE19 . . 22 E3
Thrale Almshouses SW16 . 21 E1
Thrale Rd SW16 . . . . 21 C3
Three Acres RH12 . . . . . 217 A1
Three Arch Bsns Pk RH1 140 A4
Three Arches Pk RH1 . . . 139 F5
Three Arch Rd RH1 . . . . . 140 A5
THREE BRIDGES 202 A7
Three Bridges Fst Sch
  RH10 . . . . 202 A7
Three Bridges Jun Sch
  RH10 . . . . 201 F6
Three Bridges Rd RH10 . . 202 A6
Three Bridges Sta RH10 . 202 B6
Three Gates GU1 . . . . . . 110 C3
Three Gates La GU27 . . . 208 E8
Three Pears Rd GU1 . . . . 110 E1
Threestile Corner RH12 . . 197 E1
Threestile Rd RH12 . . . . 197 F1
Three Stiles Rd GU9 . . . . 124 F3
Threeways TW1 . . . . 16 F4
Three Ways GU10 . . . . . . 166 D6
Threshfield RG12 . . . . . . 27 A4
Threshold Way GU24 . . . . 50 D1
Thriffwood SE23, SE26 . . . 23 D5
Thrift Vale GU4 . . . . 110 D4
Thrigby Rd KT9 . . . . 56 F4
Throwley Rd SM1 . . . . . . 59 B5
Throwley Way SM1 . . . . . 59 B5
Thrupp Cl CR4 . . . . 41 B7
Thrupps Ave KT12 . . . . . . 54 D5
Thrupps La KT12 . . . . 54 D5
Thundery Hill GU10 . . . . 126 F4
Thurbans Rd GU9 . . . . . . 146 A7
Thurbarn Rd SE6 . . . . . . 24 B3
Thurbarns Hill RH5 . . . . . 157 E1
Thurlby Rd SE27 . . . . 22 A4
Thurleigh Rd SW11, SW12 . 20 F8
Thurleston Ave SM4 . . . . 39 E4
Thurlestone Cl TW17 . . . . 34 C3
Thurlestone Par TW17 . . . 34 C3
Thurlestone Rd SE27 . . . . 22 A4
Thurlow GU7 . . . . 150 D3
Thurlow Hill SE21 . . . . . . 22 C6
Thurlow Ho **17** SW16 . . . 21 E5
Thurlow Park Rd SE21,
  SE24 . . . . 22 C6
Thurlow Towers SE27 . . . . 22 A5
Thurlow Wlk GU6 . . . . . . 174 E1
Thurlton Ct GU21 . . . . . . 69 E3
Thurnby Ct TW2 . . . . 16 E5
Thurne Way RH12 . . . . . 214 D7
Thurnham Way KT20 . . . . 97 D7
Thursby Rd GU21 . . . . . . 69 A1
THURSLEY 169 C4
Thursley Cres CR0 . . . . . 63 D3
Thursley Gdns SW19 . . . . 19 D6
Thursley Ho
  3 Kingston upon Thames
    KT2 . . . . 18 B1
  13 Streatham SW2 . . . . 21 F8
Thursley National Nature
  Reserve★ GU8 . . . . . . 169 C5
Thursley Rd
  Churt GU10, GU8 . . . . . . 168 C3
  Thursley GU8, GU10 . . . . 169 B6
Thurso St SW17 . . . . 20 D4
Thurstan Rd SW20 . . . . . 19 B1
Thurston Ho BR3 . . . . . . 24 B2
Thurza Ct **2** TW7 . . . . . . .5 F5
Thyme Ct
  Farnborough GU14 . . . . . 84 C5
  Guildford GU4 . . . . 110 B4
Thyme Ho RH10 . . . . 182 A1
Tibbenham Pl SE6 . . . . . . 24 A6
Tibbets Cl SW19 . . . . 19 D7
Tibbet's Cnr SW19 . . . . . 19 D8
Tibbet's Ride SW19 . . . . . 19 D8
Ticehurst Cl RH10 . . . . . 202 E6
Ticehurst Rd SE23 . . . . . 23 E6
Tichborne Cl GU17 . . . . . 64 D5
Tichborne Pl GU12 . . . . . 126 D8
Tichbourne Cl GU16 . . . . 65 F3
Tichmarsh KT19 . . . . 57 C1
Tide Cl **2** CR4 . . . . 41 A8
Tidenham Gdns CR0 . . . . 61 E7
Tides End Ct GU15 . . . . . 65 E4
Tideswell Rd CR0 . . . . . . 63 A7
Tideway Cl TW10 . . . . . . 17 C4
Tideway Yd SW13 . . . . . . .7 E5
Tidwells Lea RG12 . . . . . 27 E8
Tiepigs La BR2, BR4 . . . . 44 F1

Tierney Ct **4** CR0 . . . . . 61 F8
Tierney Rd SW2 . . . . 21 E7
Tierney Terr SW2 . . . . . . 21 E7
Tiffin Girls' Sch KT2 . . . . 17 E2
Tiffin Sch KT2 . . . . 37 F7
Tiffin Sp Ctr KT2 . . . . . . 37 F7
Tilburstow Cotts RH9 . . . 121 C3
Tilburstow Hill Rd RH9 . . 142 D5
Tile Barn Cl GU14 . . . . . . 85 A5
Tilehouse Rd GU4 . . . . . 130 E5
Tilehurst La RH3, RH5 . . . 136 F5
Tilehurst Rd
  Cheam SM3 . . . . 58 E5
  Wandsworth SW17, SW18 . 20 D7
Tilers Cl RH1 . . . . 119 C4
Tiler's Way RH2 . . . . 139 C5
Tiler's Wlk RH2 . . . . 139 C5
TILFORD 147 D3
Tilford Ave CR0 . . . . 63 C2
Tilford Gdns SW19 . . . . . 19 D7
Tilford Ho **11** SW2 . . . . . 21 F8
Tilford Rd
  Beacon Hill GU10, GU26 . 188 D7
  Farnham GU10, GU9 . . . . 146 F7
  Hindhead GU26 . . . . . . 188 B3
  Hindhead GU26 . . . . . . 188 F4
  Rushmoor GU10 . . . . . . 168 C4
  Tilford GU10 . . . . 147 C4
Tilford St GU10 . . . . 147 D5
TILGATE 201 E2
Tilgate Comm RH1 . . . . . 120 C2
Tilgate Dr RH10, RH11 . . . 201 E2
Tilgate Forest Bsns Ctr
  RH11 . . . . 201 D1
Tilgate Forest Nature
  Reserve★ RH10 . . . . . 202 B2
Tilgate Mansions RH10 . . 201 F1
Tilgate Par RH10 . . . . . . 201 E3
Tilgate Park Ctry Pk★
  RH10 . . . . 201 F1
Tilgate Pl RH10 . . . . 201 E3
Tilgates Cotts RH1 . . . . . 120 C3
Tilgate Way RH10 . . . . . 201 E3
Tilia Cl SM1 . . . . 58 F5
Tilletts La RH12 . . . . 216 E8
Tilley La KT18 . . . . 96 C4
Tillingbourne Jun Sch
  GU4 . . . . 131 B2
Tillingbourne Mews
  GU5 . . . . 132 B4
Tillingbourne Rd GU4 . . . 130 E3
Tillingdown Hill CR3 . . . . 101 A5
Tillingdown La
  Caterham CR3 . . . . 101 B2
  Caterham CR3 . . . . 101 B3
Tillman Ho **8** SW2 . . . . . 21 F7
Tillotson Ct RH10 . . . . . 202 D5
Tilly's La TW18 . . . . 12 F4
Tilney Cl KT22 . . . . 95 A7
Tilney Ct KT6 . . . . 37 D4
Tilson Gdns SW2, SW4 . . . 21 E8
Tilson Ho SW2 . . . . 21 E8
Tilt Cl KT11 . . . . 73 E3
Tilthams Corner Rd GU5,
  GU7 . . . . 151 C8
Tilthams Gn GU7 . . . . . . 151 B8
Tilt Mdw KT11 . . . . 73 E3
Tilt Rd KT11 . . . . 73 D3
Tiltview KT11 . . . . 73 C4
Tiltwood Dr RH10 . . . . . 204 C8
Timber Bank GU16 . . . . . 86 A6
Timber Cl
  Farnham GU9 . . . . 125 B2
  Great Bookham KT23 . . . 114 C8
  Pyrford GU22 . . . . 70 F5
Timbercroft KT19 . . . . . . 57 E6
Timber Ct RH12 . . . . 217 C3
Timberham Farm Rd
  RH6 . . . . 181 D8
Timberham Ho RH6 . . . . 181 E8
Timberham Way RH6 . . . 181 E8
Timber Hill KT21 . . . . 95 E8
Timber Hill Rd CR3 . . . . . 101 A3
Timber La CR3 . . . . 101 A3
Timberlands **14** RH11 . . . 201 B1
Timberling Gdns CR2 . . . . 61 D1
Timbermill Ct GU27 . . . . 207 F6
Timberslip Dr SM6 . . . . . 60 D2
Timbertop Rd TN16 . . . . . 83 C1
Times Sq SM1 . . . . 59 B5
Timline Gn RG12 . . . . . . 27 F7
Timperley Ct
  Putney SW19 . . . . 19 E7
  Redhill RH1 . . . . 118 E3
Timperley Gdns RH1 . . . . 118 E3
Timsbury Wlk **5** SW15 . . 19 A7
Timsway TW18 . . . . 12 F3
Tina Ct
  Forest Hill SE6 . . . . 23 F8
  West Norwood SW16 . . . . 22 A5
  3 Wimbledon SW20 . . . 19 D1
Tindale Cl CR2 . . . . 80 D8
Tinsey Cl TW20 . . . . 12 B3
Tinsley Cl
  Crawley RH10 . . . . 182 A1
  South Norwood SE25 . . . . 43 B6
Tinsley Gn RH10 . . . . . . 182 B4
TINSLEY GREEN 182 C4
Tinsley La RH10 . . . . 182 A1
Tinsley La N RH10 . . . . . 182 B3
Tinsley La S RH10 . . . . . 202 A8
Tintagel Cl KT17 . . . . 76 F5
Tintagel Ct RH13 . . . . . . 217 D1
Tintagel Dr GU16 . . . . . . 65 F1
Tintagel Way GU22 . . . . . 70 A3
Tintells La KT24 . . . . 112 B7
Tintern Cl SW19 . . . . 20 C2

Tintern Rd
Carshalton SM5 40 D1
Crawley RH11 201 A4
Tippits Mead RG42 26 D8
Tipton Dr CR0 61 E6
Tiree Path RH11 201 B3
Tirlemont Rd CR2 61 C3
Tirrell Rd CR0 42 C3
Tisbury Rd SW16 41 E7
TISMAN'S COMMON 214 A6
Titchfield Rd SM5 40 D1
Titchfield Wlk SM5 40 D2
Titchwell Rd SW18 20 D7
Tite Hill TW20 11 D3
Tithe Barn Cl KT2 37 F8
Tithebarns La GU23 91 B1
Tithe Barn The GU4 111 D4
Tithe Cl
Virginia Water GU25 31 D3
Walton-on-Thames KT12 35 B3
Tithe Ct RG40 25 C7
Tithe La TW19 1 A1
Tithe Mdws GU25 31 D3
Tithe Orch RH19 184 E4
Tithepit Shaw La CR6 81 B3
Tithe The RH11 181 A1
Titlarks Hill Rd SL5 30 B1
Titmus Dr RH10 201 F2
TITSEY 103 B2
Titsey Cnr RH8 123 A7
Titsey Hill CR6, RH8 103 B4
Titsey Pl & Gdns* RH8 103 B3
Titsey Rd
Limpsfield RH8 123 B8
Titsey RH8 103 B1
TITTENHURST 30 A5
Tiverton Cl CR0 42 F2
Tiverton Rd TW3 5 C5
Tiverton Way
Chessington KT9 56 D5
Frimley GU16 65 F1
Tivoli Rd
Hounslow TW4 4 E3
West Norwood SE27 22 C3
Toad La
Blackwater GU17 64 E4
10 Hounslow TW4 4 F3
Tobias Sch of Art RH19 205 E6
Tobin Cl KT19 76 B8
Toby Way KT5 57 B8
Todds Cl RH6 160 E5
Toftwood Cl RH10 202 C5
Toldene Ct CR5 99 F8
Toll Bar Ct SM2 59 B2
Tolldene Cl GU21 68 E2
Tollers La CR5 99 F8
Tollgate GU1 110 D1
Tollgate Ave RH1 139 F4
Tollgate Ct RH1 139 F4
Tollgate Dr SE21 22 E6
Tollgate Hill RH11 201 C1
Tollgate Pl 12 RH19 205 F8
Tollgate Prim Sch CR0 43 C3
Tollgate Rd RH4 136 B4
Toll Gdns RG12 27 F6
Tollhouse La SM6 60 C2
Tolson Ho 3 TW7 6 A4
Tolson Rd TW7 6 A4
Tolvaddon Cl GU21 69 A2
Tolverne Rd SW20 39 C8
TOLWORTH 57 B7
Tolworth Cl KT6 38 B1
Tolworth Court Bridge
KT19 57 C7
Tolworth Girls' Sch KT6 56 F7
Tolworth Hospl KT6 57 A8
Tolworth Inf Sch KT6 37 F1
Tolworth Jun Sch KT6 37 F1
Tolworth Park Rd KT6 56 F8
Tolworth Rd KT6 56 E8
Tolworth Rec Ctr KT6 56 F7
Tolworth Rise N KT5 38 B1
Tolworth Rise S KT5 38 B1
Tolworth Sta KT5 57 B8
Tolworth Underpass KT5,
KT6 57 B8
Tomlin Cl KT19 76 D8
Tomlin Ct KT19 76 D8
Tomlins Ave GU16 65 F2
Tomlinscote Sch & Sixth
Form Coll GU16 66 A2
Tomlinscote Sp Ctr GU16 66 A2
Tomlinscote Way GU16 66 A2
Tompset's Bank RH18 206 F1
Tomtit Cres RH10 204 C5
Tomtits La RH18 206 E1
Tonbridge Cl SM7 78 F5
Tonbridge Rd KT12, KT8 35 F5
Tonfield Rd SM3 39 F1
Tonge Cl BR3 44 A4
TONGHAM 126 F6
Tongham Mdws GU10 126 F7
Tongham Rd
Aldershot GU12 126 D8
Runfold GU10 126 C4
Tonstall Rd
Epsom KT19 76 D8
Mitcham CR4 41 A7
Tooting Bec Gdns SW16 21 D4
Tooting Bec Rd SW16 21 B4
Tooting Bec U Sta SW17 21 A5
Tooting Broadway SW17 20 F3
Tooting Broadway U Sta
SW17 20 E3
Tooting Gr SW17 20 E3
TOOTING GRAVENEY 20 D3
Tooting High St SW17,
SW19 20 E3
Tooting L Ctr SW17 20 D4
Tooting Mkt SW17 20 F4
Tooting Sta SW17 20 F2
Tootswood Rd BR2 44 E5
Topaz Ct TW13 14 F5
Topaz Ho KT4 38 D1
Topiary Sq TW9 6 F4
Topiary The
Ashtead KT21 95 E7
Farnborough GU14 84 E3
Topladly Pl GU9 125 C7
Top Pk BR3 44 E4
Topsham Rd SW17 21 A4
Top Terr Rd GU14 105 A8
Torcross Dr SE23 23 C6
Torin Ct TW20 11 C3
Tor La KT13 72 D8
Torland Dr KT22 74 D6
Tormead Cl SM1 59 A4
Tormead Rd GU1 109 F1
Tormead Sch GU1 109 F1
Toronto BR2 44 E6
Toronto Dr RH6 162 A3
Torquay Ho SM6 60 D5
Tor Rd GU9 124 F2
Torrens Cl GU2 109 A4
Torre Wlk SM5 40 E1
Torridge Rd
Brands Hill SL3 1 B8
Thornton Heath CR7 42 B4
Torridon Cl GU21 69 B2
Torridon Jun & Inf Schs
SE6 24 D6
Torridon Rd SE13, SE6 24 D7
Torrington Cl KT10 55 E4
Torrington Ct SE26 23 A3
Torrington Rd KT10 55 E4
Torrington Sq CR0 42 D2
Torrington Way SM4 40 A3
Torr Rd SE20 23 D1
Torwood La CR3 100 F8
Totford La GU10 127 E4
Totham Lodge SW20 39 B8
Totland Cl GU14 85 A6
Totnes Ho 18 TW1 6 D1
Tottenham Rd GU7 150 E6
Tottenham Wlk GU47 45 D1
Totterdown St SW17 20 F3
Totton Rd CR7 42 A6
Toulouse Cl GU15 66 B7
Tournai Cl GU11 105 E7
Toutley Rd RG41 25 A8
Tovil Cl SE20 43 B7
Tower Approach Rd RH6 181 E6
Tower Cl
East Grinstead RH19 185 E2
Hindhead GU26 188 E4
Horley RH6 160 F3
Penge SE20 23 B1
Woking GU21 69 D2
Tower Cotts KT10 54 F1
Tower Ct
East Grinstead RH19 185 E2
12 Egham TW20 12 A3
Tower Gate Bsns Ctr
GU8 190 F7
Tower Gdns KT10 56 A3
Tower Gr KT13 53 E8
TOWER HILL 136 B5
Towerhill GU5 133 C3
Tower Hill
Dorking RH4 136 B5
Farnborough GU14 85 A3
Tower Hill Prim Sch GU14 84 F3
Tower Hill Rd RH4 136 B5
Tower Hill Rise GU5 133 C3
Tower Ho KT14 71 E7
Tower Pl CR6 82 A4
Tower Rd
Faygate RH12 218 F8
Hindhead GU26 188 E4
Tadworth KT20 97 C4
Twickenham TW1 16 F5
Tower Rise TW9 6 E4
Towers Dr RG45 45 B4
Towers Pl TW10 6 E2
Towers The
Kenley CR8 80 C4
1 Richmond TW9 6 F3
Towers Wlk KT13 53 B4
Tower View CR0 43 E2
Towfield Ct TW13 15 F6
Towfield Rd TW13 15 F6
Town Barn Rd RH11 201 C7
Townend CR3 100 E5
Town End Cl
Caterham CR3 100 E5
Godalming GU7 150 E4
Townend Ct 8 BR1 44 F8
Town End St GU7 150 E4
Town Farm Prim Sch
TW19 13 D8
Town Farm Way TW19 13 D8
Townfield Ct RH4 136 A6
Townfield Rd RH4 136 A6
Town Field Way TW7 6 A5
Towngate KT11 73 E4
Town Hill RH7 164 E4
Town La TW19 13 D7
Town Mead
Bletchingley RH1 120 D2
Crawley RH11 201 D7
Town Meadow TW8 6 D7
Townmead Rd TW9 7 B5
Town Quay TW18 33 C6
Townsend Cl RG12 27 E4
Townsend Cotts GU22 90 B6
Townsend La GU22 90 B6
Townsend Mews 3 SW18 20 C6
Townsend Rd TW15 13 E3
Townsend Way RH10 202 D4
Townshend Rd TW9 6 F3
Townshend Terr TW9 6 F3
Townshott Cl KT23 94 A1
Townside Pl GU15 65 D6
Town Sq
Bracknell RG12 27 C7
Camberley GU15 65 C6
6 Woking GU21 69 F2
Town Tree Rd TW15 14 A3
Towpath Way CR0, SE25 42 F4
Towton Rd SE27 22 C6
Toynbee Rd SW19, SW20 39 E8
Tracery The SM7 78 B4
Tracious Cl GU21 69 B3
Traemore Ct SW16 22 A5
Trafalgar Ave KT4, SM3,
SM4 39 D1
Trafalgar Com Inf Sch
RH12 217 B4
Trafalgar Ct
Cobham KT11 73 A6
Farnham GU9 125 C1
Hounslow TW3 4 F4
West Barnes KT3 39 B6
Trafalgar Dr KT12 54 B7
Trafalgar Gdns RH10 202 B6
Trafalgar Inf Sch TW2 16 D6
Trafalgar Jun Sch TW2 16 D6
Trafalgar Rd
Horsham RH12 217 C4
Merton SW19 20 C1
Twickenham TW2 16 D6
Trafalgar Way
Camberley GU15 64 F4
Croydon CR0, CR9 61 A8
Trafalger Villas GU14 84 C4
Trafford Rd
Frimley GU16 85 D8
Thornton Heath CR7 41 F4
Trafford Villas CR7 41 F4
Traherne Lodge 6 TW11 16 F3
Tramsheds Ind Est The
CR0 41 D2
Tramway Cl SE20 43 C8
Tramway Path CR4 40 E5
Tranmere Ct 13 SM2 59 C3
Tranmere Rd
Twickenham TW2 16 B8
Wandsworth SW17, SW18 20 C6
Tranquil Dale RH3 116 F3
Transport Ave TW8 6 B8
Transport Police Training Ctr
KT20 97 A4
Transport Rd GU14 85 B1
Trap La RH5 176 F2
Traps La KT2, KT3 38 E8
Trasher Mead RH4 136 C4
Travellers Way TW5 4 C5
Travis La GU47 64 C7
Treadcroft Dr RH12 217 E5
Treadwell Rd KT18 76 F4
Treasury Cl SM6 60 D5
Treaty Ctr TW3 5 B4
Trebor Ave GU9 146 D8
Tredenham Cl GU14 105 C8
Tredown Rd SE26 23 C3
Tredwell Cl SW2 21 F6
Tredwell Rd SE27 22 B4
Treebourne Rd TN16 83 C1
Treebys Ave GU4 109 D7
Tree Cl TW10 17 D7
Treelands RH5 136 C4
Treemount Ct KT17 76 E6
Treen Ave SW13, SW14 7 F4
Treeside Dr GU9 125 E7
Treetops RH9 142 E6
Tree Tops CR6 81 A1
Tree Tops Ave GU15 66 B8
Treetops Ct CR7 42 C4
Treeview RH11 201 C1
Tree View Cl SE19 42 E8
Treeview Ct 3 RH2 118 D1
Treeway RH2 118 B4
Trefoil Cl
Horsham RH12 217 E5
Wokingham RG40 25 E7
Trefoil Cres RH11 201 A2
Trefusis Ct TW5 4 B6
Tregaron Gdns KT3 38 E5
Tregarthen Pl KT22 95 C6
Tregarth Pl GU21 68 F2
Treglos Ct KT13 53 E8
Tregolls Dr GU14 85 D3
Trehaven Par RH2 139 B6
Treherne Ct SW17 21 A4
Trehern Rd 13 SW14 7 D4
Trelawn Cl KT16 51 D3
Trelawne Dr GU6 174 E2
Trelawney KT12 35 D1
Trelawney Gr KT13 53 A4
Trellis Ho SW19 20 C1
Treloar Gdns SE19 22 D2
Tremaine Rd SE20 43 B7
Trematon Pl TW11 17 C1
Tremayne Wlk GU15 66 C4
Trenance GU21 69 A2
Trenchard Cl KT12 54 C5
Trenchard Ct SM4 40 A3
Trenear Cl RH13 217 E2
Trenham Dr CR6 81 C3
Trenholme Cl SE20 23 B1
Trenholme Ct CR3 101 A4
Trenholme Rd SE20 23 B1
Trenholme Terr SE20 23 B1
Trent Cl
Crawley RH11 200 F4
Farnborough GU14 84 E6
Trent Ct 1 CR2 61 C5
Trentham Cres GU22 90 A6
Trentham Rd RH1 140 A7
Trentham St SW18 20 A7
Trent Ho 8 KT2 37 D8
Trenton Cl GU16 66 A1
Trent Rd SL3 1 B8
Trent Way KT4 58 C7
Treport St SW18 20 B8
Treryn Hts GU7 150 D6
Tresco Cl BR1 24 E2
Tresidder Ho 8 SW4 21 D8
Tresillian Way GU21 69 B2
Tresta Wlk GU21 69 A3
Trevanne Plat RH10 202 D7
Trevelyan RG12 26 E2
Trevelyan Ct KT3 38 F2
Trevelyan Ho 6 TW1 6 C1
Trevelyan Rd SW17 20 F2
Trevenna Ho 13 SE23 23 D5
Trevereux Hill RH8 123 F4
Treversh Ct 9 BR1 44 F8
Treville St SW15 19 B8
Treviso Rd SE23 23 D6
Trevithick Cl TW14 14 F7
Trevor Cl
Hayes BR2 44 F2
Isleworth TW7 5 F2
Trevor Rd SW19 19 E1
Trevose Ave KT14 70 F5
Trewenna Dr KT9 56 D5
Trewince Rd SW20 39 C8
Trewint St SW18 20 C6
Trewsbury Rd SE26 23 D3
Treyford Cl RH11 200 F6
Triangle The
Kingston upon Thames
KT3 38 C7
Woking GU21 69 C1
Trickett Ho SM2 59 B2
Trident Bsns Ctr SW17 20 F3
Trident Ho TW19 13 E8
Trident Ind Est SL3 1 E4
Trieste Ct SW12 20 F7
Trigg's Cl GU22 89 D8
Trigg's La GU21, GU22 89 D8
Trigo Ct KT19 76 D8
Trig St RH5 178 F8
Trilby Rd SE23 23 D6
Trimmer Ct TW7 5 F4
Trimmer's Almshouses
GU9 125 A1
Trimmers Cl GU9 125 C7
Trimmers Field GU9 125 E1
Trimmers Wood GU26 188 E6
Trimmer Wlk 11 TW8 6 E8
Trinder Mews 11 TW11 17 A3
Trindles Rd RH1 140 F7
Tring Ct TW1 17 A4
Tringham Cl
Knaphill GU21 68 C1
Ottershaw KT16 51 C5
Tringham Cotts GU24 67 F7
Trinity GU47 45 E2
Trinity Churchyard 3
GU1 130 D7
Trinity Cl
Crawley RH10 202 C8
Hounslow TW4 4 E3
South Croydon CR2 61 E2
Stanwell TW19 2 C1
Trinity Cotts TW9 6 F4
Trinity Cres
Sunningdale SL5 30 A4
Upper Tooting SW17 21 A6
Trinity Ct
Addlestone KT15 52 B6
Bracknell RG12 26 F7
Forest Hill SE23 23 C5
Horsham RH12 217 C3
Thornton Heath SE25 42 E3
Twickenham TW2 16 E6
2 Wallington SM6 60 C3
1 Wimbledon SW19 20 A2
Trinity Fields GU9 125 A6
Trinity Gate 9 GU1 130 E8
Trinity Hill GU9 125 A6
Trinity Mews SE20 43 B8
Trinity Par TW3 5 B4
Trinity Rd
Knaphill GU21 68 B1
Richmond TW9 6 F4
Upper Tooting SW17, SW18 20 E7
Wimbledon SW19 20 A2
Trinity Rise SE24, SW2 22 B8
Trinity St Mary's Prim Sch
SW12 21 A7
Trinity Sch CR9 62 C8
Trinity Sq RH12 217 D2
Tristram Rd BR1 24 F4
Trist Way RH11 201 A8
Tritton Ave CR0 60 E6
Tritton Rd SE21 22 D5
Trittons KT20 97 D6
Triumph Cl UB7 3 C6
Trodd's La
Albury GU4 132 A8
Guildford GU1, GU4 110 E1
Trojan Way CR0 60 F7
Troon RH6 161 B2
Troon Cl RH11 200 D5
Troon Ct SL5 29 C4
Troston Ct TW18 12 F3
Trotsford Mdw GU17 64 C4
Trotsworth Ave GU25 31 E5
Trotsworth Ct GU25 31 D5
Trotters La GU24 69 B7
Trotter Way KT19 76 A7
Trotton Cl RH10 202 C3
Trotwood Cl GU47 45 E2
Troutbeck Wlk GU15 66 D3
Trout Rd GU27 207 E6
Trowers Way RH1 119 B4
Trowlock Ave TW11 17 C2
Trowlock Way TW11 17 D2
Troy Cl KT20 97 B7
Troy La TN8 144 F4
Troy Rd SE19 22 D2
TROY TOWN 144 F5
Trueman Rd CR8 100 D7
Trumpeters Inn TW9 6 C2
Trumpetshill Rd RH2 138 B7
TRUMPS GREEN 31 D3
Trumps Green Ave GU25 31 D3
Trumps Green Cl GU25 31 E4
Trumps Green Inf Sch
GU25 31 D3
Trumpsgreen Rd GU25 31 D3
Trumps Mill La GU25 31 F4
Trundle Mead RH12 217 C5
Trunk Rd GU14 84 C5
Trunley Heath Rd GU5 151 C8
Truscott Ho 3 CR0 42 A3
Truslove Rd SE27 22 B3
Truss Hill Rd SL5 29 C4
Trust Wlk SE21 22 B7
Trys Hill KT16 51 A8
Trystings Cl KT10 56 A4
Tucker Rd KT16 51 D4
Tuckers Dr GU6 174 B3
Tuckey Gr GU23 90 F3
Tudor Ave
Hampton TW12 16 A1
North Cheam KT4 58 B6
Tudor Circ GU7 150 E7
Tudor Cl
Ashford TW15 13 E4
Banstead SM7 77 E4
Cheam SM3 58 E4
Chessington KT9 56 E5
Cobham KT11 73 F6
Coulsdon CR5 80 A1
Crawley RH10 202 D5
East Grinstead RH19 205 F8
Grayshott GU26 188 D2
Hampton TW12 16 C3
Hamsey Green CR2 81 B4
Little Bookham KT23 94 A3
Smallfield RH6 162 B3
Wallington SM6 60 C3
Woking GU22 70 A2
Wokingham RG40 25 F5
Tudor Ct
Biggin Hill TN16 83 E2
19 Egham TW20 12 A3
16 Egham TW20 12 A3
Farncombe GU7 150 E5
Feltham TW13 15 C4
Haslemere GU27 208 C7
6 Knaphill GU21 68 D2
4 Purley CR8 80 A8
12 Redhill RH1 119 A2
4 Stanwell TW19 2 E1
5 Sutton SM2 59 C4
Teddington TW11 16 F2
Tudor Dr
Kingston upon Thames
KT2 17 E3
Walton-on-Thames KT12 35 D1
West Barnes SM4 39 E3
Tudor Gdns
6 Mortlake SW13, SW14 7 E4
Twickenham TW1 16 F7
West Wickham BR4 63 C7
Tudor Grange KT13 53 E8
Tudor Hall GU15 65 F6
Tudor Ho
Bracknell RG12 27 B4
Feltham TW13 15 C4
2 Horsham RH13 217 F3
Mitcham CR4 41 A8
Weybridge KT13 53 A4
Tudor La SL4 11 C8
Tudor Lodge KT20 97 F6
Tudor Lodge Sch CR8 60 E1
Tudor Pl CR4 20 E1
Tudor Rd
Ashford TW15 14 D2
Beckenham BR3 44 C6
Croydon CR0, SE25 43 B4
Farncombe GU7 150 E7
Hampton TW12 16 A1
Isleworth TW3 5 D3
Kingston upon Thames KT2 18 A1
Penge SE19 22 F1
Tudors The 2 BR3 44 B7
Tudor Way GU21 88 C8
Tudor Wlk
Leatherhead KT22 94 F7
3 Weybridge KT13 53 B7
TUESLEY 171 C8
Tuesley Cnr GU7 150 D3
Tuesley La
Godalming GU7, GU8 150 D1
Milford GU7 171 C7
Tufton Gdns KT8 36 B7
Tugela Rd CR0 42 D3
Tugela St SE6 23 F6
Tuggles Plat RH12 216 E7
Tugswood Cl CR5 99 D6

Tulip Cl
Croydon CR0 . . . . **43** D1
Hampton TW12 . . . . **15** F2
Tulip Ct RH12 . . . . **217** C4
Tulip Tree Ct SM2 . . . . **78** A8
Tulk Ho KT16 . . . . **51** B3
Tullett Rd RH10 . . . . **202** B2
Tulleys Farm* RH10 . . . . . . **203** D4
Tull St CR4 . . . . **40** F2
Tulse Cl BR3 . . . . **44** C6
TULSE HILL **22** A8
Tulse Hill SW2, SE24 . . . . . . **22** A8
Tulse Hill Sta SE27 . . . . **22** A8
Tulsemere Rd SE21, SE27 . **22** C6
Tulyar Cl KT20 . . . . **97** B7
Tumber Cl GU12 . . . . **106** A2
Tumber St KT18 . . . . **96** C2
Tumblewood Rd SM7 . . . . . **59** A4
Tumbling Bay KT12 . . . . **35** A3
Tummons Gdns SE25 . . . . . . **42** E1
Tunbridge Ct **1** SE26 . . . . . **23** A5
Tunley Rd SW12, SW17 . . . . **21** A6
Tunnel Link Rd TW6 . . . . **3** A2
Tunnel Rd GU14 . . . . **84** E1
Tunnel Rd E TW6 . . . . **3** B5
Tunnel Rd W TW6 . . . . **3** A6
Tunnel St RH12 . . . . **118** A1
Tunnmeade **7** RH11 . . . . . . **200** E5
Tunsgate GU1 . . . . **130** D7
Tunsgate Sq Sh Ctr GU1 **220** D7
Tunstall Rd CR0 . . . . **42** E1
Tunstall Wlk **10** TW8 . . . . . . **6** E8
Tunworth Cres SW15 . . . . . . **7** F1
Tupwood Ct CR3 . . . . **101** A2
Tupwood La CR3 . . . . **101** A1
Tupwood Scrubbs Rd
CR3 . . . . **121** A8
Turf Hill Rd GU15 . . . . **65** F8
Turfhouse La GU24 . . . . **49** E2
Turing Dr RG12 . . . . **27** A4
Turkey Oak Cl SE19 . . . . **42** E8
Turle Rd SW16 . . . . **41** E7
Turnberry RG12 . . . . **26** E2
Turnberry Ho SL5 . . . . **30** A1
Turner Ave
Mitcham CR4 . . . . **40** F8
Twickenham TW2 . . . . **16** C5
Westerham TN16 . . . . **83** C7
Turner Cl GU1 . . . . **109** F4
Turner Cres CR7 . . . . **42** C3
Turner Ct
East Grinstead RH19 . . . . **186** A3
Godalming GU7 . . . . **150** D4
Turner Ho
Beare Green RH5 . . . . **157** C4
12 Twickenham TW1 . . . . . **6** D1
Turner Lodge **10** SW19 . . . . **19** D7
Turner Mews SM2 . . . . **59** B3
Turner Pl GU47 . . . . **64** D6
Turner Rd KT3 . . . . **38** D2
Turners Cl TW18 . . . . **13** B3
TURNERS HILL **204** A4
Turners Hill CE Prim Sch
RH10 . . . . **204** A3
TURNERS HILL PARK **204** C5
Turners Hill Rd
Copthorne RH10 . . . . **183** F2
Crawley Down RH10 . . . . **204** A7
Crawley RH10 . . . . **203** C5
Turners Hill RH10 . . . . . . **203** F5
Turner's Hill Rd RH19 . . . **205** B6
Turners La KT12 . . . . **54** B3
Turners Mead GU8 . . . . **191** C3
Turners Meadow Way
BR3 . . . . **43** F8
Turners Way CR0, CR9 . . . . **61** A8
Turner Wlk RH10 . . . . **201** F3
Turney Rd SE21 . . . . **22** D8
Turney Sch SE21 . . . . **22** C8
Turnham Cl GU2 . . . . **130** C5
Turnoak Ave GU22 . . . . **89** E7
Turnoak La GU22 . . . . **89** E8
Turnoak Rdbt GU22 . . . . . . **89** E8
Turnpike La SM1 . . . . **59** C5
Turnpike Link CR0 . . . . **61** E8
Turnpike Pl **1** RH11 . . . . . **201** D8
Turnpike Rd RG42 . . . . **26** D7
Turnpike Way TW7 . . . . **6** A6
Turnstone Cl CR0, CR2 . . . . **62** E1
Turnville Cl GU18 . . . . **48** A1
Turpin Rd TW14 . . . . **3** F1
Turpins Rise GU20 . . . . **48** B6
Turpin Way SM6 . . . . **60** B3
Turret Ct RH19 . . . . **185** C3
Turret Ho KT2 . . . . **17** E2
Turtledove Ave RH10 . . . . . **204** C5
Turville Ct KT23 . . . . **94** B2
Tuscam Way GU15 . . . . **64** F4
Tuscany Gdns RH10 . . . . . **201** E8
Tushmore Ave RH10 . . . . . **181** E1
Tushmore Cres RH10 . . . . . **181** E1
Tushmore Ct RH10 . . . . **201** E8
Tushmore La RH10 . . . . **201** E8
Tushmore Rdbt RH11 . . . . . **201** D8
Tussock Cl RH11 . . . . **201** A4
Tuxford Cl RH10 . . . . **202** C4
Tweed Cl GU14 . . . . **84** E6
Tweeddale Prim Sch SM5 **40** D2
Tweeddale Rd SM5 . . . . **40** D1
Tweed La
Brockham RH3 . . . . **137** B5
Rusper RH11 . . . . **180** F1
Tweed Rd SL3 . . . . **1** B8
Tweedsmuir Cl GU14 . . . . . . **84** D3

Tweedy Rd **6** BR1 . . . . **44** F8
Twelve Acre Cl KT23 . . . . . . **93** F3
Twelve Acre Cres GU14 . . . **84** E5
Twelve Trees Ho RG45 . . . . **45** C4
TWICKENHAM **17** B8
Twickenham Bridge TW9 . . **6** C2
Twickenham Cl CR0 . . . . **60** F7
Twickenham Mus The★
TW1 . . . . **17** A7
Twickenham Pl KT7 . . . . **55** F8
Twickenham Prep Sch
TW12 . . . . **36** B8
Twickenham Rd
Feltham TW13 . . . . **15** F5
Isleworth TW1, TW7 . . . . . . **6** A4
Richmond TW1, TW9 . . . . . **6** C3
14 Richmond TW9 . . . . **6** E3
Teddington TW11 . . . . **17** A4
Twickenham Sta TW1 . . . . . **17** A8
Twickenham Stad (Rugby
Football Union) **5** E1
Twickenham Stoop Stad
TW2 . . . . **16** E8
Twickenham Trad Ctr TW1 . **15** F1
Twilley St SW18 . . . . **20** B8
Twining Ave TW2 . . . . **16** D5
Twinoaks KT11 . . . . **74** A6
Twitten La RH19 . . . . **184** E4
Twitten The RH11 . . . . **201** C6
Two Bridges Ind Est CR2 . **61** D3
Two Oaks KT13 . . . . **53** B6
Two Rivers Retail Pk
TW18 . . . . **12** E4
Two Ways RH14 . . . . **213** A4
Twycross Rd
Farncombe GU7 . . . . **150** D7
Wokingham RG40 . . . . **25** E7
Twyford La GU10 . . . . **146** B6
Twyford Par KT6 . . . . **38** A1
Twyford Rd
Carshalton SM5 . . . . **40** D1
Wokingham RG40 . . . . **25** B8
Twyhurst Ct RH19 . . . . **185** D3
Twyne Cl RH11 . . . . **200** F4
Twyner Cl RH6 . . . . **161** D4
Twynersh Ave KT16 . . . . **32** F3
Tybenham Rd SW19 . . . . . . **40** A6
Tychbourne Dr GU4 . . . . . . **110** C4
Tydcombe Rd CR6 . . . . **101** D8
Tyers Ho **1** SW16 . . . . **21** C3
Tylden Way RH12 . . . . **217** F6
Tylecroft Rd SW16 . . . . **41** E7
Tylehost GU2 . . . . **109** A5
Tylehurst Dr RH1 . . . . **139** F8
Tyler Gdns KT15 . . . . **52** C6
Tyler Rd RH10 . . . . **201** D3
Tylers Cl RH9 . . . . **121** B5
Tylers Ct GU6 . . . . **174** D3
TYLER'S GREEN **121** C5
Tylers Path SM5 . . . . **59** F6
Tylney Ave SE19 . . . . **22** F3
Tylney Ct KT22 . . . . **95** C6
Tylney Wood GU10 . . . . . . **187** F2
Tymperley Ct RH13 . . . . **217** E3
Tynamara KT1 . . . . **37** D5
Tynan Cl TW14 . . . . **15** A7
Tyndalls GU26 . . . . **188** F4
Tyne Cl
Crawley RH10 . . . . **202** C5
Farnborough GU14 . . . . . . **84** E6
Tynedale Rd RH3 . . . . **137** B5
Tyne Ho **4** KT2 . . . . **37** D8
Tynemouth Rd CR4 . . . . **21** A1
Tynley Gr GU4 . . . . **109** D7
Tynwald Ho **14** SE26 . . . . . . **23** A5
Typhoon Cl RG12 . . . . **27** D6
Tyrell Ct SM5 . . . . **59** F6
Tyrells Pl **15** GU1 . . . . **130** F8
Tyrolean Ct SM7 . . . . **78** B4
Tyrols Rd SE23 . . . . **23** D7
Tyrone Ct SW16 . . . . **21** D3
Tyrrell Ho RH3 . . . . **24** B3
Tyrrell Sq **9** CR4 . . . . **40** E8
Tyrwhitt Ct GU2 . . . . **109** B5
Tyson Rd SE23 . . . . **23** C8
Tythebarn Cl GU4 . . . . **110** B6
Tytherton RG12 . . . . **27** C7

U

Uckfield Rd CR4 . . . . **41** A8
Udney Park Rd TW11 . . . . . . **17** A2
Uffington Dr RG12 . . . . **27** E5
Uffington Rd SE27 . . . . **22** A4
Ujima Ct SW16 . . . . **21** E4
Ujima Ho SW16 . . . . **21** E4
Ullathorne Rd SW16 . . . . . . **21** C4
Ullswater RG12 . . . . **26** F2
Ullswater Ave GU14 . . . . . . **84** E3
Ullswater Bsns Pk CR5 . . . . **79** E3
Ullswater Cl
Bromley BR1 . . . . **24** E1
Hale GU9 . . . . **125** A6
Kingston upon Thames
SW15 . . . . **18** D4
Lightwater GU18 . . . . **48** B1
Ullswater Cres
Coulsdon CR5 . . . . **79** E3
Kingston upon Thames
SW15 . . . . **18** D4
Ullswater Rd
Lightwater GU18 . . . . **48** B1
West Norwood SE27 . . . . **22** B6
Ulstan Cl GU3 . . . . **102** A4
Ulster Ct KT2 . . . . **17** D2
Ulverstone Rd SE27 . . . . . . **22** B6
Ulwyn Ave KT14 . . . . **71** E5

Umberstone GU25 . . . . **31** D3
Underhill GU7 . . . . **150** E1
Underhill La RH2 . . . . **146** B7
Underhill Park Rd RH2 . . . **118** A4
Underhill Rd
Dulwich SE21, SE22 . . . . . **23** B8
Newdigate RH5 . . . . **158** B1
Undershaw Rd BR1 . . . . **24** F5
Underwood
Bracknell RG12 . . . . **26** E3
New Addington CR0 . . . . . **63** C5
Underwood Ave GU12 . . . . **105** F1
Underwood Cl RH10 . . . . . **204** B8
Underwood Ct CR3 . . . . . . **100** F2
Underwood Ho KT8 . . . . **36** A4
Underwood Rd
Caterham CR3 . . . . **100** E2
Haslemere GU27 . . . . **207** F7
Undine St SW17 . . . . **20** F3
Unicorn Prim Sch BR3 . . . . **44** B4
Unicorn Sch TW9 . . . . **6** E3
Unicorn Trad Est GU27 . . . **208** B7
Union Cl GU47 . . . . **45** E2
Union Ct **2** TW10 . . . . **6** E2
Union Rd
Farnham GU9 . . . . **125** C2
Frimley GU16 . . . . **86** D8
Thornton Heath CR0 . . . . **42** C2
Union St
Aldershot GU11 . . . . **105** A2
Farnborough GU14 . . . . . . **85** B4
Kingston upon Thames KT1 . **37** D7
Pirbright GU24 . . . . **87** A6
Union Terr **7** GU11 . . . . . . **105** A2
Unity Cl
New Addington CR0 . . . . . **63** B2
West Norwood SE19 . . . . **22** C3
University Ct GU2 . . . . **109** B1
University Rd SW19 . . . . **20** D2
Univ for the Creative Arts
Epsom KT18 . . . . **76** D5
Epsom KT18 . . . . **76** E5
Farnham GU9 . . . . **125** A2
Univ of Surrey The GU2 . . **109** B1
Unstead La GU5 . . . . **151** C7
Unstead Wood GU3 . . . . . **130** C1
Unwin Ave TW14 . . . . **3** D2
Unwin Rd TW7 . . . . **5** E4
Upavon Gdns RG12 . . . . **27** F4
Upchurch Cl SE20 . . . . **23** B1
Updown Hill GU20 . . . . **48** D4
Upfield
Horley RH6 . . . . **161** A1
South Croydon CR0, CR9 . . **62** B7
Upfield Cl RH6 . . . . **161** A1
Upfold Cl GU6 . . . . **174** B5
Upfold La GU6 . . . . **174** C5
Upfolds Gn GU4 . . . . **110** C5
Upgrove Manor Way 12
SE24 . . . . **22** A8
Upland Ct
Dulwich SE21, SE22 . . . . . **23** A8
Sutton SM2 . . . . **59** D3
Woldingham CR3 . . . . . . **102** B7
Uplands
Ashtead KT21 . . . . **95** D7
Beckenham BR3 . . . . **44** A7
Warlingham CR6 . . . . **81** F1
Uplands Cl
Haslemere GU27 . . . . **208** D8
Mortlake SW14 . . . . **7** B2
Sandhurst GU47 . . . . **64** B8
Uplands Ct KT22 . . . . **74** D5
Uplands Prim Sch GU47 . . . **64** B8
Uplands Rd
Farnham GU9 . . . . **125** E1
Kenley CR8 . . . . **80** C2
Upland Way KT18 . . . . **77** C1
Uppark Gdns RH12 . . . . . . **217** F6
Upper Beulah Hill SE19 . . . **42** E8
Upper Bourne La GU10 . . . **146** B5
Upper Bourne Vale
GU10 . . . . **146** A5
Upper Bridge Rd RH1 . . . . **118** A1
Upper Brighton Rd KT6 . . . . **37** E2
Upper Broadmoor Rd
RG45 . . . . **45** D5
Upper Butts TW8 . . . . **6** C8
Upper Charles St **5** GU15 **65** C6
Upper Chobham Rd GU15 . . **66** B4
Upper Church La **19** GU9 **125** B2
Upper Cl RH18 . . . . **206** F2
Upper College Ride GU15 . **65** E8
Upper Court Rd
Epsom KT19 . . . . **76** C8
Woldingham CR3 . . . . . . **102** A3
Upper Dr TN16 . . . . **83** C1
Upper Dunnymans 6
SM7 . . . . **77** F5
UPPER EASHING **150** A4
Upper Edgeborough Rd
GU1 . . . . **130** F8
UPPER ELMERS END **43** F4
Upper Elmers End Rd
BR3 . . . . **43** E4
Upper Elms Rd GU11 . . . . . **105** A1
Upper Fairfield Rd KT22 . . . **95** B6
Upper Farm Rd KT8 . . . . **35** F5
Upper Forecourt RH6 . . . . **182** B7
Upper Gordon Rd GU15 . . . **65** D5
Upper Gr SE25 . . . . **42** F5
Upper Green E CR4 . . . . **40** F6
Upper Green W CR4 . . . . . . **40** F7
Upper Grotto Rd TW1 . . . . . **16** F6

Upper Guildown Rd GU2 . . **130** C6
UPPER HALE **125** B6
Upper Hale Rd GU9 . . . . . . **125** C6
UPPER HALLIFORD **34** D5
Upper Halliford Rd TW17 . . **34** E6
Upper Halliford Sta TW16 . . **34** E7
Upper Ham Rd TW10, TW7 . **17** D4
Upper Harestone CR3 . . . . **121** A8
Upper High St KT17 . . . . **76** E6
Upper House La GU5 . . . . . **152** F1
Upper Lodge Mews TW12 . **16** C2
Upper Lodge Way CR5 . . . . **99** D5
Upper Manor Rd
Farncombe GU7 . . . . **150** E6
Milford GU8 . . . . **149** F1
Upper Mount GU27 . . . . . . **189** F1
Upper Mulgrave Rd SM2 . . . **58** E3
UPPER NORWOOD **22** E1
Upper Nursery SL5 . . . . **30** A4
Upper Old Park La GU9 . . . **125** A5
Upper Park Rd
Camberley GU15 . . . . **65** E6
Kingston upon Thames KT2 . **18** A2
Upper Pillory Down SM5 . . . **79** A7
Upper Pines SM7 . . . . **78** F2
Upper Pinewood Rd
GU12 . . . . **106** D3
Upper Queen St GU7 . . . . . **150** E4
Upper Rd SM6 . . . . **60** E5
Upper Richmond Rd SW15 . . **7** F3
Upper Richmond Road W
TW10, SW14, SW15 . . . . . . **7** C3
Upper Rose Hill RH4 . . . . . **136** B6
Upper St Michael's Rd
GU11 . . . . **126** B8
Upper Sawleywood 3
SM7 . . . . **77** F5
Upper School Dr GU27 . . . **207** F5
Upper Selsdon Rd CR2 . . . . **62** A2
UPPER SHIRLEY **62** D6
Upper Shirley Rd CR0,
CR9 . . . . **62** D7
Upper South View GU9 . . . **125** C3
Upper Springfield GU8 . . . **148** D3
Upper Sq
Forest Row RH18 . . . . **206** F3
Isleworth TW7 . . . . **6** A4
Upper St GU5 . . . . **133** A4
Upper Stanford GU24 . . . . . **87** F1
Upper Sunbury Rd TW12 . . **36** A8
Upper Sutton La TW5 . . . . . . **5** A6
UPPER SYDENHAM **23** B4
Upper Teddington Rd KT1,
KT8 . . . . **37** C8
Upperton Rd GU2 . . . . **130** C2
UPPER TOOTING **20** F6
Upper Tooting Park Mans 1
SW17 . . . . **21** A6
Upper Tooting Pk SW17 . . . **20** F6
Upper Tooting Rd SW17 . . . **20** F5
Upper Tulse Hill SW2 . . . . . . **21** F8
Upper Union St **1** GU11 . . **105** A2
Upper Union Terr 5
GU11 . . . . **105** A2
Upper Vann La GU8 . . . . . . **172** A1
Upper Vernon Rd SM1 . . . . **59** D5
Upper Verran Rd GU15 . . . . **65** D3
Upper Village Rd SL5 . . . . . **29** D4
Upper Warlingham Sta
CR6 . . . . **81** A1
Upper Way GU9 . . . . **146** B8
Upper West St RH2 . . . . . . **117** F1
Upper Weybourne La
GU9 . . . . **125** E2
Upper Wlk GU25 . . . . **31** E5
Upper Woodcote Village
CR8 . . . . **79** D7
Upshire Gdns RG12 . . . . **27** F5
Upshot La GU22 . . . . **70** F2
Upton GU21 . . . . **69** B2
Upton Cl GU14 . . . . **85** D3
Upton Ct
7 Penge SE20 . . . . **23** C1
8 Wimbledon SW20 . . . . **19** D1
Upton Dene SM2 . . . . **59** B3
Upton Rd
Hounslow TW3 . . . . **5** A4
South Norwood CR7 . . . . . **42** D7
Upwood Rd SW16 . . . . **41** E8
Urmston Dr SW19 . . . . **19** E7
Urquhart Ct BR3 . . . . **23** E5
Ursuline High Sch SW20 . . **39** D8
Usherwood Cl KT20 . . . . . . **116** C4
Uvedale Cl CR0 . . . . **82** D8
Uvedale Cres CR0 . . . . **82** E8
Uvedale Rd RH8 . . . . **122** F5
Uxbridge Rd
Feltham TW13 . . . . **15** D6
Hampton TW12 . . . . **16** B3
Kingston upon Thames KT1,
KT6 . . . . **37** D4

V

Vachery La GU6 . . . . **194** E7
Vaillant Rd KT13 . . . . **53** C6
Valan Leas BR2 . . . . **44** E6
Vale Cl
Coulsdon CR5 . . . . **79** E5
Epsom KT18 . . . . **96** E8
Farnham GU10 . . . . **146** C4
Oatlands Park KT13 . . . . . **53** D7
Twickenham TW1 . . . . **17** A5
Woking GU21 . . . . **69** E3
Vale Cres SW15 . . . . **18** E4
Vale Croft KT10 . . . . **55** F2

Vale Ct
Ash Vale GU12 . . . . **106** A7
Oatlands Park KT13 . . . . . **53** D7
Vale Dr RH12 . . . . **217** B3
Vale Farm Rd GU21 . . . . **69** E2
Vale Ho GU21 . . . . **69** E2
Vale Lodge SE23 . . . . **23** C6
Valens Ho **1** SW2 . . . . **22** A7
Valentin Ct TW12 . . . . **16** B3
Valentine Ct SE23 . . . . **23** D6
Valentyne Cl CR0 . . . . **82** E8
Vale Prim Sch The KT18 . . . **96** E8
Vale Rd
Ash Vale GU12 . . . . **106** A5
Camberley GU15 . . . . **65** A4
Claygate KT10 . . . . **55** F3
Mitcham CR4 . . . . **41** D5
Oatlands Park KT13 . . . . . **53** D7
Sutton SM1 . . . . **59** B6
Worcester Park KT4 . . . . . **57** F7
Valerie Ct SM2 . . . . **59** B3
Vale Road N KT6 . . . . **56** E5
Vale Road S **4** KT6 . . . . **56** E8
Valery Pl TW12 . . . . **16** A1
Valeswood Rd BR1 . . . . **24** F3
Vale The
Ashford TW16 . . . . **15** A2
Coulsdon CR5, CR8 . . . . . . **79** E5
Croydon CR0 . . . . **62** D8
Feltham TW14 . . . . **4** B1
Heston TW5 . . . . **4** E8
Vale Wood Dr GU10 . . . . . **146** D4
Vale Wood La GU26 . . . . . . **188** C4
Valewood Rd GU27 . . . . . . **208** C4
Valiant Dr RG12 . . . . **27** C6
Valiant Way GU14 . . . . **104** D8
Valley Cres RG41 . . . . **25** A8
Valley Ct CR3 . . . . **101** A5
Valley End CE Inf Sch
GU24 . . . . **49** A4
Valley End Rd GU24 . . . . **49** A4
Valleyfield Rd SW16 . . . . **21** F3
Valley Gdns SW19 . . . . **20** D1
Valley Gardens* TW20 . . . . **30** E7
Valley La GU10 . . . . **146** C2
Valley Mews TW1 . . . . **17** A6
Valley Mushroom Farm
TN16 . . . . **83** D1
Valley Pl KT6 . . . . **37** E3
Valley Point Ind Est CR0 . . . **41** E2
Valley Prim Sch BR2 . . . . . . **44** F7
Valley Prospect **3** SE19 . . . **22** E2
Valley Rd
Beckenham BR2 . . . . **44** F7
Frimley GU16 . . . . **86** B8
Kenley CR3, CR8 . . . . **80** D4
Streatham SW16 . . . . **21** F4
Valley The GU2 . . . . **130** C5
Valley View
Biggin Hill TN16 . . . . **83** D1
Godalming GU7 . . . . **150** D4
Sandhurst GU47 . . . . **64** A7
Valley View Gdns CR8 . . . . . **80** E4
Valley Wlk CR0 . . . . **62** C8
Vallis Way KT9 . . . . **56** D6
Valnay St SW17 . . . . **20** F3
Valroy Cl GU15 . . . . **65** D6
Vampire Way GU11, GU14 **104** E8
Vanborough Ct **3** SM2 . . . . **59** C4
Vanbrugh Cl RH11 . . . . **200** E3
Vanbrugh Dr KT12 . . . . **35** C3
Vanbrugh Mews KT12 . . . . . **35** C2
Vancouver Cl KT19 . . . . **76** C8
Vancouver Ct
Horley/Gatwick RH6 . . . . **162** A3
Smallfield RH6 . . . . **162** A3
Vancouver Dr RH11,
RH11 . . . . **181** D1
Vancouver Rd
Forest Hill SE23 . . . . **23** E6
Richmond TW10 . . . . **17** C4
Vanderbilt Rd SW18 . . . . . . **20** C7
Van Dyck Ave KT3 . . . . **38** D2
Vandyke RG12 . . . . **26** E3
Vandyke Cl
Putney SW15 . . . . **19** D8
Redhill RH1 . . . . **118** F3
Vanfame Ct KT3 . . . . **38** F6
Van Gogh Cl TW7 . . . . **6** A4
Vanguard Cl CR0 . . . . **42** B1
Vanguard Ho
7 Merton SW19 . . . . **20** C1
6 Stanwell TW19 . . . . **2** E1
Vanguard Way
Harlington TW6 . . . . **3** E5
Wallington SM6 . . . . **60** E3
Vanners RH10 . . . . **201** E7
Vanners Par KT14 . . . . **71** E6
Vann Farm Rd RH5 . . . . . . **177** E4
Vann La
Chiddingfold GU8 . . . . . . **191** E4
Hambledon GU8 . . . . **171** D1
Vann Lake RH5 . . . . **177** F4
Vann Lake Rd RH5 . . . . **178** A4
Vanquish Cl **1** TW2 . . . . . . **16** A8
Vantage Ct
Harlington UB3 . . . . **3** E7
Streatham SW16 . . . . **21** F1
Woking GU21 . . . . **69** D2
Vant Rd SW17 . . . . **20** F3
Vapery La GU24 . . . . **87** D6
Varley Way CR4 . . . . **40** D7
Varna Rd TW12 . . . . **36** B8
Varney Cl GU14 . . . . **84** E5
Varsity Dr TW1, TW7 . . . . . . **5** F1
Varsity Row SW14 . . . . **7** C5
Vaughan Almshouses
TW15 . . . . **14** B3

Vaughan Cl TW12 15 E2
Vaughan Ct GU2 109 B5
Vaughan Rd KT7 37 B2
Vaughan Way RH4 136 A7
Vaux Cres KT12 54 B4
Vauxhall Gdns CR2 61 C4
Veals Mead CR4 40 E8
Vectis Gdns SW17 21 B2
Vectis Rd SW17 21 B2
Vegal Cres TW20 11 C3
Veitch Cl TW14 14 F8
Vellum Dr SM5 60 A7
Venita Manor SE27 22 A3
Venner Cl 20 RH1 119 A2
Venner Rd SE20, SE26 23 C3
Ventnor Rd SM2 59 B3
Ventnor Terr GU12 105 C1
Venton Cl GU21 69 B2
Venture Ho TW18 13 A4
Venus Mews CR4 40 E6
Verbania Way RH19 186 B1
Verdant Ct 3 SE6 24 E8
Verdant La SE6 24 E7
Verdayne Ave CR0, CR9 62 D8
Verdayne Gdns CR6 81 C3
Vere Bank SW19 19 F7
Vereker Dr TW16 35 A6
Verge Wlk GU11 126 A7
Vermillion Ct TW13 14 F5
Vermont Hall KT4 39 B2
Vermont Rd
South Norwood SE19 22 E2
Sutton SM1 59 B7
Verney Ho TW3 5 C3
Vernon Ave SW20 39 D7
Vernon Cl
Horsham RH12 218 A4
Ottershaw KT16 51 D4
Stanwell TW19 13 E7
West Ewell KT19 57 C4
Vernon Ct
Farnham GU9 125 A2
North Ascot SL5 28 D6
Vernon Dr
Caterham CR3 100 C5
North Ascot SL5 28 E7
Vernon Rd
Carshalton SM1 59 D5
Feltham TW13 14 F6
Mortlake SW14 7 D4
Vernon Way GU2 108 F2
Vernon Wlk KT20 97 D7
Vern Pl TN16 103 C6
Verona Dr KT6 56 E8
Veronica Gdns CR4, SW16 41 C8
Veronica Rd SW17 21 B6
Verralls GU22 70 B2
Verran Rd
Balham SW12 21 B8
Camberley GU15 65 D3
Versailles Rd SE20 23 A1
Verulam Ave CR8 79 C7
Veryan GU21 69 A2
Vesey Cl GU14 85 A5
Vestris Rd SE23 23 D6
Vevers Rd RH2 139 C6
Vevey St SE23, SE6 23 F6
Vibart Gdns SW2 21 F8
Vibia Cl TW19 13 D8
Viburnum Ct GU24 67 E6
Vicarage Ave TW20 12 B3
Vicarage Cl
Farnham GU9 146 D7
Kingswood KT20 97 E3
Lingfield RH7 164 D4
Little Bookham KT23 94 A2
New Malden KT4 38 E1
Vicarage Cres TW20 12 B3
Vicarage Ct
Beckenham BR3 43 E6
East Bedfont TW14 14 C8
Egham TW20 12 B2
8 Roehampton SW15 19 A8
Vicarage Dr
Beckenham BR3 44 A8
Mortlake SW14 7 D2
Vicarage Farm Ct TW5 4 F7
Vicarage Farm Rd TW3, TW4, TW5 4 E6
Vicarage Fields KT12 35 C3
Vicarage Gate GU2 130 A7
Vicarage Gdns
Ascot SL5 29 A4
Grayshott GU26 188 C3
Mitcham CR4 40 E6
Mortlake SW14 7 D2
Vicarage Hill
Farnham GU10, GU9 146 D7
Loxwood RH14 213 A2
Vicarage Ho 2 KT1 37 F7
Vicarage La
Capel RH5 178 D6
Farnham GU9 125 B2
Farnham, Middle Bourne GU9 146 D7
Haslemere GU27 207 F6
Heath End GU9 125 C7
Horley RH6 160 F4
Laleham TW18 33 C6
Send GU23 90 D1
Wraysbury TW19 11 F7
Vicarage Rd
Ashford TW16 14 F2
Bagshot GU19 47 C3
Blackwater GU17 64 E4
Crawley Down RH10 204 A8
Croydon CR0, CR9 61 A7
Egham TW20 12 B3

Vicarage Rd *continued*
Kingston upon Thames KT1, KT2 37 D7
Lingfield RH7 164 D4
Mortlake SW14 7 D2
Staines TW18 12 E5
Sutton SM1 59 B7
Teddington, Hampton Wick KT1, KT8 37 C8
Teddington TW11 17 A3
Twickenham, Strawberry Hill TW2 16 E6
Twickenham TW2 5 C1
Woking GU22 89 F6
Vicarage Way SL3 1 D7
Vicars Oak Rd SE19 22 E2
Viceroy Ct 5 CR0 42 D1
Viceroy Lodge 6 KT6 37 E4
Vickers Cl SM6 60 F3
Vickers Ct 10 TW19 2 E1
Vickers Drive N KT13 52 E1
Vickers Drive S KT13 71 E8
Vickers Rd GU12 105 F5
Victor Ct RH10 182 D1
Victoria Almshouses
4 Redhill RH1 119 A4
1 Reigate RH2 118 C1
Victoria Ave
Camberley GU15 65 A5
East Molesey KT8 36 B6
Hackbridge SM6 60 A7
Hounslow TW3, TW4 5 A2
Kingston upon Thames KT6 37 D3
South Croydon CR2 61 C1
Victoria Cl
East Molesey KT8 36 A6
Horley RH6 161 A3
Oatlands Park KT13 53 D7
Victoria Cotts 7 TW9 7 A6
Victoria Cres SE19 22 E2
Victoria Ct
Bagshot GU19 47 E1
Guildford GU1 130 D8
9 Horsham RH13 217 D2
Penge SE26 23 C2
Redhill RH1 140 A6
Shalford GU4 130 E3
Victoria Dr
Blackwater GU17 64 C4
Putney SW15, SW19 19 D7
Victoria Gdns
Biggin Hill TN16 83 C4
Farnborough GU14 84 D4
Heston TW5 4 E6
Wokingham RG40 25 E8
Victoria Ho 4 KT22 95 C6
Victoria Jun Sch TW13 15 B7
Victoria La UB7 3 D8
Victoria Lodge SW19 19 C1
Victoria Mews
Crawley RH11 201 D6
Englefield Green TW20 11 C2
Wandsworth SW18 20 C7
2 Weybridge KT13 53 A6
Victoria Pl
Cobham KT11 73 B6
Esher KT10 55 B6
Ewell KT17 76 E7
17 Richmond TW10 6 D2
3 Woking GU21 70 A3
Victoria Rd
Addlestone KT15 52 D6
Aldershot GU11 105 A2
Ascot SL5 29 A4
Carshalton SM1 59 D5
Coulsdon CR5 79 D4
Cranleigh GU6 174 D3
Crawley RH11 201 C6
Farnborough GU14 85 B4
Farnham GU9 125 C2
Feltham TW13 15 B7
Godalming GU7 150 E4
Guildford GU1 109 E1
Horley RH6 161 B2
Kingston upon Thames KT1 37 F7
Kingston upon Thames, Seething Wells KT6 37 D3
Knaphill GU21 68 E1
Mitcham CR4, SW19 20 F1
Mortlake SW14 7 D4
Oatlands Park KT13 53 D7
Redhill RH1 140 A8
Sandhurst GU47 45 E1
Staines TW18 12 E5
Teddington TW11 17 A2
Twickenham TW1 17 B8
Woking GU22 69 F2
Victoria St
Englefield Green TW20 11 C2
Horsham RH13 217 D2
Victoria Tk GU11 104 E7
Victoria Villas TW9 6 F3
Victoria Way
East Grinstead RH19 205 F7
Oatlands Park KT13 53 D7
Woking GU21, GU22 69 E2
Victor Rd
Penge SE20 23 D1
Teddington TW11 16 E4
Victors Dr TW12 15 E2
Victor Seymour Inf Sch 3 SM5 59 F6
Victor Way GU14 84 C1
Victor Wlk RG12 27 D6
Victory Ave SM4 40 C4
Victory Bsns Ctr TW7 5 F3
Victory Cl TW19 13 E7
Victory Cotts KT24 113 E7

Victory Ct KT15 52 B6
Victory Day Sch CR7 42 C5
Victory Park Rd KT15 52 C6
Victory Pl SE19 22 E2
Victory Rd
Chertsey KT16 33 A1
Horsham RH12 217 B3
Merton SW19 20 C1
Victory Road Mews 5 SW19 20 C1
Vidler Cl KT9 56 C4
Vienna Ct GU14 85 A6
View Cl TN16 83 C3
Viewfield Rd SW18 19 F8
View Terr RH7 165 A1
Viggory La GU21 69 C4
Vigilant Cl SE26 23 A4
Viking RG12 26 E4
Viking Ct TW12 36 B8
Village Cl 3 KT13 53 D7
Village Ct SL5 29 C4
Village Gate TW17 34 B4
Village Gdns KT17 57 F1
Village Green Ave TN16 83 E2
Village Green Way TN16 83 E2
Village Mews SL5 29 C5
Village Rd TW20 32 C6
Village Row SM2 59 A3
Village Sq The CR5 99 D5
Village St RH5 158 B1
VILLAGE THE 10 B5
Village The SL4 10 B5
Village Way
Ashford TW15 14 A4
Beckenham BR3 44 A6
Sanderstead CR2 81 A6
Villas The
Blindley Heath RH7 163 E8
Woking GU21 69 F3
Villiers Ave
Kingston upon Thames KT5 37 F5
Twickenham TW2 15 F7
Villiers Cl KT5 37 F5
Villiers Gr SM2 58 D2
Villiers Mead RG41 25 A6
Villiers Rd
Hounslow TW7 5 E5
Kingston upon Thames KT1 37 F6
Penge BR3 43 D7
Vimy Cl TW4 4 F2
Vinall Gdns RH12 216 D4
Vincam Cl TW2 16 A8
Vincent Ave
Sutton SM5 78 D8
3 Tolworth KT5 38 B1
Vincent Cl
Chertsey KT16 32 E2
Esher KT10 55 B7
Fetcham KT23 94 B4
Harmondsworth UB7 3 A8
Horsham RH13 217 F2
Vincent Dr
Dorking RH4 136 A6
Upper Halliford TW17 34 E6
Vincent Ho KT3 38 F5
Vincent La RH4 136 A7
Vincent Rd
Chertsey KT16 32 E2
Coulsdon CR5 79 C3
Croydon CR0 42 E2
Dorking RH4 136 A7
Hounslow, Hounslow West TW4 4 D4
Hounslow TW7 5 D6
Kingston upon Thames KT1 38 A6
Stoke D'Abernon KT11 73 E3
Vincent Rise RG12 27 E6
Vincent Row TW12 16 C3
Vincents Cl CR5 98 F7
Vincent Sq TN16 83 C6
Vincents Wlk 10 RH4 136 A7
Vincent Walk RH4 135 A7
Vincent Works RH4 136 A7
Vine Cl
Ash Vale GU12 85 F1
Farnborough GU11 105 A6
Rowledge GU10 146 A4
Stanwell TW19 2 A2
Surbiton KT5 37 F3
Sutton SM1 59 C7
Worplesdon GU3 88 D1
Vine Cotts GU6 174 B3
Vine Ct KT12 54 C4
Vine House Cl GU16 86 A3
Vine La GU10 146 A5
Vine Pl TW3 5 B3
Vine Rd
Barnes SW13, SW15 7 F4
East Molesey KT8 36 C5
Vineries Cl UB7 3 A8
Viners Cl KT12 35 C3
Vine St GU11 105 A1
Vine Way GU10 146 A5
Vineyard Cl
Forest Hill SE6 24 A7
Kingston upon Thames KT1 37 F6
Vineyard Hill Rd SW19 20 A4
Vineyard Path SW14 7 D4
Vineyard Prim Sch The TW10 6 E1
Vineyard Rd TW13 15 A5
Vineyard Row KT1, KT8 37 C8
Vineyards The TW13 15 A5
Vineyard The TW10 6 E2
Viney Bank CR0 62 F2
Vinter Ct TW17 34 A4

Viola Ave
Feltham TW14 4 C1
Stanwell TW19 13 E7
Viola Croft RG42 27 F8
Violet Cl
Carshalton CR4 41 A1
Cheam SM3 39 E1
Violet Gdns CR0 61 B5
Violet La CR0 61 B5
Violette Szabo Ho 4 SE27 22 D4
Virginia Ave GU25 31 C4
Virginia Beeches GU25 31 C6
Virginia Cl
Ashtead KT21 75 D1
Bromley/Keston BR2 44 E6
Kingston upon Thames KT3 38 C5
Laleham TW18 33 C6
Weybridge KT13 53 C4
Virginia Ct
Ashford TW15 13 E4
Virginia Water GU25 31 D5
Virginia Dr GU25 31 C5
Virginia Gdns GU14 85 C2
Virginia Ho TW11 17 A3
Virginia Pl KT11 73 A5
Virginia Rd CR7 42 B8
VIRGINIA WATER 31 C6
Virginia Water★ SL5 30 E6
Virginia Water Sta GU25 31 E4
Virgo Fidelis Convent Senior Sch SE19 22 D2
Virgo Fidelis Prep Sch SE19 22 D2
Viridian Ct TW13 14 F5
Viscount Cl GU12 105 F5
Viscount Ct TW15 14 C1
Viscount Gdns KT14 71 E7
Viscount Ind Est SL3 1 E4
Viscount Point 6 SW19 20 A1
Viscount Rd TW19 13 E7
Viscount Way TW6 3 E3
Vista Ho 2 SW19 40 D8
Vista Hts SE23 23 E8
Vivian Ct BR3 44 A8
Vivien Cl KT9 56 E3
Vivien Ct CR0 61 F8
Vivienne Cl
Crawley RH11 181 D1
Twickenham TW1 6 D1
Vivienne Ho TW18 13 A3
Vixen Dr GU12 105 E3
Voewood Cl KT3 38 F3
Vogan Cl RH2 139 B6
Voltaire 15 TW9 6 F6
Volta Way CR0, CR9 41 F1
Voss Ct SW16 21 E2
Vowels Forest Wlk★ RH19 204 E3
Vowels La RH19 204 E2
Vulcan Bsns Ctr CR0 63 E2
Vulcan Cl
Crawley RH11 201 C2
Sandhurst GU47 64 A7
Vulcan Dr RG12 27 C6
Vulcan Way
New Addington CR0 63 E1
Sandhurst GU47 64 B7
Wallington SM6 60 E2
Vumba Ho 12 SM2 59 C4
Vyne Ho SM5 59 F4

W

Wadbrook St KT1 37 D7
Waddington Ave CR5, CR8 100 B8
Waddington Cl
Coulsdon CR5 100 B8
Crawley RH11 201 A3
Waddington Way CR7, SE19 42 D8
WADDON 61 A6
Waddon Cl CR0, CR9 61 A7
Waddon Court Rd CR0, CR9 61 A7
Waddon Marsh Halt CR0 61 A8
Waddon Marsh Way CR0, CR9 41 F1
Waddon New Rd CR0, CR9 61 B8
Waddon Park Ave CR0, CR9 61 A7
Waddon Rd CR0, CR9 61 B7
Waddon Sta CR0 61 A6
Waddon Way CR0, CR2, CR9 61 B4
Wade Ct RH18 206 F2
Wade's La TW11 17 A3
Wadham GU47 45 F1
Wadham Cl
Crawley RH10 182 C1
Shepperton TW17 34 C2
Wadhurst Cl SE20 43 B7
Wadlands Brook Rd RH19 185 D5
Wagbullock Rise RG12 27 C3
Wagg Cl RH19 186 A1
Waggon Cl GU2 108 E2
Waggoners Hollow GU19 47 E2
Waggoners Way GU26 188 A4
Waggoners Wells Rd GU26 188 A2
Wagner Mews 23 KT6 37 E4
Wagtail Cl RH12 217 D7
Wagtail Gdns CR2 62 E1
Wagtail Wlk BR3 44 C4
Waights Ct 8 KT2 37 E8

Wain End RH12 217 D5
Wainford Cl SW19 19 D7
Wainscot SL5 29 F3
Wainwright Cl RG40 26 A6
Wainwright Gr TW7 5 D3
Wainwrights RH10 201 D3
Waite Davies Rd SE12 24 F8
Waitelands Ho KT3 38 D5
Wake Cl GU2 109 B6
Wakefield Cl KT14 71 E7
Wakefield Ct
3 Horsham RH12 217 B2
Penge SE26 23 C2
Wakefield Gdns SE19 22 E1
Wakefield Ho SE22 23 B7
Wakefield Rd 21 TW10 6 D2
Wakefords Cl GU11 105 D6
Wakehams Green Dr RH10 182 D1
Wakehurst Dr RH10 201 D3
Wakehurst Mews RH12 216 F1
Wakehurst Path GU21 70 C5
Wakeling Ho 8 SE27 22 B5
Wakelin Ho SE23 23 E8
Wakely Cl TN16 83 C1
Walburton Rd CR8 79 C7
Walbury RG12 27 E5
Walcot Ct CR0 62 A8
Waldby Ct RH11 201 A3
Waldeck Gr SE27 22 B5
Waldeck Rd
Brentford W4 7 A8
Mortlake SW14 7 C4
Waldeck Terr SW14 7 C4
Waldegrave Ct 1 TW11 16 F3
Waldegrave Gdns TW1 16 F5
Waldegrave Girls Sch TW2 16 D5
Waldegrave Pk TW1 16 F4
Waldegrave Rd
Penge SE19 22 F1
Teddington TW1, TW11 16 F4
Waldegrove CR0 61 F7
Waldemar Rd SW19 20 A3
Walden Cotts GU3 107 A3
Walden Gdns CR7, SW16 41 F5
Waldenshaw Rd SE23 23 C7
Waldens Park Rd GU21 69 C3
Waldens Rd GU21 69 D2
Waldo Pl CR4 20 E1
Waldorf Cl CR2 61 B2
Waldorf Hts GU17 64 D3
Waldorf Sch of SW London SW16 21 D6
Waldram Cres SE23 23 C7
Waldram Park Rd SE23 23 D7
Waldram Pl 6 SE23 23 C7
Waldron Gdns BR2 44 D6
Waldron Hill RG12 27 F8
Waldronhyrst CR0, CR2 61 B6
Waldron Rd SW17, SW18 20 C6
Waldrons The
Croydon CR0 61 C6
Oxted RH8 122 F4
Waldy Rise GU6 174 E4
Wales Ave SM5 59 E5
Walesbeech RH10 202 A5
Waleton Acres SM6 60 C4
Waley's La RH5 177 C1
Walford Rd RH5 136 C3
Walham Rise 1 SW19 19 E2
Walhatch Cl RH18 206 F2
Walker Cl
East Bedfont TW14 14 F8
Hampton TW12 15 F2
Walker Rd RH10 202 C4
Walkerscroft Mead SE21 22 C7
Walker's Ridge GU15 65 E5
Walkfield Dr KT18 77 B2
Walking Bottom GU5 154 C6
Walk The
Ashford TW16 14 F1
Tandridge RH8 122 A2
Wallace Cl
Fairlands GU3 108 C4
Upper Halliford TW17 34 D5
Wallace Cres SM5 59 F5
Wallace Fields KT17 77 A6
Wallace Fields Cty Inf Sch KT17 77 A6
Wallace Fields Jun Sch KT17 77 A7
Wallace Sq CR5 99 D5
Wallace Way GU11 104 F3
Wallace Wlk KT15 52 C6
Wallage La RH10 203 D6
Wallbrook Bsns Ctr TW4 4 B4
Walled Garden Cl BR3 44 B5
Walled Gdn The
Betchworth RH3 137 D8
Loxwood RH14 212 F7
Tadworth KT20 97 D5
Waller La CR3 100 F4
Wall Hill Rd RH18, RH19 206 E5
Wallingford Cl RG12 27 E5
WALLINGTON 60 A4
Wallington Ct 10 SM6 60 B4
Wallington Cty Gram Sch SM6 60 B6
Wallington High Sch for Girls SM6 60 B2
Wallington Rd GU15 47 A1
Wallington Sq 4 SM6 60 C4
Wallington Sta SM6 60 B4
Wallis Ct RH10 181 F2

Wallis Ho RH19 . . . . 185 E1
Wallis Mews KT22 . . . . 95 A5
Wallis Way RH13 . . . . 218 A4
WALLIS WOOD 176 E1
Wallner Way RG40 . . . . 25 E5
Wallorton Gdns SW14 . . . . . 7 D3
Walmer Cl
　Crowthorne RG45 . . . . 45 C5
　Frimley GU16 . . . . 86 A7
Walmer Ho 10 SE20 . . . . . . 23 C1
Walmsley Ho 1 SW16 . . . . . 21 C4
Walnut Cl
　Aldershot GU11 . . . . 126 A8
　Epsom KT18 . . . . 76 F4
　Wallington SM5 . . . . 59 F5
Walnut Ct RH13 . . . . 217 E1
Walnut Dr KT20 . . . . 97 E3
Walnut Gr SM7 . . . . 77 D5
Walnut Ho RH2 . . . . 139 C7
Walnut La RH11 . . . . 181 B1
Walnut Mews
　Bracknell RG42 . . . . 26 F8
　Sutton SM2 . . . . 59 C3
Walnut Tree Ave CR4 . . . . . 40 E6
Walnut Tree Cl
　Barnes SW13 . . . . 7 F6
　Belmont SM7 . . . . 77 E7
　Guildford GU1 . . . . 130 C8
Walnut Tree Cotts SW19 . . 19 E3
Walnut Tree Gdns GU7 . . . 150 E7
Walnut Tree La KT14 . . . . . 71 D7
Walnut Tree Pk GU1 . . . . . 109 C1
Walnut Tree Pl GU23 . . . . . 90 D4
Walnut Tree Rd
　Brentford TW8 . . . . 6 E8
　Charlton TW17 . . . . 34 C7
　Heston TW5 . . . . .4 F8
Walpole Ave
　Chipstead CR5 . . . . 98 F8
　Richmond TW9 . . . . .6 F5
Walpole Cres 12 TW11 . . . 16 F3
Walpole Ct
　Twickenham TW2 . . . . . . 16 E6
　2 Wallington SM6 . . . . . 60 B5
Walpole Gdns TW2 . . . . . . 16 E5
Walpole Ho
　4 Aldershot GU11 . . . . . 105 B2
　East Molesey KT8 . . . . . . 36 A4
Walpole Pl 10 TW11 . . . . . 16 F3
Walpole Rd
　Croydon CR0, CR9 . . . . . 61 D8
　Mitcham SW19 . . . . 20 D2
　Old Windsor SL4 . . . . 11 B8
　Surbiton KT6 . . . . 37 E3
　Teddington TW11 . . . . . . 16 F3
　Twickenham TW2 . . . . . . 16 E6
Walrus Rd
　Farnborough GU14 . . . . 104 D8
　Hounslow TW6 . . . . 2 B4
Walsham Rd TW14 . . . . 15 B8
Walsh CE Jun Sch GU12 106 A1
Walsh Cres CR0 . . . . 82 E7
Walsh Memorial CE Inf Sch
　3 GU12 . . . . 105 F1
Walsingham Gdns KT19 . . 57 F5
Walsingham Ho TW2 . . . . . 16 D6
Walsingham Rd
　Mitcham CR4 . . . . 40 F4
　New Addington CR0 . . . . 63 C1
Walstead Ho 2 RH10 . . . . 201 D5
Walter Inf Sch RG41 . . . . . 25 A6
Walter's Mead KT21 . . . . . . 75 E2
Walter St 2 KT2 . . . . 37 E8
Waltham Ave GU2 . . . . . . 109 B5
Waltham Cl GU47 . . . . 45 D1
Waltham Rd
　Carshalton SM5 . . . . 40 E1
　Caterham CR3 . . . . 101 B5
Walton Ave
　Cheam SM3 . . . . 58 F7
　New Malden KT3 . . . . . . 38 F5
Walton Bridge Rd KT12,
　TW17 . . . . 34 E2
Walton Com Hospl KT12 . . 54 B8
Walton Ct
　13 Croydon CR2 . . . . 61 C5
　12 Richmond TW9 . . . . . .6 F3
　Woking GU21 . . . . 70 A3
Walton Dr
　Horsham RH13 . . . . 218 C4
　North Ascot SL5 . . . . 28 F8
Walton Gdns TW13 . . . . . . 14 F4
Walton Gn CR0 . . . . 63 C3
Walton Heath RH10 . . . . . 202 D8
Walton Ho 1 KT2 . . . . 17 E1
Walton La
　Lower Halliford TW17 . . . 34 D2
　Oatlands Park KT12 . . . . 34 E1
　Weybridge KT12, KT13 . . 53 E8
Walton Leigh Sch KT12 . . 53 F6
Walton Lodge KT12 . . . . . . 34 F1
Walton Manor KT12 . . . . . 34 F2
Walton Oak Sch KT12 . . . . 35 C1
WALTON-ON-THAMES . . . 35 C2
Walton-on-Thames Sta
　KT12 . . . . 54 A6
WALTON ON THE HILL . . . 97 A3
Walton on the Hill Prim Sch
　KT20 . . . . 97 B3
Walton Pk KT12 . . . . 54 D8
Walton Pk La KT12 . . . . . . 54 D8
Walton Rd
　Ashtead KT18 . . . . 96 C6
　East Molesey KT8, KT12 . 36 B5

Walton Rd continued
Walton-on-Thames KT12,
　KT8 . . . . 35 E4
　Woking GU21 . . . . 70 A3
Walton St KT20 . . . . 97 B3
Walton Terr GU21 . . . . 70 B4
Walton Way CR4 . . . . 41 C5
WANBOROUGH 128 C6
Wanborough Bsns Ctr
　GU3 . . . . 128 E8
Wanborough Dr SW15 . . . . 19 B7
Wanborough Hill GU3 . . . 128 C6
Wanborough La GU6 . . . . 175 A3
Wanborough Sta GU3 . . . 107 C1
Wandle Bank
　Merton SW19 . . . . 20 D1
　Wallington CR0 . . . . 60 E7
Wandle Cl
　Ash GU12 . . . . 106 A1
　Crawley RH10 . . . . 202 C5
Wandle Court Gdns CR0 . . 60 E7
Wandle Ct
　Wallington CR0 . . . . 60 E7
　West Ewell KT19 . . . . . . 57 C6
Wandle Ho
　Catford BR1 . . . . 24 D3
　5 Redhill RH1 . . . . 118 F2
　Wandsworth SW18 . . . . . 20 B8
Wandle Lodge
　Hackbridge SM6 . . . . . . 60 B8
　Wallington CR0 . . . . 60 E7
Wandle Pk Halt CR0 . . . . . 61 A8
Wandle Rd
　Croydon CR0, CR9 . . . . . 61 C7
　Hackbridge SM6 . . . . . . 60 B8
　Morden CR4, SM4, SW19 . 40 D4
　Upper Tooting SW17 . . . 20 E6
　Wallington CR0 . . . . 60 E7
Wandle Side
　Croydon CR0 . . . . 60 F7
　Hackbridge SM6 . . . . . . 60 B7
Wandle Trad Est CR4 . . . . . 40 F2
Wandle Valley Sch SM5 . . 40 E2
Wandle Way
　Mitcham CR4 . . . . 40 F4
　Wandsworth SW18 . . . . . 20 B7
WANDSWORTH 20 C7
Wandsworth Common Sta
　SW12 . . . . 20 F8
Wansbeck Ho RH2 . . . . . . 139 A6
Wansdyke Cl GU16 . . . . . . 85 F8
Wansford Gn 3 GU21 . . . . 68 F2
Wanstraw Gr RG12 . . . . . . 27 E2
Wantage Cl
　Bracknell RG12 . . . . 27 E4
　Crawley RH10 . . . . 202 C3
Wantage Rd GU47 . . . . 64 D8
Wapati Way GU14 . . . . . . 104 D8
Waplings The KT20 . . . . . . 97 B3
Wapshott Rd TW18 . . . . . . 12 E3
Warbank Cl CR0 . . . . 63 E1
Warbank Cres CR0 . . . . 63 E1
Warbank La KT2 . . . . 18 F1
Warbeck Ho KT13 . . . . 53 D5
Warblers Gn KT11 . . . . 73 F5
Warbleton Ho 6 RH11 . . . 200 F3
Warboys App KT2 . . . . 18 B2
Warboys Rd KT2 . . . . 18 B2
Warburton Cl RH19 . . . . . 206 A8
Warburton Rd TW2 . . . . . . 16 B7
Warbury La GU21 . . . . 68 C3
War Coppice Rd CR3 . . . . 120 D7
Ward Cl
　Croydon CR0 . . . . 61 E5
　Wokingham RG40 . . . . . 25 D8
Ward La CR6 . . . . 81 D2
Wardle Cl GU19 . . . . 47 E3
Wardley St SW18 . . . . 20 B8
Wardrobe The 3 TW9 . . . . 6 D2
Wards Cotts TW19 . . . . 13 F8
Wards Pl TW20 . . . . 12 C2
Wards Stone Pk RG12 . . . . 27 E2
Ward St GU1 . . . . 130 D8
Ware Ct SM1 . . . . 58 F6
Wareham Cl TW3 . . . . .5 B3
Wareham Rd RG12 . . . . . . 27 F4
Warehouse Theatre ★ 13
　CR0 . . . . 61 D8
Wareland Ho 3 RH19 . . . 185 E1
Warenne Hts RH1 . . . . 139 D7
Warenne Rd KT22 . . . . 94 C5
Warfield Ct 1 TW12 . . . . . 36 B8
Warfield Pk RG42 . . . . 28 A8
Warfield Rd
　Bracknell RG12 . . . . 27 C8
　East Bedfont TW14 . . . . . 14 E8
　Hampton TW12 . . . . 36 B8
Wargrove Dr GU47 . . . . . . 64 D8
Warham Rd CR0, CR2 . . . . 61 C5
Warkworth Gdns TW7 . . . . 6 A7
WARLINGHAM 81 C1
Warlingham Park Sch
　CR6 . . . . 82 A3
Warlingham Rd CR7 . . . . . 42 B5
Warlingham Sch CR6 . . . . 81 B3
Warlingham Village Prim
　Sch CR6 . . . . 81 E2
Warltersville Way RH6 . . . 161 C1
War Memorial Homes W4 . 7 D7
Warminster Gdns SE25 . . . 43 A7
Warminster Rd SE25 . . . . . 43 A7
Warminster Sq SE25 . . . . . 43 A7
Warminster Way CR4 . . . . . 41 B7
Warner Ave SM3 . . . . 58 E8
Warner Cl
　Crawley RH10 . . . . 202 C2
　Feltham TW12 . . . . 15 F3

Warner Cl continued
　Harlington UB3 . . . . 3 D7
Warner Ct
　Cheam SM3 . . . . 58 E8
　Sandhurst GU47 . . . . 64 E7
Warner Ho BR3 . . . . 24 B2
Warner Rd BR1 . . . . 24 F1
Warners La GU5 . . . . 132 E2
Warnford Ho SW15 . . . . . . .7 E1
WARNHAM 216 E7
Warnham CE Prim Sch
　RH12 . . . . 216 F8
Warnham Court Rd SM5 . . 59 F3
Warnham Ct RH12 . . . . . . 216 F8
Warnham Ho 9 SW2 . . . . . 21 F8
Warnham Manor RH12 . . 216 C7
Warnham Nature Reserve ★
　RH12 . . . . 217 B6
Warnham Rd
　Broadbridge Heath
　　RH12 . . . . 216 D4
　Crawley RH10 . . . . 202 B4
　Horsham RH12 . . . . 217 B5
Warnham Sta RH12 . . . . . 217 D8
Warpole Pk KT13 . . . . 53 A3
Warramill Rd GU7 . . . . . . 151 A5
Warren Ave
　Belmont SM2 . . . . 58 F1
　Bromley BR1 . . . . 24 E1
　Mortlake SW14, TW10 . . . 7 B3
　South Croydon CR2 . . . . 62 D3
Warren Cl
　Esher KT10 . . . . 55 B6
　Farnham GU9 . . . . 125 E3
　Felbridge RH19 . . . . . . 184 E3
　Sandhurst GU47 . . . . 64 A8
　West Norwood SE21 . . . . 22 C8
Warren Cnr GU10 . . . . 124 C7
WARREN CORNER 124 C7
Warren Ct
　18 Beckenham BR3 . . . . 24 A1
　6 Croydon CR0 . . . . 42 E1
Warren Cutting KT2 . . . . . . 18 D1
Warren Down RG42 . . . . . . 26 E8
Warren Dr
　Crawley RH11 . . . . 201 A8
　Kingswood KT20 . . . . . . 98 A4
Warren Drive N KT5, KT6 . . 38 E3
Warren Drive S KT5 . . . . . . 38 C1
Warreners La KT13 . . . . . . 53 D3
Warren Farm Cotts KT24 113 C5
Warren Farm Mobile Home
　Pk GU23 . . . . 91 B8
Warren Hill KT18 . . . . 76 D3
Warren House Rd RG40 . . . 25 D8
Warrenhyrst GU1 . . . . 131 A8
Warren La
　Oxshott KT22 . . . . 74 C7
　Oxted RH8 . . . . 123 A1
　Woking GU22 . . . . 71 B1
Warren Lodge KT13 . . . . . . 97 E3
Warren Lodge Dr KT20 . . . 97 E3
Warren Mead SM7 . . . . 77 C4
Warren Mead Inf Sch
　SM7 . . . . 77 D4
Warren Mead Jun Sch
　SM7 . . . . 77 D4
Warrenne Rd RH3 . . . . 137 C7
Warrenne Way RH2 . . . . . 118 A1
Warren Park Rd SM1 . . . . . 59 E4
Warren Pk
　Box Hill KT20 . . . . 116 C4
　Kingston upon Thames KT2 . 18 C2
　Warlingham CR6 . . . . 81 D1
Warren Rd
　Ashford TW15 . . . . 14 E1
　Banstead KT17, SM7 . . . 77 D5
　Croydon CR0 . . . . 42 F1
　Farncombe GU7 . . . . . . 150 E7
　Guildford GU1 . . . . 131 A8
　Kingston upon Thames KT2 . 18 C2
　Mitcham SW19 . . . . 20 E2
　Purley CR8 . . . . 80 B8
　Reigate RH2 . . . . 118 B2
　Twickenham TW2 . . . . 5 D1
　Woodham KT15 . . . . 52 A1
Warren Rise
　Frimley GU16 . . . . 65 F3
　Kingston upon Thames KT3 . 38 D8
Warren Row SL5 . . . . 28 D7
Warren The
　Aldershot GU11 . . . . . . 104 F1
　Ashtead KT21 . . . . 95 F7
　East Horsley KT24 . . . . . 112 F5
　Heath End GU9 . . . . . . 125 E8
　Heston TW5 . . . . .4 F7
　Kingswood KT20 . . . . . . 97 E4
　Leatherhead KT22 . . . . . 74 D6
　Oxshott KT22 . . . . 74 D6
　Wallington SM5 . . . . 59 E2
　Weybridge KT13 . . . . . . 53 A5
　Worcester Park KT4 . . . . 57 D7
Warren Way KT13 . . . . 53 C4
Warren Wood Cl 5 BR2 . . 63 F8
Warrington Cl RH11 . . . . . 200 E2
Warrington Ct
　11 Bromley BR1 . . . . 24 F1
　3 Croydon CR0 . . . . 61 B7
　13 Merton SW19 . . . . . . 20 A1
Warrington Mews GU11 . 125 E8
Warrington Rd
　Croydon CR0, CR9 . . . . . 61 B7
　23 Richmond TW10 . . . . .6 D2
Warrington Spur SL4 . . . . . 11 B8
Warwick Cl GU21 . . . . 27 E3
Warwick Ave
　Staines TW18 . . . . 13 C2
　Thorpe Lea TW20 . . . . . . 32 C8

Warwick Cl
　Aldershot GU11 . . . . . . 126 C8
　Frimley GU15 . . . . 66 B3
　Hampton TW12 . . . . 16 C1
　South Holmwood RH5 . . 157 B7
Warwick Ct
　1 Beckenham BR2 . . . . . 44 E7
　Kenley CR8 . . . . 80 D5
　Merton SW19 . . . . 39 F8
　Surbiton KT6 . . . . 56 E8
　Weybridge KT13 . . . . . . 53 A5
Warwick Deeping KT16 . . . 51 C5
Warwick Gdns
　Ashtead KT21 . . . . 75 C2
　Thames Ditton KT7 . . . . . 36 F4
　Thornton Heath CR7 . . . . 42 A5
Warwick Gr KT5 . . . . 37 F2
Warwick Ho
　Aldershot GU11 . . . . . . 126 C8
　6 Kingston upon Thames
　　KT2 . . . . 37 E8
　5 Merton SW19 . . . . 19 E1
　9 Redhill RH1 . . . . 119 A3
Warwick La GU21 . . . . 89 A8
Warwick Lodge SM1 . . . . . 58 F6
Warwick Pl RH2 . . . . 118 D1
Warwick Quadrant 22
　RH1 . . . . 119 A2
Warwick Rd
　Ashford TW15 . . . . 13 E3
　Ash Vale GU12 . . . . 106 A3
　Coulsdon CR5 . . . . 79 D5
　Farnborough GU14 . . . . 104 D8
　Hounslow TW4 . . . . 4 B4
　Kingston upon Thames KT3 . 38 C6
　Penge SE20 . . . . 43 B6
　Redhill RH1 . . . . 118 F2
　South Holmwood RH5 . . 157 C7
　Sutton SM1 . . . . 59 C5
　Teddington KT1 . . . . 37 C8
　Thames Ditton KT7 . . . . . 36 F4
　Thornton Heath CR7 . . . . 42 A6
　Twickenham TW2 . . . . . . 16 E7
Warwicks Bench GU1 . . . 130 D6
Warwick's Bench Rd
　GU1 . . . . 130 E6
Warwick Sch The RH1 . . . 119 A2
Warwick Villas TW20 . . . . . 32 C8
WARWICK WOLD 120 A6
Warwick Wold Rd RH1 . . . 120 A7
Wasdale Cl GU47 . . . . 45 D2
Washington Cl RH10 . . . . 202 A6
Washington Ct SW17 . . . . . 20 F2
Washington Rd
　Crawley RH11 . . . . 200 E3
　Kingston upon Thames KT1 . 38 A7
　North Cheam KT4 . . . . . 39 B1
Washpond La CR6 . . . . 82 C1
WASP GREEN 162 C7
Wasp Green La RH1 . . . . . 162 C8
Wasp Rd TW6 . . . . .2 B5
Wassand Cl RH10 . . . . . . 202 A6
Wastdale Rd SE23 . . . . 23 D7
Watcombe Cotts TW9 . . . . . 7 A8
Watcombe Rd SE25 . . . . . . 43 B4
Watchetts Dr GU15 . . . . . . 65 C2
Watchetts Jun Sch The
　GU15 . . . . 65 B2
Watchetts Lake Cl GU15 . . 65 D3
Watchetts Rd GU15 . . . . . . 65 B4
Watchmoor Pk GU15 . . . . . 65 A4
Watchmoor Rd GU15 . . . . . 65 A4
Watchmoor Trade Ctr
　GU15 . . . . 65 A3
Watcombe Cotts TW9 . . . . . 7 A8
Watcombe Rd SE25 . . . . . . 43 B4
Waterbank Rd SE6 . . . . 24 C4
Waterbourne Way CR8 . . . 80 D5
Watercress Pl 8 RH13 . . . 217 F3
Watercress Way GU21 . . . . 69 B2
Waterden Cl GU1 . . . . 130 F8
Waterden Rd GU1 . . . . 130 E8
Waterer Gdns KT20 . . . . . . 77 E1
Waterer Ho SE6 . . . . 24 C4
Waterer Rise SM6 . . . . 60 D4
Waterers Rise GU21 . . . . . . 68 D2
Waterfall Cl GU25 . . . . 31 A6
Waterfall Cotts SW19 . . . . 20 D2
Waterfall Rd SW19 . . . . . . 20 D2
Waterfall Terr SW17 . . . . . . 20 E2
Waterfield Cl RH13 . . . . . 217 E3
Waterfield Dr CR6 . . . . . . 101 C8
Waterfield Fst Sch RH11 . 200 E4
Waterfield Gdns
　Crawley RH11 . . . . 200 E4
　South Norwood SE25 . . . 42 E4
Waterfield Gn KT20 . . . . . . 97 B7
Waterfields KT22 . . . . 95 B8
Waterford Cl KT11 . . . . 73 E8
Waterford Way RG40 . . . . . 25 C6
Watergardens The KT2 . . . 18 C2
Watergate Sch SE6 . . . . . . 24 B3
Waterham Rd RG12 . . . . . . 27 B3
Waterhouse Ct 8 TW11 . . 16 F3
Waterhouse La
　Bletchingley RH1, RH9 . . 121 A3
　Coulsdon CR8 . . . . 100 C8
　Kingswood KT20 . . . . . . 97 E6
Waterhouse Mead GU47 . . 64 D7
Water La
　Abinger Common RH5 . . 155 B8
　Albury GU5 . . . . 132 B5
　Bisley GU24 . . . . 87 E8
　Cobham KT11 . . . . 73 F5
　Enton Green GU8 . . . . . 171 B4
　Farnborough GU14 . . . . 85 A7
　Farnham GU9 . . . . 125 C4
　Kingston upon Thames KT1 . 37 D8
　Limpsfield RH8 . . . . 123 A8

Water La continued
　Lingfield TN8 . . . . 165 D7
　Little Bookham KT23 . . . 93 E1
　Richmond TW10, TW9 . . . 6 D2
　South Godstone RH9 . . . 142 D5
　Twickenham TW1 . . . . . . 17 A7
Waterlands La RH12 . . . . . 196 E1
Water Lane Ho 30 TW9 . . . 6 D2
Waterlea RH10 . . . . 202 A5
WATERLOO 132 A4
Waterloo Cl
　Camberley GU15 . . . . . . 66 B7
　East Bedfont TW14 . . . . . 14 F7
Waterloo Cotts 4 SM5 . . . 59 E7
Waterloo Cres RG40 . . . . . 25 E4
Waterloo Pl
　Richmond, Kew TW9 . . . . 7 A8
　13 Richmond TW9 . . . . . 6 E3
Waterloo Rd
　Aldershot GU12 . . . . . . 105 C1
　Carshalton SM1 . . . . 59 D5
　Crowthorne RG45 . . . . . 45 B4
　Epsom KT17, KT19 . . . . . 76 D6
　Wokingham RG40 . . . . . 25 F5
Waterlow Rd RH2 . . . . 139 D8
Watermans Bsns Pk
　TW18 . . . . 12 E4
Watermans Ct 14 TW8 . . . . 6 D8
Watermead
　East Bedfont TW14 . . . . . 14 E7
　Tadworth KT20 . . . . 97 B6
　Woking GU21 . . . . 68 F3
Water Mead CR5 . . . . 78 F2
Watermead Ho 2 SM1 . . . 59 C4
Watermead La CR4 . . . . . . 40 F2
Watermead Rd SE6 . . . . . . 24 C4
Watermen's Sq 1 SE20 . . . 23 C1
Watermill Cl TW10 . . . . . . 17 C5
Watermill Way SW19 . . . . . 40 C8
Water Mill Way TW13 . . . . 16 A6
Waterperry La GU24 . . . . . . 49 F1
Waters Dr TW18 . . . . 12 F4
Watersedge KT19 . . . . 57 C6
Waters Edge KT15 . . . . 52 D6
WATERSIDE 164 E7
Waterside
　9 Beckenham BR3 . . . . . 44 A8
　East Grinstead RH19 . . . 186 B1
　East Molesey KT8 . . . . . . 36 E5
　Horley RH6 . . . . 161 A5
Waterside Ave BR3 . . . . . . 44 B4
Waterside Bsns Ctr TW1 . . .6 D3
Waterside Cl
　Crawley RH11 . . . . 200 E4
　Godalming GU7 . . . . . . 151 A5
　Surbiton KT6 . . . . 56 E8
Waterside Ct SM6 . . . . 60 A7
Waterside Dr KT12 . . . . . . 35 B4
Waterside La GU7 . . . . 150 C3
Waterside Mews GU1 . . . 109 C3
Waterside Rd GU1 . . . . . . 109 D4
Waterside Trad Est KT15 . . 52 E6
Waterside Way
　Wimbledon SW17 . . . . . 20 C3
　2 Woking GU21 . . . . . . 69 B1
Waterslade RH1 . . . . 118 E1
Watersmeet Cl GU4 . . . . . 110 A6
Watersplash Cl KT1 . . . . . . 37 E6
Water Splash La SL5 . . . . . 29 E8
Watersplash Rd TW17 . . . . 34 A5
Waters Sq KT1 . . . . 38 B6
Water Tower Hill CR0,
　CR2 . . . . 61 D6
Water View RH6 . . . . 161 C3
Waterway Rd KT22 . . . . 95 A5
Waterworks Cl RH18 . . . . 206 F3
Waterworks Cotts TW12 . . 36 A8
Waterworks Yd 2 CR0 . . . 61 C7
Watery La
　Merton SW19, SW20 . . . . 39 F7
　Woking GU24 . . . . 68 D8
Wates Way CR4 . . . . 40 F3
Watford Cl GU1 . . . . 109 F1
Wathen Rd RH4 . . . . 136 B8
Watlings Cl CR0 . . . . 43 E3
Watlington Cotts SE26 . . . 23 E3
Watlington Gr SE26 . . . . . . 23 E3
Watney Cl CR8 . . . . 79 F6
Watney Cotts SW14 . . . . . . 7 C4
Watney Rd SW14 . . . . 7 C4
Watneys Rd CR4 . . . . 41 D4
Watson Ave SM3 . . . . 58 E8
Watson Cl
　Crawley RH10 . . . . 202 C3
　Mitcham SW19 . . . . 20 E1
Watson Ho 3 SW2 . . . . . . 21 E8
Watson Rd RH4 . . . . 135 C6
Wattenden Prim Sch CR8 . 80 B3
Wattendon Rd CR8 . . . . . . 80 B3
Wattlehurst Dr RH12 . . . . 198 B7
Wattlehurst Farm &
　Deadwood Town ★
　RH12 . . . . 198 A7
Watts Gall The ★ GU3 . . . 129 B4
Watt's La
　Tadworth KT20 . . . . 97 D5
　Teddington TW11 . . . . . . 17 A3
Watts Lea GU21 . . . . 69 A4
Watt's Mead KT20 . . . . 97 D5
Watts Rd
　Farnborough GU14 . . . . 84 F5
　Thames Ditton KT7 . . . . . 37 A2
Wavel Ct
　Croydon CR2 . . . . 61 D5
　7 Streatham SW16 . . . . . 21 E5

Wavell Ct
Aldershot GU12 105 C1
Croydon CR0 61 F8
Wavell Sch The GU14 105 B7
Wavel Pl SE19, SE26 22 F4
Wavendene Ave TW20 12 C1
Waveney Ct BR3 44 C8
Waveney Ho 7 RH1 118 F1
Waveney Wlk RH10 202 B4
Waverleigh Rd GU6 174 E1
Waverley RG12 26 E4
Waverley Abbey★ GU9 147 B7
Waverley Abbey CE Sch GU10 147 D5
Waverley Ave
Kenley CR8 80 E3
Sutton SM1 59 C8
Tolworth KT5 38 C3
Twickenham TW2 16 A7
Waverley Cl
Farnham GU9 125 D2
Frimley GU15 65 F4
Waverley Ct
6 Horsham RH12 217 B2
Woking GU22 69 E1
Waverley Dr
Ash Vale GU12 106 A6
Camberley GU15 65 F5
Chertsey KT16 51 D7
Virginia Water GU25 31 A5
Waverley Gdns GU12 106 A6
Waverley Ho BR3 24 B1
Waverley Hts GU9 125 E1
Waverley La
Farnham, Compton GU9 125 E1
Farnham GU10, GU9 147 C8
Waverley Lodge TW16 35 A7
Waverley Pl KT22 95 B5
Waverley Rd
Bagshot GU19 47 E3
Croydon SE25 43 B6
Farnborough GU14 85 D3
Oxshott KT11, KT22 74 B5
Stoneleigh KT17, KT4 58 B5
Weybridge KT13 53 A5
Waverley Way SM5 59 E4
Waverton Rd SW18 20 C8
Wavertree Ct
Horley RH6 160 F2
9 Streatham SW2 21 E7
Wavertree Rd SW2 21 F7
Waye Ave TW5 4 A6
Wayfarer Rd TW6 2 B4
Wayland Cl RG12 27 F5
Waylands Mead BR3 44 B8
Waylett Pl SE27 22 B5
Wayman Rd GU14 84 E8
Wayneflete Pl KT10 55 B7
Wayneflete Tower Ave KT10 55 A7
Waynflete Ave CR0, CR9 61 B7
Waynflete Ho KT10 55 B6
Waynflete La GU9 124 F2
Waynflete St SW18 20 C6
Ways End GU15 65 E4
Wayside
Capel RH5 178 D6
Crawley RH11 200 E4
Mortlake SW14 7 C2
New Addington CR0 63 B4
Wayside Cotts
Churt GU10 167 E3
Ellen's Green GU6 195 F4
Holmbury St M RH5 155 C6
Wayside Ct
Hounslow TW7 5 E5
Twickenham TW1 6 C1
Woking GU21 68 E3
Wayswood GU15 65 E6
Way The RH2 118 D2
Weald CE Prim Sch The RH5 157 D3
Weald Cl GU4 130 E3
Weald Dr RH10 202 A4
Wealden Ho GU2 129 E8
Wealdon Ct 1 GU2 108 F1
Wealdstone Rd SM3 58 F8
Weald The RH19 185 F4
Weald View Cotts RH5 156 D3
Weald Way
Caterham CR3 120 E8
Reigate RH2 139 C5
Weall Cl CR8 79 F7
Weare St
Capel RH5 178 B4
Ockley RH5 177 F1
Weasdale Ct GU21 68 F3
Weatherall Cl KT15 52 B5
WEATHERHILL 162 A4
Weatherhill Cl RH6 161 F3
Weatherhill Cotts RH6 162 A4
Weatherhill Rd RH6 162 A3
Weatherill Ct SE25 43 B3
Weather Way RG12 27 C7
Weaver Cl
5 Crawley RH11 200 E5
Croydon CR9 61 F6
Weaver Moss GU47 64 B7
Weavers Cl TW7 5 E3
Weavers Gdns GU9 145 F7
Weavers Yd 18 GU9 125 B2
Weaver Wlk SE27 22 B4
Webb Cl
Bagshot GU19 47 E1
Crawley RH11 201 B1
Webb Ct RG40 25 E8
Webb Ho TW13 15 E5
Webb Rd GU8 170 C6
Webster Cl KT22 74 B5
Webster Ct GU5 151 F7
Websters Cl GU22 89 B7
Weddell Rd RH10 201 F3
Wedgewood Ct 1 BR2 44 F5
Wedgewood Ho KT7 36 F1
Wedgwood Pl KT11 73 A5
Wedgwoods TN16 103 C6
Wedgwood Way SE19 22 C1
Weeks Ho TW10 17 C4
Weighbridge Rd KT15 52 B2
Weighton Rd SE20 43 B7
Weihurst Ct SM1 59 E5
Weihurst Gdns SM1 59 D5
Weint The SL3 1 C7
Weir Ave GU14 85 A3
Weirbrook RH10 202 A3
Weir Cl GU14 85 A3
Weir Ho 8 SW12 21 C8
Weir Pl TW18 32 E8
Weir Rd
Chertsey KT16 33 B2
Farnborough GU14, GU51 84 A2
Streatham SW12 21 C8
Walton-on-Thames KT12 35 A3
Wimbledon SW18, SW19 20 B5
Weir Wood Resr Nature Reserve★ RH19 205 D1
Welbeck RG12 26 E4
Welbeck Cl
Ewell KT17 58 A3
Farnborough GU14 84 F3
New Malden KT3 38 F4
Welbeck Rd SM1, SM5 59 D8
Welbeck Wlk SM5 40 D1
Welcome Cotts CR3 102 A4
Welcomes Rd CR8 80 C3
Welcomes Terr CR3 80 F3
Weldon Ct
7 Carshalton SM1 59 D5
Thornton Heath CR7 42 B4
Weldon Dr KT8 35 F5
Weldon Way RH1 119 D6
Welford Pl SW19 19 E4
Welham Rd SW16, SW17 21 B2
Welhouse Rd SM5 59 E8
Welland Cl SL3 1 B8
Welland Ct SE6 23 F6
Wellburn Cl GU47 64 B7
Well Cl
Camberley GU15 65 B4
Streatham SW16 21 F4
Woking GU21 69 C2
Well Ct
North Cheam SM3 58 D8
Surbiton KT6 37 D2
Welldon Ct 1 SE21 22 D6
Weller Cl RH10 202 D5
Weller Dr GU15 65 C3
Wellers Ct GU5 133 A4
Wellesford Cl SM7 77 F2
Wellesley Cl
Ash Vale GU12 105 F7
Bagshot GU19 47 C3
Wellesley Court Rd 1 CR0, CR9 61 D8
Wellesley Cres TW2 16 E5
Wellesley Ct
Cheam SM3 39 E1
Twickenham TW2 16 E5
Wellesley Gate 3 GU12 105 B1
Wellesley Gdn GU9 125 C7
Wellesley Gr CR0, CR9 61 D8
Wellesley Ho
Epsom KT19 76 B8
12 Merton SW19 19 E1
Wellesley Par TW2 16 E5
Wellesley Rd
Aldershot GU11 104 E2
Croydon CR0 42 C1
Rushmoor GU10 168 C6
Sutton SM2 59 C4
Twickenham TW2 16 E5
Wellesley Rd Halt CR0 61 D8
Well Farm Hts CR3 101 A8
Well Farm Rd CR3, CR6 101 A8
Wellfield RH19 206 C7
Wellfield Gdns SM5 59 E2
Wellfield Rd SW16 21 E4
Well Ho SM7 78 B4
Wellhouse La RH3 137 D6
Wellhouse Rd BR3 44 A5
Wellingham Way RH12 200 C2
Wellington Ave
Aldershot GU11 104 F2
Hounslow TW3, TW4 5 A2
North Cheam KT4 58 C7
Virginia Water GU25 31 B4
Wellington Cl
Crawley RH10 182 E1
Sandhurst GU47 64 C8
Walton-on-Thames KT12 34 F1
Wellington Coll RG45 45 A3
Wellington Cotts KT24 112 E6
Wellington Cres KT3 38 C6
Wellington Ct
Ashford TW15 13 E3
Stanwell TW19 13 E8
5 Surbiton KT6 37 E3
Teddington TW11 16 D3
4 Upper Tooting SW17 20 E2
Wellington Dr
Bracknell RG12 27 E4
Wallington CR8 60 F1
Wellington Gate RH19 186 A3
Wellington Gdns
Aldershot GU11 104 F1
Teddington TW2 16 D4
Wellingtonia Ho KT15 52 A5
Wellingtonias RG42 8 A1
Wellington La GU9 125 D7
Wellington Lodge SL4 9 B6
Wellington Mews SW16 21 D5
Wellington Pl
Ash Vale GU12 105 F4
Cobham KT11 73 C7
Farncombe GU7 150 E7
Wellington Prim Sch TW3 4 F5
Wellington Rd
Ashford TW15 13 E3
Caterham CR3 100 C5
Crowthorne RG45 45 C4
Hatton TW14 3 E2
Horsham RH12 217 D2
Hounslow TW6 2 B5
Sandhurst GU47 64 C8
Teddington TW12, TW2 16 D4
Thornton Heath CR0 42 B2
Wimbledon SW19 20 A6
Wokingham RG40 25 B5
Wellington Rdbt GU11 104 E2
Wellington Road N TW4 4 F4
Wellington Road S TW4 4 F3
Wellington Sh Ctr The 21 GU11 105 A2
Wellington St 8 GU11 105 A2
Wellington Terr
6 Knaphill GU21 68 E1
Sandhurst GU47 64 C8
Wellington Town Rd RH19 185 D2
Wellington Way
Byfleet KT13 52 F1
Farnborough GU11, GU14 104 D7
Horley RH6 160 F5
Well La
Godalming GU8 190 D8
Haslemere GU27 208 D6
Mortlake SW14 7 C2
Woking GU21 69 C2
Wellmeadow Rd SE13, SE6 24 E7
Wellow Wlk SM5 40 D1
Well Path GU21 69 C2
Wells Cl
Great Bookham KT23 94 C3
Horsham RH12 216 F2
South Croydon CR2 61 E5
Wells Cotts GU9 146 A7
Wells Ct 1 CR4 40 E8
Wellside Gdns SW14 7 C2
Wells La
Ascot SL5 29 B5
Normandy GU3 107 C4
Wells Lea RH19 185 D3
Wells Mdw RH19 185 D3
Wells Park Ct SE26 23 B4
Wells Park Rd SE21, SE26 23 B4
Wells Pl
Merstham RH1 119 B6
Wandsworth SW18 20 C8
Wells Rd
Crawley RH10 201 E2
Epsom KT18 76 B4
Guildford GU4 110 C4
WELLS THE 76 A5
Wells The GU27 208 C6
Well Way KT18 76 A5
Wellwood Cl
Coulsdon CR5, CR8 79 E5
Horsham RH13 218 B4
Wellwynds Rd GU6 174 E2
Welwyn Ave TW14 3 F1
Welwyn Cl RH11 200 E2
Wembley Rd TW12 36 A8
Wembury Pk RH7 163 E1
Wendela Cl GU22 69 F1
Wenderholme CR2 61 D5
Wendley Dr KT15 51 F1
Wendling Rd SM1 59 D8
Wendon Ct SM6 60 C4
Wendover Ct
Egham TW18 12 C3
South Croydon CR2 61 D2
Wendover Dr
Frimley GU16 66 C3
New Malden KT3 38 F3
Wendover Pl TW18 12 D3
Wendover Rd TW18, TW20 12 D3
Wendron Cl 2 GU21 69 A1
Wend The CR5 79 D5
Wendy Cres GU2 109 A3
Wenlock Cl RH11 201 A4
Wenlock Edge RH4 136 C5
Wensleydale RH11 201 C3
Wensleydale Dr GU15 66 D5
Wensleydale Gdns TW12 16 B1
Wensleydale Rd TW12 16 B1
Wentland Cl SE6 24 D6
Wentland Rd SE6 24 D6
WENTWORTH 30 F3
Wentworth Ave SL5 28 C7
Wentworth Cl
Ashford TW15 14 B4
Ash Vale GU12 106 A7
Heath End GU9 125 F6
Long Ditton KT6 56 D8
Morden SM4 40 A2
Ripley GU23 91 B6
Wentworth Cres GU12 106 A6
Wentworth Ct
20 Kingston upon Thames KT6 37 E4
6 Surbiton KT6 56 E8
Twickenham TW2 16 E5
Wentworth Dene KT13 53 B5
Wentworth Dr
Crawley RH10 202 D7
Wentworth GU25 30 F5
Wentworth Golf Club GU25 31 A4
Wentworth Ho KT15 52 B6
Wentworth Pl GU15 65 A4
Wentworth Rd CR0 42 A2
Wentworth Way
Hamsey Green CR2 81 A4
North Ascot SL5 28 C7
Werndee Rd SE25 43 A5
Wesco Ct GU21 70 A3
Wescott Inf Sch RG40 25 D6
Wescott Rd RG40 25 D6
Wesley Ave TW3 4 F5
Wesley Cl
Crawley RH11 200 F3
Horley RH6 161 A5
Reigate RH2 138 F8
Wesley Dr TW20 12 A2
Wesley Pl SL4 9 B6
Wessels KT20 97 D6
Wessex Ave SW19 40 A6
Wessex Cl
Hinchley Wood KT7 55 F8
Kingston upon Thames KT1, KT2 38 B8
Wessex Ct 5 TW19 2 E1
Wessex Pl GU9 125 C1
Wessex Rd
Farnborough GU14 84 E1
Harmondsworth TW19, TW6 2 E4
Wesson Ho 3 CR0 43 A1
Westacres KT10 54 F3
West Ashtead Prim Sch KT21 95 E7
West Ave
Crawley RH10 202 A8
Heath End GU9 125 D7
Redhill RH1 140 A3
Wallington SM6 60 E5
Whiteley Village KT12, KT13 53 E2
West Bank RH4 136 A6
Westbank Rd TW12 16 C2
WEST BARNES 39 C4
West Barnes La KT3, SW20 39 B5
WEST BEDFONT 13 F8
WESTBOROUGH 108 F2
Westbourne RH4 136 C5
Westbourne Ave SM3 58 E8
Westbourne Ct SM3 58 E8
Westbourne Dr SE23 23 D6
Westbourne Ho
Heston TW5 5 A8
9 Twickenham TW1 17 B8
Westbourne Prim Sch SM1 59 A7
Westbourne Rd
Croydon CR0 42 F3
Feltham TW13 14 F5
Penge SE26 23 D2
Sandhurst GU47 64 E7
Staines TW18 13 B1
WESTBROOK 150 C5
Westbrook RH18 206 E3
Westbrook Ave TW12 15 F1
Westbrook Gdns RG12 27 D8
Westbrook Hill GU8 148 C3
Westbrook Rd
Godalming GU7 150 C5
Heston TW5 4 F7
South Norwood CR7 42 D7
Staines TW18 12 F3
Westbury Ave KT10 55 F4
Westbury Cl
1 Crowthorne RG45 45 B5
Crowthorne RG45 45 B6
Shepperton TW17 34 B3
Whyteleafe CR3 80 F1
Westbury Ct BR3 44 B8
Westbury Gdns GU9 125 E4
Westbury House Sch KT3 38 D4
Westbury Pl 2 TW8 6 D8
Westbury Rd
Beckenham BR3 43 E6
Feltham TW13 15 D6
New Malden KT3 38 D4
Penge SE20 43 D8
Thornton Heath CR0 42 D3
Westbury Way GU12 105 D2
WEST BYFLEET 71 B6
West Byfleet Cty Inf Sch KT14 71 B7
West Byfleet Jun Sch KT14 71 B7
West Byfleet Sta KT14 71 A7
Westcar La KT12 54 B5
West Cl
Ashford TW15 13 E4
Hampton TW12 15 E2
Heath End GU9 125 D7
WEST CLANDON 111 B6
Westcombe Ave CR0 41 F2
Westcombe Cl RG12 27 E2
Westcoombe Ave SW20 38 F8
Westcote Rd
Epsom KT19 57 B1
Streatham SW16 21 C3
WESTCOTT 135 D6
Westcott CE Fst Sch RH4 135 D5
Westcott Cl CR0 63 B2
Westcott Keep RH6 161 C4
Westcott Rd RH4 135 F7
West Cotts GU26 188 C6
Westcott St RH4 135 B6
Westcott Way SM2 58 C1
Westcroft SM5 60 A6
Westcroft Gdns SM4, SW20 39 F5
Westcroft Ho SM5 60 A6
Westcroft L Ctr SM5 60 A6
Westcroft Rd SM5, SM6 60 A6
West Cross Ctr TW8 6 B8
West Cross Way TW8 6 B8
West Croydon Sta/Halt CR0 42 C1
West Ct
Guildford GU4 110 B5
Hounslow TW7 5 C7
Sunbury TW16 35 B7
Wimbledon SW20 39 B7
Westdene
Godalming GU7 150 E3
Hersham KT12 54 B5
Westdene Mdws GU6 174 A3
West Dene Sch CR8 79 F6
Westdene Way KT13 53 E7
West Down KT23 114 B8
Westdown Rd SE13, SE6 24 A8
West Dr
Belmont SM2 58 E2
Burgh Heath KT20 77 D1
Streatham SW16, SW17 21 C4
Sutton SM5 59 D1
Wentworth GU25, SL5 30 E2
Woodham KT15 52 B2
WEST DULWICH 22 C6
West Dulwich Sta SE21 22 D7
WEST END
Esher 54 F4
Woking 67 F6
West End Comm Nature Reserve★ KT10 54 E3
West End Cotts GU23 91 B5
Westende RG40 25 D6
Westende Jun Sch RG40 25 D6
West End Gdns KT10 54 F5
West End Gr GU9 125 A2
West End Inf Sch GU11 104 F2
West End La
Chiddingfold GU27 190 E1
Esher KT10 54 F4
Frensham GU10 146 A1
Harlington UB7 3 C7
Westerdale Dr GU16 66 B3
Westerfolds Cl GU22 70 C2
Westerham 13 KT6 37 E4
Westerham Cl
Belmont SM2 59 A1
New Haw KT15 52 C4
Westerham Lodge 10 BR3 24 A1
Westerham Rd RH8, TN16 123 C6
Westerley Cres SE26, SE6 23 F3
Westermain KT15 52 C1
Western Ave
Brookwood GU24 88 A6
Chertsey KT16 33 A6
Thorpe TW20 32 B6
Western Cl KT16 33 A6
Western Ctr The RG12 26 F7
Western Dr TW17 34 D3
Western Hts SM1 59 A5
Western Ind Area RG12 26 F7
Western La SW12 21 A8
Western Par RH2 139 B6
Western Perimeter Rd TW19, TW6, UB7 2 B5
Western Perimeter Road Rdbt TW19 2 C2
Western Rd
Aldershot GU11 104 E1
Bracknell RG12 26 F7
Mitcham CR4, SW19 40 E7
Sutton SM1 59 A5
WEST EWELL 57 E3
West Ewell Inf Sch KT19 57 D5
West Farm Ave KT21 95 D8
West Farm Cl KT21 95 C8
West Farm Dr KT21 95 D8
WESTFIELD 89 F6
Westfield
Ashtead KT21 75 F1
Peaslake RH5 154 E8
Reigate RH2 118 B4
Westfield Ave
Sanderstead CR2 80 E6
Woking GU22 89 E7
Westfield Cl SM1 58 F6
Westfield Comm GU22 89 E5
Westfield Ct
Kingston upon Thames KT6 37 D4
New Haw KT15 52 D1
Westfield Dr KT23 94 B5
Westfield Gdns 2 RH4 136 A7
Westfield Gr GU22 89 E7
Westfield La GU10 145 E6
Westfield Par KT15 52 D1
Westfield Prim Sch GU22 89 E6
Westfield Rd
Beckenham BR3 43 F7
Camberley GU15 65 B2
Cheam SM1 58 F6
Crawley RH11 201 B6
Guildford GU1 109 E5
Kingston upon Thames KT6 37 D4
Mitcham CR4 40 F7
Thornton Heath CR0, CR9 61 B8
Walton-on-Thames KT12 35 E2
Woking GU22 89 E5

Westfields
Mortlake SW13 . . . . .7 F4
Witley GU8 . . . . 170 F5
Westfields Ave SW13, SW14 .7 E4
Westfield Way GU22 . . . . . 89 F5
West Flexford La GU3 . . 128 E8
Westgate Est TW14 . . . . . . 14 B7
Westgate Ho KT18 . . . . . . 76 D4
Westgate Rd
Beckenham BR3 . . . . 44 C8
Croydon SE25 . . . . 43 B5
West Gdns
Ewell KT17 . . . . 57 F1
Mitcham SW19 . . . . 20 E2
Westglade GU14 . . . . 84 D4
West Gr KT12 . . . . 54 B6
WEST GREEN 201 C6
West Green Dr RH11 . . . . 201 C6
Westhall Pk CR6 . . . . 101 C8
Westhall Rd CR6 . . . . 101 B8
West Hall Rd TW9 . . . . .7 B6
West Hanger Nature Trail★
GU5 . . . . 133 A7
Westhaven SM1 . . . . 59 A5
Westhay Gdns SW14 . . . . .7 B2
WEST HEATH 84 F6
West Heath GU24 . . . . 87 D5
West Heath Rd GU14 . . . . 84 F4
West Hill
Biggin Hill BR6 . . . . 83 F7
Dormans Park RH19 . . . . . 185 E6
East Grinstead RH19 . . . . . 205 D8
Elstead GU8 . . . . 148 C3
Epsom KT18, KT19 . . . . 76 C6
Oxted RH8 . . . . 122 D5
Putney SW15 . . . . 19 D8
South Croydon CR2 . . . . 61 E2
Woking GU22 . . . . 89 E8
West Hill Ave KT19 . . . . . . 76 C7
West Hill Bank RH8 . . . . 122 D5
West Hill Cl
Brookwood GU24 . . . . 88 B7
Elstead GU8 . . . . 148 C3
West Hill Ct KT19 . . . . 76 C6
West Hill Rd
Wandsworth SW18 . . . . 20 A8
Woking GU22 . . . . 89 E8
West Hill Sch KT22 . . . . . 75 A1
West Ho
Penge SE20 . . . . 23 D1
⑨ Streatham SW2 . . . . 21 C8
West Hoathly Rd RH19 . . 205 D4
WEST HORSLEY 112 B8
West House Cl SW19 . . . . . 19 E7
WESTHUMBLE 115 A4
Westhumble St RH5 . . . . 115 B4
West La
East Grinstead RH19 . . . . . 205 D8
Wotton RH5 . . . . 134 D4
Westland Cl TW19 . . . . .2 E1
Westland Dr BR2, BR4 . . . 63 F8
Westlands RH13 . . . . 217 E3
Westlands Ct
East Molesey KT8 . . . . 36 E5
Epsom KT18 . . . . 76 C4
Westlands Way RH8 . . . . 122 D8
Westleas RH6 . . . . 160 E5
Westlees Cl RH5 . . . . 136 D4
West Leigh RH19 . . . . 205 F4
Westleigh Ave CR5 . . . . . . 79 B3
Westleigh Ct ④ CR2 . . . . 61 E6
Westmacott Dr TW14 . . . . 14 F7
Westmark Point ⑬ SW15. 19 B7
Westmead
Farnborough GU14 . . . . 85 B3
⑩ Farnham GU9 . . . . 125 B2
Putney SW15 . . . . 19 B8
Woking GU21 . . . . 69 B2
West Mead KT19 . . . . 57 E4
Westmead Cnr SM1 . . . . . 59 E4
Westmead Rd SM1 . . . . . . 59 D6
Westmeads RH6 . . . . 161 C3
West Meads GU2 . . . . 129 F8
West Middlesex Univ Hosp
TW7 . . . . 6 A5
Westminster Ave CR7 . . . 42 B7
Westminster Cl
East Bedfont TW14 . . . . 15 A7
Teddington TW11 . . . . 17 A3
Westminster Ct SM3 . . . . 58 C6
Westminster Ct GU22 . . . 90 B6
Westminster Ct CR7 . . . . 42 C7
Westminster Rd
Carshalton SM1 . . . . 59 D8
Crawley RH10 . . . . 202 C5
Westmoat Cl BR3 . . . . 24 C1
WEST MOLESEY 36 A5
Westmont Rd KT10 . . . . . . 55 E8
Westmoreland Dr SM2 . . . 59 B2
Westmoreland Rd
Barnes SW13 . . . . .7 F6
Beckenham BR2 . . . . 44 F5
Westmoreland Terr SE20 . 23 B1
Westmore Rd TN16 . . . . . 103 C7
Westmorland Cl
Epsom KT19 . . . . 57 E4
③ Twickenham TW1 . . . . . . 6 B1
Westmorland Ct
⑫ Surbiton KT6 . . . . 37 D2
Sutton SM1 . . . . 59 C7
Westmorland Dr GU15 . . . 66 B3
Westmorland Sq CR4 . . . 41 E4
Westmorland Way CR4 . . 41 E4
West Mount GU2 . . . . 130 C7

WEST NORWOOD 22 C5
West Norwood Sta SE27 . 22 C4
West Oak BR3 . . . . 44 D8
Weston Ave
Addlestone KT15 . . . . 52 B6
East Molesey KT8 . . . . 35 F5
Thames Ditton KT10, KT7 . . 36 E2
Weston Cl
Coulsdon CR5 . . . . 99 F7
Farncombe GU7 . . . . 150 E6
Weston Ct
Farncombe GU7 . . . . 150 E6
❸ Kingston upon Thames
KT1 . . . . 37 E6
Weston Dr CR3 . . . . 100 C6
Weston Farm Cotts GU5 . 132 B4
Weston Farm Yard GU5 . 132 B4
Weston Fields GU5 . . . . . 132 C4
Weston Gdns
Hounslow TW7 . . . . .5 E6
Pyrford GU22 . . . . 70 E3
Weston Gn KT7 . . . . 36 E1
Weston Gr
Bagshot GU19 . . . . 47 F2
❶ Bromley BR1 . . . . 44 F8
WESTON GREEN 36 F1
Weston Green Rd KT7 . . . 36 E2
Weston Green Sch KT7 . . 36 E1
Weston Lea KT24 . . . . 92 D2
Weston Lodge KT7 . . . . . . 36 F1
Weston Park Cl KT7 . . . . . 36 F1
Weston Pk
Kingston upon Thames
KT1 . . . . 37 E7
Thames Ditton KT10, KT7 . . 36 E1
Weston Rd
Bromley BR1 . . . . 24 F1
Ewell KT17 . . . . 76 E8
Guildford GU2 . . . . 109 A2
Thames Ditton KT7 . . . . 36 E1
Westons Cl RH12 . . . . 217 D7
Weston Way GU22 . . . . . . 70 E3
Weston Yd GU5 . . . . 132 C4
Westover Cl SM2 . . . . 59 B2
Westover Rd SW18 . . . . . . 20 C8
Westow Hill SE19 . . . . 22 F2
Westow St SE19 . . . . 22 F2
West Palace Gdns KT13 . . 53 B7
West Par RH12 . . . . 217 C4
West Park Ave TW9 . . . . . . .7 B6
West Park Cl TW5 . . . . .4 F8
West Park Rd
Domewood RH10, RH7 . . . 183 F5
Epsom KT19 . . . . 75 F7
Horne RH7 . . . . 184 B7
Richmond TW9 . . . . .7 A6
West Parkside CR6 . . . . . . 82 A3
West Pl SW19 . . . . 19 C3
Westpoint BR2 . . . . 44 D6
West Ramp TW6 . . . . .3 A6
West Rd
Bracknell RG40 . . . . 26 D2
Camberley GU15 . . . . 65 D5
Chessington KT9 . . . . 75 C8
East Bedfont TW14 . . . . 14 D8
Farnborough GU14 . . . . 85 B8
Guildford GU1 . . . . 130 E8
Kingston upon Thames KT2,
KT3 . . . . 38 C8
Reigate RH2 . . . . 139 B8
Weybridge KT13 . . . . 53 B3
West Ring GU10 . . . . 126 F7
West Sheen Vale TW9 . . . .6 F3
Westside GU24 . . . . 67 E6
West Side Comm SW19 . . 19 C3
Westside Ho RH1 . . . . 140 B2
West St
Carshalton SM5 . . . . 59 F6
Crawley RH11 . . . . 201 D5
Croydon CR0, CR9 . . . . 61 C6
Dorking RH4 . . . . 136 A7
Dormansland RH7 . . . . 165 A1
East Grinstead RH19 . . . . . 205 B4
Epsom KT18, KT19 . . . . 76 C6
Ewell KT17 . . . . 57 F1
Farnham GU9 . . . . 125 A2
Haslemere GU27 . . . . 208 C6
Horsham RH12 . . . . 217 C2
Reigate RH2 . . . . 117 F1
Sutton SM1 . . . . 59 B5
Woking GU21 . . . . 69 F2
West Street La SM5 . . . . . . 59 F6
West Street Pl ❶ CR0,
CR9 . . . . 61 C6
West Surrey Est TW15 . . . 34 C8
West Sussex Ho GU2 . . . 129 E8
West Sutton Sta SM1 . . . . 59 A6
West Temple Sheen SW14 . .7 B2
West Thames Coll TW7 . . . .5 E6
West Thornton Prim Sch
CR0 . . . . 41 F3
Westview ❺ GU22 . . . . . . 69 F1
West View TW14 . . . . 14 C8
West View Ave CR3 . . . . . 80 F1
Westview Cl RH1 . . . . 139 E6
West View Cotts RH8 . . . 122 A2
West View Gdns RH19 . . 205 E8
West View Rd
Headley Down GU35 . . . . 187 C4
Warlingham CR6 . . . . 101 B8
Westville Rd KT7 . . . . 37 A2
Westward Ho GU1 . . . . . . 109 F3
Westward Prep Sch KT12. 54 B8
Westwates Cl RG12 . . . . . . 27 D8
Westway
Caterham CR3 . . . . 100 D5
Copthorne RH10 . . . . 183 A3
Crawley RH6 . . . . 182 B7

Westway continued
Guildford GU2 . . . . 108 F3
West Barnes KT3, SW20 . . . 39 C5
Wormley GU8 . . . . 190 F8
West Way
Crawley RH10 . . . . 202 A7
Croydon CR0 . . . . 62 E7
Heston TW5 . . . . .4 F6
Shepperton TW17 . . . . 34 D3
Slinfold RH13 . . . . 215 D3
Sutton SM2, SM5 . . . . 59 D1
West Wickham BR4 . . . . . . 44 E3
Westway Cl SW20 . . . . 39 B6
Westway Ct SE23 . . . . 100 D4
West Way Gdns CR0 . . . . 62 D8
Westway Gdns RH1 . . . . . 119 A4
Westways RH19 . . . . 57 F6
Westwell Rd SW16 . . . . . . 21 E2
Westwell Road App SW16 . 21 E2
Westwick Gdns TW4, TW5 . .4 B5
WEST WICKHAM 44 C2
West Wickham Sta BR4 . . 44 C2
West Wimbledon Prim Sch
SW20 . . . . 39 B6
Westwood Ave
South Norwood SE19 . . . . . 42 C8
Woodham WK15 . . . . 70 F7
Westwood Cl KT10 . . . . . . 55 C7
Westwood Ct
❸ Forest Hill SE23 . . . . 23 C7
Guildford GU2 . . . . 108 F3
❼ Wimbledon SW19 . . . . . 19 F3
Westwood Gdns SW13 . . . .7 F4
Westwood Hill SE19, SE26 . 23 B4
Westwood La
Normandy GU3 . . . . 107 A2
Wanborough GU3 . . . . 128 B7
Westwood Language Coll for
Girls SE19 . . . . 22 D1
Westwood Pk SE23 . . . . . . 23 B8
Westwood Pl SE26 . . . . . . 23 A4
Westwood Rd
Coulsdon CR5 . . . . 79 D1
Mortlake SW13, SW15 . . . . .7 F4
Windlesham GU20 . . . . 48 E6
Wetheral Ct SW17 . . . . 20 D4
Wetherby Ct SE25 . . . . 42 E7
Wetherby Gdns ❷ GU14 . 85 C1
Wetherby House GU15 . . . 65 D7
Wetherby Way KT9 . . . . . . 56 E3
Wettern Cl CR2 . . . . 61 E1
Wetton Pl TW20 . . . . 11 F3
Wexfenne Gdns GU22 . . . 71 B3
Wexford Rd SW12 . . . . 20 F8
Wey Ave KT16 . . . . 33 A6
Weybank GU23 . . . . 71 E3
Weybank Cl GU9 . . . . 125 C3
Wey Barton KT14 . . . . 71 F6
Weybourne Inf Sch GU9. 125 E6
Weybourne Pl CR2 . . . . . . 61 D1
Weybourne Rd
Aldershot GU11 . . . . 126 B7
Heath End GU11, GU9 . . . 125 E6
Weybourne St SW18 . . . . . 20 C6
WEYBRIDGE 53 A6
Weybridge Bsns Pk KT15. 52 E6
Weybridge Ho KT13 . . . . . 53 D5
Weybridge Hospl KT13 . . 53 A6
Weybridge Pk KT13 . . . . . 53 B5
Weybridge Rd
Addlestone KT15, KT13 . . . 52 E6
Thornton Heath CR7 . . . . . . 42 A5
Weybridge Sta KT13 . . . . . 53 A4
Weybrook Dr GU4 . . . . . . 110 B6
Wey Cl
Ash GU12 . . . . 106 A1
Camberley GU15 . . . . 65 B5
West Byfleet KT14 . . . . 71 B6
Weycombe Rd GU27 . . . . 208 C8
Wey Ct GU7 . . . . 151 A6
Wey Ct ❼ GU1 . . . . 130 C8
Wey Ct
New Haw KT15 . . . . 52 D2
West Ewell KT19 . . . . 57 C6
Weydon Farm La GU9 . . . 146 B8
Weydon Hill Cl GU9 . . . . . 146 B8
Weydon Hill Rd GU9 . . . . 146 C8
Weydon La
Farnham GU9 . . . . 146 A8
Wrecclesham GU9 . . . . 145 F8
Weydon Mill La GU9 . . . . 125 B1
Weydon Sch GU9 . . . . 145 F7
Weydown Cl
Guildford GU2 . . . . 109 A6
Putney SW19 . . . . 19 E7
Weydown Ct GU27 . . . . . . 208 B7
Weydown La GU2 . . . . 109 A6
Weydown Rd GU27 . . . . . . 208 B7
Weydown Rd Ind Est
GU27 . . . . 208 B7
Weyfield Prim Sch GU1 . 109 D4
Wey Gdns GU27 . . . . 207 F5
Weyhill GU27 . . . . 208 A6
Wey House Sch GU5 . . . . 151 E8
Weylands Cl KT12 . . . . 35 F1
Weylands Pk KT13 . . . . . . 53 D4
Weylea Ave GU4 . . . . 110 A4
Wey Manor Rd KT15 . . . . . 52 F5
Wey Mdws KT13 . . . . 52 F5
Weymead Cl KT16 . . . . 33 C1
Weymede KT14 . . . . 71 F7
Weymouth Ct
Belmont SM2 . . . . 59 A3
⑱ Streatham SW2 . . . . . . 21 F8
Wey Rd
Godalming GU7 . . . . 151 A5
Weybridge KT13 . . . . 52 F7

Wey Ret Pk KT14 . . . . 71 E7
Weyside
Farnham GU9 . . . . 125 C2
Weybridge KT13 . . . . 53 B8
Weyside Cl KT14 . . . . 71 F7
Weyside Gdns GU1 . . . . . 109 C3
Weyside Pk GU7 . . . . 151 A5
Weyside Rd GU1 . . . . 109 B3
Weysprings GU27 . . . . 208 A6
Weyvern Pk GU3 . . . . 130 B1
Weyview Cl GU1 . . . . 109 C3
Wey View Ct GU1 . . . . . . 130 C8
Weyview Cl GU9 . . . . 125 F7
Weywood La GU9 . . . . . . 125 E7
Whaley Rd RG40 . . . . 25 D8
Wharfedale Gdns CR7,
SW16 . . . . 41 F6
Wharfenden Way GU16 . . 85 F6
Wharf La
Send GU23 . . . . 90 C4
Twickenham TW1 . . . . 17 A7
Wharf Rd
Ash GU12 . . . . 106 A4
Frimley GU16 . . . . 86 A6
Guildford GU1 . . . . 109 C1
Wraysbury TW19 . . . . 11 D8
Wharf St GU7 . . . . 150 E4
Wharf The KT13 . . . . 53 A7
Wharf Way GU16 . . . . 86 A6
Wharncliffe Gdns SE25 . . 42 E7
Wharncliffe Rd SE25 . . . . 42 E7
Whateley Cl GU2 . . . . 109 B6
Whateley Rd SE20 . . . . 23 D1
Whateley Rd SE22 . . . . 23 B6
Whatley Ave SW20 . . . . . . 39 E6
Whatley Gn RG12 . . . . 27 B3
Whatman Rd SE23 . . . . . . 23 D8
Whatmore Cl TW19 . . . . . . .2 A1
Wheatash Rd KT15 . . . . . . 52 B8
Wheatcroft Ct SM1 . . . . . . 40 B1
Wheatcroft Ho ❸ KT3 . . . 38 E2
Wheatfield Way
Horley RH6 . . . . 161 C4
Kingston upon Thames KT1 . 37 D7
Wheathill Ho SE20 . . . . . . 43 B7
Wheathill Rd SE20 . . . . . . 43 B6
Wheat Ho TW19 . . . . 13 E7
Wheat Knoll CR8 . . . . 80 C3
Wheatlands TW5 . . . . .5 A8
Wheatlands Rd SW17 . . . . 21 A5
Wheatley RG12 . . . . 26 E4
Wheatley Ct SW2 . . . . 21 E6
Wheatley Ho ❸ SW15 . . . 19 A8
Wheatley Rd
Aldershot GU11 . . . . 104 F3
Isleworth TW7 . . . . .5 F4
Wheatsheaf Cl
Horsham RH12 . . . . 217 E5
Ottershaw KT16 . . . . 51 D4
Woking GU21 . . . . 69 F3
Wheatsheaf La TW18 . . . . 12 F1
Wheatsheaf Par ❹ BR4 . . 44 B1
Wheatstone Cl
Crawley RH10 . . . . 182 B3
Mitcham SW19 . . . . 40 E8
Wheeler Ave RH8 . . . . 122 D6
Wheeler La GU8 . . . . 170 E6
Wheeler Rd RH10 . . . . . . 202 B4
Wheelers La
Brockham RH3 . . . . 137 C7
Epsom KT18 . . . . 76 C5
Smallfield RH6 . . . . 162 B3
Wheeler's St SM1 . . . . 59 A7
WHEELERSTREET 170 F6
Wheelers Way RH19 . . . . 184 E3
Wheelwrights La GU26 . . 188 A4
Wheelwrights Pl SL3 . . . . .1 C7
Whelan Way SM6 . . . . 60 D7
Wherwell Lodge GU2 . . . 130 C7
Wherwell Rd GU2 . . . . . . 130 C7
Whetstone Rd
Farnborough GU14 . . . . 84 C4
❹ Farnborough GU14 . . . . 84 C4
Whimbrel Cl CR2, CR8 . . . 80 D8
Whinfell Cl SW16 . . . . 21 D3
Whins Cl GU15 . . . . 65 B4
Whins Dr GU15 . . . . 65 B4
Whinshill Ct SL5 . . . . 30 A1
Whipley Cl GU4 . . . . 110 B6
Whistler Cl RH10 . . . . 201 F3
Whistler Gr GU47 . . . . 64 D6
Whistley Cl RG12 . . . . 27 E6
Whitby Cl
Biggin Hill TN16 . . . . 83 B1
Farnborough GU12 . . . . 85 E1
Whitby Gdns SM1 . . . . 59 D8
Whitby Rd SM1 . . . . 59 D8
Whitchurch Cl GU11 . . . . 126 D6
Whitchurch Ct SW17 . . . . 20 D4
Whitchurch Ho SE6 . . . . . . 24 C5
Whitcome Mews TW9 . . . .7 B6
White Acres Rd GU16 . . . . 85 F4
Whitebeam Ct CR8 . . . . . . 80 B8
Whitebeam Dr RH2 . . . . . 139 B6
Whitebeam Gdns GU14 . . 84 C3
White Beam Way KT20 . . . 97 A6
Whiteberry Rd RH5 . . . . . 156 B7
Whitebines GU9 . . . . 125 D2
White Bridge Ave CR4 . . . 40 D6
White Bridge Cl TW14 . . . .3 F1
White Ct GU2 . . . . 109 A4
Whitefield Ave CR8 . . . . . . 80 B3

Whitefield Ho CR8 . . . . . . 80 B3
Whitefoot La BR1, SE6 . . . 24 D5
Whitefoot Terr BR1 . . . . . . 24 F5
Whitegates
Old Woking GU22 . . . . 89 F7
Whyteleafe CR3 . . . . 101 A8
White Gates ❹ KT7 . . . . . 37 A2
Whitegate Way KT20 . . . . 97 B7
Whitehall Cres KT9 . . . . . . 56 D5
Whitehall Ct W4 . . . . .7 B8
Whitehall Dr RH11 . . . . . . 200 E6
Whitehall Farm La GU25. . 31 E6
Whitehall Gdns W4 . . . . . .7 B8
Whitehall La
Egham TW20 . . . . 11 F1
Horton TW19 . . . . .1 A1
Reigate RH2 . . . . 138 F6
Whitehall Park Rd W4 . . . .7 B8
Whitehall Pl SM5 . . . . 60 B6
Whitehall Rd CR7 . . . . 42 A4
White Hart Ct
Horsham RH12 . . . . 217 C4
Ripley GU23 . . . . 91 C6
White Hart Ho TW12 . . . . . 36 C8
White Hart Ind Est GU17 . 64 E4
White Hart La
Mortlake SW14 . . . . .7 E4
Wood St V GU3 . . . . 108 A2
Whitehart Lo SW19 . . . . . . 20 C2
White Hart Mdws GU23 . . 91 C6
Whitehead Cl SW18 . . . . . 20 C8
White Heron Mews TW11 . 16 F2
White Hill
Kingswood CR5 . . . . 98 D4
South Croydon CR2 . . . . . . 61 D1
Windlesham GU20 . . . . 48 B6
Whitehill Cl GU15 . . . . 65 D7
Whitehill La
Bletchingley RH1 . . . . 120 D6
Martyr's Green GU23 . . . . . 92 C4
Whyteleafe/Caterham
CR3 . . . . 120 D7
Whitehill Pl GU25 . . . . 31 E4
White Ho ❷ SW4 . . . . 21 D8
White Horse Dr KT18 . . . . 76 C5
Whitehorse La SE25 . . . . . 42 E5
White Horse La GU23 . . . . 91 C6
Whitehorse Manor Inf Sch
CR7 . . . . 42 D5
Whitehorse Manor Jun Sch
CR7 . . . . 42 D5
Whitehorse Rd
Horsham RH12 . . . . 218 B6
Thornton Heath CR0, CR7,
SE25 . . . . 42 D3
White Ho The SW17 . . . . . 20 F3
Whitehouse Cl GU14 . . . . 85 B6
White House Ct BR3 . . . . . 44 C8
White House Dr GU1 . . . . 110 B1
White House La GU4 . . . . 109 D6
White House Prep Sch
RG41 . . . . 25 A3
White House Prep Sch The
SW12 . . . . 21 D7
White House Wlk GU9 . . . 125 D7
White Knights Rd KT13 . . 53 C3
White Knobs Way CR3 . . 101 A2
White La
Guildford GU4 . . . . 131 D7
Titsey RH8 . . . . 103 B3
Tongham GU10, GU12 . . . . 127 C7
Whitelands Cres SW18 . . . 19 E8
Whitelands Dr SL5 . . . . . . 28 D8
White Leaf Ho ❼ GU14 . . 85 C1
Whiteley Ct ❶ TW16 . . . . 15 F5
Whiteley Ho ❼ SW4 . . . . 21 D8
Whiteley Rd SE19 . . . . 22 D3
Whiteleys Ho TW13 . . . . . 16 A5
Whiteleys Way TW13 . . . . 16 A5
WHITELEY VILLAGE 53 E1
White Lion Gate KT11 . . . . 73 A5
White Lion Wlk ❶ GU1 . . 130 D7
White Lion Wlk Sh Ctr
GU1 . . . . 220 D7
White Lodge
Ashtead KT21 . . . . 95 E7
South Norwood SE19 . . . . . 22 B1
White Lodge Cl
Isleworth TW7 . . . . .6 A5
Sutton SM2 . . . . 59 C3
White Lodge Ct TW16 . . . 35 C8
White Lodge Gdns RH1 . . 140 A1
Whitely Hill RH10 . . . . 202 F1
Whitemore Rd GU1 . . . . . 109 D5
White Oak Dr BR3 . . . . 44 D7
Whiteoak Ho SE19 . . . . . . 22 C1
Whiteoaks SM7 . . . . 78 B6
White Pillars GU23 . . . . . . 89 B7
WHITE POST 120 E1
Whitepost Hill RH1 . . . . . 118 E1
Whitepost Ho RH1 . . . . . . 118 E1
White Post La GU10 . . . . . 146 A4
White Rd GU15 . . . . 64 F6
White Rose La
Farnham GU9, GU10 . . . . . 146 B7
Old Woking GU22 . . . . 90 A8
Woking GU22 . . . . 69 F1
White Rose La Nature
Reserve★ GU22 . . . . 90 B8
Whites Rd GU14 . . . . 85 E1
White Star Cl GU7 . . . . . . 150 F2
Whitethorn Ave CR5 . . . . . 79 B4
Whitethorn Cl GU12 . . . . 106 B1
Whitethorn Cotts GU6. . . 174 B5
Whitethorn Gdns CR0 . . . 62 B8
White Way KT23 . . . . 94 B1
Whiteways Ct TW18 . . . . . 13 B1
Whiteways End GU10. . . . 126 D4

Whitewood Cotts
Horne RH9 . . . . . 163 B7
Tatsfield TN16 . . . . . 103 C7
Whitewood La RH9 . . . . . 163 B7
Whitfield Cl
Guildford GU2 . . . . . 109 A4
Haslemere GU27 . . . . . 189 C1
Whitfield Ct
3 Dulwich SE21 . . . . . 22 E4
Merton SW20 . . . . . 39 D7
Whitfield Rd GU27 . . . . . 189 C1
Whitford Gdns CR4 . . . . . 40 F6
Whitgift Ave CR2 . . . . . 61 C5
Whitgift Ct CR2 . . . . . 61 C5
Whitgift Ctr CR9 . . . . . 61 C8
Whitgift Ho CR2 . . . . . 61 C5
Whitgift Sch CR2 . . . . . 61 C5
Whitgift St CR0, CR9 . . . . . 61 C7
Whitgift Wlk RH10 . . . . . 201 D3
Whitland Rd SM5 . . . . . 40 D1
Whitlet Cl GU9 . . . . . 125 B1
Whitley Cl TW19 . . . . . 2 E1
Whitley Ct 14 BR2 . . . . . 44 F5
Whitlock Dr SW19 . . . . . 19 E7
Whitmead Cl CR2 . . . . . 61 E4
Whitmead La GU10 . . . . . 147 E4
Whitmoor La GU4 . . . . . 89 D1
Whitmoor Rd GU19 . . . . . 47 F2
Whitmoor & Rickford Commons Nature Reserve★ GU3 . . . . . 109 A8
Whitmore Cl GU47 . . . . . 45 D1
Whitmore Gn GU9 . . . . . 125 E6
Whitmore Hill Cotts GU26 . . . . . 188 C3
Whitmore La SL5 . . . . . 30 A5
Whitmore Rd BR3 . . . . . 43 F6
Whitmores Cl KT18 . . . . . 76 C4
Whitmore Vale GU10, GU26 . . . . . 187 F7
Whitmore Vale Rd
Beacon Hill GU26 . . . . . 188 A5
Grayshott GU26 . . . . . 188 A4
Headley Down GU26 . . . . . 187 F7
Whitmore Way RH6 . . . . . 160 E3
Whitstable Cl BR3 . . . . . 43 F8
Whitstable Pl 9 CR0 . . . . . 61 C6
Whitstone La BR3 . . . . . 44 B4
Whittaker Ave TW10, TW9 . . 6 D2
Whittaker Ct KT21 . . . . . 75 D2
Whittaker Pl 29 TW10 . . . . . 6 D2
Whittaker Rd SM3 . . . . . 58 F7
Whittam Ho SE27 . . . . . 22 C3
Whittell Gdns SE26 . . . . . 23 C5
Whittingham Ct W4 . . . . . 7 E7
Whittington Coll (Almshouses) RH19 . . . . 185 A4
Whittington Ct SE20 . . . . . 43 B7
Whittington Rd RH10 . . . . . 201 E3
Whittlebury Cl SM5 . . . . . 59 F3
Whittle Cl
Ash Vale GU12 . . . . . 105 F5
Sandhurst GU47 . . . . . 45 A1
Whittle Cres GU14 . . . . . 84 F7
Whittle Rd
Heston TW5 . . . . . 4 C7
Hounslow TW6 . . . . . 2 B4
Whittle Rdbt GU14 . . . . . 84 C1
Whittle Way RH10 . . . . . 182 A3
WHITTON 16 C8
Whitton Dene TW2, TW7 . . . 5 D1
Whitton Manor Rd TW7 . . . 5 C1
Whitton Rd
Bracknell RG12 . . . . . 27 F6
Hounslow TW3 . . . . . 5 B2
Twickenham TW1 . . . . . 17 A8
Whitton Sch TW2 . . . . . 16 B6
Whitton Sta TW2 . . . . . 16 C8
Whitton Waye TW2, TW3 . . . 5 A1
Whitwell Hatch GU27 . . . . . 208 D5
Whitworth Rd
Crawley RH11 . . . . . 181 D2
South Norwood SE25 . . . . . 42 F5
Whopshott Ave GU21 . . . . . 69 C3
Whopshott Cl GU21 . . . . . 69 C3
Whopshott Dr GU21 . . . . . 69 C3
Whynstones Rd SL5 . . . . . 29 A4
Whyteacre CR3 . . . . . 101 B7
Whyte Ave GU12 . . . . . 126 D7
Whytebeam View CR3 . . . . . 80 F1
Whytecliffe Rd N CR8 . . . . . 80 B8
Whytecliffe Rd S CR8 . . . . . 80 B8
Whytecroft TW5 . . . . . 4 D7
WHYTELEAFE 80 E1
Whyteleafe Bsns Village CR3 . . . . . 80 F2
Whyteleafe Hill CR3 . . . . . 80 F1
Whyteleafe Rd CR3 . . . . . 100 F6
Whyteleafe Sch CR3 . . . . . 80 F1
Whyteleafe South Sta CR3 . . . . . 101 A8
Whyteleafe Sta CR3 . . . . . 80 F2
Whyte Mews SM3 . . . . . 58 E4
Wickers Oake SE19 . . . . . 22 F4
Wicket Hill GU10, GU9 . . . 146 A6
Wickets The TW15 . . . . . 13 E4
Wicket The CR0 . . . . . 63 A5
Wick & Grove Ho RH4 . . . 136 A6
Wickham Ave
Cheam KT4, SM3 . . . . . 58 C5
Croydon CR0 . . . . . 43 E1
Wickham Chase BR4 . . . . . 44 E2
Wickham Cl
Horley RH6 . . . . . 160 F4
New Malden KT3 . . . . . 38 F4
Wickham Comm Prim Sch BR4 . . . . . 63 F6
Wickham Court Rd BR4 . . . 63 C8
Wickham Court Sch BR4 . . 63 D6
Wickham Cres BR4 . . . . . 63 C8
Wickham La TW20 . . . . . 12 A1
Wickham Rd
Beckenham BR3 . . . . . 44 B6
Camberley GU15 . . . . . 65 E8
Croydon CR0, CR9 . . . . . 62 E8
Wickham Vale RG12 . . . . . 26 E3
Wickham Way BR3 . . . . . 44 C4
WICK HILL 27 C8
Wick Ho 1 KT1 . . . . . 37 D8
Wickhurst Gdns RH12 . . . 216 E3
Wickhurst La RH12 . . . . . 216 E3
Wick La TW20 . . . . . 10 F3
Wickland Ct RH10 . . . . . 201 D3
Wicklow Ct SE26 . . . . . 23 C3
Wick Rd
Englefield Green TW20 . . . . 11 B1
Teddington TW11 . . . . . 17 C1
Wide Way CR4, SW16 . . . . . 41 D6
Widewing Cl TW11 . . . . . 17 B1
Widgeon Way RH12 . . . . . 217 C5
Widmer Ct TW5 . . . . . 4 E5
Wigan Rd GU14 . . . . . 104 D8
Wiggie La RH1 . . . . . 119 A3
Wiggins Cotts TW10 . . . . . 17 C6
Wiggins La TW10 . . . . . 17 C6
Wighton Mews TW7 . . . . . 5 E5
Wigley Rd TW13 . . . . . 15 D7
Wigmore La RH5 . . . . . 157 C1
Wigmore Rd SM5 . . . . . 40 E1
Wigmore Wlk SM5 . . . . . 59 D8
Wilberforce Ct KT18 . . . . . 76 D5
Wilberforce Way
Bracknell RG12 . . . . . 27 D4
Wimbledon SW19 . . . . . 19 D2
Wilbury Ave SM2 . . . . . 58 F1
Wilbury Rd GU21 . . . . . 69 D2
Wilcot Cl GU24 . . . . . 68 A3
Wilcot Gdns GU24 . . . . . 68 A3
Wilcox Gdns TW17 . . . . . 33 F6
Wilcox Rd
Sutton SM1 . . . . . 59 B6
Teddington TW11 . . . . . 16 D4
Wildacre Cl RH14 . . . . . 212 D3
Wild Acres KT14 . . . . . 71 C8
Wildbank Ct 12 GU22 . . . . . 69 F1
Wildcat Rd TW6 . . . . . 2 B4
Wildcroft Dr
Dorking RH5 . . . . . 136 D4
Wokingham RG40 . . . . . 25 A1
Wildcroft Manor SW15 . . . 19 C8
Wildcroft Rd SW15 . . . . . 19 C8
Wildcroft Wood GU8 . . . . . 170 D6
Wilde Pl SW18 . . . . . 20 D8
Wilderness Ct GU2 . . . . . 129 F7
Wilderness Rd
Frimley GU16 . . . . . 65 E2
Guildford GU2 . . . . . 129 F7
Oxted RH8 . . . . . 122 E5
Wilderness Rise RH19 . . . 186 A6
Wilderness The
East Molesey KT8 . . . . . 36 C4
Hampton TW12 . . . . . 16 B4
Wilders Cl
Frimley GU16 . . . . . 65 E3
Woking GU21 . . . . . 69 C1
Wilderwick Rd RH19 . . . . . 186 A5
Wildes Cotts SM3 . . . . . 58 E4
Wildfell Rd SE6 . . . . . 24 B8
Wildfield Cl GU3 . . . . . 108 B2
Wildgoose Dr RH12 . . . . . 216 F3
WILDRIDINGS 27 A5
Wildridings Prim Sch RG12 . . . . . 27 A5
Wildridings Rd RG12 . . . . . 27 A5
Wildridings Sq RG12 . . . . . 27 A5
Wildwood Cl
Cranleigh GU6 . . . . . 174 F1
East Horsley KT24 . . . . . 92 F2
Lewisham SE12 . . . . . 24 F8
Pyrford GU22 . . . . . 70 F4
Wildwood Ct CR8 . . . . . 80 D4
Wildwood La GU6 . . . . . 194 C5
Wilford Rd CR0 . . . . . 42 C2
Wilfred Owen Cl SW19 . . . 20 C2
Wilfred St GU21 . . . . . 69 D1
Wilhelmina Ave CR5 . . . . . 99 C8
Wilkes Rd 3 TW8 . . . . . 6 E8
Wilkins Cl CR4 . . . . . 40 E8
Wilkinson Ct
4 Crawley RH11 . . . . . 201 B1
Upper Tooting SW17 . . . . . 20 D4
Wilkinson Gdns SE25 . . . . . 42 E8
Wilkinson Ho
Isleworth TW7 . . . . . 5 F4
Twickenham TW2 . . . . . 16 D6
Wilks Gdns CR0 . . . . . 43 E1
Willard Way RH19 . . . . . 185 A3
Willats Cl 5 KT16 . . . . . 33 A3
Willbury Rd GU9 . . . . . 125 E4
Willcocks Cl KT9 . . . . . 56 E7
Willems Ave GU11 . . . . . 104 F2
Willems Rdbt GU11 . . . . . 104 F2
Willerton Lodge 1 KT13 . . 53 D4
Willett Pl CR7 . . . . . 42 A4
Willett Rd CR7 . . . . . 42 A4
Willetts RH14 . . . . . 136 C4
Willetts Way RH14 . . . . . 212 F3
Willey Broom La CR3 . . . . . 100 A2
Willey Farm La CR3 . . . . . 100 C1
WILLEY GREEN 107 D4
Willey La CR3 . . . . . 100 D2
William Booth Rd SE20 . . . 43 A8
William Brown Ct SE27 . . . 22 B6
William Byrd Sch UB3 . . . . . 3 D8
William Cobbett Jun Sch GU9 . . . . . 125 E6
William Ct
Cheam SM3 . . . . . 58 C6
Farnborough GU14 . . . . . 85 B4
9 Farnborough, South Farnborough GU14 . . . . . 85 C1
South Norwood SE19 . . . . . 22 D1
William Dyce Mews SW16 21 D4
William Ellis Sch (The Mill) RH5 . . . . . 176 D8
William Evans Rd KT19 . . . 76 A8
William Evelyn Ct RH5 . . 134 F4
William Farthing Cl 17 GU11 . . . . . 105 A2
William Gdns RH6 . . . . . 162 A3
William Harvey Ho 1 SW19 . . . . . 19 E7
William Hitchcock Ho GU14 . . . . . 85 B7
William Lilly Ho KT12 . . . 54 C5
William Marden Ho 2 SE27 . . . . . 22 B4
William Morris Prim Sch CR4 . . . . . 41 D6
William Rd
Caterham CR3 . . . . . 100 D5
Guildford GU1 . . . . . 109 C1
Merton SW19 . . . . . 19 E1
Sutton SM1 . . . . . 59 C5
William Russell Ct 3 GU21 . . . . . 68 E1
Williams Cl KT15 . . . . . 52 B5
Williams Dr TW3 . . . . . 5 A3
Williams Gr KT6 . . . . . 37 C3
Williams Ho 14 SW2 . . . . . 22 A7
William Sim Wood RG42 . . . 8 B2
Williams La
Morden SM4 . . . . . 40 C4
Mortlake SW14 . . . . . 7 C5
Williamson Cl GU27 . . . . . 189 F1
Williams Pl GU6 . . . . . 175 E5
William St SM5 . . . . . 59 F7
Williams Terr CR0 . . . . . 61 A4
Williams Way RH10 . . . . . 202 B5
William Swayne Ho 1 GU1 . . . . . 130 E8
Williams Wlk GU2 . . . . . 109 B5
William Wilberforce Ho 1 SE27 . . . . . 22 B4
William Winter Ct SW2 . . . 22 A8
William Wood Ho SE26 . . . 23 C5
Willian Pl GU26 . . . . . 188 E6
Willingham Way KT1 . . . . . 38 A7
Willington Cl GU15 . . . . . 65 B6
Willington Sch SW19 . . . . . 19 F3
Willis Ave SM2 . . . . . 59 E4
Willis Cl KT18 . . . . . 76 B5
Willis Ct 5 CR7 . . . . . 42 A3
Willis Rd CR0 . . . . . 42 C2
Willlows The CR0 . . . . . 62 E8
Will Miles Ct 6 SW19 . . . . . 20 C1
Willmore End SW19 . . . . . 40 B7
Willoughby Ave CR0 . . . . . 60 F6
Willoughby Rd
Bracknell RG12 . . . . . 26 F6
Kingston upon Thames KT2 . 37 F8
Twickenham TW1 . . . . . 6 D2
Willoughbys The 8 SW15 . . 7 E4
Willow Ave SW13 . . . . . 7 F5
Willow Bank
Richmond TW10 . . . . . 17 B5
Woking GU22 . . . . . 89 F6
Willowbank Gdns KT20 . . . 97 B5
Willowbank Pl CR8 . . . . . 61 B2
Willow Brean RH6 . . . . . 160 E5
Willowbrook Ct 10 TW20 . . 12 A3
Willowbrook Rd TW19 . . . . 13 E6
Willow Bsns Ctr CR4 . . . . . 40 F3
Willow Cl
Addlestone KT16 . . . . . 51 E8
Beare Green RH5 . . . . . 157 C4
Brentford TW8 . . . . . 6 C8
Catford SE6 . . . . . 24 F7
Colnbrook SL3 . . . . . 1 C7
Crawley RH10 . . . . . 201 E8
East Grinstead RH19 . . . . . 185 D3
Mytchett GU16 . . . . . 85 E4
Woodham KT15 . . . . . 70 F8
Willow Cnr RH6 . . . . . 180 F7
Willow Cotts
Carshalton CR4 . . . . . 40 F2
Dorking RH5 . . . . . 136 D4
Feltham TW13 . . . . . 15 E5
Richmond TW9 . . . . . 7 A8
Willow Cres GU14 . . . . . 85 B7
Willow Ct
2 Ashford TW16 . . . . . 14 E1
Ash Vale GU12 . . . . . 106 A7
5 Beckenham BR3 . . . . . 44 A8
9 Chiswick W4 . . . . . 7 E7
Frimley GU16 . . . . . 65 D1
Guildford GU1 . . . . . 109 D5
Horley RH6 . . . . . 161 B6
Kingston upon Thames KT1 . 38 B6
Mitcham CR4 . . . . . 40 E5
3 Streatham SW16 . . . . . 21 F5
Thornton Heath CR7 . . . . . 42 D4
Wallington SM6 . . . . . 60 B3
Wokingham RG41 . . . . . 25 B6
Willow Ctr The CR4 . . . . . 40 F3
Willowdene Cl TW2 . . . . . 16 C8
Willow Dr
Bracknell RG12 . . . . . 27 C8
Flexford GU3 . . . . . 107 C1
Send Marsh GU23 . . . . . 91 A3
Willow End KT6 . . . . . 37 E1
Willowfield 4 RH11 . . . . . 201 D5
Willow Fields GU12 . . . . . 106 B1
Willow Gdns TW5 . . . . . 5 A6
Willow Glade RH2 . . . . . 139 B6
Willow Gn
Dorking RH5 . . . . . 136 B3
West End GU24 . . . . . 68 A6
Willowhayne Ct KT12 . . . . . 35 B2
Willowhayne Dr KT12 . . . . . 35 B2
Willowhayne Gdns KT4 . . . 58 C6
Willowherb Cl RG40 . . . . . 25 E7
Willow Ho CR6 . . . . . 82 B3
Willow Ho TW14 . . . . . 4 B2
Willow Ho TW11 . . . . . 17 C1
Willow La
Blackwater GU17 . . . . . 64 D4
Guildford GU1 . . . . . 110 A2
Mitcham CR4 . . . . . 40 F3
Willow Lodge 6 TW16 . . . . . 14 F1
Willow Manor SM1 . . . . . 58 F6
Willowmead TW18 . . . . . 33 B8
Willow Mead
6 Dorking RH4 . . . . . 136 A8
8 East Grinstead RH19 . . 205 F8
Witley GU8 . . . . . 170 E5
Willowmead Cl GU21 . . . . . 69 A3
Willowmere KT10 . . . . . 55 C6
Willow Mews GU8 . . . . . 170 F5
Willow Mount CR0 . . . . . 61 E7
Willow Pk GU12 . . . . . 105 F2
Willow Rd
Farncombe GU7 . . . . . 150 F8
Horsham RH12 . . . . . 218 B5
Kingston upon Thames KT3 . 38 C5
Poyle SL3 . . . . . 1 E5
Reigate RH1 . . . . . 139 C6
Wallington SM6 . . . . . 60 B3
Willow Ridge RH10 . . . . . 204 A3
Willows Ave SM4 . . . . . 40 B4
Willows Ct 3 SW19 . . . . . 20 A1
Willows End GU47 . . . . . 64 B8
Willows Path KT18 . . . . . 76 B5
Willows Pk The GU3 . . . . . 107 E4
Willows The
Beckenham BR3 . . . . . 44 A8
1 Bracknell RG12 . . . . . 27 F5
Byfleet KT14 . . . . . 71 E6
Chiddingfold GU8 . . . . . 191 A4
Claygate KT10 . . . . . 55 E4
Guildford, Bushy Hill GU4 . 110 D3
Guildford, Pitch Place GU2 108 F6
Horsham RH12 . . . . . 217 D5
Lightwater GU18 . . . . . 48 C1
3 Redhill RH1 . . . . . 139 F8
Runfold GU10 . . . . . 126 C4
Weybridge KT13 . . . . . 53 A7
Willow Tree Cl SW18 . . . . . 20 B7
Willowtree Way SW16 . . . . . 42 A8
Willow Vale KT23 . . . . . 94 B4
Willow View SW19 . . . . . 40 D8
Willow Way
Aldershot GU12 . . . . . 126 E8
Forest Hill SE26 . . . . . 23 C5
Godstone RH9 . . . . . 121 B3
Guildford GU1 . . . . . 109 B5
Heath End GU9 . . . . . 125 D6
Sunbury TW16 . . . . . 35 A5
Twickenham TW2 . . . . . 16 B6
West Byfleet KT14 . . . . . 71 C8
West Ewell KT19 . . . . . 57 D4
Woking GU22 . . . . . 89 E7
Willow Wlk
Box Hill KT20 . . . . . 116 B5
Cheam SM3 . . . . . 58 F7
Chertsey KT16 . . . . . 33 B2
Englefield Green TW20 . . . . 11 C3
Leatherhead KT23 . . . . . 94 C3
Redhill RH1 . . . . . 140 B7
Shere GU5 . . . . . 133 A4
Willow Wood Cres SE25 . . . 42 E3
Wills Cres TW3 . . . . . 5 B1
Willson Rd TW20 . . . . . 11 B3
Wilmar Gdns BR4 . . . . . 44 B1
Wilmer Cl TW10 . . . . . 17 F3
Wilmer Cres KT2, TW10 . . . 17 F3
Wilmerhatch La KT18, KT21 . . . . . 76 B2
Wilmer House Mus of Farnham★ 22 GU9 . . . . . 125 B2
Wilmington Ave W4 . . . . . 7 D7
Wilmington Cl RH11 . . . . . 201 C1
Wilmington Ct SW16 . . . . . 21 E1
Wilmot Ct GU14 . . . . . 85 B4
Wilmot Ho 16 SM2 . . . . . 59 C4
Wilmot Rd
Purley CR8 . . . . . 80 A7
Wallington SM5 . . . . . 59 F5
Wilmots Cl RH2 . . . . . 118 C2
Wilmot's La RH1, RH6 . . . . . 162 E5
Wilmot Way
Banstead SM7 . . . . . 78 A5
Frimley GU15 . . . . . 65 F3
Wilna Rd SW18 . . . . . 20 C8
Wilson Ave CR4, SW19 . . . 40 E8
Wilson Cl
Crawley RH10 . . . . . 202 D3
Croydon CR0 . . . . . 61 D5
Wilson Dr KT16 . . . . . 51 B5
Wilson Ho TW13 . . . . . 15 A5
Wilson Rd
Aldershot GU12 . . . . . 105 D1
Chessington KT9 . . . . . 56 F4
Farnborough GU14 . . . . . 84 F3
Wilsons KT20 . . . . . 97 D6
Wilsons Rd GU35 . . . . . 187 B5
Wilson's Sch SM6 . . . . . 60 E4
Wilson Way GU21 . . . . . 69 D3
Wilton Cl UB7 . . . . . 2 D8
Wilton Cres SW19 . . . . . 39 F8
Wilton Ct
Farnborough GU14 . . . . . 85 D3
Wilton Ct *continued*
4 Richmond TW10 . . . . . 6 E2
Wilton Gdns
East Molesey KT8 . . . . . 36 A6
Walton-on-Thames KT12 . . 35 D1
Wilton Gr
Merton SW19 . . . . . 39 F8
New Malden KT3 . . . . . 38 F3
Wilton Hill Ct 5 RH1 . . . . . 139 F8
Wilton Ho CR2 . . . . . 61 C5
Wilton Lodge KT12 . . . . . 54 C8
Wilton Par TW13 . . . . . 15 B6
Wilton Pl
Beckenham BR3 . . . . . 44 C6
New Haw KT15 . . . . . 52 D2
Wilton Rd
Camberley GU15 . . . . . 65 B3
Hounslow TW4 . . . . . 4 D4
Mitcham SW19 . . . . . 20 E1
Redhill RH1 . . . . . 139 F8
Wiltshire Ave RG45 . . . . . 45 B5
Wiltshire Ct CR2 . . . . . 61 C5
Wiltshire Dr RG40 . . . . . 25 D7
Wiltshire Gdns TW2 . . . . . 16 C7
Wiltshire Rd
Thornton Heath CR7 . . . . . 42 A6
Wokingham RG40 . . . . . 25 C7
Wilverley Cres KT3 . . . . . 38 E3
Wilwood Rd RG42 . . . . . 26 E8
Wimbart Rd SW2 . . . . . 21 F8
WIMBLEDON 19 F2
Wimbledon Bridge SW19 . 19 F2
Wimbledon Central SW19 19 F2
Wimbledon Chase Prim Sch SW20 . . . . . 39 E8
Wimbledon Chase Sta SW20 . . . . . 39 E7
Wimbledon Cl
Camberley GU15 . . . . . 46 F1
2 Wimbledon SW20 . . . . . 19 D1
Wimbledon Coll SW19 . . . 19 D1
Wimbledon Common Pre-Prep Sch SW19 . . . . . 19 D1
Wimbledon High Sch SW19 . . . . . 19 E2
Wimbledon Hill Rd SW19 . 19 F2
Wimbledon Lawn Tennis Mus★ SW19 . . . . . 19 E5
Wimbledon Mus★ SW19 . . 19 E2
Wimbledon Park Ct SW19 19 F7
Wimbledon Park Montessori Sch SW18 . . . . . 20 A6
Wimbledon Park Prim Sch SW19 . . . . . 20 B6
Wimbledon Park Rd SW18, SW19 . . . . . 19 F7
Wimbledon Park Side SW19 . . . . . 19 D7
Wimbledon Park U Sta SW19 . . . . . 20 A5
Wimbledon Rd
Camberley GU15 . . . . . 46 F1
Wandsworth SW17 . . . . . 20 C4
Wimbledon Sch of Art SW19 . . . . . 39 E8
Wimbledon Sh Ctr SW19 . 19 F2
Wimbledon Stadium SW17 . . . . . 20 C4
Wimbledon Stadium Bsns Ctr SW17 . . . . . 20 B5
Wimbledon Sta/Halt/U SW19 . . . . . 19 F2
Wimbledon Ursuline Prep Sch SW19 . . . . . 19 D1
Wimbledon Windmill Mus★ SW19 . . . . . 19 C5
Wimblehurst Ct 4 RH12 . 217 C4
Wimblehurst Rd RH12 . . . 217 C4
Wimborne Ave RH1 . . . . . 140 A4
Wimborne Cl
Epsom KT17 . . . . . 76 E6
North Cheam KT4 . . . . . 39 C1
Wimborne Ho
Croydon CR0 . . . . . 43 C4
Farnborough GU14 . . . . . 85 D2
South Norwood SE19 . . . . . 22 D2
Upper Tooting SW12 . . . . . 21 C5
Wimborne Way BR3 . . . . . 43 E5
Wimbourne Ct
Mitcham SW19 . . . . . 20 D1
South Croydon CR2 . . . . . 61 E4
Wimbourne Ho RH11 . . . . . 201 C6
Wimland Hill RH12 . . . . . 199 D2
Wimland Rd
Faygate RH12 . . . . . 199 D1
Rusper RH12 . . . . . 199 C4
Wimlands La RH12 . . . . . 199 E3
Wimpole Cl 1 KT1 . . . . . 38 A7
Wimshurst Cl CR0 . . . . . 41 E1
Wincanton Cl RH10 . . . . . 202 D6
Wincanton Rd SW18 . . . . . 19 F8
Winchcombe Rd SM5 . . . . . 40 E1
Winchelsey Rise CR2 . . . . . 61 F4
Winchendon Rd TW11 . . . . . 16 D4
Winchester Ave TW5 . . . . . 4 F8
Winchester Cl
Beckenham BR2 . . . . . 44 F6
Esher KT10 . . . . . 55 A7
Kingston upon Thames KT2 . 18 B1
Poyle SL3 . . . . . 1 E6
Winchester Ct TW9 . . . . . 6 F4
Winchester Ho
Epsom KT19 . . . . . 76 A7
Twickenham TW1 . . . . . 17 C8
Winchester Mews KT4 . . . 58 D8

Winchester Pk BR2 . . . . **44** F6
Winchester Rd
Ash GU12 . . . . **106** A3
Beckenham BR2 . . . . **44** F6
Crawley RH10 . . . . **201** E2
Feltham TW13 . . . . **15** F5
Harlington UB3 . . . . **3** E7
Rushmoor GU10 . . . . . . **168** B7
Twickenham TW1 . . . . **6** B1
Walton-on-Thames KT12 . . **35** A1
Winchester St GU14 . . . . **105** C8
Winchester Way GU17 . . **64** C6
Winchet Wlk CR0 . . . . . . **43** C3
Winchfield Ho SW15 . . . . . **7** F1
Winchfield Rd SE26 . . . . . **23** E3
Winchilsea Cres KT8 . . . . **36** C7
Winchstone Cl TW17 . . . . **33** F5
Windborough Rd SM5 . . . . **60** A3
Windermere Ave SM4,
SW19 . . . . **40** B6
Windermere Cl
East Bedfont TW14 . . . . . **14** F7
Farnborough GU14 . . . . . **84** E3
Stanwell TW19 . . . . **13** D6
1 Thorpe Lea TW20 . . . . **12** B1
Windermere Ct
Barnes SW13 . . . . **7** F8
Purley CR8 . . . . **80** B4
Wallington SM5 . . . . **60** A7
9 Woking GU21 . . . . . . **69** A1
Windermere Ho TW1 . . . . . **5** F2
Windermere Rd
Coulsdon CR5 . . . . **79** E4
Croydon CR0 . . . . **42** F1
Kingston upon Thames
SW15 . . . . **18** E3
Lightwater GU18 . . . . **48** B1
Mitcham SW16 . . . . **41** D7
West Wickham BR4 . . . . . **63** E8
Windermere Way
Hale GU9 . . . . **125** A6
Redhill RH2 . . . . **118** E2
Windermere Wlk GU15 . . **66** D5
Windfield KT22 . . . . **95** B5
Windfield Cl SE26 . . . . . . **23** D4
Windgates GU4 . . . . **110** C4
Windham Ave CR0 . . . . . . **63** D1
Windham Rd TW9 . . . . **6** F4
Windings The CR2 . . . . . . **80** F8
Winding Wood Dr GU15 . . **66** B3
Windlebrook Gn 3 RG42 . . **27** A8
Windle Cl GU20 . . . . **48** D4
WINDLESHAM **48** C4
Windlesham Cl GU20 . . . . **48** C6
Windlesham Gr SW19 . . . . **19** D7
Windlesham Rd
Bracknell RG42 . . . . **26** F8
Chobham GU24 . . . . **49** C3
West End GU24 . . . . **67** F7
Windlesham Village Inf Sch
GU20 . . . . **48** A6
Windley Cl SE23 . . . . **23** C6
Windmill Ave KT17 . . . . . . **76** F8
Windmill Bridge Ho 1
CR0 . . . . **42** E1
Windmill Bsns Village
TW16 . . . . **34** E8
Windmill Cl
Caterham CR3 . . . . **100** C6
Charlton TW16 . . . . **14** E1
Ewell KT17 . . . . **76** F7
Horley RH6 . . . . **161** B3
Horsham RH13 . . . . **218** A4
Long Ditton KT6 . . . . **37** C2
Windmill Ct
1 Aldershot GU12 . . . . **105** C1
Crawley RH10 . . . . **201** D8
Windmill Dr
Headley Down GU35 . . . . **187** B6
Leatherhead KT22 . . . . . . **95** C4
Redhill RH2 . . . . **118** E3
Windmill End KT17 . . . . . **76** F7
Windmill Field GU20 . . . . **48** D4
Windmill Gr CR0 . . . . **42** C3
Windmill La
Ashurst Wood RH19 . . . . **206** C4
East Grinstead RH19 . . . **185** D3
Ewell KT17 . . . . **76** F7
Thames Ditton KT7 . . . . . **37** B2
Windmill Lodge TW16 . . . . **34** E8
Windmill Rd
Aldershot GU12 . . . . **105** C1
Bracknell RG42 . . . . **27** A8
Brentford TW8 . . . . **6** D8
Charlton TW16 . . . . **34** E8
Hampton TW12 . . . . **16** C3
Mitcham CR4 . . . . **41** C5
Roehampton SW19 . . . . . **19** B5
Thornton Heath CR0 . . . . . **42** C2
Windmill Rd W TW16 . . . . **34** E8
Windmill Rise KT2 . . . . . . **18** B1
Windmill Shott TW20 . . . . **11** F2
Windmill Terr TW17 . . . . . **34** E2
Windmill Trad Est CR4 . . . **41** C5
Windmill Way RH2 . . . . . **118** D3
Windrush KT3 . . . . **38** C5
Windrush Cl
Bramley GU5 . . . . **151** F6
Chiswick W4 . . . . **7** C7
Crawley RH11 . . . . **200** F4
Windrush Ho 8 RH1 . . . . **118** F2
Windrush Hts GU47 . . . . . **64** B8
Windrush La SE23 . . . . . . **23** D5
Windsock Way TW6 . . . .**2** B5

Windsor Ave
Cheam SM3 . . . . **58** E7
East Molesey KT8 . . . . . . **36** A6
Merton SW19 . . . . **40** C8
New Malden KT3 . . . . . . **38** C4
Windsor Cl
Brentford TW8 . . . . **6** B8
Crawley RH11 . . . . **201** C2
Farnborough GU14 . . . . . **85** B4
Guildford GU2 . . . . **129** F7
West Norwood SE27 . . . . **22** C4
Windsor Court Rd GU24 . . **49** E2
Windsor Cres GU9 . . . . . **125** B6
Windsor Ct
Ashford TW16 . . . . **15** A1
3 Horsham RH13 . . . . **217** F3
South Norwood SE19 . . . . **42** E8
Teddington TW11 . . . . . . **16** D3
6 West Wickham BR4 . . **44** B1
Whyteleafe CR3 . . . . **80** F1
Windsor Dr TW15 . . . . . . **13** D4
Windsor Forest Ct SL5 . . . **28** D8
Windsor Gdns
Ash GU12 . . . . **105** F1
Wallington CR0 . . . . **60** E7
Windsor Gr SE27 . . . . . . **22** C4
Windsor Great Pk SL4 . . . **10** D4
Windsor Ho
5 Egham TW20 . . . . . . **12** A3
Reigate RH2 . . . . **139** B4
Windsor Lodge KT3 . . . . . **38** C4
Windsor Mews
Catford SE6 . . . . **24** C7
Forest Hill SE23 . . . . **23** E7
Windsor Park Rd UB3 . . . . . **3** F7
Windsor Pk SW19 . . . . . . **40** C8
Windsor Pl 2 KT16 . . . . . **33** A3
Windsor Pl RH10 . . . . . . **181** F2
Windsor Pl RH19 . . . . . . **206** A4
Windsor Rd
Ascot SL4, SL5 . . . . **9** B1
Ashford TW16 . . . . **15** A2
Chobham GU24 . . . . **49** D3
Cranford TW4, TW5 . . . . . . **4** C5
Englefield Green TW19,
TW20 . . . . **11** E6
Farnborough, South Farnborough
GU14 . . . . **85** D1
Kingston upon Thames KT2 . **17** E1
North Ascot SL5 . . . . **29** A8
Richmond TW9 . . . . **6** F5
South Norwood CR7 . . . . . **42** B7
Teddington TW11 . . . . . . **16** D3
Worcester Park KT4 . . . . . **58** A8
Windsor Ride
Bracknell SL5 . . . . **28** C4
Owlsmoor GU47 . . . . **45** F1
Sandhurst GU15 . . . . **65** A8
Windsor St KT16 . . . . **33** A3
Windsor Way
Aldershot GU11 . . . . **105** B2
Frimley GU16 . . . . **85** F8
Woking GU22 . . . . **70** C3
Windsor Wlk
Walton-on-Thames KT12 . . **35** D1
Weybridge KT13 . . . . **53** B5
Winds Ridge GU23 . . . . . **90** C2
Windways GU8 . . . . **192** F7
Windycroft Cl CR5, CR8 . . **79** D6
Windyridge RH11 . . . . . . **201** A5
Windy Ridge SW19 . . . . . **19** D3
Windy Wood GU7 . . . . . . **150** C3
Winern Glebe KT14 . . . . . **71** D6
Winery La KT1 . . . . **37** F6
Winey Cl KT9 . . . . **56** C3
Winfield Ct RH5 . . . . **158** B1
Winfield Gr RH5 . . . . **158** B1
Winfrith Rd SW18 . . . . . . **20** C7
Wingate Cres CR0 . . . . . . **41** E3
Wingate Ct GU11 . . . . . . **104** F2
Wingfield Cl KT15 . . . . . . **52** B1
Wingfield Ct SM7 . . . . . . **78** A4
Wingfield Gdns GU16 . . . . **66** D3
Wingfield Rd KT2 . . . . . . **18** A2
Wingham Ho 3 SE26 . . . . **23** B3
Wingrove Rd SE6 . . . . . . **24** E6
Wings Cl
Hale GU9 . . . . **125** B6
Sutton SM1 . . . . **59** A6
Wings Mus RH1 . . . . . . **140** D5
Wings Rd GU9 . . . . **125** B6
Winifred Rd
Coulsdon CR5 . . . . **79** B4
Hampton TW12 . . . . **16** A4
Merton SW19 . . . . **40** A8
WINKFIELD **8** D4
Winkfield Cl RG40, RG41 . . **25** B3
Winkfield La SL4 . . . . **8** D7
Winkfield Manor SL5 . . . . . **8** D1
Winkfield Rd
Ascot SL5 . . . . **29** B7
Windsor SL4 . . . . **9** C8
WINKFIELD ROW **8** B2
Winkfield Row RG42 . . . . . . **8** B3
Winkfield St SL4 . . . . **8** C6
WINKFIELD STREET **8** C6
Winkworth Arboretum
GU8 . . . . **172** C2
Winkworth Pl SM7 . . . . . . **78** A5
Winkworth Rd SM7 . . . . . . **78** A5
Winlaton Rd BR1, SE6 . . . . **24** D4
Winner Way RH6 . . . . . . **181** D6
Winnington Way GU21 . . . **69** C1
Winscombe RG12 . . . . . . **26** E4
Winsford Rd SE6 . . . . **23** F5
Winslade Way SE6 . . . . . . **24** B8
Winslow Way
Feltham TW13 . . . . **15** E5

Winslow Way continued
Walton-on-Thames KT12 . . **54** C7
Winstanley Cl KT11 . . . . . **73** B5
Winstanley Wlk KT11 . . . . **73** B5
Winston Churchill Sch The
GU21 . . . . **68** F1
Winston Cl GU16 . . . . **85** F6
Winston Dr
Stoke D'Abernon KT11 . . . **73** E3
Westerham TN16 . . . . . . **83** D2
Winston Way GU22 . . . . . . **90** B7
Winston Wlk GU10 . . . . . **146** C6
Winterbourne RH12 . . . . . **217** F7
Winterbourne Ct RG12 . . . **27** D7
Winterbourne Gr KT13 . . . **53** C4
Winterbourne Inf Sch
CR7 . . . . **42** A5
Winterbourne Jun Boys' Sch
CR7 . . . . **42** A5
Winterbourne Jun Girls' Sch
CR7 . . . . **42** A5
Winterbourne Mews
RH8 . . . . **122** C5
Winterbourne Rd
Forest Hill SE23, SE6 . . . . **23** F7
Thornton Heath CR7 . . . . . **42** A5
Winterbourne Wlk GU16 . . **85** F8
Winter Box Wlk TW10 . . . . . **6** F2
Winter Cl GU12 . . . . **106** A3
Winterdown Gdns KT10 . . . **54** F4
Winterdown Rd KT10 . . . . **54** F4
Winterfold RH10 . . . . **202** A3
Winterfold Cl SW19 . . . . . **19** E6
Winter Gdns RH11 . . . . . **201** C5
Winterhill Way GU4 . . . . . **110** B5
Wintersells Ind Est KT14 . . **52** D1
Wintersells Rd KT14 . . . . . **52** E1
Winters Rd KT7 . . . . **37** B2
Winterstoke Rd SE23, SE6 . **23** F7
Winterton Ct
Horsham RH13 . . . . **217** D2
Teddington KT1 . . . . **37** D8
Winton Ct
Stoneleigh KT17 . . . . **58** B4
15 Surbiton KT6 . . . . . . **37** D2
Winton Rd
Aldershot GU11 . . . . **105** A1
Farnham GU9 . . . . **125** D4
Winton Way SW16 . . . . . . **22** A3
Winward Ct 15 SM2 . . . . . **59** C4
Wire Cut GU10 . . . . **146** D1
Wireless Rd TN16 . . . . . . **83** D4
Wire Mill La RH7 . . . . . . **184** F8
Wirrall Ho 15 SE26 . . . . . **23** A5
Wisbeach Rd CR0 . . . . . . **42** D4
Wisborough Ct RH11 . . . . **200** F3
Wisborough Rd CR2 . . . . . **61** F2
Wisdom Ct 6 TW7 . . . . **6** A4
Wiseman Ct 12 SE19 . . . . **22** E3
Wiseton Rd SW17 . . . . . . **20** F7
Wishanger Farm Est
GU10 . . . . **167** A3
Wishanger La GU10 . . . . . **167** B2
Wishbone Way GU21 . . . . . **68** F3
Wishford Ct KT21 . . . . **75** F1
Wishmoor Cl GU15 . . . . . . **65** E8
Wishmoor Rd GU15 . . . . . . **65** E8
Wishmore Cross Sch
GU24 . . . . **49** F1
WISLEY **71** E3
Wisley Court Ho RH4 . . . . **136** B4
Kingston upon Thames
KT2 . . . . **17** E2
Wisley Ct CR2 . . . . **61** D1
Wisley Gdns GU14 . . . . . . **84** D2
Wisley La GU23 . . . . **71** E3
Wispers Sch GU27 . . . . . **189** C1
Wiston Ct
Crawley RH11 . . . . **200** F3
1 Horsham RH13 . . . . **217** D5
Witham Ct SW17 . . . . **20** F5
Witham Rd
Hounslow TW7 . . . . **5** D6
Penge BR3, SE20 . . . . . . **43** C6
Witherby Cl CR0, CR2 . . . . **61** E6
Wither Dale RH6 . . . . **160** E4
Withers Cl KT9 . . . . **56** C4
Witherslack Cl GU35 . . . . **187** C4
Withey Brook RH6 . . . . . **160** D1
Witheygate Ave TW18 . . . . **13** B2
Withey Mdws RH6 . . . . . **160** D1
Withies La GU3 . . . . **129** C2
Withies The
Knaphill GU21 . . . . **68** E2
Leatherhead KT22 . . . . . . **95** B6
Withybed Cnr KT20 . . . . . **97** B4
Withy Cl GU18 . . . . **48** C1
Withycombe Rd SW19 . . . . **19** D8
WITHYPITTS **204** A3
Withypitts RH10 . . . . **204** A3
Withypitts E RH10 . . . . . . **204** A3
WITLEY **170** F4
Witley CE Inf Sch GU8 . . . **170** F4
Witley Centre (Visitor Ctr)
The GU8 . . . . **170** C6
Witley Cres CR0 . . . . **63** C4
Witley Ho 5 SW2 . . . . **21** F8
Witley Point 8 SW15 . . . . **19** B7
Witley Sta GU8 . . . . **190** F8
Witney Path SE23 . . . . . . **23** D5
Wittenham Rd RG12 . . . . . **27** F8
Witten Ho KT3 . . . . **38** D1
Wittering Ct KT17 . . . . . . **17** D3
Wittersham Rd BR1 . . . . . **24** F3
Wittmead Rd GU16 . . . . . . **85** F4
Wivenhoe Ct TW4 . . . .**4** F3
Wiverton Rd SE20, SE26 . . **23** C3
Wix Hill KT24 . . . . **112** B4
Woburn Ave
Farnborough GU14 . . . . . **85** D3

Woburn Ave continued
Purley CR8 . . . . **80** A8
Woburn Cl
Frimley GU16 . . . . **66** A1
Merton SW19 . . . . **20** C2
Woburn Ct
Croydon CR0 . . . . **42** C1
Richmond TW9 . . . .**6** F4
Woburn Hill KT15 . . . . **52** D7
Woburn Ho SL5 . . . . **30** A1
Woburn Rd
Carshalton SM5 . . . . **40** E1
Crawley RH11 . . . . **201** A4
Croydon CR0 . . . . **42** C1
Wodehouse Pl GU1 . . . . . **130** E8
Wodeland Ave GU2 . . . . . **130** B7
Woffington Cl KT1, KT8 . . . **37** C8
WOKING **69** E1
Woking Bsns Pk GU21 . . . **70** B4
Woking Cl SW15 . . . .**7** F3
Woking Coll GU22 . . . . **90** A7
Woking Com Hospl GU22 . **69** F1
WOKINGHAM **25** B5
Wokingham Com Hospl
RG41 . . . . **25** A6
Wokingham Rd RG42 . . . . . **26** F8
Wokingham Sta RG40 . . . . **25** B6
Wokingham High Sch GU21 . **69** D4
Woking L Ctr GU22 . . . . . . **89** F8
Woking Nuffield Hospl
GU21 . . . . **69** E5
Woking Rd GU1, GU4 . . . . **109** D5
Woking Sta GU22 . . . . **69** F2
Wold Cl RH11 . . . . **200** F4
Woldhurstlea Cl RH11 . . . **201** A4
WOLDINGHAM **102** A4
WOLDINGHAM GARDEN
VILLAGE **101** F6
Woldingham Rd CR3,
CR6 . . . . **101** C6
Woldingham Sch CR3 . . . **101** C3
Woldingham Sta CR3 . . . . **101** D5
Wold The CR3 . . . . **102** A5
Wolfendale Cl RH1 . . . . . **119** C5
Wolfe Rd GU12 . . . . **105** C1
Wolfington Rd SE27 . . . . . **22** B4
Wolf's Cnr RH8 . . . . **123** B6
Wolf's Hill RH8 . . . . **123** A4
Wolf's Rd RH8 . . . . **123** B5
Wolfs Wood RH8 . . . . **123** A3
Wolseley Ave SW18, SW19 . **20** A6
Wolseley Ct 3 GU21 . . . . . **68** C1
Wolseley Gdns W4 . . . .**7** B8
Wolseley Rd
4 Aldershot GU11 . . . . **105** A1
Carshalton CR4 . . . . **41** A2
Farncombe GU7 . . . . **150** F6
Wolsey Ave KT7 . . . . **36** F4
Wolsey Cl
Isleworth TW3 . . . .**5** C3
Kingston upon Thames KT2 . **38** B8
Wimbledon SW20 . . . . . . **19** B1
Worcester Park KT4 . . . . . **58** A6
Wolsey Cres
New Addington CR0 . . . . . **63** C2
West Barnes SM4 . . . . . . **39** F2
Wolsey Dr
Kingston upon Thames
KT2 . . . . **17** E2
Walton-on-Thames KT12 . . **35** D1
Wolsey Gr KT10 . . . . **55** B6
Wolsey Ho 2 TW12 . . . . . . **16** B2
Wolsey Jun & Inf Schs
CR0 . . . . **63** C3
Wolsey Pl Sh Ctr GU22 . . **221** C2
Wolsey Rd
Ashford, Felthamhill TW16 . **14** F1
Ashford TW15 . . . . **13** F4
East Molesey KT8 . . . . . . **36** D5
Esher KT10 . . . . **55** B6
Hampton TW12 . . . . **16** C2
Wolsey Way KT9 . . . . **57** A5
Wolsey Wlk 7 GU21 . . . . . **69** F2
Wolsonbury Cl RH11 . . . . **201** C4
Wolvens La
Coldharbour RH5 . . . . . . **156** E5
Westcott RH4, RH5 . . . . . **135** B2
Wolverton Ave KT2 . . . . . . **38** A8
Wolverton Cl RH6 . . . . . . **160** F1
Wolverton Gdns RH6 . . . . **160** F2
Wolves Hill RH5 . . . . **178** C4
WONERSH **152** B7
Wonersh Ct GU5 . . . . **152** B7
Wonersh & Shamley Green
CE Inf Sch GU5 . . . . . . **152** D5
Wonersh Way SM2 . . . . . . **58** D2
Wonford Cl
Kingston upon Thames KT2,
KT3 . . . . **38** E8
Walton on the Hill KT20 . . . **97** A1
Wonford Ho KT20 . . . . **97** A2
Wonham La RH3 . . . . **137** F8
Wonham Pl RH9 . . . . **142** E8
Wonham Way
Gomshall GU5 . . . . **133** D3
Peaslake GU5 . . . . **133** D1
Wontford Rd CR8 . . . . **80** B4
Wontner Rd SW12, SW17 . . **20** F6
Woodall Cl KT9 . . . . **56** D4
Woodall Ho TW7 . . . .**5** F4
Woodbank Rd BR1 . . . . . . **24** F5
Woodbarn The GU9 . . . . . **125** C1
Woodbastwick Rd SE26 . . **23** E3

Woodberry Cl
Ashford TW16 . . . . **15** A2
Chiddingfold GU8 . . . . . . **191** A5
Woodbine Cl
Sandhurst GU47 . . . . **64** C7
Twickenham TW2 . . . . . . **16** D6
Woodbine Cotts
Egham TW20 . . . . **11** F2
Shalford GU4 . . . . **130** E2
Woodbine Gr SE20 . . . . . . **23** B1
Woodbine La KT4 . . . . **58** C7
Woodbines Ave KT1 . . . . . **37** D6
Woodbourne GU9 . . . . . . **125** E7
Woodbourne Ave SW16 . . . **21** D5
Woodbourne Cl SW16 . . . . **21** E5
Woodbourne Dr KT10 . . . . **55** F4
Woodbourne Gdns SM6 . . **60** B3
Woodbridge Ave KT22 . . . . **75** A1
Woodbridge Ct RH12 . . . . **218** A5
Woodbridge Dr GU15 . . . . **65** D7
Woodbridge Gr KT22 . . . . **75** A1
WOODBRIDGE HILL **109** A3
Woodbridge Hill GU2 . . . . **109** B2
Woodbridge Hill Gdns
GU2 . . . . **109** A2
Woodbridge Manor GU15 . . **65** D7
Woodbridge Mdws GU1 . . **109** C2
Woodbridge Park Est
GU1 . . . . **109** C2
Woodbridge Rd
Blackwater GU17 . . . . **64** B5
Guildford GU1, GU2 . . . . **109** C2
Woodbury Ave RH19 . . . . **186** B1
Woodbury Cl
Biggin Hill TN16 . . . . **83** F1
East Grinstead RH19 . . . **206** B8
South Croydon CR0 . . . . . **61** F8
Woodbury Dr SM2 . . . . . . **59** C1
Woodbury Ho SE26 . . . . . . **23** B5
Woodbury St SW17 . . . . . . **20** E3
Woodby Dr SL5 . . . . **29** F2
Wood Cl RH1 . . . . **161** A8
Woodcock Chase RG12 . . . **26** D5
Woodcock Cl TW19 . . . .**2** B3
Woodcock Dr GU24 . . . . . . **49** C3
Woodcock Hill RH19 . . . . **184** F6
Woodcock La GU24 . . . . . . **49** B3
Woodcombe Cres SE23 . . . **23** C7
WOODCOTE
Coulsdon **79** D4
Epsom **76** D3
Woodcote
Artington GU2 . . . . **130** B5
Cranleigh GU6 . . . . **174** B4
Farncombe GU7 . . . . **150** D6
Horley RH6 . . . . **161** C4
Woodcote Ave
Thornton Heath CR7 . . . . . **42** B5
Wallington SM6 . . . . **60** B2
Woodcote Cl
Epsom KT18 . . . . **76** D5
Kingston upon Thames KT2 . **17** F3
Woodcote Ct 14 SM6 . . . . **60** B4
Woodcote Dr CR8 . . . . **60** D1
Woodcote End KT18 . . . . . **76** D4
Woodcote Gn SM6 . . . . . . **60** C2
WOODCOTE GREEN **60** C1
Woodcote Green Rd RH18 **76** D4
Woodcote Grove Rd CR5 . . **79** C4
Woodcote Hall
Epsom KT18 . . . . **76** D5
Wallington SM6 . . . . **60** B2
Woodcote High Sch CR5 . . **79** D6
Woodcote Ho KT18 . . . . . . **76** D4
Woodcote House Ct KT18 . . **76** D4
Woodcote House Sch
GU20 . . . . **48** B5
Woodcote Hurst KT18 . . . . **76** C3
Woodcote La CR8 . . . . **79** D7
Woodcote Lo KT18 . . . . . . **76** C4
Woodcote Mews
Epsom KT18 . . . . **76** D5
Wallington SM6 . . . . **60** B4
Woodcote Park Ave CR8 . . **79** C7
Woodcote Park Rd KT18 . . **76** C4
Woodcote Pl
North Ascot SL5 . . . . **28** F8
1 West Norwood SE27 . . **22** B3
Woodcote Prim Sch CR5 . . **79** D5
Woodcote Rd
Epsom KT18 . . . . **76** D5
Forest Row RH18 . . . . . . **206** F2
Wallington SM6 . . . . **60** C2
Woodcote Side KT18 . . . . . **76** B4
Woodcote Valley Rd CR5,
CR8 . . . . **79** E7
Woodcote Villas SE27 . . . . **22** C3
Woodcot Gdns GU14 . . . . . **84** D4
Woodcott Ho 1 SW15 . . . . **19** A8
Woodcott Terr GU12 . . . . **126** D8
Woodcourt RH11 . . . . **201** C1
Wood Crest 4 SM2 . . . . . . **59** C3
Woodcrest Rd CR8 . . . . . . **79** E6
Woodcrest Wlk RH2 . . . . . **118** E3
Woodcroft 3 CR0 . . . . **61** E7
Woodcroft Rd
Crawley RH11 . . . . **200** D4
Thornton Heath CR0, CR7 . . **42** B3
Wood Ct GU2 . . . . **109** B2
Woodcut Rd GU10 . . . . . . **145** F6
Woodend
Farnborough GU14 . . . . . **85** D3
Leatherhead KT22 . . . . . . **95** C2
South Norwood SE19 . . . . **22** C2
Sutton SM1 . . . . **59** C8
Thames Ditton KT10 . . . . . **55** C8
Wood End RH12 . . . . **218** C5

Woodend Cl
Crawley RH10 . . . . 202 A8
North Ascot SL5 . . . . 28 E8
Woking GU21 . . . . 89 A8
Wood End Cl GU22 . . . . 70 F3
Woodend Dr SL5 . . . . . . 29 B4
Woodend Pk KT11 . . . . . 73 D4
Woodend Rd GU16 . . . . . 86 C7
Wood End The SM6 . . . . 60 B2
Woodenhill RG12 . . . . . . 26 E1
Wooden Hill Prim Sch
RG12 . . . . 26 E2
Wooderson Cl SE25 . . . . 42 E5
Wooderson Ct [10] BR3 . . 44 A8
Woodfield
Ashtead KT21 . . . . 75 D2
Thornton Heath SW16 . . 41 F8
Woodfield Ave
Streatham SW16 . . . . . 21 D5
Wallington SM5 . . . . . . 60 A3
Woodfield Cl
Ashtead KT21 . . . . 75 D2
Coulsdon CR5 . . . . 99 C8
Crawley RH10 . . . . 201 E7
Redhill RH1 . . . . 118 E3
South Norwood SE19 . . 22 C1
Woodfield Gdns KT3 . . . . 38 F4
Woodfield Gr SW16 . . . . 21 D5
Woodfield Hill CR5 . . . . 99 B8
Woodfield Ho
[11] Forest Hill SE23 . . . 23 D5
Hinchley Wood KT7 . . . 55 F8
[1] New Malden KT3 . . . 38 F4
Woodfield La
Ashtead KT21 . . . . 75 E2
Streatham SW16 . . . . . 21 D5
Woodfield Rd
Ashtead KT21 . . . . 75 D2
Cranford TW4, TW5 . . . . 4 B5
Crawley RH10 . . . . 201 F7
Hinchley Wood KT7 . . . 55 F8
Rudgwick RH12 . . . . . . 214 D7
Woodfield Sch RH1 . . . . 119 E6
Woodfields Ct SM1 . . . . 59 C7
Woodfields The CR2 . . . 80 F8
Woodfield Way RH1 . . . 118 E3
Woodford Gn RG12 . . . . 27 F5
Woodgate Ave KT9 . . . . 56 D5
Woodgate Cl KT11 . . . . 73 C6
Woodgate Dr SW16 . . . . 21 D1
Woodgates Cl RH13 . . . 217 F3
Woodgavil SM7 . . . . . . 77 F3
Woodger Cl GU4 . . . . . 110 C3
Woodglen SM4 . . . . 40 E4
Woodgrange Ct [1] BR2 . . 44 F1
Woodhall Ave SE21 . . . . 22 F5
Woodhall Dr SE21 . . . . . 22 F5
Woodhall La SL5 . . . . . . 48 E8
WOODHAM 52 A2
WOODHAM HALL
ESTATE 70 B5
Woodham La
New Haw KT15 . . . . . . 52 B1
Sheerwater GU21, KT15 . . 70 D7
Woodham Park Rd KT15 . . 51 F1
Woodham Park Way KT15 70 F8
Woodham Pl GU21 . . . . 69 F5
Woodham Rd
Catford SE6 . . . . 24 C5
Woking GU21 . . . . 69 F4
Woodham Rise GU21 . . . 70 A4
Woodham Waye GU21 . . 70 B5
WOODHATCH 139 B7
Woodhatch Rd RH1, RH2 . 139 E5
Woodhatch Spinney CR5 . 79 E3
Woodhaw TW20 . . . . . . 12 B4
Woodhayes [4] RH6 . . . . 161 B4
Woodhayes Rd SW19 . . . 19 C2
Woodhill GU23 . . . . 90 D2
Woodhill Ct GU23 . . . . . 90 E2
Woodhill La GU5 . . . . . 152 F4
Woodhouse La RH5 . . . 155 A8
Woodhouse St RG42 . . . 26 E8
Woodhurst La RH8 . . . . 122 E4
Woodhurst Pk RH8 . . . . 122 E5
Woodhyrst Gdns CR8 . . 80 B4
Wooding Gr [15] RH11 . . 201 B1
Wood La
Banstead KT20 . . . . . . 77 F2
Bracknell RG42 . . . . . . 26 E8
Caterham CR3 . . . . . . 100 D3
Farnborough GU14 . . . . 85 A3
Hounslow TW7 . . . . .5 F7
Knaphill GU21 . . . . 68 D1
Seale GU10 . . . . 127 B5
Weybridge KT13 . . . . . 53 C2
Woodland Ave GU6 . . . 174 F3
Woodland Cl
East Horsley KT24 . . . . 112 F8
Horsham RH13 . . . . . . 218 B4
Oatlands Park KT13 . . . 53 D6
West Ewell KT19 . . . . . 57 E4
West Norwood SE19 . . . 22 E2
Woodland Cotts GU8 . . 190 B8
Woodland Cres GU14 . . 85 C6
Woodland Ct
Ewell KT17 . . . . 76 F7
Oxted RH8 . . . . 122 E7
Sutton SM1 . . . . 59 A4
Woodland Dr
Cobham KT11 . . . . 73 F7
Crawley Down RH10 . . . 204 B8
East Horsley KT24 . . . . 112 F8
Farnham GU10 . . . . . . 146 B6
Ockley RH5 . . . . 178 A5
Woodland Gdns
Isleworth TW7 . . . . .5 E4
Selsdon CR2 . . . . 81 C8

Woodland Glade GU15 . . 65 D7
Woodland Gr KT13 . . . . 53 D6
Woodland Hill SE19 . . . 22 E2
Woodland Mews SW16 . . 21 E5
Woodland Rd
Thornton Heath CR7 . . . 42 A5
West Norwood SE19 . . . 22 F3
Woodland Rise RH8 . . . 122 E5
WOODLANDS 5 E4
Woodlands
Beckenham BR3 . . . . . 24 B1
Bromley BR2 . . . . 44 F5
Chertsey KT15 . . . . . . 52 E7
Crawley RH10 . . . . 202 D8
Horley RH6 . . . . 161 D4
Send Marsh GU23 . . . . 90 F2
West Barnes SW20 . . . 39 D5
[14] Woking GU22 . . . . 89 E8
Woodlands Ave
Heath End GU9 . . . . . . 125 F7
Kingston upon Thames KT3 . 38 D8
Redhill RH1 . . . . 139 F8
West Byfleet KT14, KT15 . . 70 F7
Worcester Park KT4 . . . 58 A8
Woodlands Cl
Ascot SL5 . . . . 28 F3
Ash GU12 . . . . 106 A5
Claygate KT10 . . . . . . 55 F3
Cranleigh GU6 . . . . . . 174 F2
Crawley Down RH10 . . . 204 B7
Farnborough GU17 . . . . 64 E1
Guildford GU1 . . . . . . 109 E5
Ottershaw KT16 . . . . . 51 B1
Woodlands Copse KT21 . . 75 D3
Woodlands Ct
[11] Bromley BR1 . . . . . 44 F8
Dulwich SE22 . . . . 23 B8
Sandhurst GU47 . . . . . 45 F1
[12] Woking, Mount Hermon
GU22 . . . . 89 E8
[7] Woking, St John's GU21. 69 A1
Woodlands Dr
South Godstone RH9 . . . 142 E6
Sunbury TW16 . . . . . . 35 C7
Woodlands Est GU18 . . . 77 C2
Woodlands Gr
Coulsdon CR5 . . . . 79 B2
Isleworth TW7 . . . . .5 E5
Woodlands Ho
Sheerwater GU21 . . . . . 70 C5
[8] West Byfleet KT14 . . . 71 A6
Woodlands Par
Haslemere GU27 . . . . . 207 F7
Stoke D'Abernon KT11. . . 74 B2
Windlesham GU20, GU24 . 48 E3
Woodlands Par TW15 . . . 14 C2
Woodlands Pk
Addlestone KT15 . . . . . 51 F5
[2] Ash GU12 . . . . 105 F1
Box Hill KT20 . . . . 116 B4
Guildford GU1 . . . . . . 110 B2
Sheerwater GU21 . . . . . 70 C5
Woodlands Pl CR3 . . . . 101 B1
Woodlands Rd
Camberley GU15 . . . . . 65 B5
East Grinstead RH19 . . . 186 A4
Effingham KT23 . . . . . 113 F6
Epsom KT18 . . . . 76 A4
Farnborough GU14 . . . . 84 D6
Guildford GU1 . . . . . . 109 D5
Hambledon GU8 . . . . . 171 D1
Isleworth TW7 . . . . .5 E5
Leatherhead KT22 . . . . 74 D1
Mortlake SW13 . . . . . . .7 F4
Pyrford KT14 . . . . 70 F5
Redhill RH1 . . . . 139 F7
Surbiton KT6 . . . . 37 D2
Virginia Water GU25 . . . 31 C5
Woodlands Rd E GU25 . . 31 C5
Woodlands Rd W GU25 . . 31 C5
Woodlands Ride SL5 . . . 29 A3
Woodlands Sch KT22 . . . 95 C5
Woodlands St SE13 . . . . 24 D8
Woodlands The
Isleworth TW7 . . . . .5 F7
Lewisham SE13 . . . . . . 24 D8
Mitcham CR4 . . . . 41 A6
Smallfield RH6 . . . . . . 162 B3
South Norwood SE19 . . 22 C1
Thames Ditton KT10 . . . 55 C8
Wallington SM6 . . . . . . 60 B2
Woodlands Way
Ashtead KT21 . . . . 76 B2
Box Hill KT20 . . . . 116 C5
Woodlands Wlk GU17 . . 64 E1
Woodland View GU7 . . 129 E1
Woodland Way
Caterham CR3 . . . . . . 120 E8
Croydon CR0, CR9 . . . . 43 E1
Horsham RH13 . . . . . . 218 B4
Kingswood KT20 . . . . . 97 E4
Merton SM4 . . . . 39 F5
Mitcham CR4 . . . . 21 A1
Purley CR8 . . . . 80 A6
Tolworth KT5 . . . . 57 B8
West Wickham BR4 . . . 63 C7
Weybridge KT13 . . . . . 53 D5
Woodland Wlk
Aldershot GU12 . . . . . 105 D3
Epsom KT19 . . . . 57 A4
Woodlawn Cres TW2 . . . 16 B6
Woodlawn Dr TW13 . . . 15 D6
Woodlawn Gr GU21 . . . 69 F4
Wood Lea Cotts RH12 . . 215 F7
Woodlea Dr BR2 . . . . . . 44 E4
Woodlea Prim Sch CR3. . 101 F5
Woodlee Cl GU25 . . . . . 31 C7
Woodleigh [1] KT5 . . . . . 37 F4

Woodleigh Gdns SW16 . . 21 E5
Woodley Cl SW17 . . . . . 20 F1
Woodley Ho [1] SW19 . . . 19 F3
Woodley La SM5 . . . . . . 59 E7
Woodlodge
Ashtead KT21 . . . . 75 E2
[4] Wimbledon SW19 . . . 19 F3
Wood Lodge La BR4 . . . 63 C7
Woodmancote Ct [5]
RH12 . . . . 217 D5
Woodmancote Gdns KT14 71 A6
Woodmancott Gr RG12 . . 27 F3
Woodmancourt GU7 . . . 150 D3
Woodman Mews TW9 . . . .7 B6
Woodman Rd CR5 . . . . . 79 D4
Woodmans Hill RH11 . . . 201 C2
WOODMANSTERNE 78 E4
Woodmansterne La
Wallington SM6, SM5 . . . 79 A7
Woodmansterne SM7 . . . 78 D4
Woodmansterne Prim Sch
Streatham SW16 . . . . . 41 D8
Woodmansterne SM7 . . . 78 F5
Woodmansterne Rd
Coulsdon CR5 . . . . 79 C4
Streatham SW16 . . . . . 41 D8
Wallington SM5 . . . . . . 59 E2
Woodmansterne St SM7 . . 78 E4
Woodmansterne Sta CR5 . 79 B3
Woodmere RG12 . . . . . . 27 E5
Woodmere Ave CR0 . . . . 43 D2
Woodmere Cl CR0 . . . . . 43 D2
Woodmere Gdns CR0 . . . 43 D2
Woodmere Way BR3 . . . 44 D4
Woodmill Cl SL5 . . . . . . 28 D6
Woodnook Rd SW16 . . . 21 B3
Woodpecker Cl
Cobham KT11 . . . . 73 E7
Crondall GU10 . . . . . . 124 D8
Woodpecker La RH5 . . . 158 C2
Woodpecker Mount CR0 . 62 F2
Woodpecker Pl RG12 . . . 26 D5
Woodpeckers
Bracknell RG12 . . . . . . 27 B5
Witley GU8 . . . . 170 E7
Woodpecker Way
Turners Hill RH10 . . . . 204 C5
Woking GU22 . . . . 89 D3
Woodplace Cl CR5 . . . . . 79 C1
Woodplace La CR5 . . . . . 99 C7
Wood Rd
Beacon Hill GU26 . . . . 188 D6
Biggin Hill TN16 . . . . . 83 C1
Camberley GU15 . . . . . 65 B1
Farncombe GU7 . . . . . 150 F7
Heath End GU9 . . . . . . 125 C7
Littleton TW17 . . . . . . 34 A5
Woodridge Cl RG12 . . . . 27 C6
Wood Riding GU22 . . . . 70 E4
Wood Rise GU3 . . . . . . 108 E3
Woodrising KT13 . . . . . . 53 C4
Woodroffe Benton Ho
RH11 . . . . 200 F6
Woodrough Copse GU5 . 152 A5
Woodrough La GU5 . . . 151 F6
Woodrow Dr RG40 . . . . . 25 F6
Woodroyd Ave RH6 . . . . 160 F2
Woodroyd Gdns RH6 . . . 160 F1
Woodruff Ave GU1 . . . . 110 B4
Woods Hill Cl RH19 . . . . 206 D6
Woods Hill La RH19 . . . . 206 D6
Woodshore Cl GU25 . . . . 31 B3
WOODSIDE
Ascot 9 C4
Croydon 43 A4
Woodside
Blackwater GU17 . . . . . 64 C3
[1] Farnborough GU14. . . 85 B7
Fetcham KT22 . . . . 94 B5
Horsham RH13 . . . . . . 218 B4
Lower Kingswood KT20 . . 117 F7
Sandhurst GU15 . . . . . 64 F7
Walton-on-Thames KT12 . . 35 A1
West Horsley KT24 . . . . 92 C1
Weybridge KT13 . . . . . 53 A5
Wimbledon SW19 . . . . 19 F3
Woodside Ave
Croydon SE25 . . . . 43 B4
Hersham KT12 . . . . . . 54 B6
Thames Ditton KT10 . . . 36 E2
Woodside Cl
Caterham CR3 . . . . . . 100 E3
Chiddingfold GU8 . . . . 191 B4
Knaphill GU21 . . . . . . 68 D2
Tolworth KT5 . . . . 38 C2
Woodside Cotts GU8 . . 148 C3
Woodside Court Rd CR0,
CR9 . . . . 43 A2
Woodside Cres RH6 . . . 162 A3
Woodside Ct GU14 . . . . 84 D5
Woodside Flats GU8 . . . 191 B4
Woodside Gn CR0, SE25 . . 43 A3
Woodside Halt SE25 . . . 43 B3
Woodside Jun & Inf Schs [1]
CR0 . . . . 43 A2
Woodside La SL4 . . . . . . .9 C3
Woodside Park Est GU7 . 150 F4
Woodside Pk SE25 . . . . . 43 B3
Woodside Rd
Beare Green RH5 . . . . . 157 D3
Chiddingfold GU8 . . . . 191 B5
Cobham KT11 . . . . 74 A6
Cranbourne SL4 . . . . . . .9 B3
Crawley RH10 . . . . 201 F8
Croydon SE25 . . . . 43 B3
Farnborough GU11 . . . 104 F7
Guildford GU2 . . . . . . 108 F2

Woodside Rd continued
Heath End GU9 . . . . . . 125 E7
Kingston upon Thames KT2. 17 E1
New Malden KT3 . . . . . 38 E7
Purley CR8 . . . . 79 E6
Sutton SM1 . . . . 59 C7
Woodside Way
Croydon CR0 . . . . 43 C3
Redhill, Earlswood RH1. . 140 A8
Redhill, South Earlswood
RH1 . . . . 140 A3
Streatham CR4 . . . . . . 41 C8
Virginia Water GU25 . . . 31 B6
Woodsome Lodge KT13 . . 53 C4
Woodspring Rd SW19 . . . 19 E6
Wood St
Ash Vale GU12 . . . . . . 106 A6
Carshalton CR4 . . . . . . 41 A2
East Grinstead RH19 . . . 185 E7
Kingston upon Thames KT2. 37 E8
Merstham RH1 . . . . . . 119 C7
Woodstock
East Grinstead RH19 . . . 185 C2
West Clandon GU4 . . . . 111 B7
Wokingham RG40 . . . . 25 C6
Woodstock Ave
Cheam SM3 . . . . 39 F2
Isleworth TW7 . . . . .6 A2
Woodstock Cl
Cranleigh GU6 . . . . . . 174 F1
Horsham RH12 . . . . . . 217 D5
Woking GU21 . . . . 69 E3
Woodstock Ct KT17 . . . . 76 D7
Woodstock Gdns BR3 . . . 24 B1
Woodstock Gr GU1 . . . . 110 A1
Woodstock La N KT6 . . . 56 C8
Woodstock La S KT10, KT6 56 C6
Woodstock Rd
Coulsdon CR5 . . . . 79 B3
Croydon CR0, CR9 . . . . 61 D7
Wallington SM5 . . . . . . 60 A5
Woodstocks GU14 . . . . . 85 D6
Woodstock Way CR4 . . . 41 C7
Woodstone Ave KT17, KT4. 58 A5
Wood Street Gn GU3 . . 108 A3
Wood Street Inf Sch
GU3 . . . . 108 C3
WOOD STREET
VILLAGE 108 B3
Woodsway KT22 . . . . . . 74 E5
Woodsyre SE19, SE26 . . . 22 F4
Woodthorpe Rd TW15 . . . 13 D4
Wood Vale SE22 . . . . . . 23 B8
Woodvale Ave SE25 . . . . 42 F7
Woodvale Ct SE25 . . . . . 42 F6
Woodvale Wlk SE27 . . . . 22 C3
Woodview KT9 . . . . 75 C8
Woodview Cl
Ashtead KT21 . . . . 76 A3
Hamsey Green CR2 . . . 81 B5
Kingston upon Thames
SW15 . . . . 18 D4
Woodview Ct KT13 . . . . . 53 C5
Woodville Cl
Blackwater GU17 . . . . . 64 B5
Teddington TW11 . . . . . 17 A4
Woodville Ct KT22 . . . . . 95 B7
Woodville Gdns KT6 . . . 37 D2
Woodville Ho SM1 . . . . . 59 B6
Woodville Rd
Leatherhead KT22 . . . . 95 B7
Merton SM4 . . . . 40 A5
Richmond TW10 . . . . . 17 C5
South Norwood CR7 . . . 42 D6
Woodward Cl KT10 . . . . 55 F4
Woodwards RH11 . . . . . 201 C1
Woodway
Camberley GU15 . . . . . 65 B5
Guildford GU1 . . . . . . 110 B2
Woodwicks GU6 . . . . . . 174 F2
Woodyard La SE21 . . . . 22 E8
Woodyers Cl GU5 . . . . . 152 B7
Woolborough Cl RH10. . . 201 E7
Woolborough La
Crawley RH10 . . . . 181 F1
Crawley, Three Bridges
RH10 . . . . 202 A8
Salfords RH1 . . . . 161 F8
Woolborough Rd RH10 . . 201 E7
Woolf Dr RG40 . . . . 25 C7
Woolf Memorial Cotts
RG40 . . . . 25 C7
Woolford Cl RG42 . . . . . .8 C1
Woolfords La GU8 . . . . . 169 B7
Woolhampton Way RG12 . 27 D4
Woolhams CR3 . . . . 101 A1
Woollards Rd GU12 . . . . 106 B4
Woolmead Ct GU9 . . . . . 125 C3
Woolmead Rd GU9 . . . . . 125 C3
Woolmead The GU9 . . . . 125 C3
Woolmead Walk GU9. . . . 125 C3
WOOLMER HILL 207 D7
Woolmer Hill Ho GU27 . . 207 C6
Woolmer Hill Rd GU27 . . 207 D6
Woolmer Hill Tech Coll
GU27 . . . . 207 D7
Woolmer View GU26 . . . 188 D3
Woolridge Cl TW14 . . . . 14 C7
Woolsack Way GU7 . . . . 150 F4
Woolstone Rd SE23, SE6 . . 23 E6
Wooshill La
Wokingham RG41 . . . . . 25 A5
Wokingham RG41 . . . . . 25 A5
Wootton KT10 . . . . 55 C6
Wootton Cl KT18 . . . . . . 76 F3
Wootton Grange [3] GU22. 89 E8

Worbeck Rd SE20 . . . . . 43 C7
Worcester Cl
Croydon CR0 . . . . 63 A8
Farnborough GU14 . . . . 85 B7
Mitcham CR4 . . . . 41 A7
Worcester Ct
Ashford TW15 . . . . 14 B3
Camberley GU15 . . . . . 65 B3
Redhill RH1 . . . . 118 E3
[9] Sutton SM2 . . . . . . 59 B4
[5] Walton-on-Thames KT12 35 C1
Worcester Park KT4 . . . 57 E7
Worcester Dr TW15 . . . . 14 B3
Worcester Gdns KT4 . . . 57 E7
Worcester Ho [6] TW3 . . . .4 F3
WORCESTER PARK 57 E6
Worcester Park Rd KT4 . . 57 D7
Worcester Park Sta KT4. . 39 A1
Worcester Rd
Belmont SM2 . . . . 59 B3
Crawley RH10 . . . . 201 E2
Guildford GU2 . . . . . . 108 F3
Reigate RH2 . . . . 118 A2
[11] Wimbledon SW19 . . . 19 F3
Wordsworth RG12 . . . . . 26 F4
Wordsworth Ave CR8. . . . 80 D4
Wordsworth Cl RH10 . . . 202 B8
Wordsworth Dr KT4, SM3 . 58 C6
Wordsworth Mead RH1. . 119 B3
Wordsworth Pl RH12 . . . 217 E7
Wordsworth Rd
Addlestone KT15 . . . . . 52 D6
Hampton TW12 . . . . . . 15 F4
Penge SE20 . . . . 23 D1
Wallington SM6 . . . . . . 60 D4
Wordsworth Rise [6]
RH19 . . . . 185 C1
Works Rd KT15 . . . . 52 B2
World Bsns Ctr TW6 . . . . . .3 C6
World Rugby Mus★ TW1 . . 5 E1
World's End KT11 . . . . . . 73 A5
Worlds End Hill RG12 . . . 27 F3
WORMLEY 170 F1
Wormley La GU8 . . . . . . 171 B1
Worple Ave
Isleworth TW7 . . . . .6 A2
Staines TW18 . . . . 13 B2
Wimbledon SW19 . . . . 19 D1
Worple Ct SW19 . . . . . . 19 D1
Worple Prim Sch TW7 . . . .6 A3
Worple Rd
Epsom KT18 . . . . 76 D4
Epsom KT18 . . . . 76 E5
Isleworth TW7 . . . . .6 A3
Leatherhead KT22 . . . . 95 B4
Staines TW18 . . . . 13 B1
Wimbledon SW19, SW20. . 39 D8
Worple Road Mews SW19 19 F2
WORPLESDON 108 D4
Worplesdon Hill GU22. . . 88 D5
Worplesdon Hill Ho GU22 88 D5
Worplesdon Prim Sch
GU3 . . . . 108 D4
Worplesdon Rd GU2 . . . . 109 A4
Worplesdon Sta GU22 . . . 89 B3
Worple St SW14 . . . . .7 D4
Worple Way TW10 . . . . . . .6 E3
Worsfold Cl GU23 . . . . . . 90 B4
Worslade Rd SW17 . . . . . 20 D4
Worsley Bridge Jun Sch
BR3 . . . . 24 A1
Worsley Bridge Rd
Beckenham BR3, SE6 . . . 24 A2
Catford SE6 . . . . 23 F3
Worsley Ho SE23 . . . . 23 B6
Worsley Rd GU16 . . . . . . 85 F7
Worsted Gn RH1 . . . . . . 119 D6
Worsted La RH19 . . . . . . 206 B8
WORTH 202 E6
Worth Abbey★ RH10 . . . 203 B1
Worthfield Cl KT19 . . . . . 57 D3
Worthing Rd
Heston TW5 . . . . .4 F8
Horsham RH12 . . . . 217 B1
Worthington Cl CR4 . . . . 41 B6
Worthington Ho [16] SW2. 22 A8
Worthington Rd KT6 . . . . 37 F1
Worth Park Ave RH10 . . . 202 C7
Worth Rd RH10 . . . . 202 C6
Worth Sch RH10 . . . . . . 203 B1
Worth Way RH10 . . . . . . 202 E5
Wortley Rd CR0 . . . . 42 A2
Worton Ct TW7 . . . . .5 E3
Worton Gdns TW7 . . . . . . .5 D5
Worton Hall Est TW7 . . . . .5 E3
Worton Rd TW7 . . . . .5 E4
Worton Way TW3, TW7 . . . .5 D5
WOTTON 134 F3
Wotton Way SM2 . . . . . . 58 C1
Wrabness Way TW18 . . . . 33 B8
Wrangthorn Wlk CR0. . . . 61 A6
Wray Cl RH19 . . . . 206 D6
Wray Common Prim Sch
RH2 . . . . 118 D2
Wray Common Rd RH2 . . 118 D2
Wrayfield Ave RH2 . . . . . 118 C2
Wrayfield Rd SM3 . . . . . . 58 D7
Wray Ho [11] SW2 . . . . . . 21 E7
Wray La RH2 . . . . 118 D4
Wraylands Dr RH2 . . . . . 118 D3
Wraymead Pl RH2 . . . . . 118 B2
Wraymill Ct [5] RH2 . . . . 118 C2
Wray Mill Ho RH2 . . . . . 118 E3
Wray Mill Pk RH2 . . . . . 118 E3
Wray Park Rd RH2 . . . . . 118 C2

Wray Rd SM2 . . . . 58 F2
WRAYS 160 B5
WRAYSBURY 11 E8
Wraysbury Cl TW4 . . . . . . 4 E2
Wraysbury Gdns TW18 . . . 12 E4
Wraysbury Rd
  Staines TW18 . . . . 12 E4
  Staines TW19 . . . . 12 B6
Wraysbury Sta TW19 . . . 1 A1
WRECCLESHAM 145 E6
Wrecclesham Hill GU10 . 145 E5
Wrecclesham Rd GU10,
  GU9 . . . . 145 F8
Wrekin The GU14 . . . . . 85 E1
Wren Cl
  Horsham RH12 . . . . . . 217 D7
  Hounslow TW6. . . . . . . 2 B4
  Selsdon CR2. . . . . 62 D2
Wren Cres KT15. . . . . . 52 D5
Wren Ct
  Ash GU12. . . . . 106 B3
  Crawley RH10 . . . . 201 E3
  South Croydon CR0 . . . . 61 D6
  Warlingham CR6 . . . . . . 81 C2
Wren Gdns RG12 . . . . . 26 D5
Wren Ho
  4 Hampton TW12. . . . . 16 B2
  Teddington KT1 . . . . . . 37 F7
Wrens Ave TW15 . . . . . 14 C4
Wren's Hill KT22 . . . . . 74 C4
Wren St RH10 . . . . 204 C5
Wrenthorpe Rd BR1. . . . 24 E4
Wren Way GU14 . . . . . . 84 F7
Wright Cl RH10 . . . . . . 202 C2
Wright Gdns TW17 . . . . 34 A4
Wrighton Ct SM1 . . . . . 58 F4
Wright Rd TW5 . . . . . . 4 C7
Wrights Rd SE25 . . . . . 42 E6
Wright's Row SM5 . . . . 60 B6
Wriotsley Way KT15 . . . 52 A4
Writers Ct GU26 . . . . . 188 C6
Wrotham Hill GU8 . . . . 192 E3
Wrotham Ho BR3 . . . . . 23 F1
Wroxham RG12 . . . . . . 26 F4
Wroxham Wlk RH10 . . . 202 B4
Wrythe Gn SM5 . . . . . . 59 F7
Wrythe Green Rd SM5. . . 59 F7
Wrythe La SM5 . . . . . . 59 F7
WRYTHE THE 59 F8
Wulwyn Ct RG45 . . . . . 45 A5
Wyatt Cl TW13 . . . . . . 15 D7
Wyatt Ct GU47 . . . . . . 64 D7
Wyatt Ho 11 TW1 . . . . . 6 D1
Wyatt Park Mans 1 SW2. 21 E6
Wyatt Park Rd SW2 . . . . 21 F6
Wyatt Rd TW18 . . . . . . 13 E4
Wyatt's Almshouses GU7 151 A6
Wyatt's Cl GU7. . . . . . . 151 A6
Wyche Gr CR2 . . . . 61 D2
Wychelm Rd GU18 . . . . 67 C8
Wych Elm Rise GU1 . . . 130 E6
Wych Hill GU22 . . . . . . 89 C8
Wych Hill La GU22 . . . . 89 E8
Wych Hill Pk GU22 . . . . 89 D8
Wych Hill Rise GU22 . . . 89 D8
Wych Hill Way GU22 . . . 89 D8

Wychwood
  Camberley GU15 . . . . . 65 D7
  Ifold RH14 . . . . 212 D3
Wychwood Ave
  Bracknell RG12 . . . . . . 27 F5
  South Norwood CR7 . . . 42 C6
Wychwood Cl
  Ashford TW16 . . . . 15 A2
  Ash GU12. . . . . 105 F2
Wychwood Pl GU15 . . . . 66 B8
Wychwood Way SE19 . . . 22 D2
Wycliffe Bldgs GU2 . . . 130 C7
Wycliffe Ct RH11 . . . . . 200 E3
Wycliffe Rd SW19 . . . . . 20 B2
Wydell Cl SM4 . . . . 39 D3
Wydenhurst Rd CR0, CR9. . 43 B2
Wye Cl TW15 . . . . 14 B4
Wyeth's Mews KT17 . . . 76 F6
Wyeth's Rd KT17 . . . . . 76 F6
WYKE. 106 E3
Wyke Ave GU12 . . . . . . 106 E3
Wyke Cl TW7 . . . . 5 F8
Wykeham Cl UB7 . . . . . 3 A4
Wykeham Ho
  Farnborough GU14 . . . . 105 C8
  Merton SW19 . . . . 40 A8
Wykeham Rd
  Farnham GU9 . . . . 125 C3
  Guildford GU1 . . . . . . 110 D2
Wykehurst Ho SW19 . . . 20 D3
Wyke La GU12 . . . . 106 D2
Wyke Prim Sch GU3. . . . 106 F4
Wyke Rd SW20 . . . . . . 39 C7
Wylam RG12 . . . . 26 F4
Wyldewood SL5. . . . . . 29 D3
Wyleu St SE23 . . . . 23 E8
Wymering Ct GU14 . . . . 85 D3
Wynash Gdns SM5 . . . . 59 E5
Wynbourne Ct SE20 . . . 43 B7
Wyncliffe Ct BR2. . . . . . 44 E5
Wyncote Way CR2 . . . . 62 D2
Wyndham Ave KT11 . . . 73 A6
Wyndham Cl SM2 . . . . . 59 A3
Wyndham Cres
  Cranleigh GU6 . . . . . . 174 A3
  Twickenham TW4. . . . . 5 A1
Wyndham Ct CR7 . . . . . 42 B3
Wyndham Lo TW7 . . . . . 5 E6
Wyndham Rd
  Kingston upon Thames
    KT2. . . . . 17 F1
  Woking GU21. . . . . . . 69 B1
Wyndham St GU12 . . . . 105 C1
Wyndhurst Cl CR2. . . . . 61 B3
Wynell Rd SE23 . . . . . . 23 D5
Wynfields GU16. . . . . . 85 F3
Wynlea Cl RH10. . . . . . 204 A8
Wynne Ct 5 TW7 . . . . . 6 A4
Wynnstow Pk RH8 . . . . 122 F4
Wynsham Way GU20 . . . 48 B6
Wynton Gdns SE25 . . . . 42 F4
Wynton Gr KT12 . . . . . 54 A7
Wyphurst Rd GU6 . . . . 174 E4
Wyresdale RG12 . . . . . 27 F2
Wysemead RH6. . . . . . 161 C4
Wythegate TW18. . . . . 12 F1
Wyvern Cl
  2 Ash Vale GU12 . . . . . 105 F5

Wyvern Cl continued
  1 East Grinstead RH19 . . 185 D2
Wyvern Ct TW15 . . . . . 13 E5
Wyvern Est The KT3. . . . 39 A5
Wyvern Pl
  Addlestone KT15 . . . . . 52 B6
  Warnham RH12 . . . . . . 216 F8
Wyvern Rd CR8 . . . . . . 61 B1

Y

Yaffle Rd KT13 . . . . 53 C1
Yale Cl
  Hounslow TW4. . . . . . . 4 F2
  Sandhurst GU47 . . . . . 45 F2
Yarborough Rd 1 SW19. . 40 D8
Yarbridge Cl SM2. . . . . 59 B1
Yardley RG12 . . . . 26 F4
Yardley Cl RH2 . . . . . . 118 B3
Yardley Ct SM3. . . . . . . 58 D6
Yard Mead TW20. . . . . . 12 A5
Yarm Cl KT20 . . . . 95 C4
Yarm Court Rd KT22 . . . 95 C4
Yarmouth Cl RH10 . . . . 202 A4
Yarnold Cl RG40 . . . . . 25 F7
Yarrow RH12 . . . . 217 E5
YATELEY. 64 A5
Yateley Ct CR8. . . . . . . 80 C5
Yatesbury Cl GU9 . . . . 145 F7
Yattendon Rd RH6 . . . . 161 B3
Yattendon Sch RH6 . . . 161 A4
Yaverland Dr GU19. . . . 47 D2
Yeats Cl RH1 . . . . 139 C6
Yeend Cl KT8 . . . . 36 A5
Yehudi Menuhin Sch
  KT11. . . . . 94 A8
Yellowcress Dr GU24. . . 68 A3
Yelverton Ct 2 KT23 . . . 94 A1
Yelverton Lodge TW1 . . 17 C8
Ye Market CR0. . . . . . . 61 D5
Yenston Cl SM4. . . . . . 40 A3
Yeoman Cl SE27 . . . . . 22 B5
Yeoman Ct
  Burgh Heath KT20 . . . . 97 E8
  6 Carshalton SM1 . . . . 59 D5
  Heston TW5. . . . . 4 F7
Yeoman Dr TW19 . . . . . 13 E7
Yeomanry Cl KT17 . . . . 76 F7
Yeomans Cl
  Ash GU10. . . . . 126 F8
  Farnborough GU14 . . . . 85 A5
Yeomans Croft KT23 . . . 94 A2
Yeomans Mews TW7 . . . 5 D2
Yeomans Way GU15. . . . 65 E5
Yeoman Way RH1. . . . . 140 B4
Yeoveney Cl TW19 . . . . 12 D6
Yeovil Cl GU14. . . . . . . 85 D1
Yeovil Rd
  Farnborough GU14 . . . . 85 E1
  Sandhurst GU47 . . . . . 45 E1
Yeovilton Pl KT2 . . . . . 17 C3
Yetminster Rd GU14. . . 85 D1
Yewbank Cl CR8 . . . . . 80 D4
Yew Close RG42 . . . . . . 8 A1
Yew Cnr RG12 . . . . 27 C6
Yew Ct
  Crawley RH11 . . . . 201 D5

Yew Ct continued
  1 East Grinstead RH19 . . 185 D2
Yewdale Cl BR1. . . . . . . 24 E2
Yewens GU8. . . . . 191 B5
Yew La RH19 . . . . 185 B3
Yewlands Cl SM7 . . . . . 78 C4
Yewlands Wlk RH11 . . . 200 D4
Yew Pl KT13 . . . . 53 F7
Yews The
  Ashford TW15 . . . . 14 B4
  West Byfleet KT14. . . . . 71 E7
Yew Tree Bottom Rd KT17,
  KT18. . . . . 77 C2
Yew Tree Cl
  Chipstead CR5. . . . . . . 98 F8
  Farnborough GU14 . . . . 84 C3
  Horley RH6 . . . . 161 A4
  New Malden KT4 . . . . . 38 E1
Yew Tree Cotts KT10 . . . 55 D8
Yew Tree Ct 10 SM2. . . . 59 C3
Yew Tree Dr
  Caterham CR3. . . . . . . 100 F2
  Guildford GU1 . . . . . . 109 C6
Yew Tree Gdns KT18 . . . 76 C4
Yew Tree Ho
  New Malden KT4 . . . . . 38 E1
  5 Surbiton KT6 . . . . . . 37 E1
Yew Tree La RH2 . . . . . 118 B4
Yew Tree Lodge 10 SW16. 21 C4
Yew Tree Rd
  Beckenham BR3. . . . . . 43 F6
  Charlwood RH6 . . . . . . 180 E7
  Dorking RH4 . . . . 115 A1
  Witley GU8. . . . . 170 D6
Yewtrees TW20 . . . . . . 32 C6
Yew Trees TW17 . . . . . 33 F5
Yew Tree Wlk
  Effingham KT24 . . . . . 113 D8
  Frimley GU16. . . . . . . 65 F1
  Hounslow TW4. . . . . . . 4 F2
  South Croydon CR8 . . . 61 C1
Yockley Cl GU15. . . . . . 66 D3
Yolland Cl GU9 . . . . . . 125 C7
York Ave
  East Grinstead RH19 . . 206 A8
  Mortlake SW14 . . . . . . 7 C2
York Cl
  Byfleet KT14 . . . . 71 E7
  Horsham RH13 . . . . . . 217 F3
  Morden SM4 . . . . 40 B5
  Staines TW18. . . . . . . 13 E2
York Cres GU11. . . . . . 104 F1
York Ct
  Beckenham BR3. . . . . . 44 D8
  Epsom KT19. . . . . 76 A7
  Kingston upon Thames KT2. 17 D2
  Wallington SM6. . . . . . 60 C4
Yorke Gate CR3. . . . . . 100 D5
Yorke Gdns RH2 . . . . . 118 A2
Yorke Rd RH2 . . . . 118 A2
York Gdns KT12. . . . . . 54 D8
York Hill SE27, SW16. . . 22 B5
York Ho
  Bracknell RG42 . . . . . . 26 F8
  Forest Hill SE26. . . . . . 23 C3
  4 Kingston upon Thames
    KT2. . . . . 17 F1
  Lower Kingswood KT20. . 117 F8
  Richmond, Kew TW9 . . . 7 A6

York Ho continued
  Richmond, North Sheen
    TW10 . . . . 7 A2
  West Norwood SE27 . . . 22 B6
York House SE25. . . . . . 42 E5
York Pl GU15 . . . . 65 D7
York Rd
  Aldershot GU11 . . . . . . 104 F1
  Ash GU12. . . . . 106 A3
  Belmont SM1, SM2. . . . 59 A3
  Biggin Hill TN16. . . . . . 103 B8
  Byfleet KT14 . . . . 71 E7
  Camberley GU15 . . . . . 65 D7
  Crawley RH10 . . . . 201 E2
  Farnborough, South Farnborough
    GU14. . . . . 85 C1
  Farnham GU9. . . . . . . 125 C1
  Guildford GU1 . . . . . . 130 D8
  Hounslow TW3. . . . . . . 5 B4
  Kingston upon Thames KT2. 17 F1
  4 Richmond TW10 . . . . 6 F2
  Selsdon CR2. . . . . 62 D1
  Teddington TW11. . . . . 16 E4
  Thornton Heath CR0 . . . 42 A2
  Weybridge KT13 . . . . . 53 C2
  Wimbledon SW19 . . . . 20 C2
  Woking GU22. . . . . . . 69 E1
Yorkshire Rd CR4 . . . . . 41 E5
York St
  Carshalton CR4 . . . . . . 41 A2
  Twickenham TW1. . . . . 17 A7
York Terr La GU15 . . . . 65 A5
YORK TOWN 65 A4
York Town Ind Est GU15. 65 A5
Yorktown Rd
  Sandhurst, College Town
    GU47. . . . . 64 E7
  Sandhurst GU47 . . . . . 64 C7
York Way
  Chessington KT9 . . . . . 56 E3
  Feltham TW13 . . . . . . 15 F5
  Sandhurst GU47 . . . . . 64 B8
Youlden Cl GU15. . . . . . 66 A5
Youlden Dr GU15 . . . . . 66 B6
Youngman RH7. . . . . . 165 B4
Youngs Dr GU12 . . . . . 105 F2
Young St
  Fetcham KT22 . . . . . . 94 F3
  Leatherhead KT22 . . . . 95 A3
Youngstroat La GU24. . . 50 E1
Yukon Rd SW12. . . . . . 21 B8

Z

Zealand Ave UB7. . . . . . 2 E7
Zenith Ct GU47 . . . . . . 45 E1
Zennor Rd SW12. . . . . . 21 C7
Zennor Rd Ind Est SW12. 21 C7
Zermatt Rd CR7. . . . . . 42 C5
Zig Zag Rd
  Kenley CR8. . . . . 80 C3
  Mickleham KT20, RH4,
    RH5. . . . . 115 D4
Zinnia Dr GU24 . . . . . . 68 A3
Zion Pl CR7. . . . . 42 D5
Zion Rd CR7, SE25 . . . . 42 D5
ZK Pk CR0. . . . . 60 F7
Zodiac Ct CR0 . . . . 42 B1